W9-BHT-989

A New Star-Rating System & Other Exciting News from Frommer's!

In our continuing effort to publish the savviest, most up-to-date, and most appealing travel guides available, we've added some great new features.

Frommer's guides now include a new **star-rating system.** Every hotel, restaurant, and attraction is rated from 0 to 3 stars to help you set priorities and organize your time.

We've also added **seven brand-new features** that point you to the great deals, in-the-know advice, and unique experiences that separate travelers from tourists. Throughout the guide, look for:

Finds	Special finds—those places only insiders know about
Fun Fact	Fun facts—details that make travelers more informed and their trips more fun
Kids	Best bets for kids—advice for the whole family
Moments	Special moments—those experiences that memories are made of
Overrated	Places or experiences not worth your time or money
Tips	Insider tips—some great ways to save time and money
Value	Great values—where to get the best deals

Here's what the critics say about Frommer's:

"Amazingly easy to use. Very portable, very complete."

—*Booklist*

"Detailed, accurate, and easy-to-read information for all price ranges."
—*Glamour Magazine*

"Hotel information is close to encyclopedic."

—*Des Moines Sunday Register*

"Frommer's Guides have a way of giving you a real feel for a place."
—*Knight Ridder Newspapers*

Other Great Guides for Your Trip:

Frommer's Southeast Asia

Frommer's Thailand

Frommer's Hong Kong

Frommer's China: The 50 Most Memorable Trips

Frommer's Beijing

Frommer's Shanghai

Frommer's Australia

Frommer's®

Singapore & Malaysia

3rd Edition

by Jennifer Eveland

WILEY

Wiley Publishing, Inc.

About the Author

Jennifer Eveland was a child when she and her family first moved to Singapore, and after returning to the United States, she was drawn again and again to the magic of Singapore, East Asia, and Southeast Asia. She is the author of *Frommer's Thailand* and a contributor to *Frommer's Southeast Asia,* and currently lives in Singapore.

Published by:

Wiley Publishing, Inc.

909 Third Ave.
New York, NY 10022

Copyright © 2003 Wiley Publishing, Inc., New York, New York. All rights reserved. No part of this publication may be reproduced, stored in a retrieval system or transmitted in any form or by any means, electronic, mechanical, photocopying, recording, scanning or otherwise, except as permitted under Sections 107 or 108 of the 1976 United States Copyright Act, without either the prior written permission of the Publisher, or authorization through payment of the appropriate per-copy fee to the Copyright Clearance Center, 222 Rosewood Drive, Danvers, MA 01923, (978) 750-8400, fax (978) 646-8700. Requests to the Publisher for permission should be addressed to the Legal Department, Wiley Publishing, Inc., 10475 Crosspoint Blvd., Indianapolis, IN 46256, (317) 572-3447, fax (317) 572-4447, E-Mail: permcoordinator@wiley.com.

Wiley and the Wiley Publishing logo are trademarks or registered trademarks of Wiley Publishing, Inc. in the United States and other countries and may not be used without written permission. Frommer's is a trademark or registered trademark of Arthur Frommer. Used under license. All other trademarks are the property of their respective owners. Wiley Publishing, Inc. is not associated with any product or vendor mentioned in this book.

ISBN 0-7645-2458-5
ISSN 1093-6971

Editor: Amy Lyons
Production Editor: M. Faunette Johnston
Cartographer: Roberta Stockwell
Photo Editor: Richard Fox
Production by Wiley Indianapolis Composition Services

For information on our other products and services or to obtain technical support, please contact our Customer Care Department within the U.S. at 800-762-2974, outside the U.S. at 317-572-3993 or fax 317-572-4002.

Wiley also publishes its books in a variety of electronic formats. Some content that appears in print may not be available in electronic formats.

Manufactured in the United States of America

5   4   3   2   1

Contents

List of Maps

I owe it all to Mom and Dad. Richard Eveland (Dad) brought me to live in Singapore when I was a child and held my little hand on the plane. The following years I spent in Singapore instilled in me a deep appreciation for the people and culture there. Linda Eveland (Mom), was there for me as I wrote this book, holding my big hand through every challenge I encountered. She kept my sense of humor alive and my sanity intact. For her help I am forever indebted.

Acknowledgments

I wish to thank Pauline Tan, who provided most of the research and wonderful insights for the Malaysia portion of this book.

For cheering me on, I would like to thank Jackie Allen, Joy Cantarella, Regina Caslin, Michelle Cavallaro, David Fix, Michele Hudak, Balkiss and Suliman Hamid, Niamani Mutima, Molly and Tay Chee Beng, and Terence Tay.

For their support, I'd like to thank the good people at the Chinatown Hotel, Tania Goh at the Singapore Tourism Board, Dan Marino at Singapore Airlines, Shu-Hana Shuib at the Malaysia Tourism Board, Bhajan Singh at the Registered Tourist Guides Association of Singapore, and Karen Wos at Spring O'Brien.

—Jennifer Eveland

An Invitation to the Reader

In researching this book, we discovered many wonderful places—hotels, restaurants, shops, and more. We're sure you'll find others. Please tell us about them, so we can share the information with your fellow travelers in upcoming editions. If you were disappointed with a recommendation, we'd love to know that, too. Please write to:

Frommer's Singapore & Malaysia, 3rd Edition
Wiley Publishing, Inc. • 909 Third Ave. • New York, NY 10022

An Additional Note

Please be advised that travel information is subject to change at any time—and this is especially true of prices. We therefore suggest that you write or call ahead for confirmation when making your travel plans. The authors, editors, and publisher cannot be held responsible for the experiences of readers while traveling. Your safety is important to us, however, so we encourage you to stay alert and be aware of your surroundings. Keep a close eye on cameras, purses, and wallets, all favorite targets of thieves and pickpockets.

New! Frommer's Star Ratings & Icons

Every hotel, restaurant, and attraction listing in this guide has been ranked for quality, value, service, amenities, and special features using a star-rating scale. In country, state, and regional guides, we also rate towns and regions to help you narrow down your choices and budget your time accordingly. Hotels and restaurants in the Very Expensive and Expensive categories are rated on a scale of one (highly recommended) to three stars (exceptional). Those in the Moderate and Inexpensive categories rate from zero (recommended) to two stars (very highly recommended). Attractions, towns, and regions are rated according to the following scale: zero stars (recommended), one star (highly recommended), two stars (very highly recommended), and three stars (must-see).

In addition to the rating system, we also use seven icons to highlight insider information, useful tips, special bargains, hidden gems, memorable experiences, kid-friendly venues, places to avoid, and other useful information:

Finds	Fun Fact	Kids	Moments	Overrated	Tips	Value

The following abbreviations are used for credit cards:

AE American Express	DISC Discover	V Visa
DC Diners Club	MC MasterCard	

FROMMERS.COM

Now that you have the guidebook to a great trip, visit our website at **www.frommers.com** for travel information on nearly 2,500 destinations. With features updated regularly, we give you instant access to the most current trip-planning information available. At Frommers.com, you'll also find the best prices on airfares, accommodations, and car rentals—and you can even book travel online through our travel booking partners. At Frommers.com, you'll also find the following:

- Online updates to our most popular guidebooks
- Vacation sweepstakes and contest giveaways
- Newsletter highlighting the hottest travel trends
- Online travel message boards with featured travel discussions

The Best of Singapore & Malaysia

I could spend a lifetime exploring Singapore. I'm in awe of the cultural mysteries and exotic beauty of the city's old mosques and temples. As I pass the facades of buildings that mark history, I get nostalgic for old tales of colonial romance. Towering overhead, present-day Singapore glistens with the wealth of modern miracles. And when I smell incense and spice and jasmine swirling in wet topical breezes, I can close my eyes and know exactly where I am.

The longer I stay in Singapore, new curiosities present themselves to me. Singapore thrives on a history that has absorbed a multitude of foreign elements over almost 2 centuries, melding them into a unique modern national identity. Beginning with the landing of Sir Stamford Raffles in 1819, add to the mix the original Malay inhabitants, immigrating waves of Chinese traders and workers, Indian businessmen and laborers, Arab merchants, British colonials, European adventure-seekers, and an assortment of Southeast Asian settlers—this tiny island rose from the ingenuity of those who worked and lived together here. Today, all recognize each group's importance to the heritage of the land, each adding unique contributions to a culture and identity we know as Singaporean.

I'll confess, many travelers complain to me about how westernized Singapore is. For many, a vacation in Asia should be filled with culture shock, unfamiliar traditions, and curious adventures. Today's travel philosophy seems to be that the more underdeveloped and obscure a country is, the more "authentic" the experience will be. But poor Singapore—all those lovely opium-stained coolies and toothless rickshaw pullers are now driving BMWs and exchanging cellular phone numbers. How could anyone possibly find this place so fascinating?

With all its shopping malls, fast-food outlets, imported fashion, and steel skyscrapers, Singapore could look like any other contemporary city you've ever visited—but to peel through the layers is to understand that life here is far more complex. While the outer layers are startlingly Western, just underneath lies a curious area where East blends with West in language, cuisine, attitude, and style. At the core, you'll find a sensibility rooted in the cultural heritage of values, religion, superstition, and memory. In Singapore, nothing is ever as it appears to be.

For me this is where the fascination begins. I detect so many things familiar in this city, only to discover how these imported ideas have been altered to fit the local identity. Like the Singaporean shophouse—a jumble of colonial architectural mandates, European tastes, Chinese superstitions, and Malay finery. Or "Singlish," the unofficial local tongue, which combines English language with Chinese grammar, common Malay phrases, and Hokkien slang to form a patois unique to this part of the world. This transformation of cultures has been going

Southeast Asia

TAIWAN

Bashi Channel

| 0 | 500 mi |
| 0 | 500 km |

N

★ National Capital

PACIFIC OCEAN

Luzon
○ Bagio City

Philippine Sea

★ Manila
THE PHILIPPINES

○ Puerto Galera
Mindoro

Samar

Panay

Cebu
○ Cebu City

Negros   *Bohol*

Sulu Sea

Mindanao

Palau

○
Isabela

Celebes Sea

Makassar Strait

Molucca Sea

Halmahera

MOLUCCAS   ○ Sorong

Sulawesi   *Ceram Sea*

I N D O N E S I A

Buru   ○   Seram

Jayapura ○

New Guinea

PAPUA NEW GUINEA

Banda Sea

Sea

Flores

Timor

Arafura Sea

Timor Sea   Darwin ○   **AUSTRALIA**

on for almost 2 centuries. So, in a sense, Singapore is no different today than it was 100 years ago. And in this I find my "authentic" travel experience.

When the urban jungle gets me crazy, I escape to Malaysia. Even Kuala Lumpur, the capital city, seems relaxed in comparison to Singapore. In fact, many Singaporeans look to their northern neighbor for the perfect vacation, taking advantage of its pristine and exciting national forests and marine parks, relaxing on picture-perfect beaches in either sophisticated resorts or quaint bungalows, taking in culture in its small towns, shopping for inexpensive handicrafts, or eating some of the finest food in Southeast Asia. Malaysia offers something for everyone—history, culture, adventure, romance, mystery, nature, and relaxation—without the glaring buzz of an overdeveloped tourism industry. It almost makes me overjoyed that few tourists venture here.

My favorite part of Malaysia, however, is the warmth of its people. I have yet to travel in this country without collecting remarkable tales of hospitality, openness, and generosity. I've found the Malaysian people to be genuine in their approach to foreign visitors, another fine byproduct of the underdeveloped tourism industry. For those who want to find a nice little corner of paradise, Malaysia could be your answer.

I've crept down alleys, wandered the streets of cities and towns, combed beaches, and trekked jungles to seek out the most exciting things that Singapore and Malaysia have to offer. In this volume I've presented the sights and attractions of these countries with insight into historical, cultural, and modern significance to bring you a complete appreciation of all you are about to experience. I've peeked in every shop door, chatting up the local characters inside. I've eaten local food until I can't move. I've stayed out all night. I've done it all and written about it here. I can only hope you will love Singapore and Malaysia as much as I do.

1 Frommer's Favorite Singapore Experiences

Sipping a Singapore Sling at the Long Bar: Ahhhh, the Long Bar, home of the Singapore Sling. I like to come in the afternoons, before the tourist rush. Sheltered by long jalousie shutters that close out the tropical sun, the air cooled by lazy *punkahs* (small fans that wave gently back and forth above), you can sit back in old rattan chairs and have your saronged waitress serve you sticky alcoholic creations while you toss back a few dainty crab cakes. Life can be so decadent. Okay, so the punkahs are electric, and, come to think of it, the place is air-conditioned (not to mention that it costs a small fortune), but it's fun to imagine the days when Somerset Maugham, Rudyard Kipling, or Charlie Chaplin would be sitting at the bar sipping Slings and spinning exotic tales

of their world travels. Drink up, my friend; it's a lovely high. See p. 180.

Witnessing Bloody Traditions: Every so often, a magical Saturday night comes around when you can witness the Kuda Kepang, which is not your average traditional dance. It features young men on wooden horses who move like warriors, whirling and spinning and slapping the horses to shake intimidating sounds out of them. Accompanied by rhythmic and repetitive traditional Malay music, the warriors dance in unison, staging battles with each other until by the end of a long series of dances, the horsemen are in a trance. A pot of burning frankincense is produced, from which they all inhale. After that, all hell breaks loose. The dancers are whipped, fed glass—which they chew and swallow hungrily—walk on glass shards, and shred entire coconuts with their teeth. While the whipping appears somewhat staged, I assure you the rest is real. It's a traditional dance that's taken very seriously both by the dancers and by the huge and mostly Malay crowds that gather for it. What's more, the next day the dancers don't recall what they did—and they're never injured. Unfortunately, the dance is not performed on a regular basis. The group works mostly for private ceremonies and gatherings, and appears at Malay Village (© **65/ 6748-4700**) on the off Saturday night when they don't have a gig. Call ahead to find out if they'll be performing. See chapters 5 and 8.

If you're not able to catch a performance, but still want a little ceremonial gore, check out the calendar of events in chapter 2. During the Thaipusam Festival, men pierce their bodies with skewers, and during the Thimithi Festival, they walk on burning coals. To celebrate the Birthday of the Monkey God, Chinese priests will slice themselves with sharp implements and write chants and prayers with their own blood.

Checking Out the Orchard Road Scene: You can't find better people-watching than on Orchard Road every Saturday afternoon, when it seems like every Singaporean crawls out of the woodwork to join the parade of shoppers, strollers, hipsters, posers, lovers,

geeks, and gabbers. Everybody is here, milling around every mall, clustered around every sidewalk bench, checking everybody out. At the corner of Scotts Road and Orchard, just under the Marriott, there's an alfresco cafe where you'll find local celebrities hanging out to see and be seen. International celebrities and models have been spotted here on occasion, too. In the mix, you're bound to see most every tourist on the island, coming around to see what all the excitement is about.

On Saturdays, school lets out early, so the malls are filled with mobs of bored teenagers, kicking around, trying to look cool, and watching the music videos in the front window of the HMV music store in The Heeren. Moms and dads also have half-days at the office, so the strip takes on the feel of an obstacle course, as all the parents race around wielding strollers, trying to run errands while they have the chance. Meanwhile, outside in the shady areas, you can see crowds of amahs (housekeepers) and workers relaxing and catching up on the latest news on their free afternoon.

For some, the scene is a madhouse to be avoided; for others, it's a chance to watch life on a typical Saturday afternoon in downtown Singapore. And it is typical, because however huge and delightful the scene is for tourists, it's just part of everyday reality for residents of the Garden City. See p. 136.

2 Frommer's Favorite Malaysia Experiences

Opening Your Mind to Good Medicine: The first time I went to Tioman Island I was appalled by the rows of A-frame shacks that passed themselves off as bungalows. "I wouldn't let my dog sleep in one of these! Who's your architect—Lassie? Call the concierge, there's been a terrible mistake! Good Lord, where's the minibar?!"

Needless to say, my first day in the doghouse was nutty. The rustic little cabin felt like it would fall apart at the first breeze. Really, I've stayed in more attractive places at summer camp. The concrete latrine in the rear was as back-to-basics as you could get, save going outside behind a tree. But I somehow survived my first night, cold shower and all.

The next day, after strolling around the kampung village, lazing about at the beach, chatting with friendly locals and fellow travelers, eating great barbecued fish and drinking some cold beer, I had to admit, the place had its charm. And I also had to admit my doghouse was starting to look rather cozy. No annoying telephones, no loud TVs, no distractions. Just peace.

By my third day, I began to redecorate. Drape a little sarong over the window here, place another mosquito candle on the table there, sweep out the sand; it was my little home. I couldn't remember the last time I'd felt so laid-back and satisfied. The hectic world I'd left behind began to look more and more insane with each passing day. And as the years of stress melted away, I couldn't imagine why anyone would ever want more from life than this. Civilization is so overrated. See p. 249.

Experiencing Kampung Hospitality: Pakcik (uncle) was just slightly older than his ancient Mercedes, but his price was right, so I hired him for the day to drive me around Kota Bharu. Sometime after lunch, during a stop at the kite-maker's house, I spotted a beautiful gasing, a wood-and-steel Malay top. It would be the perfect gift for my brother! I just had to have one.

Well, the kite-maker didn't want to give his up, but Pakcik had a few ideas. After coming up empty at the local shops, he took on my quest with personal conviction. Off we drove

through the outskirts of town, the sights becoming more and more rural. He turned down a dirt road, past grazing water buffaloes lazing near rice paddies. Soon the fields turned to jungle, and a small kampung village appeared in the trees. I watched out the window as we passed traditional wooden stilt houses where grannies fanned themselves on the porch watching the children chase chickens in the yard. Beside each house, colorful batik sarongs waved in the breeze.

The path wound to the house of Pakcik's nephew. I was welcomed inside with curiosity, perhaps the first foreigner to visit. They offered me a straw mat, which I used to join the others resting comfortably on the floor. Within minutes, an audience of neighbors gathered around, plucking fruits from the trees in the yard for me. I listened as Pakcik told them of my search for a gasing, and was surprised to see every person scatter. That afternoon I was offered every gasing in the village.

My afternoon in Pakcik's kampung is one of my most cherished memories, and a most meaningful experience. You see, as Southeast Asia becomes increasingly affluent and globalized, this way of life becomes steadily endangered. It's a lifestyle that for many urban Malaysians captures the spirit of the good life—simple days when joy was free. And everyone will be proud to show you; all you need is an open heart and a big smile. Malaysian hospitality never ceases to amaze me.

3 The Best Small Towns & Villages

Any Kampung (Tioman Island, Malaysia): Even though Tioman was developed for the tourism industry, you'll never think this place is overdeveloped. The casual and rustic nature of the island's tiny beach villages holds

firm, and those who seek escape rarely leave disappointed. See p. 249.

Malacca (Malaysia): As perhaps the oldest trading port in Malaysia, this town hosted a wide array of international traders: Arabs, Portuguese,

Dutch, English, Indian, and Chinese, all of whom left their stamp. See p. 225.

Cameron Highlands (Malaysia): When the tropical heat gets you down, head for the hills. The colonials favored this cooling retreat for growing tea and roses and for building lovely Tudor country homes. See p. 217.

4 The Best Beaches

Tanjung Rhu (Langkawi, Malaysia): Perhaps one the most stunning beach in Malaysia, this wide gorgeous stretch of white sand hugs a crystal clear, deep blue cove. Even Alex Garland would be impressed. See p. 247.

Kampung Juara (Tioman Island, Malaysia): This beach is what they mean when they say isolated. Be prepared to live like Robinson Crusoe—in tiny huts, many with no electricity at all. But, oh, the beach! Most visitors don't get to this part of the island, so many times you can have it all to yourself. See p. 253.

Central Beach (Sentosa Island, Singapore): This is just about the best beach you'll find in Singapore, which isn't really known for its beaches. It's lively, with water sports and beach activities plus food and drink. Every so often you'll find an all night dance party here. However, if you really need pristine seclusion, you'll have to head for Malaysia. See p. 151.

Cherating (Malaysia): If you're a leatherback turtle, you'll think the best beach in the world is just north of Cherating. Every spring and summer, these giant sea creatures come ashore to lay their eggs, so if you're in town from May to June you might catch a look at the hatchlings. Meanwhile, during the turtles' off-season, international windsurfing and water-board enthusiasts gather annually for competitions at this world-famous spot. See p. 256.

5 The Most Exciting Outdoor Adventures

Trekking in Taman Negara (Malaysia): With suitable options for all budgets, levels of comfort, and desired adventure, peninsular Malaysia's largest national park opens the wonders of primary rainforest and the creatures who dwell in it to everyone. From the canopy walk high atop the forest to night watches for nocturnal life, this adventure is as stunning as it is informative. See p. 253.

Sungei Buloh Nature Reserve (Singapore): Every year during the winter months, flocks of migrating birds from as far north as Siberia vacation in the warm waters of this unique mangrove swamp park. Easily traversed via wooden walkway, the park will never disappoint for some stunning wildlife shots. See p. 146-147.

6 The Most Fascinating Temples, Churches & Mosques

Thian Hock Keng (Singapore): One of Singapore's oldest Chinese temples, it is a fascinating testimony to Chinese Buddhism as it combines with traditional Confucian beliefs and natural Taoist principles. Equally fascinating is the modern world that carries on just outside the old temple's doors. See p. 130.

Jalan Tokong, Malacca (Malaysia): This street, in the historical heart of the city, supports a Malay mosque, a

Chinese temple, and a Hindu temple existing peacefully side by side—the perfect example of how the many foreign religions that came to Southeast Asia shaped its communities and learned to coexist in harmony. See p. 231.

Armenian Church (Singapore): While not the biggest Christian house of worship in the city, it is perhaps one of the most charming in its architectural simplicity, tropical practicality, and spiritual tranquility. See p. 115.

Hajjah Fatimah Mosque (Singapore): I love this mosque for its eclectic mix of religious symbols and architectural influences. To me, it represents not just the Singaporean ability to absorb so many different ideas, but also a Muslim appreciation and openness toward many cultures. See p. 133.

7 The Most Interesting Museums

Images of Singapore (Sentosa Island, Singapore): No one has done a better job than this museum in chronicling the horrors of the World War II Pacific Theater and Japanese occupation in Southeast Asia. Video and audio displays take you on a journey through Singapore's experience. The grand finale, the Surrender Chambers, features life-size wax-figure dioramas of the fateful events. See p. 152.

Penang Museum and Art Gallery (Penang, Malaysia): A slick display of Penang's colonial history and multicultural heritage, this place is chockfull of fascinating tidbits about the people, places, and events of this curious island. Plus, it doesn't hurt that the air-conditioning works very well! See p. 241.

Asian Civilisations Museum (Singapore): One of the newer displays on the block, this extremely well-presented museum documents the evolutionary and cultural history of the region's major ethnic groups. A very informative afternoon. See p. 115.

State Museums of Malacca (Malaysia): This small city has more museums than any other city in the country, with some unusual displays such as kites and Malaysian literature. See p. 230.

8 The Best Luxury Resorts & Hotels

Raffles Hotel (Singapore): For old-world opulence, Raffles is second to none. It's pure fantasy of the days when tigers still lurked around the perimeters. See p. 61.

The Four Seasons (Singapore): Elegance and warmth combine to make this place a good bet. Consider a regular room here before you book a suite elsewhere. See p. 73.

The Regent (Kuala Lumpur, Malaysia): For my money, the Regent offers the smartest decor and the best service and selection of facilities in the whole city. See p. 206.

Shangri-La's Rasa Sayang Resort (Penang, Malaysia): The oldest resort on the beach has claimed the best stretch of sand and snuggled the most imaginative modern, yet traditionally designed resort into the gardens just beyond. See p. 238.

The Datai (Langkawi, Malaysia): The Datai is as stunning as any of the best resorts Phuket and Bali have to offer, without the Phuket or Bali price tag. See p. 246.

9 The Best Hotel Bargains

RELC International Hotel (Singapore): For a safe and simple place to call home in Singapore, RELC can't be beat. One wonders how they keep costs so low when their location is so good. See p. 84.

Traders Hotel (Singapore): Value-for-money is the name of the game, with all sorts of promotional packages, self-service launderettes, vending machines, and a checkout lounge just a few of the offerings that make this the most convenient hotel in the city. See p. 81.

Swiss-Inn (Kuala Lumpur, Malaysia): Location, location, location! Right in the center of Kuala Lumpur's bustling Chinatown, the Swiss-Inn is the perennial favorite for travelers here. A comfortable choice, plus it's so close to everything. See p. 210.

Heeren House (Malacca, Malaysia): Bargain or no bargain, this boutique hotel in the heart of the old city is the place to stay in Malacca if you want to really get a feel of the local atmosphere. See p. 228.

Telang Usan Hotel (Kuching, Malaysia): An informal place, Telang Usan is homey and quaint, and within walking distance of many major attractions in Kuching. See p. 275.

10 The Best Local Dining Experiences

Hawker Centers (Singapore and Malaysia): Think of them as shopping malls for food—great food! For local cuisine, who needs a menu with pictures when you can walk around and select anything you want as it's prepared before your eyes. See chapters 4, 9, 10, and 11.

Gurney Drive (Penang, Malaysia): Penang is the king of Asian cuisine, from Chinese to Malay to Indian and everything else in between. This large hawker center by the sea is a great introduction to Penang. See p. 240.

Imperial Herbal (Singapore): In the Chinese tradition of yin and yang, dishes are prepared under the supervision of the house doctor, a traditional healer who will be glad to "prescribe" the perfect cure for whatever ails you. See p. 100.

Chile Crab at UDMC Seafood Centre (Singapore): A true Singaporean favorite, chile crabs will cause every local to rise up in argument over where you can find the best in town. Head out to UDMC to try the juicy crabs cooked in a sweet chile sauce. Prepare to get messy! See p. 111.

11 The Best Markets

Arab Street (Singapore): Even though Singapore is a shopper's paradise, it could still use more places like Arab Street. Small shops selling everything from textiles to handicrafts line the street. Bargaining is welcome. See p. 168.

Central Market (Kuala Terengganu, Malaysia): This huge bustling market turned me into a shopping freak! All of the handicrafts Terengannu is famous for come concentrated in one exciting experience: batik, songket cloth, brassware, basket weaving—the list goes on. See p. 261.

Petaling Street, (Kuala Lumpur, Malaysia): This night market gets very, very crowded and crazy with all who come for watches, handbags, computer software, video CDs (which aren't exactly DVDs but can be played on a DVD player), and all manner of blatant disregard for international copyright laws. See p. 213.

12 The Best Shopping Bargains

Silver Filigree Jewelry (Malaysia): This fine silver is worked into detailed filigree jewelry designs to make brooches, necklaces, bracelets, and other fine jewelry.

Pewter (Malaysia): Malaysia is the home of Selangor Pewter, one of the largest manufacturers of pewter in the world, and their many showrooms have all sorts of items to choose from. See the Kuala Lumpur shopping section in chapter 9 for locations there. For locations in Penang, Malacca, and Johor call the **Selangor hot line** at ℂ **03/422-1000.** See chapter 9.

Knockoffs and Pirate Goods (Singapore and Malaysia): Check out how real those watches look! And so cheap!

You can find them at any night market. Ever dream of owning a Gucci? Have I got a deal for you! Can I tell you about pirate video CDs and computer software without getting my book banned? Uh, okay, whatever you do, don't buy these items! See chapters 6 and 9.

Batik (Singapore and Malaysia): While most of the batiks you find in Singapore come from Indonesia, most in Malaysia are made at factories that you can often tour. The Indonesian prints usually show traditional motif and colors, while Malaysian designs can be far more modern. Look for batik silk as well. See chapters 6, 9, and 10.

13 The Best Nightlife

Singapore, the whole city: Nightlife is becoming increasingly sophisticated in Singapore, where locals have more money for recreation and fun. Take the time to choose the place that suits your personality. Jazz club? Techno disco? Cocktail lounge? Wine bar? Good old pub? They have it all. See p. 175.

Bangsar (near Kuala Lumpur, Malaysia): Folks in Kuala Lumpur know to go to Bangsar for nighttime excitement. A couple of blocks of concentrated restaurants, cafes, discos, pubs, and wine bars will tickle any fancy. Good people-watching, too. See p. 215.

Planning Your Trip to Singapore

The seasoned traveler usually has as many stories of travel nightmares as he does of glorious experiences—your luggage gets sent to Timbuktu, your hotel reservations get mixed up, and your taxi driver takes you to Lord-knows-where. The good news about traveling to Singapore? This place works! A seamless communications infrastructure means that you can plan your own trip, without a middleman travel agent, and still have everything go as smoothly as if you were on an organized coach tour. Reliable phone lines, fax technology, and Internet presence makes advance planning a breeze. Of course, it helps that so many Singaporeans speak English. Additionally, the **Singapore Tourism Board (STB)** is a wealthy and well-oiled machine that has anticipated the needs of travelers.

The STB is perhaps one of the most visible government agencies in Singapore, and it's impossible for any tourist to get out of the country without encountering at least one of its many publications or postings or coming face-to-face with one of its innumerable representatives. If you have access to one of its offices before your trip, it's a great source of information. (more information on STBis listed under "Visitor Information," below.)

In this chapter, I'll run through the nuts and bolts of travel to Singapore, letting you in on everything from how much your money will buy, to the best time of year to travel and what to wear, to what sea creatures to watch out for if you go swimming.

1 Singapore's Regions in Brief

Singapore thrives on a history that has absorbed a multitude of foreign elements over almost 2 centuries, melding them into a unique modern national identity. Beginning with the landing of Sir Stamford Raffles in 1819, add to the mix the original Malay inhabitants, immigrating waves of Chinese traders and workers, Indian businessmen and laborers, Arab merchants, British colonials, European adventure-seekers, and an assortment of Southeast Asian settlers—this tiny island rose from the ingenuity of those who worked and lived together here. Today, all recognize each group's importance to the heritage of the land, each adding unique contributions to a culture and identity we know as Singaporean.

With all its shopping malls, fast-food outlets, imported fashion, and steel skyscrapers, Singapore could look like any other contemporary city you've ever visited—but to peel through the layers is to understand that life here is far more complex. While the outer layers are startlingly Western, just underneath lays a curious area where East blends with West in language, cuisine, attitude, and style. At the core, you'll find a sensibility rooted in the cultural heritage of values, religion, superstition, and memory. In Singapore, nothing is ever as it appears to be.

For me this is where the fascination begins. I detect so many things familiar in this city, only to discover how these imported ideas have been altered to fit the local identity. Like the Singaporean shophouse—a jumble of colonial architectural mandates, European tastes, Chinese superstitions, and Malay finery. Or Singlish, the unofficial local tongue, combining English language with Chinese grammar, common Malay phrases, and Hokkien slang to form a patois unique to this part of the world. This transformation of cultures has been going on for almost 2 centuries. So, in a sense, Singapore is no different today than it was 100 years ago. And in this I find my "authentic" travel experience.

THE LAY OF THE LAND

The country is made up of one main island, Singapore, and around 60 smaller ones, some of which—like Sentosa, Pulau Ubin, Kusu, and St. John's Island—are popular retreats. The main island is shaped like a flat, horizontal diamond, measuring in at just over 42km (25 miles) from east to west and almost 23km (14 miles) north to south. With a total land area of only 584.8 sq. km (351 sq. miles), Singapore is almost shockingly tiny.

Singapore's geographical position, sitting approximately 137km (82 miles) north of the equator, means that its climate offers uniform temperatures, plentiful rainfall, and high, high humidity.

As a city-state, Singapore is basically a city that *is* the country. That doesn't necessarily mean that the entire country is urban, but that the whole of the country and the city is "Singapore," without provincial divisions.

Singapore does, however, have an urban center and smaller suburban neighborhoods: The urban area centers around the Singapore River at the southern point of the island, and within it are neighborhood divisions: the **Historic District** (also referred to as the city center or cultural district), **Chinatown and Tanjong Pagar** (which is oftentimes lumped together with Chinatown due to its close proximity), the **Orchard Road area, Little India,** and **Kampong Glam** (also referred to as the Arab District).

Just beyond the urban area lie suburban neighborhoods. Some older suburbs, like **Katong** and **Geylang,** date from the turn of the 20th century. Others are new, and are therefore referred to as "HDB New Towns." (HDB stands for "Housing Development Board," the government agency responsible for public housing.) HDB New Towns such as **Ang Mo Kio** or **Toa Payoh** are clusters of public housing units, each with their own network of supporting businesses: provision shops, restaurants, healthcare facilities, and sometimes shopping malls.

THE CITY   The urban center of Singapore spans quite far from edge to edge, so walking from one end to the other—say, from Tanjong Pagar to Kampong Glam—might be a bit much. However, once you become handy with local maps, you'll be constantly surprised at how close the individual districts are to one another.

The main focal point of the city is the **Singapore River,** which on a map is located at the southern point of the island, flowing west to east into the Marina. It's here that Sir Stamford Raffles, a British administrator, landed and built his settlement for the East India Trading Company. As trade prospered, the banks of the river were expanded to handle commerce, behind which neighborhoods and administrative offices took root. In 1822, Raffles developed a Town Plan, which allocated neighborhoods to each of the races who'd come in droves

Singapore

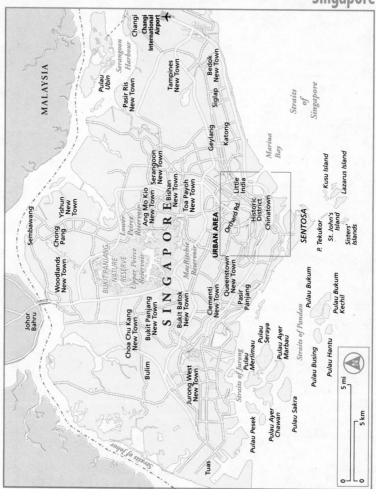

to find work and begin new lives. The lines drawn then still remain today, shaping the major ethnic enclaves within the city limits.

On the south bank of the river, godowns (warehouses) were built along the waterside, behind which offices and residences sprang up for the Chinese community of merchants and "coolie" laborers who worked the river and sea trade. Raffles named this section **Chinatown**, a name that stands today.

Neighboring Chinatown to the southwest is **Tanjong Pagar,** a small district where wealthy Chinese and Eurasians built plantations and manors. With the development of the steamship, Keppel Harbour, a deep natural harbor just off the shore of Tanjong Pagar, was built up to receive the larger vessels. Tanjong Pagar quickly developed into a commercial and residential area filled with workers who flocked there to support the industry.

Urban Singapore Neighborhoods

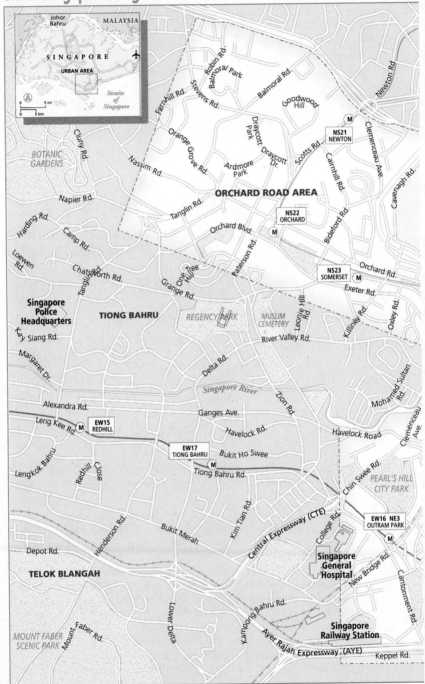

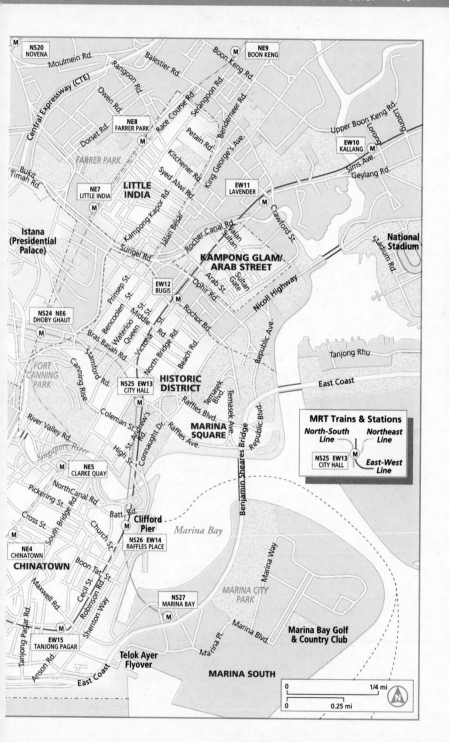

In these early days, both Chinatown and Tanjong Pagar were amazing sites of city activity. Row houses lined the streets, with shops on the bottom floors and homes on the second and third floors. Chinese coolie laborers commonly lived 16 to a room, and the area flourished with gambling casinos, clubs, and opium dens for them to spend their spare time and money. Indians also thronged to the area to work on the docks, a small reminder that although races had their own areas, they were never exclusive communities.

As recently as the 1970s, a walk down the streets in this area was an adventure: The shops housed Chinese craftsmen and artists; on the streets, hawkers peddled food and other merchandise. Calligrapher scribes set up shop on sidewalks to write letters for a fee. Housewives would bustle, running their daily errands; children would dash out of every corner; and bamboo poles hung laundry from upper stories. Today, however, both of these districts are sleepy by comparison. Modern HDB apartment buildings have siphoned residents off to the suburbs, and though the Urban Redevelopment Authority has renovated many of the old shophouses in an attempt to preserve history, they're now tenanted by law offices and architectural, public relations, and advertising firms. About the only time you'll see this place hustle anymore is during weekday lunchtime, when all the professionals dash out for a bite.

The **north bank** was originally reserved for colonial administrative buildings, and is today commonly referred to as the **Historic District.** The center point was The Padang, the field on which the Europeans would play sports and hold outdoor ceremonies. Around the field, the Parliament Building, Supreme Court, City Hall, and other municipal buildings sprang up in grand style, and behind these buildings, Government Hill—the present-day **Fort Canning Park**—was the home of the governors. The Esplanade along the waterfront was a center for European social activities and music gatherings, when colonists would don their finest Western styles and walk the park under parasols or cruise in horse-drawn carriages. These days, the Historic District is still the center of most of the government's operations, and close by high-rise hotels and shopping malls have been built. The area on the bank of the river is celebrated as Raffles's landing site.

To the northwest of the Historic District, in the areas along **Orchard Road and Tanglin,** a residential area was created for Europeans and Eurasians. Homes and plantations were eventually replaced by apartment buildings and shops, and in the early 1970s, luxury hotels ushered tourism into the area in full force. In the 1980s, huge shopping malls sprang up along the sides of Orchard Road, turning the landscape into the shopping hub it continues to be. The Tanglin area is home to most of the foreign embassies in Singapore.

The original landscape of **Little India** made it a natural location for an Indian settlement, as the Indians were the original cattle hands and traders in Singapore; the area's natural grasses and springs provided their cattle with food and water, while bamboo groves supplied necessary lumber for their pens. Later, with the establishment of a jail nearby, Indian convict laborers, and the Indian workers who supplied services to them, came to the area for work and ended up staying. Today, while fewer Indians actually reside in this district, Little India is still the heartbeat of Indian culture in Singapore; shops here sell the clothing, cultural, and religious items, and imported goods from "back home" that keep the Indian community linked to their cultural heritage. Although the Indian community in Singapore is a minority in its numbers, you wouldn't think so on Sundays, when all the workers have their day off and come to the streets here to socialize and relax.

Like Little India, the area around **Bugis Street** is adjacent to the Historic District. This neighborhood was originally allocated for the Bugis settlers who came from the island of Celebes, part of Indonesia. The Bugis were welcomed in Singapore, and because they originated from a society based on seafaring and trading, they became master shipbuilders. Today, regrettably, nothing remains of Bugis culture outside of the national museums. In fact, for most locals, Bugis Street is better remembered as a 1970s den of iniquity where transvestites, transsexuals, and other sex performers would stage seedy Bangkok-style shows and beauty contests. The government "cleaned up" Bugis Street in the 1980s, so that all that remains is a huge shopping mall and a sanitized night market.

Kampong Glam, the neighborhood beyond Bugis Street, was given to Sultan Hussein and his family as part of his agreement to turn control of Singapore over to Raffles. Here he built his *istana* (palace) and the Sultan Mosque, and the area subsequently filled with Malay and Arab Muslims who imparted a distinct Islamic flavor to the neighborhood. The presence of the Sultan Mosque assures that area remains a focal point of Singapore Muslim society, but the istana has fallen into disrepair and serves as a sad reminder of the economic condition into which Singapore's Malay community has fallen. **Arab Street** is perhaps

the most popular area attraction for tourists and locals, who come to find deals on textiles and regional crafts.

Two areas of the city center are relatively new, having been built atop huge parcels of reclaimed land. Where the eastern edges of Chinatown and Tanjong Pagar once touched the water's edge, land reclamation created the present-day downtown business district, which is named after its central thoroughfare, **Shenton Way.** This Wall Street–like district is home to the magnificent skyscrapers that grace Singapore's skyline and to the banks and businesses that have made the place an international financial capital. During weekday business hours (9am–5pm), Shenton Way is packed with scurrying businesspeople. After hours and on weekends, it's nothing more than a quiet forest of concrete, metal, and glass.

The other reclaimed area is **Marina Bay,** on the other side of the river, just east of the Historic District. **Suntec City,** Southeast Asia's largest convention and exhibition center, is located here, and has become the linchpin of a thriving hotel, shopping mall, and amusement zone.

OUTSIDE THE URBAN AREA

The heart of the city centers around the Singapore River, but outside the city proper are suburban neighborhoods and rural areas. In the immediate outskirts of the main urban area are the older suburban neighborhoods, such as **Katong, Geyland,** and **Holland Village.** Beyond these are the newer suburbs, called **HDB New Towns.** The HDB, or Housing Development Board, is responsible for creating large towns, such as **Ang Mo Kio** and **Toa Payoh,** each have their own network of supporting businesses: restaurants, schools, shops, health-care facilities, and sometimes department stores.

2 Visitor Information

The long arm of the Singapore Tourism Board (STB) reaches many overseas audiences through its branch offices, which will gladly provide brochures and booklets to help you plan your trip, and through their website, at www.newasia-singapore. com. The STB also has websites with special tips directed specifically for American and Canadian travelers, www.tourismsingapore.com.

3 Entry Requirements & Customs

ENTRY REQUIREMENTS

To enter Singapore, you must have a valid passport. Visitors from the United States, Canada, Australia, New Zealand, and the United Kingdom are not required to obtain a visa prior to their arrival. A Social Visit Pass (with combined social and business status) good for up to 30 days will be awarded upon entry for travelers arriving by plane, or for 14 days if your trip is by ship or overland from Malaysia. Good news for U.S. passport holders: In fall 1999 the United States allowed Singaporeans to travel socially in the United States without a visa, so Singapore has reciprocated by allowing Americans a 90-day social/business-class Social Visit Pass upon entry. Be advised, this and all other types of passes are at the discretion of the Immigration officer, who may not award you the full amount of time. Singapore is trying to cut down on foreigners living here without proper documentation—many make illegal "Visa Runs" to Malaysia to allow them to stay longer in Singapore. However, if this is your first trip to Singapore, you should have no problems.

FOR RESIDENTS OF THE UNITED STATES

If you're applying for a first-time passport, you need to do it in person at a U.S. passport office; a federal, state, or probate court; or a major post office (though not all post offices accept applications; call the number below to find the ones that do). You need to present a certified birth certificate as proof of citizenship, and it's wise to bring along your driver's license, state or military ID, and social security card as well. You also need two identical passport-size photos (2 in. by 2 in.), taken at any corner photo shop (not one of the strip photos, however, from a photo-vending machine).

For people 16 and over, a passport is valid for 10 years and costs $85; for those 15 and under, it's valid for 5 years and costs $70. If you have a valid passport that was issued within the past 15 years (and you were over age 16 when it was issued) and in your current name, you can renew it by mail for $55. Whether you're applying in person or by mail, you can download passport applications from the U.S. State Department website at **http://travel.state.gov**. Allow plenty of time before your trip to apply; processing normally takes 3 weeks but can take longer during busy periods (especially spring). For general information, call the **National Passport Agency** (© 202/647-0518). To find your regional passport office, either check the U.S. State Department website or call the **National Passport Information Center** (© 900/225-5674); the fee is 55¢ per minute for automated information and $1.50 per minute for operator-assisted calls.

American Passport Express (© 800/841-6778; www.american passport.com) will process your first-time passport application for you in 5 to 8 business days for $145, plus a $60 service fee; for renewals, it's $115 plus a $60 service fee. If you need the passport in 3 to 5 business days, the service fee is $100, and for a $150 service fee you can receive your passport in 24 hours.

FOR RESIDENTS OF CANADA

Canadian passports are valid for 5 years and cost $60. Children under 16 may be included on a parent's passport but need their own to travel unaccompanied by the parent. Applications, which must be accompanied by two identical passport-size photographs and proof of Canadian citizenship, are available at passport offices throughout Canada, post offices, or from the central **Passport Office, Department of Foreign Affairs and International Trade,** Ottawa, Ont. K1A 0G3 (© 800/567-6868; www.dfait-maeci.gc.ca/passport). Processing takes 5 to 10 days if you apply in person, or about 3 weeks by mail.

FOR RESIDENTS OF THE UNITED KINGDOM

As a member of the European Union, you need only an identity card, not a passport, to travel to other EU countries. However, if you already possess a passport, it's always useful to carry it. To pick up an application for a regular 10-year passport (the Visitor's Passport has been abolished), visit your nearest passport office, major post office, or travel agency. You can also contact the **United Kingdom Passport Service** at © 0870/571-0410 or search its website at www.ukpa.gov.uk. Passports are £30 for adults and £16 for children under 16.

FOR RESIDENTS OF IRELAND

You can apply for a 10-year passport, costing 57€ at the **Passport Office,** Setanta Centre, Molesworth Street, Dublin 2 (© 01/671-1633; www.irl-gov.ie/iveagh). Those under age 18 and over 65 must apply for a 3-year passport, costing 12€. You can also apply at 1A South Mall, Cork (© 021/272-525) or over the counter at most main post offices.

FOR RESIDENTS OF AUSTRALIA

Apply at your local post office or passport office or search the government website at www.passports.gov.au. Passports cost A$136 for adults and A$68 for those under 18. The **Australia State Passport Office** can be reached at © 131232; travelers must schedule an interview to submit their passport application materials.

FOR RESIDENTS OF NEW ZEALAND

You can pick up a passport application at any travel agency or Link Centre. For more info, contact the **Passport Office,** Dept. of Internal Affairs, P.O. Box 10-526, Wellington (© 0800/225-050; www.passports.govt.nz). Passports are NZ$80 for adults and NZ$40 for those under 16.

VISA INFORMATION

If you overstay your visa, report immediately to the SIR. Even the most conscientious travelers can overstay their visas. At immigration, you'll be asked to hand over your passport, departure record, your airline ticket to prove your return flight, and you'll be asked to write a letter to explain why you did not depart on time. They'll ask you to return the next day to retrieve your documents. In certain cases they may even require that you undergo an interview with an immigration official. If this happens, I strongly recommend that you act very humble, grovel, and beg forgiveness. The minimum fine for overstaying is S$50 (US$29), but the officer can charge you more. Again, it's at his discretion. If you are unfortunate enough to have overstayed for over a month or two, you may be arrested and punished, which means jail time or caning. How about that for a holiday story to take back to your friends?

If you need to replace travel documents while in Singapore, or have other problems, the foreign mission contacts are as follows: **United States,** 27 Napier Rd. (© 65/6476-9100; open Mon–Fri 8:30am–5:15pm); **Canada,** 80 Anson Rd., #14/15-00 IBM Towers (© 65/6325-3240; open Mon–Fri 8:30am–12:30pm and 1:30–4:30pm); **United Kingdom,** Tanglin Road (© 65/6473-9333; open Mon–Fri 8:30am–5pm); **Australia,** 25 Napier Rd. (© 65/6836-4100; open Mon–Fri 8:30am–12:30pm and 1:30–4:30pm); **New Zealand,** 391A Orchard Rd., Ngee Ann City Tower A #15-06 (© 65/6235-9966; open Mon–Fri 8:30am–5pm).

CUSTOMS
WHAT YOU CAN BRING INTO SINGAPORE

There's no restriction on the amount of currency you can bring into Singapore. For those over 18 years of age who have arrived from countries other than Malaysia and have spent more than 48 hours outside Singapore, allowable duty-free concessions are 1 liter of spirits; 1 liter of wine; and 1 liter of either port, sherry, or beer, all of which must be intended for personal consumption only. There are no duty-free concessions on cigarettes or other tobacco items. If you exceed the duty-free limitations, you can bring your excess items in upon payment of goods and services tax (GST) and Customs duty.

Upon departure, you'll be required to pay a **departure tax of S$15.** Nowadays, this tax is usually added onto your airfare. Ask your airline if this is the case. If not, coupons for the amount can be purchased at most hotels, travel agencies, and airline offices.

PROHIBITED ITEMS

The following items are not allowed through Customs unless you have authorization or an import permit: animals; birds and their by-products; plants; endangered species or items made from these species; arms and explosives; bulletproof clothing; toy guns of any type; weapons, including decorative swords and knives; cigarette lighters in the shape of pistols; toy coins; pornographic prerecorded videotapes and cassettes, books, or magazines; controlled substances; poisons; and materials that may be considered treasonable (plutonium, military maps—that kind of thing). For all pharmaceutical drugs, especially sleeping pills, depressants, or stimulants, you must provide a prescription from your physician authorizing personal use for your well-being.

All inquiries can be directed to the **Customs Office** at Changi International Airport (© **65/6542-7058**) or to the automated **Customs hot line** at © **65/6355-2000** (Mon–Fri 8am–5pm, Sat 8am–noon). A detailed rundown can be found on the net at the Ministry of Home Affairs home page www.mha.gov.sg.

If you do try to bring in any of the above articles, they will be confiscated and you will need to defend yourself to the relevant authorities. Pornographic materials will be confiscated, and upon occasion, videotapes will be returned with questionable scenes erased. And—my favorite part—you will be charged a small sum for the "service."

Another tip: You may be carrying items that are perfectly legal elsewhere, but aren't legal here. Keep in mind to report the following items to Customs officers upon entry: any sort of video cassette, decorative weapons (say, if you've bought a lovely antique keris dagger in Malaysia), or pornographic materials. If they find these items on you and you've failed to declare them, you could be punished with a fine. You may be ordered by Customs to unpack your bags to reveal the contents inside. As a leisure traveler, you should rarely have any problems along these lines, but it's always better to be aware. By the way, on a nice note, if you have been asked to empty your cases, the officers are required to help you repack if they're not too busy.

SINGAPORE'S DRUG POLICY

With all of the publicity surrounding the issue, Singapore's strict drug policy shouldn't need recapitulation, but here it is: Importing, selling, or using illegal narcotics is absolutely forbidden. Punishments are severe, up to and including the death penalty (automatic for morphine quantities exceeding 30g, heroin exceeding 15g, cocaine 30g, marijuana 500g, hashish 200g, opium 1.2kg, and methamphetamines 250g). If you're carrying smaller sums (anything above: morphine 3g, heroin 2g, cocaine 3g, marijuana 15g, hashish 10g, opium 100g, and methamphetamines 25g) you'll still be considered to have intent to traffic, and may face the death penalty if you can't prove otherwise. If you're crazy enough to try to bring these things into the country and you are caught, no measure of appeal to your home consulate will grant you any special attention.

It should be noted that even with these drug laws, narcotics abuse still continues in Singapore. Despite aggressive government campaigns to stop drug abuse, casual marijuana consumption continues in underground circles. I also hear many rumors about growing opiate addiction problems, and in recent years there's been trouble among Singaporean youth involving the most recent fashionable drugs, Ecstasy and methamphetamines. Do yourself a favor: If you're in an area

where you suspect illegal drug consumption is taking place, get the hell away from there as fast as you can. Consumption charges include 5 to 30 years imprisonment, up to S$20,000 (US$11,419) fine and caning. Things have become so strict that Singaporeans are even accountable for drug abuses committed overseas—a Singaporean who fails a urine analysis after an overseas trip faces the same penalties as if the offense were committed in the country.

THE TOURIST REFUND SCHEME

Singapore has a great incentive for travelers to drop big bucks: the Tourist Refund Scheme. If you purchase goods at a value of S$300 (US$171) or more at a shop that displays the Tax Free Shopping sign, Customs will reimburse the 3% GST (goods and services tax) you paid for the purchase. You are allowed to pool receipts from different retailers for purchases of S$100 (US$57) or more. Here's how it works: When you purchase the item(s), apply with the retailer for a Tax Free Shopping Check. When you're leaving Singapore, present your Shopping Checks and the items purchased at the Tax Refund Counters located in the Departure Hall at Changi Airport's terminals 1 or 2. Within 12 weeks, you'll receive a check for the GST refund—or, if you used a credit card for the purchase, your bill can be credited (a surcharge may be levied). For more information, contact the **Singapore Tourism Board** at (℗ **800/736-2000.**

WHAT YOU CAN TAKE HOME

Returning **U.S. citizens** who have been away for at least 48 hours are allowed to bring back, once every 30 days, $400 worth of merchandise duty-free. You'll be charged a flat rate of 4% duty on the next $1,000 worth of purchases. Be sure to have your receipts handy. On mailed gifts, the duty-free limit is $100. You cannot bring fresh foodstuffs into the United States; tinned foods, however, are allowed. For more information, contact the **U.S. Customs Service,** 1300 Pennsylvania Ave., NW, Washington, DC 20229 (© **877/287-8867**), and request the free pamphlet *Know Before You Go.* It's also available on the Web at www.customs.gov. (Click on "Traveler Information," then "Know Before You Go.")

For a clear summary of **Canadian** rules, write for the booklet *I Declare,* issued by the **Canada Customs and Revenue Agency** (© **800/461-9999** in Canada, or 204/983-3500; www.ccra-adrc.gc.ca). Canada allows its citizens a C$750 exemption, and you're allowed to bring back duty-free 1 carton of cigarettes, 1 can of tobacco, 40 imperial ounces of liquor, and 50 cigars. In addition, you're allowed to mail gifts to Canada valued at less than C$60 a day, provided they're unsolicited and don't contain alcohol or tobacco (write on the package "Unsolicited gift, under $60 value"). All valuables should be declared on the Y-38 form before departure from Canada, including serial numbers of valuables you already own, such as expensive foreign cameras. *Note:* The $750 exemption can only be used once a year and only after an absence of 7 days.

U.K. citizens returning from a non-EU country have a Customs allowance of 200 cigarettes; 50 cigars; 250g of smoking tobacco; 2 liters of still table wine; 1 liter of spirits or strong liqueurs (over 22% volume); 2 liters of fortified wine, sparkling wine or other liqueurs; 60cc (ml) perfume; 250cc (ml) of toilet water; and £145

worth of all other goods, including gifts and souvenirs. People under 17 cannot have the tobacco or alcohol allowance. For more information, contact **HM Customs & Excise,** Passenger Enquiry Point, 2nd Floor Wayfarer House, Great South West Road, Feltham, Middlesex, TW14 8NP (© **0181/910-3744,** or 44/181-910-3744 outside the U.K.), or consult their website at www.open.gov.uk.

The duty-free allowance in **Australia** is A$400 or, for those under 18, A$200. Upon returning to Australia, citizens can bring in 250 cigarettes or 250g of loose tobacco and 1,125ml of alcohol. If you're returning with valuable goods you already own, such as foreign-made cameras, you should file form B263. For more information, contact **Australian Customs Services,** GPO Box 8, Sydney NSW 2001 (© **02/6275-6666** in Australia, or 202/797-3189 in the U.S.), or go to **www.customs.gov.au**.

The duty-free allowance for **New Zealand** is NZ$700. Citizens over 17 can bring in 200 cigarettes, or 50 cigars, or 250g of tobacco (or a mixture of all three if their combined weight doesn't exceed 250g); plus 4.5 liters of wine and beer, or 1.125 liters of liquor. New Zealand currency does not carry import or export restrictions. Fill out a certificate of export, listing the valuables you are taking out of the country; that way, you can bring them back without paying duty. Most questions are answered in a free pamphlet available at New Zealand consulates and Customs offices: *New Zealand Customs Guide for Travellers, Notice no. 4.* For more information, contact **New Zealand Customs,** 50 Anzac Ave., P.O. Box 29, Auckland (© **09/359-6655**).

4 Money

CURRENCY

The local currency unit is the **Singapore dollar.** It's commonly referred to as the "Sing dollar," and retail prices are often marked as S$ (a designation I've used throughout this book).

Singapore Dollar Conversion Chart

S$	U.S.$	C$	A$	NZ$	U.K.£
.10	$0.06	$0.09	$0.10	$0.12	£0.04
.20	$0.11	$0.18	$0.20	$0.23	£0.07
.50	$0.28	$0.45	$0.51	$0.58	£0.18
1.00	$0.57	$0.89	$1.01	$1.15	£0.36
2.00	$1.14	$1.78	$2.03	$2.30	£0.71
5.00	$2.84	$4.46	$5.06	$5.75	£1.78
10.00	$5.68	$8.91	$10.13	$11.50	£3.57
20.00	$11.36	$17.82	$20.26	$23.00	£7.14
50.00	$28.40	$44.55	$50.65	$57.49	£17.85
100.00	$56.79	$89.10	$101.30	$115.00	£35.70
500.00	$283.97	$445.45	$506.56	$574.95	£178.49
1000.00	$567.96	$890.88	$1013.11	$1,149.78	£356.97

Notes are issued in denominations of S$1, S$2, S$5, S$10, S$50, S$100, S$500, and S$1,000. Notes vary in size and color from denomination to denomination. Coins are issued in denominations of S1¢, S5¢, S10¢, S20¢, S50¢, and the fat, gold-colored S$1. Singapore has an interchange-ability agreement with Brunei, so the Brunei dollar is accepted as equal to the Singapore dollar.

Singapore's currency weathered the Southeast Asian economic crisis in 1997 rather successfully, so if you were hoping for a more favorable exchange rate, you're looking in the wrong place; the Sing dollar has decreased in value only slightly from precrisis rates. At the time of this writing, exchange rates on the Singapore dollar were as follows: US$1 = S$1.76, C$1 = S$1.12, £1 = S$2.80, A$1 = S$.99, NZ$1 = S87¢. The exchange rate used throughout this book is US$1 = S$1.75, to use an average figure, but before you begin budgeting your trip, I suggest you obtain the latest conversions so you don't suffer any shocks at the last minute. A neat and easy customizable currency conversion program can be found on the Internet through www.xe.com.

While hotels and banks will perform currency exchanges, you'll get a better rate at any one of the many money changers that can be found in all the shopping malls and major shopping districts (look for the certificate of government authorization). Many shops are also authorized to change money, and will display signs to that effect. Money changers usually give you the official going rate for the day, and sometimes the difference in rate between hotels and money changers can be as much as US8¢ to the dollar. Last, while some hotels and shops may accept your foreign currency as payment, they will always calculate the exchange rate in their favor.

It's a good idea to exchange at least some money—just enough to cover airport incidentals and transportation to your hotel—before you leave home, so you can avoid the less-favorable rates you'll get at airport currency exchange desks. Check with you local American Express or Thomas Cook office or your bank. **American Express** cardholders can order foreign currency over the phone at ℂ **800/807-6233.**

It's best to exchange currency or traveler's checks at a bank, not a currency exchange, hotel, or shop.

What Things Cost in Singapore	S$	US$
Taxi from the airport to city center	S$22	US$12
MRT from Orchard to Chinese Garden stations	S$1.40	US$.80
Local telephone call (3 min.)	S10¢	US$.06
Double room at an expensive hotel	S$350	US$200
Double room at a moderate hotel	S$250	US$143
Double room at an inexpensive hotel	S$120	US$68
Dinner for one at an expensive restaurant	S$60	US$34
Dinner for one at a moderate restaurant	S$25	US$14
Dinner for one at an inexpensive restaurant	S$5	US$3
Glass of beer	S$9	US$5
Coca-Cola	S$1.10	US$0.63
Cup of coffee at common coffee shop	S70¢	US$40
Cup of coffee at Starbucks, Coffee Club, and so on	S$2.80	US$1.60
Roll of 36-exposure color film	S$4.50	US$2.60
Admission to the National History Museum	S$3	US$1.70
Movie ticket	S$9	US$5

ATMS

ATMs are linked to a network that most likely includes your bank at home. **Cirrus** (© **800/424-7787;** www.mastercard.com) and **PLUS** (© **800/843-7587;** www.visa.com) are the two most popular networks in the U.S.; call or check online for ATM locations at your destination. Be sure you know your four-digit PIN before you leave home and be sure to find out your daily withdrawal limit before you depart. You can also get cash advances on your credit card at an ATM. Keep in mind that credit card companies try to protect themselves from theft by limiting the funds someone can withdraw away from home. It's therefore best to call your credit card company before you leave and let them know where you're going and how much you plan to spend. You'll get the best exchange rate if you withdraw money from an ATM, but keep in mind that many banks impose a fee every time a card is used at an ATM in a different city or bank. On top of this, the bank from which you withdraw cash may charge its own fee.

Singapore has thousands of conveniently located 24-hour ATMs. Whether you're in your hotel, a shopping mall, or a suburban neighborhood, I'd be surprised if you're more than 1 or 2 blocks from an ATM—ask your concierge or any passerby and they can direct you. With debit cards on the MasterCard/Cirrus or Visa/PLUS systems, you can withdraw Singapore currency from any of these machines, and your bank will deduct the amount from your account at that day's official exchange rate. This is a very good way to access cash for the most favorable currency rate, but make sure you check with your bank before you leave home, to find out what your daily withdrawal limits are. It's also a good idea to keep track of ATM charges—your home financial institution can levy a fee of up to US$1.50 per transaction for this convenience, and rumor has it Singapore banks will be charging a fee as well.

TRAVELER'S CHECKS

Traveler's checks are something of an anachronism from the days before the ATM made cash accessible at any time. Traveler's checks used to be the only sound alternative to traveling with dangerously large amounts of cash. They were as reliable as currency, but, unlike cash, could be replaced if lost or stolen.

These days, traveler's checks seem less necessary because most cities have 24-hour ATMs that allow you to withdraw small amounts of cash as needed. However, keep in mind that you will likely be charged an ATM withdrawal fee if the bank is not your own, so if you're withdrawing money every day, you might be better off with traveler's checks—provided that you don't mind showing identification every time you want to cash one.

You can get traveler's checks at almost any bank. **American Express** offers denominations of $20, $50, $100, $500, and (for cardholders only) $1,000. You'll pay a service charge ranging from 1% to 4%. You can also get American Express traveler's checks over the phone by calling © **800/221-7282;** Amex gold and platinum cardholders who use this number are exempt from the 1% fee. AAA members can obtain checks without a fee at most AAA offices.

Visa offers traveler's checks at Citibank locations nationwide, as well as at several other banks. The service charge ranges between 1.5% and 2%;

checks come in denominations of $20, $50, $100, $500, and $1,000. Call © **800/732-1322** for information. **MasterCard** also offers traveler's checks. Call © **800/223-9920** for a location near you.

CREDIT CARDS

Credit cards are invaluable when traveling. They are a safe way to carry money and provide a convenient record of all your expenses. You can also withdraw cash advances from your credit cards at any bank (though you'll start paying hefty interest on the advance the moment you receive the cash.) At most banks, you don't even need to go to a teller; you can get a cash advance at the ATM if you know your PIN. If you've forgotten yours, or didn't even know you had one, call the number on the back of your credit card and ask the bank to send it to you. It usually takes 5 to 7 business days, though some banks will provide the number over the phone if you tell them your mother's maiden name or pass some other security clearance. Keep in mind, though, that your credit card company will likely charge a commission (1% or 2%) on every foreign purchase you make.

American Express (AE) is accepted widely, as are Diners Club (DC), MasterCard (MC), Japan Credit Bank (JCB), and Visa (V), though you'll find that some budget hotels, smaller shops, and restaurants will accept no credit cards at all. Purchases made with credit cards will appear on your bill at the exchange rate on the day your charge is posted, not what the rate was on the day the purchase was

---

(*Tips* **Small Change**

When you change money, ask for some small bills or loose change. Petty cash will come in handy for tipping and public transportation. Consider keeping the change separate from your larger bills, so it's readily accessible and you'll be less of a target for theft.

made. It's also worth noting that if your signature is slightly different on the slip than it is on your card, shop owners will make you redo the slip. They're real sticklers for signature details, so don't leave out a middle initial or forget to cross a T.

WHAT TO DO IF YOUR WALLET GETS STOLEN

Be sure to block charges against your account the minute you discover a credit card has been lost or stolen. Then be sure to file a police report.

Almost every credit card company has an emergency 800-number to call if your card is stolen. They may be able to wire you a cash advance off your credit card immediately, and in many places, they can deliver an emergency credit card in a day or two. The issuing bank's 800-number is usually on the back of your credit card—though of course, if your card has been stolen, that won't help you unless you recorded the number elsewhere.

Citicorp Visa's U.S. emergency number is ✆ **800/336-8472,** or for **Visa**'s Emergency Assistance in Singapore call ✆ **65/6435-1345. American Express** cardholders and traveler's check holders should call the Singapore office at ✆ **65/6880-1333** (✆ 800/221-7282 in the U.S.). **MasterCard** holders should call ✆ **65/ 6538-4833** (✆ 800/307-7309 in the

U.S) to reach their Global Service Emergency Assistance for International Travelers. Otherwise, call the toll-free number directory at ✆ 800/ 555-1212.

Odds are that if your wallet is gone, the police won't be able to recover it for you. However, it's still worth informing the authorities. Your credit card company or insurer may require a police report number or record of the theft.

If you choose to carry traveler's checks, be sure to keep a record of their serial numbers separate from your checks. You'll get a refund faster if you know the numbers.

If you need emergency cash over the weekend when all banks and American Express offices are closed, you can have money wired to you from **Western Union** (✆ **800/325-6000;** www.westernunion.com). You must present valid ID to pick up the cash at the Western Union office. However, in most countries, you can pick up a money transfer even if you don't have valid identification, as long as you can answer a test question provided by the sender. Be sure to let the sender know in advance that you don't have ID. If you need to use a test question instead of ID, the sender must take cash to his or her local Western Union office, rather than transferring the money over the phone or online.

5 When to Go

The busy season is from January to June. In the late summer months, business travel dies down, and in fall, even tourism drops off somewhat, making the season ripe for budget-minded visitors. These may be the best times to get a deal. Probably the worst time to negotiate will be between Christmas and the Chinese New Year.

CLIMATE

At approximately 137km (82 miles) north of the equator, with exposure to

the sea on three sides, it's a sure bet that Singapore will be hot and humid year-round. Temperatures remain uniform, with a daily average of 81°F (27°C), afternoon temperatures reaching as high as 87°F (31°C), and an average sunrise temperature as low as 75.03°F (23.9°C). Relative humidity often exceeds 90% at night and in the early morning. Even on a "dry" afternoon, don't expect it to drop much below 60%. (The daily average is 84°

relative humidity.) Rain falls year-round, much of it coming down in sudden downpours that end abruptly and are followed immediately by the sun.

The Northeast Monsoon occurs between December and March, when temperatures are slightly cooler, relatively speaking, than other times of the year. The heaviest rainfall occurs between November and January, with daily showers that sometimes last for long periods of time; at other times, it comes down in short heavy gusts and goes quickly away. Wind speeds are rarely anything more than light. The Southwest Monsoon falls between June and September. Temperatures are higher and, interestingly, it's during this time of year that Singapore gets the *least* rain (with the very least reported in July).

In between monsoons, thunder-storms are frequent. Also interesting, the number of daylight hours and number of nighttime hours remains almost constant year-round. February is the sunniest month, while December is generally more overcast.

HOLIDAYS

There are 11 official public holidays: New Year's Day, Chinese New Year or Lunar New Year (2 days), Hari Raya Puasa, Good Friday, Hari Raya Haji, Labour Day, Vesak Day, National Day, Deepavali, and Christmas Day. On these days, expect government offices, banks, and some shops to be closed.

Holidays and festivals are well pub-licized by the **Singapore Tourism Board (STB),** which loves to introduce the world to the joys of all Singapore's cultures. As with any schedule of upcoming events, the following information is subject to change; always confirm the details before you plan you trip around an event. A call or visit to an STB office either before your trip or once you arrive will let

you know the what, where, and when of all that's happening during your stay. See the listing of STB offices in the United States, Canada, the United Kingdom, and Australia under "Visitor Information," earlier in this chapter. Its website at www.newasia-singapore.com also has information about upcoming holidays and festivals.

CALENDAR OF PUBLIC HOLIDAYS & EVENTS
January/February

New Year's Day. The first day of the calendar year is celebrated in Singapore by all races and religions. New Year's Eve in Singapore is always cause for parties and celebrations similar to those in the West. Look for special events and parties at restaurants and nightclubs, but don't expect to find a lot of taxis around when you need one! January 1.

Lunar New Year or Chinese New Year. If you want to catch the biggest event in the Chinese calendar and pretty much the biggest in Singapore, come during the Chinese New Year celebrations, which include parades and festivals. Two days, late January/early February.

Thaipusam Festival. If you're lucky enough to be in Singapore during this event, you're in for a bizarre cultural treat. This annual festival is celebrated by Hindus to give thanks to Lord Subramaniam, the child god who represents virtue, youth, beauty, and valor. During Thaipusam, male Hindus who have made prayers to Subramaniam for special wishes must carry kavadis in gratitude. These huge steel racks are decorated with flowers and fruits and are held onto the men's bodies by skewers and hooks that pierce the skin. Carrying the kavadis, the devotees parade from Sri Perumal

Temple in Little India to Chettiar's Temple on Tank Road, where family members remove the heavy structures. For an additional spectacle, they will pierce their tongues and cheeks with skewers and hang fruits from hooks in their flesh. The devotees have all undergone strict diet and prayer before the festival, and it is reported that, afterward, no scars remain. Late January/early February.

Hari Raya Puasa. Hari Raya Puasa marks the end of Ramadan, the Muslim month of fasting during daylight hours. During Ramadan, food stalls line up around the Sultan Mosque in Kampong Glam, ready to sell Malay and Indian food at sundown. It's a 3-day celebration (though only the 1st day is a public holiday) of thanksgiving dinners, and non-Muslims are often invited to these feasts, as the holiday symbolizes an openness of heart and mind and a renewed sense of community. During the course of the three evenings, Geylang—the neighborhood centered around Geylang Road—is decorated with lights and banners and the whole area is open for a giant pasar malam, or night market. Late January/early February.

March/April

Good Friday. Churches and cathedrals hold special services on this Christian holiday to remember the crucifixion of Christ. St. Joseph's on Victoria Street holds an annual candlelight procession. Late March/early April.

Qing Ming (All Souls' Day). Qing Ming, or All Souls' Day, was originally a celebration of spring. On this day, Chinese families have picnics at ancestral graves, cleaning the graves and pulling weeds, lighting red candles, burning joss sticks and "Hell Money" (paper money whose smoke rises to the afterworld to be used by the ancestors), and bringing rice, wine, and flowers for the deceased in a show of ancestral piety. Early April.

The Singapore International Film Festival. This event showcases critically acclaimed works, including international films and Singaporean short productions. The year 1999 marked the 12th year this event has taken place—it's become a renowned showcase for Asian films, which constitute 40% of those featured. The festival includes competitions, workshops, and tributes to filmmakers. Information can be obtained from its website at www.filmfest.org.sg. You can order tickets through TicketCharge over the phone by calling ✆ **65/6296-2929,** via their website at www.ticketcharge.com.sg, or at many locations throughout the city. See "The Performing Arts" section in chapter 7 for exact locations. April.

Hari Raya Haji. One of the five pillars of Islam involves making a pilgrimage to Mecca at least once in a lifetime, and Hari Raya Haji is celebrated the day after pilgrims make this annual voyage to fulfill their spiritual promise. Muslims who have made the journey adopt the title of Haji (for men) and Hajjah (for women). After morning prayers, sheep and goats are sacrificed and their meat is distributed to poor families. Late April/early May.

May

Vesak Day. Buddhist shrines and temples are adorned with banners, lights, and flowers and worshippers gather to pray and chant in observance of the birth, enlightenment, and death of the Buddha, which all occurred on this day. Good places to watch the festivities, unless you're afraid of crowds, are the

Temple of a Thousand Lights in Little India or Thian Hock Keng Temple in Chinatown. On this day, Buddhists will refrain from eating meat, donate food to the poor, and set animals (especially birds) free to show kindness and generosity. It falls on the full moon of the fifth month of the lunar calendar—which means somewhere around mid-May.

June

Singapore Arts Festival. During this monthlong festival, first-class local, regional, and international music and dance performances are staged in a number of venues. The cultural performances, some modern and some traditional, are always excellent and are highly recommended. Contact the STB for a full program with details of each event, or check out www.singaporeartsfest. com. June.

Singapore World Invitational Dragon Boat Races. The annual dragon boat races are held to remember the fate of Qu Yuan, a patriot and poet during the Warring States period in Chinese history (475–221 B.C.), who threw himself into a river to end his suffering at watching his state fall into ruin under the hands of corrupt leadership. The people searched for him in boats shaped like dragons, beating gongs and throwing rice dumplings into the water to distract the River Dragon. Today, the dragon boat races are an international event, with rowing teams from 20 countries coming together to compete. Drums are still beaten, and rice dumplings are still a traditional favorite. Contact the STB for information. Late June/early July.

July

The Singapore Food Festival. Local chefs compete for honors in this monthlong exhibition of international culinary delights. It's a good time to be eating in Singapore, as restaurants feature the brand-new creations they have entered in the events. Contact the STB for details. July.

The Great Singapore Sale. This is a monthlong promotion to increase retail sales, and most shops will advertise huge savings for the entire month. It's well publicized with red banners all over Orchard Road. July.

Maulidin Nabi. Muslims celebrate the birth of the Prophet Mohammed on this day. Sultan Mosque is the center of the action for Muslims who come to chant in praise. July 17.

August

National Day. On August 9, 1965, Singapore separated from the Federation of Malaysia, becoming an independent republic. Singaporeans celebrate this as a sort of independence day, with a grand parade with spectacular floats and marching bands. They also stage a fireworks display in the evening. August 9.

Festival of the Hungry Ghosts. The Chinese believe that once a year the gates of purgatory are opened and all the souls inside are let loose to wander among the living. These are the poor souls who either died violent deaths or whose families failed to pay them respects after they died—fates that cause them to menace people as much as they can. To appease the spirits and prevent evil from falling upon themselves, the Chinese burn joss, Hell money, and paper replicas of luxury items, the latter two meant to appear in the afterworld for greedy ghosts to use. The main celebration is on the 15th day of the 7th month of the lunar calendar, and is celebrated with huge feasts to settle hungry ghosts. At markets, altars are placed under tents. Chinese operas are performed throughout the month to entertain the spirits and make them more docile. For information on these performances, call the **Chinese Theatre Circle,** 5 Smith St. (© **65/323-4862**). They perform excerpts from classic operas every Wednesday and Friday evenings year-round at Clarke Quay (see chapter 7 for more details), but may stage special full-length operas for the occasion. You can also try the STB, which will tell you if there are any visiting operas performing around the city.

September

The Mooncake and Lantern Festivals. Traditionally called the midautumn festival, it was celebrated to give thanks for a plentiful harvest. The origins date from the Sung Dynasty (A.D. 970–1279) when Chinese officials would exchange round mirrors as gifts to represent the moon and symbolize good health and success. Today, the holiday is celebrated by eating moon cakes, which are sort of like little round hockey pucks filled with lotus seeds or red bean paste and a salted duck egg yolk. Children light colorful plastic or paper lanterns shaped like fish, birds, butterflies, and, more recently, cartoon characters. There's an annual lantern display and competition out at the Chinese Garden, with acrobatic performances, lion dances, and night bazaars. Late September/early October.

Birthday of the Monkey God. In the Chinese temples ceremonies are performed by mediums who pierce their faces and tongues and write prayers with the blood. In the temple courtyards you can see Chinese operas and puppet shows. The Tan Si Chong Su Temple on Magazine Road, upriver from Boat Quay, is a good bet for seeing the ceremonies. Contact the STB for information. Late September/early October.

October/November

Pilgrimage to Kusu Island. During this monthlong period, plan your trips to Kusu Island wisely, as the place becomes a mob scene. Throughout the month (the lunar month, that is), Chinese travel to this small island to visit the temple there and pray for another year of health and wealth. See chapter 5 for more information on Kusu. October/November.

Festival of the Nine-Emperor God. During this celebration, held over the first 9 days of the ninth month of the lunar calendar (to the Chinese, the double nines are particularly auspicious), temples are packed with worshippers, hawkers sell religious items outside, and Chinese operas are performed for the Nine-Emperor God, a composite of nine former emperors who control the prosperity and health of worshippers. At the height of the festival, priests write prayers with their own blood. On the ninth day, the festival closes as the Nine-Emperor God's spirit, contained in an urn, is sent to sea on a small decorated boat. Contact the STB for information. Late October.

Navarathiri Festival. During this 9-day festival, Hindus make offerings to the wives of Shiva, Vishnu, and Brahma. The center point in the evenings is Chettiar's Temple (at 15 Tank Rd.), where dances and musical performances are staged. Performances begin around 7:30pm. Contact the STB for information. Late October/early November.

Deepavali. Hindus and Sikhs celebrate Deepavali as the first day of their calendar. The new year is ushered in with new clothing, social feasts, and gatherings. It's a beautiful holiday, with Hindu temples aglow from the tiny earthen candles placed in cutouts up the sides of the buildings. Hindus believe that the souls of the deceased come to earth during this time, and the candles help to light their way back to heaven. During the celebration, Serangoon Road in Little India is a crazy display of colored lights and decorative arches. Children love this holiday, as it is customary to hand out sweets, especially to the little ones, and many businesspeople choose this time to close their books from the year's accounts and start afresh. Late October/early November.

Thimithi Festival. Thimithi begins at the Sri Perumal Temple in Little India and makes its way in parade fashion to the Sri Mariamman Temple in Chinatown. Outside the temple, a bed of hot coals is prepared and a priest will lead the way, walking first over the coals, to be followed one at a time by devotees. Crowds gather to watch the spectacle, which begins around 5pm. Make sure you're early so you can find a good spot. Contact the STB for information.

Christmas Light-Up. Orchard Road is brilliant in bright and colorful streams of Christmas lights and garlands. All of the hotels and shopping malls participate, dressed in the usual Christmas regalia of nativity scenes and Santa Clauses. November 15 through January 2.

December

Christmas Day. On this day, Christian Singaporeans celebrate the birth of Christ. December 25.

6 Insurance, Health & Safety

TRAVEL INSURANCE AT A GLANCE

Check your existing insurance policies before you buy travel insurance to cover trip cancellation, lost luggage, medical expenses, or car-rental insurance. You're likely to have partial or complete coverage. But if you need some, ask your travel agent about a comprehensive package. The cost of travel insurance varies widely, depending on the cost and length of your trip, your age and overall health, and the type of trip you're taking. Insurance for extreme sports or adventure travel, for example, will cost more than coverage for a cruise. Some insurers provide packages for specialty vacations, such as skiing or backpacking. More dangerous activities may be excluded from basic policies.

And keep in mind that in the aftermath of the September 11, 2001 terrorist attacks, a number of airlines, cruise lines, and tour operators are no longer covered by insurers. *The bottom line:* Always, always check the fine print before you sign on; more and more policies have built-in exclusions and restrictions that may leave you out in the cold if something does go awry.

For information, contact one of the following popular insurers:

- **Access America** (© 800/284-8300; www.accessamerica.com)
- **Travel Guard International** (© 800/826-1300; www.travelguard.com)
- **Travel Insured International** (© 800/243-3174; www.travelinsured.com)
- **Travelex Insurance Services** (© 800/228-9792; www.travelexinsurance.com)

TRIP-CANCELLATION INSURANCE (TCI)

There are three major types of trip-cancellation insurance—one, in the

---

> **Tips** **Travel Warning**
>
> Under U.S. law, insurance companies are not required to cover any medical expenses incurred in countries on the **State Department's Travel Advisory List,** even if their policies indicate they will over out-of-country medical expenses. Some supplemental carriers (such as the ones listed in this chapter) will sell travelers coverage for these areas. You can view the Travel Advisory List at http://travel.state.gov/warnings_list.html).

---

event that you prepay a cruise or tour that gets cancelled, and you can't get your money back; a second when you or someone in your family gets sick or dies, and you can't travel (but beware that you may not be covered for a pre-existing condition); and a third, when bad weather makes travel impossible. Some insurers provide coverage for events like jury duty; natural disasters close to home, like floods or fire; even the loss of a job. A few have added provisions for cancellations due to terrorist activities. Always check the fine print before signing on, and don't buy trip-cancellation insurance from the tour operator that may be responsible for the cancellation; buy it only from a reputable travel insurance agency. Don't overbuy. You won't be reimbursed for more than the cost of your trip.

MEDICAL INSURANCE

Most health insurance policies cover you if you get sick away from home—but check, particularly if you're insured by an HMO. With the exception of certain HMOs and Medicare/Medic-aid, your medical insurance should cover medical treatment—even hospital care—overseas. However, most out-of-country hospitals make you pay your bills up front, and send you a refund after you've returned home and filed the necessary paperwork. Members of **Blue Cross/Blue Shield** can now use their cards at select hospitals in most major cities worldwide (© **800/810-BLUE** or www.blue-cares.com for a list of hospitals).

Some credit cards (American Express and certain gold and platinum Visa and MasterCards, for example) offer automatic flight insurance against death or dismemberment in case of an airplane crash if you charged the cost of your ticket.

If you require additional insurance, try one of the following companies:

- **MEDEX International,** 9515 Deereco Rd., Timonium, MD 21093-5375 (© **888/MEDEX-00** or 410/453-6300; fax 410/453-6301; www.medexassist.com)
- **Travel Assistance International** (© **800/821-2828;** www.travelassistance.com), 9200 Keystone Crossing, Suite 300, Indianapolis, IN 46240 (for general information on services, call the company's Worldwide Assistance Services, Inc., at © **800777-8710**).
- Only for diving destinations: **The Divers Alert Network** (DAN) (© **800/446-2671** or 919/684-8181; www.diversalertnetwork.org).

The cost of travel medical insurance varies widely. Check your existing policies before you buy additional coverage. Also, check to see if your medical insurance covers you for emergency medical evacuation: If you have to buy a one-way same-day ticket home and forfeit your nonrefundable round-trip ticket, you may be out big bucks.

LOST-LUGGAGE INSURANCE

On domestic flights, checked baggage is covered up to $2,500 per ticketed passenger. On international flights (including U.S. portions of international trips), baggage is limited to approximately $9.05 per pound, up to approximately $635 per checked bag. If you plan to check items more valuable than the standard liability, you may purchase "excess valuation" coverage from the airline, up to $5,000. Be sure to take any valuables or irreplaceable items with you in your carry-on luggage. If you file a lost luggage claim, be prepared to answer detailed questions about the contents of your baggage, and be sure to file a claim immediately, as most airlines enforce a 21-day deadline. Before you leave home, compile an inventory of all packed items and a rough estimate of the total value to ensure you're properly compensated if your luggage is lost. You will only be reimbursed for what you lost, no more. Once you've filed a complaint, persist in securing your reimbursement; there are no laws governing the length of time it takes for a carrier to reimburse you. If you arrive at a destination without your bags, ask the airline to forward them to your hotel or to your next destination; they will usually comply. If your bag is delayed or lost, the airline may reimburse you for reasonable expenses, such as a toothbrush or a set of clothes, but the airline is under no legal obligation to do so.

Lost luggage may also be covered by your homeowner's or renter's policy. Many platinum and gold credit cards cover you as well. If you choose to purchase additional lost-luggage insurance, be sure not to buy more than you need. Buy in advance from the insurer or a trusted agent (prices will be much higher at the airport).

CAR-RENTAL INSURANCE (LOSS/DAMAGE WAIVER OR COLLISION DAMAGE WAIVER)

If you hold a private auto insurance policy, you probably are covered in the U.S., but not abroad, for loss or damage to the car, and liability in case a passenger is injured. The credit card you used to rent the car also may provide some coverage.

Car-rental insurance probably does not cover liability if you caused the accident. Check your own auto insurance policy, the rental company policy, and your credit card coverage for the extent of coverage: Is your destination covered? Are other drivers covered? How much liability is covered if a passenger is injured? (If you rely on your credit card for coverage, you may want to bring a second credit card with you, as damages may be charged to your card and you may find yourself stranded with no money.)

Car-rental insurance costs about $20 a day.

THE HEALTHY TRAVELER

BEATING THE HEAT & HUMIDITY As Singapore's climate guarantees heat and humidity year-round, you should remember to take precautions. Make sure you give yourself plenty of time to relax and regroup on arrival to adjust your body to the new climate (and to the new time, if there is a time difference for you). Also, drink plenty of water. This may seem obvious, but remember that tea, coffee, colas, and alcohol dehydrate the body and should never be substituted for water if you're thirsty. Singapore's tap water is absolutely potable, so you don't have to worry about any wee beasties floating around in your glass.

Avoid overexposure to the sun. The tropical sun will burn you like thin toast in no time at all. You may also feel more lethargic than usual. This is typical in the heat, so take things easy and you'll be fine. Be careful of the air-conditioning, though. It's nice and cooling, but if you're prone to catching a chill, or find yourself moving in and out of air-conditioned buildings a lot, you can wind up with a horrible summer cold.

DIETARY PRECAUTIONS Generally speaking, you'll have no more problems with the food in Singapore than you will in your hometown, barring any digestive problems you may experience simply because you're not used to the ingredients. All the same sanitary rules apply, too—for instance, as at home, you should thoroughly wash the fruits or vegetables you buy, to rinse away any bacteria and pesticides.

Chinese restaurants in Singapore still use monosodium glutamate (MSG), the flavor enhancer that was blamed for everything from fluid retention to migraine headaches, and has been squeezed out of most Chinese restaurant cuisine in the West. The MSG connection has just started to catch on here, but not in full force. Many restaurants can now prepare dishes without MSG upon request, but smaller places will probably think you're insane for asking.

DISEASES Singapore doesn't require that you have any vaccinations to enter the country, but strongly recommends immunization against diphtheria, tetanus, hepatitis A and B, and typhoid. If you're particularly worried, follow their advice; if you're the intrepid type, ignore it.

While there's no risk of contracting malaria (the country's been declared malaria-free for decades by the World Health Organization), there is a similar deadly virus, dengue fever (also just called dengue), that's carried by mosquitoes and has no immunization. Dengue fever is a problem in the tropics around the world; however, Singapore has an aggressive campaign to prevent the responsible mosquitoes from breeding, spraying dark corners with insecticide and enforcing laws so people mop up pools of stagnant water. Symptoms of dengue fever include sudden fever and tiny red spotty rashes on the body. If you suspect you've contracted dengue, seek medical attention immediately (see the listing of hospitals under "Fast Facts," later in this chapter). If left untreated, this disease can cause internal hemorrhaging and even death. Your best protection is to wear insect repellent, especially if you're heading out to the zoo, bird park, or any of the gardens or nature preserves.

DANGEROUS ANIMALS & PLANTS Singapore has a whole slew of snakes, and they're not only in the deepest, darkest parts of the island—sometimes they're forced from their homes by construction and left to look for trouble in more populated areas. The venomous kinds are cobras, kraits, coral snakes, pit vipers, and sea snakes. If you encounter a sea snake, don't splash around, as this will just encourage an attack.

If you're bitten by a snake, keep yourself calm, try to position the wounded area below the level of your heart, and wrap a tourniquet loosely above the wound (but not on a joint). Don't take any aspirin or other medications unless it's an over-the-counter pain reliever that doesn't contain aspirin. There are only two facilities in Singapore with snake antivenin: **Singapore General Hospital,** Outram Road (© **65/6222-3322**), and **National University Hospital,** 5 Lower Kent Ridge Rd. (© **65/6779-5555**).

Dangerous insects are scorpions, spiders, centipedes, bees, and wasps. If stung, wash the area with disinfectant and apply ice to reduce the pain and prevent the venom from being absorbed further. If you have an allergic reaction, seek medical help.

There are a lot of plants in Singapore that have poisonous parts. Some of the more common ones are common bamboo, arcea palm, frangipani, mango tree, papaya, and tapioca. Only parts of these plants are poisonous. If you're unsure, just don't nibble on anything strange.

WHAT TO DO IF YOU GET SICK AWAY FROM HOME

If you worry about getting sick away from home, consider purchasing

medical travel insurance and carry your ID card in your purse or wallet. In most cases, your existing health plan will provide the coverage you need. See the section on insurance earlier in this chapter for more information.

If you suffer from a chronic illness, consult your doctor before your departure. For conditions like epilepsy, diabetes, or heart problems, wear a **Medic Alert Identification Tag** (© **800/825-3785;** www.medicalert.org), which will immediately alert doctors to your condition and give them access to your records through Medic Alert's 24-hour hot line.

Pack **prescription medications** in your carry-on luggage, and carry prescription medications in their original containers. Also bring along copies of your prescriptions in case you lose your pills or run out. Carry the generic name of prescription medicines, in case a local pharmacist is unfamiliar with the brand name.

And don't forget sunglasses and an extra pair of contact lenses or prescription glasses.

Contact the **International Association for Medical Assistance to Travelers (IAMAT)** (© **716/754-4883** or 416/652-0137; www.iamat.org) for tips on travel and health concerns in the countries you're visiting, and lists of local, English-speaking doctors. The United States **Centers for Disease Control and Prevention** (© **800/311-3435;** www.cdc.gov) provides up-to-date information on necessary vaccines and health hazards by region or country (Their booklet, *Health Information for International Travel,* is $25 by mail; on the Internet, it's free). Any foreign consulate can provide a list of area doctors who speak English. If you get sick, consider asking your hotel concierge to recommend a local doctor—even his or her own. You can also try the emergency room at a local hospital; many have walk-in clinics for emergency cases that are not life threatening. You may not get immediate attention, but you won't pay the high price of an emergency room visit (usually a minimum of $300 just for signing your name).

THE SAFE TRAVELER   Singapore is a pretty safe place by any standards. There's very little violent crime, even late at night. If you stay out, there's very little worry about making it home safe. If your children are missing, they probably aren't kidnapped, but are being consoled by a friendly passerby while you search for them. This may sound naive, but the Chinese are culturally a very family-oriented people, and most would never dream of harming a child.

In recent years, some pickpocketing has been reported. Hotel safe-deposit boxes are the best way to secure valuables, and traveler's checks solve theft problems in a jiff.

Before you go, always check the U.S. State department website to see if any warnings have been issued in this region: http://travel.state.gov/travel_warnings.html.

7 Tips for Travelers with Special Needs

TRAVELERS WITH DISABILITIES

Most disabilities shouldn't stop anyone from traveling. There are more options and resources out there than ever before.

There's a handy free guide called *The Access Singapore Physically Disabled Person's Guide to Accessible Places,* put together by the Singapore Council of Social Services, with charts to rate accessibility features of hotels, airports, places of interest, shops, and public buildings. It's published on the Net at www.dpa.org.sg/DPA/access/contents.htm.

Most hotels have accessible rooms, and some cab companies offer special van services. I've found most of the newer buildings are constructed with access ramps for wheelchairs, but older buildings are very problematic, especially the shophouses, with narrow sidewalks and many uneven steps.

AGENCIES/OPERATORS

- **Flying Wheels Travel** (© 507/451-5005; www.flyingwheels travel.com) offers escorted tours and cruises that emphasize sports and private tours in minivans with lifts.
- **Access Adventures** (© 716/889-9096), a Rochester, New York–based agency, offers customized itineraries for a variety of travelers with disabilities.
- **Accessible Journeys** (© 800/TINGLES** or 610/521-0339; www.disabilitytravel.com) caters specifically to slow walkers and wheelchair travelers and their families and friends.

ORGANIZATIONS

- **The Moss Rehab Hospital** (© 215/456-9603; www.moss resourcenet.org) provides friendly, helpful phone assistance through its **Travel Information Service.**
- **The Society for Accessible Travel and Hospitality** (© 212/447-7284; fax 212/725-8253; www.sath.org) offers a wealth of travel resources for all types of disabilities and informed recommendations on destinations, access guides, travel agents, tour operators, vehicle rentals, and companion services. Annual membership costs $45 for adults; $30 for seniors and students.
- **The American Foundation for the Blind** (© 800/232-5463; www.afb.org) provides information on traveling with Seeing Eye dogs.

PUBLICATIONS

- **Mobility International USA** (© 541/343-1284; www.miusa.org) publishes *A World of Options,* a 658-page book of resources, covering everything from biking trips to scuba outfitters, and a biannual newsletter, *Over the Rainbow.* Annual membership is $35.
- **Twin Peaks Press** (© 360/694-2462) publishes travel-related books for travelers with special needs.
- *Open World for Disability and Mature Travel* magazine, published by the Society for Accessible Travel and Hospitality (see above), is full of good resources and information. A year's subscription is $13 ($21 outside the U.S.).

GAY & LESBIAN TRAVELERS

In a highly publicized December 11, 1998, interview on CNN, Senior Minister Lee Kuan Yew was asked by an anonymous caller about the future of gays in Singapore. The senior minister responded, "Well, it's not a matter which I can decide or any government can decide. It's a question of what a society considers acceptable. And as you know, Singaporeans are by and large a very conservative, orthodox society . . . I would say, completely different from . . . the United Sates and I don't think an aggressive gay rights movement would help. But what we are doing as a government is to leave people to live their own lives as long as they don't impinge on other people. I mean, we don't harass anybody." Naturally, the conservative government doesn't support such alternative lifestyles; however, gay and lesbian culture is alive and well in Singapore. What you'll find is that older gays and lesbians are more conservative and therefore less open to discussion, while the younger generations have very few qualms about describing the local scene and their personal experiences as gay men or lesbians in Singapore.

There are tons of websites on the Internet for gays and lesbians in Singapore. Start at www.utopia-asia.com/tipsing.htm, an extremely comprehensive "insider" collection of current events, meeting places, travel tips, topical Web discussions, and links to resources. Chapter 7 lists some gay and lesbian clubs and karaoke lounges that are all nice places with friendly folks.

The International Gay & Lesbian Travel Association (IGLTA) (℗ 800/448-8550 or 954/776-2626; fax 954/776-3303; www.iglta.org) links travelers with gay-friendly hoteliers, tour operators, and airline and cruise-line representatives. It offers monthly newsletters, marketing mailings, and a membership directory that's updated once a year. Membership is $200 yearly, plus a $100 administration fee for new members.

AGENCIES/OPERATORS

- **Above and Beyond Tours** (℗ 800/397-2681; www.abovebeyondtours.com) offers gay and lesbian tours worldwide and is the exclusive gay and lesbian tour operator for United Airlines.
- **Now, Voyager** (℗ 800/255-6951; www.nowvoyager.com) is a San Francisco–based gay-owned and -operated travel service.
- **Olivia Cruises & Resorts** (℗ 800/631-6277 or 510/655-0364; http://oliviatravel.com) charters entire resorts and ships for exclusive lesbian vacations all over the world.

PUBLICATIONS

- *Frommer's Gay & Lesbian Europe* is an excellent travel resource.
- *Out and About* (℗ 800/929-2268 or 415/644-8044; www.outandabout.com) offers guidebooks and a newsletter 10 times a year packed with solid information on the global gay and lesbian scene.
- *Spartacus International Gay Guide* and *Odysseus* are good, annual English-language guidebook focused on gay men, with some information for lesbians. You can get them from most gay and lesbian bookstores, or order them from **Giovanni's Room** bookstore, 1145 Pine St., Philadelphia, PA 19107 (℗ **215/923-2960;** www.giovannisroom.com).
- *Gay Travel A to Z: The World of Gay & Lesbian Travel Options at Your Fingertips,* by Marianne Ferrari (Ferrari Publications; Box 35575, Phoenix, AZ 85069), is a very good gay and lesbian guidebook series.

SENIOR TRAVEL

Mention the fact that you're a senior citizen when you first make your travel reservations. All major airlines and many hotels offer discounts for seniors. Major airlines also offer coupons for domestic travel for seniors over sixty. Typically, a book of four coupons costs less than $700, which means you can fly anywhere in the continental U.S. for under $350 round-trip. In most cities, people over the age of 60 qualify for reduced admission to theaters, museums, and other attractions, as well as discounted fares on public transportation.

Around the world, most countries won't consider you eligible for senior citizen's discount until you reach maybe 60 or 65 years of age. However, in Singapore it's common to see 55 as the starting age for benefits. My poor mother (who's not yet old enough to qualify back home) had a shock when she was asked her age at the National Museum. She saved a few dollars, but was a bit sore about it! Most attractions and museums have discounted admission for senior citizens. Hotels, airlines, and tour operators will also quote you discounted packages if you request senior rates.

The STB will also help plan your trip, and can offer its own advice for senior travelers. Regarding this service, here's my advice: If you work out your itinerary with the help of STB, make sure you're firm about time constraints. Many of the tours and daily itineraries are rushed, with little time for a rest here and there. A common complaint is exhaustion by the end of just 1 day. In the heat, this is not only uncomfortable, but dangerous as well.

Members of **AARP** (formerly known as the American Association of Retired Persons), 601 E St. NW, Washington, DC 20049 (© **800/424-3410** or 202/434-2277; www.aarp.org), get discounts on hotels, airfares, and car rentals. AARP offers members a wide range of benefits, including *Modern Maturity* magazine and a monthly newsletter. Anyone over 50 can join.

The Alliance for Retired Americans, 8403 Colesville Rd., Suite 1200, Silver Spring, MD 20910 (© **301/ 578-8422**; www.retiredamericans.org), offers a newsletter six times a year and discounts on hotel and auto rentals; annual dues are $13 per person or couple. *Note:* Members of the former National Council of Senior Citizens receive automatic membership in the Alliance.

AGENCIES/OPERATORS
- **Grand Circle Travel** (© **800/ 221-2610** or 617/350-7500; www. gct.com) offers package deals for the 50-plus market, mostly of the tour-bus variety, with free trips thrown in for those who organize groups of 10 or more.
- **Elderhostel** (© **877/426-8056;** www.elderhostel.org) arranges study programs for those aged 55 and over (and a spouse or companion of any age) in the U.S. and in more than 80 countries around

the world. Most courses last 5 to 7 days in the U.S. (2–4 weeks abroad), and many include airfare, accommodations in university dormitories or modest inns, meals, and tuition.
- **Interhostel** (© **800/733-9753;** www.learn.unh.edu/interhostel), organized by the University of New Hampshire, also offers educational travel for seniors. On these escorted tours, the days are packed with seminars, lectures, and field trips, with sightseeing led by academic experts. **Interhostel** takes travelers 50 and over (with companions over 40), and offers 1- and 2-week trips, mostly international.

PUBLICATIONS
- *The Book of Deals* is a collection of more than 1,000 senior discounts on airlines, lodging, tours, and attractions around the country; it's available for $9.90 by calling © **800/460-6676.**
- *101 Tips for the Mature Traveler* is available from Grand Circle Travel (© **800/221-2610** or 617/ 350-7500; fax 617/346-6700).
- *The 50+ Traveler's Guidebook* (St. Martin's Press).
- *Unbelievably Good Deals and Great Adventures That You Absolutely Can't Get Unless You're Over 50* (Contemporary Publishing Co.).

FAMILY TRAVEL
The family vacation is a rite of passage for many households, one that in a split second can devolve into a *National Lampoon* farce. But as any veteran family vacationer will assure you, a family trip can be among the most pleasurable and rewarding times of your life.

However, because of their focus on business travelers, hotels in Singapore are not especially geared toward children. You can get extra beds in hotel rooms (this can cost anywhere from S$15–S$50/US$8.55–US$29), and most hotels will arrange a babysitter for you on request, though most ask for at least 24 hours notice. While almost all hotels have pools to keep the kiddies cool and happy, only two, the YMCA International House and Metro YMCA, have lifeguards on duty, and only one, Shangri-La's Rasa Sentosa Resort, has activity programs specifically for children. See chapter 3 for more information on these hotels.

Children have their own special rates of admission for just about every attraction and museum. The cutoff age for children is usually 12 years of age, but if your kids are older, be sure to ask if the attraction has a student rate for teens. If the kids get edgy during all the "boring" historical and cultural aspects of your trip, plan a morning visit to the Singapore Zoological Gardens. I can almost guarantee they (and you) will have a great time.

In Singapore, childhood innocence is revered, so you will rarely find crimes being committed against them. You can rest assured that if your child is missing, he or she is probably just around the corner looking for you— maybe even with the help of a concerned Singaporean.

Given the strictures of Muslim culture, women who are breast-feeding should strictly limit the activity to private places. In the West it may be acceptable, but here it'll just freak people out.

AGENCIES/OPERATORS

Familyhostel (© **800/733-9753;** www.learn.unh.edu/familyhostel) takes the whole family on moderately priced domestic and international learning vacations. All trip details are handled by the program staff, and lectures, fields trips, and sightseeing are guided by a team of academics. For kids ages 8 to 15 accompanied by their parents and/or grandparents.

PUBLICATIONS

- *The Unofficial Guide to the Southeast with Kids* (Wiley)
- *How to Take Great Trips with Your Kids* (The Harvard Common Press) is full of good general advice that can apply to travel anywhere.

WEBSITES

- **Family Travel Network** (www. familytravelnetwork.com) offers travel tips and reviews of family-friendly destinations, vacation deals, and thoughtful features such as "What to Do When Your Kids Are Afraid to Travel" and "Kid-Style Camping."
- **Travel with Your Children** (www. travelwithyourkids.com) is a comprehensive site offering sound advice for traveling with children.
- **The Busy Person's Guide to Travel with Children** (http:// wz.com/travel/TravelingWith Children.html) offers a "45-second newsletter" where experts weigh in on the best websites and resources for tips for traveling with children.

STUDENT TRAVEL

If you're planning to travel outside the U.S., you'd be wise to arm yourself with an **international student ID card,** which offers substantial savings on rail passes, plane tickets, and entrance fees. It also provides you with basic health and life insurance and a 24-hour help line. The card is available for $22 from the **Council on International Educational Exchange,** or CIEE (www.ciee.org). The CIEE's travel branch, **Council Travel Service** (© **800/226-8624;** www.council travel.com), is the biggest student travel agency in the world. If you're no longer a student but are still under 26, you can get a **GO 25 card** from the same people, which entitles you to insurance and some discounts (but not on museum admissions). **STA Travel**

(© **800/781-4040;** www.statravel. com) is another travel agency catering especially to young travelers, although their bargain-basement prices are available to people of all ages.

In Canada, **Travel CUTS** (© **800/ 667-2887** or 416/614-2887; www. travelcuts.com), offers similar services.

BUSINESSPEOPLE

Businesspeople, Singapore is your town. Every hotel has special accommodations for business travelers, which can include nicer rooms; higher floors; extras such as newspapers, shoe shines, and suit pressings; and club lounges where you can have a free breakfast and evening cocktails while you watch CNN or work on one of the hotel's PCs.

Most multinational corporations have accounts with major hotel chains, so your firm may tell you where to stay. If you make your arrangements on your own, though, remember that every hotel has a corporate rate, which is sometimes up to 40% off the going room rate.

Refer to "Etiquette & Customs," later in this chapter, before your first meeting, so you know how to greet people and trade business cards in the appropriate style.

8 Getting There

If you're hunting for the best airfare, there are a few things you can do. First, plan your trip for the low-volume season, which runs from September 1 to November 30. Between January 1 and May 31, you'll pay the highest fares. Plan your travel on weekdays only, and, if you can, plan to stay for at least a full week. Book your reservations in advance—waiting until the last minute can mean you'll pay sky-high rates. Also, if you have access to the Internet, there are a number of great sites that'll search out super fares for you.

FROM THE UNITED STATES Singapore Airlines (© **800/742- 3333** in the U.S., or 65/6223-6030 in Singapore; www.singaporeair.com) has a daily flight from New York, two daily flights from Los Angeles, two daily flights from San Francisco (only one on Sun), and a flight four times weekly from Newark, New Jersey. Flights originating from the East Coast travel over Europe, stopping in either Frankfurt or Amsterdam. Flights from the West Coast stop over in either Tokyo or Hong Kong. **United Airlines** (© **800/241-6522** in the U.S., or 65/6873-3533 in Singapore; www.ual.com) has daily flights connecting pretty much every major city in the United States with Singapore via the Pacific route. Expect a stopover in Tokyo en route. **Northwest Airlines** (© **800/447-4747** in the U.S., or 65/6336-3371 in Singapore; www.nwa.com) links all major U.S. airports with daily direct flights to Singapore from the following ports of exit: New York, Detroit, Minneapolis, Los Angeles, Seattle, and San Francisco, with direct flights from Las Vegas on Mondays and Thursdays only. All flights have one short stopover in Tokyo.

FROM CANADA Singapore Airlines (© **604/681-7488** in the U.S., or 65/6223-6030 in Singapore; www.singaporeair.com) has flights from Vancouver three times a week, with a stopover in Seoul.

FROM THE UNITED KINGDOM Singapore Airlines (© **181/747-0007** in London, 161/832-3346 in Manchester, or 65/6223-6030 in Singapore; www.singaporeair.com) has three daily flights departing from London's Heathrow Airport with a daily connection from Manchester. Depending on the day of departure, these flights stopover in either Amsterdam, Zurich, or Bombay. **British Airways** (✆ **0345/ 222111** local call from anywhere within the U.K., or 65/6839-7788 in Singapore; www.british-airways.com) has daily nonstop flights from London. **Quantas Airways Ltd.** (✆ **0345/ 747767** in Australia, or 65/6839-7788 in Singapore; www.quantas.com) has daily nonstop flights on weekdays and flights twice daily on weekends from London.

FROM AUSTRALIA

Singapore Airlines (✆ **65/223-6030** in Singapore; www.singaporeair.com) has twice-daily flights from Melbourne (✆ 3/9254-0300) and Sydney (✆ 2/ 9350-0100); three dailies from Perth (✆ 8/9265-0500); a daily from Brisbane (✆ 7/3259-0717); flights from Adelaide (✆ 8/8203-0800) four times a week; and from Cairns (✆ 70/317-538) three times a week. **Quantas Airways Ltd.** (✆ **2/131313** toll free, or 65/6839-7788 in Singapore; www.quantas.com) links all major airports in Australia with daily direct flights to Singapore from Sydney and Melbourne. **British Airways** (✆ **8/9425-7711** in Perth, 7/3223-3133 in Brisbane, or 65/6839-7788 in Singapore; www.british-airways.com) has daily flights from Perth and Brisbane. British Airways and Quantas work in partnership to provide routing from Australia, so be sure to consult Quantas for connecting flights form your city.

FROM NEW ZEALAND

Singapore Airlines (✆ **303-2129** in Auckland, or 366-8003 in Christchurch; www.singaporeair.com) has daily flights from Auckland and Christchurch. **Air New Zealand** (✆**0800/737000;** www.airnewzealand. co.nz) has daily flights from Christchurch and a daily flight from Auckland in partnership with Singapore Airlines (so you can still use or accumulate frequent-flier miles for this trip).

GETTING INTO TOWN FROM THE AIRPORT

Most visitors to Singapore will land at Changi International Airport, which is located toward the far eastern corner of the island. Compared to so many other international airports, Changi is a dream come true, providing clean and very efficient space and facilities. Expect to find in-transit accommodations, restaurants, duty-free shops, money-changers, ATMs, car-rental desks, accommodation assistance, and tourist information all marked with clear signs. When you arrive, keep your eyes peeled for the many Singapore Tourism Board brochures that are so handily displayed throughout the terminal.

The city is easily accessible by public transportation. A taxi trip to the city center will cost around S$22 to S$25 (US$13–US$14) and takes around 20 minutes. You'll traverse the wide Airport Boulevard to the Pan-Island Expressway (PIE) or the East Coast Parkway (ECP), past public housing estates and other residential neighborhoods in the eastern part of the island, over causeways, and into the city center.

CityCab offers an airport shuttle, a six-seater maxicab that traverses between the airport and the major hotel areas. It covers most hotels, and is very flexible about drop-offs and pickups within the central areas, including MRT (subway) stations. Bookings are made at the airport shuttle counter in the arrival terminal or by calling ✆ **65/6542-8297.** Pay S$7 (US$4) for adults and S$5 (US$2.85) for children directly to the driver.

The **MRT** now operates to the airport, linking you with the city and areas beyond. Follow signs in the terminal buildings. Trains operate roughly from 6am to midnight daily, and the trip takes about a half-hour. Pay S$1.40 (US80¢) to travel to City Hall Station.

A couple of **buses** run from the airport into the city as well. SBS bus no. 16 will take you on a route to Orchard Road and Raffles City (in the Historic District). SBS bus no. 36 runs a direct route to and from the airport and Orchard Road. Both bus stops are located in the basement of the arrival terminal. A trip to town will be about S$1.40 (US80¢).

For arrival and departure information, you can call **Changi International Airport** toll-free at ⓒ 65/ 6542-4422.

AIR TRAVEL SECURITY MEASURES

In the wake of the terrorist attacks of September 11, 2001, the airline industry implemented sweeping security measures in airports. Expect a lengthier check-in process and possible delays. Although regulations vary from airline to airline, you can expedite the process by taking the following steps:

- **Arrive early.** Arrive at the airport at least 2 hours before your scheduled flight.
- **Try not to drive your car to the airport.** Parking and curbside access to the terminal may be limited. Call ahead and check.
- **Don't count on curbside check-in.** Some airlines and airports have stopped curbside check-in altogether, whereas others offer it on a limited basis. For up-to-date information on specific regulations, check with the individual airline.
- **Be sure to carry plenty of documentation.** A government-issued photo ID (federal, state, or local) is now required. You may need to show this at various checkpoints. With an E-ticket, you may be required to have with you printed confirmation of purchase, and perhaps even the credit card with which you bought your ticket. This varies from airline to airline, so call ahead to make sure you

have the proper documentation. And be sure that your ID is **up-to-date:** An expired driver's license, for example, may keep you from boarding the plane altogether.

- **Know what you can carry on— and what you can't.** Travelers in the United States are now limited to one carry-on bag, plus one personal bag (such as a purse or a briefcase). The Transportation Security Administration (TSA) has also issued a list of newly restricted carry-on items; see the box "What You Can Carry On— and What You Can't."
- **Prepare to be searched.** Expect spot-checks. Electronic items, such as a laptop or cellphone, should be readied for additional screening. Limit the metal items you wear on your person.
- **It's no joke.** When a check-in agent asks if someone other than you packed your bag, don't decide that this is the time to be funny. The agents will not hesitate to call security.
- **No ticket, no gate access.** Only ticketed passengers will be allowed beyond the screener checkpoints, except for those people with specific medical or parental needs.

COPING WITH JET LAG

Jetlag is a pitfall of traveling across time zones. If you're flying north-south—say, from Canada to Chile— and you feel sluggish when you touch down, your symptoms will be the by-product of dehydration and the general stress of air travel. When you travel east to west or vice versa, however, the bodily functions that operate cyclically—your hormone levels, blood pressure, body temperature, digestive enzymes, kidney, heart, and brain activity—fall into a sort of time warp. This is because they are, in part, someplace else, inclined to do the things they normally would have been

MRT Transit Map

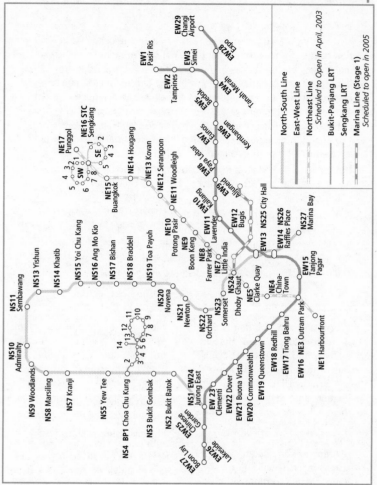

doing back home. Traveling east, say, from Chicago to Paris, is more difficult on your internal clock than traveling west, say from Atlanta to Hawaii. Traveling east, you lose time, whereas traveling west you gain time, and thus gain sleep, which will help your body recover more quickly.

Here are some tips for combating jet lag:

- **Drink lots of water** before, during, and after your flight.

- **Reset your watch** according to your destination time before you board the plane.
- **Avoid drinking alcohol** or ingesting other depressants, such as motion sickness drugs, before and during your flight.
- **Exercise, sleep well, and eat especially healthy foods** during the few days before your trip.
- **Eat more lightly** than you would, both before and during your flight.

> ## (Tips   What You Can Carry On—And What You Can't
>
> The Transportation Security Administration (TSA), the government agency that now handles all aspects of airport security, has devised new restrictions for carry-on baggage, not only to expedite the screening process but to prevent potential weapons from passing through airport security. Passengers are now limited to bringing just one carry-on bag and one personal item onto the aircraft (previous regulations allowed two carry-on bags and one personal item, like a briefcase or a purse). For more information, go to the TSA's website, www.tsa.gov. The agency has released an updated list of items passengers are not allowed to carry onto an aircraft:
>
> **Not permitted:** knives and box cutters, corkscrews, straight razors, metal scissors, golf clubs, baseball bats, pool cues, hockey sticks, ski poles, ice picks.
>
> **Permitted:** nail clippers, nail files, tweezers, eyelash curlers, safety razors (including disposable razors), syringes (with documented proof of medical need), walking canes and umbrellas (must be inspected first).
>
> The airline you fly may have **additional restrictions** on items you can and cannot carry on board. Call ahead to avoid problems.

- When you reach your destination, **don't sleep longer than you normally would** to try to "catch up."
- **Push yourself** to stay as active as you can when you reach your destination, until the normal bedtime there. Likewise, wake at the same hours that locals do. The more you expose your body to daily rhythms in your destination, the faster your body will adjust.
- **Some doctors recommend melatonin** 2 hours before bedtime. A natural, sleep-inducing hormone, it's thought that melatonin will trick your body into thinking night has fallen earlier and help you adjust to a new time zone.
- Remember that eating **carbohydrates** (such as pasta or whole-grain bread) **before bedtime** will

allow you to sleep better. High protein foods—such as meats, fish, eggs, and dairy products—eaten before bedtime will give you energy.

If you're flying to Europe and you have trouble sleeping on planes, consider taking a flight that departs in the morning and arrives in the evening, as opposed to a flight that departs in the late afternoon or evening and arrives the following morning. If you arrive in the evening, you'll be able to settle into your hotel at a reasonable hour, get a good's night sleep, and wake up refreshed the next morning. The problem with this strategy is that you waste a full day on the plane and you will likely still suffer the effects of jet lag for a few days at least.

9 Escorted Tours, Package Deals & Special-Interest Vacations

Before you start your search for the lowest airfare, you may want to consider booking your flight as part of a travel package such as an escorted tour or a package tour. What you lose in adventure, you'll gain in time and money saved when you book accommodations, and maybe even food and entertainment, along with your flight.

PACKAGE TOURS FOR INDEPENDENT TRAVELERS

Package tours are not the same thing as escorted tours. Package tours are simply a way to buy the airfare, accommodations, and other elements of your trip (such as car rentals, airport transfers, and sometimes even activities) at the same time and often at discounted prices—kind of like one-stop shopping. Packages are sold in bulk to tour operators—who resell them to the public at a cost that drastically undercuts standard rates.

RECOMMENDED PACKAGE TOUR OPERATORS

One good source of package deals is the airlines themselves. Most major airlines offer air/land packages, including **American Airlines Vacations** (© 800/ 321-2121; http://aav1.aavacations. com), **Delta Vacations** (© 800/221- 6666; www.deltavacations.com), and **US Airways Vacations** (© 800/ 455-0123 or 800/422-3861; www.us airwaysvacations.com), **Continental Airlines Vacations** (© 800/301-3800; www.coolvacations.com), and **United Vacations** (© 888/854-3899; www. unitedvacations.com).

Online Vacation Mall (© 800/ 839-9851; www.onlinevacationmall. com) allows you to search for and book packages offered by a number of tour operators and airlines. The **United States Tour Operators Association**'s website (www.ustoa.com) has a search engine that allows you to look for operators that offer packages to a specific destination. Travel packages are also listed in the travel section of your local Sunday newspaper. **Liberty Travel** (© **888/271-1584;** www.libertytravel. com), one of the biggest packagers in the Northeast, often runs full-page ads in Sunday papers. Or check ads in the national travel magazines such as *Arthur Frommer's Budget Travel Magazine, Travel & Leisure, National Geographic Traveler,* and *Condé Nast Traveler.*

THE PROS & CONS OF PACKAGE TOURS

Packages can save you money because they are sold in bulk to tour operators, who sell them to the public. They offer group prices but allow for independent travel. The disadvantages are that you're usually required to make a large payment up front; you may end up on a charter flight; and you have to deal with your own luggage and with transfers between your hotel and the airport, if transfers are not included in the package price. Packages often don't allow for a wide range of choices (the hotels may be unremarkable and are usually located more for the packager's convenience than for yours), or have a fixed itinerary that doesn't allow for an extra day of shopping. Some packages offer a better class of hotels than others. Some offer the same hotels for lower prices than their competitors. Some offer flights on scheduled airlines while others book charters. In some packages, your choices of travel days may be limited. Some packages let you choose between escorted vacations and independent vacations; others allow you to add on a few guided excursions or escorted day trips (also at prices lower than if you booked them yourself) without booking an entirely escorted tour. Your choice of travel days may be limited as well.

QUESTIONS TO ASK IF YOU BOOK A PACKAGE TOUR

- What are the **accommodations choices** available and are there price differences? Once you find out, look them up in a Frommer's guide. Most countries rate their hotels, so ask about the rating of the hotel in question. Or get this information from the government tourist office or its website.

- What **type of room** will you be staying in? Don't take whatever is thrown your way. Request a non-smoking room, a quiet room, a room with a view, or whatever you fancy.
- Look for **hidden expenses.** Ask whether airport departure fees and taxes are included in the total cost.

ESCORTED TOURS (TRIPS WITH GUIDES)

Escorted Tours are structured group tours, with a group leader. The price usually includes everything from airfare to hotels, meals, tours, admission costs, and local transportation.

RECOMMENDED ESCORTED TOUR OPERATORS

A good resource is the airlines themselves, which often package their flights together with accommodations. Fly-by-night packagers are uncommon, but they do exist; when you buy your package through the airline, however, you can be pretty sure that the company will still be in business when your departure date arrives. Singapore Airlines, in partnership with many travel-related businesses here, has a special **New Singapore Stopover Package.** If you book passage with Singapore Airlines, for an additional US$30 you can take advantage of free admission to many attractions, free transportation on the Hop-On Trolley, and special discounts on hotel rooms, dining, shopping, and more. For details, contact Singapore Airlines at the phone numbers listed under "By Plane," above, or check their website at **www.singaporeair.com**.

The biggest hotel chains and resorts also offer package deals. If you already know where you want to stay, call the resort itself and ask if they offer land/air packages.

Perhaps the most experienced and knowledgeable tour operator specializing in Southeast Asia is **Absolute Asia,** 180 Varick St., 16th Fl., New York, NY 10014 (© **800/736-8187;** www.absoluteasia.com) They offer a diverse blend of cultural and adventure travel programs and will customize tours and design itineraries to suit each individual's particular interest. People traveling with Absolute Asia have three options: follow the itinerary as is, combine it with another itinerary, or design their own trip.

Explore Worldwide, c/o the Adventure Center, 1311 63rd St., Suite 200, Emeryville, CA 94608 (© **800/227-8747;** 800/661-7265 Trek Holidays, in Canada; 800/221-931 Adventure World, in Australia), offers adventure and cultural group tours to Southeast Asia, including several to Malaysia and one that covers Singapore and Malaysia.

THE PROS & CONS OF ESCORTED TOURS

If you book an escorted tour, most everything is paid for up front, so you deal with fewer money issues. They allow you to enjoy the maximum number of sights in the shortest time, with the least amount of hassle, as all the details are arranged by others. Escorted tours give you the security of traveling in a group and are convenient for people with limited mobility. Many escorted tours are theme tours, putting people together who share the same interest or activity (such as cooking or sailing).

On the downside, if you book an escorted tour you often have to pay a lot of money up front, and your lodging and dining choices are predetermined. Escorted tours can be jam-packed with activities, leaving little room for individual sightseeing, whim, or adventure. They also often focus only on the heavily touristed sites, so you miss out on the lesser-known gems. Plus, you may not always be happy rubbing suitcases with strangers.

Frommers.com: The Complete Travel Resource

For an excellent travel-planning resource, we highly recommend **Frommers.com** (www.frommers.com). We're a little biased, of course, but we guarantee that you'll find the travel tips, reviews, monthly vacation giveaways, and online-booking capabilities thoroughly indispensable. Among the special features are our popular **Message Boards,** where Frommer's readers post queries and share advice (sometimes even our authors show up to answer questions); **Frommers.com Newsletter,** for the latest travel bargains and inside travel secrets; and Frommer's **Destinations Section,** where you'll get expert travel tips, hotel and dining recommendations, and advice on the sights to see for more than 2,500 destinations around the globe. When your research is done, the **Online Reservation System** (www.frommers.com/booktravelnow) takes you to Frommer's favorite sites for booking your vacation at affordable prices.

10 Getting Around Singapore

The many inexpensive mass transit options make getting around Singapore pretty easy. Of course, taxis always simplify the ground transportation dilemma. They're also very affordable and, by and large, drivers are helpful and honest if not downright personable. The **Mass Rapid Transit (MRT) subway service** has lines that cover the main areas of the city and out to the farther parts of the island. Buses present more of a challenge because there are so many routes snaking all over the island, but they're a great way to see the country while getting where you want to go. In the bus section, below, I've thrown in some tips that will hopefully demystify the bus experience for you.

Of course, if you're just strolling around the urban limits, many of the sights within the various neighborhoods are within walking distance, and indeed, some of the neighborhoods are only short walks from each other—getting from Chinatown to the Historic District only requires crossing over the Singapore River, and from Little India to Kampong Glam is not far at all. However, I advise against

trying to get from, say, Chinatown (in the west) to Kampong Glam (in the east). The distance can be somewhat prohibitive, especially in the heat.

Stored-fare EZ-Link fare cards can be used on both the subway and the buses, and can be purchased at TransitLink offices in the MRT stations. These save you the bother of trying to dig up exact change for bus meters. The card does carry a S$5 (US$2.85) deposit—for a S$15 (US$8.55) initial investment, you'll get S$10 (US$5.70) worth of travel credit.

BY MASS RAPID TRANSIT (MRT)

The MRT is Singapore's subway system. It's cool, clean, safe, and reliable, providing service from the far west reaches of the island to the far east parts on the east-west line and running in a loop around the north part of the island on the north-south line. The lines are color coded to make it easy to find the train you're looking for (see the MRT map in this chapter for specifics). The two lines intersect at the Raffles Place Interchange in Chinatown/Shenton Way, at City Hall in the Historic

District, and in the western part of the island at the Jurong East Interchange. (By the way, don't let the "East" fool you—Jurong East is actually in the western part of the island.) MRT operating hours vary between lines and stops, with the earliest train beginning service daily at 5:15am and the last train ending at 12:47am.

Fares range from S80¢ to S$1.80 (US45¢–US$1.05), depending on which stations you travel between. System charts are prominently displayed in all MRT stations to help you find your appropriate fare, which you pay with an EZ-Link fare card. Single-fare cards can be purchased at vending machines at MRT stations. See above for information on stored-fare cards. (*One caution:* A fare card cannot be used by 2 people for the same trip; each must have his own.)

For more information, call **TransitLink TeleInfo** at ✆ **1800/767-4333** (daily 24 hr.).

BY BUS

Singapore's bus system comprises an extensive web of routes that reach virtually everywhere on the island. It can be intimidating for newcomers, but once you get your feet wet, you'll feel right at home. There are two main bus services, SBS (Singapore Bus Service) and TIBS (Trans-Island Bus Service). Most buses are clean, but not all are air-conditioned.

Start off first by purchasing the latest edition of the *TransitLink Guide* for about S$1.50 (US85¢) at the TransitLink office in any MRT station, at a bus interchange, or at selected bookstores around the city. This tiny book is a very handy guide that details each route and stop, indicating connections with MRT stations and fares for each trip. Next to the guide, the best thing to do is simply ask people for help. At any crowded bus stop there will always be somebody who speaks English and is willing to help out a lost stranger.

You can also ask the bus driver where you need to go, and he'll tell you the fare, how to get there, and even when to get off.

All buses have a gray machine with a sensor pad close to the driver. Tap your EZ-Link care when you board and alight, and the fare will be automatically deducted. It'll be anywhere between S80¢ and S$1.60. If you're paying cash, be sure to have exact change; place the coins in the red box by the driver and announce your fare to him. He'll issue a ticket, which will pop out of a slot on one of the TransitLink machines behind him.

The **Tourist Day Ticket** is a great deal for travelers. The 1-day pass costs S$10 (US$5.70), and is good for 12 rides on either SBS or TIBS buses or the MRT. Using one of these will save you having to worry about calculating the correct fare or coming up with exact change. You can pick one up at any TransitLink office and at hotels, money-changers, provisioner shops, or travel agents. Unfortunately, there's no handy sign identifying which shops sell them, so you'll have to ask around.

For more information, contact either of the two operating bus lines during standard business hours: **Singapore Bus Service (SBS)** (✆ **1800/287-2727**) or **the Trans-Island Bus Service (TIBS)** (✆ **1800/482-5433**).

BY TROLLEY

You have a couple of trolley options; both services are offered for the convenience of travelers, making stops at most major tourist destinations. The Singapore Explorer shuttles down Orchard Road, through the Historic District and over the Singapore River, and down to Marina Square. For S$15 (US$8.50) adults and S$9.90 (US$5.65) children, you can enjoy unlimited rides for one day (this price also includes a free riverboat tour). Buy your tickets either from your hotel's front desk or directly from the driver. Call **Singapore Explorer** at 🕾 **65/6339-6833**.

Singapore Airlines hosts the **SIA Hop-on bus.** Plying between Bugis Junction, Suntec City, the Historic District, the Singapore River, Chinatown, Orchard Road and the Singapore Botanic Gardens, the Hop-on comes every 30 minutes between the hours of 8:30am and 7pm. Unlimited rides for one day cost S$6 (US$3.45) adults and S$4 (US$2.30) children. Buy your tickets from your hotel's front desk, from a Singapore Airlines office, or from the bus drivers. If you've traveled to Singapore via Singapore Airlines, you're entitled to free passage aboard the Hop-on. Just show your boarding pass to the driver. For more information call **SH Tours** 🕾 **65/6374-9923.**

BY TAXI

Taxis are a very convenient and affordable way to get around Singapore, and there's every chance you'll get a good conversation with the driver into the bargain. Despite this, I advise against relying completely on taxicabs, since Singapore's excellent public transportation system will take you practically anywhere you need to go for a fraction of the price. Even in the middle of nowhere there's always a bus route to take you to familiar territory—just remember to keep your *TransitLink Guide* (see above) handy, so you'll know where the bus you're about to hop is headed.

In town, all of the shopping malls, hotels, and major buildings have taxi queues, which you're expected to use. During lunch hours and the evening rush, the queues can be very long; though by and large taxis are convenient, don't count on finding one fast during the evening rush hours between 5pm and 7pm. Especially if it's raining, you'll be waiting for an hour, easy. Everybody wants a cab at this time, and for some strange reason

this is the time the cabbies choose to change shifts. Brilliant. During this time, I recommend you call to book a taxi pickup, but even that may mean up to a half-hour wait. You pay a little extra, but believe me, some days it can really be worth it.

Most destinations in the main parts of the island can be reached fairly inexpensively, while trips to the outlying attractions can cost from S$10 to S$15 (US$5.70–US$8.55) one-way. If you're at an attraction or restaurant outside of the central part of the city where it is more difficult to hail a cab on the street, you can ask the cashier or service counter attendant to call a taxi for you. The extra charge for pickup is between S$3 and S$3.20 (US$1.70–US$1.85) depending on the cab company (City-Cab is the cheapest). Call these main cab companies for bookings: **CityCab** (🕾 **65/6552-2222**), **Comfort** (🕾 **65/6552-1111**), and **TIBS** (🕾 **65/6552-8888**).

CityCab and Comfort charge the metered fare, which is S$2.40 (US$1.35) for the first kilometer and S10¢ (US6¢) for each additional 225m to 240m or 30 seconds of waiting. TIBS's meter starts at S$2.10 (US$1.20). Extra fares are levied on top of the metered fare depending on where you're going and when you go. At times, figuring your fare seems more like a riddle. Here's a summary:

Trips during peak hours: Between the hours of 7:30 and 9:30am Monday to Friday, 4:30 to 7pm Monday to Friday, and 11:30am to 2pm on Saturdays, trips will carry an additional S$1 (US55¢) peak-period surcharge. But if you're traveling outside the Central Business District (CBD), you won't need to pay this surcharge during the morning rush. (To accurately outline the boundaries of the CBD, I'd need to fill a couple of encyclopedic volumes, so for this purpose, let's just say it's basically Orchard Rd., the Historic District, Chinatown, and Shenton Way.)

Additional charges rack up each time you travel through an Electronic Road Pricing (ERP) scheme underpass. On the Central Expressway (CTE), Pan-Island Expressway (PIE), and selected thoroughfares in the CBD, charges from S30¢ to S$1.70 (US15¢–US95¢) are calculated by an electronic box on the driver's dashboard. The driver will add this amount to your fare.

And for special torture, here's some more charges: From midnight to 6am, add 50% to your fare. From 6pm on the eve of a public holiday to midnight the following day, you pay an additional S$1 (US.55¢). From Changi Airport add S$5 (US$2.85) if you're traveling Fridays, Saturdays, or Sundays between 5pm and midnight. Other times, it's S$3 (US$1.70). And for credit-card payments (yes, you can pay with plastic!) add 10%.

BY CAR

Singapore's public transportation systems are so extensive, efficient, and inexpensive that you shouldn't need a car to enjoy your stay. In fact, I don't advise it. While most hotels and restaurants and many attractions do have parking facilities, parking in lots can be expensive, and on-street parking is by prepurchased, color-coded parking tickets that are a pain to purchase. In addition, if you're not accustomed to driving on the left side of the road, you'll need to take the time to pick up a new skill.

Because of heavy government taxes aimed at reducing traffic congestion and air pollution, everything to do with cars in Singapore is outlandishly expensive—the going price for a Toyota Camry, for instance, can be as high as S$125,000 (US$71,429). This attempt to reduce automobile traffic is also extended to you, the traveler, through rental charges up to S$1,000 (US$571) plus taxes for 1 week's rental of the smallest car on the lot.

One of the few good reasons to rent a car is if you plan to drive into Malaysia. Back in the 1970s, driving in Malaysia was risky because of highway bandits. These days, though, it's relatively safe traveling, and thanks to the new toll road—the North-South Highway from Singapore all the way up to the Thai border—it's pretty convenient (see chapter 9 for more on this subject, and on renting a car in Malaysia rather than Singapore, which can save you some cash).

Two good places to seek out a rental car are:

- **Avis:** Changi Airport Terminal 2 (© **65/6542-8855**), #01–01 Concorde Shopping Centre (© 65/6737-1668). You must be at least 23 years old to rent, and the minimum rental period is 24 hours. Rates in Singapore run daily from S$100 (US$57) for a Mitsubishi Lancer to S$160 (US$91) for a Mitsubishi Gallant. For travel to Malaysia, the daily rates are somewhat higher One-way rentals are available, with varying drop-off fees for Malacca, Kuala Lumpur, Kuantan, Alor Setar, Ipoh, and Penang. All major credit cards are accepted.

- **Hertz:** Changi Airport Terminal 2, Arrival Meeting Hall South (© **65/542-5300**), or 125 Tanglin Rd., Tudor Court Shopping Gallery (© 1800/734-4646). You must be at least 21 years of age to rent and the minimum rental period is 24 hours. Daily rates for rental within Singapore run from S$199 (US$119) for a Mitsubishi Lancer to S$559 (US$335) for a BMW or Mercedes Benz, and S$1,194 (US$715) to S$3,354 (US$2,008) per week, respectively. Hertz does not rent luxury cars for driving to Malaysia. For Malaysia driving, Hertz will charge an extra S$25 (US$15) per day. For one-way trips to Malaysia there are varying drop-off charges for Johor Bahru, Kuala Lumpur, Kuantan, and Penang. Hertz accepts all major credit cards.

An additional solution to getting around is to hire a car and driver. A **CityCab Mercedes** can be hired for S$39 per hour, which is about the best rate available. For bookings call © **65/ 6454-2222.**

11 Etiquette & Customs

ETIQUETTE TIPS

Here's a delicate one, but there's no way to get around it: Only use your right hand in social interaction. Why? Because in Indian and Muslim society, the left hand is used only for bathroom chores. Not only should you eat with your right hand and give and receive all gifts with your right hand, but you should make sure all gestures, especially pointing (and, even more especially, pointing in temples and mosques), are made with your right hand. By the way, you should also be sure to point with your knuckle rather than your finger, to be more polite.

The other important etiquette tip is to remember to remove your shoes before entering places of worship (except for churches and synagogues) and all private residences. The private residence part is very important. I have yet to meet a local family that does not leave its shoes at the door.

A traditional Indian greeting is a slight bow with your palms pressed together in front of your chest. In these modern times, though, a handshake will usually do. When greeting an older man or especially a woman, wait for a gesture, then follow suit.

The traditional Malay greeting, called the *salaam,* is still practiced in Malaysia, but is rarely seen in Singapore. In this practice, both parties extend their hands to lightly touch each others', then touch their hearts with their fingertips. This is only done between members of the same sex. While Malay men will offer the more common handshake, always remember that Muslim women are not allowed to touch men to whom they are not related by blood or marriage. A simple smile and nod is fine.

Ladies, if seated on the floor, should never sit with their legs crossed in front of them—instead, always tuck your legs to the side. Both men and women should also be careful not to show the bottoms of their feet. If you cross your legs while on the floor or in a chair, don't point your soles toward other people—it's very rude. Also be careful not to use your foot to point or gesture, as this is also insulting.

Muslims who have traveled to Mecca take the prefix Haji, for males, and Hajjah for females, before their names. Feel free to use these titles if you know the person you're talking with has made the pilgrimage; it's a real mark of pride for them.

As for Chinese etiquette and customs, that can be rough. So many elements of Chinese culture make no sense to Westerners that I couldn't possibly cover the whole range. The younger generations are not as strict as the older folks about these points of cultural etiquette, but if you find yourself in a situation, even common sense can't make you a good judge of proper etiquette. You could give a beautiful brush painting to a Chinese as a gift, and the tiniest bird in the background could be a bad omen laying a curse on all of their future generations. Seriously.

If you are invited to a Chinese occasion or need to buy a gift for someone, the best thing you can possibly do is consult a Chinese person for advice. This is where hotel staff comes in handy. What color should I wear? What is the proper attire? Will this gift be nice? You'll thank them later.

I can give you some basic rules of thumb that will help:

- Don't wear all white or all black if you're invited to a festive occasion; these colors are for mourning. The same is pretty much true for all-blue and all-green outfits. Reds, pinks, oranges, and yellows are great for such gatherings.
- Gifts should never be knives, clocks, or handkerchiefs, and don't send anybody white flowers. (The sharp blades of knives symbolize the severing of a friendship; in Cantonese, the word for clock sounds the same as the word for funeral; handkerchiefs bring to mind tears and sadness; and white is the color of funeral mourning.)
- When giving money, an even amount in a red envelope is presented on auspicious occasions, and an odd number in a white envelope is presented at funerals.

There's no correct amount, but if there's a meal involved, the amount should at least cover the cost. By the way, the Chinese do not open gifts in public.

- The main rules regarding table manners revolve around the use of chopsticks. Don't stick them upright in any dish, don't gesture with them, and don't suck on them. Dropped chopsticks are also considered bad luck.

As for greetings, Chinese men and women are all pretty well accustomed to the standard handshake.

If you're conducting business in Singapore, you'll most likely be exchanging business cards. All Chinese Singaporeans present and receive business cards using both hands, as if giving or accepting a gift. If a card is given to you, read it and make a comment about it. "Nice card" or "You're the director of the department!" will do. Hang on to it a bit before putting it away—to stow it immediately is a sign of disrespect.

 FAST FACTS: Singapore

American Express The American Express office is located at 300 Beach Rd., #18-01 The Concourse, ℂ 65/6880-1333. It's open Monday to Friday 9am to 5pm and Saturday 9am to 1pm. There's a more convenient kiosk that handles traveler's checks and simple card transactions (including emergency check guarantee) on orchard Road just outside the Marriott Hotel at Tang Plaza ℂ 65/6735-2069. It's open daily from 9am to 9pm. An additional foreign exchange office is open at Changi Airport Terminal 2 (ℂ 65/6543-0671). It's open from noon to midnight daily. See the "Money" section earlier in this chapter for more details on member privileges.

Business Hours Shopping centers are open Monday through Saturday from 10am to 8pm, and stay open until 10pm on some public holidays. Banks are open from 9:30am to 3pm Monday through Friday, and from 9am to 11am on Saturdays. Restaurants open at lunchtime from around 11am to 2:30pm, and for dinner they reopen at around 6pm and take the last order sometime around 10pm. Nightclubs stay open until 2am on weekdays and until 3am on Fridays and Saturdays. Government offices are open from 9am to 5pm Monday through Friday and from 9am to 3pm on Saturdays. Post offices conduct business from 8:30am to 5pm on weekdays and from 8:30am to 1pm on Saturdays.

Car Rentals See "Getting Around Singapore," earlier in this chapter.

Climate See "When to Go," earlier in this chapter.

Currency See "Money," earlier in this chapter.

Documents See "Visitor Information & Entry Requirements," earlier in this chapter.

Driving Rules See "Getting Around Singapore," earlier in this chapter.

Drugstores **Guardian Pharmacies** fills prescriptions with name-brand drugs (from a licensed physician within Singapore), and carries a large selection of toiletry items. Convenient locations include #B1-05 Centrepoint Shopping Centre (© 65/737-4835), Changi International Airport Terminal 2 (© 65/545-4233), #02-139 Marina Square (© 65/333-9565), and #B1-04 Raffles Place MRT Station (© 65/535-2762).

Electricity Standard electrical current is 220 volts AC (50 cycles). Consult your concierge to see if your hotel has converters and plug adapters in-house for you to use. If you are using sensitive equipment, do not trust the cheap voltage transformers. Nowadays, a lot of electrical equipment—including portable radios and laptop computers—comes with built-in converters, so you can follow the manufacturer's directions for changing them over. FYI, videocassettes taped on different voltage currents are recorded on machines with different record and playback cycles. Prerecorded videotapes are not interchangeable between currents unless you have special equipment that can play either kind.

Embassies & Consulates See "Visitor Information & Entry Requirements," earlier in this chapter.

Emergencies For **police** dial © **999.** For **medical** or **fire** emergencies call © **995.**

Etiquette & Customs See "Etiquette & Customs," above.

Holidays See the "Calendar of Public Holidays & Events," earlier in this chapter.

Information See "Visitor Information," earlier in this chapter.

Internet Access Internet cafes are becoming common throughout the city, with usage costs between S$4 and S$5 (US$2.30 and US$2.85) per hour (keep in mind, if you use the Internet in your hotel's business center, you'll pay a much higher price). Almost every shopping mall has one, especially along Orchard Road, and there are cybercafes in both terminals at Changi Airport. In the Historic District, there are a few in Stamford House, just across from City Hall MRT Station. Check out **Chills Café,** #01-01 Stamford House, 39 Stamford Rd. (© **65/883-1016;** open 9:30am–midnight daily).

Language The official languages are Malay, Chinese (Mandarin), Tamil, and English. Malay is the national language while English is the language for government operations, law, and major financial transactions. Most Singaporeans are at least bilingual, with many speaking one or more dialects of Chinese, English, and some Malay

Liquor Laws The legal age for alcohol purchase and consumption is 18 years. Some of the smaller clubs rarely check identification, but the larger ones will, and sometimes require patrons to be 21 years old to enter, just to weed out younger crowds. Public drunk-and-disorderly behavior is against the law, and may snag you for up to S$1,000 in fines for the first offense, or even imprisonment—which is unlikely, but still a great way to ruin a vacation. There are strict drinking and driving laws, and roadblocks are set up on weekends to catch party people on their way home to the housing developments.

Mail Most hotels have mail services at the front counter. Singapore Post has centrally located offices at #04-15 Ngee Ann City/Takashimaya Shopping Centre (✆ 65/6738-6899); Tang's department store at 320 Orchard Rd. #03-00 (✆ 65/6738-5899); Chinatown Point, 133 New Bridge Rd. #02-42/43/44 (✆ 65/6538-7899); Change Alley, 16 Collyer Quay #02-02 Hitachi Tower (✆ 65/6538-6899); and at 231 Bain St. #01-03 Bras Basah Complex (✆ 65/6339-8899). Plus there are five branches at Changi International Airport.

The going rate for international airmail letters to North America and Europe is S$1 (US55¢) for 20g plus S35¢ (US20¢) for each additional 10g. For international airmail service to Australia and New Zealand, the rate is S70¢ (US40¢) for 20g plus S30¢ (US15¢) for each additional 10g. Postcards and aerograms to all destinations are S50¢ (US30¢).

Your hotel will accept mail sent for you at its address. American Express has a special mail delivery and holding deal for card members.

Maps The Singapore Street Directory, a book detailing every section of the island, is carried by most taxi drivers, and can be very helpful if you're trying to get someplace and he either doesn't know where it is or can't understand you. The street listing in the front will direct you to the corresponding map. A good cabbie can take it from there. Other good maps of the major city areas can be found in free STB publications, while there are also a few commercially produced maps sold in all major bookstores here.

Newspapers & Magazines Local English newspapers available are the International Herald Tribune, The Business Times, The Straits Times, Today, and USA Today International. Following an article criticizing the Singapore government, the Asian Wall Street Journal was banned from wide distribution in Singapore. Most of the major hotels are allowed to carry it, though, so ask around and you can find one. The New Paper is an "alternative publication" that may be a useful source for finding out what's happening around town. Major hotels, bookstores, and magazine shops sell a wide variety of international magazines.

Pets Singapore has strict quarantine regulations so don't even think about bringing a pet.

Police Given the strict law enforcement reputation in Singapore, you can bet the officers here don't have the greatest senses of humor. If you find yourself being questioned about anything, big or small, be dead serious and most respectful. For emergencies, call ✆ **999.** If you need to call the police headquarters, dial ✆ **65/6224-0000.**

If you are arrested, you have the right to legal council, but only when the police decide you can exercise that right. You get no call unless they give you permission. Bottom line: Don't get arrested.

Smoking It's against the law to smoke in public buses, elevators, theaters, cinemas, air-conditioned restaurants, shopping centers, government offices, and taxi queues.

Taxes Many hotels and restaurants will advertise rates followed by "+++." The first + is the goods and services tax (GST), which is levied at 3% of the purchase. The second + is 1% cess (a 1% tax levied by the STB on all tourism-related activities). The third is a 10% gratuity. See the "Customs Regulations" section earlier in this chapter for information on the GST Tourist Refund Scheme, which lets you recover the GST for purchases of goods over S$300 (US$171) in value.

Telephones **To call Singapore:** If you're calling Singapore from the United States:

1. Dial the international access code: 011

2. Dial the country code 65

3. Plus the 8-digit phone number. So the whole number you'd dial would be 011-65-0000-0000.

To make international calls: To place a direct international call from Singapore: Dial the international access code (001), the country code (U.S. and Canada 1, Australia 61, Republic of Ireland 353, New Zealand 64, U.K. 44), the area or city code, and the number.

For operator assistance: If you need operator assistance in making a call, dial ⓒ 104.

Time Zone Singapore Standard Time is 8 hours ahead of Greenwich mean time (GMT). International time differences will change during daylight saving or summer time. Basic time differences are: New York -13, Los Angeles -16, Montreal -13, Vancouver -16, London -8, Brisbane +3, Darwin +1, Melbourne +2, Sydney +3, and Auckland +4. For the current time within Singapore, call ⓒ 1711.

Tipping Tipping is discouraged at hotels, bars, and in taxis. Basically, the deal here is not to tip. A gratuity is automatically added into guest checks, and there's no need to slip anyone an extra buck for carrying bags or such. It's not expected.

Water Tap water in Singapore passes World Health Organization standards and is potable.

3

Where to Stay in Singapore

At last count, the number of hotels in Singapore was 196, and the number of hotel rooms was somewhere more than 60,000. Now here's another fact to chew over: On any given night, an average 75% of these rooms are occupied, mostly by business travelers. International business is the Singaporean hotel industry's bread and butter, so competition between hotels is fierce, causing them to invest in the most high-priced renovations of the most deluxe-super-royal-regal executive facilities, all in an attempt to lure business folks and—eventually, it is hoped—land lucrative corporate accounts.

Of course, this all means that budget accommodations are not a

high priority on the island. Between the business community's demand for luxury on the one hand and the inflated Singaporean real estate market on the other, room prices tend to be high. What this means for leisure travelers is that you may end up paying for a business center you'll never use or a 24-hour stress-reliever masseuse you'll never call—and all this without the benefit of a corporate discount rate.

Don't fret, though: I'm here to tell you that there's a range of accommodations out there—you just have to know where to find 'em. In this chapter, I'll help you pick the right accommodations for you, based on your vacation goals and your travel budget, so you can make the most of your stay.

CHOOSING YOUR NEIGHBORHOOD

In considering where you'll stay, think about what you'll be doing in Singapore—that way, you can choose a hotel that's close to the particular action that suits you. (On the other hand, since Singapore is a small place and public transportation is excellent, nothing's really ever too far away.)

Orchard Road has the largest cluster of hotels in the city, and is right in the heart of Singaporean shopping mania—the malls and wide sidewalks where locals and tourists stroll to see and be seen. The Historic District has hotels that are near museums and sights, while those in Marina Bay center more around the business professionals who come to Singapore for Suntec City, the giant convention and exhibition center located there. Chinatown and Tanjong Pagar have some lovely boutique hotels in quaint back streets, and Shenton Way has a couple of high-rise places for the convenience of people doing business in the downtown business district. Many hotels have free morning and evening shuttle buses to Orchard Road, Suntec City, and Shenton Way. I've also listed two hotels on Sentosa, an island to the south that's a popular day or weekend trip for many Singaporeans. (It's connected to Singapore by a causeway.)

CHOOSING YOUR HOME AWAY FROM HOME

What appeals to you? A big, flashy, internationalist palace or a smaller, homier place? Hyatt, Sheraton, Hilton, and Hotel Intercontinental are just a few of the international chain hotels you will find in Singapore. For the most part, these city hotels are nondescript towers—though the Swissôtel Stamford has the distinction of being the tallest hotel in Southeast Asia, with 71 floors. A few exceptions stand out. The Shangri-La has gorgeous landscaped grounds and pool area, making it truly a resort inside the city. Meanwhile, Shangri-La's Rasa Sentosa resort and The Beaufort on Sentosa island are out of the way, but have a real "get-away-from-it-all" ambience. In addition, a few hotels offer charming accommodations in historical premises. The most notable is Raffles, a Southeast Asian classic, and the new Fullerton Hotel, converted from the old general post office building. But you need not pay a fortune for quaint digs. Budget places like Albert Court and Regalis Court offer budget rooms in great locations with old-world charm.

The newest trend is the boutique hotel. Conceived as part of the Urban Restoration Authority's renewal plans, rows of old shophouses and buildings in ethnic areas like Chinatown and Tanjong Pagar have been restored and transformed into small, lovely hotels. Places like Albert Court Hotel, Berjaya Hotel, and the Royal Peacock are beautiful examples of local flavor turned into elegant accommodations. While these places can put you closer to the heart of Singapore, they do have their drawbacks—for one, both the hotels and their rooms are small and, due to building codes and a lack of space, they're unable to provide facilities like swimming pools, Jacuzzis, or fitness centers.

While budget hotels have very limited facilities and interior stylings that never made it much past 1979, you can always expect a clean room. What's more, service can sometimes be more personal in smaller hotels, where front desk staff has fewer faces to recognize and is accustomed to helping guests with the sorts of things a business center or concierge would handle in a larger hotel. Par for the course, many of the guests in these places are backpackers, and mostly Western backpackers at that. However, you will see some ASEAN (Association of Southeast Asian Nations) people staying in these places. *One note:* The budget accommodations listed here are places decent enough for any standards. While cheaper digs are available, the rooms can be dreary and depressing, musty and old, or downright sleazy.

Unless you choose one of the extreme budget hotels, there are some standard features you can expect to find everywhere. While no hotels offer a courtesy car or limousine, many have courtesy shuttles to popular parts of town. Security key cards are catching on, as are in-room safes (yes, even in safe and secure Singapore). You'll also see in-house movies and sometimes CNN on your TV, as well as a nifty interactive service that lets you check on your hotel bill, order room service, and get general information on Singapore with the touch of a button. Voice mail is gaining popularity, and fax services can always be provided upon request. You'll find most places have adequate fitness center facilities, almost all of which offer a range of massage treatments. Pools tend to be on the small side, and Jacuzzis are often placed in men's and women's locker rooms, making it impossible for couples to use them together. While tour desks are in some lobbies, car-rental desks are rare.

The Singapore Tourism Board (STB) recently launched a new campaign to pull hotel concierges into its loop with updated and accurate visitor information via a computer link to STB information resources. I've indicated in the text which hotels offer this service.

Many of the finest restaurants in Singapore are located in hotels, whether they are operated by the hotel directly or just inhabiting rented space. Some hotels can have up to five or six restaurants, each serving a different cuisine. Generally, you can expect these restaurants to be more expensive than places not located in

Urban Singapore Accommodations

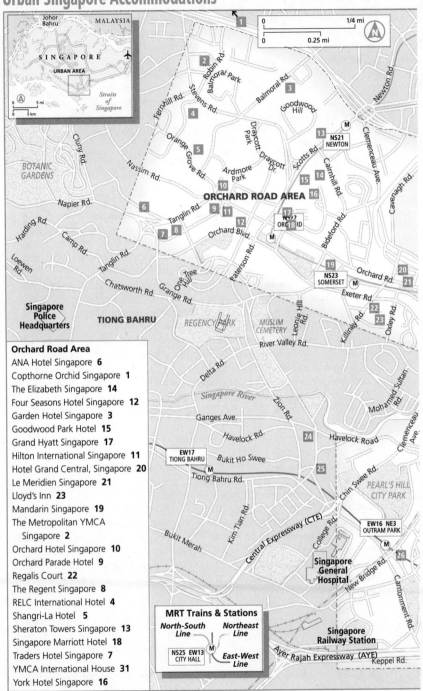

Orchard Road Area

ANA Hotel Singapore **6**
Copthorne Orchid Singapore **1**
The Elizabeth Singapore **14**
Four Seasons Hotel Singapore **12**
Garden Hotel Singapore **3**
Goodwood Park Hotel **15**
Grand Hyatt Singapore **17**
Hilton International Singapore **11**
Hotel Grand Central, Singapore **20**
Le Meridien Singapore **21**
Lloyd's Inn **23**
Mandarin Singapore **19**
The Metropolitan YMCA
  Singapore **2**
Orchard Hotel Singapore **10**
Orchard Parade Hotel **9**
Regalis Court **22**
The Regent Singapore **8**
RELC International Hotel **4**
Shangri-La Hotel **5**
Sheraton Towers Singapore **13**
Singapore Marriott Hotel **18**
Traders Hotel Singapore **7**
YMCA International House **31**
York Hotel Singapore **16**

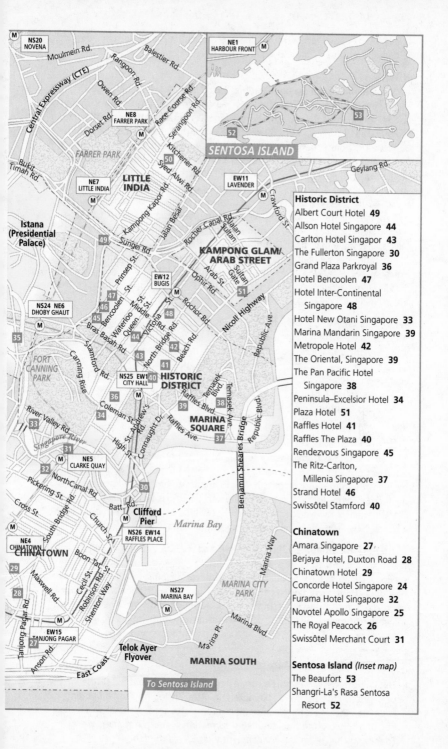

Historic District

Albert Court Hotel **49**
Allson Hotel Singapore **44**
Carlton Hotel Singapor **43**
The Fullerton Singapore **30**
Grand Plaza Parkroyal **36**
Hotel Bencoolen **47**
Hotel Inter-Continental
Singapore **48**
Hotel New Otani Singapore **33**
Marina Mandarin Singapore **39**
Metropole Hotel **42**
The Oriental, Singapore **39**
The Pan Pacific Hotel
Singapore **38**
Peninsula–Excelsior Hotel **34**
Plaza Hotel **51**
Raffles Hotel **41**
Raffles The Plaza **40**
Rendezvous Singapore **45**
The Ritz-Carlton,
Millenia Singapore **37**
Strand Hotel **46**
Swissôtel Stamford **40**

Chinatown

Amara Singapore **27**
Berjaya Hotel, Duxton Road **28**
Chinatown Hotel **29**
Concorde Hotel Singapore **24**
Furama Hotel Singapore **32**
Novotel Apollo Singapore **25**
The Royal Peacock **26**
Swissôtel Merchant Court **31**

Sentosa Island *(Inset map)*

The Beaufort **53**
Shangri-La's Rasa Sentosa
Resort **52**

hotels. In each hotel review, the distinguished restaurants have been noted; these restaurants are also fully reviewed in chapter 4.

RATES

Let's talk money. Rates for double rooms range from as low as S$95 (US$54) at the Strand on Bencoolen (a famous backpacker's strip) to as high as S$650 (US$371) a night at the exclusive Raffles Hotel. Average rooms are usually in the S$300 (US$171) range, but keep in mind that although all prices listed in this book are the going rates, they rarely represent what you'll actually pay. In fact, you should never have to pay the advertised rate in a Singapore hotel, as many offer promotional rates. When you call for your reservation, always ask what special deals they are running and how you can get the lowest price for your room. Many times hotels that have just completed renovations offer discounts, and most have special weekend or long-term stay programs. Also be sure to inquire about free add-ons. Complimentary breakfast and other services can have added value that makes a difference in the end.

For the purposes of this guide, I've divided hotels into the categories very expensive, S$450 (US$257) and up; expensive, S$350 to S$450 (US$200–US$257); moderate, S$200 to S$350 (US$114–US$200); and inexpensive, under S$200 (US$114).

TAXES & SERVICE CHARGES

All rates listed are in Singapore dollars, with U.S. dollar equivalents provided as well (remember to check the exchange rate when you're planning, though, since it may fluctuate). Most rates do not include the so-called "+++" taxes and charges: the 10% service charge, 5% goods and services tax (GST), and 1% cess (a 1% tax levied by the STB on all tourism-related activities). Keep these in mind when figuring your budget. Some budget hotels will quote discount rates inclusive of all taxes.

THE BUSY SEASON

The busy season is from January to around June. In the late summer months, business travel dies down and hotels try to make up for drooping occupancy rates by going after the leisure market. In fall, even tourism drops off somewhat, making the season ripe for budget-minded visitors. These may be the best times to get a deal. Probably the worst time to negotiate will be between Christmas and the Chinese New Year, when folks travel on vacation and to see their families.

MAKING RESERVATIONS ON THE GROUND

If you are not able to make a reservation before your trip, there is a reservation service available at Changi International Airport. The Singapore Hotel Association operates desks in both Terminals 1 and 2, with reservation services based upon room availability for many hotels. Discounts for these arrangements are sometimes as high as 30%. The desks are open daily from 7:30am to 11:30pm.

Tips **Making Hotel Reservations Online**

The website www.asia-hotels.com offers an Internet-based hotel reservation system for up to 6,500 hotels in Asia, including Singapore and Malaysia. The site offers competitive room rates through their Internet booking service, and lists detailed information on each hotel and resort. There's no charge for their service—hotels pick up the tab.

1 The Historic District

VERY EXPENSIVE

The Fullerton Singapore ★★ The newest darling of Singapore's luxury hotel market, The Fullerton is giving competitors like Ritz-Carlton and Four Seasons a run for their money. Originally built in 1928, this squat administrative building at the mouth of the Singapore River once housed the General Post Office. Today it is flanked by the urban skyline, and its classical facade, with its Doric columns and tall porticos, looks more mundane than opulent. But designers have done a superb job, restoring Italian marble floors, coffered ceilings, and cornices inside. The courtyard lobby is grand, with skylights above and Courtyard guest room windows lining the inner face of the building. Rooms have been cleverly arranged to fit the original structure, featuring vaulted ceilings and tall windows. While the architectural style is antique, the rooms are anything but. In fresh shades of champagne, they feature large writing desks, deluxe stationery kits, flat-screen TVs, SONY PlayStations, and electronic safes big enough to hold your laptop. Big bathrooms have separate bath and shower stalls, mini-Stairmasters, and stylish Philippe Starck fixtures. The attentive service here is second to none.

1 Fullerton Sq., Singapore 049178. (② **800/44-UTELL** in the U.S. and Canada, 800/221-176 in Australia, 800/933-123 in New Zealand, or 65/6733-8388. Fax 65/6735-8388. www.fullertonhotel.com. 400 units. S$450–S$650 (US$257–US$371) double, from S$800 (US$457) suite. AE, DC, MC, V. 5-min. walk to Raffles Place MRT. **Amenities:** 3 restaurants; bar and lobby lounge; outdoor infinity pool with view of the Singapore River; fitness center with Jacuzzi, sauna, and steam; spa with massage and beauty treatments; concierge; limousine service; business center; shopping arcade; salon; 24-hr. room service; babysitting; same-day laundry service/dry cleaning; nonsmoking rooms; executive-level rooms. *In room:* A/C, TV w/satellite programming and in-house movies, minibar, coffee/tea-making facilities, dataport w/direct Internet access, hair dryer, iron, safe.

Raffles Hotel ★★ Legendary since its establishment in 1887, and named after Singapore's first British colonial administrator, Sir Stamford Raffles, this posh hotel is one of the most recognizable names in Southeast Asian hospitality. Originally it was a bungalow, but by the 1920s and 1930s it had expanded to become a mecca for celebrities like Charlie Chaplin and Douglas Fairbanks, writers like Somerset Maugham and Noël Coward, and various and sundry kings, sultans, and politicians (the famous Long Bar, where the Singapore Sling was invented, is located here). Always at the center of Singapore's colonial high life, it's hosted balls, tea dances, and jazz functions, and during World War II was the last rallying point for the British in the face of Japanese occupation and the first place for refugee prisoners of war released from concentration camps. In 1987, the Raffles Hotel was declared a landmark and restored to its early-20th-century splendor, with grand arches, 4.2m (14-ft.) molded ceilings with spinning fans, tiled teak and marble floors, Oriental carpets, and period furnishings. Outside, the facade of the main building was similarly restored, complete with the elegant cast-iron portico and the verandas that encircle the upper stories.

Because it is a national landmark, thousands of people pass through the open lobby each day, so in addition there's a private inner lobby marked off for "residents" only. Nothing feels better than walking along the dark teak floors of the verandas, past little rattan-furnished relaxation areas overlooking the green tropical courtyards. Each suite entrance is like a private apartment door: Enter past the small living and dining area dressed in Oriental carpets and reproduction furniture, then pass through louvered doors into the bedroom with its four-poster bed and beautiful armoire, ceiling fan twirling high above. Now imagine you're a colonial traveler, fresh in town from a long ocean voyage. Raffles is the only hotel in Singapore where you can still fully play out this fantasy, and it can be a lot of fun. Other unique features include a hotel museum, popular theater playhouse, and an excellent culinary academy.

1 Beach Rd., Singapore 189673. ✆ **800/232-1886** in the U.S. and Canada, or 65/6337-1886. Fax 65/6339-7650. www.raffleshotel.com. 103 suites. S$650–S$6,000 (US$371–US$3,429) suite. AE, DC, MC, V. Next to City Hall MRT. **Amenities:** 8 restaurants; 2 bars and a billiard room; small outdoor pool; fitness center with Jacuzzi, sauna, steam, and spa; concierge; personal butler service; limousine service; business center; shopping arcade; salon; 24-hr. room service; babysitting; same-day laundry service/dry cleaning. *In room:* A/C, TV w/satellite programming and in-room VCR, minibar, coffee/tea-making facilities, fax, dataport w/direct Internet access, hair dryer, safe.

The Ritz-Carlton, Millenia Singapore ★★★ The ultimate in luxury hotels, The Ritz-Carlton blazes trails with sophisticated ultramodern design, sumptuous comfort, and stimulating art. Grand public spaces, lighted by futuristic window designs and splashed with artworks from the likes of Frank Stella, Dale Chihuly, David Hockney, and Andy Warhol, are a welcome change from international chain hotel design cliché. In comparison, guest rooms display a great deal of warmth and hominess. All rooms have spectacular views of either Kallang Bay or the more majestic Marina Bay. Even the bathrooms have views, as the huge tubs are placed under octagonal picture windows so you can gaze as you bathe. Oh, the decadence! Guest rooms here are about 25% larger than most five-star rooms elsewhere, providing ample space for big two-poster beds, and full walk-in closets.

7 Raffles Ave., Singapore 039799. ✆ **800/241-3333** in the U.S. and Canada, 800/241-33333 in Australia, 800/241-33333 in New Zealand, 800/234-000 in the U.K., or 65/6337-8888. Fax 65/6338-0001. www.ritz carlton.com. 610 units. S$515–S$595 (US$294–US$340) double; from S$698 (US$399) suite. AE, DC, MC, V. 10-min. walk to City Hall MRT. **Amenities:** 3 restaurants; lobby lounge; outdoor pool and Jacuzzi; outdoor, lighted tennis court; fitness center with sauna, steam, massage; concierge; limousine service; business center; shopping mall adjacent; 24-hr. room service; babysitting; same-day laundry service/dry cleaning; nonsmoking rooms; executive-level rooms. *In room:* A/C, TV w/satellite programming and in-house movie, minibar, coffee/tea-making facilities, dataport with direct Internet access, hair dryer, iron, safe.

EXPENSIVE

Carlton Hotel Singapore ★★★ In April 2002 Carlton opened its new Premier Wing, a 19-story building just next door to its 26-story Main Wing. Leisure travelers will be most interested in the newly refurbished, and lower-priced, superior and deluxe rooms in the Main Wing. While rooms in both categories are the same size and have all been smartly redone in contemporary neutral tones, deluxe rooms have broadband Internet access in-room, a flat-screen TV, plus marble bathroom decor (superiors are humble ceramic tile). The new building houses premier deluxe rooms, which, for a premium, feature larger bathrooms with separate bath and shower stall, an in-room safe to fit your laptop, and access to a coin-operated launderette. All public spaces have been upgraded as well, including the lobby entrance, alfresco coffee shop, and a tiny wine and cigar room. The location, in the center of the historic district, is terrific. Ask for a room with a view of the city.

76 Bras Basah Rd., Singapore 189558. ✆ **65/6338-8333.** Fax 65/6339-6866. www.carlton.com.sg. 627 units. S$350–S$400 (US$200–US$229) double; from S$480 (US$274) suite. AE, DC, MC, V. 5-min. walk to City Hall MRT. **Amenities:** 2 restaurants; lobby lounge; outdoor pool; fitness center with sauna, steam, and massage; concierge; tour desk; car-rental desk; limousine service; shuttle service; business center; 24-hr. room service; babysitting; same-day laundry service/dry cleaning; nonsmoking rooms; executive-level rooms. *In room:* A/C, TV w/satellite programming and in-house movie, minibar, coffee/tea-making facilities.

Hotel Inter-Continental Singapore ★ The government let Inter-Continental build a hotel in this spot with one ironclad stipulation: The hotel

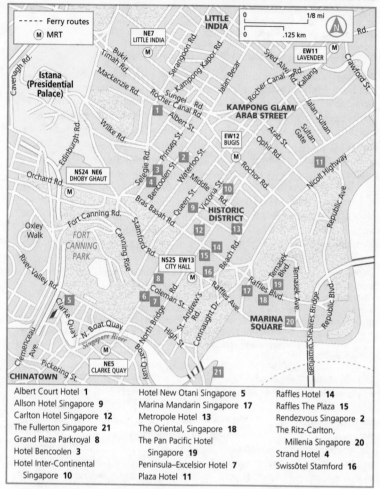

Albert Court Hotel **1**	Hotel New Otani Singapore **5**	Raffles Hotel **14**
Allson Hotel Singapore **9**	Marina Mandarin Singapore **17**	Raffles The Plaza **15**
Carlton Hotel Singapore **12**	Metropole Hotel **13**	Rendezvous Singapore **2**
The Fullerton Singapore **21**	The Oriental, Singapore **18**	The Ritz-Carlton,
Grand Plaza Parkroyal **8**	The Pan Pacific Hotel	Millenia Singapore **20**
Hotel Bencoolen **3**	Singapore **19**	Strand Hotel **4**
Hotel Inter-Continental	Peninsula–Excelsior Hotel **7**	Swissôtel Stamford **16**
Singapore **10**	Plaza Hotel **11**	

chain had to retain the original shophouses on the block and incorporate them into the hotel design. No preservation, no hotel. Reinforcing the foundation, Hotel Inter-Continental built up from there, giving touches of old architectural style to the lobby, lounge, and other public areas on the bottom floors while imbuing it with the feel of a modern hotel. Features like beamed ceilings and wooden staircases are warmly accentuated with Chinese and European antique reproductions, Oriental carpets, and local artworks. The second and third floors have "Shophouse Rooms" styled with such Peranakan trappings as carved hardwood furnishings and floral linens, and with homey touches like potted plants and carpets over wooden floors. These rooms are very unique, presenting a surprising element of local flair that you don't often find in large chain hotels. Guest rooms on higher levels are large, with formal European styling and large luxurious bathrooms.

80 Middle Rd., Singapore 188966 (near Bugis Junction). ✆ **800/327-0200** in the U.S. and Canada, 800/221-335 in Australia, 800/442-215 in New Zealand, 800/0289-387 in the U.K., or 65/6338-7600. Fax 65/6338-7366.

www.interconti.com. 406 units. S$440–S$480 (US$251–US$275) double; from S$630 (US$360) suite. AE, DC, MC, V. Bugis MRT. **Amenities:** 3 restaurants; bar and lobby lounge; outdoor pool; fitness center with Jacuzzi, sauna, and massage; concierge; limousine service; business center; shopping mall adjacent; 24-hr. room service; babysitting; same-day laundry service/dry cleaning; executive-level rooms. *In room:* A/C, TV w/satellite programming and in-house movie, minibar, coffee/tea-making facilities, hair dryer, safe.

Marina Mandarin Singapore ★★   There are a few hotels in the Marina Bay area built around the atrium concept, and of them, this one is the loveliest. The atrium lobby opens up to ceiling skylights 21 stories above, guest corridor balconies fringed with vines line the sides, and in the center hangs a glistening metal mobile sculpture in red and gold. One of the most surprising details is the melodic chirping of caged songbirds, which fills the open space every morning. In the evening, live classical music from the lobby bar drifts upward.

The guest rooms are equally impressive: large and cool, with two desk spaces and balconies standard for each room. Try to get the Marina view for that famous Shenton Way skyline towering above the bay. All bathrooms have double sinks, a separate shower and tub, and a bidet. Unique Venus Rooms, for women travelers, include potpourri, bath oils, custom pillows, and hair curler. One plus, the Marina Square Shopping Center attached to the lobby adds dozens of shops and services.

6 Raffles Blvd., Marina Square, Singapore 039594. ✆ **65/6338-3388.** Fax 65/6845-1001. www.marina-mandarin.com.sg. 575 units. S$380–S$450 (US$217–US$257) double; S$480 (US$274) executive club; from S$600 (US$343) suite. AE, DC, MC, V. 10-min. walk to City Hall MRT. **Amenities:** 3 restaurants; English pub and lobby lounge; outdoor pool; outdoor, lighted tennis courts; squash courts; fitness center with Jacuzzi, sauna, steam and massage; concierge; limousine service; business center; shopping mall adjacent; salon; 24-hr. room service; babysitting; same-day laundry service/dry cleaning; nonsmoking rooms; executive-level rooms. *In room:* A/C, TV w/satellite programming and in-house movie, minibar, coffee/tea-making facilities, hair dryer, safe.

The Oriental, Singapore ★★   Another atrium-concept hotel similar to neighboring properties Marina Mandarin and the Pan Pacific, The Oriental is one notch above the others. It has recently been honored as the official hotel for the brand-new Esplanade—Theatres on the Bay concert hall which is just opposite the hotel. Public spaces are elegant and modern, with polished black marble, leather seating and Asian decorative arts and accents. Despite its name, the hotel's guest rooms have very few Asian touches, featuring primarily Western style comforts and design. Rooms on higher floors command excellent views and are worth the extra cost.

5 Raffles Ave., Marina Sq., Singapore 039797. ✆ **800/526-6566** in the U.S. and Canada, 800/123-693 in Australia, 800/2828-3838 in New Zealand, 800/2828-3838 in the U.K., or 65/6338-0066. Fax 65/6339-9537. www.mandarinoriental.com. 524 units. S$390–S$440 (US$223–US$251) double; from S$520 (US$297) suite. AE, DC, MC, V. 10-min. walk to City Hall MRT. **Amenities:** 4 restaurants; bar and lobby lounge; outdoor pool; fitness center with Jacuzzi, sauna, and steam; concierge; limousine service; business center; salon; 24-hr. room service; babysitting; same-day laundry service/dry cleaning; nonsmoking rooms; executive-level rooms. *In room:* A/C, TV w/satellite programming and in-house movie, minibar, coffee/tea-making facilities, hair dryer, safe.

The Pan Pacific Hotel Singapore ★   Because of its location and design, the Pan Pacific Hotel competes heavily with the Marina Mandarin and The Oriental, all grabbing up their share of business travelers and Suntec City Convention Center guests. In doing so, Pan Pacific has included broadband Internet access in each room and optional mobile phones upon check-in for forwarding calls from the hotel's main number. Leisure travelers probably won't find tremendous use for these services; however, Pan Pacific is still a fine choice for comfortable and convenient accommodations. The atrium lobby has been newly renovated from its previous dark and looming presence to a brighter, more airy feel. Guest rooms are good-size and handsome, with designer fabrics in shades of tan plaids, coordinated plush carpeting, and luxurious marble bathrooms. Some have terrific views.

7 Raffles Blvd., Marina Square, Singapore 039595 (near Suntec City). (©) 800/327-8585 in the U.S. and Canada, 800/525-900 in Australia, 800/969-496 in the U.K., or 65/6336-8111. Fax 65/6339-1861. www. panpac.com. 784 units. S$440–S$480 (US$251–US$274) double; from S$780 (US$446) suite. AE, DC, MC, V. 10-min. walk to City Hall MRT. **Amenities:** 6 restaurants; lobby lounge; outdoor pool; 2 outdoor, lighted tennis court; fitness center with Jacuzzi, sauna, steam, massage and spa treatments; concierge; limousine service; shuttle service; business center; shopping arcade adjacent; 24-hr. room service; babysitting; same-day laundry service/dry cleaning; nonsmoking rooms; executive-level rooms. *In room:* A/C, TV w/satellite programming and in-house movie, minibar, coffee/tea-making facilities, dataport with direct Internet access, hair dryer, safe.

Raffles The Plaza ★★★   This has to be the best location in the city. Above an MRT hub and next to one of the largest shopping centers in Singapore, you won't find any inconveniences here. The lobby is studied serenity with soft lighting and music, a lovely escape from the crazy mall and hot streets. Perhaps the best reason to stay is the Amrita spa and fitness center, the largest of its type. A huge state-of-the-art gym with exercise and relaxation classes, a pool, hot and cold plunge pools, steam and sauna, and endless treatment rooms with Asian and European treatments from beauty and rejuvenation. Standard rooms are large and comfortable, having been recently updated with new soft goods. Premier deluxe rooms, however, are stunningly contemporary, with cushy bedding, big desk spaces, Bose Wave systems, and incredible bathrooms—crisp white tiles, glistening glass countertops, polished chrome fixtures, and a shower that simulates rainfall.

2 Stamford Road, Singapore 178882. (©) 65/6339-7777. Fax 65/6337-1554. www.raffles-theplazahotel.com. 769 units. S$390–S$430 (US$223–US$246) double; suites from S$1,100 (US$628.57). AE, DC, MC, V. **Amenities:** 10 restaurants; martini bar, lobby lounge, and a live jazz venue; outdoor pool; spa with gym, Jacuzzi, sauna, steam, and massage; concierge; limousine service; business center; shopping arcade adjacent; 24-hr. room service; babysitting; same-day laundry service/dry cleaning; nonsmoking rooms; executive-level rooms. *In room:* A/C, TV w/satellite programming and in-house movie, minibar, coffee/tea-making facilities, hair dryer, safe.

MODERATE

Allson Hotel Singapore   In 2002 and 2003, Allson will see some major renovations—just in time to save it from getting overly tatty. The facade, two-tiered lobby, and public spaces will get a complete work over, advancing the decor to the current century. Guest rooms will be upgraded floor-by-floor, with new decorator touches and sprucing in bathrooms. Even perennial Szechuan favorite Liu Hsiang Lou restaurant will be replaced with something more in keeping with current trends. The small pool area and even smaller gym will see some maintenance touch-ups as art of the scheme. Don't book a stay here until after June 2003, and make sure to inquire that renovations have actually completed, or you may be inconvenienced by construction noises. However, after completion, this sparkling hotel, with its terrific location and inexpensive rates, will be an even greater value for the leisure traveler.

101 Victoria St., Singapore 188018. (©) 65/6336-0811. Fax 65/6339-7019. www.allsonhotels.com. 450 units. S$250 (US$150) double; S$450 (US$269) suite. AE, DC, MC, V. 5-min. walk from Bugis Junction MRT. **Amenities:** 3 restaurants; lounge; small outdoor pool; fitness center with Jacuzzi, sauna, steam, massage; tour desk; business center; salon; 24-hr. room service; babysitting; same-day laundry service/dry cleaning; nonsmoking rooms; executive-level rooms. *In room:* A/C, TV w/satellite programming and in-house movie, minibar, coffee/tea-making facilities, safe.

Grand Plaza Parkroyal ⭐⭐ The Grand Plaza was built on top of (and incorporating) 2 blocks of prewar shophouses, and you can see hints of shophouse detail throughout the lobby, which is otherwise like any other hotel's. The old alleyway that ran between the shophouse blocks has been transformed into a courtyard where dinner is served alfresco. The hotel is located at the corner of Coleman and Hill streets, just across from the Armenian Church, the Asian Civilisations Museum, the Singapore Arts Museum, and Fort Canning Park—and if that's not convenient enough, a shuttle will take you to Orchard Road. Guest rooms are of smaller size, have decent closet space, and sport sharp Italian contemporary furniture in natural tones, with homey touches like snugly comforters on all the beds. This property does not stand out from the crowd, except for the St. Gregory Marine Spa, a popular and discrete full-service facility.

10 Coleman St., Singapore 179809. © **65/6336-3456.** Fax 65/6339-9311. www.plazapacifichotels.com. 326 units. S$320–S$340 (US$183–US$194) double; from S$500 (US$286) suite. AE, DC, MC, V. 5-min. walk to City Hall MRT. **Amenities:** 3 restaurants; lobby lounge; outdoor pool with view of Armenian Church across the street; fitness center; spa with Jacuzzi, sauna, steam, massage; concierge; shuttle service; business center; 24-hr. room service; babysitting; same-day laundry service/dry cleaning; executive-level rooms. *In room:* A/C, TV w/satellite programming, minibar, coffee/tea-making facilities, safe.

Hotel New Otani Singapore The Hotel New Otani sits along the Singapore River just next to Clarke Quay (a popular spot for nightlife, dining, and shopping) and a stroll away from the Historic District. At night, you have access to nearby Boat Quay bars and restaurants to one side and to the unique clubs of Mohamed Sultan Road on the other. The hotel was renovated in 1993, and unique additions (to all rooms) include multimedia PCs with Microsoft Office and tourist information. Internet access and computer games are also available for an extra charge. All rooms have small balconies with good views of the river, the financial district, Fort Canning Park, or Chinatown, and the standard rooms have large luxurious bathrooms like those you typically see in more deluxe accommodations. Facilities include a large outdoor pool and a fitness center with aerobics, a Jacuzzi, sauna, facials, and massage (you can even get a massage poolside). The hotel runs daily shuttle service to Orchard Road, Shenton Way, and Marina Square, plus a complimentary evening river cruise for all room categories.

177A River Valley Rd., Singapore 179031. © **800/421-8795** in the U.S. and Canada, or 65/6338-3333. Fax 65/6339-2854. www.newotanisingapore.com. 408 units. S$320–S$360 (US$183–US$206) double; from S$600 (US$343) suite. AE, DC, MC, V. Far from MRT stations. **Amenities:** 3 restaurants; lobby lounge; outdoor pool; fitness center; concierge; tour desk; limousine service; shuttle service; business center; shopping mall adjacent; 24-hr. room service; babysitting; same-day laundry service/dry cleaning; executive-level rooms. *In room:* A/C, TV w/satellite programming, minibar, coffee/tea-making facilities; in-room PC w/direct Internet access, safe.

Peninsula • Excelsior Hotel ⭐⭐ *Value* In 2000, two of Singapore's busiest tourist-class hotels merged, combining their lobby and facilities into one giant value-for-money property. The location is excellent, in the Historic District within walking distance to Chinatown and Boat Quay. It's a popular pick for groups, but don't let the busloads of tourists steer you away. There are some great deals to be had here, especially if you request the guest rooms in the Peninsula tower. These are large and colorful, with big picture windows, some of which have stunning views of the city, the Singapore River, and the marina. Surprisingly, these rooms are priced about S$10 lower than rooms in the Excelsior tower, which are smaller and, frankly, look like they haven't seen a decor update since the far-out 1970s. At the time of writing, they were in the process of wiring the place for in-room Internet access.

5 Coleman St., Singapore 179805. ⓒ **65/6337-2200.** Fax 65/6336-3847. www.ythotels.com.sg. 600 units. S$240–S$260 (US$144–US$156) double; S$360–S$440 (US$216–US$263) suite. AE, DC, MC, V. 5-min. walk to City Hall MRT. **Amenities:** Restaurant; bar and lobby lounge; 2 outdoor pools; fitness center with Jacuzzi; concierge; tour desk; business center; shopping mall adjacent; 24-hr. room service; babysitting; same-day laundry service/dry cleaning. *In room:* A/C, TV, minibar, coffee/tea-making facilities, hair dryer, safe.

Plaza Hotel   Situated just across from the Arab Street and Kampong Glam areas, you're a little off the beaten track at the Plaza Hotel—you'll need to take buses or taxis just about everywhere—but the trade-off is that if you stick around you can take advantage of the gorgeous and luxurious recreation and relaxation facilities, which include a half-size Olympic pool with a diving board (a rarity in Singapore), a dreamy sun deck decorated in a lazy-days Balinese-style tropical motif, and a Bali-themed poolside cafe, cooled by ceiling fans. Two gyms to the side have plenty of space and new equipment, but the most exquisite facility of all is the spa. Guest rooms are fine and exactly what you'd want for the price. Other hotel facilities include outdoor and indoor Jacuzzis, sauna, and steam room.

7500A Beach Rd., Singapore 199591. ⓒ **65/6298-0011.** Fax 65/6296-3600. www.plazapacifichotels.com. 350 units. S$270–S$370 (US$154–US$211) double; from S$390 (US$223) suite. AE, DC, MC, V. 10-min. walk to Bugis MRT. **Amenities:** 2 restaurants; lounge; outdoor pool; fitness center; spa with Jacuzzi, sauna, steam, massage; concierge; tour desk; limousine service; business center; 24-hr. room service; babysitting; same-day laundry service/dry cleaning; executive-level rooms. *In room:* A/C, TV w/satellite programming and in-house movie, minibar, coffee/tea-making facilities, dataport w/direct Internet access, hair dryer, safe.

Rendezvous Singapore ⭐   A new tourist-class hotel, this modest place run by an Australian chain occupies a block of prewar shophouses along busy Bras Basah Road between Orchard Road and Raffles City. Everything here is very scaled down, from the rear entrance that looks like a service entrance, to the small lobby, to the plain but tidy guest rooms. Standard category rooms are small compared to others in the city, but deluxe and premier rooms are larger. Mediterranean touches, royal colors, and high ceilings are standard throughout, but only higher priced category rooms have in-room broadband Internet access. Or, to save a dime, you can use the inexpensive Internet cafe off the lobby courtyard. Unless you can get a great discount, you can find better accommodations for the money.

9 Bras Basah Rd., Singapore 189559. ⓒ **800/655-147** in Australia, or 65/6336-0220. Fax 65/6337-3773. www.rendezvoushotels.com. 300 units. S$330–S$410 (US$189–US$234) double. AE, DC, MC, V. 10-min. walk to either Dhoby Ghaut or Raffles City MRT. **Amenities:** Restaurant; bar; outdoor pool and Jacuzzi; basic fitness center with sauna; concierge; shuttle service; business center; shopping arcade; 24-hr. room service; babysitting; same-day laundry service/dry cleaning; nonsmoking rooms; executive-level rooms. *In room:* A/C, TV w/satellite programming, minibar, coffee/tea-making facilities, hair dryer, safe.

Swissôtel Stamford ⭐⭐⭐ (Value)   You'd think a room in the tallest hotel in the world would cost a bundle, but this gem is reasonably priced. Besides, with an amazing location, right on top of a subway hub and a huge shopping complex, walking distance from many sights and attractions, this hotel is great value for money. On a clear day you can see Indonesia, so make sure you request a room with a view. Done in fresh white linens, cool neutral fabrics, and new furnishings in golden wood tones, these large rooms also feature private balconies and full toiletries in marble bathrooms. Executive rooms in The Stamford Crest also have Bose hi-fi systems, ergonomically designed writing tables and chairs, multifunction printer, fax and copier, plus bathrooms with a view. It's managed by Raffles international, so you can be sure of friendly and professional service.

2 Stamford Rd., Singapore 178882. ℂ 800/637-9477 in the U.S. and Canada, and 800/121-043 in Australia, or 65/6338-8585. Fax 65/6338-2862. www.swissotel-thestamford.com. 1,200 units. S$195–S$420 (US$110–US$236) double; S$600–S$3300 (US$337–US$1,854) suite. AE, DC, MC, V. City Centre MRT. **Amenities:** 10 restaurants; martini bar, lobby lounge, and a live jazz venue; outdoor pool; spa with gym, Jacuzzi, sauna, steam, and massage; concierge; limousine service; business center; shopping arcade adjacent; 24-hr. room service; babysitting; same-day laundry service/dry cleaning; nonsmoking rooms; executive-level rooms. *In room:* A/C, TV w/satellite programming and in-house movie, minibar, coffee/tea-making facilities, hair dryer, safe.

INEXPENSIVE

Albert Court Hotel ★★ (*Value*) This hotel was first conceived as part of the Urban Renewal Authority's master plan to revitalize this block, which involved the restoration of two rows of prewar shophouses. The eight-story boutique hotel that emerged has all the Western comforts but has retained the charm of its shophouse roots. Decorators placed local Peranakan touches everywhere from the carved teak furnishings in traditional floral design to the antique china cups used for tea service in the rooms. (Guaranteed: The sight of these cups brings misty-eyed nostalgia to the hearts of Singaporeans.) Guest room details like the teak molding, bathroom tiles in bright Peranakan colors, and old-time brass electrical switches give this place true local charm and distinction. A recent refurbishment, completed in 2001, gives an added freshness to the rooms.

180 Albert St., Singapore 189971. ℂ 65/6339-3939. Fax 65/6339-3252. www.albertcourt.com.sg. 136 units. S$185–S$200 (US$106–US$114) double. AE, DC, MC, V. 5-min. walk to Bugis MRT. **Amenities:** 3 restaurants; small lobby lounge; tour desk; limited room service; babysitting; same-day laundry service/dry cleaning. *In room:* A/C, TV w/satellite programming, minibar, coffee/tea-making facilities, hair dryer, safe.

Hotel Bencoolen Bencoolen is the signature backpacker hotel on the block, and it is definitely budget minded through and through: To get into the place you have to enter through the ground-level parking lot; the rooms are on the small side, and filled with old and oddly matched furnishings; and the double beds are two twins pushed together. Even the walls are strange combinations of painted concrete, tiles, and padded paneling. The showers here are a nightmare, with hand-held shower nozzles and no clips on the walls on which to hang them. Executive rooms are slightly nicer—the same size, but with bigger closets, a small desk area, and a TV set, hair dryer, and fridge in each. For only US$5 more a night, I'd say go for it. The hotel has a rooftop restaurant, and parking is available.

47 Bencoolen St., Singapore 189626. ℂ 65/6336-0822. Fax 65/6336-2250. www.hotelbencoolen.com.sg. 74 units. S$85 (US$49) double. MC, V. 10-min. walk to City Hall MRT. **Amenities:** Restaurant; sauna; same-day laundry service; nonsmoking rooms. *In room:* A/C, TV, coffee/tea-making facilities.

Metropole Hotel Located at the corner of Beach Road and Seah Street, the Metropole Hotel is right next to the Raffles Hotel, which means you'll either enjoy the proximity or feel like a passenger in steerage staring up at first class. The lobby is nothing to speak of, and the rooms are sparsely furnished and on the musty side, with desks, a stock-it-yourself fridge, radios, small windows, small closets, and no views. Babysitting and fax services are available. Sure, the rates include breakfast, but you could do better at the Strand (see below) for less money. A coffeehouse and the Imperial Herbal restaurant (reviewed in chapter 4 and a good place for the cure to what ails you) are on the premises.

41 Seah St., Singapore 188396. ℂ 65/6336-3611. Fax 65/6339-3610. www.metrohotel.com. 54 units. S$98–S$124 (US$56–US$71) standard to studio deluxe. AE, DC, MC, V. 5-min. walk to City Hall MRT. **Amenities:**

2 restaurants; babysitting; same-day laundry service; executive-level rooms. *In room:* A/C, TV, coffee/tea-making facilities.

Strand Hotel ⭐ *Value*   The Strand is by far the best of the backpacker places in Singapore. The lobby is far nicer than you'd expect, and for a promotional price of S$69, you get a clean and neat room. Although there are some hints that you really are staying in a budget hotel—older decor and uncoordinated furniture sets, for instance—the place provides some little niceties, like hotel stationery. The no-frills bathrooms are clean and adequate. There are no coffee/tea-making facilities, but there is 24-hour room service and a cafe on the premises. Free parking is available.

25 Bencoolen St., Singapore 189619. ℂ **65/6338-1866.** Fax 65/6338-1330. 130 units. S$95 (US$54) double; S$110 (US$63) triple; S$140 (US$80) 4-person sharing. AE, DC, MC, V. 10-min. walk to City Hall MRT. **Amenities:** Restaurant; 24-hr. room service; same-day laundry service. *In room:* A/C, TV.

2 Chinatown

EXPENSIVE

Swissôtel Merchant Court ⭐   Merchant Court's convenient location and facilities make it very popular with leisure travelers. Situated on the Singapore River, the hotel has easy access not only to Chinatown and the Historic District, but also to Clarke Quay and Boat Quay, with their multitude of dining and nightlife options. It will become even more convenient when the new MRT stop opens just outside its doors in early 2003. While this hotel's guest rooms aren't the biggest or most plush in the city, I never felt claustrophobic due to the large windows, uncluttered decor, and cooling atmosphere. Try to get a room with a view of the river or landscaped pool area. Convenience is provided by a self-service launderette, drink and snack vending machines on each floor, and unstocked minibar fridge, so you can buy your own provisions. The hotel touts itself as a city hotel with a resort feel, with landscaped pool area (with a view of the river).

20 Merchant Rd., Singapore 058281. ℂ **800/637-9477** in the U.S. and Canada, 800/121-043 in Australia, 800/637-94771 in the U.K., or 65/6337-2288. Fax 65/6334-0606. www.swissotel.com. 476 units. S$315–S$375 (US$180–US$214) double; from S$810 (US$463) suite. AE, DC, MC, V. 10-min. walk to Raffles Place MRT. **Amenities:** Restaurant; bar; outdoor pool; fitness center and spa with Jacuzzi, sauna, steam, massage and beauty treatments; 24-hr. room service; babysitting; same-day laundry service/dry cleaning; nonsmoking rooms; executive-level rooms. *In room:* A/C, TV w/satellite programming and in-house movie, minibar, coffee/tea-making facilities, dataport with direct Internet access, hair dryer, safe.

MODERATE

Amara Singapore   Amara, located in the Shenton Way financial district, attracts primarily business travelers, so if your vacation includes a little business too, this hotel puts you closer to the action. If you're simply in town for a vacation, though, Amara probably isn't your best choice. The top eight floors of this hotel are reserved for the corporate set—not only do they have better views, but modern decor and services attractive to business visitors as well. Rooms on the Leisure Floors have an unappealing combination of green and white painted furniture, and have very little to offer in terms of views. The hotel does have other convenience facilities like a self-service launderette and ice machines and shoe polishers on each floor, plus the usual: a large outdoor pool, a fitness center, Jacuzzi, sauna, two outdoor tennis courts, a jogging track, and a shopping arcade.

165 Tanjong Pagar Rd., Singapore 088539. ⓒ **65/6224-4488.** Fax 65/6224-3910. www.amarahotels.com. 338 units. S$360 (US$206) double; S$420 (US$240) executive club; S$600–S$800 (US$343–US$457) suite. AE, DC, MC, V. 5-min. walk to Tanjong Pagar MRT. **Amenities:** 2 restaurants; lounge; outdoor pool; outdoor, lighted tennis court; fitness center with Jacuzzi, sauna, steam, and massage; concierge; limousine service; business center; shopping arcade; salon; 24-hr. room service; babysitting; same-day laundry service/dry cleaning; nonsmoking rooms; executive-level rooms. *In room:* A/C, TV w/satellite programming and in-house movie, minibar, coffee/tea-making facilities, dataport w/direct Internet access, hair dryer, safe.

Berjaya Hotel, Duxton Road (⋆   Formerly The Duxton, this was one of the first accommodations in Singapore to experiment with the boutique hotel concept, transforming its shophouse structure into a small hotel and doing it with an elegance that earned it great international acclaim. From the outside, the place has old-world charm equal to any lamplit European cobblestone street, but step inside and there are very few details to remind you that you are in a quaint old shophouse—or in the historic Chinese district, for that matter. It's done entirely in turn-of-the-20th-century styling that includes reproduction Chippendale furniture, hand-painted wallpapers, and pen-and-ink Audubon-style drawings. Unfortunately, in recent years the hotel has dropped in service quality and the place has grown frayed around the edges. The recent take-over by Malaysian four-star hotel chain Berjaya is the first clue that this former luxury accommodation has gone downhill. Berjaya has no plans for refurbishment, which this place really needs. Each room is different (to fit the structure of the building), and some can be quite small with limited views. Garden suites feature a lovely little courtyard. Building regulations do not allow for a pool and space does not allow for fitness centers (they will arrange access to a nearby fitness center for you).

83 Duxton Rd., Singapore 089540. ⓒ **65/6227-7678.** Fax 65/6227-1232. www.berjayaresorts.com. 50 units. S$210–S$250 (US$120–US$143) double; S$290 (US$166) suite. AE, DC, MC, V. 5-min. walk to Tanjong Pagar MRT. **Amenities:** Restaurant; lobby bar; shuttle service; limited room service; babysitting; same-day laundry service/dry cleaning. *In room:* A/C, TV w/satellite programming and in-house movie, minibar, coffee/tea-making facilities, hair dryer, safe.

Concorde Hotel Singapore   This place originally opened as the Glass Hotel, a name Concorde has found difficult to shake, since its curving facades are covered to the seams with smoky windows. That famous facade recently underwent a face-lift, along with the hotel's large circular atrium and bubble lifts that take you up to guest floors. The newly refurbished rooms are airy, with new furniture in simple contemporary style. Make sure when you book that you request a newer room. Superior rooms, on lower floors, fill up faster than deluxe rooms, and really for your money there's very little difference between the two. However, the building's round shape means that rooms located in the middle are larger, while those off to the side are somewhat cramped. The Concorde's location is not exactly central, but it still remains a favorite with tour groups and leisure travelers looking for some of the lowest promotional rates in town. Make sure you bargain hard.

317 Outram Rd., Singapore 169075. ⓒ **65/6733-0188.** Fax 65/6733-0989. www.concorde.net. 515 units. S$260–S$500 (US$149–US$286) double; S$650–S$1,600 (US$371–US$914) suite. AE, DC, MC, V. **Amenities:** 2 restaurants; bar; outdoor pool; outdoor tennis court; small gym; tour desk; business center; shopping arcade; 24-hr. room service; babysitting; same-day laundry service/dry cleaning; executive-level rooms. *In room:* A/C, TV w/satellite programming, minibar, coffee/tea-making facilities, hair dryer, safe.

Furama Hotel Singapore   Located smack-dab between the heart of Chinatown and the Boat Quay and Clarke Quay areas, the Furama is a good moderately priced choice if you want to be near shopping and nightlife. The first

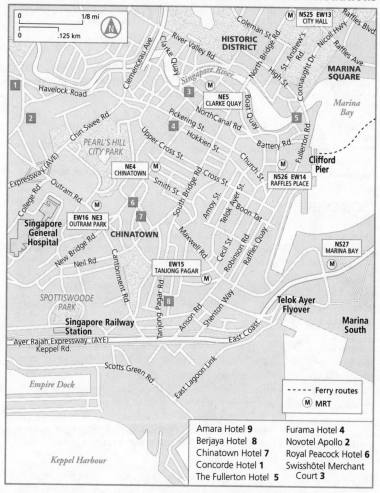

Amara Hotel **9**
Berjaya Hotel **8**
Chinatown Hotel **7**
Concorde Hotel **1**
The Fullerton Hotel **5**
Furama Hotel **4**
Novotel Apollo **2**
Royal Peacock Hotel **6**
Swisshôtel Merchant Court **3**

high-rise hotel built in Chinatown, it has a funky, arching multilevel rooftop that always attracts attention. Guest rooms are good size and as cozy as home, and the bathrooms are large, leaving you plenty of space to spread out. One small drawback is the lack of any foyer or entranceway between the corridors and the rooms themselves—the doors just open right in. Hotel facilities include a small outdoor pool, a small fitness center with Jacuzzi, and a shopping arcade.

60 Eu Tong Sen St., Singapore 059804. **℃** **65/6533-3888.** Fax 65/6534-1489. www.furama-hotels.com. 355 units. S$260–S$330 (US$149–US$189) double; from S$380 (US$217) suite. AE, DC, MC, V. 10-min. walk to Outram MRT. **Amenities:** 2 restaurants; lounge; outdoor pool; tour desk; limousine service; business center; shopping arcade; salon; 24-hr. room service; babysitting; same-day laundry service/dry cleaning; nonsmoking rooms; executive-level rooms. *In room:* A/C, TV w/satellite programming, minibar, coffee/tea-making facilities, dataport w/direct Internet access.

Novotel Apollo Singapore Novotel has just recently taken over the management of this property, an older hotel that has recently undergone construction of a new wing. Called the Tropical Wing, it caters primarily to corporate travelers, featuring a fully modern facility with large rooms and new furnishings. The construction project also included enlargement of the lobby with a comfortable lobby lounge, a new outdoor pool and Jacuzzi, outdoor tennis courts, and a huge ballroom. The old wing, called the Tower Block, has slightly less expensive rooms, and has also been recently refurbished with new plush carpeting, bedspreads, drapery and upholstery. If you're staying here, you may find yourself dependent on taxi transportation, as the MRT is a bit far, but the location is still within short taxi hops around the city.

405 Havelock Rd., Singapore 169633. ⓒ **65/6733-2081.** Fax 65/6733-1588. www.novotelapollo.com. 480 units. S$240–S$280 (US$137–US$189) double; S$450 (US$257) suite. AE, DC, MC, V. 15-min. walk to Outram MRT. **Amenities:** 2 restaurants; lounge; outdoor pool; outdoor, lighted tennis court; concierge; tour desk; business center; salon; 24-hr. room service; same-day laundry service/dry cleaning; nonsmoking rooms; executive-level rooms. *In room:* A/C, TV w/satellite programming, minibar, coffee/tea-making facilities, dataport w/direct Internet access, safe.

INEXPENSIVE

Chinatown Hotel ⭐ Chinatown Hotel definitely has its pros and cons, but for clean rooms, friendly service, and a good rate, it's one of my favorites. *Be prepared:* Because this is a boutique hotel with limited space, the rooms, though modern and well maintained, are tiny, and the bathrooms are the shower—just a shower head coming out of the wall as you stand in front of the sink. Some rooms have no windows, so specify when you make reservations if you're fond of natural light. Guest room TVs have one movie channel, and some rooms have been recently supplied with coffee/tea-making facilities, hair dryers (unique for this price category), and unstocked refrigerators. Or you can enjoy free coffee, tea, and toast in the lobby. Larger hotels will charge higher rates so you can enjoy the luxury of a pool, fitness center, and multiple food and beverage outlets; but if you're in town to get out and see Singapore, it's nice to know you won't pay for things you'll never use. Besides, the folks at the front counter will always remember your name and are very professional without being impersonal.

12–16 Teck Lim Rd., Singapore 088388. ⓒ **65/6225-5166.** Fax 65/6225-3912. www.chinatownhotel.com. 42 units. S$80–S$90 (US$48–US$54) double. AE, DC, MC, V. 5-min. walk to Outram MRT. **Amenities:** Complimentary toast, coffee, and instant noodles in the lobby; same-day laundry service/dry cleaning. *In room:* A/C, TV.

The Royal Peacock In the center of Chinatown's historic red-light district is one of Singapore' smallest boutique hotels, the Royal Peacock. Occupying 10 restored prewar shophouses, the place is tiny but colorful inside and out. As with other hotels of this type, the existing shophouse structure and strict restoration regulations make very small rooms de rigueur, but you've got to wonder about the hotel's decision to decorate them in the darkest colors they could find: Each room has one wall painted deep red, and purple carpet is used throughout. It's visually exciting, sure, but it makes you (or me, at least) feel claustrophobic. Adding to the problem is the fact that the less expensive rooms have no windows, and, where there are windows, they're just small squares. Yikes. All told, though, and even taking these criticisms into account, the rooms have flair. All have pretty wooden sleigh beds, and the bathrooms—which, due to restoration regulations, don't have tubs—are separated from the rooms with louvered shutters and are done in terra-cotta tiles. Rumor has it they're rethinking the entire design scheme. Room service is available for lunch and dinner till 10:30pm, and secretarial services are available as well.

55 Keong Saik Rd., Singapore 089158. ⓒ **65/6223-3522.** Fax 65/6221-1770. www.royalpeacockhotel.com. 79 units. S$160 (US$91) double with no window; S$230 (US$131) double with window; S$250 (US$143)

junior suite. AE, DC, MC, V. 5-min. walk to Outram MRT. **Amenities:** Restaurant; lounge; tour desk; business center; 24-hr. room service; same-day laundry service/dry cleaning. *In room:* A/C, TV w/in-house movie, minibar, coffee/tea-making facilities, dataport with direct Internet access, safe.

3 Orchard Road Area

VERY EXPENSIVE

Four Seasons Hotel Singapore ★★★   Many upmarket hotels strive to convince you that staying with them is like visiting a wealthy friend. Four Seasons delivers this promise. The guest rooms are very spacious and inviting, and even the standard rooms have creature comforts you'd expect from a suite, such as complimentary fruit, terry bathrobes and slippers, CD and video disk players, and an extensive complimentary video disk and CD library that the concierge is just waiting to deliver selections from to your room. Each room has two-line speakerphones with voice mail and an additional dataport. The Italian marble bathrooms have double vanities, deep tubs, bidets, Neutrogena amenities, and surround speakers for the TV and stereo. Did I mention remote-control drapes? Everything here is comfort and elegance done to perfection (in fact, the beds here are so comfortable that they've sold almost 100 in the gift shop.) In the waiting area off the lobby you can sink into soft sofas and appreciate the antiques and artwork selected from the owner's private collection. The fitness center has a state-of-the-art gymnasium with TV monitors, videos, tape players and CD and video disk players, a virtual-reality bike, aerobics, sauna, steam rooms, massage, facials, body wraps and aromatherapy treatments, and a staff of fitness professionals. Want more? How about a flotation tank and a Mind Gear Syncro-Energiser (a brain relaxer that uses pulsing lights), a billiards room, and an OptiGolf Indoor Pro-Golf System. Two indoor, air-conditioned tennis courts and two outdoor courts are staffed with a resident professional tennis coach to provide instruction or play a game. There are two pools: a 20m lap pool and a rooftop sun deck pool, both with adjacent Jacuzzis. Consider a standard room here before a suite in a less expensive hotel. You won't regret it.

190 Orchard Blvd., Singapore 248646. ⓒ 800/332-3442 in the U.S., 800/268-6282 in Canada, or 65/6734-1110. Fax 65/6733-0682. www.fourseasons.com 254 units. S$475–S$530 (US$271–US$303) double; S$620–S$4,500 (US$354–US$2,571) suite. AE, DC, MC, V. 5-min. walk to Orchard MRT. **Amenities:** 2 restaurants; bar; 2 outdoor pools with adjacent Jacuzzis; 2 indoor, lighted tennis courts and 2 indoor air-conditioned tennis courts; Singapore's best equipped fitness center; spa with sauna, steam, massage and full menu of beauty and relaxation treatments; billiards room; concierge; limousine service; business center; 24-hr. room service; babysitting; same-day laundry service/dry cleaning; nonsmoking rooms; executive-level rooms. *In room:* A/C, TV w/satellite programming and in-room laserdisc player with complimentary disks available, minibar, coffee/tea-making facilities, hair dryer, safe.

Goodwood Park Hotel ★   This national landmark, built in 1900, resembles a castle along the Rhine—having served originally as the Teutonia Club, a social club for the early German community. During World War II, high-ranking Japanese military used it as a residence, and later it served as a British war crimes court before being converted into a hotel. Since then the hotel has expanded from 60 rooms to 235, and has hosted a long list of international celebrities and dignitaries.

For the money, there are more luxurious facilities, but while most hotels have bigger and better business and fitness centers (Goodwood has the smallest fitness center), only the Raffles Hotel can rival Goodwood Park's historic significance. The poolside suites off the Mayfair Pool are fabulous in slate tiles and polished wood, offering direct access to the small Mayfair Pool with its lush Balinese-style landscaping. There are also suites off the main pool, which is much larger but offers little privacy from the lobby and surrounding restaurants. The original building has large and airy guest rooms in a classic European decor, but beware of the showers, which have hand-held shower heads that clip to the wall, making it difficult to aim and impossible to keep the water from splashing out all over the bathroom floor. Newer rooms in the main wing are renovated in stark contemporary style. The extremely attentive staff always serves with a smile.

22 Scotts Rd., Singapore 228221. ℂ **800/772-3890** in the U.S., 800/665-5919 in Canada, 800/89-95-20 in the U.K., or 65/6737-7411. Fax 65/6732-8558. www.goodwoodparkhotel.com.sg. 235 units. S$425–S$465 (US$243–US$266) double; S$615–S$650 (US$351–US$371) poolside suite; S$888–S$3,000 (US$507–US$1,714) suite. AE, DC, MC, V. 5-min. walk to Orchard MRT. **Amenities:** 6 restaurants; bar and lobby lounge; 2 outdoor pools; tiny fitness center; spa; concierge; limousine service; business center; 24-hr. room service; babysitting; same-day laundry service/dry cleaning. *In room:* A/C, TV w/satellite programming and in-house movie, minibar, coffee/tea-making facilities, hair dryer, safe.

Grand Hyatt Singapore ★★ Rumor has it that, despite its fantastic location, this hotel was doing pretty poorly until they had a feng shui master come in and evaluate it for redecorating. According to the Chinese monk, because the lobby entrance was a wall of flat glass doors that ran parallel to the long reception desk in front, all the hotel's money was flowing from the desk right out the doors and into the street. To correct the problem, the doors are now set at right angles to each other, a fountain was built in the rear, and the reception was moved around a corner to the right of the lobby. Since then, the hotel has enjoyed some of the highest occupancy rates in town. Feng shui or not, the new decor is modern, sleek, and sophisticated, an elegant combination of polished black marble and deep wood. Terrace Wing guest rooms invite with plush duvet and golden colors, plus unique glass-enclosed alcoves looking over the hotel gardens. Bathrooms are large, with lots of marble counter space. The Grand Wing rooms are really suites, with separate living areas, small walk-in closets and separate work area. A very deluxe choice, especially after they complete their refurbishment plans to freshen the decor in mid-2003. The pool and fitness center are amazing. Located in the center of this city hotel, a four-story waterfall provides the perfect soundscape to match a lush jungle garden hugging the free-form pool and state of the art gym.

10–12 Scotts Rd., Singapore 228211. ℂ **800/223-1234** in the U.S. and Canada, or 65/6738-1234. Fax 65/6732-1696. www.hyatt.com. 685 units. S$450–S$490 double (US$257–US$280). AE, DC, MC, V. Near Orchard MRT. **Amenities:** 3 restaurants; lobby lounge; live music bar; landscaped outdoor pool; 2 outdoor, lighted tennis courts; squash court and badminton court; excellent fitness center with Jacuzzi, sauna, steam, massage and spa treatments; concierge; limousine service; business center; 24-hr. room service; babysitting; same-day laundry service/dry cleaning; executive-level rooms. *In room:* A/C, TV w/satellite programming and in-house movie, minibar, coffee/tea-making facilities, dataport w/direct Internet access, hair dryer, iron, safe.

Shangri-La Hotel ★★★ The Shangri-La is a lovely place, with strolling gardens and an outdoor pool paradise that are great diversions from the hustle and bustle all around. Maybe that's why visiting VIPs like George Bush, Benazir Bhutto, and Nelson Mandela have all stayed here.

The hotel has three wings: The Tower Wing is the oldest, housing the lobby and most of the guest rooms, which were completely redone. Instead of the usual square block hotel rooms of typical city hotels, Shang's added unusual angles and curves, sophisticated contemporary furnishings, and a refreshing wall of glass blocks that welcomes natural light into the giant bathroom and dressing area. Balconies were melded into the rooms to become reading nooks. The Garden Wing surrounds an open-air atrium with cascading waterfall and exotic plants. Rooms here are more resortlike, with natural textured wall coverings,

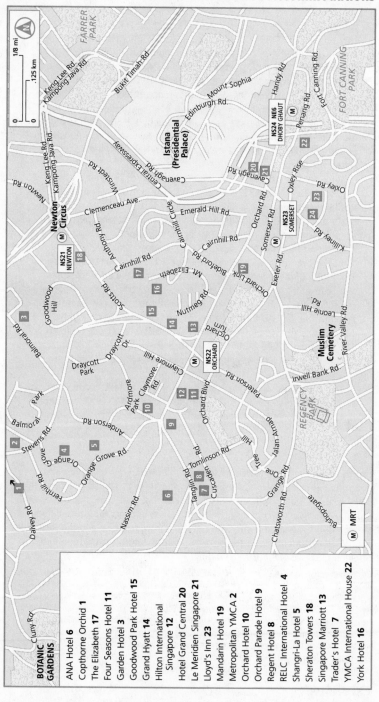

ANA Hotel **6**
Copthorne Orchid **1**
The Elizabeth **17**
Four Seasons Hotel **11**
Garden Hotel **3**
Goodwood Park Hotel **15**
Grand Hyatt **14**
Hilton International Singapore **12**
Hotel Grand Central **20**
Le Meridien Singapore **21**
Lloyd's Inn **23**
Mandarin Hotel **19**
Metropolitan YMCA **2**
Orchard Hotel **10**
Orchard Parade Hotel **9**
Regent Hotel **8**
RELC International Hotel **4**
Shangri-La Hotel **5**
Sheraton Towers **18**
Singapore Marriott **13**
Trader's Hotel **7**
YMCA International House **22**
York Hotel **16**

The Best of Singapore's Spas

In the mid-'90s, spas began making a splash in the Singapore hotel scene. By the millennium, every luxury hotel was planning either a full-blown spa facility or at least offering spa services to its residents. At the same time, day spas sprouted up in shopping centers—despite the economic downturn, these businesses have been staying afloat. Now, the STB is positioning Singapore as an urban spa hub in Southeast Asia, luring visitors from the region and beyond with luxurious facilities that go above and beyond the call of relaxation and hedonistic pampering. Here's the best:

Singapore's most celebrated spa, Amrita (Raffles The Plaza, Level 6, 2 Stamford Rd.; ✆ **65/6336-4477**; www.amritaspas.com), is operated by Raffles International, and has proven so wildly successful that the hotel chain has opened Amritas in Germany, Switzerland, and beyond. This flagship spa is the largest in Singapore, with Southeast Asia-inspired interiors and treatments—over 1,000 to choose from.

At the Grand Plaza Hotel's Saint Gregory Marine Spa (10 Coleman St. #01-23; ✆ **65/6432-5588**), even nonguests can make advance appointments to enjoy services in quiet and peaceful surroundings. Pools are snuggled amid lush green plants, with soothing sounds of waves lilting through the air. The focal treatments are the hydrotherapy baths, but you can also get jet showers, steam baths, facials and body treatments, and hand, foot, and body massage. The 20-room center has separate facilities for men and women, but couples can enjoy VIP suites for treatments for two.

The gorgeous, Bali-style spa at the **Plaza Hotel's Saint Gregory Javanese Spa** (7500 Beach Rd., Level Three; ✆ **65/6290-2028**), has exotic details right down to the floors, which are bejeweled with tiny seashells.

tweedy carpeting, and woven bedspreads. These larger-size rooms also have bougainvillea-laden balconies overlooking the tropical landscaped pool area. The exclusive Valley Wing has a private entrance and very spacious rooms, linked to the main tower by a sky bridge that looks out over the hotel's 6 hectares (15 acres) of landscaped lawns, fruit trees, and flowers. These enormous rooms, with large bathrooms and dressing areas, will be refurbished during 2003, to brighten their classical European styling.

Orange Grove Rd., Singapore 258350. ✆ **800/942-5050** in the U.S. and Canada, 800/222-448 in Australia, 800/442-179 in New Zealand, or 65/6737-3644. Fax 65/6733-3257. www.shangri-la.com. 760 units. S$480 (US$274) Tower double; S$560 (US$320) Garden double; S$520 (US$297) horizon club; S$590 (US$337) Valley double; S$1,000–S$3,200 (US$571–US$1,829) suite. AE, DC, MC, V. 10-min. walk to Orchard MRT. **Amenities:** 4 restaurants; lobby lounge; resort-style outdoor landscaped pool; 3-hole pitch and putt course; 4 outdoor, lighted tennis courts; fitness center with glass walls looking out into gardens, Jacuzzi, sauna, steam, massage; concierge; limousine service; business center; shopping arcade; salon; 24-hr. room service; babysitting; same-day laundry service/dry cleaning; nonsmoking rooms; executive-level rooms. In room: A/C, TV w/satellite programming and in-house movie, minibar, coffee/tea-making facilities, hair dryer, iron, safe.

EXPENSIVE

Hilton International Singapore ✪ If you count the luxury cars that drive up to the valet at the Hilton, you'd think this is a good address to have while

Treatments have been developed by Susan-Jane Beers, a local authority on Indonesian herbal health and beauty treatments. Enjoy aromatherapy, wet or dry herbal and floral wraps, body and facial massage, and foot reflexology.

The elegant Aspara Spa exudes Asian cosmopolitan elegance with a Zen flair that will make you forget you're in the middle of a busy city. European spa treatments for beauty and health feature prominently in this high-profile facility. Visit either **Aspara** at The Gooswood park Hotel (22 Scotts Rd.; © **65/6732-3933**) or at The Fullerton Hotel (1 Fullerton Sq.; © **65/6877-8183**).

If you can't afford a spa, you can still have a little slice of heaven. Many shopping arcades have outlets advertising foot reflexology, a technique whose popularity is just booming these days. Foot reflexology uses pressure techniques to massage the feet in spots that correspond to various parts of your body, relaxing the whole body while only touching the feet. A lot of these places aren't worth the money or time, as the certificate requirements for practitioners aren't exactly demanding. I do recommend one place, though: **Vincien Foot Reflexology** in the Tanglin Shopping Centre at 19 Tanglin Rd. #03-44 (© **65/739-9639**). Call ahead for an appointment and request Bernard, a retired businessman whose lifetime hobbies have included chi gong (Chinese energy transfer), Reiki (Japanese energy transfer), foot reflexology, and Swedish massage, to name only a few. He comes into the shop by appointment only, and because his heart and soul are in his work, he is worth every penny you pay him. Forty-minute foot reflexology treatments start at an affordable S$30. A full hour is only S$40. Full body treatments are S$80 for 1 hour.

staying in Singapore. Well, to be honest this Hilton doesn't measure up with some of their other properties worldwide and definitely can't compete with other hotels in this price category in Singapore. Probably the most famous feature of the Hilton is its shopping arcade, where you can find your Donna Karan, Louis Vuitton, Gucci—all the greats. Ask the concierge for a pager, and they'll page you for important calls while you window-shop or try some of the 45 fragrant vodkas at the lobby bar. With all this, the guest rooms should be pretty sumptuous, no? Well, no. The rooms are simpler than you'd expect, with nothing flashy or overdone. There are floor-to-ceiling windows in each, and while views in the front of the hotel are of Orchard Road and the Thai Embassy property, views in the back are not so hot. In this day and age when business-class hotels are wrestling to outdo each other, Hilton has a lot of catching up to do.

581 Orchard Rd., Singapore 238883. © **800/445-8667** in the U.S., or 65/6737-2233. Fax 65/6732-2917. www.singapore.hilton.com. 423 units. S$380–S$400 (US$217–US$229) double; S$470 (US$269) club; from S$620 (US$354) suite. AE, DC, MC, V. Near Orchard MRT. **Amenities:** 2 restaurants; lobby lounge; outdoor pool; fitness center with sauna and steam; concierge; limousine service; business center; shopping arcade; salon; 24-hr. room service; babysitting; same-day laundry service/dry cleaning; nonsmoking rooms; executive-level rooms. *In room:* A/C, TV w/satellite programming and in-house movie, minibar, coffee/tea-making facilities, hair dryer, safe.

Mandarin Singapore ⊛   Smack in the center of Orchard Road is the Mandarin Hotel, a two-tower complex with Singapore's most famous revolving restaurant topping it off like a little hat. The 39-story Main Tower opened in 1973, and with the opening of the South Wing 10 years later the number of rooms expanded to 1,200. True to its name, the hotel reflects a Chinese aesthetic, beginning in the lobby with the huge marble mural of the "87 Taoist Immortals" and the carved wood chairs lining the walls. The South Wing is predominantly for leisure travelers, who have access to the tower via a side entrance. These guest rooms are slightly smaller than average and are furnished with Chinese-style dark wood modular units. Mandarin is planning to upgrade wall, floor, bed and furniture coverings in 2003—thank God, because the old colors were dull and uninviting. New tones are promised to be warmer and more cozy. Larger Tower Wing rooms are for corporate travelers—they're larger with posh Chinois decor, including carved rosewood furnishings, silk walls, and a translucent Chinese watercolored panel separating the bathroom from the sleeping area.

333 Orchard Rd., Singapore 238867. ℭ **65/6737-4411**. Fax 65/6732-2361. www.mandarin-singapore.com. 1,200 units. US$211–US$247 double; US$264 club; from US$341 suite. AE, DC, MC, V. Near Orchard MRT. **Amenities:** 4 restaurants; revolving observation lounge and lobby lounge; outdoor pool; fitness center with Jacuzzi, sauna, steam, and massage; concierge; tour desk; limousine service; business center; shopping arcade; salon; 24-hr. room service; babysitting; same-day laundry service/dry cleaning; nonsmoking rooms; executive-level rooms. *In room:* A/C, TV w/satellite programming and in-house movie, minibar, coffee/tea-making facilities, safe.

The Regent Singapore ⊛   The Regent is tucked between Cuscaden and Tanglin roads, right across the street from the Singapore Tourism Board office—quite convenient. And check out the lobby in this place! It's a huge, three-level atrium affair with windows on three sides, a skylight, fountains, plenty of small private meeting nooks, and Jetsons-style raised walkways. The guest rooms have high ceilings and are decorated with Chinese motifs in newly refurbished fabrics, but the bathrooms are smaller than at most other comparable hotels. You have to request coffee/tea-making facilities in your room; otherwise the service is free in the tea lounge, which also serves a high tea the old-fashioned way: on silver tray service, not buffet.

1 Cuscaden Rd., Singapore 249715. ℭ **800/545-4000** in the U.S. and Canada, 800/022-800 in Australia, 800/440-800 in New Zealand, 800/917-8795 in the U.K., or 65/6733-8888. Fax 65/6732-8838. www.regent hotels.com. 441 units. S$350–S$370 (US$200–US$211) double; from S$550 (US$314) suite. 10-min. walk to Orchard MRT. **Amenities:** 2 restaurants; very cool bar; lobby tea lounge; outdoor pool; fitness center with steam and massage; concierge; limousine service; business center; 24-hr. room service; babysitting; same-day laundry service/dry cleaning; nonsmoking rooms; executive-level rooms. *In room:* A/C, TV w/satellite programming and in-house movie, minibar, dataport with direct Internet access, hair dryer, safe.

Sheraton Towers Singapore ⊛⊛   One of the first things you see when you walk into the lobby of the Sheraton Towers is the service awards the place has won; check in, and you'll begin to see why they won 'em. With the deluxe (standard) room they'll give you a suit pressing on arrival, daily newspaper delivery, shoeshine service, and complimentary movies. These newly refurbished rooms are handsome with textured walls, plush carpeting, and a bed luxuriously fitted with down pillows and dreamy 100% Egyptian cotton bedding. Upgrade to a Tower room and you get a personal butler, complimentary nightly cocktails and morning breakfast, free laundry, free local calls, your own pants press, and free use of the personal trainer in the fitness center. The cabana rooms, off the pool area, have all the services of the Tower Wing in a very private resort room. The 23 one-of-a-kind suite rooms each feature a different theme, Chinese regency,

French, Italian, jungle, you name it—very unique, with hand-picked furnishings. While Sheraton is a luxe choice, you can find better deals.

39 Scotts Rd., Singapore 228230. © **800/325-3535** in the U.S. and Canada, 800/073535 in Australia, 800/325-35353 in New Zealand, 800/353535 in the U.K., or 65/6737-6888. Fax 65/6737-1072. www.sheraton. com. 413 units. S$400 (US$229) double; S$560 (US$320) cabana room; S$1,000–S$3,000 (US$571–US$1,714) suite. AE, DC, MC, V. 5-min. walk to Newton MRT. **Amenities:** 3 restaurants; lobby lounge; outdoor landscaped pool; fitness center with sauna and massage; concierge; limousine service; 24-hr. business center; 24-hr. room service; babysitting; same-day laundry service/dry cleaning; nonsmoking rooms; executive-level rooms. In room: A/C, TV w/satellite programming and in-house movie, minibar, coffee/tea-making facilities, dataport with direct Internet access, hair dryer, safe.

Singapore Marriott Hotel ★★   You can't get a better location than at the corner of Orchard and Scotts roads. Marriott's green-roofed pagoda tower is a well-recognized landmark on Orchard Road, but guest rooms inside tend to be smaller than average to fit in the octagonal structure. Luckily the recent refurbishing scheme added lively colors to brighten the spaces with natural greens and floral fabrics. The palatial lobby has been overtaken by the Marriott Cafe, with weekend buffets that are so popular with the locals that there's a long queue. Outside, the Crossroads Café, spilling out onto the sidewalk, is a favorite place for international and Singaporean celebrities who like to be seen.

Marriott, which took over management of this property in 1995, caters to the business traveler, so the rooms on the club floors get most of the hotel's attention. The club lounge, for instance, has a great view and there's not a tacky detail in the comfortable seating and dining areas.

320 Orchard Rd., Singapore 238865. © **800/228-9290** in the U.S. and Canada, 800/251-259 in Australia, 800/22-12-22 in the U.K., or 65/6735-5800. Fax 65/6735-9800. www.marriott.com. 373 units. S$380 (US$217) double; S$420 (US$240) executive club; S$650–S$1,880 (US$371–US$1,074) suite. AE, DC, MC, V. Orchard MRT. **Amenities:** 4 restaurants; lobby lounge, bar with live jazz, and dance club with live pop bands; outdoor pool with Jacuzzi; outdoor basketball court; fitness center with Jacuzzi, sauna, steam, massage; concierge; limousine service; 24-hr. business center; shopping arcade; 24-hr. room service; babysitting; same-day laundry service/dry cleaning; nonsmoking rooms; executive-level rooms. In room: A/C, TV w/satellite programming and in-house movie, minibar, coffee/tea-making facilities, dataport w/direct Internet access, hair dryer, iron, safe.

MODERATE

ANA Hotel Singapore   ANA is located in the embassy area and a 10-minute walk from the Botanic Gardens, which is the perfect place for a morning jog or an evening stroll. From the outside, the modern building is plain, while on the inside, everything is turn-of-the-20th-century, European-style decor—no hints of Asia at all. The rooms are a fair size and have recently undergone a much-needed refurbishment, upgrading carpets, upholstery and drapes. The new look is classic European style in bright tones. All rooms sport the latest interactive system for hotel service, shopping, and video-on-demand directly through your TV. Cabana rooms, with private patios fronting the pool's new wooden sun deck, are popular. Be sure to ask for current promotions, which are priced to compete with ANA's better-situated neighbors along Orchard Road.

16 Nassim Hill, Singapore 258467. © **800/ANA-HOTELS** in the U.S. and Canada, or 65/6732-1222. Fax 65/ 6235-1516. www.anahotel.com.sg. 457 units. S$300–S$330 (US$189–US$194) double; S$360 (US$206) cabana double or executive room; S$400–S$2,000 (US$229–US$1,143) suite. AE, DC, MC, V. 15-min. walk to Orchard MRT. **Amenities:** 2 restaurants; lobby lounge plus the new and trendy Ibiza Entertainment Bar; outdoor pool; fitness center with sauna, steam, massage; concierge; limousine service; business center; 24-hr. room service; babysitting; same-day laundry service/dry cleaning; executive-level rooms. In room: A/C, TV w/satellite programming and in-house movie, minibar, coffee/tea-making facilities, hair dryer, safe.

Copthorne Orchid Singapore   The Copthorne hotel management chain has recently taken over the Orchid, which was formerly under Novotel management (so it may still be referred to as Novotel around town). Lobby renovations in 1997 redesigned the space in a very open and contemporary style, with straight lines and light wood paneling à la IKEA. Of course, the renovations were not without the addition of a lucky koi pond, full of golden fish to bring luck and fortune, and nestled in an adorable, brightly painted courtyard that can be viewed from the lobby bar. The pond runs from the courtyard under the floor of the bar to a pool and fountain inside. The newness of this part of the hotel adds contrast to the older sections—as you walk down the covered but otherwise open-air corridors, you can see signs of age. Nevertheless, guest rooms here are big and fairly pleasant, with tall stucco walls and high ceilings. The rooms in the Plymouth Wing to the back of the complex have a sofa bed in addition to the regular beds, and offer plenty of desk and counter space.

214 Dunearn Rd., Singapore 299526. ℭ 65/6250-3322. Fax 65/6250-9292. www.millennium-hotels.com. 440 units. S$260–S$380 (US$149–US$217) double; S$450 (US$257) family; S$650 (US$371) suite. AE, DC, MC, V. Far from MRT stations. **Amenities:** 2 restaurants; bar; outdoor pool; fitness center; tour desk; shuttle service; business center; salon; 24-hr. room service; babysitting; same-day laundry service/dry cleaning; non-smoking rooms. *In room:* A/C, TV w/satellite programming and in-house movie, minibar, coffee/tea-making facilities, dataport w/direct Internet access, safe.

The Elizabeth Singapore   This small, quaint hotel has cozy rooms and the most friendly and accommodating staff around. Done in dark, cool European styling throughout, from the lobby to the guest rooms, this modern hotel's most dramatic feature is the lobby area's fantastic cascading waterfalls, which drop over a vertical tropical rock-and-plant garden nestled behind three-story-high glass panels. This year the Elizabeth has seen some refurbishment to freshen the rooms. New touches include wall coverings, floral bedspreads and drapes. The burl-wood furnishings are handsome. Recreation facilities are few and small compared to similar properties. Business center services are provided by the front office staff. There is a small but imaginative gift shop specializing in feng shui, or Chinese geomancy, items. The Elizabeth has lowered rack rates since our last update, making this hotel an excellent bargain.

24 Mount Elizabeth, Singapore 228518. ℭ 65/6738-1188. Fax 65/6739-8005. www.theelizabeth.com. 256 units. S$220–S$270 (US$126–US$154) double; S$450 (US$257) suite. AE, DC, MC, V. 10-min. walk to Orchard MRT. **Amenities:** Restaurant; lobby lounge; small outdoor pool; tiny fitness center with sauna; concierge; tour desk; 24-hr. room service; babysitting; same-day laundry service/dry cleaning. *In room:* A/C, TV w/satellite programming, minibar, coffee/tea-making facilities, hair dryer, safe.

Le Meridien Singapore   Atrium lobbies are popular in Singapore, and I think Le Meridien's is the original, and one of the brightest. Long, straight corridors look out into the huge, open, skylighted space and down to the colorful lobby lounge decorated with plants and fresh flowers. Just at the southern tip of Orchard Road, Le Meridien offers good access to shopping activities, plus the attractions of the nearby Historic District. Standard rooms are light and fresh with simple European decor and subtle Chinese accents. Voice mail and extra dataports for laptop usage make for convenience, and some rooms have balconies. Bathrooms are state-of-the-art. The Jade and Opal suites are the best spaces, but the executive club facilities are not as attractive as other hotels in this category.

100 Orchard Rd., Singapore 238840. ℭ 800/543-4300 in the U.S. and Canada, 800/622240 in Australia, 800/454040 in New Zealand, 800/404040 in the U.K., or 65/6733-8855. Fax 65/6732-7886. www.lemeridien-singapore.com. 407 units. S$330 (US$189) double; S$370 (US$211) executive club; from S$400 (US$229)

suite. AE, DC, MC, V. Dhoby Ghaut/Somerset MRT. **Amenities:** 2 restaurants; lobby lounge; outdoor pool; fitness center with sauna; concierge; limousine service; business center; shopping arcade; salon; 24-hr. room service; babysitting; same-day laundry service/dry cleaning; executive-level rooms. *In room:* A/C, TV w/satellite programming and in-house movie, minibar, coffee/tea-making facilities, hair dryer, safe.

Orchard Hotel Singapore 🅰 Orchard Hotel, with its wonderful attached shopping mall, provides accommodations for leisure and business travelers in two wings. The main lobby, in Mediterranean flair, has a giant central clock with wrought iron detail and seating beneath. Between the lobby lounge to the left and coffee shop to the right, the place always feels energized. Lower priced rooms in the older Orchard Wing will undergo a (desperately needed) renovation in 2003, so make sure you ask for a newer room when booking. The Claymore Wing houses deluxe rooms in comfortable contemporary style, with large glass desktops, rosewood bed stands, neutral tone carpets and upholstery and slick chrome lamps. The friendly staff greet you with a smile always.

442 Orchard Rd., Singapore 238879. © **800/637-7200** in the U.S. and Canada, 800/655147 in Australia, 800/442519 in New Zealand, 800/252840 in the U.K., or 65/6734-7766. Fax 65/6733-5482. www.orchard hotel.com.sg. 672 units. S$320–S$360 (US$200–US$206) double; S$430 (US$246) club; S$650–S$1,800 (US$371–US$1,029) suite. AE, DC, MC, V. 5-min. walk to Orchard MRT. **Amenities:** 2 restaurants; lobby lounge; outdoor pool; fitness center with sauna; concierge; tour desk; business center; shopping mall adjacent; salon; 24-hr. room service; babysitting; same-day laundry service/dry cleaning; nonsmoking rooms; executive-level rooms. *In room:* A/C, TV w/satellite programming, minibar, coffee/tea-making facilities, safe.

Orchard Parade Hotel 🅰🅰 *Value Kids* This fine hotel, after a S$40 million, 2-year renovation, sports new swimming pool, guest rooms, lobby, driveway, front entrance, and food and beverage outlets, decorated in a Mediterranean theme integrating marble mosaics, plaster walls, beamed ceilings, and wrought-iron railings. The midsize pool on the sixth-floor roof features colorful tiles and draping arbors, a motif carried over through the new fitness center. Rooms also feature Mediterranean style in terra-cotta wall sconces, wrought iron table legs, and shades of teal and aqua. If it's important to you, you need to specify a room with a view here. For good value, the Family Studio fits a king-size bed and two twins with separate family room and dining area and plenty of space for just S$100 (US$57) extra. Just outside, a long terrace along Orchard Road hosts many restaurant choices, the most popular of which, Modestos, serves good pasta and pizzas at an affordable price.

1 Tanglin Rd., Singapore 247905. © **65/6737-1133.** Fax 65/6733-0242. www.orchardparade.com.sg. 387 units. S$260–S$290 (US$149–US$166) double; S$360–S$420 (US$206–US$240) family studio; S$400 (US$229) junior suite; from S$500 (US$286) suite. AE, DC, MC, V. Orchard MRT. **Amenities:** 5 restaurants; lobby lounge; outdoor pool; fitness center; concierge; tour desk; business center; salon; 24-hr. room service; babysitting; same-day laundry service/dry cleaning; executive-level rooms. *In room:* A/C, TV w/satellite programming, minibar, coffee/tea-making facilities, hair dryer.

Traders Hotel Singapore 🅰🅰 A fantastic bargain for leisure travelers in Singapore, Traders advertises itself as a "value-for-money" hotel. A spinoff of Shangri-La (see above), this hotel anticipates the special needs of travelers and tries on all levels to accommodate them. Rooms have an empty fridge that can be stocked from the supermarket next door (show your room card key at nearby Tanglin Mall for discounts from many of the shops); there are spanking-clean self-service launderette facilities with ironing boards on six floors; and there are vending machines and ice machines. They even provide a hospitality lounge for guests to use after checkout, with seating areas, work spaces with dataports, card phones, safe-deposit boxes, vending machines, and a shower.

Guest rooms are smaller than average, but feature child-size sofa beds and large drawers for storage. The large, landscaped pool area has a great poolside alfresco cafe, Ah Hoi's Kitchen, serving up tasty Chinese dishes at reasonable prices. Be sure to ask about promotion rates when you book your room. If you're planning to stay longer than 2 weeks, they have a long-stay program that offers discount meals, laundry and business center services, and half-price launderette tokens.

1A Cuscaden Rd., Singapore 249716. © **800/942-5050** in the U.S. and Canada, 800/222448 in Australia, 0800/442179 in New Zealand, or 65/6738-2222. Fax 65/6831-4314. www.shangri-la.com. 547 units. S$305–S$350 (US$174–US$200) double; S$385 (US$220) club; S$520–S$1,200 (US$297–US$686) studio apt. and suite. AE, DC, MC, V. 10-min. walk to Orchard MRT. **Amenities:** 2 restaurants; bar and lobby lounge; outdoor pool; fitness center with Jacuzzi, sauna, steam, massage; spa; concierge; limousine service; shuttle service; business center; salon; 24-hr. room service; babysitting; same-day laundry service/dry cleaning; self-service launderette; executive-level rooms. *In room:* A/C, TV w/satellite programming, minibar, coffee/tea-making facilities, dataport with direct Internet access, hair dryer, iron, safe.

York Hotel Singapore ★★   This small tourist-class hotel can boast some of the most consistently professional and courteous staff I've encountered. A short walk from Orchard, York is convenient though far enough removed to provide a relaxing atmosphere. A recent renovation has redressed previously flavorless rooms in a sharp contemporary style in light woods, natural tones, and simple lines. Combined with an already spacious room, the result is an airy, cooling effect. Bathrooms throughout are downright huge. Cabana rooms look out to a pool and sun deck decorated with giant palms. Despite surrounding buildings, it doesn't feel claustrophobic, as do some of the more centrally situated hotels. There's a Jacuzzi, but the business center is tiny as is the fitness center. This year, rates have been raised a bit, so make sure you ask for promotional discounts.

21 Mount Elizabeth, Singapore 228516. © **800/223-5652** in the U.S. and Canada, 800/553-549 in Australia, 800/447-555 in New Zealand, 800/89-88-52 in the U.K., or 65/6737-0511. Fax 65/6732-1217. www.york hotel.com.sg. 406 units. S$290–S$310 (US$166–US$177) double; S$310 (US$177) cabana; S$440 (US$251) split-level cabana; S$460–S$910 (US$263–US$520) suite. AE, DC, MC, V. 10-min. walk to Orchard MRT. **Amenities:** Restaurant; lobby lounge; outdoor pool; Jacuzzi; fitness center; tour desk; business center; 24-hr. room service; babysitting; same-day laundry service/dry cleaning. *In room:* A/C, TV w/satellite programming, minibar, coffee/tea-making facilities.

INEXPENSIVE

Garden Hotel Singapore   This five-story hotel is a discreet building in a quiet prime residential neighborhood north of the Orchard Road area—and that's its main downfall: It's pretty far out from where all the action is. (The hotel compensates with a free shuttle to Orchard Rd. and to the Marina area.) Other than location, this is a fine place to stay. It serves a mostly Western market of leisure travelers and families, discouraging tour groups to avoid noisy throngs loitering around the lobby area and crashing the food and beverage outlets at feeding times. The good news is that 95% of the guest rooms have balconies. The bad news is, some of them are indoors, with a view of the atrium coffee shop; so, make sure you get one with an outside view. The rooms here are aver-age-size and bright, and guest rooms in the west wing have been recently refur-bished. Garden Hotel has two pools, a rooftop pool that gets good sun and a small ground-level landscaped pool in a courtyard surrounded by large cabana rooms. In terms of services and recreation facilities offered, Garden is the best pick out of the budget choices.

14 Balmoral Rd., Singapore 259800. © **65/6235-3344.** Fax 65/6235-9730. 216 units. S$210 double; S$220 (US$120) cabana; S$260 (US$149) family; S$300 (US$194) suite. AE, DC, MC, V. 15-min. walk to Newton MRT. **Amenities:** 2 restaurants; lounge; 2 outdoor pools; fitness center with sauna; shuttle service; salon; 24-hr.

room service; babysitting; same-day laundry service/dry cleaning. *In room:* A/C, TV w/satellite programming and in-house movie, minibar, coffee/tea-making facilities.

Hotel Grand Central, Singapore

Most of the hotels in this price category are at least a 10-minute walk outside the main drag, but Hotel Grand Central is right on it, with an exclusive Orchard Road address. The hotel always runs at high occupancy, its lobby a hustle and bustle of mostly ASEAN (Association of Southeast Asian Nations) vacation travelers who, truth to tell, seem to have worn dull the front counter staff's service edge. The building was originally eight floors, but renovations added an extra floor to the top, which houses executive club rooms. The corridors are on the dreary side, and the guest rooms and bathrooms are a little run-down. Windows are positioned high, so there's not much in the way of views—although rooms in the center of the building offer views of rooms on the opposite side, if that's your idea of fun. To the side of the rooftop pool is a special corner reserved for dead hotel houseplants.

22 Cavenagh Rd./Orchard Rd., Singapore 229617. ℂ 65/6737-9944. Fax 65/6733-3175. www.grandcentral. com.sg. 390 units. S$210–S$230 (US$120–US$131) double; S$300 (US$194) suite. AE, DC, MC, V. Somerset MRT. **Amenities:** Restaurant; lounge; outdoor pool; fitness center with Jacuzzi and steam; tour desk; business center; shopping arcade; salon; same-day laundry service/dry cleaning. *In room:* A/C, TV w/in-house movie, minibar, coffee/tea-making facilities.

Lloyd's Inn

Lloyd's is a budget motel in every sense. It's a two-story building on a relatively quiet, low-traffic street. The corridors are open-air and the rooms are small, with a definite budget feeling, though all have air-conditioning and phones. Each room has its own bathroom, though they tend to be mildewy. The published rates include the "+++" taxes (see "Taxes & Service Charges," earlier in this chapter); there's no discount offered for long-term stays; you must pay for your room when you check in; and if you use a credit card, it'll cost you an extra 2%. No pool, no fitness center, no nothing—you got your room, that's what you got.

2 Lloyd Rd., Singapore 239091. ℂ 65/6737-7309. Fax 65/6737-7847. www.lloydinn.com. 34 units. S$65 (US$39) double. MC, V. 10-min. walk to Somerset MRT. **Amenities:** Same-day laundry service plus self-service launderette. *In room:* A/C, TV, minibar, coffee/tea-making facilities.

The Metropolitan YMCA Singapore

This place is a little out of the way in terms of walking distance to anywhere, and the rooms are looking a little on the older side, but they're clean and efficient. *One caution here:* The least expensive rooms have no windows; for sunlight, you'll have to pay a little extra. There are nine family rooms outfitted with either three twin beds or a double and a twin. The family rooms are the same size as the other rooms, but the bathrooms are bigger and there's a lot more closet space. In early 1998, a new multipurpose fitness center opened here, installed all new equipment, and hired a trainer. The pool is a nice size, as is the kiddie pool, and there's a lifeguard on duty from 9am to 9pm daily. No dorm rooms are available, but concierge, dry cleaning, laundry, and secretarial services are. Plus, there's a self-service launderette, a coffee shop, a tour desk, and a shuttle service to Orchard Road.

60 Stevens Rd., Singapore 257854. ℂ 65/6737-7755. Fax 65/6235-5528. www.mymca.org.sg. 91 units. S$65–S$95 (US$39–US$57) double; S$80–S$110 (US$48–US$66) family; S$125 (US$75) suite. AE, DC, MC, V. 15-min. walk to Newton MRT. **Amenities:** Restaurant; outdoor pool; fitness center; tour desk; babysitting; business center, same-day laundry service; nonsmoking rooms. *In room:* A/C, TV, minibar, coffee/tea-making facilities.

Regalis Court ★★

For a bit of local charm at an affordable price, Regalis Court is a favorite. Centrally located just a 10-minute walk from Orchard Road, this old charming bungalow has been restored beautifully and outfitted with Peranakan-inspired touches. Everything here will make you feel as if you're staying in a quaint guesthouse rather than a hotel, from the open-air lobby (under the porte-cochere) and corridors to the guest rooms, which have comforting touches like teakwood furnishings, textile wall hangings, Oriental throws over wooden floors, and bamboo blinds to keep out the sun. Although guest rooms are slightly smaller than conventional rooms, they are still quite comfortable. Facilities are few. Laundry services and car hire are also offered.

64 Lloyd Rd., Singapore 239113. ℂ 65/6734-7117. Fax 65/6736-1651. www.regalis.com.sg. 43 units. S$115–S$165 (US$66–US$94) double. AE, DC, MC, V. 10-min. walk from Somerset MRT. **Amenities:** Restaurant; car-rental desk; babysitting; same-day laundry service; nonsmoking rooms. *In room:* A/C, TV, coffee/tea-making facilities, dataport w/direct Internet access, safe.

RELC International Hotel ★★ *Value*   For real value, my money is on RELC. Sure the location is terrific (only a 10-min. walk to Orchard Rd.), but the added value is in the quality of the facility. I found the service and convenience here superior to some hotels in the higher priced categories. RELC has four types of rooms—superior twin, executive twin, Hollywood queen, and alcove suite—but no matter what the size, none of the rooms ever feel cluttered, close, or cramped. All rooms have balconies, TVs with two movie channels, and a fridge with free juice boxes and snacks. Bathrooms are large, with full-length tubs and hair dryers standard. If you're interested in the higher-priced rooms, I'd choose the Hollywood queen over the alcove suite—its decor is better and it can sleep a family very comfortably. The "superior" rooms don't have coffee/tea-making facilities. A self-service launderette is available.

30 Orange Grove Rd., Singapore 258352. ℂ 65/6885-7888. Fax 65/6733-9976. www.hotel-web.com. 128 units. S$110 (US$66) double; S$165 (US$99) suite. AE, DC, MC, V. 10-min. walk to Orchard MRT. **Amenities:** Restaurant; tour desk; same-day laundry service plus self-service launderette; nonsmoking rooms. *In room:* A/C, TV w/in-house movie, minibar, dataport w/direct Internet access.

YMCA International House *Kids*   Of the two YMCAs in Singapore, this one has the better location. At the lower end of Orchard Road, it's only a short walk to the Dhoby Ghaut MRT station, making it very convenient for getting around via mass transit. The guest rooms have been renovated and have private bathrooms that are better than I've seen at some much pricier hotels. All rooms have air-conditioning, a telephone (with free local calls), color television, and a stock-it-yourself refrigerator. The dormitories are small, dark, and quiet, with two bunk beds per room. Across the hall are men's and women's locker rooms for showering. Most of the public areas have no air-conditioning, including the old fitness facility, billiards center, and squash courts—so be warned: They can become unbearably hot. The rooftop pool is nothing to write home about, but there is a full-time lifeguard on duty. There's a coffee shop and a McDonald's in the lobby. The hotel staff is amazingly friendly.

1 Orchard Rd., Singapore 238824. ℂ 65/6336-6000. Fax 65/6337-3140. www.ymca.org.sg. 111 units. S$89 (US$53) double; S$106 (US$63) family room; S$115 (US$69) superior room; S$28 (US$17) dormitory. Non-YMCA members must pay S$5 (US$3) temporary membership fee at check-in. AE, DC, MC, V. Near Dhoby Ghaut MRT. **Amenities:** 2 restaurants; outdoor pool; small gym; game room; tour desk; Internet center; babysitting; same-day laundry service. *In room:* A/C, TV, refrigerator.

4 Sentosa Island

There are only two hotel properties on Sentosa Island, the Shangri-La Rasa Sentosa, located right on the water and designed for families and fun, and the

Beaufort, located on a cliff above the water, closer to golfing and designed for secluded, romantic getaways.

The Beaufort ✮   Designed with romance in mind, the Beaufort's small resort-style buildings, fashioned after the famous resorts of Phuket, Thailand, are connected with covered walkways encircling lily ponds and courtyard gardens. Here, the designers have done a great job combining clean modern lines with tropical touches to produce a sophisticated getaway with relaxing charm. Lazy terraces and cozy alcoves tucked all over the grounds invite guests to unwind in privacy—perfect for intimate candlelight dinners that can be requested anywhere you like. The centerpiece is the new spa, built into a garden setting—it is opulent and relaxing.

The standard guest rooms in the five-story hotel building are small but stunning, featuring camphor burl-wood doors and accents, Thai silk screens in natural browns and greens, and deep tubs and separate showers in the bathrooms, surrounded by thick celadon green tiling and sleek black granite details. Ask for views of the golf course, which are prettier than the views of the hotel courtyards and buildings. Butlers wait round the clock to serve you—a standard feature for all rooms, but if you want the ultimate, the Beaufort's Garden Villas deliver privacy and luxury in little houses with individual pools.

In a tree just behind the open-air lobby, look for Tommy the monkey, who sometimes hangs out with one or two of his wives or kids. You have to love any resort that has a resident monkey family.

2 Bukit Manis Rd., Sentosa, Singapore 099891. © **65/6275-0331.** Fax 65/6275-0228. www.beaufort. com.sg. 214 units. S$380 (US$217) double; from S$450 (US$257) suite; S$1,500 (US$857) villa. AE, DC, MC, V. See "Sentosa Island," in chapter 5 for public transportation. **Amenities:** 2 restaurants; lounge; gorgeous midnight blue-tiled outdoor pool with views of the harbor; golf at nearby facilities; 2 outdoor, lighted tennis courts with coach; 2 squash courts; fitness center with 20m lap pool, Jacuzzi, sauna; brand-new luxury spa with private pool, mud baths, steam, Jacuzzis, exercise and relaxation classes, salon, beauty treatments and massage; concierge; tour desk; limousine service; shuttle service; 24-hr. room service; babysitting; same-day laundry service/dry cleaning. *In room:* A/C, TV w/satellite programming and in-house movie, minibar, coffee/tea-making facilities, dataport w/direct Internet access, hair dryer, safe.

Shangri-La's Rasa Sentosa Resort *Kids*   Set on an immaculate white sandy beach fringed with coconut palms, Shangri-La's Rasa Sentosa Resort is Singapore's only true beachfront hotel. It's frequented by Singaporeans looking to get away from it all, but as a visitor to Singapore you may find it isolated from the city's attractions. Still, you can always take advantage of the resort's complimentary shuttle service for trips to the action, only to return to the serenity of the resort at the end of a busy day.

Great outdoor activities make the Rasa Sentosa particularly attractive. The resort's extensive recreational facilities, including a sea-sports center, offer windsurfing, sailing, and paddle skiing. Other facilities include a large outdoor freeform swimming pool, a jogging track, aqua bike rentals, an outdoor Jacuzzi, and a fully equipped spa with gym, sauna, body and facial treatments, hydromassage, and massage therapies. The hotel also organizes nature walks, cycling tours, rock-wall climbing, and beach volleyball. For children, there is a separate pool with water slides (no lifeguard, though), a playground, a nursery, and a video arcade.

As for the rooms, the decision between whether to take the hill-view room or the slightly more expensive sea-facing room is a no-brainer: The view of the sea is exceptional, and if you don't go for it, you'll be missing out on glorious mornings, throwing back the curtains, and taking in the view from the balcony.

101 Siloso Rd., Sentosa, Singapore 098970. ℭ **800/942-5050** in the U.S. and Canada, 800/222-448 in Australia, 800/442-179 in New Zealand, or 65/6275-0100. Fax 65/6275-0355. www.shangri-la.com. 459 units. Weekdays S$290 (US$166) hill-view double, S$320 (US$200) pool-view double, S$360 (US$206) cabana double and sea-facing double, from S$550 (US$314) terrace rooms and suites. Weekends S$350 (US$200) hill-view double, S$380 (US$217) pool-view double, S$420 (US$240) cabana double or sea-facing double. AE, DC, MC, V. See "Sentosa Island," in chapter 5 for public transportation. **Amenities:** 3 restaurants; poolside bar and lobby lounge; outdoor lagoon style pool with children's pool and Jacuzzi; golf at nearby facilities; fitness center; spa with sauna, steam, massage; children's center; game room; shuttle service; business center; 24-hr. room service; babysitting; same-day laundry service/dry cleaning; executive-level rooms. *In room:* A/C, TV w/satellite programming and in-house movie, minibar, coffee/tea-making facilities, dataport with direct Internet access, hair dryer, iron, safe.

Singapore Dining

Take 3 million people, put 'em on a tiny island for their whole lives, and what have you got? Three million people looking for new things to entertain them. Sure, the sights and attractions can keep visitors occupied for weeks, but how many times can you go to Sentosa before it becomes the same old same old? The locals have seen and done it all.

So what do Singaporeans do for boredom relief? They eat. Dining out in Singapore is the central focus of family quality time, the best excuse for getting together with friends, and the proper way to close that business deal. That's why you find such a huge selection of local, regional, and international cuisine here, served in settings that range from bustling hawker centers to grand and glamorous palaces of gastronomy. But to simply say, "If you like food you'll love Singapore!" doesn't do justice to the modern concept of eating in this place. The various ethnic restaurants, with their traditional decor and serving styles, hold their own special sense of theater for foreigners; but Singaporeans don't stop there, dreaming up new concepts in cuisine and ambience to add fresh dimensions to the fine art of dining. For a twist, new variations on traditions pop up, like the French-service Chinese cuisine at Chang Jiang or the East-meets-West New Asia cuisine dished up at Doc Cheng's. Theme restaurants turn regular meals into attractions. Take, for example, Imperial Herbal's intriguing predinner medical examination or House of Mao's Cultural Revolution menu.

Recent figures say Singapore has over 2,000 eating establishments, so you'll never be at a loss for a place to go. In this chapter, I'll begin by providing an overview of the main types of traditional cuisine to help you decide, and also list those signature dishes that each style has contributed to the "local cuisine," dishes that have crossed cultures to become time-honored favorites—the Singaporean equivalent to bangers and mash or burgers and fries. These suggestions are especially helpful when navigating the endless choices at hawker centers.

The restaurants I've chosen for review in this chapter offer a crosscut of cuisine and price range, and were selected for superb quality or authenticity of dishes. Some were selected for the sheer experience, whether it's a stunning view or just plain old fun. Beyond this list, you're sure to discover favorites of your own without having to look too far.

A good place to start is right in your hotel. Many of Singapore's best restaurants are in its hotels, whether they're run by the hotel itself or operated by outfits just renting the space. Hotels generally offer a wide variety of cuisine, and coffee shops almost always have Western selections. Shopping malls have everything from food courts with local fast food to midpriced and upmarket establishments. Western fast-food outlets are always easy to find—McDonald's burgers, Dunkin'

Donuts, or Starbucks coffee—but if you want something a little more local, you'll find coffee shops (called *kopitiam*) and small home-cookin' mom-and-pop joints down every back street. Then there are hawker centers, where, under one roof, the meal choices go on and on.

1 One Little Island, Lots & Lots of Choices

CHINESE CUISINE

The large Chinese population in Singapore makes this obviously the most common type of food you'll find, and by right, any good description of Singaporean food should begin with the most prevalent Chinese regional styles. Many Chinese restaurants in the West are lumped into one category—Chinese—with only mild acknowledgment of Szechuan and dim sum. But China's a big place, and its size is reflected in its many different tastes, ingredients, and preparation styles.

A very touchy topic for many Westerners: Chinese cuisine employs many a strange ingredient that sometimes makes the unaccustomed stomach queasy. A saying from way back in my family goes, "The Chinese will eat anything that doesn't eat them first," and it's almost true. Turtle, sea urchin, and sea cucumber are all popular Singaporean dishes, though their meats are unpleasantly mushy to those accustomed to more Western tastes. Many Singaporeans devour these creatures for their taste and some for their health-giving and restorative powers. In fact, some Chinese restaurants are creating dishes using unusual ingredients, which they claim balance the body's energy (its yin and yang) to promote health, beauty, and longevity. Indeed, frog's glands are pretty tasty in scrambled eggs, and the next day your skin will glow like never before!

On the more appealing side are other Chinese-inspired local favorites like carrot cake (white radishes that are steamed and pounded until soft, then fried in egg, garlic, and chile), *Hokkien bak ku teh* (boiled pork ribs in a seasoned soup), *Teochew kway teow* (stir-fried rice noodles with egg, prawns, and fish), and the number one favorite for foreigners, *Hainanese* chicken rice (boiled sliced chicken breast served over rice cooked in chicken stock).

New Asia cuisine has been hitting the market hard as globalization takes control of Singaporean palates. Also called "fusion food," this cuisine combines Eastern and Western ingredients and cooking styles for a whole new eating experience. Some of it works, some of it doesn't, but true gourmet connoisseurs consider it all a culinary atrocity.

CANTONESE CUISINE   Cantonese-style food is what you usually find in the West: Your stir-fries, wontons, and sweet-and-sour sauces all come from this southern region. Cantonese cooks emphasize freshness of ingredients, which explains why some Cantonese homemakers will shop up to three times a day for the freshest picks. Typical preparation involves quick stir-frying in light oil, or steaming for tender meats and crisp, flavorful vegetables. These are topped off with light sauces that are sometimes sweet. Cantonese-style food also includes roasted meats like suckling pig and the red-roasted pork that's ever present in Western Chinese dishes. Compared to northern styles of Chinese cuisine, Cantonese food can be bland, especially when sauces and broths are overthickened and slimy. Singaporean palates demand the standard dish of chile condiment at the table, which sometimes helps the flavor. One hearty Cantonese dish that has made it to local cuisine fame is **clay pot rice,** which is rice cooked with chicken, Chinese sausage, and mushrooms, prepared in—you guessed it—a clay pot.

The Cantonese are also responsible for **dim sum** (or *tim sum,* as you'll sometimes see it written around Singapore). Meaning "little hearts," dim sum is a variety of deep-fried or steamed buns, spring rolls, dumplings, meatballs, spare ribs, and a host of other tasty treats. It's a favorite in Singapore, especially for lunch. At a dim sum buffet wheel carts of dishes are moved from table to table and you simply point to what looks nice. Food is served in small portions, sometimes still in the steamer. Take only one item on your plate at a time, and stack the empty plates as you finish each one. Traditionally, you'd be charged by the plate, but sometimes you can find great all-you-can-eat buffets for a good price.

BEIJING CUISINE   Beijing-style food, its rich garlic and bean-paste flavoring betraying just a touch of chile, comes to us from the north of China and is the food of the emperors. Another difference is that you'll find mutton on a northern Chinese menu, but certainly not on any southern menu. The most famous Beijing-style dish is **Beijing duck** (also known as Peking duck). The crispy skin is pulled away and cut into pieces, which you then wrap in thin pancakes with spring onion and a touch of sweet plum sauce. The meat is served later in a dish that's equally scrumptious.

SHANGHAI CUISINE   Shanghai-style cuisine is similar to Beijing-style but tends to be more oily. Because of its proximity to the sea, Shanghai recipes also include more fish. The exotic **drunken prawns** and the popular **drunken chicken** are both from this regional style, as is the mysterious **bird's nest soup,** made from swift's nests.

SZECHUAN CUISINE   Szechuan-style cuisine, second only to Cantonese in the West, also relies on the rich flavors of garlic, sesame oil, and bean paste, but is heavier on the chiles than Shanghai cuisine—*much* heavier on the chiles. Sugar is also sometimes added to create tangy sauces. Some dishes can really pack a punch, but there are many Szechuan dishes that are not spicy. Popular are **chicken with dried chiles** and **hot-and-sour soup.** Another regional variation, **Hunan-style food,** is also renowned for its fiery spice, and can be distinguished from Szechuan-style by its darker sauces.

TEOCHEW CUISINE   Teochew-style cuisine uses fish as its main ingredient, and is also known for its light soups. Many dishes are steamed, and in fact **steamboat,** which is a popular poolside menu item in hotels, gets its origins from this style. For steamboat, boiling broth is brought to the table, and you dunk pieces of fish, meat, and vegetables into it, a la fondue. Other Teochew contributions to local cuisine are the **Teochew fish ball,** a springy ball made from pounded fish with salt and water served in a noodle soup, and the traditional Singaporean breakfast dish *congee* (or *moi*), which is rice porridge served with fried fish, salted vegetables, and sometimes boiled egg. Also, if you see **braised goose** on the menu, you're definitely in a Teochew restaurant.

HOKKIEN CUISINE   Although the Hokkiens are the most prevalent dialect group in Singapore, their style of cuisine rarely makes it to restaurant tables, basically because it's simple and homely. Two dishes that have made it as local cuisine favorites are the **oyster omelet,** flavored with garlic and soy, and **Hokkien mee,** which is thick wheat noodles with seafood, meat, and vegetables in a heavy sauce.

HAKKA CUISINE   If Hokkien food is simple and homely, Hakka food is the homeliest of the homely. Flavored with glutinous rice wine, many dishes feature tofu and minced seafood and meats. Hakkas are also known for not wasting an animal body part—not exactly a hallmark of haute cuisine. Good dishes to try are **salt-baked chicken** and **minced seafood** wrapped in a fried tofu cake.

MALAY CUISINE

Malay cuisine combines Indonesian and Thai flavors, blending ginger, turmeric, chiles, lemongrass, and dried shrimp paste to make unique curries. Heavy on coconut milk and peanuts, Malay food can at times be on the sweet side. The most popular Malay curries are *rendang,* a dry, dark, and heavy coconut-based curry served over meat; *sambal,* a red and spicy chile sauce; and *sambal belacan,* a condiment of fresh chiles, dried shrimp paste, and lime juice.

The ultimate Malay dish in Singapore is **satay,** sweet barbecued meat kabobs dipped in chile peanut sauce. Another popular dish is *roti john,* minced mutton and onion in French bread that's dipped in egg and fried. *Nasi lemak*— coconut rice surrounded by an assortment of fried anchovies, peanuts, prawns, egg, and sambal—is primarily a breakfast dish, but can be eaten anytime.

PERANAKAN CUISINE

Peranakan cuisine came out of the Straits-born Chinese community and combines such mainland Chinese ingredients as noodles and oyster sauces with local Malay flavors of coconut milk and peanuts. *Laksa lemak* is a great example of the combination, mixing Chinese rice flour noodles into a soup of Malay-style spicy coconut cream with chunks of seafood and tofu. And *otak otak* is all the rage. It's toasted mashed fish with coconut milk and chile, wrapped in a banana leaf and grilled over flames.

INDIAN CUISINE

SOUTHERN INDIAN CUISINE   Southern Indian food is a superhot blend of spices in a coconut milk base. Rice is the staple, along with thin breads such as prata and dosai, which are good for curling into shovels to scoop up drippy curries. Vegetarian dishes are abundant, a result of Hindu-mandated vegetarianism, and use lots of chickpeas and lentils in curry and chile gravies. **Vindaloo,** meat or poultry in a tangy and spicy sauce, is also well known.

Banana leaf restaurants, surely the most interesting way to experience southern Indian food in Singapore, serve up meals on banana leaves cut like place mats. It's very informal. Spoons and forks are provided, but if you want to act local and use your hands, remember to use your right hand only (see "Etiquette & Customs," in chapter 2), and don't forget to wash up before and after at the tap.

One tip for eating very spicy foods is to mix a larger proportion of rice to gravy. Don't drink in between bites, but eat through the burn. Your brow may sweat but your mouth will build a tolerance as you eat, and the flavors will come through more fully.

NORTHERN INDIAN CUISINE   Northern Indian food combines yogurts and creams with a milder, more delicate blend of herbs and chiles than is found in its southern neighbor. It's served most often with breads like fluffy nans and flat chapatis. Marinated meats like chicken or fish, cooked in the tandoor clay oven, are always the highlight of a northern Indian meal.

Northern Indian restaurants are more upmarket and expensive than the southern ones, but while they offer more of the comforts associated with dining out, the southern banana leaf experience is more of an adventure.

Some Singaporean variations on Indian cuisine are *mee goreng,* fried noodles with chile and curry gravy, and fish head curry, **a giant fish head** simmered in a broth of coconut curry, chiles, and fragrant seasonings.

Muslim influences on Indian food have produced the *murtabak,* a fried prata filled with minced meat, onion, and egg. Between the Muslims' dietary laws (halal) forbidding pork and the Hindus' regard for the sacred cow, Indian food is the one cuisine that can be eaten by every kind of Singaporean.

SEAFOOD

One cannot describe Singaporean food without mentioning the abundance of fresh seafood. But most important is the uniquely Singaporean **chile crab,** chopped and smothered in a thick tangy chile sauce. Restaurants hold competitions to judge who has the best, and everyone has his favorite—one local sent me all the way out to Ponggol, on the north coast, to find his pick of the best chile crab. **Pepper crabs** and **black pepper crayfish** are also a thrill. Instead of chile sauce, these shellfish are served in a thick black-pepper-and-soy sauce.

FRUITS

A walk through a wet market at any time of year will show you just what wonders the tropics can produce. Varieties of banana, fresh coconut, papaya, mango, and pineapple are just a few of the fresh and juicy fruits available year-round; in addition, Southeast Asia has an amazing selection of exotic and almost unimaginable fruits. From the light and juicy star fruit to the red and hairy rambutan, they are all worthy of a try, either whole or juiced.

Dare it if you will, the fruit to sample—the veritable king of fruits—is the *durian,* a large, green, spiky fruit that, when cut open, smells worse than old tennis shoes. The "best" ones are in season every June, when Singaporeans go wild over them. In case you're curious, the fruit has a creamy texture and tastes lightly sweet and deeply musky.

One interesting note on fruits: The Chinese believe that foods contain either yin or yang qualities with corresponding "heating" and "cooling" effects. Fried foods and hot soups are heating and therefore should be kept to a minimum in the tropics, and the same is true for some fruits. Whereas watermelon, star fruit, and oranges are cooling, mangoes, litchi, and especially durians are heating. Taking too many heating foods is believed to result in a sore throat, for which the best remedy is Chinese tea.

2 Tips on Dining

Of course, in any foreign land, the exotic cuisine isn't the only thing that keeps you guessing. Lucky for you, the following tips will make dining no problem.

HOURS   Most restaurants are open for lunch as early as 11am, but close around 2:30 or 3pm to give them a chance to set up for dinner, which begins around 6pm. Where closing times are listed, that is the time when the last order is taken.

TIPPING   Don't tip. Restaurants always add a gratuity to the bill. Sometimes I just leave the small change, but the government discourages this practice.

RESERVATIONS   Some restaurants, especially the more fashionable or upscale ones, may require that reservations be made up to a couple of days in advance. Reservations are always recommended for Saturday and Sunday lunch and dinner, as eating is a favorite national pastime and a lot of families take meals out for weekend quality time.

ATTIRE   Because Singapore is so hot, "dress casual" (meaning a shirt and slacks for men and a dress or skirt/slacks and top for women) is always a safe bet

Urban Singapore Dining

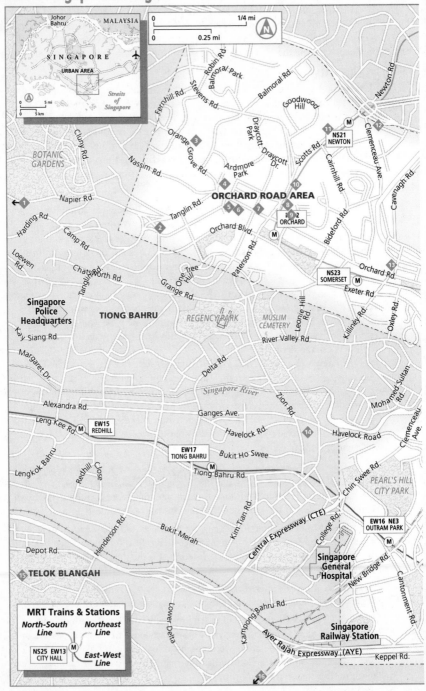

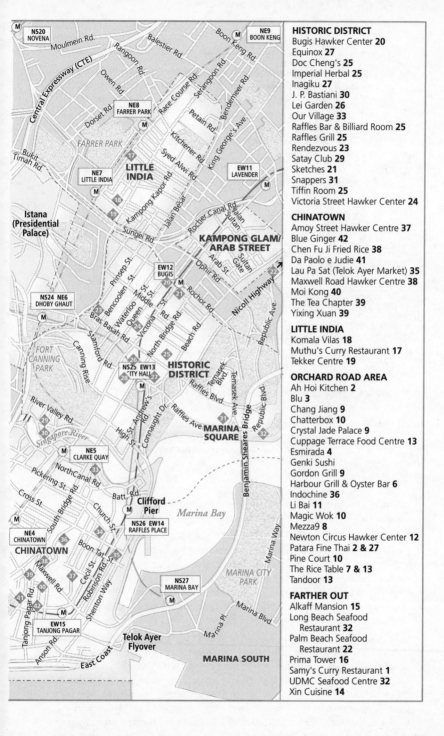

HISTORIC DISTRICT
Bugis Hawker Center **20**
Equinox **27**
Doc Cheng's **25**
Imperial Herbal **25**
Inagiku **27**
J. P. Bastiani **30**
Lei Garden **26**
Our Village **33**
Raffles Bar & Billiard Room **25**
Raffles Grill **25**
Rendezvous **23**
Satay Club **29**
Sketches **21**
Snappers **31**
Tiffin Room **25**
Victoria Street Hawker Center **24**

CHINATOWN
Amoy Street Hawker Centre **37**
Blue Ginger **42**
Chen Fu Ji Fried Rice **38**
Da Paolo e Judie **41**
Lau Pa Sat (Telok Ayer Market) **35**
Maxwell Road Hawker Centre **38**
Moi Kong **40**
The Tea Chapter **39**
Yixing Xuan **39**

LITTLE INDIA
Komala Vilas **18**
Muthu's Curry Restaurant **17**
Tekker Centre **19**

ORCHARD ROAD AREA
Ah Hoi Kitchen **2**
Blu **3**
Chang Jiang **9**
Chatterbox **10**
Crystal Jade Palace **9**
Cuppage Terrace Food Centre **13**
Esmirada **4**
Genki Sushi
Gordon Grill **9**
Harbour Grill & Oyster Bar **6**
Indochine **36**
Li Bai **11**
Magic Wok **10**
Mezza9 **8**
Newton Circus Hawker Center **12**
Patara Fine Thai **2 & 27**
Pine Court **10**
The Rice Table **7 & 13**
Tandoor **13**

FARTHER OUT
Alkaff Mansion **15**
Long Beach Seafood
  Restaurant **32**
Palm Beach Seafood
  Restaurant **22**
Prima Tower **16**
Samy's Curry Restaurant **1**
UDMC Seafood Centre **32**
Xin Cuisine **14**

Best Bets for Breakfast

The local Singaporean breakfast, available all over the island, rarely appeals to Westerners. *Congee,* a soupy rice porridge, comes with salted egg, dried anchovies, and other assorted foreign objects that make my stomach cringe at 7 in the morning (before my coffee kicks in). Still, you can pick up some in any hawker center for about S$2 (US$1.15), or pay a lot more in hotel coffee shops (read: They're overpriced).

When you're looking for a good breakfast nosh, you have to be careful in general of your hotel's coffee shop. Most hotels offer a standard buffet breakfast, and many are incredibly impressive, with an enormous selection of fruits, cereals, baked goods, eggs, meats, and dairy items. But most cost between S$15 and S$25 (US$8.55 and US$14), quite an expense for a meal that's usually "eat and run." There are many other alternatives, however. I recommend asking your concierge for the nearest cafe/coffee shop. Starbucks, The Coffee Bean & Tea Leaf, Spinelli, Seattle Coffee Company, Java Coast, and Dunkin' Donuts all have outlets in all corners of the city. A cup of coffee and scone will come to just over S$5 (US$2.85). (*Also note:* Many hotels provide an electric kettle with instant coffee and tea bags standard in every room.)

If the breakfast buffet does appeal to you, try the **Marriott Café** in the Singapore Marriott Hotel, where you can eat all you like for S$15 (US$8.55); it's one of the less expensive but better quality breakfast buffets around. Raffles Hotel's **Ah Teng's Bakery** (daily 7am–11pm) has a nice set-price breakfast for only S$6 (US$3.45), and is great if you're staying in the historic district area. For something special, every Sunday and on Public Holidays, the **Garden Seafood Restaurant** at Goodwood Park Hotel serves a massive and excellent selection of Hong Kong–style dim sum for only S$13 (US$7.30) per person (8–10:30am).

in moderate to expensive restaurants. For the very expensive restaurants, formal is required. For the cheap places, come as you are, as long as you're decent.

ORDERING WINE WITH DINNER   Singaporeans have become more wine savvy in recent years, and have begun importing estate-bottled wines from California, Australia, New Zealand, Peru, South Africa, France, and Germany. However, these bottles are heavily taxed. A bottle of wine with dinner starts at around S$50 (US$29) and a single glass runs between S$10 and S$25 (US$5.70–US$14), depending on the wine and the restaurant. Chinese restaurants usually don't charge corkage fees for bringing your own.

ORGANIZATION OF RESTAURANT LISTINGS   I've organized the restaurants in this chapter in a few different ways. First, I've grouped them in a simple list by style of cuisine, so if you decide you want a nice Peranakan dinner, for instance, you can scope out your choices all together before referring to the individual restaurant reviews. Second, I've arranged the reviews into four basic neighborhoods: the Historic District, Chinatown, Little India, and the Orchard Road area. Within these divisions, I've arranged them by price. Keep in mind that the divisions by neighborhood are almost as arbitrary as they were when Stamford Raffles created them in 1822. Everything in the city is relatively close and easily accessible, so don't think you should plan your meals by the neighborhood your hotel sits in when a short taxi ride will take you where you really want to go.

I've selected the restaurants listed here because they have some of the best food and most memorable atmospheres, but there are hundreds of other restaurants serving any kind of food in a variety of price ranges. Many magazines on dining in Singapore are available at newsstands and can help you find other favorite restaurants.

LUNCH COSTS   Lunch at a hawker center can be as cheap as S$3.50 (US$2), truly a bargain. Many places have set-price buffet lunches, but these can be as high as S$45 (US$26). Indian restaurants are great deals for inexpensive buffet lunches, which can be found as reasonably as S$10 (US$5.70) per person for all you can eat.

DINNER COSTS   In this chapter, prices for Western restaurants list the range for standard entrees and prices for Asian restaurants list the range for small dishes intended for two. As a guideline, here are the relative costs for dinner in each category of restaurant, without wine, beer, cocktails, or coffee, and ordered either a la carte or from a set-price menu:

- **Very Expensive:** At a very expensive restaurant, you can expect to pay as much as S$145 (US$83) per person. The more expensive cuisines are Continental and Japanese, but a full-course Cantonese dinner, especially if you throw in shark's fin, can be up to S$125 to S$150 (US$71–US$86) per person.
- **Expensive:** At an expensive restaurant, expect dinner to run between S$50 and S$80 (US$29–US$46) per person.
- **Moderate:** At a moderate restaurant, dinner for one can be as low as S$25 (US$14) and as high as S$50 (US$29).
- **Inexpensive:** Some inexpensive dinners can be under S$5 (US$2.85) at hawker stalls, and up to around S$15 (US$8.55) for one if you eat at local restaurants. Fortunately, Singapore is not only a haven for cultural gastric diversity, but it's also possible to eat exotic foods here to your heart's content, all while maintaining a shoestring budget.

3 Restaurants by Cuisine

CALIFORNIA
BLU ★★★ (Orchard Road, $$$, p. 104)

CHINESE
Beijing
Prima Tower Revolving Restaurant (Keppel Road, $$, p. 110)

Cantonese
Crystal Jade Palace ★ (Orchard Road, $$, p. 107)
Lei Garden ★★ (Historic District, $$$, p. 98)

Li Bai ★★★ (Orchard Road, $$$, p. 107)
Xin Cuisine (Concorde Hotel, Outram Road, $$, p. 111)

Chinese Mixed
Magic Wok (Historic District, $, p. 100)
Pine Court ★ (Orchard Road, $$, p. 108)

Hakka
Moi Kong (Chinatown, $, p. 103)

Key to Abbreviations: $$$$ = Very Expensive $$$ = Expensive $$ = Moderate $ = Inexpensive

Herbal
Imperial Herbal ★★ (Historic District, $$, p. 100)

Xin Cuisine (Concorde Hotel, Outram Road, $$, p. 111)

New Asia
Doc Cheng's (Historic District, $$, p. 99)

Equinox ★ (Historic District, $$$, p. 97)

Shanghainese
Chang Jiang ★ (Orchard Road, $$$, p. 104)

CONTINENTAL
Equinox ★ (Historic District, $$$, p. 97)

Gordon Grill ★★ (Orchard Road, $$$, p. 106)

Harbour Grill & Oyster Bar ★★★ (Orchard Road, $$$, p. 106)

FRENCH
L'Aigle d'Or ★★★ (Chinatown, $$$$, p. 101)

Raffles Grill ★★★ (Historic District, $$$$, p. 97)

FUSION
Doc Cheng's (Historic District, $$, p. 99)

Mezza9 ★★ (Orchard Road, $$$, p. 107)

INDIAN (NORTHERN)
Bukhara (Historic District, $, p. 100)

Our Village ★ (Historic District, $, p. 100)

Tandoor ★★ (Orchard Road, $$, p. 108)

INDIAN (SOUTHERN)
Komala Vilas ★ (Little India, $, p. 104)

Muthu's Curry Restaurant (Little India, $, p. 104)

Samy's Curry Restaurant ★ (Dempsey Road, $$, p. 111)

Tiffin Room ★ (Historic District, $$$, p. 98)

ITALIAN
da paolo e judie ★★★ (Chinatown, $$, p. 102)

Sketches (Historic District, $, p. 101)

JAPANESE
Genki Sushi (Orchard Road, $, p. 109)

Inagiku ★★ (Historic District, $$$$, p. 97)

MALAY/INDONESIAN
Alkaff Mansion ★ (Telok Blangah Hill Park, $$$, p. 109)

Rendezvous (Historic District, $, p. 101)

Satay Club (Historic District, $, p. 113)

The Rice Table (Orchard Road, $, p. 109)

MEDITERRANEAN
Esmirada ★ (Orchard Road, $$$, p. 106)

J. P. Bastiani ★ (Historic District, $$$, p. 97)

PERANAKAN
Blue Ginger ★ (Chinatown, $, p. 102)

SEAFOOD
Long Beach Seafood Restaurant (East Coast Parkway, $$, p. 110)

Palm Beach ★ (Stadium Walk, $$, p. 110)

Snappers ★★ (Historic District, $$$, p. 98)

UDMC Seafood Centre ★★ (East Coast Parkway, $$, p. 111)

SINGAPOREAN
Ah Hoi's Kitchen (Orchard Road, $$, p. 107)

Chatterbox (Orchard Road, $, p. 109)

Chen Fu Ji Fried Rice (Chinatown, $, p. 102)

SOUTHEAST ASIAN
Indochine (Chinatown, $, p. 102)

THAI
Patara Fine Thai (Orchard Road, $$, p. 108)

Magic Wok (Historic District, $, p. 100)

4 The Historic District

VERY EXPENSIVE

Inagiku ★★ JAPANESE   At Inagiku, you'll have excellent Japanese food that gets top marks for ingredients, preparation, and presentation. In delicately lighted and subtle decor, you can enjoy house favorites like sashimi, tempura, and teppanyaki—with separate dining areas for tempura and a sushi bar. The tokusen sashimi morikimi is masterful in its presentation: An assortment of raw fish—including salmon, prawns, and clams—is laid out in an ice-filled shell inside of which nestles the skeleton of a whole fish. It's odd and delightful at the same time. I recommend the tempura moriawase, a combination of seafood and vegetables that's very lightly deep fried. Also highly recommended are the teppanyaki prawns. In addition to sake, there is also have a good selection of wines.

The Westin Plaza Level 3, 2 Stamford Rd. ✆ 65/6431-6156. Reservations recommended. Set lunch S$30–S$50 (US$17–US$29); set dinner S$60–S$180 (US$34–US$103). AE, DC, MC, V. Daily noon–2:30pm, 6:30–10:30pm.

Raffles Grill ★★★ FRENCH   Dining in the grande dame of Singapore achieves a level of sophistication unmatched by any other five-star restaurant. The architectural charm and historic significance of the old hotel will transform dinner into a cultural event, but don't just come here for the ambience; the food is outstanding as well. Three set dinners allow you to select from the a la carte menu dishes like roasted veal tenderloin or roasted rack of suckling pig, the latter a highly recommended choice for its juicy meat under crispy mouthwatering skin. The 400-label wine list (going back to 1890 vintages) could be a history lesson, and if you'd like you can request the cellar master to select a wine to match each course. The fabulously attentive service from the wait staff will make you feel like you own the place. Formal dress is required.

Raffles Hotel, 1 Beach Rd. ✆ 65/6412-1240. Reservations recommended. Main courses S$42–S$52 (US$24–US$30); set dinner S$120 and S$130 (US$69 and US$74) per person. AE, DC, MC, V. Mon–Fri noon–2pm, 7–10pm; Sat–Sun 7–10pm.

EXPENSIVE

Equinox ★ CONTINENTAL/NEW ASIA   What a view! From the top of the tallest hotel in Southeast Asia, you can see out past the marina to Malaysia and Indonesia—and the restaurant's three-tier design and floor-to-ceiling windows means every table has a view. It's decorated in contemporary style with nice Chinese accents. Lunch is an extensive display of seafood served in a host of international recipes, with chefs searing scallops to order. Dinner is a la carte, with dishes that combine Eastern and Western ingredients and cooking styles such as *yuzu* marinated cod with braised *enoki* and *tasoi* and grilled beef tenderloin with foie gras. For dessert, order the Equinox Temptation—a sample plate of desserts.

Swissôtel Stamford, 2 Stamford Rd., Level 70. ✆ 65/6431-6156. Reservations required. Buffet lunch Mon–Sat S$36 (US$22), Sun and public holidays S$42 (US$25); dinner entrees S$41–S$45 (US$24–US$27). AE, DC, MC, V. Daily noon–2:30pm, 7–10:30pm.

J. P. Bastiani ★ MEDITERRANEAN   The real-life J. P. Bastiani owned a pineapple cannery at Clarke Quay; today, he lends his name to this cozy

Mediterranean place, with its walled courtyard patio in the back for cocktails, a wine cellar with a huge international collection on the first floor (buy your wine here for dinner), and a gorgeous dining room upstairs that's just dripping with romance. Their seafood dishes are the best, with a choice of a delicious coriander-crusted salmon with ginger and onion confit, or the pan-roasted sea bass, which is stuffed with leeks and potato. You can also try one of their excellent meat entrees such as rack of lamb or filet mignon. The dishes are rich and servings are quite large, so make a mental note in advance to save room for their fantastic tiramisu.

3A River Valley Rd., Clarke Quay Merchant's Court #01-12. ℂ **65/6433-0156.** Reservations recommended. Main courses S$29–S$42 (US$17–US$24). AE, DC, MC, V. Daily 11:30am–2:30pm, 6:30–10:30pm.

Lei Garden ★★ CANTONESE Lei Garden, with three locations in Singapore, six in Hong Kong and Kowloon, and two in Guangzhou, lives up to a great reputation for the highest quality Cantonese cuisine in one of the most elegant settings. Actually, of the three local branches, this one is special for the unique ambience of CHIJMES just outside its towering picture windows. Highly recommended dishes are the "Buddha jumps over the wall," a very popular Chinese soup made from abalone, fish maw (stomach), shark's fin, and Chinese ham. It's generally served only on special occasions. To make the beggar's chicken, they take a whole stuffed chicken and wrap and bake it in a lotus leaf covered in yam, which makes the chicken moist with a delicate flavor you'll never forget. For either of these dishes, you must place your order at least 24 hours in advance when you make your dinner reservation. Also try the barbecued Beijing duck, which is exquisite. Dim sum here is excellent. A small selection of French and Chinese wines is available.

30 Victoria St., CHIJMES #01-24. ℂ **65/6339-3822.** Reservations required. Small dishes S$18–S$58 (US$10–US$33). AE, DC, MC, V. Daily 11:30am–2:30pm, 6–10:30pm.

Snappers ★★ SEAFOOD With a view of The Ritz-Carlton's lovely pool and gardens, this restaurant is hardly your typical poolside snack bar. Snappers invents mouthwatering recipes for new ways to enjoy fresh seafood. The crispy sea bass with eggplant and walnut coriander dressing melts in your mouth. The seafood platter is awesome. But if the a la carte menu doesn't have what you're looking for, you can have your choice of live seafood prepared to your specs. This is one of the city's top choices for delicious dining with a terrific wine list and impeccable service. You will never be disappointed.

The Ritz-Carlton Millenia Singapore, Level 1, 7 Raffles Ave. ℂ **65/6434-5288.** Reservations required for dinner. Main courses S$31–S$38 (US$17–US$22).. AE, DC, MC, V. Daily noon–2:30pm, 6:30–10:30pm.

Tiffin Room ★ SOUTHERN INDIAN Tiffin curry came from India and is named after the three-tiered containers that Indian workers would use to carry their lunch. The tiffin box idea was stolen by the British colonists, who changed around the recipes a bit so they weren't as spicy. The cuisine that evolved is pretty much what you'll find served at Raffles's Tiffin Room, where a buffet spread lets you select from a variety of curries, chutneys, rice, and Indian breads. The restaurant is just inside the lobby entrance of Raffles Hotel and carries the trademark Raffles elegance throughout its decor.

Raffles Hotel, 1 Beach Rd. ℂ **65/6337-1886.** Reservations recommended. All meals served buffet style. Breakfast S$30 (US$17); lunch S$35 (US$20); high tea S$27 (US$15); dinner S$45 (US$26). AE, DC, MC, V. Daily noon–2pm, 3:30–5pm (high tea), and 7–10pm.

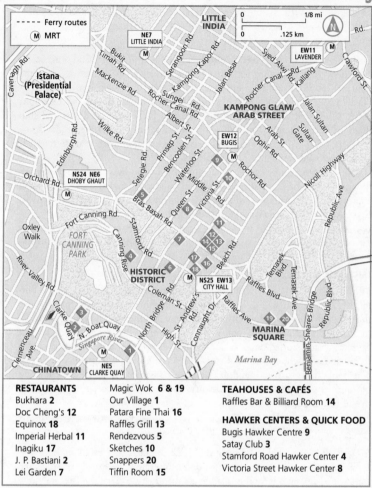

RESTAURANTS
Bukhara **2**
Doc Cheng's **12**
Equinox **18**
Imperial Herbal **11**
Inagiku **17**
J. P. Bastiani **2**
Lei Garden **7**

Magic Wok **6 & 19**
Our Village **1**
Patara Fine Thai **16**
Raffles Grill **13**
Rendezvous **5**
Sketches **10**
Snappers **20**
Tiffin Room **15**

TEAHOUSES & CAFÉS
Raffles Bar & Billiard Room **14**

HAWKER CENTERS & QUICK FOOD
Bugis Hawker Centre **9**
Satay Club **3**
Stamford Road Hawker Center **4**
Victoria Street Hawker Center **8**

MODERATE

Doc Cheng's NEW ASIA/FUSION   Doc Cheng's calls itself "The Restaurant for Restorative Foods," but you won't find any ancient Chinese secrets here. Doc Cheng, the hero of the joint, was part man and part mythological colonial figure. Educated in Western medicine in England, he was a sought-after physician who became a local celebrity and notorious drunk. His concept of restorative foods is therefore rather skewed, but the restaurant banks on the decadence of the attraction and serves up "transethnic" dishes smothered in tongue-in-cheek humor. Guest chefs make the menu ever changing—the latest and greatest, an unbelievably scrumptious tamarind charcoal beef short ribs dish on portobello mushrooms. Equally well prepared (though lighter) is the charcoal-fried shutome swordfish on risotto. The house wine is a Riesling (sweet wines are more popular with Singaporeans) from Raffles's own vineyard. Three separate dining areas allow you to dine under the veranda, on the patio, or in cozy booths inside.

Raffles Hotel Arcade #02-20, Level 2. © 65/6331-1612. Reservations recommended. Main courses S$22–S$32 (US$12–US$18). AE, DC, MC, V. Daily noon–2pm, 7–10pm.

Imperial Herbal ★★ CHINESE HERBAL   People come again and again for the healing powers of the food served here, enriched with herbs and other secret ingredients prescribed by a resident Chinese herbalist. Upon entering, go to the right, where you'll find the herb counter. The herbalist, who is also trained in Western medicine, will ask for the symptoms of what ails you and take your pulse. While you sit and order, he'll prepare a packet of ingredients and ship them off to the kitchen, where they'll be added to the food in preparation. Surprisingly, dishes turn out tasty, without the anticipated medicinal aftertaste. If all this isn't wild enough for you, order the scorpion.

The herbalist is in-house every day but Sunday. It's always good to call ahead, though, as he's the main attraction. When you leave, present him with a small ang pau—a gift of cash in a red envelope—maybe S$5 or S$7 (US$2.85–US$4). Red envelopes are available in any card or gift shop.

Metropole Hotel, 3rd Floor, 41 Seah St. (near Raffles Hotel). © 65/6337-0491. Reservations recommended for lunch, necessary for dinner. Small dishes S$14–S$24 (US$8–US$14). AE, DC, MC, V. Daily 11:30am–2:30pm, 6:30–10:30pm.

INEXPENSIVE

Bukhara NORTHERN INDIAN   I like to recommend Bukhara for the buffet, which is a great way to savor many treats without going over the top with the expense. Tandoori lamb kabobs, fish, prawns, chicken, and more will make meat lovers' eyes pop—the food just keeps coming. Plu, tandoori veggies like cauliflower and stuffed potatoes and peppers are quite good. The decor is a little bit India-kitsch, with carved stonelike accents and beat-up wooden chairs. The buffet includes breads and dal. You can also order from an a la carte menu of standard northern Indian fare. If you're in Clarke Quay, this is the best choice in this price range.

3C River Valley Rd., #01-44 Clarke Quay. © 65/6338-1411. Reservations recommended. Buffet lunch S$14 (US$7.75), buffet dinner S$20 (US$11). AE, DC, MC, V. Daily noon–2:30pm, 6:30–10:30pm.

Magic Wok *(Value* THAI/CHINESE MIXED   Here's an excellent value-for-money restaurant in town. The decor doesn't do much, it's usually crowded and staff don't pamper, but food is relaibly good and cheap. Thai favorites include a spicy tom yam seafood soup that doesn't skimp on the seafood, a mild green curry with chicken, and sweet pineapple rice. If you come too late, the yummy fried chicken chunks wrapped in pandan leaf will be sold out. If you're adventurous, the fried baby squid look like cute, tiny octopi and are crunchy and sweet. During busy times, you'll have to queue, but it moves fast. Other outlets are located at **#04-22/24 Far East Plaza** on Scotts Road (© **65/6738-3708**) and **#02-05 Marina Liesureplex** (© **65/6837-0826**).

#01–20 Capitol Building, Stamford Rd. © 65/6338-1882. Reservations not accepted. S$4–S$18 (US$2.30–US$10) small dishes. MC, V. Daily 11am–10pm.

Our Village ★ NORTHERN INDIAN   With its antique white walls stuccoed in delicate and exotic patterns and glistening with tiny silver mirrors, you'll feel like you're in an Indian fairyland here. Even the ceiling twinkles with silver stars, and hanging lanterns provide a subtle glow for the heavenly atmosphere—it's a perfect setting for a delicate dinner. Everything here is handmade from hand-selected imported ingredients, some of them coming from secret sources.

In fact, the staff is so protective of its recipes, you'd almost think their secret ingredient was opium—and you'll be floating so high after tasting the food that it might as well be. There are vegetarian selections as well as meats (no beef or pork) prepared in luscious gravies or in the tandoor oven. The dishes are light and healthy, with all natural ingredients and not too much salt.

46 Boat Quay (take elevator to 5th floor). ✆ 65/6538-3058. Reservations recommended on weekends. Main courses S$9–S$20 (US$5.15–US$11). AE, MC, V. Mon–Fri 11:30am–1:30pm, 6–10:30pm; Sat–Sun 6–10:30pm.

Rendezvous MALAY/INDONESIAN   I was sad when, after a few months away from Singapore, I couldn't find Rendezvous at its previous location in Raffles City Shopping Center, only to learn it had shifted to a nicer space at the new (coincidentally named?) Rendezvous Hotel. Line up to select from a large number of Malay dishes, cafeteria style, like sambal squid in a spicy sauce of chile and shrimp paste, and beef rendang, in a dark spicy curry gravy. The waitstaff will bring your order to your table. The coffee shop setting is as far from glamorous as the last Rendezvous, but on the wall black-and-white photos trace the restaurant's history back to its opening in the early '50s. It's a great place to experiment with a new cuisine.

#02-02 Hotel Rendezvous, 9 Bras Basah Rd. ✆ 65/339-7508. Reservations not necessary. Meat dishes sold per piece S$3–S$5 (US$1.70–US$2.85). AE, DC, MC, V. Daily 11am–9pm. Closed on public holidays.

Sketches (Value ITALIAN   Pasta is always an easy and agreeable choice, and sometimes when you're traveling, familiar tastes can be welcome from time to time. Not only is this place fast, inexpensive, and good, it's also pretty unique. The concept is "Design-a-Pasta," where they give you a menu on which is a series of boxes you check off: one set for pasta type; one set for sauce type; another for add-ins like meats, mushrooms, and garlic; and boxes for chile, Parmesan, and pine nuts. The kitchen is in the center of the restaurant, with bar seating all around. This is the best place to be if you want to watch those cooks hustle through menu card after menu card—it's a great show. You can also sit at one of the tables in the restaurant or out on the patio inside the shopping mall, but then you'd miss the fun of eating here.

200 Victoria St., #01-85/86/87 Parco Bugis Junction. ✆ 65/6339-8386. S$11 (US$6) hungry; S$14.50 (US$8.30) starving. AE, DC, MC, V. Daily 11am–10pm.

5 Chinatown

VERY EXPENSIVE

L'Aigle d'Or ✯✯✯ FRENCH   L'Aigle d'Or's reputation in Singapore is second to none, and after you dine here, you'll understand why. The French menu is perfection, the setting is classic, and the staff is extremely attentive and charming. Like many of the other European restaurants in Singapore, their menu changes regularly with the seasons, so you may find different dishes than on your last visit. This time around the menu featured a gorgeous veal rib, pan-fried and tender. For something different, try the pan-fried foie gras and rhubarb ravioli, a current house specialty and unbelievably tasty in a tangy raspberry sauce. As you would expect, the wine list is top of the line, the cheese selection is excellent, and the desserts are unmentionable. If you're looking for someplace truly special, you can't do better.

83 Duxton Rd., Berjaya Hotel Singapore. ✆ 65/6227-7678. Reservations recommended. Main courses S$75–S$96 (US$43–US$55); set lunch from S$36 (US$21). AE, DC, MC, V. Daily noon–2pm, 7–10pm.

MODERATE

da paolo e judie ★★★ ITALIAN   Beautiful ambience is created in this shophouse restaurant remodeled in contemporary elegance, with alfresco dining and a wine bar. The Italian fare features seafood in classic and modern recipes using fresh seafood — for starters, raw oysters are zesty. Also try the delicate and tangy seabass tartare with rocket salad. For your main course the lobster pasta in a tomato, olive oil, white wine and garlic sauce is perfect — the lobster is soft and juicy and the pasta a perfect al dente. The wine list features labels from Italy. For the quality of food and service, the prices can't be beat.

81 Neil Rd. ℂ 65/6225-8306. Reservations highly recommended for dinner. Main courses S$24–S$42 (US$14–US$24). AE, DC, MC, V. Mon-Sat 11:30am-3pm and 6:30-11:30pm.

Indochine ★ SOUTHEAST ASIAN (VIETNAMESE/LAOTIAN/CAMBO-DIAN)   With it's popular Club Street location close to Shenton way and Chinatown's office district, IndoChine had a steady stream of customers throughout the week. This lovely converted shophouse strikes an air of romance and mystery created by the Indochinese artifacts and subtle lighting. The cuisine here adds a French twist to popular regional favorites. I love Lao sausage, and theirs is spicy, served with a sweet and tart peanut sauce. Khmer-style deep fried seabass is another specialty here. This is definitely the place to try new things. Last year another outlet, IndoChine Waterfront opened at 1 Empress Place at the site of the soon-to-be opened new wing of the Asian Civilisations Museum. ℂ 65/6339-1720) It's lovely location and unbeatable view of the Singapore River have made it a favorite.

49 Club St. ℂ 65/6323-0503. Reservations recommended. Small dishes S$22–S$48 (US$12–US$27) AE, DC, MC, V. Daily noon–3pm and 6–10:30pm.

INEXPENSIVE

Blue Ginger ★ PERANAKAN   The standard belief is that Malay and Peranakan cooking is reserved for home-cooked meals, and therefore restaurants are not as plentiful—and where they do exist, are very informal. Not so at Blue Ginger, where traditional and modern mix beautifully in a style so fitting for Singapore. Snuggled in a shophouse, the decor combines clean and neat lines of contemporary styling with paintings by local artists and touches of Peranakan flair like carved wooden screens. The cuisine is Peranakan from traditional recipes, making for some very authentic food—definitely something you can't get back home. A good appetizer is the *ngo heong:* fried rolls of pork and prawn that are deliciously flavored with spices but not at all hot. A wonderful entree is the *ayam panggang* "Blue Ginger," really tender grilled boneless thigh and drumstick with a mild coconut-milk sauce. One of the most popular dishes is the *ayam buah keluak* (my favorite), a traditional chicken dish made with a hard black Indonesian nut with sweet meat inside. The favorite dessert here is *durian chendol,* red beans and pandan jelly in coconut milk with durian purée. Served with shaved ice on top, it smells strong.

97 Tanjong Pagar Rd. ℂ 65/6222-3928. Reservations recommended. Main courses S$6.50–S$23 (US$3.70–US$13). AE, DC, MC, V. Daily 11:30am–2:30pm, 6–10pm.

Chen Fu Ji Fried Rice SINGAPOREAN   With bright green walls glaring under fluorescent lighting, the fast-food ambience is nothing to write home about, but once you try the fried rice here, you'll never be able to eat it anywhere else again, ever. These people take loving care of each fluffy grain, frying the egg evenly throughout. The other ingredients are added abundantly, and there's no

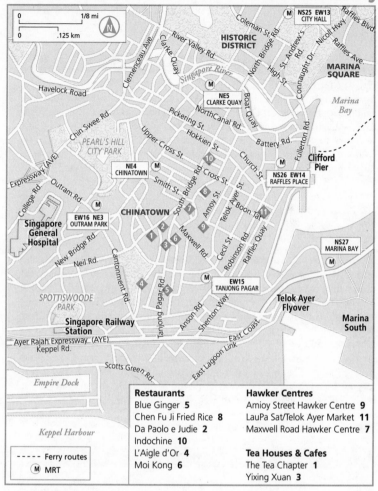

Chinatown Dining

Restaurants
Blue Ginger **5**
Chen Fu Ji Fried Rice **8**
Da Paolo e Judie **2**
Indochine **10**
L'Aigle d'Or **4**
Moi Kong **6**

Hawker Centres
Amioy Street Hawker Centre **9**
LauPa Sat/Telok Ayer Market **11**
Maxwell Road Hawker Centre **7**

Tea Houses & Cafes
The Tea Chapter **1**
Yixing Xuan **3**

----- Ferry routes
Ⓜ MRT

hint of oil. On the top is a crown of shredded crabmeat. If you've never been an aficionado, you'll be one now. Other dishes are served here to accompany the fried rice, and their soups are also very good.

7 Erskine Rd. ⓒ **65/6323-0260**. Reservations not accepted. S$10–S$20 (US$5.70–US$11). No credit cards. Daily noon–2:30pm and 6–9:45pm.

Moi Kong CHINESE HAKKA Located down a back alley called Murray Food Court, Moi Kong is a restaurant that looks more like somebody's kitchen, from the plastic tablecloths and dishes to tea served in simple glasses. The staff is very helpful about offering suggestions from the Hakka menu, dishes that are heavier on tofu and flavored more with homemade Chinese wine. Try house specialties like red wine prawn or salted chicken baked and served plain. The deep-fried bean curd stuffed with minced pork and fish is a traditional standard and can be served either dry or braised with black bean sauce. If you don't believe the food here is top rate, just ask Jackie Chan, whose happy photos are on the wall by the cash register!

22 Murray St. (between Maxwell House and Fairfield Methodist Church). ℂ **65/221-7758.** Reservations recommended on weekends. Small dishes S$4–S$30 (US$2.30–US$17). AE, MC, V. Daily 11:30am–2:30pm, 5:30–10pm.

6 Little India

INEXPENSIVE

Komala Vilas ⚑ SOUTHERN INDIAN   Komala Vilas is famous with Singaporeans of every race. Don't expect the height of ambience—it's pure fast food—but to sit here during a packed and noisy lunch hour is to see all walks of life come through the doors. Vegetarian dishes southern-Indian style, so there's nothing fancy about the food; it's just plain good. Order the dosai, a huge, thin pancake used to scoop up luscious and hearty gravies and curries. Even for carnivores, it's very satisfying. What's more, it's cheap: two samosas, dosai, and an assortment of stew-style gravies (dal) for two are only S$8 (US$4.55) with tea. For a quick fast-food meal, this place is second to none.

76/78 Serangoon Rd. ℂ **65/293-6980.** Reservations not accepted. Dosai S$2 (US$1.15); lunch for 2 S$8 (US$4.55). No credit cards. Daily 11:30am–3pm, 6:30–10:30pm.

Muthu's Curry Restaurant SOUTHERN INDIAN   We're not talking the height of dining elegance here. It's more like somebody's kitchen where the chairs don't match, but you know there's got to be a reason why this place is packed at mealtimes with a crowd of folks from construction workers to businesspeople. The list of specialties is long and includes crab masala, chicken biryani, and mutton curry, and fish cutlet and fried chicken sold by the piece. Of course you can get the local favorite, fish head curry (this is a great place to try it). The fish head floats in a huge portion of curry soup, its eye staring and teeth grinning. The cheek meat is the best part of the fish, but to be real polite, let your friend eat the eye. Go toward the end of mealtime, so you don't get lost in the rush and can find staff with more time to help you out.

76/78 Race Course Rd. ℂ **65/6293-2389.** Reservations not accepted. Main courses S$3.50–S$6.50 (US$2–US$3.70); fish head curry from S$16 (US$9.15). AE, DC, MC, V. Daily 10am–10pm.

7 Orchard Road Area

EXPENSIVE

BLU ⚑⚑⚑ CALIFORNIA   The top floor of the Shangri-La commands a lovely view of Orchard Road and the gardens of the most fashionable residential district in the city. BLU is Singapore's cutting edge in stylish dining, decorated with modern glass sculpture by Danny Lane, table lamps by Philippe Starck, and Wedgwood table settings. The Maine lobster paella with saffron, black mussel, and lobster chorizo jus is mind blowing. Even your plain old chicken is sumptuously flavored with apricots, foie gras and Swiss chard. The wine list here is excellent. After hours BLU turns into an atmospheric lounge with live jazz Monday to Thursday till 12:45am; Friday and Saturday til 1:45am. BLU is my pick for the hottest date venue.

24th floor Shangri-La Hotel, 22 Orange Grove Rd. ℂ **65/6730-2598.** Reservations required. Main courses S$48–S$59 ($27–US$34). AE, DC, MC, V. Mon–Sat 7–10:30pm.

Chang Jiang ⚑ CHINESE SHANGHAINESE   The small and elegant Chang Jiang is a unique blend of Chinese food and European style. A fine setting, which mixes refined Continental ambience with Chinese accents, has a view of the courtyard and pool of the historic Goodwood Park Hotel through

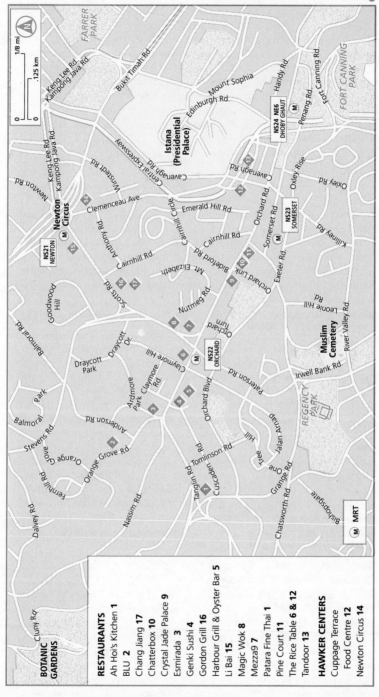

RESTAURANTS

Ah Hoi's Kitchen **1**
BLU **2**
Chang Jiang **17**
Chatterbox **10**
Crystal Jade Palace **9**
Esmirada **3**
Genki Sushi **4**
Gordon Grill **16**
Harbour Grill & Oyster Bar **5**
Li Bai **15**
Magic Wok **8**
Mezza9 **7**
Patara Fine Thai **1**
Pine Court **11**
The Rice Table **6 & 12**
Tandoor **13**

HAWKER CENTERS

Cuppage Terrace
Food Centre **12**
Newton Circus **14**

its large draped picture windows. The food is Chinese, but the service is French Gueridon style, in which dishes are presented to diners and taken to a side table to be portioned into individual servings. Some dishes are prepared while you watch, especially coffee, which is a veritable chemistry showcase. A couple of the more sumptuous dishes are the tangy and crunchy crisp eel wuxi and the sweet batter-dipped prawns with sesame seed and salad sauce. If you order the Beijing duck, after the traditional pancake dish they serve the shredded meat in a delicious sauce with green bean noodles.

Goodwood Park Hotel, 22 Scotts Rd. ℂ **65/6730-1752.** Reservations recommended. Small dishes S$15–S$58 (US$8.55–US$33). AE, DC, MC, V. Daily noon–2:30pm, 6:30–10:30pm.

Esmirada ⭐ MEDITERRANEAN   Ask any expatriate about restaurants and you'll hear about Esmirada. This place revels in the joys of good food and drink, bringing laughter and fun to the traditional act of breaking bread with friends and family. The menu is easy: There's one dish each from Italy, Spain, Greece, France, Portugal, and Morocco, and they never change. Huge portions are served family style, from big bowls of salad to shish kebab skewers hanging from a rack, all placed in the center of the table so everyone can dig in. Don't even bother with paella anywhere else—this is the best. The place is small, so make your reservations early. Stucco walls, wrought-iron details, and terra-cotta floors are mixed with wooden Indonesian tables and chairs with kilim cushions in an East-meets-West style that works very nicely.

Orchard Hotel, 442 Orchard Rd., #01-29. ℂ **65/735-3476.** Reservations recommended for dinner. Main courses S$24–S$42 (US$14–US$24). AE, DC, MC, V. Daily 11am–11pm.

Gordon Grill ⭐⭐ CONTINENTAL   Bringing meat and potatoes to the high life, Gordon Grill wheels out a carving cart full of the most tender prime rib and sirloin you could imagine, cut to your desired thickness. The menu of traditional English and Scottish fare includes house specialties like the pan-fried goose liver with apple and port wine sauce appetizer and the house recipe for (perfect) lobster bisque. Featured entrees are the mixed seafood grill of lobster, garoupa (grouper), scallops, and prawns in a lemon butter sauce and roast duck breast glazed with honey and black pepper. The traditional English sherry trifle is the dessert to order here, but if you want a little taste of everything, the dessert variation lets you have small portions of each dessert, with fresh fruit. The dining room, which is small and warmly set with dark tartan carpeting and portraits of stately Scotsmen, feels more comfortable than claustrophobic, and light piano music drifts in from the lounge next door. Dress formal.

Goodwood Park Hotel, 22 Scotts Rd. ℂ **65/6730-1744.** Reservations recommended. Main courses S$32–S$50 and up (US$18–US$29). AE, DC, MC, V. Daily noon– 2:30pm, 7–10:30pm.

Harbour Grill & Oyster Bar ⭐⭐⭐ CONTINENTAL   Grilled seafood and U.S. prime rib are perfectly prepared and served with attentive style in this award-winning restaurant. The Continental cuisine is lighter than most, with recipes that focus on the natural freshness of their ingredients rather than on creams and fat. Caesar salad is made at your table so you can request your preferred blend of ingredients, and the oyster bar serves fresh oysters from around the world. For the main course, the prime rib is the best and most requested entree, but the rack of lamb is another option worth considering—it melts in your mouth. Guest chefs from international culinary capitals are flown in for monthly specials. The place is small and cozy, with exposed brick and a finishing kitchen in the dining room. Windows have been replaced with murals of the Singapore harbor in the 1850s, but in the evenings it is still airy and fresh feeling.

Hilton International Singapore, Level 3, 581 Orchard Rd. ℂ 65/6730-3393. Reservations recommended. Main courses S$34–S$36 (US$19–US$21). 2 courses S$55 (US$31), 3 courses S$75 (US$43), or 4 courses S$90 (US$51) per person. AE, DC, MC, V. Daily noon–2:30pm,d 7–10:30pm.

Li Bai ★★★ CHINESE CANTONESE Chinese restaurants are typically unimaginative in the decor department—slapping up a landscape brush painting or two here and there is sometimes about as far as they go. Not at Li Bai, though, which is very sleekly decorated in contemporary black and red lacquer, with huge vases of soft pussy willows dotted about. Creative chefs and guest chefs turn out a constantly evolving menu, refining specialties, and jade and silver chopsticks and white bone china add opulent touches to their flawless meals. Make sure you ask for their most recent creations—they're guaranteed to please. Or, try the farm chicken smoked with jasmine tea, a succulent dish. The crab fried rice is fabulous, with generous chunks of fresh meat, and the beef in mushroom and garlic brown sauce is some of the tenderest meat you'll ever feast upon. The wine list is international, with many vintages to choose from.

Sheraton Towers, 39 Scotts Rd. ℂ 65/6839-5623. Reservations required. Main courses S$18–S$48 and up (US$10–US$27). AE, DC, MC, V. Daily 11am–2:30pm, 6:30–10:30pm.

Mezza9 ★★ FUSION This is your best bet if your party can't agree on what to eat because Mezza9 offers an extensive menu that includes Chinese steamed treats, Japanese, Thai, deli selections, Italian, fresh seafood and Continental grilled specialties. Start with big and juicy raw oysters in the half-shell. If you want to consider more raw seafood, the combination sashimi platter is also very fresh. Grilled meats include various cuts of beef, rack of lamb, and chicken dishes with a host of delicious sides to choose from. The enormous 450-seat restaurant has a warm atmosphere, with glowing wood and contemporary Zen accents. Before you head in for dinner, grab a martini in their très chic martini bar.

Grand Hyatt, 10 Scotts Rd. ℂ 65/6416-7189. Reservations required. Main courses S$25–S$40 (US$14–US$23). AE, DC, MC, V. Daily noon–3pm, 6–11:30pm.

MODERATE

Ah Hoi's Kitchen SINGAPOREAN I like Ah Hoi's for its casual charm and its selection of authentic local cuisine. The menu is extensive, specializing in local favorites like fried black pepper kuay teow (noodles), sambal kang kong (vegetable), and fabulous grilled seafood. The alfresco poolside pavilion location gives it a real "vacation in the tropics" sort of relaxed feel—think of a hawker center without the dingy florescent bulbs, greasy tables, and sludgy floor. Also good here is the chile crab—if you can't make it out to the seafood places on the east coast of the island, it's the best alternative for tasting this local treat. Make sure you order the fresh lime juice. It's very cooling.

Traders Hotel, 1A Cuscaden Rd., 4th level. ℂ 65/6831-4373. Reservations recommended. Main courses S$8–S$27 (US$4.55–US$15). AE, DC, MC, V. Daily 11:30am–2:30pm, 6:30–10:30pm.

Crystal Jade Palace ★ CHINESE CANTONESE Although Crystal Jade Palace is an upmarket choice, it's a fantastic way to try Chinese food as it was intended. From the aquariums of soon-to-be-seafood-delights at the entrance you can survey the rows of big round tables (and some small ones, too) packed with happy diners feasting away. The food here is authentic Cantonese, prepared by Hong Kong master chefs. Dim sum, fresh seafood, and barbecue dishes accompany exotic shark's fin and baby abalone. Scallop dishes are very popular and can be prepared either sautéed with cashews, chile, and soy; pan-fried with chiles, white pepper, and salt; or sautéed with green vegetables. The tender pan-fried cod in light honey sauce proves worthy of its reputation as a time-honored favorite. For a unique soup, try the double-boiled winter melon with mixed meats, mushrooms, crab, and dried scallops served in the halved melon shell. You can order Chinese or French wines to accompany your meal.

391 Orchard Rd., #04-19 Ngee Ann City. (C) **65/735-2388.** Reservations required. Small dishes S$12–S$38 (US$6.85–US$22); set lunch for 2 from S$50 (US$29). AE, DC, MC, V. Daily 11:30am–2:30pm, 6:30–10:30pm.

Patara Fine Thai THAI   Patara may say fine dining in its name, but the food here is home cooking: not too haute, not too traditional. Seafood and vegetables are big here. Deep-fried garoupa (grouper) is served in a sweet sauce with chile that can be added sparingly upon request. Curries are popular, too. The roast duck curry in red curry paste with tomatoes, rambutans, and pineapple is juicy and hot. For something really different, Patara's own invention, the Thai taco isn't exactly traditional, but is good, filled with chicken, shrimp, and sprouts. Their green curry, one of my favorites, is perhaps the best in town. Their Thai-style iced tea (which isn't on the menu, so you'll have to ask for it) is fragrant and flowery. A small selection of wines is also available. Patara has another out-let at Swissôtel Stamford Level 3, Stamford Road ((C) 65/6339-1488).

#03-14 Tanglin Mall, 163 Tanglin Rd. (C) **65/6737-0818.** Reservations recommended for lunch, required for dinner. Main courses S$17–S$30 (US$9.70–US$17). AE, DC, MC, V. Daily noon–2:30pm, 6–10:30pm.

Pine Court ⭐ CHINESE MIXED   The decor at Pine Court is stunning. Designed to emulate an elegant courtyard, the carved rosewood screens on the walls are like geometric lace, and little clusters of delicate wood and white paper lanterns cast a warm glow from the high ceilings. During dinner, and while music plays, the giant silk-screen landscape painting against the far wall is trans-formed through visual effects to represent each season. Pine Court was once a Beijing-style restaurant, and even though they now serve many different kinds of Chinese cuisine, the Beijing duck remains a favorite and will never leave the menu. The sautéed mixed seafood served in a yam basket is comprised of stir-fried scallops, prawns, and *garoupa* (grouper) with vegetables in a lightly fried basket that's very tasty—it's a great presentation. Another great dish is the spe-cialty crispy roast chicken (whole or half), with the skin left on and seasoned with soy sauce.

Mandarin Singapore, 333 Orchard Rd. (take the express elevator to the 35th floor). (C) **65/831-6262.** Reser-vations recommended. Small dishes S$16–S$46 (US$9.15–US$26). AE, DC, MC, V. Daily noon–3pm, 6:30–11pm.

Tandoor ⭐⭐ NORTHERN INDIAN   Live music takes center stage in this small restaurant, adorned with carpets, artwork, and wood floors and furnish-ings. Entrees prepared in their tandoor oven come out flavorful and not as salty as most tandoori dishes. The tandoori lobster is rich, but the chef's specialty is crab lababdar: crabmeat, onions, and tomato sautéed in a coconut gravy. Fresh cottage cheese is made in-house for fresh and light saag panir, a favorite here. Chefs keep a close eye on the spices to ensure the spice enhances the flavor rather than drowning it out—more times than not, customers ask them to add more spices. A final course of creamy masala tea perks you up and aids digestion. If you're curious, the tandoor oven is behind a glass wall in the back, so you can watch them prepare your food.

Holiday Inn Parkview, 11 Cavenagh Rd. (C) **65/730-0153.** Reservations recommended. Main courses S$11–S$40 (US$6.30–US$23). AE, DC, MC, V. Daily noon–2:30pm, 7–10:30pm.

INEXPENSIVE

Chatterbox SINGAPOREAN   If you'd like to try the local favorites but don't want to deal with street food, then Chatterbox is the place for you. Their Hainanese chicken rice is highly acclaimed, and other dishes—like nasi lemak, laksa, and carrot cake—are as close to the street as you can get. For a quick and tasty snack, order tahu goreng, deep-fried tofu in peanut chile sauce. This is also a good place to experiment with some of those really weird local drinks. Chin chow is the dark brown grass jelly drink; cendol is green jelly, red beans, palm sugar, and coconut milk; and bandung is the pink rose syrup milk with jelly. For dessert, order the ever-favorite sago pudding, made from the hearts of the sago palm. This informal and lively coffee shop dishes out room service for the Mandarin Hotel and is open 24 hours a day.

Mandarin Hotel, 333 Orchard Rd. (℗ **65/6737-4411.** Reservations recommended for lunch and dinner. Main courses S$15–S$39 (US$8.55–US$22). AE, DC, MC, V. Daily 24 hr.

Genki Sushi *Value* JAPANESE   I ducked into Genki Sushi for lunch. I sat at the counter, where a tiny conveyor belt snaked along in front of me carrying colored plates full of glistening sushi, rolls, sashimi, and other treats. Just pick and eat—and pay per plate. So the goofy Japanese guy next to me got chatty. We discussed the conveyor-belt sushi bar concept and how much we both loved it, then he poked some buttons on his electronic translator and showed me the screen. "This name in Japan." The translator spelled *revolution*. Makes sense, "revolving" sushi bar, but now I'll never shake the image of Che Guevara sitting there plucking sushi off the belt.

#01-16 Forum The Shopping Mall, Orchard Rd. (℗ **65/6734-2513.** Reservations not accepted. Revolving plates S$1.90–S$6.50 (US$1.10–US$3.70). AE, DC, MC, V. Sun–Thurs 11:30am–9pm; Fri–Sat 11:30am–10pm.

The Rice Table MALAY/INDONESIAN   Indonesian Dutch rijsttafel, meaning "rice table," is a service of many small dishes (up to almost 20) with rice. Traditionally, each dish would be brought to diners by beautiful ladies in pompous style. Here, busy waitstaff brings all the dishes out and places them in front of you—feast on favorite Indo-Malay wonders like beef rendang, chicken satay, otak otak, and sotong assam (squid) for a very reasonable price. It's an enormous amount of food and everything is terrific. Pay extra for your drinks and desserts. There's an additional outlet at Cuppage Terrace at 43-45 Cuppage Rd. H₂O Zone (℗ 65/6735-9117).

International Bldg., 360 Orchard Rd., #02-09/10. (℗ **65/6835-3783.** Reservations not necessary. Lunch set S$13 (US$7.30), dinner set S$18.50 (US$11). AE, DC, MC, V. Tues–Sun noon–2:30pm, 6–9:30pm.

8 Restaurants a Little Farther Out

Many travelers will choose to eat in town for convenience, and while there's plenty of great dining in the more central areas, there are some other really fantastic dining finds if you're willing to hop in a cab for 10 or 15 minutes. These places are worth the trip—for a chance to dine along the water at UDMC or amid lush terrace gardens at Alkaff Mansion, or to just go for superior seafood at Long Beach Seafood Restaurant. And don't worry about finding your way back: Most places always have cabs milling about. If not, restaurant staff will always help you call a taxi.

EXPENSIVE

Alkaff Mansion *★* MALAY/INDONESIAN   Alkaff Mansion was built by the wealthy Arab Alkaff family not as a home, but as a place to throw elaborate parties; and true to its mission, Alkaff Mansion is tops for elegant ambience. The mansion allows for indoor and outdoor patio dining at small tables glistening with starched white linens and small candles. The forest outside is a stunning backdrop. The dinner cuisine here is rijsttafel—home-style Indonesian fare that was influenced by Dutch tastes and is served in set menus that rotate weekly. A typical set dinner might include gado gado (a cold salad with sweet peanut sauce) and a soup. To announce the main course, a gong is sounded and ladies dressed in traditional kebaya sarongs carry out the dishes on platters. Main courses include the siakap masak asam turnis (fish in a tangy sauce); the udang kara kuning, which is a great choice for lobster; and the crayfish in chile sauce. In rijstaffel tradition, the dinner is served with rice, which is accompanied by an array of condiments like varieties of sambal and achar. Downstairs, Alkaff serves a huge buffet with nightly changing themes. I strongly recommend this place for a truly unique and memorable dining experience.

10 Telok Blangah Green (off Henderson Rd.), Telok Blangah Hill Park. © 65/6415-4888. Reservations recommended. Set rijstaffel menu S$60 (US$34) per person; buffet S$35 (US$20) per person. AE, DC, MC, V. Daily 11:30am–2:30pm, 6–10:30pm.

MODERATE

Long Beach Seafood Restaurant SEAFOOD   They really pack 'em in at this place. Tables are crammed together in what resembles a big indoor pavilion, complete with festive lights and the sounds of mighty feasting. This is one of the best places for fresh seafood of all kinds: fish like garoupa (grouper), sea bass, marble goby, and kingfish, and other creatures of the sea from prawns to crayfish. The chile crab here is good, but the house specialty is really the pepper crab, chopped and deliciously smothered in a thick concoction of black pepper and soy. Huge chunks of crayfish are also tasty in the black pepper sauce, and can be served in variations like barbecue, sambal, steamed with garlic, or in a bean sauce. Don't forget to order buns so you can sop up the sauce. You can also get vegetable, chicken, beef, or venison dishes to complement, or choose from their menu selection of local favorites.

1018 East Coast Pkwy. © 65/445-8833. Reservations recommended. Seafood is sold by weight according to seasonal prices. Most dishes S$9–S$16 (US$5.15–US$9.15). AE, DC, MC, V. Daily 5pm–1:15am.

Palm Beach ⋆ SEAFOOD   Palm Beach has two levels. Downstairs you have a dining hall that is extremely underdressed and informal, while upstairs is a lovely upscale setting. The food is great in either setting (the menu is the same), and very reasonably priced. Australian lobster graces the finest dish here—cooked in a clay pot with coconut milk and chile sauce. Their chile crab is also great, but to me seems a bit "local" if you're dining upstairs. Besides, it's very messy. A gift shop outside lets you bring home jars of hot pot sauce, achar (sweet sauce), chile sauce, and sambal. On weekends if you don't have a reservation, you'll have to queue up.

5 Stadium Walk, #01-16 Leisure Park. © 65/6344-3088. Reservations for dinner required. Seafood is sold by the gram according to seasonal prices. Most small dishes S$12–S$28 (US$6.85–US$16). AE, MC, V. Daily noon–2:30pm, 6–11:30pm.

Prima Tower Revolving Restaurant CHINESE BEIJING   One of the main attractions here is the fact that the restaurant revolves, giving you an ever-changing view of the city from your table. The other main attraction is the food, which is Beijing-style Chinese. Naturally, the best dish is the Beijing duck, which has been a house specialty since this restaurant opened 20 years ago. All of the noodles for the noodle dishes are prepared in-house using traditional recipes and techniques, so the word of the day is fresh. Try them with minced pork and chopped cucumber in a sweet sauce. The restaurant manager comes to each table to present the daily specials. It's a good time to chat him up for the best dishes and ask questions about the menu.

201 Keppel Rd. ℂ **65/6272-8822.** Reservations required. Small dishes S$14–S$50 (US$8–US$29) and up. AE, DC, MC, V. Mon-Sat 11am–2:30pm, 6:30–10:30pm; Sun 10:30am-2:30pm, 6:30-10:30pm. Closed Chinese New Year.

UDMC Seafood Centre ★★ SEAFOOD   Eight seafood restaurants are lined side by side in 2 blocks, their fronts open to the view of the sea outside. UDMC is a fantastic way to eat seafood Singapore style, in the open air, in restaurants that are more like grand stalls than anything else. Eat the famous local chile crab and pepper crab here, along with all sorts of squid, fish, and scallop dishes. Noodle dishes are also available, as are vegetable dishes and other meats. But the seafood is the thing to come for. Of the eight restaurants, there's no saying which is the best, as everyone seems to have his own opinions about this one or that one (I like Jumbo at the far eastern end of the row; call ℂ 65/6442-3435 for reservations, which are recommended for weekends). Have a nice stroll along the walkway and gaze out to the water while you decide which one to go for.

Block 1202 East Coast Pkwy. No phone. Seafood dishes are charged by weight, with dishes from around S$12 (US$6.85). AE, DC, MC, V. Daily 5pm–midnight.

Xin Cuisine CHINESE CANTONESE/CHINESE HERBAL   A recent trend is to bring back the Chinese tradition of preparing foods that have special qualities for beauty, health, and vitality, balancing the body's yin and yang and restoring energy. Xin (new) cuisine transforms these concepts into light and flavorful creations, listed in a menu that's literally a book. The chef is famous for East-meets-West creations, but be assured, the cuisine is mostly Chinese. The concentrated seafood soup with chicken and spinach is a light and delicious broth that's neither too thick nor thin and has chunks of meat and shredded spinach. Stewed Mongolian rack of lamb is obviously not Cantonese, but is as tender as butter and served in a sweet brown sauce with buns to soak up the gravy. The steamed eggplant with toasted sesame seed is fantastic, with warm tender slices served in soy sauce. For the more adventurous, they serve up a mean hasma scrambled egg whites. Hasma is frog glands, which are believed to improve the complexion. The dish is a little alarming to some, but served with a hint of ginger and scooped onto walnut melba toast, it's actually quite nice.

Concorde Hotel, 317 Outram Rd., Level 4. ℂ **65/6732-3337.** Reservations recommended. Small dishes S$10–S$30 (US$5.70–US$17). AE, DC, MC, V. Daily noon– 2.30pm and 6:30–10:30pm.

INEXPENSIVE

Samy's Curry Restaurant ★ SOUTHERN INDIAN   There are many places in Singapore to get good southern Indian banana leaf (see description under "One Little Island, Lots & Lots of Choices," earlier in this chapter), but none quite so unique as Samy's out at Dempsey Road. Because it's part of the Singapore Civil Service Clubhouse, at lunchtime nonmembers must pay S50¢ (US30¢) to get in the door. Not that there's much of a door, because Samy's is situated in a huge, high-ceilinged, open-air hall, with shutters thrown back and fans whirring above. Wash your hands at the back and have a seat, and soon someone will slap a banana leaf place mat in front of you. A blob of white rice will be placed in the center, and then buckets of vegetables, chicken, mutton, fish, prawn, and you name it will be brought out, swimming in the richest and spiciest curries to ever pass your lips. Take a peek in each bucket, shake your head yes when you see one you like, and a scoop will be dumped on your banana leaf. Eat with your right hand or with a fork and spoon. When you're done, wipe the sweat from your brow, fold the banana leaf away from you, and place your tableware on top. Samy's serves no alcohol, but the fresh lime juice is nice and cooling.

Block 25 Dempsey Rd. © 65/6472-2080. Reservations not accepted. Sold by the scoop or piece, S80¢–S$3 (US46¢–US$1.70). V. Daily 11am–3pm, 6–10pm. No alcohol served.

9 Hawker Centers

Hawker centers—large groupings of informal open-air food stalls—were Singapore's answer to fast and cheap food in the days before McDonald's came along, and are still the best way to sample every kind of Singaporean cuisine. They can be intimidating for newcomers, especially during the busy lunch or dinner rush, when they turn into fast-paced carnivals; so if it's your first time, try this: First, walk around to every stall to see what they have to offer. The stalls will have large signs displaying principal menu items, and you should feel free to ask questions, too, before placing your order. Special stalls have drinks only. The fresh lime goes with any dish, but to be truly local, grab a giant bottle of Tiger beer.

Next, find a table. Some stalls have their own tables for you to use; otherwise, sit anywhere you can and when you order let the hawker know where you are (tables usually have numbers to simplify). If it's crowded and you find a couple of free seats at an already occupied table, politely ask if they are taken; and if the answer is no, have a seat—it's perfectly customary. Your food will be brought to you, and you are expected to pay upon delivery. When you're finished, don't clear your own plates, and don't stack them. Some stalls may observe strict religious customs that require different plates for different foods, and getting other scraps on their plates may be offensive.

For the record, all hawkers are licensed by the government, which inspects them and enforces health standards.

The most notorious hawker center in Singapore is **Newton.** Located at Newton Circus, the intersection of Scotts Road, Newton Road, and Bukit Timah/Dunearn Road, this place is notorious, as opposed to famous, for being an overcommercialized tourist spectacle where busloads of foreigners come and gawk at the Singaporean fast-food experience. It's slightly more expensive than other hawker centers, and if you go, be very careful about ordering seafood—they may bring you more than you asked for, and overcharge you for it. All in all, if you want to check it out, it is a good initiation before moving on to the real places. **Lau Pa Sat Festival Village** (Telok Ayer Market) is located in Chinatown at the corner of Raffles Way and Boon Tat Street, and sometimes gets touristy, too; but for the record, both Newton and Lau Pa Sat are open 24 hours.

For a more authentic experience in **Chinatown,** try the center at the end of Amoy Street near Telok Ayer Road, or the one at the corner of Maxwell Road and South Bridge Road (though the latter is known for being frighteningly dingy).

In the **Historic District** they are fast disappearing. Try the one on Stamford Road between the National Museum and Armenian Street intersection. You'll also find one on Victoria Street next to Allson Hotel, and another at Bugis night market.

In **Little India,** Tekker Centre, formerly Zhujiao Centre, is a nice-size hawker center. On **Orchard Road,** try Cuppage Terrace, just beyond the Centrepoint Shopping Centre.

Nowadays, most hawker centers have become "food courts," the same concept, only they're located in air-conditioned shopping malls around the city. Food courts are serve-yourself. Stall operators give you your food on a tray, you pay, then carry the tray to an open table.

One place that's been near and dear to Singaporeans for years (though now they've mostly been chased away by overcommercialization) is the **Satay Club** ✺. It used to be down at the Esplanade, but constant building and land reclamation efforts moved it around a bunch of times, and so they eventually moved it to Clarke Quay off River Valley Road. Yes, it is very touristy now, but still worth a visit. Satay, by the way, is perhaps the most popular Malay dish of all time. The small kabobs of meat are skewered onto the stiff veins of palm leaves and barbecued over a hibachi. Order them by the stick. They come with cucumbers and onion on the side, and a bowl of peanut chile sauce to dunk it all in. Find yourself a table, get some beer, order yourself up a whole plate, and you'll be happy as a clam, whether you look like a tourist or not.

10 Cafe Society

In Singapore, traditions such as British high tea and the Chinese tea ceremony live side by side with a growing coffee culture. These popular hangouts are all over the city. Here are a few places to try.

BRITISH HIGH TEA

Two fabulous places to take high tea in style are at **Raffles Bar & Billiard** Room at Raffles Hotel, 1 Beach Rd. (© **65/6331-1746**), and **Equinox** at Swissôtel Stamford, 2 Stamford Rd. (© **65/6431-6156**). Both places are lovely, if pricey. The buffet will cost anywhere between S$35 and S$45 (US$20–US$26). High tea is served in the afternoons from 3pm until 5 or 5:30pm.

CHINESE TEA

There are a few places in Chinatown where tea is still as important today as it has always been in Chinese culture. **The Tea Chapter,** 11A Neil Rd. (© **65/ 6226-1175**), and **Yixing Xuan,** 30-32 Tanjong Pagar Rd. (© **65/6224-6961**), offer tranquil respites from the day and cultural insight into Chinese tea appreciation.

CAFES

Western-style coffee joints have been popping up left and right all over the island, so coffee-addicted travelers can rest assured that in the morning their favorite blends are brewing close by—as long as you don't mind spending up to S$4 (US$2.30) for a cup of brew. **Starbucks, The Coffee Bean & Tea Leaf, The Coffee Club, Spinelli,** and many more international chain cafes have outlets in just about every shopping mall in the city.

5

Singapore Attractions

Of Singapore's many sights and attractions, I enjoy the historic and cultural sights the most. The city's many old buildings and well-presented museum displays bring history to life. Chinese and Hindu temples and Muslim mosques welcome curious observers to discover their culture as they play out their daily activities, and the country's natural parks make the great outdoors easily accessible from even the most urban neighborhood. That's the best benefit of traveling in Singapore: Most attractions are situated within the heart of the city, and those that lie outside the urban center still can be easily reached.

Singapore also has a multitude of planned attractions for visitors and locals alike. Theme parks devoted to cultural heritage, sporting fun, and even kitsch amusement pop up all over the place. While some of these can be a little too Disneyland for many peoples' tastes, some are fun, especially if you're traveling with children. In this chapter, I've outlined the many attractions here, provided historic and cultural information to help you appreciate each sight in its local context, and given you the truth about those attractions I think you could really skip, so you don't waste your time and money finding out for yourself. To help you plan your activities, I've put stars next to those attractions I've enjoyed the most—either for significance, excellent planning, or just plain curiosity.

I've divided this chapter into the main sections of the urban center—the Historic District, Chinatown, Little India, Kampong Glam, and Orchard Road, where you'll find the more historic sights of the city—and those outside the city, to the west, north, and east, where you'll find large areas dedicated to nature reserves, a zoo, and other wildlife attractions, theme parks, and sprawling temple complexes, all easily accessible by public transportation or a cab ride. As a kicker, I'll take you to Sentosa (a small island to the south that's packed from shore to shore with amusements, adventure theme parks, historic exhibits, nature displays, and outdoor activities for families), and to some of the smaller outlying islands, and will fill you in on sports and recreation options.

When you're traveling to attractions outside the urban area, I recommend keeping this book handy—taxis are not always easy to find, so you may need to refer to the guide to call for a pick up or use the bus and MRT system, route numbers for which I've included with listings of most noncentral attractions.

A note: Many of the sights to see in Singapore are not of the "pay your fee and see the show" variety, but rather historic buildings, monuments, and places of religious worship. The city's historic buildings, such as City Hall or Parliament House, must be appreciated from the outside, their significance lying in their unique architecture and historical context combined with the sensual effect of the surrounding city. Monuments and statues tell the stories of events and heroes important to Singapore in both the past and the present. The places of worship listed in this chapter are open to the public and free of entrance charge. Expect temples to be open from sunup to sundown. Visiting hours are not specific to the hour, but, unless it's a holiday (when hours may be extended), you can expect these places to be open during daylight hours.

1 The Historic District

Armenian Church 🛠 Of all colonial buildings, the Armenian Church (more formally called the Church of St. Gregory the Illuminator) is one of the most beautiful examples of early architectural style here. Designed by George Coleman, one of Singapore's most prolific and talented architects, it is his finest work. Although there were many alterations in the last century, the main style of the structure still dominates. The round congregation hall is powerful in its simplicity, its long louvered windows letting in cooling breezes while keeping out the imposing sunlight. Roman Doric columns support symmetrical porticos that protect the structure from rain. All in all, it's a wonderful achievement of combined European eclectic tastes and tropical necessity.

The first permanent Christian church in Singapore, it was funded primarily by the Armenian community, which was at one time quite powerful. Today, few Singaporeans can trace their heritage back to this influential group of immigrants. The church was consecrated in 1836, and the last appointed priest serving the parish retired in 1936. Although regular Armenian services are no longer held, other religious organizations make use of the church from time to time. The cemetery in the back of the church is the burial site of many prominent Armenians, including Ashgen Agnes Joachim, discoverer of the Vanda Miss Joachim, Singapore's national flower.

60 Hill St., across from the Grand Plaza Hotel. ✆ 65/6334-0141.

Asian Civilisations Museum 🛠🛠🛠 The old Tao Nan School, which dates from 1910, was completely renovated and reopened in 1997 to house the Asian Civilisations Museum. Beautiful and clear exhibits display fine collections of jade, calligraphy, ceramics, furniture, and artworks, all offering visitors the chance to trace the archipelago's rich Chinese heritage. Changing exhibits in the temporary galleries represent the other Asian civilizations.

39 Armenian St. ✆ 65/6332-3015. Adults S$3 (US$1.70), children and seniors S$1.50 (US86¢). Tues–Sun 9am–6pm (extended hours Fri until 9pm). Free guided tours in English Tues–Fri 11am and 2pm, with an extra tour on weekends at 3:30. City Hall MRT, and follow Stamford Rd. to Armenian St.

Bugis Street/Bugis Junction If you happened to visit Singapore in the seventies, and remember Bugis as a haven for transvestites and sex shows, you're in for a big surprise: Bugis Street ain't what it used to be. In place of the decadence is a giant shopping mall, Parco Bugis Junction. There's also a night market with a few bargains on cheap chic, curio items, accessories, and video disks.

The area around Bugis Street has a more benign history. The Bugis, fierce and respected warriors, were some of the first people to settle on Singapore in its early years. Raffles took note of their boat-building skills and, as part of his master town plan, included Bugis Town to attract more of them to the island.

Bugis MRT stop, across from Parco Bugis Junction shopping mall.

Cathedral of the Good Shepherd This cathedral was Singapore's first permanent Catholic church. Built in the 1840s, it brought together many elements of a fractured parish. In the early days of the colony, the Portuguese Mission

Urban Singapore Attractions

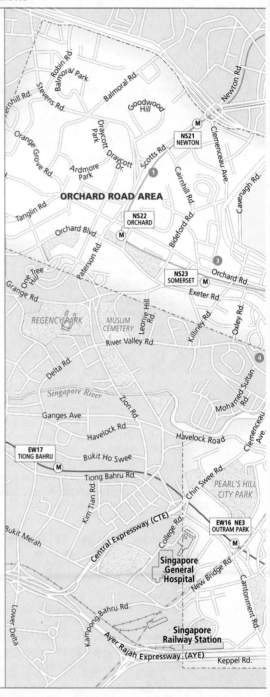

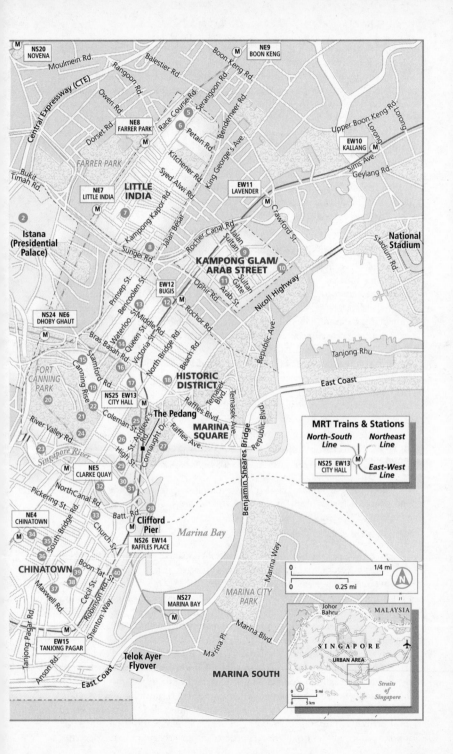

thought itself the fount of the Holy Roman Empire's presence on the island, and so the French Bishop was reduced to holding services at the home of a Mr. McSwiney on Bras Basah Road; a dissenting Portuguese priest held forth at a certain Dr. d'Ameida's residence; and the Spanish priest was so reduced that we don't even know where he held his services. These folks were none too pleased with their makeshift houses of worship and so banded together to establish their own cathedral—the Cathedral of the Good Shepherd. Designed in a Latin cross pattern, much of its architecture is reminiscent of St. Martin-In-The-Fields and St. Paul's in Covent Garden. The Archbishop's residence, in contrast, is a simple two-story bungalow with enclosed verandas and a portico. Also on the grounds are the resident's Quarters and the Priests' Residence, the latter more ornate in design, with elaborate plasterwork.

4 Queen St., at the corner of Queen St. and Bras Basah Rd. ℂ **65/6337-2036.** Open to the public during the day.

CHIJMES (Convent of the Holy Infant Jesus)   As you enter this bustling enclave of retail shops, restaurants, and nightspots, it's difficult to imagine this was once a convent which, at its founding in 1854, consisted of a lone, simply constructed bungalow. After decades of buildings and add-ons, this collection of unique yet perfectly blended structures—a school, a private residence, an orphanage, a stunning Gothic chapel, and many others—were enclosed within walls, forming peaceful courtyards and open spaces encompassing an entire city block. Legend has it the small door on the corner of Bras Basah and Victoria streets welcomed hundreds of orphan babies, girl children who were born during inauspicious years or to poor families who just appeared on the stoop each morning. In late 1983, the convent relocated to the suburbs, and some of the block was leveled to make way for the MRT Headquarters. Thankfully, most of the block survived and the Singapore government, in planning the renovation of this desirable piece of real estate, wisely kept the integrity of the architecture. For an evening out, the atmosphere at CHIJMES is exquisitely romantic. At the same time, you can enjoy a special decadence when you party in one of the popular bars here.

A note on the name: CHIJMES is pronounced "Chimes"; the "Chij," as noted, stands for Convent of the Holy Infant Jesus, and the "mes" was just added on so they could pronounce it "Chimes."

30 Victoria St. Free admission. ℂ **65/6337-7810.**

City Hall (Municipal Building)   During the Japanese occupation, City Hall was a major headquarters, and it was here in 1945 that Admiral Lord Louis Mountbatten accepted the Japanese surrender. In 1951, the Royal Proclamation from King George VI was read here declaring that Singapore would henceforth be known as a city. Fourteen years later, Prime Minister Lee Kuan Yew announced to its citizens that Singapore would henceforth be called an independent republic.

City Hall, along with the Supreme Court, was judiciously sited to take full advantage of the prime location. Magnificent Corinthian columns march across the front of the symmetrically designed building, while inside, two courtyards lend an ambience of informality to otherwise officious surroundings. For all its magnificence and historical fame, however, its architect, F. D. Meadows, relied too heavily on European influence. The many windows afford no protection from the sun, and the entrance leaves pedestrians unsheltered from the elements.

Booked seat 6A, open return.

Rented red 4-wheel drive.

Reserved cabin, no running water.

Discovered space.

With over 700 airlines, 50,000 hotels, 50 rental car companies and 5,000 cruise and vacation packages, you can create the perfect getaway for you. Choose the car, the room, even the ground you walk on.

Travelocity.com
A Sabre Company
Go Virtually Anywhere.

Travelocity,® Travelocity.com® and the Travelocity skyline logo are trademarks and/or servicemarks of Travelocity.com L.P., and Sabre® is a trademark of an affiliate of Sabre Inc. © 2002 Travelocity.com L.P. All rights reserved.

Book your air, hotel, and transportation all in one place.

Hotel or hostel? Cruise or canoe? Car? Plane? Camel? Wherever you're going, visit Yahoo! Travel and get total control over your arrangements. Even choose your seat assignment. So. One hump or two? travel.yahoo.com

powered by **COMPAQ**

YAHOO!
Travel

© 2002 Yahoo! Inc.

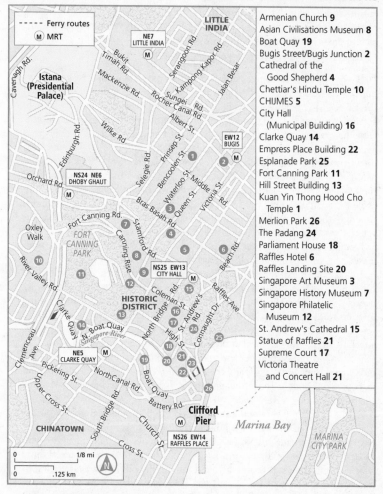

In defining the very nobility of the Singapore government, it appears the Singaporean climate wasn't taken into consideration.

St. Andrew's Rd., across from the Padang. Entrance to the visitor's gallery is permitted, but all other areas are off-limits.

Empress Place Building Standing as a symbol of British colonial authority as travelers entered the Singapore River, Empress Place Building housed almost the entire government bureaucracy around the year 1905, and was a government office until the 1980s, housing the Registry of Births and Deaths and the Citizenship Registry. Every Singaporean at some point passed through its doors. In the late 1980s, the government offices moved out and the building was restored as an historical cultural exhibition venue.

The oldest portion is the part nearest Parliament House; it was designed by colonial engineer J. F. A. McNair and built by convict labor between June 1864 and December 1867. Four major additions and other renovations have been faithful to his original design. Inside, there are many surviving details, including plaster moldings, cornices, and architraves. It is currently being renovated as the second phase of the Asian Civilisations Museum.

1 Empress Place, at the southern end of the Padang next to the Parliament Bldg.

Fort Canning Park   These days, Fort Canning Park is known for great views out over Singapore, but in days past it served as the site of Raffles's home and the island's first botanical garden. Its history goes back even farther, though: Excavations over the years have unearthed ancient brick foundations and artifacts that gave a certain credence to the island natives' belief that their royal ancestors lived and were buried on the site. Fourteenth-century Javanese gold ornaments were excavated and placed on display at the Singapore History Museum. Atop the hill, a mysterious *keramat,* or sacred grave, marks the burial site of Iskander Shah (also known as Parameswara), the Palembang ruler who came to Singapore in the late 1300s before settling in Malacca. The debate surrounding the truth of this account doesn't hinder those who come to pay homage and worship at the site, which is well maintained within the park.

From the start Raffles chose this hill to build his home (at the site of the present-day lookout point), which later became a residence for Singapore's diplomats and governors. In 1860, the house was torn down to make way for Fort Canning, which was built to quell British fears of invasion but instead quickly became the laughingstock of the island. The location was ideal for spotting invaders from the sea, but defending Singapore? Not likely. The cannons' range was such that their shells couldn't possibly have made it all the way out to an attacking ship—instead, most of the town below would have been destroyed. In 1907, the fort was demolished for a reservoir. Today, the only reminders of the old fort are some of the walls and the Fort Gate, a deep stone structure. Behind its huge wooden door you'll find a narrow staircase that leads to the roof of the structure.

Raffles also chose this as the location for the first botanical garden on the island. The garden was short-lived due to lack of funding; however, the park still has a pretty interesting selection of plants and trees, like the cannonball tree with its large round seed pods, and the cotton tree, whose pods open to reveal fluffy white "cotton" that was commonly used for stuffing pillows and mattresses. In many parts, these plants are well marked along the pathways. Also look for the ASEAN sculpture garden; five members of the Association of Southeast Asian Nations each donated a work for the park in 1982 to represent the region's unity.

Fort Canning was also the site of a **European cemetery.** To make improvements in the park, the graves were exhumed and the stones placed within the walls surrounding the outdoor performance field that slopes from the Music and Drama Society building. A large Gothic monument was erected in memory of James Napier Brooke, infant son of William Napier, Singapore's first law agent, and his wife, Maria Frances, the widow of prolific architect George Coleman. Although no records exist, Coleman probably designed the cupolas as well as two small monuments over unknown graves. The Music and Drama Society building itself was built in 1938. Close by, in the wall, are the tombstones of Coleman and of Jose D'Almeida, a wealthy Portuguese merchant.

Inside the park, The Battle Box is an old WWII bunker displaying in wax dioramas and a multimedia show the surrender of Singapore. It's open Tuesday to Sunday from 10am to 6pm; adults S$8 (US$4.55), children S$5 (US$2.85); (65/6333-0510.

© 65/3663-3307. Major entrances are from behind the MITA building, Percival Rd. (Drama Centre), Fort Canning Aquarium, National Library Carpark, and Canning Walk (behind Park Mall). Free admission. Dhoby Gaut or City Hall MRT.

Hill Street Building   Originally built to house the British Police Force, the building was sited directly across from Chinatown for easy access to quell the frequent gang fights. Later it became home to the National Archives, and it is believed that inquisitions and torture were carried out in the basement during the Japanese occupation. Former National Archive employees have claimed to have seen ghosts of tortured souls sitting at their desks.

Today, this colorful building houses the Ministry of Information, Communications and the Arts (MITA), and the National Arts Council. Inside, check out ARTrium@MITA, with six galleries displaying Singaporean, Southeast Asian, and European fine arts. It's air-conditioned!

Hill St. at the corner of River Valley Rd., on Fort Canning Park.

Kuan Yin Thong Hood Cho Temple   It's said that whatever you wish for within the walls of Kuan Yin Temple comes true, so get in line and have your wishes ready. It must work, as there's a steady stream of people on auspicious days of the Chinese calendar. The procedure is simple: Wear shoes easily slipped off before entering the temple. Light several joss sticks. Pray to the local god, pray to the sky god, then turn to the side and pray some more. Now pick up the container filled with inscriptions and shake it until one stick falls out. After that, head for the interpretation box office to get a piece of paper with verses in Mandarin and English to look up what your particular inscription means. (For a small fee, there are interpreters outside.) Now for the payback: If your wish comes true, be prepared to return to the temple and offer fruits and flowers to say thanks (oranges, pears, and apples are a thoughtful choice and jasmine petals are especially nice). Be careful what you wish for. Once you're back home and that job promotion comes through, your new manager might nix another vacation so soon. To be on the safe side, bring the goods with you when you make your wish.

Waterloo St., about 1½ blocks from Bras Basah Rd. Open to the public during the day.

The Padang   This large field—officially called Padang Besar but known as the Padang—has witnessed its share of historical events. Bordered on one end by the Singapore Recreation Club and on the other end by the Singapore Cricket Club, and flanked by City Hall, the area was once known as Raffles Plain. Upon Raffles's return to the island in 1822, he was angry that resident Farquhar had allowed merchants to move into the area he had originally intended for government buildings. All building permits were rescinded and a new site for the commercial district was planned for the area across the Singapore River. The Padang became the official center point for the government quarters, around which the Esplanade and City Hall were built. On weekends the Padang hosts cricket and rugby matches in season.

Today, the Padang is mainly used for public and sporting events—pleasant activities—but in the 1940s it felt more forlorn footsteps when the invading Japanese forced the entire European community onto the field. There they waited while the occupation officers dickered over a suitable location for the "conquered." They ordered all British, Australian, and Allied troops as well as European prisoners on the 22km (14-mile) march to Changi.

An interesting side note: Frank Ward, designer of the Supreme Court, had big plans for the Padang and surrounding buildings. He would have demolished the Cricket Club, Parliament House, and the Victoria Hall & Theatre to erect an enormous government block if World War II hadn't arrived, ruining his chances.

St. Andrew's Rd. and Connaught Dr.

Parliament House   Parliament House, built in 1826, is probably Singapore's oldest surviving structure, even though it has been renovated so many times it no longer looks the way it was originally constructed. It was designed as a home for John Argyle Maxwell, a Scottish merchant, but before it was completed, the government rented it to house the court and other government offices. In 1939, when the new Supreme Court was completed, the judiciary moved in; then, in 1953, following a major renovation, Maxwell's House was renamed Parliament House and was turned over to the legislature.

The original house was designed by architect George D. Coleman, who had helped Raffles with his Town Plan of 1822. Coleman's design was in the English neo-Palladian style. Simple and well suited to the tropics, this style was popular at the time with Calcutta merchants. Major alterations have left very little behind of Coleman's design, however, replacing it with an eclectic French classical style, but some of his work survives. Today, the building has been transformed once again, into part of a larger S$80 million Parliament Complex.

The bronze elephant in front of Parliament House was a gift to Singapore in 1872 from His Majesty Somdeth Phra Paraminda Maha Chulalongkorn (Rama V), supreme king of Siam, as a token of gratitude following his stay the previous year.

1 High St., at the south end of the Padang, next to the Supreme Court. Closed to the general public, but worth seeing from the outside.

Raffles Hotel ★★   Built in 1887 to accommodate the increasing upper-class trade, Raffles Hotel was originally only a couple of bungalows with 10 rooms, but, oh, the view of the sea was perfection. The owners, Armenian brothers named Sarkies, already had a couple of prosperous hotels in Southeast Asia (the Eastern & Oriental in Penang and The Strand in Rangoon) and were well versed in the business. It wasn't long before they added a pair of wings and completed the main building—and reading rooms, verandas, dining rooms, a grand lobby, the Bar and Billiards Room, a ballroom, and a string of shops. By 1899, electricity was turning the cooling fans and providing the pleasing glow of comfort.

As it made its madcap dash through the twenties, the hotel was the place to see and be seen. Vacancies were unheard of. Hungry Singaporeans and guests from other hotels, eager for a glimpse of the fabulous dining room, were turned away for lack of reservations. The crowded ballroom was jumping every night of the week. During this time Raffles's guest book included famous authors like Somerset Maugham, Rudyard Kipling, Joseph Conrad, and Noël Coward. These were indeed the glory years, but the lovely glimmer from the chandeliers soon faded with the stark arrival of the Great Depression. Raffles managed to limp through that dark time—and, darker still, through the Japanese occupation—and later pull back from the brink of bankruptcy to undergo modernization in the fifties. But fresher, brighter, more opulent hotels were taking root on Orchard Road, pushing the "grand old lady" to the back seat.

The hotel was in limbo for a period of time due to legal matters, and in 1961 it passed through several financial institutions to land on the doorstep of the Development Bank of Singapore (DBS). It was probably this journey that saved the Raffles from a haphazard renovation nightmare. Instead, history-minded renovators selected 1915 as a benchmark and, with a few changes here and there, faithfully restored the hotel to that era's magnificence and splendor. Today, the hotel's restaurants and nightlife draw thousands of visitors daily to its open lobby, its theater playhouse, the Raffles Hotel Museum, and 65 exclusive boutiques. Its 15 restaurants and bars—especially the Tiffin Room, Raffles Grill, and Doc Cheng's, all reviewed in chapter 4—are a wonder, as is its famous Bar and Billiards Room and Long Bar.

1 Beach Rd. ℭ 65/337-1886.

Raffles Landing Site   The polymarble statue at this site was unveiled in 1972. It was made from plaster casts of the original 1887 figure located in front of the Victoria Theatre and Concert Hall (see below) and stands on what is believed to be the site where Sir Stamford Raffles landed on January 29, 1819. North Boat Quay.

St. Andrew's Cathedral   Designed by George Coleman; erected on a site selected by Sir Stamford Raffles himself; named for the patron saint of Scotland, St. Andrew; and primarily funded by Singapore's Scottish community, the first St. Andrew's was the colonials' Anglican Church. Completed toward the end of the 1830s, its tower and spire were added several years later to accord the edifice more stature. By 1852, because of massive damage sustained from lightning strikes, the cathedral was deemed unsafe and torn down. The cathedral that now stands on the site was completed in 1860. Of English Gothic Revival design, the cathedral is one of the few standing churches of this style in the region. The spire resembles the steeple of the Salisbury Cathedral—another tribute from the colonials to Mother England. Not only English residents but Christian Chinese, Indians, continental Europeans, and Malays consider this to be their center of worship.

The plasterwork of St. Andrew's inside walls used a material called Madras chunam, which, though peculiar, was a common building material here in the 1880s. A combination of shell lime (without the sand) was mixed with egg whites and coarse sugar or jaggery until it took on the consistency of a stiff paste. The mixture was thinned to a workable consistency with water in which coconut husks had steeped, and was then applied to the surface, allowed to dry, and polished with rock crystal or smooth stones to a most lustrous patina. Who would've thought?

The original church bell was presented to the cathedral by Maria Revere Balestier, the daughter of famed American patriot Paul Revere. The bell now stands in the Singapore History Museum.

Coleman St., between North Bridge Rd. and St. Andrew's Rd., across from the Padang. ℭ 65/6337-6104. Open during daylight hours.

Singapore Art Museum ★   The Singapore Art Museum (SAM) officially opened in 1996 to house an impressive collection of over 3,000 pieces of art and sculpture, most of it by Singaporean and Malay artists. Limited space requires the curators to display only a small number at a time, but these are incorporated in interesting exhibits to illustrate particular artistic styles, social themes, or historical concepts. A large collection of Southeast Asian pieces rotates regularly, as well as visiting international exhibits. Besides the main halls, the museum offers up a gift shop with fine souvenir ideas, a cafe, a conservation laboratory, an auditorium, and the E-mage Gallery, where multimedia presentations include not only the museum's own acquisitions but other works from public and private collections in the region as well. Once a Catholic boys' school established in 1852, SAM has retained some visible reminders of its former occupants: Above the front door of the main building you can still see inscribed "St. Joseph's Institution," and a bronze-toned, cast-iron statue of St. John Baptist de la Salle with two children stands in its original place.

71 Bras Basah Rd. ① 65/6332-3222. www.museum.org.sg. Adults S$3 (US$1.70), children and seniors S$1.50 (US86¢). Tues–Sun 9am–6pm (extended hours Fri until 9pm). Free guided tours in English Tues–Fri 11am and 2pm, with additional weekend tour at 3:30pm. City Hall MRT, across Bras Basah Park from the Singapore History Museum.

Singapore History Museum ★★   Raffles Museum was opened in 1887, in a handsome example of neo-Palladian architecture designed by colonial architect Henry McCallum. It was the first of its kind in Southeast Asia, housing a superb collection of regional natural history specimens and ethnographic displays. In both 1907 and 1916, the museum outgrew its space and was enlarged. Renamed the National Museum in 1969, its collections went through a transformation, focusing on Singapore's history rather than that of the archipelago. Several years later, it became known as the Singapore History Museum. While the small museum's lack of space limits the number and size of exhibits, several are quite interesting. I always enjoy the Audubon-style pen-and-inks commissioned by first resident William Farquhar. Take the time to read the accompanying descriptions, which point out the many flaws in the artists' knowledge of basic anatomy and botany. Also interesting are 20 dioramas portraying events from the settlement's early days to modern times. An interesting note: At one time the descriptions that accompanied the dioramas raked the Japanese over the coals for the horrors committed during their World War II occupation. In recent years, the Japanese requested they change these to a less offensive account, and the museum responded with silence. Today, while other dioramas have paragraphs of description, these few have maybe one or two lines each. Period. Finally, "Rumah Baba" shows through costumes and household and ceremonial items the unique culture of the Peranakans, or Straits-born Chinese. Additional visiting exhibits change frequently.

93 Stamford Rd., across the street from Bras Basah Park. ① 65/6332-3659. National Heritage Board www.museum.org.sg/nhb.html. Adults S$3 (US$1.70), children and seniors S$1.50 (US86¢). Tues–Sun 9am–6pm (extended hours Fri until 9am). Free guided tours in English Tues–Fri 11am and 2pm, with an extra tour on weekends at 3:30pm.

Singapore Philatelic Museum   This building, constructed in 1895 to house the Methodist Book Room, recently underwent a S$7 million restoration and reopened as the Philatelic Museum in 1995. Exhibits include a fine collection of old stamps issued to commemorate historically important events, first-day covers, antique printing plates, postal service memorabilia, and private collections. Visitors can trace the development of a stamp from idea to the finished sheet, and you can even design your own. Free guided tours are available upon request.

23B Coleman St. ① 65/6337-3888. Adults S$2 (US$1.15), children and seniors S$1 (US55¢). Tues–Sun 9am–6pm. Take the MRT to City Hall and walk toward Coleman St.

Statue of Raffles   This sculpture of Sir Stamford Raffles was erected on the Padang in 1887 and moved to its present position after getting in the way of one too many cricket matches. During the Japanese occupation, the statue was placed in the Singapore History Museum (then the Raffles Museum), and was replaced here in 1945. The local joke is that Raffles's arm is outstretched to the

Bank of China building, and his pockets are empty. (Translation: In terms of wealth in Singapore, it's Chinese 1, Brits 0.)

Victoria Theatre and Concert Hall.

Supreme Court   The Supreme Court stands on the site of the old Hotel de L'Europe, a rival of the Raffles Hotel until it went bankrupt in the 1930s. The court's structure, a classical style favored for official buildings the world over, was completed in 1939. With its spare adornment and architectural simplicity, the edifice has a no-nonsense, utilitarian attitude, and the sculptures across the front, executed by the Italian sculptor Cavaliere Rodolpho Nolli, echo what transpires within. Justice is the most breathtaking, standing 2.7m (9 ft.) high and weighing almost 4 tons. Kneeling on either side of her are representations of Supplication and Thankfulness. To the far left are Deceit and Violence. To the far right, a bull represents Prosperity and two children hold wheat, to depict Abundance.

Two and a half million bricks were used in building this structure, but take a moment to note the stonework: It's fake! Really a gypsum type of plaster, it was applied by Chinese plasterers who'd fled from Shanghai during the Sino-Japanese conflict, and molded to give the appearance of granite.

While taking in the exterior, look up at the dome, which is a copy of the dome of St. Paul's Cathedral in London. The dome covers the courtyard, which is surrounded by the four major portions of the Supreme Court building.

St. Andrew's Rd., across from the Padang. Closed to visitors, but worth seeing from the outside.

Victoria Theatre and Concert Hall   Designed by colonial engineer John Bennett in a Victorian Revival style that was fashionable in Britain at the time, the theater portion was built in 1862 as the Town Hall. Victoria Memorial Hall was built in 1905 as a memorial to Queen Victoria, retaining the same style of the old building. The clock tower was added a year later. In 1909, with its name changed to Victoria Theatre, the hall opened with an amateur production of the *Pirates of Penzance*. Another notable performance occurred when Noël Coward passed through Singapore and stepped in at the last moment to help out a traveling English theatrical company that had lost a leading man. The building looks much the same as it did then, though of course the interiors have been modernized. It was completely renovated in 1979, conserving all the original details, and was renamed Victoria Concert Hall. It housed the Singapore Symphony Orchestra until the opening of The Esplanade—Theatres on the Bay, when they shifted to the larger digs.

9 Empress Place, at the southern end of the Padang. © 65/339-6120.

ALONG THE RIVER

The Singapore River had always been the heart of life in Singapore even before Raffles landed, but for many years during the 20th century life here was dead—quite literally. Rapid urban development that began in the 1950s turned the river into a giant sewer, killing all plant and animal life in it. In the mid-1980s, though, the government began a large and surprisingly successful cleanup project; and shortly thereafter, the buildings at Boat Quay and Clarke Quay were restored. Now the areas on both banks of the river offer entertainment, food, and pubs day and night.

Boat Quay ✸   Known as "the belly of the carp" by the local Chinese because of its shape, this area was once notorious for its opium dens and coolie shops.

Nowadays, thriving restaurants boast every cuisine imaginable and the rocking nightlife offers up a variety of sounds—jazz, rock, blues, Indian, and Caribe— that are lively enough to get any couch potato tapping his feet. See chapters 4 and 7 for dining and nightlife suggestions, and remember to pronounce quay *key* if you don't want people to look at you funny.

Located on the south bank of the Singapore River between Cavenagh Bridge and Elgin Bridge.

Chettiar's Hindu Temple (aka the Tank Road Temple)   One of the richest and grandest of its kind in Southeast Asia, the Tank Road Temple is most famous for a **thoonganai maadam,** a statue of an elephant's backside in a seated position. It's said that there are only four others of the kind, located in four temples in India.

The original temple was completed in 1860, restored in 1962, and practically rebuilt in 1984. The many sculptures of Hindu deities and the carved Kamalam-patterned rosewood doors, arches, and columns were executed by architect-sculptors imported from Madras, India, specifically for the job. The Hindu child god, Lord Muruga, rules over the temple and is visible in one form or another wherever you look. Also notice the statues of the god Shiva and his wife, Kali, captured in their lively dance competition. The story goes that Kali was winning the competition, so Shiva lifted his leg above his head, something a woman wasn't thought capable of doing. He won and quit dancing—good thing, too, since every time Shiva did a little jig he destroyed part of the world.

Outside in the courtyard are statues of the wedding of Lord Muruga; his brother, Ganesh; another brother, Vishnu; and their father, Shiva; along with Brahma, the creator of all.

Used daily for worship, the temple is also the culmination point of Thai-pusam, a celebration of thanks, and the Festival of Navarathiri (see chapter 2).

15 Tank Rd., close to the intersection of Clemenceau Ave. and River Valley Rd.

Clarke Quay   The largest of the waterfront developments, Clarke Quay was named for the second governor of Singapore, Sir Andrew Clarke. In the 1880s, a pineapple cannery, iron foundry, and numerous warehouses made this area bustle. Today, with 60 restored warehouses hosting restaurants and a shopping section known as Clarke Quay Factory Stores, the Quay still hops. **River House,** formerly the home of a *towkay* (company president), occupies the oldest building. The **Bar Gelateria Bellavista** ice cream parlor (River Valley Rd. at Coleman Bridge) was once the icehouse. On Thursdays and Fridays from 6:30 to 8:15pm, enthusiasts can catch a **Chinese opera performance** and makeup demonstration—it's a treat to watch. Get up early on Sunday, forgo the comics section and take in the **flea market,** which opens at 9am and lasts all day. You'll find lots of bargains on unusual finds.

River Valley Rd. west of Coleman Bridge. ✆ 65/6337-3292.

Esplanade Park   Esplanade Park and Queen Elizabeth Walk, two of the most famous parks in Singapore, were established in 1943 on land reclaimed from the sea. Several memorials are located here. The first is a fountain built in 1857 to honor **Tan Kim Seng,** who gave a great sum of money toward the building of a waterworks. Another monument, **the Cenotaph,** commemorates the 124 Singaporeans who died in World War I; it was dedicated by the Prince of Wales. On the reverse side, the names of those who died in World War II have been inscribed. The third prominent memorial is dedicated to **Major General Lim Bo Seng,** a member of the Singaporean underground resistance in World War II who was captured and killed by the Japanese. His memorial was unveiled in 1954 on the 10th anniversary of his death. At the far end of the park, the Esplanade—Theatres on the Bay opened in October 2002. Fashioned after the Sydney Opera House, the unique double-domed structure is known locally as The Durians, since their spiky domes resemble halves of durian shells (the building itself is actually smooth—the "spikes" are sun shields).

Connaught Dr., on the marina, running from the mouth of the Singapore River along the Padang to The Esplanade–Theatres on the Bay. Daily until midnight.

Merlion Park   The Merlion is Singapore's half-lion, half-fish national symbol, the lion representing Singapore's roots as the "Lion City" and the fish representing the nation's close ties to the sea. Bet you think a magical and awe-inspiring beast like this has been around in tales for hundreds of years, right? No such luck. Rather, he was the creation of some scheming mind at the Singapore Tourism Board in the early 1970s. Talk about the collision of ancient culture and the modern world. Despite the Merlion's commercial beginnings, he's been adopted as the national symbol and spouts continuously every day at the mouth of the Singapore River.

South bank, at the mouth of the Singapore River, adjacent to One Fullerton. Free admission. Daily 7am–10pm.

2 Chinatown & Tanjong Pagar

Al-Abrar Mosque   This mosque was originally erected as a thatched building in 1827 and was also called Masjid Chulia and Kuchu Palli, which in Tamil means "hut mosque." The building that stands today was built in the 1850s, and even though it faces Mecca, the complex conforms with the grid of the neighborhood's city streets. In the late 1980s, the mosque underwent major renovations that enlarged the mihrab and stripped away some of the ornamental qualities of the columns in the building. The one-story prayer hall was extended upward into a two-story gallery. Little touches like the timber window panels and fanlight windows have been carried over into the new renovations.

192 Telok Ayer St., near the corner of Telok Ayer St. and Amoy St., near Thian Hock Keng Temple.

Chinatown Heritage Centre ★★   This block of old shophouses in the center of the Chinatown heritage district has been converted into a display that tells the story of the Chinese immigrants who came to Singapore to find work in the early days of the colony. Walk through rooms filled with period antiques replicating coolie living quarters, shops, clan association houses and other places that were prominent in daily life. It reminded me of the museum on Ellis Island in New York City that walks visitors through the immigrant experience of the early 1900s. Like Ellis Island, this display also has detailed descriptions to explain each element of the immigrant experience.

48 Pagoda St. ✆ 65/6325-2878. Adults S$8 (US$4.55), children S$4.80 (US$2.75). Daily 10am-7pm. English language tour every hour.

Jamae Mosque   Jamae Mosque was built by the Chulias, Tamil Muslims who were some of the earlier immigrants to Singapore, and who had a very influential hold over Indian Muslim life centered in the Chinatown area. The Chulias built not only this mosque, but Masjid Al-Abrar and the Nagore Durgha Shrine as well. Jamae Mosque dates from 1827, but wasn't completed until the early 1830s. The mosque stands today almost exactly as it did then.

While the front gate is typical of mosques you'd see in southern India, inside most of the buildings reflect the neoclassical style of architecture introduced in administrative buildings and homes designed by George Coleman and favored by the Europeans. There are also some Malay touches in the timber work. A small shrine inside, which may be the oldest part of the mosque, was erected to memorialize a local religious leader, Muhammad Salih Valinva.

18 South Bridge Rd., at the corner of South Bridge Rd. and Mosque St.

Lau Pa Sat Festival Pavilion   Though it used to be well beloved, the locals think this place has become an atrocity. Once the happy little hawker center known as Telok Ayer Market, it began life as a wet market, selling fruits, vegetables, and other foodstuffs. Now it's part hawker center, part Western fast-food outlets, and all tourist.

It all began on Market Street in 1823, in a structure that was later torn down, redesigned, and rebuilt by G. D. Coleman. Close to the water, seafood could be unloaded fresh off the pier. After the land in Telok Ayer Basin was reclaimed in 1879, the market was moved to its present home, a James MacRitchie design that kept the original octagonal shape and was constructed of 3,000 prefab cast-iron elements brought in from Europe.

In the 1970s, as the financial district began to develop, the pavilion was dominated by hawkers who fed the lunchtime business crowd. In the mid-1980s, the structure was torn down to make way for the MRT construction and then meticulously put back together, puzzle piece by puzzle piece. By 1989, the market was once again an urban landmark, but it sat vacant until Scotts Holdings successfully tendered to convert it into a festival market. At this time, numerous changes were made to the building, which was renamed Lau Pa Sat (Old Market) in acknowledgment of the name by which the market had been known by generations of Singaporeans. By the way, Lau Pa Sat is one of the few hawker centers that's open 24 hours, in case you need a coffee or snack before retiring.

18 Raffles Quay, located in the entire block flanked by Robinson Rd., Cross St., Shenton Way, and Boon Tat St.

Nagore Durgha Shrine   Although this is a Muslim place of worship, it is not a mosque, but a shrine, built to commemorate a visit to the island by a Muslim holy man of the Chulia people (Muslim merchants and moneylenders from India's Coromandel Coast), who was traveling around Southeast Asia spreading the word of Indian Islam. The most interesting visual feature is its facade: Two arched windows flank an arched doorway, with columns in between. Above these is a "miniature palace"—a massive replica of the facade of a palace, with tiny cutout windows and a small arched doorway in the middle. The cutouts in white plaster make it look like lace. From the corners of the facade, two 14-level minarets rise, with three little domed cutouts on each level and onion domes on top. Inside, the prayer halls and two shrines are painted and decorated in shockingly tacky colors.

Controversy surrounds the dates that the shrine was built. The government, upon naming the Nagore Durgha a national monument, claimed it was built sometime in the 1820s; however, Nagoreallauddeen, who is the 15th descendant of the holy man for whom the shrine is named, claims it was built many years before. According to Nagoreallauddeen, the shrine was first built out of wood and *attap* (a thatch roof made from a type of palm), and later, in 1815, was rebuilt from limestone, 4 years before the arrival of Sir Stamford Raffles. In 1818, rebuilding materials were imported from India to construct the present shrine. The government has no historical records to prove the previous existence of the shrine at that time. Nagoreallauddeen, who sits daily in the office just to the right in the entrance hall, is fighting to have his date made official, and has

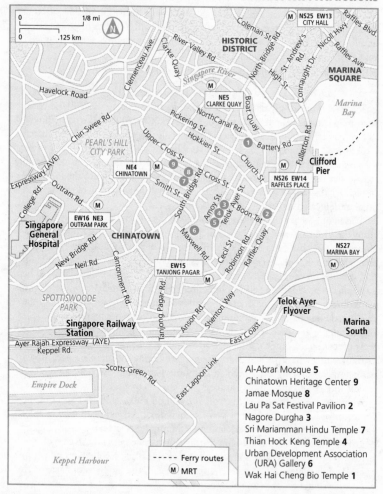

NS25 EW13
CITY HALL
Raffles Blvd.
Coleman St Rd.
HISTORIC
DISTRICT
River Valley Rd.
Clarke Quay
North Bridge Rd.
High St.
St. Andrew's
Rd.
Connaught Dr.
Nicoll Hwy.
Raffles Ave.
MARINA
SQUARE
Clemenceau Ave.
Havelock Road
Singapore River
Marina
Bay
NE5
CLARKE QUAY
Boat Quay
Chin Swee Rd.
PEARL'S HILL
CITY PARK
Pickering St.
NorthCanal Rd.
Hokkien St.
Upper Cross St.
Battery Rd.
Church St.
Fullerton Rd.
Clifford
Pier
Expressway (AYE)
College Rd.
Outram Rd.
NE4
CHINATOWN
Smith St.
South Bridge Rd.
Cross St.
Amoy St.
Telok Ayer St.
Boon Tat
NS26 EW14
RAFFLES PLACE
EW16 NE3
OUTRAM PARK
Singapore
General
Hospital
CHINATOWN
Maxwell Rd.
Cecil St.
Robinson Rd.
Raffles Quay
NS27
MARINA BAY
New Bridge Rd.
Neil Rd.
Cantonment Rd.
EW15
TANJONG PAGAR
Tanjong Pagar Rd.
Anson Rd.
Shenton Way
Telok Ayer
Flyover
SPOTTISWOODE
PARK
Marina
South
Singapore Railway
Station
East Coast
Ayer Rajah Expressway (AYE)
Keppel Rd.
Scotts Green Rd.
East Lagoon Link
Empire Dock

Keppel Harbour

Al-Abrar Mosque 5
Chinatown Heritage Center 9
Jamae Mosque 8
Lau Pa Sat Festival Pavilion 2
Nagore Durgha 3
Sri Mariamman Hindu Temple 7
Thian Hock Keng Temple 4
Urban Development Association
(URA) Gallery 6
Wak Hai Cheng Bio Temple 1

- - - - Ferry routes
Ⓜ MRT

covered the government plaque to the left of the front door, which declares the shrine a national monument. He'll tell you the whole story of the building and of his lineage if you ask, but he doesn't speak English, so try to grab a translator. 140 Telok Ayer St., at the corner of Telok Ayer St. and Boon Tat St. ⓒ 65/6324-0021.

Sri Mariamman Hindu Temple As the oldest Hindu temple in Singapore, Sri Mariamman has been the central point of Hindu tradition and culture. In its early years, the temple housed new immigrants while they established themselves and also served as social center for the community. Today, the main celebration here is the Thimithi Festival in October or November (see chapter 2). The shrine is dedicated to the goddess Sri Mariamman, who is known for curing disease (a very important goddess to have around in those days), but as is the case at all other Hindu temples, the entire pantheon of Hindu gods are present to be worshipped as well. On either side of the gopuram are statues of Shiva and Vishnu, while inside are two smaller shrines to Vinayagar and Sri Ararvan. Also note the sacred cows that lounge along the top of the temple walls.

The temple originated as a small wood-and-thatch shrine founded by Naraina Pillai, an Indian merchant who came to Singapore with Raffles's first expedition and found his fortune in trade. In the main hall of the temple is the small god that Pillai originally placed here.

244 South Bridge Rd., at the corner of South Bridge Rd. and Pagoda St.

Thian Hock Keng Temple ★★★   Thian Hock Keng, the "Temple of Heavenly Bliss," is one of the oldest Chinese temples in Singapore. Before land reclamation, when the shoreline came right up to Telok Ayer Road, the first Chinese sailors landed here and immediately built a shrine, a small wood-and-thatch structure, to pray to the goddess Ma Po Cho for allowing their voyage to be safely completed. For each subsequent boatload of Chinese sailors, the shrine was always the first stop upon landing. Ma Po Cho, the Mother of the Heavenly Sages, was the patron goddess of sailors, and every Chinese junk of the day had an altar dedicated to her.

The temple that stands today was built in 1841 over the shrine with funds from the Hokkien community, led by the efforts of two Malacca-born philanthropists, Tan Tock Seng and Tan Kim Seng. All of the building materials were imported from China, except for the gates, which came from Glasgow, Scotland, and the tiles on the facade, which are from Holland. The doorway is flanked by two lions, a male with a ball to symbolize strength and a female with a cup to symbolize fertility. On the door are door gods, mythical beasts made from the combined body parts of many animals. Note the wooden bar that sits at the foot of the temple entrance (as do similar bars in so many Chinese temples). This serves a couple of purposes: First, it keeps out wandering ghosts, who cannot cross over the barrier. Second, it forces anyone entering the temple to look down as they cross, bowing their head in humility. Just inside the door are granite tablets that record the temple's history.

Ahead at the main altar is Ma Po Cho, and on either side are statues of the Protector of Life and the God of War. To the side of the main hall is a Gambler Brother statue, prayed to for luck and riches. From here you can see the temple's construction of brackets and beams, fitting snugly together and carved with war heroes, saints, flowers, and animals, all in red and black lacquer and gilded in gold. Behind the main hall is an altar to Kuan Yin, the Goddess of Mercy. On either side of her are the sun and moon gods.

To the left of the courtyard are the ancestral tablets. In keeping with Confucian filial piety, each represents a soul. The tablets with red paper are for souls still alive. Also in the temple complex is a pagoda and a number of outer buildings that at one time housed a school and community associations.

158 Telok Ayer St., ½ block beyond Nagore Durgha Shrine. ✆ 65/6423-4626.

Urban Redevelopment Association (URA) Gallery   This enormous exhibit is perhaps of real interest only to Singaporeans and civil planners, but if you're in the neighborhood, it's worth a pop inside to see the giant plan of the city in miniature. Very cool. If you have time, sift through 48 permanent exhibits and 25 interactive displays that paint a historical picture of the development of urban Singapore.

URA Centre, 45 Maxwell Rd. ✆ 65/6321-8321. Admission free. Mon-Fri 9am-4:30pm; Sat 9am-12:30pm.

Wak Hai Cheng Bio Temple ★★   Like most of Singapore's Chinese temples, Wak Hai Cheng Bio had its start as a simple wood-and-thatch shrine where sailors, when they got off their ships, would go to express their gratitude for sailing safely to their destination. Before the major land reclamation projects shifted the shoreline outward, the temple was close to the water's edge, and so it was named "Temple of the Calm Sea Built by the Guangzhou People." It's a Teochew temple, located in a part of Chinatown populated mostly by the Teochews.

Inside the Taoist temple walls are two blocks. One is devoted to Ma Po Cho, the Mother of Heavenly Sages, who protects travelers and ensures a safe journey. The other is devoted to Siong Tek Kong, the god of business. Both are as important to the Chinese community today as they were way back when. Look for the statue of the Gambler Brother, with coins around his neck. The Chinese pray to him for wealth and luck, and in olden days would put opium on his lips. This custom is still practiced today, only now they use a black herbal paste called *koyo*, which is conveniently legal.

Inside the temple you can buy joss sticks and paper for S$2.50. Three joss sticks are for heaven, your parents, and yourself, to be burned before the altar. Three corresponding packets of elaborately decorated paper and gold leaf are to be burned outside in the gourd-shaped kilns (gourd being a symbol of health). The joss or "wishing paper," four thin sheets stamped with black and red characters, has many meanings. The red sheet is for luck (red being particularly auspicious) and the other three are to wash away your sins, for a long life, and for your wishes to be carried to heaven. Even if you are not Taoist, you're more than welcome to burn the joss.

The temple itself is quite a visual treat, with ceramic figurines and pagodas adorning the roof, and every nook and cranny of the structure adorned with tiny three-dimensional reliefs that depict scenes from Chinese operas. The spiral joss hanging in the courtyard adds an additional picturesque effect.

30-B Phillip St., at the corner of Phillip St. and Church St.

3 Little India

Abdul Gafoor Mosque   Abdul Gafoor Mosque is currently undergoing a major restoration. The grounds might be still boarded off if work has not been completed yet. It's actually a mosque complex consisting of the original mosque, a row of shophouses facing Dunlop Street, a prayer hall, and another row of houses ornamented with crescent moons and stars, facing the mosque. The original mosque was called Masjid Al-Abrar, and is commemorated on a granite plaque above what could have been either the entrance gate or the mosque itself. It still stands, and even though it is badly dilapidated, retains some of its original beauty. One beautiful detail is the sunburst above the main entrance, its rays decorated with Arabic calligraphy.

The surrounding shophouses were built in 1887 and 1903 by Sheik Abdul Gafoor, and their income paid for the start of the new mosque on the site 7 years later. Gafoor passed away before the mosque's completion, and although he'd willed the entire complex to his son, the latter's mismanagement of the affair led the government to pass control to the Mohammeden Endowments Board, who saw the mosque to completion in 1927.

Restoration of the shophouses is underway, including transformation of the facing shophouses into a religious school.

41 Dunlop St., between Perak Rd. and Jalan Besar.

Sakya Muni Buddha Gaya (Temple of a Thousand Lights)   Thai elements influence this temple, from the chedi (stupa) roofline to the huge Thai-style

An Introduction to Hindu Temples

The *gopuram* is the giveaway—the tiered roof piled high with brightly colored statues of gods and goddesses. Definitely a Hindu temple. So what are they all doing up there? It's because in India, what with the caste system and all, the lower classes were at one time not permitted inside the temple, so having these statues on the outside meant they could still pray without actually entering. Furthermore, while each temple is dedicated to a particular deity, all the gods are represented, in keeping with the Hindu belief that although there are many gods, they are all one god. So everyone is up there, in poses or scenes that depict stories from Hindu religious lore. Sometimes there are brightly colored flowers, birds, and animals as well—especially sacred cows. So why are some of them blue? It's because blue is the color of the sky, and to paint the gods blue meant that they, like the sky, are far-reaching and ever present.

There's no special way to pray in these temples, but by custom, most will pray first to Ganesh, the god with the elephant head, who is the remover of obstacles, especially those that can hinder one's closeness to god. Another interesting prayer ritual happens in the temple's main hall around a small dais that holds nine gods, one for each planet. Devotees who need a particular wish fulfilled will circle the dais, praying to their astrological planet god for their wish to come true.

The location of Hindu temples is neither by accident nor by Raffles's Town Plan. By tradition, they must always be built near a source of fresh water so that every morning, before prayer, all of the statues can be bathed. The water runs off a spout somewhere outside the main hall, from which devotees take the water and touch their heads.

Non-Hindus are welcome in the temples to walk around and explore. **Temple etiquette** asks that you first remove your shoes, and if you need to point to something, out of respect, please use your right hand, and don't point with your index finger.

Buddha image inside. Often this temple is brushed off as strange and tacky, but there are all sorts of surprises inside, making the place a veritable Buddha theme park. On the right side of the altar, statues of baby bodhisattvas receive toys and sweets from worshippers. Around the base of the altar, murals depict scenes from the life of Prince Siddhartha (Buddha) as he searches for enlightenment. Follow them around to the back of the hall and you'll find a small doorway to a chamber under the altar. Another Buddha image reclines inside, this one shown at the end of his life, beneath the Yellow Seraka tree. On the left side of the main part of the hall is a replica of a footprint left by the Buddha in Ceylon. Next to that is a wheel of fortune. For S$0.87 (US50¢) you get one spin.

336 On Race Course Rd., 1 block past Perumal Rd. ℂ 65/6294-0714. Daily 7:30am–4:45pm.

Sri Perumal Temple   Sri Perumal Temple is devoted to the worship of Vishnu. As part of the Hindu trinity, Vishnu is the sustainer balancing out Brahma the creator and Shiva the destroyer. When the world is out of whack, he rushes to its aid, reincarnating himself to show mankind that there are always new directions for development.

On the first tier to the left of the front entrance on the gopuram, statues depict Vishnu's nine reincarnations. Rama, the sixth incarnation, is with Hanuman, the monkey god, who helped him in the fierce battle to free his wife from kidnapping. Krishna, shown reclining amid devotees, is the eighth incarnation and a hero of many Hindu legends, most notably the Bhagavad-Gita. Also up there is the half-and-half bird Garuda, Vishnu's steed. Inside the temple are altars to Vishnu, his two wives, and Garuda.

The temple was built in 1855, and was most recently renovated in 1992. During Thaipusam, the main festival celebrated here (see chapter 2), male devotees who have made vows over the year carry kavadi—huge steel racks decorated with flowers and fruits and held onto their bodies by skewers and hooks— to show their thanks and devotion, while women carry milk pots in a parade from Sri Perumal Temple to Chettiar's Temple on Tank Road.

397 Serangoon Rd., ½ block past Perumal Rd. Best times to visit are daily 7–11am or 5–7:30pm.

Sri Veerama Kaliamman Temple ★★   This Hindu temple is primarily for the worship of Shiva's wife, Kali, who destroys ignorance, maintains world order, and blesses those who strive for knowledge of God. The box on the walkway to the front entrance is for smashing coconuts, a symbolic smashing of the ego, asking God to show "the humble way." The coconuts have two small "eyes" at one end so they can "see" the personal obstacles to humility they are being asked to smash.

Inside the temple in the main hall are three altars, the center one for Kali (depicted with 16 arms and wearing a necklace of human skulls) and two altars on either side for her two sons—Ganesh, the elephant god, and Murugan, the four-headed child god. To the right is an altar with nine statues representing the nine planets. Circle the altar and pray to your planet for help with a specific trouble.

Around the left side of the main hall, the first tier of the gopuram tells the story of how Ganesh got his elephant head. A small dais in the rear left corner of the temple compound is an altar to Sri Periyachi, a very mean looking woman with a heart of gold. She punishes women who say and do things to make others feel bad. She also punishes men—under her feet is an exploiter of ladies.

Here's a bit of trivia: Red ash, as opposed to white, is applied to the forehead after prayers are offered in a temple devoted to a female god.

On Serangoon Rd. at Veerasamy Rd. Daily 8am–noon, 5:30–8:30pm.

4 Arab Street & Kampong Glam

Alsagoff Arab School   Built in 1912, the school was named for Syed Ahmad Alsagoff, a wealthy Arab merchant and philanthropist who was very influential in Singapore's early colonial days and who died in 1906. It is the oldest girls' school in Singapore, and was the island's first Muslim school.

121 Jalan Sultan, across from Sultan Plaza.

Hajjah Fatimah Mosque ★★   Hajjah Fatimah was a wealthy businesswoman from Malacca and something of a local socialite. She married a Bugis prince from Celebes, and their only child, a daughter, married Syed Ahmed Alsagoff, son of Arab trader and philanthropist Syed Abdul Rahman Alsagoff. Hajjah Fatimah had originally built a home on this site, but after it had been robbed a couple of times and later set fire to, she decided to build a mosque here and moved to another home.

Inside the high walls of the compound are the prayer hall, an ablution area, gardens and mausoleums, and a few other buildings. You can walk around the main prayer halls to the garden cemeteries, where flat square headstones mark the graves of women and round ones mark the graves of men. Hajjah Fatimah is buried in a private room to the side of the main prayer hall, along with her daughter and son-in-law.

The minaret tower in the front was designed by an unknown European architect and could be a copy of the original spire of St. Andrew's Cathedral. The tower leans a little, a fact that's much more noticeable from the inside. On the outside of the tower is a bleeding heart—an unexpected place to find such a downright Christian symbol. It's a great example of what makes this mosque so charming—all the combined influences of Moorish, Chinese, and European architectural styles.

4001 Beach Rd., past Jalan Sultan.

Istana Kampong Glam   The Istana Kampong Glam hardly seems a fitting palace for Singapore's former royal family, but there's a fascinating and controversial story behind its current state of sad disrepair. In 1819, Sultan Hussein signed the original treaty that permitted the British East India Trading Company to set up operations in Singapore. Then, in 1824, he signed a new treaty in which he gave up his sovereign rights to the country in return for Kampong Glam (which became his personal residence) and an annual stipend for himself and his descendants. Shortly after his death some 11 years later, his son, Sultan Ali, built the palace. The family fortunes began to dwindle over the years that followed, and a decades-long dispute arose between Ali's descendants over ownership rights to the estate. In the late 1890s, they went to court, where it was decided that no one had the rights as the successor to the sultanate, and the land was reverted to the state, though the family was allowed to remain in the house. Trouble is, since the place had become state owned, the family lost the authority to improve the buildings of the compound, which is why they've fallen into the dilapidated condition you see today. Just recently, Sultan Hussein's family was given the boot and the place will be spruced up to house Kampong Glam cultural exhibits.

It's not known who designed the Istana, but many believe it was George Coleman who, in addition to official buildings, also contracted himself out to design personal residences. The style certainly resembles signature elements found in some of his other works.

The house to the left before the main gate of the Istana compound is called **Gedong Kuning,** or Yellow Mansion. It was the home of Tenkgu Mahmoud, the heir to Kampong Glam. When he died, it was purchased by local Javanese businessman Haji Yusof, the belt merchant.

Located at the end of Sultan Gate, 1 block past the intersection of Sultan Gate, Bagdad St., and Pahang St. This is a construction site, therefore no entry is permitted.

Sultan Mosque ⊛   Though there are more than 80 mosques on the island of Singapore, Sultan Mosque is the real center of the Muslim community. The mosque that stands today is the second Sultan Mosque to be built on this site. The first was built in 1826, partially funded by the East India Company as part of their agreement to leave Kampong Glam to Sultan Hussein and his family in

An Introduction to Mosques

To appreciate what's going on in the mosques in Singapore, here's a little background on some of the styles and symbols behind these exotic buildings. I have also included some tips that will help non-Muslims feel right at home.

The rule of thumb for Mosques is that they all face Mecca. Lucky for these buildings (and for Singaporean urban planners), most of the major mosques in Singapore have managed to fit within the grid of city streets quite nicely, with few major angles or corners jutting into the surrounding streets. One fine example of a mosque that obeys the Mecca rule but disregards zoning orders is Sultan Mosque in Kampong Glam. A peek around the back will reveal how the road is crooked to make way for the building.

The mosques in Singapore are a wonderful blend of Muslim influences from around the world. The grand Sultan Mosque has the familiar onion dome and Moorish stylings of the Arabic Muslim influence. The smaller but fascinating Hajjah Fatimah Mosque is a real blend of cultures, from Muslim to Chinese to even Christian—testimony to Islam's tolerance of other cultural symbols. On the other hand, the mosques in Chinatown, such as Jamae Mosque and the Nagore Durgha Shrine, are Saracenic in style, a style that originated in India in the late 19th century, mixing traditional styles of Indian and Muslim architecture with British conventionality.

Each mosque has typical features such as a **minaret,** a skinny tower from which the call to prayer was sounded (before recorded broadcasts), and a **mihrab,** a niche in the main hall which faces Mecca and in front of which the imam prays, his voice bouncing from inside and resonating throughout the mosque during prayers. You will also notice that there are no statues to speak of. Some mosques will have a **makam,** a burial site within the building for royalty and esteemed benefactors. This room is usually locked, but sometimes can be opened upon request. To the side of the main prayer hall there's always an **ablution area,** a place for worshippers to wash the exposed parts of their bodies before prayers, to show their respect. This is a custom for all Muslims, whether they pray in the mosque or at home. .

When visiting the mosques in Singapore, and anywhere else for that matter, there are some important rules of **etiquette** to follow. Appropriate dress is required. For both men and women, shorts are prohibited, and you must remove your shoes before you enter. For women, please do not wear short skirts or sleeveless, backless, or low-cut tops (although modern Singaporean Muslims do not require women to cover their heads before entering). *Also remember:* Never enter the main prayer hall. This area is reserved for Muslims only. Women should also tread lightly around this area, as it's forbidden for women to enter. No cameras or video cameras are allowed, and remember to turn off cellular phones and pagers. Friday is the Sabbath day, and you should not plan on going to the mosques between 11am and 2pm on this day.

return for sovereign rights to Singapore. The present mosque was built in 1928 and was funded by donations from the Muslim community. The Saracenic flavor of the onion domes, topped with crescent moons and stars, is complemented by Mogul cupolas. Funny thing, though: The mosque was designed by an Irish guy named Denis Santry, who was working for the architectural firm Swan and McLaren.

Other interesting facts about the mosque: Its dome base is a ring of black bottles; the carpeting was donated by a prince of Saudi Arabia and bears his emblem; and at the back of the compound, North Bridge Road has a kink in it, showing where the mosque invaded the nicely planned urban grid pattern. Also, if you make your way through the chink where the back of the building almost touches the compound wall, peer inside the makam to see the royal graves. They open the makam doors on Friday mornings and afternoons.

Sultan Mosque, like all the others, does not permit shorts, miniskirts, low necklines, or other revealing clothing to be worn inside. However, they do realize that non-Muslim travelers like to be comfortable as they tour around, and provide cloaks free of charge. They hang just to the right as you walk up the stairs.

3 Muscat St. Daily 9am–1pm and 2–4pm. No visiting is allowed during mass congregation Fri 11:30am–2:30pm.

5 Orchard Road Area

Goodwood Park Hotel Tower Wing   In 1861, with the Orchard Road area developing from a plantation area into a residential district popular with Europeans, Singapore's prosperous Germans purchased a piece of land on Scotts Road to build a community clubhouse, to be called the Teutonia Club. The design was entrusted to Swan and McLaren and placed in the hands of R. A. J. Bidwell, who chose for the building the lively Dutch-, French-, and English-influenced Queen Anne style, which had emerged in England in the late 19th century. The L-shaped plan enclosed two large halls linked by a prominent projecting porte-cochere at the corner. The halls had generous verandas both front and back, which separated guests from service staff and ensured adequate ventilation.

The club officially opened on September 21, 1900, but toward the end of March 1915, as the reverberations of World War I spread around the world, some 300 German nationals in Penang and Singapore were classified as enemy aliens and, together with their families, shipped to be interned in Australia. Their possessions, including the clubhouse, were confiscated and liquidated at public auction. Three brothers purchased the club, renaming it Goodwood Hall after the famous Goodwood Racecourse and using it as a performance venue (for 2 nights in December 1922, ballerina Anna Pavlova performed there with her troupe) before converting it to a hotel in the late 1920s. During the Japanese occupation the hotel was used by senior Japanese officers, and after the war, the Army War Crimes Office conducted trials on the premises. Plans in the seventies that called for the replacement of the Tower Wing with a 16-story modern building, complete with bubble lift, were abandoned when it was vocally criticized by the public. Instead, a new tower, which faintly resembles the original, was built in 1978. It's only a replica, but for the record it's an official national monument. The hotel's public areas are open to nonguests.

22 Scotts Rd., 1 block from Orchard Rd.

The Istana and Sri Temasek   In 1859, the construction of Fort Canning necessitated the demolition of the original governors' residence, and the autocratic and unpopular governor-general Sir Harry St. George Ord proposed this structure be built as the new residence. Though the construction of such a large and expensive edifice was unpopular, Ord had his way, and design and construction went through, with the building mainly performed by convicts under the supervision of Maj. J. F. A. McNair, the colonial engineer and superintendent of convicts.

In its picturesque landscaped setting, Government House echoed Anglo-Indian architecture, but its symmetrical and cross-shaped plan also echoed the form of the traditional Malay *istana* (palace). During the occupation, the house was occupied by Field Marshal Count Terauchi, commander of the Japanese Southern Army, and Major General Kawamura, commander of the Singapore Defense Forces. With independence, the building was renamed the Istana, and today serves as the official residence of the president of the Republic of Singapore. Used mainly for state and ceremonial occasions, the grounds are open to every citizen on selected public holidays, though they're not generally open for visits. The house's domain includes several other houses of senior colonial civil servants. The colonial secretary's residence, a typical 19th-century bungalow, is also gazetted a monument and is now called Sri Temasek.

Orchard Rd., between Claymore Rd. and Scotts Rd.

Peranakan Place ⚐   Emerald Hill was once nothing more than a wide treeless street along whose sides quiet families lived in typical terrace houses—residential units similar to shophouses, with a walled courtyard in the front instead of the usual "five-foot way." Toward Orchard Road, the terrace houses turned into shophouses, with their first floors occupied by small provisioners, seamstresses, and dry-goods stores. Across Orchard was Robinson's department store in a plain, boxy building.

As Orchard Road developed, so did Emerald Hill. A giant shopping mall called Centrepoint was built close to the junction of the two roads, and Robinsons moved into more glitzy digs. Meanwhile, the buildings were all renovated. The shophouses close to Orchard Road became restaurants and bars and the street was closed off to vehicular traffic. Now it's an alfresco cafe, landscaped with a veritable jungle of potted foliage and peopled by colorful tourists—much different from its humble beginnings.

But as you pass Emerald Hill, don't just blow it off as a tourist trap. Walk through the cafe area and out the back onto Emerald Hill. All of the terrace houses have been redone, and magnificently. The facades have been freshly painted and the tiles polished, and the dark wood details add a contrast that is truly elegant. When these places were renovated, they could be purchased for a song, but as Singaporeans began grasping at their heritage in recent years, their value shot up, and now these homes fetch huge sums.

For a peek inside some of these wonderful places (and who doesn't like to see how the rich live?), go to a bookstore and look at *Living Legacy: Singapore's Architectural Heritage Renewed,* by Robert Powell. Gorgeous photographs take you inside a few of these homes and some other terrace houses and bungalows around the island, showing off the traditional interior details of these buildings and bringing their heritage to life.

Located at the intersection of Emerald Hill and Orchard Rd.

Attractions Outside the Urban Area

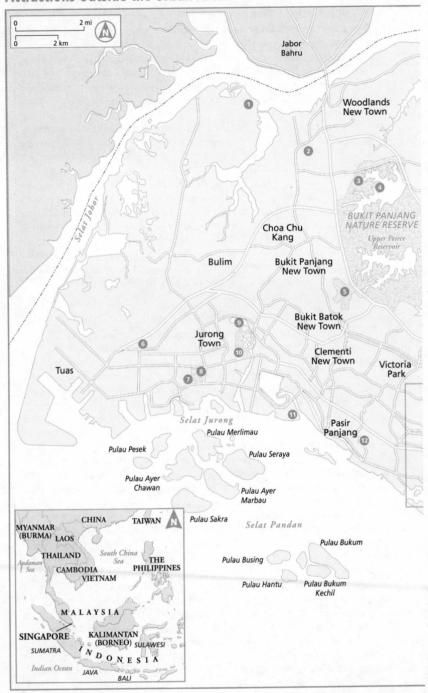

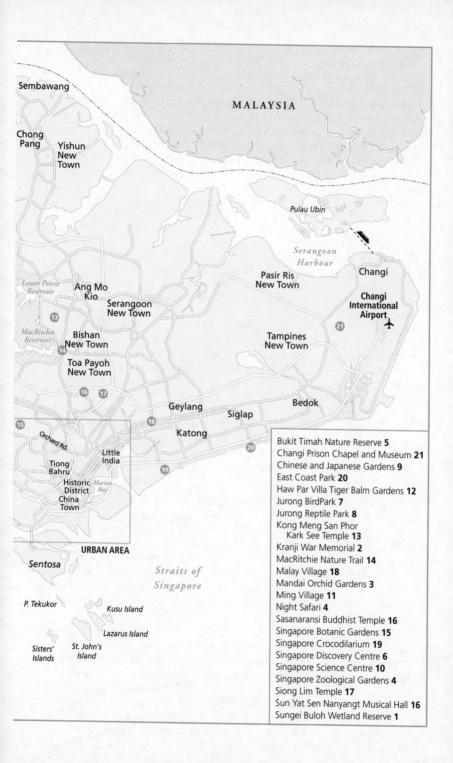

MALAYSIA

Sembawang

Chong Pang

Yishun New Town

Pulau Ubin

Serangoon Harbour

Changi

Pasir Ris New Town

Changi International Airport ✈

Lower Peirce Reservoir

Ang Mo Kio

Serangoon New Town

㉑

MacRitchie Reservoir

⑬

Bishan New Town

Tampines New Town

Toa Payoh New Town

⑭

⑯ ⑰

Geylang

Siglap

Bedok

⑮

Orchard Rd.

Little India

Katong

Tiong Bahru

⑱

Historic District

Marina Bay

China Town

⑳

⑲

URBAN AREA

Sentosa

Straits of Singapore

P. Tekukor

Kusu Island

Lazarus Island

Sisters' Islands

St. John's Island

Bukit Timah Nature Reserve **5**
Changi Prison Chapel and Museum **21**
Chinese and Japanese Gardens **9**
East Coast Park **20**
Haw Par Villa Tiger Balm Gardens **12**
Jurong BirdPark **7**
Jurong Reptile Park **8**
Kong Meng San Phor
  Kark See Temple **13**
Kranji War Memorial **2**
MacRitchie Nature Trail **14**
Malay Village **18**
Mandai Orchid Gardens **3**
Ming Village **11**
Night Safari **4**
Sasanaransi Buddhist Temple **16**
Singapore Botanic Gardens **15**
Singapore Crocodilarium **19**
Singapore Discovery Centre **6**
Singapore Science Centre **10**
Singapore Zoological Gardens **4**
Siong Lim Temple **17**
Sun Yat Sen Nanyangt Musical Hall **16**
Sungei Buloh Wetland Reserve **1**

6 Attractions Outside the Urban Area

The famous image of Singapore, promulgated by the convention board and recognizable to business travelers everywhere, is of the towering cityscape along the water's edge—but there's a reason they call this place the Garden City. Not only are there picturesque gardens and parks nestled within the urban jungle, but the urban jungle is nestled within real jungle. While it's true that most of the wooded areas have been replaced by suburban housing, it's also true that thousands of acres of secondary rainforest have survived the migration of Singaporeans to the suburbs. Better yet, there are still some areas with primary rainforest, some of which are accessible by paths.

What Singapore does have are spectacular **gardens,** from the well-groomed Botanical Garden to nature preserves like Bukit Timah and Sungei Buloh, where tropical rainforest and mangrove swamps are close enough to the city that you can visit them on a morning or afternoon visit. Outside the city center you'll also find **historic sites and temples** like the edifying Changi Prison Museum and the Siong Lim Temple, as well as **museums** and **science centers.**

In the late 1800s, the colonial government began to section off tracts of forest into **nature reserves** to preserve the habitats of local species of plants and animals. The first of these was the Bukit Timah Nature Reserve, established in 1883. In 1990, Singapore passed a national parks act, which established the National Parks Board to oversee not only the national parks, but also the Singapore Botanical Gardens and Fort Canning Park. The mission of the board is to preserve and promote the nature reserves as a sanctuary for wildlife, a place for plant conservation, and a resource for education and outdoor recreational activities. Today, in addition to Bukit Timah, the nature reserve system includes MacRitchie, Seletar, Pierce, and Upper Pierce reservoirs. With the exception of Bukit Timah, these places are located in the central part of the island (see "Central & Northern Singapore Attractions," below).

While the Sungei Buloh Wetland Reserve is not under the jurisdiction of the National Parks Board, it too serves to conserve wildlife for educational and recreational purposes.

WESTERN SINGAPORE ATTRACTIONS

The attractions grouped in this section are on the west side of Singapore, beginning from the Singapore Botanic Gardens at the edge of the urban area all the way out to the Singapore Discovery Centre past Jurong. Remember, if you're traveling around this area that transportation can be problematic, as the MRT system rarely goes direct to any of these places, taxis can be hard to find, and bus routes get more complex. Keep the telephone number for taxi booking handy. Sometimes ticket sales people at each attraction can help and make the call for you.

Bukit Timah Nature Reserve ★★   Bukit Timah Nature Reserve is pure primary rainforest. Believed to be as old as 1 million years, it's the only place on the island with vegetation that exists exactly as it was before the British settled here. The park is more than 81 hectares (202 acres) of soaring canopy teeming with mammals and birds and a lush undergrowth with more bugs, butterflies, and reptiles than you can shake a vine at. Here you can see more than 700 plant species, many of which are exotic ferns, plus mammals like long-tailed macaques, squirrels, and lemurs. There's a visitor center and four well-marked paths, one of which leads to Singapore's highest point. At 163m (535 ft.) above sea level, don't expect a nosebleed, but some of the scenic views of the island are really nice. Along another walkway is Singapore's oldest tree, estimated to be 400 years old. Also at Bukit Timah is Hindhede Quarry, which filled up with water at some point, so you can take a dip and cool off during your hike.

177 Hindhede Dr. ✆ **1800/468-5736**. Free admission. Daily 24-hours. MRT to Newton, then TIBS bus no. 171 or SBS bus no. 182 to park entrance.

Chinese and Japanese Gardens   Situated on two islands in Jurong lake, the gardens are reached by an overpass and joined by the Bridge of Double Beauty. The **Chinese Garden** dedicates most of its area to "northern style" landscape architecture. The style of Imperial gardens, the northern style integrates brightly colored buildings with the surroundings to compensate for northern China's absence of rich plant growth and natural scenery. The Stoneboat is a replica of the stone boat at the Summer Palace in Beijing. Inside the Pure Air of the Universe building are courtyards and a pond, and there is a seven-story pagoda, the odd number of floors symbolizing continuity. Around the gardens, special attention has been paid to the placement of rock formations to resemble true nature, and also to the qualities of the rocks themselves, which can represent the forces of yin and yang, male and female, passivity or activity, and so on.

I like the Garden of Beauty, in Suzhou style, representing the southern style of landscape architecture. Southern gardens were built predominantly by scholars, poets, and men of wealth. Sometimes called Black-and-White gardens, these smaller gardens had more fine detail, featuring subdued colors as the plants and elements of the rich natural landscape gave them plenty to work with. Inside the Suzhou garden are 2,000 pots of *penjiang* (bonsai) and displays of small rocks.

While the Chinese garden is more visually stimulating, the **Japanese garden** is intended to evoke feeling. Marble-chip paths lead the way so that as you walk you can hear your own footsteps and meditate on the sound. They also serve to slow the journey for better gazing upon the scenery. The Keisein, or "Dry Garden," uses white pebbles to create images of streams. Ten stone lanterns, a small traditional house, and a rest house are nestled between two ponds with smaller islands joined by bridges.

Toilets are situated at stops along the way, as well as benches to have a rest or to just take in the sights. Paddle boats can be rented for S$5 (US$2.85) per hour just outside the main entrance.

1 Chinese Garden Rd. ✆ **65/6261-3632**. Admission free; admission to bonsai garden Adult S$5 (US$2.85), children S$3 (US$1.70). Daily 9am–7pm. MRT to Chinese Garden or bus nos. 335, 180, and 154.

Haw Par Villa (Tiger Balm Gardens) ★   In 1935, brothers Haw Boon Haw and Haw Boon Par—creators of Tiger Balm, the camphor and menthol rub that comes in those cool little pots—took their fortune and opened Tiger Balm Gardens as a venue for teaching traditional Chinese values. They made more than 1,000 statues and life-size dioramas depicting Chinese legends and historic tales and illustrating morality and Confucian beliefs. Many of these were gruesome and bloody and some of them were really entertaining.

But Tiger Balm Gardens suffered a horrible fate. In 1985, it was converted into an amusement park and reopened as Haw Par Villa. Most of the statues and scenes were taken away and replaced with rides. Well, business did not exactly boom. In fact, the park has been losing money fast. But recently, in an attempt to regain some of the original Tiger Balm Garden edge, they replaced many of the old statues, some of which are a great backdrop for really kitschy vacation photos. Last year they also lowered the admission price from S$16 for adults to the more affordable S$5 they charge today. Catch the two theme rides: the Tales of China Boat Ride and the Wrath of the Water Gods Flume.

262 Pasir Panjang Rd. © 65/6872-2780. Admission free. Daily 9am–5pm. MRT to Buona Vista and transfer to bus no. 200.

Jurong BirdPark ★ *Kids*   Jurong BirdPark, with a collection of 8,000 birds from more than 600 species, showcases Southeast Asian breeds plus other colorful tropical beauties, some of which are endangered. The more than 20 hectares (50 acres) can be easily walked or, for a couple dollars extra, you can ride the panorail for a bird's-eye view (so to speak) of the grounds. I enjoy the Waterfall Aviary, the world's largest walk-in aviary. It's an up-close-and-personal experience with African and South American birds, plus a pretty walk over pathways and babbling brooks through landscaped tropical forest. This is where you'll also see the world's tallest man-made waterfall, but the true feat of engineering here is the panorail station, built inside the aviary. Another smaller walk-in aviary is for Southeast Asian endangered bird species; at noon every day this aviary experiences a man-made thunderstorm. The daily guided tours and regularly scheduled feeding times are enlightening. Other bird exhibits are the flamingo pools, the World of Darkness (featuring nocturnal birds), and the penguin parade, a favorite for Singaporeans, who adore all things Arctic.

Two shows feature birds of prey either acting out their natural instincts or performing falconry tricks. The **Fuji World of Hawks** is at 10am and the **King of the Skies** is at 4pm. The **All-Star Birdshow** takes place at 11am and 3pm, with trained parrots that race bikes and birds that perform all sorts of silliness, including staged birdie misbehaviors. Try to come between 8am and 10:30am for breakfast among hanging cages of chirping birds at the **Songbird Terrace.**

2 Jurong Hill. © 65/6265-0022. Adults S$12 (US$6.85), children under 12 S$5 (US$2.85). Daily 8am-6pm. MRT to Boon Lay Station, transfer to SBS no. 194 or 251.

Jurong Reptile Park   The newly renovated Jurong Reptile Park (fixed up just in time, as the older facility was smelling up the entire neighborhood) houses more than 50 species of reptiles from the region and around the world. Feedings are fun, as are the reptile shows (at 11:45am and 2pm daily). Snakes are happy to wrap themselves around your neck for a souvenir photo (10:30am and 5pm daily). In itself, it's no reason to trek out to Jurong, but it makes a convenient add-on to a visit to the Jurong BirdPark.

241 Jalan Ahmad Ibrahim. © 65/6261-8866. Adults S$7 (US$4), children under 12 and seniors S$3.50 (US$2.10). Daily 9am–6pm. MRT to Boon Lay Station, transfer to SBS no. 194 or 251.

Ming Village   Tour a pottery factory that employs traditional pottery-making techniques from the Ming and Qing dynasties and watch the process from mold making, hand throwing, and hand painting to glazing each piece. After the tour, shop from their large selection of beautiful antique reproduction dishes, vases, urns, and more. Certificates of authenticity are provided, which describe the history of each piece. They are happy to arrange overseas shipping for your treasures, or if you want to carry your purchase home, they'll wrap it very securely.

32 Pandan Rd. © 65/6265-7711. Admission and guided tour free. Daily 9am–5:30pm. MRT to Clementi, then SBS no. 78.

Singapore Botanic Gardens ★★   In 1822, Singapore's first botanic garden was started at Fort Canning by Sir Stamford Raffles. After it lost funding, the present Botanic Garden came into being in 1859 thanks to the efforts of a horticulture society; it was later turned over to the government for upkeep. More than just a garden, this space occupied an important place in the region's economic development when "Mad" Henry Ridley, one of the garden's directors, imported Brazilian rubber tree seedlings from Great Britain. He devised improved latex-trapping methods and led the campaign to convince reluctant coffee growers to switch plantation crops. The garden also pioneered orchid hybridization, breeding a number of internationally acclaimed varieties.

Carved out within the tropical setting lies a rose garden, sundial garden with pruned hedges, a banana plantation, a spice garden, and sculptures by international artists dotted around the area. As you wander, look for the Cannonball tree (named for its cannonball-shaped fruit), Para rubber trees, teak trees, bamboos, and a huge array of palms, including the sealing wax palm—distinguished by its bright scarlet stalks—and the rumbia palm, which bears the pearl sago. The fruit of the silk-cotton tree is a pod filled with silky stuffing that was once used for stuffing pillows. Flowers like bougainvilleas and heliconias add beautiful color.

The **National Orchid Garden** is 3 hectares (7½ acres) of gorgeous orchids growing along landscaped walks. The English Garden features hybrids developed here and named after famous visitors to the garden—there's the Margaret Thatcher, the Benazir Bhutto, the Vaclav Havel, and more. The gift shops sell live hydroponic orchids in test tubes for unique souvenirs.

The gardens have three lakes. Symphony Lake surrounds an island band shell for "Concert in the Park" performances by the local symphony and international entertainers like Chris de Burg. Call visitor services at the number below for performance schedules.

Main entrance at corner of Cluny Rd. and Holland Rd. ⓒ 65/6471-7361. Free admission. Daily 4am–11:30pm (closing at midnight on weekends). The National Orchid Garden adults S$2 (US$1.15), children under 12 and seniors S$1 (US55¢). Daily 8:30am–7pm. MRT to Orchard. Take SBS no. 7, 105, 106, or 174 from Orchard Blvd.

Singapore Discovery Centre *(Kids)* The original plan was to build a military history museum here, but then planners began to wonder if maybe the concept wouldn't bring people running. What they came up with instead is a fascinating display of the latest military technology with hands-on exhibits that cannot be resisted—one of 19 interactive information kiosks, for instance, lets you design tanks and ships. Airborne Rangers, a virtual-reality experience, lets you parachute from a plane and manipulate your landing to safety. In the motion simulator, feel your seat move in tandem with the fighter pilot on the screen. The Shooting Gallery is a computer-simulated combat firing range using real but decommissioned M16 rifles. Other attractions are an exhibit of 14 significant events in Singapore history, including the fall of Singapore, self-government, racial riots, and housing block development. And then there's Tintoy Theatre, where the robot Tintoy conducts an entertaining lecture on warfare! Tintoy fights a war, seeking the help of Sun Tzu and other ancient military tacticians. IMAX features roll at the five-story iWERKS Theatre regularly. When you get hungry, there's a fast-food court.

You can also have a 30-minute bus tour of the neighboring Singapore Air Force Training Institute free with SDC admission. Inquire about tour times at the front counter.

510 Upper Jurong Rd. ⓒ 65/6792-6188. Adults S$9 (US$5.15), children under 12 S$5 (US$2.85). Tues–Sun 9am–7pm. MRT to Boon Lay; transfer to SBS no. 192 or 193.

Singapore Science Centre Kids   The center features hands-on exhibits in true science-center spirit. You can play in the Atrium, Physical Sciences Gallery, Life Sciences Gallery, and the Hall of Science. Unfortunately, many of the exhibits are worn and tired from overuse and abuse. The Technology Gallery is one of the more interesting exhibits if you can wrestle the kids away from the machines, and the aromatics display, with blindfolded "guess the herb or spice" corner, is so popular they're thinking of upgrading it from temporary status. Singapore Airlines has redone the new "On Wings We Fly" Aviation Gallery. Also notable are the section on the cleaning of the Singapore River and showcased educational projects from university students. The Omni Theatre planetarium has a projection booth encased in glass so you can check out how it works.

15 Science Centre Rd., off Jurong Town Hall Rd. ✆ 65/6425-2500. www.sci-ctr.edu.sg. Adults S$6 (US$3.45), children under 16 S$3 (US$1.70), seniors S$2.50 (US$1.45). Tues–Sun and public holidays 10am–6pm. Take the West Coast Attractions bus (see above) or MRT to Jurong East then SBS no. 66 or 335.

CENTRAL & NORTHERN SINGAPORE ATTRACTIONS

The northern part of Singapore contains most of the island's nature reserves and parks. Here's where you'll find the Singapore Zoological Gardens, in addition to some sights with historical and religious significance. Despite the presence of the **MRT** in the area, there is not any simple way to get from attraction to attraction with ease. Bus transfers to and from MRT stops is the way to go—or you could stick to taxicabs.

Kong Meng San Phor Kark See Temple   The largest and most modern religious complex on the island, this place, called Phor Kark See for short, is comprised of prayer and meditation halls, a hospice, gardens, and a vegetarian restaurant. The largest building is the Chinese-style Hall of Great Compassion. There is also the octagonal Hall of Great Virtue and a towering pagoda. For S50¢ (US30¢) you can buy flower petals to place in a dish at the Buddha's feet. Compared to other temples on the island, Phor Kark See seems shiny—having only been built in 1981. As a result, the religious images inside carry a strange, almost artificial, cartoon air about them.

If you're curious, find the crematorium in the back of the complex. Arrive on Sundays after 1pm and wait for the funeral processions to arrive. Chairs line the side and back of the hall, and attendees do not mind if you sit quietly and observe, as long as you are respectful. The scene is not for the faint of heart, but makes for a touching moment of cultural difference and human similarity.

88 Bright Hill Dr. Located in the center of the island to the east of Bukit Panjang Nature Preserve. Bright Hill Dr. is off Ang Mo Kio Ave. ✆ 65/6453-4046. Take MRT to Bishan, then take bus No. 410.

Kranji War Memorial   Kranji Cemetery commemorates the men and women who fought and died in World War II. Prisoners of war in a camp nearby began a burial ground here, and after the war it was enlarged to provide space for all the casualties. The Kranji War Cemetery is the site of 4,000 graves of servicemen, while the Singapore State Cemetery memorializes the names of over 20,000 who died and have no known graves. Stones are laid geometrically on a slope with a view of the Strait of Johor. The memorial itself is designed to represent the three arms of the services.

Woodlands Rd., located in the very northern part of the island. ✆ 65/6269-6158. Daily 24 hr. MRT to Kranji.

MacRitchie Nature Trail   Of all the nature reserves in Singapore, the Central Catchment Nature Reserve is the largest at 2,000 hectares (5,000 acres). Located in the center of the island, it's home to four of Singapore's reservoirs:

MacRitchie, Seletar, Pierce, and Upper Pierce. The rainforest here is secondary forest, but the animals don't care; they're just as happy with the place. There's one path for walking and jogging (no bicycles allowed) that stretches 3km (1¾ miles) from its start in the southeast corner of the reserve, turning to the edge of MacRitchie Reservoir, then letting you out at the Singapore Island Country Club.

Central Catchment Nature Reserve. No phone. Free admission. From Orchard Rd. take bus no. 132 from the Orchard Parade Hotel. From Raffles City take bus no. 130. Get off at the bus stop near Little Sisters of the Poor. Next to Little Sisters of the Poor, follow the paved walkway, which turns into the trail.

Mandai Orchid Gardens Owned and operated by Singapore Orchids Pte Ltd. to breed and cultivate hybrids for international export, the gardens double as an STB tourist attraction. Arranged in English garden style, orchid varieties are separated in beds that are surrounded by grassy lawn. Tree-growing varieties prefer the shade of the covered canopy. On display is Singapore's national flower, the Vanda Miss Joaquim, a natural hybrid in shades of light purple. Behind the gift shop is the Water Garden, where a stroll will reveal many houseplants common to the West, as you would find them in the wild.

Mandai Lake Rd., on the route to the Singapore Zoological Gardens. ✆ 65/6269-1036. Adults S$2 (US$1.15), children under 12 S50¢ (US30¢). Daily 8:30am–5:30pm. MRT to Ang Mo Kio and SBS no. 138.

Night Safari ★★★ *Kids* Singapore takes advantage of its unchanging tropical climate and static ratio of daylight to night to bring you the world's first open-concept zoo for nocturnal animals. Here, as in the zoological gardens, animals live in landscaped areas, their barriers virtually unseen by visitors. These areas are dimly lit to create a moonlit effect, and a guided tram leads you through "regions" designed to resemble the Himalayan foothills, the jungles of Africa, and, naturally, Southeast Asia. Some of the free-range prairie animals come very close to the tram. The 45-minute ride covers almost 3.5km (2 miles), and has regular stops to get off and have a rest or stroll along trails for closer views of smaller creatures.

Staff, placed at regular intervals along the trails, help you find your way, though it's almost impossible to get lost along the trails; however, it is nighttime, you are in the forest, and it can be spooky. The guides are there more or less to add peace of mind (and all speak English). Flash photography is strictly prohibited, and be sure to bring plenty of insect repellent. A weirder tip: Check out the bathrooms. They're all open-air, Bali style.

Singapore Zoological Gardens, 80 Mandai Lake Rd., at the western edge of the Bukit Panjang Nature Reserve, on the Seletar Reservoir. ✆ 65/6269-3411. Adults S$15.45 (US$8.85), children under 12 S$10.30 (US$5.90). Daily 7:30pm–midnight. Ticket sales close at 11pm. Entrance Plaza, restaurant, and fast-food outlet open from 6:30pm. MRT to Ang Mo Kio and take SBS no. 138.

Sasanaransi Buddhist Temple Known simply as the Burmese Buddhist Temple, it was founded by a Burmese expatriate to serve the overseas Burmese Buddhist community. His partner, an herbal doctor also from Burma, traveled home to buy a 10-ton block of marble from which was carved the 3.3m-tall (11 ft.) Buddha image that sits in the main hall, surrounded by an aura of brightly colored lights. The original temple was off Serangoon Road in Little India, and was moved here in 1991 at the request of the Housing Development Board. On the third story is a standing Buddha image in gold, and murals of events in the Buddha's life.

14 Tai Gin Rd., located next to the Sun Yat-sen Villa near Toa Payoh New Town. Daily 6:30am–9pm. Chanting Sun 9:30am, Wed 8pm, and Sat 7:30pm. Take MRT to Toa Payoh, then take a taxi.

Singapore Zoological Gardens ★★ *Kids*　They call themselves the Open Zoo because, rather than coop the animals in jailed enclosures, they let them roam freely in landscaped areas. Beasts of the world are kept where they are supposed to be using psychological restraints and physical barriers that are disguised behind waterfalls, vegetation, and moats. Some animals are grouped with other species to show them coexisting as they would in nature. For instance, the white rhinoceros is neighborly with the wildebeest and ostrich—not that wildebeests and ostriches make the best company, but certainly contempt is better than boredom. Guinea and pea fowl, Emperor tamarins, and other creatures are free roaming and not shy; however, if you spot a water monitor or long-tailed macaque, know that they're not zoo residents—just locals looking for a free meal.

Major zoo features are the Primate Kingdom, Wild Africa, the Reptile Garden, the children's petting zoo, and underwater views of polar bears, sea lions, and penguins. Daily shows include primate and reptile shows at 10:30am and 2:30pm, and elephant and sea lion shows at 11:30am and 3:30pm. You can take your photograph with an orangutan, chimpanzee, or snake, and there are elephant and camel rides, too.

The literature provided includes half-day and full-day agendas to help you see the most while you're there. The best time to arrive, however, is at 9am, to have breakfast with an orangutan, which feasts on fruits, and puts on a hilarious and very memorable show. If you miss that, you can also have tea with it at 4pm. Another good time to go is just after a rain, when the animals cool off and get frisky.

Also see listing for "Night Safari," above

80 Mandai Lake Rd., at the western edge of the Bukit Panjang Nature Reserve, on the Seletar Reservoir. ⓒ 65/6269-3411. Adults S$12 (US$6.85), children under 12 S$5 (US$2.85). Discounts for seniors. Daily 8:30am–6pm. MRT to Ang Mo Kio and take SBS no. 138.

Siong Lim Temple　This temple, in English "the Twin Groves of the Lotus Mountain Temple," has a great story behind its founding. One night in 1898, Hokkien businessman Low Kim Pong and his son had the same dream—of a golden light shining from the West. The following day, the two went to the western shore and waited until, moments before sundown, a ship appeared carrying a group of Hokkien Buddhist monks and nuns on their way to China after a pilgrimage to India. Low Kim Pong vowed to build a monastery if they would stay in Singapore. They did.

Laid out according to feng shui principles, the buildings include the Dharma Hall, a main prayer hall, and drum and bell towers. They are arranged in cong lin style, a rare type of monastery design with a universal layout so that no matter how vast the grounds are, any monk can find his way around. The entrance hall has granite wall panels carved with scenes from Chinese history. The main prayer hall has fantastic details in the ceiling, wood panels, and other wood carvings. In the back is a shrine to Kuan Yin, goddess of mercy.

Originally built amid farmland, the temple became surrounded by suburban high-rise apartments in the 1950s and 1960s, with the Toa Payoh Housing Development Board New Town project and the Pan-Island Expressway creeping close by.

184-E Jalan Toa Payoh. ⓒ 65/6259-6924. Located in Toa Payoh New Town. Take MRT to Toa Payoh, then take SBS nos. 232, 237, 238.

Sungei Buloh Wetland Reserve ★　Located to the very north of the island and devoted to the wetland habitat and mangrove forests that are so common to the region, 87-hectare (218-acre) Sungei Buloh is out of the way, and not the easiest place to get to; but it's a beautiful park, with constructed paths and boardwalks taking you through tangles of mangroves, soupy marshes, grassy spots, and coconut groves. Of the flora and fauna, the most spectacular sights here are the birds, of which there are somewhere between 140 and 170 species in residence or just passing through for the winter. Of the migratory birds, some have traveled from as far as Siberia to escape the cold months from September to March. Bird observatories are set up at different spots along the paths. Also, even though you're in the middle of nowhere, Sungei Buloh has a visitor center, a cafeteria, and souvenirs.

301 Neo Tiew Crescent. (©) **65/6794-1401.** Adults S$1 (US55¢) children and seniors S50¢ (US30¢). Mon–Fri 7:30am–7pm; Sat–Sun and public holidays 7am–7pm. Audiovisual show Mon–Sat 9am, 11am, 1pm, 3pm and 5pm; hourly Sun and public holidays. MRT to Kranji, bus no. 925 to Kranji Reservoir Dam. Cross causeway to park entrance.

Sun Yat-sen Nanyang Memorial Hall ★ Dr. Sun Yat-sen visited Singapore eight times to raise funds for his revolution in China, and made Singapore his headquarters for gaining the support of overseas Chinese in Southeast Asia. A wealthy Chinese merchant built the villa around 1880 for his mistress, and a later owner permitted Dr. Sun Yat-sen to use it. The house reflects the classic bungalow style, which is becoming endangered in modern Singapore. Its typical bungalow features include a projecting carport with a sitting room overhead, verandas with striped blinds, second-story cast-iron railings, and first-story masonry balustrades. A covered walkway leads to the kitchen and servants' quarters in the back.

Inside, the life of Dr. Yat-sen is traced in photos and watercolors, from his birth in southern China through his creation of a revolutionary organization.

12 Tai Gin Rd., near Toa Payoh New Town. (©) **65/6256-7377.** Admission S$2 (US$1.15). Tue-Sun 9am-5pm. Take the MRT to Toa Payoh, then take bus No. 45.

EASTERN SINGAPORE ATTRACTIONS

The east coast leads from the edge of Singapore's urban area to the tip of the eastern part, at Changi Point. Eastern Singapore is home to the Changi International Airport, nearby Changi Prison, and the long stretch of East Coast Park along the shoreline. The **MRT** heads east in this region, but swerves northward at the end of the line. A popular **bus line** for east coast attractions not reached by MRT is the SBS no. 2, which takes you to Changi Prison, Changi Point, Malay Village, and East Coast Park.

Changi Chapel and Museum ★ Upon successful occupation of Singapore, the Japanese marched all British, Australian, and allied European prisoners to Changi by foot, where they lived in a prison camp for 3 years, suffering overcrowding, disease, and malnutrition. Prisoners were cut off from the outside world except to leave the camp for labor duties. The hospital conditions were terrible; some prisoners suffered public beatings, and many died. In an effort to keep hope alive, they built a small chapel from wood and attap. Years later, at the request of former POWs and their families and friends, the government built this replica.

The museum displays sketches by W. R. M. Haxworth and secret photos taken by George Aspinall—both men POWs who were imprisoned here. Displayed with descriptions, the pictures, along with writings and other objects from the camp, bring this period to life, depicting the day-to-day horror with a touch of high morale.

169 Sims Ave., off Upper Changi Rd., in the same general area as the airport. (C) **65/6543-0893**. Free admission. Daily 9:30am-4:30pm. Changi Chapel Sun Service (all are welcome) 5:30–6:30pm. MRT to Tanah Merah station, then transfer to SBS no. 2.

East Coast Park East Coast Park is a narrow strip of reclaimed land, only 8.5km (5¼ miles) long, tucked in between the shoreline and East Coast Parkway, and serves as a hangout for Singaporean families on the weekends. Moms and dads barbecue under the trees while the kids swim at the beach, which is nothing more than a narrow lump of grainy sand sloping into yellow-green water that has more seaweed than a sushi bar. Paths for bicycling, in-line skating, walking, or jogging run the length of the park, and are crowded on weekends and public and school holidays. On Sundays, you'll find kite flyers in the open grassy parts. The lagoon is the best place to go for bicycle rentals, canoeing, and windsurfing. A couple of outfits, listed in section 9, "Sports & Recreation," offer equipment rentals and instruction.

Because East Coast Park is so long, getting to the place you'd like to hang out can be a bit confusing. Many of the locators I've included sound funny (for example, McDonald's Carpark C), but are recognizable landmarks for taxi drivers. Sailing, windsurfing, and other sea sports happen at the far end of the park, at the lagoon, which is closer to Changi Airport than it is to the city. Taxi drivers are all familiar with the lagoon as a landmark. Unfortunately, public transportation to the park is tough—you should bring a good map, and expect to do a little walking from any major thoroughfare.

East Coast Park is also home to **UDMC Seafood Centre** (see chapter 4) is located not far from the lagoon.

East Coast Pkwy. No phone. Free admission. Bus no. 16 to Marine Parade and use the underpass to cross the highway.

Malay Village In 1985, Malay Village opened in Geylang as a theme village to showcase Malay culture. The Cultural Museum is a collection of artifacts from Malay culture, including household items, musical instruments, and a replica of a wedding dais and traditional beaded ceremonial bed. Kampung Days lets you walk through a kampung house (or Malay village house) as it would have looked in the 1950s and 1960s. The 25-minute **Lagenda Fantasy show** is more for kids, using multi-image projection, Surround Sound, and lights to tell tales from the Arabian Nights and the legend of Sang Nila Utama, the founder of Temasek (Singapore). The village has souvenir shops mixed with places that sell everything from antique knives to caged birds.

Two in-house groups perform **traditional Malaysian and Indonesian dances** in the late afternoons and evenings. Call during the day on Saturday to find out if they'll be performing the **Kuda Kepang** in the evening. If you're lucky enough to catch it, it's a long performance but worth the wait because at the end the dancers are put in a trance and walk on glass, eat glass, and rip coconuts to shreds with their teeth (see "Frommer's Favorite Singapore Experiences," in chapter 1 for details). Arrive early because the place gets packed with locals.

39 Geylang Serai, in the suburb of Geylang, an easy walk from the MRT station. (C) **65/6748-4700** or 65/6740-8860. Free admission to village. Kampong Days and Cultural Museum adults S$5 (US$2.85), children S$3 (US$1.70). Daily 10am–10pm. MRT to Paya Lebar.

The Singapore Crocodilarium Head to the Crocodilarium if you're interested in seeing alligators from India and four types of crocodiles—from Singapore, Africa, Louisiana, and Caiman (South Africa). Of the total 1,800

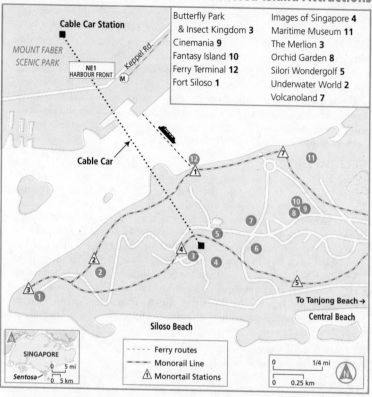

Cable Car Station

MOUNT FABER SCENIC PARK

Keppel Rd.

NE1 HARBOUR FRONT

Cable Car

Butterfly Park & Insect Kingdom **3**	Images of Singapore **4**
Cinemania **9**	Maritime Museum **11**
Fantasy Island **10**	The Merlion **3**
Ferry Terminal **12**	Orchid Garden **8**
Fort Siloso **1**	Silori Wondergolf **5**
	Underwater World **2**
	Volcanoland **7**

To Tanjong Beach →

Central Beach

Siloso Beach

SINGAPORE

0 5 mi

0 5 km

Sentosa

- - - - Ferry routes
━━━ Monorail Line
⚠ Monortail Stations

0   1/4 mi

0   0.25 km

crocodiles that reside here, 500 are on display. The Singapore crocodile, one of the largest, reaches a maximum size of 5.5m (18 ft.) and can weigh up to 500kg (1,100 lb.). They're pretty fierce because they have bigger heads, which means bigger mouths. However, midsize ones are the most dangerous to people because they have better mobility on land. Every so often the place picks up when a couple of them have a brutish fight. On a sweeter note, the Crocodilarium has approximately 400 births per year. Some young ones are on display—and they're very cute—but the Crocodilarium won't let you see the newborn babies because they're delicate and spook easily. While many of these alligators and crocodiles are intended for the booming pelt industry, some are just for show. A huge gift shop peddles crocodile products, which are made both in-house and imported from outside designers. Here you can also find ostrich hide, stingray skin, and antelope pelt goods.

The best way to get back to town is to ask the front counter to call you a cab.

730 East Coast Pkwy., running along East Coast Park. ☎ **65/447-3722.** Adults S$2 (US$1.20), children under 12 S$1 (US60¢). Daily 9am–5pm. MRT to Paya Lebar or Eunos and take a taxi.

7 Sentosa Island

In the 1880s, Sentosa, then known as Pulau Blakang Mati, was a hub of British military activity, with hilltop forts built to protect the harbor from sea invasion from all sides. Today, it has become a weekend getaway spot and Singapore's answer to Disneyland all rolled into one. You'll find a lot of people recommending Sentosa as a must-see on your vacation, and while some travelers do visit the island for some part of their trip, it might not be the best way to spend your time if you're only in town for a few days. Basically, for those who like to do hard-core cultural and historical-immersion vacations, Sentosa will seem too contrived and cartoonish.

If you're spending the day, there are numerous restaurants and a couple of food courts. For overnights, the Shangri-La's Rasa Sentosa Resort and the Beaufort Sentosa, Singapore (see chapter 3), are popular hotel options. For general **Sentosa inquiries**, call ✆ **1800/736-8672.**

GETTING THERE

Private cars are not allowed entry to the island except between the hours of 6:30pm and 3am, but there are more than a few other ways to get to Sentosa. The cable car and ferry fares are exclusive of Sentosa admission charges, which you are required to pay upon arrival; bus fares include your admission charge. **Island admission** is S$6 (US$3.45) for adults and S$4 (US$2.30) for children. Tickets can be purchased at the following booths: Mount Faber Cable Car Station, World Trade Centre Ferry Departure Hall, Cable Car Towers (next to the World Trade Centre), Cable Car Plaza (on Sentosa), Sentosa Information Booth 4 (at the start of the causeway, opposite Kentucky Fried Chicken), and at Sentosa Information Booth 3 (at the end of the causeway bridge, upon entering Sentosa). Many attractions require purchase of additional tickets, which you can get at the entrance of each.

BY CABLE CAR Cable cars depart from the top of Mount Faber and from the World Trade Centre daily from 8:30am to 9pm at a cost of S$8.50 (US$4.85) for adults and S$7.50 (US$4.30) for children, not including island admission. You can also take a glass-bottomed car for S$15 (US$8.55) adults and S$8 (US$4.55) children. The ticket is good for round-trip, and you can decide where you choose to depart and arrive (at either Mt. Faber or World Trade Centre every 5 or 10 min. on the Singapore side) for one price. Plan at least one trip on the cable car because the view of Singapore, Sentosa, and especially the container port is really fantastic from up there. The round-trip cable car ticket is also good for a return on the ferry, in case you've had enough view. Be warned: If you return to Singapore at the Mt. Faber stop, you'll have to walk down the mountain to find a cab or bus. For more information, call ✆ **65/ 6270-8855.**

BY FERRY The ferry departs from the World Trade Centre on weekdays from 9:30am to 10pm at 30-minute intervals, and on weekends and public holidays from 8:30am to 10pm at 20-minute intervals. The round-trip fare for adults S$8.30 (US$4.75) and children S$6.30 (US$3.60), includes admission.

BY BUS **Sentosa Bus Service Leisure Pte Ltd** operates bus service to and from Sentosa. Service A operates between 7am and 10:30pm daily from the World Trade Centre (WTC) Bus Terminal. Service C runs from the Tiong Bahru MRT Station. Service E stops along Orchard Road at Lucky Plaza, the Mandarin Hotel, Peranakan Place, Le Meridien Hotel, Plaza Singapura, and then Bencoolen Street, POSB Headquarters, Raffles City, and Pan Pacific Hotel, and operates from 7am to 10:35pm daily. Fares are S$7 (US$4) for adults and S$5 (US$2.85) for children. Fares are paid to the driver as you board, and the Sentosa admission fee is included in your fare. The last bus out of Sentosa is at 10:30pm.

BY TAXI   Taxis are only allowed to drop off and pick up passengers at the Beaufort Sentosa, Singapore; Shangri-La's Rasa Sentosa Resort; and NTUC Sentosa Beach Resort. The taxi surcharge is S$3 (US$1.70).

GETTING AROUND

Once on Sentosa, a free monorail operates from 9am to 10pm daily at 10-minute intervals to shuttle you around to the various areas. If you're staying at one of the island's major hotels, you can take advantage of their free shuttle services to get into Singapore's urban area.

SEEING THE SIGHTS

The attractions that you get free with your Sentosa admission are the **Fountain Gardens** and **Musical Fountain,** the **Enchanted Garden of Tembusu,** the **Dragon Trail Nature Walk,** and the **beaches.**

The **Fountain Gardens,** just behind the Ferry Terminal, are geometric European-style gardens with groomed pathways and shady arbors. In the center is an amphitheater of sorts, the focus of which is a fountain—actually three fountains—that creates water effects with patterns of sprays and varying heights. During regular shows throughout the day, the fountains burst to the sounds of everything from marches to Elton John. At night, they turn on the lights for color effects.

The **Dragon Trail Nature Walk** takes advantage of the island's natural forest for a 1.5km (1-mile) stroll through secondary rainforest. In addition to the variety of dragon sculptures, there are also local squirrels, monkeys, lizards, and wild white cockatoos to try to spot.

Sentosa has three beaches, **Siloso Beach** on the western end **and J Central Beach** and **Tanjong Beach** on the eastern end, each dressed in tall coconut palms and flowering trees. At Central Beach, deck chairs, beach umbrellas, and a variety of **watersports equipment** like pedal boats, aqua bikes, fun bugs, canoes, surfboards, and banana boats are available for hire at nominal charges. Bicycles are also available for hire at the bicycle kiosk at Siloso Beach. Shower and changing facilities, food kiosks, and snack bars are at rest stations. Siloso Beach is open at night for barbecue picnics, and has a really nice view of the tiny lights of ships anchored in the port. About once a month, rumors spread throughout the island about a full-moon party on Siloso that lasts until the sun comes up. The parties are never publicized, but are anticipated by the many folks looking for an alternative to the bar scene at night. Ask around at the bars, and they'll let you know if there's something going on.

Unless noted, all of the following Sentosa attractions have admission charges separate from the Sentosa charge, and operating hours that differ from place to place.

Butterfly Park and Insect Kingdom Museum of Singapore   This walk-in enclosure provides an up-close view of some 60 live species of native butterflies, from cocoon to adult. At the Insect Kingdom, the exhibits are mostly dead, but extensive, with its collection carrying more than 2,500 bugs.
© 65/6275-0013. Adults S$6 (US$3.45), children S$3 (US$1.70). Daily 9am–6:30pm. Monorail stop 4.

Fort Siloso   Fort Siloso guarded Keppel Harbour from invasion in the 1880s. It's one of three forts built on Sentosa, and it later became a military camp in World War II. The buildings have been decorated to resemble a barracks, kitchen, laundry, and military offices as they looked back in the day. In places, you can explore the underground tunnels and ammunition holds, but they're not as extensive as you would hope they'd be.

🕐 1800/736-8672. Adults S$3 (US$1.70), children S$2 (US$1.15). Daily 9am–7pm. Monorail stop 3.

Images of Singapore ★★   Images of Singapore is without a doubt one of the main reasons to come to Sentosa. There are three parts to this museum/exhibit: the Pioneers of Singapore and the Surrender Chambers—which date back as far as I can remember—and Festivals of Singapore, a recent addition.

Pioneers of Singapore is an exhibit of beautifully constructed life-size dioramas that place figures like Sultan Hussein, Sir Stamford Raffles, Tan Tock Seng, and Naraina Pillai, to name just a few pioneers, in the context of Singapore's timeline and note their contributions to its development. Also interesting are the dioramas depicting scenes from the daily routines of the different cultures as they lived during colonial times. It's a great stroll that brings history to life.

The powers that be have tried to change the name of the **Surrender Chambers** to the Sentosa Wax Museum, but it still hasn't caught on because the Surrender Chambers are oh so much more than just a wax museum. The gallery leads you through authentic footage, photos, maps, and recordings of survivors to chronologically tell the story of the Pacific theater activity of World War II and how the Japanese conquered Singapore. The grand finale is a wax museum depicting, first, a scene of the British surrender and, last, another of the Japanese surrender.

Recently, Images of Singapore had added the **Festivals of Singapore,** another life-size diorama exhibit depicting a few of the major festivals and traditions of the Chinese, Malay, Indian, and Peranakan cultures in Singapore. For each group, wedding traditions are shown in complete regalia, with brief explanations of the customs. While this exhibit is not quite like being there and would be dull as a stand-alone, it's not bad tacked on to the other two. Try to catch the video presentation at the end—a tribute to Singapore's strides in "cultural integration" told in true "It's a small world after all" style.

🕐 65/6275-0388. Adults S$5 (US$2.85), children S$3 (US$1.70). Daily 9am–9pm. Monorail stop 4.

The Maritime Museum   The Maritime Museum is a showcase devoted to Singapore's ever-important connection to the sea. From ship models to artifacts, sea charts, and photos, the museum tells the story of 14 centuries of maritime life.

🕐 65/6270-8855. Free admission. Daily 10am–7pm. Closest to monorail stop 7, then walk along Gateway Ave.

The Merlion   Imagine, if you will, 12 towering stories of that half-lion, half-fish creature, the Merlion. That's a lot of mythical beast. Admission buys you an elevator ride to the ninth floor, where you can peer out the mouth, and to the top of its head for a 360° view of Singapore, Sentosa, and even Indonesia. Be at the Fountain Gardens at 7:30, 8:30, and 9:30pm nightly for the "Rise of the Merlion" show, where they light up the thing with 16,000 fiber-optic lights and shoot red lasers out its eyes. Poor Merlion. Hope this never happens to the national symbol of *your* home country.

🕐 65/6275-0388. Adults S$3 (US$1.70), children S$2 (US$1.15). Daily 9am–10pm. Monorail stop 1 and 4.

Silori WonderGolf Sentosa   This place is definitely miniature golf, but without the windmill. Instead, holes are made tricky using greens landscaped with rock designs and water features set on tiny terraces up the side of a steep slope.

65/6275-2011. Adults S$8 (US$4.55), children S$4 (US$2.30). Daily 9am–9pm. Monorail stop 4.

Underwater World ★ *Kids*   Underwater World is without a doubt one of the most visited attractions on Sentosa. Everybody comes for the tunnel: 83m (272 ft.) of transparent acrylic tube through which you glide on a conveyor belt, gaping at sharks, stingrays, eels, and other creatures of the sea drifting by, above and on both sides. At 11:30am, 2:30pm, and 4:30pm daily, a scuba diver hops in and feeds them by hand. In smaller tanks you can view other unusual sea life like the puffer fish and the mysteriously weedy and leafy sea dragons. Then there's the latest display of bamboo shark embryos, developing within egg cases—what's keeping you?

ⓒ 65/6275-0030. Adults S$13 (US$7.45), children S$7 (US$4). Daily 9am–9pm. Monorail stop 2.

VolcanoLand   It's hard to say whether VolcanoLand is amusing or whether it's touristy and weird. A walk-through exhibit that takes you on a journey to the center of the Earth with a mythological explorer and his Jules Verne–style robot buddy. Inside the "volcano" there's a multimedia show about the mysteries of life and the universe and a simulated volcano eruption.

VolcanoLand. ⓒ 65/6275-1828. Adults S$12 (US$6.85), children S$6 (US$3.45). Daily 10am–7pm. Monorail stop 1 or 4.

8 The Surrounding Islands

There are 60 smaller islands ringing Singapore that are open for full- or half-day trips. The ferry rides are cool and breezy, and provide interesting up-close views of some of the larger ships docked in the harbor. The islands themselves are small and, for the most part, don't have a lot going on. The locals basically see them as little escapes from the everyday grind—peaceful respites for the family.

KUSU & ST. JOHN'S ISLANDS

Kusu Island and St. John's Island are both located to the south of Singapore proper, about a 15- to 20-minute ferry ride to Kusu from the World Trade Centre, 25 to 30 minutes to St. John's.

It's name meaning "Tortoise Island" in Chinese, there are many popular legends about how **Kusu Island** came to be. The most popular ones involve shipwrecked people, either fishermen or monks, who were rescued when a tortoise turned himself into an island. Kusu Island was originally two small islands and a reef, but in 1975, reclaimed land turned it into a (very) small getaway island. There are two places of worship: a Chinese temple and a Malay shrine. The Chinese temple becomes a zoo during "Kusu Season" in October, when thousands of Chinese devotees flock here to pray for health, prosperity, and luck. There are two swimming lagoons (the one to the north has a really beautiful view of Singapore Island), picnic tables, toilets, and public telephones.

Historically speaking, **St. John's Island** is an unlikely place for a day trip. As far back as 1874, this place was a quarantine for Chinese immigrants sick with cholera; in the 1950s, it became a deportation holding center for Chinese Mafia thugs; and later, it was a rehab center for opium addicts. Today you'll find a mosque, holiday camps, three lagoons, bungalows, a cafeteria, a huge playing field, and basketball. It's much larger than Kusu Island, but not large enough to fill a whole day of sightseeing. Toilets and public phones are available.

Ferries leave at regular intervals and make a circular route, landing on both islands. Tickets are available from the desk at the back of the **World Trade Centre** (ⓒ 65/6321-2802). Adult tickets cost S$9 (US$5.15), and tickets for children under 12 are S$6 (US$3.45). During "Kusu Season"—the month of

October—thousands of people make their way to Kusu Island to pray in the temple there, and during this month the ferry departs from **Clifford Pier** (© **65/6532-7441**). To get to the World Trade Centre, take MRT to Tanjong Pagar, then bus no. 10, 97, 100, or 131. For Clifford Pier, take the MRT to Raffles and walk through Change Alley. *A small tip:* There's a Cold Storage grocery store in the World Trade Center where you can pick up water and provisions for the trip.

PULAU UBIN ✦

My favorite island getaway has to be Ubin. Located off the northeast tip of Singapore, Pulau Ubin remains the only place in Singapore where you can find life as it used to be before urban development. Lazy kampung villages pop up along side trails perfect for a little more rugged bicycling. It's truly a great day trip for those who like to explore nature and rural scenery. Toward the end of 1999, the Singapore press carried numerous reports about government plans to develop the island for public housing, so I expect that within the next 20 years we'll see poor Ubin burdened with boxy housing estates and the hideous trappings of urban sprawl. And when they eventually extend the MRT out to the island, it's curtains for this place. See it while you can. *A side note:* Rumors have it that during the occupation the Japanese brought soldiers here to be tortured, and so some believe the place is haunted.

To get to Ubin, take bus no. 2 to Changi Village. Walk past the food court down to the water and find the ferry. There's no ticket booth, so you should just approach the captain and buy your ticket from him—it'll cost you about S$2 (US$1.15). The boats leave regularly, with the last one returning from the island at 9pm.

Once you're there, bicycle-rental places along the jetty can provide you with bikes and island maps at reasonable prices. A few coffee shops cook up rudimentary meals, and you'll also find public toilets and coin phones in the more populated areas.

9 Sports & Recreation

BEACHES

Besides the beach at East Coast Park (see "Attractions Outside the Urban Area," earlier in this chapter) and those on Sentosa Island (see above) you can try the smaller beach at Changi Village, called Changi Point. From the shore, you have a panoramic view of Malaysia, Indonesia, and several smaller islands that belong to Singapore. The beach is calm, and frequented mostly by locals who set up camps and barbecues to hang out all day. There's kayak rentals along the beach, and in Changi Village you'll find, in addition to a huge hawker center, quite a few international restaurants and pubs to hang out in and have a fresh seafood lunch when you get hungry. To get there take SBS bus no. 2 from either the Tanah Merah or Bedok MRT stations.

On Kusu and St. John's Islands there are quiet swimming lagoons, a couple of which have quite nice views of the city.

BICYCLE RENTAL

Bicycles are not for rent within the city limits, and traffic does not really allow for cycling on city streets, so sightseeing by bicycle is not recommended for city touring. If you plan a trip out to **Sentosa,** cycling provides a great alternative to that island's tram system, and gets you closer to the parks and nature there. For a little light cycling, most people head out to **East Coast Park,** where rentals are inexpensive, the scenery is nice on cooler days, and there are plenty of great stops for eating along the way. One favorite place where the locals go for mountain-biking sorts of adventures (and to cycle amidst the old kampung villages) is **Pulau Ubin,** off the northeast coast of Singapore.

AT EAST COAST PARK Bicycles can be rented at East Coast Park from **Ling Choo Hong** (℃ 65/6449-7305), near the hawker center at Carpark E; **SDK Recreation** (℃ 65/6445-2969), near McDonald's at Carpark C; or **Wimbledon Cafeteria & Bicycle Rental** (℃ 65/6444-3928), near the windsurfing rental places at the lagoon. All of these are open 7 days from about 9am to 8 or 9pm. Rentals are all in the neighborhood of S$4 to S$8 (US$2.40–US$4.80) per hour, depending on the type and quality bike you're looking for. Identification may be requested.

ON SENTOSA ISLAND Try **SDK Recreation** (℃ 65/6272-8738), located at Siloso Beach off Siloso Road, a short walk from Underwater World (see "Sentosa Island," above). Open 7 days from around 10am to 6:30 or 7pm. Rental for a standard bicycle is S$4 (US$2.40) per hour. A mountain bike goes for S$8 (US$4.80) per hour. Identification is required.

IN PULAU UBIN When you get off the ferry, there are a number of places to rent bikes. The shops are generally open between 8am and 6pm and will charge between S$5 (US$3) and S$8 (US$4.80) per hour, depending on which bike you choose. Most rental agents will have a map of the island for you—take it. Even though it doesn't look too impressive, it'll be a great help.

DEEP-SEA FISHING

For something different, but very worth your time and money, Grant Pereira, Singapore's most acclaimed salty dog, takes folks out on fantastic fishing tours. With 25 years of experience fishing the waters of Southeast Asia and the rest of the world, he uses his expertise and connections to arrange weekend trips around Singapore and to neighboring Malaysia and Indonesia for great catches. Be prepared to live the life of a seaman, though. While you'll be inundated with cockroaches and saltfish on board, Mr. Pereira guarantees you'll "catch fish 'til your arms drop off!" Everything is included with the price of the trip (he even has a cook on board), but you'll have to bring your own booze. And bring plenty of extra booze for Mr. Pereira—his awesome fish tales don't come cheap! (Trust me, he's the fishing buddy you've always dreamed of.) If you're up for a really unique local experience, with a little bit of advance notice he can arrange an overnight on a kelong—a Malay fishing shack in the middle of the sea, surrounded by bamboo traps. Your best bet is to contact him via e-mail well in advance of your visit at grant@tacklemall.com.sg. Or call or fax ℃ 65/6583-6732.

GOLF

Golf is a very popular sport in Singapore. There are quite a few clubs, and though some of them are exclusively for members only, many places are open for limited play by nonmembers. All will require you bring a par certificate.

Most hotel concierges will be glad to make arrangements for you, and this may be the best way to go. Also, it's really popular for Singaporeans go on day trips to Malaysia for the best courses. See chapters 10 and 11 for more information about golfing in Malaysia.

Changi Golf Club Nonmembers can play at this private club only on weekdays. The 9-hole course is par 34, with greens fees of S$41 (US$25), or you can play it twice for S$82 (US$49). They have club and shoe rentals for around S$20 (US$12) and S$10 (US$6) respectively. A caddy for 18 holes sets you back S$25 (US$15). While on weekdays they will accept walk-ins, the club recommends advanced booking and requires it for weekend and holiday play. They may even be able to set you up with other players. The course opens at 7:30am. Last tee is 4:30pm.

20 Netheravon Rd. ℰ 65/6545-5133.

Jurong Country Club   This private course welcomes nonmembers 7 days a week, but requests at least 48 hours advanced booking for its 18-hole, par 72 course. Greens fees cost S$95 (US$57) on weekdays and S$180 (US$108) on weekends. A caddy can be hired for S$25 (US$15) each, and shoe and club rentals are also available. First tee is between 7:15 and 8:45am. Second tee is between noon and 1:30pm. Night golf begins between 5 and 6:30pm.

9 Science Centre Rd. ℰ 65/6560-5655.

Seletar Base Golf Course   A public course, Seletar's 9-hole, par 36 course is open for everyone 7 days a week. Expect to pay greens fees of S$45 (US$27) on weekdays and S$60 (US$36) on weekends, with very low-cost golf cart and equipment rentals (all available with deposit). First tee is at 7am except for Monday through Thursday, when first tee is at 11am. Last tee is 5pm.

244 Oxford St., 3 Park Lane. ℰ 65/6481-4745.

Sentosa Golf Club   The best idea if you're traveling with your family and want to get in a game, Sentosa's many activities will keep the kids happy while you practice your swing guilt-free. This club's two 18-hole courses are each 72 par, with greens fees ranging from S$120 to S$140 (US$72–$84) on weekdays and S$220 (US$132) on weekends and holidays. It's a bit more expensive than other courses around, but the chance to get off Singapore island for the day can be quite relaxing. Advance phone bookings are required.

27 Bukit Manis Rd., Sentosa Island. ℰ 65/6275-0022.

SCUBA DIVING

The locals are crazy about scuba diving, but are more likely to travel to Malaysia and other Southeast Asian destinations for good underwater adventures. The most common complaint is that the water surrounding Singapore is really silty—sometimes to the point where you can barely see your hand before your face. If you're still interested, the best place to try for a beginner certification course is at **SEADive Adventurers** (ℰ 65/6251-0322), which also organizes diving trips and offers classes up to advanced levels. **Sharkey's Dive & Travel** (ℰ 65/6294-0168) also arranges diving trips.

TENNIS

Quite a few hotels in the city provide tennis courts for guests, many floodlit for night play (which allows you to avoid the midday heat), and even a few that can arrange lessons, so be sure to check out listings for hotel facilities in chapter 3. You'll have to travel about 15 minutes by taxi form the city center to reach the Singapore Tennis Centre on East Coast Parkway near the **East Coast Park** (ℰ 65/6442-5966). Their courts are open to the public for day and evening play. Weekdays offer discount rates of S$8.50 (US$5.10) per hour, while weekday evening peak hours (6–9pm) jump to S$13 (US$7.50). Weekends and public holidays expect to pay S$13 (US$7.50) per hour also. If you need to stay

closer to town, you can play at the **Tanglin Sports Centre** on Minden Road
(© **65/6473-7236**). Court costs are S$3.50 (US$2.10) per hour on weekdays,
with charges upped to S$9.50 (US$5.70) on weekday nights from 6 to 10pm,
on weekends, and all public holidays.

WATER-SKIING

The Kallang River, located to the east of the city, has hosted quite a few international water-skiing tournaments. If this is your sport, contact the Cowabunga
Ski Centre, the authority in Singapore. Located at **Kallang Riverside Park,** 10
Stadium Lane (© **65/6344-8813**), they'll arrange lessons for adults and children and water-skiing by the hour. Beginner courses will set you back S$140
(US$84) for five half-hour lessons, while more experienced skiers can hire a boat
plus equipment for S$80 (US$48) on weekdays and S$100 (US$60) on weekends. It's open on weekdays from noon to 7pm and weekends from 9am to 7pm.
Call in advance for a reservation.

WINDSURFING & SAILING

You'll find both windsurf boards and sailboats for rent at the lagoon in East
Coast Park, which is where these activities primarily take place. The largest and
most reputable firm to approach has to be the **Europa Sailing Club** at 1212
East Coast Pkwy. (© **65/6449-5118**). For S$20 an hour (US$12) you can rent
a small sailboat, while windsurf boards go for about the same. Expect to leave
around S$30 (US$18) deposit. While Europa does offer courses, instruction is
really not recommended for short-term visitors since classes usually occur over
extended periods of time on a set schedule.

6

Singapore Shopping

In Singapore, shopping is a sport, and from the practiced glide through haute couture boutiques to skillful back-alley bargaining to win the best prices on Asian treasures, it's always exciting, with something to satiate every pro shopper's appetite.

From its humble beginnings as an operation for the British East India Trading Company, Singapore has always been a trading mecca. When Sir Stamford Raffles first set foot on its shore, he envisioned a free port to serve as a go-between for trade from China in the north and Indonesia in the south to Europe and India in the west. In the early days of maritime trade, the northeast monsoon from November to March would blow in junks from China, Indochina, and Siam, while during the autumn months, the southwest monsoon would usher in Bugis and Indonesian traders. Boat Quay was in its trading glory, with spices, silks, gold, tin, rattan, and, of course, opium.

Today, the focal point of shopping in Singapore is **Orchard Road,** a very long stretch of glitzy shopping malls packed with Western clothing stores, from designer apparel to cheap chic, and many other mostly imported finds. Singaporeans have a love-hate relationship with Orchard Road. As the shopping malls developed, they brought hip styles into the reach of everyday Singaporeans, adding a cosmopolitan sheen to Singapore style. But Orchard Road also ushered in a new culture of obsessive consumerism. One working mother told me about her school-age son who spent a month

working at a job for S$200 (US$114) a week, only to take all his earnings down to Orchard Road and squander it on a pair of S$800 (US$457)jeans. You can see this kind of blatant image-consciousness in the throngs of teenagers that crowd the malls on weekends and school holidays.

Even to outsiders, Orchard Road is a drug; however, most of the clothing and accessories shops sell Western imports, and while the prices may be bargain-basement for Japanese visitors, the rest of us will find that the prices of Western brand-name fashions are no less expensive than at home. And it's all the same stuff you can get at home, too. I tried to find a unique gift to bring for a Singaporean friend, something she could not get in Singapore, so I went to the gift shop at the Metropolitan Museum of Art in New York City. Sure enough, as soon as I got back to Singapore I found that the Met had opened two outlets on Orchard Road.

In the seventies, before the malls, Singapore was truly a shopping heaven. Local and regional handicrafts were skillfully made by local artisans, who by now have almost all been squeezed out of their quaint shops by rising real estate prices. And who can forget Thieves' Market, a sprawling series of awning-covered back alleys that teemed on weekends with table displays of antique finds from the region; brass and gems from Thailand; jade and ivory from China; batiks from Indonesia; and knock-off luggage, clothing, watches, leather goods, and pirate recordings, all for a bargain.

The government shut down the place in the late eighties when drugs started to take the place of other goods sold, and as the government became more aware of copyright violation practices.

Nostalgia aside, there are still some nifty shopping areas around, like the places on **Arab Street,** the night market out at **Bugis Street,** and at the small flea market in **Chinatown,** where you can pick up odd items for bargains. Anybody who's been around Singapore long enough will tell you that most of the really juicy bargains went the way of the dodo when the huge shopping malls came to town, but if you know the prices of certain items that you'd like, some comparison shopping may save you a little money. In this chapter, I'll give you some tips on where to find the better merchandise, competitive prices, and memorable shopping experiences.

1 Singapore Shopping Tips

HOURS   Shopping malls are generally open from 10am to 8pm Monday through Saturday, with some stores keeping shorter Sunday hours. The malls sometimes remain open until 10pm on holidays. Smaller shops are open from around 10am to 5pm Monday through Saturday, but are almost always closed on Sundays. Hours will vary from shop to shop. Arab Street is closed on Sundays.

PRICES   Almost all of the stores in shopping malls have fixed prices. Sometimes these stores will have seasonal sales, especially in July, when they have the monthlong **Great Singapore Sale,** during which prices are marked down, sometimes up to 50% or 75%. In the smaller shops and at street vendors, prices are never marked, and vendors will quote you higher prices than the going rate, in anticipation of the bargaining ritual. These are the places to find good prices, if you negotiate well.

BARGAINING   In Singapore, many shopkeepers cling to the old tradition of not fixing prices on their merchandise, instead making every item's purchase a little performance piece by insisting their customers bargain for it. For Westerners who are unaccustomed to this tradition, bargaining can be embarrassing and frustrating at first—after all, Westerners are accustomed to accepting fixed prices without an argument, and if you don't know the protocol, you can't be sure what to do. All it takes is a little practice, though, and soon you'll be bargaining with the best of 'em. I've seen many travelers go into their first market like lambs to the slaughter, only to loosen up after a few encounters and begin to enjoy the process for the sport it really is.

The most important thing to remember when bargaining is to keep a friendly, good-natured banter between you and the seller. Getting him or her mad won't save you a dime, and if you get 'em really riled up, they won't sell you anything at any price and will just throw you out. But don't let that scare you; just be nice and patient, and you'll get where you want to go.

One important tip for bargaining is to first have an idea of the value of what you're buying. This can be difficult for unusual items, but a little comparison shopping here may help you out. Try to look like you live in Singapore. A lot of the local European and North American residents shop at these places, so you won't look out of place. If a salesperson asks you where you are from, don't smile and say London or San Francisco, but toss out a blasé "Katong" or "Holland Village" without even looking up. If they think you're a local, they'll try to get away with less.

Urban Singapore Shopping

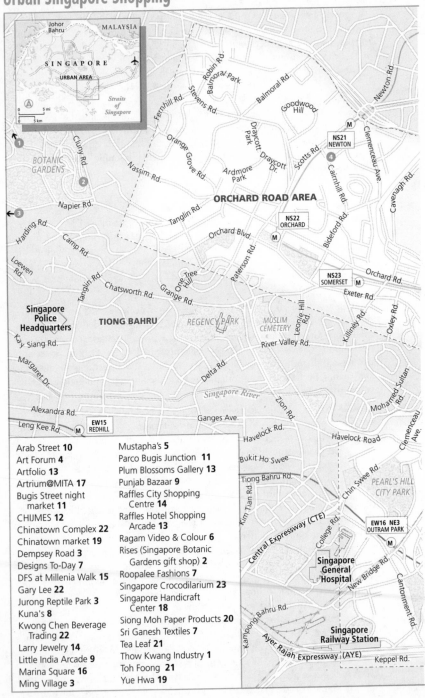

Arab Street **10**
Art Forum **4**
Artfolio **13**
Artrium@MITA **17**
Bugis Street night market **11**
CHIJMES **12**
Chinatown Complex **22**
Chinatown market **19**
Dempsey Road **3**
Designs To-Day **7**
DFS at Millenia Walk **15**
Gary Lee **22**
Jurong Reptile Park **3**
Kuna's **8**
Kwong Chen Beverage Trading **22**
Larry Jewelry **14**
Little India Arcade **9**
Marina Square **16**
Ming Village **3**

Mustapha's **5**
Parco Bugis Junction **11**
Plum Blossoms Gallery **13**
Punjab Bazaar **9**
Raffles City Shopping Centre **14**
Raffles Hotel Shopping Arcade **13**
Ragam Video & Colour **6**
Rises (Singapore Botanic Gardens gift shop) **2**
Roopalee Fashions **7**
Singapore Crocodilarium **23**
Singapore Handicraft Center **18**
Siong Moh Paper Products **20**
Sri Ganesh Textiles **7**
Tea Leaf **21**
Thow Kwang Industry **1**
Toh Foong **21**
Yue Hwa **19**

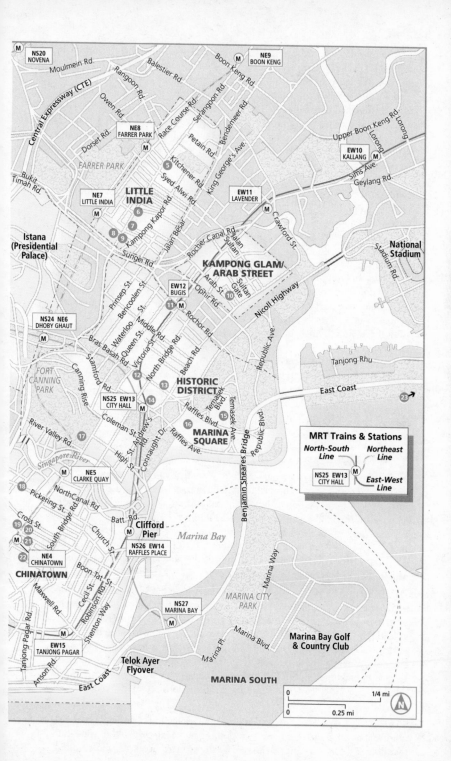

A simple "How much?" is the place to start, to which they'll reply with their top price. Let the bidding begin! It's always good to come back with a little smile and ask, "Is that your best price?" They'll probably come down a bit, but if it's obvious they're trying to soak you, tell them you'll pay a price that's about half of what they had originally offered; otherwise, just knock about 30% or 40% off. The standard reaction from them will always be to look at you like you're a crazy person for even suggesting such a discount—but don't falter! This is standard technique. For each little bit their price comes down, bring yours up just a bit until you reach a price you like. If you're having trouble talking them down, try these strategies: When buying more than one item, ask for a generous discount on the less expensive item. If you've seen it cheaper elsewhere, tell them. Or you can pull the old, "But I only have $20" ploy. (Just make sure you don't turn around and ask them to change a $50!) Try anything, even if it's just a wink and a little, "Don't you have any special discounts for ladies shopping on Wednesdays?"

Some people have said that once you start the bargaining ritual, it's rude to walk away and not purchase the item. Well, I see it this way: It's my money, and if I still don't feel comfortable shelling it out, then I won't do it under any feeling of obligation. (However, if you've spent hours negotiating over a high-priced item, and the owner agrees to your offer, it may be considered harsh to walk away after going through all that trouble.) Besides, the final bargaining strategy is to just politely say, "No, thank-you" and walk away. You'll be surprised at how fast prices can come down as you're walking out the door.

GLOBAL REFUND SCHEME When you shop in stores that display the blue "Tax Free Shopping" logo, the government will refund the goods and services tax (GST) you pay on purchases totaling S$300 (US$180) or more. Upon request, the sales clerk will fill out a Tax Free Shopping Cheque, which you retain with your receipt. If you've purchased up to S$300 at the same store, but on different dates, you can still claim the refund for all of the items. When you leave Singapore, present your checks at Customs along with your passport, and let them see the goods you've purchased to show that you're taking them out of the country with you. Customs will stamp the forms, which you then present at any of the Global Refund Counters in the airport for an on-the-spot cash refund—or, if you like, you can mail in the stamped form to receive a check or a direct transfer of the amount to your bank account. Certain restrictions apply—if you've been working in Singapore, for instance, or fail to take the items out of the country within 2 months of the purchase date. For complete details, call the Singapore Tourism Board at © **1800/736-2000.**

DUTY-FREE ITEMS Changi International Airport has a large duty-free shop that carries cigarettes, liquor, wine, perfumes, cosmetics, watches, jewelry, and other designer accessories. There's also a chain of duty-free stores in Singapore called **DFS.** Their main branch is at #01-58 Millenia Walk, 9 Raffles Blvd., next to the Pan Pacific Hotel (© **65/6332-2188**). The store is huge and impressive, but unfortunately, the only truly duty-free items are liquor, which you can arrange to pick up at the airport before you depart—everything else carries the standard 5% GST. Feel free to apply for the Tourist Refund Scheme here, though.

CLOTHING SIZES Those of you used to shopping in big-and-tall stores will unfortunately find little ready-to-wear clothing in Singapore that'll fit you—but that doesn't mean you can't take advantage of the many excellent tailors around town. If you wear a standard size, however, this chart will help you convert your size to local measures.

Ladies' Dress Sizes						
U.S.	8	10	12	14	16	18
U.K.	30	32	34	36	38	40
Continental	36	38	40	42	44	46

Ladies' Shoes									
U.S.	5	5½	6	6½	7	7½	8	8½	9
U.K.	3½	4	4½	5	5½	6	6½	7	7½
Continental	35	35	36	37	38	38	38	39	40

Men's Suits								
U.S. & U.K.	34	36	38	40	42	44	46	48
Continental	44	46	48	50	52	54	56	58

Men's Shirts								
U.S. & U.K.	14	14½	15	15½	16	16½	17	17½
Continental	36	37	38	39	40	41	42	43

Men's Shoes										
U.S.	7	7½	8	8½	9	9½	10	10½	11	11½
U.K.	6½	7	7½	8	8½	9	9½	10	10½	11
Continental	39	40	41	42	43	43	44	44	45	45

Children's Clothes						
U.S.	2	4	6	8	10	13	15
U.K.	1	2	5	7	9	10	12
Continental	1	2	5	7	9	10	12

2 The Shopping Scene, Part 1: Western-Style Malls

Orchard Road is the biggie, as I've said, but other good mall spots are at Marina Bay, Bugis Junction, Raffles City, and at Raffles Hotel. In this section, I'll give you the lowdown on the hot spots.

ORCHARD ROAD AREA

The malls on Orchard Road are a tourist attraction in their own right, with smaller boutiques and specialty shops intermingled with huge department stores. Takashimaya and Isetan have been imported from Japan. **John Little Pte. Ltd.** is one of the oldest department stores in Singapore, followed by **Robinson's. Tang's** is historic, having grown from a cart-full of merchandise nurtured by the business savvy of local entrepreneur C. K. Tang. Boutiques range from the younger styles of Stussy and Guess? to the sophisticated fashions of Chanel and Salvatore Ferragamo. You'll also find antiques, Oriental carpets, art galleries and curio shops, Tower Records and HMV music stores, Kinokuniya and Borders bookstores, video arcades, and scores of restaurants, local food courts, fast-food joints, and coffeehouses—even a few discos, which open in the evenings (see chapter 7). It's hard to say when Orchard Road is not crowded, but it's definitely a mob scene on weekends, when folks have the free time to come and hang around, looking for fun.

Centrepoint   Centrepoint is home to Robinson's department store, which first opened in Singapore in 1858. Here you'll find about 150 other shops, plus fast-food outlets, and on the sixth level is the huge new Times bookstore. 176 Orchard Rd. ✆ 65/6235-6629.

Far East Plaza   At this crowded mall, the bustle of little shops will sell everything from CDs to punk fashions, luggage to camera equipment, eyewear to souvenirs. Mind yourself here: Most of these shops do not display prices, but rather gauge the price depending on how wealthy the customer appears. If you must shop here, use your shrewdest bargaining powers. It may pay off to wear an outfit that's seen better days. 14 Scotts Rd. ✆ 65/6374-2325.

The Heeren   Thanks to the opening of a Singapore branch of Britain's HMV music stores, the Heeren is the latest hangout joint for teens. The front entrance of the mall hums with towers of video monitors flashing and blaring the latest in American and British chart toppers. There is also a nice cafe to the side, with a garden for enjoying a cup of coffee, tea, or a snack. At the midway point along the Orchard Road stretch, it's a recommended stop for a break. 260 Orchard Rd. ✆ 65/6733-4725.

Hilton Shopping Gallery   The shopping arcade at the Hilton International Hotel is the most exclusive shopping in Singapore. Gucci, Donna Karan, Missoni, and Luis Vuitton are just a few of the international design houses that have made this their Singapore home. 581 Orchard Rd. ✆ 65/6737-2233.

Lucky Plaza   The map of this place will take hours to decipher, as there are more than 400 stores here (no kidding). It's basically known for sportswear, camera equipment, watches, and luggage. If you buy electronics, please make sure you get an international warranty with your purchase. Also, like Far East Plaza, Lucky Plaza is a notorious rip-off problem for travelers. Make sure you come here prepared to fend off slick sales techniques. It may also help to take the government's advice and avoid touts and offers that sound too good to be true. 304 Orchard Plaza. ✆ 65/6235-3294.

Ngee Ann City/Takashimaya Shopping Centre   Takashimaya, a major Japanese department store import, anchors Ngee Ann City's many smaller boutiques. Alfred Dunhill, Chanel, Coach, Tiffany & Co., Royal Copenhagen, and a Waterford and Wedgwood boutique are found here, along with many other local and international fashion shops. 391 Orchard Rd. ✆ 65/6739-9323.

Palais Renaissance   Shops here include upmarket boutiques like Prada, Versus, and DKNY. 390 Orchard Rd. ✆ 65/6737-1520.

Paragon   Another upmarket shopping mall, Paragon houses Diesel, Emanuel Ungaro, Escada, and Ferragamo. 290 Orchard Rd. ✆ 65/6238-5535.

Shaw House   The main floors of Shaw House are taken up by Isetan, a large Japanese department store with designer boutiques for men's and women's fashions, accessories, and cosmetics. On the fifth level, the Lido Theatre screens new releases from Hollywood and around the world. 350 Orchard Rd. ✆ 65/6235-1150.

Specialists' Shopping Centre   The anchor store in this smaller shopping mall is John Little, Singapore's oldest department store, which opened in 1845. The prices, however, are very up-to-date. 277 Orchard Rd. ✆ 65/6737-8222.

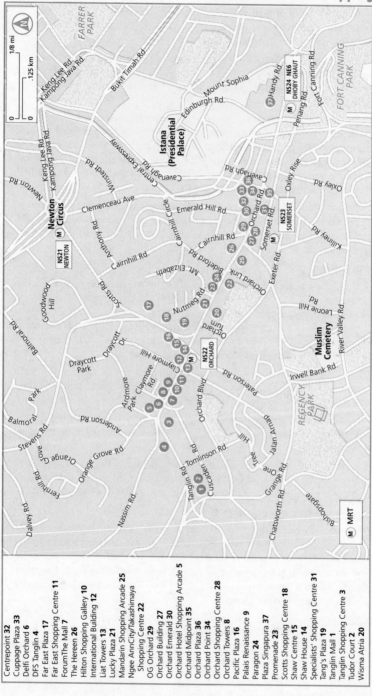

FARRER PARK

FORT CANNING PARK

Keng Lee Rd.
Kampong Java Rd.

Bukit Timah Rd.

Mount Sophia

Edinburgh Rd.

37 Handy Rd.

NS24 NE6
DHOBY GHAUT

M Penang Rd.

Fort Canning Rd.

Keng Lee Rd.
Kampong Java Rd.

Newton Rd.

Winstedt Rd.

Central Expressway

Clemenceau Ave.

Cavenagh Rd.

Cavenagh Rd.

Oxley Rise

Oxley Rd.

Newton
Circus

M NS21
NEWTON

Anthony Rd.

Cairnhill Rd.

Cairnhill Circle

Emerald Hill Rd.

Orchard Rd.

NS23
SOMERSET

Killiney Rd.

Cairnhill Rd.

Somerset Rd.

M

27 28

29

Bideford Rd.

25

Exeter Rd.

Leonie Hill Rd.

Goodwood Hill

Scotts Rd.

Mt. Elizabeth

24

Orchard Link

22

21

23

26

Nutmeg Rd.

17

18

19

20

Orchard Turn

NS22
ORCHARD

Patterson Rd.

River Valley Rd.

Muslim Cemetery

Irwell Bank Rd.

Balmoral Rd.

Draycott Park

Draycott Dr.

Claymore Hill

Claymore Rd.

16

15

14

12

13

11

10

9

8

7

6

5

Ardmore Park

3

4

REGENCY PARK

Park

Balmoral

Stevens Rd.

Anderson Rd.

Orange Grove Rd.

Orchard Blvd.

Cuscaden Rd.

Tomlinson Rd.

Tanglin Rd.

Jalan Arnap

Grange Rd.

One Tree Hill

Fernhill Rd.

Dalvey Rd.

Nassim Rd.

1 2

Chatsworth Rd.

Bishopsgate

M MRT

Tanglin Mall   This mall has a few charming boutiques filled with regional handicrafts crafts for home and neat ethnic fashions from Singapore's neighboring countries. 163 Tanglin Rd. ℂ 65/6736-4922.

Tanglin Shopping Centre   Tanglin Shopping Centre is unique and fun. You won't find many clothing stores here, but you'll find shop after shop selling antiques, art, and collectibles—from curios to carpets. 19 Tanglin Rd. ℂ 65/6373-0849.

Tang's Plaza   Once upon a time, C. K. Tang peddled goods from an old cart in the streets of Singapore. An industrious fellow, he parlayed his business into a small department store. A hit from the start, Tang's has grown exponentially over the decades, and now competes with all the other international megastores that have moved in. The beauty is that Tang's is truly Singaporean, and its history is a local legend. 320 Orchard Rd. ℂ 65/6737-5500.

Wisma Atria   Wisma Atria caters to the younger set. Here you'll find everything from Nine West to a Levi's store mixed in with numerous eyewear, cosmetics, and high- and low-fashion boutiques, all under one roof. 435 Orchard Rd. ℂ 65/6235-2103.

MARINA BAY

The Marina Bay area arose from a plot of reclaimed land, and now boasts the giant Suntec City convention center and all the hotels, restaurants, and shopping malls that have grown up around it. Shopping in the Marina Bay area is popular for everyone because of its convenience, with the major malls and hotels all interconnected by covered walkways and pedestrian bridges, making it easy to get around with minimal exposure to the elements.

Marina Square   Marina Square is a huge complex that, in addition to a wide variety of shops, has a cinema, fast-food outlets and cafes, pharmacies, and convenience stores. 6 Raffles Blvd. ℂ 65/6335-2613.

Millenia Walk   Smaller than Marina Square, Millenia Walk has more upmarket boutiques like Fendi, Guess?, and Liz Claiborne, to name a few. 9 Raffles Blvd. ℂ 65/6383-1122.

Suntec City Mall   Singapore's largest mall has tons of shops selling fashion, sports equipment, books, CDs, plus restaurants and food courts, and a cinema adjacent to the Suntec Convention Centre. 3 Temasek Blvd. ℂ 65/6821-3668.

AROUND THE CITY CENTER

While the Historic District doesn't have as many malls as the Orchard Road area, it still has some good shopping. Raffles City can be overwhelming in its size, but convenient because it sits right atop the City Hall MRT stop. One of my favorite places to go, however, is the very upmarket Raffles Hotel Shopping Arcade, where I like to window-shop and dream about actually being able to afford some of the stuff on display.

Parco Bugis Junction   Here you'll find restaurants—both fast food and fine dining—mixed in with clothing retailers, most of which sell fun fashions for younger tastes. Victoria St. ℂ 65/6334-8831.

Raffles City Shopping Centre   Raffles City sits right on top of the City Hall MRT station, which makes it a very well visited mall. Men's and women's fashions, books, cosmetics, and accessories are sold in shops here, along with gifts. 252 North Bridge Rd. ℂ 65/6338-7766.

Raffles Hotel Shopping Arcade   These shops are mostly haute couture; however, there is the Raffles Hotel gift shop for interesting souvenirs. For golfers, there's a Jack Nicklaus signature store. 328 North Bridge Rd.

3 The Shopping Scene, Part 2: Multicultural Shopping

The most exciting shopping has got to be in all the ethnic enclaves throughout the city. Down narrow streets, bargains are to be had on all sorts of unusual items, many of which are perfect for gifts to take back home. If you're stuck for a gift idea, read on. Chances are I'll mention something for even the most difficult person on your list.

CHINATOWN

In Chinatown, I've stumbled on some of my most precious treasures. My all-time favorite gift idea? Spend an afternoon learning the traditional Chinese tea ceremony at **The Tea Chapter,** 9A Neil Rd. (© **65/6226-1175**), then head down to the **Tea Leaf,** 65 Pagoda St. (© **65/6225-8307**), to pick up a good quality tea set and accessories. After a stop at **Kwong Chen Beverage** Trading, 16 Smith St. (© **65/6223-6927**), for some Chinese teas in handsome tins, you'll be ready to give a fabulous gift—not just a tea set, but your own cultural performance as well, as you teach your friends a new art. While the teas are really inexpensive, they're packed in lovely tins—great to buy lots to bring back as smaller gifts.

Another neat place, **Gary Lee,** 20 Smith St. (© **65/221-8129**), carries a fantastic selection of linens imported from China. These hand-embroidered gems include bedding, dining linens, tea towels and handkerchiefs, and other decorative items for the home. They're priced right, and won't break on the trip back home. For something a little more unusual, check out **Siong Moh Paper Products,** 39 Mosque St. (© **65/6224-3125**), both of which carry a full line of ceremonial items. Pick up some joss sticks (temple incense) or joss paper (books of thin sheets of paper, stamped in reds and yellows with bits of gold and silver leaf). Definitely a conversation piece, as is the Hell Money, stacks of "money" that believers burn at the temple for their ancestors to use in the afterlife. Perfect for that friend who has everything? Also, if you duck over to **Sago Lane** while you're in the neighborhood, there are a few souvenir shops that sell Chinese kites and Cantonese Opera masks—cool for kids.

For one-stop souvenir shopping, you can tick off half your shopping list at **Chinatown Point,** aka the **Singapore Handicraft Center,** 133 New Bridge Rd. The best gifts there include hand-carved chops, or Chinese seals. **Chinatown Seal Carving Souvenir,** #03-72 (© **65/6534-0761**), has an absolutely enormous selection of carved stone, wood, bone, glass, and ivory chops ready to be carved to your specifications. Simple designs are really quite affordable, while some of the more elaborate chops and carvings fetch a handsome sum. At **Inherited Arts & Crafts,** #03-69 (© **65/6534-1197**), you can commission a personalized Chinese scroll painting or calligraphy piece. The handiwork is quite beautiful. Amid the many jade and gold shops at Chinatown Point, **La Belle Collection,** #04-53 (© **65/6534-0231**), stands out for its jewelry crafted from orchids. The coating lets the flowers' natural colors show, while delicate gold touches add a little extra sparkle.

For Chinese goods, however, nothing beats **Yue Hwa,** 70 Eu Tong Sen St. (© **65/6538-4222**). This five-story Chinese Emporium is an attraction in its own right. The superb inventory includes all manner of silk wear (robes, underwear, blouses), embroidery and house linens, bolt silks, tailoring services (for perfect mandarin dresses!), cloisonné (enamel work) jewelry and gifts, lacquerware, pottery, musical instruments, traditional Chinese clothing for men and women (from scholars' robes to coolie duds!), jade and gold, cashmere, traditional items, art supplies, herbs, home furnishings—I could go on and on. Plan to spend some time here.

ARAB STREET

Over on Arab Street, shop for handicrafts from Malaysia and Indonesia. I go for sarongs at **Hadjee Textiles,** 75 Arab St. (© **65/6298-1943**), for their stacks of folded sarongs in beautiful colors and traditional patterns. They're perfect for traveling, as they're lightweight, but can serve you well as a dressy skirt, a bedsheet, beach blanket, window shade, bath towel, or whatever you need—when I'm on the road I can't live without mine. Buy a few here and the prices really drop. If you're in the market for a more masculine sarong, **Goodwill Trading,** 56 Arab St. (© **65/6298-3205**), specializes in pulicat, or the plaid sarongs worn by Malay men. For modern styles of batik, check out **Basharahil Brothers,** 99-101 Arab St. (© **65/6296-0432**), for their very interesting designs, but don't forget to see their collection of fine silk batiks in the back. For batik household linens, you can't beat **Maruti Textiles,** 93 Arab St. (© **65/6392-0253**), where you'll find high-quality place mats and napkins, tablecloths, pillow covers, and quilts from India. The buyer for this shop has a good eye for style.

I've also found a few shops on Arab Street that carry handicrafts from other countries in **Southeast Asia. Memoirs,** 18 Baghdad St. (© **65/6294-5900**), sells mostly Indonesian crafts, from carved and hand-painted decorative items to scored leather shadow puppets and unusual teak gifts. For antiques and curios, try **Gim Joo Trading,** 16 Baghdad St. (© **65/6293-5638**), a jumble of the unusual, some of it old. A departure from the more packed and dusty places here, **Suraya Betawj,** 67 Arab St. (© **65/6398-1607**), carries gorgeous Indonesian and Malaysian crafted housewares in contemporary design—the type you normally find for huge prices in shopping catalogues back home.

Other unique treasures include the large assortment of fragrance oils at **Aljunied Brothers,** 91 Arab St. (© **65/6293-2751**). Muslims are forbidden from consuming alcohol in any form (a proscription that includes the wearing of alcohol-based perfumes as well), so these oil-based perfumes re-create designer scents plus other floral and wood creations. Check out their delicate cut-glass bottles and atomizers as well. Finally, for the crafter in your life, **Kin Lee & Co.,** 109 Arab St. (© **65/6291-1411**), carries a complete line of patterns and accessories to make local Peranakan beaded slippers. In vivid colors and floral designs, these traditional slippers were always made by hand, to be attached later to a wooden sole. The finished versions are exquisite, plus they're fun to make.

LITTLE INDIA

I have a ball shopping the crowded streets of Little India. The best shopping is on Serangoon Road, where Singapore's Indian community shops for Indian imports and cultural items. If you fancy casual lightweight cottons, many ready-to-wear outfits are on hand at **Designs To-Day,** 81 Serangoon Rd. (© **65/6292-1641**), from dresses and skirts to blouses and shirts. Vegetable-dyed cotton prints feature embroidery and other Indian-style adornment. Prices are just right, too.

For something more traditional, you can pick up a sari or a Punjabi suit. Punjab Bazaar, #01-07 **Little India Arcade,** 48 Serangoon Rd. (© **65/6296-0067**), carries a larger choice of salwar kameez, also called Punjabi suits, in many styles and fabrics. These graceful three-piece outfits, consisting of a pair of drawstring pants worn under a flowing dress with a long coordinated scarf wrapped over the shoulders, translate elegantly in any culture. If nothing strikes your fancy at Punjab Bazaar, try **Roopalee Fashions,** a little farther down at 84 Serangoon Rd. (© **65/6298-0558**). Their selection is a bit smaller, but you may find something there you like. Both shops carry sandals, bags, and other accessories to complement your new outfit.

Of the multitude of shops that sell saris, I like the selection at **Sri Ganesh Textiles,** 100 Serangoon Rd. (© **65/6298-2029**). Choose your favorite colors and patterns from the many bolts stacked on the counters, and the staff will cut the required 6m (20 ft.) length for you. They keep the less expensive polyesters in the front of the shop, but wander to the back to find the gorgeous silk ones. A sari is worn over a choli (a tiny tight-fitting blouse) and a cotton petticoat. These can also be purchased at Sri Ganesh for a very small sum. The absolute largest selection of saris, however, has to be at **Mohamed Mustapha & Samsuddin Co.,** locally known simply as **Mustapha's,** 320 Serangoon Rd./145 Syed Alwi Rd., at the corner of Serangoon and Syed Alwi (© **65/6299-2603**). Down in the basement, the piles of sari fabric bolts go as far as the eye can see. The best part about buying your sari at Mustapha's is their free pamphlet on how to tie the things! It's pretty easy to follow (I actually didn't do too bad with mine!)

Little India offers all sorts of small finds, especially throughout **Little India Arcade** (48 Serangoon Rd.) and just across the street on Campbell Lane at Kuna's, #3 Campbell Lane (© **65/6294-2700**). Here you can buy inexpensive Indian costume jewelry like bangles, earrings, and necklaces in exotic designs, and a wide assortment of decorative dots (called *pottu* in Tamil) to grace your forehead. Indian handicrafts include brass work, wood carvings, dyed tapestries, woven cotton household linens, small curio items, very inexpensive incense, colorful pictures of Hindu gods, and other ceremonial items. Look here also for Indian cooking pots and household items. If after you pick up these items you care to try your hand at making your own curry, head for **Mannan Impex,** 118 Serangoon (© **65/6299-8424**), to peruse all the necessary spices.

Oh, and if you've never seen a Bollywood production, now's your chance. These Indian megahit movies feature amazingly huge music and dance numbers, fabulous costumes, and time-honored stories of danger and romance. At **Ragam Video & Colour,** 124 Serangoon Rd. (© **65/6291-5760**), shop for the latest releases and old favorites on video CD with English subtitles. (*Note:* Video CDs—or VCDs—are not technically DVDs, but you can play them on a DVD player.)

OUTDOOR MARKETS

A few outdoor markets still exist in Singapore, though it ain't like the old days. At the Bugis MRT station, across from Parco Bugis Junction, a well-established **night market** (which is also open during the day) delivers overpriced cheap chic, some curio items, accessories, and video compact discs (VCDs) to tourists. In **Chinatown,** on the corner of South Bridge Road and Cross Street look for the old guys who come out with blankets full of odd merchandise—old watches, coins, jewelry, Mao paraphernalia, Peranakan pottery, and local artifacts from decades past. There's not many of these guys there, but for impromptu markets, I thought their merchandise was far more imaginative than at Bugis. If you're really desperate for a **flea market,** you can always head for the field between

Little India and Arab Street (just behind the Johor bus terminal), where you'll find about five times more vendors than at Chinatown, **but be warned:** The goods are weird. Old nasty shoes, Barry Gibb records, broken radios—the same junk you'd see at garage sales back home, only local style. It could be interesting culturally . . . if you're in the mood.

4 Best Buys A to Z

Basically, you can buy most things in Singapore that you can buy at home for a comparable price. There are, however, some items available here that are real steals. Following is a list of some of your better buys in Singapore.

ANTIQUES At the northern tip of Orchard Road is the mellow **Tanglin Shopping Centre** (Tanglin Rd.), whose quiet halls are just packed with little antiques boutiques. Tanglin is a quiet place, which adds to the museum feel as you stroll past window displays of paintings, pottery, tapestries, and curios made of jade or brass—all kinds of excellent, quality collectibles and gifts. A couple of good shops to visit are **Tzen Gallery,** Basement 1 (① **65/6734-4339**), and **Naga Arts & Antiques,** #01-34 (① **65/6835-2330**). There are many, many more, though. This is a place to really explore.

Just next to Tanglin Shopping Centre you'll find Tanglin Place, with many gallery-quality shops. I can browse forever in **Lopburi Arts & Antiques,** #01-04 Tanglin Place, 91 Tanglin Rd. (① **65/6735-2579**), which features a large selection of beautiful Buddha sculptures from around the world, but most particularly Thailand.

To get an eyeful of some local furnishings in antique Indonesian, Chinese, and Peranakan styles, take a taxi out to **Dempsey Road** and walk up the hill to the warehouses. Inside each warehouse are dealers like the **Woody Antique House,** full of Chinese antiques and Burmese teak at Blk. 7, #01-01/02 Dempsey Rd. (① **65/6471-1770**), and the **Renaissance Art Gallery,** with displays of Chinese figurines, Southeast Asian Buddha images, and chests at Blk. 15, #01-06 Dempsey Rd. (① **65/6474-0338**). There are more than a dozen places here, each specializing in different wares. Some have large furniture pieces, from carved teak Indonesian-style reproduction furniture to authentic pieces from mainland China. Some have smaller collectible items, like antique baskets, carved scale weights from the old opium trade, or collections of Buddha images. There are also Oriental carpet shops mixed in. The stores on Dempsey Road are all open daily from around 10:30am to 6:30pm, though they close for a short lunch break at midday. As with all of the antiques shops in Singapore, they'll help you locate a reliable shipper to send your purchases home.

ELECTRONICS At **Funan–The IT Mall,** 109 North Bridge Rd., you can find computers and accessories—there are many, many shops, each with special offers and deals, so compare when you shop. At Sim Lim Square, 1 Rochor Canal Rd., not only can you find computers, but office and home electronics as well. Bargain hard here—prices are not marked.

If you're in the market for photographic equipment, the best place to go is **Cathay Photo,** #01-05, #01-07/08, #01-11/14 Peninsula Plaza, 111 North Bridge Rd. (① **65/6337-4274**).

EYEGLASSES Eyeglasses? Why would anyone want to buy eyeglasses on his vacation? Because in Singapore they're dirt cheap, that's why. For the price of one pair of frames with prescription lenses in the United States, I can get a pair of prescription glasses, a pair of prescription sunglasses, contact lenses, and even have my old frames relensed. If you can beat that at home, do it. If not, take advantage while you can.

They're so inexpensive because the government does not have as strict regulations on optometry as do countries in the West. However, I assure you the larger prescription firms are very good at what they do, and many shops carry the latest frames from international designers. At **Capitol Optical** you'll get the best price on generic frames, but not cheap quality in the lenses. Centrally located branches are at #03-132 **Far East Plaza** (© 65/6736-0365); #01-77 Lucky Plaza (© 65/734-4166); and 435 Orchard Rd. #03-39 Wisma Atria (© 65/732-2401).

FABRICS   Exquisite fabrics like Chinese silk, Thai silk, batiks, and inexpensive gingham are very affordable and the selections are extensive. If you have time, see if you can have something tailored. There are many fine men's tailors for suits and slacks made to fit. For women, the ultimate souvenir is to order a **cheongsam,** the Chinese dress with the mandarin collar, frog clasps, and high slits up the side. Ready-made ones of lesser-quality silk and sateens are really cheap and kitsch, but a tailored full-length dress from rich Chinese silk makes for an elegant addition to your formal wardrobe.

On another note, if you've ever dreamed of owning a sarong or sari, you can get them in Singapore for great prices. *A suggestion:* I buy the traditional Asian prints and have them tailored into Western designs for my own East-meets-West styles.

Most fabrics are sold by the meter and there is no standard width, so make sure you inquire when you're purchasing off the bolt. Silk dealers are in almost every mall in the Orchard Road area.

You should also check out **Arab Street.** I love the selection of silks from India, Thailand, Japan, and Europe at **Poppy Fabric,** 111 Arab St. (© 65/6296-6352). Buy modern batik fabrics at **Basharahil Bros.,** 101 Arab St. (© 65/6296-0432), and be sure to take a peek at their batik silks in the back—just gorgeous! For bolt batik cottons in traditional patterns, the following shops have good selections: **Hadjee Textiles,** 75 Arab St. (© 65/6298-1943); **Bian Swee Hin & Co.,** 107 Arab St. (© 65/6293-4763); and **Aik Joo Textiles,** 68 Arab St. (© 65/6293-7580).

For other finds, a few shops along Serangoon Road in Little India have some fine Indian silks. The largest selection is at **Mohd Mustapha & Samsuddin Co., Pte. Ltd.,** more commonly known as **Mustapha's,** 320 Serangoon Rd. (© 65/6299-2603).

FINE ART   As Singaporeans' wealth increases, so does appreciation of the arts, so you'll get to see a multitude of successful galleries cropping up, many of which feature the works of local and regional artists. Late 19th-century Chinese oil paintings, watercolors, and brush paintings blend agreeably with contemporary artworks by well-known and new-to-the-scene artists from ASEAN (Association of Southeast Asian Nations) countries as well as the United States and Europe. Rich antique embroideries, carved jade and wooden pieces, and calligraphy (an art unto itself) beg to be admired for their excellent craftsmanship.

Six Galleries are packed into the **Artrium@MITA** (The Ministry of Information, Communications and The Arts), 140 Hill St., including Gajah Gallery, with regional fine arts (© 65/6737-4202) and Soobin Gallery (© 65/837-2777).

Artfolio's exhibits at #02-25 Raffles Hotel Arcade, 328 North Bridge Rd. (© **65/6334-4677**), always make me wish I were rich enough to collect. **Art Forum,** 82 Cairnhill Rd. (© **65/6737-3448**), operated by a diva of the local scene, also features contemporary Singaporean and ASEAN artworks. If you're in the market for fine arts from the mainland (China, that is), Plum Blossoms, #02-37 **Raffles Hotel Shopping Arcade,** 328 North Bridge Rd. (© **65/6334-1198**), showcases contemporary works.

With the burgeoning collecting mania for Oriental artifacts, paintings, sculpture, calligraphy, and antique furniture, prominent international auction houses **Christie's,** Goodwood Park Hotel, 22 Scotts Rd. (© **65/6235-3828**), and **Sotheby's,** The Regent Singapore, 1 Cuscaden Rd. (© **65/6732-8239**), have established themselves in Singapore.

JEWELRY & ACCESSORIES Crocodile skin products are well made and affordable at **Jurong Reptile Park,** 241 Jalan Ahmad Ibrahim (© **65/6261-8866**), and The Singapore Crocodilarium, 730 East Coast Pkwy., running along East Coast Park (© **65/6447-3722**). They both have showrooms filled with crocodile goods, as well as pelts from other exotic beasts. Jewelry is also a bargain. Gold, which is sold at the day's rate, is fashioned into modern Western styles and into styles that suit Chinese and Indian tastes. Loose stones, either precious or semiprecious, are abundant in many reputable shops, and can be set for you during your stay.

For upmarket jewels and settings, the most trusted dealer in Singapore is **Larry Jewelry (S) Pte. Ltd.,** #01-38 Raffles City Shopping Centre, 252 North Bridge Rd. (© **65/6336-9648**), but be prepared to drop some serious cash.

Peek in the window displays of the gold shops along Serangoon Road and you'll see all kinds of Indian-style gold necklaces and bangles. Each Indian ethnic group has its own traditional patterns, all of them featuring intricate filigree. Indian gold is more reddish in color, and the delicate designs are brilliant and very unusual. The selection at **Mustapha's,** 320 Serangoon Rd. (© **65/6299-2603**), is absolutely mind-blowing. I can't imagine the staggering value of all their merchandise. Enter from the Serangoon Road entrance, which will put you in the jewelry department.

ORIENTAL RUGS Once you've walked on a hand-knotted **Turkoman** in your bare feet, trailed your fingers along the pile of an antique **Heriz,** or admired the sensuous colors of a **Daghostani,** you'll never look at broadloom again with the same forbearance. And best yet, they come in a range of sizes and prices to suit most any room and wallet. Think of your purchase as an investment—even the new carpets coming out of Turkey and other Middle Eastern countries increase in value. (Ask that of your wall-to-wall.) Still don't want to splurge? Check out the "minirugs," which measure about a foot square. They're very inexpensive, fit in your luggage, and, once home, drape nicely over the arm of a sofa or look elegant on the hall table.

Many shops also carry **kilims** (woven carpets). These tribals lend a primitive elegant ambience to most any decorating scheme. Antique camel bags, tent door hangings (how did you think the nomads maintain their privacy?), and other colorful pieces are offered at reasonable prices.

Ask anyone in Singapore where to shop for carpets, and he'll send you to **Hassan's Carpets,** #03-01/06 Tanglin Shopping Centre (© **65/6737-5626**), which has been a fixture in Singapore for generations with a stock of more than US$5 million worth of museum-quality carpets. Proprietor Suliman Hamid is the local authority on carpets, having advised on and supplied the carpets for the restoration of Raffles Hotel. He and his staff know the background of every rug and have wonderful stories to tell. They forego the hard sales pitch for more civilized discourse on carpet appreciation. It's an afternoon well spent.

If you still want to see more carpets, you can take a taxi out to Dempsey Road where you'll find a few warehouses filled with stock.

OUTLET SHOPPING   I've found a couple of shops that sell clothing manufactured locally at prices that make outlet mall in the States seem overpriced—and they sell American sizes. At **Export Fashions**, #01-144 Suntec City Mall (© 65/6333-6106), I've bought **Talbots** dresses, **J. Crew** and **Ungaro** skirts and **CK** tops for between S$17 and S$35 (US$10–US$20). At **Pace Fashions Outlet,** #03-64 Far East Plaza, 14 Scotts Rd. (© 65/6738-7160), I've gotten **Ann Taylor, Saks,** and **Nordstrom** originals—suits, separates, and dresses for anywhere between S$9 and S$61(US$5–US$35).

Cheap shoes are a real find here, you can get sandals and flats for under S$19 (US$11) and dress shoes for as low as S$29 (US$17), in tons of styles. Bargain shoe stores are everywhere, you can begin your search at Far East Plaza, Lucky Plaza and Suntec City.

Discount sporting goods are a find at **Why Pay More?,** #02-57 Suntec City Mall (© 65/6336-7568).

PEWTER   Royal Selangor, the famous Malaysian pewter manufacturer since 1885, rode high on the Malaysian tin business at the turn of the 20th century, pewter being a tin alloy. This firm is based in Kuala Lumpur and has eight showrooms in Singapore. The most centrally located are at #02-38 Raffles City Shopping Centre (© 65/6339-3958), #02-40 Paragon, 290 Orchard Rd. (© 65/6235-6633), and #02-127 Marina Square (© 65/6339-3115).

POTTERY   Antique porcelain items can be found in the many small shops along Pagoda and Trenagganu streets in Chinatown. Beautiful examples of antique reproductions are to be had at the showroom at **Ming Village,** 32 Pandan Rd. (© 65/6265-7711), which is also written up in chapter 5. For modern table settings in traditional Chinese designs, plus numerous curios, check out Toh Foong, 5 Temple St. (© 65/6223-1343).

The ultimate in pottery shopping, however, is a place the locals refer to as the "pottery jungle." **Thow Kwang Industry Pte. Ltd.** is a taxi ride away at 85 Lorong Tawas off Jalan Bahar (© 65/6265-5808). This backwoods place has row after row of pots, lamps, umbrella stands—you name it. There's even a room with antique pieces.

SOUTHEAST ASIAN HANDICRAFTS   Naturally, Southeast Asian handicrafts are all cheaper here than as imports available in the West. I've covered a lot of ground with regard to local and regional handicrafts in "The Shopping Scene, Part 2: Multicultural Shopping" section earlier in this chapter. I've found the best shopping for local treasures is within Chinatown, Kampong Glam, and Little India. Outside of the ethnic quarters, there are a few other interesting places to see. Note, though, that if you'll be traveling to other countries in Southeast Asia, you should probably wait to do your shopping there. The downside of doing this, however, is that sometimes these countries export the finest quality merchandise, saving only the shoddier varieties for domestic sales.

A gold-plated orchid is something you don't find every day, but you do find them every day at **RISIS, Singapore Botanic Gardens** gift shop, Cluny Road (© 65/6475-2319), and #01-084 Suntec City Mall, 3 Temasek Blvd.

(© 65/6338-8250); see "Attractions Outside the Urban Area," in chapter 5 for full gardens information. The process was developed in the 1970s and is exclusive to Singapore. Different orchid species make up the pins, earrings, and pendants, and the choices are extensive.

If unique and comfortable batik fashions sound good to you, head for local clothing designer **Peter Hoe's** boutique, at 30 Victoria St., #01-05 CHIJMES (© 65/6339-6880). This Malaysian fabric and clothing designer fashions very handsome individual fabric patterns pieced together in styles to suit Western wardrobes. His collection of regional silver jewelry is also worth noting.

Singapore After Dark

What do you want to do tonight? Do you want to go out for a cultural experience and find a traditional dance or music performance or a Chinese opera, or do you want to put on your finery and rub elbows with society at the symphony? If it's live performance you're looking for, you have your choice not only of the local dance and theater troupes but of the many West End and Broadway shows that come through on international tours. Or you may want to try a local performance—smaller theater groups have lately been hitting nerves and funny bones through stage portrayals of life in the Garden City. Singapore has been transforming itself into a center for the arts in this part of the world, and is beginning to achieve the level of sophistication you'd come to expect from a Western city.

If partying it up is more your speed, there's all kinds of nighttime revelry going on. Society may seem puritanical during the daylight hours, but once the night comes, the clubs get crazy.

Start at **Boat Quay.** This strip of renovated shophouses turns into a veritable parade of bars, karaoke lounges, discos, and cafes after 9pm. As you stroll along the river, you can hear the hip-hop, reggae, jazz, blues, rap, techno, disco—you name it—pouring from each door. It seems like there's a million places here, and you're bound to find at least some of them appealing.

Upriver you'll find a few more places at Clarke Quay, then further near Robinson Quay until you reach **Mohamed Sultan Road,** a hub of clubs and bars that popped up in the mid-'90s.

Then there's **Orchard Road.** The area around the Scotts Road and Orchard Road intersection has a tremendous number of nightclubs, each with its own favorite clientele and all with high prices of admission. Another fun place with a high concentration of nightlife options is **CHIJMES,** but for the latest trendy joints, check out **Club Street** in Chinatown.

1 Tips on Singapore Nightlife

INFORMATION   Major cultural festivals are highly publicized by the **Singapore Tourism Board (STB),** so one stop by their office will probably provide enough info to fill your evening agenda for your whole trip. Another source is the *Straits Times,* which lists events around town, as well as the *New Paper,* which also lists musical events like local bands and international rock and pop tours. Both of these papers also provide cinema listings and theater reviews.

Theartsmagazine, a bimonthly publication with articles about the local scene plus coming events, is on sale at bookstores and magazine stands for S$5.80 (US$3.30).

TICKETS   Two ticket agents, **TicketCharge** and **Sistic,** handle bookings for almost all theater performances, concert dates, and special events. You can find

Urban Singapore Nightlife

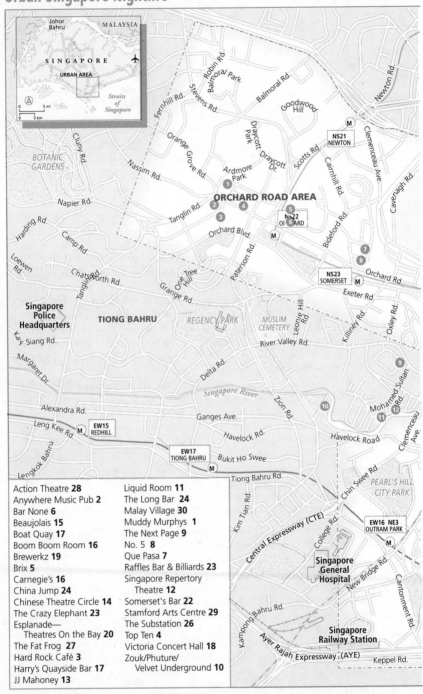

Action Theatre **28**
Anywhere Music Pub **2**
Bar None **6**
Beaujolais **15**
Boat Quay **17**
Boom Boom Room **16**
Brewerkz **19**
Brix **5**
Carnegie's **16**
China Jump **24**
Chinese Theatre Circle **14**
The Crazy Elephant **23**
Esplanade—
   Theatres On the Bay **20**
The Fat Frog **27**
Hard Rock Café **3**
Harry's Quayside Bar **17**
JJ Mahoney **13**

Liquid Room **11**
The Long Bar **24**
Malay Village **30**
Muddy Murphys **1**
The Next Page **9**
No. 5 **8**
Que Pasa **7**
Raffles Bar & Billiards **23**
Singapore Repertory
   Theatre **12**
Somerset's Bar **22**
Stamford Arts Centre **29**
The Substation **26**
Top Ten **4**
Victoria Concert Hall **18**
Zouk/Phuture/
   Velvet Underground **10**

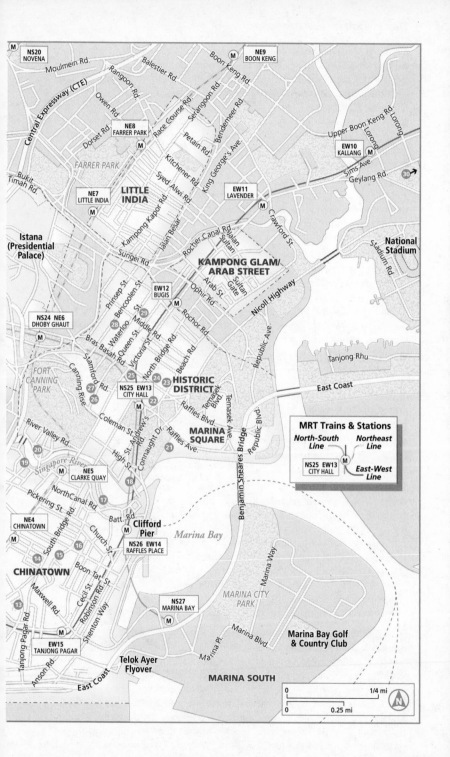

out about schedules before your visit through their websites: www.ticketcharge. net and www.sistic.com.sg. When in Singapore, stop by one of their centrally located outlets to pick up a schedule, or call them for more information. Call TicketCharge at ℂ **65/6296-2929** or head for Centrepoint, Forum—The Shopping Mall, Funan—The IT Mall, Marina Square Shopping Centre, or Tanglin Mall. For **Sistic** bookings call ℂ **65/6348-5555,** or see them at the Victoria Concert Hall Box Office, Parco Bugis Junction, Raffles Shopping Centre, Scotts, Specialists' Shopping Center, Suntec Mall, or Wisma Atria. The STB also carries information about current and coming events.

HOURS   Theater and dance performances can begin anywhere between 7:30 and 9pm. Be sure to call for the exact time. Many bars open in the late afternoon, a few as early as lunchtime. Disco and entertainment clubs usually open around 6pm, but generally don't get lively until 10 or 11pm. Closing time for bars and clubs is at 1 or 2am on weekdays, 3am on weekends.

DRINK PRICES   Because of the government's added tariff, alcoholic beverage prices are high everywhere, whether in a hotel bar or a neighborhood pub. "House pour" drinks (generics) are between S$8 and S$14 (US$4.55–US$8). A glass of house wine will cost between S$10 and S$15 (US$5.70–US$8.55), depending if it's a red or a white. Local draft beer (Tiger), brewed in Singapore, is on average S$10 (US$5.70). Hotel establishments are, on average, the most expensive venues, while stand-alone pubs and cafes are better value. Almost every bar and club has a happy hour in the early evenings and discounts can be up to 50% off for house pours and drafts. Most of the disco and entertainment clubs charge covers, but they will usually include one drink. Hooray for ladies' nights—at least 1 night during the week—when those of the feminine persuasion get in for free.

DRESS CODE   Many clubs will require smart casual attire. Feel free to be trendy, but stay away from shorts, T-shirts, sneakers, and torn jeans. Be forewarned that you may be turned away if not properly dressed. Many locals dress up for their night on the town, either in elegant garb or fashionista threads.

SAFETY   You'll be fairly safe out during the wee hours in most parts of the city, and even a single woman alone has little to worry about. Occasionally, groups of young men may catcall, but by and large those groups are not hanging out in the more cosmopolitan areas. On the weekends, police set up barricades around the city to pick up drunk drivers, so if you rent a car, be careful about your alcohol intake, or appoint a designated driver. Otherwise, you can get home safely in a taxi, which fortunately isn't too hard to find even late at night, with one exception: When Boat Quay clubs close, there's usually a mob of revelers scrambling for cabs. (Note that after midnight, a 50% surcharge is added to the fare, so make sure you don't drink away your ride home!)

2 The Bar & Club Scene

Singaporeans love to go out at night, whether it's to lounge around in a cozy wine bar or to jump around on a dance floor until 3am. And this city has become pretty eclectic in its entertainment choices, so you'll find everything from live jazz to Elvis, from garage rock to techno, world beat, or just plain rock. The truth is, the nightlife is happening. Local celebrities and the young, wealthy, and beautiful are the heroes of the scene, and their quest for the "coolest" spot keeps the club scene on its toes. The listings here are keyed in to help you find the latest or most interesting place. *A tip:* At press time, the most happening bars and clubs were anything on Mohamed Sultan Road and the new Chinese-chic Lan Kwai Fong. Start from there.

BARS

Anywhere Music Pub   This perennial favorite has weathered fashion trends and the economic crisis to become one of the oldest and most established bars in the city. Resident band Tania plays pop and rock covers to packed crowds Monday through Saturday. It's a casual joint, come as you are, and a mixed crowd of mostly 30s and up, locals and foreign expatriates. Hours are Sun–Thurs 6pm–2am; Fri–Sat 6pm–3am. Happy hours held on weekdays 6–9pm. 19 Tanglin Rd. #04-08/08, Tanglin Shopping Centre. ✆ **65/6734-8233.**

Brix   In the basement of the Grand Hyatt Regency, Brix has inherited the spot once reserved for Brannigan's, a rowdy upmarket watering hole and pickup joint. Grand Hyatt decided to clean up its act, and had Brix move in instead. Decidedly more sophisticated than its predecessor, Brix has a new air of class, but somehow lacks a certain seedy spontaneity. Still, it's a nice new place on the scene for those who prefer a more discriminating kind of fun. The Music Bar features live jazz and R&B, while the Wine & Whiskey Bar serves up a fine selection of wines, Scotch, and cognacs. Hours are Sun–Thurs 7pm–2am; Fri–Sat 7pm–3am and there is a nightly happy hour from 7–9pm. Basement, Grand Hyatt Singapore, 10–12 Scotts Rd. ✆ **65/6416-7108.** Cover charge Thurs, Fri, and Sat S$20 (US$11.45) that includes one standard drink.

Carnegie's   Carnegies Rocks. Here's the place where you'll hear rowdy old favorites to make to room shake from dancing and roar with singing, everything from the latest hot pop songs to cheesy old Grease medleys, disco and drinking favorites. Time was, the rowdier girls would jump up on the bar to dance (including yours truly), but a recent controverisal law banning bartop dancing in the city has put a damper on that (at least for now). It's a great time, but it's also a notorious "ang moh" place, *ang moh* being Hokkien for Westerners, so don't count on rubbing elbows with too many locals here. On busy nights sometimes the doorman will charge 10 bucks to let you jump the queue). Hours are Sun–Thurs 11am–2am; Fri–Sat 11am–3am. There is a happy hour daily 11am–9pm and a crazy hour 6–7pm except Sat and Sun. 44-45 Pekin St., #01-01 Far East Sq. ✆ **65/6534-0850.**

The Crazy Elephant   Crazy Elephant is the city's address for blues. Hang out in cooling breezes blowing off the river while listening to classic rock and blues by resident bands. This place has hosted, in addition to the best local and regional guitarists, international great such as Rick Derringer, Eric Burdon, and Walter Trout. It's an unpretentious place to chill out and have a cold one. Beer is reasonably priced as well. Hours are Sun–Thurs 5pm–1am, Fri–Sat 5pm–2am with daily happy hour 5–9pm. 3E River Valley Road, #01-06/07 Traders Market, Clarke Quay. ✆ **65/6337-1990.**

The Fat Frog Café   More a cafe than a bar, Fat Frog draws folks who prefer conversation without intrusive music. The patio at the back of this place stays quiet in the afternoons, and at night fills up, but rarely becomes overcrowded. The main attraction is its location—behind the Substation, a hub for Singapore's visual and performing-arts scene, making this place a good stop after a show. Sometimes you can even run into performers and other majors from the local scene. Inside you'll find a bulletin board promoting current shows, performances, and openings. Around the patio courtyard walls local painters contribute mural work to the decor. There is a limited menu available. Hours are Sun–Thurs 11:30am–midnight; Fri–Sat 11:30am–1am. 45 Armenian St. (behind the Substation). ℂ **65/6338-6201.**

Hard Rock Cafe   The Hard Rock Cafe in Singapore is like the Hard Rock Cafe in your hometown. You probably don't go to that one, so don't bother spending your vacation time in this one either. Not that it's all bad—the Filipino bands are usually pretty good and, of course, so are the burgers. Other than that it's not much more than a tourist pickup joint. Bring mace. There is a cover charge of S$23 (US$13) Fri–Sat only, and includes your first drink. Sun–Mon 1 drink minimum charge. Hours are Sun–Thurs 11am–2am; Fri–Sat 11am–3am. Happy hour is Mon–Sat 4–6pm, Sun 4–6pm and 10:30–2am. #02-01 HPL House, 50 Cuscaden Rd. ℂ **65/6235-5232.**

IndoChine   Richly atmospheric, with graceful Southeast Asian decor, this fashionable lounge drips with exotic charm. Seating areas feel almost like cushiony opium dens, with low benches piled with pillows surrounding small candlelit tables. Music is moody and not too loud to talk over. This is a good place to start exploring all the watering holes along Club Street, and there are a few, all of them pretty hip. 49 Club St. ℂ **65/6323-0503.**

JJ Mahoney   If you're looking for a real bar-type bar, JJ Mahoney comes pretty close. You have the tile floor, the dark wood bar and paneling, stools lining the sides, and everyday people sidling up for another round. The first floor is a nice place to hang out and meet people (until about 10:30pm, when the band kicks in with contemporary but rather loud music), and will broadcast soccer games from time to time. The second floor, up a wide hardwood staircase, has small tables where you can order drinks and play games like Scrabble, Yahtzee, chess, and checkers. The third floor is reserved for KTV, a karaoke lounge where you can sing without worrying about con-women hitting you up for overpriced and watered-down drinks. Hours are Sun–Thurs 5pm–1am; Fri–Sat and the eve of public holidays 5pm–2am. Happy hour is held nightly 5–8pm. 58 Duxton Rd. ℂ **65/6225-6225.**

The Long Bar   Here's a nice little gem of a bar, even if it is touristy and expensive. With tiled mosaic floors, large shuttered windows, electric fans, and punkah fans moving in waves above, Raffles Hotel has tried to retain much of the charm of yesteryear, so you can enjoy a Singapore Sling in its birthplace and take yourself back to when history was made. And truly, the thrill at the Long Bar is tossing back one of these sweet juicy drinks while pondering the Singapore adventures of all the famous actors, writers, and artists who came through here in the first decades of the 20th century. If you're not inspired by the poetry of the moment, stick around and get juiced for the pop/reggae band at 9pm, which is quite good. Hours are Sun–Thurs 11am–1am; Fri–Sat 11am–2am. Happy hour nightly 6–9pm, with special deals on pitchers of beer and some mixed drinks. A Singapore Sling is S$18.30 (US$10), and a Sling with souvenir glass costs S$28 (US$16). Raffles Hotel Arcade, Raffles Hotel, 1 Beach Rd. ℂ **65/6337-1886.**

Muddy Murphys   This is one of a few Irish bars in Singapore. Located on two levels in the shopping mall, on the upper level you have the more conservative business set having drinks after their 9-to-5 gigs, while downstairs the party lasts a little longer and gets a little more lively. Irish music rounds out the ambience created by the mostly Irish imported trappings around the place. Occasionally they'll even have an Irish band. There is a limited menu for lunch, dinner, and snacks. Hours are Sun–Thurs 11am–1am; Fri–Sat 11am–3am. Happy hour is daily 11am–7:30pm (happy hour begins earlier, but the discount is not as great as other places). #B1-01/01-06 Orchard Hotel Shopping Arcade, 442 Orchard Rd. ℂ 65/6735-0400.

The Next Page Few bars stand out for ambience like The Next Page, which is a freaky Chinese dream in an old Singaporean shophouse. Creep through the pintu pagar front door into the main room, its old walls of crumbling stucco washed in sexy Chinese red, and lanterns glowing crimson in the air shaft rising above the island bar. The crowd is mainly young professionals who by late night have been known to dance on the bar (and not only on weekends). The back has a bit more space for seating, darts, and a pool table. There is a small snack menu available. Open daily 3pm–3am. Happy hour daily 3–9pm. 17 Mohamed Sultan Rd. ℂ 65/6235-6967.

No. 5 Down Peranakan Place there are a few bars, one of which is No. 5, a cool, dark place just dripping with Southeast Asian ambience, from its old shophouse exterior to its partially crumbling interior walls hung with rich wood carvings. The hardwood floors and beamed ceilings are complemented by seating areas cozied with Oriental carpets and kilim throw pillows. Upstairs is more conventional table-and-chair seating. The glow of the skylighted air shaft and the whirring fans above make this an ideal place to stop for a cool drink on a hot afternoon. In the evenings, be prepared for a lively mix of people. Open Mon–Thurs noon–2am, Fri–Sat noon–3am, Sun 5pm–2am. Happy hour daily noon–9pm. 5 Emerald Hill. ℂ 65/6732-0818.

MICROBREWERIES

Brewerkz Brewerkz, with outside seating along the river and an airy contemporary style inside—like a giant IKEA room built around brewing kettles and copper pipes—brews the best house beer in Singapore. The bar menu features five tasty brew selections from recipes created by their English brew master: Nut Brown Ale, Red Ale, Wiesen, Bitter, and Indian Pale Ale (which, by the way, has the highest alcohol content). Their American cuisine lunch, dinner, and snack menu is also very good—I recommend planning a meal here as well. Open Sun–Thurs 5pm–1am; Fri–Sat 5pm–3am. Happy hour is held daily 3–9pm with 2-for-1 beers. #01-05 Riverside Point, 30 Merchant Rd. ℂ 65/438-7438.

JAZZ BARS

Harry's Quayside Bar & Upstairs at Harry's Wine Bar The official after-work drink stop for finance professionals from nearby Shenton Way, Harry's biggest claim to fame is that it was bank-buster Nick Leeson's favorite bar. But don't let the power ties put you off. Harry's is a cool place, from airy riverside seating, to cozy tables next to the stage. Harry's is known for its live jazz and R&B music, which is always good. Of all the choices along Boat Quay, Harry's remains the most classy; and even though it's also the most popular, you can usually get a seat. Dig their Sunday jazz brunches. Upstairs, the wine bar is very laid back, with plush sofas and dimly lit seating areas. Look for Harry's latest installment, scheduled to open in early 2003 at The Esplanade. It's being touted as the hottest hub for musicians and other artiste-types. Open Sun–Thurs 11am–1am; Fri–Sat 11am–2am. Happy hour daily 11am–9pm. 28 Boat Quay. ℂ 65/6538-3029.

Raffles Bar & Billiards   Talk about a place rich with the kind of elegance only history can provide. Raffles Bar & Billiards began as a bar in 1896 and over the decades has been transformed to perform various functions as the hotel's needs dictated. In its early days, legend has it that a patron shot the last tiger in Singapore under a pool table here. Whether or not the tiger part is true, one of its two billiards tables is an original piece, still in use after 100 years. In fact, many of the fixtures and furniture here are original Raffles antiques, including the lights above the billiards tables and the scoreboards, and are marked with small brass placards. In the evenings, a jazzy little trio shakes the ghosts out of the rafters, while from 6pm to 1am nightly people lounge around enjoying single malts, cognacs, coffee, port, Champagne, chocolates, and imported cigars. Expect to drop a small fortune. Open daily 11:30am–12:30am. Raffles Hotel, 1 Beach Rd. © 65/6331-1746.

Somerset's Bar   This huge hotel lounge can accommodate large crowds very comfortably. Good thing, as the place serves quite a lot of patrons, mostly jazz lovers who come for the best live jazz in the city. They feature at least two sets of live music every night: country, pop, and rock from 6:15 to 8:15pm except Saturday, and a jazz set from 9pm to around 1am every night. From time to time they've hosted internationally renowned performers like bassist Eldee Young, pianist Judy Roberts, and vocalist Nancy Kelly. Call ahead to find out their schedule of performances, and plan some time here for a nice evening in their relaxing environment. Open daily 5pm–2am. Happy hour 5–8:30pm daily. The Westin Stamford and Westin Plaza hotels, 2 Stamford Rd. © 65/6431-5332.

CLUBS

Bar None   In Singapore's trendy club scene, nightclubs have been known to come and go. Bar None is one place that has enjoyed steady success, probably because they do a great job keeping up with their patrons' needs, with regularly scheduled theme parties and comedy nights. Resident band Energy is the best club band in town, playing a high-voltage mix of R&B, Top-40 and rock. Be prepared to queue up on weekends. Hours are Tue–Sun 7pm–3am, Mon 7pm–2am. Happy hour is 7–9pm. Basement Marriott Hotel, 320 Orchard Road. © 65/ 6831-4656. Cover Fri–Sat S$26 (US$15), includes 1 drink.

China Jump Bar & Grill   China Jump combines a disco, bar, and restaurant—sounds tame, but this place has been known to hop. It's especially famous for its Wednesday "Babe Central Night" that draws hordes of women after office hours. On any night, however, you can count on a fun crowd, dancing to pop and dance music. Restaurant cuisine is a passable American and Mexican grill offering, with huge portions. Open daily 5pm–3am. No happy hour. 30 Victoria St., #B1-07/08 CHIJMES Fountain Court. © 65/6338-9388. Cover Wed Ladies' Night, men pay S$18 (US$10). Cover Fri–Sat S$18 (US$10) for everybody.

Liquid Room   Liquid Room was one of the first dance clubs in Singapore to spin techno, trance, and house music nightly. Local and guest DJs are very selective about the music they play, highlighting the best of each genre. The upstairs dance floor is only open Wednesdays through Saturdays. Downstairs, a moody lounge provides some down time. The crowd here is young and energetic. Open daily 7pm–3am. There is a happy hour daily 7–9pm. 76 Robertson Quay, Evason Hotel. © 65/6333-8117.

Top Ten   It's one of the sleazier joints in Singapore, and does a booming business. The huge space is like an auditorium, with a stage and dance floor at one end, seating areas on levels grading up to the top of the other end, and a lighted cityscape scene surrounding the whole thing. A cover band plays three sets of pop 7 days a week, but people don't come here for the decor or even the music: Top Ten is a notorious pickup joint for Asian women. Gentlemen, you'll be buying drinks all night. Open daily 5pm–3am with a happy hour daily 9–11pm. #04-35/36 Orchard Towers, 400 Orchard Rd. © 65/6732-3077. Cover Fri–Sat S$18 (US$10), includes 1 drink.

Zouk/Phuture/Velvet Underground   Singapore's first innovative danceteria, Zouk introduced the city to house music, which throbs nightly in its cavernous disco, comprised of three warehouses joined together. They play the best in modern music, so even if you're not much of a groover you can still have fun watching the party from the many levels that tower above the dance floor. If you need a bit more intimacy in your nightlife, Velvet Underground, within the Zouk complex, drips in red velvet and soft lighting—a good complement to the more soulful sounds spinning here. The newer addition to Zouk, Phuture, draws a younger, more hip-hop-loving crowd than VU. Including the wine bar outside, Zouk is basically your one-stop shopping for a party; and in Singapore, this place is legendary. Call for cover charges. All clubs are open 6pm–3am. Jiak Kim St. © 65/738-2988. Payment of highest cover charge among the 3 clubs in the complex allows admission to the other clubs as well; otherwise, additional charges will incur when moving between clubs.

CABARET

Boom Boom Room   Singapore's fun night out with female impersonators and somewhat bawdy vaudeville-style acts. Local TV stars Kumar and Leena perform regularly, in elaborate costumes, to Japanese and Bollywood hits in between bawdy jokes and audience participation. Drinks are moderately priced. Hours are Sun–Thurs 8:30pm–2am; Fri–Sat 8:30pm–3am. 130-132 Amoy St., Far East Square, © 65/6435-0030. Cover S$20 (US$11) weekdays; S$25 (US$14) weekends.

GAY NIGHTSPOTS

It seems a few of Singapore's better known gay and lesbian spots have closed down in the past couple of years, but new places are popping up regularly. The Web has listings at www.utopia-asia.com/tipsing.htm. For the latest info, I'd recommend one of the chat rooms suggested at the address above, and talk to the experts. Velvet Underground, part of the Zouk complex (see above), welcomes a mixed clientele of gays, lesbians, and straight folks. In addition to the places I've listed below, there are a couple of gay bars that have asked to remain unlisted in this book, so ask around for a better sense of the scene in Singapore.

WINE BARS

Beaujolais   This little gem of a place, in a shophouse built on a hill, is smaller than small, but its charm makes it a favorite for loyal regulars. Two tables outside (on the Five-Foot-Way, which serves more as a patio than a sidewalk) and two tables inside doesn't seem like much room, but there's more seating upstairs. They believe that wine should be affordable, and so their many labels tend to be more moderately priced per glass and bottle. Hours are Mon–Thurs 11am–midnight; Fri 11am–2am; Sat 6pm–2am. Happy hour is held from opening until 9pm. 1 Ann Siang Hill. © 65/6224-2227.

Que Pasa   One of the more mellow stops along Peranakan Place, this little wine bar serves up a collection of some 70 to 100 labels with plenty of atmosphere and a nice central location. It's another bar in a shophouse, but this one has as its centerpiece a very unusual winding stairway up the air shaft to the level above. Wine bottles and artwork line the walls. In the front you can order Spanish-style finger food—tapas, anyone?—and cigars. The VIP club on the upper floor has the look and feel of a formal living room, complete with wing chairs and board games. Hours are Sun–Thurs 6pm–2am; Fri–Sat 6pm–3am. 7 Emerald Hill. © 65/235-6626.

3 The Performing Arts

Singapore is not a cultural backwater. Professional and amateur theater companies, dance troupes, opera companies, and musical groups offer a wide variety of not only Asian performances, but Western as well. Broadway road shows don't stop in San Francisco, where the road ends, but continue on to include Singapore in their itineraries, and international stars like Domingo, Pavarotti, Yo Yo Ma, Winston Marsalis, Tito Puente, and Michael Jackson have come to town. International stars make up only a small portion of the performance scene, though. Singapore theater comprises four distinct language groups—English, Chinese, Malay, and Tamil—and each maintains its own voice and culture.

CLASSICAL PERFORMANCES

The **Singapore Symphony Orchestra** performs regularly in its new home at Esplanade—Theatres On the Bay, with regular special guest appearances by international celebrities. For information about the orchestra, check out www.sso.org.sg, or for performance dates see www.esplanade.som.

The **Singapore Lyric Opera,** Stamford Arts Centre, 155 Waterloo St. #03-06 (© 65/336-1929), also appears regularly. For the millennium, they staged the ever-popular **Die Fledermaus** with local talents. Call them for upcoming schedules, or call Sistic.

The **Singapore Chinese Orchestra,** the only professional Chinese orchestra in Singapore, has won several awards for its classic Chinese interpretations. They perform every 2 weeks at a variety of venues (including outdoor concerts at the Botanic Gardens). Contact them c/o People's Association, Block B, Room 5, No. 9 Stadium Link (© 65/440-3839; www.sco-music.org.sg). Ticket sales are handled by Sistic.

THEATER

Most international companies will perform at the new **Esplanade—Theatres On the Bay** (1 Esplanade Dr., 10-min. walk from City Hall MRT; © 65/6828-8222; www.esplanade.com). Smaller shows are staged at the **Victoria Concert Hall,** 2nd floor Victoria Memorial Hall, 11 Empress Place, (© 65/338-6125). **Sistic** (© 65/6348-5555) handles bookings for both venues.

A few local companies are quite noteworthy. Granted, theater is new to Singaporeans; however, many local playwrights have emerged to capture life here (with some hilarious interpretations), using local stage talents. **ACTION Theatre,** 42 Waterloo St. (© 65/6837-0842), is one of the best companies to capture poignant and funny social themes, many of which cross-cultural barriers. **The Necessary Stage,** 126 Cairnhill Arts Centre, Cairnhill Road (© 65/6738-6355), blazed trails for the local performing arts scene after staging productions that touched tender nerves for the community, including a startlingly frank monologue by the first Singaporean to publicly declare his struggle with AIDS.

The **Singapore Repertory Theatre**, DBS Arts Centre, 20 Merbau Rd., Robertson Quay (© **65/6733-0005**), is another company to watch; in 2002 they staged Art, the award-winning West End and Broadway hit. Also check out the many events at **The Substation,** 45 Armenian St. (© **65/6337-7800;** www.sub station.org), which offers its space to many smaller troupes, plus performance artists.

CULTURAL SHOWS

Once upon a time, **Cantonese opera** could be seen under tents on street corners throughout the city. These days, local and visiting companies still perform, but very sporadically. For a performance you can count on, the **Chinese Theatre Circle,** #5 Smith St. (© **65/6323-4862**), has a 2-hour show on Friday and Saturdays with excerpts from the most famous and beloved tales and explanations of the craft. Come at 7pm for the 2-hour show with dinner, or at 8pm to catch the last half with tea only. Tickets are S$35 (US$20) for the former and S$20 (US$11) for the latter.

If you're looking for something with a little Malay flavor, head for **Malay Village,** 39 Geylang Serai (© **65/748-4700**), on weekends. Every Saturday and Sunday at 5pm (except during the fasting month of Ramadan), you can enjoy Indo-Malay dancers performing in traditional costume accompanied by a live gamelan orchestra. Come on Saturdays for the Kuda Kepang, a traditional dance from Johor in southern Malaysia. Featuring male dancers on wooden horses, this long performance is well worth the wait. During the grand finale, the dancers walk on glass, eat glass, and tear coconuts with their teeth. It's all real, and highly recommended.

8

Planning Your Trip to Malaysia

Compared with spicy Thailand to the north and cosmopolitan Singapore to the south, Malaysia is a relative secret to many from the West, and most travelers to Southeast Asia skip over it, opting for more heavily traversed routes.

Boy, are they missing out. Those who venture here wander through streets awash with international influences from colonial times and trek through mysterious rainforests and caves, often without another tourist in sight. They relax peacefully under palms on lazy white beaches that fade into blue, blue waters. They spy the bright colors of batik sarongs hanging to dry in the breeze. They hear the melodic drone of the Muslim call to prayer seeping from exotic mosques. They taste culinary masterpieces served in modest local shops—from Malay with its deep mellow spices to succulent seafood punctuated by brilliant chili sauces. In Malaysia, I'm always thrilled to witness life without the distracting glare of the tourism industry, and I leave impressed by how accessible Malaysia is to outsiders while remaining true to its heritage.

Malaysia just doesn't get the tourism press it deserves, but it's not because foreign travelers aren't welcome. True, the Malaysian Tourism Board has almost no international advertising campaign—and you'll be hard-pressed to get any useful information out of them—but everyone from government officials in Kuala Lumpur to boat hands in Penang seems delighted to see the smiling face of a traveler who has discovered just how beautiful their country is.

Chapter 9 covers the major destinations of peninsular Malaysia. We begin with the country's capital, Kuala Lumpur, then tour the peninsula's west coast—the cities of Johor Bahru, Malacca (Melaka), the hill resorts at Cameron and Genting Highlands, plus islands like the popular Penang and the luxurious Langkawi. Chapter 10 takes you up the east coast of the peninsula, through resort areas such as Desaru, Mersing, Kuantan, Cherating, and the small and charming Tioman Island, all the way north to the culturally stimulating cities of Kuala Terengganu and Kota Bharu. My coverage also includes Taman Negara National Park, peninsular Malaysia's largest national forest. Finally, in chapter 11, we cross the South China Sea to the island of Borneo, where the Malaysian states of Sarawak and Sabah feature Malaysia's most impressive forests as well as unique and diverse cultures.

Malaysia is easily accessible to the rest of the world through its international airport in Kuala Lumpur. Or if you want to hop from another country in the region, daily flights to Malaysia's many smaller airports give you access to all parts of the country, and you can also travel by car, bus, or train from Singapore or Thailand. In this section, I'll run through your options and get you started.

1 Malaysia's Regions in Brief

Malaysia's territory covers peninsular Malaysia—bordering Thailand in the north just across from Singapore in the south—and two states on the island of Borneo, Sabah and Sarawak, approximately 240km (150 miles) east

Peninsular Malaysia

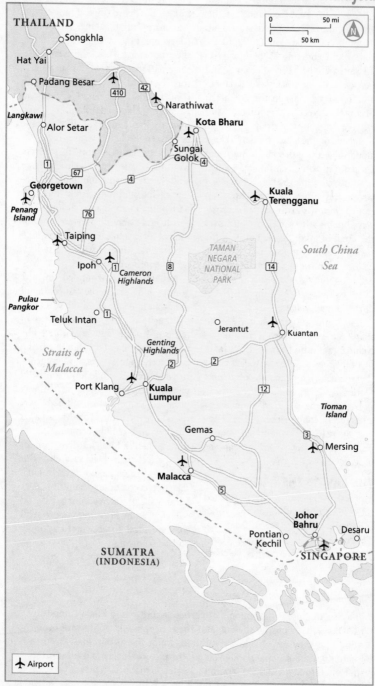

THAILAND

Songkhla

Hat Yai

Padang Besar

410 42

Langkawi

Narathiwat

Alor Setar

Kota Bharu

Sungai Golok

1 67 4

4

Georgetown

Kuala Terengganu

Penang Island

76

Taiping

South China Sea

Ipoh

Cameron Highlands

1

8

TAMAN NEGARA NATIONAL PARK

14

Pulau Pangkor

1

Teluk Intan

Jerantut

Kuantan

Straits of Malacca

Genting Highlands

2

2

12

Port Klang

Kuala Lumpur

Tioman Island

Gemas

3

Mersing

Malacca

5

Johor Bahru

Desaru

Pontian Kechil

SUMATRA (INDONESIA)

SINGAPORE

✈ Airport

across the South China Sea. All thirteen of its states total 336,700 sq. km (202,020 sq. miles) of land. Of this area, Peninsular Malaysia makes up about 465,000 sq. km (134,680 sq. miles) and contains 11 of Malaysia's 13 states: Kedah, Perlis, Penang, and Perak are in the northwest; Kelantan and Terengganu are in the northeast; Selangor, Negeri Sembilan, and Melaka are about midway down the peninsula on the western side; Pahang, along the east coast, sprawls inward to cover most of the central area (which is mostly forest preserve); and Johor covers the entire southern tip from east to west, with two vehicular causeways linking it to Singapore, just over the Strait of Johor. Kuala Lumpur, the nation's capital, appears on a map to be located in the center of the state of Selangor, but it is actually a federal district similar to Washington, D.C., in the United States.

On Borneo, Sarawak and Sabah share the landmass with Indonesia's Kalimantan. Also sharing the island, in a tiny nook on the Sarawak coast, is the tiny oil-rich Sultanate of Brunei Darussalam.

Back on the peninsula, the major cities can be found closer to the coastline, many having built on old trade or mining settlements, usually near one of Malaysia's many rivers.

THE LAY OF THE LAND

Tropical evergreen forests, estimated to be some of the oldest in the world, cover more than 70% of Malaysia. The country's diverse terrain allows for a range of forest types, such as montane forests, sparsely wooded tangles at higher elevations; lowland forests, the dense tropical jungle type; mangrove forests along the waters' edge; and peat swamp forests along the waterways. On the peninsula, three national forests—Taman Negara (or "National Forest") and Kenong Rimba Park, both inland, and Endau Rompin National Park, located toward the southern end of the peninsula—welcome visitors regularly, for quiet nature walks to observe wildlife or hearty adventures like white-water rafting, mountain climbing, caving, and jungle trekking. Similarly, the many national forests of Sabah and Sarawak provide a multitude of memorable experiences, which can include brushes with the indigenous peoples of the forests.

Malaysia is surrounded by the South China Sea on the east coast and the Strait of Malacca on the west, and the waters off the peninsula vary in terms of sea life (and beach life). The waters off the east coast house a living coral reef, good waters, and gorgeous tropical beaches, while more southerly parts host beach resort areas. By way of contrast, the surf in southern portions of the Strait of Malacca is choppy and cloudy from shipping traffic—hardly ideal for diving or for the perfect Bali Hai vacation. But once you get as far north as Penang, the waters become beautiful again. Meanwhile, the sea coast of Sabah and Sarawak count numerous resort areas that are ideal for beach vacationing and scuba diving.

Tips **Abbreviating Malaysia**

The first tip here is that people are always abbreviating Kuala Lumpur to KL. Okay, that's pretty obvious. But these people will abbreviate everything else they can get away with. So, Johor Bahru becomes JB, Kota Bharu KB, Kota Kinabalu, KK—you get the picture. Malaysia itself is often shortened to M'sia and Singapore to S'pore. To make it easier for you, the only shortened version I've used in this book is KL.

East Malaysia

2 Visitor Information

The **Malaysia Tourism Board (MTB)** can provide some information by way of pamphlets and advice before your trip, but keep in mind they are not yet as sophisticated as the Singapore Tourism Board. Much of the information they provide is vague, broad-stroke descriptions with few concrete details that are useful for the traveler. Overseas offices are located as follows.

The nationwide tourist hot line is ℰ **1300/88-5776.** The official website of the Malaysia Tourism Board is www.tourismmalaysia.gov.my.

3 Entry Requirements & Customs

ENTRY REQUIREMENTS

To enter the country you must have a valid passport. Citizens of the United States do not need visas for tourism and business visits, and upon entry are granted a Social/Business Visit Pass good for up to 3 months. Citizens of Canada, Australia, New Zealand, and the United Kingdom can also enter the country without a visa, and will be granted up to 30 days pass upon entry. For other countries, please consult the nearest Malaysian consulate before your trip for visa regulations. Also note: Travelers holding Israeli passports are not permitted to travel within Malaysia (likewise, Malaysians are forbidden from traveling to Israel).

While in Malaysia, should you need to contact an official representative from your home country, the following contact information in Kuala Lumpur can help you out: **United States Embassy** © 03/2168-5000; **Canadian High Commission** © 03/2718-8333; **Australian High Commission** © 03/2146-5555; **New Zealand High Commission** © 03/2078-2533; and **the British High Commission** © 03/2148-2122.

If you are arriving from an area in which yellow fever has been reported, you will be required to show proof of yellow fever vaccination. Contact your nearest MTB office to research the specific areas that fall into this category.

CUSTOMS REGULATIONS

With regard to currency, you can bring into the country as many foreign currency notes or traveler's checks as you please, but you are not allowed to leave the country with more foreign currency or traveler's checks than you had when you arrived.

Social visitors can enter Malaysia with 1 liter of hard alcohol and one carton of cigarettes without paying duty—anything over that amount is subject to local taxes. Prohibited items include firearms and ammunition, daggers and knives, and pornographic materials. Be advised that, similar to Singapore, Malaysia enforces a very strict drug abuse policy that includes the death sentence for convicted drug traffickers.

4 Money

CURRENCY

Malaysia's currency is the **Malaysian ringgit.** It's also commonly referred to as the Malaysian dollar, but prices are marked as RM (a designation I've used throughout this book). Notes are issued in denominations of RM2, RM5, RM10, RM20, RM50, RM100, RM500, and RM1000. One ringgit is equal to 100 sen. Coins come in denominations of 1, 5, 10, 20, and 50 sen, and there's also a 1-ringgit coin.

Following the dramatic decline in the value of its currency during the Southeast Asian economic crisis, the Malaysian government has sought to stabilize the ringgit to ward off currency speculation by pegging the ringgit at an artificial exchange rate. At the

Malaysian Ringgit Conversion Chart

RM	US$	C$	A$	NZ$	U.K£
.10	.03	.04	.05	.05	.02
.20	.05	.08	.09	.11	.03
.50	.13	.20	.24	.26	.08
1.00	.26	.41	.47	.53	.17
2.00	.53	.82	.94	1.05	.34
5.00	1.32	2.05	2.35	2.64	.84
10.00	2.63	4.10	4.70	5.27	1.68
20.00	5.26	8.19	9.41	10.54	3.36
50.00	13.16	20.48	23.52	26.36	8.41
100.00	26.32	40.96	47.04	52.72	16.82
500.00	131.58	204.81	235.20	263.59	84.11
1000.00	263.16	409.60	470.40	527.15	168.23

What Things Cost in Kuala Lumpur	RM	US$
Taxi from the airport to city center	RM63–RM88	US$16–US$23
Local telephone call (3 min.)	RM20	US$5
Double room at an expensive hotel (J. W. Marriott)	RM300	US$79
Double room at a moderate hotel (Concorde Hotel)	RM200	US$53
Double room at an inexpensive hotel (Swiss-Inn)	RM140	US$37
Dinner for one at an expensive restaurant (Ching Yuen Lai)	RM70–RM100	US$18–US$26
Dinner for one at a moderate restaurant (Legends Natural Cuisine)	RM50–RM70	US$13–US$18
Dinner for one at an inexpensive restaurant (Top Hats)	RM25	US$6.60
Glass of beer	RM15–RM20	US$4–US$5
Coca-Cola	RM2–RM6	US$.50–US$1.60
Cup of coffee at common coffee shop	RM1.50	US$.40
Cup of coffee in a hotel	RM6	US$1.60
Roll of 36-exposure color film	RM15	US$4
Admission to the National Museum		
Movie ticket	RM8	US$2.10

time of writing, exchange rates were RM3.80 to US$1.

Currency can be changed at banks and hotels, but you'll get a more favorable rate if you go to one of the money-changers that seem to be everywhere; in shopping centers, in little lanes, and in small stores—just look for signs. They are often men in tiny booths with a lit display on the wall behind them showing the exchange rate. All major currencies are generally accepted, and there is never a problem with the U.S. dollar.

ATMS

Kuala Lumpur, Penang, and Johor Bahru have quite a few automated teller machines (ATMs) scattered around, but they are few and far between in the smaller towns. In addition, some ATMs do not accept credit cards or debit cards from your home

bank. I have found that debit cards on the MasterCard/Cirrus or VISA/PLUS networks are almost always accepted at **Maybank,** with at least one location in every major town. Cash is dispensed in ringgit deducted from your account at the day's rate.

TRAVELER'S CHECKS

Generally, travelers to Malaysia will never go wrong with American Express and Thomas Cook traveler's checks, which can be cashed at banks, hotels, and licensed money changers. Unfortunately, they are often not accepted at smaller shops. Even in some big restaurants and department stores, many cashiers don't know how to process these checks, which might lead to a long and frustrating wait. For more on traveler's checks see chapter 2, "Planning Your Trip to Singapore."

CREDIT CARDS

Credit cards are widely accepted at hotels and restaurants, and at many shops as well. Most popular are American Express, MasterCard, and Visa. Some banks may also be willing to advance cash against your credit card, but you have to ask around because this service is not available everywhere.

In Malaysia, to report a lost or stolen card, call American Express via the nearest **American Express** representative office (see individual city listings), or the head office in Kuala Lumpur (© 603/2026-1770); for **MasterCard Emergency Assistance for International Visitors** call © 800/88-4594; and for **Visa Emergency Assistance** call © 800/80-1066. Both numbers are toll-free from anywhere in the country. For more on credit cards and what to do if your wallet gets stolen, see chapter 2.

5 When to Go

There are **two peak seasons** in Malaysia, one in winter and another in summer. The peak winter tourist season falls roughly from the beginning of December to the end of January, covering the major winter holidays—Christmas, New Year's Day, Chinese New Year, and Hari Raya. These dates can change according to the full moon, which dictates the exact dates of the Chinese New year and Hari Raya holidays. Note that due to the monsoon at this time (Nov–Mar), the east coast of peninsular Malaysia is rainy and the waters are rough. Resort areas, especially Tioman, are deserted and oftentimes closed. Tourist traffic slows down from February through the end of May, then picks up again in June. The peak summer season falls in the months of June, July, and August, and can last into mid-September. During this period hotels are booked solid with families from the Middle East as this is school holiday season for many of the region's countries. After September it's quiet again until December. Both seasons experience approximately equal tourist traffic, but in summer months that traffic may ebb and flow.

CLIMATE

Climate considerations will play a role in your plans. If you plan to visit any of the east coast resort areas, the low season is between November and March, when the monsoon tides make the water too choppy for water sports and beach activities. On the west coast, the rainy season is from April through May, and again from October through November.

The temperature is basically static year-round. Daily averages are between 67°F and 90°F (21°C and 32°C). Temperatures in the hill resorts get a little cooler, averaging 67°F (21°C) during the day and 50°F (10°C) at night.

HOLIDAYS

During Malaysia's official public holidays, expect government offices to be closed, as well as some shops and restaurants, depending on the ethnicity of the shop owner or restaurant owner. **Hari Raya Puasa** and **Chinese New Year** fall within a month or two of each other, during these holidays can expect many shop and restaurant closings. However, during these holidays, look out for special sales and celebrations. Also count on public parks, shopping malls, and beaches to be more crowded during public holidays, as locals will be taking advantage of their time off.

Official public holidays fall as follows: Hari Raya Aidil Fitri (Dec or Jan), New Year's Day (Jan 1), Chinese New Year (Jan or Feb), Hari-Raya Aidil-Adha (Mar or Apr), Wesak Day (May), Prophet Muhammad's

Birthday (June 26), National Day (Aug 31), Deepavali (Oct or Nov) and Christmas (Dec 25). Where general dates are given above, expect these holidays to shift from year to year depending on the lunar calendar. The MTB can help you with exact dates as you plan your trip. In addition, each state has a public holiday to celebrate the birthday of the state sultan.

6 Insurance, Health & Safety

HEALTH

The **tap water** in Kuala Lumpur is supposedly potable, but I don't recommend drinking it—in fact, I don't recommend drinking tap water anywhere in Malaysia. Bottled water is inexpensive enough and readily available at convenience stores and food stalls. Food prepared in hawker centers is generally safe—I have yet to experience trouble and I'll eat almost anywhere. If you buy fresh fruit, wash it well with bottled water and carefully peel the skin off before eating it.

Malaria has not been a major threat in most parts of Malaysia, even Malaysian Borneo. **Dengue fever,** on the other hand, which is also carried by mosquitoes, remains a constant threat in most areas, especially rural parts. Dengue, if left untreated, can cause fatal internal hemorrhaging, so if you come down with a sudden fever or skin rash, consult a physician immediately. There are no prophylactic treatments for dengue; the best protection is to wear plenty of insect repellent. Choose a product that contains DEET or is specifically formulated to be effective in the tropics.

SAFETY/CRIME

While you'll find occasional news reports about robberies in the countryside, there's not a whole lot of crime going on, especially crime that would impact your trip. There's very little crime against tourists like pickpocketing and purse slashing. Still, hotels without in-room safes will keep valuables in the hotel safe for you. Be careful when traveling on overnight trains and buses where there are great opportunities for theft (many times by fellow tourists, believe it or not). Keep your valuables close to you as you sleep.

For further health and insurance and safety information, see chapter 2.

7 Getting There

BY PLANE

Malaysia has five international airports—at Kuala Lumpur, Penang, Langkawi, Kota Kinabalu and Kuching—and 14 domestic airports at locations that include Johor Bahru, Kota Bharu, Kuantan, and Kuala Terengganu. Specific airport information is listed with coverage of each city.

A passenger service charge, or **airport departure tax,** is levied on all

---

Tips **Travel Warning**

Under U.S. law, insurance companies are not required to cover any medical expenses incurred in countries on the **State Department's Travel Advisory List,** even if their policies indicate they will over out-of-country medical expenses. Some supplemental carriers (such as the ones listed in this chapter) will sell travelers coverage for these areas. You can view the Travel Advisory List at http://travel.state.gov/warnings_list.html).

flights. A tax of RM6 (US$1.58) for domestic flights and RM45 (US$12) for international flights is usually included when you pay for your ticket.

Few Western carriers fly directly to Malaysia. If Malaysian Airlines does not have suitable routes directly from your home country, you'll have to contact another airline to work out a route that connects to one of Malaysia Airline's routes. I have found Malaysia Airlines service to be of a very good standard, not to mention they have possibly the lowest rates to Southeast Asia from North American destinations.

FROM THE UNITED STATES Malaysia Airlines (© 800/552-9264) flies at least once daily from Los Angeles to Kuala Lumpur, and three times a week from New York.

FROM CANADA North American carriers will have to connect with a Malaysian Airlines flight, either in East Asia or in Europe.

FROM THE UNITED KINGDOM Malaysia Airlines (© 0171/341-2020) has two daily nonstop flights from London Heathrow airport, operating domestic connections from Glasgow, Edinburgh, Teesside, Leeds Bradford, and Manchester. **British Airways** (© 0345/222111, a local call from anywhere within the U.K.) departs London to KL daily, except on Mondays and Fridays.

FROM AUSTRALIA Malaysia Airlines (© 02/132627) flies directly to Kuala Lumpur from Perth, Adelaide, Brisbane, Darwin, Sydney and Melbourne, and Cairns. **Quantas Airlines** (© 02/131211) provides service from Sydney to KL on Tuesday, Friday, and Saturday.

FROM NEW ZEALAND Malaysia Airlines (© 09/373-2741 or 0800/657-472) flies a direct route from Auckland.

BY TRAIN

FROM SINGAPORE The Keretapi Tanah Melayu Berhad (KTM), Malaysia's rail system, runs express and local trains that connect the cities along the west coast of Malaysia with Singapore to the south and Thailand to the north. Trains depart three times daily from the **Singapore Railway Station** (© 65/6222-5165), on Keppel Road in Tanjong Pagar, not far from the city center. About five daily trains to Johor Bahru cost S$4.20 (US$2.50) for first-class passage, S$1.90 (US$1.15) for second class, and S$1.10 (US65¢) for third class for the half-hour journey. **Johor Bahru's train station** is very centrally located at Jalan Campbell (© 07/223-4727), and taxis are easy to find. Trains to Kuala Lumpur depart five times daily for fares from S$60 (US$36) for first class, S$26 (US$16) for second class, and S$15 (US$8.90) for third. The trip takes around 6 hours. Kuala Lumpur's KL Sentral railway station is a 10-minute taxi ride from the center of town, and is connected to the Putra LRT, KL Monorail city public transportation trains, and the Express Rail Link (ERL) to Kuala Lumpur International Airport (KLIA).

FROM THAILAND KTM's international service departs from the **Hua Lamphong Railway Station** (© 662/223-7010 or 662/223-7020) in Bangkok, with operations to Hua Hin, Surat Thani, Nakhon Si Thammarat, and Hat Yai in Thailand's southern peninsula. The final stop in Malaysia is at Butterworth (Penang), so passage to KL will require you to catch a connecting train onward. The daily service departs at 3:15pm and takes approximately 22 hours from Bangkok to Butterworth. There is no first- or third-class service on this train, only air-conditioned second class; upper birth goes for about US$20, and lower is US$23.

For a fascinating journey from Thailand, you can catch the **Eastern & Orient Express (E&O),** which operates a route between Bangkok, Kuala Lumpur, and Singapore. Traveling in the luxurious style for which the Orient Express is renowned, you'll finish the entire journey in about 42 hours. Compartments are classed as Sleeper (approximately US$1,490 per person double occupancy), State (US$2,200 per person double occupancy), and Presidential (US$3,000 per person double occupancy). All fares include meals on the train. Overseas reservations for the E&O Express can be made through a travel agent or, from the United States and Canada call ✆ **800/524-2420,** from Australia ✆ 3/9699-9766, and from the United Kingdom ✆ 0207/805-5100. From Singapore, Malaysia, and Thailand contact the E&O office in Singapore at ✆ 65/6392-3500.

BY BUS

From Singapore, there are many bus routes to Malaysia. The easiest depart from the Johor-Singapore bus terminal at the corner of Queen and Arab streets. Buses to Kuala Lumpur leave three times daily and cost S$25. Contact **The Singapore-KL bus service** at ✆ 65/6292-8254. Buses to Johor Bahru and Malacca can also be picked up at this terminal, leaving at regular intervals throughout the day. Call ✆ 65/6292-8149 for buses to Johor Bahru (S$2.10/US$1.20)) and ✆ 65/6293-5915 for buses to Malacca (S$11/US$6.30). If you wish to travel by bus to a smaller destination, the best way is to hop a bus to Johor Bahru and then transfer to a bus to your final stop.

By the way, it is possible to take local SBS bus service #170 between Singapore and Johor Bahru, which is the cheapest way to go, but really I don't recommend it. During peak travel hours I've seen the bus queues snaking for miles at the immigration checkpoints and thought, "Thank God I'm not those guys."

From Thailand, you can grab a bus in either Bangkok or Hat Yai (in the southern part of the country) heading for Malaysia. I don't recommend the bus trip from Bangkok. It's just far too long a journey to be confined to a bus. You're better off taking the train. From Hat Yai, many buses leave regularly to northern Malaysian destinations, particularly Butterworth (Penang).

BY TAXI (FROM SINGAPORE)

From the Johor-Singapore bus terminal at Queen and Arab streets, the **Singapore Johor Taxi Operators Association** (✆ **65/6296-7054**) can drive you to Johor Bahru for S$28 (US$16) if you get to the terminal yourself, or S$40 (US$23) if you ask to be picked up at your hotel.

BY CAR

For convenience, driving to Malaysia from Singapore can't be beat. You can go where you want to go, when you want to go, and without the hassle of public transportation—but it is quite expensive. Cars can be rented in Singapore (see chapter 2 for details), then driven to and even dropped off in Malaysia. A slightly cheaper option is taking the ferry from Singapore to Johor and renting there.

8 Getting Around

The modernization of Malaysia has made travel here—whether it's by plane, train, bus, taxi, or self-driven car—easier and more convenient than ever. Malaysia Airlines has service to every major destination within the peninsula and East Malaysia. Buses have a massive web of routes between every city and town. Train service up the western coast and out to the east provides even more options. And a unique travel offering—the outstation taxi—is available to and from every city on the peninsula. All the options make it convenient enough for you to plan to hop from city to city and not waste too much precious vacation time.

By and large, all the modes of transportation between cities are reasonably comfortable. Air travel can be the most costly of the alternatives, followed by outstation taxis, then buses and trains.

BY PLANE

Malaysia Airlines links from its hub in Kuala Lumpur to the cities of Johor Bahru, Kota Bharu, Kota Kinabalu, Kuala Terengganu, Kuantan, Kuching, Langkawi, Penang, and other smaller cities not covered in this volume. Malaysian Airline's national hot line ✆ **1300/88-3000** can be dialed from anywhere in the country. Individual airport information is provided in sections for each city that follows. One-way domestic fares can average RM100 to RM372 (US$26–US$98).

A new domestic airline competes with incredibly affordable rates. AirAsia links all the country's major cities with fares that average run from RM35 to RM180 (US$9.20–US$47). Call their KL office at ✆ **03/7651-2222,** or visit their website at www.airasia.com.

BY TRAIN

The **Keretapi Tanah Melayu Berhad (KTM)** provides train service throughout peninsular Malaysia. Trains run from north to south between the Thai border and Singapore, with stops between including Butterworth (Penang), Kuala Lumpur, and Johor Bahru. There is a second line that branches off this line at Gemas, midway between Johor Bahru and KL, and heads northeast to Tempas near Kota Bharu. Fares range from RM64 (US$17) for first-class between Johor

Bahru and KL, to RM158 (US$42) for first-class passage between Johor Bahru and Butterworth. Train station information is provided for each city in individual city headings in the following chapters.

BY BUS

Malaysia's intercity coach system is extensive, reliable, and inexpensive. Buses depart several times daily for many destinations on the peninsula, and fares are charged according to the distance you travel. Air-conditioned express bus service (called Executive Coach service or Business Class) will cost you more, but since the fares are so inexpensive, it's well worth your while to spend the couple of extra dollars for the comfort. For an idea of price, it costs about RM50 (US$13) for business class service from KL to Johor Bahru, and RM27 (US$7.10) from KL to Penang. While there are more than a few independent bus companies around, for this book I've stuck to only the two major route providers, **Transnasional** and **Park May** (which operate the NiCE and Plusliner buses). I've found these companies to be more reliable and comfortable than the others. For each city covered, I've listed bus terminal locations, but scheduling information must be obtained from the bus company itself.

BY TAXI

You can take special hired cars, called **outstation taxis,** between every city and state on the peninsula. Rates depend on the distance you plan to travel. They are fixed, and stated at the beginning of the trip, but many times can be bargained down. In Kuala Lumpur, go to the second level of the Puduraya Bus Terminal to find cabs that will take you outside the city or call the **Kuala Lumpur Outstation Taxi Service Station,** 123 Jalan Sultan, Kuala Lumpur (✆ **03/2078-0213**). A taxi from KL to Malacca will cost you approximately RM120 (US$32), KL to Cameron Highlands RM180 (US$47), KL to Butterworth or Johor Bahru RM220 (US$58). Outstation taxi stand locations are included under each individual city heading.

Also, within each of the smaller cities, feel free to negotiate with unmetered taxis for hourly, half-day, or daily rates. It's an excellent way to get around for sightseeing and shopping without transportation hassles. Hourly rates are anywhere from RM15 to RM25 (US$3.95–US$6.60).

BY CAR

As recently as the 1970s, there was trouble with roadside crime—bandits stopping cars and holding up the travelers inside. Fortunately for drivers in Malaysia, this is a thing of the past. In the mid-1990s, Malaysia opened the North-South Highway, running from Bukit Kayu Hitam in the north on the Thai border to Johor Bahru at the southern tip of the peninsula. The highway (and the lack of bandits) has made travel along the west coast of Malaysia easy. There are rest areas with toilets, food outlets, and emergency telephones at intervals along the way. There is also a toll that varies depending on the distance you're traveling.

Driving along the east coast of Malaysia is actually much more pleasant than driving along the west coast. The highway is narrower and older, but it takes you through oil palm and rubber plantations, and the essence of kampung Malaysia permeates throughout. As you near villages you'll often have to slow down and swerve past cows and goats, which are really quite oblivious to oncoming traffic. You have to get very close to honk at them before they move.

The speed limit on highways is 110 kmph. On the minor highways the limit ranges from 70 to 90 kmph. Do not speed, as there are traffic police strategically situated around certain bends.

Distances between major towns are: from KL to Johor Bahru, 368km (221 miles); from KL to Malacca, 144km (86 miles); from KL to Kuantan, 259km (155 miles); from KL to Butterworth, 369km (221 miles); from Johor Bahru to Malacca, 224km (134 miles); from Johor Bahru to Kuantan, 325km (195 miles); from Johor Bahru to Mersing, 134km (80 miles); from Johor Bahru to Butterworth, 737km (442 miles).

To rent a car in Malaysia, you must produce a driver's license from your home country that shows you have been driving at least 2 years. There are desks for major car-rental services at the international airports in Kuala Lumpur and Penang, and additional outlets throughout the country (see individual city sections for this information).

Hitchhiking is not common among locals and I don't really think it's advisable for you either. The buses between cities are very affordable, so it's a much better idea to opt for those instead.

9 Etiquette & Customs

The mix of cultural influences in Malaysia is the result of centuries of immigration and trade with the outside world, particularly with Arab nations, China, and India. Early groups of incoming foreigners brought wealth from around the world, plus their own unique cultural heritages and religions. Further, once imported, each culture remained largely intact; that is, none have truly been homogenized. Traditional temples and churches exist side by side with mosques.

Likewise, **traditional art forms** of various cultures are still practiced in

Malaysia, most notably in the areas of dance and performance art. Chinese opera, Indian dance, and Malay martial arts are all very popular cultural activities. Silat, originating from a martial arts form (and still practiced as such by many), is a dance performed by men and women. Religious and cultural festivals are open for everyone to appreciate and enjoy. Unique arts and traditions of indigenous people distinguish Sabah and Sarawak from the rest of the country.

Traditional **Malaysian music** is very similar to Indonesian music. Heavy on rhythms, its constant drum beats underneath the light repetitive melodies of the stringed gamelan (no relation at all to the Indonesian metallophone gamelan, with its gongs and xylophones), will entrance you with its simple beauty.

Questions of etiquette in Malaysia are very similar to those in Singapore, so see chapter 2 for more information.

 FAST FACTS: **Malaysia**

American Express See individual city sections for offices.

Business Hours Banks are open from 10am to 3pm Monday through Friday and 9:30 to 11:30am on Saturday. Government offices are open from 8am to 12:45pm and 2 to 4:15pm Monday through Friday and from 8am to 12:45pm on Saturday. Smaller shops like provision stores may open as early as 6 or 6:30am and close as late as 9pm, especially those near the wet markets. Many such stores are closed on Saturday evenings and Sunday afternoons and are busiest before lunch. Other shops are open 9:30am to 7pm. Department stores and shops in malls tend to open later, about 10:30am or 11am till 8:30pm or 9pm throughout the week. Bars, except for those in Penang and the seedier bars in Johor Bahru, must close at 1am. Note that in Kuala Terengganu and Kota Bharu the weekday runs from Saturday to Wednesday. The above hours generally apply to that part of the country too.

Dentists & Doctors Consultation and treatment fees vary greatly depending on whether the practitioner you have visited operates from a private or public clinic. Your best bet is at a private medical center if your ailment appears serious. These are often expensive but, being virtual minihospitals, they have the latest equipment. If you just have a flu, it's quite safe to go to a normal M.D.—most doctors have been trained overseas, and will display diplomas on their walls. The fee at a private center ranges from RM20 to RM45 (US$5.25–$12). Call © **999** for emergencies.

Drug Laws As in Singapore, the death sentence is mandatory for drug trafficking (defined as being in possession of more than 15g of heroin or morphine, 200g of marijuana or hashish, or 40g of cocaine). For lesser quantities you'll be thrown in jail for a very long time and flogged with a cane.

Electricity The voltage used in Malaysia is 220–240 volts AC (50 cycles). The three-point square plugs are used, so buy an adapter if you plan to bring any appliances. Also, many larger hotels can provide adapters upon request.

Internet Service is available to all of the nation, and I have found Internet cafes in the most surprisingly remote places. While the major international hotels will have access for their guests in the business center, charges can be very steep. Still, most locally operated hotels do not offer this service for their guests. For each city I have listed at least one alternative, usually for a very inexpensive hourly cost of RM5 to RM10 (US$1.30–$2.65).

Language The national language is Bahasa Malaysia, although English is widely spoken. Chinese dialects and Tamil are also spoken.

Liquor Laws Liquor is sold in pubs and supermarkets in all big cities, or in provision stores. You'll hardly find any sold at Tioman though, so bring your own if you're headed there and wish to imbibe. In Terengganu and Kelantan, liquor is strictly limited to a handful of Chinese restaurants. Hotels are having an increasingly difficult time keeping their bars open. A recent ruling requires pubs and other nightspots to officially close by 1am nationwide.

Newspapers & Magazines English-language papers the *New Straits Times, The Star, The Sun,* and *The Edge* can be bought in hotel lobbies and magazine stands. Of the local KL magazines, *Day & Night* has great listings and local "what's happening" information for travelers.

Postal Services Post office locations in each city covered are provided in each section. Overseas airmail postage rates are as follows: RM.50 (US15¢) for postcards and RM1.50 (US40¢) for a 100g letter.

Taxes Hotels add a 5% government tax to all hotel rates, plus an additional 10% service charge. Larger restaurants also figure the same 5% tax into your bill, plus a 10% service charge, whereas small coffee shops and hawker stalls don't charge anything above the cost of the meal. While most tourist goods (such as crafts, camera equipment, sports equipment, cosmetics, and select small electronic items) are tax-free, a small, scaled tax is issued on various other goods such as clothing, shoes, and accessories that you'd buy in the larger shopping malls and department stores.

Telephone   **To place a call from your home country to Malaysia:** Dial the international access code (011 in the U.S., 0011 in Australia, or 00 in the U.K., Ireland, and New Zealand), plus the country code (60), plus the Malaysia area code (Cameron Highlands 5, Desaru 7, Genting Highlands 9, Johor Bahru 7, Kuala Lumpur 3, Kuala Terengganu 9, Kota Bharu 9, Kota Kinabalu 88, Kuantan 9, Kuching 82, Langkawi 4, Malacca 6, Mersing 7, Penang 4, Tioman 9), followed by the six-, seven-, or eight-digit phone number (for example, from the U.S. to Kuala Lumpur, you'd dial 011-60-3/0000-0000).

To place a direct international call from Malaysia: Dial the international access code (00), plus the country code of the place you are dialing (U.S. and Canada 1, Australia 61, Republic of Ireland 353, New Zealand 64, U.K. 44), plus the area/city code and the residential number.

To reach the international operator: Dial ✆ 108.

To place a call within Malaysia: You must use area codes if calling between states. Note that for calls within the country, area codes are preceded by a zero (Cameron Highlands 05, Desaru 07, Genting Highlands 09, Johor Bahru 07, Kuala Lumpur 03, Kuala Terengganu 09, Kota Bharu 09, Kota Kinabalu 088, Kuantan 09, Kuching 082, Langkawi 04, Malacca 06, Mersing 07, Penang 04, Tioman 09).

Television Guests in larger hotels will sometimes get satellite channels such as HBO, Star TV, or CNN. Another in-house movie alternative, Vision Four, preprograms videos throughout the day. Local TV stations TV2, TV5, and TV7 show English-language comedies, movies, and documentaries.

Time Malaysia is 8 hours ahead of Greenwich mean time, 16 hours ahead of U.S. Pacific Standard Time, 13 ahead of Eastern Standard Time, and 2 hours behind Sydney. It is in the same zone as Singapore. There is no daylight saving time.

Tipping People don't tip, except to bellhops and car jockeys. For these, an amount not less than RM4 is okay.

Toilets To find a public toilet, ask for the tandas. In Malay, lelaki is male and perempuan is female. Be prepared for pay toilets. Coin collectors sit outside almost every public facility, taking RM20 per person, RM30 if you want paper. Once inside, you'll find it obvious that the money doesn't go for cleaning crews.

Water Water in Kuala Lumpur is supposed to be potable, but most locals boil the water before drinking it—and if that's not a tip-off, I don't know what is. I advise against drinking the tap water anywhere in Malaysia. Hotels will supply bottled water in your room. If they charge you for it, expect inflated prices. A 1.5-liter bottle goes for RM7 (US$1.85) in a hotel minibar, but RM2 (US55¢) at 7-Eleven.

9

Peninsular Malaysia: Kuala Lumpur & the West Coast

The most popular destinations in Malaysia dot the west coast of the peninsula where the main rail line passes through, connecting Singapore with Kuala Lumpur and on to Bangkok.

The convenience of train travel isn't the only draw of this part of the country; it also holds some of Malaysia's most significant historical towns. As you travel north from Singapore, **Johor Bahru** makes for a great day trip for those with only a short time to experience Malaysia. Three hours north of Johor Bahru, the sleepy town of **Malacca** reveals the evidence of hundreds of years of Western conquest and rule. Three hours north of Malacca, and you're in **Kuala Lumpur,** the cosmopolitan capital of

the country, full of shopping, culture, history, and nightlife. Close by, **Genting Highlands** draws tourists from all over the region for the casino excitement, while the more relaxed **Cameron Highlands** offers a cool and charming respite from Southeast Asia's blaring heat. Still farther north, **Penang,** possibly Malaysia's most popular destination, retains all the charm of an old-time Southeast Asian waterfront town, full of romance (and great food!), with the added advantage of beach resorts nearby. Still farther north, just before you reach the Thai border, **Langkawi** proves that there are still a few tropical paradise islands left on the planet that are not swarming with tourists.

1 Kuala Lumpur

Kuala Lumpur (or KL as it is commonly known) is more often than not a traveler's point of entry to Malaysia. As the capital it is the most modern and developed city in the country, with contemporary high-rises and world-class hotels, glitzy shopping malls and international cuisine.

The city began sometime around 1857 as a small mining town at the spot where the Gombak and Klang rivers meet, at the spot where the Masjid Jame sits in the center of the city. Fueled by tin mining in the nearby Klang River valley, the town grew under the business interests of three officials: a local Malay raja Abdullah, a British resident, and a Chinese headman (Kapitan China). The industry and village attracted Chinese laborers, Malays from nearby villages, and Indian immigrants who followed the British, and as the town grew, colonial buildings that housed local administrative offices were erected around Merdeka Square, close to Masjid Jame and bounded by Jalan Sultan Hishamuddin and Jalan Kuching. The town, and later the city, spread outward from this center.

Life in KL had many difficult starts and stops then—tin was subject to price fluctuations, the Chinese were involved in clan "wars," but worst of all, malaria was killing thousands. Still, in the late 1800s KL overcame its hurdles to become the capital of the state of Selangor, and later the capital of the Federated Malay States (Perak, Selangor, Negeri Sembilan, and Pahang) and got its big break as the hub of the Malayan network of rail lines. Its development continued to accelerate, save for during the Japanese occupation (1942–45), and in 1957, with newly won independence from Britain, Malaysia declared Kuala Lumpur its national capital.

Today the original city center at **Merdeka Square** is the core of KL's history. Buildings like the Sultan Abdul Samad Building, the Royal Selangor Club, and the Kuala Lumpur Railway Station are gorgeous examples of British style peppered with Moorish flavor. South of this area is KL's **Chinatown.** Along Jalan Petaling and surrounding areas are markets, shops, food stalls, and the bustling life of the Chinese community. There's also a **Little India** in KL, around the area occupied by Masjid Jame, where you'll find flower stalls, Indian Muslim and Malay costumes, and traditional items. Across the river you'll find **Lake Gardens,** a large sanctuary that houses Kuala Lumpur's bird park, butterfly park, and other attractions and gardens. Modern Kuala Lumpur is rooted in the city's **"Golden Triangle,"** bounded by Jalan Ampang, Jalan Tun Razak, and Jalan Imbi. This section is home to most of KL's hotels, office complexes, shopping malls, and sights like the KL Tower and the Petronas Twin Towers, the tallest buildings in the world.

ESSENTIALS
VISITOR INFORMATION
In Kuala Lumpur, the Malaysia Tourism Board has several offices. The largest is at the **MATIC,** the **Malaysia Tourist Information Complex** (see "Attractions," later in this chapter), located on 109 Jalan Ampang (© **03/2164-3929**). In addition to a tourist information desk, MATIC also has a money exchanger, tourist police post, travel agent booking for Taman Negara trips, souvenir shops, an amphitheater, and Transnasional bus ticket bookings.

Vision KL Magazine is offered for free in many hotel rooms and has listings for events in KL and around the country, plus ads for restaurants and shops.

GETTING THERE
BY PLANE The new **Kuala Lumpur International Airport (KLIA)** (© **03/ 8776-2000**) opened in June 1998. Located in Sepang, 53km (32 miles) outside the city, KLIA is a huge complex with business centers, dining facilities, a fitness center, medical services, shopping, post offices, and an airport hotel operated by **Pan Pacific** (© **03/8787-3333**). While there are money changers, they are few and far between, so hop on the first line you see, and don't assume there's another one just around the corner.

From KLIA, domestic flights can be taken to almost every major city in the country.

GETTING INTO TOWN FROM THE AIRPORT
By Taxi City taxis are not permitted to pick up fares from the airport, but **special airport taxis** (© **03/8787-3030**) operate round the clock, charging RM88 (US$23) for a premier car (Mercedes) and RM63 (US$17) for a standard vehicle (locally-built Proton). Coupons must be purchased at the arrival concourse.

An **express coach** connects KLIA to most of the city's major hotels. Operating every 30 minutes from 5:30am to 10:15pm daily, the trip takes 1 hour and costs RM25 (US$6.60) adult and RM13 (US$3.40) child.

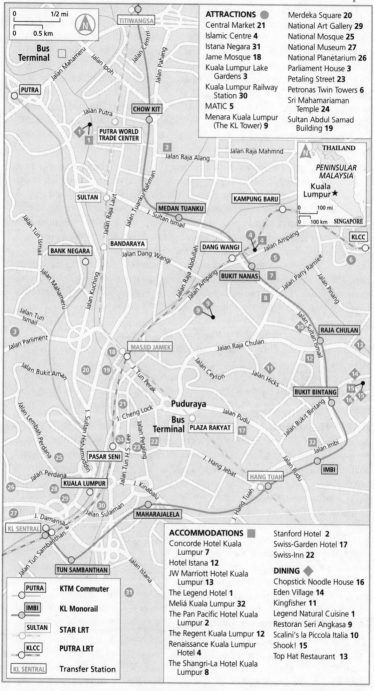

Kuala Lumpur

Bus Terminal □

ATTRACTIONS ●

Central Market **21**
Islamic Centre **4**
Istana Negara **31**
Jame Mosque **18**
Kuala Lumpur Lake
  Gardens **3**
Kuala Lumpur Railway
  Station **30**
MATIC **5**
Menara Kuala Lumpur
  (The KL Tower) **9**

Merdeka Square **20**
National Art Gallery **29**
National Mosque **25**
National Museum **27**
National Planetarium **26**
Parliament House **3**
Petaling Street **23**
Petronas Twin Towers **6**
Sri Mahamariaman
  Temple **24**
Sultan Abdul Samad
  Building **19**

THAILAND

PENINSULAR MALAYSIA

Kuala Lumpur ★

0   100 mi
0   100 km   **SINGAPORE**

ACCOMMODATIONS ■

Concorde Hotel Kuala
  Lumpur **7**
Hotel Istana **12**
JW Marriott Hotel Kuala
  Lumpur **13**
The Legend Hotel **1**
Meliá Kuala Lumpur **32**
The Pan Pacific Hotel Kuala
  Lumpur **2**
The Regent Kuala Lumpur **12**
Renaissance Kuala Lumpur
  Hotel **4**
The Shangri-La Hotel Kuala
  Lumpur **8**

Stanford Hotel **2**
Swiss-Garden Hotel **17**
Swiss-Inn **22**

DINING ◆

Chopstick Noodle House **16**
Eden Village **14**
Kingfisher **11**
Legend Natural Cuisine **1**
Restoran Seri Angkasa **9**
Scalini's la Piccola Italia **10**
Shook! **15**
Top Hat Restaurant **13**

PUTRA   **KTM Commuter**
IMBI   **KL Monorail**
SULTAN   **STAR LRT**
KLCC   **PUTRA LRT**
KL SENTRAL **Transfer Station**

The **Express Rail Link** runs between KLIA and KL Sentral train station from 5am to 1am daily. Trains depart every 15 minutes and take 28 minutes to complete the journey. Tickets cost RM35 (US$9.20) for adults and RM15 (US$3.95) for children. From KL Sentral you can catch one of the city's commuter trains to a station near your hotel.

The outstation taxi stand in Kuala Lumpur is located at **Puduraya Bus Terminal** on Jalan Pudu. Call ✆ **03/2078-0213** for booking to any city on the peninsula. Fares will run you about RM180 (US$47) to Cameron Highlands, RM120 (US$32) to Malacca, RM220 (US$58) to Johor Bahru, and RM220 (US$58) to Penang and to Kuantan. These taxis can pick you up at your hotel for an additional RM10 (US$2.65) upon request.

BY BUS   There's more than one bus terminal in Kuala Lumpur, and it can be somewhat confusing. The main bus terminal, **Puduraya Bus Terminal,** is on Jalan Pudu right in the center of town—literally. Buses heading in and out of the station block traffic along already congested city streets, spewing noxious gasses. The terminal itself is hot, filthy, and noisy; the heavy-metal boom box wars between the provision shops is amusing for about 30 seconds. This terminal handles bus routes to all over the country, but more specifically to areas on the west coast from north to south. Buses to Penang or Malacca will leave from here. I think Puduraya is a mess to be avoided at all costs. It is a well-kept secret that many business-class and executive coaches to Penang, Johor Bahru, and Singapore depart peacefully from the **KL Railway Station,** which is a far saner alternative.

The other main terminals are the **Putra Bus Terminal** on Jalan Tun Ismail just across from the Putra World Trade Centre and the **Pekililing terminal** on Jalan Ipoh, also not far from Putra WTC. Both terminals deal primarily with buses to east coast cities such as Kota Bharu, Kuala Terengganu, and Kuantan.

The bus terminals have no general telephone inquiry numbers in their own right. Inquiries must be made directly to individual bus companies.

GETTING AROUND

Kuala Lumpur is a prime example of a city that was not planned, per se, from a master graph of streets. Rather, because of its beginnings as an outpost, it grew as it needed to, expanding outward and swallowing up suburbs. The result is a tangled web of streets too narrow to support the traffic of a capital city. Cars and buses weave through one-way lanes, with countless motorbikes sneaking in and out, sometimes in the opposite direction of traffic or up on the sidewalks. Expect traffic jams in the morning rush between 6 and 9am, and again between 4 and 7pm. At other times, taxis are a convenient way of getting around, but the commuter train systems, if they're going where you need to, is perhaps the best value and easiest route. City buses are hot and crowded with some very confusing routes. Walking can also be frustrating. Many sidewalks are in poor condition, with buckled tiles and gaping gutters. The heat can be prohibitive as well. However, areas within the colonial heart of the city, Chinatown, Little India, and some areas in the Golden Triangle are within walking distance of each other.

BY TAXI   Taxis around town can be waved down by the side of the road, or can be caught at taxi stands outside shopping complexes or hotels. The metered fare is RM2 (US55¢) for the first 2km and an additional 10 sen for each 200m after that. Between midnight and 6am you'll be charged an extra 50% of the total fare. If you call ahead for a cab, there's an extra charge of RM1 (US25¢).

Truth be told, many cabbies in KL are really lousy. Government regulations have made it compulsory for cabbies to charge the metered fare, but many still try to fix a price, which is invariably higher than what the metered fare would be. The worst is during peak hours or if it's raining, when they'll jack up the price depending on how badly they think you need their services. There are times when empty cabs will just pass you right by, or when cabbies will refuse to take you to your destination if it's "out of their way." The city's been trying to crack down on the poor quality of service; as a matter of fact, a government minister got into some hot water when in late 2002 he suggested errant cabbies be shot! But I haven't noticed any change for the better.

To request a cab pickup, call **KL Teksi** at © **03/9221-8999** or **Comfort** at © **03/8024-2727**. Maybe they'll show up. Maybe they won't.

BY BUS   There are regular city buses and minibuses to take you around the city. The fare is 20 sen for the first kilometer and 5 sen for each additional kilometer. Know, however, that the buses in Kuala Lumpur are not dependable. You can wait at a stop for a long time only to find when the bus arrives that it's hot and packed so full that passengers seem to be hanging out every window. It's not the most relaxing way to get around.

BY RAIL   KL has a network of mass transit trains that snake through the city and out to the suburbs, and it'll be worth your time to become familiar with them, since taxis are sometimes unreliable and traffic jams can be unbearable. Trouble is, there are five train routes and each one is operated by a different company. How confusing! The lines don't seem to connect in any logical way.

The four lines that are most useful to visitors are the **Putra LRT,** the **Star LRT,** the **KL Monorail** and the **ERL Express Rail Link** to the airport. The latter route is explained under "Getting into Town from the Airport," earlier in this chapter.

Putra LRT has stops at Bangsar (featured in the nightlife section), KL Sentral (train station), Pasar Seni (Chinatown), Masjid Jamek, Dang Wangi, and KLCC shopping center. An average fare would be about RM1.40 (US35¢).

The **Star LRT** is only convenient if you need to get to the Putra World Trade Centre. It also stops at Masjid Jamek and Plaza Rayat. An average trip will cost well under RM2 (US55¢).

The newly opened **KL Monorail** provides good access through the main hotel and shopping areas of the city, including stops at KL Sentral, Imbi, Bukit Bintang (the main shopping strip), and Raja Chulan (along Jalan Sultan Ismail, where many hotels are). Fares run between RM1.20 (US30¢) and RM 2.50 (US65¢).

As a rough guide all lines operate between 5 or 6am till around midnight, with trains coming every 10 minutes or so. Tickets can be purchased at any station either from the stationmaster or from single-fare electronic ticket booths.

ON FOOT   The heat and humidity can make walking between attractions pretty uncomfortable. However, sometimes the traffic is so unbearable that you'll get where you're going much faster by strapping on your tennis shoes and hiking it.

FAST FACTS: KUALA LUMPUR

The main office for **American Express** is located in KL at The Weld, 18th floor, Jalan Raja Chulan (© **03/2050-0888**). You'll also find headquarters for all Malaysian and many international banks, most of which have outlets along Jalan

Sultan Ismail plus ATMs at countless locations thought the city. Look for money exchangers in just about every shopping mall, they're a better bargain than banks or hotel cashiers.

KL's **General Post Office,** on Jalan Sultan Hishamuddin (✆ **03/2274-1122**), can be pretty overwhelming. If you can, try to use your hotel's mail service for a much easier time. Internet service in KL will run about RM6 (US$1.60) per hour for usage. I like **Master-World SurfNet Café,** 23 Jalan Petaling, M floor (technically it's on Jalan Cheng Lock around the corner; ✆ **03/2031-0133**), which charges RM6 (US$1.60) per hour. If you're near the KL City Centre, try **Café Caravali,** Lot 346, third floor next to the cinema (✆ **03/382-9033**). It's a bit more expensive (RM10/US$2.65 per hour), but is a nice setting.

If you have a medical **emergency,** the number to dial is ✆ **999.** This is the same number for **police and fire emergencie**s as well.

ACCOMMODATIONS

There are dozens of hotels in Kuala Lumpur, most of them within city limits; an especially large number of them are in the Golden Triangle area. Other hotels listed in this chapter are located in the Chinatown area, within walking distance of plenty of shopping attractions and nightlife.

VERY EXPENSIVE

The Regent Kuala Lumpur ★★★ *Value*   Of the best five-star properties in Kuala Lumpur, nobody delivers first-class accommodations with the finesse of The Regent. The lobby and guest rooms are contemporary and elegant, without a single sacrifice to comfort. Touches like soft armchairs and cozy comforters in each room will make you want to check in and never leave, and the large marble bathrooms will make you feel like a million bucks even on a bad-hair day. The outdoor pool is a palm-lined free-form escape, and the fitness center is state-of-the-art, with sauna, steam, spa, and Jacuzzi.

160 Jalan Bukit Bintang, 55100 Kuala Lumpur. ✆ **800/545-4000** in the U.S. and Canada, 800/022-800 in Australia, 800/440-800 in New Zealand, 800/917-8795 in the U.K., or 03/2141-8000. Fax 03/2142-1441. 468 units. RM550 (US$145) double; from RM880 (US$232) suite. AE, DC, MC, V. **Amenities:** 3 restaurants (international, Italian, Cantonese); bar and lobby lounge; outdoor pool; 2 squash courts; 24-hr. fitness center with Jacuzzi, sauna, steam and massage; concierge; limousine service; business center; 24-hr. room service; babysitting; same-day laundry service/dry cleaning; nonsmoking rooms; executive-level rooms. *In room:* A/C, TV w/satellite programming and in-house movie, minibar, coffee/tea-making facilities, hair dryer, safe.

Renaissance Kuala Lumpur Hotel ★★   The Renaissance has become a very elegant address in KL, its most recent claim to fame was hosting the U.S. secretary of state during his last visit to the city. It's actually two hotels in one, since the Renaissance absorbed its neighbor, The New World. Renaissance's lobby is a huge oval colonnade with a domed ceiling and massive marble columns rising from the sides of a geometric star burst on the floor. Guest rooms in the Renaissance Wing have an equally "official" feel to them—very bold and impressive, and completely European in style. In fact, you'll never know you're in Malaysia. The New World Wing is less opulent, with plain furnishings and bathrooms devoid of luxurious touches. Renaissance is essentially two hotels in one, with facilities sharing, so expect restaurants and leisure facilities to be more crowded than at other places, and service to be less personalized.

Corner of Jalan Sultan Ismail and Jalan Ampang, 50450 Kuala Lumpur. ✆ **800/HOTELS-1** in the U.S. and Canada, 800/251-259 in Australia, 800/441-035 in New Zealand, or 03/2162-2233. Fax 03/2163-1122. 910 units. RM460–RM535 (US$121–US$141) double, RM755 (US$199) executive double; from RM955 (US$251) suite. AE, DC, MC, V. **Amenities:** 3 restaurants (Pan-Asian, Japanese, Mediterranean); lounge; large, landscaped outdoor pool; outdoor, lighted tennis court; fitness center with sauna and massage; concierge; limousine service; business center; shopping arcade; salon; 24-hr. room service; babysitting; same-day laundry service/dry cleaning; nonsmoking rooms; executive-level rooms. *In room:* A/C, TV w/satellite programming and in-house movie, minibar, coffee/tea-making facilities, hair dryer, safe.

EXPENSIVE

Hotel Istana ★ Fashioned after a Malay palace, Hotel Istana is rich with Moorish architectural elements, and songket weaving patterns are featured in decor elements throughout. The guest rooms have Malaysian touches like handwoven carpets and upholstery in local fabric designs, capturing the exotic flavor of the culture without sacrificing modern comfort and convenience. Located on Jalan Raja Chulan, Istana is in a favorable Golden Triangle location, within walking distance to shopping and some of the sights in that area. Ask about big-rate discounts in the summer months.

73 Jalan Raja Chulan, 50200 Kuala Lumpur. ⓒ **03/2141-9988.** Fax 03/2144-0111. 516 units. RM550–RM575 (US$145–US$151) double; RM690 (US$182) executive club; RM1,095 (US$288) suite. AE, DC, MC, V. **Amenities:** 4 restaurants (international, Japanese, Cantonese, and Italian); lobby lounge; outdoor pool; 2 outdoor, lighted tennis courts; 2 squash courts; fitness center with Jacuzzi, sauna, steam, and massage; concierge; limousine service; business center; 24-hr. room service; babysitting; same-day laundry service/dry cleaning; executive-level rooms. *In room:* A/C, TV w/satellite programming and in-house movie, minibar, coffee/tea-making facilities, hair dryer, safe.

JW Marriott Hotel Kuala Lumpur ★ Opened in July 1997, the Marriott is one of the newer hotels in town. The smallish lobby area still allows for a very dramatic entrance, complete with wrought-iron filigree and marble. The modern guest rooms have a European flavor, decorated in deep greens and reds with plush carpeting, large desks, and a leather executive chair that are all beginning to show some wear. If you've stayed at Marriotts in other locations, this one might disappoint you. It's not their hottest property, however, the staff is very motivated and enthusiastic. Another great plus: The hotel is next door to some of the most upmarket and trendy shopping complexes in the city.

183 Jalan Bukit Bintang, 55100 Kuala Lumpur. ⓒ **800/228-9290** in the U.S. and Canada, 800/251-259 in Australia, 800/221-222 in the U.K., or 03/2715-9000. 518 units. RM300 (US$79) double, from RM500 (US$132) suite. AE, DC, MC, V. **Amenities:** 4 restaurants (Malay, international, Shanghainese, delicatessen); lounge and cigar bar; outdoor pool; outdoor lighted tennis court; fitness center with Jacuzzi, sauna, and steam; new spa with massage and beauty treatments; concierge; limousine service; business center; shopping mall with designer boutiques adjacent; salon; 24-hr. room service; babysitting; same-day laundry service/dry cleaning; executive-level rooms. *In room:* A/C, TV w/satellite programming, minibar, coffee/tea-making facilities, dataport, hair dryer, safe.

The Pan Pacific Hotel Kuala Lumpur ★ One thing you'll love about staying at the Pan Pacific is the view from the glass elevator as you drift up to your floor. The atrium lobby inside the main entrance is bright and airy and filled with the scent of jasmine. The hotel staff handles the demands of its international clientele with courtesy and professionalism, but when Pan Pac's running a full house, help can be a little weary and hard to find. The rooms are spacious and stately, in pale pastels. Sunken windows with lattice work frame each view. The large shopping mall across the street makes this hotel more convenient, otherwise it's a bit out of the city center—the inconvenience is felt during rush hour when it can take 30 minutes to make an otherwise 10-minute taxi hop. A recent dramatic drop in rates makes this an especially good choice for value.

Jalan Putra, P.O. Box 11468, 50746 Kuala Lumpur. ⓒ **800/327-8585** in the U.S. and Canada, 800/252-900 in Australia, 800/969-496 in the U.K., or 03/4042-5555. Fax 03/4041-7236. 565 units. RM199–RM259 (US$52–US$68) double. AE, DC, MC, V. **Amenities:** 3 restaurants (international, Chinese, Japanese); lobby lounge; outdoor pool; outdoor, lighted tennis court; squash court; fitness center with Jacuzzi, sauna, and massage; concierge; limousine service; business center; 24-hr. room service; babysitting; same-day laundry service/dry cleaning; nonsmoking rooms; executive-level rooms. *In room:* A/C, TV w/satellite programming and in-house movie, minibar, coffee/tea-making facilities, iron, safe.

The Shangri-La Hotel Kuala Lumpur   I don't know how they do it, but Shangri-La can always take what could easily be a dull building in a busy city and turn it into a resort-style garden oasis. Their property in KL is no different. With attention paid to landscaping and greenery, the hotel is one of the more attractive places to stay in town. The guest rooms are large with cooling colors and nice views of the city. Shangri-La hotels always have great choices for dining. This one offers Restaurant Lafite for classic French cuisine, Nadaman Japanese restaurant, Shang Palace Cantonese restaurant, and a coffee garden and pool cafe. Also check out their pub, cigar bar, and wine shop.

11 Jalan Sultan Ismail, 50250 Kuala Lumpur. ⓒ 800/942-5050 in the U.S. and Canada, 800/222-448 in Australia, 0800/442-179 in New Zealand, or 03/232-2388. Fax 03/202-1245. 681 units. RM420–RM505 (US$111–US$133) double; RM575 (US$151) executive club room; RM1,300 (US$342) suite. AE, DC, MC, V. **Amenities:** 5 restaurants (international, Continental, delicatessen, Chinese and Japanese); outdoor pool; outdoor lighted tennis courts; fitness center with Jacuzzi, steam, sauna and massage; concierge; limousine service; salon; babysitting; 24-hour room service; same day dry cleaning/laundry service; nonsmoking rooms; executive level rooms. *In room:* A/C; TV w/ satellite programming and in-house movie; Internet access; minibar; coffee/tea-making facilities; hair dryer, in-room safe.

MODERATE

Concorde Hotel Kuala Lumpur ★★ *Value*   Jalan Sultan Ismail is the address for the big names in hotels, like Shangri-La and Hilton, but tucked alongside the giants is the Concorde, a very reasonably priced choice. What's best about staying here is that you don't sacrifice amenities and services for the lower cost. Although rooms are not as large as those in the major hotels, they're well outfitted in an up-to-date style that can compete with the best of them. Choose Concorde if you'd like location and comfort for less. It also has a small outdoor pool facing a fitness center. A well-equipped business center adds additional value. Better yet, the Hard Rock Cafe, located on the premises, is one of the more fun clubs in town.

2 Jalan Sultan Ismail, 50250 Kuala Lumpur. ⓒ 03/2144-2200. Fax 03/2144-1628. 570 units. RM200–RM350 (US$53–US$92) double; from RM800 (US$211) suite. AE, DC, MC, V. **Amenities:** 3 restaurants (international, Cantonese); lobby lounge and Hard Rock Cafe; small outdoor pool; fitness center with sauna, steam, massage; concierge; limousine service; business center; shopping arcade; salon; 24-hr. room service; babysitting; same-day laundry service/dry cleaning; executive-level rooms. *In room:* A/C, TV w/satellite programming and in-house movie, minibar, coffee/tea-making facilities, safe.

The Legend Hotel   Sitting on top of a very large shopping complex, this hotel doesn't actually start until you reach the ninth story. From an unimpressive entrance, you're whisked on an express elevator to the vast lobby, which features earthy toned marble Chinese touches such as carved wood furniture and terra-cotta warrior statues. Guest rooms are spacious, and all overlook the city, but ask to face the Twin Towers for the best view. Also, the less expensive rooms seem to have the nicest decor, with softer tones and modern touches. The executive rooms are rather strange—mine had a bright pink frilly bedcover and amenities included a packet of generic made in China pantyhose. Facilities are highlighted by an outdoor pool with a great view, and the convenience off the shopping mall beneath. Another good features to consider here is free Internet in-room via your flat-screen interactive TV. The hotel is, however, located a little outside the main shopping and dining action of the city.

Putra Place, 100 Jalan Putra, 50350 Kuala Lumpur. ℂ **800/573-8483** in the U.S., 800/126-533 in Australia, 800/894351 in the U.K., or 03/4042-9888. Fax 03/4043-0700. 400 units. RM435–RM525 (US$114–US$138) double; from RM785 (US$207) suite. AE, DC, MC, V. **Amenities:** 4 restaurants (international, Chinese, Japanese, and haute cuisine vegetarian); bar and lobby lounge; outdoor pool and Jacuzzi with good views; squash courts; concierge; limousine service; business center and Internet cafe; large shopping mall; salon; 24-hr. room service; babysitting; same-day laundry service/dry cleaning; executive-level rooms. *In room:* A/C, TV w/satellite programming and in-house movie, minibar, coffee/tea-making facilities, Internet access, hair dryer, safe.

Meliá Kuala Lumpur ★ *Value*   This tourist-class hotel had nothing special to boast until recently. The opening of a KL Monorail station just outside, combined with a giant shopping and entertainment complex across the street, has certainly added great value. The small lobby is functional, with space for tour groups and a very active and efficient tour desk. Newly renovated guest rooms have light wood furnishings, contemporary decorator fixtures, wall desks with a swivel arm for extra space, and large-screen TVs. Bathrooms, while small, are well maintained with good counter space. Mealtimes in the hotel's coffee shop can be a little crowded.

16 Jalan Imbi, 55100 Kuala Lumpur ℂ 03/2142-8333. Fax 03/2142-6623. www.solmelia.com. 301 units. RM280–RM380 (US$74–US$100) double; from RM500 (US$132) suite. AE, DC, MC, V. **Amenities:** 2 restaurants (international, Chinese); bar and karaoke lounge; small outdoor pool; health center with massage; tour desk; small business center; shopping arcade; salon; 24-hr. room service; babysitting; same-day laundry service/dry cleaning; nonsmoking rooms. *In room:* A/C, TV w/satellite programming and in-house movie, minibar, coffee/tea-making facilities, iron.

Swiss-Garden Hotel   For midrange prices, Swiss-Garden offers reliable comfort, good location, and affordability that attracts many leisure travelers to its doors. It also knows how to make you feel right at home, with a friendly staff (the concierge is on the ball) and a hotel lobby bar that actually gets patronized (by travelers having cool cocktails at the end of a busy day of sightseeing). The guest rooms are simply furnished, but are neat and comfortable. Swiss-Garden is just walking distance from KL's lively Chinatown district, and close to the Puduraya bus station. Facilities include an outdoor pool, a brand-new spa, and a fitness center.

117 Jalan Pudu, 55100 Kuala Lumpur. ℂ **03/2141-3333.** Fax 03/2141-5555. www.swissgarden.com. 310 units. RM350–RM425 (US$92–US$112) double; from RM580 (US$153) suite. AE, DC, MC, V. **Amenities:** 2 restaurants (international, Cantonese); lobby lounge; small outdoor pool; small fitness center; spa with massage; concierge; limousine service; business center; 24-hr. room service; babysitting; same-day laundry service/dry cleaning; nonsmoking rooms. *In room:* A/C, TV w/satellite programming and in-house movie, minibar, coffee/tea-making facilities, hair dryer, safe.

INEXPENSIVE

Stanford Hotel ★ *Value*   The Stanford Hotel is a good alternative for the budget-conscious traveler. The lobby feels like a miniversion of a more upmarket hotel, a tiny marble room with glass front facing the street. A small stairway leads to the tiny business center, coffee shop and lifts to guest floors. Guest rooms have new carpeting, fresh paint, and refurbished furnishings and bathrooms, the place provides accommodations that are good value for your money. And some of the rooms even have lovely views of the Petronas Twin Towers. Discounted rates as low as RM100 (US$26) can be had if you ask about promotions. Facilities are thin, but if you plan to spend most of your time out and about, you won't notice.

449 Jalan Tuanku Abdul Rahman, 50100 Kuala Lumpur. ℂ **03/2691-9833.** Fax 03/2691-3103. 168 units. RM150 (US$39) double. AE, MC, V. **Amenities:** Restaurant (international); tour desk; limousine service; business center; limited room service; same-day laundry service; nonsmoking rooms. *In room:* A/C, TV, refrigerator, coffee/tea-making facilities.

Swiss-Inn This mini-size hotel is one of KL's better bargains. Tucked away in the heart of Chinatown, Swiss-Inn's best asset is its location, amid the jumble of vibrant night market hawkers. The place is small, and offers almost no facilities. Higher priced rooms have a small window, a bit more space (but are still compact) and are somewhat better maintained. Budget rooms, on lower floors, are very small, the cheapest having no windows at all. Beige carpeting can use a deep cleaning, the walls can use a fresh coat of paint, and the bathrooms some new grout work. On my last visit, housekeeping wasn't up to snuff, which added to the problem. Still, these rooms can be had for as little as RM80 per night, which comes to about US$20. Make sure you reserve your room early, because this place runs at high occupancy year round.

62 Jalan Sultan, 50000 Kuala Lumpur. ✆ 03/2072-3333. Fax 03/2031-6699. www.swissgarden.com. 110 units. RM150–RM184 (US$39–US$48) double. AE, DC, MC, V. **Amenities:** Restaurant (international); bar; tour desk; Internet terminals for guest use (extra charge); limited room service; babysitting; same-day laundry service/dry cleaning; nonsmoking rooms. *In room:* A/C, TV w/in-house movie, coffee/tea-making facilities.

DINING

Kuala Lumpur, like Singapore, is very cosmopolitan. Here you'll not only find delicious and exotic cuisine, but you'll find it served in some pretty trendy settings.

Chopstick Noodle House ★ *Value* CANTONESE I was in the mood for something cheap and good in the center of town, and was thrilled to find this place. The menu is vast, with no fewer than 20 kinds of noodles, served either in soup or dry (with soup on the side). The fresh prawn won ton noodle is light and flavorful and you can also get them fried. They have barbecue dishes—duck, pork, honey spare ribs, and seafood dishes are reasonably priced. Also good are the clay-pot dishes, with rice and meats baked in a clay pot with dark soy, mushrooms, and crunchy onions. A good alternative to formal dining.

Lot F 003, First Floor, KL Plaza, 179 Jalan Bukit Bintang, ✆ 03/2148-2221. Main courses RM9–RM22 (US$2.35–US$5.80). AE, MC, V. Daily 11:30am–midnight.

Eden Village SEAFOOD Uniquely designed inside and out to resemble a Malay house, Eden Village has great local atmosphere. Waitresses are clad in traditional sarong kebaya, and serve up popular dishes like braised shark's fin in a clay pot with crabmeat and roe, and the Kingdom of the Sea (a half lobster baked with prawns, crab, and cuttlefish). The terrace seating is the best in the house.

260 Jalan Raja Chulan. ✆ 03/2141-4027. Reservations recommended. Main courses RM18–RM100 and up (US$4.75–US$26). AE, MC, V. Daily noon–3pm, 7pm–midnight, closed for lunch on Sun.

Kingfisher ★★ SEAFOOD This street, lined with simple low-rise houses and commercial buildings in the center of KL's fashionable shopping and hotel district, has in recent years become a hot address for trendy restaurants and bars, the best of which is Kingfisher. The very freshest fishes are crafted into lovely haute cuisine dishes with delicate Asian accents for flavor. With the help of the friendly waitstaff, you select your fish of choice, then decide the best preparation style in a "one from column A, one from column B" approach. Everything is fresh and delicious—a good pick.

20 Changkat Bukit Bintang. ✆ 03/2141-9266. Reservations recommended. Main courses RM 58–128 (US$15–US$33). MC, V. Mon–Sat noon–2:30pm, 6:30–10:30pm.

Legend Natural Cuisine INTERNATIONAL Legend Natural Cuisine's menu is selected by dieticians, its dishes incorporating organically grown produce and calorie-conscious recipes with a mind toward health awareness. Off the Legend Hotel's lobby, the restaurant is spacious and cozy, and the food is so good you'll never know it's healthy. It's easy to forget about dieting when you're traveling, but Legend Natural Cuisine makes it incredibly easy to stick to one. Try the rack of lamb, and the forest mushroom soup is an unbelievably good appetizer.

The Legend Hotel and Apartments, 100 Jalan Putra. (C) 03/4042-9888. Reservations recommended for lunch and dinner; required for high tea. Main courses RM38–RM55 (US$10–US$14). AE, DC, MC, V. Daily 6:30am–1am.

Restoran Seri Angkasa MALAYSIAN   At the top of the Menara KL (KL Tower) is Restoran Seri Angkasa, a revolving restaurant with the best view in the city. Better still, it's a great way to try all the Malay-, Chinese-, and Indian-inspired local dishes at a convenient buffet, with a chance to taste just about everything you have room for—like nasi goreng, clay-pot noodles, or beef rendang

Jalan Punchak, off Jalan P. Ramlee. (C) 03/2020-5055. Reservations recommended. Lunch buffet RM55 (US$14); dinner buffet RM75 (US$20). AE, DC, MC, V. Daily noon–2:30pm lunch; 3:30–5:30pm high tea; 6:30–11pm dinner.

Scalini's la Piccola Italia ★★★ ITALIAN   Four chefs from Italy create the dishes that make Scalini's a favorite among KL locals and expatriates. From a very extensive menu you can select pasta, fish, and meat, as well as a large selection of pizzas. The specials are superb and change all the time. Some of the best dishes are salmon with creamed asparagus sauce and ravioli with goat cheese and zucchini. Scalini's has a large wine selection (that is actually part of the romantic decor) with labels from California, Australia, New Zealand, France, and, of course, Italy.

19 Jalan Sultan Ismail. (C) 03/2145-3211. Reservations recommended. Main courses RM26–RM58 (US$6.85–US$15). AE, DC, MC, V. Sun–Thurs noon–2:30pm, 6–10:30pm; Fri noon–2:30pm, 6–11pm; Sat 6–11pm.

Shook! JAPANESE/CHINESE/ITALIAN/WESTERN GRILL   This place is unique for a number of reasons. First, Shook! is located on the ground floor of a shopping center, in a cavernous space decorated in a sort of Zen minimalism with splashes of color. Above, escalators glide shoppers to floors over the glass stage where the pop and jazz band plays nightly. Second, the menu features four different types of cuisine that are prepared in four separate show kitchens. It will take a few minutes to read the menu, which offers a mind-boggling selection of Japanese, Chinese, Italian, and Western grill specialties. Very inventive. A good spot if your party can't agree on where to eat—something for everyone. One caveat: The waitstaff sometimes seem lost in Shook's enormity.

Starhill Centre, Lower Ground Floor, 181 Jalan Bukit Bintang, (C) 03/2716-8535. Main courses RM20–RM200 (US$5–US$53). AE, DC, MC, V. Daily noon–2:30pm and 6:3–10:30pm..

Top Hat Restaurant ★★★ *Finds* ASIAN MIX   Let me tell you about my favorite restaurant in Kuala Lumpur. First, Top Hat has a unique atmosphere. In a 1930s bungalow that was once a school, the place winds through room after room, its walls painted in bright hues and furnished with an assortment of mix-and-matched teak tables, chairs, and antiques. Second, the menu is fabulous. While a la carte is available, Top Hat puts together set meals featuring nonya, Malacca Portuguese, traditional Malay, Thai, western, even vegetarian recipes. They're all brilliant. Desserts are huge and full of sin.

No.7 Jalan Kia Peng. © 03/2141-8611. Reservations recommended. Main courses RM30–RM88 (US$7.90–US$23). Set meals RM37–RM123 (US$9.75–US$32). AE, DC, MC, V. Lunch Mon–Fri noon–2:30pm; dinner daily 6–10:30pm.

ATTRACTIONS

Most of Kuala Lumpur's historic sights are located in the area around Merdeka Square/Jalan Hishamuddin area, while many of the gardens, parks, and museums are out at Lake Gardens. Taxi fare between the two areas will run you about RM5 (US$1.30).

Central Market ★   The original Central Market, built in 1936, used to be a wet market, but the place is now a cultural center (air-conditioned!) for local artists and craftspeople selling antiques, crafts, and curios. It is a fantastic place for buying Malaysian crafts and souvenirs, with two floors of shops to chose from. The Central Market also stages evening performances (7:45pm on weekends) of Malay martial arts, Indian classical dance, or Chinese orchestra. Call the number above for performance information.

Jalan Benteng. © 03/2274-6542. Daily 10am–10pm. Shops until 8pm.

Islamic Arts Museum ★★   The seat of Islamic learning in Kuala Lumpur, the center has displays of Islamic texts, artifacts, porcelain, and weaponry.

Jalan Perdana. © 03/2274-2020. Admission RM8 (US$2.10). Tues–Sun 10am–6pm.

Istana Negara   Closed to the public, this is the official residence of the king. You can peek through the gates at the istana (palace) and its lovely grounds.

Jalan Negara. No phone.

Jame Mosque (Masjid Jame)   The first settlers landed in Kuala Lumpur at the spot where the Gombak and Klang rivers meet, and in 1909 a mosque was built here. Styled after an Indian Muslim design, it is one of the oldest mosques in the city.

Jalan Tun Terak. No phone.

Kuala Lumpur Lake Gardens (Taman Tasik Perdana)   Built around an artificial lake, the 91.6-hectare (229-acre) park has plenty of space for jogging and rowing, and has a playground for the kids. It's the most popular park in Kuala Lumpur. Inside the Lake Gardens find the Kuala Lumpur Orchid Garden (Jalan Perdana; weekend and public holiday admission adults RM1/US25¢, children RM.50/US15¢; weekdays free; daily 9am–6pm) with a collection of over 800 orchid species from Malaysia, and it also contains thousands of international varieties. The **Kuala Lumpur Bird Park** (Jalan Perdana; © **03/2273-5423;** adults RM1/US$3.15, children RM6/US$1.60; daily 9am–6:30pm) is nestled in beautifully landscaped gardens, and has over 2,000 birds within its 3.2 hectares (8 acres). The **Kuala Lumpur Butterfly Park** (Jalan Cenderasari; © **03/2693-4799;** adults RM5/US$1.30, children RM1/US25¢; daily 9am–6pm) has over 6,000 butterflies belonging to 120 species make their home in this park, which has been landscaped with more than 15,000 plants to simulate the butterflies' natural rainforest environment. There are also other small animals and an insect museum.

Enter via Jalan Parliament. No phone. Free admission. Daily 9am–6pm.

Kuala Lumpur Railway Station   Built in 1910, the KL Railway Station is a beautiful example of Moorish architecture.

Jalan Sultan Hishamuddin. © 03/2274-6542. Daily 7:30am–10:30pm.

MATIC (Malaysia Tourist Information Complex) At MATIC you'll find an exhibit hall, tourist information services for Kuala Lumpur and Malaysia, and other travel-planning services. On Tuesdays, Thursdays, Saturdays, and Sundays there are cultural shows at 3pm, featuring Malaysian dance and music. Shows are RM5 (US$1.30) for adults, free for children.

Jalan Ampang. © 03/2164-3929. Daily 9am–6pm.

Menara Kuala Lumpur Standing 421m (1,389 ft.) tall, this concrete structure is the third tallest tower in the world, and the views from the top reach to the far corners of the city and beyond. At the top, the glass windows are fashioned after the Shah Mosque in Isfahan, Iran.

Bukit Nanas. © 03/2020-5448. Adults RM8 (US$2.10); children RM3 (US80¢). Daily 9am–10pm.

Merdeka Square Surrounded by colonial architecture with an exotic local flair, the square is a large field that was once the site of British social and sporting events. These days, Malaysia holds its spectacular Independence Day celebrations on the field, which is home to the world's tallest flagpole, standing at 100m (330 ft.).

Jalan Raja. No phone.

National Art Gallery The building that now houses the National Art Gallery was built as the Majestic Hotel in 1932 and has been restored to display contemporary works by Malaysian artists. There are international exhibits as well.

Jalan Sultan Hishamuddin. © 03/4025-4990. Free admission. Daily 10am–6pm.

National Mosque (Masjid Negara) Built in a modern design, the most distinguishing features of the mosque are its 73m (243-ft.) minaret and the umbrella-shaped roof, which is said to symbolize a newly independent Malaysia's aspirations for the future. Could be true, as the place was built in 1965, the year Singapore split from Malaysia.

Jalan Sultan Hishamuddin (near the KL Railway Station). No phone. Daily 9am–6pm.

National Museum (Muzim Negara) ★★ Located at Lake Gardens, the museum has more than 1,000 items of historic, cultural, and traditional significance, including art, weapons, musical instruments, and costumes.

Jalan Damansara. © 03/2282-6255. Admission RM1 (US25¢), children under 12 free. Daily 9am–6pm.

National Planetarium *Kids* The National Planetarium has a Space Hall with touch-screen interactive computers and hands-on experiments, a Viewing Gallery with binoculars for a panoramic view of the city, and an Ancient Observatory Park with models of Chinese and Indian astronomy systems. The Space Theatre has two different outer-space shows at 11am, 2pm, and 4pm for an extra charge of RM6 (US$1.60) for adults and RM4 (US$1.05) for children.

Lake Gardens. © 03/2273-5484. Admission to exhibition hall RM3 (US80¢), children RM2 (US55¢). Sat–Thurs 10am–4pm.

Parliament House In the Lake Gardens area, the Parliament House is a modern building housing the country's administrative offices, which were once in the Sultan Abdul Samad Building at Merdeka Square.

Jalan Parliament. Parliament sessions are not open to the public. No phone.

Petaling Street ★ This is the center of KL's Chinatown district. By day, stroll past hawker stalls, dim sum shops, wet markets, and all sorts of shops, from pawn shops to coffin makers. At night, a crazy bazaar (which is terribly crowded) pops up—look for designer knockoffs, fake watches, and pirate VCDs (Video CDs) here.

Petronas Twin Towers ✷   After 5 years of planning and building, Petronas Twin Towers has been completed. Standing at a whopping 451.9m (1,482 ft.) above street level, with 88 stories, the towers are the tallest buildings in the world. From the outside, the structures are designed with the kind of geometric patterns common to Islamic architecture, and on levels 41 and 42 the two towers are linked by a bridge. Visitors are permitted on the sky bridge daily from 10am to 12:45pm and 3 to 4:45pm every day except Mondays and public holidays.
Kuala Lumpur City Centre. No phone.

Sri Mahamariaman Temple   With a recent face-lift (Hindu temples must renovate every 12 years), this bright temple livens the gray street scene around. It's a beautiful temple tucked away in a narrow street in KL's Chinatown area, which was built by Thambusamy Pillai, a pillar of old KL's Indian community.
Jalan Bandar. No phone.

Sultan Abdul Samad Building   In 1897 this exotic building was designed by Regent Alfred John Bidwell, a colonial architect responsible for many of the buildings in Singapore. He chose a style called "Muhammadan" or "neo-Saracenic," which combines Indian Muslim architecture with Gothic and other Western elements. Built to house government administrative offices, today it is the home of Malaysia's Supreme Court and High Court.
Jalan Raja. No phone.

GOLF GREENS FEES

People from all over Asia flock to Malaysia for its golf courses, many of which are excellent standard courses designed by pros. The **Bangi Golf Resort,** No. 1 Persiaran Bandar, Bandar Baru Bangi, 43650 Selangor (℃ **03/8925-3728;** fax 03/8925-3726), has 18 holes, par 72, designed by Ronald Fream, with greens fees of RM100 (US$26) weekdays, RM170 (US$45) weekends and holidays. The **Mines Resort & Golf Club,** 101/5 mile, Jalan Sungei Besi, 43300 Seri Kembangan, Selangor (℃ **03/8943-2288**), features 18 holes, par 71, designed by Robert Trent Jones Jr., with greens fees of RM280 (US$74) weekdays, RM350 (US$92) weekend and holidays. **Suajana Golf & Country Club,** km 3, Jalan Lapangan Terbang Sultan Abdul Aziz Shah, 46783 Subang Selangor (℃ **03/7846-1466;** fax 03/7846-7818), has two 18-hole courses, each par 72, deigned by Robert Trent Jones Jr., with greens fees of RM170 (US$45) weekdays, RM290 (US$76) weekends and holidays.

SHOPPING

Kuala Lumpur is a truly great place to shop. In recent years, mall after mall has risen from city lots, filled with hundreds of retail outlets selling everything from haute couture to cheap chic clothing, electronic goods, jewelry, and arts and crafts. The **major shopping malls** are located in the area around Jalan Bukit Bintang and Jalan Sultan Ismail. There are also a few malls along Jalan Ampang. Suria KLCC, located just beneath the Petronas Twin Towers, has to be KLs best and brightest mall, and its largest. If you purchase electronics, make sure you get an international warranty.

Still the best place for Malaysian handicrafts, the huge **Central Market** on Jalan Benteng (℃ **03/2274-6542**) keeps any shopper saturated for hours. There you'll find a jumble of local artists and craftspeople selling their wares in the heart of town. It's also a good place to find Malaysian handicrafts from other regions of the country. One specific shop I like to recommend for Malaysian handicrafts is **Karyaneka,** Lot B, Kompleks Budaya Kraf (© **03/2164-4344**), with a warehouse selection of assorted goods from around the country, all of it fine quality.

Another favorite shopping haunt in KL is **Chinatown,** along Petaling Street. Day and night, it's a great place to wander and bargain for knockoff designer clothing and accessories, sunglasses, T-shirts, souvenirs, fake watches, and pirated videos.

Pasar malam (night markets) are very popular evening activities in KL. Whole blocks are taken up with these brightly lit and bustling markets packed with stalls selling everything you can dream of. They are likely to pop up anywhere in the city. Two good bets for catching one: Go to Jalan Haji Taib after dark until 10pm. On Saturday nights, head for Jalan Tuanku Abdul Rahman.

NIGHTLIFE

There's nightlife to spare in KL, from fashionable lounges to sprawling discos to pubs perfect for lounging. Basically, you can expect to pay about RM11 to RM20 (US$2.90–US$5.25) for a pint of beer, depending on what and where you order. While quite a few pubs are open for lunch, most clubs won't open until about 6 or 7pm. These places must all close by 1am, so don't plan on staying out too late. Nearly all have a happy hour, usually between 5 and 7pm, when drink discounts apply on draft beers and "house-pour" (lower shelf) mixed drinks. Generally, you're expected to wear dress casual clothing for these places, but avoid old jeans, tennis shoes, and very revealing outfits.

While there are some very good places in Kuala Lumpur, the true nightlife spot is in a place called **Bangsar,** just outside the city limits. It's 2 or 3 blocks of bars, cafes, and restaurants that cater to a variety of tastes (in fact, so many expatriates hang out there, they call it Kweiloh Lumpur, "Foreigner Lumpur" in Mandarin). Every taxi driver knows where it is. Get in and ask to go to Jalan Telawi Tiga in Bangsar (fare should be no more than RM5 or RM6/US$1.30 or US$1.60), and once there it's very easy to catch a cab back to town. Begin at **The Roof** (2 Jalan Telawi 4; © **03/2282-7168**), a three-story open-air cafe/bar that looks like a crazy Louisiana cathouse (you really can't miss it). From there you can try **La Bodega** (16 Jalan Telawi 2; © **03/2287-8318**) for some funky dance music; or **Finnegan's** (© **03/284-0187**), a very rowdy Irish bar. And that's only the beginning.

Back in Kuala Lumpur, there are some fun bars and pubs that I'd recommend. If you just want to hop around and see different places, I'd suggest heading for the corner of Jalan Sultan Ismail and Jalan P. Ramlee, and head down P. Ramlee and check out the colorful pubs, clubs and tiki bars along this stretch. For a reliable Irish pub, **Delaney's,** ground floor, Park Royal Hotel, Jalan Sultan Ismail (© **03/2141-5195**), has a good selection of draft beers.

For a little live music with your drinks, the **Hard Rock Cafe,** Jalan Sultan Ismail next to Concorde Hotel (© **03/2144-4062**), hosts the best of the regional bands, which play nightly for a crowd of locals, tourists, and expatriates who take their parties very seriously.

SIDE TRIPS FROM KUALA LUMPUR
TAMAN NEGARA NATIONAL PARK ✶✶✶

Malaysia's most famous national park, **Taman Negara,** covers 434,300 hectares (1,085,750 acres) of primary rainforest estimated to be as old as 130 million years, and encompasses within its borders **Gunung Tahan,** peninsular Malaysia's highest peak at 2,187m (2,392 ft.) above sea level.

Prepare to see lush vegetation and rare orchids, some 250 bird species, and maybe, if you're lucky, some barking deer, tapir, elephants, tigers, leopards, and rhinos. As for primates, there are long-tailed macaques, leaf monkeys, gibbons, and more. Malaysia has taken the preservation of this forest seriously since the early part of the century, so Taman Negara showcases efforts to keep this land in as pristine a state as possible while still allowing humans to appreciate the splendor.

There are outdoor activities for any level of adventurer. Short **jungle walks** to observe nature are lovely, but then so are the hardcore 9-day treks or climbs up Gunung Tahan. There are also overnight trips to night hides where you can observe animals up close. The jungle canopy walk is the longest in the world, and at 25m (83 ft.) above ground, the view is spectacular. There are also rivers for rafting and swimming, fishing spots, and a couple of caves.

If you plan your trip through one of the main resort operators, they can arrange, in addition to accommodations, all meals, treks and a coach transfer to and from Kuala Lumpur. Prices vary wildly, depending on the time of season you plan your visit, your level of comfort desired, and the extent to which you wish to explore the forests. The best time to visit the park is between the months of April to September, other times it will be a tad wet, and that's why it's called a rainforest.

Mutiara Taman Negara Resort ✿, well established in the business of hosting visitors to the park, is the best accommodation in the park in terms of comfort. It organizes trips for 3 days and 2 nights or for 4 days and 3 nights, as well as an a la carte deal where you pay for lodging (see above) and activities separately. Accommodations come in many styles: a bungalow suite for families, chalet and chalet suite, both good for couples; standard guesthouse rooms in a motel-style longhouse; and dormitory hostels for budget travelers. Explorer visitors check into the chalets, which are air-conditioned with attached bathroom, and enjoy a full itinerary of activities included in the package price. A la carte activities include a 3-hour jungle trek, a 1½-hour night jungle walk, the half-day Lata Berkoh river trip with swimming, a 2-hour cave exploration, and a trip down the rapids in a rubber raft (Kuala Tahan, Jerantut, 27000 Pahang; © 09/266-3500; fax 09/266-1500; Kuala Lumpur Sales Office 03/2721-8888; fax 03/2721-3388).

Nusa Camp will send you to the park, put you up in their own kampung house, chalet, or hostel accommodations, and guide your activities. Once there, they have numerous guided trips out into the wilds: a night safari, night walk, a trip to see an orang asli village, tubing down rapids, overnight hikes, overnight river fishing trips, a trip to the canopy walkway, or an overnight trip to explore caves. This outfit is just slightly less expensive than Taman Negara Resort, above, but Taman Negara Resort is a better facility. Bookings through Kuala Lumpur Office: **Malaysia Tourist Information Centre (MATIC),** 109 Jalan Ampang (© 03/2162-7682; fax 03/2162-7682).

GENTING HIGHLANDS

The "City of Entertainment," as Genting is known locally, serves as Malaysia's answer to Las Vegas, complete with bright lights (that can be seen from Kuala Lumpur) and gambling. And while most people come here for the casino, there's a wide range of other activities, although most of them seem to serve the purpose of entertaining the kids while you bet their college funds at the roulette wheel.

Genting has four hotels of varying prices within the resort. Rates vary depending on the season, so be prepared for higher rates during the winter holidays.

Genting Hotel is a newer property in the resort complex, and is linked directly to the casino. Promotional rates can be as low as RM97 (US$26) for low period weekdays. The Highlands Hotel's main attraction is its direct link to the casino. You'll pay the highest rate here, as promotional rates in this hotel are very rare. **Resort Hotel** is comparable to the Theme Park Hotel below, but it's a little newer and the double occupancy rooms all have two double beds and standing showers only. The **Theme Park Hotel** is a little less expensive than the others, primarily because it's a little older and you must walk outside to reach the casino. Promotional rates during the week can be as low as RM62 for up to three people in one room. All properties share the same address and contact numbers at Genting Highlands 69000, Pahang Darul Makmur (✆ 03/211-1118; fax 03/211-1888).

The Resort casino is open 24 hours. Entry is a refundable deposit of RM200 (US$53) whether you're a guest at the resort or just visiting for the day. By the way, you must be at least 21 years old to enter the casino. Outside of the casino, there's also a pond, a bowling alley and an indoor heated pool. The **Awana Golf and Country Club** (✆ 03/6101-3025; fax 03/6101-3535) is the premier golf course in these hills. For children, there's the huge Genting Theme Park, covering 100,000 square feet and mostly filled with rides, plus many Western fast-food eating outlets, games, and other attractions. At night Gentings dinner theaters stage pop concerts by international (mostly Asian) performers, and everything from lion dance competitions to Wild West and magic shows. For dining, the most highly recommended place is **The Peak Restaurant & Lounge,** Genting's fine-dining restaurant on the 17th floor of the Genting Hotel.

For buses from Kuala Lumpur, call **Genting Highlands Transport,** operating buses every half-hour from 6:30am to 9pm daily from the Pekeliling Bus Terminal on Jalan Ipoh. The cost for one way is RM2.60 (US70¢) and the trip takes 1 hour. The bus lets you off at the foot of the hill, where you take the cable car to the top for RM3 (US80¢). For bus information, call ✆ 03/4041-0173.

You can also get there by hiring an outstation **taxi.** The cost is RM40 (US$11) and can be arranged by calling the **Puduraya** outstation taxi stand at ✆ 03/2078-0213.

The **Genting Highlands Resort** is owned and operated by Resorts World Berhad, who'll be glad to provide you with hotel reservations if you call ✆ 03/2162-3555 or fax 03/2161-6611. You can also visit their central office at Wisma Genting on Jalan Sultan Ismail in KL.

CAMERON HIGHLANDS

Located in the hills, this colonial-era resort town has a cool climate, which makes it the perfect place for weekend getaways by Malaysians and Singaporeans who are sick of the heat. If you've been in the region awhile, you might also appreciate the respite.

The climate is also very conducive to agriculture. After the area's discovery by British surveyor William Cameron in 1885, the major crop here became tea, which is still grown today. The area's lovely gardens supply cities throughout the region with vegetables, flowers, and fruit year-round. Among the favorites here are the strawberries, which can be eaten fresh or transformed into yummy desserts in the local restaurants. At the many commercial flower nurseries you can see chrysanthemums, fuchsias, and roses growing on the terraces. Rose gardens are prominent here.

Ringlet is the first town you see as you make your way up the highlands, and the main agricultural center. Travel farther up the elevation to **Tanah Rata,** the major tourism town in the Highlands, where you'll find chalets, cottages, and bungalows. The town basically consists of shops along one side of the main street (Jalan Sultan Ahmad Shah) and food stalls and the bus terminal on the other. **Brinchang,** at 1,524m (5,029 ft.) above sea level, is the highest town, surrounding a market square where there are shops, Tudor inns, rose gardens, and a Buddhist temple.

Temperatures in the Cameron Highlands average 70°F (21°C) during the day and 50°F (10°C) at night. There are paths for treks though the countryside and to peaks of surrounding mountains. Two waterfalls, the Robinson Falls and Parit Falls, have pools at their feet where you can have a swim.

There are **no visitor information services** here. They've been closed for a very long time, and have no immediate plans for reopening. Walking in each town is a snap because the places are so small, but the towns are far apart, so a walk between them could take up much time. There are local buses that ply at odd times between them for around RM3 (US80¢), or you could pick up one of the ancient, unmarked taxis and cruise between towns for RM4 (US$1.05). You'll find banks with ATMs and money-changing services along the main road in Tanah Rata.

The best choice for accommodations here is **The Smokehouse Hotel.** Situated between Tanah Rata and Brinchang, this picturesque Tudor mansion has pretty gardens outside and a charming old-world ambience inside. Built in 1937 as a country house in the heyday of colonial British getaways, the conversion into a hotel has kept the place happily in the 1930s. Guest suites have four-poster beds and antique furnishings, and are stocked with plush amenities. The hotel encourages guests to play golf at the neighboring course, sit for afternoon tea with strawberry confections, or trek along nearby paths (for which they'll provide a picnic basket). It's all a bizarre escape from Malaysia, but an extremely charming one (Tanah Rata, Cameron Highlands, Pahang Darul Makmur; ✆ **05/491-1215;** fax 05/491-1214; RM400–RM600/US$105–US$158 suite).

For a more economical place to stay try **The Cool Point Hotel** (891 Persiaran Dayang Endah, 39000 Tanah Rata, Cameron Highlands, Pahang Darul Makmur; ✆ **05/491-4914;** fax 05/491-4070; RM125–RM180/US$33–US$47 double). Cool Point has an outstanding location, a 2-minute walk to Tanah Rata. While the modern building has some Tudor-like styling on the outside, the rooms inside are pretty standard, but the place is very clean. Make sure you book your room early. This place is always a sellout.

Most of the sights can be seen in a day, but it's difficult to plan your time well. In Cameron Highlands I recommend trying one of the sightseeing outfits in either Brinchang or Tanah Rata. **C. S. Travel & Tours,** 47 Main Rd., Tanah Rata (✆ 05/491-1200; fax 05/491-2390), is a highly reputable agency that will plan half-day tours for RM15 (US$3.95) or full days starting from RM80 (US$21). On your average tour you'll see the Boh tea plantation and factory, flower nurseries, rose gardens, strawberry farms, butterfly farms and the Sam Poh Buddhist Temple. You're required to pay admission to each attraction yourself. They also provide trekking and overnight camping tours in the surrounding hills with local trail guides. Treks are RM30 (US$7.90), camping RM150 (US$39) for 2 days and 1 night. Bookings are requested at least 1 day in advance. Also, pretty much every hotel can arrange these services for you.

If you want to hit around some balls, **Padang Golf,** Main Road between Tanah Rata and Brinchang (© 05/491-1126), has 18 holes at par 71, with greens fees around RM42 (US$11) on weekdays and RM63 (US$17) on weekends. They also provide club rentals, caddies, shoes, and carts.

To get to Cameron Highlands, **Kurnia Bistari Express Bus** (© 05/491-2978) operates between Kuala Lumpur and Tanah Rata four times daily for RM10 (US$2.65) one way. They don't accept bookings in Kuala Lumpur, asking you to just show up at Puduraya bus terminal to buy your ticket and board the next bus. The bus terminal is in the center of town along the main drag. Just next to it is the taxi stand. It's a two-horse town; you can't miss either of them. Outstation taxis from KL will cost RM180 (US$47) for the trip. Call © 03/2078-0213 for booking. For trips from Cameron Highlands call © 05/491-2355. Taxis are cheaper on the way back because they don't have to climb the mountains.

2 Johor Bahru

Johor Bahru, the capital of the state of Johor, is at the southern tip of the Malaysian peninsula, where Malaysia's north-south highway comes to its southern terminus. Since it's just over the causeway from Singapore, a very short jump by car, bus, or train, it's a popular point of entry to Malaysia. Johor Bahru, or "JB," is not the most fascinating destination in Malaysia, but for a quick day visit from Singapore or as a stopover en route to other Malaysian destinations, it offers some good shopping, sightseeing, and dining.

Johor's early beginnings were very closely entwined with nearby Malacca's. The Portuguese and Dutch, who each had their eye on the successful city-port, used Johor as a stepping-stone—the Portuguese pummeled the place to get to Malacca in 1511, and in 1641 the Dutch formed a strategic alliance with Johor to overthrow the Portuguese. In an ironic twist, Malacca's success did not continue under the Portuguese or the Dutch. In fact, by the 1700s, favorable rights bestowed upon Johor turned the state into a powerful threat to Malacca's trade. Eventually the envious Dutch attacked Johor, driving its leaders to establish a capital on the island of Riau, just south of the peninsula.

Under the successful administration of the Temenggong and Bendahara families (ministerial agents for the sultanate), Riau grew into a very successful entry port. But conflict between the two families led to the assassination of the sultan. The city was weakened, as the Malays believed the sultan to be the last direct descendent of Raja Iskander Zul-karnain, Alexander the Great, and his passing left a great void. This fragile state left the city vulnerable to the Bugis, who came to settle to escape conflict in their home in southern Sulawesi. The Bugis, master navigators and skilled traders with countless allies, catapulted Riau's status ever higher, but in meddling with affairs of the leadership won few supporters among the local Malays. By 1721, the Bugis were ruling under a puppet sultan, yet intermarriage secured the Bugis bloodline that many Malays carry with them to this day.

In 1757 the Malays once again aligned themselves with the Dutch to overthrow the Bugis, and by 1760 all foreign-born Bugis were expelled. However, the economic success of Riau waned in the decades to follow. The Bugis-controlled sultan was deposed, and the Dutch appointed one of his sons, Abdul Rahman, as his successor.

Temmenggong Ibrahim, under Sultan Abdul Rahman, signed a treaty in 1819 with Sir Stamford Raffles, allowing the British East India Company to set up shop on Singapore. During the 1800s Singapore's success greatly overshadowed Riau's former glory. In the mid-1800s under Sultan Abu Bakar (who was raised and educated in Singapore), Johor became an administerial extension of Singapore. In 1866 Johor Bahru was named the state capital, and it was developed with a Western-style government. Hence, today Abu Bakar is known as "The Father of Modern Johor." Finally, in 1914 Johor was placed under the Federated States of Malaya. The sultan lost his power, except to perform ceremonial duties—for example, his successors could retain the official yellow costume of the sultanate. To this day no one (including you) is permitted to wear yellow at the sultan's favorite golf courses (especially at the Royal Johor Golf Club). The present sultan is His Majesty Sultan Iskander, who has held the title since 1981.

ESSENTIALS
VISITOR INFORMATION
The Malaysia Tourism Board office in Johor Bahru is at the **Johor Tourist Information Centre (JOTIC),** centrally located on Jalan Ayer Molek, on the second floor (© 07/222-4935). Information is available not only for Johor Bahru, but for the state of Johor as well.

GETTING THERE
BY CAR If you arrive by car via the causeway you will clear the immigration checkpoint upon entering the Malaysia side.

BY BUS Buses to and from other parts of Malaysia are based at the Larkin Bus Terminal off Jalan Garuda in the northern part of the city. Taxis are available at the terminal to take you to the city. The easiest way to catch a bus from KL is at the old KL Railway Station. **Plusliner** (© 03/2274-9601) runs service 12 times daily for RM20 (US$5.30). The trip takes just under 6 hours. Most all other cities in Malaysia have service to Johor Bahru. Consult each city section for bus terminal information. From Singapore, the **Singapore-Johor Express** (© 65/6292-8149) operates every 10 minutes between 6:30am and midnight from the Ban Sen Terminal at Queen Street near Arab Street, Singapore. The cost for the half-hour trip is S$2.10 (US$1.20).

If you're looking to depart Johor Bahru via bus, contact one of the following companies at Larkin for route information: **Transnasional** (© 07/224-5182) or **Plusliner/NICE** (© 07/222-3317).

BY TRAIN The **Keretapi Tanah Melayu Berhad (KTM)** trains arrive and depart from the Johor Bahru Railway Station at Jalan Tun Abdul Razak, opposite Merlin Tower (© 07/223-4727). Catch trains from **KL Sentral** (© 03/2730-2000) four times daily for a cost between RM14 and RM56 (US$3.60 and US$15), depending on the class you travel. From the **Singapore Railway Station** (© 65/6222-5165), on Keppel Road in Tanjong Pagar, the short trip is between S$1.10 and S$4.20 (US65¢ and US$2.50).

BY PLANE The **Sultan Ismail Airport,** 30 to 40 minutes outside the city (© 07/599-4737), has regular flights to and from major cities in Malaysia and also from Singapore. The airport tax is RM20 (US$5.25) for international flights and RM5 (US$1.30) for domestic, but this is usually reflected in the price of the ticket. For reservations on **Malaysian Airlines** flights call © **1300/88-3000** in Johor Bahru. A taxi from the airport to the city center will run you RM20 to RM25 (US$5.25–US$6.60) per person. There's also a **Hertz** counter, but to make your reservation you must call their downtown office at © **07/223-7520.** A RM4 (US$1.05) coach service runs between the airport and the

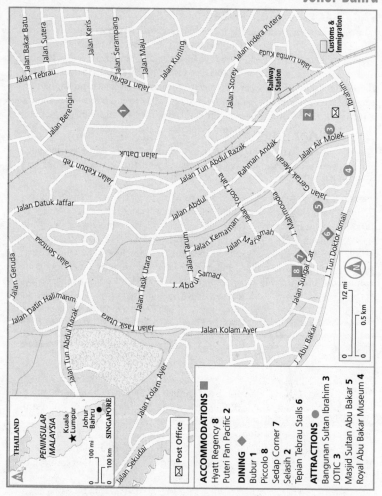

Customs & Immigration

Railway Station

Jalan Bakar Batu
Jalan Sutera
Jalan Keris
Jalan Serampang
Jalan Maju
Jalan Kuning
Jalan Storey
Jalan Indera Putera
Jalan Lumba Kuda
Jalan Tebrau
Jalan Tebrau
Jalan Berengin
Jalan Datuk
Jalan Kebun Teh
Jalan Tun Abdul Razak
Rahman Andak
Jalan Air Molek
Jalan Gertak Merah
Jalan Datuk Jaffar
Jalan Abdul
Jalan Yusof Taha
Jalan Mahmoodia
J. Ibrahim
Jalan Geruda
Jalan Sentosa
Jalan Tarum
Jalan Kemaman
Jalan Mariamah
J. Tun Doktor Ismail
Jalan Datin Halimanm
Jalan Tasik Utara
J. Abdul Samad
Jalan Sungai Cat
Jalan Tun Abdul Razak
Jalan Tasik Utara
Jalan Kolam Ayer
J. Abu Bakar
Jalan Kolam Ayer
Jalan Sekudai

1/2 mi
0.5 km
N

THAILAND
PENINSULAR MALAYSIA
Kuala Lumpur ★
Johor Bahru ●
SINGAPORE
100 mi
100 km

⊠ Post Office

ACCOMMODATIONS ■
Hyatt Regency **8**
Puteri Pan Pacific **2**

DINING ◆
Bubur **1**
Piccolo **8**
Sedap Corner **7**
Selasih **2**
Tepian Tebrau Stalls **6**

ATTRACTIONS ●
Bangunan Sultan Ibrahim **3**
JOTIC **3**
Masjid Sultan Abu Bakar **5**
Royal Abu Bakar Museum **4**

JOTIC tourist information center in town. If you use this service for departures, make sure you catch the coach at least 2 hours before departure time. Call ✆ **07/221-7481** for more information.

BY TAXI   Outstation taxis can bring you to Johor Bahru from any major city on the peninsula. From KL's **Puduraya Bus Terminal** (✆ **03/2078-0213** Outstation Taxi) the cost is about RM220 (US$58). For taxi stands in other cities please refer to each city's section. For taxi hiring from **Johor Bahru** call ✆ **07/223-4494**. The outstation taxi stand is located at Larkin Bus Terminal, but for an extra RM10 (US$2.65) they'll pick you up at your hotel.

GETTING AROUND

As in Kuala Lumpur, taxis charge a metered fare, RM2.05 (US55¢) for the first kilometer and an additional 10 sen for each 200m after that. Between midnight and 6am you'll be charged an extra 50% of the total fare. For taxi pickup there's an extra RM1 (US25¢) charge. Call **Citycab** at ✆ **07/354-0007**.

FAST FACTS: JOHOR BAHRU

The **American Express** office is located at **Overseas Express Travel & Tours,** Wisma Overseas Express, 29 Jalan Meldrum (② **07/224-6611**). Major banks are located in the city center, and money changers at shopping malls and at JOTIC.

The main post office is on **Jalan Dato Onn** (② **07/223-2555**), just around the corner from JOTIC. For Internet connection, I recommend the conveniently located Weblinks Connexions in the JOTIC center on Jalan Ayer Molek, L1-2 (② **07/225-1387**). They charge RM2.50 (US65¢) per hour.

ACCOMMODATIONS

Several international chains have accommodations in JB. Most are intended for the business set, but holiday travelers will find the accommodations very comfortable.

Mutiara Hotel Johor Bahru   Formerly the Holiday Inn, this property has gotten a recent upgrading as Mutiara, but that still does not compensate for its location—a bit far from the major attractions. Still, discounts here are good, so be sure to inquire. The big modern hotel block serves groups and conferences better than independent travelers. The handsome two-level lobby has polished marble floors and a domed ceiling supported by fat wood columns. Guest rooms are comfortable enough, with furniture in traditional fabrics, wood paneling details.

Jalan Dato Sulaiman, Century Garden, 80990 Johor Bahru, Johor. ② **07/332-3800**. Fax 07/331-8884. 330 units. RM370 (US$97) double; RM550 (US$145) suite. AE, DC, MC, V. **Amenities:** 4 restaurants (international, Szechuan, Italian, local); lobby lounge; outdoor pool; squash court; fitness center with Jacuzzi, sauna, steam, and massage; concierge; business center; 24-hr. room service; same-day laundry service/dry cleaning; nonsmoking rooms; executive-level rooms. *In room:* A/C, TV w/satellite programming, minibar, coffee/tea-making facilities, hair dryer, safe.

The Hyatt Regency   he Hyatt is near the City Square, but likes to fancy itself as a city resort, focusing on landscaped gardens and greenery around the premises—the private lagoon-style pool, with gardens seen from the glass windows of the main lobby, is surely spectacular. The deluxe rooms are located better than the others, with views of Singapore and fabulous sunsets. Rooms are bland, with typical amenities common to this type of international chain hotel. However, this is without a doubt the best accommodation in town in terms of comfort; its rival Pan Pacific has the better location, though.

Jalan Sungai Chat, P.O. Box 222, 80720 Johor Bahru, Johor. ② **800/233-1234** or 07/222-1234. Fax 07/223-2718. 406 units. RM420–RM480 (US$111–US$126) double; RM500–RM600 (US$132–US$158) Executive Floor; from RM800 (US$211) suite. AE, DC, MC, V. **Amenities:** 3 restaurants (international, Japanese, Italian); lounge; outdoor lagoon-style pool on 2 levels; outdoor, lighted tennis courts; fitness center; spa with Jacuzzi, sauna, steam, and massage; concierge; limousine service; business center; 24-hr. room service; babysitting; same-day laundry service/dry cleaning; nonsmoking rooms; executive-level rooms. *In room:* A/C, TV w/satellite programming and in-house movie, minibar, coffee/tea-making facilities, hair dryer, safe.

The Puteri Pan Pacific   The good news about the Puteri is it's located in the heart of the city, near attractions, shopping, dining and entertainment. The bad news is it is a very busy hotel and human traffic makes it noisy and somewhat on the run-down side. Nevertheless, little traditional touches to the decor make the Pan Pacific unique. Be sure to ask about special discounts, which can bring the price down by as much as half.

"The Kotaraya," P.O. Box 293, 80730 Johor Bahru, Johor. ② **07/223-3333**. Fax 07/223-6622. 500 units. RM330–RM400 (US$87–US$105) double; RM450–RM2,000 (US$118–US$526) suite. AE, DC, MC, V. **Amenities:** 4 restaurants (international, local, Mediterranean, Chinese); lobby lounge; outdoor pool; outdoor, lighted tennis court; squash court; well-managed and popular fitness center with Jacuzzi, sauna, steam, and massage; concierge; limousine service; business center; shopping arcade adjacent; 24-hr. room service; babysitting; same-day laundry service/dry cleaning; nonsmoking rooms; executive-level rooms. *In room:* A/C, TV w/satellite programming and in-house movie, minibar, coffee/tea-making facilities, hair dryer.

DINING

The majority of fine dining in Johor Bahru is in the hotels. Outside the hotels you can sample some great local cuisine, both Malay and Chinese, and wonderful seafood from the city's hawker stalls.

Bubur TAIWAN CHINESE   For fast, inexpensive eats you can even order for takeout, try this place. It's a family restaurant, so it can get pretty lively. The staff is quick and attentive without being imposing. Best dishes are the traditional braised pork in soy sauce and the grilled butterfish in black-bean sauce.

191 Jalan Harimau, Century Garden. ✆ 07/335-5891. Reservations held for a half-hour only. Main courses RM7–RM12 (US$1.85–US$3.15). AE, MC, V. Daily 11am–5am except 4 days into the Chinese New Year.

Piccolo ITALIAN   Perhaps the most popular restaurant for the expatriate community in Johor Bahru, Piccolo's lush lagoon-style poolside ambience has a very tropical and relaxed feel. Under the timber awning, the high ceiling and bamboo chick blinds make for romantic terrace dining. The antipasto is wonderful, as are dishes like chicken with shrimp and spinach. The grilled seafood is outstanding.

Hyatt Regency, Jalan Sungai Chat. ✆ 07/222-1234. Main courses RM20–RM58 (US$5.25–US$15). AE, DC, MC, V. Daily 11:30am–2:30pm, 6:30–10:30pm.

Sedap Corner THAI/CHINESE/MALAY   Sedap Corner is very popular with the locals. It's dressed down in metal chairs and Formica-top tables, with a coffee shop feel. Local dishes like sambal sabah, otak-otak, and fish head curry are house specials, and you don't have to worry about them being too spicy.

11 Jalan Abdul Samad. ✆ 07/224-6566. Reservations recommended. Main courses RM4.50–RM24 (US$1.20–US$6.30), though most dishes no more than RM6 (US$1.60). No credit cards. Daily 9am–9:45pm.

Selasih MALAY   For a broad-range sampling of Malaysian cuisine, try Selasih, which has a daily buffet spread of more than 70 items featuring regional dishes from all over the country. Each night, the dinner buffet is accompanied by traditional Malay music and dance performances. Children and seniors receive a 50% discount.

The Puteri Pan Pacific, "The Kotaraya." ✆ 07/223-3333, ext. 3151. Reservations recommended. Buffet lunch RM28 (US$7.35); buffet dinner RM40 (US$11). AE, DC, MC, V. Daily 11:30am–2:30pm; Fri–Sat 6:30–10:30pm (no dinner on weekdays).

HAWKER CENTERS

The Tepian Tebrau Stalls in Jalan Skudai (along the seafront) and the stalls near the Central Market offer cheap local eats in hawker-center style. The dish that puts Johor Bahru on the map, ikan bakar (barbecued fish with chiles), is out of this world at the Tepian Tebrau stalls.

ATTRACTIONS

The sights in Johor Bahru are few, but there are some interesting museums and a beautiful istana and mosque. It's a fabulous place to stay for a day, especially if it's a day trip from Singapore, but to stay for longer may be stretching the point.

Bangunan Sultan Ibrahim (State Secretariat Building)   The saracenic flavor of this building makes it feel older than it truly is. Built in 1940, today it houses the State Secretariat.

Jalan Abdul Ibrahim. No phone.

Masjid Sultan Abu Bakar This mosque was commissioned by Sultan Ibrahim in 1890 after the death of his father, Sultan Abu Bakar. It took 8 years and RM400,000 to build, and is one of the most beautiful mosques in Malaysia—at least from the outside. The inside? I can't tell you. I showed up in "good Muslim woman" clothing, took off my shoes, and crept up to the outer area (where I know women are allowed), and a Haji flew out of an office and shooed me off in a flurry. He asked if I was Muslim, I said no, and he said I wasn't allowed in. When I reported this to the tourism office at JOTIC, they thought I was nuts, and said anyone with proper attire could enter the appropriate sections. Let me know if you get in.

Jalan Masjid. No phone.

Royal Abu Bakar Museum Also called the Istana Bakar, this gorgeous royal palace was built by Sultan Abu Bakar in 1866. Today it houses the royal collection of international treasures, costumes, historical documents, fine art from the family collection, and relics of the Sultanate.

Grand Palace, Johor. Jalan Tun Dr Ismail. © 07/223-0555. Adults RM27 (US$7); children under 12 RM11 (US$3). Sat–Thurs 9am–4pm.

SPORTS & THE OUTDOORS

In addition to its cities and towns, Johor also has some beautiful nature to take in, which is doubly good if you have only a short time to see Malaysia and can't afford to travel north to some of the larger national parks.

Johor Endau Rompin National Park is about 488 sq. km (293 sq. miles) of lowland forest. There's jungle trekking through 26km (16 miles) of trails and over rivers to see diverse tropical plant species, colorful birds, and wild animals. Unfortunately, you'll have to be a camper to really enjoy the park, as this is the only accommodation you'll get. Still, for those who love the great outdoors, first contact the National Parks (Johor) Corporation, JKR 475, Bukit Timbalan, Johor Bahru (© 07/223-7471), for entry permission. You'll have to take an out-station taxi from Johor Bahru (cost: RM60/US$16); for booking, call © 07/223-4494 to Kluang. The taxi driver will drop you at the shuttle to the park entrance. Take this shuttle (which you'll need to prearrange through the National Parks Board) to the park entrance at Kahang. The 3-hour trip costs RM350 (US$92) for two people, then you'll have to pay the RM20 (US$5.25) per-person entrance fee to the park. They can rent you all the gear you'll need, but you must bring your own food, and remember to boil your drinking water at least 10 minutes to get it into a potable condition.

The **Waterfalls at Lombong,** near Kota Tinggi, measuring about 34m (112 ft.) high, are about 56km (34 miles) northeast of Johor Bahru. You can cool off in the pools below the falls and enjoy the area's chalets, camping facilities, restaurant, and food stalls. An outstation taxi will also take you to the falls, which are a little off the track on your way east to Desaru. The cost would also be around RM60 (US$16).

Johor is a favorite destination for **golf** enthusiasts. The Royal Johor Country Club and Pulai Springs Country Club are just outside Johor Bahru and offer a range of country club facilities, while other courses require a bit more traveling time, but offer resort-style accommodations. *One note of caution:* If you play in Johor, especially at the Royal Johor Country Club, don't wear yellow. It is the official color of the sultan, and is worn only by him when he visits the courses.

The most famous course has to be the **Royal Johor Country Club,** 3211 Jalan Larkin, 80200 Johor Bahru, Johor ((© 07/223-3322; fax 07/224-0729).

This 18-hole, par-72 course provides the favored game of the sultan of Johor, so they don't accept walk-ins. You must contact the club manager beforehand to obtain admission. Once you've received his okay, expect to pay RM105 (US$28) for weekday play and RM210 (US$55) for weekends. Other courses to try include **Palm Resort Golf & Country Club,** Jalan Persiaran Golf, off Jalan Jumbo, 81250 Senai, Johor (© **07/599-6222;** fax 07/599-6001), with two 18-hole courses, par 72 and 74, and greens fees RM150 (US$39) weekdays, RM250 to RM325 (US$66–US$86) weekends; **Pulai Springs Country Club,** km 20 Jalan Pontian Lama, 81110 Pulai, Johor (© **07/521-2121;** fax 07/521-1818), with two 18-hole courses (both par 72) and greens fees of RM105 (US$28) weekdays, RM210 (US$55) weekends); or the **Ponderosa Golf & Country Club,** 10-C Jalan Bumi Hijau 3, Taman Molek, 81100 Johor Bahru, Johor (© **07/354-9999;** fax 07/355-7400), with 18 holes, par 72, and greens fees of RM80 (US$21) weekdays, RM180 (US$47) weekends).

SHOPPING

The **Johor Craftown Handicraft Centre,** 36 Jalan Skudai, off Jalan Abu Bakar (© **07/236-7346**), has, in addition to a collection of local crafts, demonstration performances of handicrafts techniques. **JOTIC,** 2 Jalan Ayer Molek (© **07/224-2000**), is a shopping mall with tourist information, cultural performances, exhibits, demonstrations of crafts, and restaurants.

3 Malacca

While the destinations on the east coast are ideal for resort-style beach getaways, the cities on the west coast are perfect for vacations filled with culture and history, and Malacca is one of the best places to start. The attraction here is the city's cultural heritage, around which a substantial tourism industry has grown. If you're visiting, a little knowledge of this history will help you understand and appreciate all there is to see.

Malacca was founded around 1400 by Parameswara, called **Iskander Shah** in the Malay Annals. After he was chased from Palembang in southern Sumatra by invading Javanese, he set up a kingdom in Singapore (Temasek), and after being overthrown by invaders there, ran up the west coast of the Malay peninsula to Malacca, where he settled and established a port city. The site was an ideal midpoint in the east-west trade route and was in a favorable spot to take advantage of the two monsoons that dominated shipping routes. Malacca soon drew the attention of the Chinese, and the city maintained very close relations with the mainland as a trading partner and a political ally. The Japanese were also eager to trade in Malacca, as were Muslim merchants. After Parameswara's death in 1414, his son, Mahkota Iskander Shah, converted to Islam and became the first sultan of Malacca. The word of Islam quickly spread throughout the local population.

During the 15th century, Malacca was ruled by a succession of wise sultans who expanded the wealth and stability of the economy, built up the administration's coffers, extended the sultanate to the far reaches of the Malay peninsula, Singapore, and parts of northern Sumatra, and thwarted repeated attacks by the Siamese. The success of the empire was drawing international attention.

The Portuguese were one of the powers eyeing the port and formulating plans to dominate the east-west trade route, establish the naval supremacy of Portugal, and promote Christianity in the region. They struck in 1511 and conquered Malacca in a battle that lasted only a month. It is believed the local Malaccans had become accustomed to the comforts of affluence and turned soft and vulnerable. After the defeat, the sultanate fled to Johor, where it reestablished the seat of Malay power. Malacca would never again be ruled by a sultan. The Portuguese looted the city and sent its riches off to Lisbon.

The Portuguese were also the first of a chain of ruling foreign powers who would struggle in vain to retain the early economic success of the city. The foreign conquerors had a major strike against them: Their Christianity alienated the locals and repelled Muslim traders. The city quickly became nothing more than a sleepy outpost.

In 1641, the Dutch, with the help of Johor, conquered Malacca and controlled the city until 1795. Again, the Dutch were unsuccessful in rebuilding the glory of past prosperity in Malacca, and the city continued to sleep.

In 1795, the Dutch traded Malacca to the British in return for Bencoolen in Sumatra, being far more concerned with their Indonesian interests anyway. Malacca became a permanent British settlement in 1811, but by this time had become so poor and alienated that it was impossible to bring it back to life.

The final blow came in 1941, when the city fell under Japanese occupation for 4 years. It wasn't until 1957 that Malacca, along with the rest of Malaysia, gained full independence.

ESSENTIALS
VISITOR INFORMATION
Surprisingly, there is no Malaysia Tourism Board office in Malacca, but there is a locally operated **Malacca Tourism Centre** in the Town Square (© 06/283-6538).

GETTING THERE
While there is an airport in Malacca, it's not open for any flights due to lack of demand. And while Malacca doesn't have a proper train station, the **KTM** stops at Tampin (© 06/441-1034), 38km (23¾ miles) north of the city. It's not the most convenient way in and out of Malacca, but if you decide to stop en route between Kuala Lumpur and Johor Bahru, you can easily catch a waiting taxi to your hotel in town for RM35 to RM40 (US$9.20–US$11).

BY BUS From Singapore, contact **Malacca-Singapore Express** at © 65/6293-5915. Buses depart seven times daily for the 4½-hour trip (S$11/(US$6.30). From **KL's Puduraya Bus Terminal** on Jalan Pudu, Transnasional (© 03/230-5044) has hourly buses between 8am and 10pm for RM6.80 (US$1.80).

The bus station in Malacca is at Jalan Kilang, within the city. Taxis are easy to find from here.

BY TAXI Outstation **taxis** can bring you here from any major city, including Johor Bahru (about RM120/US$32) and Kuala Lumpur (RM120/US$32). Taxi reservation numbers are listed in each city's section. The outstation taxi stand in Malacca is at the bus terminal on Jalan Kilang. There's no number for reservations.

GETTING AROUND
Most of the historic sights around the town square are well within walking distance. For other trips **taxis** are the most convenient way around, but are at times difficult to find. They're also not as clearly marked as in KL or Johor Bahru. They are also not metered, so be prepared to bargain. Basically, no matter what you do, you'll always be charged a higher rate than a local. Tourists are almost

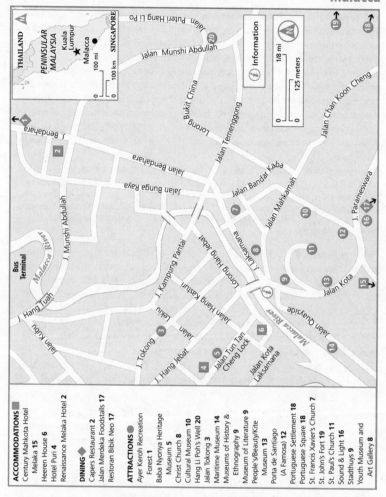

always quoted at RM10 (US$2.65) for local trips. Malaysians pay RM5 (US$1.30). If you're feeling sporty, you can bargain for a price somewhere in between. Trips to Ayer Keroh will cost about RM20 (US$5.25).

Trishaws (bicycle rickshaw) are all over the historic areas of town, and in Malacca they're renowned for being very, very garishly decorated (which adds to the fun!). Negotiate for hourly rates of about RM20 (US$5.25) for two people.

FAST FACTS: MALACCA

Major **banks** are located in the historic center of town, with a couple along Jalan Putra. The most convenient post office location is on Jalan Laksamana (© **06/ 284-8440**). For centrally located **Internet,** try **Internet Booth Café,** No. 3A Jalan Kota Lakshamana (© **06/281-3266**).

ACCOMMODATIONS

Malacca is not very large, and most of the places to stay are well within walking distance of attractions, shopping, and restaurants.

Century Mahkota Hotel Melaka   Located along the waterfront, the hotel is walking distance from sightseeing, historical areas, shopping, and commercial centers. Rooms are more like holiday apartments, with minikitchens and up to three bedrooms for family living—a big hit with Malaysian and Singaporean families. Each apartment has a tiled main room with clean cooking space at one end and simple rattan furnishings at the other—only bedrooms are air-conditioned. The views are of either the pools, the shopping mall across the street, or the muddy reclaimed seafront. The sprawling complex includes two outdoor pools, facilities for children, and is across from the largest shopping mall in Malacca. This place gets especially crowded during the school holidays in June and December.

Jalan Merdeka, 75000 Malacca. ℂ 06/281-2828. Fax 06/281-2323. 617 units. RM198–RM428 (US$52–US$113) 1- to 3-bedroom apt. AE, DC, MC, V. **Amenities:** 3 restaurants (international, Asian, pizza); lounge and piano bar; 2 outdoor pools; outdoor, lighted tennis courts; squash courts; fitness center with sauna and massage; children's playground; game room; shuttle; tour desk; car-rental desk; business center; 24-hr. room service; babysitting; same-day laundry service/dry cleaning. *In room:* TV w/satellite programming, coffee/tea-making facilities, hair dryer.

Heeren House ★★   This is the place to stay in Malacca for a taste of the local culture. Started by a local family, the guesthouse is a renovated 100-year-old building furnished in traditional Peranakan and colonial style and located right in the heart of historical European Malacca. All the bedrooms have views of the Malacca River, and outside the front door of the hotel is a winding stretch of old buildings housing antiques shops. Just walk out and wander. The rooms on the higher floors are somewhat larger. Laundry service is available, and there's a cafe and gift shop on the premises. Reserve well in advance.

1 Jalan Tun Tan Cheng Lock, 75200 Malacca. ℂ 06/281-4241. Fax 06/281-4239. 7 units. RM139 (US$37) double; RM299 (US$79) family suite. No credit cards. **Amenities:** Restaurant (local and international); souvenir shop; same-day laundry service. *In room:* A/C, TV.

Hotel Puri *Value*   In the olden days, Jalan Tun Tan Cheng Lock was known as "Millionaire Row" for all the wealthy families that lived here. This old "mansion" has been converted into a guesthouse, its tiled parlor has become a lobby, and the courtyard is where breakfast is served each morning. While Hotel Puri isn't big on space, it is big on value (discount rates can be pretty low). Rooms are very clean, and while not overly stylish, are comfortable enough for any weary traveler. Friendly and responsive staff add to the appeal.

118 Jalan Tun Tan Cheng Lock, 75200 Malacca. ℂ 06/282-5588. Fax 06/281-5588. 50 units. RM110–RM200 (US$29–US$53) double; RM230 (US$61) triple; suites from RM305 (US$80). AE, MC, V. **Amenities:** Restaurant (international); tour desk; limited room service; babysitting; same-day laundry service. *In room:* A/C, TV w/satellite programming, refrigerator, coffee/tea-making facilities, hair dryer.

Renaissance Melaka Hotel ★   Renaissance is one of the more posh hotels in Malacca, and, according to business travelers, is the most reliable place for quality accommodations—but aside from the pieces of Peranakan porcelain and art in the public areas, you could almost believe you weren't in Malacca at all. The hotel is, however, situated in a good location, though you'll still need a taxi to most of the sights. Renovations were completed 2 years ago to upgrade the guest rooms, which are fairly large and filled with Western comforts. Don't expect much from the views, as the hotel is in a more business-minded part of the city. No historical landmarks to gaze upon here. Facilities include an outdoor pool, fitness center with massage, sauna, and steam, two indoor squash courts, a tour operator desk, and a beauty salon. Golf is located nearby.

Jalan Bendahara, 75100 Malacca. ⓒ **800/228-9898** in the U.S. and Canada, 800/251-259 in Australia, 800/441-035 in New Zealand, 800/181-737 in the U.K., or 06/284-8888. Fax 06/284-9269. 294 units. RM450–RM510 (US$118–US$134) double; from RM570 (US$150) suite. AE, MC, V. **Amenities:** 3 restaurants (international, Chinese, fusion cuisine); bar and lobby lounge; outdoor pool; golf nearby; squash courts; fitness center with sauna, steam, and massage; concierge; tour desk; limousine service; business center; salon; 24-hr. room service; babysitting; same-day laundry service/dry cleaning; executive-level rooms. *In room:* A/C, TV w/satellite programming and in-house movie, minibar, coffee/tea-making facilities, safe.

DINING

In Malacca you'll find the typical mix of authentic Malay and Chinese food, and as the city was the major settling place for the Peranakans in Malaysia, their unique style of food is featured in many of the local restaurants.

A good recommendation for a quick bite at lunch or dinner if you're strolling in the historical area is the long string of open-air food stalls along Jalan Merdeka, just between Mahkota Plaza Shopping and Warrior Square. Mama Fatso's is especially good for Chinese style seafood and Malay sambal curry. A good meal will run you about RM35 to RM40 (US$9.20–US$11) per person. And believe me, it's a good meal.

Capers Restaurant CONTINENTAL   This is the nicest fine-dining establishment in Malacca at the moment, which means it is quite formal and pricey compared to the rest. Warm lighting and crystal and silver flatware are only a few of the many details that add to the elegant and romantic atmosphere. The signature dishes, like grilled tenderloin, come from the charcoal grill. The pan-fried sea bass is served quite artfully in a ginger and dill sauce over bok choy and potatoes. Their wine list is large and international (including Portuguese selections, in keeping with the Malacca theme).

Renaissance Melaka Hotel, Jalan Bendahara. ⓒ **06/284-8888.** Reservations recommended. Main courses RM20–RM48 (US$5.25–US$13). AE, DC, MC, V. Mon–Sat 6:30–10:30pm.

Portuguese Settlement PORTUGUESE   For a taste of Portuguese Malacca head down to the Portuguese Settlement where open-air food stalls by the water sell an assortment of dishes inspired by these former colonial rulers, including many fresh seafood offerings. Saturday nights are best when, at 8pm, there's a cultural show with music and dancing.

Jalan d'Albuquerque off Jalan Ujon Pasir. No phone. Dinner from RM15–RM20 (US$3.95–US$5.25) per person. No credit cards. Open nightly from 6pm onward.

Restoran Bibik Neo PERANAKAN   For a taste of the local cuisine, the traditional Nyonya food here is delicious and very reasonably priced. And while the restaurant isn't exactly tops in terms of decor, be assured that the food here is excellent and authentic. Ikan assam with eggplant is a tasty mild fish curry that's very rich and tasty, but I always go for the otak-otak (pounded fish and spices baked in a banana leaf).

No. 6, ground floor, Jalan Merdeka, Taman Melaka Raya. ⓒ **06/281-7054.** Reservations recommended. Main courses RM5–RM15 (US$1.30–US$3.95). AE, DC, MC, V. Daily 11am–3pm, 6–10pm.

ATTRACTIONS

To really understand what you're seeing in Malacca you have to understand a bit about the history, so be sure to read the introduction at the beginning of this section. Most of the really great historical places are on either side of the Malacca River. Start at Stadthuys (the old town hall) and you'll see most of Malacca pretty quickly.

MUSEUMS

Baba Nyonya Heritage Museum ★ Called Millionaire's Row, Jalan Tun Ten Cheng Lock is lined with row houses that were built by the Dutch and later bought by wealthy Peranakans; the architectural style reflects their East-meets-West lifestyle. The Baba Nyonya Heritage Museum sits at nos. 48 and 50 as a museum of Peranakan heritage. The entrance fee includes a guided tour.

48/50 Jalan Tun Tan Cheng Lock. ℂ 06/283-1273. Admission RM8 (US$2.10) adults, RM 4 (US$1.05) children. Daily 10am–12:30pm, 2–4:30pm.

The Cultural Museum (Muzium Budaya) ★ A replica of the former palace of Sultan Mansur Syah (1456–77), this museum was rebuilt according to historical descriptions to house a fine collection of cultural artifacts such as clothing, weaponry, and royal items.

Kota Rd., next to Porta de Santiago. ℂ 06/282-0769. Admission RM1.50 (US40¢) adults, RM.50 (US15¢) children. Sat–Thurs 9am–6pm; Fri 9am–12:15pm, 2:45–6pm.

The Maritime Museum and the Royal Malaysian Navy Museum These two museums are located across the street from one another but share admission fees. The Maritime Museum is in a restored 16th-century Portuguese ship, with exhibits dedicated to Malacca's history with the sea. The Navy Museum is a modern display of Malaysia's less-pleasant relationship with the sea.

Quayside Rd. ℂ 06/282-6526. Admission RM2 (US55¢) adults, RM.50 (US15¢) children. Sat–Thurs 9am–6pm; Fri 9am–12:15pm, 2:45–6pm.

The People's Museum, the Museum of Beauty, the Kite Museum, and the Governor of Melaka's Gallery This strange collection of displays is housed under one roof. The People's Museum is the story of development in Malacca. The Museum of Beauty is a look at cultural differences of beauty throughout time and around the world. The Kite Museum features the traditions of making and flying wau (kites) in Malaysia, and the governor's personal collection is on exhibit at the Governor's Gallery.

Kota Rd. ℂ 06/282-6526. Admission RM2 (US55¢) adults, RM.50 (US15¢) children. Sat–Thurs 9am–6pm; Fri 9am–12:15pm, 2:45–6pm.

Stadthuys—The Museums of History & Ethnography and the Museum of Literature ★ The Stadthuys Town Hall was built by the Dutch in 1650, and it's now home to the Malacca Ethnographical and Historical Museum, which displays customs and traditions of all the peoples of Malacca, and takes you through the rich history of this city. Behind Stadthuys, the Museum of Literature includes old historical accounts and local legends. Admission price is for both exhibits.

Located at the circle intersection of Jalan Quayside, Jalan Laksamana, and Jalan Chan Koon Cheng. ℂ 06/282-6526. Admission RM2 (US55¢) adults, RM.50 (US15¢) children. Sat–Thurs 9am–6pm; Fri 9am–12:15pm, 2:45–6pm.

The Youth Museums and Art Gallery In the old General Post office are these displays dedicated to Malaysia's youth organizations and to the nation's finest artists. An unusual combination.

Laksamana Rd. ℂ 06/282-6526. Admission RM1 (US25¢) adults, RM.50 (US15¢) children. Sat–Thurs 9am–6pm; Fri 9am–12:15pm, 2:45–6pm.

HISTORICAL SITES

Christ Church The Dutch built this place in 1753 as a Dutch Reform Church, and its architectural details include such wonders as ceiling beams cut from a single tree and a Last Supper glazed tile motif above the altar. It was later consecrated as an Anglican church, and mass is still performed today in English, Chinese, and Tamil.

Located on Jalan Laksamana. No phone.

Hang Li Poh's Well   Also called "Sultan's Well," Hang Li Poh's Well was built in 1495 to commemorate the marriage of Chinese Princess Hang Li Poh to Sultan Mansor Shah. It is now a wishing well, and folks say that if you toss in a coin, you'll someday return to Malacca.

Located off Jalan Laksamana Cheng Ho (Jalan Panjang). No phone.

Jalan Tokong ⋆   Not far from Jalan Tun Tan Cheng Lock is Jalan Tokong, called the "Street of Harmony" by the locals because it has three coexisting places of worship: the Kampong Kling Mosque, the Cheng Hoon Teng Temple, and the Sri Poyyatha Vinayar Moorthi Temple.

Porta de Santiago (A Famosa) ⋆   Once the site of a Portuguese fortress called A Famosa, all that remains today of the fortress is the entrance gate, which was saved from demolition by Sir Stamford Raffles. When the British East India Company demolished the place, Raffles realized the arch's historical value and saved it. The fort was built in 1512, but the inscription above the arch, "Anno 1607," marks the date when the Dutch overthrew the Portuguese.

Located on Jalan Kota, at the intersection of Jalan Parameswara. No phone.

Portuguese Settlement and Portuguese Square   The Portuguese Settlement is an enclave once designated for Portuguese settlers after they conquered Malacca in 1511. Some elements of their presence remain in the Lisbon-style architecture. Later, in 1920, the area was a Eurasian neighborhood. In the center of the settlement, Portuguese Square is a modern attraction with Portuguese restaurants, handicrafts, souvenirs, and cultural shows. It was built in 1985 in an architectural style to reflect the surrounding flavor of Portugal.

Located down Jalan d'Albuquerque off of Jalan Ujon Pasir in the southern part of the city.

St. Francis Xavier's Church   This church was built in 1849 and dedicated to St. Francis Xavier, a Jesuit who brought Catholicism to Malacca and other parts of Southeast Asia.

Located on Jalan Laksamana. No phone.

St. John's Fort   The fort, built by the Dutch in the late 18th century, sits on top of St. John's Hill. Funny how the cannons point inland, huh? At the time, threats to the city came from land. It was named after a Portuguese church to St. John the Baptist, which originally occupied the site.

Located off Lorong Bukit Senjuang. No phone.

St. Paul's Church   The church was built by the Portuguese in 1521, but when the Dutch came in, they made it part of A Famosa, converting the altar into a cannon mount. The open tomb inside was once the resting place of St. Francis Xavier, a missionary who spread Catholicism throughout Southeast Asia, and whose remains were later moved to Goa.

Located behind Porta de Santiago. No phone.

Sound & Light   The Museums Department has developed a sound-and-light show at the Warrior Square, the large field in the historical center of the city, which narrates the story of Malacca's early history, lighting up the historical buildings in the area for added punch. This is a good activity when you first arrive to help you get your historical bearings.

Warrior Sq., Jalan Kota. © 06/282-6526. Admission RM5 (US$1.30) adults, RM3 (US80¢) children. Shows nightly at 9:30pm.

OTHER ATTRACTIONS

Outside of Malacca is the 202 hectares (500 acres) of forest that make up **Ayer Keroh Recreational Forest,** where many attractions have been built. A taxi from Malacca will run you about RM20 (US$5.25). See the **Reptile Park** (© 06/231-9136), admission RM4 (US$1.05) adults, RM2 (US55¢) children, open daily 9am to 6pm; the **Butterfly & Reptile Sanctuary** (© 06/232-0033), admission RM5 (US$1.30) adults, RM3 (US80¢) children, open daily 8:30am to 5:30pm; the **Malacca Zoo** (© 06/232-4053), admission RM3 (US80¢) adults, RM1 (US25¢) children, open daily 9am to 6pm; and the **Taman Mini Malaysia/Mini ASEAN** (© 06/231-6087), admission RM5 (US$1.30) adults, RM2 (US55¢) children, open 9am to 5pm daily.

SHOPPING

Antique hunting has been a major draw to Malacca for decades. Distinct Peranakan and teak furniture, porcelain, and household items fetch quite a price these days, due to a steady increase in demand for these rare treasures. The area down and around Jalan Tun Tan Cheng Lok called **Jonker Walk,** sports many little antiques shops that are filled with as many gorgeous items as any local museum. Whether you're buying or just looking, it's a fun way to spend an afternoon.

Modern **shopping malls** are sprouting up in Malacca, the biggest being the Mahkota Parade on Jalan Merdeka, just south of the field (Warrior Square) in the historic district. Two hundred retail stores sell everything from books to clothing.

For crafts, start at **Karyaneka** (© 06/284-3270) on Jalan Laksamana close to the Town Square. If you travel down Laksamana you'll find all sorts of small crafts and souvenir shops.

4 Penang

Penang is unique in Malaysia because, for all intents and purposes, Penang has it all. Tioman Island (see chapter 10) may have beaches and nature, but it has no shopping or historical sights to speak of. And while Malacca has historical sights and museums, it hasn't a good beach for miles. Similarly, while KL has shopping, nightlife, and attractions, it also has no beach resorts. Penang has all of it: beaches, history, diverse culture, shopping, food—you name it, it has it. If you only have a short time to visit Malaysia but want to take in as wide an experience as you can, Penang is your place.

Penang gets its name from the Malay word *pinang,* in reference to the areca plant, which grew on the island in abundance. The nut of the tree, commonly called *betel,* was chewed habitually in the East. In the 15th century it was a quiet place populated by small Malay communities, attracting the interest of some southern Indian betel merchants. By the time Francis Light, an agent for the British East India Company, arrived in 1786, the island was already on the maps of European, Indian, and Chinese traders. Light landed on the northeast part of the island, where he began a settlement after an agreement with the sultan of Kedah, on the mainland. He called the town **Georgetown,** after George III. To

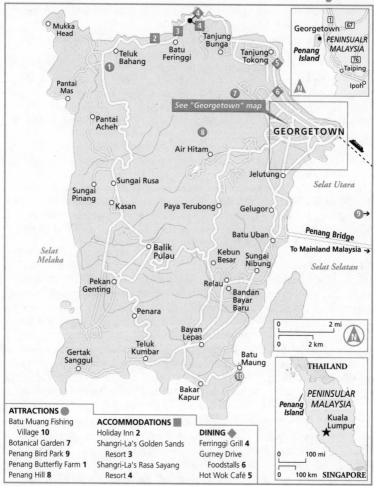

Georgetown · PENINSUALR MALAYSIA · Penang Island · Taiping · Ipoh

Tanjung Bunga · Tanjung Tokong · Mukka Head · Teluk Bahang · Batu Feringgi · Pantai Mas · Pantai Acheh

See "Georgetown" map

GEORGETOWN

Air Hitam · Jelutong · Selat Utara · Sungai Rusa · Sungai Pinang · Kasan · Paya Terubong · Gelugor · Batu Uban · Penang Bridge · To Mainland Malaysia → · Selat Selatan · Balik Pulau · Kebun Besar · Sungai Nibung · Selat Melaka · Pekan Genting · Relau · Bandan Bayar Baru · Penara · Bayan Lepas · Gertak Sanggul · Teluk Kumbar · Batu Maung · Bakar Kapur

THAILAND · PENINSULAR MALAYSIA · Penang Island · Kuala Lumpur · SINGAPORE

0   2 mi
0   2 km

0   100 mi
0   100 km

ATTRACTIONS ●
Batu Muang Fishing
    Village 10
Botanical Garden 7
Penang Bird Park 9
Penang Butterfly Farm 1
Penang Hill 8

ACCOMMODATIONS ■
Holiday Inn 2
Shangri-La's Golden Sands
    Resort 3
Shangri-La's Rasa Sayang
    Resort 4

DINING ◆
Ferringgi Grill 4
Gurney Drive
    Foodstalls 6
Hot Wok Café 5

gain the help of local inhabitants for clearing the spot, he shot a cannon-load of coins into the jungle.

Georgetown became Britain's principal post in Malaya, attracting traders and settlers from all over the world. Europeans, Arabs, northern and southern Indians, southern Chinese, and Malays from the mainland and Sumatra flocked to the port. But it was never extremely profitable for England, especially when in 1819 Sir Stamford Raffles founded a new trading post in Singapore. Penang couldn't keep up with the new port's success.

In 1826 Penang, along with Malacca and Singapore, formed a unit called the Straits Settlements, and Penang was narrowly declared the seat of government over the other two. Finally in 1832, Singapore stole its thunder when authority shifted there. In the late 1800s Penang got a big break. Tin mines and rubber plantations on mainland Malaya were booming, and with the opening of the railway between KL and **Butterworth** (the town on the mainland just opposite the island), Penang once again thrived. Singapore firms scrambled to open offices in Butterworth.

The Great Depression hit Penang hard. So did the Japanese occupation from 1941 to 1945. The island had been badly bombed. But since Malaysia's independence in 1957, Penang has had relatively good financial success. Today the state of Penang is made up of the island and a small strip of land on the Malaysian mainland. Georgetown is the seat of government for the state. Penang Island is 285 sq. km (171 sq. miles) and has a population of a little more than one million. Surprisingly, the population is mostly Chinese (59%), followed by Malays (32%) and Indians (7%).

ESSENTIALS
VISITOR INFORMATION
The main **Malaysia Tourism Board (MTB)** office is located at No. 10 Jalan Tun Syed Sheh Barakbah (© **04/261-9067**), just across from the clock tower by Fort Cornwallis. There's another information center at **Penang International Airport** (© **04/643-0501**) and a branch on the third level at **KOMTAR (Kompleks Tun Abdul Razak)** on Jalan Penang (© **04/261-4461**).

GETTING THERE
BY PLANE   Penang International Airport (© **04/643-0811**) has direct flights from Singapore about seven times daily (**Singapore Airlines** toll-free in Singapore © 1800/223-8888; **Malaysia Airlines** © 65/336-6777). From KL, Malaysia Airlines has two flights daily (© 1300/88-3000). The airport is 20km (12 miles) from the city. To get into town, you must purchase fixed-rate coupons for taxis (RM23/US$6.05 to Georgetown; RM35/US$9.20 to Batu Feringgi). There's also the **Penang Yellow Bus Company** bus no. 83, which will take you to Weld Quay in Georgetown.

There are also car rentals at the airport. Talk to **Hertz** (© **04/643-0208**) or **Budget** (© **04/643-6025**).

BY TRAIN   By rail, the trip from KL to Butterworth takes 6 hours and costs RM59 (US$15) first-class passage, RM25.40 (US$6.70) for second class, and RM14 (US$3.80) for third class. Three trains leave daily. Call **KL Sentral** (© **03/2730-2000**) for schedule information.

The train will let you off at the **Butterworth Railway Station** (© **04/323-7962**), on Jalan Bagan Dalam (near the ferry terminal) in Butterworth, on the Malaysian mainland. From there, you can take a taxi to the island or head for the ferry close by.

BY BUS   Many buses will bring you only to Butterworth, so if you want the trip to take you all the way onto the island, make sure you buy a ticket that specifically says Penang. These buses will let you out at **KOMTAR** on Jalan Gladstone across from the Shangri-La Hotel. If you're dropped in Butterworth at the bus terminal on Jalan Bagan Dalam (next to the ferry terminal), you'll need to grab a taxi or take the ferry to the island.

In KL, **Plusliner/NICE** (© **03/2722-2760**) departs from the KL Train Station regularly. The NICE Executive Express coaches leave six times daily, costing RM50 (US$13). The trip takes about 4½ hours.

For buses back to KL call their counter at the **Garden Inn Hotel,** 41 Jalan Ansor © **04/227-7370.**

BY FERRY   The ferry to Penang is nestled between the Butterworth Railway Station and the Butterworth bus terminal. It operates 24 hours a day and takes

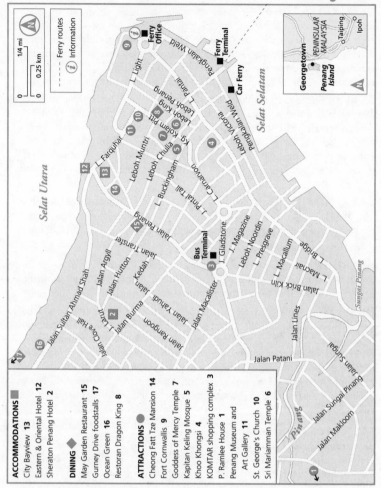

20 minutes from pier to pier. From 6am to midnight ferries leave every 10 minutes. From midnight to 1:20am boats run every half-hour, and from 1:20 to 6am they run hourly. Purchase your passage by dropping 60 sen (US15¢) exact change in the turnstile (there's a change booth if you don't have it). Fare is paid only on the trip to Penang. The return is free. The ferry lets you off at **Pengalan Raja Tun Udah,** Weld Quay (© **04/210-2363**).

The ferry will also take cars for a fee of RM7 (US$1.85), which includes passenger fees.

BY TAXI   The outstation taxi stand is in Butterworth next to the bus terminal (© **04/323-2045**). Fares to Butterworth from KL will be about RM240 (US$63).

BY CAR   If you're driving you can cross over the 13.5km (8-mile) Penang Bridge, the longest bridge in Southeast Asia. All cars are charged RM7 (US$1.85) for the trip to Penang. It's free on the return.

GETTING AROUND

BY TAXI Taxis are abundant, but be warned they do not use meters, so you must agree on the price before you ride. Most trips within the city are between RM3 and RM6. If you're staying out at the Batu Feringgi beach resort area, expect taxis to town to run RM20 (US$5.25); RM30 (US$7.90) at night. The ride is about 15 or 20 minutes, but can take 30 minutes during rush hour.

BY BUS Buses also run all over the island, and are well used by tourists, who don't want to spring RM20 every time they want to go to the beach. The most popular route is the **Hin Bus Co. (Blue Bus)** no. 93, which operates every 10 minutes between Pengkalan Weld (Weld Quay) in Georgetown and the beach resorts at Batu Feringgi. It makes stops at KOMTAR Shopping Plaza and also at the ferry terminal. Fare is RM1 (US25¢). Give your money to the nice ticket person on board.

CAR RENTAL **Hertz** has an office in Georgetown at 38 Farquhar St. (© 04/ 263-5914).

BY BICYCLE & MOTORCYCLE Along Batu Feringgi there are bicycles and motorcycles available for rent.

BY TRISHAW In Georgetown it's possible to find some trishaw action for about RM20 (US$3.95) an hour. It's fun and I recommend it for traveling between sights, at least for an hour or two.

ON FOOT I think everyone should walk at least part of the time to see the sights of Georgetown, because in between each landmark and exhibit there's so much more to see. A taxi, even a trishaw, will whisk you right by back alleys where elderly haircutters set up alfresco shops, bicycle repairmen sit fixing tubes in front of their stores, and Chinese grannies fan themselves in the shade. The streets of Georgetown are stimulating, with the sights of old trades still being plied on these living streets, the noise of everyday life, and the exotic smells of an old Southeast Asian port. Give yourself at least a day here.

FAST FACTS: PENANG

American Express has an office in Georgetown at **Mayflower Acme Tours,** 10th floor, Unit 10-05 MWE Plaza, No. 8 Lebuh Farquhar (© **04/262-8196**). The **banking center** of Georgetown is in the downtown area (close to Ft. Cornwallis) on Leboh Pantai, Leboh Union and Leboh Downing. For **Internet** service in town, try **STC Net Café,** 221 Chulia St. (© **04/264-3378**), which charges RM6 (US$1.60) per hour. Out on Batu Feringgi head for Cyber By the Beach, **Golden Sands Resort** (© **04/881-2096**), with fees of RM5 (US$1.30) per hour.

The main post **office** in Georgetown is on Leboh Downing (© **04/261-9222**). Another convenient location is out on Jalan Batu Feringgi (© **04/ 881-2555**).

ACCOMMODATIONS

While Georgetown has many hotels right in the city for convenient sightseeing, many visitors choose to stay at one of the beach resorts 30 minutes away at Batu Feringgi. Trips back and forth can be a bother (regardless of the resorts' free shuttle services), but if you're not staying in a resort, most of the finer beaches are off-limits.

The City Bayview Hotel, Penang This city hotel is perfect for those who visit Penang for its cultural treasures rather than its beaches. A good budget choice, it has a number of fair dining venues, including a rooftop revolving restaurant with excellent views of the island. Choose from guest rooms in the new wing, completed in 1999, or those in the old wing, which have been recently refurbished. Either choice offers cool rooms in neutral tones, not as elegant as many, but comfortable and definitely value for money.

25-A Farquhar St., Georgetown, 10200 Penang. ℭ **04/263-3161.** Fax 04/263-4124. 320 units. RM350–RM450 (US$92–US$118) double. AE, DC, MC, V. **Amenities:** 3 restaurants (international, Chinese); club with live entertainment, lobby lounge; outdoor pool; concierge; limousine service; business center; 24-hr. room service; babysitting; same-day laundry service/dry cleaning; nonsmoking rooms. *In room:* A/C, TV w/in-house movie, minibar, coffee/tea-making facilities, hair dryer, safe.

Eastern & Oriental Hotel (E&O) ★★ E&O first opened in 1884, established by the same Sarkies brothers who were behind the Raffles Hotel in Singapore. Closed for many, many years (it was desperately in need of an overhaul) it reopened in April 2001. It is without a doubt the most atmospheric hotel in Penang, with its manicured lawns and tropical gardens flanking a white colonial-style mansion, with a lacelike facade and Moorish minarets. Accommodations are all suites, with little sitting areas and sleeping quarters separated with pocket sliding doors. You can expect molding details around every door and paned window, Oriental carpets over polished plank floorboards, and Egyptian cotton linens dressing each poster bed. Dining along the hotel's many verandas is gorgeous. One caveat—no beach, but the pool in the seafront garden is very pretty.

10 Farquhar St., 10200 Penang. ℭ **04/222-2000.** Fax 04/261-6333. www.e-o-hotel.com. 101 units. RM1635–RM33,440 (US$430–US$8800). AE, DC, MC, V. **Amenities:** 2 restaurants (Continental, Chinese); English-style pub; outdoor pool; small fitness center with sauna; concierge; limousine service; 24-hr. room service; same-day laundry service/dry cleaning. *In room:* A/C, TV w/satellite programming, minibar, coffee/tea-making facilities.

Holiday Inn Resort Penang *(Kids)* This is a recommended choice for families, but be warned this resort has little appeal for vacationing couples or singles sans children. For families it has everything—special KidSuites have a separate room for the wee ones with TV, video and PlayStation, some with bunk beds—choose from jungle, treasure island or outer space themes. Holiday Inn also has a Kids Club, fully supervised day care with activities and games and a lifeguard. Older kids can join in beach volleyball, water polo, bike tours, and an assortment of watersports arranged by the staff. Guest rooms are in two blocks: a low-rise structure near the beach and a high-rise tower along the hillside, connected by a second-story walkway. Naturally, the beachside rooms command the greater rate. Beachside rooms also have better ambience and slightly larger rooms with wood floors and details, while tower rooms have less charm. The lack of dining options gets tiring.

72 Batu Ferringhi, 11100 Penang. ℭ **04/881-1601.** Fax 04/881-1389. www.penang.holiday-inn.com 362 units. RM400-RM850 (US$105–US$224) double; RM700–RM750 (US$184–US$197) KidSuite; from RM1,400 (US$368) suite. AE, DC, MC, V. **Amenities:** Restaurant (international); lobby lounge; outdoor pool and children's pool; outdoor, lighted tennis courts; fitness center; massage; children's club; game room; watersports equipment rentals; concierge; tour desk; limousine service; 24-hr. room service; babysitting; same-day laundry service/dry cleaning. *In room:* A/C, TV w/satellite programming and in-house movie, minibar, coffee/tea-making facilities, hair dryer, iron, safe.

Shangri-La's Golden Sands Resort ★ *(Kids)* Rasa Sayang's little sister property is located just next door. A newer resort, it is priced lower than the Rasa Sayang, so it attracts more families. The beach, pool area, and public spaces fill up fast in the morning, and folks are occupied all day with beach sports like parasailing and jet-skiing, and pool games. For the younger set, a kids' club keeps small ones busy while Mom and Dad do "boring stuff." Rooms are large with full amenities, and the higher priced categories have views of the pool and sea. Better still, guests here can use the facilities at Rasa Sayang.

Batu Feringgi Beach, 11100 Penang. ℂ **800/942-5050** in the U.S. and Canada, 800/222448 in Australia, 800/442179 in New Zealand, or 04/881-1911. Fax 04/881-1880. www.shangri-la.com. 395 units. RM415–RM590 (US$109–US$155) double; RM1,295 (US$341) suite. AE, DC, MC, V. **Amenities:** 3 restaurants (international, Italian, seafood); lobby lounge; 2 outdoor lagoon-style pools; outdoor, lighted tennis courts; children's center; game room; concierge; tour desk; watersports equipment and activities; car-rental desk; limousine service; shuttle service to Shangri-La Hotel in Georgetown; business center; salon; 24-hr. room service; babysitting; same-day laundry service/dry cleaning; self-service launderette. *In room:* A/C, TV w/satellite programming and in-house movie, fridge, coffee/tea-making facilities, hair dryer, safe.

Shangri-La's Rasa Sayang Resort ★★★

Of all the beachfront resorts on Penang, Rasa Sayang is the finest. It has been here the longest, celebrating its 25-year anniversary in 1998, so it had the first pick of beachfront property and plenty of space to create lush gardens and pool areas. Get a room looking over the pool area, and your private balcony will be facing the picturesque palm-lined beach. The free-form pool is sprawled amid tropical landscaping and cafes, and the rest of the grounds have strolling gardens that are romantically illuminated in the evenings. The hotel is both elegant and relaxed, with Malay-style decor in the public areas and rooms. You'll also appreciate the good seafood restaurants nearby. Facilities include an outdoor pool, fitness center, small putting green, and table tennis. Guests have access to nearby tennis courts, sailing, boating, and waterskiing. Make sure to ask about the incredible bargain packages.

Batu Feringgi Beach, 11100 Penang. ℂ **800/942-5050** in the U.S. and Canada, 800/222448 in Australia, 800/442179 in New Zealand, or 04/881-1811. Fax 04/881-1984. www.shangri-la.com. 514 units. RM515–RM670 (US$136–US$176) double; RM750 (US$197) deluxe sea-facing double; from RM970 (US$255) suite. AE, DC, MC, V. **Amenities:** 5 restaurants (Continental grill, 2 international cafes, Chinese, Japanese); lobby lounge and beachfront bar; 4 outdoor pools, including children's pool; outdoor, lighted tennis courts; fitness center with Jacuzzi, sauna, steam, and massage; children's center; game room; concierge; tour desk; watersports equipment and activities; car-rental desk; limousine service; shuttle service to Shangri-La Hotel in Georgetown; business center; salon; 24-hr. room service; babysitting; same-day laundry service/dry cleaning. *In room:* A/C, TV w/satellite programming and in-house movie, minibar, coffee/tea-making facilities, hair dryer, safe.

Sheraton Penang Hotel ★★

If you prefer to stay in town, Sheraton's Penang offering is hard to beat. Its 20-story high-rise is filled with elegance throughout, from the contemporary lobby and public rooms filled with modern art, to the discreet and professional service of its staff. Guest rooms are well appointed with stately furnishings of European design with local decorator touches. Many good views of the city and ocean are to be had. Marble bathrooms have separate shower stall and bathtub plus fine toiletries. You can expect excellence from this hotel, which is used to catering to the demands of the international business traveler.

3 Jalan Larut, 10050 Georgetown, Penang. ℂ **04/226-7888**; fax 04/226-6615. www.sheraton.com 237 units. RM460 (US$121) double; from RM575 (US$151) suite. AE, DC, MC, V. **Amenities:** 2 restaurants (international, Korean); bar and lobby lounge; outdoor pool; fitness center with sauna and massage; concierge; tour desk; limousine service; 24-hr. business center; shopping arcade adjacent; 24-hr. room service; babysitting; same-day laundry service/dry cleaning; nonsmoking rooms; executive-level rooms. *In room:* A/C, TV w/satellite programming and in-house movie, minibar, coffee/tea-making facilities, hair dryer, iron, safe.

DINING

Feringgi Grill ★★ CONTINENTAL The Feringgi Grill is comparable to any five-star hotel grill anywhere. From the dreamy lobster bisque to the carving cart of perfectly grilled top-quality meats flown in from all over the world, you'll be living the good life with each bite. A good wine selection will help revive you when you think you've died and gone to heaven. And don't even mention the desserts—the whole cart is a sore temptation sent straight from hell. Feringgi is perfect for a romantic dinner, or a change from all that char koay teow you've been eating in town.

Shangri-La's Rasa Sayang Resort, Batu Feringgi Beach. © **04/881-1811.** Reservations recommended. Main courses RM50–RM68 (US$13–US$18). AE, DC, MC, V. Daily 7–10:30pm.

Hot Wok Café ★ PERANAKAN   This place is the number one recommended Peranakan restaurant in the city, and small wonder: The food is great and the atmosphere is fabulous. Filled with local treasures such as wooden lattice work, wooden lanterns, carved Peranakan cabinets, tapestries, and carved wood panels, the decor will make you want to just sit back, relax, and take in sights you'd only ever see in a Peranakan home. Their curry capitan, a famous local dish, is curry chicken stuffed with potatoes, with a thick delicious coconut-based gravy. The house specialty is a mean perut ikan (fish intestine with roe and vegetable).

125-D Desa Tanjung, Jalan Tanjung. © **04/899-0858.** Reservations recommended for weekends. Main courses RM9–RM15 (US$2.35–US$3.95). AE, DC, MC, V. Daily 11am–3pm, 6–11pm.

May Garden Restaurant CANTONESE   This is a top Cantonese restaurant in Georgetown, and while it's noisy and not too big on ambience, it has excellent food. But how many Chinese do you know who go to places for ambience? It's the food that counts! Outstanding dishes include the tofu and broccoli topped with sea snail slices or the fresh steamed live prawns. They also have suckling pig and Peking duck. Don't agree to all the daily specials or you'll be paying a fortune.

70 Jalan Penang. © **04/261-6806.** Reservations recommended. Main courses start at RM8 (US$2.10). Seafood is priced by weight in kilograms. AE, DC, MC, V. Daily noon–3pm, 6–10:30pm.

Ocean Green ★★ SEAFOOD   I can't rave enough about Ocean Green. If the beautiful sea view and ocean breezes don't make you weep with joy, the food certainly will. A long list of fresh seafood is prepared steamed or fried, with your choice of chile, black-bean, sweet-and-sour, or curry sauces. On the advice of a local food expert, I tried the lobster thermidor, expensive but divine, and the chicken wings stuffed with minced chicken, prawns, and gravy.

48F Jalan Sultan Ahmad Shah. © **04/226-2681.** Reservations recommended. Main courses starting from RM12 (US$3.15); seafood priced according to market value. AE, MC, V. Daily 9am–11pm.

Restoran Dragon King PERANAKAN   Penang is famous around the world for delicious local Peranakan dishes, and Dragon King is a good place to sample the local cuisine at its finest. It was opened 20 years ago by a group of local teachers who wanted to revive the traditional dishes cooked by their mothers. In terms of decor, the place is nothing to shout about—just a coffee shop with tile floors and folding chairs—but all the curries are hand blended to perfection. Their curry capitan will make you weep with joy, it's so rich. But come early for the otak-otak, or it might sell out. While Dragon King is hopping at lunchtime, dinner is quiet.

99 Leboh Bishop. © **04/261-8035.** Main courses RM8–RM20 (US$2.10–US$5.25). No credit cards. Daily 11am–3pm, 6–10pm.

FOOD STALL DINING

No section on Penang dining would be complete without full coverage of the local food stall scene, which is famous. Penang hawkers can make any dish you've had in Malaysia, Singapore, or even southern Thailand better. I had slimy char koay teow in Singapore and swore off the stuff forever. After being forced to try it in Penang (where the fried flat noodles and seafood are a specialty dish), I was completely addicted. Penang may be attractive for many things—history, culture, nature—but it is loved for its food.

Gurney Drive Foodstalls, toward the water just down from the intersection with Jalan Kelawai, is the biggest and most popular hawker center. It has all kinds of food, including local dishes with every influence: Chinese, Malay, Indian. In addition to the above-mentioned char koay teow, there's char bee hoon (a fried thin rice noodle), laksa (fish soup with noodles), murtabak (a sort of curry mutton burrito), oh chien (oyster omelette with chile dip), and rojak (a spicy fruit and seafood salad). After you've eaten your way through Gurney Drive, you can try the stalls on Jalan Burmah near the Lai Lai Supermarket.

ATTRACTIONS
IN GEORGETOWN

Cheong Fatt Tze Mansion ✦ Cheong Fatt Tze (1840–1917), once dubbed as "China's Rockefeller" by the *New York Times*, built a vast commercial empire in Southeast Asia, first in Indonesia, then in Singapore. He came to Penang in 1890 and continued his success, giving some of his spoils to build schools throughout the region. His mansion, where he lived with his eight wives, was built between 1896 and 1904. Inside are lavish adornments—stained glass, crown moldings, gilded wood-carved doors, ceramic ornaments, and seven staircases.

Lebuhraya Leith. ✆ **04/261-0076**. Admission RM10 (US$2.65) adults and children. Open for guided tours Mon, Wed, Fri–Sat at 11am.

Fort Cornwallis Fort Cornwallis is built on the site where Capt. Francis Light, founder of Penang, first landed in 1786. The fort was first built in 1793, but this site was an unlikely spot to defend the city from invasion. In 1810 it was rebuilt in an attempt to make up for initial strategic planning errors. In the shape of a star, the only actual buildings still standing are the outer walls, a gunpowder magazine, and a small Christian chapel. The magazine houses an exhibit of old photos and historical accounts of the old fort.

Lebuhraya Leith. ✆ **04/262-9461**. Admission RM1 (US25¢) adults, RM.50 (US15¢) children. Daily 8am–7pm.

Goddess of Mercy Temple Dedicated jointly to Kuan Yin, the goddess of mercy, and Ma Po Cho, the patron saint of sea travelers, this is the oldest Chinese temple in Penang. On the 19th of each second, sixth, and ninth month of the lunar calendar, Kuan Yin is celebrated with Chinese operas and puppet shows.

Leboh Pitt. No phone.

Kapitan Keling Mosque Captain Light donated a large parcel of land on this spot for the settlement's sizable Indian Muslim community to build a mosque and graveyard. The leader of the community, known as Kapitan Keling (or Kling, which ironically was once a racial slur against Indians in the region), built a brick mosque here. Later, in 1801, he imported builders and materials from India for a new, brilliant mosque. Expansions in the 1900s topped the mosque with stunning domes and turrets, adding extensions and new roofs.

Jalan Masjid Kapitan Keling (Leboh Pitt). No phone.

Khoo Khongsi ✦ The Chinese who migrated to Southeast Asia created clan associations in their new homes. Based on common heritage, these social groups formed the core of Chinese life in the new homelands. The Khoo clan, who immigrated from Hokkien province in China, acquired this spot in 1851 and set to work building row houses, administrative buildings, and a clan temple around a large square. The temple here now was actually built in 1906 after a fire destroyed its predecessor. It was believed the original was too ornate, provoking the wrath of the gods. One look at the current temple, a Chinese baroque masterpiece, and you'll wonder how that could possibly be. Come here in August for Chinese operas.

Leburaya Cannon. (📞) **04/261-4609.** Free admission. Daily 9am–5pm.

P. Ramlee House   This is the house where legendary Malaysian actor, director, singer, composer, and prominent figurehead of the Malaysian film industry P. Ramlee (1928–73) was born and raised. A gallery of photos from his life and personal memorabilia offer a glimpse of local culture even those who've never heard of him can appreciate.

No phone. Free admission. Daily 9am–5pm.

Penang Museum and Art Gallery ⭐⭐   The historical society has put together this marvelous collection of ethnological and historical findings from Penang, tracing the port's history and diverse cultures through time. It's filled with paintings, photos, costumes, and antiques among much more, all presented with fascinating facts and trivia. Upstairs is an art gallery. Originally the Penang Free School, the building was built in two phases, the first half in 1896 and the second in 1906. Only half of the building remains; the other was bombed to the ground in World War II. It's a favorite stop on a sightseeing itinerary because it's air-conditioned!

Leburaya Farquhar. (📞) **04/261-3144.** Free admission. Sat–Thurs 9am–5pm.

St. George's Church   Built by Rev. R. S. Hutchins (who was also responsible for the Free School next door, home of the Penang Museum) and Capt. Robert N. Smith, whose paintings hang in the museum, this church was completed in 1818. While the outside is almost as it was then, the contents were completely looted during World War II. All that remains are the font and the bishop's chair.

Farquhar St. No phone.

Sri Mariamman Temple   This Hindu temple was built in 1833 by a Chettiar, a group of southern Indian Muslims, and received a major face-lift in 1978 with the help of Madras sculptors. The Hindu Navarithri festival is held here, whereby devotees parade Sri Mariamman, a Hindu goddess worshipped for her powers to cure disease, through the streets in a night procession. It is also the starting point of the Thaipusam Festival, which leads to a temple on Jalan Waterfall.

Leburaya Queen. No phone

OUTSIDE GEORGETOWN

Batu Muang Fishing Village   If you'd like to see a local fishing village, here's a good one. This village is special for its shrine to Admiral Cheng Ho, the early Chinese sea adventurer.

Southeast tip of Penang. No central phone.

Botanical Gardens   Covering 30 hectares (70 acres) of landscaped grounds, this botanical garden was established by the British in 1884, with grounds that are perfect for a shady walk and a ton of fun if you love monkeys. They're crawling all over the place and will think nothing of stepping forward for a peanut (which you can buy beneath the DO NOT FEED THE MONKEYS sign). Also in the gardens is a jogging track and kiddie park.

About a 5- or 10-min. drive west of Georgetown. ✆ 04/228-6248. Free admission. Daily 7am–7pm.

Penang Bird Park   The Bird Park is not on Penang Island, but on the mainland part of Penang state. The 2-hectare (5-acre) park is home to some 200 bird species from Malaysia and around the world.

Jalan Teluk, Seberang Jaya. ✆ 04/399-1899. Admission RM5 (US$1.30) adult, RM2 (US55¢) child. Daily 9am–7pm.

Penang Butterfly Farm   The Penang Butterfly Farm, located toward the northwest corner of the island, is the largest in the world. On its 0.8-hectare (2-acre) landscaped grounds there are more than 4,000 flying butterflies from 120 species. At 10am and 3pm there are informative butterfly shows. Don't forget the insect exhibit—there are about 2,000 or so bugs.

Jalan Teluk Bahang. ✆ 04/881-1253. Admission RM5 (US$1.30) adult, RM2 (US55¢) child over 5; free for children under 4. Mon–Fri 9am–5pm; Sat–Sun 9am–6pm.

Penang Hill   Covered with jungle growth and 20 nature trails, the hill is great for trekking. Or, you can go to Ayer Hitam, a town in the central part of Penang, and take the Keretapi Bukit Bendera funicular railway to the top. It sends trains up and down the hill every half-hour from 6:30am to 9:30pm weekdays and until midnight on weekends, and costs RM4 (US$1.05) for adults and RM2 (US55¢) for children. If you prefer to make the trek on foot, go to the "Moon Gate" at the entrance to the Botanical Garden for a 5.5km (9-mile), 3-hour hike to the summit.

A 20- to 30-min. drive southwest from Georgetown. The funicular station is on Jalan Stesen Keretapi Bukit.

SHOPPING

The first place anyone here will recommend you to go for shopping is **KOMTAR.** Short for "Kompleks Tun Abdul Razak," it is the largest shopping complex in Penang, a full 65 stories of clothing shops, restaurants, and a couple of large department stores. There's a **duty-free shop** on the 57th floor. On the third floor is a **tourist information center.**

Good shopping finds in Penang are batik, pewter products, locally produced curios, paintings, antiques, pottery, and jewelry. If you care to walk around in search of finds, there are a few streets in Georgetown that are the hub of shopping activity. In the city center, the area around Jalan Penang, Leburhaya Campbell, Lebuhraya Kapitan Keling, Lebuhraya Chulia, and Lebuhraya Pantai is near the Sri Mariamman Temple, the Penang Museum, the Kapitan Keling Mosque, and other sites of historic interest. Here you'll find everything from local crafts to souvenirs and fashion, and maybe even a bargain or two. Most of these shops are open from 10am to 10pm daily.

Out at Batu Feringgi, the main road turns into a fun **night bazaar** every evening just at dark. During the day, there are also some good shops for batik and souvenirs.

NIGHTLIFE

Clubs in Penang stay open a little later than in the rest of Malaysia, and some even stay open until 3am on the weekends.

If you're looking for a bar that's a little out of the ordinary, visit **20 Leith Street,** 11-A Lebuh Leith (✆ 04/261-8873). Located in an old 1930s house, the place has seating areas fitted with traditional antique furniture in each room of the house. Possibly the most notorious bar in Penang is the **Hong Kong Bar,** 371 Lebuh Chulia (© **04/261-9796**), which opened in 1920 and was a regular hangout for military personnel based in Butterworth. It has an extraordinary archive of photos of the servicemen who have patronized the place throughout the years, plus a collection of medals, plaques, and buoys from ships.

For dancing, the resorts in Batu Feringgi have the better discos. **Zulu's Seaside Paradise,** Paradise Tanjung Bungah (© **04/890-8808**), is a world-beat dance club, spinning African, reggae, and other danceable international music.

Hard Life Café, 363 Lebuh Chulia (© **04/262-1740**), is an interesting alternative hangout. Decorated with Rastafarian paraphernalia, the place fills up with backpackers, who sometimes aren't as laid-back as Mr. Marley would hope they'd be. Still, it's fun to check out the books where guests comment on their favorite (or least favorite) travel haunts in Southeast Asia.

5 Langkawi

Where the beautiful Andaman Sea meets the Strait of Malacca, Langkawi Island positions itself as one of the best emerging island paradise destinations in the region. Since 1990, the Malaysian Tourism Board has dedicated itself to promoting the island and developing it as an ideal travel spot. Now, after a decade of work, the island has proven itself as one of this country's holiday gems.

Its biggest competition comes from Phuket, Thailand's beach-lover fantasy to the north. But, day for day and dollar for dollar, I'd take Langkawi over Phuket hands down. Why? Well, despite being pumped up by government money and promotional campaigns, Langkawi remains relatively unheard of on the travel scene. So, while you get the same balmy weather, gorgeous beaches, fun watersports, and great seafood, you also avoid the horrible effects of tourism gone awry—inflated prices, annoying touts, and overcrowding. Besides, I've stayed in almost every luxury property on Phuket, and can testify that Langkawi's finest resorts can compete with pride.

This small island also claims a Hollywood credit, starring in the 1999 film *Anna and the King.* Langkawi played the part of Thailand to Jodie Foster's Anna Leonowens and Chow Young Fatt's King Mongkut (Rama IV). The Thais wouldn't allow the filmmakers to shoot on location in their kingdom (and rightly so, as King Mongkut, their revered father of modern Thailand, has been continuously portrayed in the West as a stubborn, immature fop who got all his great ideas from a common English tutor—indeed, historians agree that according to many well-documented sources, Anna Leonowens's famous account of her time at the Royal Palace had more basis in her imagination than in reality), so Hollywood turned to neighboring Malaysia for location filming. The palatial Thai-style buildings constructed for the set have never been torn down, and you can still hear all kinds of local gossip about the film's stars.

Technically, Langkawi is a cluster of islands, the largest of which serves as the main focal point. Ask how many islands actually make up Langkawi and you'll hear either 104 or 99. The official MTB response? "Both are correct. It depends on the tide!" On Langkawi Island itself, the main town, **Kuah,** provides the island's administrative needs, while on the western and northern shores, the beaches have been developed with resorts. The west-coast beaches of **Pantai Cenang** and **Pantai Tengah** are the most developed; however, the concept of development here should be taken in relative terms. To the north, **Datai Bay** and **Tanjung Rhu** host the island's two finest, and most secluded, resorts.

One final note: Malaysia has declared Langkawi a duty-free zone, so take a peek at some of the shopping in town, and enjoy RM4 (US$1.05) beers!

ESSENTIALS
GETTING THERE

BY PLANE   Malaysia Airways makes Langkawi very convenient from either mainland Malaysia or Singapore. From KL, two daily flights depart for **Langkawi's International Airport** (℗ **04/955-1322**). Call Malaysia Airline's ticketing office in KL or Langkawi at (℗ **1300/88-3000**). From Singapore, Malaysian Airlines flies direct daily, but has numerous other flights with stops in either KL or Penang. For Singapore reservations call ℗ **65/6336-6777.**

The best thing to do is prearrange a shuttle pickup from your resort, otherwise you can just grab a taxi out in front of the airport. To Pantai Cenang or Pantai Tengah, the fare should be about RM25 (US$6.60), while to the farther resorts at Tanjung Rhu and Datai Bay it will be as high as RM40 (US$11). To call for a pickup from the airport dial ℗ **04/955-1800.**

BY TRAIN   Taking the train can be a bit of a hassle, because the nearest stop (in Alor Setar) is quite far from the jetty to the island, requiring a cab transfer. Still, if you prefer rail, hop on the overnight train from KL (the only train), which will put you in to Alor Setar at around 6am. Just outside the train station you can find the taxi stand, with cabs to take you to the Kuala Kedah jetty for RM10 (US$2.65). Call KL Sentral at ℗ **03/2730-2000** or the Alor Setar Railway Station at ℗ **04/731-4045** for further details.

BY BUS   To be honest, I don't really recommend using this route. If you're coming from KL, the bus ride is long and uncomfortable, catching the taxi transfer to the jetty can be problematic, and by the time you reach the island you'll need a vacation from your vacation. Fly or use the train. If you're coming from Penang, the direct ferry is wonderfully convenient.

BY FERRY   From the jetty at Kuala Kedah, there are about five companies that provide ferry service to the island (trip time: about 1 hr. and 45 min.; cost: RM15/US$3.95). Contact **LADA Holdings** at ℗ 04/762-3823 in Kuala Kedah or 04/966-8823 in Langkawi; Langkawi Ferry Services at ℗ 04/762-4524 in Kuala Kedah or 04/966-9439; or Nautica Ferries at ℗ 04/762-1201 in Kuala Kedah or 04/966-7868 in Langkawi. Ferries let you off at the main ferry terminal in Kuah, where you can hop a taxi to your resort for RM30 to RM40 (US$7.90–US$11).

If you're coming from Penang, the ferry is the way to go. **Bahagia Express** has a morning and afternoon speedboat from Weld Quay in Georgetown for RM35 (US$9.20). Call them in Penang at ℗ **04/263-1943** or visit their office across from the clock tower, just next to the main tourism board office. If you're heading from Langkawi to Penang, you can call Bahagia in Langkawi at ℗ **04/966-5784.**

VISITOR INFORMATION

The MTB office is unfortunately situated in Kuah town on Jalan Persiaran Putra, so most travelers miss it completely, instead heading straight for the beach areas. If you'd like to pick up some of their information, ask your taxi driver to stop on the way to your resort. For specific queries, you can also call them at ℗ **04/966-7789.** If you're arriving by plane, there's another MTB office at the airport (℗ **04/955-7155**).

Langkawi

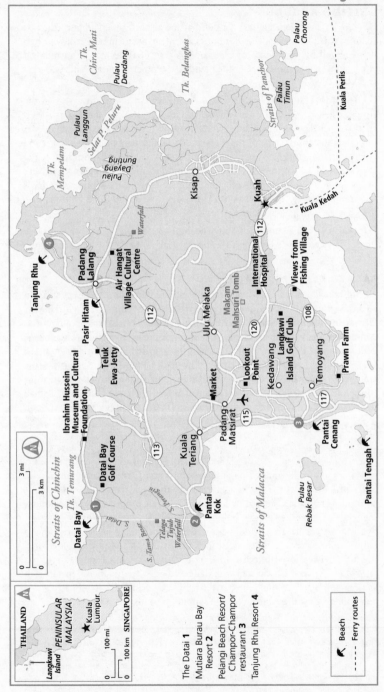

The Datai **1**
Mutiara Burau Bay Resort **2**
Pelangi Beach Resort/ Champor-Champor restaurant **3**
Tanjung Rhu Resort **4**

Beach
Ferry routes

GETTING AROUND

BY TAXI Taxis generally hang around at the airport, the main jetty, the taxi stand in Kuah, and at some major hotels. From anywhere in between, your best bet is to call the taxi stand for a pickup (© **04/966-5249**). Keep in mind, if you're going as far as one side of the island to the other, your fare can go as high as RM40 (US$11).

CAR & MOTORCYCLE RENTAL At the airport and from agents in the complex behind the main jetty, car rentals can be arranged starting at RM60 (US$16) per day. This is for the standard, no-frills model—actually, mine was more reminiscent of some of the junkers I drove throughout college, but it still got me around. Insurance policies are lax, as are rental regulations. My rental guys seemed more concerned with my passport documents than with my driver's license. If you're out on the beach at Cenang or Tengah, a few places rent Jeeps and motorcycles from RM80 (US$21) per day and RM30 (US$7.90) per day, respectively. Pick a good helmet.

BY FOOT The main beaches at Cenang and Tengah can be walked quite nicely; however, don't expect to be able to walk around to other parts of the island.

FAST FACTS: LANGKAWI

The only major **bank** branches seem sadly located far from the beach areas, in Kuah town, mostly around the blocks across the street from the Night Hawker Center (off Jalan Persiaran Putra). Money exchangers keep long hours out at Pantai Cenang and Pantai Tengah, but for other resorts you'll have to change your money at the resort itself. The main **post office** is in Kuah town at the LADA Kompleks on Jalan Persiaran Putra (© **04/966-7271**). Otherwise, use your resort's mail services. Along the Pantai Cenang and Pantai Tengah main road, you'll find at least a half dozen small **Internet** places. **The Shop,** a small convenience store along the strip, provides service for RM6 (US$1.60) per hour.

ACCOMMODATIONS

The Datai ★★★ Aesthetically speaking, this is one of my favorite resorts in Southeast Asia, coming damn close to heaven. Datai is the epitome of sublime, its tropical resort design incorporating nature at every turn. Beyond the graceful open air lobby, pass the lily pond courtyard, to the Datai's brilliant lounge— a hillside veranda surrounded by lush jungle and suspended above a breathtaking bay. Rooms and villas, also built into the hillside, are expert in their studied Southeast Asian elegance. Minimalist in design, the color schemes stick close to nature, with rosewood tones, deep local tapestries, and regal celadon-colored upholstery. Even lower-priced deluxe rooms have a quaint seating area with a view, plus an oversize bathroom with designer body-care products, separate stall shower, and long bathtub. Guest facilities, which include two pools, a spa, and golf course, show the same meticulous attention to luxury. A top pick.

Jalan Teluk Datai, Langkawi, Kedah. © **800/223-6800** in the U.S. and Canada, 800/181-123 in the U.K., or 04/959-2500. Fax 04/959-2600. RM1,325 (US$349) double; RM1,520–RM1,890 (US$400–US$497) villa; RM2,135–RM5,880 (US$562–US$1,547) suite. Prices jump about 50% from Dec–Jan. AE, DC, MC, V. **Amenities:** 3 restaurants (international, Thai, Malaysian); lounge; library; golf course; 2 outdoor pools surrounded by jungle; 2 outdoor, lighted tennis court; fitness center with Jacuzzi, sauna, steam and massage; spa; concierge; watersports equipment; jungle trekking; mountain bike rental; limousine service; limited room service; babysitting; same-day laundry service/dry cleaning. *In room:* A/C, TV w/satellite programming and in-house movie, minibar, coffee/tea-making facilities, hair dryer, safe.

Mutiara Burau Bay Beach Resort   Burau offers beachside resort accommodations for less money than its upscale neighbors. Not nearly as ritzy, this place feels more like summer camp than a resort. All guest rooms are contained in cabanas, with simple decor that's a bit on the older side. For the price, though, they offer value for money. Burau also organizes golf, massage, Jeep treks, jungle treks, mountain biking, tennis, canoeing, catamaran sailing, jet skiing, scuba diving, snorkeling, fishing, water-skiing, windsurfing, and yachting.

Teluk Burau, 07000 Langkawi, Kedah. ℂ **04/959-1061.** Fax 04/959-1172. 150 units. RM250 (US$66) garden-view chalet; RM280 (US$74) sea-view chalet; RM370 (US$97) family chalet; RM735 (US$193) royal chalet. AE, DC, MC, V. **Amenities:** 3 restaurants (international, seafood); beach bar; outdoor pool; outdoor, lighted tennis courts; massage; children's center; concierge; activities desk; game room; car-rental desk; shuttle service; business center; 24-hr. room service; babysitting; same-day laundry service; nonsmoking rooms. *In room:* A/C, TV w/satellite programming and in-house movie, minibar, coffee/tea-making facilities.

Pelangi Beach Resort ⭐   For those who prefer a more active vacation or are looking for a resort that's more family-oriented, I recommend Pelangi. A top-quality resort, this place stands out from neighboring five-star resorts for its sheer fun. A long list of organized sports and leisure pastimes make it especially attractive for families, but surprisingly I never found children to be a distraction here. Pelangi's 51 ethnic wooden chalets are huge inside, and are divided into either one, two, or four guest rooms. You'll be welcomed by vaulted ceilings, modern bathrooms, and large living spaces. But it's the little things you'll love—I didn't want to get out of bed and leave my squishy down pillows and snuggly bedding! In addition, Pelangi's location, near the central beach strip for island life, means you're not cloistered away from the rest of civilization.

Pantai Cenang, 07000 Langkawi, Kedah ℂ **04/952-8888.** Fax 04/952-8899. 350 units. RM620–RM690 (US$163–US$182) double; from RM1,100 (US$289) suite. AE, DC, MC, V. **Amenities:** 3 restaurants (international, Thai, barbecue); 3 bars; 2 large outdoor pools with swim-up bar; Jacuzzi; golf nearby; mini-golf course; outdoor, lighted tennis courts; squash courts; fitness center with sauna, steam, and massage; concierge; tour desk and watersports center with equipment rental, boating excursions, and jungle trekking; car-rental desk; limousine service; shuttle service; business center; 24-hr. room service; babysitting; same-day laundry service/dry cleaning. *In room:* A/C, TV w/satellite programming and in-house movie, minibar, coffee/tea-making facilities, hair dryer, safe.

Tanjung Rhu Resort ⭐⭐   Everyone on the island will agree that the beach at Tanjung Rhu wins first prize, no contest. It's a wide crescent of dazzlingly pure sand wrapped around a perfect crystal azure bay. Tree-lined karst islets jut up from the sea, dotting the horizon. Just gorgeous. This resort claims 440 hectares (1,100 acres) of jungle in this part of the island, monopolizing the scene for extra privacy, but it has its pros and cons. The pros? Guest rooms are enormous and decorated with a sensitivity to the environment, from natural materials to organic recycled-paper wrapped toiletries. The cons? Make sure you don't book your vacation during the months of June or December when Malaysia and Singapore celebrate school holidays, since the place draws families like flies. Still, during between-holiday downtime, I love this resort's friendly and casual atmosphere—and, of course, the beach.

Tanjung Rhu, Mukim Ayer Hangat, Langkawi, Kedah 07000. ℂ **04/959-1033.** Fax 04/959-1899. 138 units. RM980–RM1,950 (US$258–US$513) double. AE, DC, MC, V. **Amenities:** 3 restaurants (international, Mediterranean); bar and library; golf nearby; 2 outdoor pools, 1 saltwater and 1 freshwater; outdoor, lighted tennis courts; fitness center with Jacuzzi, sauna, steam, massage; spa with Jacuzzi, sauna, steam, massage; concierge; activity desk with watersports (nonmotorized), trekking, and boat tours; limousine service; shuttle service; 24-hr. room service; babysitting; same-day laundry service/dry cleaning. *In room:* A/C, TV w/satellite programming and in-room video with movie library, compact disc player, minibar, coffee/tea-making facilities, hair dryer, safe.

DINING

If you're out at one of the more secluded resorts, chances are you'll stay there for most of your meals. However, if you're at Pantai Cenang or Pantai Tengah, I strongly recommend taking a stroll down to **Champor-Champor** ✦, just across the road in the Pelangi Resort (© **04/955-1449**), which serves magnificently creative dishes at lunch and dinner—a local roti canai served like a pizza, and local fish catches doused in sweet sauces. Everything is incredibly fresh, wildly delicious, and amazingly inexpensive. As for decor, the imaginative catchall beach shack atmosphere really relaxes. After dinner, hang around the bar for the best fun on the island. Since Langkawi is an official duty-free port, one beer costs a wee RM4 (US$1.05)! If you're in Kuah town looking for something good to eat, the best local dining experience can be found at the evening **hawker stalls** just along the waterfront near the taxi stand. A long row of hawkers cook up every kind of local favorite, including seafood dishes. You can't get any cheaper or more laid-back. After dinner, from here it's easy to flag down a taxi back to your resort.

Finally, I'm not one to bash places, but I got suckered by a glossy brochure for **Barn Thai,** a Thai restaurant on the eastern side of the island built deep inside a thick mangrove forest. Sound interesting? The food was terrible and overpriced while the atmosphere was destroyed by busloads of tourists. Stay away.

ATTRACTIONS

Most visitors will come for the **beaches.** All resorts are pretty much self-contained units, planning numerous water-sports activities, trekking, sports, and tours.

For a fun day trip I recommend taking one of the local boat trips to some of Langkawi's other islands. Most diving trips take you out to **Payar Marine Park** for two dives per day. Off Payar Island, a floating platform drifts above a stunning coral reef, where dive operators and snorkel gear rentals are available (there's also a glass-bottom boat if you don't want to get wet). Day trips to other **surrounding islands** such as Pulau Singa Besar, Pulau Langgun, Pulau Rebak, or Pulau Beras Basah give you a day of peaceful sun-soaking and swimming. The full day trip to Payar Island floating reef platform costs RM170 (US$45), but dives and rental of snorkel gear cost extra. If you want to hop around to nice secluded island beaches, the half-day island hopping tour costs RM45 (US$12). The half-day **round-island tour** also stops at a few attractions, including the **Batik Art Village** (RM30/US$7.90). In Langkawi call Asian Overland at © **04/955-2002,** or talk to your hotel tour desk operator.

Perhaps one of the loveliest additions to Langkawi's attractions is the **Ibrahim Hussein Museum and Cultural Foundation,** Pasir Tengkorak, Jalan Datai (© **04/959-4669**). The artistic devotion of the foundation's namesake fueled the creation of this enchanting modern space designed to showcase Malaysia's contribution to the international fine-arts scene. If you can pull yourself from the beach for any one activity in Langkawi, this is the one I recommend. Mr. Hussein has created a museum worthy of international attention. Truly a gem. It's open daily from 10am to 5pm; adults RM7 (US$1.85), children free.

SHOPPING

Langkawi's designated Duty Free Port status makes shopping here quite fun and very popular. In Kuah town, the **Sime Darby Duty Free Shop,** Langkawi Duty Free, 64 Persiaran Putra, Pekan Kuah (© **04/966-6052**), carries the largest selection.

Peninsular Malaysia:
The East Coast

Over the past 200 years, while the cities on the western coast of peninsular Malaysia preoccupied themselves with waves of foreign domination, those on the eastern coast developed in relative seclusion. Today, this part of the country remains true to its Malay heritage, from the small fishing kampungs in the south to the Islamic strongholds of the north. The southern parts of the coastline see quite a few visitors each year, mostly Singaporeans who come to unwind on the long palm-fringed beaches of **Kuantan** and **Cherating,** and islands such as **Tioman, Redang,** and **Perhentian,** lapped by the South China Sea. However, few travelers explore the northern cities, **Kuala Terengganu** and **Kota Bharu,** where you'll find some of the most developed cottage industries producing Malaysia handicrafts, plus an orthodox Muslim history and way of life. For visitors who prefer a less plodded path, these areas prove quite a joy.

One note before you plan your trip: If you're looking for beach fun, the monsoon from November through February makes the waters too choppy, so avoid the island resorts and take care by the seaside. Meanwhile in the north, with the exception of a few beach resorts and islands, Muslim modesty will probably make you uncomfortable wearing a Western-style bathing suit at a public beach (the locals swim fully clothed).

1 Tioman Island

Tioman Island (pronounced Tee-oh-mahn) is arguably the most popular destination on Malaysia's east coast. The island is only 39km (23½ miles) long and 12km (7¼ miles) wide, with sandy beaches, clear water with sea life and coral reefs, and jungle mountain-trekking trails with streams and waterfalls. So idyllic is the setting that Tioman was the location for the 1950s Hollywood film *South Pacific.*

At almost any given time there are fewer locals than tourists here, most of whom come from Singapore and other parts of Malaysia. Most come for the scuba and beaches. In fact, many dive books claim the best scuba is to the north at Redang and Perhentian Islands (which are not as easy to get to as Tioman), but to be honest, I have many friends who have taken dive trips all over Southeast Asia, and claim that Tioman is the same, if not better, than sister sites to the north. Don't plan your trip from November through February. Monsoon tides make Tioman inaccessible by ferry, and not the most perfect vacation in the tropics.

Despite the tourist traffic, Tioman has retained much of its tropical island charm, perhaps by virtue of the fact that only one resort has been built on it. **Kampung Tekek,** which is the village where you arrive by either sea or air, has the only paved road on the island connecting it with Berjaya Tioman Beach Resort (the only resort on Tioman). This area is more built up than the rest of the island—built up is really a relative term; trust me, it's a one-horse town.

Activity is spread throughout the *kampungs* (villages), which spring up in the various bays of the island. Besides **Tekek,** the main ones are **Kampung Air Batang,** aka ABC, and **Kampung Salang.** Each kampung has some sort of accommodation facilities, most of them very, very basic wooden chalets, with some access to canteens or restaurants.

ESSENTIALS
GETTING THERE
BY PLANE   Flights to Tioman originate from Kuala Lumpur and Singapore, operated by a private airline, Berjaya Air, and coordinated by the folks at the Berjaya Tioman Beach Resort. However, you need not stay at the resort to book passage on these flights. When considering travel to Tioman, keep in mind the monsoon. Berjaya Air does operate a daily flight during low season, but many times flights are cancelled due to inclement weather conditions. During the lovely months of March through October, Berjaya flies twice daily. Call their KL office for reservations at © 03/746-8228. Their office in Tioman is at the **Berjaya Resort** (© 09/419-1000). The airport in Tioman is in Kampung Tekek, just across from the main jetty. If you're staying at Berjaya Tioman, a shuttle will fetch you; however, if you plan to stay elsewhere, you're on your own. See "Getting Around," below.

BY BUS   SPM Ekspress operates daily bus service from KL's Puduraya Bus Terminal to Mersing, which is the mainland hopping off point to the island (© 03/202-5255 in KL). From Johor Bharu take Johora Express from the Larkin Terminal (© 07/224-8280). They have a daily bus costing RM7 (US$1.85) for the trip. All buses arrive at and depart from the R&R Plaza, which is just next to the jetty where you'll find speedboats to Tioman.

BY FERRY   Ten speedboats depart from Mersing each day. Book passage from the many agents huddled around the dock near Mersing's R&R Plaza. They're basically all the same, each reserving trips on the same boats. Boats leave Mersing Jetty at intervals that depend on the tide. The trip takes around 1½ hours and can cost between RM20 and RM25 (US$5.25–US$6.60), depending on the power of the boat you hire. Boats drop you at either the Berjaya Resort or at the main jetty in Kampung Tekek. The last boat leaves for Tioman between 5 and 6pm every evening. If you miss this boat, you're stuck in Mersing for the night.

From Singapore, **Auto Batam Ferries & Tours** (© 65/6524-7105) operates a daily ferry at 8:30am from the Tanah Merah Ferry Terminal for S$168 (US$44) adults and S$93 (US$25) for children. The ferry takes 4 hours and travels directly to the Berjaya resort, which is also where you catch the ferry back to Singapore at 2:30pm each day.

GETTING AROUND
There are hiking trails between kampungs along the west coast, and another trail overland to the one beach on the east coast. Other than footing it, the most popular mode of transport is **water taxi.** Each village has a jetty; you can pay your fare either at tour offices located near the foot of the pier, or pay the captain directly. The taxis stop operating past nightfall, so make sure you get home before 6 or 7pm. A few sample fares: from Tekek to ABC is RM12 (US$3.15)

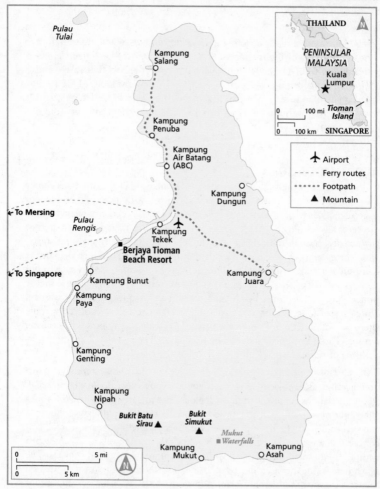

per person, to Salang RM20 (US$5.25), to Juara RM60 (US$16). Also, these guys don't like to shuttle around only one person, so if there's only one of you, be prepared to pay double.

FAST FACTS

You'll find **money exchangers** who accept traveler's checks in Tekek at the airport, by the jetty, and at Berjaya Tioman Resort. Other places will take traveler's checks, and some of the smaller accommodations now accept them as payment. The best idea for a better rate is to cash them at a bank on the mainland before you go.

There are **public phones** at Tekek, ABC, and Salang, which you can use with Telekom phone cards bought on the island. Most guesthouses have nothing more than cellular phones that they will allow guests to use—at a price. These days you can find reliable **Internet access** in Tekek or from the couple of small shops in Salang. Rates run between RM5 and RM10 (US$1.30–US$2.65) per hour.

> **Tips Island Travel**
>
> If you have not already acquired a good mosquito repellent, do so before heading to any of the islands on Malaysia's east coast. You'll need something with DEET (an active ingredient used in repellents that safely and effectively keeps bugs away from your skin). These mosquitoes are hungry. If you plan to stay in one of the smaller chalet places, you might want to invest in a mosquito net. Also, bring a flashlight to help you get around after sunset.

ACCOMMODATIONS

Unless you stay at the Best Western Berjaya Tioman Beach Resort, expect to be roughing it. For some travelers, the Berjaya Tioman, with its wonderful modern conveniences, is what it takes to make a tropical island experience relaxing. Your shower is always warm, you can order food to your room, and you can arrange any activity through the concierge in the lobby. For others, though, real relaxation comes from an escape from modern distractions. The **small chalets in the kampungs** have very minimal facilities and few or no conveniences such as hot showers and telephones. Why would you want to stay in them? Because they're simple, quiet, close to the beach, and less touristy than the resort. Be warned, however, that touts at the jetty in Mersing will offer you all sorts of really, really cheap accommodations, many of which are so rustic they're beyond Robinson Crusoe. Those I've listed under "The Kampungs," below, are all on the habitable side of rustic.

Berjaya Tioman Beach Resort ⭐   This is the only true Western-style resort on the island, and provides all the conveniences you'd expect from a chain hotel. Accommodations are provided in small blocks and private chalets, some with sea views, but most facing gardens. Inside, wood floors, flowery drapes, upholstery, and bedspreads brighten simple rattan furnishings. Each room has a small balcony, but guests are advised against hanging clothes and towels to dry. Attached bathrooms are small, tiled affairs, with combination bathtub and showers. The beach here is fine, however don't expect much surf since the resort if located on the west coast of the island, protected form the open sea. One benefit, an on-site PADI center, but don't come all this way for Berjaya's ho-hum golf course.

Tioman Island, Pahang Darul Makmur. © **09/419-1000.** Fax 09/419-1718. www.berjayaresorts.com.my. 400 units. Mar–Oct RM550–700 (US$145–US$184) chalet; RM800 (US$211) suite. Nov–Feb rates discounted 50%. AE, DC, MC, V. **Amenities:** 4 restaurants (international, local, Chinese, steamboat); beach bar and karaoke lounge; 2 outdoor pools; 18-hole golf course; outdoor, lighted tennis courts; tiny fitness center; sauna; game room; activities desk; watersports equipment rentals; PADI scuba center; shuttle service; limited room service; babysitting; same-day laundry service. *In room:* A/C, TV w/satellite programming, minibar, coffee/tea-making facilities, hair dryer.

THE KAMPUNGS

Each kampung (with the exception of Juara) has, in addition to bungalow accommodations, some sort of eating arrangements, and a PADI dive center that organizes scuba trips as well as snorkel outings. These companies are all internationally accredited with excellent dive masters on hand.

Kampung Tekek is the center of life on Tioman, which means it's the busiest spot, and while there are small accommodations here—as well as some convenience stores (7am–11pm), souvenir shops, and restaurants—you're better off in one of the other kampungs. The best dining is to the side of the main jetty, where you'll find open-air seafood stalls selling soups, noodle dishes, and seafood and vegetable dishes, at very inexpensive prices.

Kampung ABC lines a long rocky beach that is not the best for swimming in spots, but ABC is very laid-back and comfortable in other ways. Chalets line the pathway along the beach, where you'll find small shady picnic areas and hammocks to swing in. While ABC is well populated by travelers, the people here tend to be more relaxed.

The nicest place to stay is **Air Batang Beach Cabanas,** Kampung Air Batang, 86800 Mersing (no phone). Creeping up the side of the hill, these chalets, many with views of the sea, are the largest and newest in the kampung. Rates go from RM120 (US$32) for units with air-conditioning and RM70 (US$18) for those without. All cabins have private toilets with cold shower. Cash is accepted, but not credit cards or traveler's checks. Really the only place to eat here is Nazri's Place in the south end of the beach, which serves breakfast, lunch, and fish or chicken barbecue dinner daily.

Kampung Salang is a happening spot. Snuggled in a big cove of lovely beach and blue water, the village has relatively more conveniences for visitors, such as a choice of eating places serving Continental and local seafood dishes for a song, a few bars, money exchangers, convenience stores, and places to make international calls. It is not a metropolis by any standard, though, and accommodations remain basic.

A better place to stay is at Salang Indah Resorts, **Kampung Salang, Tioman** (© **09/419-5015;** fax 09/419-5024). Choices of rooms vary from fan-cooled hillside chalets at RM25 (US$6.55), to air-conditioned hillside chalets at RM90 (US$24) and sea-view chalets for between RM130 (US$34) and RM150 (US$39). Air-conditioned chalets also feature hot-water showers.

Kampung Juara is where to go if you really want to get away from it all. A gorgeous cove of crystal blue waters and wide clean sand make for the best beach on the island. Most of the chalets here are terrible, some only slightly more accommodating than dog houses. There are no phones, only one TV, one place to eat (The Happy Café, which has the one TV and a few small convenience store items), and no air-conditioning anywhere.

TIOMAN OUTDOORS

After you're waterlogged, you can trek the trail from Tekek to Juara, and some of the paths along the west coast. The hike across the island will take around 2 hours. Bring water and mosquito repellent, and don't try it unless you are reasonably fit.

At the southern part of the island are Bukit Batu Sirau and Bukit Simukut, **"The Famous Twin Peaks,"** and closer to the water near Kampung Mukut are the **Mukut Waterfalls.** There are two smallish pools for taking a dip. Some regular trails exist, but it's inadvisable to venture too far from them because the forest gets dense and it can be tough to find your way back. Negotiate with water taxis to bring you down and pick you up.

2 Kuantan

Kuantan is the capital of Pahang Darul Makmur, the largest state in Malaysia, covering about 35,960 sq. km (22,475 sq. miles). Travelers come to Pahang for the beautiful beaches, which stretch all the way up the east coast, and for inland jungle forests that promise adventures in trekking, climbing, and river rafting. Much of **Taman Negara,** Malaysia's national forest preserve, is in this state, although most people access the forest via Kuala Lumpur (see "Side Trips from Kuala Lumpur," in chapter 9). Kuantan, although it's the capital, doesn't have the feel of a big city. If you're staying at the beach at Telok Chempedak, 5km (3 miles) north of Kuantan, the atmosphere is even more relaxed.

Here's an interesting piece of trivia. Kuantan has the highest property values in the country, higher than the capital city and cosmopolitan Panang. Why? The discovery of offshore oil reserves means all the big oil companies have operations in this region, and I can assure you, their executives ain't livin' in no wooden bungalows on stilts.

ESSENTIALS
VISITOR INFORMATION
A **Tourist Information Centre** (℡ 09/517-1624) is located on Jalan Penjara in the center of town. Staff here are exceptionally helpful and good at answering specific inquiries.

GETTING THERE
BY AIR   **Malaysia Airlines** has a daily flight from KL. For reservations call (℡ 1300/88-3000). Flights arrive at the **Sultan Ahmad Shah Airport** (℡ 09/538-1291). Just outside the airport is a taxi stand where you can get a cab to Kuantan for RM25 (US$6.60) or to Cherating for RM60 (US$16).

BY BUS   Bus routes service Kuantan from all parts of the peninsula. From KL, **Plusliner** (℡ 03/4042-1256) departs from the Pekeliling Bus Terminal, off Jalan Tun Razak. Five daily buses make the trip for RM14 (US$3.75). The bus terminal in Kuantan is in Kompleks Makmur. Taxis at the stand just outside the terminal can take you to town for RM10 (US$2.65).

For buses from Kuantan to other destinations call **Plusliner** at ℡ 09/515-0991 or **Transnasional** at ℡ 09/515-6740.

BY TAXI   Outstation taxis from KL (℡ 03/2078-0213) will cost RM220 (US$58). The outstation taxi stand in Kuantan is at the bus terminal.

GETTING AROUND
The areas in the town's center are nice for walking. Otherwise stick with taxis, which can be waved down on any street. If you need to arrange for a pickup, call the **taxi stand** at the bus terminal at ℡ 09/513-4478. There's also a stand behind the Tourist Information Centre where you'll be sure to find a cab in a pinch. Taxis here are not metered, so you must negotiate the fare before you set out. This is a good deal when you want to hire someone for a few hours to take you around the city. Rates are from RM15 (US$3.95) per hour. Use taxis to travel to areas of interest outside the city that are covered later in this section.

FAST FACTS
The **American Express** office is at Mayflower Acme Tours, Ground Floor, Sultan Ahmad Shah Airport (℡ 09/538-3490). Most major banks are located appropriately along Jalan Bank, near the State Mosque.

The central **post office** (℡ 09/552-1078) is near the State Mosque on Jln. Haji Abdul Aziz. **Internet service** is available from a couple of cafes at the Kompleks Makmur; check the shopping mall adjacent to the bus terminal.

ACCOMMODATIONS
Kuantan is not a very large place, and most of those who vacation here prefer to stay just a little farther north, in **Cherating,** which is more established as a resort destination. If staying in Kuantan is important to you, though, the Hotel Grand

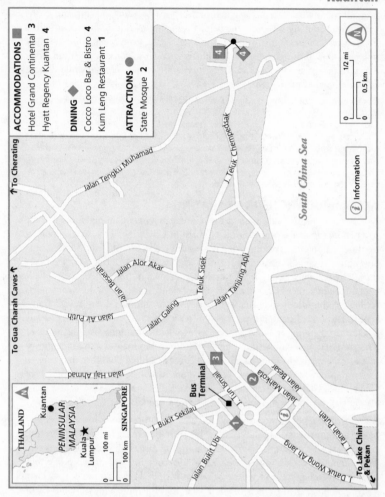

ACCOMMODATIONS ■
Hotel Grand Continental **3**
Hyatt Regency Kuantan **4**

DINING ◆
Cocco Loco Bar & Bistro **4**
Kum Leng Restaurant **1**

ATTRACTIONS ●
State Mosque **2**

↑ To Cherating

Jalan Tengku Muhamad

J. Teluk Chempedak

South China Sea

ⓘ Information

← To Gua Charah Caves

Jalan Alor Akar

Jalan Beserah

Jalan Air Putih

Jalan Galing

J. Teluk Sisek

Jalan Tanjung Apli

Jalan Haji Ahmad

Jalan Mankota

Jalan Besar

Bus Terminal

J. Tun Ismail

J. Bukit Sekilau

Jalan Bukit Ubi

J. Dauk Wong Ah Jang

J. Tanah Putih

To Lake Chini & Pekan ↓

THAILAND
Kuantan
PENINSULAR MALAYSIA
Kuala Lumpur ★
SINGAPORE
100 mi
100 km

1/2 mi
0.5 km

Continental is a decent, centrally located place. Near the beach at Telok Chempedak, the Hyatt Regency is as romantic and relaxing as any place at Cherating.

Hotel Grand Continental   Located in the heart of Kuantan, this hotel is near the central mosque. It's a simple three-star hotel, run by a budget hotel chain from Down Under. New and adequate facilities are somewhat reminiscent of the 1970s. The front view of the bridge and river is more pleasant than the view in the rear rooms.

Jalan Gambut, 25000 Kuantan, Pahang Darul Makmur. ✆ **09/515-8888**. Fax 09/515-9999. www.grand continental.com.my. 202 units. RM222 (US$58) double; RM360 (US$95) suite. AE, DC, MC, V. **Amenities:** Restaurant (international); outdoor pool; small fitness center; business center; limited room service; babysitting; same-day laundry service/dry cleaning. *In room:* A/C, TV w/satellite programming and in-house movie, minibar, coffee/tea-making facilities, hair dryer.

Hyatt Regency Kuantan ⋇   The Hyatt Regency is located on the beach at Telok Chempedak, about 10 minutes outside of Kuantan proper. The long stretch of sandy beach bordering it is perfect for relaxation and fun, and in the evening the crashing waves are the perfect romantic backdrop. Hyatt has built a five-star resort here, and it is five-star in every sense, from outstanding facilities to large well-appointed rooms. The lobby is open-air so you can practically look out onto the sea as you check in. Guest rooms are in two blocks—while all have balconies, higher priced rooms have sea views.

Telok Chempedak, 25050 Kuantan, Pahang. ℂ **800/233-1234** in the U.S., or 09/566-1234. Fax 09/567-7577. http://kuantan.regency.hyatt.com. 336 units. RM391–RM450 (US$103–US$118) double; RM841–RM956 (US$221–US$252) suite. AE, DC, MC, V. **Amenities:** 3 restaurants (Chinese, Italian, Malaysian/international); 3 bars including a pub with live entertainment; 2 outdoor pools; 3 outdoor, lighted tennis courts; 2 squash courts; fitness center; spa with sauna, steam, and massage; children's center; concierge; tour desk; limousine service; business center; 24-hr. room service; babysitting; same-day laundry service/dry cleaning; nonsmoking rooms on the top floors; executive-level rooms. *In room:* A/C, TV w/satellite programming and in-house movie, minibar, coffee/tea-making facilities, hair dryer, safe.

ACCOMMODATIONS IN CHERATING

Because Kuantan is such a small town, some travelers coming through these parts choose to stay 47km (28 miles) north in Cherating. This area supports a few international-class resorts along the beautiful beachfront of the South China Sea. Funny thing: Compared to Kuantan, the town of Cherating has even fewer things to do, and guests tend not to stray too far from their resort. Self-contained units, they each offer a few dining choices, arrange all the water-sports facilities and outdoor activities you have time for, and can even provide transport to and from Kuantan if you need to see a little "big city life." Windsurfers take note: Cherating is world famous for excellent conditions, and the home of a few international competitions and exhibitions. Resorts can also arrange trips through the mangroves up the Cherating River in a hired bumboat, and trips to crafts shops and cultural shows. A little more than 11km (6¾ miles) north of Cherating is Chendor Beach, one of the peninsula's special beaches where giant leatherback turtles lay their eggs from May to October.

Club Med *Kids*   The world-renowned Club Med occupies a lovely stretch of beachfront property along the coastline here. On 80 private hectares (200 acres), you can expect this resort chain to take complete care of all your holiday needs. The compound of Malay-style wooden houses contains very contemporary but natural furnishings, and nice little balconies with each. Everything is absolutely spotless. *A note:* If you're new to Club Med, they'll require a membership fee of RM80 (US$21) for adults only, added on to your booking (Club Med really is a club, you see). They'll also be happy to arrange all your transportation from KL for an additional cost. For fun, try their outdoor swimming pool, sailing activities, windsurfing, kayaking, tennis (6 lighted courts), squash, badminton, cricket, archery, volleyball, wall-scaling, and a circus school with flying trapeze. They also coordinate jungle walks and batik lessons. Almost all above activities are included in your daily rate. At extra cost, there's also a nearby golf course. A daily international buffet features Malay, Indian, Korean, Japanese, and Chinese cuisine, while the Pantai features grilled seafood and meats and Vesuvio opens in the evenings for Italian fare. After that, head for the nightclub and bar.

Correspondence through KL office only via Vacances, Suite 1.1, 1st Floor Bangunan MAS, Jalan Sultan Ismail, 50250 Kuala Lumpur. ℂ 03/261-4599. Fax 03/261-7229. www.clubmed.com. 315 units. Weekdays (Sun–Fri) RM300 (US$79) per adult, RM30–RM180 (US$7.90–US$47) per child; weekends (Sat) RM350 (US$92) per adult, RM35–RM210 (US$9.20–US$55) per child. Peak season (Christmas, New Year's, and Chinese New Year) RM420 (US$111) per adult, RM42–RM252 (US$11–US$66) per child. AE, DC, MC, V. **Amenities:** 3 restaurants (international, barbecue, Italian); 2 bars; outdoor pool; outdoor, lighted tennis courts; squash courts, fitness center; massage; children's center; game room; tour desk; watersports equipment rentals; car-rental desk; shuttle service; babysitting; same-day laundry service. *In room:* A/C, hair dryer, safe.

Holiday Villa Cherating ★ This 4-hectare (10-acre) coastline property has three different wings to choose from: The Capital Wing houses deluxe rooms in a longhouse building. The Palace Wing has superior and deluxe chalets. All categories in both wings have views facing one of the resorts two pools. Be warned that not all categories have double beds, so make sure you specify when booking if this is important to you. Holiday Villa's best accommodations, however, are the Eastern Pavilion Wing—two-room and three-room villas with their own private pool and Jacuzzi. In contrast to the other categories of rooms, which are a bit dark with older style decor, these villas are very pretty with polished teak furnishings and Oriental carpets. You will pay a premium, however.

Lot 1303, Mukin Sungai Karang, 26080 Kuantan, Pahang Darul Makmur. © **09/581-9500.** Fax 09/581-9178. www.holidayvillacherating.com. 150 units. RM110–RM190 (US$29–US$50) double; RM230–RM295 (US$61–US$78) suite. AE, DC, MC, V. **Amenities:** 3 restaurants (international, steakhouse, Chinese); 2 pubs; 2 outdoor pools; 3 outdoor, lighted tennis courts; badminton; fitness center; spa with massage; tour desk; watersports equipment rental; 24-hr. room service; babysitting; same-day laundry service. *In room:* A/C, TV w/satellite programming and in-house movie, minibar, coffee/tea-making facilities.

DINING

You can find both seafood and local food in Kuantan, but like the other smaller destinations in Malaysia, you'll be hard-pressed to find fine dining outside of the larger hotels. The best evening activities are centered around the beach area at Telok Chempedak.

Cocco Loco Bistro & Bar ITALIAN For a little fine dining in Kuantan, your best bet is at the Hyatt's Italian restaurant, Cocco Loco. Local seafood like sea bass and prawns is transformed into beautiful entrees, with light sauces and the freshest ingredients. There is a good wine list with many international labels. If you arrive early, you can still see the ocean from huge glass windows. However, even after dark, Cocco Loco has a beautiful atmosphere enhanced by romantic lights, terra-cotta floors, and bright table linens.

Hyatt Regency Kuantan, Telok Chempedak. © **09/566-1234,** ext. 7700. Reservations recommended. Entrees RM20–RM48 (US$5.25–US$13). AE, DC, MC, V. Daily noon–2:30pm, 6–10:30pm.

Kum Leng Restoran CANTONESE Kum Leng is one of the top restaurants in Kuantan. A bit cramped, it's always doing a good business but there's rarely a wait. Try the fried chicken with dry chile topped with onions and cashew nuts, or the fried chile prawns with shells. They're very fresh and not too spicy.

E–897/899/901 Jalan Bukit Ubi, Kuantan. © **09/513-4446.** Seafood priced according to seasonal availability; other dishes can be as low as RM5 (US$1.30) for fried tofu or as high as RM100 (US$26) for shark's fin. No credit cards. Daily 11:30am–2:30pm, 5:30–10:30pm.

ATTRACTIONS

Kuantan can really be seen in a day. While there are a few fun crafts shops, the place is not exactly a hotbed of culture. The main attraction in town is the huge State Mosque, which is quite beautiful inside and out, with a distinct dome, minarets, and stained glass. Late afternoon is the best time to see it, when the light really shines through the glass.

SHOPPING

You can have a nice walk down **Jalan Besar,** sampling local delicacies sold on the street and shopping in the smaller craft and souvenir shops. Visit **HM Batik**

& Handicraft, 45 N-1, Bangunan LKNP, Jalan Besar (℃ **09/552-8477**), and **Kedai Mat Jais B. Talib,** 45N-8, Bangunan LKNP, Jalan Besar (℃ **09/555-2860**), for good selections of batiks and crafts. **Batik RM** has a showroom on Jalan Besar (2–C Medan Pelancung; ℃ **09/514-2008**), but the showroom out on Jalan Tanah Puteh (℃ **09/513-9631**) is much more fun. Tours around the back allow you to watch the waxing and dyeing processes. Their showroom has some great batik fashions—more stylish than so much of the batik clothing that you find in the markets.

ATTRACTIONS OUTSIDE KUANTAN

Pahang is home to peninsular Malaysia's most stunning forests. With Kuantan as your starting point, it's easy jump out to these spots for a day or half-day trip.

Gua Charah caves are about 25km (15⅔ miles) outside of Kuantan. Also called Pancing caves (they're located in a town called Pancing), one of the caves in the network is a temple, home to a huge reclining Buddha. It is said that the monk caretaker, who has grown very old, is having difficulty finding another monk who will take over his duties at the caves. An outstation taxi can take you there for RM80 (US$21).

Also fun is **Lake Chini,** 12 freshwater lakes that have local legends that rival Loch Ness. They say that there once was an ancient Khmer city at the site of the lakes, but it is now buried deep under the water, protected by monsters. Some have tried to find both city and monsters, but have come up with nothing. Boats are there to take you across the lake to an *orang asli* (indigenous peoples) kampung to see the native way of life. Lake Chini is 60km (38 miles) southwest of Kuantan, and an outstation taxi can take you there for RM80 (US$21).

Just south of Kuantan is **Pekan,** which for history and culture buffs is far more interesting then Kuantan. Pekan is called "the Royal City" because it is where the Sultan of Pahang resides in a beautiful Malay-style istana. The **State Museum** on Jalan Sultan Ahmad has displays depicting the history of Pahang and its royal family, as well as sunken treasures from old Chinese junks. Outstation taxis to Pekan are RM20 (US$5.25).

GOLF

The **Royal Pahang Golf Club** is near Kuantan's beach resort area on Jalan Teluk Chempedak (℃ **09/567-5811;** fax 09/567-1170). Your hotel will be happy to make all necessary reservations for you.

3 Kuala Terengganu

The capital of the state of Terengganu, Kuala Terengganu has far more exciting activities to offer a visitor than its southern capital neighbor, Kuantan. And yet, many travelers to Malaysia often skip this part of the country for the more beaten paths. So why should you consider coming here? **Malaysian crafts.** Kuala Terengganu has the best cottage industries for Malaysian crafts—better than anywhere else on the peninsula. Terengganu artisans specialize in everything from boatbuilding to kite making, and it is here that you can see how these things are made, in warehouse workshops and private backyards.

In recent years Terengganu has become somewhat controversial, since the 1999 elections when the Pan Malaysian Islamic Party (PAS) gained control of the state, giving them control of 2 out of 13 Malaysian states—the other is Kelantan, covered in the next section. PAS leaders toyed with the idea of initiating syariah law, the old "you get caught stealing, I chop off your hand" business. They have

Kuala Terengganu

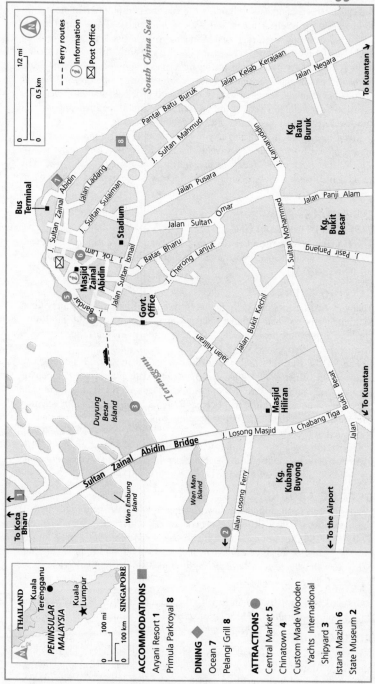

ACCOMMODATIONS ■

Aryani Resort **1**
Primula Parkroyal **8**

DINING ◆

Ocean **7**
Pelangi Grill **8**

ATTRACTIONS ●

Central Market **5**
Chinatown **4**
Custom Made Wooden
   Yachts International
   Shipyard **3**
Istana Maziah **6**
State Museum **2**

been successful passing laws forbidding the sale and consumption of alcohol (in all but a few Chinese restaurants and Western hotels), banning women's images used for advertising, requiring establishments to have two separate swimming pools, one for men and one for women, although nobody's really dug any second pools as of yet. They have even made separate lanes in grocery stores for men and women, even though everyone basically ignores them. To be honest I haven't noticed big changes. Traveling here is as peaceful as it ever was. However, I do advise while traveling in Terengganu (as well as Kelantan) that men and women dress conservatively so as not to draw unfavorable reactions.

Kuala Terengganu is small and easy to navigate, clustered around a port at the mouth of the Terengganu River. Many livelihoods revolve around the sea, so most of the activity, even today, focuses on the areas closest to the jetties. The local business week is from Saturday to Wednesday, so be prepared for that when you plan your time here.

ESSENTIALS

VISITOR INFORMATION

The **Tourism Information Centre** is on Jalan Sultan Zainal Abidin just next to the post office and across from the central market. The phone number there is (© **09/622-1553**).

GETTING THERE

Malaysia Airlines has two daily flights from KL to Kuala Terengganu's Sultan Mahmud Airport. Their national reservations number is (© **1300/88-3000**). For local airport information call © **09/666-4204.** From the airport, a taxi to town is about RM15 (US$3.95).

The **MPKT Bus Terminal** is located on Jalan Sultan Zainal Abidin next to the water. **Plusliner** (© **03/4043-4285**) has two daily buses from KL, departing from the Putra Bus Terminal opposite the Putra World Trade Centre. The trip time is 8 hours, with tickets priced at RM25.70 (US$6.75). From Kuantan you can also catch the Plusliner bus heading from KL to Kuala Terengganu via Kuantan. For buses out of Kuala Terengganu call Plusliner at (© **09/622-7076**).

Outstation taxis from Kuantan will cost RM90 (US$24). Call © **09/513-6950** for booking. Outstation taxi bookings from Kuala Terengganu can be arranged by calling © **09/622-1581.**

GETTING AROUND

While you can stroll around the downtown areas with ease, getting to many of the bigger attractions will require a **taxi.** To call and arrange for a taxi, dial © **09/622-1581,** or arrange through your hotel concierge. It's a good idea to hire these guys for a half or whole day, so you can go around to places and not worry how you'll get back. Rates will be around RM15 (US$3.95) per hour.

FAST FACTS

Most **banks** are on Jalan Sultan Ismail. The main **post office** is on Jalan Sultan Zainal Abidin (© **09/622-7555**), next to the Tourist Information Centre.

ACCOMMODATIONS

The Aryani Resort ★★ *Finds* Two and a half years ago, Raja Dato' Bahrin Shah Raja Ahmad (a most royal name) opened his dream resort. An internationally celebrated architect, he'd previously designed the State Museum (see below) and wished to translate the beautiful lines of Terengganu style into a special resort. The resulting Aryani is stunning—organic, stimulating, unique, and best of all, peaceful. In a rural 3.6-hectare (9-acre) spot by the sea, the rooms are private bungalows situated like a village. Inside, each is masterfully decorated to suit both traditional style and modern comfort. The Heritage Suite wins the prize: a 100-year-old timber palace, restored and rebuilt on the site, it's appointed with fine antiques. The design of the outdoor pool is practically an optical illusion, and the spa (for massage and beauty treatments) is in its own Malay house. The resort's rural location has both a plus and a minus: On the plus side it's secluded; on the minus side it's 45 minutes from Kuala Terengganu. The resort can arrange boat trips, tours to town, and golfing.

Jalan Rhu Tapai–Merang, 21010 Setiu, Terengganu, Malaysia. © **09/624-1111** or 09/624-4489. Fax 09/624-8007. www.malaysia-hotels-online.com/hotels/merang/aryaniresort.htm. 20 units. RM418–RM475 (US$110–US$125) double; RM740 (US$195) modern suite; RM930 (US$245) heritage suite. AE, DC, MC, V. **Amenities:** 2 restaurants (local, international); library; outdoor infinity pool; spa with massage; concierge; nonmotorized watersports equipment rental; limousine service; same-day laundry service. *In room:* A/C, TV w/satellite programming, minibar, coffee/tea-making facilities.

Primula Parkroyal Kuala Terengganu   A top pick for accommodations in Kuala Terengganu is the Parkroyal. The first resort to open in this area, it commands the best section of beach the city has to offer and still is very close to the downtown area. It has full resort facilities, which include three excellent restaurants and the only bar in the city (perhaps even in the state). Make sure you get a room facing the sea—the view is dreamy. Other facilities include an outdoor pool with grassy lawn, water-sports facilities, a lobby shop, and a kid's club.

Jalan Persinggahan, P.O. Box 43, 20904, Kuala Terengganu, Terengganu Darul Iman, Malaysia. © **800/835-7742** in the U.S. and Canada, 800/363-300 in Australia, 0800/801-111 in New Zealand, 09/622-2100, or 09/623-3722. Fax 09/623-3360. www.asiatravel.com/malaysia/primula/v4.html. 249 units. RM320 (US$84) double; RM400 (US$105) suite. AE, DC, MC, V. **Amenities:** 3 restaurants; pub; outdoor pool; children's center; concierge; tour desk; limousine service; business center; 24-hr. room service; babysitting; same-day laundry service/dry cleaning. *In room:* A/C, TV w/satellite programming and in-house movie, minibar, coffee/tea-making facilities, hair dryer.

DINING

Ocean CHINESE/SEAFOOD   One of the most celebrated seafood restaurants in town, Ocean prepares tender prawns, light butterfish, and juicy crab in local and Chinese recipes that are very good. Don't count on much from the alfresco decor. To be honest, the place looks more or less like a warehouse, but the views of the sea help. So does the beer, which Ocean is permitted to serve.

Lot 2679 Jalan Sultan Janah Apitin (by the waterfront). © **09/623-9154.** Reservations not accepted. RM10–RM25 (US$2.65–US$6.60); seafood sold according to market prices. MC, V. Daily noon–2:30pm, 5:30pm–midnight.

Pelangi Grill LOCAL/CONTINENTAL   In an open-air lanai facing the sea and the resort's gardens, this delightful multilevel outdoor cafe is good for either family meals or romantic dinners. The main level is set for standard menu items, which include the house specialties, sizzling dishes of prawn or beef, plus pizzas and a great assortment of local and Western entrees. The lower patio is set for steamboat, a fondue-style dinner where you place chunks of fish and meats into boiling broth at your table. A small assortment of international wines is available.

Primula Parkroyal, Jalan Persinggahan. © **09/622-2100.** Reservations not necessary. RM10–RM24 (US$2.65–US$6.30). AE, DC, MC, V. Daily noon–11pm.

ATTRACTIONS

Central Market ★   Open daily from very early until about 7pm, the central market is a huge maze of shops selling every craft made in the region. There's basket weaving for everything from place mats to beach mats. Batik comes in sarongs (with some very unique patterns), ready-made clothing, and household linens. Songet, beautiful fabric woven with gold and silver threads, is sold by the piece or sarong. Brass-ware pots, candlesticks, and curios are piled high and glistening. Every handicraft item you can think of is here, waiting for you to bargain and bring it home. And when you're done, venture to the back of the market and check out the produce, dried goods, and seafood in the wet market.

Jalan Sultan Zainal Abidin.

Chinatown While Terengganu has only a small Chinese population, its Chinatown is still quite interesting. This street of shophouses close to the water is still alive, only today many of the shops are art galleries and boutiques, showcasing only the finest regional arts. Also along Jalan Bandar you can find travel agents for trips to nearby islands.

Jalan Bandar.

Custom Made Wooden Yachts International Shipyard ★ Abdullah bin Muda's family has been building ships by hand for generations. Now Mr. Abdullah is an old-timer, but he gets around, balancing on the planks that surround the dry-docked hulls of his latest masterpieces. He makes fishing boats in western and Asian styles, as well as luxury yachts—all handmade, all from wood. While Mr. Abdullah doesn't speak any English, he'll let you explore the boats on your own, and even tell you how much money he's getting for them. You'll weep when you hear how inexpensive his fine work is.

3592 Duyong Besar. ✆ 09/623-2072.

Istana Maziah Probably one of the least ornate istanas in Malaysia, this lovely yellow and white royal palace, built in 1897, is today mainly only used for state and royal ceremonies. It is not open to the public. Tucked away down the narrow winding street is its neighbor, the Masjid (mosque) Abidin.

Jalan Masji. No phone.

State Museum ★★ The buildings that house the museum's collection were built specifically for this purpose. Designed by a member of the Terengganu royal family, an internationally renowned architect who also built the nearby Aryani resort, it reflects the stunning Terengganu architectural style. Atop stilts (16 of them, the traditional number) with high sloping roofs, the three main buildings are connected by elevated walkways. Inside are fine collections that illustrate the history and cultural traditions of the state.

Bukit Losong. ✆ 09/622-1444. Admission RM5 (US$1.30) adults; RM2 (US55¢) children. Sat–Thurs 9am–5pm. Closed Fri.

TERENGGANU'S HANDICRAFTS

Chendering, an industrial town about 40 minutes' drive south of Kuala Terengganu, is where you'll find major handicraft production—factories and showrooms of batiks and other lovely items. All these places are located along one stretch of highway, but all are too far apart to walk. Plan to hire a taxi by the hour to shuttle you between them; they're about a 5-minute hop between each if you're driving. Also, while you're in the area, stop by the **Masjid Tengku Tengah Zahara,** which is only 5km (3 miles) outside of the town. The mosque is more commonly referred to as the "Floating Mosque," as it is built in a lake and appears to be floating on the top.

Noor Arfa Noor Arfa is Malaysia's largest producer of hand-painted batik. This former cottage-industry business now employs 200 workers to create ready-to-wear fashions that are esteemed as designer labels throughout the country. There's also a shop in town at Aked Mara, A3 Jalan Sultan Zainal Abidin (© 09/623-5173).

Lot 1048 K Kawasan Perindustrian Chendering. © **09/617-5700**. Sat–Thurs 8am–5pm. Closed Fri.

Suteramas Suteramas specializes in batik painting on fine quality silks. At this, their factory showroom, you can buy their latest creations or just watch them being made. Not only do they dye the cloth, they make it from their own worm stock.

Zkawasan Perindustrian Chendering. © **09/617-1355**. Free admission. Sat–Wed 9am–5pm. Closed Thurs–Fri.

Terengganu Craft Cultural Centre Operated by the Malaysian Handicraft Development Corporation, The Craft Cultural Center, also called Budaya Craft, not only sells handicrafts, but also has blocks of warehouses where artisans create the work. See batik painting, brass casting, basket weaving, and wood carving as well as other local crafts in progress.

Lot 2195 Kawasan Perindustrian Chendering. © **09/617-1033**. Sat–Wed 8am–5pm; Thurs 8am–12:45pm. Closed Fri.

TERANGGANU'S OUTDOORS

If you are in Terengganu between May and August, you've arrived just in time to see the **baby leatherback turtles.** For hundreds of years, possibly more, giant leatherback turtles have come to the shore here by the thousands. The females crawl to the beaches where they dig holes in which to lay their eggs. Sixty days later, the small turtles hatch and scurry for the water. In recent decades the turtles have had trouble carrying out their ritual, with development and poaching putting severe hardships on the population. Of the babies that are hatched, many never make it to the deep sea. At the **Department of Fisheries of the State of Terengganu** (Taman Perikanan Chendering; © **09/917-3353**) there is a sanctuary that collects the eggs from the beaches, incubates them in hatcheries, then sets the babies free. They welcome visitors to their exhibits about turtles and the sanctuary's activities, and to midnight watches to see mothers lay eggs and babies hatch. These activities are free of charge.

TERENGGANU MARINE PARK

The first marine park in Malaysia, the Terengganu Marine Park, is situated around the nine islands of the Redang archipelago, 45km (28 miles) northeast of Kuala Terengganu and 27km (17 miles) out to sea. Sporting the best coral reefs and dive conditions off peninsular Malaysia, the park attracts divers with its many excellent sites. The largest of the islands is Pulau Redang (Redang Island), where most people stay in resorts on overnight diving excursions. Begin with an hour's drive to the northern jetty town of Merang (not to be confused with Marang, which is in the south), followed by an overwater trip to any one of the islands for scuba, snorkeling, and swimming.

The best place to stay on Redang is the **Berjaya Redang Beach Resort** ⚘. It's the best, mainly because they can arrange your entire trip and activities for you—transfers to and from the airport, speedboat trip to and from the island, accommodations, meals, and activities including scuba. Very no-muss-no-fuss. It also happens to be the most comfortable place on the island, with 152 Malay-style chalets all with en suite bathroom, air-conditioning, phones, TVs with satellite programs and in-house movies, and minibars. Of their three restaurants, the beach seafood grill is the favorite. In addition to scuba and snorkeling trips to the coral reefs, they'll plan other watersports activities plus treks around the island. Their pool is a gorgeous lagoon-style affair by the beach. Very pretty. Contact Berjaya Redang Beach Resort at © **800/88-8818** or 09/697-3988, fax 09/697-3899 or online at www.berjayaresorts.com. Rates are RM600–RM800 (US$158–US$210) double.

At the time of printing, Berjaya was in the midst of completing another resort on the island, a spa resort. If this option interests you, ask about it when you make your booking inquiries.

PERHENTIAN ISLANDS

The Perhentian Islands (two islands, one big, one small) are part of this same archipelago within the Terengganu Marine Park. Located to the north of Redang, they are easier accessed via Kota Bharu in Kelantan. It's about a 45-minute ride to the jetty from Kota Bharu airport—you can take a taxi easily.

There are many bungalow operators on these islands—some of these places are terrible, shoddy huts with poor excuses for beds and scarcely anything else. But the worst part is the piles of garbage that accumulate. One place I saw had a stinking garbage heap knee high at the foot of the path that lead from the beach to reception. For some reason these small bungalow operators have not realized that if they turn their own beaches into compost heaps, people will stop coming.

Perhentian Island Resort is your best option here. They have a private beach and are managed properly. Their 106 rooms, housed in cabanas offer comfortable beds in air-conditioning. Their one restaurant serves buffet meals three times daily. Activities are organized through their PADI dive center, plus there's snorkeling, tennis, trekking and non-motorized sea sports. They will arrange your speedboat transfers to and from the jetty.

Note: The resort is closed during the rainy season from December through January. Contact Perhentian Island Resort at © **010/903-0100,** fax 010/903-0106 (these are mobile numbers), www.jaring.my/perhentian. It may be more practical to make your arrangements from their **KL sales office** at © **3/244-8530,** fax 03/243-4984. Rates are as follows: RM200–RM350 (US$53–US$92) double.

4 Kota Bharu

In the northeast corner of peninsular Malaysia, bordering Thailand, is the state of **Kelantan.** Few tourists head this far north up the east coast, but it's a fascinating journey for those interested in seeing Malaysia as it might have been without so many foreign influences. The state is populated mostly by Malays and Bumiputeras, with only tiny factions of Chinese and Indian residents and almost no traces of British colonialism. Not surprisingly, Kelantan is the heart of traditional Islam in modern Malaysia. While the government in KL constructs social policies based upon a more open and tolerant Islam, religious and government leaders in Kelantan can be counted on for putting forth a strong Muslim ideal where they feel they may have influence.

Kelantan owes its character to the mountain range that runs north to south through the interior, slicing the peninsula in half. Isolated from other Malay areas, Kelantan for most of its history was aligned with Siam, which didn't care

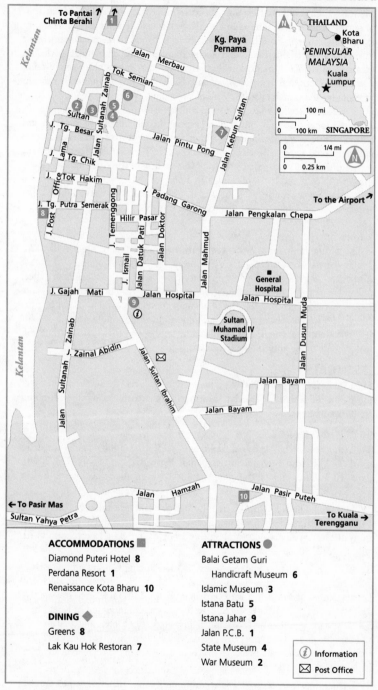

Kota Bharu

THAILAND
● Kota Bharu

PENINSULAR MALAYSIA

Kuala Lumpur ★

SINGAPORE

0 — 100 mi
0 — 100 km

0 — 1/4 mi
0 — 0.25 km

Kelantan

To Pantai Chinta Berahi

Kg. Paya Pernama

Jalan Merbau

Tok Semian

Jalan Sultanah Zainab

Sultan

J. Tg. Besar

J. Tg. Chik

J. Lama

J. e Tok Hakim

J. Tg. Putra Semerak

J. Post Office

Jalan Pintu Pong

Jalan Kebun Sultan

J. Padang Garong

Hilir Pasar

J. Temenggong

J. Ismail

J. Datuk Pati

Jalan Doktor

J. Gajah Mati

Jalan Hospital

Jalan Padang Garong

Jalan Pengkalan Chepa

To the Airport

General Hospital

Jalan Hospital

Sultan Muhamad IV Stadium

Jalan Mahmud

Jalan Dusun Muda

Zainab

Sultanah

J. Zainal Abidin

Jalan Sultan Ibrahim

Jalan Bayam

Jalan Bayam

Jalan Hamzah

Jalan Pasir Puteh

To Pasir Mas →

Sultan Yahya Petra

To Kuala Terengganu →

Kelantan

ACCOMMODATIONS ■
Diamond Puteri Hotel **8**
Perdana Resort **1**
Renaissance Kota Bharu **10**

DINING ◆
Greens **8**
Lak Kau Hok Restoran **7**

ATTRACTIONS ●
Balai Getam Guri
   Handicraft Museum **6**
Islamic Museum **3**
Istana Batu **5**
Istana Jahar **9**
Jalan P.C.B. **1**
State Museum **4**
War Museum **2**

ⓘ Information
✉ Post Office

one way or another how Kelantan ran its territory. Cut off from the trade traffic on the other side of the mountains, Kelantan, and to some extent its southern neighbor Terengganu, had sufficient peace of mind to form its own Islamic bureaucracy, judicial system, and societal institutions, emphasizing Muslim standards of scholarship and learning. Trade in gold, mined from the interior, provided for business with Chinese and Thais, but Europeans, their mouths watering for the mineral wealth, were not welcome.

But Kelantan couldn't keep away the British in 1900. Not only were the Brits interested in all that gold, but also in keeping the region free from French and German interests. Arguments were had and agreements made between London and Siam, and eventually Kelantan came under British rule. Several peasant uprisings disturbed the peace, and the Muslim elite in the cities took to developing their own modern knowledge in hopes of overcoming their Christian infiltrators. Some time after World War II, Malaysia went the way of most other British colonies, and gained independence. However, its strong Muslim roots remain to this day.

Kota Bharu, the state capital, is the heart of the region. The area is rich in Malay cultural heritage, as evidenced in the continuing interest in arts like *silat* (Malay martial arts), *wayang kulit* (puppetry), *gasing* (top spinning), and *wau* (kite flying). For the record, you won't find too much traditional music or dance, as women are forbidden from entertaining in public. Also beware that the state has strict laws controlling the sale of alcoholic beverages, which cannot be purchased in stores, hotels, or most restaurants. You will not find a single bar. Chinese restaurants, however, are permitted to sell beer to their patrons, but will probably not allow you to take any away.

ESSENTIALS
VISITOR INFORMATION
You'll find the **Kelantan Tourist Information Centre** at Jalan Sultan Ibrahim (© **09/748-5534**).

GETTING THERE
BY AIR From KL, **Malaysia Airlines** (© **1300/88-3000**) flies twice daily. You'll land at **Kota Bharu's Sultan Ismail Petra Airport** (© **09/773-7000**), about 20 minutes outside the city. A taxi to town shouldn't be any more than RM25 (US$6.60).

BY TRAIN The KTM runs a line through the center of the peninsula all the way to the Thai border. The Wakaf Bharu station is closest to the city, and taxis are available, or you can take local bus no. 19 or 27. For train information in KL call ((© **03/2730-2000**).

BY BUS Kota Bharu's bus terminal is at Jalan Padang Garong off Jalan Doktor. Buses bring you here from all corners of the peninsula. From KL call **Transnasional at Puduraya Bus Terminal** (© **03/230-3300**). They've got two dailies at a cost of RM22 (US$5.80). To find out about buses out of Kota Bharu call © 09/747-4330. The taxi stand is just across the street, and you may be hounded by all sorts of gypsy cabs, people with cars who are not proper taxi drivers but who will take you places to make some extra cash. They're basically honest Joes trying to make a buck.

BY TAXI The local taxi stand across from the bus terminal also acts as the outstation taxi stand. To reserve a car the number is © **09/748-1386.** Taxis from Kuala Terengganu run about RM80 (US$21).

GETTING AROUND

One thing I like about Kota Bharu is how most of the major museums are located in one central area, so walking to them is very easy. For the beach and cottage industry areas you'll need to hire a **taxi.** The main taxi stand is at Jalan Padang Garong; call ✆ **09/748-1386** for booking. Daily and half-day rates can be negotiated for about RM15 (US$3.95) per hour. Trips around town will be between RM5 and RM10 (US$1.30–US$2.65).

FAST FACTS

Banks are at Jalan Pitum Pong and Jalan Kebun Sultan. The main **post office** is at Jalan Sultan Ismail (✆ **09/748-4033**). Look for **Internet service** at **Perdana Cyber Café,** just inside Perdana Superbowl next to (naturally) the Hotel Perdana.

ACCOMMODATIONS

Diamond Puteri Hotel   This recent addition to the skyline still retains its original shine, it is second only to the Renaissance, however it enjoys a superior location to the international chain heavy hitter. Guest rooms are welcoming and bright, with modern conveniences geared toward the business traveler. The location by the Kelantan River isn't the fabulous view you'd hope for, which makes the outdoor pool area not as inviting. They also have a fitness center with a sauna.

Jalan Post Office Lama, 1500 Kota Bharu, Kelantan. ✆ 09/743-9988. Kuala Lumpur sales office 03/413-0448. Fax 09/743-8388. www.diamond-puteri-hotel.h-2696.travelmall.com. 311 units. RM220–RM255 (US$58–US$67) double; RM320 (US$84) suite. AE, DC, MC, V. **Amenities:** Restaurant; coffee shop; lounge; foreign currency exchange; pool; gymnasium; sauna; valet and pressing service. *In room:* A/C, TV, dataport, minibar, coffee/tea-making facilities, hair dryer, safe.

Perdana Resort   Mmmmmmm, I'll be honest with you. Hanging out at a resort in Kelantan just isn't fun. Go to any beach and you'll see locals swimming fully clothed. At this resort, the atmosphere is less conservative, but the thought of baring skin in a bikini somehow felt too trashy to bear. I've included it in this edition just so you know all the options, but I really prefer staying in town in Kota Bharu. At Perdana Resort the individual chalets make for great privacy, each with its own balcony outside and bathroom inside. They're also spacious, so if you want to put in an extra bed or two for an additional RM30 (US$8), you'll still have ample room to get around.

Jalan Kuala Pa'Amat, Pantai Cahaya Bulan, P.O. Box 121, 15710 Kota Bharu, Kelantan, Malaysia. ✆ 09/774-4000. Fax 09/774-4980. 117 units. RM170–RM210 (US$45–US$55) chalet. AE, DC, MC, V. **Amenities:** Restaurant; coffee shop; outdoor pool; mini-golf course; tennis court; horseback riding; watersports equipment (including canoes, water skiing, windsurfing); 24-hr. room service. *In room:* A/C, TV, minibar, coffee/tea-making facilities.

Renaissance Kota Bharu Hotel ★   Are you as surprised as I am to find a Renaissance in a hardship posting like Kota Bharu? While it's nice to experience exotic cultures, sometimes you just want creature comforts. Catering primarily to the oil industry execs who come for business trips, you'll find this hotel is the most efficient place in the whole state. Guest rooms do little to distinguish themselves from Renaissance rooms in other cities worldwide. You'd almost never know you were in deepest darkest Malaysia here—a plus and a minus. Another minus, if you're here for the sights, you're a bit farther from the action.

Kota Sri Mutiara, Jalan Sultan Yahya Petra, Kota Bharu 15150, Kelantan, Malaysia. ✆ 09/746-2233. Fax 09/746-1122. 335 units. RM195 (US$50) and up for a double. AE, DC, MC, V. **Amenities:** 2 restaurants (international, Chinese); lounge; outdoor pool; outdoor, lighted tennis courts; squash courts; fitness center with Jacuzzi and sauna; concierge; limousine service; business center; 24-hr. room service; babysitting; same-day laundry service/dry cleaning; executive-level rooms. *In room:* A/C, TV w/satellite programming and in-house movie, minibar, coffee/tea-making facilities, hair dryer, iron, safe.

DINING

Greens WESTERN/LOCAL   Done up in a simple cafe style, Greens has yet to grow into its surroundings in the new Diamond Puteri Hotel. Serving as the coffee shop for the hotel, it is open from early in the morning till late at night and features a wide range of dishes. Choose from familiar western favorites or try their specialty local Kelantanese selections (which are the best dishes), such as *ayam perchik* (chicken in a coconut and fish stock gravy), a favorite in these parts.

Diamond Puteri Hotel, Jalan Post Office Lama. ℂ 09/743-9988. Reservations not necessary. RM10–RM38 (US$2.65–US$10). AE, DC, MC, V. Daily 7am–midnight.

Lak Kau Hok Restoran CHINESE/SEAFOOD   Kota Bharu isn't all that boring a town at night. Head down to Chinatown's Jalan Kebun Sultan where the streets get lively. Walk past glowing restaurants, hawker stalls, and friends out for a chat and a stroll, and when you reach the little house that is Lak Kau Hok, head inside. The smells of garlic and chiles will seduce you from the moment you enter, and after specialties like steamed garlic prawns and steamed fish Teochew style (with vegetables and mushrooms sautéed in a rich gravy), you'll be very happy you came. Did I mention they serve beer?

2959 Jalan Kebun Sultan. ℂ 09/748-3762. Reservations not necessary. RM8–RM25 (US$2.10–US$6.60). No credit cards. Daily 11am–2:30pm and 6–10pm.

ATTRACTIONS

Padang ⭐   Centered around the Padang Merdeka are five of the most significant sights in Kota Bharu, run by the Kelantan State Museum Corporation. At the **Istana Jahar** (adults RM3/US80¢, children RM1.50/US40¢), Kelantan traditional costumes, antiques, and musical instruments are displayed in context of their usage in royal ceremonies. **Istana Batu** (adults RM2/US55¢, children RM1/US25¢) takes you through a photographic journey of Kelantan's royal family, and offers a peek at their lifestyle through the past 200 years. The **Balai Getam Guri handicraft museum** (adults RM1/US25¢, children RM.50/US15¢) showcases the finest in Kelantanese textiles, basketry, embroidery, batik printing, and silversmithing. You'll also be able to buy crafts in the shops within the compound. The **Islamic Museum** (Muzium Islam) (adults RM1/US25¢, children RM.50/US15¢) teaches everything you might want to know about Islam in this state, with a focus on Islamic arts and Kelantan's role in spreading Islam in the region. Finally there is the **War Museum (Bank Kerapu)** (adults RM2/US55¢, children RM1/US25¢), which tells the story of Kelantan during World War II in a 1912 bank building that survived the invasion.

Merdeka museums. At the end of Jalan Hilir Kota. ℂ 09/744-4666. Sat–Thurs 8:30am–4:45pm. Closed Fri.

State Museum (Muzium Negeri)   It's been a long time since this old building served as the colonial land office, but in 1990 major renovations gave it a new life. It now houses the Kelantan Art Gallery, including ceramics, traditional musical instruments, and cultural pastimes exhibits.

Jalan Hospital. ℂ 09/744-4666. Adults RM2 (US55¢), children RM1 (US25¢). Daily 8:30am–4:45pm. Closed Fri.

SHOPPING

For great local handicrafts shopping, visitors to Kelantan need go no further than **Jalan P.C.B.,** the road that leads to P.C.B. beach from Kota Bharu's

Chinatown area. Hire a taxi and stop at every roadside factory, showroom, shop, and crafts house (the place crawls with them!) and you'll satisfy every shopping itch that needs scratching. Some wonderful places to try are **Wisma Songket Kampung Penambang,** Jalan P.C.B. (© **09/744-7757**), for songket cloth and clothing, and to see the ladies weaving the fine cloth. The local kite man, **Haji Wan Hussen bin Haji Ibrahim,** makes and sells kites out of his home at 328-A Kampong Redong Tikat, Jalan P.C.B. (© **09/744-0462**), and will invite you in for a look. He'll pack them sturdily so you can airmail them home. Also, **Pantas Songet & Batik Manufacturer,** Kampung Penambang, Jalan P.C.B. (© **09/744-1616**), has a nice selection of batik clothing and sarongs, plus some pieces of songket cloth.

In town, if you'd like to buy some silver, good (and inexpensive) filigree jewelry collections and silver housewares are to be had at **Mohamed Salleh & Sons,** 1260B Jalan Sultanah Zainab (© **09/748-3401**), and **K. B. Permai,** 5406-C Jalan Sultanah Zainab (© **09/748-5661**). In the small but lively Chinatown area look for **A. Zahari Antik,** 3953-B Jalan Kebin Sultan (© **09/744-3548**), where you can shop for old treasures like keris (Malay daggers with wavy blades, of which this place has a great selection) as well as pottery, carvings, and brass. Finally, for a little local shopping experience, check out the giant **Pasar Besar wet market** on Jalan Parit Dalam. Behind the produce and fish stands are shops for cheap bargains.

11

East Malaysia: Borneo

Borneo for the past 2 centuries has been the epitome of adventure travel. While bustling ports like Penang, Malacca, and Singapore attracted early travelers with dollars in their eyes, Borneo attracted those with adventure in their hearts. Today, the island still draws visitors who seek new and unusual experiences, and few leave disappointed. Rivers meander through dense tropical rainforests, beaches stretch for miles, and caves snake out longer than any in the world. All sorts of creatures you'd never imagine live in the rainforest: deer the size of house cats, owls only 6 inches tall, the odd proboscis monkey, and the orangutan, whose only other natural home is Sumatra. It's also home to the largest flower in the world, the Rafflesia, spanning up to a meter wide. Small wonder this place has special interest for scientists and researchers the world around.

The people of Borneo can be credited for most of the alluring tales of early travels. The exotically adorned tribes of warring headhunters and pirates of yesteryear, some of whom still live lifestyles little changed (though both headhunting and piracy are now illegal), today share their mysterious cultures and colorful traditions openly with outsiders.

Add to all of this the fabulous tale of the White Raja of Sarawak, Sir James Brooke, whose family ruled the state for just over 100 years, and you have a land filled with allure, mystery, and romance unlike any other.

Malaysia, Brunei Darussalam, and Indonesia have divided the island of Borneo. Indonesia claims Kalimantan to the south and east, and the Malaysian states of **Sarawak** and **Sabah** lie to the north and northwest. The small sultanate of Brunei is nestled between the two Malaysian states on the western coastline.

1 Sarawak

Tropical rainforest accounts for more than 70% of Sarawak's total land mass, providing homes for not only exotic species of plants and animals, but for the different ethnic groups who are indigenous to the area. With more than 10 national parks and four wildlife preserves, Malaysia shows its commitment to conserving the delicate balance of life here, while allowing small gateways for travelers to appreciate Sarawak's natural wonders. A network of rivers connects the inland areas to the rest of the world, and a boat trip to visit tribal communities and trek into caves and jungles can prove to be the most memorable attraction going.

The indigenous peoples of Sarawak make up more than half the state's population. Early explorers and settlers referred to these people with the catch-all term Dyaks, which didn't account for the variations between the more than 25 different ethnicities. Of these groups, the Iban are the largest, with more than 30% of the population of the state. A nomadic people by tradition, the Ibans

were once located all over the region, existing on agriculture, hunting, and fishing. They were also notorious warriors who would behead enemies—a practice now outlawed but that has retained its cultural significance. The Ibans fought not only with other tribes, but within their own separate tribal units as well.

The next largest group, the Bidayuh, live peacefully in the hills. Their longhouse communities are the most accessible to travelers from Kuching. The Melanu are a coastal people who excel in fishing and boatbuilding. Finally, the Orang Ulu is an association of smaller tribes mostly in the northern parts of the state. Tribes like the Kayah, Kenyah, Kelabit, and Penan, while culturally separate entities, formed an umbrella organization to loosely govern all groups and provide representation. These groups are perhaps the least accessible to outsiders.

The indigenous people who still stay in the forest live in longhouse communities, some of which are open for visitors. Most travelers access these places with the help of local tour operators, who have trips that last from an overnight excursion to a weeklong adventure. While some tours take you to well-trampled villages for the standard "gawk at the funny costumes" trips, many operators can take you to more remote places to meet people in an environment of cultural learning with a sensitivity that is appreciated by all involved. A few adventuresome souls travel solo into these areas, but I recommend that you stick with an operator. I don't care much for visitors who pop in unexpectedly, and I can't imagine why people in one of these villages wouldn't feel the same way.

Every visitor to Sarawak starts out from **Kuching,** the capital city. With a population of some 400,000 people, it's small but oddly cosmopolitan. In addition to local tribes that gave up forest living, the city has large populations of Malays, Chinese, Indians, and Europeans, most of whom migrated in the last 2 centuries. The city sits at the mouth of the Kuching River, which will be your main artery for trips inland. Before you head off for the river, though, check out the many delights of this mysterious colonial kingdom.

Sarawak was introduced to the Western world by James Brooke, an English adventurer who in 1839 came to Southeast Asia to follow in the footsteps of his idol, Sir Stamford Raffles. Like Raffles's Singapore, there was a region waiting for Brooke to settle and start a bustling community. His wanderings brought him to Borneo, where he was introduced to the sultan of Brunei. The sultan was deeply troubled by warring tribes to the south of his kingdom, who were in constant revolt, sometimes to the point of pirating ships to Brunei's port. Brooke provided the solution, initiating a campaign to befriend some of the warring tribes, uniting them to conquer the others. Soon the tribes were calmed. The sultan, delighted by Brooke, ceded Kuching to him for a small annual fee. In 1841, James Brooke became raja and set about claiming the land that is now Sarawak.

Raja Sir James Brooke became a colonial legend. Known as "The White Raja of Sarawak," he and his family ruled the territory and its people with a firm but compassionate hand. Tribal leaders were appointed to leadership and administrative positions within his government and militia, and as a result, the Brookes were highly respected by the populations they led. However, Brooke was a bit of a renegade, turning his nose up at London's attempts to include Sarawak under the crown. He took no money from the British and closed the doors to British commercial interests in Sarawak. Instead, he dealt in local trade and trade with Singapore. Still, Kuching was understood to be a British holding, though the city never flourished as did other British ports in Southeast Asia.

After his death in 1868, Raja James Brooke was succeeded by his nephew, Charles Brooke. In 1917, Charles's son, Vyner Brooke, became the last ruling Raja, a position he held until World War II, when the territory was conquered by invading Japanese. After the war Raja Vyner Brooke returned briefly, but soon after, the territory was declared a crown colony. Eventually Malaya was granted independence by Britain, prompting Prime Minister Tunku Abdul Rahman to form Malaysia in 1963, uniting peninsular Malaya with Singapore, Sarawak, and Sabah. Singapore departed from the union 2 years later, but Sarawak and Sabah happily remained.

KUCHING

The perfect introduction to Sarawak begins in its capital. Kuching's museums, cultural exhibits, and historical attractions will help you form an overview of the history, people, and natural wonders of the state. In Kuching your introduction to Sarawak will be comfortable and fun; culture by day and good food and fun by night. Kuching, meaning "cat" in Malay, also has a wonderful sense of humor, featuring monuments and exhibits to its feline mascot on almost every corner.

ESSENTIALS

VISITOR INFORMATION The Sarawak Tourism Board's Visitor Information Centre has literature and staff that can answer any question about activities in the state and city. This is actually the best place to start planning any trips

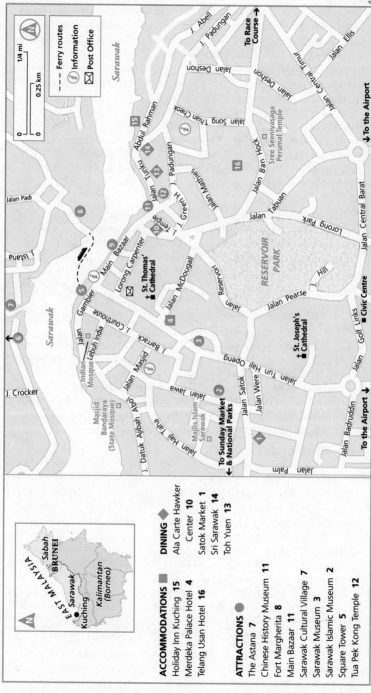

Kuching

N

1/4 mi
0.25 km
0

--- Ferry routes
i Information
☒ Post Office

Sarawak
Sarawak
Sarawak

J. Abell
J. Padungan
To Race Course →
Jalan Ellis
Jalan Deshon
Jalan Deshon
Jalan Central Timur
↓ To the Airport
Jalan Song Thian Check
Abdul Rahman
Tunku
Jalan
Jalan Matmies
Padungan
Jalan Ban Hock
Sree Seenivasaga Perumal Temple
16
Jalan Tabuan
J. Green
J. Temple
Jalan Padi
Jalan Padi
J. Istana
J. Crocker
Jalan Gambier
Main Bazaar
Lorong Carpenter
St. Thomas' Cathedral
Jalan McDougall
Jalan Reservoir
RESERVOIR PARK
Lorong Park
J. Hill
J. Courthouse
Jalan
Indian Mosque Lebuh India
J. Barrack
Jalan Masjid
Jalan Werе
Jalan Satok
Jalan Tun Haji Openg
Jalan Pearse
St. Joseph's Cathedral
Jalan Golf Links
■ Civic Centre
Jalan Central Barat
To the Airport →
Jalan Badruddin
Jalan Palm
Jalan Hali Taha
Majlis Islam Sarawak
Jalan Jawa
Masjid Bandaraya (State Mosque)
J. Datuk Ajibah Abol
To Sunday Market & National Parks ←

5 15 14 13 12 11 10 9 8 7 6 5 4 3 2 1 16

N
EAST MALAYSIA
Sabah
BRUNEI
Sarawak
● Kuching
Kalimantan (Borneo)

to Sarawak's wonderful national parks, as the main office for the parks board operates from here. Really, they're just incredibly informed and are so welcoming, so feel free to take advantage. You'll find them at the Padang Merdeka next to the Sarawak Museum (© 082/423-600).

GETTING THERE Almost all travelers to Sarawak enter via Kuching International Airport, just outside the city. **Malaysia Airlines** (© 1300/88-3000) flies here about 10 times daily from KL. In addition, there are nonstop flights from the Malaysian cities of Johor Bahru and Kota Kinabalu. Malaysia Airlines also connects Kuching with direct flights from Singapore, Bandar Seri Bagawan in Brunei, Hong Kong, and Manila. The number for Malaysia Airlines in Kuching is © 082/246-622. For airport information call © 082/454-255.

Taxis from the airport use coupons that you purchase outside the arrival hall. Priced according to zones, most trips to the central parts of town will be RM16 (US$4.20).

GETTING AROUND Centered around a padang, or large ceremonial field, Kuching resembles many other Malaysian cities. Buildings of beautiful Colonial style rise on the edges of the field; many of these today house Sarawak's museums. The main sights, as well as the Chinatown area and the riverfront, are easily accessible on foot. Taxis are also available, and do not use meters; most rides around town are quoted at RM6 (US$1.60). Taxis can be waved down from the side of the road, or if you're in the Chinatown area, the main taxi stand is near Gambier Road near the end of the India Street Pedestrian Mall. For a taxi call © 082/348-898.

FAST FACTS The **American Express** office is located at Cph Travel Agencies, 70 Padungan Rd. (© 082/242-289). Major **banks** have branches on Tunku Abdul Rahman Road near Holiday Inn Kuching, or in the downtown area around Khoo Hun Yeang Road. The central **post office** is on Jalan Tun Abang Haji Openg (© 082/245-952). For a good **Internet cafe** try **Cyber City,** No. 46 Ground Floor Block D (© 082/428-318), just behind Riverside Complex Shopping Mall, charging RM6 (US$1.60) per hour.

ACCOMMODATIONS

Holiday Inn Kuching Holiday Inn offers Western-style accommodations at a moderate price, and you'll appreciate its location in an excellent part of town. It sits along the bank of the Kuching River, so to get to the main riverside area you need only stroll 10 minutes past some of the city's unique historical and cultural sights, shopping, and good places to dine. Catering to a diverse group of leisure travelers and businesspeople, the hotel has spacious, modern, and comfortable rooms; and while there are few bells and whistles, you won't want for convenience. The outdoor swimming pool and excellent fitness center facility will help you unwind, and the small shopping arcade has one of the best collections of books on Sarawak that can be found in the city.

P.O. Box 2362, Jalan Tunku Abdul Rahman, 93100 Kuching, Sarawak, Malaysia. © 082/423-111. Fax 082/426-169. www.holidayinn-sarawak.com. 305 units. RM310–RM350 double (US$82–US$92); RM510 (US$134) and up suite. AE, DC, MC V. **Amenities:** 3 restaurants (international, Indian, Chinese); bar; outdoor pool; fitness center with sauna; concierge; tour desk; limousine service; business center; 24-hr. room service; babysitting; same-day laundry service/dry cleaning; nonsmoking rooms; executive-level rooms. *In room:* A/C, TV w/satellite programming and in-house movie, minibar, coffee/tea-making facilities, hair dryer.

Merdeka Palace Hotel ⭑ Towering over the Padang Merdeka in the center of town is the Merdeka Palace, practically a landmark in its own right (as soon as you see the easily distinguishable tower, you'll always know where you are).

This is one of the most fashionable addresses in the city, for guests as well as banquets and functions. From the large marble lobby to the mezzanine shopping arcade stuffed with designer tenants, its reputation for elegance is justified. Large rooms come dressed in European-inspired furnishings and fabrics. Try to get a view of the padang, as the less expensive rooms face the parking lot. The rooftop outdoor swimming pool is small, but the fully equipped fitness center has sauna and steam rooms, plus massage. The pub here is perhaps the most happening one in town

Jalan Tun Abang Haji Openg, 93000 Kuching, Sarawak, Malaysia. © 082/258-000. Fax 082/425-400. www.merdekapalace.com. 214 units. RM255–RM440 (US$67–US$116) double. AE, DC, MC, V. **Amenities:** 2 restaurants (international, Italian); bar; outdoor pool; fitness center with Jacuzzi, sauna, steam, massage; concierge; limousine service; business center; shopping arcade; salon; 24-hr. room service; babysitting; same-day laundry service/dry cleaning; nonsmoking rooms; executive-level rooms. *In room:* A/C, TV w/satellite programming, minibar, coffee/tea-making facilities, safe.

Telang Usan Hotel ★★ (Value)   While in Kuching I like to stay at the Telang Usan Hotel. It's not as flashy as the higher priced places, but it's a fantastic bargain for a good room. Most guests here are leisure travelers, and in fact, many are repeat visitors. The small public areas sport murals in local Iban style, revealing the origin of the hotel's owner and operator. While rooms are small and decor is not completely up-to-date, they're spotless. Some rooms have only standing showers, so be sure to specify when making your reservation if a bathtub is important to you. The coffee shop serves local and Western food from 7am to midnight, and the higher category rooms have minibars. There is an excellent tour agency under the same ownership at the hotel.

Ban Hock Rd., P.O. Box 1579, 93732 Kuching, Sarawak, Malaysia. © 082/415-588. Fax 082/245-316. www. telangusan.com. 66 units. RM140–RM200 (US$37–US$53) double. AE, DC, MC, V. **Amenities:** Restaurant (international); Internet service; limited room service; same-day laundry service. *In room:* A/C, TV.

DINING

In addition to the two conventional restaurants listed below, Kuching's **hawker center** food stalls offer a culinary adventure at affordable prices. A good centrally located center is at **Ala Carte** on Lebuh Temple. It's indoors and air-conditioned. Also try the food stalls at **Satok Market** out at Jalan Satok for excellent Malay, Chinese, and Sarawakian cuisine.

Sri Sarawak MALAY   Sri Sarawak is the only place to find Malay food in a fine-dining establishment. The restaurant occupies the 18th floor of the Crowne Plaza hotel, with views all around to the city below. The friendly and helpful staff is more than happy to help you navigate the menu, which includes Sarawak specialties such as umai, raw fish that's "cooked" in lime juice with onion, ginger, and chile. I'm addicted and want everyone to try it!

Crowne Plaza Riverside Kuching, Jalan Tunku Abdul Rahman. © 082/247-777. Reservations not necessary. Entrees RM8– RM22 (US$2.10–US$5.80). AE, DC, MC, V. Daily noon–2:30pm, 6–10:30pm.

Toh Yuen CHINESE   One of the premier Chinese restaurants in Kuching, Toh Yueh serves excellently prepared dishes that are as pleasing to the eye as they are to the palate. Chef's specialties like butter prawns melt in your mouth, as do any of the many bean curd selections and crunchy vegetable dishes. Beware, portions are huge! Call ahead for special promotions for weekend lunch and dinner, which can be surprisingly low priced.

Kuching Hilton, Jalan Tunku Abdul Rahman. © 082/248-200. Reservations recommended on weekends. RM14–RM48 (US$3.70–US$13). AE, DC, MC, V. Daily 11:30am–2:30pm, 6:30–10:30pm.

ATTRACTIONS

The Astana and Fort Margherita   At the waterfront by the Square Tower you'll find water taxis to take you across the river to see these two reminders of the White Rajas of Sarawak. The Astana, built in 1870 by Raja Charles Brooke, the second raja of Sarawak, is now the official residence of the governor. It is not open to the public, but visitors may still walk in the gardens. The best view of the Astana, however is from the water.

Raja Charles Brooke's wife, Ranee Margaret, gave her name to Fort Margherita, which was erected in 1870 to protect the city of Kuching. Inside the great castlelike building is a police museum, the most interesting sights of which are the depictions of criminal punishment.

Across the Sarawak River from town. Museum: no phone. Fort: © **082/244-232**. Free admission. Tues–Sun 9am–5pm.

Chinese History Museum   Built in 1912, this old Chinese Chamber of Commerce Building is the perfect venue for a museum that traces the history of Chinese communities in Sarawak. Though small, it's centrally located and a convenient stop while you're in the area.

Corner of Main Bazaar and Jalan Tunku Abdul Rahman. No phone. Free admission. Daily 9am–5pm.

Main Bazaar   Main Bazaar, the major thoroughfare along the river, is home to Kuching's antiques and handicraft shops. If you're walking along the river, a little time in these shops is like a walk through a traditional handicrafts art gallery. You'll also find souvenir shops and some nice T-shirt silk screeners.

Along the river.

Sarawak Cultural Village ✧   What appears to be a contrived theme park turns out to be a really fun place to learn about Sarawak's indigenous people. Built around a lagoon, the park re-creates the various styles of longhouse dwellings of each of the major tribes. Inside each house are representative members of each tribe displaying cultural artifacts and performing music, teaching dart blowing, and showing off carving talents. Give yourself plenty of time to stick around and talk with the people, who are recruited from villages inland and love to tell stories about their homes and traditions. Performers dance and display costumes at 11:30am and 4:30pm daily. A shuttle bus leaves at regular intervals from the Holiday Inn Kuching on Jalan Abell.

Kampung Budaya Sarawak, Pantai Damai, Santubong. © **082/846-411**. Adults RM45 (US$12), children RM23 (US$5.90). Daily 9am–5pm.

Sarawak Islamic Museum   A splendid array of Muslim artifacts at this quiet and serene museum depicts the history of Islam and its spread to Southeast Asia. Local customs and history are also highlighted. While women are not required to cover their heads, respectable attire that covers the legs and arms is requested.

Jalan P. Ramlee. © **082/244-232**. Free admission. Sat–Thurs 9am–5pm; Fri 9am–12:45pm, 3–5pm.

Sarawak Museum ✧   Two branches, one old and one new, display exhibits of the natural history, indigenous peoples, and culture of Sarawak, plus the state's colonial and modern history. The two branches are connected by an overhead walkway above Jalan Tun Haji Openg. The wildlife exhibit is a bit musty, but the arts and artifacts in the other sections are well tended. A tiny aquarium sits neglected behind the old branch, but the gardens here are lovely.

Jalan Tun Haji Openg. © **082/244-232**. Free admission. Sat–Thurs 9am–5pm; Fri 9am–12:45pm, 3–5pm.

Square Tower   The tower, built in 1879, served as a prison camp, but today the waterfront real estate is better served by a tourist information center. The Square tower is also a prime starting place for a stroll along the riverside, and is where you'll also find out about cultural performances and exhibitions held at the waterfront, or call the number above for performance schedules. Jalan Gambier near the riverfront. © 082/426-093.

Tua Pek Kong Temple   At a main crossroads near the river stands the oldest Chinese temple in Sarawak. While officially it is dated at 1876, most locals acknowledge the true date of its beginnings as 1843. It's still lively in form and spirit, with colorful dragons tumbling along the walls and incense filling the air. Junction of Jalan Tunku Abdul Rahman and Jalan Padungan. No phone.

TOURING LOCAL CULTURE ★★★

When you come to Sarawak, everyone will tell you that you must take a trip to witness **life in a longhouse.** It is perhaps one of the most unique experiences you'll have, and is a lot easier to arrange than it sounds. Many good tour operators in Kuching take visitors out to longhouse communities, where guests are invited to stay for one or more nights. You'll eat local food, experience daily culture, and view traditional pastimes and ceremonies. On longer tours you may stop at more than one village to get a cross-cultural comparison of two or more different tribes. Good tour operators to speak to about arranging a trip are **Borneo Adventure,** 55 Main Bazaar (© **082/245-175;** fax 082/422-626), and **Telang Usan Travel & Tours,** Ban Hock Rd. (© **082/236-945;** fax 082/236-589). These agencies can also arrange trips into Sarawak's national parks.

TOURING SARAWAK'S NATIONAL PARKS

Before planning any trip into the national parks, travelers must contact the **National Parks Booking Office** at the Visitors Information Centre next to the Sarawak Museum (© **082/248-088;** fax 082/256-301). You will need to acquire permission to enter any park, and be advised on park safety and regulations. I recommend you visit the office itself. Situated inside the Tourism Board office, the staff here knows about every trip activity and can advise on accommodations options and all forms of transportation to and from the parks, and can even book your trip for you. They'll also screen tourism videos of the parks for you in their conference room, to help you decide which parks are best for your interests.

Bako National Park ★★★, established in 1957, is Sarawak's oldest national park. An area of 2,728 hectares (6,820 acres) combines mangrove forest, lowland jungle, and high plains covered in scrub. Throughout the park you'll see the pitcher plant and other strange carnivorous plants, plus long-tailed macaques, monitor lizards, bearded pigs, and the unique proboscis monkey. Because the park is only 37km (22 miles) from Kuching, trips here are extremely convenient.

A new project, the **Matang Wildlife Centre,** about an hour outside of Kuching, gives endangered wildlife a home, provides researchers with insights into wildlife conservation, and educates visitors about the animals and their habitat. For day trips, no parks department permission is required.

Gunung Gading National Park, about a 2-hour drive west of Kuching, sprawls 4,106 hectares (10,265 acres) over rugged mountains to beautiful beach spots along the coast. Day-trippers and overnighters come to get a glimpse of the Rafflesia, the largest flower in the world. The flowers are short-lived and temperamental, but the national parks office will let you know if there are any in bloom.

Gunung Mulu National Park provides an amazing adventure with its astounding underground network of caves. The park claims the world's largest cave passage (Deer Cave), the world's largest natural chamber (Sarawak Chamber), and Southeast Asia's longest cave (Clearwater Cave). No fewer than 18 caves offer explorers trips of varying degrees of difficulty, from simple treks with minimal gear to technically difficult caves that require specialized equipment and skills. Aboveground is 544 sq. km (326 sq. miles) of primary rainforest, peat swamps, and mountainous forests teeming with mammals, birds, and unusual insects. Located in the north of Sarawak, Mulu is very close to the Brunei border.

Niah National Park, while interesting to nature buffs, is more fascinating for those interested in archaeology. From 1954 to 1967 explorers excavated a prehistoric site inside Niah's extensive cave network. The site dates as far back as 40,000 years, and is believed to have been continuously occupied until some 2,000 years ago. The **Niah Great Cave,** which contains the site, revealed sharp stone implements, pottery vessels, and animal and botanical remains. Near the mouth of the cave is a burial ground dating from Paleolithic times. The Painted Cave, also within Niah's cave network, is a magnificent gallery of mystical cave paintings and coffins that were buried here between A.D. 1 and A.D. 780. While a visit to the park requires parks department permission, further information on the excavation sites can be obtained from the **Sarawak Museum (© 082/244-232;** fax 082/246-680).

2 Sabah

Of all the outdoor destinations in Southeast Asia, Sabah by far proves the most exciting. Covering 73,711 sq. km (48,480 sq. miles) in the northern part of Borneo, the world's third largest island, Sabah stretches from the South China Sea in the west to the Sulu Sea in the east, both seas containing an abundance of uninhabited islands and pristine coral reefs and marine life. In between, more than half of the state is covered in primary rainforest that's protected in national parks and forest and wildlife reserves. In these forests, some **rare species of mammals** like the Sumatran rhino and Asian elephant (herds of them) are hard to spot, but other animals, such as the orangutan, proboscis monkey, gibbon, lemur, civet, Malaysian sun bear, and a host of others can be seen on jungle treks if you search them out. Of the **hundreds of bird species** here, the hornbills and herons steal the show.

Sabah's tallest peak also happens to be the highest mountain between the Himalayas and Irian Jaya. At 4,095m (13,432 ft.), it's the tallest in Southeast Asia, and a thrill to trek or climb. Sabah's rivers are also open for **river rafters,** providing white-water thrills for every level of excitement, from soft adventure to extreme sports.

Not only does this state hold mysterious wildlife and geography, but people as well. Many visitors are attracted to Sabah by the region's **32 different ethnic groups,** whose cultures and traditions are so different from the Western norm. Divided into four major linguistic families—Kadazandusun, Murutic, Tidong, and Paitanic—certain of these groups were the headhunters that filled past travelers' tales with much intrigue.

The largest group, the Kadazandusun, live on the west coast and in the interior. They are one of the first groups you'll come into contact with, especially if you're in town during their Pesta Kaamatan, or harvest festival, held during May, where the high priest or priestess presides over a ceremony designed to appease the rice spirit. Although it's a Kadazandusun tradition, it is celebrated by all cultures in the state. While this group is the main agricultural producer of the state, these days most members hold everyday jobs and live in cities. The exception to this trend is the Runggus, the last group of Kadazandusun to live in a traditional longhouse community, where they're famous for exquisite basket weaving, fabric weaving, and beadwork.

The Bajau migrated from the Philippines. On the eastern coast of Sabah, these people live their lives as sea gypsies, coming to shore only for burials. On the west coast, they live on land as farmers and cattle raisers. Known as the cowboys of the east, their men are very skilled equestrians, and are usually pictured on horseback. During festivals, their brilliant costumes and decorated ponies almost always take center stage.

The third most prominent tribal group, the Murut, shares the southwest corner of Sabah with the Bajau. Skilled hunters, they use spears, blowpipes, poisoned darts, and trained dogs to hunt their prey. In past days, these skills were used for headhunting, which thankfully is not practiced today (although many skulls can still be seen during visits to their longhouse settlements). One nonlethal Murat tradition involves a trampoline competition. The *lansaran* (the trampoline itself), situated in the community longhouse, is made of split bamboo. During Murut ceremonies, contestants drink rice wine and jump on the trampoline to see who can reach the farthest. A prize is hung above for the winner to grab.

KOTA KINABALU

The best place to begin exploring Sabah's marine wonders, wildlife and forests, adventure opportunities, and indigenous peoples is from its capital, Kota Kinabalu. A speck of a city on the west coast, it's where you'll find the headquarters for all of Sabah's adventure tour operators and package excursion planners. I recommend you spend at least a day here to explore all your options, then set out to the wilds for the adventure of a lifetime.

ESSENTIALS

VISITOR INFORMATION The best information here can be gotten at the **Sabah Tourism Promotion Corporation,** operated by the state government, at 51 Jalan Gaya (*C* **088/212-121**). While the national MTB has a small office on Jalan Gaya a block down from the Sabah Tourism office, almost all of their information promotes travel in other parts of the country. Still, if you're interested, stop by Ground Floor Bangunan EON, CMG Life, No 1 Jalan Sagunting (*C* **088/242-064**).

GETTING THERE Because of Sabah's remote location, just about everybody will arrive by air via the **Kota Kinabalu International Airport** in the capital city (*C* **088/238-555**), about a 20-minute drive south of the central part of the city. Malaysia Airlines makes the flight from KL at least five times daily. For reservations information in KL, call the airlines at *C* **1300/88-3000,** or in Kota Kinabalu visit their office at 10th floor, Block C, Kompleks Karamunsing (*C* **088/213-555**).

The most efficient way to get into town from the airport is via taxi. The cars line up outside the arrival hall and are supposed to use a coupon system—look for the coupon sales and taxi-booking counter close by. You'll pay about RM12 (US$3.10) for a trip to town. On my last trip, I noticed the drivers trying to wave me over to negotiate a ride without the ticket counter middleman. I didn't go chat them up, but I'm pretty sure they would have quoted me a higher rate if I had.

GETTING AROUND   In the downtown area, you can get around quite easily on foot between hotels, restaurants, tour operators, markets, and the tourism office. For longer trips, a taxi will be necessary. They're easy enough to find cruising the town, or you can go to one of the regular stands around town—the most centrally located one at Jalan Datuk Saleh Sulong between Jalan Haji Saman and Jalan Pantai. I suggest you talk to your hotel concierge before you head out to ask how much you should expect to pay for your particular destination.

FAST FACTS   You'll find your **banks** conveniently located in the downtown area around Jalan Limabelas and along Jalan Gaya and Jalan Pantai. The **post office** (✆ **088/210-855**) is on Jalan Tun Razak. Look for Internet at K. K. **Internet** on Jalan Haji Saman across from Wisma Merdeka (✆ **088/235-219**).

ACCOMMODATIONS

Hyatt Regency Kota Kinabalu ✦   The only international business-class hotel in town, in some ways the Hyatt seems a little out of place in cozy Kota Kinabalu. Still, it's located close to the waterfront, near all major shopping and travel operators, and has a fantastic assortment of restaurants to choose from. Even if you're staying elsewhere in town, you may appreciate one of their dining options. As modern as you would expect the Hyatt chain to be, rooms here are large, and are presented in up-to-date furnishing styles that are not so Western that they take all the charm away from the room. Local tour and car-rental booking in the lobby make the place convenient for leisure travelers. One of the high points is Shenanigan's, the best bar in Kota Kinabalu, with live entertainment. It gets packed, mostly with locals and expatriates out for a sip.

Jalan Datuk Salleh Sulong, 88994 Kota Kinabalu, Sabah. ✆ **800/233-1234** in the U.S. and Canada, 131234 in Australia, 800/441-234 in New Zealand, or 088/221-234. Fax 088/225-972. http://kinabalu.hyatt.com. 288 units. RM403–RM448 (US$105–$117) double; RM863–RM3,450 (US$224–US$897) suite. AE, DC, MC, V. **Amenities:** 3 restaurants (international, Chinese, Japanese); bar; outdoor pool; fitness center; concierge; tour desk; car-rental desk; limousine service; business center; 24-hr. room service; babysitting; same-day laundry service/dry cleaning; nonsmoking rooms; executive-level rooms. *In room:* A/C, TV w/satellite programming and in-house movie, minibar, coffee/tea-making facilities, hair dryer, safe.

The Jesselton Hotel ✦✦   Listen to me rave about The Jesselton. It's such a nice surprise to find this quaint boutique hotel in the center of Kota Kinabalu, just about the last real reminder in this city of a colonial presence. Even more lovely is the level of personalized service you receive, and the comfort of the rooms, which, though completely modern, retain their charm with lovely Audubon-style inks and attractive wallpapers and fabrics—sort of a cross between a cozy guesthouse and a top-class hotel. Due to lack of space in the building, there's no pool, fitness center, or business center, but the staff at the front desk can help you with tour information and transportation. The coffee house serves local and Western food, which is quite good. The Gardenia Restaurant looks more upmarket than it really is.

69 Jalan Gaya, 88000 Kota Kinabalu, Sabah. ✆ **088/223-333**. Fax 088/240-401. www.asia-hotels.com/ hotelinfo/Jesselton_Hotel_The. 32 units. RM390 (US$103) double; RM910 (US$240) suite. AE, DC, MC, V. **Amenities:** Restaurant; bar & lounge; coffee shop; tour desk; foreign currency exchange; limousine service; 24-hr. room service; babysitting; same-day laundry service; complimentary clothes pressing and shoe polishing; nonsmoking rooms. *In room:* A/C, TV (movies available), minibar, coffee/tea-making facilities, hair dryer, safe.

Shangri-La's Tanjung Aru Resort ✦✦✦   A short ride southwest of Kota Kinabalu and you're at Tanjung Aru, an amazingly gorgeous beach resort area— Sabah's Riviera. The Shangri-La here is located in a most impressive tropical ocean-side setting, it serves the finest local Sabahian cuisine and freshest seafood

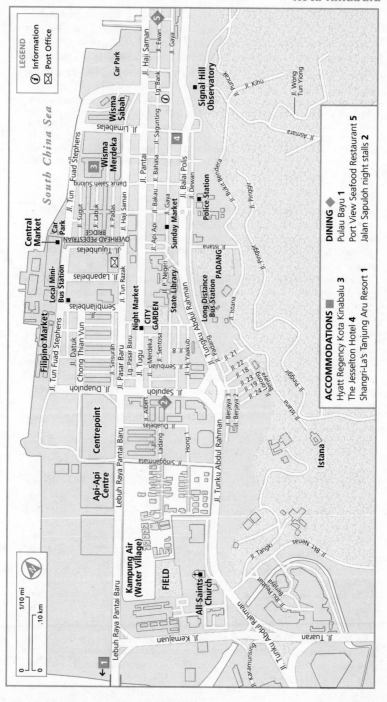

Kota Kinabalu

LEGEND

ⓘ Information

☒ Post Office

South China Sea

Central Market

Car Park

Wisma Sabah

Wisma Merdeka

Filipino Market

Local Mini-Bus Station

OVERHEAD PEDESTRIAN BRIDGE

Jl. Tuinbelas

Jl. Lapanbelas

Sembilanbelas

Night Market

CITY GARDEN

State Library

Signal Hill Observatory

Police Station

Sunday Market

PADANG

Long Distance Bus Station

Centrepoint

Api-Api Centre

Kampung Air (Water Village)

FIELD

All-Saints Church

Istana

Jl. Haji Saman

Jl. Ewan

Jl. Gaya

Jl. Bank

Lg. Bank

Jl. Saguting

Jl. Bahasa

Jl. Bakau

Jl. Api-Api

Jl. Gaya

Jl. Dewan

Jl. Balai Polis

Jl. Pantai

Jl. Limabelas

Fuad Stephens

Datuk Saleh Suong

Jl. Tun

Jl. Sugut

Jl. Labuk

Jl. Padas

Jl. Haji Saman

Jl. Tun Razak

Jl. Datuk Chong Thian Vun

Jl. Sinsurah

Jl. Pasar Baru

Lg. Pasar Baru

Jl. Merdeka

Jl. Sembulan

Jl. Sentosa

Jl. Hj Yaakub

Jl. P. Negeri

Jl. Tunku Abdul Rahman

Jl. Istana

Jl. Istana

Jl. Istana

Jl. Duapuloh

Jl. Tun Fuad Stephens

Lebuh Raya Pantai Baru

Jl. Ladang

Hong 1

Jl. Singgahmata

Jl. Albert

Jl. Duabelas

Jl. Sapuloh

Jl. Beriaja 3

Jl. Beriaja 2

Jl. 21

Jl. 22

Jl. 18

Jl. 23

Jl. 19

Jl. 24

Jl. Beriaja 1

Jl. Tuaran

Jl. Tunku Abdul Rahman

Jl. Kemajuan

Jl. Bt. Nenas

Jl. Tangki

Jl. Katamunsing

Jl. Ibu Pejabat

Jl. Beriaya

Jl. Pinggir

Jl. Istana

Jl. Pinggir

Jl. Bukit Bendera

Jl. Asmara

Jl. Kihu

Jl. Wong Tun Yiong

Jl. Puncak

0   1/10 mi

0   .10 km

ACCOMMODATIONS ■
Hyatt Regency Kota Kinabalu **3**
The Jesselton Hotel **4**
Shangri-La's Tanjung Aru Resort **1**

DINING ◆
Pulau Bayu **1**
Port View Seafood Restaurant **5**
Jalan Sapuloh night stalls **2**

you can get in the region. Book a room in the Tanjung Wing as the Kinabalu Wing, while newer, is more like a hotel block. Every room has a stunning view of either the sea or Mount Kinabalu, with a balcony for full appreciation. Tropical touches include rattan furnishings in cool colors and local fabrics with wood details. Their tour desk can arrange everything from scuba to trekking and rafting, and their free shuttle gives you convenient access to town.

Locked Bag 174, 88744 Kota Kinabalu, Sabah. © **088/225-800.** Fax 088/217-155. www.shangri-la.com. 499 units. RM505–RM570 (US$131–$148) double; RM740 (US$192) suite. **Amenities:** 3 restaurants (international and local, Cantonese, Italian); beach bar and lounge lounge; 2 outdoor lagoon-style pools; 4 outdoor, lighted tennis courts; fitness center with Jacuzzi, sauna, steam, massage; tour desk; shuttle service; salon; 24-hr. room service; babysitting; same-day laundry service/dry cleaning; nonsmoking rooms. *In room:* A/C, TV w/satellite programming and in-house movie, minibar, coffee/tea-making facilities, dataport with direct Internet access, hair dryer, safe.

DINING
Pulau Bayu at Shangri-La's Tanjung Aru Resort (© **088/225-800**) serves all varieties of the freshest fish, lobsters, prawns, squid, crabs, scallops, and clams can be ordered in a great many styles, especially prepared from local recipes or barbecue. My mouth waters just thinking about the hinava (raw fish marinated in lime juice, ginger, shallots, herbs, and chile).

If you're in town, you can also get fresh seafood (selected from tanks on the back wall) at **Port View Seafood Restaurant,** Jalan Haji Saman across from the old Custom's Wharf (© **088/221-753**). Prepared primarily in Chinese and Malay styles, dishes are moderately priced and always succulent.

For a more local experience, food stalls provide the most authentic local cuisine at the best prices. Check out the night stalls on Jalan Sapuloh. Walk through and peek at all the offerings before ordering, and check for the most popular stalls and dishes. (When approaching a new hawker center, I always stroll around checking out what everybody else is eating. Locals always seem to know what's best.)

ATTRACTIONS
Basically, here in Sabah there's enough to keep you busy for about 6 months solid. Every time I leave, I have a list of about 50 million things I'm dying to do when I return.

We'll start with **scuba diving.** Off the eastern coast of Sabah lies the tiny island of **Sipadan** ★★★. If you're a real scuba fanatic, then you already know about it. It is, after all, one of the top-five dive sites in the world. This giant coral "garden" just can't be beat by any other site in Southeast Asia. Many outfits in Kota Kinabalu organize short-term and long-term stays out at the dive site, but **Borneo Action** ★★★, G19 Ground Floor, Wisma Sabah (© and fax **088/246-701;** www.borneoaction.com), in my opinion, is the most exciting and professionally run. They'll take you out for trips either on a live-aboard boat or with night stays at one of the resorts on Sipadan island, and will arrange all transportation and dives. Their special 7-day/6-night live-aboard trip includes not only Sipadan sites but trips all around the region to places other divers don't go. One note about reservations: You're better off booking a Sipadan trip through this local agency rather than through an agent at home. Regulations allow only 150 guests on the island each night, and overseas agents constantly overbook. The local firms make sure there's space available before booking.

For shorter trips, **Layang Layang,** while not as incredible as Sipadan, also has some great diving. Borneo Action can take you on this trip as well. Contact them at the address above.

For **snorkeling** and **beach activities,** pick up a boat at the Sabah Parks Jetty just behind the Hyatt to take you out to nearby **Tunku Abdul Rahman Park.** Only 8km (12¾ miles) from Kota Kinabalu, you can head out for RM10 (US$2.60) round-trip, and spend the day on one of the park's five islands, snorkeling and swimming (you can rent snorkel gear once you're there). Accommodations are available on Pulau Manukan and Pulau Mumutik, and can be booked in advance through any of the tour operators in Sabah.

Meanwhile, back on dry land, Sabah's spectacular geography draws trekkers, hikers, climbers, rafters, and all sorts of others seeking **adventure travel.** There are a great number of firms that coordinate these trips, but the very creative folks at **Borneo Action Adventure Center,** Lot 3-0-9, Api Api Centre, Lorog Api Api (© **088/267-190;** fax 088/267-194; info@borneoaction.com), put together the most challenging and fascinating trips, designed for all levels of outdoor achievers, with the area's most acclaimed local guides. You can head out to the Crocker Range, Sabah's mountainous range southeast of Kota Kinabalu for either 2 days and 1 night or 5 days and 4 nights of trekking in primary rainforest to kampung villages inhabited by indigenous tribes, either camping in the jungle or staying in the villages. Their 6-day/5-night Jungle Experience includes not only trekking and camping, but educational sessions on the jungle's medicinal plants, fruits, and vegetables, plus wildlife observation and visits to local tribal villages. If that's not enough for you, try their Eco-Challenge: 9 days and 8 nights where you'll learn jungle navigation and survival skills, including the construction of bamboo rafts (that you'll be using to get yourself home!). It's a tough and exciting challenge.

Borneo Action Adventure Center also puts together great **mountain-biking** trips. The Kinabalu and Borneo 6-day/5-night trip takes you to the deepest interior village in Sabah and to many sights along the way. If you're up to it, their Hardcore Mountain Bike Adventure will really kick your butt with 14 days of biking all over the territory, interspersed with a climb up Mount Kinabalu and white-water rafting on the Padas River.

If you prefer a **softer adventure,** talk to the people at **Discovery Tours,** Lot G 22, 433-435 Wisma Sabah (© **088/221-244;** fax 088/221-600), with another office at Shangri-La's Tanjung Aru Resort (© **088/216-26**). They take groups on either 2-day/1-night or 3-day/2-night trips to **hike Mt. Kinabalu** (RM380/US$99 and RM540/US$140 per person, respectively). They also plan regular trips out to Sandakan, on the eastern coast of Sabah, for 2-day/1-night trips to see the **Sepilok Orang Utan Rehabilitation Center,** the largest orangutan sanctuary in the world, and take a boat trip to see probiscus monkeys and swallows nest caves (RM556/US$145 per person). Or, for about the same price, you can see the orangutan center with a stop at the **Marine Turtle Conservation Park and Hatchery.**

River rafting is also a popular sport here, especially along the Kiulu River, which is an exciting trip for all levels of experience and fitness. A day trip can

---

(Tips **Customized Adventure**

Borneo Action, with both scuba dive and land-adventure divisions, can arrange any activity at any level of extremism you'd like in Sabah, customized to the activities you wish to take advantage of. For further details, see their website at **www.borneoaction.com,** or call © **088/246-701.**

be arranged through Discovery Tours and costs only RM150 (US$39) per person. Keep in mind, the best time for rafting in Sabah is between March and September.

Finally, the indigenous peoples of Sabah are happy to welcome visitors to their villages to witness their daily lives and traditions. Discovery Tours offers coach trips to see the Runggus, Bajau, and other tribes in the Kota Kinabalu area. Half-day and day trips cost between RM60 and RM250 (US$16–US$65) per person.

Appendix: Singapore & Malaysia in Depth

By the 1800s, European powers had already explored much of the world, staking their authority over major trade routes. Southeast Asia's initial attraction was its position in between two seasonal monsoons—one half of the year saw winds that carried sailing vessels from China to Southeast Asia, while the other half of the year favored ships coming from India and Arabia. The English, Dutch, Portuguese, French, and Spanish, recognizing Southeast Asia's advantage, scrambled to set up trading posts to receive valuable tea, opium, silk, spices, and other goods from China.

The British East India Company, in its rivalry with the Dutch East Indies Company, sought to control the Strait of Malacca, the narrow passage between Indonesian Sumatra and the Malay peninsula. They already had a port at Penang, an island in the north of the Strait, but it was proving an economic failure. The company charged one of its officers, Sir Stamford Raffles with the task of locating a new post. Raffles, who knew the area well, had his heart set on a small island at the tip of the Malay peninsula.

At the time of its "discovery," Singapore was occupied by only 1,000 people, mainly Malay residents, orang laut (sea nomads), a handful of Chinese farmers, plus assorted pirates in hiding. The island had little known historical significance. An early settlement on the island, called Temasek, had been visited regularly by Chinese merchants, and later the settlement came under the rule of the far-reaching Srivijaya

Dateline

- **3rd century** A.D. Singapore mentioned by Chinese sailors.
- **5th century** Tamil (Indian) and Persian traders arrive.
- **1295** Marco Polo visits Sumatra; has a swell time.
- **1349** Siam (Thailand) attacks Temasek (Singapore).
- **1390** Iskander Shah establishes sultanate on Singapura and ascends the "lion throne," but is eventually ousted.
- **1613** Portuguese report having torched a Malay outpost on Singapura.
- **1700s** Temenggongs rule Singapura.
- **1819** Sir Stamford Raffles lands on Singapura, likes what he sees.
- **1820s** First billiards club, first newspaper, first judicial system, first census (counting 4,727 souls).
- **1824** East India Trading Company buys the island.
- **1826** Raffles dies in London.
- **1827** Straits Settlements is formed, which includes Malaysia and Singapore; first steamship seen in Singapore.
- **1830** The British rule Singapore from India.
- **1833** East India Trading Company loses its foothold in Southeast Asia; population now 20,978.
- **1834** First New Year Regatta.
- **1837** First Chamber of Commerce formed.
- **1839** Launching of first Singapore vessel.
- **1840** First bank opened, Union Bank of Calcutta; population 33,969.
- **1845** First Masonic Lodge; arrival of first P&O mail boat.

continues

Empire (9th–13th centuries A.D.), which was based in Palembang in Sumatra. It was the Srivijayas who named the island Singapura, or Lion City, after its leader claimed to have seen a strange lion on its shores. However, the Srivijayas were eventually overtaken by a neighboring power, the Java-based Majapahits. Sometime around 1390, a young Palembang ruler, Iskander Shah (aka Parameswara), rebelled against the Majapahits and fled to Singapura, where he set up independent rule. The Majapahits were quick to chase him out, and Iskander fled up the Malay peninsula to Malacca, where he founded what would be one of the most successful trading ports in the region at the time.

When Raffles arrived in 1819, Singapura had been asleep for nearly 400 years under the rule of the sultan of Johor, of the southernmost province in Malaya, with local administration handled by a Temenggong, or senior minister. It was Temenggong Abdu'r Rahman who, on February 6, 1819, signed a treaty with Raffles to set up a trading post on the island in return for an annual payment to the Sultanate. After this, Raffles didn't stay around for too long, handing over the Residency of the port to his friend and colleague, Colonel William Farquhar.

When Raffles returned 3 years later, Singapore was fast becoming a success story. The ideally situated port was inspired by Raffles's own dream of free trade and Farquhar's skill at orderly administration. The population had grown to more than 11,000—Malays, Chinese, Bugis (from Celebes in Indonesia), Indians, Arabs, Armenians, Europeans, and Eurasians. The haphazard sprawl convinced Raffles to draft the Town Plan of 1822, assigning specific neighborhoods to the many ethnic groups that had settled. These ethnic enclaves remain much the same today—Singapore's Chinatown, the

- 1850 Population 52,891.
- 1854 First Singapore postage stamp printed.
- 1860 Telegraph opened between Singapore and Batavia; population 81,734.
- 1864 First use of gas street lighting.
- 1867 Singapore is declared a British colony.
- 1869 Suez Canal opens; Singapore leaps to prominence.
- 1871 Singapore's population reaches 94,816; visit of the King of Siam; telegraph opened between Singapore and Hong Kong.
- 1877 Experimental rubber seeds smuggled from Brazil; planted at the Botanic Gardens.
- 1877 Chinese Protectorate is formed to curb violence among rival Chinese gangs.
- 1879 First telephone; Gen. Ulysses Grant visits Singapore; first official postcards issued.
- 1881 Population now 137,722.
- 1886 Steam trams begin operation.
- 1887 Statue of Raffles unveiled.
- 1888 Rubber trees introduced into Malaysia as a commercial crop.
- 1891 Singapore Golf Club formed; population 181,602; first concert by Philharmonic Society.
- 1896 First automobile.
- 1901 Population 226,842.
- 1903 Singapore-Kranji Railway opens.
- 1904 Motor vehicle registration and drivers' licensing introduced.
- 1905 First frozen foods arrive in Singapore; electric trams introduced.
- 1907 Singapore Automobile Club founded.
- 1911 Population now 303,321.
- 1914 Outbreak of the Great War in Europe.
- 1915 Singapore Sling invented at the Long Bar in the Raffles Hotel (becomes a smashing success).
- 1916 Slavery abolished.
- 1919 First airplane arrives in Singapore.
- 1921 Britain severs its defense alliance with Japan; population 418,358.
- 1922 Prince of Wales visits.
- 1926 First trolley bus service.
- 1928 Singapore Flying Club formed.

continues

administrative center or Historic District, Little India, Kampong Glam, and other neighborhoods are still the ethnic centers they originally were (of course, with many modern alterations).

This would be the last trip Raffles would make to the island that credits him with its founding. His visit in 1822 was merely a stop on his way back to London to retire. Raffles had had big plans for his career with the East India Company, but never saw any of his ambitions come to fruition. While Singaporeans celebrate him with statues and street names, the truth is he eventually succumbed to syphilis in London, dying a failed and penniless man. He remains, however, a hero to modern day Singaporeans.

In 1824, the Dutch finally signed a treaty with Britain acknowledging Singapore as a permanent British possession, and Sultan Hussein of Johor ceded the island to the East India Trading Company in perpetuity. Three years later, Singapore was incorporated, along with Malacca and Penang, to form the Straits Settlements. Penang was acknowledged as the settlements' seat of government, with direction from the Presidency of Bengal in India.

Singapore's first 40 years were filled with all the magic of an Oriental trading port. Chinese coolie laborers came to Singapore in droves to escape economic hardship at home. Most were from one of four major dialect groups: Hokkien, Teochew, Cantonese, and Hakka, all from southern China. Living in crowded bunks in the buildings that sprang up behind the go-downs, these immigrants formed secret societies, social and political organizations made up of residents who shared similar ancestry or Chinese hometowns. These clan groups helped new arrivals get settled and find work, and carried money and messages back to workers' families in China. But it was the secret societies' other contribution—to gambling,

- **1929** Direct Singapore-London telegraph link.
- **1931** Population 570,128.
- **1932** Last tiger on island killed.
- **1936** Anti-Japanese riots by Chinese in Singapore; start of wireless broadcasting.
- **1937** Sultan Mosque installs loudspeakers for muezzin's call to prayer; Kallang Aerodrome opens; opium sales proceeds still providing 25% of Straits Settlements' budget.
- **1938** First set of synchronized traffic lights installed.
- **1939** World War II begins in Europe.
- **1942** Japanese invade Singapore from the north.
- **1945** Japanese surrender; British rule restored.
- **1946** Singapore becomes a Crown Colony.
- **1948** Communist Party of Malaya attempts to take control of the peninsula; emergency powers instituted to discourage such activities.
- **1955** Constitution allows a freely elected parliament; People's Action Party (PAP) is formed; concessions won toward greater political autonomy.
- **1958** Singapore granted internal self-government.
- **1959** People's Action Party (PAP) wins general election; Lee Kuan Yew becomes first prime minister.
- **1961** First oil refinery.
- **1963** Singapore is admitted to the Federation of Malaysia; Internal Security Act passed.
- **1965** Singapore expelled from Federation and becomes an independent state; Singapore admitted into the United Nations.
- **1967** Singapore issues its own currency.
- **1981** PAP monopoly ends; Changi International Airport opens, named the best service in Southeast Asia; East Coast Expressway completed; Pan-Island Expressway opens.
- **1987** Singapore's policy of limiting families to two children reversed due to declining birth rate; hefty incentives given for third children.

continues

street crime, and violence—that helped fuel Singapore's image as a lawless boomtown, filled with all the excitement and danger of a frontier town in the Wild West.

Indians were quick to become Singapore's second largest community. Most were traders or laborers, but many others were troops carried with the Brits. Most came from southern India, from the mostly Tamil-speaking population, including the Chettiars, Muslim moneylenders who financed the building of many places of worship in the early neighborhoods. After 1825, the British turned possession of Bencoolen on Sumatra to the Dutch, transferring the thousands of Indian prisoners incarcerated there to Singapore, where they were put to work constructing the buildings and clearing the land that the fledgling settlement needed. After they'd worked off their sentences, many stayed in Singapore instead of returning home to work their trade as free men.

During this period The Istana Kampong Glam was built in Raffles's designated Malay enclave, along with the Sultan Mosque. The surrounding streets supported a large but modest Malay settlement of businesses and residences.

1988 The Mass Rapid Transit System (MRT), an intra-island subway network built to the tune of S$5 billion, opens.

1990 Singapore celebrates 25 years of independence; Prime Minister Lee steps down and Goh Chok Tong takes over the reins; Ministry for Information and the Arts formed; Placido Domingo first opera star to play Singapore.

1992 Chewing gum banned due to vandals plugging up elevator buttons and subway doors.

1993 First Christie's auction; Michael Jackson World Tour sellout; *Cats* opens to rave notices and becomes the first of several Broadway road shows in Southeast Asia.

1994 Rogue securities trader Nick Leeson turns fugitive and is eventually captured after the US$1.4 billion collapse of Britain's Barings Bank.

1996 Passage of Maintenance of Parents Bill, which mandates that children provide for the care of their older parents.

1997 Asian Economic Crisis hits. Compared with the economic troubles in neighboring Southeast Asian nations, Singapore weathers the storm effectively.

1999 S. R. Nathan declared president without election. No other candidates were certified eligible.

Despite early successes, Singapore was almost entirely dependent on entrepôt trade, which was literally dependent on the whim of the winds. Dutch trading power still threatened its economic health, and the opening of Chinese trading ports to Western trade placed Singapore in a precarious position. The soil on the island barely supported a small sago palm industry, and with the lack of natural resources Singapore had to constantly look to trade for survival. True economic stability wouldn't arrive until the 1860s.

Major changes around the globe had an enormous effect on Singapore in the second half of the 19th century. In 1869, the Suez Canal opened, linking the Mediterranean and the Red Sea and putting Singapore in a prime position on the Europe–East Asia route. In addition, steamship travel made the trip to Singapore less dependent on trade winds. The shorter travel time not only saw entrepôt trade leap to new heights but also allowed leisure travelers to consider Singapore a viable stop on their itinerary.

The blossoming Industrial Revolution thirsted for raw materials, namely tin and rubber. Malaya was already being mined for tin, much of which changed hands in Singapore. Rubber didn't enter the scene until 1877, when "Mad" Henry Ridley, director of the Botanical Gardens, smuggled the first rubber seedlings from Brazil to Singapore. After developing a new way to tap latex, he finally convinced planters in Malaya to begin plantations. To this day rubber remains a major industry for Malaysia.

WORLD WAR II   Although the British maintained a military base of operations on the island, Singapore was virtually untouched by World War I. Just before the Great Depression, however, Britain bowed to U.S. pressure and broke off relations with Japan due to that country's increasing military power. Singapore's defense became a primary concern, and the British, thinking any invasion would come by sea, installed heavy artillery along the southern coastline, leaving the north of the island virtually unprotected.

In 1941, on the night of December 7, the Japanese attacked Pearl Harbor, invaded the Philippines and Hong Kong, landed in southern Thailand, and dropped the first bombs on Singapore.

Japanese Lieutenant General Yamashita, fresh from battles in Mongolia, saw a definite advantage in Singapore's unprotected northern flank, and stealthily moved three divisions—almost 20,000 troops—down the Malay Peninsula on bicycles. From Johor Bahru, across the Johor Strait, he had a direct view of Singapore and on the evening of February 8th the army quietly invaded the island. For days, the British tried to hold off their attackers, but bit by bit they lost ground. Within days, the Japanese were firmly entrenched.

The occupation brought terrible conditions to multiethnic Singapore, as the Japanese ruled harshly and punished any word of dissent with prison or worse. Mass executions were commonplace, prisoners of war were tortured and killed, and it was said that the beaches at Changi ran red with blood. The prisoners that survived were sent to Thailand to work on the railway. Conditions were worst for the island's Chinese, many of whom were arrested indiscriminately just because of their ethnicity, rowed out to sea, and dumped overboard. Little information from the outside world reached Singapore's citizens during this time except when the Japanese were victorious.

Mercifully, the Japanese surrender came before Singapore became a battleground once again. On September 5, 1945, British warships arrived, and a week later, the Japanese officially surrendered to Lord Louis Mountbatten, supreme Allied commander in Southeast Asia.

THE POSTWAR YEARS   Now back under British rule, Singapore spent the next 10 years revitalizing itself, while efforts to become a fully self-governing country were tantamount. Resentment against the British was still very strong for the way they'd abandoned the island to the Japanese in 1941.

The British Military Administration (BMA), set up to efficiently organize and systematically administrate Singapore's postoccupation reconstruction, was neither efficient nor systematic. On the streets, conditions were terrible. The BMA eventually got itself under control and proceeded to clean up the port and harbor and return them to civilian control, restore public utilities, and overhaul the distrusted police force. Although food was still scarce, rice was available at a reasonable price.

THE RISE OF LEE KUAN YEW & SINGAPOREAN INDEPENDENCE
In 1949, just 3 years after the British military regime turned Singapore over to a civil administration as a crown colony once again, six Singaporean students in London formed a discussion group aimed at bringing together Malayan overseas students. A third-generation Straits Chinese, Lee Kuan Yew, was a formidable member of the group. Returning to Singapore, his education completed, Lee

made a name for himself as an effective courtroom lawyer during the trials of Chinese students arrested during the anti–national service riots of May 1954. Around this time, he had decided that, although he detested their politics, an alliance with the illegal Malayan Communist Party would best serve his aims, and so a new combined party, the People's Action Party (PAP), was inaugurated.

By 1957, the Federation of Malaysia had won its independence, and around the same time Britain agreed to allow the establishment of a fully elected, 51-seat Legislative Assembly in Singapore. In the first elections for this body, in 1959, the PAP swept 43 of the seats and Lee Kuan Yew became the country's first prime minister.

Lee's agenda was met with distrust by the Federation of Malaysia. His aim was to have Singapore admitted to the Federation, but the Malaysian government was fearful of a dominant Chinese influence and fought to keep Singapore out. In 1963, however, they broke down and admitted Singapore as a member. It was a short-lived marriage. When the PAP looked to becoming a national entity rather than a local Singaporean party, an alarmed Federation demanded Singapore be expelled, and so, on August 9, 1965, Singapore found itself a newly independent country. Lee's tearful television broadcast announcing Singapore's expulsion from the Federation and simultaneous gain of independence is one of the most famous in Singapore's history. In 1971, the last British military forces left the island.

SINGAPORE TODAY

Who would have believed that Singapore would rise to such international fame and become the vaunted "Asian Tiger" it has in recent decades? This small country's political stability and effective government have inspired many other nations to study its methods, and former prime minister (and current senior minister) Lee Kuan Yew is counted among the most renowned political figures in the world. When asked to explain how Singapore's astounding economic, political, and social success was made possible, Lee always takes the credit—and deservedly so—but in the face of international criticism for dictatorial policies, absolutist law enforcement, and human rights violations, he also stands first in line to receive the blame.

THE GOVERNMNENT   Since Mr. Lee's election, and without debate, it has been his unfailing vision of a First World Singapore that's inspired the policies and plans that created the political and economic miracle we see today. During his tenure he mobilized government, industry, and citizens toward fulfilling his vision, establishing a government almost devoid of corruption, a strong economy built from practically no resources save labor, and a nation of racial and religious harmony from a multiethnic melting pot.

Both critics and admirers refer to Lee Kuan Yew as a strict yet generous "father" to the "children" of Singapore, raising them to a high position on the world stage yet dictating policies that have cost citizens many of their personal freedoms. You'll find that the average Singaporean expresses some duality about this: He or she will be outwardly critical of the government's invasion of privacy and disregard for personal freedoms, and of policies that have driven up the cost of housing and health care, but will also recognize all that Lee has done to raise Singaporeans' standard of living, expand their opportunities for the future, and ensure tranquillity at home—achievements for which many are willing to sacrifice a certain amount of freedom to enjoy. By and large, they wish to see the current government continue its work.

Lee stepped down from the prime minister's chair in 1990, assuming the position of senior minister. Although the new prime minister, Mr. Goh Chok Tong, has created some policies of his own to promote more openness in the political system, it is understood that Lee still drives the car. To his credit, Goh has been a popular leader. In addition to initiating more citizen participation in the politics of the country, he is supporting local visual and performing arts and encouraging an effort to draw internationally acclaimed arts performances and exhibits to Singapore, all in an attempt to solve Singapore's current brain drain by encouraging more creative and educated Singaporeans to stay in-country rather than emigrate. Unfortunately, he also has to face suspicion that he's nothing more than a seat warmer for Lee's son, Lee Hsien Loong, who is currently deputy prime minister.

THE CENSORSHIP QUESTION   One infamous feature of Singapore's government is its control over media, both domestic and international. All national news publications have ties to the government, whose philosophy holds that the role of the media is to promote the government's goals. Articles are censored for any content that might threaten national security, incite riot, or promote disobedience or racism. Offenders face stiff fines.

It doesn't stop at the print media, either. Television is also censored, satellite dishes are banned, and there's only one cable provider, which the government keeps a close eye on for anything resembling pornography.

The Internet provided Singapore with a tough dilemma. By design, the Net promotes freedom of communication, which is taken advantage of by, among others, every political dissident and pornographer who can get his little hands on a PC. This thought so concerned the Singapore government that it debated long and hard about allowing access to its citizens. However, the possibilities for communications and commerce and their implications for the future of Singapore's economy won, and the government paved the way for all Singaporeans to have access by the year 2000—though it goes without saying, of course, that access will be heavily censored. Private- and public-sector organizations must register with the government, which clears all content, and Internet providers must block questionable sites and monitor hits to websites, reporting to the government who's accessing what.

THE ECONOMY   Singapore's economy is a bizarre marriage between free trade and government control. Lee Kuan Yew's vision and resulting policies have created annual national growth rates of 8.9% going on 3 decades now. Singapore survived the East Asian Economic Crisis that began in July 1997 because of its firm bank-lending regulations and transparent government and business dealings. The biggest moneymakers are the electronics industry, financial and business services, transportation and communications, petroleum refining and shipping, construction, and tourism. Seventy-six percent of Singapore's exports, exclusive of oil exports, go to the United States, Malaysia, the European Union, Hong Kong, and Japan.

Singaporeans enjoy a high standard of living, with average annual incomes reaching US$23,000. The most commonly heard complaint? The rising cost of real estate.

TOURISM   The Singapore Tourism Board has far-reaching influence that has helped to turn Singapore into a veritable machine for raising foreign cash. More than 7.5 million tourists visit Singapore annually, spending over S$12 billion during their stays.

Not content to rest on its laurels, Singapore has big plans to dramatically increase these numbers in the new century through implementation of its new Tourism 21 Plan, which will restore landmarks and create Thematic Zones, areas within the ethnic neighborhoods where the URA (Urban Redevelopment Authority) plans to restore old buildings and block off vehicular traffic to create pedestrian avenues. Neighborhoods like Chinatown have become more like China-World, as local shops and colorful street life are replaced by tidy restored buildings, glitzy souvenir shops, and ironic little exhibits describing the vibrant community that once thrived in the neighborhood but was run out by high rents.

2 Malaysian History

If Malaysia can trace its success to one element, it would be geographic location. Placed strategically at a major crossroads between the Eastern and Western worlds and enforced by the northeast and southwest monsoons, Malaysia (formerly known as Malaya) was the ideal center for East-West trade activities. The character of the indigenous Malays is credited to their relationship with the sea, while centuries of outside influences shaped their culture.

The earliest inhabitants of the peninsula were the orang asli, who are believed to have migrated from China and Tibet as early as 5,000 years ago. The first Malays were established by 1000 B.C., having migrated not only to Malaya, but throughout the entire Indonesian archipelago as well, including Sumatra and Borneo. They brought with them knowledge of agriculture and metalwork, as well as beliefs in a spirit world (attitudes that are still practiced by many groups today).

Malaysia's earliest trading contacts were established by the 1st century B.C., with China and India. India proved most influential, impacting local culture with Buddhist and Hindu beliefs that are evidenced today in the Malay language, in literature, and in many customs.

Recorded history didn't come around until the Malay Annals of the 17th century, which tell the story of Parameswara, also known as Iskander Shah, ruler of Temasek (Singapore), who was forced to flee to Malacca around A.D. 1400. He set up a trading port and, taking advantage of the favorable geographic location, led it to world-renowned financial success. Malacca grew in population and prosperity, attracting Chinese, Indian, and Arab traders.

With Arabs and Muslim Indians came Islam, and Iskander Shah's son, who took leadership of Malacca after his father's death, is credited as the first Malay to convert to the new religion. The rule of Malacca was transformed into a sultanate, and the word of Islam won converts not only in Malaya, but throughout Borneo and the Indonesian archipelago. Today the people of this region are very proud to be Muslim by conversion, as opposed to conquest.

Malacca's success was not without admirers, and in 1511 the Portuguese decided they wanted a piece of the action. They conquered the city in 30 days, chased the sultanate south to Johor, built a fortress that forestalled any trouble from the populace, and set up Christian missions. The Portuguese stuck around until 1641, when the Dutch came to town, looking to expand their trading power in the region. For the record, after Malacca's fall to the Portuguese, its success plummeted, and has never been regained.

The British came sniffing around in the late 1700s, when Francis Light of the British East India Company landed on the island of Penang and cut a deal with the Sultan of Kedah to cede it to the British. By 1805, Penang had become the seat of British authority in Southeast Asia, but the establishment served less as a trading cash cow and more as political leverage in the race to beat out the Dutch for control of the Southeast Asian trade routes. In 1824, the British and Dutch finally signed a treaty dividing Southeast Asia. The British would have Malaya and the Dutch Indonesia. Dutch-ruled Malacca was traded for British-ruled Bencoolen in Sumatra. In 1826, the British East India Company formed the Straits Settlements, uniting Penang, Malacca, and Singapore under Penang's control. In 1867, power over the Straits Settlements shifted from the British East India Company to British colonial rule in London.

The Anglo-Dutch treaty never provided for the island of Borneo. The Dutch sort of took over Kalimantan, but the areas to the northwest were generally held under the rule of the Sultan of Brunei. Sabah was ceded for an annual sum to the British North Borneo Company, ruled by London until the Japanese invaded during World War II. In 1839, Englishman James Brooke arrived in Sarawak. The Sultan of Brunei had been having a hard time with warring factions in this territory, and was happy to hand over control of it to Brooke. In 1841, after winning allies and subjugating enemies, Brook became the Raja of Sarawak, building his capital in Kuching.

Meanwhile, back on the peninsula, Kuala Lumpur sprang to life in 1857 as a settlement at the crook of the Klang and Gombak rivers, about 35 km (21 miles) inland from the west coast. Tin miners from India, China, and other parts of Malaya came inland to prospect and set up a trading post, which flourished. In 1896, it became the capital of the British Malayan territory.

In 1941, the Japanese conquered Malaya en route to Singapore. Life for Malayans during the 4-year occupation was a constant and almost unbearable struggle to survive hunger, disease, and separation from the world. After the war, when the British sought to reclaim their colonial sovereignty over Malaya, they found the people thoroughly fed up with foreign rule. The struggle for independence served to unite Malay and non-Malay residents throughout the country. By the time the British agreed to Malayan independence, the states were already united. On August 31, 1957, Malaya was cut loose, and Kuala Lumpur became its official capital. For a brief moment in the early 1960s, the peninsula was united with Singapore and the Borneo states of Sabah and Sarawak. Singapore was ejected from the federation in 1965, and today Malaysia continues on its own path.

MALAYSIA TODAY

The Malaysia of today is a peaceful nation of many races and ethnicities. The Census 2000 placed the population at roughly 23.27 million. Of this number, bumiputeras are the most numerous ethnic group (broadly speaking), and are defined as those with cultural affinities indigenous to the region and to one another. Technically, this group includes people of the aboriginal groups native to the peninsula. A smaller segment of the population is nonbumiputera groups such as the Chinese, Indians, Arabs, and Eurasians, most of whom are descended from settlers to the region in the past 150 years. It is important to know the difference between the bumiputera and nonbumiputera groups to understand Malaysian politics, which favors the first group in every policy. It is equally important to understand that despite ethnic divisions, each group is considered no less Malaysian.

The state religion is Islam. The Muslim way of life is reflected in almost every element of Malaysian life. The strict adherence to Islam will most likely affect your vacation plans in some way. If you're traveling to Malaysia for an extended period of time, or are planning to work there, I highly recommend *Malaysian Customs & Etiquette: A Practical Handbook,* by Datin Noor Aini Syed Amir (Times Books), for its great advice on how to negotiate any situation.

As for the non-Muslim, life goes on under the government's very serious policy to protect freedom of religion. ***Note:*** Despite its "freedom of religion" policy, Malaysia is very anti-Zionist. Almost daily the local papers report anti-Semitic news, and Israel is the only country in the world to which Malaysian citizens may not travel. If you carry an Israeli passport, you will need to consult your home embassy before considering travel to Malaysia. Jewish people from other countries who still wish to visit are advised to downplay their religion and culture.

THE GOVERNMENT   The government is headed by a prime minister, a post that for the past 21 years has been held by Dato' Seri Dr. Mahathir Bin Mohamad. Dr. Mahathir has been both criticized and praised for his unique efforts to solve his country's economic troubles.

In September 1998, Dr. Mahathir's administration came under international scrutiny when he ousted his deputy prime minister, Dato' Seri Anwar Bin Ibrahim, for alleged sexual misconduct and corruption. While there were brief moments of civil unrest in the nation's capital, the situation never placed travelers in danger. In 1999, Anwar stood trial for corruption and sodomy charges, was found guilty of all counts and was sentenced to 15 years imprisonment. As a result, Malaysians began to raise questions about the role of government and the press. Dr. Mahathir's United Malay National Organization (UMNO) lost some footing to its opposition, the Pan Malaysian Islamic Party (PAS), who during elections in 1999 gained control of the state of Terengganu giving them control of 2 out of 13 Malaysian states. In June 2002, Mahathir announced his resignation to a shocked public, issuing a statement that he will hand power to his current deputy, Abdullah Ahmad Badawi in late 2003. PAS leaders accuse him of playing out a drama to swing popularity back to his party.

THE ECONOMY   Until the Asian Economic Crisis that began in July 1997, Malaysia was one of the rising stars of the East Asian Miracle, with an economy built upon the manufacturing sector in electronics and rubber products, as well as on agriculture and mining. Though the crisis hit the country hard, the most recent economic reports show that Malaysia's recovery has been one of the strongest in the region.

TOURISM   Malaysia has remained helpful to the US in the war against terrorism. The leading UMNO party has denounced extremists who commit crimes in the name of religion. However, the local PAS governments in Kelantan and Terengganu are moving toward strict Islamic-oriented rule to counter UMNO's moderate state policies. At the time of writing, Malaysia has been arguing a U.S. Department of State travel advisory that warns travelers in the state of Sabah on Borneo. This is in response to the kidnapping 3 years ago of tourists off an island resort in east Sabah by the Abu-Sayaff, a Philippine based, Al Qaeda-linked terrorist group. The Bali bombings of late 2002 stepped up the alert, but Malaysia would like the world to know that terrorist activities have not been carried out by Malaysians in Malaysia and the government has taken every effort to keep the country stable and safe.

Index

See also Accommodations and Restaurant indexes, below.

Frommer's® Complete Travel Guides

Alaska
Alaska Cruises & Ports of Call
Amsterdam
Argentina & Chile
Arizona
Atlanta
Australia
Austria
Bahamas
Barcelona, Madrid & Seville
Beijing
Belgium, Holland & Luxembourg
Bermuda
Boston
Brazil
British Columbia & the Canadian Rockies
Budapest & the Best of Hungary
California
Canada
Cancún, Cozumel & the Yucatán
Cape Cod, Nantucket & Martha's Vineyard
Caribbean
Caribbean Cruises & Ports of Call
Caribbean Ports of Call
Carolinas & Georgia
Chicago
China
Colorado
Costa Rica
Denmark
Denver, Boulder & Colorado Springs
England
Europe
European Cruises & Ports of Call
Florida

France
Germany
Great Britain
Greece
Greek Islands
Hawaii
Hong Kong
Honolulu, Waikiki & Oahu
Ireland
Israel
Italy
Jamaica
Japan
Las Vegas
London
Los Angeles
Maryland & Delaware
Maui
Mexico
Montana & Wyoming
Montréal & Québec City
Munich & the Bavarian Alps
Nashville & Memphis
Nepal
New England
New Mexico
New Orleans
New York City
New Zealand
Northern Italy
Nova Scotia, New Brunswick & Prince Edward Island
Oregon
Paris
Philadelphia & the Amish Country
Portugal
Prague & the Best of the Czech Republic

Provence & the Riviera
Puerto Rico
Rome
San Antonio & Austin
San Diego
San Francisco
Santa Fe, Taos & Albuquerque
Scandinavia
Scotland
Seattle & Portland
Shanghai
Singapore & Malaysia
South Africa
South America
South Florida
South Pacific
Southeast Asia
Spain
Sweden
Switzerland
Texas
Thailand
Tokyo
Toronto
Tuscany & Umbria
USA
Utah
Vancouver & Victoria
Vermont, New Hampshire & Maine
Vienna & the Danube Valley
Virgin Islands
Virginia
Walt Disney World® & Orlando
Washington, D.C.
Washington State

Frommer's® Dollar-a-Day Guides

Australia from $50 a Day
California from $70 a Day
Caribbean from $70 a Day
England from $75 a Day
Europe from $70 a Day

Florida from $70 a Day
Hawaii from $80 a Day
Ireland from $60 a Day
Italy from $70 a Day
London from $85 a Day

New York from $90 a Day
Paris from $80 a Day
San Francisco from $70 a Day
Washington, D.C. from $80 a Day

Frommer's® Portable Guides

Acapulco, Ixtapa & Zihuatanejo
Amsterdam
Aruba
Australia's Great Barrier Reef
Bahamas
Berlin
Big Island of Hawaii
Boston
California Wine Country
Cancún
Charleston & Savannah
Chicago
Disneyland®
Dublin
Florence

Frankfurt
Hong Kong
Houston
Las Vegas
London
Los Angeles
Los Cabos & Baja
Maine Coast
Maui
Miami
New Orleans
New York City
Paris
Phoenix & Scottsdale

Portland
Puerto Rico
Puerto Vallarta, Manzanillo & Guadalajara
Rio de Janeiro
San Diego
San Francisco
Seattle
Sydney
Tampa & St. Petersburg
Vancouver
Venice
Virgin Islands
Washington, D.C.

Frommer's® National Park Guides

Banff & Jasper
Family Vacations in the National Parks
Grand Canyon

National Parks of the American West
Rocky Mountain

Yellowstone & Grand Teton
Yosemite & Sequoia/ Kings Canyon
Zion & Bryce Canyon

FROMMER'S® MEMORABLE WALKS

Chicago
London

New York
Paris

San Francisco
Washington, D.C.

FROMMER'S® GREAT OUTDOOR GUIDES

Arizona & New Mexico
New England

Northern California
Southern New England

Vermont & New Hampshire

SUZY GERSHMAN'S BORN TO SHOP GUIDES

Born to Shop: France
Born to Shop: Hong Kong,
  Shanghai & Beijing

Born to Shop: Italy
Born to Shop: London

Born to Shop: New York
Born to Shop: Paris

FROMMER'S® IRREVERENT GUIDES

Amsterdam
Boston
Chicago
Las Vegas
London

Los Angeles
Manhattan
New Orleans
Paris
Rome

San Francisco
Seattle & Portland
Vancouver
Walt Disney World®
Washington, D.C.

FROMMER'S® BEST-LOVED DRIVING TOURS

Britain
California
Florida
France

Germany
Ireland
Italy
New England

Northern Italy
Scotland
Spain
Tuscany & Umbria

HANGING OUT™ GUIDES

Hanging Out in England
Hanging Out in Europe

Hanging Out in France
Hanging Out in Ireland

Hanging Out in Italy
Hanging Out in Spain

THE UNOFFICIAL GUIDES®

Bed & Breakfasts and Country
  Inns in:
  California
  Great Lakes States
  Mid-Atlantic
  New England
  Northwest
  Rockies
  Southeast
  Southwest
Best RV & Tent Campgrounds in:
  California & the West
  Florida & the Southeast
  Great Lakes States
  Mid-Atlantic
  Northeast
  Northwest & Central Plains

Southwest & South Central
  Plains
  U.S.A.
Beyond Disney
Branson, Missouri
California with Kids
Chicago
Cruises
Disneyland®
Florida with Kids
Golf Vacations in the Eastern U.S.
Great Smoky & Blue Ridge Region
Inside Disney
Hawaii
Las Vegas
London

Mid-Atlantic with Kids
Mini Las Vegas
Mini-Mickey
New England and New York with
  Kids
New Orleans
New York City
Paris
San Francisco
Skiing in the West
Southeast with Kids
Walt Disney World®
Walt Disney World® for Grown-ups
Walt Disney World® with Kids
Washington, D.C.
World's Best Diving Vacations

SPECIAL-INTEREST TITLES

Frommer's Adventure Guide to Australia &
  New Zealand
Frommer's Adventure Guide to Central America
Frommer's Adventure Guide to India & Pakistan
Frommer's Adventure Guide to South America
Frommer's Adventure Guide to Southeast Asia
Frommer's Adventure Guide to Southern Africa
Frommer's Britain's Best Bed & Breakfasts and
  Country Inns
Frommer's Caribbean Hideaways
Frommer's Exploring America by RV
Frommer's Fly Safe, Fly Smart
Frommer's France's Best Bed & Breakfasts and
  Country Inns
Frommer's Gay & Lesbian Europe

Frommer's Italy's Best Bed & Breakfasts and
  Country Inns
Frommer's New York City with Kids
Frommer's Ottawa with Kids
Frommer's Road Atlas Britain
Frommer's Road Atlas Europe
Frommer's Road Atlas France
Frommer's Toronto with Kids
Frommer's Vancouver with Kids
Frommer's Washington, D.C., with Kids
Israel Past & Present
The New York Times' Guide to Unforgettable
  Weekends
Places Rated Almanac
Retirement Places Rated

America Online Keyword: Travel

Booked seat 6A, open return.

Rented red 4-wheel drive.

Reserved cabin, no running water.

Discovered space.

With over 700 airlines, 50,000 hotels, 50 rental car companies and 5,000 cruise and vacation packages, you can create the perfect getaway for you. Choose the car, the room, even the ground you walk on.

Travelocity.com
A Sabre Company
Go Virtually Anywhere.

Travelocity,® Travelocity.com® and the Travelocity skyline logo are trademarks and/or servicemarks of Travelocity.com L.P., and Sabre® is a trademark of an affiliate of Sabre Inc. © 2002 Travelocity.com L.P. All rights reserved.

America Online Keyword: Travel

You Need A Vacation.

700 Airlines, 50,000 Hotels, 50 Rental Car
Companies, And A Million Ways To Save Money.

Travelocity.com
A Sabre Company
Go Virtually Anywhere.

Travelocity,® Travelocity.com® and the Travelocity skyline logo are trademarks and/or servicemarks of Travelocity.com L.P.,
and Sabre® is a trademark of an affiliate of Sabre Inc. © 2002 Travelocity.com L.P. All rights reserved.

P9-CCG-269

In 1977, Stephen King's *The Shining* gave us a new kind of
horror novel—one that played out in the mind of a psychi-
cally gifted young boy, Danny Torrance, and his alcoholic
father, in the corridors of a snowbound hotel.

Now, Dan Torrance has grown up. So have his demons. . . .

"Almost 40 years later, I've changed, the world has
changed, the planet has changed—and Stephen King
is still scaring the hell out of me. . . . I could hardly
find the courage to turn the page."
—Alan Cheuse, NPR

STEPHEN KING

DOCTOR SLEEP

The acclaimed sequel to *The Shining*

"King's inventiveness and skill show no sign of slacking: *Doctor Sleep* has all the virtues of his best work. . . . King is right
at the center of the American literary taproot that goes all
the way down . . . to Hawthorne, to Poe, to Melville, to the
Henry James of *The Turn of the Screw*, and then to later exem-
plars like Ray Bradbury. What will King do next? Perhaps
Abra will grow up, and become a writer, and use her 'shining'
talents to divine the minds and souls of others. For that, of
course, is yet another interpretation of King's eerie, lumines-
cent metaphor."
—Margaret Atwood, *The New York Times Book Review*

"King at his best . . . thoroughly terrifying. It's impossible to
close the cover on *Doctor Sleep* and not immediately yearn for a
sequel to this sequel."
—*New York Daily News*

"A gripping, taut read."

—*Publishers Weekly*

"King found there was indeed a reason to revisit Daniel Torrance in adulthood. . . . The temptation toward the bottle that destroyed his father—and the Overlook Hotel—remains at all times, adding remarkable tension. . . ."

—*The Toledo Free Press*

"Chilling scenes. . . . *Doctor Sleep* has its own trajectory and cast of characters, and they come fully alive. As with so many of King's characters over the years, we root for them, love them, hate them, fear them, and remember them. . . . It's not simple horror King is after, but thematic resonance: the manacles of the past, the fear of death, the brutality of alcoholism, and the remorse that lingers from bad choices. King offers hope that good can outweigh evil, with some work, commitment, and a little (*lots and lots of*) blood and guts."

—*The Cleveland Plain Dealer*

"*Doctor Sleep* has its own vivid frightscape . . . the red mist secreted by the dying is terrifying to imagine. And the steam of those who shine is one of Mr. King's best surreal inventions."

—Janet Maslin, *The New York Times*

"*Doctor Sleep* doesn't disappoint."

—*The Wall Street Journal*

"Like Poe, King works at the blurry boundary between supernatural horrors and psychological ones. King is excellent on addiction and its attendant dysfunctions: deception, self-justification, disregard of others, new-leaf fantasies and their near-instant collapse, the next fix as the North Star. . . . As for *Doctor Sleep*: It refers to Dan Torrance, hospice worker—who, in his sober, shining kindness, comforts his elderly patients as they're dying. Stephen King has given us a work of horror that promises, of all things, a good night's sleep."

—*New York Magazine*

Praise for
STEPHEN KING

"A master storyteller."

—*Los Angeles Times*

"The most wonderfully gruesome man on the planet."

—*USA Today*

"Stephen King knows exactly what scares you most. . . ."

—*Esquire*

"An undisputed master of suspense and terror."

—*The Washington Post*

"King probably knows more about scary goings-on in confined, isolated places than anybody since Edgar Allan Poe."

—*Entertainment Weekly*

"Peerless imagination."

—*The Observer*

"America's greatest living novelist."

—Lee Child

STEPHEN KING

DOCTOR SLEEP

A NOVEL

GALLERY BOOKS

New York   London   Toronto   Sydney   New Delhi

Gallery Books
A Division of Simon & Schuster, Inc.
1230 Avenue of the Americas
New York, NY 10020

This book is a work of fiction. Any references to historical events, real people, or real places
are used fictitiously. Other names, characters, places, and events are products of the author's
imagination, and any resemblance to actual events or places or persons, living or dead,
is entirely coincidental.

Copyright © 2013 by Stephen King

All rights reserved, including the right to reproduce this book or portions thereof
in any form whatsoever. For information address Gallery Subsidiary Rights Department,
1230 Avenue of the Americas, New York, NY 10020.

This Gallery Books export edition June 2014

GALLERY BOOKS and colophon are registered trademarks of Simon & Schuster, Inc.

For information about special discounts for bulk purchases,
please contact Simon & Schuster Special Sales at 1-866-506-1949
or business@simonandschuster.com.

The Simon & Schuster Speakers Bureau can bring authors to your live event.
For more information or to book an event, contact the Simon & Schuster Speakers Bureau
at 1-866-248-3049 or visit our website at www.simonspeakers.com.

DESIGNED BY ERICH HOBBING
Jacket design by Tal Goretsky
Front jacket illustration by Sean Freeman
Back cover photograph by MacGregor and Gordon

Manufactured in the United States of America

1   3   5   7   9   10   8   6   4   2

Library of Congress Control Number: 2013000431

ISBN 978-1-4767-7941-6
ISBN 978-1-4767-2766-0 (ebook)

Permissions: *Epigraph: The Big Book* of Alcoholics Anonymous © 1939, 1955, 1976, 2001 by Alcoholics Anonymous World Services, Inc. All rights reserved. *Page 80:* "Y.M.C.A.," written by Henri Belolo, Jacques Morali & Victor Willis © Can't Stop Music/Scorpio Music, S.A. *Pages 139 and 422:* "A Game of Chess" from *The Waste Land* by T. S. Eliot © The Estate of T. S. Eliot. Reprinted by permission of Faber & Faber Ltd. Publishing Company. *Collected Poems 1909–1962* by T. S. Eliot. Copyright ©1936 by Houghton Mifflin Harcourt Publishing Company. Copyright © renewed 1964 by Thomas Stearns Eliot. Reprinted by permission of Houghton Mifflin Harcourt Publishing Company. All rights reserved. *Pages 249–250:* Keeley, Edmund: *George Sefaris.* ©1967 Princeton University Press, 1995 renewed PUP/revised edition. Reprinted by permission of Princeton University Press. *Page 251:* "Shorts" © 1940 by W. H. Auden, renewed © 1974 by The Estate of W. H. Auden, from COLLECTED POEMS OF W. H. AUDEN by W. H. Auden. Used by permission of Random House, Inc., and Curtis Brown, Ltd. Any third party use of this material, outside of this publication, is prohibited. Interested parties must apply directly to Random House, Inc., for permission. *Page 263:* THE WRECK OF THE EDMUND FITZGERALD. Words and music by GORDON LIGHTFOOT © 1976 (Renewed) MOOSE MUSIC LTD. Used by Permission of ALFRED MUSIC PUBLISHING CO., INC. All Rights Reserved. *Page 517:* "Ancient Music" by Ezra Pound, from PERSONAE, copyright ©1926 by Ezra Pound. Reprinted by permission of New Directions Publishing Corp. and Faber & Faber Ltd.

When I was playing my primitive brand of rhythm guitar with a group called the Rock Bottom Remainders, Warren Zevon used to gig with us. Warren loved gray t-shirts and movies like *Kingdom of the Spiders*. He insisted I sing lead on his signature tune, "Werewolves of London," during the encore portion of our shows. I said I was not worthy. He insisted that I was. "Key of G," Warren told me, "and howl like you mean it. Most important of all, *play like Keith*."

I'll never be able to play like Keith Richards, but I always did my best, and with Warren beside me, matching me note for note and laughing his fool head off, I always had a blast.

Warren, this howl is for you, wherever you are. I miss you, buddy.

We stood at the turning point. Half-measures availed us nothing.

> —The Big Book of Alcoholics Anonymous

If we were to live, we had to be free of anger. [It is] the dubious luxury of normal men and women.

> —The Big Book of Alcoholics Anonymous

PREFATORY MATTERS

FEAR stands for fuck everything and run.
—Old AA saying

LOCKBOX

1

On the second day of December in a year when a Georgia peanut farmer was doing business in the White House, one of Colorado's great resort hotels burned to the ground. The Overlook was declared a total loss. After an investigation, the fire marshal of Jicarilla County ruled the cause had been a defective boiler. The hotel was closed for the winter when the accident occurred, and only four people were present. Three survived. The hotel's off-season caretaker, John Torrance, was killed during an unsuccessful (and heroic) effort to dump the boiler's steam pressure, which had mounted to disastrously high levels due to an inoperative relief valve.

Two of the survivors were the caretaker's wife and young son. The third was the Overlook's chef, Richard Hallorann, who had left his seasonal job in Florida and come to check on the Torrances because of what he called "a powerful hunch" that the family was in trouble. Both surviving adults were quite badly injured in the explosion. Only the child was unhurt.

Physically, at least.

2

Wendy Torrance and her son received a settlement from the corporation that owned the Overlook. It wasn't huge, but enough

3

to get them by for the three years she was unable to work because of back injuries. A lawyer she consulted told her that if she were willing to hold out and play tough, she might get a great deal more, because the corporation was anxious to avoid a court case. But she, like the corporation, wanted only to put that disastrous winter in Colorado behind her. She would convalesce, she said, and she did, although back injuries plagued her until the end of her life. Shattered vertebrae and broken ribs heal, but they never cease crying out.

Winifred and Daniel Torrance lived in the mid-South for awhile, then drifted down to Tampa. Sometimes Dick Hallorann (he of the powerful hunches) came up from Key West to visit with them. To visit with young Danny especially. They shared a bond.

One early morning in March of 1981, Wendy called Dick and asked if he could come. Danny, she said, had awakened her in the night and told her not to go in the bathroom.

After that, he refused to talk at all.

3

He woke up needing to pee. Outside, a strong wind was blowing. It was warm—in Florida it almost always was—but he did not like that sound, and supposed he never would. It reminded him of the Overlook, where the defective boiler had been the very least of the dangers.

He and his mother lived in a cramped second-floor tenement apartment. Danny left the little room next to his mother's and crossed the hall. The wind gusted and a dying palm tree beside the building clattered its leaves. The sound was skeletal. They always left the bathroom door open when no one was using the shower or the toilet, because the lock was broken. Tonight the door was closed. Not because his mother was in there, however. Thanks to facial injuries she'd suffered at the Overlook, she now snored—a soft *queep-queep* sound—and he could hear it coming from her bedroom.

Well, she closed it by accident, that's all.

He knew better, even then (he was possessed of powerful hunches and intuitions himself), but sometimes you had to know. Sometimes you had to *see*. This was something he had found out at the Overlook, in a room on the second floor.

Reaching with an arm that seemed too long, too stretchy, too *boneless,* he turned the knob and opened the door.

The woman from Room 217 was there, as he had known she would be. She was sitting naked on the toilet with her legs spread and her pallid thighs bulging. Her greenish breasts hung down like deflated balloons. The patch of hair below her stomach was gray. Her eyes were also gray, like steel mirrors. She saw him, and her lips stretched back in a grin.

Close your eyes, Dick Hallorann had told him once upon a time. *If you see something bad, close your eyes and tell yourself it's not there and when you open them again, it will be gone.*

But it hadn't worked in Room 217 when he was five, and it wouldn't work now. He knew it. He could *smell* her. She was decaying.

The woman—he knew her name, it was Mrs. Massey—lumbered to her purple feet, holding out her hands to him. The flesh on her arms hung down, almost dripping. She was smiling the way you do when you see an old friend. Or, perhaps, something good to eat.

With an expression that could have been mistaken for calmness, Danny closed the door softly and stepped back. He watched as the knob turned right . . . left . . . right again . . . then stilled.

He was eight now, and capable of at least some rational thought even in his horror. Partly because, in a deep part of his mind, he had been expecting this. Although he had always thought it would be Horace Derwent who would eventually show up. Or perhaps the bartender, the one his father had called Lloyd. He supposed he should have known it would be Mrs. Massey, though, even before it finally happened. Because of all the undead things in the Overlook, she had been the worst.

The rational part of his mind told him she was just a fragment of unremembered bad dream that had followed him out of sleep and across the hall to the bathroom. That part insisted that if he opened the door again, there would be nothing there. Surely there wouldn't be, now that he was awake. But another part of him, a part that *shone,* knew better. The Overlook wasn't done with him. At least one of its vengeful spirits had followed him all the way to Florida. Once he had come upon that woman sprawled in a bathtub. She had gotten out and tried to choke him with her fishy (but terribly strong) fingers. If he opened the bathroom door now, she would finish the job.

He compromised by putting his ear against the door. At first there was nothing. Then he heard a faint sound.

Dead fingernails scratching on wood.

Danny walked into the kitchen on not-there legs, stood on a chair, and peed into the sink. Then he woke his mother and told her not to go into the bathroom because there was a bad thing there. Once that was done, he went back to bed and sank deep beneath the covers. He wanted to stay there forever, only getting up to pee in the sink. Now that he had warned his mother, he had no interest in talking to her.

His mother knew about the no-talking thing. It had happened after Danny had ventured into Room 217 at the Overlook.

"Will you talk to Dick?"

Lying in his bed, looking up at her, he nodded. His mother called, even though it was four in the morning.

Late the next day, Dick came. He brought something with him. A present.

4

After Wendy called Dick—she made sure Danny heard her doing it—Danny went back to sleep. Although he was now eight and in the third grade, he was sucking his thumb. It hurt her to see him do that. She went to the bathroom door and stood looking at it. She was afraid—Danny had made her afraid—but she had to go, and she had no intention of using the sink as he had. The image of how she would look teetering on the edge of the counter with her butt hanging over the porcelain (even if there was no one there to see) made her wrinkle her nose.

In one hand she had the hammer from her little box of widow's tools. As she turned the knob and pushed the bathroom door open, she raised it. The bathroom was empty, of course, but the ring of the toilet seat was down. She never left it that way before going to bed, because she knew if Danny wandered in, only ten percent awake, he was apt to forget to put it up and piss all over it. Also, there was a smell. A bad one. As if a rat had died in the walls.

She took a step in, then two. She saw movement and whirled, hammer upraised, to hit whoever

(*whatever*)

was hiding behind the door. But it was only her shadow. Scared of her own shadow, people sometimes sneered, but who had a better right than Wendy Torrance? After the things she had seen and been through, she knew that shadows could be dangerous. They could have teeth.

No one was in the bathroom, but there was a discolored smear on the toilet seat and another on the shower curtain. Excrement was her first thought, but shit wasn't yellowish-purple. She looked more closely and saw bits of flesh and decayed skin. There was more on the bathmat, in the shape of footprints. She thought them too small—too *dainty*—to be a man's.

"Oh God," she whispered.

She ended up using the sink after all.

5

Wendy nagged her son out of bed at noon. She managed to get a little soup and half a peanut butter sandwich into him, but then he went back to bed. He still wouldn't speak. Hallorann arrived shortly after five in the afternoon, behind the wheel of his now ancient (but perfectly maintained and blindingly polished) red Cadillac. Wendy had been standing at the window, waiting and watching as she had once waited and watched for her husband, hoping Jack would come home in a good mood. And sober.

She rushed down the stairs and opened the door just as Dick was about to ring the bell marked TORRANCE 2A. He held out his arms and she rushed into them at once, wishing she could be enfolded there for at least an hour. Maybe two.

He let go and held her at arm's length by her shoulders. "You're lookin fine, Wendy. How's the little man? He talkin again?"

"No, but he'll talk to you. Even if he won't do it out loud to start with, you can—" Instead of finishing, she made a finger-gun and pointed it at his forehead.

"Not necessarily," Dick said. His smile revealed a bright new pair of false teeth. The Overlook had taken most of the last set on the night the boiler blew. Jack Torrance swung the mallet that took Dick's dentures and Wendy's ability to walk without a hitch in her stride, but they both understood it had really been the Overlook. "He's very powerful, Wendy. If he wants to block me out, he will. I know from my own experience. Besides, it'd be better if we talk with our mouths. Better for him. Now tell me everything that happened."

After she did that, Wendy took him into the bathroom. She had left the stains for him to see, like a beat cop preserving the scene of a crime for the forensic team. And there *had* been a crime. One against her boy.

Dick looked for a long time, not touching, then nodded. "Let's see if Danny's up and in the doins."

He wasn't, but Wendy's heart was lightened by the look of gladness that came into her son's face when he saw who was sitting beside him on the bed and shaking his shoulder.

(*hey Danny I brought you a present*)

(*it's not my birthday*)

Wendy watched them, knowing they were speaking but not knowing what it was about.

8

Dick said, "Get on up, honey. We're gonna take a walk on the beach."

(*Dick she came back Mrs. Massey from Room 217 came back*)

Dick gave his shoulder another shake. "Talk out loud, Dan. You're scarin your ma."

Danny said, "What's my present?"

Dick smiled. "That's better. I like to hear you, and Wendy does, too."

"Yes." It was all she dared say. Otherwise they'd hear the tremble in her voice and be concerned. She didn't want that.

"While we're gone, you might want to give the bathroom a cleaning," Dick said to her. "Have you got kitchen gloves?"

She nodded.

"Good. Wear them."

6

The beach was two miles away. The parking lot was surrounded by tawdry beachfront attractions—funnel cake concessions, hotdog stands, souvenir shops—but this was the tag end of the season, and none were doing much business. They had the beach itself almost entirely to themselves. On the ride from the apartment, Danny had held his present—an oblong package, quite heavy, wrapped in silver paper—on his lap.

"You can open it after we talk a bit," Dick said.

They walked just above the waves, where the sand was hard and gleaming. Danny walked slowly, because Dick was pretty old. Someday he'd die. Maybe even soon.

"I'm good to go another few years," Dick said. "Don't you worry about that. Now tell me about last night. Don't leave anything out."

It didn't take long. The hard part would have been finding words to explain the terror he now felt, and how it was mingled with a suffocating sense of certainty: now that she'd found him, she'd never leave. But because it was Dick, he didn't need words, although he found some.

"She'll come back. I know she will. She'll come back and come back until she gets me."

"Do you remember when we met?"

Although surprised at the change of direction, Danny nodded. It had been Hallorann who gave him and his parents the guided tour on their first day at the Overlook. Very long ago, that seemed.

"And do you remember the first time I spoke up inside your head?"

"I sure do."

"What did I say?"

"You asked me if I wanted to go to Florida with you."

"That's right. And how did it make you feel, to know you wasn't alone anymore? That you wasn't the only one?"

"It was great," Danny said. "It was so great."

"Yeah," Hallorann said. "Yeah, course it was."

They walked in silence for a bit. Little birds—peeps, Danny's mother called them—ran in and out of the waves.

"Did it ever strike you funny, how I showed up when you needed me?" He looked down at Danny and smiled. "No. It didn't. Why would it? You was just a child, but you're a little older now. A *lot* older in some ways. Listen to me, Danny. The world has a way of keeping things in balance. I believe that. There's a saying: When the pupil is ready, the teacher will appear. I was your teacher."

"You were a lot more than that," Danny said. He took Dick's hand. "You were my friend. You saved us."

Dick ignored this . . . or seemed to. "My gramma also had the shining—do you remember me telling you that?"

"Yeah. You said you and her could have long conversations without even opening your mouths."

"That's right. She taught me. And it was her *great*-gramma that taught her, way back in the slave days. Someday, Danny, it will be your turn to be the teacher. The pupil will come."

"If Mrs. Massey doesn't get me first," Danny said morosely.

They came to a bench. Dick sat down. "I don't dare go any further; I might not make it back. Sit beside me. I want to tell you a story."

"I don't want stories," Danny said. "She'll come back, don't you get it? She'll come *back* and come *back* and come *back*."

"Shut your mouth and open your ears. Take some instruction." Then Dick grinned, displaying his gleaming new dentures. "I think you'll get the point. You're far from stupid, honey."

7

Dick's mother's mother—the one with the shining—lived in Clearwater. She was the White Gramma. Not because she was Caucasian, of course, but because she was *good*. His father's father lived in Dunbrie, Mississippi, a rural community not far from Oxford. His wife had died long before Dick was born. For a man of color in that place and time, he was wealthy. He owned a funeral parlor. Dick and his parents visited four times a year, and young Dick Hallorann hated those visits. He was terrified of Andy Hallorann, and called him—only in his own mind, to speak it aloud would have earned him a smack across the chops—the Black Grampa.

"You know about kiddie-fiddlers?" Dick asked Danny. "Guys who want children for sex?"

"Sort of," Danny said cautiously. Certainly he knew not to talk to strangers, and never to get into a car with one. Because they might do stuff to you.

"Well, old Andy was more than a kiddie-fiddler. He was a damn sadist, as well."

"What's that?"

"Someone who enjoys giving pain."

Danny nodded in immediate understanding. "Like Frankie Listrone at school. He gives kids Indian burns and Dutch rubs. If he can't make you cry, he stops. If he can, he *never* stops."

"That's bad, but this was worse."

Dick lapsed into what would have looked like silence to a passerby, but the story went forward in a series of pictures and connecting phrases. Danny saw the Black Grampa, a tall man in a suit as black as he was, who wore a special kind of

(*fedora*)

hat on his head. He saw how there were always little buds of spittle at the corners of his mouth, and how his eyes were red-rimmed, like he was tired or had just gotten over crying. He saw how he would take Dick—younger than Danny was now, probably the same age he'd been that winter at the Overlook—on his lap. If they weren't alone, he might only tickle. If they were, he'd put his hand between Dick's legs and squeeze his balls until Dick thought he'd faint with the pain.

"Do you like that?" Grampa Andy would pant in his ear. He smelled of cigarettes and White Horse scotch. "Coss you do, every boy likes that. But even if you don't, you dassn't tell. If you do, I'll hurt you. I'll burn you."

"Holy shit," Danny said. "That's gross."

"There were other things, too," Dick said, "but I'll just tell you one. Grampy hired a woman to help out around the house after his wife died. She cleaned and cooked. At dinnertime, she'd slat out everything on the table at once, from salad to dessert, because that's the way ole Black Grampa liked it. Dessert was always cake or puddin. It was put down on a little plate or in a little dish next to your dinnerplate so you could look at it and want it while you plowed through the other muck. Grampa's hard and fast rule was you could *look* at dessert but you couldn't *eat* dessert unless you finished every bite of fried meat and boiled greens and mashed potatoes. You even had to clean up the gravy, which was lumpy and didn't have much taste. If it wasn't all gone, Black Grampa'd hand me a hunk of bread and say 'Sop er up with that, Dickie-Bird, make that plate shine like the dog licked it.' That's what he called me, Dickie-Bird.

"Sometimes I couldn't finish no matter what, and then I didn't get the cake or the puddin. He'd take it and eat it himself. And sometimes when I *could* finish all my dinner, I'd find he'd smashed a cigarette butt into my piece of cake or my vanilla puddin. He could do that because he always sat next to me. He'd make like it was a big joke. 'Whoops, missed the ashtray,' he'd say. My ma and pa never put a stop to it, although they must have known that even if it was a joke, it wasn't a fair one to play on a child. They just made out like it was a joke, too."

"That's really bad," Danny said. "Your folks should have stood up for you. My mom does. My daddy would, too."

"They were scairt of him. And they were right to be scairt. Andy Halloran was a bad, bad motorcycle. He'd say, 'Go on, Dickie, eat around it, that won't poison ya.' If I took a bite, he'd have Nonnie—that was his housekeeper's name—bring me a fresh dessert. If I wouldn't, it just sat there. It got so I could never finish my meal, because my stomach would get all upset."

"You should have moved your cake or puddin to the other side of your plate," Danny said.

"I tried that, sure, I wasn't born foolish. He'd just move it back, saying dessert went on the right." Dick paused, looking out at the water, where a long white boat was trundling slowly across the dividing line between the sky and the Gulf of Mexico. "Sometimes when he got me alone he bit me. And once, when I said I'd tell my pa if he didn't leave me alone, he put a cigarette out on my bare foot. He said, 'Tell him that, too, and see what good it does you. Your daddy knows my ways already and he'll never say a word, because he yella and because he wants the money I got in the bank when I die, which I ain't fixing to do soon.'"

Danny listened in wide-eyed fascination. He had always thought the story of Bluebeard was the scariest of all time, the scariest there ever could be, but this one was worse. Because it was true.

"Sometimes he said that he knew a bad man named Charlie Manx, and if I didn't do what he wanted, he'd call Charlie Manx on the long-distance and he'd come in his fancy car and take me away to a place for bad children. Then Grampa would put his hand between my legs and commence squeezing. 'So you ain't gonna say a thing, Dickie-Bird. If you do, ole Charlie will come and keep you with the other children he done stole until you die. And when you do, you'll go to hell and your body will burn forever. Because you peached. It don't matter if anybody believes you or not, peaching is peaching.'

"For a long time I believed the old bastard. I didn't even tell my White Gramma, the one with the shining, because I was afraid she'd think it was my fault. If I'd been older I would've known better, but I was just a kid." He paused. "There was something else, too. Do you know what it was, Danny?"

Danny looked into Dick's face for a long time, probing the thoughts and images behind his forehead. At last he said, "You wanted your father to get the money. But he never did."

"No. Black Grampa left it all to a home for Negro orphans in Alabama, and I bet I know why, too. But that's neither here nor there."

"And your good gramma never knew? She never guessed?"

"She knew there was *something,* but I kep it blocked away, and she left me alone about it. Just told me that when I was ready to talk, she was ready to listen. Danny, when Andy Halloran died—it was a stroke—I was the happiest boy on earth. My ma said I didn't have to go to the funeral, that I could stay with Gramma Rose—my White Gramma—if I wanted to, but I wanted to go. You bet I did. I wanted to make sure old Black Grampa was really dead.

"It rained that day. Everybody stood around the grave under black umbrellas. I watched his coffin—the biggest and best one in his shop, I have no doubt—go into the ground, and I thought about all the times he'd twisted my balls and all the cigarette butts in my cake and the one he put out on my foot and how he ruled the dinner table like the crazy old king in that Shakespeare play. But most of all I thought about Charlie Manx—who Grampa had no doubt made up out of whole cloth—and how Black Grampa could never call Charlie Manx on the long-distance to come in the night and take me away in his fancy car to live with the other stolen boys and girls.

"I peeped over the edge of the grave—'Let the boy see,' my pa said when my ma tried to pull me back—and I scoped the coffin down in that wet hole and I thought, 'Down there you're six feet closer to hell, Black Grampa, and pretty soon you'll be all the way, and I hope the devil gives you a thousand with a hand that's on fire.'"

Dick reached into his pants pocket and brought out a pack of Marlboros with a book of matches tucked under the cellophane. He put a cigarette in his mouth and then had to chase it with the match because his hand was trembling and his lips were trembling, too. Danny was astounded to see tears standing in Dick's eyes.

Now knowing where this story was headed, Danny asked: "When did he come back?"

Dick dragged deep on his cigarette and exhaled smoke through a smile. "You didn't need to peek inside my head to get that, did you?"

"Nope."

"Six months later. I came home from school one day and he was laying naked on my bed with his half-rotted prick all rared up. He said, 'You come on and sit on this, Dickie-Bird. You give me a thousand and I'll give you *two* thousand.' I screamed but there was no one there to hear it. My ma and pa, they was both working, my ma in a restaurant and my dad at a printing press. I ran out and slammed the door. And I heard Black Grampa get up . . . *thump* . . . and cross the room . . . *thump-thump-thump* . . . and what I heard next . . ."

"Fingernails," Danny said in a voice that was hardly there. "Scratching on the door."

"That's right. I didn't go in again until that night, when my ma and pa were both home. He was gone, but there were . . . leavings."

"Sure. Like in our bathroom. Because he was going bad."

"That's right. I changed the bed myself, which I could do because my ma showed me how two years before. She said I was too old to need a housekeeper anymore, that housekeepers were for little white boys and girls like the ones she took care of before she got her hostessing job at Berkin's Steak House. About a week later, I see ole Black Grampa in the park, a-settin in a swing. He had his suit on, but it was all covered with gray stuff—the mold that was growing on it down in his coffin, I think."

"Yeah," Danny said. He spoke in a glassy whisper. It was all he could manage.

"His fly was open, though, with his works stickin out. I'm sorry to tell you all this, Danny, you're too young to hear about such things, but you need to know."

"Did you go to the White Gramma then?"

"Had to. Because I knew what you know: he'd just keep comin back. Not like . . . Danny, have you ever seen dead people? *Regular* dead people, I mean." He laughed because that sounded funny. It did to Danny, too. "Ghosts."

"A few times. Once there were three of them standing around a railroad crossing. Two boys and a girl. Teenagers. I think . . . maybe they got killed there."

Dick nodded. "Mostly they stick close to where they crossed over until they finally get used to bein dead and move on. Some of the folks you saw in the Overlook were like that."

"I know." The relief in being able to talk about these things—to someone who *knew*—was indescribable. "And this one time there was a woman at a restaurant. The kind, you know, where they have tables outside?"

Dick nodded again.

"I couldn't see through that one, but no one else saw her, and when a waitress pushed in the chair she was sitting in, the ghost lady disappeared. Do you see them sometimes?"

"Not for years, but you're stronger in the shining than I was. It goes back some as you get older—"

"Good," Danny said fervently.

"—but you'll have plenty left even when you're grown up, I think, because you started with so much. Regular ghosts aren't like the woman you saw in Room 217 and again in your bathroom. That's right, isn't it?"

"Yes," Danny said. "Mrs. Massey's *real*. She leaves pieces of herself. You saw them. So did Mom . . . and she doesn't shine."

"Let's walk back," Dick said. "It's time you saw what I brought you."

8

The return to the parking lot was even slower, because Dick was winded. "Cigarettes," he said. "Don't ever start, Danny."

"Mom smokes. She doesn't think I know, but I do. Dick, what did your White Gramma do? She must have done something, because your Black Grampa never got you."

"She gave me a present, same like I'm gonna give you. That's what a teacher does when the pupil is ready. Learning itself is a present, you know. The best one anybody can give or get.

"She wouldn't call Grampa Andy by his name, she just called him"—Dick grinned—"the *preevert*. I said what you said, that he wasn't a ghost, he was real. And she said yes, that was true, because I was *making* him real. With the shining. She said that some spirits—angry spirits, mostly—won't go on from this world, because they know what's waiting for them is even worse. Most eventually starve away to nothing, but some of them find food. 'That's what the shining is to them, Dick,' she told me. 'Food. You're feeding that preevert. You don't mean to, but you are. He's like a mosquito who'll keep circling and then landing for more blood. Can't do nothing about that. What you *can* do is turn what he came for against him.'"

They were back at the Cadillac. Dick unlocked the doors, then slid behind the steering wheel with a sigh of relief. "Once upon a time I could've walked ten miles and run another five. Nowadays, a little walk down the beach and my back feels like a hoss kicked it. Go on, Danny. Open your present."

Danny stripped off the silver paper and discovered a box made of green-painted metal. On the front, below the latch, was a little keypad.

"Hey, neat!"

"Yeah? You like it? Good. I got it at the Western Auto. Pure American steel. The one White Gramma Rose gave me had a padlock, with a little key I wore around my neck, but that was long ago. This is the nineteen eighties, the modern age. See the number pad? What you do is put in five numbers you're sure you won't forget, then push the little button that says SET. Then, anytime you want to open the box, you punch your code."

Danny was delighted. "Thanks, Dick! I'll keep my special things in it!" These would include his best baseball cards, his Cub Scouts Compass Badge, his lucky green rock, and a picture of him and his father, taken on the front lawn of the apartment building where they'd lived in Boulder, before the Overlook. Before things turned bad.

"That's fine, Danny, I want you to do that, but I want you to do something else."

"What?"

"I want you to know this box, inside and out. Don't just look at it; touch it. Feel it all over. Then stick your nose inside and see if there's a smell. It needs to be your closest friend, at least for awhile."

"Why?"

"Because you're going to put another one just like it in your mind. One that's even more special. And the next time that Massey bitch comes around, you'll be ready for her. I'll tell you how, just like ole White Gramma told me."

Danny didn't talk much on the ride back to the apartment. He had a lot to think about. He held his present—a lockbox made of strong metal—on his lap.

9

Mrs. Massey returned a week later. She was in the bathroom again, this time in the tub. Danny wasn't surprised. A tub was where she had died, after all. This time he didn't run. This time he went inside and closed the door. She beckoned him forward, smiling.

Danny came, also smiling. In the other room, he could hear the television. His mother was watching *Three's Company*.

"Hello, Mrs. Massey," Danny said. "I brought you something."

At the last moment she understood and began to scream.

10

Moments later, his mom was knocking at the bathroom door. "Danny? Are you all right?"

"Fine, Mom." The tub was empty. There was some goo in it, but Danny thought he could clean that up. A little water would send it right down the drain. "Do you have to go? I'll be out pretty soon."

"No. I just . . . I thought I heard you call."

Danny grabbed his toothbrush and opened the door. "I'm a hundred percent cool. See?" He gave her a big smile. It wasn't hard, now that Mrs. Massey was gone.

The troubled look left her face. "Good. Make sure you brush the back ones. That's where the food goes to hide."

"I will, Mom."

From inside his head, far inside, where the twin of his special lockbox was stored on a special shelf, Danny could hear muffled screaming. He didn't mind. He thought it would stop soon enough, and he was right.

11

Two years later, on the day before the Thanksgiving break, halfway up a deserted stairwell in Alafia Elementary, Horace Derwent appeared to Danny Torrance. There was confetti on the shoulders of his suit. A little black mask hung from one decaying hand. He reeked of the grave. "Great party, isn't it?" he asked.

Danny turned and walked away, very quickly.

When school was over, he called Dick long-distance at the

restaurant where Dick worked in Key West. "Another one of the Overlook People found me. How many boxes can I have, Dick? In my head, I mean."

Dick chuckled. "As many as you need, honey. That's the beauty of the shining. You think my Black Grampa's the only one *I* ever had to lock away?"

"Do they die in there?"

This time there was no chuckle. This time there was a coldness in Dick's voice the boy had never heard before. "Do you care?"

Danny didn't.

When the onetime owner of the Overlook showed up again shortly after New Year's—this time in Danny's bedroom closet—Danny was ready. He went into the closet and closed the door. Shortly afterward, a second mental lockbox went up on the high mental shelf beside the one that held Mrs. Massey. There was more pounding, and some inventive cursing that Danny saved for his own later use. Pretty soon it stopped. There was silence from the Derwent lockbox as well as the Massey lockbox. Whether or not they were alive (in their undead fashion) no longer mattered.

What mattered was they were never getting out. He was safe.

That was what he thought then. Of course, he also thought he would never take a drink, not after seeing what it had done to his father.

Sometimes we just get it wrong.

RATTLESNAKE

Her name was Andrea Steiner, and she liked movies but she didn't like men. This wasn't surprising, since her father had raped her for the first time when she was eight. He had gone on raping her for that same number of years. Then she had put a stop to it, first popping his balls, one after the other, with one of her mother's knitting needles, and then putting that same needle, red and dripping, in her rapist-sire's left eyesocket. The balls had been easy, because he was sleeping, but the pain had been enough to wake him in spite of her special talent. She was a big girl, though, and he was drunk. She had been able to hold him down with her body just long enough to administer the coup de grâce.

Now she had years eight times four, she was a wanderer on the face of America, and an ex-actor had replaced the peanut farmer in the White House. The new fellow had an actor's unlikely black hair and an actor's charming, untrustworthy smile. Andi had seen one of his movies on TV. In it, the man who would be president played a guy who lost his legs when a train ran over them. She liked the idea of a man without legs; a man without legs couldn't chase you down and rape you.

Movies, they were the thing. Movies took you away. You could count on popcorn and happy endings. You got a man to go with you, that way it was a date and he paid. This movie was a good one, with fighting and kissing and loud music. It was called *Raiders of the Lost Ark.* Her current date had his hand under her skirt, high up on her bare thigh, but that was all right; a hand wasn't a prick. She had met him in a bar. She met most of the men she went on dates with in bars. He bought her a drink, but a free drink wasn't a date; it was just a pickup.

What's this about? he'd asked her, running the tip of his finger over her upper left arm. She was wearing a sleeveless blouse, so the tattoo showed. She liked the tattoo to show when she was out looking for a date. She wanted men to see it. They thought it was kinky. She had gotten it in San Diego the year after she killed her father.

It's a snake, she said. *A rattler. Don't you see the fangs?*

Of course he did. They were *big* fangs, out of all proportion to the head. A drop of poison hung from one.

He was a businessman type in an expensive suit, with lots of combed-back presidential hair and the afternoon off from whatever paper-pushing crap he did for work. His hair was mostly white instead of black and he looked about sixty. Close to twice her age. But that didn't matter to men. He wouldn't have cared if she was sixteen instead of thirty-two. Or eight. She remembered something her father had said once: *If they're old enough to pee, they're old enough for me.*

Of course I see them, the man who was now sitting beside her had said, *but what does it mean?*

Maybe you'll find out, Andi replied. She touched her upper lip with her tongue. *I have another tattoo. Somewhere else.*

Can I see it?

Maybe. Do you like movies?

He had frowned. *What do you mean?*

You want to date me, don't you?

He knew what that meant—or what it was supposed to mean. There were other girls in this place, and when they spoke of dates, they meant one thing. But it was not what Andi meant.

Sure. You're cute.

Then take me on a date. A real date. Raiders of the Lost Ark *is playing at the Rialto.*

I was thinking more of that little hotel two blocks down, darlin. A room with a wetbar and a balcony, how does that sound?

She had put her lips close to his ear and let her breasts press against his arm. *Maybe later. Take me to the movies first. Pay my way and buy me popcorn. The dark makes me amorous.*

And here they were, with Harrison Ford on the screen, big as a skyscraper and snapping a bullwhip in the desert dust. The old guy with the presidential hair had his hand under her skirt but she had a tub of popcorn placed firmly on her lap, making sure he could get most of the way down the third base line but not quite to home plate. He was trying to go higher, which was annoying because she wanted to see the end of the movie and find out what was in the Lost Ark. So . . .

2

At 2 p.m. on a weekday, the movie theater was almost deserted, but three people sat two rows back from Andi Steiner and her date. Two men, one quite old and one appearing on the edge of middle age (but appearances could be deceiving), flanked a woman of startling beauty. Her cheekbones were high, her eyes were gray, her complexion creamy. Her masses of black hair were tied back with a broad velvet ribbon. Usually she wore a hat—an old and battered tophat—but she had left it in her motorhome this day. You didn't wear a tall topper in a movie theater. Her name was Rose O'Hara, but the nomadic family she traveled with called her Rose the Hat.

The man edging into middle age was Barry Smith. Although one hundred percent Caucasian, he was known in this same family as Barry the Chink, because of his slightly upturned eyes.

"Now watch this," he said. "It's interesting."

"The *movie's* interesting," the old man—Grampa Flick—grunted. But that was just his usual contrariness. He was also watching the couple two rows down.

"It better be interesting," Rose said, "because the woman's not all that steamy. A little, but—"

"There she goes, there she goes," Barry said as Andi leaned over and put her lips to her date's ear. Barry was grinning, the box of gummy bears in his hand forgotten. "I've watched her do it three times and I still get a kick out of it."

3

Mr. Businessman's ear was filled with a thatch of wiry white hairs and clotted with wax the color of shit, but Andi didn't let that stop her; she wanted to blow this town and her finances were at a dangerously low ebb. "Aren't you tired?" she whispered in the disgusting ear. "Don't you want to go to sleep?"

The man's head immediately dropped onto his chest and he began to snore. Andi reached under her skirt, plucked up the relaxing hand, and placed it on the armrest. Then she reached into Mr. Businessman's expensive-looking suitcoat and began to rummage. His wallet was in the inside left pocket. That was good. She wouldn't have to make him get up off his fat ass. Once they were asleep, moving them could be tricky.

She opened the wallet, tossed the credit cards on the floor, and looked for a few moments at the pictures—Mr. Businessman with a bunch of other overweight Mr. Businessmen on the golf course; Mr. Businessman with his wife; a much younger Mr. Businessman standing in front of a Christmas tree with his son and two daughters. The daughters were wearing Santa hats and matching dresses. He probably hadn't been raping them, but it was not out of the question. Men would rape when they could get away with it, this she had learned. At her father's knee, so to speak.

There was over two hundred dollars in the bill compartment. She had been hoping for even more—the bar where she had met him catered to a better class of whore than those out by the airport—but it wasn't bad for a Thursday matinee, and there were always men who wanted to take a good-looking girl to the movies, where a little heavy petting would only be the appetizer. Or so they hoped.

4

"Okay," Rose murmured, and started to get up. "I'm convinced. Let's give it a shot."

But Barry put a hand on her arm, restraining her. "No, wait. Watch. This is the best part."

5

Andi leaned close to the disgusting ear again and whispered, "Sleep deeper. As deep as you can. The pain you feel will only be a dream." She opened her purse and took out a pearl-handled knife. It was small, but the blade was razor-sharp. "What will the pain be?"

"Only a dream," Mr. Businessman muttered into the knot of his tie.

"That's right, sweetie." She put an arm around him and quickly slashed double Vs into his right cheek—a cheek so fat it would soon be a jowl. She took a moment to admire her work in the chancy light of the projector's colored dream-beam. Then the blood sheeted down. He would wake up with his face on fire, the right arm of his expensive suitcoat drenched, and in need of an emergency room.

And how will you explain it to your wife? You'll think of something, I'm sure. But unless you have plastic surgery, you'll see my marks every time you look in the mirror. And every time you go looking for a little strange in one of the bars, you'll remember how you got bitten by a rattlesnake. One in a blue skirt and a white sleeveless blouse.

She tucked the two fifties and five twenties into her purse, clicked it shut, and was about to get up when a hand fell on her shoulder and a woman murmured in her ear. "Hello, dear. You can see the rest of the movie another time. Right now you're coming with us."

Andi tried to turn, but hands seized her head. The terrible thing about them was that they were *inside*.

After that—until she found herself in Rose's EarthCruiser in a going-to-seed campground on the outskirts of this Midwestern city—all was darkness.

6

When she woke up, Rose gave her a cup of tea and talked to her for a long time. Andi heard everything, but most of her attention was taken up by the woman who had abducted her. She was a presence, and that was putting it mildly. Rose the Hat was six feet tall, with long legs in tapered white slacks and high breasts inside a t-shirt branded with the UNICEF logo and motto: *Whatever It Takes To Save a Child*. Her face was that of a calm queen, serene and untroubled. Her hair, now unbound, tumbled halfway down her back. The scuffed tophat cocked on her head was jarring, but otherwise she was the most beautiful woman Andi Steiner had ever seen.

"Do you understand what I've been telling you? I'm giving you an opportunity here, Andi, and you should not take it lightly. It's been twenty years or more since we've offered anyone what I'm offering you."

"And if I say no? What then? Do you kill me? And take this . . ." What had she called it? "This steam?"

Rose smiled. Her lips were rich and coral pink. Andi, who considered herself asexual, nonetheless wondered what that lipstick would taste like.

"You don't have enough steam to bother with, dear, and what you *do* have would be far from yummy. It would taste the way the meat from a tough old cow tastes to a rube."

"To a what?"

"Never mind, just listen. We won't kill you. What we'll do if you say no is to wipe out all memory of this little conversation. You will find yourself on the side of the road outside some nothing town—

Topeka, maybe, or Fargo—with no money, no identification, and no memory of how you got there. The last thing you'll remember is going into that movie theater with the man you robbed and mutilated."

"He deserved to be mutilated!" Andi spat out.

Rose stood on her tiptoes and stretched, her fingers touching the roof of the RV. "That's your business, honeydoll, I'm not your psychiatrist." She wasn't wearing a bra; Andi could see the shifting punctuation marks of her nipples against her shirt. "But here's something to consider: we'll take your talent as well as your money and your no doubt bogus identification. The next time you suggest that a man go to sleep in a darkened movie theater, he'll turn to you and ask what the fuck you're talking about."

Andi felt a cold trickle of fear. "You can't do that." But she remembered the terribly strong hands that had reached inside her brain and felt quite sure this woman could. She might need a little help from her friends, the ones in the RVs and motorhomes gathered around this one like piglets at a sow's teats, but oh yes— she could.

Rose ignored this. "How old are you, dear?"

"Twenty-eight." She had been shading her age since hitting the big three-oh.

Rose looked at her, smiling, saying nothing. Andi met those beautiful gray eyes for five seconds, then had to drop her gaze. But what her eyes fell upon when she did were those smooth breasts, unharnessed but with no sign of a sag. And when she looked up again, her eyes only got as far as the woman's lips. Those coral-pink lips.

"You're thirty-two," Rose said. "Oh, it only shows a little— because you've led a hard life. A life on the run. But you're still pretty. Stay with us, live with us, and ten years from now you really will be twenty-eight."

"That's impossible."

Rose smiled. "A hundred years from now, you'll look and feel thirty-five. Until you take steam, that is. Then you'll be twenty-eight again, only you'll feel ten years younger. And you'll take steam often. Live long, stay young, and eat well: those are the things I'm offering. How do they sound?"

"Too good to be true," Andi said. "Like those ads about how you can get life insurance for ten dollars."

She wasn't entirely wrong. Rose hadn't told any lies (at least not yet), but there were things she wasn't saying. Like how steam was sometimes in short supply. Like how not everyone lived through the Turning. Rose judged this one might, and Walnut, the True's jackleg doctor, had cautiously concurred, but nothing was sure.

"And you and your friends call yourself—?"

"They're not my friends, they're my family. We're the True Knot." Rose laced her fingers together and held them in front of Andi's face. "And what's tied can never be untied. You need to understand that."

Andi, who already knew that a girl who has been raped can never be unraped, understood perfectly.

"Do I really have any other choice?"

Rose shrugged. "Only bad ones, dear. But it's better if you want it. It will make the Turning easier."

"Does it hurt? This Turning?"

Rose smiled and told the first outright lie. "Not at all."

7

A summer night on the outskirts of a Midwestern city.

Somewhere people were watching Harrison Ford snap his bullwhip; somewhere the Actor President was no doubt smiling his untrustworthy smile; here, in this campground, Andi Steiner was lying on a discount-store lawn recliner, bathed in the headlights of Rose's EarthCruiser and someone else's Winnebago. Rose had explained to her that, while the True Knot owned several campgrounds, this wasn't one of them. But their advance man was able to four-wall places like this, businesses tottering on the edge of insolvency. America was suffering a recession, but for the True, money was not a problem.

"Who is this advance man?" Andi had asked.

"Oh, he's a very winning fellow," Rose had said, smiling. "Able to charm the birdies down from the trees. You'll meet him soon."

"Is he your special guy?"

Rose had laughed at that and caressed Andi's cheek. The touch of her fingers caused a hot little worm of excitement in Andi's stomach. Crazy, but there it was. "You've got a twinkle, don't you? I think you'll be fine."

Maybe, but as she lay here, Andi was no longer excited, only scared. News stories slipped through her mind, ones about bodies found in ditches, bodies found in wooded clearings, bodies found at the bottom of dry wells. Women and girls. Almost always women and girls. It wasn't Rose who scared her—not exactly—and there were other women here, but there were also men.

Rose knelt beside her. The glare of the headlights should have turned her face into a harsh and ugly landscape of blacks and whites, but the opposite was true: it only made her more beautiful. Once again she caressed Andi's cheek. "No fear," she said. "No fear."

She turned to one of the other women, a pallidly pretty creature Rose called Silent Sarey, and nodded. Sarey nodded back and went into Rose's monster RV. The others, meanwhile, began to form a circle around the lawn recliner. Andi didn't like that. There was something *sacrificial* about it.

"No fear. Soon you'll be one of us, Andi. One *with* us."

Unless, Rose thought, *you cycle out. In which case, we'll just burn your clothes in the incinerator behind the comfort stations and move on tomorrow. Nothing ventured, nothing gained.*

But she hoped that wouldn't happen. She liked this one, and a sleeper talent would come in handy.

Sarey returned with a steel canister that looked like a thermos bottle. She handed it to Rose, who removed the red cap. Beneath was a nozzle and a valve. To Andi the canister looked like an unlabeled can of bug spray. She thought about bolting up from the recliner and running for it, then remembered the movie theater. The hands that had reached inside her head, holding her in place.

"Grampa Flick?" Rose asked. "Will you lead us?"

"Happy to." It was the old man from the theater. Tonight he was wearing baggy pink Bermuda shorts, white socks that climbed all the way up his scrawny shins to his knees, and Jesus sandals. To Andi he looked like Grandpa Walton after two years in a concentration camp. He raised his hands, and the rest raised theirs with him. Linked that way and silhouetted in the crisscrossing headlight beams, they looked like a chain of weird paperdolls.

"We are the True Knot," he said. The voice coming from that sunken chest no longer trembled; it was the deep and resonant voice of a much younger and stronger man.

"We are the True Knot," they responded. *"What is tied may never be untied."*

"Here is a woman," Grampa Flick said. "Would she join us? Would she tie her life to our life and be one with us?"

"Say yes," Rose said.

"Y-Yes," Andi managed. Her heart was no longer beating; it was thrumming like a wire.

Rose turned the valve on her canister. There was a small, rueful sigh, and a puff of silver mist escaped. Instead of dissipating on the light evening breeze, it hung just above the canister until Rose leaned forward, pursed those fascinating coral lips, and blew gently. The puff of mist—looking a bit like a comic-strip dialogue balloon without any words in it—drifted until it hovered above Andi's upturned face and wide eyes.

"We are the True Knot, and we endure," Grampa Flick proclaimed.

"Sabbatha hanti," the others responded.

The mist began to descend, very slowly.

"We are the chosen ones."

"Lodsam hanti," they responded.

"Breathe deep," Rose said, and kissed Andi softly on the cheek. "I'll see you on the other side."

Maybe.

"We are the fortunate ones."

"Cahanna risone hanti."

Then, all together: "We are the True Knot, and we . . ."

But Andi lost track of it there. The silvery stuff settled over her face and it was cold, cold. When she inhaled, it came to some sort of tenebrous life and began screaming inside her. A child made of mist—whether boy or girl she didn't know—was struggling to get away but someone was cutting. *Rose* was cutting, while the others stood close around her (in a knot), shining down a dozen flashlights, illuminating a slow-motion murder.

Andi tried to bolt up from the recliner, but she had no body to bolt with. Her body was gone. Where it had been was only pain in the shape of a human being. The pain of the child's dying, and of her own.

Embrace it. The thought was like a cool cloth pressed on the burning wound that was her body. *That's the only way through.*

I can't, I've been running from this pain my whole life.

Perhaps so, but you're all out of running room. Embrace it. Swallow it. Take steam or die.

8

The True stood with hands upraised, chanting the old words: *sabbatha hanti, lodsam hanti, cahanna risone hanti.* They watched as Andi Steiner's blouse flattened where her breasts had been, as her skirt puffed shut like a closing mouth. They watched as her face turned to milk-glass. Her eyes remained, though, floating like tiny balloons on gauzy strings of nerve.

But they're going to go, too, Walnut thought. *She's not strong enough. I thought maybe she was, but I was wrong. She may come back a time or two, but then she'll cycle out. Nothing left but her clothes.* He tried to recall his own Turning, and could only remember that the moon had been full and there had been a bonfire instead of headlights. A bonfire, the whicker of horses . . . and the pain. Could you actually remember pain? He didn't think so. You knew there was such a thing, and that you had suffered it, but that wasn't the same.

Andi's face swam back into existence like the face of a ghost above a medium's table. The front of her blouse plumped up in curves; her skirt swelled as her hips and thighs returned to the world. She shrieked in agony.

"We are the True Knot and we endure," they chanted in the crisscrossing beams of the RVs. "Sabbatha hanti. *We are the chosen ones,* lodsam hanti. *We are the fortunate ones,* cahanna risone hanti."* They would go on until it was over. One way or the other, it wouldn't take long.

Andi began to disappear again. Her flesh became cloudy glass through which the True could see her skeleton and the bone grin of her skull. A few silver fillings gleamed in that grin. Her disembodied eyes rolled wildly in sockets that were no longer there. She was still screaming, but now the sound was thin and echoing, as if it came from far down a distant hall.

9

Rose thought she'd give up, that was what they did when the pain became too much, but this was one tough babe. She came swirling back into existence, screaming all the way. Her newly arrived hands seized Rose's with mad strength and bore down. Rose leaned forward, hardly noticing the pain.

"I know what you want, honeydoll. Come back and you can have it." She lowered her mouth to Andi's, caressing Andi's upper lip with her tongue until the lip turned to mist. But the eyes stayed, fixed on Rose's.

"Sabbatha hanti," they chanted. *"Lodsam hanti. Cahanna risone hanti."*

Andi came back, growing a face around her staring, pain-filled eyes. Her body followed. For a moment Rose could see the bones of her arms, the bones in the fingers clutching hers, then they were once more dressed in flesh.

Rose kissed her again. Even in her pain Andi responded, and Rose breathed her own essence down the younger woman's throat.

I want this one. And what I want, I get.

Andi began to fade again, but Rose could feel her fighting it. Getting on top of it. Feeding herself with the screaming life-force she had breathed down her throat and into her lungs instead of trying to push it away.

Taking steam for the first time.

10

The newest member of the True Knot spent that night in Rose O'Hara's bed, and for the first time in her life found something in sex besides horror and pain. Her throat was raw from the screaming she'd done on the lawn recliner, but she screamed again as this new sensation—pleasure to match the pain of her Turning—took her body and once more seemed to render it transparent.

"Scream all you want," Rose said, looking up from between her thighs. "They've heard plenty of them. The good as well as the bad."

"Is sex like this for everybody?" If so, what she had missed! What her bastard father had stolen from her! And people thought *she* was a thief?

"It's like this for us, when we've taken steam," Rose said. "That's all you need to know."

She lowered her head and it began again.

11

Not long before midnight, Token Charlie and Baba the Russian were sitting on the lower step of Token Charlie's Bounder, sharing a joint and looking up at the moon. From Rose's EarthCruiser came more screams.

Charlie and Baba turned to each other and grinned.

"Someone is likin it," Baba remarked.

"What's not to like?" Charlie said.

12

Andi woke in the day's first early light with her head pillowed on Rose's breasts. She felt entirely different; she felt no different at all. She lifted her head and saw Rose looking at her with those remarkable gray eyes.

"You saved me," Andi said. "You brought me back."

"I couldn't have done it alone. You wanted to come." *In more ways than one, honeydoll.*

"What we did after . . . we can't do it again, can we?"

Rose shook her head, smiling. "No. And that's okay. Some experiences absolutely cannot be topped. Besides, my man will be back today."

"What's his name?"

"He answers to Henry Rothman, but that's just for the rubes. His True name is Crow Daddy."

"Do you love him? You do, don't you?"

Rose smiled, drew Andi closer, kissed her. But she did not answer.

"Rose?"

"Yes?"

"Am I . . . am I still human?"

To this Rose gave the same answer Dick Hallorann had once given young Danny Torrance, and in the same cold tone of voice: "Do you care?"

Andi decided she didn't. She decided she was home.

MAMA

1

There was a muddle of bad dreams—someone swinging a hammer and chasing him down endless halls, an elevator that ran by itself, hedges in the shapes of animals that came to life and closed in on him—and finally one clear thought: *I wish I were dead.*

Dan Torrance opened his eyes. Sunlight shot through them and into his aching head, threatening to set his brains on fire. The hangover to end all hangovers. His face was throbbing. His nostrils were clogged shut except for a tiny pinhole in the left one that allowed in a thread of air. Left one? No, it was the right. He could breathe through his mouth, but it was foul with the taste of whiskey and cigarettes. His stomach was a ball of lead, full of all the wrong things. *Morning-after junkbelly,* some old drinking buddy or other had called that woeful sensation.

Loud snoring from beside him. Dan turned his head that way, although his neck screamed in protest and another bolt of agony shot him through the temple. He opened his eyes again, but just a little; no more of that blazing sun, please. Not yet. He was lying on a bare mattress on a bare floor. A bare woman lay sprawled on her back beside him. Dan looked down and saw that he was also alfresco.

Her name is . . . Dolores? No. Debbie? That's closer, but not quite—

Deenie. Her name was Deenie. He had met her in a bar called the Milky Way, and it had all been quite hilarious until . . .

35

He couldn't remember, and one look at his hands—both swollen, the knuckles of the right scuffed and scabbed—made him decide he didn't want to remember. And what did it matter? The basic scenario never changed. He got drunk, someone said the wrong thing, chaos and bar-carnage followed. There was a dangerous dog inside his head. Sober, he could keep it on a leash. When he drank, the leash disappeared. *Sooner or later I'll kill someone.* For all he knew, he had last night.

Hey Deenie, squeeze my weenie.

Had he actually said that? He was terribly afraid he had. Some of it was coming back to him now, and even some was too much. Playing eightball. Trying to put a little extra spin on the cue and scratching it right off the table, the little chalk-smudged sonofabitch bouncing and rolling all the way to the jukebox that was playing—what else?—country music. He seemed to remember Joe Diffie. Why had he scratched so outrageously? Because he was drunk, and because Deenie was standing behind him, Deenie had been squeezing his weenie just below the line of the table and he was showing off for her. All in good fun. But then the guy in the Case cap and the fancy silk cowboy shirt had laughed, and that was his mistake.

Chaos and bar-carnage.

Dan touched his mouth and felt plump sausages where normal lips had been when he left that check-cashing joint yesterday afternoon with a little over five hundred bucks in his front pants pocket.

At least all my teeth seem to be—

His stomach gave a liquid lurch. He burped up a mouthful of sour gunk that tasted of whiskey and swallowed it back. It burned going down. He rolled off the mattress onto his knees, staggered to his feet, then swayed as the room began to do a gentle tango. He was hungover, his head was bursting, his gut was filled with whatever cheap food he'd put in it last night to tamp down the booze . . . but he was also still drunk.

He hooked his underpants off the floor and left the bedroom

with them clutched in his hand, not quite limping but definitely favoring his left leg. He had a vague memory—one he hoped would never sharpen—of the Case cowboy throwing a chair. That was when he and Deenie-squeeze-my-weenie had left, not quite running but laughing like loons.

Another lurch from his unhappy gut. This time it was accompanied by a clench that felt like a hand in a slick rubber glove. That released all the puke triggers: the vinegar smell of hardcooked eggs in a big glass jar, the taste of barbecue-flavored pork rinds, the sight of french fries drowning in a ketchup nosebleed. All the crap he'd crammed into his mouth last night between shots. He was going to spew, but the images just kept on coming, revolving on some nightmare gameshow prize wheel.

What have we got for our next contestant, Johnny? Well, Bob, it's a great big platter of GREASY SARDINES!

The bathroom was directly across a short stub of hall. The door was open, the toilet seat up. Dan lunged, fell on his knees, and spewed a great flood of brownish-yellow stuff on top of a floating turd. He looked away, groped for the flush, found it, pushed it. Water cascaded, but there was no accompanying sound of draining water. He looked back and saw something alarming: the turd, probably his own, rising toward the pee-splashed rim of the toilet bowl on a sea of half-digested bar-snacks. Just before the toilet could overspill, making this morning's banal horrors complete, something cleared its throat in the pipe and the whole mess flushed away. Dan threw up again, then sat on his heels with his back against the bathroom wall and his throbbing head lowered, waiting for the tank to refill so he could flush a second time.

No more. I swear it. No more booze, no more bars, no more fights. Promising himself this for the hundredth time. Or the thousandth.

One thing was certain: he had to get out of this town or he might be in trouble. *Serious* trouble was not out of the question.

Johnny, what have we got for today's grand prize winner? Bob, it's TWO YEARS IN STATE FOR ASSAULT AND BATTERY!

And . . . the studio audience goes wild.

The toilet tank had quieted its noisy refill. He reached for the handle to flush away The Morning After, Part Two, then paused, regarding the black hole of his short-term memory. Did he know his name? Yes! Daniel Anthony Torrance. Did he know the name of the chick snoring on the mattress in the other room? Yes! Deenie. He didn't recall her last name, but it was likely she had never told him. Did he know the current president's name?

To Dan's horror, he didn't, not at first. The guy had a funky Elvis haircut and played the sax—quite badly. But the name . . . ?

Do you even know where you are?

Cleveland? Charleston? It was one or the other.

As he flushed the toilet, the president's name arrived in his head with splendid clarity. And Dan wasn't in either Cleveland *or* Charleston. He was in Wilmington, North Carolina. He worked as an orderly at Grace of Mary Hospital. Or had. It was time to move on. If he got to some other place, some *good* place, he might be able to quit the drinking and start over.

He got up and looked in the mirror. The damage wasn't as bad as he'd feared. Nose swelled but not actually broken—at least he didn't think so. Crusts of dried blood above his puffy upper lip. There was a bruise on his right cheekbone (the Case cowboy must have been a lefty) with the bloody imprint of a ring sitting in the middle of it. Another bruise, a big one, was spreading in the cup of his left shoulder. That, he seemed to remember, had been from a pool cue.

He looked in the medicine cabinet. Amid tubes of makeup and cluttered bottles of over-the-counter medicine, he found three prescription bottles. The first was Diflucan, commonly prescribed for yeast infections. It made him glad he was circumcised. The second was Darvon Comp 65. He opened it, saw half a dozen capsules, and put three in his pocket for later reference. The last scrip was for Fioricet, and the bottle—thankfully—was almost full. He swallowed three with cold water. Bending over the basin made his headache worse than ever, but he thought he would soon get relief. Fioricet, intended for migraine and tension headaches, was a guaranteed hangover killer. Well . . . almost guaranteed.

He started to close the cabinet, then took another look. He moved some of the crap around. No birth control ring. Maybe it was in her purse. He hoped so, because he hadn't been carrying a rubber. If he'd fucked her—and although he couldn't remember for sure, he probably had—he'd ridden in bareback.

He put on his underwear and shuffled back to the bedroom, standing in the doorway for a moment and looking at the woman who had brought him home last night. Arms and legs splayed, everything showing. Last night she had looked like the goddess of the Western world in her thigh-high leather skirt and cork sandals, her cropped top and hoop earrings. This morning he saw the sagging white dough of a growing boozegut, and the second chin starting to appear under the first.

He saw something worse: she wasn't a woman, after all. Probably not jailbait (please God not jailbait), but surely no more than twenty and maybe still in her late teens. On one wall, chillingly childish, was a poster of KISS with Gene Simmons spewing fire. On another was a cute kitten with startled eyes, dangling from a tree branch. HANG IN THERE, BABY, this poster advised.

He needed to get out of here.

Their clothes were tangled together at the foot of the mattress. He separated his t-shirt from her panties, yanked it over his head, then stepped into his jeans. He froze with the zipper halfway up, realizing that his left front pocket was much flatter than it had been when he left the check-cashing joint the previous afternoon.

No. It can't be.

His head, which had begun to feel the teeniest bit better, started to throb again as his heartbeat picked up speed, and when he shoved his hand into the pocket, it brought up nothing but a ten-dollar bill and two toothpicks, one of which poked under his index fingernail and into the sensitive meat beneath. He hardly noticed.

We didn't drink up five hundred dollars. No way we did. We'd be dead if we drank up that much.

His wallet was still at home in his hip pocket. He pulled it out, hoping against hope, but no joy. He must have transferred the ten he usually kept there to his front pocket at some point. The front pocket made it tougher for barroom dips, which now seemed like quite the joke.

He looked at the snoring, splayed girl-woman on the mattress and started for her, meaning to shake her awake and ask her what she'd done with his fucking money. *Choke* her awake, if that was what it took. But if she'd stolen from him, why had she brought him home? And hadn't there been something else? Some other adventure after they left the Milky Way? Now that his head was clearing, he had a memory—hazy, but probably valid—of them taking a cab to the train station.

I know a guy who hangs out there, honey.

Had she really said that, or was it only his imagination?

She said it, all right. I'm in Wilmington, Bill Clinton's the president, and we went to the train station. Where there was indeed a guy. The kind who likes to do his deals in the men's room, especially when the customer has a slightly rearranged face. When he asked who teed off on me, I told him—

"I told him he should mind his beeswax," Dan muttered.

When the two of them went in, Dan had been meaning to buy a gram to keep his date happy, no more than that, and only if it wasn't half Manitol. Coke might be Deenie's thing but it wasn't his. Rich man's Anacin, he'd heard it called, and he was far from rich. But then someone had come out of one of the stalls. A business type with a briefcase banging his knee. And when Mr. Businessman went to wash his hands at one of the basins, Dan had seen flies crawling all over his face.

Deathflies. Mr. Businessman was a dead man walking and didn't know it.

So instead of going small, he was pretty sure he'd gone big. Maybe he'd changed his mind at the last moment, though. It was possible; he could remember so little.

I remember the flies, though.

Yes. He remembered those. Booze tamped down the shining, knocked it unconscious, but he wasn't sure the flies were even a part of the shining. They came when they would, drunk or sober.

He thought again: *I need to get out of here.*
He thought again: *I wish I were dead.*

2

Deenie made a soft snorting sound and turned away from the merciless morning light. Except for the mattress on the floor, the room was devoid of furniture; there wasn't even a thrift-shop bureau. The closet stood open, and Dan could see the majority of Deenie's meager wardrobe heaped in two plastic laundry baskets. The few items on hangers looked like barhopping clothes. He could see a red t-shirt with SEXY GIRL printed in spangles on the front, and a denim skirt with a fashionably frayed hem. There were two pairs of sneakers, two pairs of flats, and one pair of strappy high-heel fuck-me shoes. No cork sandals, though. No sign of his own beat-up Reeboks, for that matter.

Dan couldn't remember them kicking off their shoes when they came in, but if they had, they'd be in the living room, which he *could* remember—vaguely. Her purse might be there, too. He might have given her whatever remained of his cash for safekeeping. It was unlikely but not impossible.

He walked his throbbing head down the short hall to what he assumed was the apartment's only other room. On the far side was a kitchenette, the amenities consisting of a hotplate and a bar refrigerator tucked under the counter. In the living area was a sofa hemorrhaging stuffing and propped up at one end with a couple of bricks. It faced a big TV with a crack running down the middle of the glass. The crack had been mended with a strip of packing tape that now dangled by one corner. A couple of flies were stuck to the tape, one still struggling feebly. Dan eyed it with morbid fascination, reflecting (not for the first time) that the hungover eye had a weird ability to find the ugliest things in any given landscape.

There was a coffee table in front of the sofa. On it was an ashtray filled with butts, a baggie filled with white powder, and a *People* magazine with more blow scattered across it. Beside it, completing the picture, was a dollar bill, still partly rolled up. He didn't know how much they had snorted, but judging by how much still remained, he could kiss his five hundred dollars goodbye.

Fuck. I don't even like *coke. And how did I snort it, anyway? I can hardly breathe.*

He hadn't. *She* had snorted it. He had rubbed it on his gums. It was all starting to come back to him. He would have preferred it stay away, but too late.

The deathflies in the restroom, crawling in and out of Mr. Businessman's mouth and over the wet surfaces of his eyes. Mr. Dealerman asking what Dan was looking at. Dan telling him it was nothing, it didn't matter, let's see what you've got. It turned out Mr. Dealerman had plenty. They usually did. Next came the ride back to her place in another taxi, Deenie already snorting from the back of her hand, too greedy—or too needy—to wait. The two of them trying to sing "Mr. Roboto."

He spied her sandals and his Reeboks right inside the door, and here were more golden memories. She hadn't kicked the sandals off, only dropped them from her feet, because by then he'd had his hands planted firmly on her ass and she had her legs wrapped around his waist. Her neck smelled of perfume, her breath of barbecue-flavored pork rinds. They had been gobbling them by the handful before moving on to the pool table.

Dan put on his sneakers, then walked across to the kitchenette, thinking there might be instant coffee in the single cupboard. He didn't find coffee, but he did see her purse, lying on the floor. He thought he could remember her tossing it at the sofa and laughing when it missed. Half the crap had spilled out, including a red imitation leather wallet. He scooped everything back inside and took it over to the kitchenette. Although he knew damned well that his money was now living in the pocket of Mr. Dealerman's designer jeans, part of him insisted that there must be *some* left, if only because he needed some to be left. Ten dollars was enough for three drinks or two six-packs, but it was going to take more than that today.

He fished out her wallet and opened it. There were some pictures—a couple of Deenie with some guy who looked too much like her not to be a relative, a couple of Deenie holding a baby, one of Deenie in a prom dress next to a bucktoothed kid in a gruesome blue tux. The bill compartment was bulging. This gave him hope until he pulled it open and saw a swatch of food stamps. There was also some currency: two twenties and three tens.

That's my money. What's left of it, anyway.

He knew better. He never would have given some shitfaced pickup his week's pay for safekeeping. It was hers.

Yes, but hadn't the coke been her idea? Wasn't she the reason he was broke as well as hungover this morning?

No. You're hungover because you're a drunk. You're broke because you saw the deathflies.

It might be true, but if she hadn't insisted they go to the train station and score, he never would have *seen* the deathflies.

She might need that seventy bucks for groceries.

Right. A jar of peanut butter and a jar of strawberry jam. Also a loaf of bread to spread it on. She had food stamps for the rest.

Or rent. She might need it for that.

If she needed rent money, she could peddle the TV. Maybe her dealer would take it, crack and all. Seventy dollars wouldn't go very far on a month's rent, anyway, he reasoned, even for a dump like this one.

That's not yours, doc. It was his mother's voice, the last one he needed to hear when he was savagely hungover and in desperate need of a drink.

"Fuck you, Ma." His voice was low but sincere. He took the money, stuffed it in his pocket, put the billfold back in the purse, and turned around.

A kid was standing there.

He looked about eighteen months old. He was wearing an Atlanta Braves t-shirt. It came down to his knees, but the diaper underneath showed anyway, because it was loaded and hanging just above his ankles. Dan's heart took an enormous leap in his chest and his head gave a sudden terrific whammo, as if Thor had swung his hammer in there. For a moment he was absolutely sure he was going to stroke out, have a heart attack, or both.

Then he drew in a deep breath and exhaled. "Where did *you* come from, little hero?"

"Mama," the kid said.

Which in a way made perfect sense—Dan, too, had come from his mama—but it didn't help. A terrible deduction was trying to form itself in his thumping head, but he didn't want anything to do with it.

He saw you take the money.

Maybe so, but that wasn't the deduction. If the kid saw him take it, so what? He wasn't even two. Kids that young accepted everything adults did. If he saw his mama walking on the ceiling with fire shooting from her fingertips, he'd accept that.

"What's your name, hero?" His voice was throbbing in time with his heart, which still hadn't settled down.

"Mama."

Really? The other kids are gonna have fun with that when you get to high school.

"Did you come from next door? Or down the hall?"

Please say yes. Because here's the deduction: if this kid is Deenie's, then she went out barhopping and left him locked in this shitty apartment. Alone.

"Mama!"

Then the kid spied the coke on the coffee table and trotted toward it with the sodden crotch of his diaper swinging.

"Canny!"

"No, that's not candy," Dan said, although of course it was: nose candy.

Paying no attention, the kid reached for the white powder with one hand. As he did, Dan saw bruises on his upper arm. The kind left by a squeezing hand.

He grabbed the kid around the waist and between the legs. As he swung him up and away from the table (the sodden diaper squeezing pee through his fingers to patter on the floor), Dan's head filled with an image that was brief but excruciatingly clear: the Deenie look-alike in the wallet photo, picking the kid up and shaking him. Leaving the marks of his fingers.

(*Hey Tommy what part of* get the fuck out *don't you understand?*)

(*Randy don't he's just a baby*)

Then it was gone. But that second voice, weak and remonstrating, had been Deenie's, and he understood that Randy was her older brother. It made sense. Not every abuser was the boyfriend. Sometimes it was the brother. Sometimes the uncle. Sometimes

(*come out you worthless pup come out and take your medicine*)

it was even dear old Dad.

He carried the baby—Tommy, his name was Tommy—into the bedroom. The kid saw his mother and immediately began wriggling. "Mama! Mama! *Mama!*"

When Dan set him down, Tommy trotted to the mattress and crawled up beside her. Although sleeping, Deenie put her arm around him and hugged him to her. The Braves shirt pulled up, and Dan saw more bruises on the kid's legs.

The brother's name is Randy. I could find him.

This thought was as cold and clear as lake ice in January. If he handled the picture from the wallet and concentrated, ignoring the pounding of his head, he probably *could* find the big brother. He had done such things before.

I could leave a few bruises of my own. Tell him the next time I'll kill him.

Only there wasn't going to be a next time. Wilmington was done. He was never going to see Deenie or this desperate little apartment again. He was never going to think of last night or this morning again.

This time it was Dick Hallorann's voice. *No, honey. Maybe you can put the things from the Overlook away in lockboxes, but not memories. Never those. They're the* real *ghosts.*

He stood in the doorway, looking at Deenie and her bruised boy. The kid had gone back to sleep, and in the morning sun, the two of them looked almost angelic.

She's no angel. Maybe she didn't leave the bruises, but she went out partying and left him alone. If you hadn't been there when he woke up and walked into the living room . . .

Canny, the kid had said, reaching for the blow. Not good. Something needed to be done.

Maybe, but not by me. I'd look good showing up at DHS to complain about child neglect with this face, wouldn't I? Reeking of booze and puke. Just an upstanding citizen doing his civic duty.

You can put her money back, Wendy said. *You can do that much.*

He almost did. Really. He took it out of his pocket and had it right there in his hand. He even strolled it over to her purse, and the walk must have done him good, because he had an idea.

Take the coke, if you've got to take something. You can sell what's left for a hundred bucks. Maybe even two hundred, if it hasn't been stomped on too much.

Only, if his potential buyer turned out to be a narc—it would be just his luck—he'd wind up in jail. Where he might also find himself nailed for whatever stupid shit had gone down in the Milky Way. The cash was way safer. Seventy bucks in all.

I'll split it, he decided. *Forty for her and thirty for me.*

Only, thirty wouldn't do him much good. And there were the food stamps—a wad big enough to choke a horse. She could feed the kid with those.

He picked up the coke and the dusty *People* magazine and put them on the kitchenette counter, safely out of the kid's reach. There was a scrubbie in the sink, and he used it on the coffee table, cleaning up the leftover shake. Telling himself that if she came stumbling out while he was doing it, he would give her back her goddam money. Telling himself that if she went on snoozing, she deserved whatever she got.

Deenie didn't come out. She went on snoozing.

Dan finished cleaning up, tossed the scrubbie back in the sink, and thought briefly about leaving a note. But what would it say? *Take better care of your kid, and by the way, I took your cash?*

Okay, no note.

He left with the money in his left front pocket, being careful not to slam the door on his way out. He told himself he was being considerate.

3

Around noon—his hangover headache a thing of the past thanks to Deenie's Fioricet and a Darvon chaser—he approached an establishment called Golden's Discount Liquors & Import Beers. This was in the old part of town, where the establishments were brick, the sidewalks were largely empty, and the pawnshops (each displaying an admirable selection of straight razors) were many. His intention was to buy a very large bottle of very cheap whiskey, but what he saw out front changed his mind. It was a shopping cart loaded with a bum's crazy assortment of possessions. The bum in question was inside, haranguing the clerk. There was a blanket, rolled up and tied with twine, on top of the cart. Dan could see a couple of stains, but on the whole it didn't look bad. He took it and walked briskly away with it under his arm. After stealing seventy dollars from a single mother with a substance abuse problem, taking a bum's magic carpet seemed like small shit indeed. Which might have been why he felt smaller than ever.

I am the Incredible Shrinking Man, he thought, hurrying around the corner with his new prize. *Steal a few more things and I will vanish entirely from sight.*

He was listening for the outraged caws of the bum—the crazier they were, the louder they cawed—but there was nothing. One more corner and he could congratulate himself on a clean getaway.

Dan turned it.

4

That evening found him sitting at the mouth of a large stormdrain on the slope beneath the Cape Fear Memorial Bridge. He had a room, but there was the small matter of stacked-up back rent, which he had absolutely promised to pay as of 5 p.m. yesterday. Nor was that all. If he returned to his room, he might be invited to visit a certain fortresslike municipal building on Bess Street, to answer questions about a certain bar altercation. On the whole, it seemed safer to stay away.

There was a downtown shelter called Hope House (which the winos of course called Hopeless House), but Dan had no intention of going there. You could sleep free, but if you had a bottle they'd take it away. Wilmington was full of by-the-night flops and cheap motels where nobody gave a shit what you drank, snorted, or injected, but why would you waste good drinking money on a bed and a roof when the weather was warm and dry? He could worry about beds and roofs when he headed north. Not to mention getting his few possessions out of the room on Burney Street without his landlady's notice.

The moon was rising over the river. The blanket was spread out behind him. Soon he would lie down on it, pull it around him in a cocoon, and sleep. He was just high enough to be happy. The takeoff and the climb-out had been rough, but now all that low-altitude turbulence was behind him. He supposed he wasn't leading what straight America would call an exemplary life, but for the time being, all was fine. He had a bottle of Old Sun (purchased at a liquor store a prudent distance from Golden's Discount) and half a hero sandwich for breakfast tomorrow. The future was cloudy, but tonight the moon was bright. All was as it should be.

(*Canny*)

Suddenly the kid was with him. Tommy. Right here with him. Reaching for the blow. Bruises on his arm. Blue eyes.

(*Canny*)

He saw this with an excruciating clarity that had nothing to do with the shining. And more. Deenie lying on her back, snoring. The red imitation leather wallet. The wad of food stamps with U.S. DEPARTMENT OF AGRICULTURE printed on them. The money. The seventy dollars. Which he had taken.

Think about the moon. Think about how serene it looks rising over the water.

For awhile he did, but then he saw Deenie on her back, the red imitation leather wallet, the wad of food stamps, the pitiful crumple of cash (much of it now gone). Most clearly of all he saw the kid reaching for the blow with a hand that looked like a starfish. Blue eyes. Bruised arm.

Canny, he said.

Mama, he said.

Dan had learned the trick of measuring out his drinks; that way the booze lasted longer, the high was mellower, and the next day's headache lighter and more manageable. Sometimes, though, the measuring thing went wrong. Shit happened. Like at the Milky Way. That had been more or less an accident, but tonight, finishing the bottle in four long swallows, was on purpose. Your mind was a blackboard. Booze was the eraser.

He lay down and pulled the stolen blanket around him. He waited for unconsciousness, and it came, but Tommy came first. Atlanta Braves shirt. Sagging diaper. Blue eyes, bruised arm, starfish hand.

Canny. Mama.

I will never speak of this, he told himself. *Not to anyone.*

As the moon rose over Wilmington, North Carolina, Dan Torrance lapsed into unconsciousness. There were dreams of the Overlook, but he would not remember them upon waking. What he remembered upon waking were the blue eyes, the bruised arm, the reaching hand.

He managed to get his possessions and went north, first to upstate New York, then to Massachusetts. Two years passed. Sometimes he helped people, mostly old people. He had a way of doing that. On too many drunk nights, the kid would be the last thing he thought of and the first thing that came to mind on the hungover mornings-after. It was the kid he always thought of when he told himself he was going to quit the drinking. Maybe next week; next month for sure. The kid. The eyes. The arm. The reaching starfish hand.

Canny.

Mama.

PART ONE

ABRA

CHAPTER ONE

WELCOME TO TEENYTOWN

1

After Wilmington, the daily drinking stopped.

He'd go a week, sometimes two, without anything stronger than diet soda. He'd wake up without a hangover, which was good. He'd wake up thirsty and miserable—*wanting*—which wasn't. Then there would come a night. Or a weekend. Sometimes it was a Budweiser ad on TV that set him off—fresh-faced young people with nary a beergut among them, having cold ones after a vigorous volleyball game. Sometimes it was seeing a couple of nice-looking women having after-work drinks outside some pleasant little café, the kind of place with a French name and lots of hanging plants. The drinks were almost always the kind that came with little umbrellas. Sometimes it was a song on the radio. Once it was Styx, singing "Mr. Roboto." When he was dry, he was completely dry. When he drank, he got drunk. If he woke up next to a woman, he thought of Deenie and the kid in the Braves t-shirt. He thought of the seventy dollars. He even thought of the stolen blanket, which he had left in the stormdrain. Maybe it was still there. If so, it would be moldy now.

Sometimes he got drunk and missed work. They'd keep him on for awhile—he was good at what he did—but then would come a day. When it did, he would say thank you very much and board a bus. Wilmington became Albany and Albany became Utica. Utica became New Paltz. New Paltz gave way to Sturbridge, where he got drunk at an outdoor folk concert and woke up the next day in jail with a broken wrist. Next up was Weston, after that came a nursing home on Martha's Vineyard, and boy, *that* gig didn't last long. On his third day the head nurse smelled booze on his breath and it was seeya, wouldn't want to beya. Once he crossed the path of the True Knot without realizing it. Not in the top part of his mind, anyway, although lower down—in the part that *shone*—there was something. A smell, fading and unpleasant, like the smell of burned rubber on a stretch of turnpike where there has been a bad accident not long before.

From Martha's Vineyard he took MassLines to Newburyport. There he found work in a don't-give-much-of-a-shit veterans' home, the kind of place where old soldiers were sometimes left in wheelchairs outside empty consulting rooms until their peebags overflowed onto the floor. A lousy place for patients, a better one for frequent fuckups like himself, although Dan and a few others did as well by the old soldiers as they could. He even helped a couple get over when their time came. That job lasted awhile, long enough for the Saxophone President to turn the White House keys over to the Cowboy President.

Dan had a few wet nights in Newburyport, but always with the next day off, so it was okay. After one of these mini-sprees, he woke up thinking *at least I left the food stamps.* That brought on the old psychotic gameshow duo.

Sorry, Deenie, you lose, but nobody leaves empty-handed. What have we got for her, Johnny?

Well, Bob, Deenie didn't win any money, but she's leaving with our new home game, several grams of cocaine, and a great big wad of FOOD STAMPS!

What Dan got was a whole month without booze. He did it, he guessed, as a weird kind of penance. It occurred to him more than once that if he'd had Deenie's address, he would have sent her that crappy seventy bucks long ago. He would have sent her twice that much if it could have ended the memories of the kid in the Braves t-shirt and the reaching starfish hand. But he didn't have the address, so he stayed sober instead. Scourging himself with whips. *Dry* ones.

Then one night he passed a drinking establishment called the Fisherman's Rest and through the window spied a good-looking blonde sitting alone at the bar. She was wearing a tartan skirt that ended at mid-thigh and she looked lonely and he went in and it turned out she was newly divorced and wow, that was a shame, maybe she'd like some company, and three days later he woke up with that same old black hole in his memory. He went to the veterans' center where he had been mopping floors and changing lightbulbs, hoping for a break, but no dice. Don't-give-much-of-a-shit wasn't quite the same as don't-give-*any*-shit; close but no cigar. Leaving with the few items that had been in his locker, he recalled an old Bobcat Goldthwait line: "My job was still there, but somebody else was doing it." So he boarded another bus, this one headed for New Hampshire, and before he got on, he bought a glass container of intoxicating liquid.

He sat all the way in back in the Drunk Seat, the one by the toilet. Experience had taught him that if you intended to spend a bus trip getting smashed, that was the seat to take. He reached into the brown paper sack, loosened the cap on the glass container of intoxicating liquid, and smelled the brown smell. That smell could talk, although it only had one thing to say: *Hello, old friend.*

He thought *Canny.*

He thought *Mama.*

He thought of Tommy going to school by now. Always assuming good old Uncle Randy hadn't killed him.

He thought, *The only one who can put on the brakes is you.*

This thought had come to him many times before, but now it was followed by a new one. *You don't have to live this way if you don't want to. You* can, *of course . . . but you don't have to.*

That voice was so strange, so unlike any of his usual mental dialogues, that he thought at first he must be picking it up from someone else—he could do that, but he rarely got uninvited transmissions anymore. He had learned to shut them off.

Nevertheless he looked up the aisle, almost positive he would see someone looking back at him. No one was. Everyone was sleeping, talking with their seatmates, or staring out at the gray New England day.

You don't have to live this way if you don't want to.

If only that were true. Nevertheless, he tightened the cap on the bottle and put it on the seat beside him. Twice he picked it up. The first time he put it down. The second time he reached into the bag and unscrewed the cap again, but as he did, the bus pulled into the New Hampshire welcome area just across the state line. Dan filed into the Burger King with the rest of the passengers, pausing only long enough to toss the paper bag into one of the trash containers. Stenciled on the side of the tall green can were the words IF YOU NO LONGER NEED IT, LEAVE IT HERE.

Wouldn't that be nice, Dan thought, hearing the clink as it landed. *Oh God, wouldn't that be nice.*

2

An hour and a half later, the bus passed a sign reading WELCOME TO FRAZIER, WHERE THERE'S A REASON FOR EVERY SEASON! And, below that, HOME OF TEENYTOWN!

The bus stopped at the Frazier Community Center to take on passengers, and from the empty seat next to Dan, where the bottle had rested for the first part of the trip, Tony spoke up. Here was a voice Dan recognized, although Tony hadn't spoken so clearly in years.

(this is the place)

As good as any, Dan thought.

He grabbed his duffel from the overhead rack and got off. He stood on the sidewalk and watched the bus pull away. To the west, the White Mountains sawed at the horizon. In all his wanderings he had avoided mountains, especially the jagged monsters that broke the country in two. Now he thought, *I've come back to the high country*

56

after all. I guess I always knew I would. But these mountains were gentler than the ones that still sometimes haunted his dreams, and he thought he could live with them, at least for a little while. If he could stop thinking about the kid in the Braves t-shirt, that is. If he could stop using the booze. There came a time when you realized that moving on was pointless. That you took yourself with you wherever you went.

A snow flurry, fine as wedding lace, danced across the air. He could see that the shops lining the wide main street catered mostly to the skiers who'd come in December and the summer people who'd come in June. There would probably be leaf-peepers in September and October, too, but this was what passed for spring in northern New England, an edgy eight weeks chrome-plated with cold and damp. Frazier apparently hadn't figured out a reason for this season yet, because the main drag—Cranmore Avenue—was all but deserted.

Dan slung the duffel over his shoulder and strolled slowly north. He stopped outside a wrought-iron fence to look at a rambling Victorian home flanked on both sides by newer brick buildings. These were connected to the Victorian by covered walkways. There was a turret at the top of the mansion on the left side, but none on the right, giving the place a queerly unbalanced look that Dan sort of liked. It was as if the big old girl were saying *Yeah, part of me fell off. What the fuck. Someday it'll happen to you.* He started to smile. Then the smile died.

Tony was in the window of the turret room, looking down at him. He saw Dan looking up and waved. The same solemn wave Dan remembered from his childhood, when Tony had come often. Dan closed his eyes, then opened them. Tony was gone. Had never been there in the first place, how could he have been? The window was boarded up.

The sign on the lawn, gold letters on a green background the same shade as the house itself, read HELEN RIVINGTON HOUSE.

They have a cat in there, he thought. *A gray cat named Audrey.*

This turned out to be partly right and partly wrong. There *was* a cat, and it was gray, but it was a neutered tom and its name wasn't Audrey.

Dan looked at the sign for a long time—long enough for the clouds to part and send down a biblical beam—and then he walked on. Although the sun was now bright enough to twinkle the chrome of the few slant-parked cars in front of Olympia Sports and the Fresh Day Spa, the snow still swirled, making Dan think of something his mother had said during similar spring weather, long ago, when they had lived in Vermont: *The devil's beating his wife.*

3

A block or two up from the hospice, Dan stopped again. Across the street from the town municipal building was the Frazier town common. There was an acre or two of lawn, just beginning to show green, a bandstand, a softball field, a paved basketball half-court, picnic tables, even a putting green. All very nice, but what interested him was a sign reading

VISIT TEENYTOWN
FRAZIER'S "SMALL WONDER"
AND RIDE THE TEENYTOWN RAILWAY!

It didn't take a genius to see that Teenytown was a teeny replica of Cranmore Avenue. There was the Methodist church he had passed, its steeple rising all of seven feet into the air; there was the Music Box Theater; Spondulicks Ice Cream; Mountain Books; Shirts & Stuff; the Frazier Gallery, Fine Prints Our Specialty. There was also a perfect waist-high miniature of the single-turreted Helen Rivington House, although the two flanking brick buildings had been omitted. Perhaps, Dan thought, because they were butt-ugly, especially compared to the centerpiece.

Beyond Teenytown was a miniature train with TEENYTOWN RAILWAY painted on passenger cars that were surely too small to hold anyone larger than toddler size. Smoke was puffing from the stack of a bright red locomotive about the size of a Honda Gold Wing motorcycle. He could hear the rumble of a diesel engine. Printed on the side of the loco, in old-fashioned gold flake letters, was THE HELEN RIVINGTON. Town patroness, Dan supposed. Somewhere in Frazier there was probably a street named after her, too.

He stood where he was for a bit, although the sun had gone back in and the day had grown cold enough for him to see his breath. As a kid he'd always wanted an electric train set and had never had one. Yonder in Teenytown was a jumbo version kids of all ages could love.

He shifted his duffel bag to his other shoulder and crossed the street. Hearing Tony again—and seeing him—was unsettling, but right now he was glad he'd stopped here. Maybe this really was the place he'd been looking for, the one where he'd finally find a way to right his dangerously tipped life.

You take yourself with you, wherever you go.

He pushed the thought into a mental closet. It was a thing he was good at. There was all sorts of stuff in that closet.

4

A cowling surrounded the locomotive on both sides, but he spied a footstool standing beneath one low eave of the Teenytown Station, carried it over, and stood on it. The driver's cockpit contained two sheepskin-covered bucket seats. It looked to Dan as if they had been scavenged from an old Detroit muscle car. The cockpit and controls also looked like modified Detroit stock, with the exception of an old-fashioned Z-shaped shifter jutting up from the floor. There was no shift pattern; the original knob had been replaced with a grinning skull wearing a bandanna faded from red to pallid pink by years of gripping hands. The top half of the steering wheel had been cut off, so that what remained looked like the steering yoke of a light plane. Painted in black on the dashboard, fading but legible, was TOP SPEED 40 DO NOT EXCEED.

"Like it?" The voice came from directly behind him.

Dan wheeled around, almost falling off the stool. A big weathered hand gripped his forearm, steadying him. It was a guy who looked to be in his late fifties or early sixties, wearing a padded denim jacket and a red-checked hunting cap with the earflaps down. In his free hand was a toolkit with PROPERTY OF FRAZIER MUNICIPAL DEPT Dymo-taped across the top.

"Hey, sorry," Dan said, stepping off the stool. "I didn't mean to—"

"S'all right. People stop to look all the time. Usually model-train buffs. It's like a dream come true for em. We keep em away in the summer when the place is jumpin and the *Riv* runs every hour or so, but this time of year there's no we, just me. And I don't mind." He stuck out his hand. "Billy Freeman. Town maintenance crew. The *Riv*'s my baby."

Dan took the offered hand. "Dan Torrance."

Billy Freeman eyed the duffel. "Just got off the bus, I 'magine. Or are you ridin your thumb?"

"Bus," Dan said. "What does this thing have for an engine?"

"Well now, that's interesting. Probably never heard of the Chevrolet Veraneio, didja?"

He hadn't, but knew anyway. Because *Freeman* knew. Dan didn't think he'd had such a clear shine in years. It brought a ghost of delight that went back to earliest childhood, before he had discovered how dangerous the shining could be.

"Brazilian Suburban, wasn't it? Turbodiesel."

Freeman's bushy eyebrows shot up and he grinned. "Goddam right! Casey Kingsley, he's the boss, bought it at an auction last year. It's a corker. Pulls like a sonofabitch. The instrument panel's from a Suburban, too. The seats I put in myself."

The shine was fading now, but Dan got one last thing. "From a GTO Judge."

Freeman beamed. "That's right. Found em in a junkyard over

Sunapee way. The shifter's a high-hat from a 1961 Mack. Nine-speed. Nice, huh? You lookin for work or just lookin?"

Dan blinked at the sudden change of direction. *Was* he looking for work? He supposed he was. The hospice he'd passed on his amble up Cranmore Avenue would be the logical place to start, and he had an idea—didn't know if it was the shining or just ordinary intuition—that they'd be hiring, but he wasn't sure he wanted to go there just yet. Seeing Tony in the turret window had been unsettling.

Also, Danny, you want to be a little bit farther down the road from your last drink before you show up there askin for a job application form. Even if the only thing they got is runnin a buffer on the night shift.

Dick Hallorann's voice. Christ. Dan hadn't thought of Dick in a long time. Maybe not since Wilmington.

With summer coming—a season for which Frazier most definitely had a reason—people would be hiring for all sorts of things. But if he had to choose between a Chili's at the local mall and Teenytown, he definitely chose Teenytown. He opened his mouth to answer Freeman's question, but Hallorann spoke up again before he could.

You're closing in on the big three-oh, honey. You could be runnin out of chances.

Meanwhile, Billy Freeman was looking at him with open and artless curiosity.

"Yes," he said. "I'm looking for work."

"Workin in Teenytown, wouldn't last long, y'know. Once summer comes and the schools let out, Mr. Kingsley hires local. Eighteen to twenty-two, mostly. The selectmen expect it. Also, kids work cheap." He grinned, exposing holes where a couple of teeth had once resided. "Still, there are worse places to make a buck. Outdoor work don't look so good today, but it won't be cold like this much longer."

No, it wouldn't be. There were tarps over a lot of stuff on the common, but they'd be coming off soon, exposing the superstructure of small-town resort summer: hotdog stands, ice cream booths, a circular something that looked to Dan like a merry-go-round. And there was the train, of course, the one with the teeny passenger cars and the big turbodiesel engine. If he could stay off the sauce and prove trustworthy, Freeman or the boss—Kingsley—might let him drive it a time or two. He'd like that. Farther down the line, when the municipal department hired the just-out-of-school local kids, there was always the hospice.

If he decided to stay, that was.

You better stay somewhere, Hallorann said—this was Dan's day for hearing voices and seeing visions, it seemed. *You better stay somewhere soon, or you won't be able to stay anywhere.*

He surprised himself by laughing. "It sounds good to me, Mr. Freeman. It sounds really good."

5

"Done any grounds maintenance?" Billy Freeman asked. They were walking slowly along the flank of the train. The tops of the cars only came up to Dan's chest, making him feel like a giant.

"I can weed, plant, and paint. I know how to run a leaf blower and a chainsaw. I can fix small engines if the problem isn't too complicated. And I can manage a riding mower without running over any little kids. The train, now . . . that I don't know about."

"You'd need to get cleared by Kingsley for that. Insurance and shit. Listen, have you got references? Mr. Kingsley won't hire without em."

"A few. Mostly janitorial and hospital orderly stuff. Mr. Freeman—"

"Just Billy'll do."

"Your train doesn't look like it could carry passengers, Billy. Where would they sit?"

Billy grinned. "Wait here. See if you think this is as funny as I do. I never get tired of it."

Freeman went back to the locomotive and leaned in. The engine, which had been idling lazily, began to rev and send up rhythmic jets of dark smoke. There was a hydraulic whine along the whole length of *The Helen Rivington*. Suddenly the roofs of the passenger wagons and the yellow caboose—nine cars in all—began to rise. To Dan it looked like the tops of nine identical convertibles all going up at the same time. He bent down to look in the windows and saw hard plastic seats running down the center of each car. Six in the passenger wagons and two in the caboose. Fifty in all.

When Billy came back, Dan was grinning. "Your train must look very weird when it's full of passengers."

"Oh yeah. People laugh their asses off and burn yea film, takin pitchers. Watch this."

There was a steel-plated step at the end of each passenger car. Billy used one, walked down the aisle, and sat. A peculiar optical illusion took hold, making him look larger than life. He waved grandly to Dan, who could imagine fifty Brobdingnagians, dwarfing the train upon which they rode, pulling grandly out of Teenytown Station.

As Billy Freeman rose and stepped back down, Dan applauded. "I'll bet you sell about a billion postcards between Memorial Day and Labor Day."

"Bet your ass." Billy rummaged in his coat pocket, brought out a battered pack of Duke cigarettes—a cut-rate brand Dan knew well, sold in bus stations and convenience stores all over America—and held it out. Dan took one. Billy lit them up.

"I better enjoy it while I can," Billy said, looking at his cigarette. "Smoking'll be banned here before too many more years. Frazier Women's Club's already talkin about it. Bunch of old biddies if you ask me, but you know what they say—the hand that rocks the fuckin cradle rules the fuckin world." He jetted smoke from his nostrils. "Not that most of *them* have rocked a cradle since Nixon was president. Or needed a Tampax, for that matter."

"Might not be the worst thing," Dan said. "Kids copy what they see in their elders." He thought of his father. The only thing Jack Torrance had liked better than a drink, his mother had once said, not long before she died, was a dozen drinks. Of course what

Wendy had liked was her cigarettes, and they had killed her. Once upon a time Dan had promised himself he'd never get going with that habit, either. He had come to believe that life was a series of ironic ambushes.

Billy Freeman looked at him, one eye squinted mostly shut. "I get feelins about people sometimes, and I got one about you." He pronounced *got* as *gut,* in the New England fashion. "Had it even before you turned around and I saw your face. I think you might be the right guy for the spring cleanin I'm lookin at between now and the end of May. That's how it feels to me, and I trust my feelins. Prob'ly crazy."

Dan didn't think it was crazy at all, and now he understood why he had heard Billy Freeman's thoughts so clearly, and without even trying. He remembered something Dick Hallorann had told him once—Dick, who had been his first adult friend. *Lots of people have got a little of what I call the shining, but mostly it's just a twinkle—the kind of thing that lets em know what the DJ's going to play next on the radio or that the phone's gonna ring pretty soon.*

Billy Freeman had that little twinkle. That gleam.

"I guess this Cary Kingsley would be the one to talk to, huh?"

"Casey, not Cary. But yeah, he's the man. He's run municipal services in this town for twenty-five years."

"When would be a good time?"

"Right about now, I sh'd think." Billy pointed. "Yonder pile of bricks across the street's the Frazier Municipal Building and town offices. Mr. Kingsley's in the basement, end of the hall. You'll know you're there when you hear disco music comin down through the ceiling. There's a ladies' aerobics class in the gym every Tuesday and Thursday."

"All right," Dan said, "that's just what I'm going to do."

"Got your references?"

"Yes." Dan patted the duffel, which he had leaned against Teenytown Station.

"And you didn't write them yourself, nor nothin?"

Danny smiled. "No, they're straight goods."

"Then go get im, tiger."

"Okay."

"One other thing," Billy said as Dan started away. "He's death on drinkin. If you're a drinkin man and he asts you, my advice is . . . lie."

Dan nodded and raised his hand to show he understood. That was a lie he had told before.

6

Judging by his vein-congested nose, Casey Kingsley had not always been death on drinkin. He was a big man who didn't so much inhabit his small, cluttered office as wear it. Right now he was rocked back in the chair behind his desk, going through Dan's references, which were neatly kept in a blue folder. The back of Kingsley's head almost touched the downstroke of a plain wooden cross hanging on the wall beside a framed photo of his family. In the picture, a younger, slimmer Kingsley posed with his wife and three bathing-suited kiddos on a beach somewhere. Through the ceiling, only slightly muted, came the sound of the Village People singing "YMCA," accompanied by the enthusiastic stomp of many feet. Dan imagined a gigantic centipede. One that had recently been to the local hairdresser and was wearing a bright red leotard about nine yards long.

"Uh-huh," Kingsley said. "Uh-huh . . . yeah . . . right, right, right . . ."

There was a glass jar filled with hard candies on the corner of his desk. Without looking up from Dan's thin sheaf of references, he took off the top, fished one out, and popped it into his mouth. "Help yourself," he said.

"No, thank you," Dan said.

A queer thought came to him. Once upon a time, his father had probably sat in a room like this, being interviewed for the position of caretaker at the Overlook Hotel. What had he been thinking? That he really needed a job? That it was his last chance? Maybe. Probably. But of course, Jack Torrance had had hostages to fortune. Dan did not. He could drift on for awhile if this didn't work out. Or try his luck at the hospice. But . . . he liked the town common. He liked the train, which made adults of ordinary size look like Goliaths. He liked Teenytown, which was absurd and cheerful and somehow brave in its self-important small-town-America way. And he liked Billy Freeman, who had a pinch of the shining and probably didn't even know it.

Above them, "YMCA" was replaced by "I Will Survive." As if he had just been waiting for a new tune, Kingsley slipped Dan's references back into the folder's pocket and passed them across the desk.

He's going to turn me down.

But after a day of accurate intuitions, this one was off the mark. "These look fine, but it strikes me that you'd be a lot more comfortable working at Central New Hampshire Hospital or the hospice here in town. You might even qualify for Home Helpers—I see you've got a few medical and first aid qualifications. Know your way around a defibrillator, according to these. Heard of Home Helpers?"

"Yes. And I thought about the hospice. Then I saw the town common, and Teenytown, and the train."

Kingsley grunted. "Probably wouldn't mind taking a turn at the controls, would you?"

Dan lied without hesitation. "No, sir, I don't think I'd care for that." To admit he'd like to sit in the scavenged GTO driver's seat and lay his hands on that cut-down steering wheel would almost certainly lead to a discussion of his driver's license, then to a further discussion of how he'd lost it, and then to an invitation to leave Mr. Casey Kingsley's office forthwith. "I'm more of a rake-and-lawnmower guy."

"More of a short-term employment guy, too, from the looks of this paperwork."

"I'll settle someplace soon. I've worked most of the wanderlust out of my system, I think." He wondered if that sounded as bullshitty to Kingsley as it did to him.

"Short term's about all I can offer you," Kingsley said. "Once the schools are out for the summer—"

"Billy told me. If I decide to stay once summer comes, I'll try the hospice. In fact, I might put in an early application, unless you'd rather I don't do that."

"I don't care either way." Kingsley looked at him curiously. "Dying people don't bother you?"

Your mother died there, Danny thought. The shine wasn't gone after all, it seemed; it was hardly even hiding. *You were holding her hand when she passed. Her name was Ellen.*

"No," he said. Then, with no reason why, he added: "We're all dying. The world's just a hospice with fresh air."

"A philosopher, yet. Well, Mr. Torrance, I think I'm going to take you on. I trust Billy's judgment—he rarely makes a mistake about people. Just don't show up late, don't show up drunk, and don't show up with red eyes and smelling of weed. If you do any of those things, down the road you'll go, because the Rivington House won't have a thing to do with you—I'll make sure of it. Are we clear on that?"

Dan felt a throb of resentment

(*officious prick*)

but suppressed it. This was Kingsley's playing field and Kingsley's ball. "Crystal."

"You can start tomorrow, if that suits. There are plenty of rooming houses in town. I'll make a call or two if you want. Can you stand paying ninety a week until your first paycheck comes in?"

"Yes. Thank you, Mr. Kingsley."

Kingsley waved a hand. "In the meantime, I'd recommend the Red Roof Inn. My ex-brother-in-law runs it, he'll give you a rate. We good?"

"We are." It had all happened with remarkable speed, the way the last few pieces drop into a complicated thousand-piece jigsaw puzzle. Dan told himself not to trust the feeling.

Kingsley rose. He was a big man and it was a slow process. Dan also got to his feet, and when Kingsley stuck his ham of a hand over the cluttered desk, Dan shook it. Now from overhead came the sound of KC and the Sunshine Band telling the world that's the way they liked it, oh-ho, uh-huh.

"I hate that boogie-down shit," Kingsley said.

No, Danny thought. *You don't. It reminds you of your daughter, the one who doesn't come around much anymore. Because she still hasn't forgiven you.*

"You all right?" Kingsley asked. "You look a little pale."

"Just tired. It was a long bus ride."

The shining was back, and strong. The question was, why now?

7

Three days into the job, ones Dan spent painting the bandstand and blowing last fall's dead leaves off the common, Kingsley ambled across Cranmore Avenue and told him he had a room on Eliot Street, if he wanted it. Private bathroom part of the deal, tub and shower. Eighty-five a week. Dan wanted it.

"Go on over on your lunch break," Kingsley said. "Ask for Mrs. Robertson." He pointed a finger that was showing the first gnarls of arthritis. "And don't you fuck up, Sunny Jim, because she's an old pal of mine. Remember that I vouched for you on some pretty thin paper and Billy Freeman's intuition."

Dan said he wouldn't fuck up, but the extra sincerity he tried to inject into his voice sounded phony to his own ears. He was thinking of his father again, reduced to begging jobs from a wealthy old friend after losing his teaching position in Vermont. It was strange to feel sympathy for a man who had almost killed you, but the sympathy was there. Had people felt it necessary to tell his father not to fuck up? Probably. And Jack Torrance had fucked up anyway. Spectacularly. Five stars. Drinking was undoubtedly a part of it, but when you were down, some guys just seemed to feel an urge to walk up your back and plant a foot on your neck instead of helping you to stand. It was lousy, but so much of human nature was. Of course when you were running with the bottom dogs, what you mostly saw were paws, claws, and assholes.

"And see if Billy can find some boots that'll fit you. He's squirreled away about a dozen pairs in the equipment shed, although the last time I looked, only half of them matched."

The day was sunny, the air balmy. Dan, who was working in jeans and a Utica Blue Sox t-shirt, looked up at the nearly cloudless sky and then back at Casey Kingsley.

"Yeah, I know how it looks, but this is mountain country, pal. NOAA claims we're going to have a nor'easter, and it'll drop maybe a foot. Won't last long—poor man's fertilizer is what New Hampshire folks call April snow—but there's also gonna be gale-force winds. So they say. I hope you can use a snowblower as well as a leaf blower." He paused. "I also hope your back's okay, because you and Billy'll be picking up plenty of dead limbs tomorrow. Might be cutting up some fallen trees, too. You okay with a chainsaw?"

"Yes, sir," Dan said.

"Good."

8

Dan and Mrs. Robertson came to amicable terms; she even offered him an egg salad sandwich and a cup of coffee in the communal kitchen. He took her up on it, expecting all the usual questions about what had brought him to Frazier and where he had been before. Refreshingly, there were none. Instead she asked him if he had time to help her close the shutters on the downstairs windows in case they really did get what she called "a cap o' wind." Dan agreed. There weren't many mottoes he lived by, but one was always get in good with the landlady; you never know when you might have to ask her for a rent extension.

Back on the common, Billy was waiting with a list of chores.

The day before, the two of them had taken the tarps off all the kiddie rides. That afternoon they put them back on, and shuttered the various booths and concessions. The day's final job was backing the *Riv* into her shed. Then they sat in folding chairs beside the Teenytown station, smoking.

"Tell you what, Danno," Billy said, "I'm one tired hired man."

"You're not the only one." But he felt okay, muscles limber and tingling. He'd forgotten how good outdoors work could be when you weren't also working off a hangover.

The sky had scummed over with clouds. Billy looked up at them and sighed. "I hope to God it don't snow n blow as hard as the radio says, but it probably will. I found you some boots. They don't look like much, but at least they match."

Dan took the boots with him when he walked across town to his new accommodations. By then the wind was picking up and the day was growing dark. That morning, Frazier had felt on the edge of summer. This evening the air held the face-freezing dampness of coming snow. The side streets were deserted and the houses buttoned up.

Dan turned the corner from Morehead Street onto Eliot and paused. Blowing down the sidewalk, attended by a skeletal scutter of last year's autumn leaves, was a battered tophat, such as a magician might wear. *Or maybe an actor in an old musical comedy,* he thought. Looking at it made him feel cold in his bones, because it wasn't there. Not really.

He closed his eyes, slow-counted to five with the strengthening wind flapping the legs of his jeans around his shins, then opened them again. The leaves were still there, but the tophat was gone. It had just been the shining, producing one of its vivid, unsettling, and usually senseless visions. It was always stronger when he'd been sober for a little while, but never as strong as it had been since coming to Frazier. It was as if the air here were different, somehow. More conducive to those strange transmissions from Planet Elsewhere. Special.

The way the Overlook was special.

"No," he said. "No, I don't believe that."

A few drinks and it all goes away, Danny. Do you believe that*?*

Unfortunately, he did.

9

Mrs. Robertson's was a rambling old Colonial, and Dan's third-floor room had a view of the mountains to the west. That was a panorama he could have done without. His recollections of the Overlook had faded to hazy gray over the years, but as he unpacked his few things, a memory surfaced . . . and it *was* a kind of surfacing, like some nasty organic artifact (the decayed body of a small animal, say) floating to the surface of a deep lake.

It was dusk when the first real snow came. We stood on the porch of that big old empty hotel, my dad in the middle, my mom on one side, me on the other. He had his arms around us. It was okay then. He wasn't drinking then. At first the snow fell in perfectly straight lines, but then the wind picked up and it started to blow sideways, drifting against the sides of the porch and coating those—

He tried to block it off, but it got through.

—those hedge animals. The ones that sometimes moved around when you weren't looking.

He turned away from the window, his arms rashed out in gooseflesh. He'd gotten a sandwich from the Red Apple store and had planned to eat it while he started the John Sandford paperback he'd also picked up at the Red Apple, but after a few bites he rewrapped the sandwich and put it on the windowsill, where it would stay cold. He might eat the rest later, although he didn't think he'd be staying up much past nine tonight; if he got a hundred pages into the book, he'd be doing well.

Outside, the wind continued to rise. Every now and then it gave a bloodcurdling scream around the eaves that made him look up from his book. Around eight thirty, the snow began. It was heavy and wet, quickly coating his window and blocking his view of the mountains. In a way, that was worse. The snow had blocked the windows in the Overlook, too. First just on the first floor . . . then on the second . . . and finally on the third.

Then they had been entombed with the lively dead.

My father thought they'd make him the manager. All he had to do was show his loyalty. By giving them his son.

"His only begotten son," Dan muttered, then looked around as if someone else had spoken . . . and indeed, he did not feel alone. Not quite alone. The wind shrieked down the side of the building again, and he shuddered.

Not too late to go back down to the Red Apple. Grab a bottle of something. Put all these unpleasant thoughts to bed.

No. He was going to read his book. Lucas Davenport was on the case, and he was going to read his book.

He closed it at quarter past nine and got into another rooming-house bed. *I won't sleep,* he thought. *Not with the wind screaming like that.*

But he did.

10

He was sitting at the mouth of the stormdrain, looking down a scrubgrass slope at the Cape Fear River and the bridge that spanned it. The night was clear and the moon was full. There was no wind, no snow. And the Overlook was gone. Even if it hadn't burned to the ground during the tenure of the Peanut Farmer President, it would have been over a thousand miles from here. So why was he so frightened?

Because he wasn't alone, that was why. There was someone behind him.

"Want some advice, Honeybear?"

The voice was liquid, wavering. Dan felt a chill go rushing down his back. His legs were colder still, prickled out in starpoints of gooseflesh. He could see those white bumps because he was wearing shorts. Of course he was wearing shorts. His brain might be that of a grown man, but it was currently sitting on top of a five-year-old's body.

Honeybear. Who—?

But he knew. He had told Deenie his name, but she didn't use it, just called him Honeybear instead.

You don't remember that, and besides, this is just a dream.

Of course it was. He was in Frazier, New Hampshire, sleeping while a spring snowstorm howled outside Mrs. Robertson's rooming house. Still, it seemed wiser not to turn around. And safer—that, too.

"No advice," he said, looking out at the river and the full moon. "I've been advised by experts. The bars and barbershops are full of them."

"Stay away from the woman in the hat, Honeybear."

What hat? he could have asked, but really, why bother? He knew the hat she was talking about, because he had seen it blowing down the sidewalk. Black as sin on the outside, lined with white silk on the inside.

"She's the Queen Bitch of Castle Hell. If you mess with her, she'll eat you alive."

He turned his head. He couldn't help it. Deenie was sitting behind him in the stormdrain with the bum's blanket wrapped around her naked shoulders. Her hair was plastered to her cheeks. Her face was bloated and dripping. Her eyes were cloudy. She was dead, probably years in her grave.

You're not real, Dan tried to say, but no words came out. He was five again, Danny was five, the Overlook was ashes and bones, but here was a dead woman, one he had stolen from.

"It's all right," she said. Bubbling voice coming from a swollen throat. "I sold the coke. Stepped on it first with a little sugar and got two hundred." She grinned, and water spilled through her teeth. "I liked you, Honeybear. That's why I came to warn you. *Stay away from the woman in the hat.*"

"False face," Dan said . . . but it was Danny's voice, the high, frail, chanting voice of a child. "False face, not there, not real."

He closed his eyes as he had often closed them when he had seen terrible things in the Overlook. The woman began to scream, but he wouldn't open his eyes. The screaming went on, rising and falling, and he realized it was the scream of the wind. He wasn't in Colorado and he wasn't in North Carolina. He was in New Hampshire. He'd had a bad dream, but the dream was over.

11

According to his Timex, it was two in the morning. The room was cold, but his arms and chest were slimy with sweat.

Want some advice, Honeybear?

"No," he said. "Not from you."

She's dead.

There was no way he could know that, but he did. Deenie—who had looked like the goddess of the Western world in her thigh-high leather skirt and cork sandals—was dead. He even knew how she had done it. Took pills, pinned up her hair, climbed into a bathtub filled with warm water, went to sleep, slid under, drowned.

The roar of the wind was dreadfully familiar, loaded with hollow threat. Winds blew everywhere, but it only sounded like this in the high country. It was as if some angry god were pounding the world with an air mallet.

I used to call his booze the Bad Stuff, Dan thought. *Only sometimes it's the Good Stuff. When you wake up from a nightmare that you know is at least fifty percent shining, it's the Very Good Stuff.*

One drink would send him back to sleep. Three would guarantee not just sleep but dreamless sleep. Sleep was nature's doctor, and right now Dan Torrance felt sick and in need of strong medicine.

Nothing's open. You lucked out there.

Well. Maybe.

He turned on his side, and something rolled against his back when he did. No, not something. Some*one*. Someone had gotten into bed with him. *Deenie* had gotten into bed with him. Only it felt too small to be Deenie. It felt more like a—

He scrambled out of bed, landed awkwardly on the floor, and looked over his shoulder. It was Deenie's little boy, Tommy. The right side of his skull was caved in. Bone splinters protruded through bloodstained fair hair. Gray scaly muck—brains—was drying on one cheek. He couldn't be alive with such a hellacious wound, but he was. He reached out to Dan with one starfish hand.

"Canny," he said.

The screaming began again, only this time it wasn't Deenie and it wasn't the wind.

This time it was him.

12

When he woke for the second time—real waking, this time—he wasn't screaming at all, only making a kind of low growling deep in his chest. He sat up, gasping, the bedclothes puddled around his waist. There was no one else in his bed, but the dream hadn't yet dissolved, and looking wasn't enough. He threw back the bedclothes, and that still wasn't enough. He ran his hands down the bottom sheet, feeling for fugitive warmth, or a dent that might have been made by small hips and buttocks. Nothing. Of course not. So then he looked under the bed and saw only his borrowed boots.

The wind was blowing less strongly now. The storm wasn't over, but it was winding down.

He went to the bathroom, then whirled and looked back, as if expecting to surprise someone. There was just the bed, with the covers now lying on the floor at the foot. He turned on the light over the sink, splashed his face with cold water, and sat down on the closed lid of the commode, taking long breaths, one after the other. He thought about getting up and grabbing a cigarette from the pack lying beside his book on the room's one small table, but his legs felt rubbery and he wasn't sure they'd hold him. Not yet, anyway. So he sat. He could see the bed and the bed was empty. The whole room was empty. No problem there.

Only . . . it didn't *feel* empty. Not yet. When it did, he supposed he would go back to bed. But not to sleep. For this night, sleep was done.

13

Seven years before, working as an orderly in a Tulsa hospice, Dan had made friends with an elderly psychiatrist who was suffering from terminal liver cancer. One day, when Emil Kemmer had been reminiscing (not very discreetly) about a few of his more interesting cases, Dan had confessed that ever since childhood, he had suffered from what he called double dreaming. Was Kemmer familiar with the phenomenon? Was there a name for it?

Kemmer had been a large man in his prime—the old black-and-white wedding photo he kept on his bedside table attested to that—but cancer is the ultimate diet program, and on the day of this conversation, his weight had been approximately the same as his age, which was ninety-one. His mind had still been sharp, however, and now, sitting on the closed toilet and listening to the dying storm outside, Dan remembered the old man's sly smile.

"Usually," he had said in his heavy German accent, "I am paid for my diagnoses, Daniel."

Dan had grinned. "Guess I'm out of luck, then."

"Perhaps not." Kemmer studied Dan. His eyes were bright blue. Although he knew it was outrageously unfair, Dan couldn't help imagining those eyes under a Waffen-SS coal-scuttle helmet. "There's a rumor in this deathhouse that you are a kid with a talent for helping people die. Is this true?"

"Sometimes," Dan said cautiously. "Not always." The truth was *almost* always.

"When the time comes, will you help me?"

"If I can, of course."

"Good." Kemmer sat up, a laboriously painful process, but when Dan moved to help, Kemmer had waved him away. "What you call double dreaming is well known to psychiatrists, and of particular interest to Jungians, who call it *false awakening*. The first dream is usually a lucid dream, meaning the dreamer knows he is dreaming—"

"Yes!" Dan cried. "But the second one—"

"The dreamer believes he is awake," Kemmer said. "Jung made much of this, even ascribing precognitive powers to these dreams . . . but of course we know better, don't we, Dan?"

"Of course," Dan had agreed.

"The poet Edgar Allan Poe described the false awakening phenomenon long before Carl Jung was born. He wrote, 'All that we see or seem is but a dream within a dream.' Have I answered your question?"

"I think so. Thanks."

"You're welcome. Now I believe I could drink a little juice. Apple, please."

14

Precognitive powers . . . but of course we know better.

Even if he hadn't kept the shining almost entirely to himself over the years, Dan would not have presumed to contradict a dying man . . . especially one with such coldly inquisitive blue eyes. The truth, however, was that one or both of his double dreams were often predictive, usually in ways he only half understood or did not understand at all. But as he sat on the toilet seat in his underwear, now shivering (and not just because the room was cold), he understood much more than he wanted to.

Tommy was dead. Murdered by his abusive uncle, most likely. The mother had committed suicide not long after. As for the rest of the dream . . . or the phantom hat he'd seen earlier, spinning down the sidewalk . . .

Stay away from the woman in the hat. She's the Queen Bitch of Castle Hell.

"I don't care," Dan said.

If you mess with her, she'll eat you alive.

He had no intention of meeting her, let alone messing with her. As for Deenie, he wasn't responsible for either her short-fused brother or her child neglect. He didn't even have to carry around the guilt about her lousy seventy dollars anymore; she had sold the cocaine—he was sure that part of the dream was absolutely true—and they were square. More than square, actually.

What he cared about was getting a drink. Getting drunk, not to put too fine a point on it. Standing-up, falling-down, pissy-assed drunk. Warm morning sunshine was good, and the pleasant feeling of muscles that had been worked hard, and waking up in the morning without a hangover, but the price—all these crazy dreams and visions, not to mention the random thoughts of passing strangers that sometimes found their way past his defenses—was too high.

Too high to bear.

15

He sat in the room's only chair and read his John Sandford novel by the light of the room's only lamp until the two town churches with bells rang in seven o'clock. Then he pulled on his new (new to him, anyway) boots and duffel coat. He headed out into a world that had changed and softened. There wasn't a sharp edge anywhere. The snow was still falling, but gently now.

I should get out of here. Go back to Florida. Fuck New Hampshire, where it probably even snows on the Fourth of July in odd-numbered years.

Hallorann's voice answered him, the tone as kind as he remembered from his childhood, when Dan had been Danny, but there was hard steel underneath. *You better stay somewhere, honey, or you won't be able to stay anywhere.*

"Fuck you, oldtimer," he muttered.

He went back to the Red Apple because the stores that sold hard liquor wouldn't be open for at least another hour. He walked slowly back and forth between the wine cooler and the beer cooler, debating, and finally decided if he was going to get drunk, he might as well do it as nastily as possible. He grabbed two bottles of Thunderbird (eighteen percent alcohol, a good enough number when whiskey was temporarily out of reach), started up the aisle to the register, then stopped.

Give it one more day. Give yourself one more chance.

He supposed he could do that, but why? So he could wake up in bed with Tommy again? Tommy with half of his skull caved in? Or maybe next time it would be Deenie, who had lain in that tub for two days before the super finally got tired of knocking, used his passkey, and found her. He couldn't know that, if Emil Kemmer had been here he would have agreed most emphatically, but he did. He did know. So why bother?

Maybe this hyperawareness will pass. Maybe it's just a phase, the psychic equivalent of the DTs. Maybe if you just give it a little more time . . .

But time changed. That was something only drunks and junkies understood. When you couldn't sleep, when you were afraid to look around because of what you might see, time elongated and grew sharp teeth.

"Help you?" the clerk asked, and Dan knew

(*fucking shining fucking thing*)

that he was making the clerk nervous. Why not? With his bed head, dark-circled eyes, and jerky, unsure movements, he probably looked like a meth freak who was deciding whether or not to pull out his trusty Saturday night special and ask for everything in the register.

"No," Dan said. "I just realized I left my wallet home."

He put the green bottles back in the cooler. As he closed it, they spoke to him gently, as one friend speaks to another: *See you soon, Danny.*

16

Billy Freeman was waiting for him, bundled up to the eyebrows. He held out an old-fashioned ski hat with ANNISTON CYCLONES embroidered on the front.

"What the hell are the Anniston Cyclones?" Dan asked.

"Anniston's twenty miles north of here. When it comes to football, basketball, and baseball, they're our archrivals. Someone sees that on ya, you'll probably get a snowball upside your head, but it's the only one I've got."

Dan hauled it on. "Then go, Cyclones."

"Right, fuck you and the hoss you rode in on." Billy looked him over. "You all right, Danno?"

"Didn't get much sleep last night."

"I hear that. Damn wind really screamed, didn't it? Sounded like my ex when I suggested a little Monday night lovin might do us good. Ready to go to work?"

"Ready as I'll ever be."

"Good. Let's dig in. Gonna be a busy day."

17

It was indeed a busy day, but by noon the sun had come out and the temperature had climbed back into the mid-fifties. Teenytown was filled with the sound of a hundred small waterfalls as the snow melted. Dan's spirits rose with the temperature, and he even caught himself singing ("Young man! I was once in your shoes!") as he followed his snowblower back and forth in the courtyard of the little shopping center adjacent to the common. Overhead, flapping in a mild breeze far removed from the shrieking wind of the night before, was a banner reading HUGE SPRING BARGAINS AT TEENYTOWN PRICES!

There were no visions.

After they clocked out, he took Billy to the Chuck Wagon and ordered them steak dinners. Billy offered to buy the beer. Dan shook his head. "Staying away from alcohol. Reason being, once I start, it's sometimes hard to stop."

"You could talk to Kingsley about that," Billy said. "He got himself a booze divorce about fifteen years ago. He's all right now, but his daughter still don't talk to him."

They drank coffee with the meal. A lot of it.

Dan went back to his third-floor Eliot Street lair tired, full of hot food and glad to be sober. There was no TV in his room, but he had the last part of the Sandford novel, and lost himself in it for a couple of hours. He kept an ear out for the wind, but it did not rise. He had an idea that last night's storm had been winter's final shot. Which was fine with him. He turned in at ten and fell asleep almost immediately. His early morning visit to the Red Apple now seemed hazy, as if he had gone there in a fever delirium and the fever had now passed.

18

He woke in the small hours, not because the wind was blowing but because he had to piss like a racehorse. He got up, shuffled to the bathroom, and turned on the light inside the door.

The tophat was in the tub, and full of blood.

"No," he said. "I'm dreaming."

Maybe double dreaming. Or triple. Quadruple, even. There was something he hadn't told Emil Kemmer: he was afraid that eventually he would get lost in a maze of phantom nightlife and never be able to find his way out again.

All that we see or seem is but a dream within a dream.

Only this was real. So was the hat. No one else would see it, but that changed nothing. The hat was real. It was somewhere in the world. He knew it.

From the corner of his eye, he saw something written on the mirror over the sink. Something written in lipstick.

I must not look at it.

Too late. His head was turning; he could hear the tendons in his neck creaking like old doorhinges. And what did it matter? He knew what it said. Mrs. Massey was gone, Horace Derwent was gone, they were securely locked away in the boxes he kept far back in his mind, but the Overlook was still not done with him. Written on the mirror, not in lipstick but in blood, was a single word:

REDRUM

Beneath it, lying in the sink, was a bloodstained Atlanta Braves t-shirt.

It will never stop, Danny thought. *The Overlook burned and the most terrible of its revenants went into the lockboxes, but I can't lock away the shining, because it isn't just inside me, it* is *me. Without booze to at least stun it, these visions will go on until they drive me insane.*

He could see his face in the mirror with **REDRUM** floating in front of it, stamped on his forehead like a brand. This was not a dream. There was a murdered child's shirt in his washbasin and a hatful of blood in his tub. Insanity was coming. He could see its approach in his own bulging eyes.

Then, like a flashlight beam in the dark, Hallorann's voice: *Son, you may see things, but they're like pictures in a book. You weren't helpless in the Overlook when you were a child, and you're not helpless now. Far from it. Close your eyes and when you open them, all this crap will be gone.*

He closed his eyes and waited. He tried to count off the seconds, but only made it to fourteen before the numbers were lost in the roaring confusion of his thoughts. He half expected hands—perhaps those of whoever owned the hat—to close around his neck. But he stood there. There was really nowhere else to go.

Summoning all his courage, Dan opened his eyes. The tub was empty. The washbasin was empty. There was nothing written on the mirror.

But it will be back. Next time maybe it'll be her shoes—those cork sandals. Or I'll see her in the tub. Why not? That's where I saw Mrs.

Massey, and they died the same way. Except I never stole Mrs. Massey's money and ran out on her.

"I gave it a day," he told the empty room. "I did that much."

Yes, and although it had been a busy day, it had also been a good day, he'd be the first to admit it. The *days* weren't the problem. As for the nights . . .

The mind was a blackboard. Booze was the eraser.

19

Dan lay awake until six. Then he dressed and once more made the trek to the Red Apple. This time he did not hesitate, only instead of extracting two bottles of Bird from the cooler, he took three. What was it they used to say? Go big or go home. The clerk bagged the bottles without comment; he was used to early wine purchasers. Dan strolled to the town common, sat on one of the benches in Teenytown, and took one of the bottles out of the bag, looking down at it like Hamlet with Yorick's skull. Through the green glass, what was inside looked like rat poison instead of wine.

"You say that like it's a bad thing," Dan said, and loosened the cap.

This time it was his mother who spoke up. Wendy Torrance, who had smoked right to the bitter end. Because if suicide was the only option, you could at least choose your weapon.

Is this how it ends, Danny? Is this what it was all for?

He turned the cap widdershins. Then tightened it. Then back the other way. This time he took it off. The smell of the wine was sour, the smell of jukebox music and crappy bars and pointless arguments followed by fistfights in parking lots. In the end, life was as stupid as one of those fights. The world wasn't a hospice with fresh air, the world was the Overlook Hotel, where the party never ended. Where the dead were alive forever. He raised the bottle to his lips.

Is this why we fought so hard to get out of that damned hotel, Danny? Why we fought to make a new life for ourselves? There was no reproach in her voice, only sadness.

Danny tightened the cap again. Then loosened it. Tightened it. Loosened it.

He thought: *If I drink, the Overlook wins. Even though it burned to the ground when the boiler exploded, it wins. If I don't drink, I go crazy.*

He thought: *All that we see or seem is but a dream within a dream.*

He was still tightening the cap and loosening it when Billy Freeman, who had awakened early with the vague, alarmed sense that something was wrong, found him.

"Are you going to drink that, Dan, or just keep jerking it off?"

"Drink it, I guess. I don't know what else to do."

So Billy told him.

20

Casey Kingsley wasn't entirely surprised to see his new hire sitting outside his office when he arrived at quarter past eight that morning. Nor was he surprised to see the bottle Torrance was holding in his hands, first twisting the cap off, then putting it back on and turning it tight again—he'd had that special look from the start, the thousand-yard Kappy's Discount Liquor Store stare.

Billy Freeman didn't have as much shine as Dan himself, not even close, but a bit more than just a twinkle. On that first day he had called Kingsley from the equipment shed as soon as Dan headed across the street to the Municipal Building. There was a young fella looking for work, Billy said. He wasn't apt to have much in the way of references, but Billy thought he was the right man to help out until Memorial Day. Kingsley, who'd had experiences—good ones—with Billy's intuitions before, had agreed. *I know we've got to have someone,* he said.

Billy's reply had been peculiar, but then *Billy* was peculiar. Once, two years ago, he had called an ambulance five minutes *before* that little kid had fallen off the swings and fractured his skull.

He needs us more than we need him, Billy had said.

And here he was, sitting hunched forward as if he were already riding his next bus or barstool, and Kingsley could smell the wine from twelve yards down the hallway. He had a gourmet's nose for such scents, and could name each one. This was Thunderbird, as in the old saloon rhyme: *What's the word? Thunderbird! . . . What's the price? Fifty twice!* But when the young guy looked up at him, Kingsley saw the eyes were clear of everything but desperation.

"Billy sent me."

Kingsley said nothing. He could see the kid gathering himself, struggling with it. It was in his eyes; it was in the way his mouth turned down at the corners; mostly it was the way he held the bottle, hating it and loving it and needing it all at the same time.

At last Dan brought out the words he had been running from all his life.

"I need help."

He swiped an arm across his eyes. As he did, Kingsley bent down and grasped the bottle of wine. The kid held on for a moment . . . then let go.

"You're sick and you're tired," Kingsley said. "I can see that much. But are you sick and tired of being sick and tired?"

Dan looked up at him, throat working. He struggled some more, then said, "You don't know how much."

"Maybe I do." Kingsley produced a vast key ring from his vast trousers. He stuck one in the lock of the door with FRAZIER MUNICIPAL SERVICES painted on the frosted glass. "Come on in. Let's talk about it."

CHAPTER TWO

BAD NUMBERS

1

The elderly poet with the Italian given name and the absolutely American surname sat with her sleeping great-granddaughter in her lap and watched the video her granddaughter's husband had shot in the delivery room three weeks before. It began with a title card: ABRA ENTERS THE WORLD! The footage was jerky, and David had kept away from anything too clinical (thank God), but Concetta Reynolds saw the sweat-plastered hair on Lucia's brow, heard her cry out *"I am!"* when one of the nurses exhorted her to push, and saw the droplets of blood on the blue drape—not many, just enough to make what Chetta's own grandmother would have called "a fair show." But not in English, of course.

The picture jiggled when the baby finally came into view and she felt gooseflesh chase up her back and arms when Lucy screamed, *"She has no face!"*

Sitting beside Lucy now, David chuckled. Because of course Abra *did* have a face, a very sweet one. Chetta looked down at it as if to reassure herself of that. When she looked back up, the new baby was being placed in the new mother's arms. Thirty or forty jerky seconds later, another title card appeared: HAPPY BIRTHDAY ABRA RAFAELLA STONE!

David pushed STOP on the remote.

"You're one of the very few people who will ever get to see that," Lucy announced in a firm, take-no-prisoners voice. "It's embarrassing."

"It's wonderful," Dave said. "And there's one person who gets to see it for sure, and that's Abra herself." He glanced at his wife, sitting next to him on the couch. "When she's old enough. And if she wants to, of course." He patted Lucy's thigh, then grinned at his granny-in-law, a woman for whom he had respect but no great love. "Until then, it goes in the safe deposit box with the insurance papers, the house papers, and my millions in drug money."

Concetta smiled to show she got the joke but thinly, to show she didn't find it particularly funny. In her lap, Abra slept and slept. In a way, all babies were born with a caul, she thought, their tiny faces drapes of mystery and possibility. Perhaps it was a thing to write about. Perhaps not.

Concetta had come to America when she was twelve and spoke perfect idiomatic English—not surprising, since she was a graduate of Vassar and professor (now emeritus) of that very subject—but in her head every superstition and old wives' tale still lived. Sometimes they gave orders, and they always spoke Italian when they did. Chetta believed that most people who worked in the arts were high-functioning schizophrenics, and she was no different. She knew superstition was shit; she also spat between her fingers if a crow or black cat crossed her path.

For much of her own schizophrenia she had the Sisters of Mercy to thank. They believed in God; they believed in the divinity of Jesus; they believed mirrors were bewitching pools and the child who looked into one too long would grow warts. These were the women who had been the greatest influence on her life between the ages of seven and twelve. They carried rulers in their belts—for hitting, not measuring—and never saw a child's ear they did not desire to twist in passing.

Lucy held out her arms for the baby. Chetta handed her over, not without reluctance. The kid was one sweet bundle.

2

Twenty miles southeast of where Abra slept in Concetta Reynolds's arms, Dan Torrance was attending an AA meeting while some chick droned on about sex with her ex. Casey Kingsley had ordered him to attend ninety meetings in ninety days, and this one, a nooner in the basement of Frazier Methodist Church, was his eighth. He was sitting in the first row, because Casey—known in the halls as Big Casey—had ordered him to do that, too.

"Sick people who want to get well sit in front, Danny. We call the back row at AA meetings the Denial Aisle."

Casey had given him a little notebook with a photo on the front that showed ocean waves crashing into a rock promontory. Printed above the picture was a motto Dan understood but didn't much care for: NO GREAT THING IS CREATED SUDDENLY.

"You write down every meeting you go to in that book. And anytime I ask to see it, you better be able to haul it out of your back pocket and show me perfect attendance."

"Don't I even get a sick day?"

Casey laughed. "You're sick *every* day, my friend—you're a drunk-ass alcoholic. Want to know something my sponsor told me?"

"I think you already did. You can't turn a pickle back into a cucumber, right?"

"Don't be a smartass, just listen."

Dan sighed. "Listening."

"'Get your ass to a meeting,' he said. 'If your ass falls off, put it in a bag and take it to a meeting.'"

"Charming. What if I just forget?"

Casey had shrugged. "Then you find yourself another sponsor, one who believes in forgetfulness. I don't."

Dan, who felt like some breakable object that has skittered to the edge of a high shelf but hasn't quite fallen off, didn't want another sponsor or changes of any kind. He felt okay, but tender. Very tender. Almost skinless. The visions that had plagued him following his arrival in Frazier had ceased, and although he often thought of Deenie and her little boy, the thoughts were not as painful. At the end of almost every AA meeting, someone read the Promises. One of these was *We will not regret the past nor wish to shut the door on it*. Dan thought he would *always* regret the past, but he had quit trying to shut the door. Why bother, when it would just come open again? The fucking thing had no latch, let alone a lock.

Now he began to print a single word on the current page of the little book Casey had given him. He made large, careful letters. He had no idea why he was doing it, or what it meant. The word was **ABRA**.

Meanwhile, the speaker reached the end of her qualification and burst into tears, through them declaring that even though her ex was a shit and she loved him still, she was grateful to be straight and sober. Dan applauded along with the rest of the Lunch Bunch, then began to color in the letters with his pen. Fattening them. Making them stand out.

Do I know this name? I think I do.

As the next speaker began and he went to the urn for a fresh cup of coffee, it came to him. Abra was the name of a girl in a John Steinbeck novel. *East of Eden*. He'd read it . . . he couldn't remember where. At some stop along the way. Some somewhere. It didn't matter.

Another thought

(*did you save it*)

rose to the top of his mind like a bubble and popped.

Save what?

Frankie P., the Lunch Bunch oldtimer who was chairing the meeting, asked if someone wanted to do the Chip Club. When no one raised a hand, Frankie pointed. "How about you, lurking back there by the coffee?"

Feeling self-conscious, Dan walked to the front of the room, hoping he could remember the order of the chips. The first—white for beginners—he had. As he took the battered cookie tin with the chips and medallions scattered inside it, the thought came again.

Did you save it?

3

That was the day the True Knot, which had been wintering at a KOA campground in Arizona, packed up and began meandering back east. They drove along Route 77 toward Show Low in the usual caravan: fourteen campers, some towing cars, some with lawn chairs or bicycles clamped to the backs. There were Southwinds and Winnebagos, Monacos and Bounders. Rose's EarthCruiser—seven hundred thousand dollars' worth of imported rolling steel, the best RV money could buy—led the parade. But slowly, just double-nickeling it.

They were in no hurry. There was plenty of time. The feast was still months away.

4

"Did you save it?" Concetta asked as Lucy opened her blouse and offered Abra the breast. Abby blinked sleepily, rooted a little, then lost interest. *Once your nipples get sore, you won't offer until she asks,* Chetta thought. *And at the top of her lungs.*

"Save what?" David asked.

Lucy knew. "I passed out right after they put her in my arms. Dave says I almost dropped her. There was no time, Momo."

"Oh, that goop over her face." David said it dismissively. "They stripped it off and threw it away. Damn good thing, if you ask me." He was smiling, but his eyes challenged her. *You know better than to go on with this,* they said. *You know better, so just drop it.*

She *did* know better . . . and didn't. Had she been this two-minded when she was younger? She couldn't remember, although it seemed she could remember every lecture on the Blessed Mysteries and the everlasting pain of hell administered by the Sisters of Mercy, those banditti in black. The story of the girl who had been struck blind for peeping at her brother while he was naked in the tub and the one about the man who had been struck dead for blaspheming against the pope.

Give them to us when they're young and it doesn't matter how many honors classes they've taught, or how many books of poetry they've written, or even that one of those books won all the big prizes. Give them to us when they're young . . . and they're ours forever.

"You should have saved *il amnio*. It's good luck."

She spoke directly to her granddaughter, cutting David out entirely. He was a good man, a good husband to her Lucia, but fuck his dismissive tone. And double-fuck his challenging eyes.

"I would have, but I didn't have a chance, Momo. And Dave didn't know." Buttoning her blouse again.

Chetta leaned forward and touched the fine skin of Abra's cheek with the tip of her finger, old flesh sliding across new. "Those born with *il amnio* are supposed to have double sight."

"You don't actually believe that, do you?" David asked. "A caul is nothing but a scrap of fetal membrane. It . . ."

He was saying more, but Concetta paid no attention. Abra had opened her eyes. In them was a universe of poetry, lines too great to ever be written. Or even remembered.

"Never mind," Concetta said. She raised the baby and kissed the smooth skull where the fontanelle pulsed, the magic of the mind so close beneath. "What's done is done."

5

One night about five months after the not-quite-argument over Abra's caul, Lucy dreamed her daughter was crying—crying as if her heart would break. In this dream, Abby was no longer in the master bedroom of the house on Richland Court but somewhere down a long corridor. Lucy ran in the direction of the weeping. At first there were doors on both sides, then seats. Blue ones with high backs. She was on a plane or maybe an Amtrak train. After running for what seemed like miles, she came to a bathroom door. Her baby was crying behind it. Not a hungry cry, but a frightened cry. Maybe

(*oh God, oh Mary*)

a hurt cry.

Lucy was terribly afraid the door would be locked and she would have to break it down—wasn't that the kind of thing that always happened in bad dreams?—but the knob twisted and she opened it. As she did, a new fear struck her: What if Abra was in the toilet? You read about that happening. Babies in toilets, babies in Dumpsters. What if she were drowning in one of those ugly steel bowls they had on public conveyances, up to her mouth and nose in disinfected blue water?

But Abra lay on the floor. She was naked. Her eyes, swimming with tears, stared at her mother. Written on her chest in what looked like blood was the number 11.

6

David Stone dreamed he was chasing his daughter's cries up an endless escalator that was running—slowly but inexorably—in the wrong direction. Worse, the escalator was in a mall, and the mall was on fire. He should have been choking and out of breath long before he reached the top, but there was no smoke from the fire, only a hell of flames. Nor was there any sound other than Abra's cries, although he saw people burning like kerosene-soaked torches. When he finally made it to the top, he saw Abby lying on the floor like someone's cast-off garbage. Men and women ran all around her, unheeding, and in spite of the flames, no one tried to use the escalator even though it was going down. They simply sprinted aimlessly in all directions, like ants whose hill has been torn open by a farmer's harrow. One woman in stilettos almost stepped on his daughter, a thing that would almost surely have killed her.

Abra was naked. Written on her chest was the number 175.

7

The Stones woke together, both initially convinced that the cries they heard were a remnant of the dreams they had been having. But no, the cries were in the room with them. Abby lay in her crib beneath her Shrek mobile, eyes wide, cheeks red, tiny fists pumping, howling her head off.

A change of diapers did not quiet her, nor did the breast, nor did what felt like miles of laps up and down the hall and at least a thousand verses of "The Wheels on the Bus." At last, very frightened now—Abby was her first, and Lucy was at her wits' end—she called Concetta in Boston. Although it was two in the morning, Momo answered on the second ring. She was eighty-five, and her sleep was as thin as her skin. She listened more closely to her wailing great-granddaughter than to Lucy's confused recital of all the ordinary remedies they had tried, then asked the pertinent questions. "Is she running a fever? Pulling at one of her ears? Jerking her legs like she has to make *merda*?"

"No," Lucy said, "none of that. She's a little warm from crying, but I don't think it's a fever. Momo, what should I do?"

Chetta, now sitting at her desk, didn't hesitate. "Give her another fifteen minutes. If she doesn't quiet and begin feeding, take her to the hospital."

"What? Brigham and Women's?" Confused and upset, it was all Lucy could think of. It was where she had given birth. "That's a hundred and fifty miles!"

"No, no. Bridgton. Across the border in Maine. That's a little closer than CNH."

"Are you sure?"

"Am I looking at my computer right now?"

Abra did not quiet. The crying was monotonous, maddening, terrifying. When they arrived at Bridgton Hospital, it was quarter of four, and Abra was still at full volume. Rides in the Acura were usually better than a sleeping pill, but not this morning. David thought about brain aneurysms and told himself he was out of his mind. Babies didn't have strokes . . . did they?

"Davey?" Lucy asked in a small voice as they pulled up to the sign reading EMERGENCY DROP-OFF ONLY. "Babies don't have strokes or heart attacks . . . do they?"

"No, I'm sure they don't."

But a new idea occurred to him then. Suppose the kiddo had somehow swallowed a safety pin, and it had popped open in her stomach? *That's stupid, we use Huggies, she's never even been near a safety pin.*

Something else, then. A bobby pin from Lucy's hair. An errant tack that had fallen into the crib. Maybe even, God help them, a broken-off piece of plastic from Shrek, Donkey, or Princess Fiona.

"Davey? What are you thinking?"

"Nothing."

The mobile was fine. He was sure of it.

Almost sure.

Abra continued to scream.

8

David hoped the doc on duty would give his daughter a sedative, but it was against protocol for infants who could not be diagnosed, and Abra Rafaella Stone seemed to have nothing wrong with her. She wasn't running a fever, she wasn't showing a rash, and ultrasound had ruled out pyloric stenosis. An X-ray showed no foreign objects in her throat or stomach, or a bowel obstruction. Basically, she just wouldn't shut up. The Stones were the only patients in the ER at that hour on a Tuesday morning, and each of the three nurses on duty had a try at quieting her. Nothing worked.

"Shouldn't you give her something to eat?" Lucy asked the doctor when he came back to check. The phrase *Ringer's lactate* occurred to her, something she'd heard on one of the doctor shows she'd watched ever since her teenage crush on George Clooney. But for all she knew, Ringer's lactate was foot lotion, or an anticoagulant, or something for stomach ulcers. "She won't take the breast *or* the bottle."

"When she gets hungry enough, she'll eat," the doctor said, but neither Lucy nor David was much comforted. For one thing, the doctor looked younger than they were. For another (this was far worse), he didn't sound completely sure. "Have you called your pediatrician?" He checked the paperwork. "Dr. Dalton?"

"Left a message with his service," David said. "We probably won't hear from him until mid-morning, and by then this will be over."

One way or the other, he thought, and his mind—made ungovernable by too little sleep and too much anxiety—presented him with a picture as clear as it was horrifying: mourners standing around a small grave. And an even smaller coffin.

9

At seven thirty, Chetta Reynolds blew into the examining room where the Stones and their ceaselessly screaming baby daughter had been stashed. The poet rumored to be on the short list for a Presidential Medal of Freedom was dressed in straight-leg jeans and a BU sweatshirt with a hole in one elbow. The outfit showed just how thin she'd become over the last three or four years. *No cancer, if that's what you're thinking,* she'd say if anyone commented on her runway-model thinness, which she ordinarily disguised with billowing dresses or caftans. *I'm just in training for the final lap around the track.*

Her hair, as a rule braided or put up in complicated swoops arranged to showcase her collection of vintage hair clips, stood out around her head in an unkempt Einstein cloud. She wore no makeup, and even in her distress, Lucy was shocked by how old Concetta looked. Well, of course she was old, eighty-five was *very* old, but until this morning she had looked like a woman in her late sixties at most. "I would have been here an hour earlier if I'd found someone to come in and take care of Betty." Betty was her elderly, ailing boxer.

Chetta caught David's reproachful glance.

"Bets is *dying,* David. And based on what you could tell me over the phone, I wasn't all that concerned about Abra."

"Are you concerned now?" David asked.

Lucy flashed him a warning glance, but Chetta seemed willing to accept the implied rebuke. "Yes." She held out her hands. "Give her to me, Lucy. Let's see if she'll quiet for Momo."

But Abra would not quiet for Momo, no matter how she was rocked. Nor did a soft and surprisingly tuneful lullabye (for all David knew, it was "The Wheels on the Bus" in Italian) do the job. They all tried the walking cure again, first squiring her around the small exam room, then down the hall, then back to the exam room. The screaming went on and on. At some point there was a commotion outside—someone with actual visible injuries being wheeled in, David assumed—but those in exam room 4 took little notice.

At five to nine, the exam room door opened and the Stones' pediatrician walked in. Dr. John Dalton was a fellow Dan Torrance would have recognized, although not by last name. To Dan he was just Doctor John, who made the coffee at the Thursday night Big Book meeting in North Conway.

"Thank God!" Lucy said, thrusting her howling child into the pediatrician's arms. "We've been left on our own for *hours!*"

"I was on my way when I got the message." Dalton hoisted Abra onto his shoulder. "Rounds here, then over in Castle Rock. You've heard about what's happened, haven't you?"

"Heard what?" David asked. With the door open, he was for the first time consciously aware of a moderate uproar outside. People were talking in loud voices. Some were crying. The nurse who had admitted them walked by, her face red and blotchy, her cheeks wet. She didn't even glance at the screaming infant.

"A passenger jet hit the World Trade Center," Dalton said. "And no one thinks it was an accident."

That was American Airlines Flight 11. United Airlines Flight 175 struck the Trade Center's South Tower seventeen minutes later, at 9:03 a.m. At 9:03, Abra Stone abruptly stopped crying. By 9:04, she was sound asleep.

On their ride back to Anniston, David and Lucy listened to the radio while Abra slept peacefully in her car seat behind them. The news was unbearable, but turning it off was unthinkable . . . at least until a newscaster announced the names of the airlines and the flight numbers of the aircraft: two in New York, one near Washington, one cratered in rural Pennsylvania. Then David finally reached over and silenced the flood of disaster.

"Lucy, I have to tell you something. I dreamed—"

"I know." She spoke in the flat tone of one who has just suffered a shock. "So did I."

By the time they crossed back into New Hampshire, David had begun to believe there might be something to that caul business, after all.

10

In a New Jersey town, on the west bank of the Hudson River, there's a park named for the town's most famous resident. On a clear day, it offers a perfect view of Lower Manhattan. The True Knot arrived in Hoboken on September eighth, parking in a private lot which they had four-walled for ten days. Crow Daddy did the deal. Handsome and gregarious, looking about forty, Crow's favorite t-shirt read I'M A PEOPLE PERSON! Not that he ever wore a tee when negotiating for the True Knot; then it was strictly suit and tie. It was what the rubes expected. His straight name was Henry Rothman. He was a Harvard-educated lawyer (class of '38), and he always carried cash. The True had over a billion dollars in various accounts across the world—some in gold, some in diamonds, some in rare books, stamps, and paintings—but never paid by check or credit card. Everyone, even Pea and Pod, who looked like kids, carried a roll of ten and twenties.

As Jimmy Numbers had once said, "We're a cash-and-carry outfit. We pay cash and the rubes carry us." Jimmy was the True's accountant. In his rube days he had once ridden with an outfit that became known (long after their war was over) as Quantrill's Raiders. Back then he had been a wild kid who wore a buffalo coat and carried a Sharps, but in the years since, he had mellowed. These days he had a framed, autographed picture of Ronald Reagan in his RV.

On the morning of September eleventh, the True watched the attacks on the Twin Towers from the parking lot, passing around four pairs of binoculars. They would have had a better view from Sinatra Park, but Rose didn't need to tell them that gathering early might attract suspicion . . . and in the months and years ahead, America was going to be a very suspicious nation: if you see something, say something.

Around ten that morning—when crowds had gathered all along the riverbank and it was safe—they made their way to the park. The Little twins, Pea and Pod, pushed Grampa Flick in his wheelchair. Grampa wore his cap stating I AM A VET. His long, baby-fine white hair floated around the cap's edges like milkweed. There had been a time when he'd told folks he was a veteran of the Spanish-American War. Then it was World War I. Nowadays it was World War II. In another twenty years or so, he expected to switch his story to Vietnam. Verisimilitude had never been a problem; Grampa was a military history buff.

Sinatra Park was jammed. Most folks were silent, but some wept. Apron Annie and Black-Eyed Sue helped in this respect; both were able to cry on demand. The others put on suitable expressions of sorrow, solemnity, and amazement.

Basically, the True Knot fit right in. It was how they rolled.

Spectators came and went, but the True stayed for most of the day, which was cloudless and beautiful (except for the thick billows of dreck rising in Lower Manhattan, that is). They stood at the iron rail, not talking among themselves, just watching. And taking long slow deep breaths, like tourists from the Midwest standing for the first time on Pemaquid Point or Quoddy Head in Maine, breathing deep of the fresh sea air. As a sign of respect, Rose took off her tophat and held it by her side.

At four o'clock they trooped back to their encampment in the parking lot, invigorated. They would return the next day, and the day after that, and the day after that. They would return until the good steam was exhausted, and then they would move on again.

By then, Grampa Flick's white hair would have become iron gray, and he would no longer need the wheelchair.

CHAPTER THREE

SPOONS

1

It was a twenty-mile drive from Frazier to North Conway, but Dan Torrance made it every Thursday night, partly because he could. He was now working at Helen Rivington House, making a decent salary, and he had his driver's license back. The car he'd bought to go with it wasn't much, just a three-year-old Caprice with blackwall tires and an iffy radio, but the engine was good and every time he started it up, he felt like the luckiest man in New Hampshire. He thought if he never had to ride another bus, he could die happy. It was January of 2004. Except for a few random thoughts and images—plus the extra work he sometimes did at the hospice, of course—the shining had been quiet. He would have done that volunteer work in any case, but after his time in AA, he also saw it as making amends, which recovering people considered almost as important as staying away from the first drink. If he could manage to keep the plug in the jug another three months, he would be able to celebrate three years sober.

Driving again figured large in the daily gratitude meditations upon which Casey K. insisted (because, he said—and with all the dour certainty of the Program long-timer—a grateful alcoholic doesn't get drunk), but mostly Dan went on Thursday nights because the Big Book gathering was soothing. Intimate, really. Some of the open discussion meetings in the area were uncomfortably large, but that was never true on Thursday nights in North Conway. There was an old AA saying that went, *If you want to hide something from an alcoholic, stick it in the Big Book,* and attendance at the North Conway Thursday night meeting suggested that there was some truth in it. Even during the weeks between the Fourth of July and Labor Day—the height of the tourist season—it was rare to have more than a dozen people in the Amvets hall when the gavel fell. As a result, Dan had heard things he suspected would never have been spoken aloud in the meetings that drew fifty or even seventy recovering alkies and druggies. In those, speakers had a tendency to take refuge in the platitudes (of which there were hundreds) and avoid the personal. You'd hear *Serenity pays dividends* and *You can take my inventory if you're willing to make my amends,* but never *I fucked my brother's wife one night when we were both drunk.*

At the Thursday night We Study Sobriety meetings, the little enclave read Bill Wilson's big blue how-to manual from cover to cover, each new meeting picking up where the last meeting had left off. When they got to the end of the book, they went back to "The Doctor's Statement" and started all over again. Most meetings covered ten pages or so. That took about half an hour. In the remaining half hour, the group was supposed to talk about the material just read. Sometimes they actually did. Quite often, however, the discussion veered off in other directions, like an unruly planchette scurrying around a Ouija board beneath the fingers of neurotic teenagers.

Dan remembered a Thursday night meeting he'd attended when he was about eight months sober. The chapter under discussion, "To Wives," was full of antique assumptions that almost always provoked a hot response from the younger women in the Program. They wanted to know why, in the sixty-five years or so since the Big Book's original publication, no one had ever added a chapter called "To Husbands."

When Gemma T.—a thirtysomething whose only two emotional settings seemed to be Angry and Profoundly Pissed Off—raised her hand on that particular night, Dan had expected a fem-lib tirade. Instead she said, much more quietly than usual, "I need to share something. I've been holding onto it ever since I was seventeen, and unless I let go, I'll never be able to stay away from coke and wine."

The group waited.

"I hit a man with my car when I was coming home drunk from a party," Gemma said. "This was back in Somerville. I left him lying by the side of the road. I didn't know if he was dead or alive. I still don't. I waited for the cops to come and arrest me, but they never did. I got away with it."

She had laughed at this the way people do when the joke's an especially good one, then put her head down on the table and burst into sobs so deep that they shook her rail-thin body. It had been Dan's first experience with how terrifying "honesty in all our affairs" could be when it was actually put into practice. He thought, as he still did every so often, of how he had stripped Deenie's wallet of cash, and how the little boy had reached for the cocaine on the coffee table. He was a little in awe of Gemma, but that much raw honesty wasn't in him. If it came down to a choice between telling that story and taking a drink . . .

I'd take the drink. No question.

2

Tonight the reading was "Gutter Bravado," one of the stories from the section of the Big Book cheerily titled "They Lost Nearly All." The tale followed a pattern with which Dan had become familiar: good family, church on Sundays, first drink, first binge, business success spoiled by booze, escalating lies, first arrest, broken promises to reform, institutionalization, and the final happy ending. All the stories in the Big Book had happy endings. That was part of its charm.

It was a cold night but overwarm inside, and Dan was edging into a doze when Doctor John raised his hand and said, "I've been lying to my wife about something, and I don't know how to stop."

That woke Dan up. He liked DJ a lot.

It turned out that John's wife had given him a watch for

Christmas, quite an expensive one, and when she had asked him a couple of nights ago why he wasn't wearing it, John said he'd left it at the office.

"Only it's not there. I looked everywhere, and it's just not. I do a lot of hospital rounds, and if I have to change into scrubs, I use one of the lockers in the doctors' lounge. There are combo locks, but I hardly ever use them, because I don't carry much cash and I don't have anything else worth stealing. Except for the watch, I guess. I can't remember taking it off and leaving it in a locker—not at CNH or over in Bridgton—but I think I must have. It's not the expense. It just brings back a lot of the old stuff from the days when I was drinking myself stupid every night and chipping speed the next morning to get going."

There were nodding heads at this, followed by similar stories of guilt-driven deceit. No one gave advice; that was called "crosstalk," and frowned on. They simply told their tales. John listened with his head down and his hands clasped between his knees. After the basket was passed ("We are self-supporting through our own contributions"), he thanked everyone for their input. From the look of him, Dan didn't think said input had helped a whole hell of a lot.

After the Lord's Prayer, Dan put away the leftover cookies and stacked the group's tattered Big Books in the cabinet marked FOR AA USE. A few people were still hanging around the butt-can outside—the so-called meeting after the meeting—but he and John had the kitchen to themselves. Dan hadn't spoken during the discussion; he was too busy having an interior debate with himself.

The shining had been quiet, but that didn't mean it was absent. He knew from his volunteer work that it was actually stronger than it had been since childhood, though now he seemed to have a greater degree of control over it. That made it less frightening and more useful. His co-workers at Rivington House knew he had *something,* but most of them called it empathy and let it go at that. The last thing he wanted, now that his life had begun to settle down, was to get a reputation as some sort of parlor psychic. Best to keep the freaky shit to himself.

Doctor John was a good guy, though. And he was hurting.

DJ placed the coffee urn upside down in the dish drainer, used a length of towel hanging from the stove handle to dry his hands, then turned to Dan, offering a smile that looked as real as the Coffee-mate Dan had stored away next to the cookies and the sugar bowl. "Well, I'm off. See you next week, I guess."

In the end, the decision made itself; Dan simply could not let the guy go looking like that. He held his arms out. "Give it up."

The fabled AA manhug. Dan had seen many but never given a single one. John looked dubious for a moment, then stepped forward. Dan drew him in, thinking *There'll probably be nothing.*

But there was. It came as quickly as it had when, as a child, he had sometimes helped his mother and father find lost things.

"Listen to me, Doc," he said, letting John go. "You were worried about the kid with Goocher's."

John stepped back. "What are you talking about?"

"I'm not saying it right, I know that. Goocher's? Glutcher's? It's some sort of bone thing."

John's mouth dropped open. "Are you talking about Norman Lloyd?"

"You tell me."

"Normie's got Gaucher's disease. It's a lipid disorder. Hereditary and very rare. Causes an enlarged spleen, neurologic disorders, and usually an early, unpleasant death. Poor kid's basically got a glass skeleton, and he'll probably die before he's ten. But how do you know that? From his parents? The Lloyds live way the hell down in Nashua."

"You were worried about talking to him—the terminal ones drive you crazy. That's why you stopped in the Tigger bathroom to wash your hands even though your hands didn't need washing. You took off your watch and put it up on the shelf where they keep that dark red disinfectant shit that comes in the plastic squeeze bottles. I don't know the name."

John D. was staring at him as though he had gone mad.

"Which hospital is this kid in?" Dan asked.

"Elliot. The time-frame's about right, and I did stop in the bathroom near the Pedes nursing station to wash my hands." He paused, frowning. "And yeah, I guess there are Milne characters on the walls in that one. But if I'd taken off my watch, I'd remem . . ." He trailed off.

"You *do* remember," Dan said, and smiled. "*Now* you do. Don't you?"

John said, "I checked the Elliot lost and found. Bridgton and CNH, too, for that matter. Nothing."

"Okay, so maybe somebody came along, saw it, and stole it. If so, you're shit out of luck . . . but at least you can tell your wife what happened. And *why* it happened. You were thinking about the kid, *worrying* about the kid, and you forgot to put your watch back on before you left the can. Simple as that. And hey, maybe it's still there. That's a high shelf, and hardly anybody uses what's in those plastic bottles, because there's a soap dispenser right beside the sink."

"It's Betadine on that shelf," John said, "and up high so the kids can't reach it. I never noticed. But . . . Dan, have you ever *been* in Elliot?"

This wasn't a question he wanted to answer. "Just check the shelf, Doc. Maybe you'll get lucky."

3

Dan arrived early at the following Thursday's We Study Sobriety meeting. If Doctor John had decided to trash his marriage and possibly his career over a missing seven-hundred-dollar watch (alkies routinely trashed marriages and careers over far less), someone would have to make the coffee. But John was there. So was the watch.

This time it was John who initiated the manhug. An extremely hearty one. Dan almost expected to receive a pair of Gallic kisses on the cheeks before DJ let him go.

"It was right where you said it would be. Ten days, and still there. It's like a miracle."

"Nah," Dan said. "Most people rarely look above their own eyeline. It's a proven fact."

"How did you *know*?"

Dan shook his head. "I can't explain it. Sometimes I just do."

"How can I thank you?"

This was the question Dan had been waiting and hoping for. "By working the Twelfth Step, dummocks."

John D. raised his eyebrows.

"Anonymity. In words of one syllable, keep ya fuckin mouth shut."

Understanding broke on John's face. He grinned. "I can do that."

"Good. Now make the coffee. I'll put out the books."

4

In most New England AA groups, anniversaries are called birthdays and celebrated with a cake and an after-meeting party. Shortly before Dan was due to celebrate his third year of sobriety in this fashion, David Stone and Abra's great-grandmother came to see John Dalton—known in some circles as either Doctor John or DJ—and invite him to another third birthday party. This was the one the Stones were throwing for Abra.

"That's very kind," John said, "and I'll be more than happy to drop by if I can. Only why do I feel there's a little more to it?"

"Because there is," Chetta said. "And Mr. Stubborn here has decided that it's finally time to talk about it."

"Is there a problem with Abra? If there is, fill me in. Based on her last checkup, she's fine. Fearsomely bright. Social skills terrific. Verbal skills through the roof. Reading, ditto. Last time she was here she read me *Alligators All Around*. Probably rote memory, but still remarkable for a child who's not yet three. Does Lucy know you're here?"

"Lucy and Chetta are the ones who ganged up on me," David said. "Lucy's home with Abra, making cupcakes for the party. When I left, the kitchen looked like hell in a high wind."

"So what are we saying here? That you want me at her party in an observational capacity?"

"That's right," Concetta said. "None of us can say for sure that something will happen, but it's more likely to when she's excited, and she's *very* excited about her party. All her little pals from daycare are coming, and there's going to be a fellow who does magic tricks."

John opened a desk drawer and took out a yellow legal pad. "What kind of something are you expecting?"

David hesitated. "That's . . . hard to say."

Chetta turned to face him. "Go on, *caro.* Too late to back out now." Her tone was light, almost gay, but John Dalton thought she looked worried. He thought they both did. "Begin with the night she started crying and wouldn't stop."

5

David Stone had been teaching American history and twentieth-century European history to undergraduates for ten years, and knew how to organize a story so the interior logic was hard to miss. He began this one by pointing out that their infant daughter's marathon crying spree had ended almost immediately after the second jetliner had struck the World Trade Center. Then he doubled back to the dreams in which his wife had seen the American Airlines flight number on Abra's chest and he had seen the United Airlines number.

"In Lucy's dream, she found Abra in an airplane bathroom. In mine, I found her in a mall that was on fire. Draw your own conclusions about that part. Or not. To me, those flight numbers seem pretty conclusive. But of what, I don't know." He laughed without much humor, raised his hands, then dropped them again. "Maybe I'm afraid to know."

John Dalton remembered the morning of 9/11—and Abra's

nonstop crying jag—very well. "Let me get this straight. You believe your daughter—who was then only five months old—had a premonition of those attacks and somehow sent word to you telepathically."

"Yes," Chetta said. "Put very succinctly. Bravo."

"I know how it sounds," David said. "Which is why Lucy and I kept it to ourselves. Except for Chetta, that is. Lucy told her that night. Lucy tells her momo everything." He sighed. Concetta gave him a cool look.

"You didn't get one of these dreams?" John asked her.

She shook her head. "I was in Boston. Out of her . . . I don't know . . . transmitting range?"

"It's been almost three years since 9/11," John said. "I assume other stuff has happened since then."

A lot of other stuff had happened, and now that he had managed to speak of the first (and most unbelievable) thing, Dave found himself able to talk about the rest easily enough.

"The piano. That was next. You know Lucy plays?"

John shook his head.

"Well, she does. Since she was in grammar school. She's not great or anything, but she's pretty good. We've got a Vogel that my parents gave her as a wedding present. It's in the living room, which is also where Abra's playpen used to be. Well, one of the presents I gave Lucy for Christmas in 2001 was a book of Beatles tunes arranged for piano. Abra used to lie in her playpen, goofing with her toys and listening. You could tell by the way she smiled and kicked her feet that she liked the music."

John didn't question this. Most babies loved music, and they had their ways of letting you know.

"The book had all the hits—'Hey Jude,' 'Lady Madonna,' 'Let It Be'—but the one Abra liked best was one of the minor songs, a B-side called 'Not a Second Time.' Do you know it?"

"Not offhand," John said. "I might if I heard it."

"It's upbeat, but unlike most of the Beatles' fast stuff, it's built around a piano riff rather than the usual guitar sound. It isn't a boogie-woogie, but close. Abra loved it. She wouldn't just kick her feet when Lucy played that one, she'd actually bicycle them." Dave smiled at the memory of Abra on her back in her bright purple onesie, not yet able to walk but crib-dancing like a disco queen. "The instrumental break is almost all piano, and it's simple as pie. The left hand just picks out the notes. There are only twenty-nine—I counted. A kid could play it. And our kid did."

John raised his eyebrows until they almost met his hairline.

"It started in the spring of 2002. Lucy and I were in bed, reading. The weather report was on TV, and that comes about halfway through the eleven p.m. newscast. Abra was in her room—fast asleep, as far as we knew. Lucy asked me to turn off the TV because she wanted to go to sleep. I clicked the remote, and that's when we heard it. The piano break of 'Not a Second Time,' those twenty-nine notes. Perfect. Not a single miss, and coming from downstairs.

"Doc, we were scared shitless. We thought we had an intruder in the house, only what kind of burglar stops to play a little Beatles before grabbing the silverware? I don't have a gun and my golf clubs were in the garage, so I just picked up the biggest book I could find and went down to confront whoever was there. Pretty stupid, I know. I told Lucy to grab the phone and dial 911 if I yelled. But there was no one, and all the doors were locked. Also, the cover was down over the piano keys.

"I went back upstairs and told Lucy I hadn't found anything or anyone. We went down the hall to check the baby. We didn't talk about it, we just did it. I think we knew it was Abra, but neither of us wanted to say it right out loud. She was awake, just lying there in her crib and looking at us. You know the wise little eyes that they have?"

John knew. As if they could tell you all the secrets of the universe, if they were only able to talk. There were times when he thought that might even be so, only God had arranged things in such a way so that by the time they *could* get beyond goo-goo-ga-ga, they had forgotten it all, the way we forget even our most vivid dreams a couple of hours after waking.

"She smiled when she saw us, closed her eyes, and dropped off. The next night it happened again. Same time. Those twenty-nine notes from the living room . . . then silence . . . then down to Abra's room and finding her awake. Not fussing, not even sucking her bink, just looking at us through the bars of her crib. Then off to sleep."

"This is the truth," John said. Not really questioning, only wanting to get it straight. "You're not pulling my leg."

David didn't smile. "Not even twitching the cuff of your pants."

John turned to Chetta. "Have you heard it yourself?"

"No. Let David finish."

"We got a couple of nights off, and . . . you know how you say that the secret of successful parenting is always make a plan?"

"Sure." This was John Dalton's chief sermon to new parents. How are you going to handle night feedings? Draw up a schedule so someone's always on call and no one gets too ragged. How are you going to handle bathing and feeding and dressing and playtime so the kid has a regular—and hence comforting—routine? Draw up a schedule. Make a plan. Do you know how to handle an emergency? Anything from a collapsed crib to a choking incident? If you make a plan, you will, and nineteen times out of twenty, things will turn out fine.

"So that's what we did. For the next three nights I slept on the sofa right across from the piano. On the third night the music started just as I was snugging down for the night. The cover on the Vogel was closed, so I hustled over and raised it. The keys weren't moving. Which didn't surprise me much, because I could tell the music wasn't coming from the piano."

"Beg pardon?"

"It was coming from *above* it. From thin air. By then, Lucy was in Abra's room. The other times we hadn't said anything, we were too stunned, but this time she was ready. She told Abra to play it again. There was a little pause . . . and then she did. I was standing so close I almost could have snatched those notes out of the air."

Silence in John Dalton's office. He had stopped writing on the pad. Chetta was looking at him gravely. At last he said, "Is this still going on?"

"No. Lucy took Abra on her lap and told her not to play anymore at night, because we couldn't sleep. And that was the end of it." He paused to consider. "*Almost* the end. Once, about three weeks later, we heard the music again, but very soft and coming from upstairs this time. From her room."

"She was playing to herself," Concetta said. "She woke up . . . she couldn't get back to sleep right away . . . so she played herself a little lullaby."

6

One Monday afternoon just about a year after the fall of the Twin Towers, Abra—walking by now and with recognizable words beginning to emerge from her all-but-constant gabble—teetered her way to the front door and plopped down there with her favorite doll in her lap.

"Whatcha doon, sweetheart?" Lucy asked. She was sitting at the piano, playing a Scott Joplin rag.

"Dada!" Abra announced.

"Honey, Dada won't be home until supper," Lucy said, but fifteen minutes later the Acura pulled up the drive and Dave got out, hauling his briefcase. There had been a water-main break in the building where he taught his Monday-Wednesday-Friday classes, and everything had been canceled.

"Lucy told me about that," Concetta said, "and of course I already knew about the 9/11 crying jag and the phantom piano. I took a run up there a week or two later. I told Lucy not to say a word to Abra about my visit. But Abra knew. She planted herself in front of the door ten minutes before I showed up. When Lucy asked who was coming, Abra said, 'Momo.'"

"She does that a lot," David said. "Not every time someone's coming, but if it's someone she knows and likes . . . almost always."

In the late spring of 2003, Lucy found her daughter in their bedroom, tugging at the second drawer of Lucy's dresser.

"Mun!" she told her mother. "Mun, mun!"

"I don't get you, sweetie," Lucy said, "but you can look in the drawer if you want to. It's just some old underwear and leftover cosmetics."

But Abra had no interest in the drawer, it seemed; didn't even look in it when Lucy pulled it out to show her what was inside.

"Hind! Mun!" Then, drawing a deep breath. "Mun hind, Mama!"

Parents never become absolutely fluent in Baby—there's not enough time—but most learn to speak it to some degree, and Lucy finally understood that her daughter's interest wasn't in the contents of the dresser but in something behind it.

Curious, she pulled it out. Abra darted into the space immediately. Lucy, thinking that it would be dusty in there even if there weren't bugs or mice, made a swipe for the back of the baby's shirt and missed. By the time she got the dresser out far enough to slip into the gap herself, Abra was holding up a twenty-dollar bill that had found its way through the hole between the dresser's surface and the bottom of the mirror. "Look!" she said gleefully. "Mun! *My* mun!"

"Nope," Lucy said, plucking it out of the small fist, "babies don't get mun because they don't need mun. But you did just earn yourself an ice cream cone."

"I-keem!" Abra shouted. "*My* i-keem!"

"Now tell Doctor John about Mrs. Judkins," David said. "You were there for that."

"Indeed I was," Concetta said. "That was some Fourth of July weekend."

By the summer of 2003, Abra had begun speaking in—more or less—full sentences. Concetta had come to spend the holiday weekend with the Stones. On the Sunday, which happened to be July sixth, Dave had gone to the 7-Eleven to buy a fresh canister of Blue Rhino for the backyard barbecue. Abra was playing with blocks in the living room. Lucy and Chetta were in the kitchen, one of them checking periodically on Abra to make sure she hadn't decided to pull out the plug on the TV and chew it or go climbing Mount Sofa. But Abra showed no interest in those things; she was busy constructing what looked like a Stonehenge made out of her plastic toddler blocks.

Lucy and Chetta were unloading the dishwasher when Abra began to scream.

"She sounded like she was dying," Chetta said. "You know how scary that is, right?"

John nodded. He knew.

"Running doesn't come naturally to me at my age, but I ran like Wilma Rudolph that day. Beat Lucy to the living room by half a length. I was so convinced the kid was hurt that for a second or two I actually *saw* blood. But she was okay. Physically, anyhow. She ran to me and threw her arms around my legs. I picked her up. Lucy was with me by then, and we managed to get her soothed a little. 'Wannie!' she said. 'Help Wannie, Momo! Wannie fall down!' I didn't know who Wannie was, but Lucy did—Wanda Judkins, the lady across the street."

"She's Abra's favorite neighbor," David said, "because she makes cookies and usually brings one over for Abra with her name written on it. Sometimes in raisins, sometimes in frosting. She's a widow. Lives alone."

"So we went across," Chetta resumed, "me in the lead and Lucy holding Abra. I knocked. No one answered. 'Wannie in the dinner room!' Abra said. 'Help Wannie, Momo! Help Wannie, Mama! She hurted herself and blood is coming out!'

"The door was unlocked. We went in. First thing I smelled was burning cookies. Mrs. Judkins was lying on the dining room floor next to a stepladder. The rag she'd been using to dust out the moldings was still in her hand, and there was blood, all right—a puddle of it around her head in a kind of halo. I thought she was finished—I couldn't see her breathing—but Lucy found a pulse. The fall fractured her skull, and there was a small brain-bleed, but she woke up the next day. She'll be at Abra's birthday party. You can say hello to her, if you come." She looked at Abra Stone's pediatrician unflinchingly. "The doctor at the ER said that if she'd lain there much longer, she would have either died or ended up in a persistent vegetative state . . . far worse than death, in my humble opinion. Either way, the kid saved her life."

John tossed his pen on top of the legal pad. "I don't know what to say."

"There's more," Dave said, "but the other stuff's hard to quantify. Maybe just because Lucy and I have gotten used to it. The way, I guess, you'd get used to living with a kid who was born blind. Except this is almost the opposite of that. I think we knew even before the 9/11 thing. I think we knew there was *something* almost from the time we brought her home from the hospital. It's like . . ."

He huffed out a breath and looked at the ceiling, as if for inspiration. Concetta squeezed his arm. "Go on. At least he hasn't called for the men with the butterfly nets yet."

"Okay, it's like there's always a wind blowing through the house, only you can't exactly feel it or see what it's doing. I keep thinking the curtains are going to billow and the pictures are going to fly off the walls, but they never do. Other stuff does happen, though. Two or three times a week—sometimes two or three times a *day*— the circuit breakers trip. We've had two different electricians out, on four different occasions. They check the circuits and tell us everything is hunky-dory. Some mornings we come downstairs and the cushions from the chairs and the sofa are on the floor. We tell Abra to put her toys away before bed and unless she's overtired and cranky, she's very good about it. But sometimes the toybox will be open the next morning and some of the toys will be back on the floor. Usually the blocks. They're her favorites."

He paused for a moment, now looking at the eye chart on the far wall. John thought Concetta would prod him to go on, but she kept silent.

"Okay, this is totally weird, but I swear to you it happened. One night when we turned on the TV, *The Simpsons* were on every channel. Abra laughed like it was the biggest joke in the world. Lucy freaked out. She said, 'Abra Rafaella Stone, if you're doing that, stop it right now!' Lucy hardly ever speaks sharply to her, and when she does, Abra just dissolves. Which is what happened that night. I turned off the TV, and when I turned it on again, everything was back to normal. I could give you half a dozen other things . . . incidents . . . phenomena . . . but most of it's so small you'd hardly even notice." He shrugged. "Like I say, you get used to it."

John said, "I'll come to the party. After all that, how can I resist?"

"Probably nothing will happen," Dave said. "You know the old joke about how to stop a leaky faucet, don't you? Call the plumber."

Concetta snorted. "If you really believe that, sonny-boy, I think you might get a surprise." And, to Dalton: "Just getting him here was like pulling teeth."

"Give it a rest, Momo." Color had begun to rise in Dave's cheeks.

John sighed. He had sensed the antagonism between these two before. He didn't know the cause of it—some kind of competition for Lucy, perhaps—but he didn't want it breaking out into the open now. Their bizarre errand had turned them into temporary allies, and that was the way he wanted to keep it.

"Save the sniping." He spoke sharply enough so they looked away from each other and back at him, surprised. "I believe you. I've never heard of anything remotely like this before . . ."

Or had he? He trailed off, thinking of his lost watch.

"Doc?" David said.

"Sorry. Brain cramp."

At this they both smiled. Allies again. Good.

"Anyway, no one's going to send for the men in the white coats. I accept you both as level-headed folks, not prone to hysteria or hallucination. I might guess some bizarre form of Munchausen syndrome was at work if it was just one person claiming these . . . these psychic outbreaks . . . but it's not. It's all three of you. Which raises the question, what do you want me to do?"

Dave seemed at a loss, but his grandmother-in-law was not. "Observe her, the way you would any child with a disease—"

The color had begun to leave David Stone's cheeks, but now it rushed back. *Slammed* back. "Abra is not sick," he snapped.

She turned to him. "I know that! *Cristo!* Will you let me finish?"

Dave put on a longsuffering expression and raised his hands. "Sorry, sorry, sorry."

"Just don't jump down my throat, David."

John said, "If you insist on bickering, children, I'll have to send you to the Quiet Room."

Concetta sighed. "This is very stressful. For all of us. I'm sorry, Davey, I used the wrong word."

"No prob, *cara*. We're in this together."

She smiled briefly. "Yes. Yes, we are. Observe her as you'd observe any child with an undiagnosed condition, Dr. Dalton. That's all we can ask, and I think it's enough for now. You may have some ideas. I hope so. You see . . ."

She turned to David Stone with an expression of helplessness that John thought was probably rare on that firm face.

"We're afraid," Dave said. "Me, Lucy, Chetta—scared to death. Not of her, but for her. Because she's just *little,* do you see? What if this power of hers . . . I don't know what else to call it . . . what if it hasn't topped out yet? What if it's still growing? What do we do then? She could . . . I don't know . . ."

"He *does* know," Chetta said. "She could lose her temper and hurt herself or someone else. I don't know how likely that is, but just thinking it *could* happen . . ." She touched John's hand. "It's awful."

7

Dan Torrance knew he would be living in the turret room of the Helen Rivington House from the moment he had seen his old friend Tony waving to him from a window that on second look turned out to be boarded shut. He asked Mrs. Clausen, the Rivington's chief supervisor, about the room six months or so after going to work at the hospice as janitor/orderly . . . and unofficial doctor in residence. Along with his faithful sidekick Azzie, of course.

"That room's junk from one end to the other," Mrs. Clausen

had said. She was a sixtysomething with implausibly red hair. She was possessed of a sarcastic, often dirty mouth, but she was a smart and compassionate administrator. Even better, from the standpoint of HRH's board of directors, she was a tremendously effective fund-raiser. Dan wasn't sure he liked her, but he had come to respect her.

"I'll clean it out. On my own time. It would be better for me to be right here, don't you think? On call?"

"Danny, tell me something. How come you're so good at what you do?"

"I don't really know." This was at least half true. Maybe even seventy percent. He had lived with the shining all his life and still didn't understand it.

"Junk aside, the turret's hot in the summer and cold enough to freeze the balls off a brass monkey in the winter."

"That can be rectified," Dan had said.

"Don't talk to *me* about your rectum." Mrs. Clausen peered sternly at him from above her half-glasses. "If the board knew what I was letting you do, they'd probably have me weaving baskets in that assisted living home down in Nashua. The one with the pink walls and the piped-in Mantovani." She snorted. "Doctor Sleep, indeed."

"I'm not the doctor," Dan said mildly. He knew he was going to get what he wanted. "Azzie's the doctor. I'm just his assistant."

"Azreel's the fucking *cat*," she said. "A raggedy-ass stray that wandered in off the street and got adopted by guests who have now all gone to the Great Who Knows. All he cares about is his twice-daily bowl of Friskies."

To this Dan hadn't responded. There was no need, because they both knew it wasn't true.

"I thought you had a perfectly good place on Eliot Street. Pauline Robertson thinks the sun shines out of your asshole. I know because I sing with her in the church choir."

"What's your favorite hymn?" Dan asked. "'What a Fucking Friend We Have in Jesus'?"

She showed the Rebecca Clausen version of a smile. "Oh, very well. Clean out the room. Move in. Have it wired for cable, put in quadraphonic sound, set up a wetbar. What the hell do I care, I'm only the boss."

"Thanks, Mrs. C."

"Oh, and don't forget the space heater, okay? See if you can't find something from a yard sale with a nice frayed cord. Burn the fucking place down some cold February night. Then they can put up a brick monstrosity to match the abortions on either side of us."

Dan stood up and raised the back of his hand to his forehead in a half-assed British salute. "Whatever you say, boss."

She waved a hand at him. "Get outta here before I change my mind, doc."

8

He *did* put in a space heater, but the cord wasn't frayed and it was the kind that shut off immediately if it tipped over. There was never going to be any air-conditioning in the third-floor turret room, but a couple of fans from Walmart placed in the open windows provided a nice cross-draft. It got plenty hot just the same on summer days, but Dan was almost never there in the daytime. And summer nights in New Hampshire were usually cool.

Most of the stuff that had been stashed up there was disposable junk, but he kept a big grammar school–style blackboard he found leaning against one wall. It had been hidden for fifty years or more behind an ironmongery of ancient and grievously wounded wheelchairs. The blackboard was useful. On it he listed the hospice's patients and their room numbers, erasing the names of the folks who passed away and adding names as new folks checked in. In the spring of 2004, there were thirty-two names on the board. Ten were in Rivington One and twelve in Rivington Two—these were the ugly brick buildings flanking the Victorian home where the famous Helen Rivington had once lived and written thrilling romance novels under the pulsating name of Jeannette Montparsse.

The rest of the patients were housed on the two floors below Dan's cramped but serviceable turret apartment.

Was Mrs. Rivington famous for anything besides writing bad novels? Dan had asked Claudette Albertson not long after starting work at the hospice. They were in the smoking area at the time, practicing their nasty habit. Claudette, a cheerful African American RN with the shoulders of an NFL left tackle, threw back her head and laughed.

"You bet! For leaving this town a shitload of money, honey! And giving away this house, of course. She thought old folks should have a place where they could die with dignity."

And in Rivington House, most of them did. Dan—with Azzie to assist—was now a part of that. He thought he had found his calling. The hospice now felt like home.

9

On the morning of Abra's birthday party, Dan got out of bed and saw that all the names on his blackboard had been erased. Written where they had been, in large and straggling letters, was a single word:

hEll☺

Dan sat on the edge of the bed in his underwear for a long time, just looking. Then he got up and put one hand on the letters, smudging them a little, hoping for a shine. Even a little twinkle. At last he took his hand away, rubbing chalkdust on his bare thigh.

"Hello yourself," he said . . . and then: "Would your name be Abra, by any chance?"

Nothing. He put on his robe, got his soap and towel, and went down to the staff shower on two. When he came back, he picked up the eraser he'd found to go with the board and began erasing the word. Halfway through, a thought

(*daddy says we'll have balloons*)

came to him, and he stopped, waiting for more. But no more came, so he finished erasing the board and then began replacing the names and room numbers, working from that Monday's attendance memo. When he came back upstairs at noon, he half expected the board to be erased again, the names and numbers replaced by *hEll☺*, but all was as he had left it.

10

Abra's birthday party was in the Stones' backyard, a restful sweep of green grass with apple and dogwood trees that were just coming into blossom. At the foot of the yard was a chainlink fence and a gate secured by a combination padlock. The fence was decidedly unbeautiful, but neither David nor Lucy cared, because beyond it was the Saco River, which wound its way southeast, through Frazier, through North Conway, and across the border into Maine. Rivers and small children did not mix, in the Stones' opinion, especially in the spring, when this one was wide and turbulent with melting snows. Each year the local weekly reported at least one drowning.

Today the kids had enough to occupy them on the lawn. The only organized game they could manage was a brief round of follow-the-leader, but they weren't too young to run around (and sometimes roll around) on the grass, to climb like monkeys on Abra's playset, to crawl through the Fun Tunnels David and a couple of the other dads had set up, and to bat around the balloons now drifting everywhere. These were all yellow (Abra's professed favorite color), and there were at least six dozen, as John Dalton could attest. He had helped Lucy and her grandmother blow them up. For a woman in her eighties, Chetta had an awesome set of lungs.

There were nine kids, counting Abra, and because at least one of every parental set had come, there was plenty of adult supervision. Lawn chairs had been set up on the back deck, and as the party hit cruising speed, John sat in one of these next to Concetta, who was dolled up in designer jeans and her WORLD'S BEST GREAT-GRAMMA sweatshirt. She was working her way through a giant slice of birthday cake. John, who had taken on a few pounds of ballast during the winter, settled for a single scoop of strawberry ice cream.

"I don't know where you put it," he said, nodding at the rapidly disappearing cake on her paper plate. "There's nothing to you. You're a stuffed string."

"Maybe so, *caro,* but I've got a hollow leg." She surveyed the roistering children and fetched a deep sigh. "I wish my daughter could have lived to see this. I don't have many regrets, but that's one of them."

John decided not to venture out on this conversational limb. Lucy's mother had died in a car accident when Lucy was younger than Abra was now. This he knew from the family history the Stones had filled out jointly.

In any case, Chetta turned the conversation herself. "Do you know what I like about em at this age?"

"Nope." John liked them at all ages . . . at least until they turned fourteen. When they turned fourteen their glands went into hyperdrive, and most of them felt obliged to spend the next five years being boogersnots.

"Look at them, Johnny. It's the kiddie version of that Edward Hicks painting, *The Peaceable Kingdom.* You've got six white ones—of course you do, it's New Hampshire—but you've also got two black ones and one gorgeous Korean American baby who looks like she should be modeling clothes in the Hanna Andersson catalogue. You know the Sunday school song that goes 'Red and yellow, black and white, they are precious in His sight'? That's what we have here. Two hours, and not one of them has raised a fist or given a push in anger."

John—who had seen plenty of toddlers who kicked, pushed, punched, and bit—gave a smile in which cynicism and wistfulness were exactly balanced. "I wouldn't expect anything different. They all go to L'il Chums. It's the smart-set daycare in these parts, and they charge smart-set prices. That means their parents are all at least upper-middle, they're all college grads, and they all practice the gospel of Go Along to Get Along. These kids are your basic domesticated social animals."

John stopped there because she was frowning at him, but he could have gone farther. He could have said that, until the age of seven or thereabouts—the so-called age of reason—most children were emotional echo chambers. If they grew up around people who got along and didn't raise their voices, they did the same. If they were raised by biters and shouters . . . well . . .

Twenty years of treating little ones (not to mention raising two of his own, now away at good Go Along to Get Along prep schools) hadn't destroyed all the romantic notions he'd held when first deciding to specialize in pediatric medicine, but those years had tempered them. Perhaps kids really did come into the world trailing clouds of glory, as Wordsworth had so confidently proclaimed, but they also shit in their pants until they learned better.

11

A silvery run of bells—like those on an ice cream truck—sounded in the afternoon air. The kids turned to see what was up.

Riding onto the lawn from the Stones' driveway was an amiable apparition: a young man on a wildly oversize red tricycle. He was wearing white gloves and a zoot suit with comically wide shoulders. In one lapel was a boutonniere the size of a hothouse orchid. His pants (also oversize) were currently hiked up to his knees as he worked the pedals. The handlebars were hung with bells, which he rang with one finger. The trike rocked from side to side but never quite fell over. On the newcomer's head, beneath a huge brown derby, was a crazy blue wig. David Stone was walking behind him, carrying a large suitcase in one hand and a fold-up table in the other. He looked bemused.

"Hey, kids! Hey, kids!" the man on the trike shouted. "Gather round, gather round, because the *show* is about to *start*!" He didn't need to ask them twice; they were already flocking toward the trike, laughing and shouting.

Lucy came over to John and Chetta, sat down, and blew hair out of her eyes with a comical *foof* of her lower lip. She had a smudge of chocolate frosting on her chin. "Behold the magician. He's a street performer in Frazier and North Conway during the summer season. Dave saw an ad in one of those freebie newspapers, auditioned the guy, and hired him. His name is Reggie Pelletier, but he styles himself The Great Mysterio. Let's see how long he can hold their attention once they've all had a good close look at the fancy trike. I'm thinking three minutes, tops."

John thought she might be wrong about that. The guy's entrance had been perfectly calculated to capture the imaginations of little ones, and his wig was funny rather than scary. His cheerful face was unmarked by greasepaint, and that was also good. Clowns, in John's opinion, were highly overrated. They scared the shit out of kids under six. Kids over that age merely found them boring.

My, you're in a bilious mood today.

Maybe because he'd come ready to observe some sort of freaky-deaky, and nothing had transpired. To him, Abra seemed like a perfectly ordinary little kid. Cheerier than most, maybe, but good cheer seemed to run in the family. Except when Chetta and Dave were sniping at each other, that was.

"Don't underestimate the attention spans of the wee folk." He leaned past Chetta and used his napkin to wipe the smudge of frosting from Lucy's chin. "If he has an act, he'll hold them for fifteen minutes, at least. Maybe twenty."

"*If* he does," Lucy said skeptically.

It turned out that Reggie Pelletier, aka The Great Mysterio, *did* have an act, and a good one. While his faithful assistant, The Not-So-Great Dave, set up his table and opened the suitcase, Mysterio asked the birthday girl and her guests to admire his flower. When they drew close, it shot water into their faces: first red, then green, then blue. They screamed with sugar-fueled laughter.

"Now, boys and girls . . . *ooh! Ahh! Yike!* That tickles!"

He took off his derby and pulled out a white rabbit. The kids gasped. Mysterio passed the bunny to Abra, who stroked it and then passed it on without having to be told. The rabbit didn't seem to mind the attention. Maybe, John thought, it had snarked up a few Valium-laced pellets before the show. The last kid handed it back to Mysterio, who popped it into his hat, passed a hand over it, and then showed them the inside of the derby. Except for the American flag lining, it was empty.

"Where did the bunny go?" little Susie Soong-Bartlett asked.

"Into your dreams, darlin," Mysterio said. "It'll hop there tonight. Now who wants a magic scarf?"

There were cries of *I do, I do* from boys and girls alike. Mysterio produced them from his fists and passed them out. This was followed by more tricks in rapid-fire succession. By Dalton's watch, the kids stood around Mysterio in a bug-eyed semicircle for at least twenty-five minutes. And just as the first signs of restiveness began to appear in the audience, Mysterio wrapped things up. He produced five plates from his suitcase (which, when he showed it, had appeared to be as empty as his hat) and juggled them, singing "Happy Birthday to You" as he did it. All the kids joined in, and Abra seemed almost to levitate with joy.

The plates went back into the suitcase. He showed it to them again so they could see it was empty, then produced half a dozen spoons from it. These he proceeded to hang on his face, finishing with one on the tip of his nose. The birthday girl liked that one; she sat down on the grass, laughing and hugging herself with glee.

"Abba can do that," she said (she was currently fond of referring to herself in the third person—it was what David called her "Rickey Henderson phase"). "Abba can do spoongs."

"Good for you, honey," Mysterio said. He wasn't really paying attention, and John couldn't blame him for that; he had just put on one hell of a kiddie matinee, his face was red and damp with sweat in spite of the cool breeze blowing up from the river, and he still had his big exit to make, this time pedaling the oversize trike uphill.

He bent and patted Abra's head with one white-gloved hand. "Happy birthday to you, and thank all you kids for being such a good aud—"

From inside the house came a large and musical jangling, not unlike the sound of the bells hanging from the Godzilla-trike's handlebars. The kids only glanced in that direction before turning to watch Mysterio pedal away, but Lucy got up to see what had fallen over in the kitchen.

Two minutes later she came back outside. "John," she said. "You better look at this. I think it's what you came to see."

12

John, Lucy, and Concetta stood in the kitchen, looking up at the ceiling and saying nothing. None of them turned when Dave joined them; they were hypnotized. "What—" he began, then saw what. "Holy shit."

To this no one replied. David stared a little longer, trying to get the sense of what he was seeing, then left. A minute or two later he returned, leading his daughter by the hand. Abra was holding a balloon. Around her waist, worn like a sash, was the scarf she'd received from The Great Mysterio.

John Dalton dropped to one knee beside her. "Did you do that, honey?" It was a question to which he felt sure he knew the answer, but he wanted to hear what she had to say. He wanted to know how much she was aware of.

Abra first looked at the floor, where the silverware drawer lay. Some of the knives and forks had bounced free when the drawer shot from its socket, but they were all there. Not the spoons, however. The spoons were hanging from the ceiling, as if drawn upward and held by some exotic magnetic attraction. A couple swung lazily from the overhead light fixtures. The biggest, a serving spoon, dangled from the exhaust hood of the stove.

All kids had their own self-comforting mechanisms. John knew from long experience that for most it was a thumb socked securely in the mouth. Abra's was a little different. She cupped her right hand over the lower half of her face and rubbed her lips with her palm. As a result, her words were muffled. John took the hand away—gently. "What, honey?"

In a small voice she said, "Am I in trouble? I . . . I . . ." Her small chest began to hitch. She tried to put her comfort-hand back, but John held it. "I wanted to be like Minstrosio." She began to weep. John let her hand go and it went to her mouth, rubbing furiously.

David picked her up and kissed her cheek. Lucy put her arms around them both and kissed the top of her daughter's head. "No, honey, no. No trouble. You're fine."

Abra buried her face against her mother's neck. As she did it, the spoons fell. The clatter made them all jump.

13

Two months later, with summer just beginning in the White Mountains of New Hampshire, David and Lucy Stone sat in John Dalton's office, where the walls were papered with smiling photographs of the children he had treated over the years—many now old enough to have kids of their own.

John said, "I hired a computer-savvy nephew of mine—at my own expense, and don't worry about it, he works cheap—to see if there were any other documented cases like your daughter's, and to research them if there were. He restricted his search to the last thirty years and found over nine hundred."

David whistled. "That many!"

John shook his head. "*Not* that many. If it *were* a disease—and we don't need to revisit that discussion, because it's not—it would be as rare as elephantiasis. Or Blaschko's lines, which basically turns those who have it into human zebras. Blaschko's affects about one in every seven million. This thing of Abra's would be on that order."

"What exactly *is* Abra's thing?" Lucy had taken her husband's hand and was holding it tightly. "Telepathy? Telekinesis? Some other *tele*?"

"Those things clearly play a part. Is she telepathic? Since she knows when people are coming to visit, and knew Mrs. Judkins had been hurt, the answer seems to be yes. Is she telekinetic? Based on what we saw in your kitchen on the day of her birthday party, the answer is a hard yes. Is she psychic? A precognate, if you want to fancy it up? We can't be so sure of that, although the 9/11 thing and the story of the twenty-dollar bill behind the dresser are both suggestive. But what about the night your television showed *The Simpsons* on all the channels? What do you call that? Or what about the phantom Beatles tune? It would be telekinesis if the notes came from the piano . . . but you say they didn't."

"So what's next?" Lucy asked. "What do we watch out for?"

"I don't know. There's no predictive path to follow. The trouble with the field of psychic phenomena is that it isn't a field at all. There's too much charlatanry and too many people who are just off their damn rockers."

"So you can't tell us what to do," Lucy said. "That's the long and short of it."

John smiled. "I can tell you exactly what to do: keep on loving her. If my nephew is right—and you have to remember that A, he's only seventeen, and B, he's basing his conclusions on unstable data—you're apt to keep seeing weird stuff until she's a teenager. Some of it may be *gaudy* weird stuff. Around thirteen or fourteen, it'll plateau and then start to subside. By the time she's in her twenties, the various phenomena she's generating will probably be negligible." He smiled. "But she'll be a terrific poker player all her life."

"What if she starts seeing dead people, like the little boy in that movie?" Lucy asked. "What do we do then?"

"Then I guess you'd have proof of life after death. In the meantime, don't buy trouble. And keep your mouths shut, right?"

"Oh, you bet," Lucy said. She managed a smile, but given the fact she'd nibbled most of her lipstick off, it didn't look very confident. "The last thing we want is our daughter on the cover of *Inside View*."

"Thank God none of the other parents saw that thing with the spoons," David said.

"Here's a question," John said. "Do you think she knows how special she is?"

The Stones exchanged a look.

"I . . . don't think so," Lucy said at last. "Although after the spoons . . . we made sort of a big deal about it . . ."

"A big deal in *your* mind," John said. "Probably not hers. She cried a little, then went back out with a smile on her face. There was no shouting, scolding, spanking, or shaming. My advice is to let it ride for the time being. When she gets a little older, you can caution her about not doing any of her special tricks at school. Treat her as normal, because mostly she is. Right?"

"Right," David said. "And it's not like she's got spots, or swellings, or a third eye."

"Oh yes she does," Lucy said. She was thinking of the caul. "She does so have a third eye. You can't see it—but it's there."

John stood up. "I'll get all my nephew's printouts and send them to you, if you'd like that."

"I would," David said. "Very much. I think dear old Momo would, too." He wrinkled his nose a bit at this. Lucy saw it and frowned.

"In the meantime, enjoy your daughter," John told them. "From everything I've seen, she's a very enjoyable child. You're going to get through this."

For awhile, it seemed he was right.

CHAPTER FOUR

PAGING DOCTOR SLEEP

1

It was January of 2007. In the turret room of Rivington House, Dan's space heater was running full blast, but the room was still cold. A nor'easter, driven by a fifty-mile-an-hour gale, had blown down from the mountains, piling five inches of snow an hour on the sleeping town of Frazier. When the storm finally eased the following afternoon, some of the drifts against the north and east sides of the buildings on Cranmore Avenue would be twelve feet deep.

Dan wasn't bothered by the cold; nestled beneath two down comforters, he was warm as tea and toast. Yet the wind had found its way inside his head just as it found its way under the sashes and doorsills of the old Victorian he now called home. In his dream, he could hear it moaning around the hotel where he had spent one winter as a little boy. In his dream, he *was* that little boy.

He's on the second floor of the Overlook. Mommy is sleeping and Daddy's in the basement, looking at old papers. He's doing RESEARCH. The RESEARCH is for the book he's going to write. Danny isn't supposed to be up here, and he's not supposed to have the passkey that's clutched in one hand, but he hasn't been able to stay away. Right now he's staring at a firehose that's bolted to the wall. It's folded over and over on itself, and it looks like a snake with a brass head. A sleeping snake. Of course it's not a snake—that's canvas he's looking at, not scales—but it sure does look like a snake.

Sometimes it *is* a snake.

"Go on," he whispers to it in this dream. He's trembling with terror, but something drives him on. And why? Because he's doing his own RESEARCH, that's why. "Go on, bite me! You can't, can you? Because you're just a stupid HOSE!"

The nozzle of the stupid hose stirs, and all at once, instead of looking at it sideways, Danny is looking into its bore. Or maybe into its mouth. A single clear drop appears below the black hole, elongating. In it he can see his own wide eyes reflected back at him.

A drop of water or a drop of poison?

Is it a snake or a hose?

Who can say, my dear Redrum, Redrum my dear? Who can say?

It buzzes at him, and terror jumps up his throat from his rapidly beating heart. Rattlesnakes buzz like that.

Now the nozzle of the hose-snake rolls away from the stack of canvas it's lying on and drops to the carpet with a dull thud. It buzzes again and he knows he should step back before it can rush forward and bite him, but he's frozen he can't move and it's buzzing—

"Wake up, Danny!" Tony calls from somewhere. "Wake up, wake up!"

But he can wake up no more than he can move, this is the Overlook, they are snowed in, and things are different now. Hoses become snakes, dead women open their eyes, and his father . . . oh dear God WE HAVE TO GET OUT OF HERE BECAUSE MY FATHER IS GOING CRAZY.

The rattlesnake buzzes. It buzzes. It

2

Dan heard the wind howling, but not outside the Overlook. No, outside the turret of Rivington House. He heard snow rattle against the north-facing window. It sounded like sand. And he heard the intercom giving off its low buzz.

He threw back the comforters and swung his legs out, wincing as his warm toes met the cold floor. He crossed the room, almost prancing on the balls of his feet. He turned on the desk lamp and blew out his breath. No visible vapor, but even with the space heater's element coils glowing a dull red, the room temperature tonight had to be in the mid-forties.

Buzz.

He pushed TALK on the intercom and said, "I'm here. Who's there?"

"Claudette. I think you've got one, doc."

"Mrs. Winnick?" He was pretty sure it was her, and that would mean putting on his parka, because Vera Winnick was in Rivington Two, and the walkway between here and there would be colder than a witch's belt buckle. Or a well-digger's tit. Or whatever the saying was. Vera had been hanging by a thread for a week now, comatose, in and out of Cheyne-Stokes respiration, and this was exactly the sort of night the frail ones picked to go out on. Usually at 4 a.m. He checked his watch. Only 3:20, but that was close enough for government work.

Claudette Albertson surprised him. "No, it's Mr. Hayes, right down here on the first floor with us."

"Are you sure?" Dan had played a game of checkers with Charlie Hayes just that afternoon, and for a man with acute myelogenous leukemia, he'd seemed as lively as a cricket.

"Nope, but Azzie's in there. And you know what you say."

What he said was Azzie was never wrong, and he had almost six years' worth of experience on which to base that conclusion. Azreel wandered freely around the three buildings that made up the Rivington complex, spending most of his afternoons curled up on a sofa in the rec room, although it wasn't unusual to see him draped across one of the card tables—with or without a half-completed jigsaw puzzle on it—like a carelessly thrown stole. All the residents seemed to like him (if there had been complaints about the House housecat, they hadn't reached Dan's ears), and Azzie liked them all right back. Sometimes he would jump up in some half-dead oldster's lap . . . but lightly, never seeming to hurt. Which was remarkable, given his size. Azzie was a twelve-pounder.

Other than during his afternoon naps, Az rarely stayed in one location for long; he always had places to go, people to see, things to do. ("That cat's a *playa*," Claudette had once told Danny.) You might see him visiting the spa, licking a paw and taking a little heat. Relaxing on a stopped treadmill in the Health Suite. Sitting atop an abandoned gurney and staring into thin air at those things only cats can see. Sometimes he stalked the back lawn with his ears flattened against his skull, the very picture of feline predation, but if he caught birds and chipmunks, he took them into one of the neighboring yards or across to the town common and dismembered them there.

The rec room was open round-the-clock, but Azzie rarely visited there once the TV was off and the residents were gone. When evening gave way to night and the pulse of Rivington House slowed, Azzie became restless, patrolling the corridors like a sentry on the edge of enemy territory. Once the lights dimmed, you might not even see him unless you were looking right at him; his unremarkable mouse-colored fur blended in with the shadows.

He never went into the guest rooms unless one of the guests was dying.

Then he would either slip in (if the door was unlatched) or sit outside with his tail curled around his haunches, *waowing* in a low, polite voice to be admitted. When he was, he would jump up on the guest's bed (they were always guests at Rivington House, never patients) and settle there, purring. If the person so chosen happened to be awake, he or she might stroke the cat. To Dan's knowledge, no one had ever demanded that Azzie be evicted. They seemed to know he was there as a friend.

"Who's the doctor on call?" Dan asked.

"You," Claudette promptly came back.

"You know what I mean. The real doctor."

"Emerson, but when I phoned his service, the woman told me not to be silly. Everything's socked in from Berlin to Manchester. She said that except for the ones on the turnpikes, even the plows are waiting for daylight."

"All right," Dan said. "I'm on my way."

3

After working at the hospice for awhile, Dan had come to realize there was a class system even for the dying. The guest accommodations in the main house were bigger and more expensive than those in Rivington One and Two. In the Victorian manse where Helen Rivington had once hung her hat and written her romances, the rooms were called suites and named after famous New Hampshire residents. Charlie Hayes was in Alan Shepard. To get there, Dan had to pass the snack alcove at the foot of the stairs, where there were vending machines and a few hard plastic chairs. Fred Carling was plopped down in one of these, munching peanut butter crackers and reading an old issue of *Popular Mechanics*. Carling was one of three orderlies on the midnight-to-eight shift. The other two rotated to days twice a month; Carling never did. A self-proclaimed night owl, he was a beefy time-server whose arms, sleeved out in a tangle of tats, suggested a biker past.

"Well lookit here," he said. "It's Danny-boy. Or are you in your secret identity tonight?"

Dan was still only half awake and in no mood for joshing. "What do you know about Mr. Hayes?"

"Nothing except the cat's in there, and that usually means they're going to go tits-up."

"No bleeding?"

The big man shrugged. "Well yeah, he had a little noser. I put the bloody towels in a plague-bag, just like I'm s'posed to. They're in Laundry A, if you want to check."

Dan thought of asking how a nosebleed that took more than one towel to clean up could be characterized as little, and decided to let it go. Carling was an unfeeling dolt, and how he'd gotten a job here—even on the night shift, when most of the guests were either asleep or trying to be quiet so they wouldn't disturb anyone else—was beyond Dan. He suspected somebody might have pulled a wire or two. It was how the world worked. Hadn't his own father pulled a wire to get his final job, as caretaker at the Overlook Hotel?

Maybe that wasn't proof positive that who you knew was a lousy way to get a job, but it certainly seemed suggestive.

"Enjoy your evening, Doctor *Sleeeep*," Carling called after him, making no effort to keep his voice down.

At the nurses' station, Claudette was charting meds while Janice Barker watched a small TV with the sound turned down low. The current program was one of those endless ads for colon cleanser, but Jan was watching with her eyes wide and her mouth hung ajar. She started when Dan tapped his fingernails on the counter and he realized she hadn't been fascinated but half asleep.

"Can either of you tell me anything substantive about Charlie? Carling knows from nothing."

Claudette glanced down the hall to make sure Fred Carling wasn't in view, then lowered her voice, anyway. "That man's as useless as boobs on a bull. I keep hoping he'll get fired."

Dan kept his similar opinion to himself. Constant sobriety, he had discovered, did wonders for one's powers of discretion.

"I checked him fifteen minutes ago," Jan said. "We check them a lot when Mr. Pussycat comes to visit."

"How long's Azzie been in there?"

"He was meowing outside the door when we came on duty at midnight," Claudette said, "so I opened it for him. He jumped right up on the bed. You know how he does. I almost called you then, but Charlie was awake and responsive. When I said hi, he hi'd me right back and started petting Azzie. So I decided to wait. About an hour later, he had a nosebleed. Fred cleaned him up. I had to tell him to put the towels in a plague-bag."

Plague-bags were what the staff called the dissolvable plastic sacks in which clothing, linen, and towels contaminated with bodily fluids or tissue were stored. It was a state regulation that was supposed to minimize the spread of blood-borne pathogens.

"When I checked him forty or fifty minutes ago," Jan said, "he was asleep. I gave him a shake. He opened his eyes, and they were all bloodshot."

"That's when I called Emerson," Claudette said. "And after I got the big no-way-Jose from the girl on service, I called you. Are you going down now?"

"Yes."

"Good luck," Jan said. "Ring if you need something."

"I will. Why are you watching an infomercial for colon cleanser, Jannie? Or is that too personal?"

She yawned. "At this hour, the only other thing on is an infomercial for the Ahh Bra. I already have one of those."

4

The door of the Alan Shepard Suite was standing half open, but Dan knocked anyway. When there was no response, he pushed it all the way open. Someone (probably one of the nurses; it almost certainly hadn't been Fred Carling) had cranked up the bed a little. The sheet was pulled to Charlie Hayes's chest. He was ninety-one, painfully thin, and so pale he hardly seemed to be there at all. Dan had to stand still for thirty seconds before he could be absolutely sure the old man's pajama top was going up and down. Azzie was curled beside the scant bulge of one hip. When Dan came in, the cat surveyed him with those inscrutable eyes.

"Mr. Hayes? Charlie?"

Charlie's eyes didn't open. The lids were bluish. The skin beneath them was darker, a purple-black. When Dan got to the side of the bed, he saw more color: a little crust of blood beneath each nostril and in one corner of the folded mouth.

Dan went into the bathroom, took a facecloth, wetted it in warm water, wrung it out. When he returned to Charlie's bedside, Azzie got to his feet and delicately stepped to the other side of the sleeping man, leaving Dan a place to sit down. The sheet was still warm from Azzie's body. Gently, Dan wiped the blood from beneath Charlie's nose. As he was doing the mouth, Charlie opened his eyes. "Dan. It's you, isn't it? My eyes are a little blurry."

Bloody was what they were.

"How are you feeling, Charlie? Any pain? If you're in pain, I can get Claudette to bring you a pill."

"No pain," Charlie said. His eyes shifted to Azzie, then went back to Dan. "I know why he's here. And I know why *you're* here."

"I'm here because the wind woke me up. Azzie was probably just looking for some company. Cats are nocturnal, you know."

Dan pushed up the sleeve of Charlie's pajama top to take a pulse, and saw four purple bruises lined up on the old man's stick of a forearm. Late-stage leukemia patients bruised if you even breathed on them, but these were finger-bruises, and Dan knew perfectly well where they had come from. He had more control over his temper now that he was sober, but it was still there, just like the occasional strong urge to take a drink.

Carling, you bastard. Wouldn't he move quick enough for you? Or were you just mad to have to be cleaning up a nosebleed when all you wanted to do was read magazines and eat those fucking yellow crackers?

He tried not to show what he was feeling, but Azzie seemed to sense it; he gave a small, troubled meow. Under other circumstances, Dan might have asked questions, but now he had more pressing matters to deal with. Azzie was right again. He only had to touch the old man to know.

"I'm pretty scared," Charlie said. His voice was little more than a whisper. The low, steady moan of the wind outside was louder. "I didn't think I would be, but I am."

"There's nothing to be scared of."

Instead of taking Charlie's pulse—there was really no point—he took one of the old man's hands in his. He saw Charlie's twin sons at four, on swings. He saw Charlie's wife pulling down a shade in the bedroom, wearing nothing but the slip of Belgian lace he'd bought her for their first anniversary; saw how her ponytail swung over one shoulder when she turned to look at him, her face lit in a smile that was all *yes*. He saw a Farmall tractor with a striped umbrella raised over the seat. He smelled bacon and heard Frank Sinatra singing "Come Fly with Me" from a cracked Motorola radio sitting on a worktable littered with tools. He saw a hubcap full of rain reflecting a red barn. He tasted blueberries and gutted a deer and fished in some distant lake whose surface was dappled by steady autumn rain. He was sixty, dancing with his wife in the American Legion hall. He was thirty, splitting wood. He was five, wearing shorts and pulling a red wagon. Then the pictures blurred together, the way cards do when they're shuffled in the hands of an expert, and the wind was blowing big snow down from the mountains, and in here was the silence and Azzie's solemn watching eyes. At times like this, Dan knew what he was for. At times like this he regretted none of the pain and sorrow and anger and horror, because they had brought him here to this room while the wind whooped outside. Charlie Hayes had come to the border.

"I'm not scared of hell. I lived a decent life, and I don't think there is such a place, anyway. I'm scared there's *nothing*." He struggled for breath. A pearl of blood was swelling in the corner of his right eye. "There was nothing *before*, we all know that, so doesn't it stand to reason that there's nothing after?"

"But there is." Dan wiped Charlie's face with the damp cloth. "We never really end, Charlie. I don't know how that can be, or what it means, I only know that it is."

"Can you help me get over? They say you can help people."

"Yes. I can help." He took Charlie's other hand, as well. "It's just going to sleep. And when you wake up—you *will* wake up—everything is going to be better."

"Heaven? Do you mean heaven?"

"I don't know, Charlie."

The power was very strong tonight. He could feel it flowing through their clasped hands like an electric current and cautioned himself to be gentle. Part of him was inhabiting the faltering body that was shutting down and the failing senses

(*hurry up please*)

that were turning off. He was inhabiting a mind

(*hurry up please it's time*)

that was still as sharp as ever, and aware it was thinking its last thoughts . . . at least as Charlie Hayes.

The bloodshot eyes closed, then opened again. Very slowly.

"Everything's all right," Dan said. "You only need sleep. Sleep will make you better."

"Is that what you call it?"

"Yes. I call it sleep, and it's safe to sleep."

"Don't go."

"I won't. I'm with you." So he was. It was his terrible privilege.

Charlie's eyes closed again. Dan closed his own and saw a slow blue pulse in the darkness. Once . . . twice . . . stop. Once . . . twice . . . stop. Outside the wind was blowing.

"Sleep, Charlie. You're doing fine, but you're tired and you need to sleep."

"I see my wife." The faintest of whispers.

"Do you?"

"She says . . ."

There was no more, just a final blue pulse behind Dan's eyes and a final exhalation from the man on the bed. Dan opened his eyes, listened to the wind, and waited for the last thing. It came a few seconds later: a dull red mist that rose from Charlie's nose, mouth, and eyes. This was what an old nurse in Tampa—one who had about the same twinkle as Billy Freeman—called "the gasp." She said she had seen it many times.

Dan saw it *every* time.

It rose and hung above the old man's body. Then it faded.

Dan slid up the right sleeve of Charlie's pajamas, and felt for a pulse. It was just a formality.

5

Azzie usually left before it was over, but not tonight. He was standing on the counterpane beside Charlie's hip, staring at the door. Dan turned, expecting to see Claudette or Jan, but no one was there.

Except there was.

"Hello?"

Nothing.

"Are you the little girl who writes on my blackboard sometimes?"

No response. But someone was there, all right.

"Is your name Abra?"

Faint, almost inaudible because of the wind, there came a ripple of piano notes. Dan might have believed it was his imagination (he could not always tell the difference between that and the shining) if not for Azzie, whose ears twitched and whose eyes never left the empty doorway. Someone was there, watching.

"Are you Abra?"

There was another ripple of notes, then silence again. Except this time it was absence. Whatever her name was, she was gone. Azzie stretched, leaped down from the bed, and left without a look back.

Dan sat where he was a little longer, listening to the wind. Then he lowered the bed, pulled the sheet up over Charlie's face, and went back to the nurses' station to tell them there had been a death on the floor.

6

When his part of the paperwork was complete, Dan walked down to the snack alcove. There was a time he would have gone there on the run, fists already clenched, but those days were gone. Now he walked, taking long slow breaths to calm his heart and mind. There was a saying in AA, "Think before you drink," but what Casey K. told him during their once-a-week tête-à-têtes was to think before he did anything. *You didn't get sober to be stupid, Danny. Keep it in mind the next time you start listening to that itty-bitty shitty committee inside your head.*

But those goddam fingermarks.

Carling was rocked back in his chair, now eating Junior Mints. He had swapped *Popular Mechanics* for a photo mag with the latest bad-boy sitcom star on the cover.

"Mr. Hayes has passed on," Dan said mildly.

"Sorry to hear it." Not looking up from the magazine. "But that *is* what they're here for, isn't i—"

Dan lifted one foot, hooked it behind one of the tilted front legs of Carling's chair, and yanked. The chair spun away and Carling landed on the floor. The box of Junior Mints flew out of his hand. He stared up at Dan unbelievingly.

"Have I got your attention?"

"You sonofa—" Carling started to get up. Dan put his foot on the man's chest and pushed him back against the wall.

"I see I have. Good. It would be better right now if you didn't get up. Just sit there and listen to me." Dan bent forward and clasped his knees with his hands. Tight, because all those hands wanted to do right now was hit. And hit. And hit. His temples were throbbing. *Slow,* he told himself. *Don't let it get the better of you.*

But it was hard.

"The next time I see your fingermarks on a patient, I'll photograph them and go to Mrs. Clausen and you'll be out on the street no matter who you know. And once you're no longer a part of this institution, I'll find you and beat the living shit out of you."

Carling got to his feet, using the wall to support his back and keeping a close eye on Dan as he did it. He was taller, and outweighed Dan by a hundred pounds at least. He balled his fists. "I'd like to see you try. How about now?"

"Sure, but not here," Dan said. "Too many people trying to sleep, and we've got a dead man down the hall. One with your marks on him."

"I didn't do nothing but go to take his pulse. You know how easy they bruise when they got the leukemia."

"I do," Dan agreed, "but you hurt him on purpose. I don't know why, but I know you did."

There was a flicker in Carling's muddy eyes. Not shame; Dan didn't think the man was capable of feeling that. Just unease at being seen through. And fear of being caught. "Big man. Doctor *Sleeeep*. Think your shit don't stink?"

"Come on, Fred, let's go outside. More than happy to." And this was true. There was a second Dan inside. He wasn't as close to the surface anymore, but he was still there and still the same ugly, irrational sonofabitch he'd always been. Out of the corner of his eye Dan could see Claudette and Jan standing halfway down the hall, their eyes wide and their arms around each other.

Carling thought it over. Yes, he was bigger, and yes, he had more reach. But he was also out of shape—too many overstuffed burritos, too many beers, much shorter wind than he'd had in his twenties—and there was something worrisome in the skinny guy's face. He'd seen it before, back in his Road Saints days. Some guys had lousy circuit breakers in their heads. They tripped easy, and once they did, those guys would burn on until they burned out. He had taken Torrance for some mousy little geek who wouldn't say shit if he had a mouthful, but he saw that he'd been wrong about that. His secret identity wasn't Doctor Sleep, it was Doctor Crazy.

After considering this carefully, Fred said, "I wouldn't waste my time."

Dan nodded. "Good. Save us both getting frostbite. Just remember what I said. If you don't want to go to the hospital, keep your hands to yourself from now on."

"Who died and left you in charge?"

"I don't know," Dan said. "I really don't."

7

Dan went back to his room and back to bed, but he couldn't sleep. He had made roughly four dozen deathbed visits during his time at Rivington House, and usually they left him calm. Not tonight. He was still trembling with rage. His conscious mind hated that red storm, but some lower part of him loved it. Probably it went back to plain old genetics; nature triumphing over nurture. The longer he stayed sober, the more old memories surfaced. Some of the clearest were of his father's rages. He had been hoping that Carling would take him up on it. Would go outside into the snow and wind, where Dan Torrance, son of Jack, would give that worthless puppy his medicine.

God knew he didn't want to be his father, whose bouts of sobriety had been the white-knuckle kind. AA was supposed to help with anger, and mostly it did, but there were times like tonight when Dan realized what a flimsy barrier it was. Times when he felt worthless, and the booze seemed like all he deserved. At times like that he felt very close to his father.

He thought: *Mama.*

He thought: *Canny.*

He thought: *Worthless pups need to take their medicine. And you know where they sell it, don't you? Damn near everywhere.*

The wind rose in a furious gust, making the turret groan. When it died, the blackboard girl was there. He could almost hear her breathing.

He lifted one hand out from beneath the comforters. For a moment it only hung there in the cold air, and then he felt hers— small, warm—slip into it. "Abra," he said. "Your name is Abra, but sometimes people call you Abby. Isn't that right?"

No answer came, but he didn't really need one. All he needed was the sensation of that warm hand in his. It only lasted for a few seconds, but it was long enough to soothe him. He closed his eyes and slept.

8

Twenty miles away, in the little town of Anniston, Abra Stone lay awake. The hand that had enfolded hers held on for a moment or two. Then it turned to mist and was gone. But it had been there. *He* had been there. She had found him in a dream, but when she woke, she had discovered the dream was real. She was standing in the doorway of a room. What she had seen there was terrible and wonderful at the same time. There was death, and death was scary, but there had also been helping. The man who was helping hadn't been able to see her, but the cat had. The cat had a name like hers, but not exactly.

He didn't see me but he felt me. And we were together just now. I think I helped him, like he helped the man who died.

That was a good thought. Holding onto it (as she had held the phantom hand), Abra rolled over on her side, hugged her stuffed rabbit to her chest, and went to sleep.

CHAPTER FIVE

THE TRUE KNOT

1

The True Knot wasn't incorporated, but if it had been, certain side o' the road communities in Maine, Florida, Colorado, and New Mexico would have been referred to as "company towns." These were places where all the major businesses and large plots of land could be traced back, through a tangle of holding companies, to them. The True's towns, with colorful names like Dry Bend, Jerusalem's Lot, Oree, and Sidewinder, were safe havens, but they never stayed in those places for long; mostly they were migratory. If you drive the turnpikes and main-traveled highways of America, you may have seen them. Maybe it was on I-95 in South Carolina, somewhere south of Dillon and north of Santee. Maybe it was on I-80 in Nevada, in the mountain country west of Draper. Or in Georgia, while negotiating—slowly, if you know what's good for you—that notorious Highway 41 speedtrap outside Tifton.

How many times have you found yourself behind a lumbering RV, eating exhaust and waiting impatiently for your chance to pass? Creeping along at forty when you could be doing a perfectly legal sixty-five or even seventy? And when there's finally a hole in the fast lane and you pull out, holy God, you see a long line of those damn things, gas hogs driven at exactly ten miles an hour below the legal speed limit by bespectacled golden oldies who hunch over their steering wheels, gripping them like they think they're going to fly away.

Or maybe you've encountered them in the turnpike rest areas, when you stop to stretch your legs and maybe drop a few quarters into one of the vending machines. The entrance ramps to those rest stops always divide in two, don't they? Cars in one parking lot, long-haul trucks and RVs in another. Usually the lot for the big rigs and RVs is a little farther away. You might have seen the True's rolling motorhomes parked in that lot, all in a cluster. You might have seen their owners walking up to the main building—slow, because many of them look old and some of them are pretty darn fat—always in a group, always keeping to themselves.

Sometimes they pull off at one of the exits loaded with gas stations, motels, and fast-food joints. And if you see those RVs parked at McDonald's or Burger King, you keep on going because you know they'll all be lined up at the counter, the men wearing floppy golf hats or long-billed fishing caps, the women in stretch pants (usually powder-blue) and shirts that say things like ASK ME ABOUT MY GRANDCHILDREN! or JESUS IS KING or HAPPY WANDERER. You'd rather go half a mile farther down the road, to the Waffle House or Shoney's, wouldn't you? Because you know they'll take forever to order, mooning over the menu, always wanting their Quarter Pounders without the pickles or their Whoppers without the sauce. Asking if there are any interesting tourist attractions in the area, even though anyone can see this is just another nothing three-stoplight burg where the kids leave as soon as they graduate from the nearest high school.

You hardly see them, right? Why would you? They're just the RV People, elderly retirees and a few younger compatriots living their rootless lives on the turnpikes and blue highways, staying at campgrounds where they sit around in their Walmart lawnchairs and cook on their hibachis while they talk about investments and fishing tournaments and hotpot recipes and God knows what. They're the ones who always stop at fleamarkets and yardsales, parking their damn dinosaurs nose-to-tail half on the shoulder and half on the road, so you have to slow to a crawl in order to creep by. They are the opposite of the motorcycle clubs you sometimes see on those same turnpikes and blue highways; the Mild Angels instead of the wild ones.

They're annoying as hell when they descend en masse on a rest area and fill up all the toilets, but once their balky, road-stunned bowels finally work and you're able to take a pew yourself, you put them out of your mind, don't you? They're no more remarkable than a flock of birds on a telephone wire or a herd of cows grazing in a field beside the road. Oh, you might wonder how they can afford to fill those fuel-guzzling monstrosities (because they *must* be on comfy fixed incomes, how else could they spend all their time driving around like they do), and you might puzzle over why anyone would want to spend their golden years cruising all those endless American miles between Hoot and Holler, but beyond that, you probably never spare them a thought.

And if you happen to be one of those unfortunate people who's ever lost a kid—nothing left but a bike in the vacant lot down the street, or a little cap lying in the bushes at the edge of a nearby stream—you probably never thought of *them*. Why would you? No, it was probably some hobo. Or (worse to consider, but horribly plausible) some sick fuck from your very own town, maybe your very own neighborhood, maybe even *your very own street,* some sick killer pervo who's very good at looking normal and will go on looking normal until someone finds a clatter of bones in the guy's basement or buried in his backyard. You'd never think of the RV People, those midlife pensioners and cheery older folks in their golf hats and sun visors with appliquéd flowers on them.

And mostly you'd be right. There are thousands of RV People, but by 2011 there was only one Knot left in America: the *True* Knot. They liked moving around, and that was good, because they had to. If they stayed in one place, they'd eventually attract attention, because they don't age like other people. Apron Annie or Dirty Phil (rube names Anne Lamont and Phil Caputo) might appear to grow twenty years older overnight. The Little twins (Pea and Pod) might snap back from twenty-two to twelve (or almost), the age at which they Turned, but their Turning was long ago. The only member of the True who's actually young is Andrea Steiner, now known as Snakebite Andi . . . and even she's not as young as she looks.

A tottery, grumpy old lady of eighty suddenly becomes sixty again. A leathery old gent of seventy is able to put away his cane; the skin-tumors on his arms and face disappear.

Black-Eyed Susie loses her hitching limp.

Diesel Doug goes from half blind with cataracts to sharp-eyed, his bald spot magically gone. All at once, hey presto, he's forty-five again.

Steamhead Steve's crooked back straightens. His wife, Baba the Red, ditches those uncomfortable continence pants, puts on her rhinestone-studded Ariat boots, and says she wants to go out line dancing.

Given time to observe such changes, people would wonder and people would talk. Eventually some reporter would turn up, and the True Knot shied away from publicity the way vampires supposedly shy away from sunlight.

But since they *don't* live in one place (and when they stop for an extended period in one of their company towns, they keep to themselves), they fit right in. Why not? They wear the same clothes as the other RV People, they wear the same el cheapo sunglasses, they buy the same souvenir t-shirts and consult the same AAA roadmaps. They put the same decals on their Bounders and 'Bagos, touting all the peculiar places they've visited (I HELPED TRIM THE WORLD'S BIGGEST TREE IN CHRISTMASLAND!), and you find yourself looking at the same bumper stickers while you're stuck behind them (OLD BUT NOT DEAD, SAVE MEDICARE, I'M A CONSERVATIVE AND I VOTE!!), waiting for a chance to pass. They eat fried chicken from the Colonel and buy the occasional scratch ticket in those EZ-on, EZ-off convenience stores where they sell beer, bait, ammo, *Motor Trend* magazine, and ten thousand kinds of candybars. If there's a bingo hall in the town where they stop, a bunch of them are apt to go on over, take a table, and play until the last cover-all game is finished. At one of those games, Greedy G (rube name Greta Moore) won five hundred dollars. She gloated over that for *months,* and although the members of the True have all the money they need, it pissed off some of the other ladies to no end. Token Charlie wasn't too pleased, either. He said he'd been waiting on B7 for five pulls from the hopper when the G finally bingoed.

"Greedy, you're one lucky bitch," he said.

"And you're one unlucky bastard," she replied. "One unlucky *black* bastard." And went off chortling.

If one of them happens to get speed-trapped or stopped for some minor traffic offense—it's rare, but it does happen—the cop finds nothing but valid licenses, up-to-date insurance cards, and paperwork in apple-pie order. No voices are raised while the cop's standing there with his citation book, even if it's an obvious scam. The charges are never disputed, and all fines are paid promptly. America is a living body, the highways are its arteries, and the True Knot slips along them like a silent virus.

But there are no dogs.

Ordinary RV People travel with lots of canine company, usually those little shit-machines with white fur, gaudy collars, and nasty tempers. You know the kind; they have irritating barks that hurt your ears and ratty little eyes full of disturbing intelligence. You see them sniffing their way through the grass in the designated pet-walking areas of the turnpike rest stops, their owners trailing behind, pooper-scoopers at the ready. In addition to the usual decals and bumper stickers on the motorhomes of these ordinary RV People, you're apt to see yellow diamond-shaped signs reading POMERANIAN ON BOARD or I ♥ MY POODLE.

Not the True Knot. They don't like dogs, and dogs don't like them. You might say dogs see *through* them. To the sharp and watchful eyes behind the cut-rate sunglasses. To the strong and long-muscled hunters' legs beneath the polyester slacks from Walmart. To the sharp teeth beneath the dentures, waiting to come out.

They don't like dogs, but they like certain children.

Oh yes, they like certain children very much.

2

In May of 2011, not long after Abra Stone celebrated her tenth birthday and Dan Torrance his tenth year of AA sobriety, Crow Daddy knocked on the door of Rosie the Hat's EarthCruiser. The True was currently staying at the Kozy Kampground outside Lexington, Kentucky. They were on their way to Colorado, where they would spend most of the summer in one of their bespoke towns, this one a place Dan sometimes revisited in his dreams. Usually they were in no hurry to get anywhere, but there was some urgency this summer. All of them knew it but none of them talked about it.

Rose would take care of it. She always had.

"Come," she said, and Crow Daddy stepped in.

When on a business errand, he always stepped out in good suits and expensive shoes polished to a mirror gloss. If he was feeling particularly old-school, he might even carry a walking stick. This morning he was wearing baggy pants held up by suspenders, a strappy t-shirt with a fish on it (KISS MY BASS printed beneath), and a flat workman's cap, which he swept off as he closed the door behind him. He was her sometime lover as well as her second-in-command, but he never failed to show respect. It was one of many things Rose liked about him. She had no doubt that the True could carry on under his leadership if she died. For awhile, at least. But for another hundred years? Perhaps not. *Probably* not. He had a silver tongue and cleaned up well when he had to deal with the rubes, but Crow had only rudimentary planning skills, and no real vision.

This morning he looked troubled.

Rose was sitting on the sofa in capri pants and a plain white bra, smoking a cigarette and watching the third hour of *Today* on her big wall-mounted TV. That was the "soft" hour, when they featured celebrity chefs and actors doing PR for their new movies. Her tophat was cocked back on her head. Crow Daddy had known her for more years than the rubes lived, and he still didn't know what magic held it at that gravity-defying angle.

She picked up the remote and muted the sound. "Why, it's Henry Rothman, as I live and breathe. Looking remarkably tasty, too, although I doubt you came to be tasted. Not at quarter of ten in the morning, and not with that look on your face. Who died?"

She meant it as a joke, but the wincing frown that tightened his forehead told her it wasn't one. She turned the TV off and made a business of butting her cigarette, not wanting him to see the dismay she felt. Once the True had been over two hundred strong. As of yesterday, they numbered forty-one. If she was right about the meaning of that wince, they were one less today.

"Tommy the Truck," he said. "Went in his sleep. Cycled once, and then boom. Didn't suffer at all. Which is fucking rare, as you know."

"Did Nut see him?" *While he was still there to be seen,* she thought but did not add. Walnut, whose rube driver's license and various rube credit cards identified him as Peter Wallis of Little Rock, Arkansas, was the True's sawbones.

"No, it was too quick. Heavy Mary was with him. Tommy woke her up, thrashing. She thought it was a bad dream and gave him an elbow . . . only by then there was nothing left to poke but his pajamas. It was probably a heart attack. Tommy had a bad cold. Nut thinks that might have been a contributing factor. And you know the sonofabitch always smoked like a chimney."

"We don't *get* heart attacks." Then, reluctantly: "Of course, we usually don't get colds, either. He was really wheezing the last few days, wasn't he? Poor old TT."

"Yeah, poor old TT. Nut says it'd be impossible to tell anything for sure without an autopsy."

Which couldn't happen. By now there would be no body left to cut up.

"How's Mary taking it?"

"How do you think? She's broken-fucking-hearted. They go back to when Tommy the Truck was Tommy the Wagon. Almost ninety years. She was the one who took care of him after he Turned. Gave him his first steam when he woke up the next day. Now she says she wants to kill herself."

Rose was rarely shocked, but this did the job. No one in the True had ever killed themselves. Life was—to coin a phrase—their only reason for living.

"Probably just talk," Crow Daddy said. "Only . . ."

"Only what?"

"You're right about us not usually getting colds, but there have been quite a few just lately. Mostly just sniffles that come and go. Nut says it may be malnutrition. Of course he's just guessing."

Rose sat in thought, tapping her fingers against her bare midriff and staring at the blank rectangle of the TV. At last she said, "Okay, I agree that nourishment's been a bit thin lately, but we took steam in Delaware just a month ago, and Tommy was fine then. Plumped right up."

"Yeah, but Rosie—the kid from Delaware wasn't much. More hunchhead than steamhead."

She'd never thought of it just that way, but it was true. Also, he'd been nineteen, according to his driver's license. Well past whatever stunted prime he might have had around puberty. In another ten years he'd have been just another rube. Maybe even five. He hadn't been much of a meal, point taken. But you couldn't always have steak. Sometimes you had to settle for bean sprouts and tofu. At least they kept body and soul together until you could butcher the next cow.

Except psychic tofu and bean sprouts hadn't kept Tommy the Truck's body and soul together, had they?

"There used to be more steam," Crow said.

"Don't be daft. That's like the rubes saying that fifty years ago people were more neighborly. It's a myth, and I don't want you spreading it around. People are nervous enough already."

"You know me better than that. And I don't think it *is* a myth, darlin. If you think about it, it stands to reason. Fifty years ago there was more of *everything*—oil, wildlife, arable land, clean air. There were even a few honest politicians."

"Yes!" Rose cried. "Richard Nixon, remember him? Prince of the Rubes?"

But he wouldn't go chasing up this false trail. Crow might be a bit lacking in the vision department, but he was rarely distracted. That was why he was her second. He might even have a point. Who was to say that humans capable of providing the nourishment the True needed weren't dwindling, just like schools of tuna in the Pacific?

"You better bust open one of the canisters, Rosie." He saw her eyes widen and raised a hand to stop her from speaking. "Nobody's saying that out loud, but the whole family's thinking about it."

Rose had no doubt they were, and the idea that Tommy had died of complications resulting from malnutrition had a certain horrid plausibility. When steam was in short supply, life grew hard and lost its savor. They weren't vampires from one of those old Hammer horror pictures, but they still needed to eat.

"And how long since we've had a seventh wave?" Crow asked.

He knew the answer to that, and so did she. The True Knot had limited precognitive skills, but when a truly big rube disaster was approaching—a seventh wave—they all felt it. Although the details of the attack on the World Trade Center had only begun to clarify for them in the late summer of 2001, they had known *something* was going to happen in New York City for months in advance. She could still remember the joy and anticipation. She supposed hungry rubes felt the same way when they smelled a particularly savory meal cooking in the kitchen.

There had been plenty for everybody that day, and in the days following. There might only have been a couple of true steamheads among those who died when the Towers fell, but when the disaster was big enough, agony and violent death had an enriching quality. Which was why the True was drawn to such sites, like insects to a bright light. Locating single rube steamheads was far more difficult, and there were only three of them now with that specialized sonar in their heads: Grampa Flick, Barry the Chink, and Rose herself.

She got up, grabbed a neatly folded boatneck top from the counter, and pulled it over her head. As always, she looked gorgeous in a way that was a bit unearthly (those high cheekbones and slightly tipped eyes) but extremely sexy. She put her hat back on and gave it a tap for good luck. "How many full canisters do you think are left, Crow?"

He shrugged. "A dozen? Fifteen?"

"In that neighborhood," she agreed. Better that none of them knew the truth, not even her second. The last thing she needed was for the current unease to become outright panic. When people panicked, they ran in all directions. If that happened, the True might disintegrate.

Meanwhile, Crow was looking at her, and closely. Before he could see too much, she said, "Can you four-wall this place tonight?"

"You kidding? With the price of gas and diesel what it is, the guy who owns it can't fill half his spots, even on weekends. He'll jump at the chance."

"Then do it. We're going to take canister steam. Spread the word."

"You've got it." He kissed her, caressing one of her breasts as he did so. "This is my favorite top."

She laughed and pushed him away. "Any top with tits in it is your favorite top. Go on."

But he lingered, a grin tipping one corner of his mouth. "Is Rattlesnake Girl still sniffin around your door, beautiful?"

She reached down and briefly squeezed him below the belt. "Oh my gosh. Is that your jealous bone I'm feeling?"

"Say it is."

She doubted it, but was flattered, anyway. "She's with Sarey now, and the two of them are perfectly happy. But since we're on the subject of Andi, she can help us. You know how. Spread the word but speak to her first."

After he left, she locked the EarthCruiser, went to the cockpit, and dropped to her knees. She worked her fingers into the carpet between the driver's seat and the control pedals. A strip of it came up. Beneath was a square of metal with an embedded keypad. Rose ran the numbers, and the safe popped open an inch or two. She lifted the door the rest of the way and looked inside.

Fifteen or a dozen full canisters left. That had been Crow's guess, and although she couldn't read members of the True the way she could read the rubes, Rose was sure he had been purposely lowballing to cheer her up.

If he only knew, she thought.

The safe was lined with Styrofoam to protect the canisters in case of a road accident, and there were forty built-in cradles. On this fine May morning in Kentucky, thirty-seven of the canisters in those cradles were empty.

Rose took one of the remaining full ones and held it up. It was light; if you hefted it, you would have guessed it too was empty. She took the cap off, inspected the valve beneath to make sure the seal was still intact, then reclosed the safe and put the canister carefully—almost reverently—on the counter where her top had been folded.

After tonight there would only be two.

They had to find some big steam and refill at least a few of those empty canisters, and they had to do it soon. The True's back wasn't to the wall, not quite yet, but it was only inches away.

3

The Kozy Kampground owner and his wife had their own trailer, a permanent job set up on painted concrete blocks. April showers had brought lots of May flowers, and Mr. and Mrs. Kozy's front yard was full of them. Andrea Steiner paused a moment to admire the tulips and pansies before mounting the three steps to the door of the big Redman trailer, where she knocked.

Mr. Kozy opened up eventually. He was a small man with a big belly currently encased in a bright red strappy undershirt. In one hand he held a can of Pabst Blue Ribbon. In the other was a mustard-smeared brat wrapped in a slice of spongy white bread. Because his wife was currently in the other room, he paused for a moment to do a visual inventory of the young woman before him, ponytail to sneakers. "Yeah?"

Several in the True had a bit of sleeper talent, but Andi was by far the best, and her Turning had proved of enormous benefit to the True. She still used the ability on occasion to lift cash from the wallets of certain older rube gentlemen who were attracted to her. Rose found this risky and childish, but knew from experience that in time, what Andi called her *issues* would fade away. For the True Knot, the only issue was survival.

"I just had a quick question," Andi said.

"If it's about the toilets, darlin, the caca sucker don't come until Thursday."

"It's not about that."

"What, then?"

"Aren't you tired? Don't you want to go to sleep?"

Mr. Kozy immediately closed his eyes. The beer and the brat tumbled out of his hands, leaving a mess on the rug. *Oh well,* Andi thought, *Crow fronted the guy twelve hundred. Mr. Kozy can afford a bottle of carpet cleaner. Maybe even two.*

Andi took him by the arm and led him into the living room. Here was a pair of chintz-covered Kozy armchairs with TV trays set up in front of them.

"Sit," she said.

Mr. Kozy sat, eyes shut.

"You like to mess with young girls?" Andi asked him. "You would if you could, wouldn't you? If you could run fast enough to catch them, anyway." She surveyed him, hands on hips. "You're disgusting. Can you say that?"

"I'm disgusting," Mr. Kozy agreed. Then he began to snore.

Mrs. Kozy came in from the kitchen. She was gnawing on an ice cream sandwich. "Here, now, who are you? What are you telling him? What do you want?"

"For you to sleep," Andi told her.

Mrs. Kozy dropped her ice cream. Then her knees unhinged and she sat on it.

"Ah, fuck," Andi said. "I didn't mean there. Get up."

Mrs. Kozy got up with the squashed ice cream sandwich sticking to the back of her dress. Snakebite Andi put her arm around the woman's mostly nonexistent waist and led her to the other Kozy chair, pausing long enough to pull the melting ice cream sandwich off her butt. Soon the two of them sat side by side, eyes shut.

"You'll sleep all night," Andi instructed them. "Mister can dream about chasing young girls. Missus, you can dream he died of a heart attack and left you a million-dollar insurance policy. How's that sound? Sound good?"

She snapped on the TV and turned it up loud. Pat Sajak was being embraced by a woman with enormous jahoobies who had just finished solving the puzzle, which was NEVER REST ON YOUR LAURELS. Andi took a moment to admire the mammoth mammaries, then turned back to the Kozys.

"When the eleven o'clock news is over, you can turn off the TV and go to bed. When you wake up tomorrow, you won't remember I was here. Any questions?"

They had none. Andi left them and hurried back to the cluster of RVs. She was hungry, had been for weeks, and tonight there would be plenty for everybody. As for tomorrow . . . it was Rose's job to worry about that, and as far as Snakebite Andi was concerned, she was welcome to it.

4

It was full dark by eight o'clock. At nine, the True gathered in the Kozy Kampground's picnic area. Rose the Hat came last, carrying the canister. A small, greedy murmur went up at the sight of it. Rose knew how they felt. She was plenty hungry herself.

She mounted one of the initial-scarred picnic tables and looked at them one by one. "We are the True Knot."

"We are the True Knot," they responded. Their faces were solemn, their eyes avid and hungry. *"What is tied may never be untied."*

"We are the True Knot, and we endure."

"We endure."

"We are the chosen ones. We are the fortunate ones."

"We are chosen and fortunate."

"They are the makers; we are the takers."

"We take what they make."

"Take this and use it well."

"We will use it well."

Once, early in the last decade of the twentieth century, there had been a boy from Enid, Oklahoma, named Richard Gaylesworthy. *I swear that child can read my mind,* his mother sometimes said. People smiled at this, but she wasn't kidding. And maybe not just *her* mind. Richard got A's on tests he hadn't even studied for. He knew when his father was going to come home in a good mood and when he was going to come home fuming about something at the plumbing supply company he owned. Once the boy begged his mother to play the Pick Six lottery because he swore he knew the winning numbers. Mrs. Gaylesworthy refused—they were good Baptists— but later she was sorry. Not all six of the numbers Richard wrote down on the kitchen note-minder board came up, but five did. Her religious convictions had cost them seventy thousand dollars. She had begged the boy not to tell his father, and Richard had promised he wouldn't. He was a good boy, a lovely boy.

Two months or so after the lottery win that wasn't, Mrs. Gaylesworthy was shot to death in her kitchen and the good and lovely boy disappeared. His body had long since rotted away beneath the gone-to-seed back field of an abandoned farm, but when Rose the Hat opened the valve on the silver canister, his essence— his *steam*—escaped in a cloud of sparkling silver mist. It rose to a height of about three feet above the canister, and spread out in a plane. The True stood looking up at it with expectant faces. Most were trembling. Several were actually weeping.

"Take nourishment and endure," Rose said, and raised her hands until her spread fingers were just below the flat plane of mist. She beckoned. The mist immediately began to sink, taking on an umbrella shape as it descended toward those waiting below. When it enveloped their heads, they began to breathe deeply. This went on for five minutes, during which several of them hyperventilated and swooned to the ground.

Rose felt herself swelling physically and sharpening mentally. Every fragrant odor of this spring night declared itself. She knew that the faint lines around her eyes and mouth were disappearing. The white strands in her hair were turning dark again. Later tonight, Crow would come to her camper, and in her bed they would burn like torches.

They inhaled Richard Gaylesworthy until he was gone—really and truly gone. The white mist thinned and then disappeared. Those who had fainted sat up and looked around, smiling. Grampa Flick grabbed Petty the Chink, Barry's wife, and did a nimble little jig with her.

"Let go of me, you old donkey!" she snapped, but she was laughing.

Snakebite Andi and Silent Sarey were kissing deeply, Andi's hands plunged into Sarey's mouse-colored hair.

Rose leaped down from the picnic table and turned to Crow. He made a circle with his thumb and forefinger, grinning back at her.

Everything's cool, that grin said, and so it was. For now. But in spite of her euphoria, Rose thought of the canisters in her safe. Now there were thirty-eight empties instead of thirty-seven. Their backs were a step closer to the wall.

5

The True rolled out the next morning just after first light. They took Route 12 to I-64, the fourteen RVs in a nose-to-tail caravan. When they reached the interstate they would spread out so they weren't quite so obviously together, staying in touch by radio in case trouble arose.

Or if opportunity knocked.

Ernie and Maureen Salkowicz, fresh from a wonderful night's sleep, agreed those RV folks were just about the best they'd ever had. Not only did they pay cash and bus up their sites neat as a pin, someone left an apple bread pudding on the top step of their trailer, with a sweet thank-you note on top. With any luck, the Salkowiczes told each other as they ate their gift dessert for breakfast, they'd come back next year.

"Do you know what?" Maureen said. "I dreamed that lady on the insurance commercials—Flo—sold you a big insurance policy. Wasn't that a crazy dream?"

Ernie grunted and splooshed more whipped cream onto his bread pudding.

"Did you dream, honey?"

"Nope."

But his eyes slid away from hers as he said it.

6

The True Knot's luck turned for the better on a hot July day in Iowa. Rose was leading the caravan, as she always did, and just west of Adair, the sonar in her head gave a ping. Not a head-blaster by any means, but moderately loud. She hopped on the CB at once to Barry the Chink, who was about as Asian as Tom Cruise.

"Barry, did you feel that? Come back."

"Yuh." Barry was not the garrulous type.

"Who's Grampa Flick riding with today?"

Before Barry could answer, there was a double break on the CB and Apron Annie said, "He's with me and Long Paul, sweetie. Is it . . . is it a good one?" Annie sounded anxious, and Rose could understand that. Richard Gaylesworthy had been a *very* good one, but six weeks was a long time between meals, and he was beginning to wear off.

"Is the old feller *compos*, Annie?"

Before she could answer, a raspy voice came back, "I'm fine, woman." And for a guy who sometimes couldn't remember his own name, Grampa Flick did sound pretty much okay. Testy, sure, but testy was a lot better than befuddled.

A second ping hit her, this one not as strong. As if to underline a point that needed no underlining, Grampa said, "We're going the wrong fuckin way."

Rose didn't bother answering, just clicked another double break on her mike. "Crow? Come back, honeybunch."

"I'm here." Prompt as always. Just waiting to be called.

"Pull em in at the next rest area. Except for me, Barry, and Flick. We'll take the next exit and double back."

"Will you need a crew?"

"I won't know until we get closer, but . . . I don't think so."

"Okay." A pause, then he added: "Shit."

Rose racked the mike and looked out at the unending acres of corn on both sides of the fourlane. Crow was disappointed, of course. They all would be. Big steamheads presented problems because they were all but immune to suggestion. That meant taking them by force. Friends or family members often tried to interfere. They could sometimes be put to sleep, but not always; a kid with big steam could block even Snakebite Andi's best efforts in that regard. So sometimes people had to be killed. Not good, but the prize was always worth it: life and strength stored away in a steel canister. Stored for a rainy day. In many cases there was even a residual benefit. Steam was hereditary, and often everyone in the target's family had at least a little.

7

While most of the True Knot waited in a pleasantly shady rest area forty miles east of Council Bluffs, the RVs containing the three finders turned around, left the turnpike at Adair, and headed north. Once away from I-80 and out in the toolies, they spread apart and begin working the grid of graveled, well-maintained farm roads that parceled this part of Iowa into big squares. Moving in on the ping from different directions. Triangulating.

It got stronger . . . a little stronger still . . . then leveled off. Good steam but not *great* steam. Ah, well. Beggars couldn't be choosers.

8

Bradley Trevor had been given the day off from his usual farm chores to practice with the local Little League All-Star team. If his pa had refused him this, the coach probably would have led the rest of the boys in a lynch party, because Brad was the team's best hitter. You wouldn't think it to look at him—he was skinny as a rake handle, and only eleven—but he was able to tag even the District's best pitchers for singles and doubles. The meatballers he almost always took deep. Some of it was plain farmboy strength, but by no means all of it. Brad just seemed to know what pitch was coming next. It wasn't a case of stealing signs (a possibility upon which some of the other District coaches had speculated darkly). He just *knew*. The way he knew the best location for a new stock well, or where the occasional lost cow had gotten off to, or where Ma's engagement ring was the time she'd lost it. *Look under the floormat of the Suburban,* he'd said, and there it was.

That day's practice was an especially good one, but Brad seemed lost in the ozone during the debriefing afterward, and declined to take a soda from the tub filled with ice when it was offered. He said he thought he better get home and help his ma take in the clothes.

"Is it gonna rain?" Micah Johnson, the coach, asked. They'd all come to trust him on such things.

"Dunno," Brad said listlessly.

"You feel okay, son? You look a little peaked."

In fact, Brad *didn't* feel well, had gotten up that morning headachey and a bit feverish. That wasn't why he wanted to go home now, though; he just had a strong sense that he no longer wanted to be at the baseball field. His mind didn't seem . . . quite his own. He wasn't sure if he was here or only dreaming he was— how crazy was that? He scratched absently at a red spot on his forearm. "Same time tomorrow, right?"

Coach Johnson said that was the plan, and Brad walked off with his glove trailing from one hand. Usually he jogged—they all did—but today he didn't feel like it. His head still ached, and now his legs did, too. He disappeared into the corn behind the bleachers, meaning to take a shortcut back to the farm, two miles away. When he emerged onto Town Road D, brushing silk from his hair with a slow and dreamy hand, a midsize WanderKing was idling on the gravel. Standing beside it, smiling, was Barry the Chink.

"Well, there you are," Barry said.

"Who are you?"

"A friend. Hop in. I'll take you home."

"Sure," Brad said. Feeling the way he did, a ride would be fine. He scratched at the red spot on his arm. "You're Barry Smith. You're a friend. I'll hop in and you'll take me home."

He stepped into the RV. The door closed. The WanderKing drove away.

By the next day the whole county would be mobilized in a hunt for the Adair All-Stars' centerfielder and best hitter. A State Police spokesman asked residents to report any strange cars or vans. There were many such reports, but they all came to nothing. And although the three RVs carrying the finders were much bigger than vans (and Rose the Hat's was truly huge), nobody reported them. They were the RV People, after all, and traveling together. Brad was just . . . gone.

Like thousands of other unfortunate children, he had been swallowed up, seemingly in a single bite.

9

They took him north to an abandoned ethanol-processing plant that was miles from the nearest farmhouse. Crow carried the boy out of Rose's EarthCruiser and laid him gently on the ground. Brad was bound with duct tape and weeping. As the True Knot gathered around him (like mourners over an open grave), he said, "Please take me home. I'll never tell."

Rose dropped to one knee beside him and sighed. "I would if I could, son, but I can't."

His eyes found Barry. "You said you were one of the good guys! I heard you! You *said* so!"

"Sorry, pal." Barry didn't look sorry. What he looked was hungry. "It's not personal."

Brad shifted his eyes back to Rose. "Are you going to hurt me? Please don't hurt me."

Of course they were going to hurt him. It was regrettable, but pain purified steam, and the True had to eat. Lobsters also felt pain when they were dropped into pots of boiling water, but that didn't stop the rubes from doing it. Food was food, and survival was survival.

Rose put her hands behind her back. Into one of these, Greedy G placed a knife. It was short but very sharp. Rose smiled down at the boy and said, "As little as possible."

The boy lasted a long time. He screamed until his vocal cords ruptured and his cries became husky barks. At one point, Rose paused and looked around. Her hands, long and strong, wore bloody red gloves.

"Something?" Crow asked.

"We'll talk later," Rose said, and went back to work. The light of a dozen flashlights had turned a piece of ground behind the ethanol plant into a makeshift operating theater.

Brad Trevor whispered, "Please kill me."

Rose the Hat gave him a comforting smile. "Soon."

But it wasn't.

Those husky barks recommenced, and eventually they turned to steam.

At dawn, they buried the boy's body. Then they moved on.

CHAPTER SIX

WEIRD RADIO

1

It hadn't happened in at least three years, but some things you don't forget. Like when your child begins screaming in the middle of the night. Lucy was on her own because David was attending a two-day conference in Boston, but she knew if he'd been there, he would have raced her down the hall to Abra's room. He hadn't forgotten, either.

Their daughter was sitting up in bed, her face pale, her hair standing out in a sleep-scruff all around her head, her eyes wide and staring blankly into space. The sheet—all she needed to sleep under during warm weather—had been pulled free and was balled up around her like a crazy cocoon.

Lucy sat beside her and put an arm around Abra's shoulders. It was like hugging stone. This was the worst part, before she came all the way out of it. Being ripped from sleep by your daughter's screams was terrifying, but the nonresponsiveness was worse. Between the ages of five and seven, these night terrors had been fairly common, and Lucy was always afraid that sooner or later the child's mind would break under the strain. She would continue to breathe, but her eyes would never unlock from whatever world it was that she saw and they couldn't.

It won't happen, David had assured her, and John Dalton had doubled down on that. *Kids are resilient. If she's not showing any lingering after-effects—withdrawal, isolation, obsessional behavior, bedwetting—you're probably okay.*

But it wasn't okay for children to wake themselves, shrieking, from nightmares. It wasn't okay that sometimes wild piano chords sounded from downstairs in the aftermath, or that the faucets in the bathroom at the end of the hall might turn themselves on, or that the light over Abra's bed sometimes blew out when she or David flipped the switch.

Then her invisible friend had come, and intervals between nightmares had grown longer. Eventually they stopped. Until tonight. Not that it *was* night anymore, exactly; Lucy could see the first faint glow on the eastern horizon, and thank God for that.

"Abs? It's Mommy. Talk to me."

There was still nothing for five or ten seconds. Then, at last, the statue Lucy had her arm around relaxed and became a little girl again. Abra took a long, shuddering breath.

"I had one of my bad dreams. Like in the old days."

"I kind of figured that, honey."

Abra could hardly ever remember more than a little, it seemed. Sometimes it was people yelling at each other or hitting with their fists. *He knocked the table over chasing after her,* she might say. Another time the dream had been of a one-eyed Raggedy Ann doll lying on a highway. Once, when Abra was only four, she told them she had seen ghostie people riding *The Helen Rivington,* which was a popular tourist attraction in Frazier. It ran a loop from Teenytown out to Cloud Gap, and then back again. *I could see them because of the moonlight,* Abra told her parents that time. Lucy and David were sitting on either side of her, their arms around her. Lucy still remembered the dank feel of Abra's pajama top, which was soaked with sweat. *I knew they were ghostie people because they had faces like old apples and the moon shone right through.*

By the following afternoon Abra had been running and playing and laughing with her friends again, but Lucy had never forgotten the image: dead people riding that little train through the woods, their faces like transparent apples in the moonlight. She had asked Concetta if she had ever taken Abra on the train during one of their "girl days." Chetta said no. They had been to Teenytown, but the train had been under repairs that day so they rode the carousel instead.

Now Abra looked up at her mother and said, "When will Daddy be back?"

"Day after tomorrow. He said he'd be in time for lunch."

"That's not soon enough," Abra said. A tear spilled from her eye, rolled down her cheek, and plopped onto her pajama top.

"Soon enough for what? What do you remember, Abba-Doo?"

"They were hurting the boy."

Lucy didn't want to pursue this, but felt she had to. There had been too many correlations between Abra's earlier dreams and things that had actually happened. It was David who had spotted the picture of the one-eyed Raggedy Ann in the North Conway *Sun,* under the heading THREE KILLED IN OSSIPEE CRASH. It was Lucy who had hunted out police blotter items about domestic violence arrests in the days following two of Abra's *people were yelling and hitting* dreams. Even John Dalton agreed that Abra might be picking up transmissions on what he called "the weird radio in her head."

So now she said, "What boy? Does he live around here? Do you know?"

Abra shook her head. "Far away. I can't remember." Then she brightened. The speed at which she came out of these fugues was to Lucy almost as eerie as the fugues themselves. "But I think I told Tony. He might tell *his* daddy."

Tony, her invisible friend. She hadn't mentioned him in a couple of years, and Lucy hoped this wasn't some sort of regression. Ten was a little old for invisible friends.

"Tony's daddy might be able to stop it." Then Abra's face clouded. "I think it's too late, though."

"Tony hasn't been around in awhile, has he?" Lucy got up and fluffed out the displaced sheet. Abra giggled when it floated against her face. The best sound in the world, as far as Lucy was concerned. A *sane* sound. And the room was brightening all the time. Soon the first birds would begin to sing.

"Mommy, that tickles!"

"Mommies like to tickle. It's part of their charm. Now, what about Tony?"

"He said he'd come any time I needed him," Abra said, settling back under the sheet. She patted the bed beside her, and Lucy lay down, sharing the pillow. "That was a bad dream and I needed him. I think he came, but I can't really remember. His daddy works in a hot spice."

This was new. "Is that like a chili factory?"

"No, silly, it's for people who are going to die." Abra sounded indulgent, almost teacherly, but a shiver went up Lucy's back.

"Tony says that when people get so sick they can't get well, they go to the hot spice and his daddy tries to make them feel better. Tony's daddy has a cat with a name like mine. I'm Abra and the cat is Azzie. Isn't that *weird,* but in a funny way?"

"Yes. Weird but funny."

John and David would both probably say, based on the similarity of the names, that the stuff about the cat was the confabulation of a very bright little ten-year-old girl. But they would only half believe it, and Lucy hardly believed it at all. How many ten-year-olds knew what a hospice was, even if they mispronounced it?

"Tell me about the boy in your dream." Now that Abra was calmed down, this conversation seemed safer. "Tell me who was hurting him, Abba-Doo."

"I don't remember, except he thought Barney was supposed to be his friend. Or maybe it was Barry. Momma, can I have Hoppy?"

Her stuffed rabbit, now sitting in lop-eared exile on the highest shelf in her room. Abra hadn't slept with him in at least two years. Lucy got the Hopster and put him in her daughter's arms. Abra hugged the rabbit to her pink pajama top and was asleep almost at once. With luck, she'd be out for another hour, maybe even two. Lucy sat beside her, looking down.

Let this stop for good in another few years, just like John said it would. Better yet, let it stop today, this very morning. No more, please. No more hunting through the local papers to see if some little boy was killed by his stepfather or beaten to death by bullies who were high on glue, or something. Let it end.

"God," she said in a very low voice, "if you're there, would you do something for me? Would you break the radio in my little girl's head?"

2

When the True headed west again along I-80, rolling toward the town in the Colorado high country where they would spend the summer (always assuming the opportunity to collect some nearby big steam did not come up), Crow Daddy was riding in the shotgun seat of Rose's EarthCruiser. Jimmy Numbers, the True's whizbang accountant, was piloting Crow's Affinity Country Coach for the time being. Rose's satellite radio was tuned to Outlaw Country and currently playing Hank Jr.'s "Whiskey Bent and Hell Bound." It was a good tune, and Crow let it run its course before pushing the OFF button.

"You said we'd talk later. This is later. What happened back there?"

"We had a looker," Rose said.

"Really?" Crow raised his eyebrows. He had taken as much of the Trevor kid's steam as any of them, but he looked no younger. He rarely did after eating. On the other hand, he rarely looked older between meals, unless the gap was very long. Rose thought it was a good trade-off. Probably something in his genes. Assuming they still *had* genes. Nut said they almost certainly did. "A steamhead, you mean."

She nodded. Ahead of them, I-80 unrolled under a faded blue denim sky dotted with drifting cumulus clouds.

"Big steam?"

"Oh yeah. Huge."

"How far away?"

"East Coast. I think."

"You're saying someone looked in from what, almost fifteen hundred miles away?"

"Could have been even further. Could have been way the hell and gone up in Canada."

"Boy or girl?"

"Probably a girl, but it was only a flash. Three seconds at most. Does it matter?"

It didn't. "How many canisters could you fill from a kid with that much steam in the boiler?"

"Hard to say. Three, at least." This time it was Rose who was lowballing. She guessed the unknown looker might fill ten canisters, maybe even a dozen. The presence had been brief but muscular. The looker had seen what they were doing, and her horror (if it *was* a her) had been strong enough to freeze Rose's hands and make her feel a momentary loathing. It wasn't her own feeling, of course—gutting a rube was no more loathsome than gutting a deer—but a kind of psychic ricochet.

"Maybe we ought to turn around," Crow said. "Get her while the getting's good."

"No. I think this one's still getting stronger. We'll let her ripen a bit."

"Is that something you know or just intuition?"

Rose waggled her hand in the air.

"An intuition strong enough to risk her getting killed by a hit-and-run driver or grabbed by some child-molesting perv?" Crow said this without irony. "Or what about leukemia, or some other cancer? You know they're susceptible to stuff like that."

"If you asked Jimmy Numbers, he'd say the actuarial tables are on our side." Rose smiled and gave his thigh an affectionate pat. "You worry too much, Daddy. We'll go on to Sidewinder, as planned, then head down to Florida in a couple of months. Both Barry and Grampa Flick think this might be a big year for hurricanes."

Crow made a face. "That's like scavenging out of Dumpsters."

"Maybe, but the scraps in some of those Dumpsters are pretty tasty. And nourishing. I'm still kicking myself that we missed that tornado in Joplin. But of course we get less warning on sudden storms like that."

"This kid. She *saw* us."

"Yes."

"And what we were doing."

"Your point, Crow?"

"Could she nail us?"

"Honey, if she's more than eleven, I'll eat my hat." Rose tapped it for emphasis. "Her parents probably don't know what she is or what she can do. Even if they do, they're probably minimizing it like hell in their own minds so they don't have to think about it too much."

"Or they'll send her to a psychiatrist who'll give her pills," Crow said. "Which will muffle her and make her harder to find."

Rose smiled. "If I got it right, and I'm pretty sure I did, giving Paxil to this kid would be like throwing a piece of Saran Wrap over a searchlight. We'll find her when it's time. Don't worry."

"If you say so. You're the boss."

"That's right, honeybunch." This time instead of patting his thigh, she squeezed his basket. "Omaha tonight?"

"It's a La Quinta Inn. I reserved the entire back end of the first floor."

"Good. My intent is to ride you like a roller coaster."

"We'll see who rides who," Crow said. He was feeling frisky from the Trevor kid. So was Rose. So were they all. He turned the radio on again. Got Cross Canadian Ragweed singing about the boys from Oklahoma who rolled their joints all wrong.

The True rolled west.

3

There were easy AA sponsors, and hard AA sponsors, and then there were ones like Casey Kingsley, who took absolutely zero shit from their pigeons. At the beginning of their relationship, Casey ordered Dan to do ninety-in-ninety, and instructed him to telephone every morning at seven o'clock. When Dan completed his ninety consecutive meetings, he was allowed to drop the morning calls. Then they met three times a week for coffee at the Sunspot Café.

Casey was sitting in a booth when Dan came in on a July afternoon in 2011, and although Casey hadn't made it to retirement just yet, to Dan his longtime AA sponsor (and first New Hampshire employer) looked very old. Most of his hair was gone, and he walked with a pronounced limp. He needed a hip replacement, but kept putting it off.

Dan said hi, sat down, folded his hands, and waited for what Casey called The Catechism.

"You sober today, Danno?"

"Yes."

"How did that miracle of restraint happen?"

He recited, "Thanks to the program of Alcoholics Anonymous and the God of my understanding. My sponsor may also have played a small part."

"Lovely compliment, but don't blow smoke up my dress and I won't blow any up yours."

Patty Noyes came over with the coffeepot and poured Dan a cup, unasked. "How are you, handsome?"

Dan grinned at her. "I'm good."

She ruffled his hair, then headed back to the counter, with a little extra swing in her stride. The men followed the sweet tick-tock of her hips, as men do, then Casey returned his gaze to Dan.

"Made any progress with that God-of-my-understanding stuff?"

"Not much," Dan said. "I've got an idea it may be a lifetime work."

"But you ask for help to stay away from a drink in the morning?"

"Yes."

"On your knees?"

"Yes."

"Say thank you at night?"

"Yes, and on my knees."

"Why?"

"Because I need to remember the drink put me there," Dan said. It was the absolute truth.

Casey nodded. "That's the first three steps. Give me the short form."

"'I can't, God can, I think I'll let Him.'" He added: "The God of my understanding."

"Which you *don't* understand."

"Right."

"Now tell me why you drank."

"Because I'm a drunk."

"Not because Mommy didn't give you no love?"

"No." Wendy had had failings, but her love for him—and his for her—had never wavered.

"Because Daddy didn't give you no love?"

"No." *Although once he broke my arm, and at the end he almost killed me.*

"Because it's hereditary?"

"No." Dan sipped his coffee. "But it is. You know that, right?"

"Sure. I also know it doesn't matter. We drank because we're drunks. We never get better. We get a daily reprieve based on our spiritual condition, and that's *it*."

"Yes, boss. Are we through with this part?"

"Almost. Did you think about taking a drink today?"

"No. Did you?"

"No." Casey grinned. It filled his face with light and made him young again. "It's a miracle. Would you say it's a miracle, Danny?"

"Yes. I would."

Patty came back with a big dish of vanilla pudding—not just one cherry on top but two—and stuck it in front of Dan. "Eat that. On the house. You're too thin."

"What about me, sweetheart?" Casey asked.

Patty sniffed. "You're a horse. I'll bring you a pine tree float, if you want. That's a glass of water with a toothpick in it." Having gotten the last word, she sashayed off.

"You still hitting that?" Casey asked as Dan began to eat his pudding.

"Charming," Dan said. "Very sensitive and New Age."

"Thanks. Are you still hitting it?"

"We had a thing that lasted maybe four months, and that was three years ago, Case. Patty's engaged to a very nice boy from Grafton."

"Grafton," Casey said dismissively. "Pretty views, shit town. She doesn't act so engaged when you're in the house."

"Casey—"

"No, don't get me wrong. I'd never advise a pidge of mine to stick his nose—or his dick—into an ongoing relationship. That's a terrific setup for a drink. But . . . are you seeing *anybody*?"

"Is it your business?"

"Happens it is."

"Not currently. There was a nurse from Rivington House—I told you about her . . ."

"Sarah something."

"Olson. We talked a little about moving in together, then she got a great job down at Mass General. We email sometimes."

"No relationships for the first year, that's the rule of thumb," Casey said. "Very few recovering alkies take it seriously. You did. But Danno . . . it's time you got regular with *somebody*."

"Oh gee, my sponsor just turned into Dr. Phil," Dan said.

"Is your life better? Better than it was when you showed up here fresh off the bus with your ass dragging and your eyes bleeding?"

"You know it is. Better than I ever could have imagined."

"Then think about sharing it with somebody. All I'm saying."

"I'll make a note of it. Now can we discuss other things? The Red Sox, maybe?"

"I need to ask you something else as your sponsor first. Then we can just be friends again, having a coffee."

"Okay . . ." Dan looked at him warily.

"We've never talked much about what you do at the hospice. How you help people."

"No," Dan said, "and I'd just as soon keep it that way. You know what they say at the end of every meeting, right? 'What you saw here, what you heard here, when you leave here, let it stay here.' That's how I am about the other part of my life."

"How many parts of your life were affected by your drinking?"

Dan sighed. "You know the answer to that. All of them."

"So?" And when Dan said nothing: "The Rivington staff calls you Doctor Sleep. Word gets around, Danno."

Dan was silent. Some of the pudding was left, and Patty would rag him about it if he didn't eat it, but his appetite had flown. He supposed he'd known this conversation had been coming, and he also knew that, after ten years without a drink (and with a pigeon or two of his own to watch over these days), Casey would respect his boundaries, but he still didn't want to have it.

"You help people to die. Not by putting pillows over their faces, or anything, nobody thinks that, but just by . . . I don't know. *Nobody* seems to know."

"I sit with them, that's all. Talk to them a little. If it's what they want."

"Do you work the Steps, Danno?"

If Dan had believed this was a new conversational tack he would have welcomed it, but he knew it was not. "You know I do. You're my sponsor."

"Yeah, you ask for help in the morning and say thanks at night. You do it on your knees. So that's the first three. Four is all that moral inventory shit. How about number five?"

There were twelve in all. After hearing them read aloud at the beginning of every meeting he'd attended, Dan knew them by heart. "'Admitted to God, ourselves, and another human being the exact nature of our wrongs.'"

"Yuh." Casey lifted his coffee cup, sipped, and looked at Dan over the rim. "Have you done that one?"

"Most of it." Dan found himself wishing he were somewhere else. Almost anywhere else. Also—for the first time in quite awhile—he found himself wishing for a drink.

"Let me guess. You've told *yourself* all of your wrongs, and you've told the God of your not-understanding all of your wrongs, and you've told one other person—that would be me—*most* of your wrongs. Would that be a bingo?"

Dan said nothing.

"Here's what I think," Casey said, "and you're welcome to correct me if I'm wrong. Steps eight and nine are about cleaning up the wreckage we left behind when we were drunk on our asses pretty much twenty-four/seven. I think at least part of your work at the hospice, the *important* part, is about making those amends. And I think there's one wrong you can't quite get past because you're too fucking ashamed to talk about it. If that's the case, you wouldn't be the first, believe me."

Dan thought: *Mama*.

Dan thought: *Canny*.

He saw the red wallet and the pathetic wad of food stamps. He also saw a little money. Seventy dollars, enough for a four-day drunk. Five if it was parceled out carefully and food was kept to a bare nutritional minimum. He saw the money first in his hand and then going into his pocket. He saw the kid in the Braves shirt and the sagging diaper.

He thought: *The kid's name was Tommy*.

He thought, not for the first time or the last: *I will never speak of this*.

"Danno? Is there anything you want to tell me? I think there is. I don't know how long you've been dragging the motherfucker around, but you can leave it with me and walk out of here a hundred pounds lighter. That's how it works."

He thought of how the kid had trotted to his mother

(*Deenie her name was Deenie*)

and how, even deep in her drunken slumber, she had put an arm around him and hugged him close. They had been face-to-face in the morning sun shafting through the bedroom's dirty window.

"There's nothing," he said.

"Let it go, Dan. I'm telling you that as your friend as well as your sponsor."

Dan gazed at the other man steadily and said nothing.

Casey sighed. "How many meetings have you been at where someone said you're only as sick as your secrets? A hundred? Probably a thousand. Of all the old AA chestnuts, that's just about the oldest."

Dan said nothing.

"We all have a bottom," Casey said. "Someday you're going to have to tell somebody about yours. If you don't, somewhere down the line you're going to find yourself in a bar with a drink in your hand."

"Message received," Dan said. "Now can we talk about the Red Sox?"

Casey looked at his watch. "Another time. I've got to get home."

Right, Dan thought. *To your dog and your goldfish.*

"Okay." He grabbed the check before Casey could. "Another time."

4

When Dan got back to his turret room, he looked at his blackboard for a long time before slowly erasing what was written there:

They are killing the baseball boy!

When the board was blank again, he asked, "What baseball boy would that be?"

No answer.

"Abra? Are you still here?"

No. But she had been; if he'd come back from his uncomfortable coffee meeting with Casey ten minutes earlier, he might have seen her phantom shape. But had she come for him? Dan didn't think so. It was undeniably crazy, but he thought she might have come for Tony. Who had been *his* invisible friend, once upon a time. The one who sometimes brought visions. The one who sometimes warned.

The one who had turned out to be a deeper and wiser version of himself.

For the scared little boy trying to survive in the Overlook Hotel, Tony had been a protective older brother. The irony was that now, with the booze behind him, Daniel Anthony Torrance had become an authentic adult and Tony was still a kid. Maybe even the fabled inner child the New Age gurus were always going on about. Dan felt sure that inner-child stuff was brought into service to excuse a lot of selfish and destructive behavior (what Casey liked to call the Gotta-Have-It-Now Syndrome), but he also had no doubt that grown men and women held every stage of their development somewhere in their brains—not just the inner child, but the inner infant, the inner teenager, and the inner young adult. And if the mysterious Abra came to him, wasn't it natural that she'd hunt past his adult mind, looking for someone her own age?

A playmate?

A protector, even?

If so, it was a job Tony had done before. But did she need protection? Certainly there had been anguish

(*they are killing the baseball boy*)

in her message, but anguish went naturally with the shining, as Dan had found out long ago. Mere children were not meant to know and see so much. He could seek her out, maybe try to discover more, but what would he say to the parents? *Hi, you don't know me, but I know your daughter, she visits my room sometimes and we've gotten to be pretty good pals?*

Dan didn't think they'd sic the county sheriff on him, but he wouldn't blame them if they did, and given his checkered past, he had no urge to find out. Better to let Tony be her long-distance friend, if that was what was really going on. Tony might be invisible, but at least he was more or less age-appropriate.

Later, he could replace the names and room numbers that belonged on his blackboard. For now he picked the stub of chalk out of the ledge and wrote: **Tony and I wish you a happy summer day, Abra! Your OTHER friend, Dan.**

He studied this for a moment, nodded, and went to the window. A beautiful late summer afternoon, and still his day off. He decided to go for a walk and try to get the troubling conversation with Casey out of his mind. Yes, he supposed Deenie's apartment in Wilmington had been his bottom, but if keeping to himself what had happened there hadn't stopped him from piling up ten years of sobriety, he didn't see why keeping it to himself should stop him from getting another ten. Or twenty. And why think about years anyway, when the AA motto was one day at a time?

Wilmington was a long time ago. That part of his life was done.

He locked his room when he left, as he always did, but a lock wouldn't keep the mysterious Abra out if she wanted to visit. When he came back, there might be another message from her on the blackboard.

Maybe we can become pen pals.

Sure, and maybe a cabal of Victoria's Secret lingerie models would crack the secret of hydrogen fusion.

Grinning, Dan went out.

5

The Anniston Public Library was having its annual summer book sale, and when Abra asked to go, Lucy was delighted to put aside her afternoon chores and walk down to Main Street with her daughter. Card tables loaded with various donated volumes had been set up on the lawn, and while Lucy browsed the paperback table ($1 EACH, 6 FOR $5, YOU PICK 'EM), looking for Jodi Picoults she hadn't read, Abra checked out the selections on the tables marked YOUNG ADULTS. She was still a long way from adulthood of even the youngest sort, but she was a voracious (and precocious) reader with a particular love of fantasy and science fiction. Her favorite t-shirt had a huge, complicated machine on the front above the declaration STEAMPUNK RULES.

Just as Lucy was deciding she'd have to settle for an old Dean

Koontz and a slightly newer Lisa Gardner, Abra came running over to her. She was smiling. "Mom! Mommy! His name is Dan!"

"Whose name is Dan, sweetheart?"

"Tony's father! He told me to have a happy summer day!"

Lucy looked around, almost expecting to see a strange man with a boy Abra's age in tow. There were plenty of strangers—it was summer, after all—but no pairs like that.

Abra saw what she was doing and giggled. "Oh, he's not here."

"Then where is he?"

"I don't know, exactly. But close."

"Well . . . I guess that's good, hon."

Lucy had just enough time to tousle her daughter's hair before Abra ran back to renew her hunt for rocketeers, time travelers, and sorcerers. Lucy stood watching her, her own choices hanging forgotten in her hand. Tell David about this when he called from Boston, or not? She thought not.

Weird radio, that was all.

Better to let it pass.

6

Dan decided to pop into Java Express, buy a couple of coffees, and take one to Billy Freeman over in Teenytown. Although Dan's employment by the Frazier Municipal Department had been extremely short, the two men had remained friendly over the last ten years. Part of that was having Casey in common—Billy's boss, Dan's sponsor—but mostly it was simple liking. Dan enjoyed Billy's no-bullshit attitude.

He also enjoyed driving *The Helen Rivington*. Probably that inner-child thing again; he was sure a psychiatrist would say so. Billy was usually willing to turn over the controls, and during the summer season he often did so with relief. Between the Fourth of July and Labor Day, the *Riv* made the ten-mile loop out to Cloud Gap and back ten times a day, and Billy wasn't getting any younger.

s he crossed the lawn to Cranmore Avenue, Dan spied Fred
ing sitting on a shady bench in the walkway between Rivington
se proper and Rivington Two. The orderly who had once left a
f fingermarks on poor old Charlie Hayes still worked the night
, and was as lazy and ill-tempered as ever, but he had at least
ned to stay clear of Doctor Sleep. That was fine with Dan.

arling, soon to go on shift, had a grease-spotted McDonald's
on his lap and was munching a Big Mac. The two men locked
for a moment. Neither said hello. Dan thought Fred Carling
a lazy bastard with a sadistic streak and Carling thought Dan
a holier-than-thou meddler, so *that* balanced. As long as they
ed out of each other's way, all would be well and all would be
and all manner of things would be well.

an got the coffees (Billy's with four sugars), then crossed to
common, which was busy in the golden early-evening light.
bees soared. Mothers and dads pushed toddlers on swings or
ght them as they flew off the slides. A game was in progress on
softball field, kids from the Frazier YMCA against a team with
NISTON REC DEPARTMENT on their orange shirts. He
d Billy in the train station, standing on a stool and polishing
Riv's chrome. It all looked good. It looked like home.

f it isn't, Dan thought, *it's as close as I'm ever going to get. All I need
is a wife named Sally, a kid named Pete, and a dog named Rover.*

Ie strolled up the Teenytown version of Cranmore Avenue and
the shade of Teenytown Station. "Hey Billy, I brought you
e of that coffee-flavored sugar you like."

t the sound of his voice, the first person to offer Dan a friendly
d in the town of Frazier turned around. "Why, ain't you the
ghborly one. I was just thinking I could use—oh shitsky, there
oes."

he cardboard tray had dropped from Danny's hands. He felt
mth as hot coffee splattered his tennis shoes, but it seemed
way, unimportant.

here were flies crawling on Billy Freeman's face.

7

Billy didn't want to go see Casey Kingsley the following morn
didn't want to take the day off, and *certainly* didn't want to go
no doctor. He kept telling Dan he felt fine, in the pink, absolu
tip-top. He'd even missed the summer cold that usually hit hir
June or July.

Dan, however, had lain sleepless most of the previous ni
and wouldn't take no for an answer. He might have if he'd b
convinced it was too late, but he didn't think it was. He had
the flies before, and had learned to gauge their meaning. A sw
of them—enough to obscure the person's features behind a ve
nasty, jostling bodies—and you knew there was no hope. A d
or so meant something *might* be done. Only a few, and there
time. There had only been three or four on Billy's face.

He never saw any at all on the faces of the terminal patient
the hospice.

Dan remembered visiting his mother nine months before
death, on a day when she had also claimed to feel fine, in the p
absolutely tickety-boo. *What are you looking at, Danny?* We
Torrance had asked. *Have I got a smudge?* She had swiped comic
at the tip of her nose, her fingers passing right through the hund
of deathflies that were covering her from chin to hairline, like a c

8

Casey was used to mediating. Fond of irony, he liked to tell pe
it was why he made that enormous six-figure annual salary.

First he listened to Dan. Then he listened to Billy's prot
about how there was no way he could leave, not at the height of
season with people already lining up to ride the *Riv* on its 8
run. Besides, no doctor would see him on such short notice. It
the height of the season for them, too.

"When's the last time you had a checkup?" Casey asked once Billy finally ran down. Dan and Billy were standing in front of his desk. Casey was rocked back in his office chair, head resting in its accustomed place just below the cross on the wall, fingers laced together across his belly.

Billy looked defensive. "I guess back in oh-six. But I was fine then, Case. Doc said my blood pressure was ten points lower'n his."

Casey's eyes shifted to Dan. They held speculation and curiosity but no disbelief. AA members mostly kept their lips zipped during their various interactions with the wider world, but inside the groups, people talked—and sometimes gossiped—quite freely. Casey therefore knew that Dan Torrance's talent for helping terminal patients die easily was not his *only* talent. According to the grapevine, Dan T. had certain helpful insights from time to time. The kind that can't exactly be explained.

"You're tight with Johnny Dalton, aren't you?" he asked Dan now. "The pediatrician?"

"Yes. I see him most Thursday nights, in North Conway."

"Got his number?"

"As a matter of fact, I do." Dan had a whole list of AA contact numbers in the back of the little notebook Casey had given him, which he still carried.

"Call him. Tell him it's important this yobbo here sees someone right away. Don't suppose you know what kind of a doctor it is he needs, do you? Sure as hell isn't a pediatrician at his age."

"Casey—" Billy began.

"Hush," Casey said, and returned his attention to Dan. "I think you do know, by God. Is it his lungs? That seems the most likely, the way he smokes."

Dan decided he had come too far to turn back now. He sighed and said, "No, I think it's something in his guts."

"Except for a little indigestion, my guts are—"

"*Hush* I said." Then, turning back to Dan: "A gut doctor, then. Tell Johnny D. it's important." He paused. "Will he believe you?"

This was a question Dan was glad to hear. He had helped several

AAs during his time in New Hampshire, and although he asked them all not to talk, he knew perfectly well that some had, and still did. He was happy to know John Dalton hadn't been one of them.

"I think so."

"Okay." Casey pointed at Billy. "You got the day off, and with pay. Medical leave."

"The *Riv*—"

"There's a dozen people in this town that can drive the *Riv*. I'll make some calls, then take the first two runs myself."

"Your bad hip—"

"Balls to my bad hip. Do me good to get out of this office."

"But Casey, I feel f—"

"I don't care if you feel good enough to run a footrace all the way to Lake Winnipesaukee. You're going to see the doctor and that's the end of it."

Billy looked resentfully at Dan. "See the trouble you got me in? I didn't even get my morning coffee."

The flies were gone this morning—except they were still there. Dan knew that if he concentrated, he could see them again if he wanted to . . . but who in Christ's name would *want* to?

"I know," Dan said. "There is no gravity, life just sucks. Can I use your phone, Casey?"

"Be my guest." Casey stood up. "Guess I'll toddle on over to the train station and punch a few tickets. You got an engineer's cap that'll fit me, Billy?"

"No."

"Mine will," Dan said.

9

For an organization that didn't advertise its presence, sold no goods, and supported itself with crumpled dollar bills thrown into passed baskets or baseball caps, Alcoholics Anonymous exerted a quietly powerful influence that stretched far beyond the doors of the various rented halls and church basements where it did its business. It wasn't the old boys' network, Dan thought, but the old drunks' network.

He called John Dalton, and John called an internal medicine specialist named Greg Fellerton. Fellerton wasn't in the Program, but he owed Johnny D. a favor. Dan didn't know why, and didn't care. All that mattered was that later that day, Billy Freeman was on the examining table in Fellerton's Lewiston office. Said office was a seventy-mile drive from Frazier, and Billy bitched the whole way.

"Are you sure indigestion's all that's been bothering you?" Dan asked as they pulled into Fellerton's little parking area on Pine Street.

"Yuh," Billy said. Then he reluctantly added, "It's been a little worse lately, but nothin that keeps me up at night."

Liar, Dan thought, but let it pass. He'd gotten the contrary old sonofabitch here, and that was the hard part.

Dan was sitting in the waiting room, leafing through a copy of *OK!* with Prince William and his pretty but skinny new bride on the cover, when he heard a lusty cry of pain from down the hall. Ten minutes later, Fellerton came out and sat down beside Dan. He looked at the cover of *OK!* and said, "That guy may be heir to the British throne, but he's still going to be as bald as a nine ball by the time he's forty."

"You're probably right."

"Of course I'm right. In human affairs, the only real king is genetics. I'm sending your friend up to Central Maine General for a CT scan. I'm pretty sure what it'll show. If I'm right, I'll schedule Mr. Freeman to see a vascular surgeon for a little cut-and-splice early tomorrow morning."

"What's wrong with him?"

Billy was walking up the hall, buckling his belt. His tanned face was now sallow and wet with sweat. "He says there's a bulge in my aorta. Like a bubble on a car tire. Only car tires don't yell when you poke em."

"An aneurysm," Fellerton said. "Oh, there's a chance it's a tumor, but I don't think so. In any case, time's of the essence. Damn thing's the size of a Ping-Pong ball. It's good you got him in for a look-see. If it had burst without a hospital nearby . . ." Fellerton shook his head.

10

The CT scan confirmed Fellerton's aneurysm diagnosis, and by six that evening, Billy was in a hospital bed, where he looked considerably diminished. Dan sat beside him.

"I'd kill for a cigarette," Billy said wistfully.

"Can't help you there."

Billy sighed. "High time I quit, anyway. Won't they be missin you at Rivington House?"

"Day off."

"And ain't this one hell of a way to spend it. Tell you what, if they don't murder me with their knives and forks tomorrow morning, I guess I'm going to owe you my life. I don't know how you knew, but if there's anything I can ever do for you—I mean anything at all—you just have to ask."

Dan thought of how he'd descended the steps of an interstate bus ten years ago, stepping into a snow flurry as fine as wedding lace. He thought of his delight when he had spotted the bright red locomotive that pulled *The Helen Rivington*. Also of how this man had asked him if he liked the little train instead of telling him to get the fuck away from what he had no business touching. Just a small kindness, but it had opened the door to all he had now.

"Billy-boy, I'm the one who owes you, and more than I could ever repay."

11

He had noticed an odd fact during his years of sobriety. When things in his life weren't going so well—the morning in 2008 when he had discovered someone had smashed in the rear window of his car with a rock came to mind—he rarely thought of a drink. When they were going well, however, the old dry thirst had a way of coming back on him. That night after saying goodbye to Billy, on the way home from Lewiston with everything okey-doke, he spied a roadhouse bar called the Cowboy Boot and felt a nearly insurmountable urge to go in. To buy a pitcher of beer and get enough quarters to fill the jukebox for at least an hour. To sit there listening to Jennings and Jackson and Haggard, not talking to anyone, not causing any trouble, just getting high. Feeling the weight of sobriety—sometimes it was like wearing lead shoes—fall away. When he got down to his last five quarters, he'd play "Whiskey Bent and Hell Bound" six times straight.

He passed the roadhouse, turned in at the gigantic Walmart parking lot just beyond, and opened his phone. He let his finger hover over Casey's number, then remembered their difficult conversation in the café. Casey might want to revisit that discussion, especially the subject of whatever Dan might be holding back. That was a nonstarter.

Feeling like a man having an out-of-body experience, he returned to the roadhouse and parked in the back of the dirt lot. He felt good about this. He also felt like a man who has just picked up a loaded gun and put it to his temple. His window was open and he could hear a live band playing an old Derailers tune: "Lover's Lie." They didn't sound too bad, and with a few drinks in him, they would sound great. There would be ladies in there who would want to dance. Ladies with curls, ladies with pearls, ladies in skirts, ladies in cowboy shirts. There always were. He wondered what kind of whiskey they had in the well, and God, God, great God, he was so thirsty. He opened the car door, put one foot out on the ground, then sat there with his head lowered.

Ten years. Ten *good* years, and he could toss them away in the next ten minutes. It would be easy enough to do. *Like honey to the bee.*

We all have a bottom. Someday you're going to have to tell somebody about yours. If you don't, somewhere down the line, you're going to find yourself in a bar with a drink in your hand.

And I can blame you, Casey, he thought coldly. *I can say you put the idea in my head while we were having coffee in the Sunspot.*

There was a flashing red arrow over the door, and a sign reading PITCHERS $2 UNTIL 9 PM MILLER LITE COME ON IN.

Dan closed the car door, opened his phone again, and called John Dalton.

"Is your buddy okay?" John asked.

"Tucked up and ready to go tomorrow morning at seven a.m. John, I feel like drinking."

"Oh, nooo!" John cried in a trembling falsetto. "Not *booooze!*"

And just like that the urge was gone. Dan laughed. "Okay, I needed that. But if you ever do the Michael Jackson voice again, I *will* drink."

"You should hear me on 'Billie Jean.' I'm a karaoke monster. Can I ask you something?"

"Sure." Through the windshield, Dan could see the Cowboy Boot patrons come and go, probably not talking of Michelangelo.

"Whatever you've got, did drinking . . . I don't know . . . shut it up?"

"Muffled it. Put a pillow over its face and made it struggle for air."

"And now?"

"Like Superman, I use my powers to promote truth, justice, and the American Way."

"Meaning you don't want to talk about it."

"No," Dan said. "I don't. But it's better now. Better than I ever thought it could be. When I was a teenager . . ." He trailed off. When he'd been a teenager, every day had been a struggle for sanity. The voices in his head were bad; the pictures were frequently worse. He had promised both his mother and himself that he would never drink like his father, but when he finally began, as a freshman in high school, it had been such a huge relief that he had—at first—only wished he'd started sooner. Morning hangovers were a thousand times better than nightmares all night long. All of which sort of led to a question: How much of his father's son *was* he? In how many ways?

"When you were a teenager, what?" John asked.

"Nothing. It doesn't matter. Listen, I better get moving. I'm sitting in a bar parking lot."

"Really?" John sounded interested. "Which bar?"

"Place called the Cowboy Boot. It's two-buck pitchers until nine o'clock."

"Dan."

"Yes, John."

"I know that place from the old days. If you're going to flush your life down the toilet, don't start there. The ladies are skanks with meth-mouth and the men's room smells like moldy jockstraps. The Boot is strictly for when you hit your bottom."

There it was, that phrase again.

"We all have a bottom," Dan said. "Don't we?"

"Get out of there, Dan." John sounded dead serious now. "Right this second. No more fucking around. And stay on the phone with me until that big neon cowboy boot on the roof is out of your rearview mirror."

Dan started his car, pulled out of the lot, and back onto Route 11.

"It's going," he said. "It's going . . . annnd . . . it's gone." He felt inexpressible relief. He also felt bitter regret—how many two-buck pitchers could he have gotten through before nine o'clock?

"Not going to pick up a six or a bottle of wine before you get back to Frazier, are you?"

"No. I'm good."

"Then I'll see you Thursday night. Come early, I'm making the coffee. Folgers, from my special stash."

"I'll be there," Dan said.

12

When he got back to his turret room and flipped on the light, there was a new message on the blackboard.

I had a wonderful day!
Your friend,
ABRA

"That's good, honey," Dan said. "I'm glad."

Buzz. The intercom. He went over and hit TALK.

"Hey there, Doctor Sleep," Loretta Ames said. "I thought I saw you come in. I guess it's still technically your day off, but do you want to pay a house call?"

"On who? Mr. Cameron or Mr. Murray?"

"Cameron. Azzie's been visiting with him since just after dinner."

Ben Cameron was in Rivington One. Second floor. An eighty-three-year-old retired accountant with congestive heart failure. Hell of a nice guy. Good Scrabble player and an absolute pest at Parcheesi, always setting up blockades that drove his opponents crazy.

"I'll be right over," Dan said. On his way out, he paused for a single backward glance at the blackboard. "Goodnight, hon," he said.

He didn't hear from Abra Stone for another two years.

During those same two years, something slept in the True Knot's bloodstream. A little parting gift from Bradley Trevor, aka the baseball boy.

PART TWO

EMPTY DEVILS

CHAPTER SEVEN

"HAVE YOU SEEN ME?"

1

On an August morning in 2013, Concetta Reynolds awoke early in her Boston condo apartment. As always, the first thing she was aware of was that there was no dog curled up in the corner, by the dresser. Betty had been gone for years now, but Chetta still missed her. She put on her robe and headed for the kitchen, where she intended to make her morning coffee. This was a trip she had made thousands of times before, and she had no reason to believe this one would be any different. Certainly it never crossed her mind to think it would prove to be the first link in a chain of malignant events. She didn't stumble, she would tell her granddaughter, Lucy, later that day, nor did she bump into anything. She just heard an unimportant snapping sound from about halfway down her body on the right-hand side and then she was on the floor with warm agony rushing up and down her leg.

She lay there for three minutes or so, staring at her faint reflection in the polished hardwood floor, willing the pain to subside. At the same time she talked to herself. *Stupid old woman, not to have a companion. David's been telling you for the last five years that you're too old to live alone and now he'll never let you hear the end of it.*

But a live-in companion would have needed the room she'd set aside for Lucy and Abra, and Chetta lived for their visits. More than ever, now that Betty was gone and all the poetry seemed to be written out of her. And ninety-seven or not, she'd been getting around well and feeling fine. Good genes on the female side. Hadn't her own momo buried four husbands and seven children and lived to be a hundred and two?

Although, truth be told (if only to herself), she hadn't felt quite so fine this summer. This summer things had been . . . difficult.

When the pain finally did abate—a bit—she began crawling down the short hall toward the kitchen, which was now filling up with dawn. She found it was harder to appreciate that lovely rose light from floor level. Each time the pain became too great, she stopped with her head laid on one bony arm, panting. During these rest stops she reflected on the seven ages of man, and how they described a perfect (and perfectly stupid) circle. This had been her mode of locomotion long ago, during the fourth year of World War I, also known as—how funny—the War to End All Wars. Then she had been Concetta Abruzzi, crawling across the dooryard of her parents' farm in Davoli, intent on capturing chickens that easily outpaced her. From those dusty beginnings she had gone on to lead a fruitful and interesting life. She had published twenty books of poetry, taken tea with Graham Greene, dined with two presidents, and—best of all—had been gifted with a lovely, brilliant, and strangely talented great-granddaughter. And what did all those wonderful things lead to?

More crawling, that was what. Back to the beginning. *Dio mi benedica*.

She reached the kitchen and eeled her way through an oblong of sun to the little table where she took most of her meals. Her cell phone was on it. Chetta grabbed one leg of the table and shook it until her phone slid to the edge and dropped off. And, *meno male*, landed unbroken. She punched in the number they told you to call when shit like this happened, then waited while a recorded voice summed up all the absurdity of the twenty-first century by telling her that her call was being recorded.

And finally, praise Mary, an actual human voice.

"This is 911, what is your emergency?"

The woman on the floor who had once crawled after the chickens in southern Italy spoke clearly and coherently in spite of the pain. "My name is Concetta Reynolds, and I live on the third floor of a condominium at Two nineteen Marlborough Street. I seem to have broken my hip. Can you send an ambulance?"

"Is there anyone with you, Mrs. Reynolds?"

"For my sins, no. You're speaking to a stupid old lady who insisted she was fine to live alone. And by the way, these days I prefer *Ms.*"

2

Lucy got the call from her grandmother shortly before Concetta was wheeled into surgery. "I've broken my hip, but they can fix it," she told Lucy. "I believe they put in pins and such."

"Momo, did you fall?" Lucy's first thought was for Abra, who was away at summer camp for another week.

"Oh yes, but the break that *caused* the fall was completely spontaneous. Apparently this is quite common in people my age, and since there are ever so many more people my age than there used to be, the doctors see a lot of it. There's no need for you to come immediately, but I think you'll want to come quite soon. It seems that we'll need to have a talk about various arrangements."

Lucy felt a coldness in the pit of her stomach. "What sort of arrangements?"

Now that she was loaded with Valium or morphine or whatever it was they'd given her, Concetta felt quite serene. "It seems that a broken hip is the least of my problems." She explained. It didn't take long. She finished by saying, "Don't tell Abra, *cara*. I've had dozens of emails from her, even an actual *letter*, and it sounds like she's enjoying her summer camp a great deal. Time enough later for her to find her old momo's circling the drain."

Lucy thought, *If you really believe I'll have to tell her—*

"I can guess what you're thinking without being psychic, *amore*, but maybe this time bad news will give her a miss."

"Maybe," Lucy said.

She had barely hung up when the phone rang. "Mom? Mommy?" It was Abra, and she was crying. "I want to come home. Momo's got cancer and I want to come home."

3

Following her early return from Camp Tapawingo in Maine, Abra got an idea of what it would be like to shuttle between divorced parents. She and her mother spent the last two weeks of August and the first week of September in Chetta's Marlborough Street condo. The old woman had come through her hip surgery quite nicely, and had decided against a longer hospital stay, or any sort of treatment for the pancreatic cancer the doctors had discovered.

"No pills, no chemotherapy. Ninety-seven years are enough. As for you, Lucia, I refuse to allow you to spend the next six months bringing me meals and pills and the bedpan. You have a family, and I can afford round-the-clock care."

"You're not going to live the end of your life among strangers," Lucy said, speaking in her she-who-must-be-obeyed voice. It was the one both Abra and her father knew not to argue with. Not even Concetta could do that.

There was no discussion about Abra staying; on September ninth, she was scheduled to start the eighth grade at Anniston Middle School. It was David Stone's sabbatical year, which he was using to write a book comparing the Roaring Twenties to the Go-Go Sixties, and so—like a good many of the girls with whom she'd gone to Camp Tap—Abra shuttled from one parent to the other. During the week, she was with her father. On the weekends, she shipped down to Boston, to be with her mom and Momo. She thought that things could not get worse . . . but they always can, and often do.

4

Although he was working at home now, David Stone never bothered to walk down the driveway and get the mail. He claimed the U.S. Postal Service was a self-perpetuating bureaucracy that had ceased to have any relevance around the turn of the century. Every now and then a package turned up, sometimes books he'd ordered to help with his work, more often something Lucy had ordered from a catalogue, but otherwise he claimed it was all junkola.

When Lucy was home, she retrieved the post from the mailbox by the gate and looked the stuff over while she had her mid-morning coffee. It *was* mostly crap, and it went directly into what Dave called the Circular File. But she wasn't home that early September, so it was Abra—now the nominal woman of the house—who checked the box when she got off the school bus. She also washed the dishes, did a load of laundry for herself and her dad twice a week, and set the Roomba robo-vac going, if she remembered. She did these chores without complaint because she knew that her mother was helping Momo and that her father's book was very important. He said this one was POPULAR instead of ACADEMIC. If it was successful, he might be able to stop teaching and write full-time, at least for awhile.

On this day, the seventeenth of September, the mailbox contained a Walmart circular, a postcard announcing the opening of a new dental office in town (WE GUARANTEE MILES OF SMILES!), and two glossy come-ons from local Realtors selling time shares at the Mount Thunder ski resort.

There was also a local bulk-mail rag called *The Anniston Shopper*. This had a few wire-service stories on the front two pages and a few local stories (heavy on regional sports) in the middle. The rest was ads and coupons. If she had been home, Lucy would have saved a few of these latter and then tossed the rest of the *Shopper* into the recycling bin. Her daughter would never have seen it. On this day, with Lucy away in Boston, Abra did.

She thumbed through it as she idled her way up the driveway, then turned it over. On the back page there were forty or fifty photographs not much bigger than postage stamps, most in color, a few in black and white. Above them was this heading:

HAVE YOU SEEN ME?
A Weekly Service Of Your *Anniston Shopper*

For a moment Abra thought it was some sort of contest, like a scavenger hunt. Then she realized these were missing children, and it was as if a hand had grasped the soft lining of her stomach and squeezed it like a washcloth. She had bought a three-pack of Oreos in the caf at lunch, and had saved them for the bus ride home. Now she seemed to feel them being wadded up toward her throat by that clutching hand.

Don't look at it if it bothers you, she told herself. It was the stern and lecturely voice she often employed when she was upset or confused (a Momo-voice, although she had never consciously realized this). *Just toss it in the garage trashcan with the rest of this gluck.* Only she seemed unable *not* to look at it.

Here was Cynthia Abelard, DOB June 9, 2005. After a moment's thought, Abra realized DOB stood for date of birth. So Cynthia would be eight now. If she was still alive, that is. She had been missing since 2009. *How does somebody lose track of a four-year-old?* Abra wondered. *She must have really crappy parents.* But of course, the parents probably *hadn't* lost her. Probably some weirdo had been cruising around the neighborhood, seen his chance, and stolen her.

Here was Merton Askew, DOB September 4, 1998. He had disappeared in 2010.

Here, halfway down the page, was a beautiful little Hispanic girl named Angel Barbera, who had disappeared from her Kansas City home at the age of seven and had already been gone for nine years. Abra wondered if her parents really thought this tiny picture would help them get her back. And if they did, would they still even know her? For that matter, would *she* know *them*?

Get rid of that thing, the Momo-voice said. *You've got enough to ~~wo~~rry about without looking at a lot of missing ki—*

Her eyes found a picture in the very bottom row, and a little ~~sou~~nd escaped her. Probably it was a moan. At first she didn't even ~~kn~~ow why, although she almost did; it was like how you sometimes ~~kn~~ew the word you wanted to use in an English composition but ~~yo~~u still couldn't quite get it, the damn thing just sat there on the ~~tip~~ of your tongue.

This photo was of a white kid with short hair and a great big ~~go~~ofy-ass grin. It looked like he had freckles on his cheeks. The ~~pic~~ture was too small to tell for sure, but

(they're freckles you know they are)

Abra was somehow sure, anyway. Yes, they were freckles and his ~~big~~ brothers had teased him about them and his mother told him ~~th~~ey would go away in time.

"She told him freckles are good luck," Abra whispered.

Bradley Trevor, DOB March 2, 2000. Missing since July 12, 2011. ~~Ra~~ce: Caucasian. Location: Bankerton, Iowa. Current Age: 13. And ~~be~~low this—below all these pictures of mostly smiling children: *If ~~you~~ think you have seen Bradley Trevor, contact The National Center for ~~Mi~~ssing & Exploited Children.*

Only no one was going to contact them about Bradley, because ~~no~~ one was going to see him. His current age wasn't thirteen, either. ~~Br~~adley Trevor had stopped at eleven. He had stopped like a busted ~~wr~~istwatch that shows the same time twenty-four hours a day. Abra ~~fou~~nd herself wondering if freckles faded underground.

"The baseball boy," she whispered.

There were flowers lining the driveway. Abra leaned over, hands ~~on~~ her knees, pack all at once far too heavy on her back, and threw ~~up~~ her Oreos and the undigested portion of her school lunch into ~~he~~r mother's asters. When she was sure she wasn't going to puke a ~~sec~~ond time, she went into the garage and tossed the mail into the ~~tra~~sh. *All* the mail.

Her father was right, it was junkola.

5

The door of the little room her dad used as his study was ope
and when Abra stopped at the kitchen sink for a glass of water
rinse the sour-chocolate taste of used Oreos out of her mouth, s
heard the keyboard of his computer clicking steadily away. Th
was good. When it slowed down or stopped completely, he had
tendency to be grumpy. Also, he was more apt to notice her. Tod
she didn't want to be noticed.

"Abba-Doo, is that you?" her father half sang.

Ordinarily she would have asked him to *please* stop using th
baby name, but not today. "Yup, it's me."

"School go okay?"

The steady *click-click-click* had stopped. *Please don't come out he*
Abra prayed. *Don't come out and look at me and ask me why I'm so p*
or something.

"Fine. How's the book?"

"Having a great day," he said. "Writing about the Charleston a
the Black Bottom. Vo-doe-dee-oh-doe." Whatever *that* meant. T
important thing was the *click-click-click* started up again. Than
God.

"Terrific," she said, rinsing her glass and putting it in the drain
"I'm going upstairs to start my homework."

"That's my girl. Think Harvard in '18."

"Okay, Dad." And maybe she would. Anything to keep hers
from thinking about Bankerton, Iowa, in '11.

6

Only she couldn't stop.

Because.

Because what? Because why? Because . . . well . . .

Because there are things I can do.

She IM'ed with Jessica for awhile, but then Jessica went to the mall in North Conway to have dinner at Panda Garden with her parents, so Abra opened her social studies book. She meant to go to chapter four, a majorly boresome twenty pages titled "How Our Government Works," but instead the book had fallen open to chapter five: "Your Responsibilities As a Citizen."

Oh God, if there was a word she didn't want to see this afternoon, it was *responsibilities*. She went into the bathroom for another glass of water because her mouth still tasted blick and found herself staring at her own freckles in the mirror. There were exactly three, one on her left cheek and two on her schnozz. Not bad. She had lucked out in the freckles department. Nor did she have a birthmark, like Bethany Stevens, or a cocked eye like Norman McGinley, or a stutter like Ginny Whitlaw, or a horrible name like poor picked-on Pence Effersham. Abra was a little strange, of course, but Abra was fine, people thought it was interesting instead of just weird, like Pence, who was known among the boys (but girls always somehow found these things out) as Pence the Penis.

And the biggie, I didn't get cut apart by crazy people who paid no attention when I screamed and begged them to stop. I didn't have to see some of the crazy people licking my blood off the palms of their hands before I died. Abba-Doo is one lucky ducky.

But maybe not such a lucky ducky after all. Lucky duckies didn't know things they had no business knowing.

She closed the lid of the toilet, sat on it, and cried quietly with her hands over her face. Being forced to think of Bradley Trevor again and how he died was bad enough, but it wasn't just him. There were all those other kids to think about, so many pictures that they were crammed together on the last page of the *Shopper* like the school assembly from hell. All those gap-toothed smiles and all those eyes that knew even less of the world than Abra did herself, and what did *she* know? Not even "How Our Government Works."

What did the parents of those missing children think? How did they go on with their lives? Was Cynthia or Merton or Angel the first thing they thought about in the morning and the last thing they thought about at night? Did they keep their rooms ready for them in case they came home, or did they give all their clothes and toys away to the Goodwill? Abra had heard that was what Lennie O'Meara's parents did after Lennie fell out of a tree and hit his head on a rock and died. Lennie O'Meara, who got as far as the fifth grade and then just . . . stopped. But of course Lennie's parents *knew* he was dead, there was a grave where they could go and put flowers, and maybe that made it different. Maybe not, but Abra thought it would. Because otherwise you'd pretty much have to wonder, wouldn't you? Like when you were eating breakfast, you'd wonder if your missing

(*Cynthia Merton Angel*)

was also eating breakfast somewhere, or flying a kite, or picking oranges with a bunch of migrants, or whatever. In the back of your mind you'd have to be pretty sure he or she was dead, that's what happened to most of them (you only had to watch Action News at Six to know), but you couldn't be sure.

There was nothing she could do about that uncertainty for the parents of Cynthia Abelard or Merton Askew or Angel Barbera, she had no idea what had happened to them, but that wasn't true of Bradley Trevor.

She had almost forgotten him, then that stupid *newspaper* . . . those stupid *pictures* . . . and the stuff that had come back to her, stuff she didn't even know she knew, as if the pictures had been startled out of her subconscious . . .

And those things she could do. Things she had never told her parents about because it would worry them, the way she guessed it would worry them if they knew she had made out with Bobby Flannagan—just a little, no sucking face or anything gross like that—one day after school. That was something they wouldn't *want* to know. Abra guessed (and about this she wasn't entirely wrong, although there was no telepathy involved) that in her parents' minds, she was sort of frozen at eight and would probably stay that way at least until she got boobs, which she sure hadn't yet—not that you'd notice, anyway.

So far they hadn't even had THE TALK with her. Julie Vandover said it was almost always your mom who gave you the lowdown, but the only lowdown Abra had gotten lately was on how important it was for her to get the trash out on Thursday mornings before the bus came. "We don't ask you to do many chores," Lucy had said, "and this fall it's especially important for all of us to pitch in."

Momo had at least approached THE TALK. In the spring, she had taken Abra aside one day and said, "Do you know what boys want from girls, once boys and girls get to be about your age?"

"Sex, I guess," Abra had said . . . although all that humble, scurrying Pence Effersham ever seemed to want was one of her cookies, or to borrow a quarter for the vending machines, or to tell her how many times he'd seen *The Avengers*.

Momo had nodded. "You can't blame human nature, it is what it is, but don't give it to them. Period. End of discussion. You can rethink things when you're nineteen, if you want."

That had been a little embarrassing, but at least it was straight and clear. There was nothing clear about the thing in her head. That was *her* birthmark, invisible but real. Her parents no longer talked about the crazy shit that had happened when she was little. Maybe they thought the thing that had caused that stuff was almost gone. Sure, she'd known Momo was sick, but that wasn't the same as the crazy piano music, or turning on the water in the bathroom, or the birthday party (which she barely remembered) when she had hung spoons all over the kitchen ceiling. She had just learned to control it. Not completely, but mostly.

And it had changed. Now she rarely saw things before they happened. Or take moving stuff around. When she was six or seven, she could have concentrated on her pile of schoolbooks and lifted them all the way to the ceiling. Nothing to it. Easy as knitting kitten-britches, as Momo liked to say. Now, even if it was only a single book, she could concentrate until it felt like her brains were going to come splooshing out her ears, and she might only be able to shove it a few inches across her desk. That was on a good day. On many, she couldn't even flutter the pages.

But there were other things she *could* do, and in many cases far better than she'd been able to as a little kid. Looking into people's heads, for instance. She couldn't do it with everyone—some people were entirely enclosed, others only gave off intermittent flashes—but many people were like windows with the curtains pulled back. She could look in anytime she felt like it. Mostly she didn't want to, because the things she discovered were sometimes sad and often shocking. Finding out that Mrs. Moran, her beloved sixth-grade teacher, was having AN AFFAIR had been the biggest mind-blower so far, and not in a good way.

These days she mostly kept the *seeing* part of her mind shut down. Learning to do that had been difficult at first, like learning to skate backwards or print with her left hand, but she *had* learned. Practice didn't make perfect (not yet, at least), but it sure helped. She still sometimes looked, but always tentatively, ready to pull back at the first sign of something weird or disgusting. And she *never* peeked into her parents' minds, or into Momo's. It would have been wrong. Probably it was wrong with everyone, but it was like Momo herself had said: You can't blame human nature, and there was nothing more human than curiosity.

Sometimes she could make people do things. Not everyone, not even *half* of everyone, but a lot of people were *very* open to suggestions. (Probably they were the same ones who thought the stuff they sold on TV really would take away their wrinkles or make their hair grow back.) Abra knew this was a talent that could grow if she exercised it like a muscle, but she didn't. It scared her.

There were other things, too, some for which she had no name, but the one she was thinking about now did have one. She called it far-seeing. Like the other aspects of her special talent, it came and went, but if she really wanted it—and if she had an object to fix upon—she could usually summon it.

I could do that now.

"Shut up, Abba-Doo," she said in a low, strained voice. "Shut up, Abba-Doo-Doo."

She opened *Early Algebra* to tonight's homework page, which she

ad bookmarked with a sheet on which she had written the names
Boyd, Steve, Cam, and Pete at least twenty times each. Collectively
hey were 'Round Here, her favorite boy band. *So* hot, especially
Cam. Her best friend, Emma Deane, thought so, too. Those blue
yes, that careless tumble of blond hair.

Maybe I could help. His parents would be sad, but at least they'd know.
"Shut up, Abba-Doo. Shut up, Abba-Doo-Doo-For-Brains."
If 5x - 4 = 26, what does x equal?
"Sixty zillion!" she said. "Who cares?"

Her eyes fell on the names of the cute boys in 'Round Here,
written in the pudgy cursive she and Emma affected ("Writing
oks more romantic that way," Emma had decreed), and all at once
ey looked stupid and babyish and all wrong. *They cut him up and
ked his blood and then they did something even worse to him.* In a world
here something like that could happen, mooning over a boy band
emed worse than wrong.

Abra slammed her book shut, went downstairs (the *click-click-
ck* from her dad's study continued unabated) and out to the
rage. She retrieved the *Shopper* from the trash, brought it up to
r room, and smoothed it flat on her desk.

All those faces, but right now she cared about only one.

7

r heart was thumping hard-hard-hard. She had been scared
fore when she consciously tried to far-see or thought-read, but
ver scared like this. Never even close.

What are you going to do if you find out?
That was a question for later, because she might not be able to.
sneaking, cowardly part of her mind hoped for that.

Abra put the first two fingers of her left hand on the picture of
adley Trevor because her left hand was the one that saw better.
would have liked to get all her fingers on it (and if it had been
object, she would have held it), but the picture was too small.

Once her fingers were on it she couldn't even see it anymore. Exce
she could. She saw it very well.

Blue eyes, like Cam Knowles's in 'Round Here. You couldn't t
from the picture, but they were that same deep shade. She *knew*.

Right-handed, like me. But left-handed like me, too. It was the
hand that knew what pitch was coming next, fastball or curveb—

Abra gave a little gasp. The baseball boy had *known* things.

The baseball boy really had been like her.

Yes, that's right. That's why they took him.

She closed her eyes and saw his face. Bradley Trevor. Brad,
his friends. The baseball boy. Sometimes he turned his cap arou
because that way it was a rally cap. His father was a farmer. H
mother cooked pies and sold them at a local restaurant, also at t
family farmstand. When his big brother went away to college, B
took all his AC/DC discs. He and his best friend, Al, especia
liked the song "Big Balls." They'd sit on Brad's bed and sing
together and laugh and laugh.

He walked through the corn and a man was waiting for him. B
thought he was a nice man, one of the good guys, because the man—

"Barry," Abra whispered in a low voice. Behind her closed li
her eyes moved rapidly back and forth like those of a sleeper in
grip of a vivid dream. "His name was Barry the Chunk. He foo
you, Brad. Didn't he?"

But not just Barry. If it had been just him, Brad might ha
known. It had to be all of the Flashlight People working togeth
sending the same thought: that it would be okay to get into Ba
the Chunk's truck or camper-van or whatever it was, because Ba
was good. One of the good guys. A friend.

And they took him . . .

Abra went deeper. She didn't bother with what Brad had se
because he hadn't seen anything but a gray rug. He was tied
with tape and lying facedown on the floor of whatever Barry
Chunk was driving. That was okay, though. Now that she w
tuned in, she could see wider than him. She could see—

His glove. A Wilson baseball glove. And Barry the Chunk—

Then that part flew away. It might swoop back or it might not. It was night. She could smell manure. There was a factory. Some kind of

(*it's busted*)

factory. There was a whole line of vehicles going there, some small, most big, a couple of them enormous. The headlights were off in case someone was looking, but there was a three-quarters moon in the sky. Enough light to see by. They went down a potholed and bumpy tar road, they went past a water tower, they went past a shed with a broken roof, they went through a rusty gate that was standing open, they went past a sign. It went by so fast she couldn't read it. Then the factory. A busted factory with busted smokestacks and busted windows. There was another sign and thanks to the moonlight this one she *could* read: NO TRESPASSING BY ORDER OF THE CANTON COUNTY SHERIFF'S DEPT.

They were going around the back, and when they got there they were going to hurt Brad the baseball boy and go on hurting him until he was dead. Abra didn't want to see that part so she made everything go backwards. That was a little hard, like opening a jar with a really tight cap, but she could do it. When she got back where she wanted, she let go.

Barry the Chunk liked that glove because it reminded him of when he was a little boy. That's why he tried it on. Tried it on and smelled the oil Brad used to keep it from getting stiff and bopped his fist in the pocket a few ti—

But now things were reeling forward and she forgot about Brad's baseball glove again.

Water tower. Shed with broken roof. Rusty gate. And then the first sign. What did it say?

Nope. Still too quick, even with the moonlight. She rewound again (now beads of sweat were standing out on her forehead) and let go. Water tower. Shed with broken roof. *Get ready, here it comes.* Rusty gate. Then the sign. This time she could read it, although she wasn't sure she understood it.

Abra grabbed the sheet of notepaper on which she had curlicued all those stupid boy names and turned it over. Quickly, before she forgot, she scrawled down everything she had seen on that sign: ORGANIC INDUSTRIES and ETHANOL PLANT #4 and FREEMAN, IOWA and CLOSED UNTIL FURTHER NOTICE.

Okay, now she knew where they had killed him, and where—she was sure—they had buried him, baseball glove and all. What next? If she called the number for Missing and Exploited Children, they would hear a little kid's voice and pay no attention . . . except maybe to give her telephone number to the police, who would probably have her arrested for trying to prank on people who were already sad and unhappy. She thought of her mother next, but with Momo sick and getting ready to die, it was out of the question. Mom had enough to worry about without this.

Abra got up, went to the window, and stared out at her street, at the Lickety-Split convenience store on the corner (which the older kids called the Lickety-Spliff, because of all the dope that got smoked behind it, where the Dumpsters were), and the White Mountains poking up at a clear blue late summer sky. She had begun to rub her mouth, an anxiety tic her parents were trying to break her of, but they weren't here, so boo on that. Boo all *over* that.

Dad's right downstairs.

She didn't want to tell him, either. Not because he had to finish his book, but because he wouldn't want to get involved in something like this even if he believed her. Abra didn't have to read his mind to know that.

So who?

Before she could think of the logical answer, the world beyond her window began to turn, as if it were mounted on a gigantic disc. A low cry escaped her and she clutched at the sides of the window, bunching the curtains in her fists. This had happened before, always without warning, and she was terrified each time it did, because it was like having a seizure. She was no longer in her own body, she was far-*being* instead of far-*seeing,* and what if she couldn't get back?

The turntable slowed, then stopped. Now instead of being in her bedroom, she was in a supermarket. She knew because ahead of her was the meat counter. Over it (this sign easy to read, thanks to bright fluorescents) was a promise: AT SAM'S, EVERY CUT IS A BLUE RIBBON **COWBOY** CUT! For a moment or two the meat counter drew closer because the turntable had slid her into someone who was walking. Walking and *shopping*. Barry the Chunk? No, not him, although Barry was near; Barry was how she had *gotten* here. Only she had been drawn away from him by someone much more powerful. Abra could see a cart loaded with groceries at the bottom of her vision. Then the forward movement stopped and there was this sensation, this

(*rummaging prying*)

crazy feeling of someone INSIDE HER, and Abra suddenly understood that for once she wasn't alone on the turntable. She was looking toward a meat counter at the end of a supermarket aisle, and the other person was looking out her window at Richland Court and the White Mountains beyond.

Panic exploded inside her; it was as if gasoline had been poured on a fire. Not a sound escaped her lips, which were pressed together so tightly that her mouth was only a stitch, but inside her head she produced a scream louder than anything of which she would ever have believed herself capable:

(*NO! GET OUT OF MY HEAD!*)

8

When David felt the house rumble and saw the overhead light fixture in his study swaying on its chain, his first thought was

(*Abra*)

that his daughter had had one of her psychic outbursts, though there hadn't been any of that telekinetic crap in years, and never anything like this. As things settled back to normal, his second—and, to his mind, far more reasonable—thought was that he had just experienced his first New Hampshire earthquake. He knew they happened from time to time, but . . . wow!

He got up from his desk (not neglecting to hit SAVE before he did), and ran into the hall. From the foot of the stairs he called, "Abra! Did you feel that?"

She came out of her room, looking pale and a little scared. "Yeah, sorta. I . . . I think I . . ."

"It was an earthquake!" David told her, beaming. "Your first earthquake! Isn't that neat?"

"Yes," Abra said, not sounding very thrilled. "Neat."

He looked out the living room window and saw people standing on their stoops and lawns. His good friend Matt Renfrew was among them. "I'm gonna go across the street and talk to Matt, hon. You want to come with?"

"I guess I better finish my math."

David started toward the front door, then turned to look up at her. "You're not scared, are you? You don't have to be. It's over."

Abra only wished it was.

9

Rose the Hat was doing a double shop, because Grampa Flick was feeling poorly again. She saw a few other members of the True in Sam's, and nodded to them. She stopped awhile in canned goods to talk to Barry the Chink, who had his wife's list in one hand. Barry was concerned about Flick.

"He'll bounce back," Rose said. "You know Grampa."

Barry grinned. "Tougher'n a boiled owl."

Rose nodded and got her cart rolling again. "You bet he is."

Just an ordinary weekday afternoon at the supermarket, and as she took her leave of Barry, she at first mistook what was happening to her for something mundane, maybe low sugar. She was prone to sugar crashes, and usually kept a candybar in her purse. Then she realized someone was inside her head. Someone was *looking*.

Rose had not risen to her position as head of the True Knot

by being indecisive. She halted with her cart pointed toward the meat counter (her planned next stop) and immediately leaped into the conduit some nosy and potentially dangerous person had established. Not a member of the True, she would have known any one of them immediately, but not an ordinary rube, either.

No, this was far from ordinary.

The market swung away and suddenly she was looking out at a mountain range. Not the Rockies, she would have recognized those. These were smaller. The Catskills? The Adirondacks? It could have been either, or some other. As for the looker . . . Rose thought it was a child. Almost certainly a girl, and one she had encountered before.

I have to see what she looks like, then I can find her anytime I want to. I have to get her to look in a mir—

But then a thought as loud as a shotgun blast in a closed room (*NO! GET OUT OF MY HEAD!*)

wiped her mind clean and sent her staggering against shelves of canned soups and vegetables. They went cascading to the floor, rolling everywhere. For a moment or two Rose thought she was going to follow them, swooning like the dewy heroine of a romance novel. Then she was back. The girl had broken the connection, and in rather spectacular fashion.

Was her nose bleeding? She wiped it with her fingers and checked. No. Good.

One of the stockboys came rushing up. "Are you okay, ma'am?"

"Fine. Just felt a little faint for a second or two. Probably from the tooth extraction I had yesterday. It's passed off now. I've made a mess, haven't I? Sorry. Good thing it was cans instead of bottles."

"No problem, no problem at all. Would you like to come up front and sit down on the taxi bench?"

"That won't be necessary," Rose said. And it wasn't, but she was done shopping for the day. She rolled her cart two aisles over and left it there.

10

She had brought her Tacoma (old but reliable) down from the high-country campground west of Sidewinder, and once she was in the cab, she pulled her phone out of her purse and hit speed dial. It rang at the other end just a single time.

"What's up, Rosie-girl?" Crow Daddy.

"We've got a problem."

Of course it was also an opportunity. A kid with enough in her boiler to set off a blast like that—to not only detect Rose but send her reeling—wasn't just a steamhead but the find of the century. She felt like Captain Ahab, for the first time sighting his great white whale.

"Talk to me." All business now.

"A little over two years ago. The kid in Iowa. Remember him?"

"Sure."

"You also remember me telling you we had a looker?"

"Yeah. East Coast. You thought it was probably a girl."

"It was a girl, all right. She just found me again. I was in Sam's, minding my own business, and then all at once there she was."

"Why, after all this time?"

"I don't know and I don't care. But we have to have her, Crow. We *have* to have her."

"Does she know who you are? Where *we* are?"

Rose had thought about this while walking to the truck. The intruder hadn't seen her, of that much she was sure. The kid had been on the inside looking out. As to what she *had* seen? A supermarket aisle. How many of those were there in America? Probably a million.

"I don't think so, but that's not the important part."

"Then what is?"

"Remember me telling you she was big steam? *Huge* steam? Well, she's even bigger than that. When I tried to turn it around on her, she blew me out of her head like I was a piece of milkweed fluff. Nothing like that's ever happened to me before. I would have said it was impossible."

"Is she potential True or potential food?"

"I don't know." But she did. They needed steam—*stored* steam—a lot more than they needed fresh recruits. Besides, Rose wanted no one in the True with that much power.

"Okay, how do we find her? Any ideas?"

Rose thought of what she'd seen through the girl's eyes before she had been so unceremoniously booted back to Sam's Supermarket in Sidewinder. Not much, but there had been a store . . .

She said, "The kids call it the Lickety-Spliff."

"Huh?"

"Nothing, never mind. I need to think about it. But we're going to have her, Crow. We've *got* to have her."

There was a pause. When he spoke again, Crow sounded cautious. "The way you're talking, there might be enough to fill a dozen canisters. If, that is, you really don't want to try Turning her."

Rose gave a distracted, yapping laugh. "If I'm right, we don't *have* enough canisters to store the steam from this one. If she was a mountain, she'd be Everest." He made no reply. Rose didn't need to see him or poke into his mind to know he was flabbergasted. "Maybe we don't have to do either one."

"I don't follow."

Of course he didn't. Long-think had never been Crow's specialty. "Maybe we don't have to Turn her *or* kill her. Think cows."

"Cows."

"You can butcher one and get a couple of months' worth of steaks and hamburgers. But if you keep it alive and take care of it, it will give milk for six years. Maybe even eight."

Silence. Long. She let it stretch. When he replied, he sounded more cautious than ever. "I've never heard of anything like that. We kill em once we've got the steam or if they've got something we need and they're strong enough to survive the Turn, we Turn em. The way we Turned Andi back in the eighties. Grampa Flick might say different, if you believe him he remembers all the way back to when Henry the Eighth was killing his wives, but I don't think the True has ever tried just holding onto a steamhead. If she's as strong as you say, it could be dangerous."

Tell me something I don't know. If you'd felt what I did, you'd call me crazy to even think about it. And maybe I am. But . . .

But she was tired of spending so much of her time—the whole family's time—scrambling for nourishment. Of living like tenth-century Gypsies when they should have been living like the kings and queens of creation. Which was what they were.

"Talk to Grampa, if he's feeling better. And Heavy Mary, she's been around almost as long as Flick. Snakebite Andi. She's new, but she's got a good head on her shoulders. Anyone else you think might have valuable input."

"Jesus, Rosie. I don't know—"

"Neither do I, not yet. I'm still reeling. All I'm asking right now is for you to do some spadework. You are the advance man, after all."

"Okay . . ."

"Oh, and make sure you talk to Walnut. Ask him what drugs might keep a rube child nice and docile for a long period of time."

"This girl doesn't sound like much of a rube to me."

"Oh, she is. A big old fat rube milk-cow."

Not exactly true. A great big white whale, that's what she is.

Rose ended the call without waiting to see if Crow Daddy had anything else to say. She was the boss, and as far as she was concerned, the discussion was over.

She's a white whale, and I want her.

But Ahab hadn't wanted *his* whale just because Moby would provide tons of blubber and almost endless barrels of oil, and Rose didn't want the girl because she might—given the right drug cocktails and a lot of powerful psychic soothing—provide a nearly endless supply of steam. It was more personal than that. Turn her? Make her part of the True Knot? Never. The kid had kicked Rose the Hat out of her head as if she were some annoying religious goofball going door-to-door and handing out end-of-the-world tracts. No one had ever given her that kind of bum's rush before. No matter how powerful she was, she had to be taught a lesson.

And I'm just the woman for the job.

Rose the Hat started her truck, pulled out of the supermarket parking lot, and headed for the family-owned Bluebell Campground. It was a really beautiful location, and why not? One of the world's great resort hotels had once stood there.

But of course, the Overlook had burned to the ground long ago.

11

The Renfrews, Matt and Cassie, were the neighborhood's party people, and they decided on the spur of the moment to have an Earthquake Barbecue. They invited everyone on Richland Court, and almost everyone came. Matt got a case of soda, a few bottles of cheap wine, and a beer-ball from the Lickety-Split up the street. It was a lot of fun, and David Stone enjoyed himself tremendously. As far as he could tell, Abra did, too. She hung with her friends Julie and Emma, and he made sure that she ate a hamburger and some salad. Lucy had told him they had to be vigilant about their daughter's eating habits, because she'd reached the age when girls started to be very conscious about their weight and looks—the age at which anorexia or bulimia were apt to show their skinny, starveling faces.

What he didn't notice (although Lucy might have, had she been there) was that Abra wasn't joining in her friends' apparently nonstop gigglefest. And, after eating a bowl of ice cream (a *small* bowl), she asked her father if she could go back across the street and finish her homework.

"Okay," David said, "but thank Mr. and Mrs. Renfrew first."

This Abra would have done without having to be reminded, but she agreed without saying so.

"You're very welcome, Abby," Mrs. Renfrew said. Her eyes were almost preternaturally bright from three glasses of white wine. "Isn't this cool? We should have earthquakes more often. Although I was talking to Vicky Fenton—you know the Fentons, on Pond Street? That's just a block over and she said they didn't feel anything. Isn't that *weird*?"

"Sure is," Abra agreed, thinking that when it came to weird, Mrs. Renfrew didn't know the half of it.

12

She finished her homework and was downstairs watching TV with her dad when Mom called. Abra talked to her awhile, then turned the phone over to her father. Lucy said something, and Abra knew what it had been even before Dave glanced at her and said, "Yeah, she's fine, just blitzed from homework, I think. They give the kids so much now. Did she tell you we had a little earthquake?"

"Going upstairs, Dad," Abra said, and he gave her an absent wave.

She sat at her desk, turned on her computer, then turned it off again. She didn't want to play Fruit Ninja and she certainly didn't want to IM with anyone. She had to think about what to do, because she had to do *something*.

She put her schoolbooks in her backpack, then looked up and the woman from the supermarket was staring in at her from the window. That was impossible because the window was on the second floor, but she was there. Her skin was unblemished and purest white, her cheekbones high, her dark eyes wide-set and slightly tilted at the corners. Abra thought she might be the most beautiful woman she had ever seen. Also, she realized at once, and without a shadow of a doubt, she was insane. Masses of black hair framed her perfect, somehow arrogant face, and streamed down over her shoulders. Staying in place on this wealth of hair in spite of the crazy angle at which it was cocked, was a jaunty tophat of scuffed velvet.

She's not really there, and she's not in my head, either. I don't know how I can be seeing her but I am and I don't think she kn—

The madwoman in the darkening window grinned, and when her lips spread apart, Abra saw she only had one tooth on top, a monstrous discolored tusk. She understood it had been the last thing Bradley Trevor had ever seen, and she screamed, screamed as loudly as she could . . . but only inside, because her throat was locked and her vocal cords were frozen.

Abra shut her eyes. When she opened them again, the grinning white-faced woman was gone.

Not there. But she could come. She knows about me and she could come.

In that moment, she realized what she should have known as soon as she saw the abandoned factory. There was really only one person she could call on. Only one who could help her. She closed her eyes again, this time not to hide from a horrible vision looking in at her from the window, but to summon help.

(TONY, I NEED YOUR DAD! PLEASE, TONY, PLEASE!)

Still with her eyes shut—but now feeling the warmth of tears on her lashes and cheeks—she whispered, "Help me, Tony. I'm scared."

CHAPTER EIGHT

ABRA'S THEORY OF RELATIVITY

1

The last run of the day on *The Helen Rivington* was called the Sunset Cruise, and many evenings when Dan wasn't on shift at the hospice, he took the controls. Billy Freeman, who had made the run roughly twenty-five thousand times during his years as a town employee, was delighted to turn them over.

"You never get tired of it, do you?" he asked Dan once.

"Put it down to a deprived childhood."

It hadn't been, not really, but he and his mother had moved around a lot after the settlement money ran out, and she had worked a lot of jobs. With no college degree, most of them had been low-paying. She'd kept a roof over their heads and food on the table, but there had never been much extra.

Once—he'd been in high school, the two of them living in Bradenton, not far from Tampa—he'd asked her why she never dated. By then he was old enough to know she was still a very good-looking woman. Wendy Torrance had given him a crooked smile and said, "One man was enough for me, Danny. Besides, now I've got you."

"How much did she know about your drinking?" Casey K. had asked him during one of their meetings at the Sunspot. "You started pretty young, right?"

Dan had needed to give that one some thought. "Probably more than I knew at the time, but we never talked about it. I think she was afraid to bring it up. Besides, I never got in trouble with the law—not then, anyway—and I graduated high school with honors." He had smiled grimly at Casey over his coffee cup. "And of course I never beat her up. I suppose that made a difference."

Never got that train set, either, but the basic tenet AAs lived by was don't drink and things will get better. They did, too. Now he had the biggest little choo-choo a boy could wish for, and Billy was right, it never got old. He supposed it might in another ten or twenty years, but even then Dan thought he'd probably still offer to drive the last circuit of the day, just to pilot the *Riv* at sunset, out to the turnaround at Cloud Gap. The view was spectacular, and when the Saco was calm (which it usually was once its spring convulsions had subsided), you could see all the colors twice, once above and once below. Everything was silence at the far end of the *Riv*'s run; it was as if God was holding His breath.

The trips between Labor Day and Columbus Day, when the *Riv* shut down for the winter, were the best of all. The tourists were gone, and the few riders were locals, many of whom Dan could now call by name. On weeknights like tonight, there were less than a dozen paying customers. Which was fine by him.

It was fully dark when he eased the *Riv* back into its dock at Teenytown Station. He leaned against the side of the first passenger car with his cap (ENGINEER DAN stitched in red above the bill) tipped back on his head, wishing his handful of riders a very good night. Billy was sitting on a bench, the glowing tip of his cigarette intermittently lighting his face. He had to be nearly seventy, but he looked good, had made a complete recovery from his abdominal surgery two years before, and said he had no plans to retire.

"What would I do?" he'd asked on the single occasion Dan had brought the subject up. "Retire to that deathfarm where you work? Wait for your pet cat to pay me a visit? Thanks but no thanks."

When the last two or three riders had ambled on their way, probably in search of dinner, Billy butted his cigarette and joined him. "I'll put er in the barn. Unless you want to do that, too."

"No, go right ahead. You've been sitting on your ass long enough.

When are you going to give up the smokes, Billy? You know the doctor said they contributed to your little gut problem."

"I've cut down to almost nothing," Billy said, but with a telltale downward shift in his gaze. Dan could have found out just how much Billy had cut down—he probably wouldn't even need to touch the guy in order to get that much info—but he didn't. One day in the summer just past, he'd seen a kid wearing a t-shirt with an octagonal road sign printed on it. Instead of STOP, the sign said TMI. When Danny asked him what it meant, the kid had given him a sympathetic smile he probably reserved strictly for gentlemen of a fortyish persuasion. "Too much information," he'd said. Dan thanked him, thinking: *Story of my life, young fellow.*

Everyone had secrets. This he had known from earliest childhood. Decent people deserved to keep theirs, and Billy Freeman was decency personified.

"Want to go for a coffee, Danno? You got time? Won't take me ten minutes to put this bitch to bed."

Dan touched the side of the engine lovingly. "Sure, but watch your mouth. This is no bitch, this is a la—"

That was when his head exploded.

2

When he came back to himself, he was sprawled on the bench where Billy had been smoking. Billy was sitting beside him, looking worried. Hell, looking scared half to death. He had his phone in one hand, with his finger poised over the buttons.

"Put it away," Dan said. The words came out in a dusty croak. He cleared his throat and tried again. "I'm okay."

"You sure? Jesus Christ, I thought you was havin a stroke. I thought it for sure."

That's what it felt like.

For the first time in years Dan thought of Dick Halloran, the Overlook Hotel's chef extraordinaire back in the day. Dick had known almost at once that Jack Torrance's little boy shared his own talent. Dan wondered now if Dick might still be alive. Almost certainly not; he'd been pushing sixty back then.

"Who's Tony?" Billy asked.

"Huh?"

"You said 'Please, Tony, please.' Who's Tony?"

"A guy I used to know back in my drinking days." As an improvisation it wasn't much, but it was the first thing to come into his still-dazed mind. "A good friend."

Billy looked at the lighted rectangle of his cell a few seconds longer, then slowly folded the phone and put it away. "You know, I don't believe that for a minute. I think you had one of your flashes. Like on the day you found out about my . . ." He tapped his stomach.

"Well . . ."

Billy raised a hand. "Say nummore. As long as you're okay, that is. And as long as it isn't somethin bad about me. Because I'd want to know if it was. I don't s'pose that's true of everyone, but it is with me."

"Nothing about you." Dan stood up and was pleased to discover his legs held him just fine. "But I'm going to take a raincheck on that coffee, if you don't mind."

"Not a bit. You need to go back to your place and lie down. You're still pale. Whatever it was, it hit you hard." Billy glanced at the *Riv*. "Glad it didn't happen while you were up there in the peak-seat, rolling along at forty."

"Tell me about it," Dan said.

3

He crossed Cranmore Avenue to the Rivington House side, meaning to take Billy's advice and lie down, but instead of turning in at the gate giving on the big old Victorian's flower-bordered walk, he decided to stroll a little while. He was getting his wind back now—getting *himself* back—and the night air was sweet. Besides, he needed to consider what had just happened, and very carefully.

Whatever it was, it hit you hard.

That made him think again of Dick Hallorann, and of all the things he had never told Casey Kingsley. Nor would he. The harm he had done to Deenie—and to her son, he supposed, simply by doing nothing—was lodged deep inside, like an impacted wisdom tooth, and there it would stay. But at five, Danny Torrance had been the one harmed—along with his mother, of course—and his father had not been the only culprit. About that Dick *had* done something. If not, Dan and his mother would have died in the Overlook. Those old things were still painful to think about, still bright with the childish primary colors of fear and horror. He would have preferred never to think of them again, but now he had to. Because . . . well . . .

Because everything that goes around comes around. Maybe it's luck or maybe it's fate, but either way, it comes back around. What was it Dick said that day he gave me the lockbox? When the pupil is ready, the teacher will appear. Not that I'm equipped to teach anyone anything, except maybe that if you don't take a drink, you won't get drunk.

He'd reached the end of the block; now he turned around and headed back. He had the sidewalk entirely to himself. It was eerie how fast Frazier emptied out once the summer was over, and that made him think of the way the Overlook had emptied out. How quickly the little Torrance family had had the place entirely to themselves.

Except for the ghosts, of course. *They* never left.

4

Hallorann had told Danny he was headed to Denver, and from there he'd fly south to Florida. He had asked if Danny would like to help him down to the Overlook's parking lot with his bags, and Danny had carried one to the cook's rental car. Just a little thing, hardly more than a briefcase, but he'd needed to use both hands to tote it. When the bags were safely stowed in the trunk and they were sitting in the car, Hallorann had put a name to the thing in Danny Torrance's head, the thing his parents only half believed in.

You got a knack. Me, I've always called it the shining. That's what my grandmother called it, too. Get you kinda lonely, thinkin you were the only one?

Yes, he had been lonely, and yes, he had believed he was the only one. Hallorann had disabused him of that notion. In the years since, Dan had run across a lot of people who had, in the cook's words, "a little bit of shine to them." Billy, for one.

But never anyone like the girl who had screamed into his head tonight. It had felt like that cry might tear him apart.

Had *he* been that strong? He thought he had been, or almost. On closing day at the Overlook, Hallorann had told the troubled little boy sitting beside him to . . . what had he said?

He said to give him a blast.

Dan had arrived back at Rivington House and was standing outside the gate. The first leaves had begun to fall, and an evening breeze whisked them around his feet.

And when I asked him what I should think about, he told me anything. "Just think it hard," *he said. So I did, but at the last second I softened it, at least a little. If I hadn't, I think I might have killed him. He jerked back—no, he* slammed *back—and bit his lip. I remember the blood. He called me a pistol. And later, he asked about Tony. My invisible friend. So I told him.*

Tony was back, it seemed, but he was no longer Dan's friend. Now he was the friend of a little girl named Abra. She was in trouble just as Dan had been, but grown men who sought out little girls attracted attention and suspicion. He had a good life here in Frazier, and he felt it was one he deserved after all the lost years.

But . . .

But when he needed Dick—at the Overlook, and later, in Florida, when Mrs. Massey had come back—Dick had come. In AA, people called that kind of thing a Twelfth Step call. Because when the pupil was ready, the teacher would appear.

On several occasions, Dan had gone with Casey Kingsley and

some other guys in the Program to pay Twelfth Step calls on men who were over their heads in drugs or booze. Sometimes it was friends or bosses who asked for this service; more often it was relatives who had exhausted every other resource and were at their wits' end. They'd had a few successes over the years, but most visits ended with slammed doors or an invitation for Casey and his friends to stick their sanctimonious, quasireligious bullshit up their asses. One fellow, a meth-addled veteran of George Bush's splendid Iraq adventure, had actually waved a pistol at them. Heading back from the Chocorua hole-in-the-wall shack where the vet was denned up with his terrified wife, Dan had said, *"That* was a waste of time."

"It would be if we did it for them," Casey said, "but we don't. We do it for us. You like the life you're living, Danny-boy?" It wasn't the first time he had asked this question, and it wouldn't be the last.

"Yes." No hesitation on that score. Maybe he wasn't the president of General Motors or doing nude love scenes with Kate Winslet, but in Dan's mind, he had it all.

"Think you earned it?"

"No," Dan said, smiling. "Not really. Can't earn this."

"So what was it that got you back to a place where you like getting up in the morning? Was it luck or grace?"

He'd believed that Casey wanted him to say it was grace, but during the sober years he had learned the sometimes uncomfortable habit of honesty. "I don't know."

"That's okay, because when your back's against the wall, there's no difference."

5

"Abra, Abra, Abra," he said as he walked up the path to Rivington House. "What have you gotten yourself into, girl? And what are you getting *me* into?"

He was thinking he'd have to try to get in touch with her by using the shining, which was never completely reliable, but when he stepped into his turret room, he saw that wouldn't be necessary. Written neatly on his blackboard was this:

cadabra@nhmlx.com

He puzzled over her screen name for a few seconds, then got it and laughed. "Good one, kid, good one."

He powered up his laptop. A moment later, he was looking at a blank email form. He typed in her address and then sat watching the blinking cursor. How old was she? As far as he could calculate by their few previous communications, somewhere between a wise twelve and a slightly naïve sixteen. Probably closer to the former. And here he was, a man old enough to have salt speckles in his stubble if he skipped shaving. Here he was, getting ready to start compu-chatting with her. *To Catch a Predator,* anyone?

Maybe it's nothing. It could be; she's just a kid, after all.

Yes, but one who was damn scared. Plus, he was curious about her. Had been for some time. The same way, he supposed, that Hallorann had been curious about him.

I could use a little bit of grace right now. And a whole lot of luck.

In the SUBJECT box at the top of the email form, Dan wrote *Hello Abra.* He dropped the cursor, took a deep breath, and typed four words: *Tell me what's wrong.*

6

On the following Saturday afternoon, Dan was sitting in bright sunshine on one of the benches outside the ivy-covered stone building that housed the Anniston Public Library. He had a copy of the *Union Leader* open in front of him, and there were words on the page, but he had no idea what they said. He was too nervous.

Promptly at two o'clock, a girl in jeans rode up on her bike and lodged it in the rack at the foot of the lawn. She gave him a wave and a big smile.

So. Abra. As in Cadabra.

She was tall for her age, most of that height in her legs. Masses of curly blond hair were held back in a thick ponytail that looked ready to rebel and spray everywhere. The day was a bit chilly, and she was wearing a light jacket with ANNISTON CYCLONES screen-printed on the back. She grabbed a couple of books that were bungee-corded to the rear bumper of her bike, then ran up to him, still with that open smile. Pretty but not beautiful. Except for her wide-set blue eyes. *They* were beautiful.

"Uncle Dan! Gee, it's good to see you!" And she gave him a hearty smack on the cheek. That hadn't been in the script. Her confidence in his basic okayness was terrifying.

"Good to see you, too, Abra. Sit down."

He had told her they would have to be careful, and Abra—a child of her culture—understood at once. They had agreed that the best thing would be to meet in the open, and there were few places in Anniston more open than the front lawn of the library, which was situated near the middle of the small downtown district.

She was looking at him with frank interest, perhaps even hunger. He could feel something like tiny fingers patting lightly at the inside of his head.

(*where's Tony?*)

Dan touched a finger to his temple.

Abra smiled, and that completed her beauty, turned her into a girl who would break hearts in another four or five years.

(*HI TONY!*)

That was loud enough to make him wince, and he thought again of how Dick Halloraan had recoiled behind the wheel of his rental car, his eyes going momentarily blank.

(*we need to talk out loud*)

(*okay yes*)

"I'm your father's cousin, okay? Not really an uncle, but that's what you call me."

"Right, right, you're Uncle Dan. We'll be fine as long as my mother's best friend doesn't come along. Her name's Gretchen

Silverlake. I think she knows our whole family tree, and there isn't very much of it."

Oh, great, Dan thought. *The nosy best friend.*

"It's okay," Abra said. "Her older son's on the football team, and she never misses a Cyclones game. Almost *everyone* goes to the game, so stop worrying that someone will think you're—"

She finished the sentence with a mental picture—a cartoon, really. It blossomed in an instant, crude but clear. A little girl in a dark alley was being menaced by a hulking man in a trenchcoat. The little girl's knees were knocking together, and just before the picture faded, Dan saw a word balloon form over her head: *Eeek, a freak!*

"Actually not that funny."

He made his own picture and sent it back to her: Dan Torrance in jail-stripes, being led away by two big policemen. He had never tried anything like this, and it wasn't as good as hers, but he was delighted to find he could do it at all. Then, almost before he knew what was happening, she appropriated his picture and made it her own. Dan pulled a gun from his waistband, pointed it at one of the cops, and pulled the trigger. A handkerchief with the word POW! on it shot from the barrel of the gun.

Dan stared at her, mouth open.

Abra put fisted hands to her mouth and giggled. "Sorry. Couldn't resist. We could do this all afternoon, couldn't we? And it would be fun."

He guessed it would also be a relief. She had spent years with a splendid ball but no one to play catch with. And of course it was the same with him. For the first time since childhood—since Hallorann—he was sending as well as receiving.

"You're right, it would be, but now's not the time. You need to run through this whole thing again. The email you sent only hit the high spots."

"Where should I start?"

"How about with your last name? Since I'm your honorary uncle, I probably should know."

That made her laugh. Dan tried to keep a straight face and couldn't. God help him, he liked her already.

"I'm Abra Rafaella Stone," she said. Suddenly the laughter was gone. "I just hope the lady in the hat never finds that out."

7

They sat together on the bench outside the library for forty-five minutes, with the autumn sun warm on their faces. For the first time in her life Abra felt unconditional pleasure—joy, even—in the talent that had always puzzled and sometimes terrified her. Thanks to this man, she even had a name for it: the shining. It was a good name, a comforting name, because she had always thought of it as a dark thing.

There was plenty to talk about—volumes of notes to compare—and they had hardly gotten started when a stout fiftyish woman in a tweed skirt came over to say hello. She looked at Dan with curiosity, but not *untoward* curiosity.

"Hi, Mrs. Gerard. This is my uncle Dan. I had Mrs. Gerard for Language Arts last year."

"Pleased to meet you, ma'am. Dan Torrance."

Mrs. Gerard took his offered hand and gave it a single no-nonsense pump. Abra could feel Dan—*Uncle* Dan—relaxing. That was good.

"Are you in the area, Mr. Torrance?"

"Just down the road, in Frazier. I work in the hospice there. Helen Rivington House?"

"Ah. That's good work you do. Abra, have you read *The Fixer* yet? The Malamud novel I recommended?"

Abra looked glum. "It's on my Nook—I got a gift card for my birthday—but I haven't started it yet. It looks hard."

"You're ready for hard things," Mrs. Gerard said. "More than ready. High school will be here sooner than you think, and then college. I suggest you get started today. Nice to have met you, Mr. Torrance. You have an extremely smart niece. But Abra—with

233

brains comes responsibility." She tapped Abra's temple to emphasize this point, then mounted the library steps and went inside.

She turned to Dan. "That wasn't so bad, was it?"

"So far, so good," Dan agreed. "Of course, if she talks to your parents . . ."

"She won't. Mom's in Boston, helping with my momo. She's got cancer."

"I'm very sorry to hear it. Is Momo your"

(*grandmother*)

(*great-grandmother*)

"Besides," Abra said, "we're not really lying about you being my uncle. In science last year, Mr. Staley told us that all humans share the same genetic plan. He said that the things that make us different are very small things. Did you know that we share something like ninety-nine percent of our genetic makeup with *dogs*?"

"No," Dan said, "but it explains why Alpo has always looked so good to me."

She laughed. "So you *could* be my uncle or cousin or whatever. All I'm saying."

"That's Abra's theory of relativity, is it?"

"I guess so. And do we need the same color eyes or hairline to be related? We've got something else in common that hardly anyone has. That makes us a special kind of relatives. Do you think it's a gene, like the one for blue eyes or red hair? And by the way, did you know that Scotland has the highest ratio of people with red hair?"

"I didn't," Dan said. "You're a font of information."

Her smile faded a little. "Is that a put-down?"

"Not at all. I guess the shining might be a gene, but I really don't think so. I think it's unquantifiable."

"Does that mean you can't figure it out? Like God and heaven and stuff like that?"

"Yes." He found himself thinking of Charlie Hayes, and all those before and after Charlie whom he'd seen out of this world in his Doctor Sleep persona. Some people called the moment of death *passing on*. Dan liked that, because it seemed just about right.

When you saw men and women pass on before your eyes—leaving the Teenytown people called reality for some Cloud Gap of an afterlife—it changed your way of thinking. For those in mortal extremis, it was the world that was passing on. In those gateway moments, Dan had always felt in the presence of some not-quite-seen enormity. They slept, they woke, they went *somewhere*. They went on. He'd had reason to believe that, even as a child.

"What are you thinking?" Abra asked. "I can see it, but I don't understand it. And I want to."

"I don't know how to explain it," he said.

"It was partly about the ghostie people, wasn't it? I saw them once, on the little train in Frazier. It was a dream but I think it was real."

His eyes widened. "Did you really?"

"Yes. I don't think they wanted to hurt me—they just looked at me—but they were kind of scary. I think maybe they were people who rode the train in olden days. Have you seen ghostie people? You have, haven't you?"

"Yes, but not for a very long time." And some that were a lot more than ghosts. Ghosts didn't leave residue on toilet seats and shower curtains. "Abra, how much do your parents know about your shine?"

"My dad thinks it's gone except for a few things—like me calling from camp because I knew Momo was sick—and he's glad. My mom knows it's still there, because sometimes she'll ask me to help her find something she's lost—last month it was her car keys, she left them on Dad's worktable in the garage—but she doesn't know how *much* is still there. They don't talk about it anymore." She paused. "Momo knows. She's not scared of it like Mom and Dad, but she told me I have to be careful. Because if people found out—" She made a comic face, rolling her eyes and poking her tongue out the corner of her mouth. "Eeek, a freak. You know?"

(*yes*)

She smiled gratefully. "Sure you do."

"Nobody else?"

"Well . . . Momo said I should talk to Dr. John, because he

already knew about some of the stuff. He, um, saw something I did with spoons when I was just a little kid. I kind of hung them on the ceiling."

"This wouldn't by chance be John Dalton, would it?"

Her face lit up. "You know him?"

"As a matter of fact, I do. I found something once for *him*. Something he lost."

(*a watch!*)

(*that's right*)

"I don't tell him everything," Abra said. She looked uneasy. "I sure didn't tell him about the baseball boy, and I'd *never* tell him about the woman in the hat. Because he'd tell my folks, and they've got a lot on their minds already. Besides, what could they do?"

"Let's just file that away for now. Who's the baseball boy?"

"Bradley Trevor. Brad. Sometimes he used to turn his hat around and call it a rally cap. Do you know what that is?"

Dan nodded.

"He's dead. *They* killed him. But they hurt him first. They hurt him so *bad*." Her lower lip began to tremble, and all at once she looked closer to nine than almost thirteen.

(*don't cry Abra we can't afford to attract*)

(*I know, I know*)

She lowered her head, took several deep breaths, and looked up at him again. Her eyes were overbright, but her mouth had stopped trembling. "I'm okay," she said. "Really. I'm just glad not to be alone with this inside my head."

8

He listened carefully as she described what she remembered of her initial encounter with Bradley Trevor two years ago. It wasn't much. The clearest image she retained was of many crisscrossing flashlight beams illuminating him as he lay on the ground. And his screams. She remembered those.

"They had to light him up because they were doing some kind of operation," Abra said. "That's what they called it, anyway, but all they were really doing was torturing him."

She told him about finding Bradley again on the back page of *The Anniston Shopper,* with all the other missing children. How she had touched his picture to see if she could find out about him.

"Can you do that?" she asked. "Touch things and get pictures in your head? Find things out?"

"Sometimes. Not always. I used to be able to do it more—and more reliably—when I was a kid."

"Do you think I'll grow out of it? I wouldn't mind that." She paused, thinking. "Except I sort of would. It's hard to explain."

"I know what you mean. It's our thing, isn't it? What we can do." Abra smiled.

"You're pretty sure you know where they killed this boy?"

"Yes, and they buried him there. They even buried his baseball glove." Abra handed him a piece of notebook paper. It was a copy, not the original. She would have been embarrassed for anyone to see how she had written the names of the boys in 'Round Here, not just once but over and over again. Even the *way* they had been written now seemed all wrong, those big fat letters that were supposed to express not love but *luv.*

"Don't get bent out of shape about it," Dan said absently, studying what she'd printed on the sheet. "I had a thing for Stevie Nicks when I was your age. Also for Ann Wilson, of Heart. You've probably never even heard of her, she's old-school, but I used to daydream about inviting her to one of the Friday night dances at Glenwood Junior High. How's that for stupid?"

She was staring at him, openmouthed.

"Stupid but normal. Most normal thing in the world, so cut yourself some slack. And I wasn't peeking, Abra. It was just there. Kind of jumped out in my face."

"Oh God." Abra's cheeks had gone bright red. "This is going to take some getting used to, isn't it?"

"For both of us, kiddo." He looked back down at the sheet.

NO TRESPASSING BY ORDER OF THE CANTON
COUNTY SHERIFF'S DEPARTMENT

ORGANIC INDUSTRIES
ETHANOL PLANT #4
FREEMAN, IOWA

CLOSED UNTIL FURTHER NOTICE

"You got this by . . . what? Watching it over and over? Rerunning it like a movie?"

"The NO TRESPASSING sign was easy, but the stuff about Organic Industries and the ethanol plant, yeah. Can't you do that?"

"I never tried. Maybe once, but probably not anymore."

"I found Freeman, Iowa, on the computer," she said. "And when I ran Google Earth, I could see the factory. Those places are really there."

Dan's thoughts returned to John Dalton. Others in the Program had talked about Dan's peculiar ability to find things; John never had. Not surprising, really. Doctors took a vow of confidentiality similar to the one in AA, didn't they? Which in John's case made it a kind of double coverage.

Abra was saying, "You could call Bradley Trevor's parents, couldn't you? Or the sheriff's office in Canton County? They wouldn't believe me, but they'd believe a grown-up."

"I suppose I could." But of course a man who knew where the body was buried would automatically go to the head of the suspect list, so if he did it, he would have to be very, very careful about the *way* he did it.

Abra, the trouble you're getting me into.

"Sorry," she whispered.

He put his hand over hers and gave it a gentle squeeze. "Don't be. That's one *you* weren't supposed to hear."

She straightened. "Oh God, here comes Yvonne Stroud. She's in my class."

Dan pulled his hand back in a hurry. He saw a plump, brown-haired girl about Abra's age coming up the sidewalk. She was wearing a backpack and carrying a looseleaf notebook curled against her chest. Her eyes were bright and inquisitive.

"She'll want to know everything about you," Abra said. "I mean *everything*. And she *talks*."

Uh-oh.

Dan looked at the oncoming girl.

(*we're not interesting*)

"Help me, Abra," he said, and felt her join in. Once they were together, the thought instantly gained depth and strength.

(*WE'RE NOT A BIT INTERESTING*)

"That's good," Abra said. "A little more. Do it with me. Like singing."

(*YOU HARDLY SEE US WE'RE NOT INTERESTING AND BESIDES YOU HAVE BETTER THINGS TO DO*)

Yvonne Stroud hurried along the walk, flipping one hand to Abra in a vague hello gesture but not slowing down. She ran up the library steps and disappeared inside.

"I'll be a monkey's uncle," Dan said.

She looked at him seriously. "According to Abra's theory of relativity, you really could be. Very similar—" She sent a picture of pants flapping on a clothesline.

(*jeans*)

Then they were both laughing.

9

Dan made her go over the turntable thing three times, wanting to make sure he was getting it right.

"You never did that, either?" Abra asked. "The far-seeing thing?"

"Astral projection? No. Does it happen to you a lot?"

"Only once or twice." She considered. "Maybe three times. Once I went into a girl who was swimming in the river. I was looking at her from the bottom of our backyard. I was nine or ten. I don't know why it happened, she wasn't in trouble or anything, just swimming with her friends. That one lasted the longest. It went on for at least three minutes. Is astral projection what you call it? Like outer space?"

"It's an old term, from séances back a hundred years ago, and probably not a very good one. All it means is an out-of-body experience." If you could label anything like that at all. "But—I want to make sure I've got this straight—the swimming girl didn't go into you?"

Abra shook her head emphatically, making her ponytail fly. "She didn't even know I was there. The only time it worked both ways was with that woman. The one who wears the hat. Only I didn't see the hat *then,* because I was inside her."

Dan used one finger to describe a circle. "You went into her, she went into you."

"Yes." Abra shivered. "She was the one who cut Bradley Trevor until he was dead. When she smiles she has one big long tooth on top."

Something about the hat struck a chord, something that made him think of Deenie from Wilmington. Because Deenie had worn a hat? Nope, at least not that he remembered; he'd been pretty blitzed. It probably meant nothing—sometimes the brain made phantom associations, that was all, especially when it was under stress, and the truth (little as he liked to admit it) was that Deenie was never far from his thoughts. Something as random as a display of cork-soled sandals in a store window could bring her to mind.

"Who's Deenie?" Abra asked. Then she blinked rapidly and drew back a little, as if Dan had suddenly flapped a hand in front of her eyes. "Oops. Not supposed to go there, I guess. Sorry."

"It's okay," he said. "Let's go back to your hat woman. When you saw her later—in your window—that wasn't the same?"

"No. I'm not even sure that was a shining. I think it was a *remembering,* from when I saw her hurting the boy."

"So she didn't see you then, either. She's *never* seen you." If the woman was as dangerous as Abra believed, this was important.

"No. I'm sure she hasn't. But she wants to." She looked at him, her eyes wide, her mouth trembling again. "When the turntable thing happened, she was thinking *mirror*. She wanted me to look at myself. She wanted to use my eyes to see me."

"What *did* she see through your eyes? Could she find you that way?"

Abra thought it over carefully. At last she said, "I was looking out my window when it happened. All I can see from there is the street. And the mountains, of course, but there are lots of mountains in America, right?"

"Right." Could the woman in the hat match the mountains she'd seen through Abra's eyes to a photo, if she did an exhaustive computer search? Like so much else in this business, there was just no way to be sure.

"Why did they kill him, Dan? Why did they kill the baseball boy?"

He thought he knew, and he would have hidden it from her if he could, but even this short meeting was enough to tell him he would never have that sort of relationship with Abra Rafaella Stone. Recovering alcoholics strove for "complete honesty in all our affairs," but rarely achieved it; he and Abra could not avoid it.

(*food*)

She stared at him, aghast. "They ate his *shining*?"

(*I think so*)

(*they're VAMPIRES?*)

Then, aloud: "Like in *Twilight*?"

"Not like them," Dan said. "And for God's sake, Abra, I'm only guessing." The library door opened. Dan looked around, afraid it might be the overly curious Yvonne Stroud, but it was a boy-girl couple that only had eyes for each other. He turned back to Abra. "We have to wrap this up."

"I know." She raised a hand, rubbed at her lips, realized what she was doing, and put it back in her lap. "But I have so many questions. There's so much I want to know. It would take *hours*."

"Which we don't have. You're sure it was a Sam's?"

"Huh?"

"She was in a Sam's Supermarket?"

241

"Oh. Yes."

"I know the chain. I've even shopped in one or two, but not around here."

She grinned. "Course not, Uncle Dan, there aren't any. They're all out west. I went on Google for that, too." The grin faded. "There are hundreds of them, all the way from Nebraska to California."

"I need to think about this some more, and so do you. You can stay in touch with me by email if it's important, but it would be better if we just"—he tapped his forehead—"zip-zip. You know?"

"Yes," she said, and smiled. "The only good part of this is having a friend who knows how to zip-zip. And what it's like."

"Can you use the blackboard?"

"Sure. It's pretty easy."

"You need to keep one thing in mind, one above all others. The hat woman probably doesn't know how to find you, but she knows you're out there someplace."

She had grown very still. He reached for her thoughts, but Abra was guarding them.

"Can you set a burglar alarm in your mind? So that if she's someplace near, either mentally or in person, you'll know?"

"You think she's going to come for me, don't you?"

"She might try. Two reasons. First, just because you know she exists."

"And her friends," Abra whispered. "She has lots of friends."

(*with flashlights*)

"What's the other reason?" And before he could reply: "Because I'd be good to eat. Like the baseball boy was good to eat. Right?"

There was no point denying it; to Abra his forehead was a window. "*Can* you set an alarm? A proximity alarm? That's—"

"I know what *proximity* means. I don't know, but I'll try."

He knew what she was going to say next before she said it, and there was no mind-reading involved. She was only a child, after all. This time when she took his hand, he didn't pull away. "Promise you won't let her get me, Dan. *Promise.*"

He did, because she was a kid and needed comforting. But of

242

course there was only one way to keep such a promise, and that was to make the threat go away.

He thought it again: *Abra, the trouble you're getting me into.*

And she said it again, but this time not out loud:

(*sorry*)

"Not your fault, kid. You didn't

(*ask for this*)

"any more than I did. Go on in with your books. I have to get back to Frazier. I'm on shift tonight."

"Okay. But we're friends, right?"

"Totally friends."

"I'm glad."

"And I bet you'll like *The Fixer*. I think you'll get it. Because you've fixed a few things in your time, haven't you?"

Pretty dimples deepened the corners of her mouth. "You'd know."

"Oh, believe me," Dan said.

He watched her start up the steps, then pause and come back. "I don't know who the woman in the hat is, but I know one of her friends. His name is Barry the Chunk, or something like that. I bet wherever she is, Barry the Chunk is someplace close. And I could find him, if I had the baseball boy's glove." She looked at him, a steady level glance from those beautiful blue eyes. "I'd know, because for a little while, *Barry the Chunk was wearing it.*"

10

Halfway back to Frazier, mulling over Abra's hat woman, Dan remembered something that sent a jolt straight through him. He almost swerved over the double yellow line, and an oncoming truck westbound on Route 16 honked at him irritably.

Twelve years ago it had been, when Frazier was still new to him and his sobriety had been extremely shaky. He'd been walking back to Mrs. Robertson's, where he had just that day secured a room. A storm was coming, so Billy Freeman had sent him off with a pair of boots. *They don't look like much, but at least they match.* And as he turned the corner from Morehead onto Eliot, he'd seen—

Just ahead was a rest area. Dan pulled in and walked toward the sound of running water. It was the Saco, of course; it ran through two dozen little New Hampshire towns between North Conway and Crawford Notch, connecting them like beads on a string.

I saw a hat blowing up the gutter. A battered old tophat like a magician might wear. Or an actor in an old musical comedy. Only it wasn't really there, because when I closed my eyes and counted to five, it was gone.

"Okay, it was a shining," he told the running water. "But that doesn't necessarily make it the hat Abra saw."

Only he couldn't believe that, because later that night he'd dreamed of Deenie. She had been dead, her face hanging off her skull like dough on a stick. Dead and wearing the blanket Dan had stolen from a bum's shopping cart. *Stay away from the woman in the hat, Honeybear.* That was what she'd said. And something else . . . what?

She's the Queen Bitch of Castle Hell.

"You don't remember that," he told the running water. "Nobody remembers dreams twelve years later."

But he did. And now he remembered the rest of what the dead woman from Wilmington had said: *If you mess with her, she'll eat you alive.*

11

He let himself into his turret room shortly after six, carrying a tray of food from the caf. He looked first at the blackboard, and smiled at what was printed there:

Thank you for believing me.

As if I had any choice, hon.

He erased Abra's message, then sat down at his desk with his dinner. After leaving the rest area, his thoughts had turned back to Dick Hallorann. He supposed it was natural enough; when someone finally asked you to teach them, you went to your own teacher to find out how to do it. Dan had fallen out of touch with Dick during the drinking years (mostly out of shame), but he thought it might just be possible to find out what had happened to the old fellow. Possibly even to get in touch, if Dick was still alive. And hey, lots of people lived into their nineties, if they took care of themselves. Abra's great-gramma, for instance—she had to be really getting up there.

I need some answers, Dick, and you're the only person I know who might have a few. So do me a favor, my friend, and still be alive.

He fired up his computer and opened Firefox. He knew that Dick had spent his winters cooking at a series of Florida resort hotels, but he couldn't remember the names or even which coast they had been on. Probably both—Naples one year, Palm Beach the next, Sarasota or Key West the year after that. There was always work for a man who could tickle palates, especially rich palates, and Dick had been able to tickle them like nobody's business. Dan had an idea that his best shot might be the quirky spelling of Dick's last name— not Halloran but Hallorann. He typed **Richard Hallorann** and **Florida** into the search box, then punched ENTER. He got back thousands of hits, but he was pretty sure the one he wanted was third from the top, and a soft sigh of disappointment escaped him. He clicked the link, and an article from *The Miami Herald* appeared. No question. When the age as well as the name appeared in the headline, you knew exactly what you were looking at.

Noted South Beach Chef Richard "Dick" Hallorann, 81.

There was a photo. It was small, but Dan would have recognized that cheerful, knowing face anywhere. Had he died alone? Dan doubted it. The man had been too gregarious . . . and too fond of women. His deathbed had probably been well attended, but the two people he'd saved that winter in Colorado hadn't been there.

Wendy Torrance had a valid excuse: she'd predeceased him. Her son, however . . .

Had he been in some dive, full of whiskey and playing truck-driving songs on the jukebox, when Dick passed on? Maybe in jail for the night on a drunk-and-disorderly?

Cause of death had been a heart attack. He scrolled back up and checked the date: January 19, 1999. The man who had saved Dan's life and the life of his mother had been dead almost fifteen years. There would be no help from that quarter.

From behind him, he heard the soft squeak of chalk on slate. He sat where he was for a moment, with his cooling food and his laptop before him. Then, slowly, he turned around.

The chalk was still on the ledge at the bottom of the blackboard, but a picture was appearing, anyway. It was crude but recognizable. It was a baseball glove. When it was done, her chalk—invisible, but still making that low squeaking sound—drew a question mark in the glove's pocket.

"I need to think about it," he said, but before he could do so, the intercom buzzed, paging Doctor Sleep.

CHAPTER NINE

THE VOICES OF OUR DEAD FRIENDS

1

At a hundred and two, Eleanor Ouellette was the oldest resident of Rivington House in that fall of 2013, old enough so her last name had never been Americanized. She answered not to *Wil-LET* but to a much more elegant French pronunciation: *Oooh-LAY*. Dan sometimes called her Miss Oooh-La-La, which always made her smile. Ron Stimson, one of four docs who made regular day-rounds at the hospice, once told Dan that Eleanor was proof that living was sometimes stronger than dying. "Her liver function is nil, her lungs are shot from eighty years of smoking, she has colorectal cancer—moving at a snail's pace, but extremely malignant—and the walls of her heart are as thin as a cat's whisker. Yet she continues."

If Azreel was right (and in Dan's experience, he was never wrong), Eleanor's long-term lease on life was about to expire, but she certainly didn't look like a woman on the threshold. She was sitting up in bed, stroking the cat, when Dan walked in. Her hair was beautifully permed—the hairdresser had been in just the day before—and her pink nightie was as immaculate as always, the top half giving a bit of color to her bloodless cheeks, the bottom half spread away from the sticks of her legs like a ballgown.

Dan raised his hands to the sides of his face, the fingers spread and wiggling. *"Ooh-la-la! Une belle femme! Je suis amoureux!"*

She rolled her eyes, then cocked her head and smiled at him. "Maurice Chevalier you ain't, but I like you, *cher*. You're cheery, which is important, you're cheeky, which is more important, and you've got a lovely bottom, which is *all*-important. The ass of a man is the piston that drives the world, and you have a good one. In my prime, I would have corked it with my thumb and then eaten you alive. Preferably by the pool of Le Meridien in Monte Carlo, with an admiring audience to applaud my frontside and backside efforts."

Her voice, hoarse but cadenced, managed to render this image charming rather than vulgar. To Dan, Eleanor's cigarette rasp was the voice of a cabaret singer who had seen and done it all even before the German army goose-stepped down the Champs-Élysées in the spring of 1940. Washed up, maybe, but far from washed out. And while it was true she looked like the death of God in spite of the faint color reflected onto her face by her craftily chosen nightgown, she had looked like the death of God since 2009, the year she had moved into Room 15 of Rivington One. Only Azzie's attendance said that tonight was different.

"I'm sure you would have been marvelous," he said.

"Are you seeing any ladies, *cher*?"

"Not currently, no." With one exception, and she was years too young for *amour*.

"A shame. Because in later years, *this*"—she raised a bony forefinger, then let it dip—"becomes *this*. You'll see."

He smiled and sat on her bed. As he had sat on so many. "How are you feeling, Eleanor?"

"Not bad." She watched Azzie jump down and oil out the door, his work for the evening done. "I've had many visitors. They made your cat nervous, but he stuck it out until you came."

"He's not my cat, Eleanor. He belongs to the house."

"No," she said, as if the subject no longer interested her much, "he's yours."

Dan doubted if Eleanor had had even one visitor—other than Azreel, that was. Not tonight, not in the last week or month, not in the last year. She was alone in the world. Even the dinosaur of an accountant who had overseen her money matters for so many years, lumbering in to visit her once every quarter and toting a briefcase the size of a Saab's trunk, had now gone to his reward. Miss Ooh-La-La claimed to have relatives in Montreal, "but I have not quite enough money left to make visiting me worthwhile, *cher.*"

"Who's been in, then?" Thinking she might mean Gina Weems or Andrea Bottstein, the two nurses working the three-to-eleven in Riv One tonight. Or possibly Poul Larson, a slow-moving but decent orderly whom Dan thought of as the anti–Fred Carling, had stopped by for a natter.

"As I said, many. They are passing even now. An endless parade of them. They smile, they bow, a child wags his tongue like a dog's tail. Some of them speak. Do you know the poet George Seferis?"

"No, ma'am, I don't." *Were* there others here? He had reason to believe it was possible, but he had no sense of them. Not that he always did.

"Mr. Seferis asks, 'Are these the voices of our dead friends, or just the gramophone?' The children are the saddest. There was a boy here who fell down a well."

"Is that so?"

"Yes, and a woman who committed suicide with a bedspring."

He felt not even the slightest hint of a presence. Could his encounter with Abra Stone have sapped him? It was possible, and in any case, the shining came and went in tides he had never been able to chart. He didn't think that was it, however. He thought Eleanor had probably lapsed into dementia. Or she might be having him on. It wasn't impossible. Quite the wag was Eleanor Ooh-La-La. Someone—was it Oscar Wilde?—was reputed to have made a joke on his deathbed: *Either that wallpaper goes, or I do.*

"You are to wait," Eleanor said. There was no humor in her voice now. "The lights will announce an arrival. There may be other disturbances. The door will open. Then *your* visitor will come."

Dan looked doubtfully at the door to the hall, which was open already. He always left it open, so Azzie could leave if he wanted to. He usually did, once Dan showed up to take over.

"Eleanor, would you like some cold juice?"

"I would if there were ti—" she began, and then the life ran out of her face like water from a basin with a hole in it. Her eyes fixed at a point over his head and her mouth fell open. Her cheeks sagged and her chin dropped almost to her scrawny chest. The top plate of her dentures also dropped, slid over her lower lip, and hung in an unsettling open-air grin.

Fuck, that was quick.

Carefully, he hooked a finger beneath the denture plate and removed it. Her lip pulled out, then snapped back with a tiny *plip* sound. Dan put the plate on her night table, started to get up, then settled back. He waited for the red mist the old Tampa nurse had called the gasp . . . as though it were a pulling-in instead of a letting-out. It didn't come.

You are to wait.

All right, he could do that, at least for awhile. He reached for Abra's mind and found nothing. Maybe that was good. She might already be taking pains to guard her thoughts. Or maybe his own ability—his *sensitivity*—had departed. If so, it didn't matter. It would be back. It always had been, at any rate.

He wondered (as he had before) why he had never seen flies on the face of any Rivington House guest. Maybe because he didn't need to. He had Azzie, after all. Did Azzie see something with those wise green eyes of his? Maybe not flies, but *something*? He must.

Are these the voices of our dead friends, or just the gramophone?

It was so quiet on this floor tonight, and still so early! There was no sound of conversation from the common room at the end of the hall. No TV or radio played. He couldn't hear the squeak of Poul's sneakers or the low voices of Gina and Andrea down at the nurses' station. No phone rang. As for his watch—

Dan raised it. No wonder he couldn't hear its faint ticking. It had stopped.

The overhead fluorescent bar went off, leaving only Eleanor's table lamp. The fluorescent came back on, and the lamp flickered out. It came on again and then it and the overhead went off together. On . . . off . . . on.

"Is someone here?"

The pitcher on the night table rattled, then stilled. The dentures he had removed gave a single unsettling clack. A queer ripple ran along the sheet of Eleanor's bed, as if something beneath it had been startled into sudden motion. A puff of warm air pressed a quick kiss against Dan's cheek, then was gone.

"Who is it?" His heartbeat remained regular, but he could feel it in his neck and wrists. The hair on the back of his neck felt thick and stiff. He suddenly knew what Eleanor had been seeing in her last moments: a parade of

(*ghostie people*)

the dead, passing into her room from one wall and passing out through the other. Passing out? No, passing on. He didn't know Seferis, but he knew Auden: *Death takes the rolling-in-money, the screamingly funny, and those who are very well hung.* She had seen them all and they were here n—

But they weren't. He knew they weren't. The ghosts Eleanor had seen were gone and she had joined their parade. He had been told to wait. He was waiting.

The door to the hall swung slowly shut. Then the bathroom door opened.

From Eleanor Ouellette's dead mouth came a single word: "*Danny.*"

2

When you enter the town of Sidewinder, you pass a sign reading WELCOME TO THE TOP OF AMERICA! It isn't, but it's close. Twenty miles from the place where the Eastern Slope becomes the Western, a dirt road splits off from the main highway, winding north. The burned-in-wood sign arched over this byway reads WELCOME TO THE BLUEBELL CAMPGROUND! STAY AWHILE, PARTNER!

That sounds like good old western hospitality, but locals know that more often than not the road is gated shut, and when it is, a less friendly sign hangs from it: CLOSED UNTIL FURTHER NOTICE. How they do business is a mystery to the folks in Sidewinder, who'd like to see the Bluebell open every day the upcountry roads aren't snowed in. They miss the commerce the Overlook used to bring in, and hoped the campground would at least partially make up for it (although they know that Camper People don't have the kind of money the Hotel People used to pump into the local economy). That hasn't been the case. The general consensus is that the campground is some rich corporation's tax haven, a designated money-loser.

It's a haven, all right, but the corporation it shelters is the True Knot, and when they are in residence, the only RVs in the big parking lot are their RVs, with Rose the Hat's EarthCruiser standing tallest among them.

On that September evening, nine members of the True were gathered in the high-ceilinged, pleasantly rustic building known as Overlook Lodge. When the campground was open to the public, the Lodge served as a restaurant that put on two meals a day, breakfast and dinner. The food was prepared by Short Eddie and Big Mo (rube names Ed and Maureen Higgins). Neither was up to Dick Hallorann's culinary standards—few were!—but it's hard to screw up too badly on the things Camper People like to eat: meatloaf, macaroni and cheese, meatloaf, pancakes drenched in Log Cabin syrup, meatloaf, chicken stew, meatloaf, Tuna Surprise, and meatloaf with mushroom gravy. After dinner, the tables were cleared for bingo or card parties. On weekends, there were dances. These festivities took place only when the campground was open. This evening—as, three time zones east, Dan Torrance sat beside a dead woman and waited for his visitor—there was business of a different sort to transact in Overlook Lodge.

Jimmy Numbers was at the head of a single table that had been set up in the middle of the polished bird's-eye maple floor. His PowerBook was open, the desktop displaying a photograph of his hometown, which happened to be deep in the Carpathian

Mountains. (Jimmy liked to joke that his grandfather had once entertained a young London solicitor named Jonathan Harker.)

Clustered around him, looking down at the screen, were Rose, Crow Daddy, Barry the Chink, Snakebite Andi, Token Charlie, Apron Annie, Diesel Doug, and Grampa Flick. None of them wanted to stand next to Grampa, who smelled as if he might have had a minor disaster in his pants and then forgotten to shower it off (a thing that happened more and more frequently these days), but this was important and they put up with him.

Jimmy Numbers was an unassuming guy with a receding hairline and a pleasant if vaguely simian face. He looked about fifty, which was one-third of his actual age. "I googled Lickety-Spliff and got nothing useful, which is what I expected. In case you care, lickety-spliff is teenage slang that means to do something really slow instead of really fast—"

"We don't," Diesel Doug said. "And by the way, you smell a trifle rank, Gramps. No offense, but when was the last time you wiped your ass?"

Grampa Flick bared his teeth—eroded and yellow, but all his own—at Doug. "Your wife wiped it for me just this morning, Deez. With her face, as it happens. Kinda nasty, but she seems to like that kind of thi—"

"Shut your heads, both of you," Rose said. Her voice was toneless and unthreatening, but Doug and Grampa both shrank away from her, their faces those of chastened schoolboys. "Go on, Jimmy. But stay on point. I want to have a concrete plan, and soon."

"The rest of them are going to be reluctant no matter how concrete the plan is," Crow said. "They're going to say it's been a good year for steam. That movie theater thing, the church fire in Little Rock, and the terrorist thing in Austin. Not to mention Juárez. I was dubious about going south of the border, but it was good."

Better than good, actually. Juárez had become known as the murder capital of the world, earning its sobriquet with over twenty-five hundred homicides a year. Many were torture-killings. The pervading atmosphere had been exceedingly rich. It wasn't pure steam, and it made you feel a little whoopsy in the stomach, but it did the job.

"All those fucking beans gave me the runs," Token Charlie said, "but I have to admit that the pickings were excellent."

"It *was* a good year," Rose agreed, "but we can't make a business of Mexico—we're too conspicuous. Down there, we're rich *americanos*. Up here, we fade into the woodwork. And aren't you tired of living from year to year? Always on the move and always counting canisters? This is different. This is the motherlode."

None of them replied. She was their leader and in the end they would do what she said, but they didn't understand about the girl. That was all right. When they encountered her for themselves, they would. And when they had her locked up and producing steam pretty much to order, they'd offer to get down on their knees and kiss Rose's feet. She might even take them up on it.

"Go on, Jimmy, but get to the point."

"I'm pretty sure what you picked up was a teen-slang version of Lickety-Split. It's a chain of New England convenience stores. There are seventy-three in all, from Providence to Presque Isle. A grammar school kid with an iPad could have nailed that in about two minutes. I printed out the locations and used Whirl 360 to get pix. I found six that have mountain views. Two in Vermont, two in New Hampshire, and two in Maine."

His laptop case was under his chair. He grabbed it, fumbled in the flap pocket, brought out a folder, and handed it to Rose. "These aren't pictures of the stores, they're pictures of various mountain views that can be seen from the neighborhoods the stores are in. Once more courtesy of Whirl 360, which is far better than Google Earth, and God bless its nosy little heart. Take a look and see if any ring a bell. If not, see if there are any you can definitely eliminate."

Rose opened the folder and slowly went through the photographs. The two showing Vermont's Green Mountains she put aside at once. One of the Maine locations was also wrong; it showed only one mountain, and she had seen a whole range of them. The other three she looked at longer. Finally she handed them back to Jimmy Numbers.

"One of these."

He turned the pictures over. "Fryeburg, Maine . . . Madison, New Hampshire . . . Anniston, New Hampshire. Got a feel for which one of the three?"

Rose took them again, then held up the photos of the White Mountains as seen from Fryeburg and Anniston. "I think it's one of these, but I'm going to make sure."

"How are you going to do that?" Crow asked.

"I'm going to visit her."

"If everything you say is true, that could be dangerous."

"I'll do it when she's asleep. Young girls sleep deeply. She'll never know I was there."

"Are you sure you need to do that? These three places are pretty close together. We could check them all."

"Yes!" Rose cried. "We'll just cruise around and say, 'We're looking for a local girl, but we can't seem to read her location the way we normally can, so give us a little help. Have you noticed any junior high girls around here with precognition or mind-reading talents?'"

Crow Daddy gave a sigh, stuck his big hands deep in his pockets, and looked at her.

"I'm sorry," Rose said. "I'm a little on edge, all right? I want to do this and get it done. And you don't have to worry about me. I can take care of myself."

3

Dan sat looking at the late Eleanor Ouellette. The open eyes, now beginning to glaze. The tiny hands with their palms upturned. Most of all at the open mouth. Inside was all the clockless silence of death.

"Who are you?" Thinking: *As if I didn't know*. Hadn't he wished for answers?

"You grew up fine." The lips didn't move, and there seemed to be no emotion in the words. Perhaps death had robbed his old friend of his human feelings, and what a bitter shame that would be. Or perhaps it was someone else, masquerading as Dick. *Something* else.

"If you're Dick, prove it. Tell me something only he and I could know."

Silence. But the presence was still here. He felt it. Then:

"You asked me why Mrs. Brant wanted the car-park man's pants."

Dan at first had no idea what the voice was talking about. Then he did. The memory was on one of the high shelves where he kept all the bad Overlook memories. And his lockboxes, of course. Mrs. Brant had been a checkout on the day Danny arrived with his parents, and he had caught a random thought from her as the Overlook's valet delivered her car: *I'd sure like to get into his pants.*

"You were just a little boy with a great big radio inside your head. I felt sorry for you. I was scared for you, too. And I was right to be scared, wasn't I?"

In that there was a faint echo of his old friend's kindness and humor. It was Dick, all right. Dan looked at the dead woman, dumbfounded. The lights in the room flickered on and off again. The water pitcher gave another brief jitter.

"I can't stay long, son. It hurts to be here."

"Dick, there's a little girl—"

"Abra." Almost a sigh. *"She's like you. It all comes around."*

"She thinks there's a woman who may be after her. She wears a hat. It's an old-fashioned tophat. Sometimes she only has one long tooth on top. When she's hungry. This is what she told me, anyway."

"Ask your question, son. I can't stay. This world is a dream of a dream to me now."

"There are others. The tophat woman's friends. Abra saw them with flashlights. Who are they?"

Silence again. But Dick was still there. Changed, but there. Dan could feel him in his nerve endings, and as a kind of electricity skating on the damp surfaces of his eyes.

"They are the empty devils. They are sick and don't know it."

"I don't understand."

"No. And that's good. If you had ever met them—if they had ever gotten so much as a sniff of you—you'd be long dead, used and thrown away like an empty carton. That's what happened to the one Abra calls the baseball boy. And many others. Children who shine are prey to them, but you already guessed that, didn't you? The empty devils are on the land like a cancer on the skin. Once they rode camels in the desert; once they drove caravans across eastern Europe. They eat screams and drink pain. You had your horrors at the Overlook, Danny, but at least you were spared these folks. Now that the strange woman has her mind fixed on the girl, they won't stop until they have her. They might kill her. They might Turn her. Or they might keep her and use her until she's all used up, and that would be worst of all."

"I don't understand."

"Scoop her out. Make her empty like them." From the dead mouth there came an autumnal sigh.

"Dick, what the hell am I supposed to do?"

"Get the girl what she asked for."

"Where are they, these empty devils?"

"In your childhood, where every devil comes from. I'm not allowed to say more."

"How do I stop them?"

"The only way is to kill them. Make them eat their own poison. Do that and they disappear."

"The woman in the hat, the strange woman, what's her name? Do you know?"

From down the hall came the clash of a mop-bucket squeegee, and Poul Larson began to whistle. The air in the room changed. Something that had been delicately balanced now began to swing out of true.

"Go to your friends. The ones who know what you are. It seems to me you grew up fine, son, but you still owe a debt." There was a pause, and then the voice that both was and wasn't Dick Hallorann's spoke one final time, in a tone of flat command: *"Pay it."*

Red mist rose from Eleanor's eyes, nose, and open mouth. It hung over her for perhaps five seconds, then disappeared. The lights were steady. So was the water in the pitcher. Dick was gone. Dan was here with only a corpse.

Empty devils.

If he had ever heard a more terrible phrase, he couldn't remember it. But it made sense . . . if you had seen the Overlook for what it really was. That place had been full of devils, but at least they had been *dead* devils. He didn't think that was true of the woman in the tophat and her friends.

You still owe a debt. Pay it.

Yes. He had left the little boy in the sagging diaper and the Braves t-shirt to fend for himself. He would not do that with the girl.

4

Dan waited at the nurses' station for the funeral hack from Geordie & Sons, and saw the covered gurney out the back door of Rivington One. Then he went to his room and sat looking down at Cranmore Avenue, now perfectly deserted. A night wind blew, stripping the early-turning leaves from the oaks and sending them dancing and pirouetting up the street. On the far side of the town common, Teenytown was equally deserted beneath a couple of orange hi-intensity security lights.

Go to your friends. The ones who know what you are.

Billy Freeman knew, had almost from the first, because Billy had some of what Dan had. And if Dan owed a debt, he supposed Billy did, too, because Dan's larger and brighter shining had saved Billy's life.

Not that I'd put it that way to him.

Not that he'd have to.

Then there was John Dalton, who had lost a watch and who just happened to be Abra's pediatrician. What had Dick said through Eleanor Ooh-La-La's dead mouth? *It all comes around.*

As for the thing Abra had asked for, that was even easier. Getting it, though . . . that might be a little complicated.

5

When Abra got up on Sunday morning, there was an email message from dtor36@nhmlx.com.

> Abra: I have spoken to a friend using the talent we share, and am convinced that you are in danger. I want to speak about your situation to another friend, one we have in common: John Dalton. I will not do so unless I have your permission. I believe John and I can retrieve the object you drew on my blackboard.
>
> Have you set your burglar alarm? Certain people may be looking for you, and it's very important they not find you. You must be careful. Good wishes and STAY SAFE. Delete this email.
>
> Uncle D.

She was more convinced by the fact of his email than its content, because she knew he didn't like communicating that way; he was afraid her parents would snoop in her mail and think she was exchanging notes with Chester the Molester.

If they only knew about the molesters she *really* had to worry about.

She was frightened, but also—now that it was bright daylight and there was no beautiful lunatic in a tophat peering in the window at her—rather excited. It was sort of like being in one of those love-and-horror supernatural novels, the kind Mrs. Robinson in the school library sniffily called "tweenager porn." In those books the girls dallied with werewolves, vampires—even zombies—but hardly ever *became* those things.

It was also nice to have a grown man stand up for her, and it didn't hurt that he was handsome, in a scruffy kind of way that reminded her a little of Jax Teller on *Sons of Anarchy,* a show she and Emma Deane secretly watched on Em's computer.

She sent Uncle Dan's email not just to her trash but to the *permanent* trash, which Emma called "the nuclear boyfriend file."

(*As if you had any, Em,* Abra thought snidely.) Then she turned off her computer and closed the lid. She didn't email him back. She didn't have to. She just had to close her eyes.

Zip-zip.

Message sent, Abra headed for the shower.

6

When Dan came back with his morning coffee, there was a new communiqué on his blackboard.

You can tell Dr. John but NOT MY PARENTS.

No. Not her parents. At least not yet. But Dan had no doubt they'd find out *something* was going on, and probably sooner rather than later. He would cross that bridge (or burn it) when he came to it. Right now he had a lot of other things to do, beginning with a call.

A child answered, and when he asked for Rebecca, the phone was dropped with a clunk and there was a distant, going-away cry of *"Gramma! It's for you!"* A few seconds later, Rebecca Clausen was on the line.

"Hi, Becka, it's Dan Torrance."

"If it's about Mrs. Ouellette, I had an email this morning from—"

"That's not it. I need to ask for some time off."

"Doctor Sleep wants time off? I don't believe it. I had to practically kick you out the door last spring to take your vacation, and you were still in once or twice a day. Is it a family matter?"

Dan, with Abra's theory of relativity in mind, said it was.

CHAPTER TEN

GLASS ORNAMENTS

1

Abra's father was standing at the kitchen counter in his bathrobe and beating eggs in a bowl when the kitchen phone rang. Upstairs, the shower was pounding. If Abra followed her usual Sunday morning MO, it would continue to pound until the hot water gave out.

He checked the incoming call window. It was a 617 area code, but the number following wasn't the one in Boston he knew, the one that rang the landline in his grandmother-in-law's condo. "Hello?"

"Oh, David, I'm so glad I got you." It was Lucy, and she sounded utterly exhausted.

"Where are you? Why aren't you calling from your cell?"

"Mass General, on a pay phone. You can't use cells in here, there are signs everywhere."

"Is Momo all right? Are you?"

"I am. As for Momes, she's stable . . . now . . . but for awhile it was pretty bad." A gulp. "It still is." That was when Lucy broke down. Not just crying, but sobbing her heart out.

David waited. He was glad Abra was in the shower, and hoped the hot water would hold out for a long time. This sounded bad.

At last Lucy was able to talk again. "This time she broke her arm."

"Oh. Okay. Is that all?"

"No, it is not *all*!" Nearly shouting at him in that why-are-men-so-stupid voice that he absolutely loathed, the one he told himself was a part of her Italian heritage without ever considering that he might, on occasion, actually *be* quite stupid.

He took a steadying breath. "Tell me, honey."

She did, although twice she broke into sobs again, and David had to wait her out. She was dead beat, but that was only part of the problem. Mostly, he realized, she was just accepting in her gut what her head had known for weeks: her momo was really going to die. Maybe not peacefully.

Concetta, who slept in only the thinnest of dozes now, had awakened after midnight and needed the toilet. Instead of buzzing for Lucy to bring the bedpan, she had tried to get up and go to the bathroom by herself. She had managed to swing her legs out onto the floor and sit up, but then dizziness had overcome her and she had tumbled off the bed, landing on her left arm. It hadn't just broken, it had shattered. Lucy, tired out from weeks of night nursing that she had never been trained to do, awoke to the sound of her grandmother's cries.

"She wasn't just calling for help," Lucy said, "and she wasn't screaming, either. She was *shrieking,* like a fox that's had a limb torn off in one of those terrible leghold traps."

"Honey, that must have been awful."

Standing in a first-floor alcove where there were snack machines and—mirabile dictu—a few working phones, her body aching and covered with drying sweat (she could smell herself, and it sure wasn't Dolce & Gabbana Light Blue), her head pounding with the first migraine she'd had in four years, Lucia Stone knew she could never tell him how awful it had really been. What a stinking revelation it had been. You thought you understood the basic fact—woman grows old, woman grows feeble, woman dies—and then you discovered there was quite a lot more to it. You found that out when you found the woman who had written some of the greatest poetry of her generation lying in a puddle of her own piss, shrieking at her granddaughter to make the pain *stop,* make it *stop,* oh *madre de Cristo,* make it *stop.* When you saw the formerly smooth forearm twisted like a washrag and heard the poet call it a cunting thing and then wish herself dead so the hurting would stop.

Could you tell your husband how you were still half asleep, and frozen with the fear that anything you did would be the wrong thing? Could you tell him that she scratched your face when you tried to move her and howled like a dog that had been run over in the street? Could you explain what it was like to leave your beloved grandmother sprawled on the floor while you dialed 911, and then sat beside her waiting for the ambulance, making her drink Oxycodone dissolved in water through a bendy-straw? How the ambulance didn't come and didn't come and you thought of that Gordon Lightfoot song, "The Wreck of the *Edmund Fitzgerald*," the one that asks if anyone knows where the love of God goes when the waves turn the minutes to hours? The waves rolling over Momo were waves of pain, and she was foundering, and they just kept coming.

When she began to scream again, Lucy had gotten both arms under her and lifted her onto her bed in a clumsy clean-and-jerk that she knew she'd feel in her shoulders and lower back for days, if not weeks. Stopping her ears to Momo's cries of *put me down, you're killing me.* Then Lucy sat against the wall, gasping, her hair plastered to her cheeks in strings while Momo wept and cradled her hideously deformed arm and asked why Lucia would hurt her like that and why this was happening to her.

At last the ambulance had come, and a man—Lucy didn't know his name but blessed him in her incoherent prayers—had given Momes a shot that put her out. Could you tell your husband you wished the shot had killed her?

"It was pretty awful," was all she said. "I'm so glad Abra didn't want to come down this weekend."

"She did, but she had lots of homework, and said she had to go to the library yesterday. It must have been a big deal, because you know how she usually pesters me about going to the football game." Babbling. Stupid. But what else was there? "Luce, I'm so goddamned sorry you had to go through that alone."

"It's just . . . if you could have heard her screaming. Then you might understand. I never want to hear anyone scream like that again. She's always been so great at staying calm . . . keeping her head when all about her are losing theirs . . ."

"I know—"

"And then to be reduced to what she was last night. The only words she could remember were *cunt* and *shit* and *piss* and *fuck* and *meretrice* and—"

"Let it go, honey." Upstairs, the shower had quit. It would only take Abra a few minutes to dry off and jump into her Sunday grubs; she'd be down soon enough, shirttail flying and sneaker laces flapping.

But Lucy wasn't quite ready to let it go. "I remember a poem she wrote once. I can't quote it word for word, but it started something like this: 'God's a connoisseur of fragile things, and decorates His cloudy outlook with ornaments of finest glass.' I used to think that was a rather conventionally pretty idea for a Concetta Reynolds poem, almost twee."

And here was his Abba-Doo—*their* Abba-Doo—with her skin flushed from the shower. "Everything all right, Daddy?"

David held up a hand: *Wait a minute.*

"Now I know what she really meant, and I'll never be able to read that poem again."

"Abby's here, hon," he said in a falsely jolly voice.

"Good. I'll need to talk to her. I'm not going to bawl anymore, so don't worry, but we can't protect her from this."

"Maybe from the worst of it?" he asked gently. Abra was standing by the table, her wet hair pulled into a couple of horsetails that made her look ten again. Her expression was grave.

"Maybe," she agreed, "but I can't do this anymore, Davey. Not even with day help. I thought I could, but I can't. There's a hospice in Frazier, just a little way down the road. The intake nurse told me about it. I think hospitals must keep a list for just this type of situation. Anyway, the place is called Helen Rivington House. I called them before I called you, and they have a vacancy as of today.

I guess God pushed another of His ornaments off the mantelpiece last night."

"Is Chetta awake? Have you discussed this—"

"She came around a couple of hours ago, but she was muddy. Had the past and present all mixed together in a kind of salad."

While I was still fast asleep, David thought guiltily. *Dreaming about my book, no doubt.*

"When she clears up—I'm assuming she will—I'll tell her, as gently as I can, that the decision isn't hers to make. It's time for hospice care."

"All right." When Lucy decided something—really decided— the best thing was to stand clear and let her work her will.

"Dad? Is Mom okay? Is Momo?"

Abra knew her mother was and her great-grandmother wasn't. Most of what Lucy had told her husband had come to her while she was still in the shower, standing there with shampoo and tears running down her cheeks. But she had gotten good at putting on happy faces until someone told her out loud that it was time to put on a sad one. She wondered if her new friend Dan had learned about the happy-face thing as a kid. She bet he had.

"Chia, I think Abby wants to talk to you."

Lucy sighed and said, "Put her on."

David held out the phone to his daughter.

2

At 2 p.m. on that Sunday, Rose the Hat hung a sign reading DO NOT DISTURB ME UNLESS ABSOLUTELY NECESSARY on the door of her plus-size RV. The coming hours had been carefully scheduled. She would eat no food today, and drink only water. Instead of mid-morning coffee, she had taken an emetic. When the time came to go after the girl's mind, she would be as clear as an empty glass.

With no bodily functions to distract her, Rose would be able to find out everything she needed: the girl's name, her exact location, how much she knew, and—this was very important—who she might have talked to. Rose would lie still on her double bed in the EarthCruiser from four in the afternoon until ten in the evening, looking up at the ceiling and meditating. When her mind was as clear as her body, she would take steam from one of the canisters in the hidden compartment—just a whiff would be enough—and once again turn the world until she was in the girl and the girl was in her. At one in the morning Eastern Time, her quarry would be dead asleep and Rose could pick through the contents of her mind at will. It might even be possible to plant a suggestion: *Some men will come. They will help you. Go with them.*

But as that old-school farmer-poet Bobbie Burns pointed out more than two hundred years before, the best laid plans of mice and men gang aft agley, and she had barely begun to recite the beginning phrases of her relaxation mantra when an agley came hammering at her door.

"Go away!" she shouted. "Can't you read the sign?"

"Rose, I've got Nut with me," Crow called. "I think he's got what you asked for, but he needs a go-ahead, and the timing on this thing is a bitch."

She lay there for a moment, then blew out an angry breath and got up, snatching a Sidewinder t-shirt (KISS ME AT THE ROOF O' THE WORLD!) and pulling it over her head. It dropped to the tops of her thighs. She opened the door. "This better be good."

"We can come back," Walnut said. He was a little man with a bald pate and Brillo pads of gray hair fluffing out above the tops of his ears. He held a sheet of paper in one hand.

"No, just make it quick."

They sat at the table in the combined kitchen/living room. Rose snatched the paper from Nut's hand and gave it a cursory glance. It was some sort of complicated chemical diagram filled with hexagons. It meant nothing to her. "What is it?"

"A powerful sedative," Nut said. "It's new, and it's clean. Jimmy got this chem sheet from one of our assets in the NSA. It'll put her out with no chance of ODing her."

"It could be what we need, all right." Rose knew she sounded grudging. "But couldn't it have waited until tomorrow?"

"Sorry, sorry," Nut said meekly.

"I'm not," Crow said. "If you want to move fast on this girl and snatch her clean, I'll not only have to make sure we can get some of this, I'll have to arrange for it to be shipped to one of our mail drops."

The True had hundreds of these across America, most of them at Mail Boxes Etc. and various UPS stores. Using them meant planning days ahead, because they always traveled in their RVs. Members of the True would no more get on public transport than they would slit their own throats. Private air travel was possible but unpleasant; they suffered extreme altitude sickness. Walnut believed it had something to do with their nervous systems, which differed radically from those of the rubes. Rose's concern was with a certain taxpayer-funded nervous system. *Very* nervous. Homeland Security had been monitoring even private flights very closely since 9/11, and the True Knot's first rule of survival was never attract attention.

Thanks to the interstate highway system, the RVs had always served their purposes, and would this time. A small raiding party, with new drivers taking the wheel every six hours, could get from Sidewinder to northern New England in less than thirty hours.

"All right," she said, mollified. "What have we got along I-90 in upstate New York or Massachusetts?"

Crow didn't hem and haw or tell her he'd have to get back to her on that. "EZ Mail Services, in Sturbridge, Massachusetts."

She flapped her fingers at the edge of the sheet of incomprehensible chemistry Nut was holding in his hand. "Have this stuff sent there. Use at least three cutouts so we have complete deniability if something goes wrong. Really bounce it around."

"Do we have that much time?" Crow asked.

"I don't see why not," Rose said—a remark that would come back to haunt her. "Send it south, then into the Midwest, then into New England. Just get it to Sturbridge by Thursday. Use Express Mail, *not* FedEx or UPS."

"I can do that," Crow said. No hesitation.

Rose turned her attention to the True's doctor. "You better be right, Walnut. If you *do* OD her instead of just putting her to sleep, I'll see you're the first True to be sent into exile since Little Big Horn."

Walnut paled a little. Good. She had no intention of exiling anyone, but she still resented being interrupted.

"We'll get the drug to Sturbridge, and Nut will know how to use it," Crow said. "No problem."

"There's nothing simpler? Something we can get around here?"

Nut said, "Not if you want to be sure she doesn't go Michael Jackson on us. This stuff is safe, and it hits fast. If she's as powerful as you seem to think, fast is going to be impor—"

"Okay, okay, I get it. Are we done here?"

"There's one more thing," Walnut said. "I suppose it could wait, but . . ."

She looked out the window and, ye gods and little fishes, here came Jimmy Numbers, bustling across the parking lot adjacent to the Overlook Lodge with his own sheet of paper. Why had she hung the DO NOT DISTURB sign on her doorknob? Why not one that said Y'ALL COME?

Rose gathered all her bad temper, stuffed it in a sack, stored it at the back of her mind, and smiled gamely. "What is it?"

"Grampa Flick," Crow said, "is no longer holding his fudge."

"He hasn't been able to hold it for the last twenty years," Rose said. "He won't wear diapers, and I can't make him. No one can make him."

"This is different," Nut said. "He can barely get out of bed. Baba and Black-Eyed Susie are taking care of him as well as they can, but that camper of his smells like the wrath of God—"

"He'll get better. We'll feed him some steam." But she didn't like the look on Nut's face. Tommy the Truck had passed two years ago, and by the way the True measured time, that might have been two weeks ago. Now Grampa Flick?

"His mind's breaking down," Crow said bluntly. "And . . ." He looked at Walnut.

"Petty was taking care of him this morning, and she says she thinks she saw him cycle."

"*Thinks*," Rose said. She didn't want to believe it. "Has anyone else seen it happen? Baba? Sue?"

"No."

She shrugged as if to say *there you are*. Jimmy knocked before they could discuss it farther, and this time she was glad for the interruption.

"Come in!"

Jimmy poked his head through. "Sure it's okay?"

"Yes! Why don't you bring the Rockettes and the UCLA marching band while you're at it? Hell, I was only trying to get in a meditation groove after a few pleasant hours of spewing my guts."

Crow was giving her a look of mild reproof, and maybe she deserved it—*probably* she deserved it, these people were only doing the True's work as she had asked them to do it—but if Crow ever stepped up to the captain's chair, he'd understand. Never a moment to yourself, unless you threatened them with pain of death. And in many cases, not even then.

"I got something you may want to see," Jimmy said. "And since Crow and Nut were already here, I figured—"

"I know what you figured. What is it?"

"I went hunting around on the internet for news about those two towns you zeroed in on—Fryeburg and Anniston. Found this in the *Union Leader*. It's from last Thursday's paper. Maybe it's nothing."

She took the sheet. The main item was about some podunk school shutting down their football program because of budget cuts. Beneath it was a shorter item, which Jimmy had circled.

"POCKET EARTHQUAKE" REPORTED IN ANNISTON

How small can an earthquake be? Pretty small, if the people of Richland Court, a short Anniston street that dead-ends at the Saco River, are to be believed. Late Tuesday afternoon, several residents of the street reported a tremor that rattled windows, shook floors, and sent glassware tumbling from shelves. Dane Borland, a retiree who lives at the end of the street, pointed out a crack running the width of his newly asphalted driveway. "If you want proof, there it is," he said.

Although the Geological Survey Center in Wrentham, MA, reports there were no temblors in New England last Tuesday afternoon, Matt and Cassie Renfrew took the opportunity to throw an "earthquake party," which most of the street's residents attended.

Andrew Sittenfeld of the Geological Survey Center says the shaking felt by Richland Court residents might have been a surge of water through the sewer system, or possibly a military plane breaking the sound barrier. When these suggestions were made to Mr. Renfrew, he laughed cheerfully. "We know what we felt," he said. "It was an earthquake. And there's really no downside. The damage was minor, and hey, we got a terrific party out of it."

(Andrew Gould)

Rose read it twice, then looked up, eyes bright. "Good catch, Jimmy."

He grinned. "Thanks. I'll leave you guys to it, then."

"Take Nut with you, he needs to check on Grampa. Crow, you stay a minute."

When they were gone, he closed the door. "You think the girl caused that shake in New Hampshire?"

"I do. Not a hundred percent certain, but at least eighty. And having a place to focus on—not just a town but a *street*—will make things a hell of a lot easier for me tonight, when I go looking for her."

"If you can stick a come-along worm in her head, Rosie, we may not even need to knock her out."

She smiled, thinking again that Crow had no idea how special this one was. Later she would think, *Neither did I. I only thought I did.* "There's no law against hoping, I suppose. But once we have her, we'll need something a little more sophisticated than a Mickey Finn, even if it's a high-tech one. We'll need some wonder drug that'll keep her nice and cooperative until she decides it's in her best interest to cooperate on her own."

"Will you be coming with us when we go to grab her?"

Rose had assumed so, but now she hesitated, thinking of Grampa Flick. "I'm not sure."

He didn't ask questions—which she appreciated—and turned to the door. "I'll see that you're not disturbed again."

"Good. And you make sure Walnut gives Grampa a complete exam—I mean from asshole to appetite. If he really *is* cycling, I want to know tomorrow, when I come out of purdah." She opened the compartment under the floor and brought out one of the canisters. "And give him what's left in this."

Crow was shocked. "*All* of it? Rose, if he's cycling, there's no point."

"Give it to him. We've had a good year, as several of you have pointed out to me lately. We can afford a little extravagance. Besides, the True Knot only has one grampa. He remembers when the people of Europe worshipped trees instead of time-share condos. We're not going to lose him if we can help it. We're not savages."

"The rubes might beg to differ."

"That's why they're rubes. Now get out of here."

3

After Labor Day, Teenytown closed at 3 p.m. on Sundays. This afternoon, at quarter to six, three giants sat on benches near the end of the mini–Cranmore Avenue, dwarfing Teenytown Drug and the Teenytown Music Box Theater (where, during tourist season, you could peek in the window and see teeny film clips playing on a teeny screen). John Dalton had come to the meeting wearing a Red Sox hat, which he placed on the head of the teeny Helen Rivington statue in the teeny courthouse square. "I'm sure she was a fan," he said. "Everybody up this way is a fan. Nobody spares a little admiration for the Yankees except exiles like me. What can I do for you, Dan? I'm missing supper with the family for this. My wife's an understanding woman, but her patience only stretches so far."

"How would she feel about you spending a few days with me in Iowa?" Dan asked. "Strictly on my dime, you understand. I have to make a Twelfth Step call on an uncle who's killing himself with booze and cocaine. My family's begging me to step in, and I can't do it alone."

AA had no rules but many traditions (that were, in fact, rules). One of the most ironclad was that you never made a Twelfth Step call on an active alcoholic by yourself, unless the alkie in question was safely incarcerated in a hospital, detox, or the local bughouse. If you did, you were apt to end up matching him drink for drink and line for line. Addiction, Casey Kingsley liked to say, was the gift that kept on giving.

Dan looked at Billy Freeman and smiled. "Got something to say? Go ahead, feel free."

"I don't think you got an uncle. I'm not sure you've got any family left at all."

"Is that it? You're just not sure?"

"Well . . . you never talk about em."

"Plenty of people have family and don't talk about them. But you *know* I don't have anyone, don't you, Billy?"

Billy said nothing, but looked uneasy.

"Danny, I can't go to Iowa," John said. "I'm booked right into the weekend."

Dan was still focused on Billy. Now he reached into his pocket, grabbed something, and held out his closed fist. "What have I got?"

Billy looked more uneasy than ever. He glanced at John, saw no help there, then back to Dan.

"John knows what I am," Dan said. "I helped him once, and he knows I've helped a few others in the Program. You're among friends here."

Billy thought about it, then said: "Might be a coin, but I think it's one of your AA medals. The kind they give you every time you get in another year sober."

"What year's this one?"

Billy hesitated, looking at Dan's fisted hand.

"Let me help you out," John said. "He's been sober since the spring of 2001, so if he's carrying a medallion around, it's probably a Year Twelve."

"Makes sense, but it ain't." Billy was concentrating now, two deep vertical lines grooving his forehead just about his eyes. "I think it might be . . . a seven?"

Dan opened his palm. The medallion had a big **VI** on it.

"Fuckaroo," Billy said. "I'm usually good at guessing."

"You were close enough," Dan said. "And it's not guessing, it's shining."

Billy took out his cigarettes, looked at the doctor sitting on the bench next to him, and put them back. "If you say so."

"Let me tell you a little about yourself, Billy. When you were small, you were *great* at guessing things. You knew when your mother was in a good mood and you could hit her for an extra buck or two. You knew when your dad was in a bad one, and you steered clear of him."

"I sure knew there were nights when bitchin about having to eat leftover pot roast would be a goddam bad idea," Billy said.

"Did you gamble?"

"Hoss-races down Salem. Made a bundle. Then, when I was twenty-five or so, I kinda lost the knack of picking winners. I had a month when I had to beg an extension on the rent, and that cured me of railbirding."

"Yes, the talent fades as people grow older, but you still have some."

"You got more," Billy said. No hesitation now.

"This is real, isn't it?" John said. It really wasn't a question; it was an observation.

"You've only got one appointment this coming week you really feel you can't miss or hand off," Dan said. "It's a little girl with stomach cancer. Her name is Felicity—"

"Frederika," John said. "Frederika Bimmel. She's at Merrimack

Valley Hospital. I'm supposed to have a consult with her oncologist and her parents."

"Saturday morning."

"Yeah. Saturday morning." He gave Dan an amazed look. "Jesus. Jesus Christ. What you have . . . I had no idea there was so *much* of it."

"I'll have you back from Iowa by Thursday. Friday at the latest."

Unless we get arrested, he thought. *Then we might be there awhile longer.* He looked to see if Billy had picked up that less-than-encouraging thought. There was no sign that he had.

"What's this about?"

"Another patient of yours. Abra Stone. She's like Billy and me, John, but I think you already know that. Only she's much, much more powerful. I've got quite a lot more than Billy, and she makes me look like a fortune-teller at a county fair."

"Oh my God, the spoons."

It took Dan a second, then he remembered. "She hung them on the ceiling."

John stared at him, wide-eyed. "You read that in my *mind?*"

"A little more mundane than that, I'm afraid. She told me."

"When? *When?*"

"We'll get there, but not yet. First, let's try for some authentic mind-reading." Dan took John's hand. That helped; contact almost always did. "Her parents came to see you when she was just a toddler. Or maybe it was an aunt or her great-gram. They were concerned about her even before she decorated the kitchen with silverware, because there was all sorts of psychic phenomena going on in that house. There was something about the piano . . . Billy, help me out here."

Billy grabbed John's free hand. Dan took Billy's, making a connected circle. A teeny séance in Teenytown.

"Beatles music," Billy said. "On the piano instead of the guitar. It was . . . I dunno. It made em crazy for awhile."

John stared at him.

"Listen," Dan said, "you have her permission to talk. She wants you to. Trust me on this, John."

John Dalton considered for almost a full minute. Then he told them everything, with one exception.

That stuff about *The Simpsons* being on all the TV channels was just too weird.

4

When he was finished, John asked the obvious question: How did Dan know Abra Stone?

From his back pocket Dan produced a small, battered notebook. On the cover was a photo of waves crashing against a headland and the motto NO GREAT THING IS CREATED SUDDENLY.

"You used to carry this, didn't you?" John asked.

"Yes. You know Casey K.'s my sponsor, right?"

John rolled his eyes. "Who could forget, when every time you open your mouth in a meeting, you start with 'My sponsor, Casey K., always says.'"

"John, nobody loves a smartass."

"My wife does," he said. "Because I'm a *studly* smartass."

Dan sighed. "Look in the book."

John paged through it. "These are meetings. From 2001."

"Casey told me I had to do ninety-in-ninety, and keep track. Look at the eighth one."

John found it. Frazier Methodist Church. A meeting he didn't often go to, but one he knew. Printed below the notation, in elaborate capital letters, was the word ABRA.

John looked up at Dan not quite unbelievingly. "She got in touch with you when she was *two months old?*"

"You see my next meeting just below it," Dan said, "so I couldn't have added her name later just to impress you. Unless I faked the whole book, that is, and there are plenty of people in the Program who'll remember seeing me with it."

"Including me," John said.

"Yeah, including you. In those days, I always had my meeting book in one hand and a cup of coffee in the other. They were my security blankets. I didn't know who she was then, and I didn't much care. It was just one of those random touchings. The way a baby in a crib might reach out and brush your nose.

"Then, two or three years later, she wrote a word on a scheduling blackboard I keep in my room. The word was *hello*. She kept in contact after that, every once in awhile. Kind of touching base. I'm not even sure she was aware she was doing it. But I was there. When she needed help, I was the one she knew, and the one she reached out to."

"What kind of help does she need? What kind of trouble is she in?" John turned to Billy. "Do *you* know?"

Billy shook his head. "I never heard of her, and I hardly ever go to Anniston."

"Who said Abra lives in Anniston?"

Billy cocked a thumb at Dan. "*He* did. Didn't he?"

John turned back to Dan. "All right. Say I'm convinced. Let's have the whole thing."

Dan told them about Abra's nightmare of the baseball boy. The shapes holding flashlights on him. The woman with the knife, the one who had licked the boy's blood off her palms. About how, much later, Abra had come across the boy's picture in the *Shopper*.

"And she could do this why? Because the kid they killed was another one of these shiners?"

"I'm pretty sure that's how the initial contact happened. He must have reached out while these people were torturing him—Abra has no doubt that's what they did—and that created a link."

"One that continued even after the boy, this Brad Trevor, was dead?"

"I think her later point of contact may have been something the Trevor kid owned—his baseball glove. And she was able to link to his killers because one of them put it on. She doesn't know how she does it, and neither do I. All I know for sure is that she's immensely powerful."

"The way you are."

"Here's the thing," Dan said. "These people—if they *are* people—are led by the woman who did the actual killing. On the day Abra came across the picture of Brad Trevor on a missing-children page in the local rag, she got in this woman's head. And the woman got in Abra's. For a few seconds they looked through each other's eyes." He held up his hands, made fists, and rotated them. "Turn and turn about. Abra thinks they may come for her, and so do I. Because she could be a danger to them."

"There's more to it than that, isn't there?" Billy asked.

Dan looked at him, waiting.

"People who can do this shining thing *have* something, right? Something these people want. Something they can only get by killing."

"Yes."

John said, "Does this woman know where Abra is?"

"Abra doesn't think so, but you have to remember she's only thirteen. She could be wrong."

"Does Abra know where the woman is?"

"All she knows is that when this contact—this mutual seeing—occurred, the woman was in a Sam's Supermarket. That puts it somewhere out West, but there are Sams in at least nine states."

"Including Iowa?"

Dan shook his head.

"Then I don't see what we can accomplish by going there."

"We can get the glove," Dan said. "Abra thinks if she has the glove, she can link to the man who had it on his hand for a little while. She calls him Barry the Chunk."

John sat with his head lowered, thinking. Dan let him do it.

"All right," John said at last. "This is crazy, but I'll buy it. Given what I know of Abra's history and given my own history with you, it's actually kind of hard not to. But if this woman doesn't know where Abra is, might it not be wiser to leave things alone? Don't kick a sleeping dog and all that?"

"I don't think this dog's asleep," Dan said. "These
(*empty devils*)
freaks want her for the same reason they wanted the Trevor
boy—I'm sure Billy's right about that. Also, they know she's
a danger to them. To put it in AA terms, she has the power to
break their anonymity. And they may have resources we can only
guess at. Would you want a patient of yours to live in fear, month
after month and maybe year after year, always expecting some sort
of paranormal Manson Family to show up and snatch her off the
street?"

"Of course not."

"These assholes *live* on children like her. Children like I was.
Kids with the shining." He stared grimly into John Dalton's face.
"If it's true, they need to be stopped."

Billy said, "If I'm not going to Iowa, what am I supposed to do?"

"Let's put it this way," Dan said. "You're going to get very
familiar with Anniston in the week ahead. In fact, if Casey will
give you time off, you're going to stay at a motel there."

5

Rose finally entered the meditative state she had been seeking. The
hardest thing to let go of had been her worries about Grampa Flick,
but she finally got past them. Got *above* them. Now she cruised
within herself, repeating the old phrases—*sabbatha hanti* and *lodsam
hanti* and *cahanna risone hanti*—over and over again, her lips barely
moving. It was too early to seek the troublesome girl, but now that
she'd been left alone and the world was quiet, both inside and out,
she was in no hurry. Meditation for its own sake was a fine thing.
Rose went about gathering her tools and focusing her concentration,
working slowly and meticulously.

Sabbatha hanti, lodsam hanti, cahanna risone hanti: words that had
been old when the True Knot moved across Europe in wagons,
selling peat turves and trinkets. They had probably been old when

Babylon was young. The girl was powerful, but the True was *all*-powerful, and Rose anticipated no real problem. The girl would be asleep, and Rose would move with quiet stealth, picking up information and planting suggestions like small explosives. Not just one worm, but a whole nest of them. Some the girl might detect, and disable.

Others, not.

6

Abra spoke with her mother on the phone for almost forty-five minutes that night after she'd finished her homework. The conversation had two levels. On the top one, they talked about Abra's day, the school week ahead, and her costume for the upcoming Halloween Dance; they discussed the ongoing plans to have Momo moved north to the Frazier hospice (which Abra still thought of as the "hot spice"); Lucy brought Abra up-to-date on Momo's condition, which she said was "actually pretty good, all things considered."

On another level, Abra listened to Lucy's nagging worry that she had somehow failed her grandmother, and to the truth of Momo's condition: frightened, addled, racked with pain. Abra tried to send her mother soothing thoughts: *it's all right, Mom* and *we love you, Mom* and *you did the best you could, for as long as you were able*. She liked to believe that some of these thoughts got through, but didn't really believe it. She had many talents—the kind that were wonderful and scary at the same time—but changing another person's emotional temperature had never been one of them.

Could Dan do that? She thought maybe he could. She thought he used that part of his shining to help people in the hot spice. If he could really do that, maybe he would help Momo when she got there. That would be good.

She came downstairs wearing the pink flannel pajamas Momo had given her last Christmas. Her father was watching the Red Sox and drinking a glass of beer. She put a big smackeroo on his nose (he always said he hated that, but she knew he sort of liked it) and told him she was off to bed.

"*La homework est complète, mademoiselle?*"

"Yes, Daddy, but the French word for homework is *devoirs.*"

"Good to know, good to know. How was your mother? I ask because I only had about ninety seconds with her before you snatched the phone."

"She's doing okay." Abra knew this was the truth, but she also knew *okay* was a relative term. She started for the hall, then turned back. "She said Momo was like a glass ornament." She hadn't, not out loud, but she'd been thinking it. "She says we all are."

Dave muted the TV. "Well, I guess that's true, but some of us are made of surprisingly tough glass. Remember, your momo's been up on the shelf, safe and sound, for many, many years. Now come over here, Abba-Doo, and give your Dad a hug. I don't know if you need it, but I could use one."

7

Twenty minutes later she was in bed with Mr. Pooh Bear Nightlight, a holdover from earliest childhood, glowing on the dresser. She reached for Dan and found him in an activities room where there were jigsaw puzzles, magazines, a Ping-Pong table, and a big TV on the wall. He was playing cards with a couple of hot spice residents.

(*did you talk to Doctor John?*)

(*yes we're going to Iowa day after tomorrow*)

This thought was accompanied by a brief picture of an old biplane. Inside were two men wearing old-fashioned flying helmets, scarves, and goggles. It made Abra smile.

(*if we bring you*)

Picture of a catcher's mitt. That wasn't what the baseball boy's glove really looked like, but Abra knew what Dan was trying to say.

(*will you freak out*)

(*no*)

She better not. Holding the dead boy's glove would be terrible, but she would have to do it.

8

In the common room of Rivington One, Mr. Braddock was staring at Dan with that look of monumental but slightly puzzled irritation which only the very old and borderline senile can bring off successfully. "Are you gonna discard something, Danny, or just sit there starin into the corner until the icecaps melt?"

(*goodnight Abra*)

(*goodnight Dan say goodnight to Tony for me*)

"Danny?" Mr. Braddock knocked his swollen knuckles on the table. "Danny Torrance, come in, Danny Torrance, over?"

(*don't forget to set your alarm*)

"Hoo-hoo, Danny," Cora Willingham said.

Dan looked at them. "Did I discard, or is it still my turn?"

Mr. Braddock rolled his eyes at Cora; Cora rolled hers right back. "And my daughters think *I'm* the one losing my marbles," she said.

9

Abra had set the alarm on her iPad because tomorrow was not only a schoolday but one of her days to make breakfast—scrambled eggs with mushrooms, peppers, and Jack cheese was the plan. But that wasn't the alarm Dan had been talking about. She closed her eyes and concentrated, her brow furrowing. One hand crept out from under the covers and began wiping at her lips. What she was doing was tricky, but maybe it would be worth it.

Alarms were all well and good, but if the woman in the hat came looking for her, a trap might be even better.

After five minutes or so, the lines on her forehead smoothed out and her hand fell away from her mouth. She rolled over on her side and pulled the duvet up to her chin. She was visualizing herself riding a white stallion in full warrior garb when she fell asleep. Mr. Pooh Bear Nightlight watched from his place on the dresser as he had since Abra was four, casting a dim radiance on her left cheek. That and her hair were the only parts of her that still showed.

In her dreams, she galloped over long fields under four billion stars.

10

Rose continued her meditations until one thirty that Monday morning. The rest of the True (with the exception of Apron Annie and Big Mo, currently watching over Grampa Flick) were sleeping deeply when she decided she was ready. In one hand she held a picture, printed off her computer, of Anniston, New Hampshire's not-very-impressive downtown. In the other she held one of the canisters. Although there was nothing left inside but the faintest whiff of steam, she had no doubt it would be enough. She put her fingers on the valve, preparing to loosen it.

We are the True Knot, and we endure: Sabbatha hanti.

We are the chosen ones: Lodsam hanti.

We are the fortunate ones: Cahanna risone hanti.

"Take this and use it well, Rosie-girl," she said. When she turned the valve, a short sigh of silver mist escaped. She inhaled, fell back on her pillow, and let the canister drop to the carpet with a soft thud. She lifted the picture of Anniston's Main Street in front of her eyes. Her arm and hand were no longer precisely there, and so the picture seemed to float. Not far from that Main Street, a little girl lived down a lane that was probably called Richland Court. She would be fast asleep, but somewhere in her mind was Rose the Hat. She assumed the little girl didn't know what Rose the Hat looked like (any more than Rose knew what the girl looked like . . . at least not yet), but she knew what Rose the Hat *felt* like. Also, she knew what Rose had been looking at in Sam's yesterday. That was her marker, her way in.

Rose stared at the picture of Anniston with fixed and dreaming eyes, but what she was really looking for was Sam's meat counter, where EVERY CUT IS A BLUE RIBBON **COWBOY** CUT. She was looking for herself. And, after a gratifyingly short search, found her. At first just an auditory trace: the sound of supermarket Muzak. Then a shopping cart. Beyond it, all was still dark. That was all right; the rest would come. Rose followed the Muzak, now echoing and distant.

It was dark, it was dark, it was dark, then a little light and a little more. Here was the supermarket aisle, then it became a hallway and she knew she was almost in. Her heartbeat kicked up a notch.

Lying on her bed, she closed her eyes so if the kid realized what was happening—unlikely but not impossible—she would see nothing. Rose took a few seconds to review her primary goals: name, exact location, extent of knowledge, anyone she might have told.

(turn, world)

She gathered her strength and pushed. This time the sensation of *revolving* wasn't a surprise but something she had planned for and over which she had complete control. For a moment she was still in that hallway—the conduit between their two minds—and then she was in a large room where a little girl in pigtails was riding a bike and lilting a nonsense song. It was the little girl's dream and Rose was watching it. But she had better things to do. The walls of the room weren't real walls, but file drawers. She could open them at will now that she was inside. The little girl was safely dreaming in Rose's head, dreaming she was five and riding her first bicycle. That was very fine. *Dream on, little princess.*

The child rode past her, singing *la-la-la* and seeing nothing. There were training wheels on her bike, but they flickered on and off. Rose guessed the princess was dreaming of the day when she had finally learned to ride without them. Always a very fine day in a child's life.

Enjoy your bicycle, dear, while I find out all about you.

Moving with confidence, Rose opened one of the drawers.

The instant she reached inside, an earsplitting alarm began to bray and brilliant white spotlights blazed on all around the room, beating down on her with heat as well as light. For the first time in a great many years, Rose the Hat, once Rose O'Hara from County Antrim in Northern Ireland, was caught completely off-guard. Before she could pull her hand out of the drawer, it slammed shut. The pain was enormous. She screamed and jerked backward, but she was held fast.

Her shadow jumped high on the wall, but not just hers. She turned her head and saw the little girl bearing down on her. Only she wasn't little anymore. Now she was a young woman wearing a leather jerkin with a dragon on her blooming chest and a blue band to hold back her hair. The bike had become a white stallion. Its eyes, like those of the warrior-woman, were blazing.

The warrior-woman had a lance.

(*You came back Dan said you would and you did*)

And then—unbelievable in a rube, even one loaded with big steam—*pleasure.*

(*GOOD*)

The child who was no longer a child had been lying in wait for her. She had laid a trap, she meant to kill Rose . . . and considering Rose's state of mental vulnerability, she probably could.

Summoning every bit of her strength, Rose fought back, not with some comic-book lance, but with a blunt battering ram that had all her years and will behind it.

(*GET AWAY FROM ME! GET THE FUCK BACK! NO MATTER WHAT YOU THINK YOU ARE YOU'RE JUST A LITTLE GIRL!*)

The girl's grown-up vision of herself—her avatar—kept coming, but she flinched as Rose's thought hit her, and the lance crashed into the wall of file drawers to Rose's immediate left instead of into her side, which was where it had been aimed.

The kid (*that's all she is,* Rose kept telling herself) wheeled her horse away and Rose turned to the drawer that had caught her. She braced her free hand above it and pulled with all her might, ignoring the pain. At first the drawer held. Then it gave a little and she was able to pull out the heel of her hand. It was scraped and bleeding.

Something else was happening. There was a fluttering sensation in her head, as if a bird were flying around up there. What new shit was this?

Expecting that goddamned lance to drive into her back at any moment, Rose yanked with all her might. Her hand slipped all the way out and she curled her fingers into a fist just in time. If she'd waited even an instant, the drawer would have cut them off when it slammed shut. Her nails throbbed, and she knew when she had a chance to look at them, they would be plum-colored with trapped blood.

She turned. The girl was gone. The room was empty. But that fluttering sensation continued. If anything, it had intensified. Suddenly the pain in her hand and wrist was the last thing on Rose's mind. She wasn't the only one who had ridden the turntable, and it didn't matter that her eyes were still shut back in the real world, where she lay on her double bed.

The fucking brat was in another room filled with file drawers.

Her room. Her head.

Instead of the burglar, Rose had become the burgled.

(*GET OUT GET OUT GET OUT GET OUT*)

The fluttering didn't stop; it sped up. Rose shoved away her panic, fought for clarity and focus, found some. Just enough to set the turntable in motion again, even though it had become weirdly heavy.

(*turn, world*)

As it did, she felt the maddening flutter in her head first diminish and then cease as the little girl was rotated back to wherever she came from.

Except that's not right, and this is far too serious for you to indulge in the luxury of lying to yourself. You *came to* her. *And walked right into a trap. Why? Because in spite of all you knew, you underestimated.*

Rose opened her eyes, sat up, and swung her feet onto the carpet. One of them struck the empty canister and she kicked it away. The Sidewinder t-shirt she had pulled on before lying down was damp; she reeked of sweat. It was a piggy smell, entirely unattractive. She looked unbelievingly at her hand, which was scraped and bruised and swelling. Her fingernails were going from purple to black, and she guessed she might lose at least two of them.

"But I *didn't* know," she said. "There was no way I could." She hated the whine she heard in her voice. It was the voice of a querulous old woman. "No way at all."

She had to get out of this goddam camper. It might be the biggest, luxiest one in the world, but right now it felt the size of a coffin. She made her way to the door, holding onto things to keep her balance. She glanced at the clock on the dashboard before she went out. Ten to two. Everything had happened in just twenty minutes. Incredible.

How much did she find out before I got free of her? How much does she know?

No way of telling for sure, but even a little could be dangerous. The brat had to be taken care of, and soon.

Rose stepped out into the pale early moonlight and took half a dozen long, steadying breaths of fresh air. She began to feel a little better, a little more herself, but she couldn't let go of that *fluttering* sensation. The feeling of having someone else inside her—a rube, no less—looking at her private things. The pain had been bad, and the surprise of being trapped that way was worse, but the worst thing of all was the humiliation and sense of violation. She had been *stolen* from.

You are going to pay for that, princess. You just messed in with the wrong bitch.

A shape was moving toward her. Rose had settled on the top step of her RV, but now she stood up, tense, ready for anything. Then the shape got closer and she saw it was Crow. He was dressed in pajama bottoms and slippers.

"Rose, I think you better—" He stopped. "What the hell happened to your hand?"

"Never mind my fucking hand," she snapped. "What are you doing here at two in the morning? Especially when you knew I was apt to be busy?"

"It's Grampa Flick," Crow said. "Apron Annie says he's dying."

THOME 25

1

Instead of pine-scented air freshener and Alcazar cigars, Grampa Flick's Fleetwood this morning smelled of shit, disease, and death. It was also crowded. There were at least a dozen members of the True Knot present, some gathered around the old man's bed, many more sitting or standing in the living room, drinking coffee. The rest were outside. Everyone looked stunned and uneasy. The True wasn't used to death among their own.

"Clear out," Rose said. "Crow and Nut—you stay."

"Look at him," Petty the Chink said in a trembling voice. "Them spots! And 'e's cycling like crazy, Rose! Oh, this is 'orrible!"

"Go on," Rose said. She spoke gently and gave Petty a comforting squeeze on the shoulder when what she felt like doing was kicking her fat Cockney ass right out the door. She was a lazy gossip, good for nothing but warming Barry's bed, and probably not very good at that. Rose guessed that nagging was more Petty's specialty. When she wasn't scared out of her mind, that is.

"Come on, folks," Crow said. "If he *is* going to die, he doesn't need to do it with an audience."

"He'll pull through," Harpman Sam said. "Tougher'n a boiled owl, that's Grampa Flick." But he put his arm around Baba the Russian, who looked devastated, and hugged her tight against him for a moment.

They got moving, some taking a last look back over their

shoulders before going down the steps to join the others. When it was just the three of them, Rose approached the bed.

Grampa Flick stared up at her without seeing her. His lips had pulled back from his gums. Great patches of his fine white hair had fallen out on the pillowcase, giving him the look of a distempered dog. His eyes were huge and wet and filled with pain. He was naked except for a pair of boxer shorts, and his scrawny body was stippled with red marks that looked like pimples or insect bites.

She turned to Walnut and said, "What in hell are those?"

"Koplik's spots," he said. "That's what they look like to me, anyway. Although Koplik's are usually just inside the mouth."

"Talk English."

Nut ran his hands through his thinning hair. "I think he's got the measles."

Rose gaped in shock, then barked laughter. She didn't want to stand here listening to this shit; she wanted some aspirin for her hand, which sent out a pain-pulse with every beat of her heart. She kept thinking about how the hands of cartoon characters looked when they got whopped with a mallet. "We don't catch rube diseases!"

"Well . . . we never used to."

She stared at him furiously. She wanted her hat, she felt naked without it, but it was back in the EarthCruiser.

Nut said, "I can only tell you what I see, which is red measles, also known as rubeola."

A rube disease called rubeola. How too fucking perfect.

"That is just . . . *horseshit*!"

He flinched, and why not? She sounded strident even to herself, but . . . ah, Jesus God, *measles*? The oldest member of the True Knot dying of a childhood disease even children didn't catch anymore?

"That baseball-playing kid from Iowa had a few spots on him, but I never thought . . . because yeah, it's like you say. We don't catch their diseases."

"He was *years* ago!"

"I know. All I can think is that it was in the steam, and it kind of hibernated. There are diseases that do that, you know. Lie passive, sometimes for years, then break out."

"Maybe with rubes!" She kept coming back to that.

Walnut only shook his head.

"If Gramp's got it, why don't we all have it? Because those childhood diseases—chicken pox, measles, mumps—run through rube kids like shit through a goose. It doesn't make sense." Then she turned to Crow Daddy and promptly contradicted herself. "What the fuck were you thinking when you let a bunch of them in to stand around and breathe his air?"

Crow just shrugged, his eyes never leaving the shivering old man on the bed. Crow's narrow, handsome face was pensive.

"Things change," Nut said. "Just because we had immunity to rube diseases fifty or a hundred years ago doesn't mean we have it now. For all we know, this could be part of a natural process."

"Are you telling me there's anything natural about *that*?" She pointed to Grampa Flick.

"A single case doesn't make an epidemic," Nut said, "and it *could* be something else. But if this happens again, we'll have to put whoever it happens to in complete quarantine."

"Would it help?"

He hesitated a long time. "I don't know. Maybe we do have it, all of us. Maybe it's like an alarm clock set to go off or dynamite on a timer. According to the latest scientific thinking, that's sort of how rubes age. They go along and go along, pretty much the same, and then something turns off in their genes. The wrinkles start showing up and all at once they need canes to walk with."

Crow had been watching Grampa. "There he goes. *Fuck*."

Grampa Flick's skin was turning milky. Then translucent. As it moved toward complete transparency, Rose could see his liver, the shriveled gray-black bags of his lungs, the pulsing red knot of his heart. She could see his veins and arteries like the highways and turnpikes on her in-dash GPS. She could see the optic nerves that connected his eyes to his brain. They looked like ghostly strings.

Then he came back. His eyes moved, caught Rosie's, held them.

He reached out and took her unhurt hand. Her first impulse was to pull away—if he had what Nut said he had, he was contagious—but what the hell. If Nut was right, they had all been exposed.

"Rose," he whispered. "Don't leave me."

"I won't." She sat down beside him on the bed, her fingers entwined in his. "Crow?"

"Yes, Rose."

"The package you had sent to Sturbridge—they'll hold it, won't they?"

"Sure."

"All right, we'll see this through. But we can't afford to wait too long. The little girl is a lot more dangerous than I thought." She sighed. "Why do problems always come in bunches?"

"Did she do that to your hand, somehow?"

That was a question she didn't want to answer directly. "I won't be able to go with you, because she knows me now." *Also,* she thought but didn't say, *because if this is what Walnut thinks it is, the rest will need me here to play Mother Courage.* "But we have to have her. It's more important than ever."

"Because?"

"If she's had the measles, she'll have the rube immunity to catching it again. That might make her steam useful in all sorts of ways."

"The kids get vaccinated against all that crap now," Crow said.

Rose nodded. "That could work, too."

Grampa Flick once more began to cycle. It was hard to watch, but Rose made herself to do it. When she could no longer see the old fellow's organs through his fragile skin, she looked at Crow and held up her bruised and scraped hand.

"Also . . . she needs to be taught a lesson."

2

When Dan woke up in his turret room on Monday, the schedule had once more been wiped from his blackboard and replaced with a message from Abra. At the top was a smiley-face. All the teeth were showing, which gave it a gleeful look.

> She came! I was ready and I hurt her!
> ### I REALLY DID!!
> She deserves it, so HOORAY!!!
> I need to talk to you, not this way or 'Net.
> Same place as before 3PM

Dan lay back on his bed, covered his eyes, and went looking for her. He found her walking to school with three of her friends, which struck him as dangerous in itself. For the friends as well as for Abra. He hoped Billy was there and on the job. He also hoped Billy would be discreet and not get tagged by some zealous Neighborhood Watch type as a suspicious character.

(*I can come John and I don't leave until tomorrow but it has to be fast and we have to be careful*)

(*yes okay good*)

3

Dan was once more seated on a bench outside the ivy-covered Anniston Library when Abra emerged, dressed for school in a red jumper and snazzy red sneakers. She held a knapsack by one strap. To Dan she looked as if she'd grown an inch since the last time he'd seen her.

She waved. "Hi, Uncle Dan!"

"Hello, Abra. How was school?"

"Great! I got an A on my biology report!"

"Sit down a minute and tell me about it."

She crossed to the bench, so filled with grace and energy she almost seemed to dance. Eyes bright, color high: a healthy after-school teenager with all systems showing green. Everything about her said ready-steady-go. There was no reason for this to make Dan feel uneasy, but it did. One very good thing: a nondescript Ford pickup was parked half a block down, the old guy behind the wheel sipping a take-out coffee and reading a magazine. Appearing to read a magazine, at least.

(*Billy?*)

No answer, but he looked up from his magazine for a moment, and that was enough.

"Okay," Dan said in a lower voice. "I want to hear exactly what happened."

She told him about the trap she had set, and how well it had worked. Dan listened with amazement, admiration . . . and that growing sense of unease. Her confidence in her abilities worried him. It was a kid's confidence, and the people they were dealing with weren't kids.

"I just told you to set an alarm," he said when she had finished.

"This was better. I don't know if I could have gone at her that way if I wasn't pretending to be Daenerys in the *Game of Thrones* books, but I think so. Because she killed the baseball boy and lots of others. Also because . . ." For the first time her smile faltered a little. As she was telling her story, Dan had seen what she would look like at eighteen. Now he saw what she had looked like at nine.

"Because what?"

"She's not human. None of them are. Maybe they were once, but not anymore." She straightened her shoulders and tossed her hair back. "But I'm stronger. She knew it, too."

(*I thought she pushed you away*)

She frowned at him, annoyed, wiped at her mouth, then caught her hand doing it and returned it to her lap. Once it was there, the other one clasped it to keep it still. There was something familiar about this gesture, but why wouldn't there be? He'd seen her do it before. Right now he had bigger things to worry about.

(*next time I'll be ready if there* is *a next time*)

That might be true. But if there was a next time, the woman in the hat would be ready, too.

(*I only want you to be careful*)

"I will. For sure." This, of course, was what all kids said in order to placate the adults in their lives, but it still made Dan feel better. A little, anyway. Besides, there was Billy in his F-150 with the faded red paint.

Her eyes were dancing again. "I found lots of stuff out. That's why I needed to see you."

"What stuff?"

"Not where she is, I didn't get that far, but I did find . . . see, when she was in my head, I was in hers. Like swapsies, you know? It was full of drawers, like being in the world's biggest library reference room, although maybe I only saw it that way because *she* did. If she had been looking at computer screens in my head, *I* might have seen computer screens."

"How many of her drawers did you get into?"

"Three. Maybe four. They call themselves the True Knot. Most of them are old, and they really are like vampires. They look for kids like me. And like you were, I guess. Only they don't drink blood, they breathe in the stuff that comes out when the special kids die." She winced in disgust. "The more they hurt them before, the stronger that stuff is. They call it steam."

"It's red, right? Red or reddish-pink?"

He felt sure of this, but Abra frowned and shook her head. "No, white. A bright white cloud. Nothing red about it. And listen: they can store it! What they don't use they put it in these thermos bottle thingies. But they never have enough. I saw this show once, about sharks? It said they're always on the move, because they never have enough to eat. I think the True Knot is like that." She grimaced. "They're naughty, all right."

White stuff. Not red but white. It still had to be what the old nurse had called the gasp, but a different kind. Because it came from healthy young people instead of old ones dying of almost every disease the flesh was heir to? Because they were what Abra called "the special kids?" Both?

She was nodding. "Both, probably."

"Okay. But the thing that matters most is that they know about you. *She* knows."

"They're a little scared I might tell someone about them, but not too scared."

"Because you're just a kid, and no one believes kids."

"Right." She blew her bangs off her forehead. "Momo would believe me, but she's going to die. She's going to your hot spice, Dan. Hospice, I mean. You'll help her, won't you? If you're not in Iowa?"

"All I can. Abra—are they coming for you?"

"Maybe, but if they do it won't be because of what I know. It will be because of what I *am*." Her happiness was gone now that she was facing this head-on. She rubbed at her mouth again, and when she dropped her hand, her lips were parted in an angry smile. *This girl has a temper,* Dan thought. He could relate to that. He had a temper himself. It had gotten him in trouble more than once.

"*She* won't come, though. That bitch. She knows I know her now, and I'll sense her if she gets close, because we're sort of tied together. But there are others. If they come for me, they'll hurt anyone who gets in their way."

Abra took his hands in hers, squeezing hard. This worried Dan, but he didn't make her let go. Right now she needed to touch someone she trusted.

"We have to stop them so they can't hurt my daddy, or my mom, or any of my friends. And so they won't kill any more kids."

For a moment Dan caught a clear picture from her thoughts— not sent, just there in the foreground. It was a collage of photos. Children, dozens of them, under the heading HAVE YOU SEEN ME? She was wondering how many of them had been taken by the True Knot, murdered for their final psychic gasp—the obscene delicacy this bunch lived on—and left in unmarked graves.

"*You have to get that baseball glove.* If I have it, I'll be able to find out where Barry the Chunk is. I know I will. And the rest of them will be where he is. If you can't kill them, at least you can report them to the police. Get me that glove, Dan, *please.*"

"If it's where you say it is, we'll get it. But in the meantime, Abra, you have to watch yourself."

"I will, but I don't think she'll try sneaking into my head again."

Abra's smile reemerged. In it, Dan saw the take-no-prisoners warrior woman she sometimes pretended to be—Daenerys, or whoever. "If she does, she'll be sorry."

Dan decided to let this go. They had been together on this bench as long as he dared. Longer, really. "I've set up my own security system on your behalf. If you looked into me, I imagine you could find out what it is, but I don't want you to do that. If someone else from this Knot tries to go prospecting in your head—not the woman in the hat, but someone else—they can't find out what you don't know."

"Oh. Okay." He could see her thinking that anyone else who tried that would be sorry, too, and this increased his sense of unease.

"Just . . . if you get in a tight place, yell *Billy* with all your might. Got that?"

(*yes the way you once called for your friend Dick*)

He jumped a little. Abra smiled. "I wasn't peeking; I just—"

"I understand. Now tell me one thing before you go."

"What?"

"Did you really get an A on your bio report?"

4

At quarter to eight on that Monday evening, Rose got a double break on her walkie. It was Crow. "Better get over here, " he said. "It's happening."

The True was standing around Grampa's RV in a silent circle. Rose (now wearing her hat at its accustomed gravity-defying angle) cut through them, pausing to give Andi a hug, then went up the steps, rapped once, and let herself in. Nut was standing with Big Mo and Apron Annie, Grampa's two reluctant nurses. Crow was sitting on the end of the bed. He stood up when Rose came in. He was showing his age this evening. Lines bracketed his mouth, and there were a few threads of white silk in his black hair.

We need to take steam, Rose thought. *And when this is over, we will.*

Grampa Flick was cycling rapidly now: first transparent, then solid again, then transparent. But each transparency was longer, and more of him disappeared. He knew what was happening, Rose saw. His eyes were wide and terrified; his body writhed with the pain of the changes it was going through. She had always allowed herself to believe, on some deep level of her mind, in the True Knot's immortality. Yes, every fifty or a hundred years or so, someone died—like that big dumb Dutchman, Hands-Off Hans, who had been electrocuted by a falling powerline in an Arkansas windstorm not long after World War II ended, or Katie Patches, who had drowned, or Tommy the Truck—but those were exceptions. Usually the ones who fell were taken down by their own carelessness. So she had always believed. Now she saw she had been as foolish as rube children clinging to their belief in Santa Claus and the Easter Bunny.

He cycled back to solidity, moaning and crying and shivering. "Make it stop, Rosie-girl, make it stop. It *hurts*—"

Before she could answer—and really, what could she have said?— he was fading again until there was nothing left of him but a sketch of bones and his staring, floating eyes. They were the worst.

Rose tried to contact him with her mind and comfort him that way, but there was nothing to hold onto. Where Grampa Flick had always been—often grumpy, sometimes sweet—there was now only a roaring windstorm of broken images. Rose withdrew from him, shaken. Again she thought, *This can't be happening.*

"Maybe we should put him out of his miz'y," Big Mo said. She was digging her fingernails into Annie's forearm, but Annie didn't seem to feel it. "Give him a shot, or something. You got something in your bag, don't you, Nut? You must."

"What good would it do?" Walnut's voice was hoarse. "Maybe earlier, but it's going too fast now. He's got no system for any drug to circulate in. If I gave him a hypo in the arm, we'd see it soaking into the bed five seconds later. Best to just let it happen. It won't be long."

Nor was it. Rose counted four more full cycles. On the fifth, even his bones disappeared. For a moment the eyeballs remained, staring first at her and then rolling to look at Crow Daddy. They hung above the pillow, which was still indented by the weight of his head and stained with Wildroot Cream-Oil hair tonic, of which he seemed to have an endless supply. She thought she remembered Greedy G telling her once that he bought it on eBay. eBay, for fuck's sweet sake!

Then, slowly, the eyes disappeared, too. Except of course they weren't really gone; Rose knew she'd be seeing them in her dreams later tonight. So would the others in attendance at Grampa Flick's deathbed. If they got any sleep at all.

They waited, none of them entirely convinced that the old man wouldn't appear before them again like the ghost of Hamlet's father or Jacob Marley or some other, but there was only the shape of his disappeared head, the stains left by his hair tonic, and the deflated pee- and shit-stained boxers he had been wearing.

Mo burst into wild sobs and buried her head in Apron Annie's generous bosom. Those waiting outside heard, and one voice (Rose would never know whose) began to speak. Another joined in, then a third and a fourth. Soon they were all chanting under the stars, and Rose felt a wild chill go zigzagging up her back. She reached out, found Crow's hand, and squeezed it.

Annie joined in. Mo next, her words muffled. Nut. Then Crow. Rose the Hat took a deep breath and added her voice to theirs.

Lodsam hanti, *we are the chosen ones.*

Cahanna risone hanti, *we are the fortunate ones.*

Sabbatha hanti, sabbatha hanti, sabbatha hanti.

We are the True Knot, and we endure.

5

Later, Crow joined her in her EarthCruiser. "You really won't be going east, will you?"

"No. You'll be in charge."

"What do we do now?"

"Mourn him, of course. Unfortunately, we can only give him two days."

The traditional period was seven: no fucking, no idle talk, no steam. Just meditation. Then a circle of farewell where everyone would step forward and say one memory of Grampa Jonas Flick and give up one object they had from him, or that they associated with him (Rose had already picked hers, a ring with a Celtic design Grampa had given her when this part of America had still been Indian country and she had been known as the Irish Rose). There was never a body when a member of the True died, so the objects of remembrance had to serve the purpose. Those things were wrapped in white linen and buried.

"So my group leaves when? Wednesday night or Thursday morning?"

"Wednesday night." Rose wanted the girl as soon as possible. "Drive straight through. And you're positive they'll hold the knockout stuff at the mail drop in Sturbridge?"

"Yes. Set your mind at ease on that."

My mind won't be at ease until I can look at that little bitch lying in the room right across from mine, drugged to the gills, handcuffed, and full of tasty, suckable steam.

"Who are you taking? Name them off."

"Me, Nut, Jimmy Numbers, if you can spare him—"

"I can spare him. Who else?"

"Snakebite Andi. If we need to put someone to sleep, she can get it done. And the Chink. Him for sure. He's the best locator we've got now that Grampa's gone. Other than you, that is."

"By all means take him, but you won't need a locator to find this one," Rose said. "That's not going to be the problem. And just one vehicle will be enough. Take Steamhead Steve's Winnebago."

"Already spoke to him about it."

She nodded, pleased. "One other thing. There's a little hole-in-the-wall store in Sidewinder called District X."

Crow raised his eyebrows. "The porno palace with the inflatable nurse doll in the window?"

"You know it, I see." Rose's tone was dry. "Now listen to me, Daddy."

Crow listened.

6

Dan and John Dalton flew out of Logan on Tuesday morning just as the sun was rising. They changed planes in Memphis and touched down in Des Moines at 11:15 CDT on a day that felt more like mid-July than late September.

Dan spent the first part of the Boston-to-Memphis leg pretending to sleep so he wouldn't have to deal with the doubts and second thoughts he felt sprouting like weeds in John's mind. Somewhere over upstate New York, pretending ceased and he fell asleep for real. It was John who slept between Memphis and Des Moines, so *that* was all right. And once they were actually in Iowa, rolling toward the town of Freeman in a totally unobtrusive Ford Focus from Hertz, Dan sensed that John had put his doubts to bed. For the time being, at least. What had replaced them was curiosity and uneasy excitement.

"Boys on a treasure hunt," Dan said. He'd had the longer nap, and so he was behind the wheel. High corn, now more yellow than green, flowed past them on either side.

John jumped a little. "Huh?"

Dan smiled. "Isn't that what you were thinking? That we're like boys on a treasure hunt?"

"You're pretty goddam spooky, Daniel."

"I suppose. I've gotten used to it." This was not precisely true.

"When did you find out you could read minds?"

"It isn't just mind-reading. The shining's a uniquely variable talent. If it *is* a talent. Sometimes—lots of times—it feels more like a disfiguring birthmark. I'm sure Abra would say the same. As for when I found out . . . I never did. I just always had it. It came with the original equipment."

"And you drank to blot it out."

A fat woodchuck trundled with leisurely fearlessness across Route 150. Dan swerved to avoid it and the chuck disappeared into the corn, still not hurrying. It was nice out here, the sky looking a thousand miles deep and nary a mountain in sight. New Hampshire was fine, and he'd come to think of it as home, but Dan thought he was always going to feel more comfortable in the flatlands. Safer.

"You know better than that, Johnny. Why does any alcoholic drink?"

"Because he's an alcoholic?"

"Bingo. Simple as can be. Cut through the psychobabble and you're left with the stark truth. We drank because we're drunks."

John laughed. "Casey K. has truly indoctrinated you."

"Well, there's also the heredity thing," Dan said. "Casey always kicks that part to the curb, but it's there. Did your father drink?"

"Him and mother dearest both. They could have kept the Nineteenth Hole at the country club in business all by themselves. I remember the day my mother took off her tennis dress and jumped into the pool with us kids. The men applauded. My dad thought it was a scream. Me, not so much. I was nine, and until I went to college I was the boy with the Striptease Mommy. Yours?"

"My mother could take it or leave it alone. Sometimes she used to call herself Two Beers Wendy. My dad, however . . . one glass of wine or can of Bud and he was off to the races." Dan glanced at the odometer and saw they still had forty miles to go. "You want to hear a story? One I've never told anybody? I should warn you, it's a weird one. If you think the shining begins and ends with paltry shit like telepathy, you're way short." He paused. "There are other worlds than these."

"You've . . . um . . . seen these other worlds?" Dan had lost track of John's mind, but DJ suddenly looked a little nervous. As if he thought the guy sitting next to him might suddenly stick his hand in his shirt and declare himself the reincarnation of Napoleon Bonaparte.

"No, just some of the people who live there. Abra calls them the ghostie people. Do you want to hear, or not?"

"I'm not sure I do, but maybe I better."

Dan didn't know how much this New England pediatrician would believe about the winter the Torrance family had spent at the Overlook Hotel, but found he didn't particularly care. Telling it in this nondescript car, under this bright Midwestern sky, would be good enough. There was one person who would have believed it all, but Abra was too young, and the story was too scary. John Dalton would have to do. But how to begin? With Jack Torrance, he supposed. A deeply unhappy man who had failed at teaching, writing, and husbanding. What did the baseball players call three strikeouts in a row? The Golden Sombrero? Dan's father had had only one notable success: when the moment finally came—the one the Overlook had been pushing him toward from their first day in the hotel—he had refused to kill his little boy. If there was a fitting epitaph for him, it would be . . .

"Dan?"

"My father tried," he said. "That's the best I can say for him. The most malevolent spirits in his life came in bottles. If he'd tried AA, things might have been a lot different. But he didn't. I don't think my mother even knew there was such a thing, or she would have suggested he give it a shot. By the time we went up to the Overlook Hotel, where a friend of his got him a job as the winter caretaker, his picture could have been next to *dry drunk* in the dictionary."

"That's where the ghosts were?"

"Yes. I saw them. He didn't, but he felt them. Maybe he had his own shining. Probably he did. Lots of things are hereditary, after all, not just a tendency toward alcoholism. And they worked on him. He thought they—the ghostie people—wanted him, but that was just another lie. What they wanted was the little boy with the great big shine. The same way this True Knot bunch wants Abra."

He stopped, remembering how Dick, speaking through Eleanor

Ouellette's dead mouth, had answered when Dan had asked where the empty devils were. *In your childhood, where every devil comes from.*

"Dan? Are you okay?"

"Yes," Dan said. "Anyway, I knew something was wrong in that goddam hotel even before I stepped through the door. I knew when the three of us were still living pretty much hand-to-mouth down in Boulder, on the Eastern Slope. But my father needed a job so he could finish a play he was working on . . ."

7

By the time they reached Adair, he was telling John how the Overlook's boiler had exploded, and how the old hotel had burned to the ground in a driving blizzard. Adair was a two-stoplight town, but there was a Holiday Inn Express, and Dan noted the location.

"That's where we'll be checking in a couple of hours from now," he told John. "We can't go digging for treasure in broad daylight, and besides, I'm dead for sleep. Haven't been getting much lately."

"All that really happened to you?" John asked in a subdued voice.

"It really did." Dan smiled. "Think you can believe it?"

"If we find the baseball glove where she says it is, I'll have to believe a lot of things. Why did you tell me?"

"Because part of you thinks we're crazy to be here, in spite of what you know about Abra. Also because you deserve to know that there are . . . forces. I've encountered them before; you haven't. All you've seen is a little girl who can do assorted psychic parlor tricks like hanging spoons on the ceiling. This isn't a boys' treasure hunt game, John. If the True Knot finds out what we're up to, we'll be pinned to the target right along with Abra Stone. If you decided to bail on this business, I'd make the sign of the cross in front of you and say go with God."

"And continue on by yourself."

Dan tipped him a grin. "Well . . . there's Billy."

"Billy's seventy-three if he's a day."

"He'd say that's a plus. Billy likes to tell people that the good thing about being old is that you don't have to worry about dying young."

John pointed. "Freeman town line." He gave Dan a small, tight smile. "I can't completely believe I'm doing this. What are you going to think if that ethanol plant is gone? If it's been torn down since Google Earth snapped its picture, and planted over with corn?"

"It'll still be there," Dan said.

8

And so it was: a series of soot-gray concrete blocks roofed in rusty corrugated metal. One smokestack still stood; two others had fallen and lay on the ground like broken snakes. The windows had been smashed and the walls were covered in blotchy spray-paint graffiti that would have been laughed at by the pro taggers in any big city. A potholed service road split off from the two-lane, ending in a parking lot that had sprouted with errant seed corn. The water tower Abra had seen stood nearby, rearing against the horizon like an H. G. Wells Martian war machine. FREEMAN, IOWA was printed on the side. The shed with the broken roof was also present and accounted for.

"Satisfied?" Dan asked. They had slowed to a crawl. "Factory, water tower, shed, No Trespassing sign. All just like she said it would be."

John pointed to the rusty gate at the end of the service road. "What if that's locked? I haven't climbed a chainlink fence since I was in junior high."

"It wasn't locked when killers brought that kid here, or Abra would have said."

"Are you sure of that?"

A farm truck was coming the other way. Dan sped up a little and lifted a hand as they passed. The guy behind the wheel—green John Deere cap, sunglasses, bib overalls—raised his in return but hardly glanced at them. That was a good thing.

"I asked if—"

"I know what you asked," Dan said. "If it's locked, we'll deal with it. Somehow. Now let's go back to that motel and check in. I'm whipped."

9

While John got adjoining rooms at the Holiday Inn—paying cash—Dan sought out the Adair True Value Hardware. He bought a spade, a rake, two hoes, a garden trowel, two pairs of gloves, and a duffel to hold his new purchases. The only tool he actually wanted was the spade, but it seemed best to buy in bulk.

"What brings you to Adair, may I ask?" the clerk asked as he rang up Dan's stuff.

"Just passing through. My sister's in Des Moines, and she's got quite the garden patch. She probably owns most of this stuff, but presents always seem to improve her hospitality."

"I hear *that,* brother. And she'll thank you for this short-handle hoe. No tool comes in handier, and most amateur gardeners never think to get one. We take MasterCard, Visa—"

"I think I'll give the plastic a rest," Dan said, taking out his wallet. "Just give me a receipt for Uncle Sugar."

"You bet. And if you give me your name and address—or your sister's—we'll send our catalogue."

"You know what, I'm going to pass on that today," Dan said, and put a little fan of twenties on the counter.

10

At eleven o'clock that night, there came a soft rap on Dan's door. He opened it and let John inside. Abra's pediatrician was pale and keyed-up. "Did you sleep?"

"Some," Dan said. "You?"

"In and out. Mostly out. I'm nervous as a goddam cat. If a cop stops us, what are we going to say?"

"That we heard there was a juke joint in Freeman and decided to go looking for it."

"There's nothing in Freeman but corn. About nine billion acres of it."

"*We* don't know that," Dan said mildly. "We're just passing through. Besides, no cop's going to stop us, John. Nobody's even going to notice us. But if you want to stay here—"

"I didn't come halfway across the country to sit in a motel watching Jay Leno. Just let me use the toilet. I used mine before I left the room, but now I need to go again. *Christ,* am I nervous."

The drive to Freeman seemed very long to Dan, but once they left Adair behind, they didn't meet a single car. Farmers went to bed early, and they were off the trucking routes.

When they reached the ethanol plant, Dan doused the rental car's lights, turned in to the service road, and rolled slowly up to the closed gate. The two men got out. John cursed when the Ford's dome light came on. "I should have turned that thing off before we left the motel. Or smashed the bulb, if it doesn't have a switch."

"Relax," Dan said. "There's no one out here but us chickens." Still, his heart was beating hard in his chest as they walked to the gate. If Abra was right, a little boy had been murdered and buried out here after being miserably tortured. If ever a place should be haunted—

John tried the gate, and when pushing didn't work, he tried pulling. "Nothing. What now? Climb, I guess. I'm willing to try, but I'll probably break my fucking—"

"Wait." Dan took a penlight from his jacket pocket and shone it on the gate, first noting the broken padlock, then the heavy twists of wire above and below it. He went back to the car, and it was his turn to wince when the trunk light came on. Well, shit. You couldn't think of everything. He yanked out the new duffel, and slammed the trunk lid down. Dark returned.

"Here," he told John, holding out a pair of gloves. "Put these on."

Dan put on his own, untwisted the wire, and hung both pieces in one of the chainlink diamonds for later reference. "Okay, let's go."

"I have to pee again."

"Oh, man. Hold it."

11

Dan drove the Hertz Ford slowly and carefully around to the loading dock. There were plenty of potholes, some deep, all hard to see with the headlights off. The last thing in the world he wanted was to drop the Focus into one and smash an axle. Behind the plant, the surface was a mixture of bare earth and crumbling asphalt. Fifty feet away was another chainlink fence, and beyond that, endless leagues of corn. The dock area wasn't as big as the parking lot, but it was plenty big.

"Dan? How will we know where—"

"Be quiet." Dan bent his head until his brow touched the steering wheel and closed his eyes.

(*Abra*)

Nothing. She was asleep, of course. Back in Anniston it was already Wednesday morning. John sat beside him, chewing his lips.

(*Abra*)

A faint stirring. It could have been his imagination. Dan hoped it was more.

(*ABRA!*)

Eyes opened in his head. There was a moment of disorientation, a kind of double vision, and then Abra was looking with him. The loading dock and the crumbled remains of the smokestacks were suddenly clearer, even though there was only starlight to see by.

Her vision's a hell of a lot better than mine.

Dan got out of the car. So did John, but Dan barely noticed. He had ceded control to the girl who was now lying awake in her bed eleven hundred miles away. He felt like a human metal detector. Only it wasn't metal that he—*they*—were looking for.

(*walk over to that concrete thing*)

Dan walked to the loading dock and stood with his back to it.

(*now start going back and forth*)

A pause as she hunted for a way to clarify what she wanted.

(*like on* CSI)

He coursed fifty feet or so to the left, then turned right, moving out from the dock on opposing diagonals. John had gotten the spade out of the duffel bag and stood by the rental car, watching.

(*here is where they parked their RVs*)

Dan cut back left again, walking slowly, occasionally kicking a loose brick or chunk of concrete out of his way.

(*you're close*)

Dan stopped. He smelled something unpleasant. A gassy whiff of decay.

(*Abra? do you*)

(*yes oh God Dan*)

(*take it easy hon*)

(*you went too far turn around go slow*)

Dan turned on one heel, like a soldier doing a sloppy about-face. He started back toward the loading dock.

(*left a little to your left slower*)

He went that way, now pausing after each small step. Here was that smell again, a little stronger. Suddenly the preternaturally sharp nighttime world began to blur as his eyes filled with Abra's tears.

(*there the baseball boy you're standing right on top of him*)

Dan took a deep breath and wiped at his cheeks. He was shivering. Not because he was cold, but because she was. Sitting up in her bed, clutching her lumpy stuffed rabbit, and shaking like an old leaf on a dead tree.

(*get out of here Abra*)

(*Dan are you*)

(*yes fine but you don't need to see this*)

Suddenly that absolute clarity of vision was gone. Abra had broken the connection, and that was good.

"Dan?" John called, low. "All right?"

"Yes." His voice was still clogged with Abra's tears. "Bring that spade."

12

It took them twenty minutes. Dan dug for the first ten, then passed the spade to John, who actually found Brad Trevor. He turned away from the hole, covering his mouth and nose. His words were muffled but understandable. "Okay, there's a body. *Jesus!*"

"You didn't smell it before?"

"Buried that deep, and after two years? Are you saying that you did?"

Dan didn't reply, so John addressed the hole again, but without conviction this time. He stood for a few seconds with his back bent as if he still meant to use the spade, then straightened and drew back when Dan shone the penlight into the little excavation they had made. "I can't," he said. "I thought I could, but I can't. Not with . . . that. My arms feel like rubber."

Dan handed him the light. John shone it into the hole, centering the beam on what had freaked him out: a dirt-clotted sneaker. Working slowly, not wanting to disturb the earthly remains of Abra's baseball boy any more than necessary, Dan scraped dirt away from the sides of the body. Little by little, an earth-covered shape emerged. It reminded him of the carvings on sarcophagi he had seen in *National Geographic*.

The smell of decay was now very strong.

Dan stepped away and hyperventilated, ending with the deepest breath he could manage. Then he dropped into the end of the shallow grave, where both of Brad Trevor's sneakers now protruded in a V. He knee-walked up to about where he thought the boy's waist must be, then held up a hand for the penlight. John handed it over and turned away. He was sobbing audibly.

Dan clamped the slim flashlight between his lips and began

brushing away more dirt. A child's t-shirt came into view, clinging to a sunken chest. Then hands. The fingers, now little more than bones wrapped in yellow skin, were clasped over something. Dan's chest was starting to pound for air now, but he pried the Trevor boy's fingers apart as gently as he could. Still, one of them snapped with a dry crunching sound.

They had buried him holding his baseball glove to his chest. Its lovingly oiled pocket was full of squirming bugs.

The air escaped Dan's lungs in a shocked *whoosh,* and the breath he inhaled to replace it was rich with rot. He lunged out of the grave to his right, managing to vomit on the dirt they'd taken out of the hole instead of on the wasted remains of Bradley Trevor, whose only crime had been to be born with something a tribe of monsters wanted. And had stolen from him on the very wind of his dying shrieks.

13

They reburied the body, John doing most of the work this time, and covered the spot with a makeshift crypt of broken asphalt chunks. Neither of them wanted to think of foxes or stray dogs feasting on what scant meat was left.

When they were done, they got back into the car and sat without speaking. At last John said, "What are we going to do about him, Danno? We can't just leave him. He's got parents. Grandparents. Probably brothers and sisters. All of them still wondering."

"He has to stay awhile. Long enough so nobody's going to say, 'Gee, that anonymous call came in just after some stranger bought a spade in the Adair hardware store.' That probably wouldn't happen, but we can't take the chance."

"How long's awhile?"

"Maybe a month."

John considered this, then sighed. "Maybe even two. Give his folks that long to go on thinking he might just have run off. Give them that long before we break their hearts." He shook his head. "If I'd had to look at his face, I don't think I ever could have slept again."

"You'd be surprised what a person can live with," Dan said. He was thinking of Mrs. Massey, now safely stored away in the back of his head, her haunting days over. He started the car, powered down his window, and beat the baseball glove several times against the door to dislodge the dirt. Then he put it on, sliding his fingers into the places where the child's had been on so many sunlit afternoons. He closed his eyes. After thirty seconds or so, he opened them again.

"Anything?"

"'You're Barry. You're one of the good guys.'"

"What does that mean?"

"I don't know, except I'm betting he's the one Abra calls Barry the Chunk."

"Nothing else?"

"Abra will be able to get more."

"Are you sure of that?"

Dan thought of the way his vision had sharpened when Abra opened her eyes inside his head. "I am. Shine your light on the pocket of the glove for a sec, will you? There's something written there."

John did it, revealing a child's careful printing: **THOME 25**.

"What does that mean?" John asked. "I thought his name was Trevor."

"Jim Thome's a baseball player. His number is twenty-five." He stared into the pocket of the glove for a moment, then laid it gently on the seat between them. "He was that kid's favorite Major Leaguer. He named his glove after him. I'm going to get these fuckers. I swear before God Almighty, I'm going to get them and make them sorry."

14

Rose the Hat shone—the entire True shone—but not in the way Dan or Billy did. Neither Rose nor Crow had any sense, as they said their goodbyes, that the child they had taken years ago in Iowa was at that moment being uncovered by two men who knew far too much about them already. Rose could have caught the communications flying between Dan and Abra if she had been in a state of deep meditation, but of course then the little girl would have noticed her presence immediately. Besides, the goodbyes going on in Rose's EarthCruiser that night were of an especially intimate sort.

She lay with her fingers laced together behind her head and watched Crow dress. "You visited that store, right? District X?"

"Not me personally, I have a reputation to protect. I sent Jimmy Numbers." Crow grinned as he buckled his belt. "He could've gotten what we needed in fifteen minutes, but he was gone for two hours. I think Jimmy's found a new home."

"Well, that's good. I hope you boys enjoy yourselves." Trying to keep it light, but after two days of mourning Grampa Flick, climaxed by the circle of farewell, keeping anything light was an effort.

"He didn't get anything that compares to you."

She raised her eyebrows. "Had a preview, did you, Henry?"

"Didn't need one." He eyed her as she lay naked with her hair spread out in a dark fan. She was tall, even lying down. He had ever liked tall women. "You're the feature attraction in my home theater and always will be."

Overblown—just a bit of Crow's patented razzle-dazzle—but it pleased her just the same. She got up and pressed against him, her hands in his hair. "Be careful. Bring everyone back. And bring *her*."

"We will."

"Then you better get a wiggle on."

"Relax. We'll be in Sturbridge when EZ Mail Services opens on Friday morning. In New Hampshire by noon. By then, Barry will have located her."

"As long as *she* doesn't locate *him*."

"I'm not worried about that."

Fine, Rose thought. *I'll worry for both of us. I'll worry until I'm looking at her wearing cuffs on her wrists and clamps on her ankles.*

"The beauty of it," Crow said, "is that if she *does* sense us and tries to put up an interference wall, Barry will key on that."

"If she's scared enough, she might go to the police."

He flashed a grin. "You think? 'Yes, little girl,' they'd say, 'we're sure these awful people are after you. So tell us if they're from outer space or just your ordinary garden variety zombies. That way we'll know what to look for.'"

"Don't joke, and don't take this lightly. Get in clean and get out the same way, that's how it has to be. No outsiders involved. No innocent bystanders. Kill the parents if you need to, kill *anyone* who tries to interfere, but keep it quiet."

Crow snapped off a comic salute. "Yes, my captain."

"Get out of here, idiot. But give me another kiss first. Maybe a little of that educated tongue, for good measure."

He gave her what she asked for. Rose held him tight, and for a long time.

15

Dan and John rode in silence most of the way back to the motel in Adair. The spade was in the trunk. The baseball glove was in the backseat, wrapped in a Holiday Inn towel. At last John said, "We've got to bring Abra's folks into this now. She's going to hate it and Lucy and David won't want to believe it, but it has to be done."

Dan looked at him, straight-faced, and said: "What are you, a mind-reader?"

John wasn't, but Abra was, and her sudden loud voice in Dan's head made him glad that this time John was driving. If he had been behind the wheel, they very likely would have ended up in some farmer's cornpatch.

(*NOOOOO!*)

"Abra." He spoke aloud so that John could hear at least his half of the conversation. "Abra, listen to me."

(*NO, DAN! THEY THINK I'M ALL RIGHT! THEY THINK I'M ALMOST NORMAL NOW!*)

"Honey, if these people had to kill your mom and dad to get to you, do you think they'd hesitate? I sure don't. Not after what we found back there."

There was no counterargument she could make to this, and Abra didn't try . . . but suddenly Dan's head was filled with her sorrow and her fear. His eyes welled up again and spilled tears down his cheeks.

Shit.

Shit, shit, *shit.*

16

Early Thursday morning.

Steamhead Steve's Winnebago, with Snakebite Andi currently behind the wheel, was cruising eastbound on I-80 in western Nebraska at a perfectly legal sixty-five miles an hour. The first streaks of dawn had just begun to show on the horizon. In Anniston it was two hours later. Dave Stone was in his bathrobe making coffee when the phone rang. It was Lucy, calling from Concetta's Marlborough Street condo. She sounded like a woman who had nearly reached the end of her resources.

"If nothing changes for the worse—although I guess that's the only way things *can* change now—they'll be releasing Momo from the hospital first thing next week. I talked with the two doctors on her case last night."

"Why didn't you call me, sweetheart?"

"Too tired. And too depressed. I thought I'd feel better after a night's sleep, but I didn't get much. Honey, this place is just so full of her. Not just her work, her *vitality* . . ."

Her voice wavered. David waited. They had been together for

over fifteen years, and he knew that when Lucy was upset, waiting was sometimes better than talking.

"I don't know what we're going to *do* with it all. Just looking at the books makes me tired. There are thousands on the shelves and stacked in her study, and the super says there are thousands more in storage."

"We don't have to decide right now."

"He says there's also a trunk marked *Alessandra*. That was my mother's real name, you know, although I guess she always called herself Sandra or Sandy. I never knew Momo had her stuff."

"For someone who let it all hang out in her poetry, Chetta could be one closemouthed lady when she wanted to."

Lucy seemed not to hear him, only continued in the same dull, slightly nagging, tired-to-death tone. "Everything's arranged, although I'll have to reschedule the private ambulance if they decide to let her go Sunday. They said they might. Thank God she's got good insurance. That goes back to her teaching days at Tufts, you know. She never made a dime from poetry. Who in this fucked-up country would pay a dime to *read* it anymore?"

"Lucy—"

"She's got a good place in the main building at Rivington House—a little suite. I took the online tour. Not that she'll be using it long. I made friends with the head nurse on her floor here, and she says Momo's just about at the end of her—"

"Chia, I love you, honey."

That—Concetta's old nickname for her—finally stopped her.

"With all my admittedly non-Italian heart and soul."

"I know, and thank God you do. This has been so hard, but it's almost over. I'll be there Monday at the very latest."

"We can't wait to see you."

"How are you? How's Abra?"

"We're both fine." David would be allowed to go on believing this for another sixty seconds or so.

He heard Lucy yawn. "I might go back to bed for an hour or two. I think I can sleep now."

"You do that. I've got to get Abs up for school."

They said their goodbyes, and when Dave turned away from the kitchen wall phone, he saw that Abra was already up. She was still in her pajamas. Her hair was every whichway, her eyes were red, and her face was pale. She was clutching Hoppy, her old stuffed rabbit.

"Abba-Doo? Honey? Are you sick?"

Yes. No. I don't know. But you will be, when you hear what I'm going to tell you.

"I need to talk to you, Daddy. And I don't want to go to school today. Tomorrow, either. Maybe not for awhile." She hesitated. "I'm in trouble."

The first thing that phrase brought to mind was so awful that he pushed it away at once, but not before Abra caught it.

She smiled wanly. "No, I'm not pregnant."

He stopped on his way to her, halfway across the kitchen, his mouth falling open. "You . . . did you just—"

"Yes," she said. "I just read your mind. Although anyone could have guessed what you were thinking that time, Daddy—it was all over your face. And it's called shining, not mind-reading. I can still do most of the things that used to scare you when I was little. Not all, but most."

He spoke very slowly. "I know you still sometimes have premonitions. Your mom and I both know."

"It's a lot more than that. I have a friend. His name is Dan. He and Dr. John have been in Iowa—"

"John Dalton?"

"Yes—"

"Who's this Dan? Is he a kid Dr. John treats?"

"No, he's a grown-up." She took his hand and led him to the kitchen table. There they sat down, Abra still holding Hoppy. "But when he was a kid, he was like me."

"Abs, I'm not understanding any of this."

"There are bad people, Daddy." She knew she couldn't tell him they were more than people, *worse* than people, until Dan and John were here to help her explain. "They might want to hurt me."

315

"Why would anyone want to hurt you? You're not making sense. As for all those things you used to do, if you could still do them, we'd kn—"

The drawer below the hanging pots flew open, then shut, then opened again. She could no longer lift the spoons, but the drawer was enough to get his attention.

"Once I understood how much it worried you guys—how much it scared you—I hid it. But I can't hide it anymore. Dan says I have to tell."

She pressed her face against Hoppy's threadbare fur and began to cry.

CHAPTER TWELVE

THEY CALL IT STEAM

1

John turned on his cell as soon as he and Dan emerged from the jetway at Logan Airport late Thursday afternoon. He had no more than registered the fact that he had well over a dozen missed calls when the phone rang in his hand. He glanced down at the window.

"Stone?" Dan asked.

"I've got a lot of missed calls from the same number, so I'd say it has to be."

"Don't answer. Call him back when we're on the expressway north and tell him we'll be there by—" Dan glanced at his watch, which he had never changed from Eastern Time. "By six. When we get there, we'll tell him everything."

John reluctantly pocketed his cell. "I spent the flight back hoping I'm not going to lose my license to practice over this. Now I'm just hoping the cops don't grab us as soon as we park in front of Dave Stone's house."

Dan, who had consulted several times with Abra on their way back across the country, shook his head. "She's convinced him to wait, but there's a lot going on in that family just now, and Mr. Stone is one confused American."

To this, John offered a smile of singular bleakness. "He's not the only one."

2

Abra was sitting on the front step with her father when Dan swung into the Stones' driveway. They had made good time; it was only five thirty.

Abra was up before Dave could grab her and came running down the walk with her hair flying out behind her. Dan saw she was heading for him, and handed the towel-wrapped fielder's mitt to John. She threw herself into his arms. She was trembling all over.

(*you found him you found him and you found the glove give it to me*)

"Not yet," Dan said, setting her down. "We need to thrash this out with your dad first."

"Thrash what out?" Dave asked. He took Abra by the wrist and pulled her away from Dan. "Who are these bad people she's talking about? And who the hell are you?" His gaze shifted to John, and there was nothing friendly in his eyes. "What in the name of sweet Jesus is going on here?"

"This is Dan, Daddy. He's like me. I *told* you."

John said, "Where's Lucy? Does she know about this?"

"I'm not telling you anything until I find out what's going on."

Abra said, "She's still in Boston, with Momo. Daddy wanted to call her, but I persuaded him to wait until you got here." Her eyes remained pinned on the towel-wrapped glove.

"Dan Torrance," Dave said. "That your name?"

"Yes."

"You work at the hospice in Frazier?"

"That's right."

"How long have you been meeting my daughter?" His hands were clenching and unclenching. "Did you meet her on the internet? I'm betting that's it." He switched his gaze to John. "If you hadn't been Abra's pediatrician from the day she was born, I would have called the police six hours ago, when you didn't answer your phone."

"I was in an airplane," John said. "I couldn't."

"Mr. Stone," Dan said. "I haven't known your daughter as long as

John has, but almost. The first time I met her, she was just a baby. And it was she who reached out to me."

Dave shook his head. He looked perplexed, angry, and little inclined to believe anything Dan told him.

"Let's go in the house," John said. "I think we can explain everything—*almost* everything—and if that's the case, you'll be very happy that we're here, and that we went to Iowa to do what we did."

"I damn well hope so, John, but I've got my doubts."

They went inside, Dave with his arm around Abra's shoulders— at that moment they looked more like jailer and prisoner than father and daughter—John Dalton next, Dan last. He looked across the street at the rusty red pickup parked there. Billy gave him a quick thumbs-up . . . then crossed his fingers. Dan returned the gesture, and followed the others through the front door.

3

As Dave was sitting down in his Richland Court living room with his puzzling daughter and his even more puzzling guests, the Winnebago containing the True raiding party was southeast of Toledo. Walnut was at the wheel. Andi Steiner and Barry were sleeping—Andi like the dead, Barry rolling from side to side and muttering. Crow was in the parlor area, paging through *The New Yorker*. The only things he really liked were the cartoons and the tiny ads for weird items like yak-fur sweaters, Vietnamese coolie hats, and faux Cuban cigars.

Jimmy Numbers plunked down next to him with his laptop in hand. "I've been combing the 'net. Had to hack and back with a couple of sites, but . . . can I show you something?"

"How can you surf the 'net from an interstate highway?"

Jimmy gave him a patronizing smile. "4G connection, baby. This is the modern age."

"If you say so." Crow put his magazine aside. "What've you got?"

"School pictures from Anniston Middle School." Jimmy tapped

the touchpad and a photo appeared. No grainy newsprint job, but a high-res school portrait of a girl in a red dress with puffed sleeves. Her braided hair was chestnut brown, her smile wide and confident.

"Julianne Cross," Jimmy said. He tapped the touchpad again and a redhead with a mischievous grin popped up. "Emma Deane." Another tap, and an even prettier girl appeared. Blue eyes, blond hair framing her face and spilling over her shoulders. Serious expression, but dimples hinting at a smile. "This one's Abra Stone."

"Abra?"

"Yeah, they name em anything these days. Remember when Jane and Mabel used to be good enough for the rubes? I read somewhere that Sly Stallone named his kid Sage Moonblood, how fucked up is that?"

"You think one of these three is Rose's girl."

"If she's right about the girl being a young teenager, it just about has to be. Probably Deane or Stone, they're the two who actually live on the street where the little earthquake was, but you can't count the Cross girl out completely. She's just around the corner." Jimmy Numbers made a swirling gesture on the touchpad and the three pictures zipped into a row. Written below each in curly script was **MY SCHOOL MEMORIES**.

Crow studied them. "Is anyone going to tip to the fact that you've been filching pictures of little girls off of Facebook, or something? Because that sets off all kinds of warning bells in Rubeland."

Jimmy looked offended. "Facebook, my ass. These came from the Frazier Middle School files, pipelined direct from their computer to mine." He made an unlovely sucking sound. "And guess what, a guy with access to a whole bank of NSA computers couldn't follow my tracks on this one. Who rocks?"

"You do," Crow said. "I guess."

"Which one do you think it is?"

"If I had to pick . . ." Crow tapped Abra's picture. "She's got a certain look in her eyes. A *steamy* look."

Jimmy puzzled over this for a moment, decided it was dirty, and guffawed. "Does it help?"

"Yes. Can you print these pictures and make sure the others have copies? Particularly Barry. He's Locator in Chief on this one."

"I'll do it right now. I'm packing a Fujitsu ScanSnap. Great little on-the-go machine. I used to have the S1100, but I swapped it when I read in *Computerworld*—"

"Just do it, okay?"

"Sure."

Crow picked up the magazine again and turned to the cartoon on the last page, the one where you were supposed to fill in the caption. This week's showed an elderly woman walking into a bar with a bear on a chain. She had her mouth open, so the caption had to be her dialogue. Crow considered carefully, then printed: *"Okay, which one of you assholes called me a cunt?"*

Probably not a winner.

The Winnebago rolled on through the deepening evening. In the cockpit, Nut turned on the headlights. In one of the bunks, Barry the Chink turned and scratched at his wrist in his sleep. A red spot had appeared there.

4

The three men sat in silence while Abra went upstairs to get something in her room. Dave thought of suggesting coffee—they looked tired, and both men needed a shave—but decided he wasn't going to offer either of them so much as a dry Saltine until he got an explanation. He and Lucy had discussed what they were going to do when Abra came home some day in the not-too-distant future and announced that a boy had asked her out, but these were men, *men,* and it seemed that the one he didn't know had been dating his daughter for quite some time. After a fashion, anyway . . . and wasn't that really the question: What *sort* of fashion?

Before any of them could risk starting a conversation that was bound to be awkward—and perhaps acrimonious—there came the muted thunder of Abra's sneakers on the stairs. She came into the room with a copy of *The Anniston Shopper*. "Look at the back page."

Dave turned the newspaper over and grimaced. "What's this brown dreck?"

"Dried coffee grounds. I threw the newspaper in the trash, but I couldn't stop thinking about it, so I fished it out again. I couldn't stop thinking about *him*." She pointed to the picture of Bradley Trevor in the bottom row. "And his parents. And his brothers and sisters, if he had them." Her eyes filled with tears. "He had freckles, Daddy. He hated them, but his mother said they were good luck."

"You can't know that," Dave said with no conviction at all.

"She knows," John said, "and so do you. Get with us on this, Dave. Please. It's important."

"I want to know about you and my daughter," Dave said to Dan. "Tell me about that."

Dan went through it again. Doodling Abra's name in his AA meeting book. The first chalked hello. His clear sense of Abra's presence on the night Charlie Hayes died. "I asked if she was the little girl who sometimes wrote on my blackboard. She didn't answer in words, but there was a little run of piano music. Some old Beatles tune, I think."

Dave looked at John. "You told him about that!"

John shook his head.

Dan said, "Two years ago I got a blackboard message from her that said, 'They are killing the baseball boy.' I didn't know what it meant, and I'm not sure Abra did, either. That might have been the end of it, but then she saw *that*." He pointed to the back page of *The Anniston Shopper* with all those postage-stamp portraits.

Abra told the rest.

When she was done, Dave said: "So you flew to Iowa on a thirteen-year-old girl's sayso."

"A very special thirteen-year-old girl," John said. "With some very special talents."

"We thought all that was over." Dave shot Abra an accusing look. "Except for a few little premonitions, we thought she outgrew it."

"I'm sorry, Daddy." Her voice was little more than a whisper.

"Maybe she shouldn't *have* to be sorry," Dan said, hoping he didn't sound as angry as he felt. "She hid her ability because she knew you and your wife wanted it to be gone. She hid it because she loves you and wanted to be a good daughter."

"She told you that, I suppose?"

"We never even discussed it," Dan said. "But I had a mother I loved dearly, and because I did, I did the same thing."

Abra shot him a look of naked gratitude. As she lowered her eyes again, she sent him a thought. Something she was embarrassed to say out loud.

"She also didn't want her friends to know. She thought they wouldn't like her anymore. That they'd be scared of her. She was probably right about that, too."

"Let's not lose sight of the major issue," John said. "We flew to Iowa, yes. We found the ethanol plant in the town of Freeman, just where Abra said it would be. We found the boy's body. And his glove. He wrote the name of his favorite baseball player in the pocket, but *his* name—Brad Trevor—is written on the strap."

"He was murdered. That's what you're saying. By a bunch of wandering lunatics."

"They ride in campers and Winnebagos," Abra said. Her voice was low and dreamy. She was looking at the towel-wrapped baseball glove as she spoke. She was afraid of it, and she wanted to put her hands on it. These conflicting emotions came through to Dan so clearly that they made him feel sick to his stomach. "They have funny names, like pirate names."

Almost plaintively, Dave asked, "Are you *sure* the kid was murdered?"

"The woman in the hat licked his blood off her hands," Abra said. She had been sitting on the stairs. Now she went to her father and put her face against his chest. "When she wants it, she has a special tooth. All of them do."

"This kid was really like you?"

"Yes." Abra's voice was muffled but understandable. "He could see through his hand."

"What does that mean?"

"Like when certain pitches would come, he could hit them because his hand saw them first. And when his mother lost something, he'd put his hand over his eyes and look through it to see where the thing was. I think. I don't know that part for sure, but sometimes I use my hand that way."

"And that's why they killed him?"

"I'm sure of it," Dan said.

"For what? Some kind of ESP vitamin? Do you know how ridiculous that sounds?"

No one replied.

"And they know Abra's on to them?"

"They know." She raised her head. Her cheeks were flushed and wet with tears. "They don't know my name or where I live, but they know there *is* a me."

"Then we need to go to the police," Dave said. "Or maybe . . . I guess we'd want the FBI in a case like this. They might have trouble believing it at first, but if the body's there—"

Dan said, "I won't tell you that's a bad idea until we see what Abra can do with the baseball glove, but you need to think pretty carefully about the consequences. For me, for John, for you and your wife, and most of all for Abra."

"I don't see what kind of trouble you and John could possibly—"

John shifted impatiently in his chair. "Come on, David. Who found the body? Who dug it up and then buried it again, after taking a piece of evidence the forensics people would no doubt consider vital? Who brought that piece of evidence halfway across the country so an eighth-grader could use it like a Ouija board?"

Although he hadn't meant to, Dan joined in. They were ganging up, and in other circumstances he might have felt bad about that, but not in these. "Your family's already in crisis, Mr. Stone. Your grandmother-in-law is dying, your wife's grieving and exhausted. This thing will hit the newspapers and the internet like a bomb. Wandering clan of murderers versus a supposedly psychic little girl. They'll want her on TV, you'll say no, and that will just make them hungrier. Your street will turn into an open-air studio, Nancy Grace will probably move in next door, and in a week or two the whole media mob will be yelling *hoax* at the top of its lungs. Remember Balloon Boy Dad? That's apt to be you. Meanwhile, these folks will still be out there."

"So who's supposed to protect my little girl if they come after her? You two? A doctor and a hospice orderly? Or are you just a janitor?"

You don't even know about the seventy-three-year-old groundskeeper standing watch down the street, Dan thought, and had to smile. "I'm a little of both. Look, Mr. Stone—"

"Seeing as how you and my daughter are great pals, I guess you better call me Dave."

"Okay, Dave it is. I guess what you do next depends on whether or not you're willing to gamble on law enforcement believing her. Especially when she tells them that the Winnebago People are life-sucking vampires."

"Christ," Dave said. "I can't tell Lucy about this. She'll blow a fuse. *All* her fuses."

"That would seem to answer the question about whether or not to call the police," John remarked.

There was silence for a moment. Somewhere in the house a clock was ticking. Somewhere outside, a dog was barking.

"The earthquake," Dave said suddenly. "That little earthquake. Was that you, Abby?"

"I'm pretty sure," she whispered.

Dave hugged her, then stood up and took the towel off the baseball glove. He held it, looking it over. "They buried him with it," he said. "They abducted him, tortured him, murdered him, and then buried him with his baseball glove."

"Yes," Dan said.

Dave turned to his daughter. "Do you really want to touch this thing, Abra?"

She held out her hands and said, "No. But give it to me anyway."

5

David Stone hesitated, then handed it over. Abra took it in her hands and looked into the pocket. "Jim Thome," she said, and although Dan would have been willing to bet his savings (after twelve years of steady work and steady sobriety, he actually had some) that she had never encountered the name before, she said it correctly: *Toe-me*. "He's in the Six Hundred Club."

"That's right," Dave said. "He—"

"Hush," Dan said.

They watched her. She raised the glove to her face and sniffed the pocket. (Dan, remembering the bugs, had to restrain a wince.) She said, "Not Barry the Chunk, Barry the *Chink*. Only he's not Chinese. They call him that because his eyes slant up at the corners. He's their . . . their . . . I don't know . . . wait . . ."

She held the glove to her chest, like a baby. She began to breathe faster. Her mouth dropped open and she moaned. Dave, alarmed, put a hand on her shoulder. Abra shook him off. "No, Daddy, *no!*" She closed her eyes and hugged the glove. They waited.

At last her eyes opened and she said, "They're coming for me."

Dan got up, knelt beside her, and put one hand over both of hers.

(*how many is it some or is it all of them*)

"Just some. Barry's with them. That's why I can see. There are three others. Maybe four. One is a lady with a snake tattoo. They call us rubes. We're rubes to them."

(*is the woman with the hat*)

(*no*)

"When will they get here?" John asked. "Do you know?"

"Tomorrow. They have to stop first and get . . ." She paused. Her eyes searched the room, not seeing it. One hand slipped out from beneath Dan's and began to rub her mouth. The other clasped the glove. "They have to . . . I don't know . . ." Tears began to ooze from the corners of her eyes, not of sadness but of effort. "Is it medicine? Is it . . . wait, wait, let go of me, Dan, I have to . . . you have to let me . . ."

He took his hand away. There was a brisk snap and a blue flick of static electricity. The piano played a discordant run of notes. On an occasional table by the door to the hall, a number of ceramic Hummel figures were jittering and rapping. Abra slipped the glove on her hand. Her eyes flew wide open.

"One is a crow! One is a doctor and that's lucky for them because Barry is sick! He's sick!" She stared around at them wildly, then laughed. The sound of it made Dan's neck hairs stiffen. He thought it was the way lunatics must laugh when their medication is late. It was all he could do not to snatch the glove off her hand.

"He's got the measles! He's caught the measles from Grampa Flick and he'll start to cycle soon! It was that fucking kid! He must never have gotten the shot! We have to tell Rose! We have to—"

That was enough for Dan. He pulled the glove from her hand and threw it across the room. The piano ceased. The Hummels gave one final clatter and grew still, one of them on the verge of tumbling from the table. Dave was staring at his daughter with his mouth open. John had risen to his feet, but seemed incapable of moving any further.

Dan took Abra by the shoulders and gave her a hard shake. "Abra, snap out of it."

She stared at him with huge, floating eyes.

(come back Abra it's okay)

Her shoulders, which had been almost up to her ears, gradually relaxed. Her eyes were seeing him again. She let out a long breath and fell back against her father's encircling arm. The collar of her t-shirt was dark with sweat.

"Abby?" Dave asked. "Abba-Doo? Are you all right?"

"Yes, but don't call me that." She drew in air and let it out in another long sigh. "God, that was intense." She looked at her father. "I didn't drop the f-bomb, Daddy, that was one of them. I think it was the crow. He's the leader of the ones who are coming."

Dan sat down beside Abra on the couch. "Sure you're okay?"

"Yes. Now. But I never want to touch that glove again. They're not like us. They look like people and I think they used to be people, but now they have lizardy thoughts."

"You said Barry has measles. Do you remember that?"

"Barry, yes. The one they call the Chink. I remember everything. I'm so thirsty."

"I'll get you water," John said.

"No, something with sugar in it. Please."

"There are Cokes in the fridge," Dave said. He stroked Abra's hair, then the side of her face, then the back of her neck. As if to reassure himself that she was still there.

They waited until John came back with a can of Coke. Abra seized it, drank greedily, then belched. "Sorry," she said, and giggled.

Dan had never been so happy to hear a giggle in his life. "John. Measles are more serious in adults, yes?"

"You bet. It can lead to pneumonia, even blindness, due to corneal scarring."

"Death?"

"Sure, but it's rare."

"It's different for them," Abra said, "because I don't think they usually get sick. Only Barry *is*. They're going to stop and get a package. It must be medicine for him. The kind you give in shots."

"What did you mean about cycling?" Dave asked.

"I don't know."

"If Barry's sick, will that stop them?" John asked. "Will they maybe turn around and go back to wherever they came from?"

"I don't think so. They might already be sick from Barry, and they know it. They have nothing to lose and everything to gain, that's what Crow says." She drank more Coke, holding the can in both hands, then looked around at each of the three men in turn, ending with her father. "They know my street. And they might know my name, after all. They might even have a picture. I'm not sure. Barry's mind is all messed up. But they think . . . they think if I can't catch the measles . . ."

"Then your essence might be able to cure them," Dan said. "Or at least inoculate the others."

"They don't call it essence," Abra said. "They call it steam."

Dave clapped his hands once, briskly. "That's it. I'm calling the police. We'll have these people arrested."

"You can't." Abra spoke in the dull voice of a depressed fifty-year-old woman. *Do what you want,* that voice said. *I'm only telling you.*

He had taken his cell out of his pocket, but instead of opening it, he held it. "Why not?"

"They'll have a good story for why they're traveling to New Hampshire and lots of good identity things. Also, they're rich. *Really* rich, the way banks and oil companies and Walmart are rich. They might go away, but they'll come back. They always come back for what they want. They kill people who get in their way, and people who try to tell on them, and if they need to buy their way out of trouble, that's what they do." She put her Coke down on the coffee table and put her arms around her father. "Please, Daddy, don't tell *anybody*. I'd rather go with them than have them hurt Mom or you."

Dan said, "But right now there are only four or five of them."

"Yes."

"Where are the rest? Do you know that now?"

"At a place called the Bluebird Campground. Or maybe it's Bluebell. They own it. There's a town nearby. That's where the supermarket is, the Sam's. The town is called Sidewinder. Rose is there, and the True. That's what they call themselves, the . . . Dan? What's wrong?"

Dan made no reply. For the moment, at least, he was incapable of speech. He was remembering Dick Hallorann's voice coming from Eleanor Ouellette's dead mouth. He had asked Dick where the empty devils were, and now the answer made sense.

In your childhood.

"Dan?" That was John. He sounded far away. "You're as white as a sheet."

It all made a weird kind of sense. He had known from the first—even before he actually saw it—that the Overlook Hotel was an evil place. It was gone now, burned flat, but who was to say the evil had also been burned away? Certainly not him. As a child, he had been visited by revenants who had escaped.

This campground they own—it stands where the hotel stood. I know it. And sooner or later, I'll have to go back there. I know that, too. Probably sooner. But first—

"I'm all right," he said.

"Want a Coke?" Abra asked. "Sugar solves lots of problems, that's what I think."

"Later. I have an idea. It's sketchy, but maybe the four of us working together can turn it into a plan."

6

Snakebite Andi parked in the truckers' lot of a turnpike rest area near Westfield, New York. Nut went into the service plaza to get juice for Barry, who was now running a fever and had a painfully sore throat. While they waited for him to come back, Crow put through a call to Rose. She answered on the first ring. He filled her in as quickly as he could, then waited.

"What's that I hear in the background?" she asked.

Crow sighed and rubbed one hand up a stubbled cheek. "That's Jimmy Numbers. He's crying."

"Tell him to shut up. Tell him there's no crying in baseball."

Crow conveyed this, omitting Rose's peculiar sense of humor. Jimmy, at the moment wiping Barry's face with a damp cloth, managed to muffle his loud and (Crow had to admit it) annoying sobs.

"That's better," Rose said.

"What do you want us to do?"

"Give me a second, I'm trying to think."

Crow found the idea of Rose having to *try* to think almost as disturbing as the red spots that had now broken out all over Barry's face and body, but he did as he was told, holding the iPhone to his ear but saying nothing. He was sweating. Fever, or just hot in here? Crow scanned his arms for red blemishes and saw none. Yet.

"Are you on schedule?" Rose asked.

"So far, yes. A little ahead, even."

There was a brisk double rap at the door. Andi looked out, then opened it.

"Crow? Still there?"

"Yes. Nut just came back with some juice for Barry. He's got a bad sore throat."

"Try this," Walnut said to Barry, unscrewing the cap. "It's apple. Still cold from the cooler. It'll soothe your gullet something grand."

Barry got up on his elbows and gulped when Nut tipped the small glass bottle to his lips. Crow found it hard to look at. He'd seen baby lambs drink from nursing bottles in that same weak, I-can't-do-it-myself way.

"Can he talk, Crow? If he can, give him the phone."

Crow elbowed Jimmy aside and sat down beside Barry. "Rose. She wants to talk to you."

He attempted to hold the phone next to Barry's ear, but the Chink took it from him. Either the juice or the aspirin Nut had made him swallow seemed to have given him some strength.

"Rose," he croaked. "Sorry about this, darlin." He listened, nodding. "I know. I get that. I . . ." He listened some more. "No, not yet, but . . . yeah. I can. I will. Yeah. I love you, too. Here he is." He handed the phone to Crow, then collapsed back onto the stacked pillows, his temporary burst of strength exhausted.

"I'm here," Crow said.

"Has he started cycling yet?"

Crow glanced at Barry. "No."

"Thank God for small favors. He says he can still locate her. I hope he's right. If he can't, you'll have to find her yourselves. *We have to have that girl.*"

Crow knew she wanted the kid—maybe Julianne, maybe Emma, probably Abra—for her own reasons, and for him that was enough, but there was more at stake. Maybe the True's continued survival. In a whispered consultation at the back of the Winnebago, Nut had told Crow that the girl had probably *never* had the measles, but her steam might still serve to protect them, because of the inoculations she would have been given as a baby. It wasn't a sure bet, but a hell of a lot better than no bet at all.

"Crow? Talk to me, honey."

"We'll find her." He shot the True's computer maven a look. "Jimmy's got it narrowed down to three possibles, all in a one-block radius. We've got pictures."

"That's *excellent*." She paused, and when she spoke again her voice was lower, warmer, and perhaps the slightest bit shaky. Crow hated the idea of Rose being afraid, but he thought she was. Not for herself, but for the True Knot it was her duty to protect. "You know I'd never send you on with Barry sick if I didn't think it was absolutely vital."

"Yeah."

"Get her, knock her the fuck out, bring her back. Okay?"

"Okay."

"If the rest of you get sick, if you feel you have to charter a jet and fly her back—"

"We'll do that, too." But Crow dreaded the prospect. Any of them not sick when they got on the plane would be when they got off—equilibrium shot, hearing screwed blue for a month or more, palsy, vomiting. And of course flying left a paper trail. Not good for passengers escorting a drugged and kidnapped little girl. Still: needs must when the devil drives.

"Time you got back on the road," Rose said. "You take care of my Barry, big man. The rest of them, too."

"Is everyone okay at your end?"

"Sure," Rose said, and hung up before he could ask her anything else. That was okay. Sometimes you didn't need telepathy to tell when someone was lying. Even the rubes knew that.

He tossed the phone on the table and clapped his hands briskly. "Okay, let's gas and go. Next stop, Sturbridge, Massachusetts. Nut, you stick with Barry. I'll drive the next six hours, then you're up, Jimmy."

"I want to go home," Jimmy Numbers said morosely. He was about to say more, but a hot hand grabbed his wrist before he could.

"We got no choice about this," Barry said. His eyes were glittering with fever, but they were sane and aware. In that moment, Crow was very proud of him. "No choice at all, Computer Boy, so man up. True comes first. Always."

Crow sat down behind the wheel and turned the key. "Jimmy," he said. "Sit with me a minute. Want to have a little gab."

Jimmy Numbers sat down in the passenger seat.

"These three girls, how old are they? Do you know?"

"That and a lot of other stuff. I hacked their school records when I got the pictures. In for a penny, in for a pound, right? Deane and Cross are fourteen. The Stone girl is a year younger. She skipped a grade in elementary school."

"I find that suggestive of steam," Crow said.

"Yeah."

"And they all live in the same neighborhood."

"Right."

"I find *that* suggestive of chumminess."

Jimmy's eyes were still swollen with tears, but he laughed. "Yeah. Girls, y'know. All three of them probably wear the same lipstick and moan over the same bands. What's your point?"

"No point," Crow said. "Just information. Information is power, or so they say."

Two minutes later, Steamhead Steve's 'Bago was merging back onto Interstate 90. When the speedometer was pegged at sixty-five, Crow put on the cruise control and let it ride.

7

Dan outlined what he had in mind, then waited for Dave Stone to respond. For a long time he only sat beside Abra with his head lowered and his hands clasped between his knees.

"Daddy?" Abra asked. "Please say something."

Dave looked up and said, "Who wants a beer?"

Dan and John exchanged a brief bemused glance and declined.

"Well, I do. What I really want is a double shot of Jack, but I'm willing to stipulate with no input from you gentlemen that sippin whiskey might not be such a good idea tonight."

"I'll get it, Dad."

Abra bounced into the kitchen. They heard the snap of the flip-top and the hiss of the carbonation—sounds that brought back memories for Dan, many of them treacherously happy. She returned with a can of Coors and a pilsner glass.

"Can I pour it?"

"Knock yourself out."

Dan and John watched with silent fascination as Abra tilted the glass and slid the beer down the side to minimize the foam, operating with the casual expertise of a good bartender. She handed the glass to her father and set the can on a coaster beside him. Dave took a deep swallow, sighed, closed his eyes, then opened them again.

"That's good," he said.

I bet it is, Dan thought, and saw Abra watching him. Her face, usually so open, was inscrutable, and for the moment he could not read the thoughts behind it.

Dave said, "What you're proposing is crazy, but it has its attractions. Chief among them would be a chance to see these . . . creatures . . . with my own eyes. I think I need to, because—in spite of everything you've told me—I find it impossible to believe in them. Even with the glove, and the body you say you found."

Abra opened her mouth to speak. Her father stayed her with a raised hand.

"I believe that *you* believe," he went on. "All three of you. And I believe that some group of dangerously deranged individuals might—I say *might*—be after my daughter. I'd certainly go along with your idea, Mr. Torrance, if it didn't mean bringing Abra. I won't use my kid as bait."

"You wouldn't have to," Dan said. He was remembering how Abra's presence in the loading dock area behind the ethanol plant had turned him into a kind of human cadaver dog, and the way his vision had sharpened when Abra opened her eyes inside his head. He had even cried her tears, although a DNA test might not have shown it.

"What do you mean?"

"Your daughter doesn't have to be with us to be with us. She's unique that way. Abra, do you have a friend you could visit tomorrow after school? Maybe even stay with overnight?"

"Sure, Emma Deane." He could see by the excited sparkle in her eyes that she already understood what he had in mind.

"Bad idea," Dave said. "I won't leave her unguarded."

"Abra was being guarded all the time we were in Iowa," John said.

Abra's eyebrows shot up and her mouth dropped open a little. Dan was glad to see this. He was sure she could have picked his brain any old time she wanted to, but she had done as he asked.

Dan took out his cell and speed-dialed. "Billy? Why don't you come on in here and join the party."

Three minutes later, Billy Freeman stepped into the Stone house. He was wearing jeans, a red flannel shirt with tails hanging almost to his knees, and a Teenytown Railroad cap, which he doffed before shaking hands with Dave and Abra.

"You helped him with his stomach," Abra said, turning to Dan. "I remember that."

"You've been picking my brains after all," Dan said.

She flushed. "Not on purpose. Never. Sometimes it just happens."

"Don't I know it."

"All respect to you, Mr. Freeman," Dave said, "but you're a little old for bodyguard duty, and this is my daughter we're talking about."

Billy raised his shirttails and revealed an automatic pistol in a battered black holster. "One-nine-one-one Colt," he said. "Full auto. World War II vintage. This is old, too, but it'll do the job."

"Abra?" John asked. "Do you think bullets can kill these things, or is it only childhood diseases?"

Abra was looking at the gun. "Oh yes," she said. "Bullets would work. They're not ghostie people. They're as real as we are."

John looked at Dan and said, "I don't suppose you have a gun?"

Dan shook his head and looked at Billy. "I've got a deer rifle I could loan you," Billy said.

"That . . . might not be good enough," Dan said.

Billy considered. "Okay, I know a guy down in Madison. He buys and sells bigger stuff. Some of it much bigger."

"Oh Jesus," Dave said. "This just gets worse." But he didn't say anything else.

Dan said, "Billy, could we reserve the train tomorrow, if we wanted to have a sunset picnic at Cloud Gap?"

"Sure. People do it all the time, 'specially after Labor Day, when the rates go down."

Abra smiled. It was one Dan had seen before. It was her angry smile. He wondered if the True Knot might have had second thoughts if they knew their target had a smile like that in her repertoire.

"Good," she said. *"Good."*

"Abra?" Dave looked bewildered and a little frightened. "What?"

Abra ignored him for the moment. It was Dan she spoke to. "They deserve it for what they did to the baseball boy." She wiped at her mouth with her cupped hand, as if to erase that smile, but when she pulled the hand away the smile was still there, her thinned lips showing the tips of her teeth. She clenched the hand into a fist.

"They deserve it."

PART THREE

MATTERS OF LIFE AND DEATH

CHAPTER THIRTEEN

CLOUD GAP

1

EZ Mail Services was in a strip mall, between a Starbucks and O'Reilly Auto Parts. Crow entered just after 10 a.m., presented his Henry Rothman ID, signed for a package the size of a shoebox, and walked back out with it under his arm. In spite of the air-conditioning, the Winnebago was rank with the stench of Barry's sickness, but they had grown used to it and hardly smelled it at all. The box bore the return address of a plumbing supply company in Flushing, New York. There actually was such a company, but it had had no hand in this particular delivery. Crow, Snake, and Jimmy Numbers watched as Nut sliced the tape with his Swiss Army Knife and lifted the flaps. He pulled out a wad of inflated plastic packing, then a double fold of cotton fluff. Beneath it, set in Styrofoam, was a large, unlabeled bottle of straw-colored fluid, eight syringes, eight darts, and a skeletal pistol.

"Holy shit, there's enough stuff there to send her whole class to Middle Earth," Jimmy said.

"Rose has a great deal of respect for this little *chiquita*," Crow said. He took the tranquilizer gun out of its Styrofoam cradle, examined it, put it back. "We will, too."

"Crow!" Barry's voice was clotted and hoarse. "Come here!"

Crow left the contents of the box to Walnut and went to the man sweating on the bed. Barry was now covered with hundreds of bright red blemishes, his eyes swollen almost shut, his hair matted to his forehead. Crow could feel the fever baking off him, but the Chink was a hell of a lot stronger than Grampa Flick had been. He still wasn't cycling.

"You guys okay?" Barry asked. "No fever? No spots?"

"We're fine. Never mind us, you need to rest. Maybe get some sleep."

"I'll sleep when I'm dead, and I ain't dead yet." Barry's red-streaked eyes gleamed. "I'm picking her up."

Crow grabbed his hand without thinking about it, reminded himself to wash it with hot water and plenty of soap, then wondered what good *that* would do. They were all breathing his air, had all taken turns helping him to the jakes. Their hands had been all over him. "Do you know which one of the three girls she is? Have you got her name?"

"No."

"Does she know we're coming for her?"

"No. Stop asking questions and let me tell you what I do know. She's thinking about Rose, that's how I homed in, but she's not thinking about her by name. 'The woman in the hat with the one long tooth,' that's what she calls her. The kid's . . ." Barry leaned to one side and coughed into a damp handkerchief. "The kid's afraid of her."

"She ought to be," Crow said grimly. "Anything else?"

"Ham sandwiches. Deviled eggs."

Crow waited.

"I'm not sure yet, but I think . . . she's planning a picnic. Maybe with her parents. They're going on a . . . toy train?" Barry frowned.

"What toy train? Where?"

"Don't know. Get me closer and I will. I'm sure I will." Barry's hand turned in Crow's, and suddenly bore down almost hard enough to hurt. "She might be able to help me, Daddy. If I can hold on and you can get her . . . hurt her enough to make her breathe out some steam . . . then maybe . . ."

"Maybe," Crow said, but when he looked down he could see— just for a second—the bones inside Barry's clutching fingers.

2

Abra was extraordinarily quiet at school that Friday. None of the faculty found this strange, although she was ordinarily vivacious and something of a chatterbox. Her father had called the school nurse that morning, and asked if she would tell Abra's teachers to take it a bit easy on her. She wanted to go to school, but they had gotten some bad news about Abra's great-grandmother the day before. "She's still processing," Dave said.

The nurse said she understood, and would pass on the message.

What Abra was actually doing that day was concentrating on being in two places at the same time. It was like simultaneously patting your head and rubbing your stomach: hard at first, but not too difficult once you got the hang of it.

Part of her had to stay with her physical body, answering the occasional question in class (a veteran hand-raiser since first grade, today she found it annoying to be called on when she was just sitting with them neatly folded on her desk), talking with her friends at lunch, and asking Coach Rennie if she could be excused from gym and go to the library instead. "I've got a stomachache," she said, which was middle-school femcode for *I've got my period*.

She was equally quiet at Emma's house after school, but that wasn't a big problem. Emma came from a bookish family, and she was currently reading her way through the *Hunger Games* for the third time. Mr. Deane tried to chat Abra up when he came home from work, but quit and dove into the latest issue of *The Economist* when Abra answered in monosyllables and Mrs. Deane gave him a warning look.

Abra was vaguely aware of Emma putting her book aside and asking if she wanted to go out in the backyard for awhile, but most of her was with Dan: seeing through his eyes, feeling his hands and feet on the controls of *The Helen Rivington*'s little engine, tasting the ham sandwich he ate and the lemonade he chased it down with. When Dan spoke to her father, it was actually Abra speaking.

As for Dr. John? He was riding at the very back of the train, and consequently there *was* no Dr. John. Just the two of them in the cab, a little father-and-daughter bonding in the wake of the bad news about Momo, cozy as could be.

Occasionally her thoughts turned to the woman in the hat, the one who had hurt the baseball boy until he died and then licked up his blood with her deformed and craving mouth. Abra couldn't help it, but wasn't sure it mattered. If she were being touched by Barry's mind, her fear of Rose wouldn't surprise him, would it?

She had an idea she couldn't have fooled the True Knot's locator if he had been healthy, but Barry was extremely sick. He didn't know she knew Rose's name. It hadn't even occurred to him to wonder why a girl who wouldn't be eligible for a driver's license until 2015 was piloting the Teenytown train through the woods west of Frazier. If it had, he probably would have assumed the train didn't really need a driver.

Because he thinks it's a toy.

"—Scrabble?"

"Hmmm?" She looked around at Emma, at first not even sure where they were. Then she saw she was holding a basketball. Okay, the backyard. They were playing HORSE.

"I asked if you wanted to play Scrabble with me and my mom, because this is totally boring."

"You're winning, right?"

"Duh! All three games. Are you here at all?"

"Sorry, I'm just worried about my momo. Scrabble sounds good." It sounded great, in fact. Emma and her mom were the slowest Scrabble players in the known universe, and would have shit large bricks if anyone had suggested playing with a timer. This would give Abra plenty of opportunity to continue minimizing her presence here. Barry was sick but he wasn't dead, and if he got wise to the fact that Abra was performing a kind of telepathic ventriloquism, the results could be very bad. He might figure out where she really was.

Not much longer. Pretty soon they'll all come together. God, please let it go okay.

While Emma cleared the crap off the table in the downstairs rec room and Mrs. Deane set up the board, Abra excused herself to use the toilet. She did need to go, but first she made a quick detour into the living room and peeked out the bow window. Billy's truck was parked across the street. He saw the curtains twitch and flashed her a thumbs-up. Abra returned the gesture. Then the small part of her that was here went to the bathroom while the rest of her sat in the cab of *The Helen Rivington*.

We'll eat our picnic, pick up our trash, watch the sunset, and then we'll go back.

(eat our picnic, pick up our trash, watch the sunset, and then)

Something unpleasant and unexpected broke into her thoughts, and hard enough to snap her head back. A man and two women. The man had an eagle on his back, and both women had tramp stamps. Abra could see the tattoos because they were having naked sex beside a pool while stupid old disco music played. The women were letting out a lot of fake moans. What in hell had she stumbled across?

The shock of what those people were doing destroyed her delicate balancing act, and for a moment Abra was all in one place, all *here.* Cautiously, she looked again, and saw the people by the pool were all blurry. Not real. Almost ghostie people. And why? Because Barry was almost a ghostie person himself and had no interest in watching people have sex by the—

Those people aren't by a pool, they're on TV.

Did Barry the Chink know she was watching him watch some porno TV show? Him and the others? Abra wasn't sure, but she didn't think so. They had taken the possibility into account, though. Oh, yes. If she was there, they were trying to shock her into going away, or into revealing herself, or both.

"Abra?" Emma called. "We're ready to play!"

We're playing already, and it's a much bigger game than Scrabble.

She had to get her balance back, and quickly. Never mind the porno TV with the crappy disco music. She was in the little train. She was *driving* the little train. It was her special treat. She was having fun.

We're going to eat, we're going to pick up our trash, we're going to watch the sunset, and then we're going to go back. I'm afraid of the woman in the hat but not too afraid, because I'm not home, I'm going to Cloud Gap with my dad.

"Abra! Did you fall in?"

"Coming!" she called. "Just want to wash my hands!"

I'm with my dad. I'm with my dad, and that's all.

Looking at herself in the mirror, Abra whispered, "Hold that thought."

3

Jimmy Numbers was behind the wheel when they pulled into the Bretton Woods rest stop, which was quite close to Anniston, the town where the troublesome girl lived. Only she wasn't there. According to Barry, she was in a town called Frazier, a little further southeast. On a picnic with her dad. Making herself scarce. Much good it would do her.

Snake inserted the first video in the DVD player. It was called *Kenny's Poolside Adventure*. "If the kid's watching this, she's gonna get an education," she said, and pushed PLAY.

Nut was sitting beside Barry and feeding him more juice . . . when he could, that was. Barry had begun to cycle for real. He had little interest in juice and none at all in the poolside ménage à trois. He only looked at the screen because those were their orders. Each time he came back to his solid form, he groaned louder.

"Crow," he said. "Get with me, Daddy."

Crow was beside him in an instant, elbowing Walnut aside.

"Lean close," Barry whispered, and—after one uneasy moment—Crow did as he was asked.

Barry opened his mouth, but the next cycle started before he could speak. His skin turned milky, then thinned to transparency. Crow could see his teeth locked together, the sockets that held his pain-filled eyes, and—worst of all—the shadowy crenellations of his brain. He waited, holding a hand that was no longer a hand but only a nestle of bones. Somewhere, at a great distance, that twanky disco music went on and on. Crow thought, *They must be on drugs. You couldn't fuck to music like that unless you were.*

Slowly, slowly, Barry the Chink grew dense again. This time he screamed as he came back. Sweat stood out on his brow. So did the red spots, now so bright they looked like beads of blood.

He wet his lips and said, "Listen to me."

Crow listened.

4

Dan did his best to empty his mind so Abra could fill it. He had driven the *Riv* out to Cloud Gap often enough for it to be almost automatic, and John was riding back by the caboose with the guns (two automatic pistols and Billy's deer rifle). Out of sight, out of mind. Or almost. You couldn't completely lose yourself even while you were asleep, but Abra's presence was large enough to be a little scary. Dan thought if she stayed inside his head long enough, and kept broadcasting at her current power, he would soon be shopping for snappy sandals and matching accessories. Not to mention mooning over the groovy boys who made up the band 'Round Here.

It helped that she had insisted—at the last minute—that he take Hoppy, her old stuffed rabbit. "It will give me something to focus on," she had said, all of them unaware that a not-quite-human gentleman whose rube name was Barry Smith would have understood perfectly. He had learned the trick from Grampa Flick, and used it many times.

It also helped that Dave Stone kept up a constant stream of family stories, many of which Abra had never heard before. And still, Dan wasn't convinced any of this would have worked if the one in charge of finding her hadn't been sick.

"Can't the others do this location thing?" he had asked her.

"The lady in the hat could, even from halfway across the country, but she's staying out of it." That unsettling smile had once more curved Abra's lips and exposed the tips of her teeth. It made her look far older than her years. "Rose is scared of me."

Abra's presence in Dan's head wasn't constant. Every now and then he would feel her leave as she went the other way, reaching out—oh so carefully—to the one who had been foolish enough to slip Bradley Trevor's baseball glove on his hand. She said they had stopped in a town called Starbridge (Dan was pretty sure she meant Sturbridge) and left the turnpike there, moving along the secondary roads toward the bright blip of her consciousness. Later on they had stopped at a roadside café for lunch, not hurrying, making the final leg of the trip last. They knew where she was going now, and were perfectly willing to let her get there, because Cloud Gap was isolated. They thought she was making their job easier, and that was fine, but this was delicate work, a kind of telepathic laser surgery.

There had been one unsettling moment when a pornographic image filled Dan's mind—some kind of group sex by a pool—but it had been gone almost at once. He supposed he had gotten a peek into her undermind, where—if you believed Dr. Freud—all sorts of primal images lurked. This was an assumption he would come to regret, although never to blame himself for; he had taught himself not to snoop into people's most private things.

Dan held the *Riv*'s steering-yoke with one hand. The other was on the mangy stuffed bunny in his lap. Deep woods, now starting to flame with serious color, flowed by on both sides. In the right-hand seat—the so-called conductor's seat—Dave rambled on, telling his daughter family stories and dancing at least one family skeleton out of the closet.

"When your mom called yesterday morning, she told me there's a trunk stored in the basement of Momo's building. It's marked *Alessandra*. You know who that is, don't you?"

"Gramma Sandy," Dan said. Christ, even his voice sounded higher. Younger.

"Right you are. Now here's something you might *not* know, and if that's the case, you didn't hear it from me. Right?"

"No, Daddy." Dan felt his lips curve up as, some miles away, Abra smiled down at her current collection of Scrabble tiles: S P O N D L A.

"Your Gramma Sandy graduated from SUNY Albany—the State University of New York—and was doing her student teaching at a prep school, okay? Vermont, Massachusetts, or New Hampshire, I forget which. Halfway through her eight weeks, she up and quit. But she hung around for awhile, maybe picking up some part-time work, waitressing or something, for sure going to a lot of concerts and parties. She was . . ."

5

(*a good-time girl*)

That made Abra think of the three sex maniacs by the pool, smooching and gobbling to oldtime disco music. Uck. Some people had very strange ideas of what was a good time.

"Abra?" That was Mrs. Deane. "It's your turn, honey."

If she had to keep this up for long, she'd have a nervous breakdown. It would have been so much easier at home, by herself. She had even floated the idea to her father, but he wouldn't hear of it. Not even with Mr. Freeman watching over her.

She used a U on the board to make POUND.

"Thanks, Abba-Doofus, I was going there," Emma said. She turned the board and began to study it with beady-eyed final-exam concentration that would go on for another five minutes, at least. Maybe even ten. Then she would make something totally lame, like RAP or PAD.

Abra returned to the *Riv*. What her father was saying was sort of interesting, although she knew more about it than he thought she did.

(*Abby? Are you*)

6

"Abby? Are you listening?"

"Sure," Dan said. *I just had to take a little time-out to play a word.* "This is interesting."

"Anyway, Momo was living in Manhattan at that time, and when Alessandra came to see her that June, she was pregnant."

"Pregnant with Mom?"

"That's right, Abba-Doo."

"So Mom was born out of *wedlock?*"

Total surprise, and maybe the tiniest bit overdone. Dan, in the peculiar position of both participating and eavesdropping on the discussion, now realized something he found touching and sweetly comic: Abra knew perfectly well that her mother was illegitimate. Lucy had told her the year before. What Abra was doing now, strange but true, was protecting her father's innocence.

"That's right, honey. But it's no crime. Sometimes people get . . . I don't know . . . confused. Family trees can grow strange branches, and there's no reason for you not to know that."

"Gramma Sandy died a couple of months after Mom was born, right? In a car wreck."

"That's right. Momo was babysitting Lucy for the afternoon, and ended up raising her. That's the reason they're so close, and why Momo getting old and sick has been so hard on your mom."

"Who was the man who got Gramma Sandy pregnant? Did she ever say?"

"Tell you what," Dave said, "that's an interesting question. If Alessandra ever told, Momo kept it to herself." He pointed ahead, at the lane cutting through the woods. "Look, honey, almost there!"

They were passing a sign reading CLOUD GAP PICNIC AREA, 2 MI.

7

Crow's party made a brief stop in Anniston to gas up the Winnebago, but on lower Main Street, at least a mile from Richland Court. As they left town—Snake now at the wheel and an epic called *Swinging Sorority Sisters* on the DVD player—Barry called Jimmy Numbers to his bed.

"You guys got to step it up a notch," Barry said. "They're almost there. It's a place called Cloud Gap. Did I tell you that?"

"Yeah, you did." Jimmy almost patted Barry's hand, then thought better of it.

"They'll be spreading their picnic in no time. That's when you should take them, while they're sat down and eating."

"We'll get it done," Jimmy promised. "And in time to twist enough steam out of her to help you. Rose can't object to that."

"She never would," Barry agreed, "but it's too late for me. Maybe not for you, though."

"Huh?"

"Look at your arms."

Jimmy did, and saw the first spots blooming on the soft white skin below his elbows. Red death. His mouth went dry at the sight of them.

"Oh Christ, here I go," Barry moaned, and suddenly his clothes were collapsing in on a body that was no longer there. Jimmy saw him swallow . . . and then his throat was gone.

"Move," Nut said. "Let me at him."

"Yeah? What are you going to do? He's cooked."

Jimmy went up front and dropped into the passenger seat, which Crow had vacated. "Take Route 14-A around Frazier," he said. "That's quicker than going through the downtown. You'll connect with the Saco River Road—"

Snake tapped the GPS. "I got all that programmed. You think I'm blind or just stupid?"

Jimmy barely heard her. All he knew was that he could not die.

He was too young to die, especially with all the incredible computer developments just over the horizon. And the thought of cycling, the crushing pain every time he came back . . .

No. *No*. Absolutely not. Impossible.

Late-afternoon light slanted in through the 'Bago's big front windows. Beautiful autumn sunlight. Fall was Jimmy's favorite season, and he intended to still be alive and traveling with the True Knot when it came around again. And again. And again. Luckily, he was with the right bunch to get this done. Crow Daddy was brave, resourceful, and cunning. The True had been in tough spots before. He would bring them through this one.

"Watch for the sign pointing to the Cloud Gap picnic area. Don't miss it. Barry says they're almost there."

"Jimmy, you're giving me a headache," Snake said. "Go sit down. We'll be there in an hour, maybe less."

"Goose it," Jimmy Numbers said.

Snakebite Andi grinned and did so.

They were just turning onto the Saco River Road when Barry the Chink cycled out, leaving only his clothes. They were still warm from the fever that had baked him.

8

(Barry's dead)

There was no horror in this thought when it reached Dan. Nor even an ounce of compassion. Only satisfaction. Abra Stone might look like an ordinary American girl, prettier than some and brighter than most, but when you got below the surface—and not that far below, either—there was a young Viking woman with a fierce and bloodthirsty soul. Dan thought it was a shame that she'd never had brothers and sisters. She would have protected them with her life.

Dan dropped the *Riv* into its lowest gear as the train came out of the deep woods and ran along a fenced drop. Below them, the Saco shone bright gold in the declining sun. The woods, sloping steeply down to the water on both sides, were a bonfire of orange, red, yellow, and purple. Above them, the puffy clouds drifting by seemed almost close enough to touch.

He pulled up to the sign reading CLOUD GAP STATION in a chuff of airbrakes, then turned the diesel off. For a moment he had no idea what to say, but Abra said it for him, using his mouth. "Thanks for letting me drive, Daddy. Now let's have our plunder." In the Deane rec room, Abra had just made this word. "Our picnic, I mean."

"I can't believe you're hungry after all you ate on the train," Dave teased.

"I am, though. Aren't you glad I'm not anorexic?"

"Yes," Dave said. "Actually, I am."

Dan saw John Dalton from the corner of his eye, crossing the picnic area clearing, head down, feet noiseless on the thick pine duff. He was carrying a pistol in one hand and Billy Freeman's rifle in the other. Trees bordered a parking lot for motor traffic; after a single look back, John disappeared into them. During summer, the little lot and all the picnic tables would have been full. On this weekday afternoon in late September, Cloud Gap was dead empty except for them.

Dave looked at Dan. Dan nodded. Abra's father—an agnostic by inclination but a Catholic by association—made the sign of the cross in the air and then followed John into the woods.

"It's so beautiful here, Daddy," Dan said. His invisible passenger was now talking to Hoppy, because Hoppy was the only one left. Dan set the lumpy, balding, one-eyed rabbit on one of the picnic tables, then went back to the first passenger car for the wicker picnic basket. "That's okay," he said to the empty clearing, "I can get it, Dad."

9

In the Deanes' rec room, Abra pushed back her chair and stood up. "I have to go to the bathroom again. I feel sick to my stomach. And after that, I think I better go home."

Emma rolled her eyes, but Mrs. Deane was all sympathy. "Oh, honey, is it your you-know?"

"Yes, and it's pretty bad."

"Do you have the things you need?"

"In my backpack. I'll be fine. Excuse me."

"That's right," Emma said, "quit while you're winning."

"*Em-ma!*" her mother cried.

"That's okay, Mrs. Deane. She beat me at HORSE." Abra went up the stairs, one hand pressed to her stomach in a way she hoped didn't look too fakey. She glanced outside again, saw Mr. Freeman's truck, but didn't bother with the thumbs-up this time. Once in the bathroom, she locked the door and sat down on the closed toilet lid. It was such a relief to be done juggling so many different selves. Barry was dead; Emma and her mom were downstairs; now it was just the Abra in this bathroom and the Abra at Cloud Gap. She closed her eyes.

(*Dan*)

(*I'm here*)

(*you don't have to pretend to be me anymore*)

She felt his relief, and smiled. Uncle Dan had tried hard, but he wasn't cut out to be a chick.

A light, tentative knock at the door. "Girlfriend?" Emma. "You all right? I'm sorry if I was mean."

"I'm okay, but I'm going to go home and take a Motrin and lie down."

"I thought you were going to stay the night."

"I'll be fine."

"Isn't your dad gone?"

"I'll lock the doors until he gets back."

"Well . . . want me to walk with you?"

"That's okay."

She wanted to be alone so she could cheer when Dan and her father and Dr. John took those *things* out. They would, too. Now that Barry was dead, the others were blind. Nothing could go wrong.

10

There was no breeze to rattle the brittle leaves, and with the *Riv* shut down, the picnic area at Cloud Gap was very quiet. There was only the muted conversation of the river below, the squall of a crow, and the sound of an approaching engine. Them. The ones the hat woman had sent. Rose. Dan flipped up one side of the wicker basket, reached in, and gripped the Glock .22 Billy had provided him with—from what source Dan didn't know or care. What he cared about was that it could fire fifteen rounds without reloading, and if fifteen rounds weren't enough, he was in a world of hurt. A ghost memory of his father came, Jack Torrance smiling his charming, crooked grin and saying, *If that don't work, I don't know what to tellya.* Dan looked at Abra's old stuffed toy.

"Ready, Hoppy? I hope so. I hope we both are."

11

Billy Freeman was slouched behind the wheel of his truck, but sat up in a hurry when Abra came out of the Deane house. Her friend—Emma—stood in the doorway. The two girls said goodbye, slapping palms first in an overhead high five, then down low. Abra started for her own house, across the street and four doors down. *That* wasn't in the plan, and when she glanced at him, he raised both hands in a *what gives* gesture.

She smiled and shot him another quick thumbs-up. She thought everything was okay, he got that loud and clear, but seeing her outside and on her own made Billy uneasy, even if the freaks were twenty miles south of here. She was a powerhouse, and maybe she knew what she was doing, but she was also only thirteen.

As he watched her go up the walk to her house, pack on her back and rummaging in her pocket for her key, Billy leaned over and thumbed the button on his glove compartment. His own Glock .22

was inside. The pistols were rented firepower from a guy who was an emeritus member of the Road Saints, New Hampshire chapter. In his younger years, Billy had sometimes ridden with them but had never joined. On the whole he was glad, but he understood the pull. The camaraderie. He supposed it was the way Dan and John felt about the drinking.

Abra slipped into her house and closed the door. Billy didn't take either the Glock or his cell phone out of the glove compartment—not yet—but he didn't close the compartment, either. He didn't know if it was what Dan called the shining, but he had a bad feeling about this. Abra should have stayed with her friend.

She should have stuck to the plan.

12

They ride in campers and Winnebagos, Abra had said, and it was a Winnebago that pulled into the parking lot where the Cloud Gap access road dead-ended. Dan sat watching with his hand in the picnic basket. Now that the time had come, he felt calm enough. He turned the basket so one end faced the newly arrived RV and flicked off the Glock's safety with his thumb. The 'Bago's door opened and Abra's would-be kidnappers spilled out, one after the other.

She had also said they had funny names—pirate names—but these looked like ordinary people to Dan. The men were the going-on-elderly kind you always saw pooting around in campers and RVs; the woman was young and good-looking in an all-American way that made him think of cheerleaders who still had their figures ten years after high school, and maybe after a kid or two. She could have been the daughter of one of the men. He felt a moment's doubt. This was, after all, a tourist spot, and it was the beginning of leaf-peeping season in New England. He hoped John and David would hold their fire; it would be horrible if they were just innocent by—

Then he saw the rattlesnake baring its fangs on the woman's left arm, and the syringe in her right hand. The man crowding in close beside her had another syringe. And the man in the lead had what looked very much like a pistol in his belt. They stopped just inside the birch poles marking the entrance to the picnic area. The one in the lead disabused Dan of any lingering doubts he might have had by drawing the pistol. It didn't look like a regular gun. It was too thin to be a regular gun.

"Where's the girl?"

With the hand not in the picnic basket, Dan pointed to Hoppy the stuffed rabbit. "That's as close to her as you're ever going to get."

The man with the funny gun was short, with a widow's peak above a mild-mannered accountant's face. A soft pod of well-fed stomach hung over his belt. He was wearing chinos and a t-shirt reading GOD DOES NOT DEDUCT FROM MAN'S ALLOTED SPAN THE HOURS SPENT FISHING.

"I have a question for you, honeybunch," the woman said.

Dan raised his eyebrows. "Go ahead."

"Aren't you tired? Don't you want to go to sleep?"

He did. All at once his eyelids were as heavy as sashweights. The hand holding the gun began to relax. Two more seconds and he would have been crashed out and snoring with his head on the initial-carved surface of the picnic table. But that was when Abra screamed.

(WHERE'S THE CROW? I DON'T SEE THE CROW!)

13

Dan jerked as a man will when he is badly startled on the edge of sleep. The hand in the picnic basket spasmed, the Glock went off, and a cloud of wickerwork fragments flew. The bullet went wild but the people from the Winnebago jumped, and the sleepiness left Dan's head like the illusion that it was. The woman with the snake tattoo and the man with the popcorny fringe of white hair flinched back, but the one with the odd-looking pistol charged forward, yelling *"Get him! Get him!"*

"Get *this,* you kidnapping fuckers!" Dave Stone shouted. He stepped out of the woods and began to spray bullets. Most of them went wild, but one hit Walnut in the neck and the True's doctor went down on the pine duff, the hypo spilling from his fingers.

14

Leading the True had its responsibilities, but also its perks. Rose's gigantic EarthCruiser, imported from Australia at paralyzing expense and then converted to left-hand drive, was one. Having the ladies' shower room at the Bluebell Campground all to herself whenever she wanted it was another. After months on the road, there was nothing like a long hot shower in a big tiled room where you could hold your arms out or even dance around, if the spirit moved you. And where the hot water didn't run out after four minutes.

Rose liked to turn off the lights and shower in darkness. She found she did her best thinking that way, and for just that reason she had headed to the shower immediately after the troubling cell phone call she'd gotten at 1 p.m., Mountain Time. She still believed everything was all right, but a few doubts had begun to sprout, like dandelions on a previously flawless lawn. If the girl was even smarter than they thought . . . or if she had enlisted help . . .

No. It couldn't be. She was a steamhead for sure—the steamhead of all steamheads—but she was still only a child. A *rube* child. In any case, all Rose could do for the time being was wait on developments.

After fifteen refreshing minutes, she stepped out, dried off, wrapped herself in a fluffy bath sheet, and headed back to her RV, carrying her clothes. Short Eddie and Big Mo were cleaning up the open-air barbecue area following another excellent lunch. Not their fault that nobody felt much like eating, with two more of the True showing those goddamned red spots. They waved to her. Rose was raising her own hand in return when a bundle of dynamite went off in her head. She went sprawling, her pants and shirt spilling from her hand. Her bath sheet unraveled.

Rose barely noticed. Something had happened to the raiding party. Something bad. She was digging for her cell in the pocket of her crumpled jeans as soon as her head began to clear. Never in her life had she wished so strongly (and so bitterly) that Crow Daddy was capable of long-distance telepathy, but—with a few exceptions, like herself—that gift seemed reserved for rube steamheads like the girl in New Hampshire.

Eddie and Mo were running toward her. Behind them came Long Paul, Silent Sarey, Token Charlie, and Harpman Sam. Rose hit speed dial on her phone. A thousand miles away, Crow's gave just half a ring.

"Hello, you've reached Henry Rothman. I can't talk to you right now, but if you leave your number and a brief message—"

Fucking voice mail. Which meant his phone was either turned off or getting no service. Rose was betting the latter. Naked and on her knees in the dirt, her heels digging into the backs of her thighs, Rose smacked the center of her forehead with the hand not holding her cell.

Crow, where are you? What are you doing? What's happening?

15

The man in the chinos and t-shirt fired his weird pistol at Dan. There was a chuff of compressed air, and suddenly a dart was sticking out of Hoppy's back. Dan raised the Glock from the ruins of the picnic basket and fired again. Chinos Guy took it in the chest and went over backwards, grunting, as fine droplets of blood blew out through the back of his shirt.

Andi Steiner was the last one standing. She turned, saw Dave Stone frozen there, looking dazed, and charged at him with her hypodermic needle clutched in her fist like a dagger. Her ponytail swung like a pendulum. She was screaming. To Dan, everything seemed to have slowed down and gained clarity. He had time to see that the plastic protector-sleeve was still on the end of the needle and had time to think, *What kind of clowns* are *these guys?* The answer, of course, was that they weren't clowns at all. They were hunters completely unused to resistance from their prey. But of course children were their usual targets, and unsuspecting ones, at that.

Dave only stared at the howling harpy coming toward him. Perhaps his gun was empty; more likely that one burst had been his limit. Dan raised his own gun but didn't shoot. The chances of missing the tattooed lady and hitting Abra's father were just too great.

That was when John ran out of the woods and slammed into Dave's back, shoving him forward into the charging woman. Her screams (fury? dismay?) were driven out of her in a gust of violently expelled air. They both tumbled over. The needle flew. As Tattoo Woman went scrabbling for it on her hands and knees, John brought the stock of Billy's deer rifle down on the side of her head. It was a full-force, adrenaline-fueled blow. There was a crunch as her jaw broke. Her features twisted to the left, one eye bulging from its socket in a startled glare. She sprawled and rolled over on her back. Blood trickled from the corners of her mouth. Her hands clenched and opened, clenched and opened.

John dropped the rifle and turned to Dan, stricken. "I didn't mean to hit her that hard! Christ, I was just so *scared*!"

"Look at the one with the frizzy hair," Dan said. He got up on legs that felt too long and not all there. "Look at him, John."

John looked. Walnut lay in a pool of blood, one hand clutching his torn neck. He was cycling rapidly. His clothes fell in, then puffed out. The blood flowing through his fingers disappeared, then reappeared again. The fingers themselves were doing the same. The man had become an insane X-ray.

John stepped back with his hands plastered over his mouth and nose. Dan still had that sense of slowness and perfect clarity. There was time to see Tattoo Woman's blood and a snarl of her blond hair on the stock of the Remington pump also appearing and disappearing. It made him think of how her ponytail had pendulumed back and forth when she

(*Dan where's the Crow WHERE'S THE CROW???*)

ran at Abra's father. She had told them that Barry was cycling. Now Dan understood what she meant.

"The one in the fishing shirt is doing it, too," Dave Stone said. His voice was only slightly shaky, and Dan guessed he knew where some of his daughter's steel had come from. But he didn't have time to think about that now. Abra was telling him they hadn't gotten the whole crew.

He sprinted to the Winnebago. The door was still open. He ran up the steps, threw himself on the carpeted floor, and managed to bang his head hard enough on the post under the eating table to send bright specks shooting across his field of vision. *Never happens that way in the movies,* he thought, and rolled over, expecting to be shot or stomped or injected by the one who had stayed behind to provide the rearguard. The one Abra called the crow. They weren't totally stupid and complacent after all, it seemed.

The Winnebago was empty.

Appeared empty.

Dan got to his feet and hurried through the kitchenette. He passed a foldout bed, rumpled from frequent occupancy. Part of his mind registered the fact that the RV smelled like the wrath of God in spite of the air-conditioner that was still running. There was a closet, but the door stood open on its track and he saw nothing inside but clothes. He bent, looking for feet. No feet. He went on to the rear of the Winnebago and stood beside the bathroom door.

He thought *more movie shit,* and pulled it open, crouching as he did it. The Winnebago's can was empty, and he wasn't surprised. If anyone had tried hiding in there, he'd be dead by now. The smell alone would have killed him.

(*maybe someone did die in here maybe this Crow*)

Abra came back at once, full of panic, broadcasting so powerfully that she scattered his own thoughts.

(*no Barry's the one who died* WHERE'S THE CROW FIND THE CROW)

Dan left the RV. Both of the men who had come after Abra were gone; only their clothes were left. The woman—the one who had tried to send him to sleep—was still there, but wouldn't be for long. She had crawled to the picnic table with the ruined wicker basket on it and now lay propped against one of the bench seats, staring at Dan, John, and Dave from her newly crooked face. Blood ran from her nose and mouth, giving her a red goatee. The front of her blouse was soaked. As Dan approached, her skin melted from her face and her clothes fell inward against the strutwork of her skeleton. No longer held in place by her shoulders, the straps of her bra flopped in loops. Of her soft parts, only her eyes remained, watching Dan. Then her skin reknit itself and her clothes plumped up around her body. The fallen bra straps bit into her upper arms, the strap on the left gagging the rattlesnake so it couldn't bite. The fingerbones clutching her shattered jaw grew a hand.

"You fucked us," Snakebite Andi said. Her voice was slurred. "Fucked by a bunch of rubes. I don't believe it."

Dan pointed at Dave. "That rube there is the father of the girl you came to kidnap. Just in case you're wondering."

Snake managed a painful grin. Her teeth were rimmed with blood. "You think I give a tin shit? To me he's just another swinging dick. Even the Pope of Rome's got one, and not one of you care where you put it. Fucking *men*. Have to win, don't you? Always have to w—"

"Where's the other one? Where's Crow?"

Andi coughed. Blood bubbled from the corners of her mouth. Once she had been lost, then she had been found. In a darkened movie theater she had been found, by a goddess with a thundercloud of dark hair. Now she was dying, and she wouldn't have changed a thing. The years between the ex-actor president and the black president had been good; that one magic night with Rose had been even better. She grinned brightly up at the tall good-looking one. It hurt to grin, but she did it, anyway.

"Oh, him. He's in Reno. Fucking rube showgirls."

She began to disappear again. Dan heard John Dalton whisper, "Oh my God, look at that. Brain bleed. I can actually see it."

Dan waited to see if Tat Woman would come back. Eventually she did, with a long groan from between her clenched and bloody teeth. The cycling seemed to hurt even more than the blow that had caused it, but Dan thought he could remedy that. He pulled Tat Woman's hand away from her shattered jaw and dug in with his fingers. He could feel her entire skull shift as he did; it was like pushing the side of a badly cracked vase held together by a few strips of tape. This time Tat Woman did more than groan. She howled and pawed weakly at Dan, who paid no attention.

"Where's Crow?"

"Anniston!" Snake screamed. *"He got off in Anniston! Please don't hurt me anymore, Daddy! Please don't, I'll do whatever you want!"*

Dan thought of what Abra said these monsters had done to Brad Trevor in Iowa, how they had tortured him and God only knew how many others, and felt an almost ungovernable urge to tear the lower half of this murdering bitch's face entirely off. To beat her bleeding, shattered skull with her own jawbone until both skull and bone disappeared.

Then—absurdly, given the circumstances—he thought of the kid in the Braves t-shirt reaching for the left-over coke piled on the shiny magazine cover. *Canny,* he'd said. This woman was nothing like that kid, *nothing,* but telling himself so did no good. His anger was suddenly gone, leaving him feeling sick and weak and empty.

Don't hurt me anymore, Daddy.

He got up, wiping his hand on his shirt, and walked blindly toward the *Riv.*

(*Abra are you there*)

(*yes*)

Not so panicky now, and that was good.

(*you need to have your friend's mom call the police and tell them you're in danger Crow's in Anniston*)

Bringing the police into a business that was, at bottom,

supernatural was the last thing Dan wanted, but at this moment he saw no choice.

(*I'm not*)

Before she could finish, her thought was blotted out by a powerful shriek of female rage.

(YOU LITTLE BITCH)

Suddenly the hat woman was in Dan's head again, this time not as part of a dream but behind his waking eyes, her image burning: a creature of terrible beauty who was now naked, her wet hair lying on her shoulders in Medusa coils. Then her mouth yawned open and the beauty was torn away. There was only a dark hole with one jutting, discolored tooth. Almost a tusk.

(WHAT HAVE YOU DONE)

Dan staggered and put a hand against the *Riv*'s lead passenger car to hold himself up. The world inside his head was revolving. The hat woman disappeared and suddenly a crowd of concerned faces was gathered around him. They were asking if he was all right.

He remembered Abra trying to explain how the world had revolved on the day she had discovered Brad Trevor's picture in *The Anniston Shopper*; how all at once Abra had been looking out of the hat woman's eyes and the hat woman had been looking out of hers. Now he understood. It was happening again, and this time he was along for the ride.

Rose was on the ground. He could see a broad swatch of evening sky overhead. The people crowding around her were no doubt her tribe of child-killers. This was what Abra was seeing.

The question was, what was *Rose* seeing?

16

Snake cycled, then came back. It *burned*. She looked at the man kneeling in front of her.

"Is there anything I can do for you?" John asked. "I'm a doctor."

In spite of the pain, Snake laughed. This doctor, who belonged to the men who had just shot the *True*'s doctor to death, was now offering to help. What would Hippocrates make of that one? "Put a bullet in me, assface. That's the only thing I can think of."

The nerdy one, the bastard who'd actually pulled the trigger on Walnut, joined the one who said he was a doctor. "You'd deserve it," Dave said. "Did you think I was just going to let you take my daughter? Torture and kill her like you did that poor little boy in Iowa?"

They knew about that? How could they? But it didn't matter now, at least not to Andi. "Your people slaughter pigs and cows and sheep. Is what we do any different?"

"In my humble opinion, killing human beings is a lot different," John said. "Call me silly and sentimental."

Snake's mouth was full of blood and some lumpy shit. Teeth, probably. That didn't matter, either. In the end, this might be more merciful than what Barry had gone through. It would certainly be quicker. But one thing needed straightening out. Just so they'd know. "*We're* the human beings. Your kind . . . just rubes."

Dave smiled, but his eyes were hard. "And yet you're the one lying on the ground with dirt in your hair and blood all down the front of your shirt. I hope hell's hot enough for you."

Snake could feel the next cycle coming on. With luck it would be the last one, but for now she held tight to her physical form. "You don't understand how it was with me. Before. Or how is with us. We're only a few, and we're sick. We've got—"

"I know what you've got," Dave said. "Fucking measles. I hope they rot your whole miserable Knot from the inside out."

Snake said, "We didn't choose to be what we are any more than you did. In our shoes, you'd do the same."

John shook his head slowly from side to side. "Never. *Never.*"

Snake began to cycle out. She managed four more words, however. *"Fucking men."* A final gasp as she stared up at them from her disappearing face. *"Fucking rubes."*

Then she was gone.

17

Dan walked to John and Dave slowly and carefully, putting his hand on several of the picnic tables to keep his balance. He had picked up Abra's stuffed rabbit without even realizing it. His head was clearing, but that was a decidedly mixed blessing.

"We have to go back to Anniston, and fast. I can't touch Billy. I could before, but now he's gone."

"Abra?" Dave asked. "What about Abra?"

Dan didn't want to look at him—Dave's face was naked with fear—but he made himself do it. "She's gone, too. So's the woman in the hat. They've both dropped out of the mix."

"Meaning what?" Dave grabbed Dan's shirt in both hands. "Meaning *what*?"

"I don't know."

This was the truth, but he was afraid.

CHAPTER FOURTEEN

CROW

1

Get with me, Daddy, Barry the Chink had said. *Lean close.*

This was just after Snake had started the first of the porn DVDs. Crow got with Barry, even held his hand while the dying man struggled through his next cycle. And when he came back . . .

Listen to me. She's been watching, all right. Only when that porno started up . . .

Explaining to someone who couldn't do the locator thing was hard, especially when the one doing the talking was mortally ill, but Crow got the gist of it. The fucksome frolickers by the pool had shocked the girl, just as Rose had hoped they might, but they had done more than make her quit spying and pull back. For a moment or two, Barry's sense of her location seemed to double. She was still on the midget train with her dad, riding to the place where they were going to have their picnic, but her shock had produced a ghost image that made no sense. In this she was in a bathroom, taking a leak.

"Maybe you were seeing a memory," Crow said. "Could that be?"

"Yeah," Barry said. "Rubes think all kinds of crazy shit. Most likely it's nothing. But for a minute it was like she was twins, you know?"

Crow didn't, exactly, but he nodded.

"Only if that's not it, she might be running some kind of game. Gimme the map."

Jimmy Numbers had all of New Hampshire on his laptop. Crow held it up in front of Barry.

"Here's where she is," Barry said, tapping the screen. "On her way to this Cloud Glen place with her dad."

"Gap," Crow said. "Cloud Gap."

"Whatever the fuck." Barry moved his finger northeast. "And this is where the ghost-blip came from."

Crow took the laptop and looked through the bead of no doubt infected sweat Barry had left on the screen. "Anniston? That's her hometown, Bar. She's probably left psychic traces of herself all over it. Like dead skin."

"Sure. Memories. Daydreams. All kinds of crazy shit. What I said."

"And it's gone now."

"Yeah, but . . ." Barry grasped Crow's wrist. "If she's as strong as Rose says, it's just possible that she really *is* gaming us. Throwing her voice, like."

"Have you ever run across a steamhead that could do that?"

"No, but there's a first time for everything. I'm almost positive she's with her father, but you're the one who has to decide if almost positive is good enough for . . ."

That was when Barry began cycling again, and all meaningful communication ceased. Crow was left with a difficult decision. It was his mission, and he was confident he could handle it, but it was Rose's plan and—more important—Rose's obsession. If he screwed up, there would be hell to pay.

Crow glanced at his watch. Three p.m. here in New Hampshire, one o'clock in Sidewinder. At the Bluebell Campground, lunch would just be finishing up, and Rose would be available. That decided him. He made the call. He almost expected her to laugh and call him an old woman, but she didn't.

"You know we can't entirely trust Barry anymore," she said, "but I trust you. What's your gut feeling?"

His gut felt nothing one way or the other; that was why he had made the call. He told her so, and waited.

"I leave it with you," she said. "Just don't screw up."

Thanks for nothing, Rosie darlin. He thought this . . . then hoped she hadn't caught it.

He sat with the closed cell phone still in his hand, swaying from side to side with the motion of the RV, inhaling the smell of Barry's sickness, wondering how long it would be before the first spots started showing up on his own arms and legs and chest. At last he went forward and put his hand on Jimmy's shoulder.

"When you get to Anniston, stop."

"Why?"

"Because I'm getting off."

2

Crow Daddy watched them pull away from the Gas 'n Go on Anniston's lower Main Street, resisting an urge to send a short-range thought (all the ESP of which he was capable) to Snake before they got out of range: *Come back and pick me up, this is a mistake*.

Only what if it wasn't?

When they were gone, he looked briefly and longingly at the sad little line of used cars for sale at the car wash adjacent to the gas station. No matter what transpired in Anniston, he was going to need transpo out of town. He had more than enough cash in his wallet to buy something that would carry him to their agreed-on rendezvous point near Albany on I-87; the problem was time. It would take at least half an hour to transact a car deal, and that might be too long. Until he was sure this was a false alarm, he would just have to improvise and rely on his powers of persuasion. They had never let him down yet.

Crow did take time enough to step into the Gas 'n Go, where he bought a Red Sox hat. When in Bosox country, dress as the Bosox fans do. He debated adding a pair of sunglasses and decided against them. Thanks to TV, a fit middle-aged man in sunglasses always looked like a hit man to a certain part of the population. The hat would have to do.

He walked up Main Street to the library where Abra and Dan had once held a council of war. He had to go no farther than the lobby to find what he was looking for. There, under the heading of TAKE A LOOK AT OUR TOWN, was a map of Anniston with every street and lane carefully marked. He refreshed himself on the location of the girl's street.

"Great game last night, wasn't it?" a man asked. He was carrying an armload of books.

For a moment Crow had no idea what he was talking about, then remembered his new hat. "It sure was," he agreed, still looking at the map.

He gave the Sox fan time to depart before leaving the lobby. The hat was fine, but he had no desire to discuss baseball. He thought it was a stupid game.

3

Richland Court was a short street of pleasant New England saltboxes and Cape Cods ending in a circular turnaround. Crow had grabbed a free newspaper called *The Anniston Shopper* on his walk from the library and now stood at the corner, leaning against a handy oak tree and pretending to study it. The oak shielded him from the street, and maybe that was a good thing, because there was a red truck with a guy sitting behind the wheel parked about halfway down. The truck was an oldie, with some hand-tools and what looked like a Rototiller in the bed, so the guy could be a groundskeeper—this was the kind of street where people could afford them—but if so, why was he just sitting there?

*Baby*sitting, maybe?

Crow was suddenly glad he had taken Barry seriously enough to jump ship. The question was, what to do now? He could call Rose, but their last conversation hadn't netted anything he couldn't have gotten from a Magic 8 Ball.

He was still standing half-hidden behind the fine old oak and debating his next move when the providence that favored the True Knot above rubes stepped in. A door partway down the street opened, and two girls came out. Crow's eyes were every bit as sharp as those of his namesake bird, and he ID'd them at once as two of the three girls in Billy's computer pix. The one in the brown skirt was Emma Deane. The one in the black pants was Abra Stone.

He glanced back at the truck. The driver, also an oldie, had been slouched behind the wheel. Now he was sitting up. Bright-eyed and bushy-tailed. On the alert. So she *had* been gaming them. Crow still didn't know for sure which of the two was the steamhead, but one thing he was sure of: the men in the Winnebago were on a wild goosechase.

Crow took out his cell but only held it in his hand for a moment, watching the girl in the black pants go down the walk to the street. The girl in the skirt watched her for a second, then went back inside. The girl in the pants—Abra—crossed Richland Court, and as she did, the man in the truck raised his hands in a *what gives* gesture. She responded with a thumbs-up: *Don't worry, everything's okay.* Crow felt a surge of triumph as hot as a knock of whiskey. Question answered. Abra Stone was the steamhead. No question about it. She was being guarded, and the guard was an old geezer with a perfectly good pickup truck. Crow felt confident it would take him and a certain young passenger as far as Albany.

He hit Snake on the speed dial, and wasn't surprised or uneasy when he got a CALL FAILED message. Cloud Gap was a local beauty spot, and God forbid there should be any cell phone towers to clutter up the tourists' snapshots. But that was okay. If he couldn't take care of an old man and a young girl, it was time to turn in his badge. He considered his phone for a moment, then turned it off. For the next twenty minutes or so, there was no one he wanted to talk to, and that included Rose.

His mission, his responsibility.

He had four loaded syringes, two in the left pocket of his light jacket, two in the right. Putting his best Henry Rothman smile on his face—the one he wore when reserving campground space or four-walling motels for the True—Crow stepped from behind the tree and strolled down the street. In his left hand he still held his folded copy of *The Anniston Shopper*. His right hand was in his jacket pocket, easing the plastic cap off one of the needles.

4

"Pardon me, sir, I seem to be a little lost. I wonder if you could give me some directions."

Billy Freeman was nervous, on edge, filled with something that was not quite foreboding . . . and still that cheerful voice and bright you-can-trust-me smile took him in. Only for two seconds, but that was enough. As he reached toward the open glove compartment, he felt a small sting on the side of his neck.

Bug bit me, he thought, and then slumped sideways, his eyes rolling up to the whites.

Crow opened the door and shoved the driver across the seat. The old guy's head bonked the passenger-side window. Crow lifted limp legs over the transmission hump, batting the glove compartment closed to make a little more room, then slid behind the wheel and slammed the door. He took a deep breath and looked around, ready for anything, but there was nothing to be ready for. Richland Court was dozing the afternoon away, and that was lovely.

The key was in the ignition. Crow started the engine and the radio came on in a yahoo roar of Toby Keith: God bless America and pour the beer. As he reached to turn it off, a terrible white light momentarily washed out his vision. Crow had very little telepathic ability, but he was firmly linked to his tribe; in a way, the members were appendages of a single organism, and one of their number had just died. Cloud Gap hadn't been just misdirection, it had been a fucking ambush.

Before he could decide what to do next, the white light came again, and, after a pause, yet again.

All of them?

Good Christ, *all three*? It wasn't possible . . . was it?

He took a deep breath, then another. Forced himself to face the fact that yes, it could be. And if so, he knew who was to blame.

Fucking steamhead girl.

He looked at Abra's house. All quiet there. Thank God for small favors. He had expected to drive the truck up the street and into her driveway, but all at once that seemed like a bad idea, at least for now. He got out, leaned back in, and grabbed the unconscious geezer by his shirt and belt. Crow yanked him back behind the wheel, pausing just long enough to give him a patdown. No gun. Too bad. He wouldn't have minded having one, at least for awhile.

He fastened the geezer's seatbelt so he couldn't tilt forward and blare the horn. Then he walked down the street to the girl's house, not hurrying. If he'd seen her face at one of the windows—or so much as a single twitch of a single curtain—he would have broken into a sprint, but nothing moved.

It was possible he could still make this work, but that consideration had been rendered strictly secondary by those terrible white flashes. What he mostly wanted was to get his hands on the miserable bitch that had caused them so much trouble and shake her until she rattled.

5

Abra sleepwalked down the front hall. The Stones had a family room in the basement, but the kitchen was their comfort place, and she headed there without thinking about it. She stood with her hands splayed out on the table where she and her parents had eaten thousands of meals, staring at the window over the kitchen sink with wide blank eyes. She wasn't really here at all. She was in Cloud Gap, watching bad guys spill out of the Winnebago: the Snake and the Nut and Jimmy Numbers. She knew their names from Barry. But something was wrong. One of them was missing.

(*WHERE'S THE CROW DAN I DON'T SEE THE CROW!*)

No answer, because Dan and her father and Dr. John were busy. They took the bad guys down, one after the other: the Walnut first—that was her father's work, and good for him—then Jimmy Numbers, then the Snake. She felt each mortal injury as a thudding deep in her head. Those thuds, like a heavy mallet repeatedly coming down on an oak plank, were terrible in their finality, but not entirely unpleasant. Because . . .

Because they deserve it, they kill kids, and nothing else would have stopped them. Only—

(*Dan where's the Crow? WHERE'S THE CROW???*)

Now Dan heard her. Thank God. She saw the Winnebago. Dan thought the Crow was in there, and maybe he was right. Still—

She hurried back down the hall and peered out one of the windows beside the front door. The sidewalk was deserted, but Mr. Freeman's truck was parked right where it belonged. She couldn't see his face because of the way the sun was shining on the windshield, but she could see *him* behind the wheel, and that meant everything was still okay.

Probably okay.

(*Abra are you there*)

Dan. It was so great to hear him. She wished he was with her, but having him inside her head was almost as good.

(*yes*)

She took one more reassuring look at the empty sidewalk and Mr. Freeman's truck, checked to make sure she had locked the door after coming in, and started back down to the kitchen.

(*you need to have your friend's mom call the police and tell them you're in danger Crow's in Anniston*)

She stopped halfway down the hall. Her comfort-hand came up and began to rub her mouth. Dan didn't know she had left the Deanes' house. How could he? He'd been very busy.

(*I'm not*)

Before she could finish, Rose the Hat's mental voice blasted through her head, wiping away all thought.

(YOU LITTLE BITCH WHAT HAVE YOU DONE)

The familiar hallway between the front door and the kitchen began to sideslip. The last time this revolving thing happened, she'd been prepared. This time she wasn't. Abra tried to stop it and couldn't. Her house was gone. Anniston was gone. She was lying on the ground and looking up at the sky. Abra realized the loss of those three in Cloud Gap had literally knocked Rose off her feet, and she had a moment to be savagely glad. She struggled for something to defend herself with. There wasn't much time.

6

Rose's body lay sprawled halfway between the showers and the Overlook Lodge, but her mind was in New Hampshire, swarming through the girl's head. There was no daydream horsewoman with a stallion and lance this time, oh no. This time it was just one surprised little chickadee and old Rosie, and Rosie wanted revenge. She would kill the girl only as a last resort, she was much too valuable for that, but Rose could give her a taste of what was coming. A taste of what Rose's friends had already suffered. There were plenty of soft, vulnerable places in the minds of rubes, and she knew them all very w—

(GET AWAY YOU BITCH LEAVE ME ALONE
OR I'LL FUCKING KILL YOU!)

It was like having a flash-bang go off behind her eyes. Rose jerked and cried out. Big Mo, who had been reaching down to touch her, recoiled in surprise. Rose didn't notice, didn't even see her. She kept underestimating the girl's power. She tried to keep her footing in the girl's head, but the little bitch was actually pushing her out. It was incredible and infuriating and terrifying, but it was true.

Worse, she could feel her physical hands rising toward her face. If Mo and Short Eddie hadn't restrained her, the little girl might have made Rose claw her own eyes out.

For the time being, at least, she had to give up and leave. But before she did, she saw something through the girl's eyes that flooded her with relief. It was Crow Daddy, and in one hand he was holding a needle.

7

Abra used all the psychic force she could muster, more than she had used on the day she had gone hunting for Brad Trevor, more than she had ever used in her life, and it was still barely enough. Just when she started to think she wouldn't be able to get the hat woman out of her head, the world began to revolve again. She was *making* it revolve, but it was so hard—like pushing a great stone wheel. The sky and the faces staring down at her slid away. There was a moment of darkness when she was

(*between*)

nowhere, and then her own front hall slid back into view. But she was no longer alone. A man was standing in the kitchen doorway.

No, not a man. A Crow.

"Hello, Abra," he said, smiling, and leaped at her. Still mentally reeling from her encounter with Rose, Abra made no attempt to push him away with her mind. She simply turned and ran.

8

In their moments of highest stress, Dan Torrance and Crow Daddy were very much alike, although neither would ever know it. The same clarity came over Crow's vision, the same sense that all of this was happening in beautiful slow motion. He saw the pink rubber bracelet on Abra's left wrist and had time to think *breast cancer awareness*. He saw the girl's backpack slew to the left as she whirled to her right and knew it was full of books. He even had time to admire her hair as it flew out behind her in a bright sheaf.

He caught her at the door as she was trying to turn the thumb lock. When he put his left arm around her throat and yanked her back, he felt her first efforts—confused, weak—to push him away with her mind.

Not the whole hypo, it might kill her, she can't weigh more than a hundred and fifteen pounds max.

Crow injected her just south of the collarbone as she twisted and struggled. He needn't have worried about losing control and shooting the whole dose into her, because her left arm came up and thumped against his right hand, knocking the hypo free. It fell to the floor and rolled. But providence favors True above rubes, it had always been that way and was now. He got just enough into her. He felt her little handhold on his mind first slip, then fall away. Her hands did the same. She stared at him with shocked, floating eyes.

Crow patted her shoulder. "We're going for a ride, Abra. You're going to meet exciting new people."

Incredibly, she managed a smile. A rather frightening one for a girl so young that with her hair piled up under a cap, she could still have passed for a boy. "Those monsters you call your friends are all dead. Theyyy . . ."

The last word was only an unwinding slur as her eyes rolled up and her knees came unhinged. Crow was tempted to let her drop—it would serve her too right—but restrained the impulse and caught her under the arms instead. She was valuable property, after all.

True property.

9

He had come in through the rear door, snapping back the next-to-useless spring lock with a single downward flick of Henry Rothman's American Express Platinum Card, but he had no intention of leaving that way. There was nothing but a high fence at the foot of the sloping backyard, and beyond that a river. Also, his transportation was in the other direction. He carried Abra through the kitchen and into the empty garage. Both parents at work, maybe . . . unless they were out at Cloud Gap, gloating over Andi, Billy, and Nut. For now he didn't give much of a shit about that end of things; whoever had been helping the girl could wait. Their time would come.

He slid her limp body under a table holding her father's few tools. Then he thumbed the button that opened the garage door and stepped out, being sure to slap on that big old Henry Rothman smile before he did. The key to survival in the world of rubes was to look as if you belonged, as if you were always on the goodfoot, and no one was better at it than Crow. He walked briskly down to the truck and moved the geezer again, this time to the middle of the bench seat. As Crow turned in to the Stone driveway, Billy's head lolled against his shoulder.

"Gettin a little chummy there, aren't you, oldtimer?" Crow asked, and laughed as he drove the red truck into the garage. His friends were dead and this situation was horribly dangerous, but there was one big compensation: he felt totally alive and aware for the first time in a great many years, the world bursting with color and humming like a powerline. He had her, by God. In spite of all her weird strength and nasty tricks, he had her. Now he would bring her to Rose. A love offering.

"Jackpot," he said, and gave the dashboard one hard, exultant hit.

He stripped off Abra's backpack, left it under the worktable, and lifted her into the truck on the passenger side. He seatbelted both of his snoozing passengers. It had certainly occurred to him to snap the geezer's neck and leave his body in the garage, but the geezer might come in handy. If the drug didn't kill him, that was. Crow checked for a pulse on the side of the grizzled old neck and felt it, slow but strong. There was no question about the girl; she was leaning against the passenger window and he could see her breath fogging the glass. Excellent.

Crow took a second to inventory his stock. No gun—the True Knot never traveled with firearms—but he still had two full hypos of the noddy-time night-night stuff. He didn't know how far two would get him, but the girl was his priority. Crow had an idea that the geezer's period of usefulness might prove to be extremely limited. Oh, well. Rubes came and rubes went.

He took out his cell and this time it was Rose he hit on the speed dial. She answered just as he had resigned himself to leaving a message. Her voice was slow, her pronunciation slurry. It was a little like talking to a drunk.

"Rose? What's up with you?"

"The girl messed with me a trifle more than I expected, but I'm all right. I don't hear her anymore. Tell me you have her."

"I do, and she's having a nice nap, but she's got friends. I don't want to meet them. I'll head west immediately, and I've got no time to be fucking with maps. I need secondary roads that'll take me across Vermont and into New York."

"I'll put Toady Slim on it."

"You need to send someone east to meet me *immediately,* Rosie, and with whatever you can lay your hands on that'll keep Little Miss Nitro pacified, because I don't have much left. Look in Nut's supplies. He must have *something*—"

"Don't tell me my business," she snapped. "Toady will coordinate everything. You know enough to get started?"

"Yes. Rosie darlin, that picnic area was a trap. The little girl fucking deked us. What if her friends call the cops? I'm riding in an old F-150 with a couple of zombies next to me in the cab. I might as well have KIDNAPPER tattooed on my forehead."

But he was grinning. Damned if he wasn't grinning. There was a pause at the other end. Crow sat behind the wheel in the Stones' garage, waiting.

At last Rose said, "If you see blue lights behind you or a roadblock ahead of you, strangle the girl and suck out as much of her steam as you can while she goes. Then surrender. We'll take care of you eventually, you know that."

It was Crow's turn to pause. At last he said, "Are you sure that's the right way to go, darlin?"

"I am." Her voice was stony. "She's responsible for the deaths of Jimmy, Nut, and Snakebite. I mourn them all, but it's Andi I feel the worst about, because I Turned her myself and she only had a taste of the life. Then there's Sarey . . ."

She trailed off with a sigh. Crow said nothing. There was really nothing to say. Andi Steiner had been with a lot of women during her early years with the True—not a surprise, steam always made newbies especially randy—but she and Sarah Carter had been a couple for the last ten years, and devoted to each other. In some ways, Andi had seemed more like Silent Sarey's daughter than her lover.

"Sarey's inconsolable," Rose said, "and Black-Eyed Susie's not much better about Nut. That little girl is going to answer for taking those three from us. One way or the other, her rube life is over. Any more questions?"

Crow had none.

10

No one paid any particular attention to Crow Daddy and his snoozing passengers as they left Anniston on the old Granite State Highway, headed west. With a few notable exceptions (sharp-eyed old ladies and little kids were the worst), Rube America was staggeringly unobservant even twelve years into the Dark Age of Terrorism. *If you see something, say something* was a hell of a slogan, but first you had to see something.

By the time they crossed into Vermont it was growing dark, and cars passing by in the other direction saw only Crow's headlights, which he purposely left on hi-beam. Toady Slim had called three times already, feeding him route information. Most were byroads, many unmarked. Toady had also told Crow that Diesel Doug, Dirty Phil, and Apron Annie were on their way. They were riding in an '06 Caprice that looked like a dog but had four hundred horses under the hood. Speeding would not be a problem; they were also carrying Homeland Security creds that would check out all the way up the line, thanks to the late Jimmy Numbers.

The Little twins, Pea and Pod, were using the True's sophisticated satellite communications gear to monitor police chatter in the Northeast, and so far there had been nothing about the possible kidnapping of a young girl. This was good news, but not unexpected. Friends smart enough to set up an ambush were probably smart enough to know what could happen to their chickadee if they went public.

Another phone rang, this one muffled. Without taking his eyes off the road, Crow leaned across his sleeping passengers, reached into the glove compartment, and found a cell. The geezer's, no doubt. He held it up to his eyes. There was no name, so the caller wasn't in the phone's memory, but the number had a New Hampshire area code. One of the ambushers, wanting to know if Billy and the girl were all right? Very likely. Crow considered answering it and decided not to. He would check later to see if the caller had left a message, though. Information was power.

When he leaned over again to return the cell to the glove compartment, his fingers touched metal. He stowed the phone and brought out an automatic pistol. A nice bonus, and a lucky find. If the geezer had awakened a little sooner than expected, he might have gotten to it before Crow could read his intentions. Crow slid the Glock under his seat, then flipped the glove compartment closed.

Guns were also power.

11

It was full dark and they were deep into the Green Mountains on Highway 108 when Abra began to stir. Crow, still feeling brilliantly alive and aware, wasn't sorry. For one thing, he was curious about her. For another, the old truck's gas gauge was touching empty, and someone was going to have to fill the tank.

But it wouldn't do to take chances.

With his right hand he removed one of the two remaining hypos from his pocket and held it on his thigh. He waited until the girl's eyes—still soft and muzzy—opened. Then he said, "Good evening, little lady. I'm Henry Rothman. Do you understand me?"

"You're . . ." Abra cleared her throat, wet her lips, tried again. "You're not Henry anything. You're the Crow."

"So you do understand. That's good. You feel woolly-headed just now, I imagine, and you're going to stay that way, because that's just how I like you. But there will be no need to knock you all the way out again as long as you mind your Ps and Qs. Have you got that?"

"Where are we going?"

"Hogwarts, to watch the International Quidditch Tourney. I'll buy you a magic hotdog and a cone of magic cotton candy. Answer my question. Are you going to mind your Ps and Qs?"

"Yes."

"Such instant agreement is pleasing to the ear, but you'll have to pardon me if I don't completely trust it. I need to give you some vital information before you try something foolish that you might regret. Do you see the needle I have?"

"Yes." Abra's head was still resting against the window, but she looked down at the hypo. Her eyes drifted shut then opened again, very slowly. "I'm thirsty."

"From the drug, no doubt. I don't have anything to drink with me, we left in a bit of a hurry—"

"I think there's a juice box in my pack." Husky. Low and slow. The eyes still opening with great effort after every blink.

"Afraid that's back in your garage. You may get something to drink in the next town we come to—if you're a good little Goldilocks. If you're a bad little Goldilocks, you can spend the night swallowing your own spit. Clear?"

"Yes . . ."

"If I feel you fiddling around inside my head—yes, I know you can do it—or if you try attracting attention when we stop, I'll inject this old gentleman. On top of what I already gave him, it will kill him as dead as Amy Winehouse. Are we clear on that, as well?"

"Yes." She licked her lips again, then rubbed them with her hand. "Don't hurt him."

"That's up to you."

"Where are you taking me?"

"Goldilocks? Dear?"

"What?" She blinked at him dazedly.

"Just shut up and enjoy the ride."

"Hogwarts," she said. "Cotton . . . candy." This time when her eyes closed, the lids stayed down. She began to snore lightly. It was a breezy sound, sort of pleasant. Crow didn't think she was shamming, but he continued to hold the hypo next to the geezer's leg just to be sure. As Gollum had once said about Frodo Baggins, it was tricksy, precious. It was very tricksy.

12

Abra didn't go under completely; she still heard the truck's motor, but it was far away. It seemed to be above her. It made her remember when she and her parents went to Lake Winnipesaukee on hot summer afternoons, and how you could hear the distant drone of the motorboats if you ducked your head underwater. She knew she was being kidnapped, and she knew this should concern her, but she felt serene, content to float between sleep and waking. The dryness in her mouth and throat was horrible, though. Her tongue felt like a strip of dusty carpet.

I have to do something. He's taking me to the hat woman and I have to do something. If I don't, they'll kill me like they killed the baseball boy. Or something even worse.

She *would* do something. After she got something to drink. And after she slept a little more . . .

The engine sound had faded from a drone to a distant hum when light penetrated her closed eyelids. Then the sound stopped completely and the Crow was poking her in the leg. Easy at first, then harder. Hard enough to hurt.

"Wake up, Goldilocks. You can go back to sleep later."

She struggled her eyes open, wincing at the brightness. They were parked beside some gas pumps. There were fluorescents over them. She shielded her eyes from the glare. Now she had a headache to go with her thirst. It was like . . .

"What's funny, Goldilocks?"

"Huh?"

"You're smiling."

"I just figured out what's wrong with me. I'm hungover."

Crow considered this, and grinned. "I suppose you are at that, and you didn't even get to prance around with a lampshade on your head. Are you awake enough to understand me?"

"Yes." At least she thought she was. Oh, but the thudding in her head. Awful.

"Take this."

He was holding something in front of her face, reaching across his body with his left hand to do it. His right one still held the hypodermic, the needle resting next to Mr. Freeman's leg.

She squinted. It was a credit card. She reached up with a hand that felt too heavy and took it. Her eyes started to close and he slapped her face. Her eyes flew open, wide and shocked. She had never been hit in her life, not by an adult, anyway. Of course she had never been kidnapped, either.

"Ow! *Ow!*"

"Get out of the truck. Follow the instructions on the pump— you're a bright kid, I'm sure you can do that—and fill the tank.

Then replace the nozzle and get back in. If you do all that like a good little Goldilocks, we'll drive over to yonder Coke machine." He pointed to the far corner of the store. "You can get a nice big twenty-ounce soda. Or a water, if that's what you want; I spy with my little eye that they have Dasani. If you're a *bad* little Goldilocks, I'll kill the old man, then go into the store and kill the kid at the register. No problem there. Your friend had a gun, which is now in my possession. I'll take you with me and you can watch the kid's head go splat. It's up to you, okay? You get it?"

"Yes," Abra said. A little more awake now. "Can I have a Coke *and* a water?"

His grin this time was high, wide, and handsome. In spite of her situation, in spite of the headache, even in spite of the slap he'd administered, Abra found it charming. She guessed lots of people found it charming, especially women. "A little greedy, but that's not always a bad thing. Let's see how you mind those Ps and Qs."

She unbuckled her belt—it took three tries, but she finally managed—and grabbed the doorhandle. Before she got out, she said: "Stop calling me Goldilocks. You know my name, and I know yours."

She slammed the door and headed for the gas island (weaving a little) before he could reply. She had spunk as well as steam. He could almost admire her. But, given what had happened to Snake, Nut, and Jimmy, almost was as far as it went.

13

At first Abra couldn't read the instructions because the words kept doubling and sliding around. She squinted and they came into focus. The Crow was watching her. She could feel his eyes like tiny warm weights on the back of her neck.

(*Dan?*)

Nothing, and she wasn't surprised. How could she hope to reach Dan when she could barely figure out how to run this stupid pump? She had never felt less shiny in her life.

Eventually she managed to start the gas, although the first time she tried his credit card, she put it in upside-down and had to begin all over again. The pumping seemed to go on forever, but there was a rubber sleeve over the nozzle to keep the stench of the fumes down, and the night air was clearing her head a little. There were billions of stars. Usually they awed her with their beauty and profusion, but tonight looking at them only made her feel scared. They were far away. They didn't see Abra Stone.

When the tank was full, she squinted at the new message in the pump's window and turned to Crow. "Do you want a receipt?"

"I think we can crutch along without that, don't you?" Again came his dazzling grin, the kind that made you happy if you were the one who caused it to break out. Abra bet he had lots of girlfriends.

No. He just has one. The hat woman is his girlfriend. Rose. If he had another one, Rose would kill her. Probably with her teeth and fingernails.

She trudged back to the truck and got in.

"That was very good," Crow said. "You win the grand prize—a Coke *and* a water. So . . . what do you say to your Daddy?"

"Thank you," Abra said listlessly. "But you're not my daddy."

"I could be, though. I can be a very good daddy to little girls who are good to me. The ones who mind their Ps and Qs." He drove to the machine and gave her a five-dollar bill. "Get me a Fanta if they have it. A Coke if they don't."

"You drink sodas, like anyone else?"

He made a comical wounded face. "If you prick us, do we not bleed? If you tickle us, do we not laugh?"

"Shakespeare, right?" She wiped her mouth again. *"Romeo and Juliet."*

"Merchant of Venice, dummocks," Crow said . . . but with a smile. "Don't know the rest of it, I bet."

She shook her head. A mistake. It refreshed the throbbing, which had begun to diminish.

"If you poison us, do we not die?" He tapped the needle against Mr. Freeman's leg. "Meditate on that while you get our drinks."

14

He watched closely as she operated the machine. This gas stop was on the wooded outskirts of some little town, and there was always a chance she might decide to hell with the geezer and run for the trees. He thought of the gun, but left it where it was. Chasing her down would be no great task, given her current soupy condition. But she didn't even look in that direction. She slid the five-spot into the machine and got the drinks, one after the other, pausing only to drink deeply from the water. She came back and gave him his Fanta, but didn't get in. Instead she pointed farther down the side of the building.

"I need to pee."

Crow was flummoxed. This was something he hadn't foreseen, although he should have. She had been drugged, and her body needed to purge itself of toxins. "Can't you hold it awhile?" He was thinking that a few more miles down the road, he could find a turnout and pull in. Let her go behind a bush. As long as he could see the top of her head, they'd be fine.

But she shook her head. Of course she did.

He thought it over. "Okay, listen up. You can use the ladies' toilet if the door's unlocked. If it's not, you'll have to take your leak around back. There's no way I'm letting you go inside and ask the counterboy for the key."

"And if I have to go in back, you'll watch me, I suppose. Pervo."

"There'll be a Dumpster or something you can squat behind. It would break my heart not to get a look at your precious little buns, but I'd try to survive. Now get in the truck."

"But you said—"

"Get in, or I'll start calling you Goldilocks again."

She got in, and he pulled the truck up next to the bathroom doors, not quite blocking them. "Now hold out your hand."

"Why?"

"Just do it."

Very reluctantly, she held out her hand. He took it. When she saw the needle, she tried to pull back.

"Don't worry, just a drop. We can't have you thinking bad thoughts, now can we? Or broadcasting them. This is going to happen one way or the other, so why make a production of it?"

She stopped trying to pull away. It was easier just to let it happen. There was a brief sting on the back of her hand, then he released her. "Go on, now. Make wee-wee and make it quick. As the old song says, sand is a-runnin through the hourglass back home."

"I don't know any song like that."

"Not surprised. You don't even know *The Merchant of Venice* from *Romeo and Juliet.*"

"You're mean."

"I don't have to be," he said.

She got out and just stood beside the truck for a moment, taking deep breaths.

"Abra?"

She looked at him.

"Don't try locking yourself in. You know who'd pay for that, don't you?" He patted Billy Freeman's leg.

She knew.

Her head, which had begun to clear, was fogging in again. Horrible man—horrible *thing*—behind that charming grin. And smart. He thought of everything. She tried the bathroom door and it opened. At least she wouldn't have to whizz out back in the weeds, and that was something. She went inside, shut the door, and took care of her business. Then she simply sat there on the toilet with her swimming head hung down. She thought of being in the bathroom at Emma's house, when she had foolishly believed everything was going to turn out all right. How long ago that seemed.

I have to do something.

But she was doped up, woozy.

(Dan)

She sent this with all the force she could muster . . . which wasn't much. And how much time would the Crow give her? She felt despair wash over her, undermining what little will to resist was left. All she wanted to do was button her pants, get into the truck again, and go back to sleep. Yet she tried one more time.

(*Dan! Dan, please!*)

And waited for a miracle.

What she got instead was a single brief tap of the pickup truck's horn. The message was clear: *time's up*.

CHAPTER FIFTEEN

SWAPSIES

1

You will remember what was forgotten.

In the aftermath of the Pyrrhic victory at Cloud Gap, the phrase haunted Dan, like a snatch of irritating and nonsensical music that gets in your head and won't let go, the kind you find yourself humming even as you stumble to the bathroom in the middle of the night. This one was plenty irritating, but not quite nonsensical. For some reason he associated it with Tony.

You will remember what was forgotten.

There was no question of taking the True Knot's Winnebago back to their cars, which were parked at Teenytown Station on the Frazier town common. Even if they hadn't been afraid of being observed getting out of it or leaving forensic evidence inside it, they would have refused without needing to take a vote on the matter. It smelled of more than sickness and death; it smelled of evil. Dan had another reason. He didn't know if members of the True Knot came back as ghostie people or not, but he didn't want to find out.

So they threw the abandoned clothes and the drug paraphernalia into the Saco, where the stuff that didn't sink would float downstream to Maine, and went back as they had come, in *The Helen Rivington*.

David Stone dropped into the conductor's seat, saw that Dan was still holding Abra's stuffed rabbit, and held out his hand for it. Dan passed it over willingly enough, taking note of what Abra's father held in his other hand: his BlackBerry.

"What are you going to do with that?"

Dave looked at the woods flowing by on both sides of the narrow-gauge tracks, then back at Dan. "As soon as we get to where there's cell coverage, I'm going to call the Deanes' house. If there's no answer, I'm going to call the police. If there *is* an answer, and either Emma or her mother tells me that Abra's gone, I'm going to call the police. Assuming they haven't already." His gaze was cool and measuring and far from friendly, but at least he was keeping his fear for his daughter—his terror, more likely—at bay, and Dan respected him for that. Also, it would make him easier to reason with.

"I hold you responsible for this, Mr. Torrance. It was your plan. Your crazy plan."

No use pointing out that they had all signed on to the crazy plan. Or that he and John were almost as sick about Abra's continued silence as her father. Basically, the man was right.

You will remember what was forgotten.

Was that another Overlook memory? Dan thought it was. But why now? Why here?

"Dave, she's almost *certainly* been taken." That was John Dalton. He had moved up to the car just behind them. The last of the lowering sun came through the trees and flickered on his face. "If that's the case and you tell the police, what do you think will happen to Abra?"

God bless you, Dan thought. *If I'd been the one to say it, I doubt if he would have listened. Because, at bottom, I'm the stranger who was conspiring with his daughter. He'll never be completely convinced that I'm not the one who got her into this mess.*

"What else can we do?" Dave asked, and then his fragile calm broke. He began to weep, and held Abra's stuffed rabbit to his face. "What am I going to tell my wife? That I was shooting people in Cloud Gap while some bogeyman was stealing our daughter?"

"First things first," Dan said. He didn't think AA slogans like *Let go and let God* or *Take it easy* would fly with Abra's dad right now. "You *should* call the Deanes when you get cell coverage. I think you'll reach them, and they'll be fine."

"You think this why?"

"In my last communication with Abra, I told her to have her friend's mom call the police."

Dave blinked. "You really did? Or are you just saying that now to cover your ass?"

"I really did. Abra started to answer. She said 'I'm not,' and then I lost her. I think she was going to tell me she wasn't at the Deanes' anymore."

"Is she alive?" Dave grasped Dan's elbow with a hand that was dead cold. "Is my daughter still alive?"

"I haven't heard from her, but I'm sure she is."

"Of course you'd say that," Dave whispered. "CYA, right?"

Dan bit back a retort. If they started squabbling, any thin chance of getting Abra back would become no chance.

"It makes sense," John said. Although he was still pale and his hands weren't quite steady, he was using his calm bedside manner voice. "Dead, she's no good to the one who's left. The one who grabbed her. Alive, she's a hostage. Also, they want her for . . . well . . ."

"They want her for her essence," Dan said. "The steam."

"Another thing," John said. "What are you going to tell the cops about the men we killed? That they started cycling in and out of invisibility until they disappeared completely? And then we got rid of their . . . their leavings?"

"I can't believe I let you get me into this." Dave was twisting the rabbit from side to side. Soon the old toy would split open and spill its stuffing. Dan wasn't sure he could bear to see that.

John said, "Listen, Dave. For your daughter's sake, you have to clear your mind. She's been in this ever since she saw that boy's picture in the *Shopper* and tried to find out about him. As soon as the one Abra calls the hat woman was aware of her, she almost had to come after her. I don't know about steam, and I know very little about what Dan calls the shining, but I know people like the ones we're dealing with don't leave witnesses. And when it comes to the Iowa boy, that's what your daughter was."

"Call the Deanes but keep it light," Dan said.

"Light? *Light?*" He looked like a man trying out a word in Swedish.

"Say you want to ask Abra if there's anything you should pick up at the store—bread or milk or something like that. If they say she went home, just say fine, you'll reach her there."

"Then what?"

Dan didn't know. All he knew was that he needed to think. He needed to think about what was forgotten.

John *did* know. "Then you try to reach Billy Freeman."

It was dusk, with the *Riv's* headlight cutting a visible cone up the aisle of the tracks, before Dave got bars on his phone. He called the Deanes', and although he was clutching the now-deformed Hoppy in a mighty grip and large beads of sweat were trickling down his face, Dan thought he did a pretty good job. Could Abby come to the phone for a minute and tell him if they needed anything at the Stop & Shop? Oh? She did? Then he'd try her at home. He listened a moment longer, said he'd be sure to do that, and ended the call. He looked at Dan, his eyes white-rimmed holes in his face.

"Mrs. Deane wanted me to find out how Abra's feeling. Apparently she went home complaining of menstrual cramps." He hung his head. "I didn't even know she'd started having periods. Lucy never said."

"There are things dads don't need to know," John said. "Now try Billy."

"I don't have his number." He gave a single chop of a laugh—*HA!* "We're one fucked-up posse."

Dan recited it from memory. Up ahead the trees were thinning, and he could see the glow of the streetlights along Frazier's main drag.

Dave punched in the number and listened. Listened some more, then killed the call. "Voice mail."

The three men were silent as the *Riv* broke out of the trees and rolled the last two miles toward Teenytown. Dan tried again to reach Abra, throwing his mental voice with all the energy he could muster, and got nothing back. The one she called the Crow had probably knocked her out somehow. The tattoo woman had been carrying a needle. Probably the Crow had another one.

You will remember what was forgotten.

The origin of that thought arose from the very back of his mind, where he kept the lockboxes containing all the terrible memories of the Overlook Hotel and the ghosts who had infested it.

"It was the boiler."

In the conductor's seat, Dave glanced at him. "Huh?"

"Nothing."

The Overlook's heating system had been ancient. The steam pressure had to be dumped at regular intervals or it crept up and up to the point where the boiler could explode and send the whole hotel sky-high. In his steepening descent into dementia, Jack Torrance had forgotten this, but his young son had been warned. By Tony.

Was this another warning, or just a maddening mnemonic brought on by stress and guilt? Because he *did* feel guilty. John was right, Abra was going to be a True target no matter what, but feelings were invulnerable to rational thought. It had been his plan, the plan had gone wrong, and he was on the hook.

You will remember what was forgotten.

Was it the voice of his old friend, trying to tell him something about their current situation, or just the gramophone?

2

Dave and John went back to the Stone house together. Dan followed in his own car, delighted to be alone with his thoughts. Not that it seemed to help. He was almost positive there was something there, something *real,* but it wouldn't come. He even tried to summon Tony, a thing he hadn't attempted since his teenage years, and had no luck.

Billy's truck was no longer parked on Richland Court. To Dan, that made sense. The True Knot raiding party had come in the

Winnebago. If they dropped the Crow off in Anniston, he would have been on foot and in need of a vehicle.

The garage was open. Dave got out of John's car before it pulled completely to a stop and ran inside, calling Abra's name. Then, spotlighted in the headlights of John's Suburban like an actor on a stage, he lifted something up and uttered a sound somewhere between a groan and a scream. As Dan pulled up next to the Suburban, he saw what it was: Abra's backpack.

The urge to drink came on Dan then, even stronger than the night he'd called John from the parking lot of the cowboy-boogie bar, stronger than in all the years since he'd picked up a white chip at his first meeting. The urge to simply reverse down the driveway, ignoring their shouts, and drive back to Frazier. There was a bar there called the Bull Moose. He'd been past it many times, always with the recovered drunk's reflexive speculations—what was it like inside? What was on draft? What kind of music was on the juke? What whiskey was on the shelf and what kind in the well? Were there any good-looking ladies? And what would that first drink taste like? Would it taste like home? Like finally coming home? He could answer at least some of those questions before Dave Stone called the cops and the cops took him in for questioning in the matter of a certain little girl's disappearance.

A time will come, Casey had told him in those early white-knuckle days, *when your mental defenses will fail and the only thing left standing between you and a drink will be your Higher Power.*

Dan had no problem with the Higher Power thing, because he had a bit of inside information. God remained an unproven hypothesis, but he knew there really was another plane of existence. Like Abra, Dan had seen the ghostie people. So sure, God was possible. Given his glimpses of the world beyond the world, Dan thought it even likely . . . although what kind of God only sat by while shit like this played out?

As if you're the first one to ask that question, he thought.

Casey Kingsley had told him to get down on his knees twice a day, asking for help in the morning and saying thanks at night. *It's the first three steps: I can't, God can, I think I'll let Him. Don't think too much about it.*

To newcomers reluctant to take this advice, Casey was wont to offer a story about the film director John Waters. In one of his early movies, *Pink Flamingos,* Waters's drag-queen star, Divine, had eaten a bit of dog excrement off a suburban lawn. Years later, Waters was still being asked about that glorious moment of cinematic history. Finally he snapped. "It was just a *little* piece of dogshit," he told a reporter, "and it made her a star."

So get down on your knees and ask for help even if you don't like it, Casey always finished. *After all, it's just a* little *piece of dogshit.*

Dan couldn't very well get on his knees behind the steering wheel of his car, but he assumed the automatic default position of his morning and nightly prayers—eyes closed and one palm pressed against his lips, as if to keep out even a trickle of the seductive poison that had scarred twenty years of his life.

God, help me not to dri—

He got that far and the light broke.

It was what Dave had said on their way to Cloud Gap. It was Abra's angry smile (Dan wondered if the Crow had seen that smile yet, and what he made of it, if so). Most of all, it was the feel of his own skin, pressing his lips back against his teeth.

"Oh my God," he whispered. He got out of the car and his legs gave way. He fell on his knees after all, but got up and ran into the garage, where the two men were standing and looking at Abra's abandoned pack.

He grabbed Dave Stone's shoulder. "Call your wife. Tell her you're coming to see her."

"She'll want to know what it's about," Dave said. It was clear from his quivering mouth and downcast eyes how little he wanted to have that conversation. "She's staying at Chetta's apartment. I'll tell her . . . Christ, I don't know what I'll tell her."

Dan gripped tighter, increasing the pressure until the lowered eyes came up and met his. "We're all going to Boston, but John and I have other business to take care of there."

"What other business? I don't understand."

Dan did. Not everything, but a lot.

3

They took John's Suburban. Dave rode shotgun. Dan lay in the back with his head on an armrest and his feet on the floor.

"Lucy kept trying to get me to tell her what it was about," Dave said. "She told me I was scaring her. And of course she thought it was Abra, because she's got a little of what Abra's got. I've always known it. I told her Abby was staying the night at Emma's house. Do you know how many times I've lied to my wife in the years we've been married? I could count them on one hand, and three of them would be about how much I lost in the Thursday night poker games the head of my department runs. Nothing like this. And in just three hours, I'm going to have to eat it."

Of course Dan and John knew what he'd said about Abra, and how upset Lucy had been at her husband's continued insistence that the matter was too important and complex to go into on the telephone. They had both been in the kitchen when he made the call. But he needed to talk. To *share,* in AA-speak. John took care of any responses that needed to be made, saying *uh-huh* and *I know* and *I understand.*

At some point, Dave broke off and looked into the backseat. "Jesus God, are you *sleeping?*"

"No," Dan said without opening his eyes. "I'm trying to get in touch with your daughter."

That ended Dave's monologue. Now there was only the hum of the tires as the Suburban ran south on Route 16 through a dozen little towns. Traffic was light and John kept the speedometer pegged at a steady sixty miles an hour once the two lanes broadened to four.

Dan made no effort to call Abra; he wasn't sure that would work. Instead he tried to open his mind completely. To turn himself into a listening post. He had never attempted anything like this before, and the result was eerie. It was like wearing the world's most powerful set of headphones. He seemed to hear a steady low rushing sound, and believed it was the hum of human thoughts. He held himself ready to hear her voice somewhere in that steady surf, not really expecting it, but what else could he do?

It was shortly after they went through the first tolls on the Spaulding Turnpike, now only sixty miles from Boston, that he finally picked her up.

(*Dan*)

Low. Barely there. At first he thought it was just imagination—wish fulfillment—but he turned in that direction anyway, trying to narrow his concentration down to a single searchlight beam. And it came again, a bit louder this time. It was real. It was *her*.

(*Dan, please!*)

She was drugged, all right, and he'd never tried anything remotely like what had to be done next . . . but Abra had. She would have to show him the way, doped up or not.

(*Abra push you have to help me*)

(*help what help how*)

(*swapsies*)

(*???*)

(*help me turn the world*)

4

Dave was in the passenger seat, going through the change in the cup holder for the next toll, when Dan spoke from behind him. Only it most certainly wasn't Dan.

"Just give me another minute, I have to change my tampon!"

The Suburban swerved as John sat up straight and jerked the wheel. "What the *hell?*"

Dave unsnapped his seatbelt and got on his knees, twisting around to peer at the man lying on the backseat. Dan's eyes were half-lidded, but when Dave spoke Abra's name, they opened.

"No, Daddy, not now, I have to help . . . I have to try . . ." Dan's body twisted. One hand came up, wiped his mouth in a gesture Dave had seen a thousand times, then fell away. "Tell him I said not to call me that. Tell him—"

Dan's head cocked sideways until it was lying on his shoulder. He groaned. His hands twitched aimlessly.

"What's going on?" John shouted. "What do I do?"

"I don't know," Dave said. He reached between the seats, took one of the twitching hands, and held it tight.

"Drive," Dan said. "Just drive."

Then the body on the backseat began to buck and twist. Abra began to scream with Dan's voice.

5

He found the conduit between them by following the sluggish current of her thoughts. He saw the stone wheel because Abra was visualizing it, but she was far too weak and disoriented to turn it. She was using all the mental force she could muster just to keep her end of the link open. So he could enter her mind and she could enter his. But he was still mostly in the Suburban, with the lights of the cars headed in the other direction running across the padded roof. Light . . . dark . . . light . . . dark.

The wheel was so heavy.

There was a sudden hammering from somewhere, and a voice. "Come out, Abra. Time's up. We have to roll."

That frightened her, and she found a little extra strength. The wheel began to move, pulling him deeper into the umbilicus that connected them. It was the strangest sensation Dan had ever had in his life, exhilarating even in the horror of the situation.

Somewhere, distant, he heard Abra say, "Just give me another minute, I have to change my tampon!"

The roof of John's Suburban was sliding away. *Turning* away. There was darkness, the sense of being in a tunnel, and he had time to think, *If I get lost in here, I'll never be able to get back. I'll wind up in a mental hospital somewhere, labeled a hopeless catatonic.*

But then the world was sliding back into place, only it wasn't the same place. The Suburban was gone. He was in a smelly bathroom with dingy blue tiles on the floor and a sign beside the washbasin reading SORRY COLD WATER ONLY. He was sitting on the toilet.

Before he could even think about getting up, the door bammed open hard enough to crack some of the old tiles, and a man strode in. He looked about thirty-five, his hair dead black and combed away from his forehead, his face angular but handsome in a rough-hewn, bony way. In one hand he held a pistol.

"Change your tampon, sure," he said. "Where'd you have it, Goldilocks, in your pants pocket? Must have been, because your backpack's a long way from here."

(*tell him I said not to call me that*)

Dan said, "I told you not to call me that."

Crow paused, looking at the girl sitting on the toilet seat, swaying a little from side to side. Swaying because of the dope. Sure. But what about the way she sounded? Was *that* because of the dope?

"What happened to your voice? You don't sound like yourself."

Dan tried to shrug the girl's shoulders and only succeeded in twitching one of them. Crow grabbed Abra's arm and yanked Dan to Abra's feet. It hurt, and he cried out.

Somewhere—miles from here—a faint voice shouted, *What's going on? What do I do?*

"Drive," he told John as Crow pulled him out the door. "Just drive."

"Oh, I'll drive, all right," Crow said, and muscled Abra into the truck next to the snoring Billy Freeman. Then he grabbed a sheaf of her hair, wound it in his fist, and pulled. Dan screamed with Abra's voice, knowing it wasn't *quite* her voice. Almost, but not quite. Crow heard the difference, but didn't know what it was. The hat woman would have; it was the hat woman who had unwittingly shown Abra this mindswap trick.

"But before we get rolling, we're going to have an understanding. No more lies, that's the understanding. The next time you lie to your Daddy, this old geezer snoring beside me is dead meat. I won't use the dope, either. I'll pull in at a camp road and put a bullet in his belly. That way it takes awhile. You'll get to listen to him scream. Do you understand?"

"Yes," Dan whispered.

"Little girl, I fucking hope so, because I don't chew my cabbage twice."

Crow slammed the door and walked quickly around to the driver's side. Dan closed Abra's eyes. He was thinking about the spoons at the birthday party. About opening and shutting drawers—that, too. Abra was too physically weak to grapple with the man now getting behind the wheel and starting the engine, but part of her was strong. If he could find that part . . . the part that had moved the spoons and opened drawers and played air-music . . . the part that had written on his blackboard from miles away . . . if he could find it and then take control of it . . .

As Abra had visualized a female warrior's lance and a stallion, Dan now visualized a bank of switches on a control room wall. Some worked her hands, some her legs, some the shrug of her shoulders. Others, though, were more important. He should be able to pull them; he had at least some of the same circuits.

The truck was moving, first reversing, then turning. A moment later they were back on the road.

"That's right," Crow said grimly. "Go to sleep. What the hell did you think you were going to do back there? Jump in the toilet and flush yourself away to . . ."

His words faded, because here were the switches Dan was looking for. The special switches, the ones with the red handles. He didn't know if they were really there, and actually connected to Abra's powers, or if this was just some mental game of solitaire he was playing. He only knew that he had to try.

Shine on, he thought, and pulled them all.

6

Billy Freeman's pickup was six or eight miles west of the gas station and rolling through rural Vermont darkness on 108 when Crow first felt the pain. It was like a small silver band circling his left eye. It was cold, pressing. He reached up to touch it, but before he could, it slithered right, freezing the bridge of his nose like a shot of novocaine. Then it circled his other eye as well. It was like wearing metal binoculars.

Or eyecuffs.

Now his left ear began to ring, and suddenly his left cheek was numb. He turned his head and saw the little girl looking at him. Her eyes were wide and unblinking. They didn't look doped in the slightest. For that matter, they didn't look like her eyes. They looked older. Wiser. And as cold as his face now felt.

(*stop the truck*)

Crow had capped the hypo and put it away, but he was still holding the gun he'd taken from beneath the seat when he decided she was spending way too much time in the crapper. He raised it, meaning to threaten the geezer and make her stop whatever it was she was doing, but all at once his hand felt as if it had been plunged into freezing water. The gun put on weight: five pounds, ten pounds, what felt like twenty-five. Twenty-five at least. And while he was struggling to raise it, his right foot came off the F-150's gas pedal and his left hand turned the wheel so that the truck veered off the road and rolled along the soft shoulder—gently, slowing—with the right-side wheels tilting toward the ditch.

"What are you doing to me?"

"What you deserve. *Daddy*."

The truck bumped a downed birch tree, snapped it in two, and stopped. The girl and the geezer were seatbelted in, but Crow had forgotten his. He jolted forward into the steering wheel, honking the horn. When he looked down, he saw the geezer's automatic turning in his fist. Very slowly turning toward him. This shouldn't be happening. The dope was supposed to stop it. Hell, the dope *had* stopped it. But something had changed in that bathroom. Whoever was behind those eyes now was cold fucking sober.

And horribly strong.

Rose! Rose, I need you!

"I don't think she can hear," the voice that wasn't Abra's said. "You may have some talents, you son of a bitch, but I don't think you have much in the way of telepathy. I think when you want to talk to your girlfriend, you use the phone."

Exerting all his strength, Crow began to turn the Glock back toward the girl. Now it seemed to weigh fifty pounds. The tendons of his neck stood out like cables. Drops of perspiration beaded on his forehead. One ran into his eye, stinging, and Crow blinked it away.

"I'll . . . shoot . . . your friend," he said.

"No," the person inside Abra said. "I won't let you."

But Crow could see she was straining now, and that gave him hope. He put everything he had into pointing the muzzle at Rip Van Winkle's midsection, and had almost gotten there when the gun started to rotate back again. Now he could hear the little bitch panting. Hell, he was, too. They sounded like marathoners approaching the end of a race side by side.

A car went by, not slowing. Neither of them noticed. They were looking at each other.

Crow brought his left hand down to join his right on the gun. Now it turned a little more easily. He was beating her, by God. But his eyes! Jesus!

"Billy!" Abra shouted. "Billy, little help here!"

Billy snorted. His eyes opened. "Wha—"

For a moment Crow was distracted. The force he was exerting slackened, and the gun immediately began to turn back toward him. His hands were cold, cold. Those metal rings were pressing into his eyes, threatening to turn them to jelly.

The gun went off for the first time when it was between them, blowing a hole in the dashboard just above the radio. Billy jerked awake, arms flailing to either side like a man pulling himself out of a nightmare. One of them struck Abra's temple, the other Crow's chest. The cab of the truck was filled with blue haze and the smell of burnt gunpowder.

"What was that? What the hell was tha—"

Crow snarled, *"No, you bitch! No!"*

He swung the gun back toward Abra, and as he did it, he felt her control slip. It was the blow to the head. Crow could see dismay and terror in her eyes, and was savagely glad.

Have to kill her. Can't give her another chance. But not a headshot. In the gut. Then I'll suck the stea—

Billy slammed his shoulder into Crow's side. The gun jerked up and went off again, this time putting a hole in the roof just above Abra's head. Before Crow could bring it down again, huge hands laid themselves over his. He had time to realize that his adversary had only been tapping a fraction of the force at its command. Panic had unlocked a great, perhaps even unknowable, reserve. This time when the gun turned toward him, Crow's wrists snapped like bundles of twigs. For a moment he saw a single black eye staring up at him, and there was time for half a thought:

(*Rose I love y*)

There was a brilliant flash of white, then darkness. Four seconds later, there was nothing left of Crow Daddy but his clothes.

7

Steamhead Steve, Baba the Red, Bent Dick, and Greedy G were playing a desultory game of canasta in the Bounder that Greedy and Dirty Phil shared when the shrieks began. All four of them had been on edge—the whole True was on edge—and they dropped their cards immediately and ran for the door.

Everyone was emerging from their campers and RVs to see what the matter was, but they stopped when they saw Rose the Hat standing in the brilliant yellow-white glare of the security lights surrounding the Overlook Lodge. Her eyes were wild. She was pulling at her hair like an Old Testament prophet in the throes of a violent vision.

"That fucking little bitch killed my Crow!" she shrieked. *"I'll kill her! I'LL KILL HER AND EAT HER HEART!"*

At last she sank to her knees, sobbing into her hands.

The True Knot stood, stunned. No one knew what to say or do. At last Silent Sarey went to her. Rose shoved her violently away. Sarey landed on her back, got up, and returned to Rose without hesitation. This time Rose looked up and saw her would-be comforter, a woman who had also lost someone dear on this unbelievable night. She embraced Sarey, hugging so hard that the watching True heard bones crack. But Sarey didn't struggle, and after a few moments, the two women helped each other to their feet. Rose looked from Silent Sarey to Big Mo, then to Heavy Mary and Token Charlie. It was as if she had never seen any of them.

"Come on, Rosie," Mo said. "You've had a shock. You need to lie d—"

"NO!"

She stepped away from Silent Sarey and clapped her hands to the sides of her face in a huge double slap that knocked off her hat. She bent down to pick it up, and when she looked around at the gathered True again, some sanity had come back into her eyes. She was thinking of Diesel Doug and the crew she had sent to meet Daddy and the girl.

"I need to get hold of Deez. Tell him and Phil and Annie to turn around. We need to be together. We need to take steam. A lot of it. Once we're loaded, *we're going to get that bitch.*"

They only looked at her, their faces worried and unsure. The sight of those frightened eyes and stupid gaping mouths infuriated her.

"Do you doubt me?" Silent Sarey had crept back to her side. Rose pushed her away from her so hard Sarey almost fell down again. "Whoever doubts me, let him step forward."

"No one doubts you, Rose," Steamhead Steve said, "but maybe

we ought to let her alone." He spoke carefully, and couldn't quite meet Rose's eyes. "If Crow's really gone, that's five dead. We've never lost five in one day. We've never even lost t—"

Rose stepped forward and Steve immediately stepped back, hunching his shoulders up around his ears like a child expecting a blow. "You want to run away from one little steamhead girl? After all these years, you want to turn tail and run from a *rube?*"

No one answered her, least of all Steve, but Rose saw the truth in their eyes. They did. They actually did. They'd had a lot of good years. Fat years. Easy-hunting years. Now they had run across someone who not only had extraordinary steam but knew them for who they were and what they did. Instead of avenging Crow Daddy—who had, along with Rose, seen them through good times and bad—they wanted to put their tails between their legs and go yipping away. In that moment she wanted to kill them all. They felt it and shuffled further back, giving her room.

All but Silent Sarey, who was staring at Rose as if hypnotized, her mouth hung on a hinge. Rose seized her by her scrawny shoulders.

"No, Rosie!" Mo squealed. "Don't hurt her!"

"What about you, Sarey? That little girl was responsible for murdering the woman you loved. Do you want to run away?"

"Nup," Sarey said. Her eyes looked up into Rose's. Even now, with everyone looking at her, Sarey seemed little more than a shadow.

"Do you want payback?"

"Lup," Sarey said. Then: *"Levenge."*

She had a low voice (almost a no-voice) and a speech impediment, but they all heard her, and they all knew what she was saying.

Rose looked around at the others. "For those of you who don't want what Sarey wants, who just want to get down on your bellies and squirm away . . ."

She turned to Big Mo and seized the woman's flabby arm. Mo screeched in fear and surprise and tried to draw away. Rose held her in place and lifted her arm so the others could see it. It was covered with red spots. "Can you squirm away from this?"

They muttered and took another step or two back.

Rose said, "It's in us."

"Most of us are fine!" Sweet Terri Pickford shouted. "*I'm* fine! Not a mark on me!" She held her smooth arms out for inspection.

Rose turned her burning, tear-filled eyes on Terri. "*Now*. But for how long?" Sweet Terri made no reply, but turned her face away.

Rose put her arm around Silent Sarey and surveyed the others. "Nut said that girl may be our only chance of getting rid of the sickness before it infects us all. Does anyone here know better? If you do, speak up."

No one did.

"We're going to wait until Deez, Annie, and Dirty Phil get back, then we'll take steam. Biggest steam ever. We're going to empty the canisters."

Looks of surprise and more uneasy mutters greeted this. Did they think she was crazy? Let them. It wasn't just measles eating into the True Knot; it was terror, and that was far worse.

"When we're all together, we're going to circle. We're going to grow strong. *Lodsam hanti,* we are the chosen ones—have you forgotten that? *Sabbatha hanti,* we are the True Knot, and we endure. Say it with me." Her eyes raked them. "*Say it.*"

They said it, joining hands, making a ring. *We are the True Knot, and we endure.* A little resolution came into their eyes. A little belief. Only half a dozen of them were showing the spots, after all; there was still time.

Rose and Silent Sarey stepped to the circle. Terri and Baba let go of each other to make a place for them, but Rose escorted Sarey to the center. Under the security lights, the bodies of the two women radiated multiple shadows, like the spokes of a wheel. "When we're strong—when we're one again—we're going to find her and take her. I tell you that as your leader. And even if her steam doesn't cure the sickness that's eating us, it'll be the end of the rotten—"

That was when the girl spoke inside her head. Rose could not see Abra Stone's angry smile, but she could feel it.

(*don't bother coming to me, Rose*)

8

In the back of John Dalton's Suburban, Dan Torrance spoke four clear words in Abra's voice.

"I'll come to you."

9

"Billy? *Billy!*"

Billy Freeman looked at the girl who didn't exactly *sound* like a girl. She doubled, came together, and doubled again. He passed a hand over his face. His eyelids felt heavy and his thoughts seemed somehow glued together. He couldn't make sense of this. It wasn't daylight anymore, and they sure as hell weren't on Abra's street anymore. "Who's shooting? And who took a shit in my mouth? *Christ.*"

"Billy, you have to wake up. You have to . . ."

You have to drive was what Dan meant to say, but Billy Freeman wasn't going to be driving anywhere. Not for awhile. His eyes were drifting shut again, the lids out of sync. Dan threw one of Abra's elbows into the old guy's side and got his attention again. For the time being, at least.

Headlights flooded the cab of the truck as another car approached. Dan held Abra's breath, but this one also went by without slowing. Maybe a woman on her own, maybe a salesman in a hurry to get home. A bad Samaritan, whoever it was, and bad was good for them, but they might not be lucky a third time. Rural people tended to be neighborly. Not to mention nosy.

"Stay awake," he said.

"Who *are* you?" Billy tried to focus on the kid, but it was impossible. "Because you sure don't sound like Abra."

"It's complicated. For now, just concentrate on staying awake."

Dan got out and walked around to the driver's side of the truck, stumbling several times. Her legs, which had seemed so long on the day he met her, were too damned short. He only hoped he wouldn't have enough time to get used to them.

Crow's clothes were lying on the seat. His canvas shoes were on the dirty floormat with the socks trailing out of them. The blood and brains that had splattered his shirt and jacket had cycled out of existence, but they had left damp spots. Dan gathered everything up and, after a moment's consideration, added the gun. He didn't want to give it up, but if they were stopped . . .

He took the bundle to the front of the truck and buried it beneath a drift of old leaves. Then he grabbed a piece of the downed birch the F-150 had struck and dragged it over the burial site. It was hard work with Abra's arms, but he managed.

He found he couldn't just step into the cab; he had to pull himself up by the steering wheel. And once he was finally behind the wheel, her feet barely reached the pedals. *Fuck.*

Billy gave a galumphing snore, and Dan threw another elbow. Billy opened his eyes and looked around. "Where are we? Did that guy drug me?" Then: "I think I have to go back to sleep."

At some point during the final life-or-death struggle for the gun, Crow's unopened bottle of Fanta had fallen to the floor. Dan bent over, grabbed it, then paused with Abra's hand on the cap, remembering what happens to soda when it takes a hard thump. From somewhere, Abra spoke to him

(*oh dear*)

and she was smiling, but it wasn't the angry smile. Dan thought that was good.

10

You can't let me go to sleep, the voice coming from Dan's mouth said, so John took the Fox Run exit and parked in the lot farthest from Kohl's. There he and Dave walked Dan's body up and down, one on each side. He was like a drunk at the end of a hard night—every now and then his head sagged to his chest before snapping back up again. Both men took a turn at asking what had happened, what was happening now, and *where* it was happening, but Abra only shook Dan's head. "The Crow shot me in my hand before he let me go in the bathroom. The rest is all fuzzy. Now shh, I have to concentrate."

On the third wide circle of John's Suburban, Dan's mouth broke into a grin, and a very Abra-like giggle issued from him. Dave looked a question at John across the body of their shambling, stumbling charge. John shrugged and shook his head.

"Oh, dear," Abra said. "Soda."

11

Dan tilted the soda and removed the cap. A high-pressure spray of orange pop hit Billy full in the face. He coughed and spluttered, for the time being wide awake.

"Jesus, kid! Why'd you do that?"

"It worked, didn't it?" Dan handed him the still-fizzing soda. "Put the rest inside you. I'm sorry, but you can't go back to sleep, no matter how much you want to."

While Billy tilted the bottle and chugged soda, Dan leaned over and found the seat adjustment lever. He pulled it with one hand and yanked on the steering wheel with the other. The seat jolted forward. It caused Billy to spill Fanta down his chin (and to utter a phrase not generally used by adults around young girls from New Hampshire), but now Abra's feet could reach the pedals. Barely. Dan put the truck in reverse and backed up slowly, angling toward the road as he went. When they were on the pavement, he breathed a sigh of relief. Getting stuck in a ditch beside a little-used Vermont highway would not have advanced their cause much.

"Do you know what you're doing?" Billy asked.

"Yes. Been doing it for years . . . although there was a little lag time when the state of Florida took away my license. I was in another state at the time, but there's a little thing called reciprocity. The bane of traveling drunks all across this great country of ours."

"You're Dan."

"Guilty as charged," he said, peering over the top of the steering wheel. He wished he had a book to sit on, but since he didn't, he would just have to do the best he could. He dropped the transmission into drive and got rolling.

"How'd you get inside her?"

"Don't ask."

The Crow had said something (or only thought it, Dan didn't know which) about camp roads, and about four miles up Route 108, they came to a lane with a rustic wooden sign nailed to a pine tree: BOB AND DOT'S HAPPY PLACE. If that wasn't a camp road, nothing was. Dan turned in, Abra's arms glad for the power steering, and flicked on the high beams. A quarter of a mile up, the lane was barred by a heavy chain with another sign hanging from it, this one less rustic: NO TRESPASSING. The chain was good. It meant Bob and Dot hadn't decided on a getaway weekend at their happy place, and a quarter of a mile from the highway was enough to assure them of some privacy. There was another bonus: a culvert with water trickling out of it.

He killed the lights and engine, then turned to Billy. "See that culvert? Go wash the soda off your face. Splash up good. You need to be as wide awake as you can get."

"I'm awake," Billy said.

"Not enough. Try to keep your shirt dry. And when you're done, comb your hair. You're going to have to meet the public."

"Where are we?"

"Vermont."

"Where's the guy who hijacked me?"

"Dead."

"Good goddam riddance!" Billy exclaimed. Then, after a moment's thought: "How about the body? Where's that?"

An excellent question, but not one Dan wanted to answer. What he wanted was for this to be over. It was exhausting, and disorienting in a thousand ways. "Gone. That's really all you need to know."

"But—"

"Not now. Wash your face, then walk up and down this road a few times. Swing your arms, take deep breaths, and get as clear as you can."

"I've got one *bitch* of a headache."

Dan wasn't surprised. "When you come back, the girl is probably going to be the girl again, which means you'll have to drive. If you feel sober enough to be plausible, go to the next town that has a motel and check in. You're traveling with your granddaughter, got it?"

"Yeah," Billy said. "My granddaughter. Abby Freeman."

"Once you're in, call me on my cell."

"Because you'll be wherever . . . wherever the rest of you is."

"Right."

"This is fucked to the sky, buddy."

"Yes," Dan said. "It certainly is. Our job now is to unfuck it."

"Okay. What *is* the next town?"

"No idea. I don't want you having an accident, Billy. If you can't get clear enough to drive twenty or thirty miles and then check into a motel without having the guy on the counter call the cops, you and Abra will have to spend the night in the cab of this truck. It won't be comfortable, but it should be safe."

Billy opened the passenger-side door. "Give me ten minutes. I'll be able to pass for sober. Done it before." He gave the girl behind the steering wheel a wink. "I work for Casey Kingsley. Death on drinkin, remember?"

Dan watched him go to the culvert and kneel there, then closed Abra's eyes.

In a parking lot outside the Fox Run Mall, Abra closed Dan's.

(*Abra*)

(*I'm here*)

(*are you awake*)

(*yes sort of*)

(*we need to turn the wheel again can you help me*)

This time, she could.

12

"Let go of me, you guys," Dan said. His voice was his own again. "I'm all right. I think."

John and Dave let go, ready to grab him again if he staggered, but he didn't. What he did was touch himself: hair, face, chest, legs. Then he nodded. "Yeah," he said. "I'm here." He looked around. "Which is where?"

"Fox Run Mall," John said. "Sixty miles or so from Boston."

"Okay, let's get back on the road."

"Abra," Dave said. "What about Abra?"

"Abra's fine. Back where she belongs."

"She *belongs* at home," Dave said, and with more than a touch of resentment. "In her room. IM'ing with her friends or listening to those stupid 'Round Here kids on her iPod."

She is *at home,* Dan thought. *If a person's body is their home, she's there.*

"She's with Billy. Billy will take care of her."

"What about the one who kidnapped her? This Crow?"

Dan paused beside the back door of John's Suburban. "You don't have to worry about him anymore. The one we have to worry about now is Rose."

13

The Crown Motel was actually over the state line, in Crownville, New York. It was a rattletrap place with a flickering sign out front reading VAC NCY and M NY CAB E CHAN ELS! Only four cars were parked in the thirty or so slots. The man behind the counter was a descending mountain of fat, with a ponytail that trickled to a stop halfway down his back. He ran Billy's Visa and gave him the keys to two rooms without taking his eyes from the TV, where two women on a red velvet sofa were engaged in strenuous osculation.

"Do they connect?" Billy asked. And, looking at the women: "The rooms, I mean."

"Yeah, yeah, they all connect, just open the doors."

"Thanks."

He drove down the rank of units to twenty-three and twenty-four, and parked the truck. Abra was curled up on the seat with her head pillowed on one arm, fast asleep. Billy unlocked the rooms, turned on the lights, and opened the connecting doors. He judged the accommodations shabby but not quite desperate. All he wanted now was to get the two of them inside and go to sleep himself. Preferably for about ten hours. He rarely felt old, but tonight he felt ancient.

Abra woke up a little as he laid her on the bed. "Where are we?"

"Crownville, New York. We're safe. I'll be in the next room."

"I want my dad. And I want Dan."

"Soon." Hoping he was right about that.

Her eyes closed, then slowly opened again. "I talked to that woman. That *bitch*."

"Did you?" Billy had no idea what she meant.

"She knows what we did. She felt it. And it *hurt*." A harsh light gleamed momentarily in Abra's eyes. Billy thought it was like seeing a peek of sun at the end of a cold, overcast day in February. "I'm glad."

"Go to sleep, hon."

That cold winter light still shone out of the pale and tired face. "She knows I'm coming for her."

Billy thought of brushing her hair out of her eyes, but what if she bit? Probably that was silly, but . . . the light in her eyes. His mother had looked like that sometimes, just before she lost her temper and whopped one of the kids. "You'll feel better in the morning. I'd like it if we could go back tonight—I'm sure your dad feels that way, too—but I'm in no shape to drive. I was lucky to get this far without running off the road."

"I wish I could talk to my mom and dad."

Billy's own mother and father—never candidates for Parents of the Year, even at their best—were long dead and he wished only for sleep. He looked longingly through the open door at the bed in the other room. Soon, but not quite yet. He took out his cell phone and flipped it open. It rang twice, and then he was talking to Dan. After a few moments, he handed the phone to Abra. "Your father. Knock yourself out."

Abra seized the phone. "Dad? *Dad?*" Tears began to fill her eyes. "Yes, I'm . . . stop, Dad, I'm *all right*. Just so sleepy I can hardly—" Her eyes widened as a thought struck her. "Are *you* okay?"

She listened. Billy's eyes drifted shut and he snapped them open with an effort. The girl was crying hard now, and he was sort of glad. The tears had doused that light in her eyes.

She handed the phone back. "It's Dan. He wants to talk to you again."

He took the phone and listened. Then he said, "Abra, Dan wants to know if you think there are any other bad guys. Ones close enough to get here tonight."

"No. I think the Crow was going to meet some others, but they're still a long way away. And they can't figure out where we are"—she broke off for a huge yawn—"without him to tell them. Tell Dan we're safe. And tell him to make sure my dad gets that."

Billy relayed this message. When he ended the call, Abra was curled up on the bed, knees to chest, snoring softly. Billy covered her with a blanket from the closet, then went to the door and ran the chain. He considered, then propped the desk chair under the knob for good measure. *Always safe, never sorry,* his father had liked to say.

14

Rose opened the compartment under the floor and took out one of the canisters. Still on her knees between the EarthCruiser's front seats, she cracked it and put her mouth over the hissing lid. Her jaw unhinged all the way to her chest, and the bottom of her head became a dark hole in which a single tooth jutted. Her eyes, ordinarily uptilted, bled downward and darkened. Her face became a doleful deathmask with the skull standing out clear beneath.

She took steam.

When she was done, she replaced the canister and sat behind the wheel of her RV, looking straight ahead. *Don't bother coming to me, Rose—I'll come to you.* That was what she had said. What she had *dared* to say to her, Rose O'Hara, Rose the Hat. Not just strong, then; strong and *vengeful*. Angry.

"Come ahead, darling," she said. "And stay angry. The angrier you are, the more foolhardy you'll be. Come and see your auntie Rose."

There was a snap. She looked down and saw she had broken off the lower half of the EarthCruiser's steering wheel. Steam conveyed strength. Her hands were bleeding. Rose threw the jagged arc of plastic aside, raised her palms to her face, and began to lick them.

CHAPTER SIXTEEN

THAT WHICH WAS FORGOTTEN

1

The moment Dan closed his phone, Dave said, "Let's pick up Lucy and go get her."

Dan shook his head. "She says they're okay, and I believe her."

"She's been drugged, though," John said. "Her judgment might not be the best right now."

"She was clear enough to help me take care of the one she calls the Crow," Dan said, "and I trust her on this. Let them sleep off whatever the bastard drugged them with. We have other things to do. Important things. You've got to trust me a little here. You'll be with your daughter soon enough, David. For the moment, though, listen to me carefully. We're going to drop you off at your grandmother-in-law's place. You're going to bring your wife to the hospital."

"I don't know if she'll believe me when I tell her what happened today. I don't know how convincing I can be when I hardly believe it myself."

"Tell her the story has to wait until we're all together. And that includes Abra's momo."

"I doubt if they'll let you in to see her." Dave glanced at his watch. "Visiting hours are long over, and she's very ill."

"Floor staff doesn't pay much attention to the visiting rules when patients are near the end," Dan said.

Dave looked at John, who shrugged. "The man works in a hospice. I think you can trust him on that."

"She may not even be conscious," Dave said.

"Let's worry about one thing at a time."

"What does Chetta have to do with this, anyway? She doesn't know anything about it!"

Dan said, "I'm pretty sure she knows more than you think."

2

They dropped Dave off at the condo on Marlborough Street and watched from the curb as he mounted the steps and rang one of the bells.

"He looks like a little kid who knows he's going to the woodshed for a pants-down butt whippin," John said. "This is going to strain the hell out of his marriage, no matter how it turns out."

"When a natural disaster happens, no one's to blame."

"Try to make Lucy Stone see that. She's going to think, 'You left your daughter alone and a crazy guy snatched her.' On some level, she's always going to think it."

"Abra might change her mind about that. As for today, we did what we could, and so far we're not doing too badly."

"But it's not over."

"Not by a long shot."

Dave was ringing the bell again and peering into the little lobby when the elevator opened and Lucy Stone came rushing out. Her face was strained and pale. Dave started to talk as soon as she opened the door. So did she. Lucy pulled him in—*yanked* him in—by both arms.

"Ah, man," John said softly. "That reminds me of too many nights when I rolled in drunk at three in the morning."

"Either he'll convince her or he won't," Dan said. "We've got other business."

3

Dan Torrance and John Dalton arrived at Massachusetts General Hospital shortly after ten thirty. It was slack tide on the intensive care floor. A deflating helium balloon with FEEL BETTER SOON printed on it in particolored letters drifted halfheartedly along the hallway ceiling, casting a jellyfish shadow. Dan approached the nurses' station, identified himself as a staffer at the hospice to which Ms. Reynolds was scheduled to be moved, showed his Helen Rivington House ID, and introduced John Dalton as the family doctor (a stretch, but not an actual lie).

"We need to assess her condition prior to the transfer," Dan said, "and two family members have asked to be present. They are Ms. Reynolds's granddaughter and her granddaughter's husband. I'm sorry about the lateness of the hour, but it was unavoidable. They'll be here shortly."

"I've met the Stones," the head nurse said. "They're lovely people. Lucy in particular has been very attentive to her gran. Concetta's special. I've been reading her poems, and they're wonderful. But if you're expecting any input from her, gentlemen, you're going to be disappointed. She's slipped into a coma."

We'll see about that, Dan thought.

"And . . ." The nurse looked at John doubtfully. "Well . . . it's really not my place to say . . ."

"Go on," John said. "I've never met a head nurse who didn't know what the score was."

She smiled at him, then turned her attention back to Dan. "I've heard wonderful things about the Rivington hospice, but I doubt very much if Concetta will be going there. Even if she lasts until Monday, I'm not sure there's any point in moving her. It might be kinder to let her finish her journey here. If I'm stepping out of line, I'm sorry."

"You're not," Dan said, "and we'll take that into consideration. John, would you go down to the lobby and escort the Stones up when they arrive? I can start without you."

"Are you sure—"

"Yes," Dan said, holding his eyes. "I am."

"She's in Room Nine," the head nurse said. "It's the single at the end of the hall. If you need me, ring her call bell."

4

Concetta's name was on the Room 9 door, but the slot for medical orders was empty and the vitals monitor overhead showed nothing hopeful. Dan stepped into aromas he knew well: air freshener, antiseptic, and mortal illness. The last was a high smell that sang in his head like a violin that knows only one note. The walls were covered with photographs, many featuring Abra at various ages. One showed a gapemouthed cluster of little folks watching a magician pull a white rabbit from a hat. Dan was sure it had been taken at the famous birthday party, the Day of the Spoons.

Surrounded by these pictures, a skeleton woman slept with her mouth open and a pearl rosary twined in her fingers. Her remaining hair was so fine it almost disappeared against the pillow. Her skin, once olive-toned, was now yellow. The rise and fall of her thin bosom was hardly there. One look was enough to tell Dan that the head nurse had indeed known what the score was. If Azzie were here, he would have been curled up next to the woman in this room, waiting for Doctor Sleep to arrive so he could resume his late-night patrol of corridors empty save for the things only cats could see.

Dan sat down on the side of the bed, noting that the single IV going into her was a saline drip. There was only one medicine that could help her now, and the hospital pharmacy didn't stock it. Her cannula had come askew. He straightened it. Then he took her hand and looked into the sleeping face.

(*Concetta*)

There was a slight hitch in her breathing.

(*Concetta come back*)

Beneath the thin, bruised lids, the eyes moved. She might have been listening; she might have been dreaming her last dreams. Of Italy, perhaps. Bending over the household well and hauling up a bucket of cool water. Bending over in the hot summer sun.

(*Abra needs you to come back and so do I*)

It was all he could do, and he wasn't sure it would be enough until, slowly, her eyes opened. They were vacant at first, but they gained perception. Dan had seen this before. The miracle of returning consciousness. Not for the first time he wondered where it came from, and where it went when it departed. Death was no less a miracle than birth.

The hand he was holding tightened. The eyes remained on Dan's, and Concetta smiled. It was a timid smile, but it was there.

"*Oh mio caro! Sei tu? Sei tu? Come e possibile? Sei morto? Sono morta anch'io? . . . Siamo fantasmi?*"

Dan didn't speak Italian, and he didn't have to. He heard what she was saying with perfect clarity in his head.

Oh my dear one, is it you? How can it be you? Are you dead? Am I?

Then, after a pause:

Are we ghosts?

Dan leaned toward her until his cheek lay against hers.

In her ear, he whispered.

In time, she whispered back.

5

Their conversation was short but illuminating. Concetta spoke mostly in Italian. At last she lifted a hand—it took great effort, but she managed—and caressed his stubbly cheek. She smiled.

"Are you ready?" he asked.

"*Sì*. Ready."

"There's nothing to be afraid of."

"*Sì*, I know that. I'm so glad you come. Tell me again your name, *signor*."

"Daniel Torrance."

"*Sì*. You are a gift from God, Daniel Torrance. *Sei un dono di Dio*."

Dan hoped it was true. "Will you give to me?"

"*Sì*, of course. What you need *per* Abra."

"And I'll give to you, Chetta. We'll drink from the well together."

She closed her eyes.

(*I know*)

"You'll go to sleep, and when you wake up—"

(*everything will be better*)

The power was even stronger than it had been on the night Charlie Hayes passed; he could feel it between them as he gently clasped her hands in his and felt the smooth pebbles of her rosary against his palms. Somewhere, lights were being turned off, one by one. It was all right. In Italy a little girl in a brown dress and sandals was drawing water from the cool throat of a well. She looked like Abra, that little girl. The dog was barking. *Il cane. Ginata. Il cane si rotolava sull'erba*. Barking and rolling in the grass. Funny Ginata!

Concetta was sixteen and in love, or thirty and writing a poem at the kitchen table of a hot apartment in Queens while children shouted on the street below; she was sixty and standing in the rain and looking up at a hundred thousand lines of purest falling silver. She was her mother and her great-granddaughter and it was time for her great change, her great voyage. Ginata was rolling in the grass and the lights

(*hurry up please*)

were going out one by one. A door was opening

(*hurry up please it's time*)

and beyond it they could both smell all the mysterious, fragrant respiration of the night. Above were all the stars that ever were.

He kissed her cool forehead. "Everything's all right, *cara*. You only need to sleep. Sleep will make you better."

Then he waited for her final breath.

It came.

6

He was still sitting there, holding her hands in his, when the door burst open and Lucy Stone came striding in. Her husband and her daughter's pediatrician followed, but not too closely; it was as if they feared being burned by the fear, fury, and confused outrage that surrounded her in a crackling aura so strong it was almost visible.

She seized Dan by the shoulder, her fingernails digging like claws into the shoulder beneath his shirt. "Get away from her. You don't know her. You have no more business with my grandmother than you do with my daugh—"

"Lower your voice," Dan said without turning. "You're in the presence of death."

The rage that had stiffened her ran out all at once, loosening her joints. She sagged to the bed beside Dan and looked at the waxen cameo that was now her grandmother's face. Then she looked at the haggard, beard-scruffy man who sat holding the dead hands, in which the rosary was still entwined. Unnoticed tears began rolling down Lucy's cheeks in big clear drops.

"I can't make out half of what they've been trying to tell me. Just that Abra was kidnapped, but now she's all right—supposedly—and she's in a motel with some man named Billy and they're both sleeping."

"All that's true," Dan said.

"Then spare me your holier-than-thou pronouncements, if you please. I'll mourn my momo after I see Abra. When I've got my arms around her. For now, I want to know . . . I want . . ." She trailed off, looking from Dan to her dead grandmother and back to Dan again. Her husband stood behind her. John had closed the door of Room 9 and was leaning against it. "Your name is Torrance? Daniel Torrance?"

"Yes."

Again that slow look from her grandmother's still profile to the man who had been present when she died. "Who are you, Mr. Torrance?"

Dan let go of Chetta's hands and took Lucy's. "Walk with me. Not far. Just across the room."

She stood up without protest, still looking into his face. He led her to the bathroom door, which was standing open. He turned on the light and pointed to the mirror above the washbasin, where they were framed as if in a photograph. Seen that way, there could be little doubt. None, really.

He said, "My father was your father, Lucy. I'm your half brother."

7

After notifying the head nurse that there had been a death on the floor, they went to the hospital's small nondenominational chapel. Lucy knew the way; although not much of a believer, she had spent a good many hours there, thinking and remembering. It was a comforting place to do those things, which are necessary when a loved one nears the end. At this hour, they had it all to themselves.

"First things first," Dan said. "I have to ask if you believe me. We can do the DNA test when there's time, but . . . do we need to?"

Lucy shook her head dazedly, never taking her eyes from his face. She seemed to be trying to memorize it. "Dear Jesus. I can hardly get my breath."

"I thought you looked familiar the first time I saw you," Dave said to Dan. "Now I know why. I would have gotten it sooner, I think, if it hadn't been . . . you know . . ."

"So right in front of you," John said. "Dan, does Abra know?"

"Sure." Dan smiled, remembering Abra's theory of relativity.

"She got it from your mind?" Lucy asked. "Using her telepathy thing?"

"No, because *I* didn't know. Even someone as talented as Abra can't read something that isn't there. But on a deeper level, we both knew. Hell, we even said it out loud. If anyone asked what we were doing together, we were going to say I was her uncle. Which I am. I should have realized consciously sooner than I did."

"This is coincidence beyond coincidence," Dave said, shaking his head.

"It's not. It's the farthest thing in the world from coincidence. Lucy, I understand that you're confused and angry. I'll tell you everything I know, but it will take some time. Thanks to John and your husband and Abra—her most of all—we've got some."

"On the way," Lucy said. "You can tell me on the way to Abra."

"All right," Dan said, "on the way. But three hours' sleep first."

She was shaking her head before he finished. "No, now. I have to see her as soon as I possibly can. Don't you understand? She's my daughter, she's been kidnapped, and *I have to see her*!"

"She's been kidnapped, but now she's safe," Dan said.

"You say that, of course you do, but you don't know."

"*Abra* says it," he replied. "And she *does* know. Listen, Mrs. Stone—Lucy—she's asleep right now, and she needs her sleep." *I do, too. I've got a long trip ahead of me, and I think it's going to be a hard one. Very hard.*

Lucy was looking at him closely. "Are you all right?"

"Just tired."

"We all are," John said. "It's been . . . a stressful day." He uttered a brief yap of laughter, then pressed both hands over his mouth like a child who's said a naughty word.

"I can't even call her and hear her voice," Lucy said. She spoke slowly, as if trying to articulate a difficult precept. "Because they're sleeping off the drugs this man . . . the one you say she calls the Crow . . . put into her."

"Soon," Dave said. "You'll see her soon." He put his hand over hers. For a moment Lucy looked as if she would shake it off. She clasped it instead.

"I can start on the way back to your grandmother's," Dan said. He got up. It was an effort. "Come on."

8

He had time to tell her how a lost man had ridden a northbound bus out of Massachusetts, and how—just over the New Hampshire state line—he'd tossed what would turn out to be his last bottle of booze into a trash can with IF YOU NO LONGER NEED IT, LEAVE IT HERE stenciled on the side. He told them how his childhood friend Tony had spoken up for the first time in years when the bus had rolled into Frazier. *This is the place,* Tony had said.

From there he doubled back to a time when he had been Danny instead of Dan (and sometimes doc, as in *what's up, doc*), and his invisible friend Tony had been an absolute necessity. The shining was only one of the burdens that Tony helped him bear, and not the major one. The major one was his alcoholic father, a troubled and ultimately dangerous man whom both Danny and his mother had loved deeply—perhaps as much because of his flaws as in spite of them.

"He had a terrible temper, and you didn't have to be a telepath to know when it was getting the best of him. For one thing, he was usually drunk when it happened. I know he was loaded on the night he caught me in his study, messing with his papers. He broke my arm."

"How old were you?" Dave asked. He was riding in the backseat with his wife.

"Four, I think. Maybe even younger. When he was on the warpath, he had this habit of rubbing his mouth." Danny demonstrated. "Do you know anyone else who does that when she's upset?"

"Abra," Lucy said. "I thought she got it from me." She raised her right hand toward her mouth, then captured it with her left and returned it to her lap. Dan had seen Abra do exactly the same thing on the bench outside the Anniston Public Library, on the day they'd met in person for the first time. "I thought she got her temper from me, too. I can be . . . pretty ragged sometimes."

"I thought of my father the first time I saw her do the mouth-rubbing thing," Dan said, "but I had other things on my mind. So I forgot." This made him think of Watson, the caretaker at the Overlook, who had first shown the hotel's untrustworthy furnace boiler to his father. *You have to watch it,* Watson had said. *Because she creeps.* But in the end, Jack Torrance had forgotten. It was the reason Dan was still alive.

"Are you telling me you figured out this family relationship from one little habit? That's quite a deductive leap, especially when it's you and I who look alike, not you and Abra—she gets most of her looks from her father." Lucy paused, thinking. "But of course you share another family trait—Dave says you call it the shining. *That's* how you knew, isn't it?"

Dan shook his head. "I made a friend the year my father died. His name was Dick Hallorann, and he was the cook at the Overlook Hotel. He also had the shining, and he told me lots of people had a little bit of it. He was right. I've met plenty of people along the way who shine to a greater or lesser degree. Billy Freeman, for one. Which is why he's with Abra right now."

John swung the Suburban into the little parking area behind Concetta's condo, but for the time being, none of them got out. In spite of her worry about her daughter, Lucy was fascinated by this history lesson. Dan didn't have to look at her to know it.

"If it wasn't the shining, what was it?"

"When we were going out to Cloud Gap on the *Riv,* Dave mentioned that you found a trunk in storage at Concetta's building."

"Yes. My mother's. I had no idea Momo had saved some of her things."

"Dave told John and me that she was quite the party girl, back in the day." It was actually Abra that Dave had been talking to, via telepathic link, but this was something Dan felt it might be better for his newly discovered half sister not to know, at least for the time being.

Lucy flashed Dave the reproachful look reserved for spouses who have been telling tales out of school, but said nothing.

"He also said that when Alessandra dropped out of SUNY Albany, she was doing her student teaching at a prep school in Vermont or Massachusetts. My father taught English—until he lost his job for hurting a student, that is—in Vermont. At a school called Stovington Prep. And according to my mother, he was quite the party *boy* in those days. Once I knew that Abra and Billy were safe, I ran some numbers in my head. They seemed to add up, but I felt if anyone knew for sure, it would be Alessandra Anderson's mother."

"*Did* she?" Lucy asked. She was leaning forward now, her hands on the console between the front seats.

"Not everything, and we didn't have long together, but she knew enough. She didn't remember the name of the school where your mother student-taught, but she knew it was in Vermont. And that she'd had a brief affair with her supervising teacher. Who was, she said, a published writer." Dan paused. "My father was a published writer. Only a few stories, but some of them were in very good magazines, like the *Atlantic Monthly*. Concetta never asked her for the man's name, and Alessandra never volunteered it, but if her college transcript is in that trunk, I'm pretty sure you'll find that her supervisor was John Edward Torrance." He yawned and looked at his watch. "That's all I can do right now. Let's go upstairs. Three hours' sleep for all of us, then on to upstate New York. The roads will be empty, and we should be able to make great time."

"Do you swear she's safe?" Lucy asked.

Dan nodded.

"All right, I'll wait. But only for three hours. As for sleeping . . ." She laughed. The sound had no humor in it.

9

When they entered Concetta's condo, Lucy strode directly to the microwave in the kitchen, set the timer, and showed it to Dan. He nodded, then yawned again. "Three thirty a.m., we're out of here."

She studied him gravely. "I'd like to go without you, you know. Right this minute."

He smiled a little. "I think you better hear the rest of the story first."

She nodded grimly.

"That and the fact that my daughter needs to sleep off whatever is in her system are the only things holding me here. Now go lie down before you fall down."

Dan and John took the guest room. The wallpaper and furnishings made it clear that it had been mostly kept for one special little girl, but Chetta must have had other guests from time to time, because there were twin beds.

As they lay in the dark, John said: "It's not a coincidence that this hotel you stayed in as a child is also in Colorado, is it?"

"No."

"This True Knot is in the same town?"

"They are."

"And the hotel was haunted?"

The ghostie people, Dan thought. "Yes."

Then John said something that surprised Dan and temporarily brought him back from the edge of sleep. Dave had been right—the easiest things to miss were the ones right in front of you. "It makes sense, I suppose . . . once you accept the idea there could be supernatural beings among us and feeding on us. An evil place would call evil creatures. They'd feel right at home there. Do you suppose this Knot has other places like that, in other parts of the country? Other . . . I don't know . . . cold spots?"

"I'm sure they do." Dan put an arm over his eyes. His body ached and his head was pounding. "Johnny, I'd love to do the boys-having-a-sleepover thing with you, but I have to get some shuteye."

"Okay, but . . ." John got up on one elbow. "All things being equal, you would have gone right from the hospital, like Lucy wanted. Because you care almost as much about Abra as they do. You think she's safe, but you could be wrong."

"I'm not." Hoping that was the truth. He had to hope so, because the simple fact was that he couldn't go, not now. If it had only been to New York, maybe. But it wasn't, and he had to sleep. His whole body cried for it.

"What's wrong with you, Dan? Because you look terrible."

"Nothing. Just tired."

Then he was gone, first into darkness and then into a confused nightmare of running down endless halls while some Shape followed him, swinging a mallet from side to side, splitting wallpaper and driving up puffs of plaster dust. *Come out, you little shit!* the Shape yelled. *Come out, you worthless pup, and take your medicine!*

Then Abra was with him. They were sitting on the bench in front of the Anniston Public Library, in the late-summer sun. She was holding his hand. *It's all right, Uncle Dan. It's all right. Before he died, your father turned that Shape out. You don't have to—*

The library door banged open and a woman stepped into the sunlight. Great clouds of dark hair billowed around her head, yet her jauntily cocked tophat stayed on. It stayed on like magic.

"Oh, look," she said. "It's Dan Torrance, the man who stole a woman's money while she was sleeping one off and then left her kid to be beaten to death."

She smiled at Abra, revealing a single tooth. It looked as long and sharp as a bayonet.

"What will he do to you, little sweetie? What will he do to *you?*"

10

Lucy woke him promptly at three thirty, but shook her head when Dan moved to wake John. "Let him sleep a bit longer. And my husband is snoring on the couch." She actually smiled. "It makes me think of the Garden of Gethsemane, you know. Jesus reproaching Peter, saying, 'So you could not watch with me even one hour?' Or something like that. But I have no reason to reproach David, I guess—he saw it, too. Come on. I've made scrambled eggs. You look like you could use some. You're skinny as a rail." She paused and added: "Brother."

Dan wasn't particularly hungry, but he followed her into the kitchen. "Saw what, too?"

"I was going through Momo's papers—anything to keep my hands busy and pass the time—and I heard a clunk from the kitchen."

She took his hand and led him to the counter between the stove and the fridge. There was a row of old-fashioned apothecary jars here, and the one containing sugar had been overturned. A message had been written in the spill.

I'm OK
Going back to sleep
Love U
☺

In spite of how he felt, Dan thought of his blackboard and had to smile. It was so perfectly Abra.

"She must have woken up just enough to do that," Lucy said.

"Don't think so," Dan said.

She looked at him from the stove, where she was dishing up scrambled eggs.

"*You* woke her up. She heard your worry."

"Do you really believe that?"

"Yes."

"Sit down." She paused. "Sit down, *Dan*. I guess I better get used to calling you that. Sit down and eat."

Dan wasn't hungry, but he needed the fuel. He did as she said.

11

She sat across from him, sipping a glass of juice from the last carafe Concetta Reynolds would ever have delivered from Dean & DeLuca. "Older man with booze issues, starstruck younger woman. That's the picture I'm getting."

"It's the one I got, too." Dan shoveled the eggs in steadily and methodically, not tasting them.

"Coffee, Mr. . . . Dan?"

"Please."

She went past the spilled sugar to the Bunn. "He's married, but his job takes him to a lot of faculty parties where there are a lot of pretty young gals. Not to mention a fair amount of blooming libido when the hour gets late and the music gets loud."

"Sounds about right," Dan said. "Maybe my mom used to go along to those parties, but then there was a kid to take care of at home and no money for babysitters." She passed him a cup of coffee. He sipped it black before she could ask what he took in it. "Thanks. Anyway, they had a thing. Probably at one of the local motels. It sure wasn't in the back of his car—we had a VW Bug. Even a couple of horny acrobats couldn't have managed that."

"Blackout screwing," John said, coming into the room. His hair was standing up in sleep-quills at the back of his head. "That's what the oldtimers call it. Are there any more of those eggs?"

"Plenty," Lucy said. "Abra left a message on the counter."

"Really?" John went to look at it. "That was her?"

"Yes. I'd know her printing anywhere."

"Holy shit, this could put Verizon out of business."

She didn't smile. "Sit down and eat, John. You've got ten minutes, then I'm going to wake up Sleeping Beauty in there on the couch." She sat down. "Go on, Dan."

"I don't know if she thought my dad would leave my mom for her or not, and I doubt if you'll find the answer to that one in her trunk. Unless maybe she left a diary. All I know—based on what Dave said and what Concetta told me later—is that she hung around for awhile. Maybe hoping, maybe just partying, maybe both. But by the time she found out she was pregnant, she must have given up. For all I know, we might have been in Colorado by then."

"Do you suppose your mother ever found out?"

"I don't know, but she must have wondered how faithful he was, especially on the nights when he came in late and shitfaced. I'm sure she knew that drunks don't limit their bad behavior to betting the ponies or tucking five-spots into the cleavages of the waitresses down at the Twist and Shout."

She put a hand on his arm. "Are you all right? You look exhausted."

"I'm okay. But you're not the only one who's trying to process all this."

"She died in a car accident," Lucy said. She had turned from Dan and was looking fixedly at the bulletin board on the fridge. In the middle was a photograph of Concetta and Abra, who looked about four, walking hand in hand through a field of daisies. "The man with her was a lot older. And drunk. They were going fast. Momo didn't want to tell me, but around the time I turned eighteen, I got curious and nagged her into giving me at least some of the details. When I asked if my mother was drunk, too, Chetta said she didn't know. She said the police have no reason to test passengers who are killed in fatal accidents, only the driver." She sighed. "It doesn't matter. We'll leave the family stories for another day. Tell me what's happened to my daughter."

He did. At some point, he turned around and saw Dave Stone standing in the doorway, tucking his shirt into his pants and watching him.

12

Dan started with how Abra had gotten in touch with him, first using Tony as a kind of intermediary. Then how Abra had come in contact with the True Knot: a nightmare vision of the one she called "the baseball boy."

"I remember that nightmare," Lucy said. "She woke me up, screaming. It had happened before, but it was the first time in two or three years."

Dave frowned. "I don't remember that at all."

"You were in Boston, at a conference." She turned to Dan. "Let me see if I've got this. These people aren't people, they're . . . what? Some kind of vampires?"

"In a way, I suppose. They don't sleep in coffins during the day or turn into bats by moonlight, and I doubt if crosses and garlic bother them, but they're parasites, and they're certainly not human."

"Human beings don't disappear when they die," John said flatly. "You really saw that happen?"

"We did. All three of us."

"In any case," Dan said, "the True Knot isn't interested in ordinary children, only those who have the shining."

"Children like Abra," Lucy said.

"Yes. They torture them before killing them—to purify the steam, Abra says. I keep picturing moonshiners making white lightning."

"They want to . . . inhale her," Lucy said. Still trying to get it straight in her head. "Because she has the shining."

"Not just the shining, but a *great* shining. I'm a flashlight. She's a lighthouse. And she *knows* about them. She knows what they are."

"There's more," John said. "What we did to those men at Cloud Gap . . . as far as this Rose is concerned, that's down to Abra, no matter who actually did the killing."

"What else could she expect?" Lucy asked indignantly. "Don't they understand self-defense? *Survival?*"

"What Rose understands," Dan said, "is that there's a little girl who has challenged her."

"Challenged—?"

"Abra got in touch telepathically. She told Rose that she was coming after her."

"She *what?*"

"That temper of hers," Dave said quietly. "I've told her a hundred times it would get her in trouble."

"She's not going anywhere *near* that woman, or her child-killing friends," Lucy said.

Dan thought: *Yes . . . and no.* He took Lucy's hand. She started to pull away, then didn't.

"The thing you have to understand is really quite simple," he said. *"They will never stop."*

"But—"

"No buts, Lucy. Under other circumstances, Rose still might have decided to disengage—this is one crafty old she-wolf—but there's one other factor."

"Which is?"

"They're sick," John said. "Abra says it's the measles. They might even have caught it from the Trevor boy. I don't know if you'd call that divine retribution or just irony."

"Measles?"

"I know it doesn't sound like much, but believe me, it is. You know how, in the old days, measles could run through a whole family of kids? If that's happening to this True Knot, it could wipe them out."

"Good!" Lucy cried. The angry smile on her face was one Dan knew well.

"Not if they think Abra's supersteam will cure them," Dave said. "That's what you need to understand, hon. This isn't just a skirmish. To this bitch it's a fight to the death." He struggled and then brought out the rest of it. Because it had to be said. "If Rose gets the chance, she'll eat our daughter alive."

13

Lucy asked, "Where are they? This True Knot, where are they?"

"Colorado," Dan said. "At a place called the Bluebell Campground in the town of Sidewinder." That the site of the campground was the very place where he had once almost died at his father's hands was a thing he didn't want to say, because it would lead to more questions and more cries of coincidence. The one thing of which Dan was sure was that there were no coincidences.

"This Sidewinder must have a police department," Lucy said. "We'll call them and get them on this."

"By telling them what?" John's tone was gentle, nonargumentative.

"Well . . . that . . ."

"If you actually got the cops to go up there to the campground," Dan said, "they'd find nothing but a bunch of middle-aged-going-on-older Americans. Harmless RV folks, the kind who always want to show you pictures of their grandkids. Their papers would all be in apple-pie order, from dog licenses to land deeds. The police wouldn't find guns if they managed to get a search warrant—which they wouldn't, no probable cause—because the True Knot doesn't need guns. Their weapons are up here." Dan tapped his forehead. "You'd be the crazy lady from New Hampshire, Abra would be your crazy daughter who ran away from home, and we'd be your crazy friends."

Lucy pressed her palms to her temples. "I can't believe this is happening."

"If you did a search of records, I think you'd find that the True Knot—under whatever name they might be incorporated—has been very generous to that particular Colorado town. You don't shit in your nest, you feather it. Then, if bad times come, you have lots of friends."

"These bastards have been around a long time," John said. "Haven't they? Because the main thing they take from this steam is longevity."

"I'm pretty sure that's right," Dan said. "And as good Americans, I'm sure they've been busy making money the whole time. Enough to grease wheels a lot bigger than the ones that turn in Sidewinder. State wheels. Federal wheels."

"And this Rose . . . she'll never stop."

"No." Dan was thinking of the precognitive vision he'd had of her. The cocked hat. The yawning mouth. The single tooth. "Her heart is set on your daughter."

"A woman who stays alive by killing children *has* no heart," Dave said.

"Oh, she has one," Dan said. "But it's black."

Lucy stood up. "No more talking. I want to go to her *now*.

Everybody use the bathroom, because once we leave, we're not stopping until we get to that motel."

Dan said, "Does Concetta have a computer? If she does, I need to take a quick peek at something before we go."

Lucy sighed. "It's in her study, and I think you can guess the password. But if you take more than five minutes, we're going without you."

14

Rose lay awake in her bed, stiff as a poker, trembling with steam and fury.

When an engine started up at quarter past two, she heard it. Steamhead Steve and Baba the Russian. When another started at twenty till four, she heard that one, too. This time it was the Little twins, Pea and Pod. Sweet Terri Pickford was with them, no doubt looking nervously through the back window for any sign of Rose. Big Mo had asked to go along—*begged* to go along—but they had turned her down because Mo was carrying the disease.

Rose could have stopped them, but why bother? Let them discover what life was like in America on their own, with no True Knot to protect them in camp or watch their backs while they were on the road. *Especially when I tell Toady Slim to kill their credit cards and empty their rich bank accounts,* she thought.

Toady was no Jimmy Numbers, but he could still take care of it, and at the touch of a button. And he'd be there to do it. Toady would stick. So would all the good ones . . . or *almost* all the good ones. Dirty Phil, Apron Annie, and Diesel Doug were no longer on their way back. They had taken a vote and decided to head south instead. Deez had told them Rose was no longer to be trusted, and besides, it was long past time to cut the Knot.

Good luck with that, darling boy, she thought, clenching and unclenching her fists.

Splitting the True was a *terrible* idea, but thinning the herd was a good one. So let the weaklings run and the sicklings die. When the bitchgirl was also dead and they had swallowed her steam (Rose had no more illusions of keeping her prisoner), the twenty-five or so who were left would be stronger than ever. She mourned Crow, and knew she had no one who could step into his shoes, but Token Charlie would do the best he could. So would Harpman Sam . . . Bent Dick . . . Fat Fannie and Long Paul . . . Greedy G, not the brightest bulb, but loyal and unquestioning.

Besides, with the others gone, the steam she still had in storage would go farther and make them stronger. They would need to be strong.

Come to me, little bitchgirl, Rose thought. *See how strong you are when there are two dozen against you. See how you like it when it's just you against the True. We'll eat your steam and lap up your blood. But first, we'll drink your screams.*

Rose stared up into the darkness, hearing the fading voices of the runners, the faithless ones.

At the door came a soft, timid knock. Rose lay silent for a moment or two, considering, then swung her legs out of bed.

"Come."

She was naked but made no attempt to cover herself when Silent Sarey crept in, shapeless inside one of her flannel nightgowns, her mouse-colored bangs covering her brows and almost hanging in her eyes. As always, Sarey seemed hardly there even when she was.

"I'm sad, Loze."

"I know you are. I'm sad, too."

She wasn't—she was furious—but it sounded good.

"I miss Andi."

Andi, yes—rube name Andrea Steiner, whose father had fucked the humanity out of her long before the True Knot had found her. Rose remembered watching her that day in the movie theater, and how, later, she had fought her way through the Turning with sheer guts and willpower. Snakebite Andi would have stuck. Snake would have walked through fire, if Rose said the True Knot needed her to.

She held out her arms. Sarey scurried to her and laid her head against Rose's breast.

"Wivvout her I lunt to die."

"No, honey, I don't think so." Rose pulled the little thing into bed and hugged her tight. She was nothing but a rack of bones held together by scant meat. "Tell me what you really want."

Beneath the shaggy bangs, two eyes gleamed, feral. *"Levenge."*

Rose kissed one cheek, then the other, then the thin dry lips. She drew back a little and said, "Yes. And you'll have it. Open your mouth, Sarey."

Sarey obediently did so. Their lips came together again. Rose the Hat, still full of steam, breathed down Silent Sarey's throat.

15

The walls of Concetta's study were papered with memos, fragments of poems, and correspondence that would never be answered. Dan typed in the four-letter password, launched Firefox, and googled the Bluebell Campground. They had a website that wasn't terribly informative, probably because the owners didn't care that much about attracting visitors; the place was your basic front. But there were photos of the property, and these Dan studied with the fascination people reserve for recently discovered old family albums.

The Overlook was long gone, but he recognized the terrain. Once, just before the first of the snowstorms that closed them in for the winter, he and his mother and father had stood together on the hotel's broad front porch (seeming even broader with the lawn gliders and wicker furniture in storage), looking down the long, smooth slope of the front lawn. At the bottom, where the deer and the antelope often came out to play, there was now a long rustic building called the Overlook Lodge. Here, the caption said, visitors could dine, play bingo, and dance to live music on Friday and

Saturday nights. On Sundays there were church services, overseen by a rotating cadre of Sidewinder's men and women of the cloth.

Until the snow came, my father mowed that lawn and trimmed the topiary that used to be there. He said he'd trimmed lots of ladies' topiaries in his time. I didn't get the joke, but it used to make Mom laugh.

"Some joke," he said, low.

He saw rows of sparkling RV hookups, lux mod cons that supplied LP gas as well as electricity. There were men's and women's shower buildings big enough to service mega-truckstops like Little America or Pedro's South of the Border. There was a playground for the wee folks. (Dan wondered if the kiddies who played there ever saw or sensed unsettling things, as Danny "Doc" Torrance once had in the Overlook's playground.) There was a softball field, a shuffleboard area, a couple of tennis courts, even bocce.

No roque, though—not that. Not anymore.

Halfway up the slope—where the Overlook's hedge animals had once congregated—there was a row of clean white satellite dishes. At the crest of the hill, where the hotel itself had stood, was a wooden platform with a long flight of steps leading up to it. This site, now owned and administered by the State of Colorado, was identified as Roof O' the World. Visitors to the Bluebell Campground were welcome to use it, or to hike the trails beyond, free of charge. *The trails are recommended only for the more experienced hiker,* the caption read, *but Roof O' the World is for everyone. The views are spectacular!*

Dan was sure they were. Certainly they had been spectacular from the dining room and ballroom of the Overlook . . . at least until the steadily mounting snow blocked off the windows. To the west were the highest peaks of the Rocky Mountains, sawing at the sky like spears. To the east, you could see all the way to Boulder. Hell, all the way to Denver and Arvada on rare days when the pollution wasn't too bad.

The state had taken that particular piece of land, and Dan wasn't surprised. Who would have wanted to build there? The ground was rotten, and he doubted if you had to be telepathic to sense it. But the True had gotten as close as it could, and Dan had an idea that their wandering guests—the normal ones—rarely came back for a second visit, or recommended the Bluebell to their friends. *An evil place would call evil creatures,* John had said. If so, the converse would also be true: it would tend to repel good ones.

"Dan?" Dave called. "Bus is leaving."

"I need another minute!"

He closed his eyes and propped the heel of his palm against his forehead.

(*Abra*)

His voice awoke her at once.

CHAPTER SEVENTEEN

BITCHGIRL

1

It was dark outside the Crown Motel, dawn still an hour or more away, when the door of unit 24 opened and a girl stepped out. Heavy fog had moved in, and the world was hardly there at all. The girl was wearing black pants and a white shirt. She had put her hair up in pigtails, and the face they framed looked very young. She breathed deeply, the coolness and the hanging moisture in the air doing wonders for her lingering headache but not much for her unhappy heart. Momo was dead.

Yet, if Uncle Dan was right, not really dead; just somewhere else. Perhaps a ghostie person; perhaps not. In any case, it wasn't a thing she could spend time thinking about. Later, perhaps, she would meditate on these matters.

Dan had asked if Billy was asleep. Yes, she had told him, still fast asleep. Through the open door she could see Mr. Freeman's feet and legs under the blankets and hear his steady snoring. He sounded like an idling motorboat.

Dan had asked if Rose or any of the others had tried to touch her mind. No. She would have known. Her traps were set. Rose would guess that. She wasn't stupid.

He had asked if there was a telephone in her room. Yes, there was a phone. Uncle Dan told her what he wanted her to do. It was pretty simple. The scary part was what she had to say to the strange woman in Colorado. And yet she wanted to. Part of her had wanted that ever since she'd heard the baseball boy's dying screams.

(*you understand the word you have to keep saying?*)

Yes, of course.

(*because you have to goad her do you know what that*)

(*yes I know what it means*)

Make her mad. Infuriate her.

Abra stood breathing into the fog. The road they'd driven in on was nothing but a scratch, the trees on the other side completely gone. So was the motel office. Sometimes she wished *she* was like that, all white on the inside. But only sometimes. In her deepest heart, she had never regretted what she was.

When she felt ready—as ready as she could be—Abra went back into her room and closed the door on her side so she wouldn't disturb Mr. Freeman if she had to talk loud. She examined the instructions on the phone, pushed 9 to get an outside line, then dialed directory assistance and asked for the number of the Overlook Lodge at the Bluebell Campground, in Sidewinder, Colorado. *I could give you the main number,* Dan had said, *but you'd only get an answering machine.*

In the place where the guests ate meals and played games, the telephone rang for a long time. Dan said it probably would, and that she should just wait it out. It was, after all, two hours earlier there.

At last a grumpy voice said, "Hello? If you want the office, you called the wrong num—"

"I don't want the office," Abra said. She hoped the rapid heavy beating of her heart wasn't audible in her voice. "I want Rose. Rose the Hat."

A pause. Then: "Who is this?"

"Abra Stone. You know my name, don't you? I'm the girl she's looking for. Tell her I'll call back in five minutes. If she's there, we'll talk. If she's not, tell her she can go fuck herself. I won't call back again."

Abra hung up, then lowered her head, cupped her burning face in her palms, and took long deep breaths.

2

Rose was drinking coffee behind the wheel of her EarthCruiser, her feet on the secret compartment with the stored canisters of steam inside, when the knock came at her door. A knock this early could only mean more trouble.

"Yes," she said. "Come in."

It was Long Paul, wearing a robe over childish pajamas with racing cars on them. "The pay phone in the Lodge started ringing. At first I let it go, thought it was a wrong number, and besides, I was making coffee in the kitchen. But it kept on, so I answered. It was that girl. She wanted to talk to you. She said she'd call back in five minutes."

Silent Sarey sat up in bed, blinking through her bangs, the covers clutched around her shoulders like a shawl.

"Go," Rose told her.

Sarey did so, without a word. Rose watched through the EarthCruiser's wide windshield as Sarey trudged barefooted back to the Bounder she had shared with Snake.

That girl.

Instead of running and hiding, the bitchgirl was making telephone calls. Talk about brassbound nerve. Her own idea? That was a little hard to believe, wasn't it?

"What were you doing up and bustling in the kitchen so early?"

"I couldn't sleep."

She turned toward him. Just a tall, elderly fellow with thinning hair and bifocals sitting at the end of his nose. A rube could pass him on the street every day for a year without seeing him, but he wasn't without certain abilities. Paul didn't have Snake's sleeper talent, or the late Grampa Flick's locator talent, but he was a decent persuader. If he happened to suggest that a rube slap his wife's face—or a stranger's, for that matter—that face would be slapped, and briskly. Everyone in the True had their little skills; it was how they got along.

"Let me see your arms, Paulie."

He sighed and brushed the sleeves of his robe and pajamas up to his wrinkly elbows. The red spots were there.

"When did they break?"

"Saw the first couple yesterday afternoon."

"Fever?"

"Yuh. Some."

She gazed into his honest, trusting eyes and felt like hugging him. Some had run, but Long Paul was still here. So were most of the others. Surely enough to take care of the bitchgirl if she were really foolish enough to show her face. And she might be. What girl of thirteen *wasn't* foolish?

"You're going to be all right," she said.

He sighed again. "Hope so. If not, it's been a damn good run."

"None of that talk. Everyone who sticks is going to be all right. It's my promise, and I keep my promises. Now let's see what our little friend from New Hampshire has to say for herself."

3

Less than a minute after Rose settled into a chair next to the big plastic bingo drum (with her cooling mug of coffee beside it), the Lodge's pay telephone exploded with a twentieth-century clatter that made her jump. She let it ring twice before lifting the receiver from the cradle and speaking in her most modulated voice. "Hello, dear. You could have reached out to my mind, you know. It would have saved you long-distance charges."

A thing the bitchgirl would have been very unwise to try. Abra Stone wasn't the only one who could lay traps.

"I'm coming for you," the girl said. The voice was so young, so fresh! Rose thought of all the useful steam that would come with that freshness and felt greed rise in her like an unslaked thirst.

"So you've said. Are you sure you really want to do that, dear?"

"Will you be there if I do? Or only your trained rats?"

Rose felt a trill of anger. Not helpful, but of course she had never been much of a morning person.

"Why would I not be, dear?" She kept her voice calm and slightly indulgent—the voice of a mother (or so she imagined; she had never been one) speaking to a tantrum-prone toddler.

"Because you're a coward."

"I'm curious to know what you base that assumption on," Rose said. Her tone was the same—indulgent, slightly amused—but her hand had tightened on the phone, and pressed it harder against her ear. "Never having met me."

"Sure I have. Inside my head, and I sent you running with your tail between your legs. And you kill kids. Only cowards kill kids."

You don't need to justify yourself to a child, she told herself. *Especially not a rube.* But she heard herself saying, "You know nothing about us. What we are, or what we have to do in order to survive."

"A tribe of cowards is what you are," the bitchgirl said. "You think you're so talented and so strong, but the only thing you're really good at is eating and living long lives. You're like hyenas. You kill the weak and then run away. Cowards."

The contempt in her voice was like acid in Rose's ear. "That's not true!"

"And you're the chief coward. You wouldn't come after me, would you? No, not you. You sent those others instead."

"Are we going to have a reasonable conversation, or—"

"What's reasonable about killing kids so you can steal the stuff in their minds? What's reasonable about that, you cowardly old whore? You sent your friends to do your work, you hid behind them, and I guess that was smart, because now they're all dead."

"You stupid little bitch, you don't know anything!" Rose leaped to her feet. Her thighs bumped the table and her coffee spilled, running beneath the bingo drum. Long Paul peeked through the kitchen doorway, took one look at her face, and pulled back. "Who's the coward? Who's the real coward? You can say such things over the phone, but you could never say them looking into my face!"

"How many will you have to have with you when I come?" Abra taunted. "How many, you yellow bitch?"

Rose said nothing. She had to get herself under control, she knew it, but to be talked to this way by a rube girl with a mouthful of filthy schoolyard language . . . and she knew too much. *Much* too much.

"Would you even dare to face me alone?" the bitchgirl asked.

"Try me," Rose spat.

There was a pause on the other end, and when the bitchgirl next spoke, she sounded thoughtful. "One-on-one? No, you wouldn't dare. A coward like you would never dare. Not even against a kid. You're a cheater and a liar. You look pretty sometimes, but I've seen your real face. You're nothing but an old chickenshit whore."

"You . . . you . . ." But she could say no more. Her rage was so great it felt like it was strangling her. Some of it was shock at finding herself—Rose the Hat—dressed down by a kid whose idea of transportation was a bicycle and whose major concern before these last weeks had probably been when she might get breasts bigger than mosquito bumps.

"But maybe I'll give you a chance," the bitchgirl said. Her confidence and breezy temerity were unbelievable. "Of course, if you take me up on it, I'll wipe the floor with you. I won't bother with the others, they're dying already." She actually laughed. "Choking on the baseball boy, and good for him."

"If you come, I'll kill you," Rose said. One hand found her throat, closed on it, and began to squeeze rhythmically. Later there would be bruises. "If you run, I'll find you. And when I do, you'll scream for hours before you die."

"I won't run," the girl said. "And we'll see who does the screaming."

"How many will *you* have to back you up? *Dear?*"

"I'll be alone."

"I don't believe you."

"Read my mind," the girl said. "Or are you afraid to do that, too?"

Rose said nothing.

"Sure you are. You remember what happened last time you tried it. I gave you a taste of your own medicine, and you didn't like it, did you? Hyena. Child-killer. *Coward.*"

"Stop . . . calling . . . me that."

"There's a place up the hill from where you are. A lookout. It's called Roof O' the World. I found it on the internet. Be there at five o'clock Monday afternoon. Be there alone. If you're not, if the rest of your pack of hyenas doesn't stay in that meeting-hall place while we do our business, I'll know. And I'll go away."

"I'd find you," Rose repeated.

"You think?" Actually *jeering* at her.

Rose shut her eyes and saw the girl. She saw her writhing on the ground, her mouth stuffed with stinging hornets and hot sticks jutting out of her eyes. *No one talks to me like this. Not ever.*

"I suppose you *might* find me. But by the time you did, how many of your stinking True Knot would be left to back you up? A dozen? Ten? Maybe only three or four?"

This idea had already occurred to Rose. For a child she'd never even seen face-to-face to reach the same conclusion was, in many ways, the most infuriating thing of all.

"The Crow knew Shakespeare," the bitchgirl said. "He quoted some to me not too long before I killed him. I know a little, too, because we had a Shakespeare unit in school. We only read one play, *Romeo and Juliet,* but Ms. Franklin gave us a printout with a whole list of famous lines from his other plays. Things like 'To be or not to be' and 'It was Greek to me.' Did you know those were from Shakespeare? I didn't. Don't you think it's interesting?"

Rose said nothing.

"You're not thinking about Shakespeare at all," the bitchgirl said. "You're thinking about how much you'd like to kill me. I don't have to read your mind to know that."

"If I were you, I'd run," Rose said thoughtfully. "As fast and as far as your baby legs can carry you. It wouldn't do you any good, but you'd live a little longer."

The bitchgirl was not to be turned. "There was another saying.

I can't remember it exactly, but it was something like 'Hoisted on your own petard.' Ms. Franklin said a petard was a bomb on a stick. I think that's sort of what's happening to your tribe of cowards. You sucked the wrong kind of steam, and got stuck on a petard, and now the bomb is going off." She paused. "Are you still there, Rose? Or did you run away?"

"Come to me, dear," Rose said. She had regained her calm. "If you want to meet me on the lookout, that's where I'll be. We'll take in the view together, shall we? And see who's the stronger."

She hung up before the bitchgirl could say anything else. She'd lost the temper she had vowed to keep, but she had at least gotten the last word.

Or maybe not, because the one the bitchgirl kept using played over and over in her head, like a gramophone record stuck in a bad groove.

Coward. Coward. Coward.

4

Abra replaced the telephone receiver carefully in its cradle. She looked at it; she even stroked its plastic surface, which was hot from her hand and wet with her sweat. Then, before she realized it was going to happen, she burst into loud, braying sobs. They stormed through her, cramping her stomach and shaking her body. She rushed to the bathroom, still crying, knelt in front of the toilet, and threw up.

When she came out, Mr. Freeman was standing in the connecting doorway with his shirttail hanging down and his gray hair in corkscrews. "What's wrong? Are you sick from the dope he gave you?"

"It wasn't that."

He went to the window and peered out into the pressing fog. "Is it *them*? Are they coming for us?"

Temporarily incapable of speech, she could only shake her head so vehemently her pigtails flew. It was *she* who was coming for *them,* and that was what terrified her.

And not just for herself.

5

Rose sat still, taking long steadying breaths. When she had herself under control again, she called for Long Paul. After a moment or two, he poked his head cautiously through the swing door that gave on the kitchen. The look on his face brought a ghost of a smile to her lips. "It's safe. You can come in. I won't bite you."

He stepped in and saw the spilled coffee. "I'll clean that up."

"Leave it. Who's the best locator we've got left?"

"You, Rose." No hesitation.

Rose had no intention of approaching the bitchgirl mentally, not even in a touch-and-go. "Aside from me."

"Well . . . with Grampa Flick gone . . . and Barry . . ." He considered. "Sue's got a touch of locator, and so does Greedy G. But I think Token Charlie's got a bit more."

"Is he sick?"

"He wasn't yesterday."

"Send him to me. I'll wipe up the coffee while I'm waiting. Because—this is important, Paulie—the person who makes the mess is the one who should have to clean it up."

After he left, Rose sat where she was for awhile, fingers steepled under her chin. Clear thinking had returned, and with it the ability to plan. They wouldn't be taking steam today after all, it seemed. That could wait until Monday morning.

At last she went into the galley for a wad of paper towels. And cleaned up her mess.

6

"Dan!" This time it was John. "Gotta go!"

"Right there," he said. "I just want to splash some cold water on my face."

He went down the hall listening to Abra, nodding his head slightly as if she were there.

(*Mr. Freeman wants to know why I was crying why I threw up what should I tell him*)

(*for now just that when we get there I'll want to borrow his truck*)

(*because we're going on going west*)

(*. . . well . . .*)

It was complicated, but she understood. The understanding wasn't in words and didn't need to be.

Beside the bathroom washbasin was a rack holding several wrapped toothbrushes. The smallest—not wrapped—had **ABRA** printed on the handle in rainbow letters. On one wall was a small plaque reading A LIFE WITHOUT LOVE IS LIKE A TREE WITHOUT FRUIT. He looked at it for a few seconds, wondering if there was anything in the AA program to that effect. The only thing he could think of was *If you can't love anybody today, at least try not to hurt anybody*. Didn't really compare.

He turned on the cold water and splashed his face several times, hard. Then he grabbed a towel and raised his head. No Lucy in the portrait with him this time; just Dan Torrance, son of Jack and Wendy, who had always believed himself to be an only child.

His face was covered with flies.

PART FOUR

ROOF O' THE WORLD

CHAPTER EIGHTEEN

GOING WEST

1

What Dan remembered best about that Saturday wasn't the ride from Boston to the Crown Motel, because the four people in John Dalton's SUV said very little. The silence wasn't uncomfortable or hostile but exhausted—the quiet of people who have a great deal to think about but not a hell of a lot to say. What he remembered best was what happened when they reached their destination.

Dan knew she was waiting, because he had been in touch with her for most of the trip, talking in a way that had become comfortable for them—half words and half pictures. When they pulled in, she was sitting on the back bumper of Billy's old truck. She saw them and jumped to her feet, waving. At that moment the cloud cover, which had been thinning, broke apart and a ray of sun spotlighted her. It was as if God had given her a high five.

Lucy gave a cry that was not quite a scream. She had her seatbelt unbuckled and her door open before John could bring his Suburban to a complete stop. Five seconds later she had her daughter in her arms and was kissing the top of her head—the best she could do, with Abra's face crushed between her breasts. Now the sun spotlighted them both.

Mother and child reunion, Dan thought. The smile that brought felt strange on his face. It had been a long time between smiles.

2

Lucy and David wanted to take Abra back to New Hampshire. Dan had no problem with that, but now that they were together, the six of them needed to talk. The fat man with the ponytail was back on duty, today watching a cage-fighting match instead of porn. He was happy to re-rent them Room 24; it was nothing to him whether they spent the night or not. Billy went into Crownville proper to pick up a couple of pizzas. Then they settled in, Dan and Abra talking turn and turn about, filling in the others on everything that had happened and everything that was going to happen. If things went as they hoped, that was.

"No," Lucy said at once. "It's far too dangerous. For both of you."

John offered a bleak grin. "The most dangerous thing would be to ignore these . . . these *things*. Rose says that if Abra doesn't come to her, she'll come to Abra."

"She's, like, fixated on her," Billy said, and selected a slice of pepperoni-and-mushroom. "Happens lots of times with crazy people. All you have to do to know that is watch *Dr. Phil.*"

Lucy fixed her daughter with a reproachful glance. "You goaded her. That was a dangerous thing to do, but when she has a chance to settle down . . ."

Although no one interrupted, she trailed off. Maybe, Dan thought, she heard how implausible that sounded when it was actually articulated.

"They won't stop, Mom," Abra said. "*She* won't stop."

"Abra will be safe enough," Dan said. "There's a wheel. I don't know how to explain it any better than that. If things get bad—if they go wrong—Abra will use the wheel to get away. To pull out. She's promised me that."

"That's right," Abra said. "I promised."

Dan fixed her with a hard look. "And you'll keep it, won't you?"

"Yes," Abra said. She spoke firmly enough, although with obvious reluctance. "I will."

"There's all those kids to consider, too," John said. "We'll never know how many this True Knot has taken over the years. Hundreds, maybe."

Dan thought that if they lived as long as Abra believed, the number was probably in the thousands. He said, "Or how many they *will* take, even if they leave Abra alone."

"That's assuming the measles doesn't kill them all," Dave said hopefully. He turned to John. "You said that really might happen."

"They want me because they think I can *cure* the measles," Abra said. "*Duh.*"

"Keep a civil tongue, miss," Lucy said, but she spoke absently. She picked up the last slice of pizza, looked at it, then threw it back in the box. "I don't care about the other kids. I care about Abra. I know how horrible that sounds, but it's the truth."

"You wouldn't feel that way if you'd seen all those little pictures in the *Shopper,*" Abra said. "I can't get them out of my head. I dream about them sometimes."

"If this crazy woman has half a brain, she'll know Abra isn't coming alone," Dave said. "What's she going to do, fly to Denver and then rent a car? A thirteen-year-old?" And, with a half-humorous look at his daughter: *"Duh."*

Dan said, "Rose already knows from what happened at Cloud Gap that Abra's got friends. What she doesn't know is that she has at least one with the shining." He looked at Abra for confirmation. She nodded. "Listen, Lucy. Dave. Together, I think that Abra and I can put an end to this"—he searched for the right word and found only one that fit—"plague. Either of us alone . . ." He shook his head.

"Besides," Abra said, "you and Dad can't really stop me. You can lock me in my room, but you can't lock up my head."

Lucy gave her the Death Stare, the one mothers save especially for rebellious young daughters. It had always worked with Abra, even when she was in one of her furies, but it didn't this time. She looked back at her mother calmly. And with a sadness that made Lucy's heart feel cold.

Dave took Lucy's hand. "I think this has to be done."

There was silence in the room. Abra was the one who broke it. "If nobody's going to eat that last slice, I am. I'm *starving*."

3

They went over it several more times, and at a couple of points voices were raised, but essentially, everything had been said. Except, it turned out, for one thing. When they left the room, Billy refused to get into John's Suburban.

"I'm goin," he told Dan.

"Billy, I appreciate the thought, but it's not a good idea."

"My truck, my rules. Besides, are you really gonna make the Colorado high country by Monday afternoon on your own? Don't make me laugh. You look like shit on a stick."

Dan said, "Several people have told me that lately, but none have put it so elegantly."

Billy didn't smile. "I can help you. I'm old, but I ain't dead."

"Take him," Abra said. "He's right."

Dan looked at her closely.

(*do you know something Abra*)

The reply was quick.

(*no* feel *something*)

That was good enough for Dan. He held out his arms and Abra hugged him hard, the side of her face pressed against his chest. Dan could have held her like that for a long time, but he let her go and stepped back.

(*let me know when you get close Uncle Dan I'll come*)

(*just little touches remember*)

She sent an image instead of a thought in words: a smoke detector beeping the way they did when they wanted a battery change. She remembered perfectly.

As she went to the car, Abra said to her father, "We need to stop on the way back for a get-well card. Julie Cross broke her wrist yesterday in soccer practice."

He frowned at her. "How do you know that?"

"I know," she said.

He gently pulled one of her pigtails. "You really could do it all along, couldn't you? I don't understand why you didn't just tell us, Abba-Doo."

Dan, who had grown up with the shining, could have answered that question.

Sometimes parents needed to be protected.

4

So they parted. John's SUV went east and Billy's pickup truck went west, with Billy behind the wheel. Dan said, "Are you really okay to drive, Billy?"

"After all the sleep I got last night? Sweetheart, I could drive to California."

"Do you know where we're going?"

"I bought a road atlas in town while I was waitin for the pizza."

"So you'd made up your mind even then. And you knew what Abra and I were planning."

"Well . . . sorta."

"When you need me to take over, just yell," Dan said, and promptly fell asleep with his head against the passenger window. He descended through a deepening depth of unpleasant images. First the hedge animals at the Overlook, the ones that moved when you weren't looking. This was followed by Mrs. Massey from Room 217, who now wore a cocked tophat. Still descending, he revisited the battle at Cloud Gap. Only this time when he burst into the Winnebago, he found Abra lying on the floor with her throat cut and Rose standing over her with a dripping straight razor. Rose saw Dan and the bottom half of her face dropped away in an obscene grin where one long tooth gleamed. *I told her it would end this way but she wouldn't listen,* she said. *Children so rarely do.*

Below this there was only darkness.

When he woke it was to twilight with a broken white line running down the middle of it. They were on an interstate highway.

"How long did I sleep?"

Billy glanced at his watch. "A good long while. Feel better?"

"Yes." He did and didn't. His head was clear, but his stomach hurt like hell. Considering what he had seen that morning in the mirror, he wasn't surprised. "Where are we?"

"Hunnert-n-fifty miles east of Cincinnati, give or take. You slept through two gas stops. And you snore."

Dan sat up straight. "We're in *Ohio*? Christ! What time is it?"

Billy glanced at his watch. "Quarter past six. Wasn't no big thing; light traffic and no rain. I think we got an angel ridin with us."

"Well, let's find a motel. You need to sleep and I have to piss like a racehorse."

"Not surprised."

Billy pulled off at the next exit showing signs for gas, food, and motels. He pulled into a Wendy's and got a bag of burgers while Dan used the men's. When they got back into the truck, Dan took one bite of his double, put it back in the bag, and sipped cautiously at a coffee milkshake. That his stomach seemed willing to take.

Billy looked shocked. "Man, you gotta eat! What's wrong with you?"

"I guess pizza for breakfast was a bad idea." And because Billy was still looking at him: "The shake's fine. All I need. Eyes on the road, Billy. We can't help Abra if we're getting patched up in some emergency room."

Five minutes later, Billy pulled the truck under the canopy of a Fairfield Inn with a blinking ROOMS AVAILABLE sign over the door. He turned off the engine but didn't get out. "Since I'm riskin my life with you, chief, I want to know what ails you."

Dan almost pointed out that taking the risk had been Billy's idea, not his, but that wasn't fair. He explained. Billy listened in round-eyed silence.

"Jesus jumped-up Christ," he said when Dan had finished.

"Unless I missed it," Dan said, "there's nothing in the New

Testament about Jesus jumping. Although I guess He might've, as a child. Most of them do. You want to check us in, or should I do it?"

Billy continued to sit where he was. "Does Abra know?"

Dan shook his head.

"But she could find out."

"Could but won't. She knows it's wrong to peek, especially when it's someone you care about. She'd no more do it than she'd spy on her parents when they were making love."

"You know that from when you were a kid?"

"Yes. Sometimes you see a little—you can't help it—but then you turn away."

"Are you gonna be all right, Danny?"

"For awhile." He thought of the sluggish flies on his lips and cheeks and forehead. "Long enough."

"What about after?"

"I'll worry about after after. One day at a time. Let's check in. We need to get an early start."

"Have you heard from Abra?"

Dan smiled. "She's fine."

At least so far.

5

But she wasn't, not really.

She sat at her desk with a half-read copy of *The Fixer* in her hand, trying not to look at her bedroom window, lest she should see a certain someone looking in at her. She knew something was wrong with Dan, and she knew he didn't want her to know what it was, but had been tempted to look anyway, in spite of all the years she'd taught herself to steer clear of APB: adult private business. Two things held her back. One was the knowledge that, like it or not, she couldn't help him with it now. The other (this was stronger) was knowing he might sense her in his head. If so, he would be disappointed in her.

It's probably locked up, anyway, she thought. *He can do that. He's pretty strong.*

Not as strong as she was, though . . . or, if you put it in terms of the shining, as bright. She could open his mental lockboxes and peer at the things inside, but she thought doing so might be dangerous for both of them. There was no concrete reason for this, it was just a feeling—like the one she'd had about how it would be a good idea for Mr. Freeman to go with Dan—but she trusted it. Besides, maybe it was something that could help them. She could hope for that. *True hope is swift, and flies on swallow's wings*—that was another line from Shakespeare.

Don't you look at that window, either. Don't you dare.

No. Absolutely not. Never. So she did, and there was Rose, grinning in at her from below her rakishly tilted hat. All billowing hair and pale porcelain skin and dark mad eyes and rich red lips masking that one snaggle tooth. That *tusk.*

You're going to die screaming, bitchgirl.

Abra closed her eyes and thought hard

(*not there not there not there*)

and opened them again. The grinning face at the window was gone. But not really. Somewhere high in the mountains—at the roof of the world—Rose was thinking about her. And waiting.

6

The motel had a breakfast buffet. Because his traveling companion was watching him, Dan made a point of eating some cereal and yogurt. Billy looked relieved. While he checked them out, Dan strolled to the lobby men's room. Once inside, he turned the lock, fell to his knees, and vomited up everything he'd eaten. The undigested cereal and yogurt floated in a red foam.

"All right?" Billy asked when Dan rejoined him at the desk.

"Fine," Dan said. "Let's roll."

7

According to Billy's road atlas, it was about twelve hundred miles from Cincinnati to Denver. Sidewinder lay roughly seventy-five miles further west, along roads full of switchbacks and lined with steep drops. Dan tried driving for awhile on that Sunday afternoon, but tired quickly and turned the wheel over to Billy again. He fell asleep, and when he woke up, the sun was going down. They were in Iowa—home of the late Brad Trevor.

(*Abra?*)

He had been afraid distance would make mental communication difficult or even impossible, but she came back promptly, and as strong as ever; if she'd been a radio station, she would have been broadcasting at 100,000 watts. She was in her room, pecking away on her computer at some homework assignment or other. He was both amused and saddened to realize she had Hoppy, her stuffed rabbit, on her lap. The strain of what they were doing had regressed her to a younger Abra, at least on the emotional side.

With the line between them wide open, she caught this.

(*don't worry about me I'm all right*)

(*good because you have a call to make*)

(*yes okay are* you *all right*)

(*fine*)

She knew better but didn't ask, and that was just the way he wanted it.

(*have you got the*)

She made a picture.

(*not yet it's Sunday stores not open*)

Another picture, one that made him smile. A Walmart . . . except the sign out front read ABRA'S SUPERSTORE.

(*they wouldn't sell us what we need we'll find one that will*)

(*okay   I guess*)

(*you know what to say to her?*)

(*yes*)

(*she'll try to suck you into a long conversation try to snoop don't let her*)

(*I won't*)

(*let me hear from you after so I won't worry*)

Of course he would worry plenty.

(*I will I love you Uncle Dan*)

(*love you too*)

He made a kiss. Abra made one back: big red cartoon lips. He could almost feel them on his cheek. Then she was gone.

Billy was staring at him. "You were just talkin to her, weren't you?"

"Indeed I was. Eyes on the road, Billy."

"Yeah, yeah. You sound like my ex-wife."

Billy put on his blinker, switched to the passing lane, and rolled past a huge and lumbering Fleetwood Pace Arrow motorhome. Dan stared at it, wondering who was inside and if they were looking out the tinted windows.

"I want to make another hundred or so miles before we quit for the night," Billy said. "Way I got tomorrow figured, that should give us an hour to do your errand and still put us in the high country about the time you and Abra set for the showdown. But we'll want to get on the road before daybreak."

"Fine. You understand how this will go?"

"I get how it's *supposed* to go." Billy glanced at him. "You better hope that if they have binoculars, they don't use them. Do you think we might come back alive? Tell me the truth. If the answer's no, I'm gonna order me the biggest steak dinner you ever saw when we stop for the night. MasterCard can chase my relatives for the last credit card bill, and guess what? I ain't *got* any relatives. Unless you count the ex, and if I was on fire she wouldn't piss on me to put me out."

"We'll come back," Dan said, but it sounded pale. He felt too sick to put up much of a front.

"Yeah? Well, maybe I'll have that steak dinner, anyway. What about you?"

"I think I could manage a little soup. As long as it's clear." The thought of eating anything too thick to read a newspaper through—tomato bisque, cream of mushroom—made his stomach cringe.

"Okay. Why don't you close your eyes again?"

Dan knew he couldn't sleep deeply, no matter how tired and sick he felt—not while Abra was dealing with the ancient horror that looked like a woman—but he managed a doze. It was thin but rich enough to grow more dreams, first of the Overlook (today's version featured the elevator that ran by itself in the middle of the night), then of his niece. This time Abra had been strangled with a length of electrical cord. She stared at Dan with bulging, accusing eyes. It was all too easy to read what was in them. *You said you'd help me. You said you'd save me. Where were you?*

8

Abra kept putting off the thing she had to do until she realized her mother would soon be pestering her to go to bed. She wasn't going to school in the morning, but it was still going to be a big day. And, perhaps, a very long night.

Putting things off only makes them worse, cara mia.

That was the gospel according to Momo. Abra looked toward her window, wishing she could see her great-grandma there instead of Rose. That would be good.

"Momes, I'm so scared," she said. But after two long and steadying breaths, she picked up her iPhone and dialed the Overlook Lodge at Bluebell Campground. A man answered, and when Abra said she wanted to talk to Rose, he asked who she was.

"You know who I am," she said. And—with what she hoped was irritating inquisitiveness: "Are you sick yet, mister?"

The man on the other end (it was Toady Slim) didn't answer that, but she heard him murmur to someone. A moment later, Rose was on, her composure once more firmly in place.

"Hello, dear. Where are you?"

"On my way," Abra said.

"Are you really? That's nice, dear. So I don't suppose that I'd find this call came from a New Hampshire area code if I star-sixty-nined it?"

"Of course you would," Abra said. "I'm using my cell. You need to get with the twenty-first century, bitch."

"What do you want?" The voice on the other end was now curt.

"To make sure you know the rules," Abra said. "I'll be there at five tomorrow. I'll be in an old red truck."

"Driven by whom?"

"My uncle Billy," Abra said.

"Was he one of the ones from the ambush?"

"He's the one who was with me and the Crow. Stop asking questions. Just shut up and listen."

"So rude," Rose said sadly.

"He'll park way at the end of the lot, by the sign that says KIDS EAT FREE WHEN COLORADO PRO TEAMS WIN."

"I see you've been on our website. That's sweet. Or was it your uncle, perhaps? He's very brave to act as your chauffeur. Is he your father's brother or your mother's? Rube families are a hobby of mine. I make family trees."

She'll try to snoop, Dan had told her, and how right he was.

"What part of 'shut up and listen' don't you understand? Do you want this to happen or not?"

No reply, just waiting silence. *Creepy* waiting silence.

"From the parking lot, we'll be able to see everything: the campground, the Lodge, and Roof O' the World on top of the hill. My uncle and me better see you up there, and we better not see the people from your True Knot *anywhere*. They're going to stay in that meeting-hall thingy while we do our business. In the big room, got it? Uncle Billy won't know if they're not where they're supposed to be, but I will. If I pick up a single one somewhere else, we'll be gone."

"Your uncle will stay in his truck?"

"No. *I'll* stay in the truck, until we're sure. Then he'll get back in and I'll come to you. I don't want him anywhere near you."

"All right, dear. It will be as you say."

No, it won't. You're lying.

But so was Abra, which kind of made them even.

"I have one really important question, dear," Rose said pleasantly.

Abra almost asked what it was, then remembered her uncle's advice. Her *real* uncle. One question, right. Which would lead to another . . . and another . . . and another.

"Choke on it," she said, and hung up. Her hands began to tremble. Then her legs and arms and shoulders.

"Abra?" Mom. Calling from the foot of the stairs. *She feels it. Just a little, but she does feel it. Is that a mom thing or a shining thing?* "Honey, are you okay?"

"Fine, Mom! Getting ready for bed!"

"Ten minutes, then we're coming up for kisses. Be in your PJs."

"I will."

If they knew who I was just talking to, Abra thought. But they didn't. They only thought they knew what was going on. She was here in her bedroom, every door and window in the house was locked, and they believed that made her safe. Even her father, who had seen the True Knot in action.

But Dan knew. She closed her eyes and reached out to him.

9

Dan and Billy were under another motel canopy. And still nothing from Abra. That was bad.

"Come on, chief," Billy said. "Let's get you inside and—"

Then she was there. Thank God.

"Hush a minute," Dan said, and listened. Two minutes later he turned to Billy, who thought the smile on his face finally made him look like Dan Torrance again.

"Was it her?"

"Yes."

"How'd it go?"

"Abra says it went fine. We're in business."

"No questions about me?"

"Just which side of the family you were on. Listen, Billy, the uncle thing was a bit of a mistake. You're *way* too old to be Lucy's or David's brother. When we stop tomorrow to do our errand, you need to buy sunglasses. Big ones. And keep that ball cap of yours jammed down all the way to your ears, so your hair doesn't show."

"Maybe I should get some Just For Men, while I'm at it."

"Don't sass me, you old fart."

That made Billy grin. "Let's get registered and get some food. You look better. Like you could actually eat."

"Soup," Dan said. "No sense pressing my luck."

"Soup. Right."

He ate it all. Slowly. And—reminding himself that this would be over one way or the other in less than twenty-four hours—he managed to keep it down. They dined in Billy's room and when he was finally finished, Dan stretched out on the carpet. It eased the pain in his gut a little.

"What's that?" Billy asked. "Some kind of yogi shit?"

"Exactly. I learned it watching Yogi Bear cartoons. Run it down for me again."

"I got it, chief, don't worry. Now you're starting to sound like Casey Kingsley."

"A scary thought. Now run it down again."

"Abra starts pinging around Denver. If they have someone who can listen, they'll know she's coming. And that she's in the neighborhood. We get to Sidewinder early—say four instead of five—and drive right past the road to the campground. They won't see the truck. Unless they post a sentry down by the highway, that is."

"I don't think they will." Dan thought of another AA aphorism: *We're powerless over people, places, and things.* Like most alkie nuggets, it was seventy percent true and thirty percent rah-rah bullshit. "In any case, we can't control everything. Carry on."

"There's a picnic area about a mile further up the road. You went there a couple of times with your mom, before you guys got snowed in for the winter." Billy paused. "Just her and you? Never your dad?"

"He was writing. Working on a play. Go on."

Billy did. Dan listened closely, then nodded. "Okay. You've got it."

"Didn't I say? Now can I ask a question?"

"Sure."

"By tomorrow afternoon, will you still be able to walk a mile?"

"I'll be able to."

I better be.

10

Thanks to an early start—4 a.m., long before first light—Dan Torrance and Billy Freeman began to see a horizon-spanning cloud shortly after 9 a.m. An hour later, by which time the blue-gray cloud had resolved itself into a mountain range, they stopped in the town of Martenville, Colorado. There, on the short (and mostly deserted) main street, Dan saw not what he was hoping for, but something even better: a children's clothing store called Kids' Stuff. Half a block down was a drugstore flanked by a dusty-looking hockshop and a Video Express with CLOSING MUST SELL ALL STOCK AT BARGAIN PRICES soaped in the window. He sent Billy to Martenville Drugs & Sundries to get sunglasses and stepped through the door of Kids' Stuff.

The place had an unhappy, losing-hope vibe. He was the only customer. Here was somebody's good idea going bad, probably thanks to the big-box mall stores in Sterling or Fort Morgan. Why buy local when you could drive a little and get cheaper pants and dresses for back-to-school? So what if they were made in Mexico or Costa Rica? A tired-looking woman with a tired-looking hairdo came out from behind the counter and gave Dan a tired-looking smile. She asked if she could help him. Dan said she could. When he told her what he wanted, her eyes went round.

"I know it's unusual," Dan said, "but get with me on this a little. I'll pay cash."

He got what he wanted. In little losing-hope stores off the turnpike, the C-word went a long way.

11

As they neared Denver, Dan got in touch with Abra. He closed his eyes and visualized the wheel they both now knew about. In the town of Anniston, Abra did the same. It was easier this time. When he opened his eyes again, he was looking down the slope of the Stones' back lawn at the Saco River, gleaming in the afternoon sun. Abra opened hers on a view of the Rockies.

"Wow, Uncle Billy, they're beautiful, aren't they?"

Billy glanced at the man sitting beside him. Dan had crossed his legs in a way that was utterly unlike him, and was bouncing one foot. Color had come back into his cheeks, and there was a bright clarity in his eyes that had been missing on their run west.

"They sure are, honey," he said.

Dan smiled and closed his eyes. When he opened them again, the health Abra had brought to his face was fading. *Like a rose without water,* Billy thought.

"Anything?"

"Ping," Dan said. He smiled again, but this one was weary. "Like a smoke detector that needs a battery change."

"Do you think they heard it?"

"I sure hope so," Dan said.

12

Rose was pacing back and forth near her EarthCruiser when Token Charlie came running up. The True had taken steam that morning, all but one of the canisters she had in storage, and on top of what

Rose had taken on her own over the last couple of days, she was too wired even to think about sitting down.

"What?" she asked. "Tell me something good."

"I got her, how's that for good?" Wired himself, Charlie grabbed Rose by the arms and whirled her around, making her hair fly. "I *got* her! Just for a few seconds, but it was her!"

"Did you see the uncle?"

"No, she was looking out the windshield at the mountains. She said they were beautiful—"

"They are," Rose said. A grin was spreading on her lips. "Don't you agree, Charlie?"

"—and he said they sure were. They're coming, Rosie! They really are!"

"Did she know you were there?"

He let go of her, frowning. "I can't say for sure . . . Grampa Flick probably could . . ."

"Just tell me what you think."

"Probably not."

"That's good enough for me. Go someplace quiet. Someplace where you can concentrate without being disturbed. Sit and listen. If—*when*—you pick her up again, let me know. I don't want to lose track of her if I can help it. If you need more steam, ask for it. I saved a little."

"No, no, I'm fine. I'll listen. I'll listen *hard*!" Token Charlie gave a rather wild laugh and rushed off. Rose didn't think he had any idea where he was going, and she didn't care. As long as he kept listening.

13

Dan and Billy were at the foot of the Flatirons by noon. As he watched the Rockies draw closer, Dan thought of all the wandering years he had avoided them. That in turn made him think of some poem or other, one about how you could spend years running, but in the end you always wound up facing yourself in a hotel room, with a naked bulb hanging overhead and a revolver on the table.

Because they had time, they left the freeway and drove into Boulder. Billy was hungry. Dan wasn't . . . but he was curious. Billy pulled the truck into a sandwich shop parking lot, but when he asked Dan what he could get him, Dan only shook his head.

"Sure? You got a lot ahead of you."

"I'll eat when this is over."

"Well . . ."

Billy went into the Subway for a Buffalo Chicken. Dan got in touch with Abra. The wheel turned.

Ping.

When Billy came out, Dan nodded to his wrapped footlong. "Save that a couple of minutes. As long as we're in Boulder, there's something I want to check out."

Five minutes later, they were on Arapahoe Street. Two blocks from the seedy little bar-and-café district, he told Billy to pull over. "Go on and chow that chicken. I won't be long. "

Dan got out of the truck and stood on the cracked sidewalk, looking at a slumped three-story building with a sign in the window reading EFFICIENCY APTS GOOD STUDENT VALUE. The lawn was balding. Weeds grew up through the cracks in the sidewalk. He had doubted that this place would still be here, had believed that Arapahoe would now be a street of condos populated by well-to-do slackers who drank lattes from Starbucks, checked their Facebook pages half a dozen times a day, and Twittered like mad bastards. But here it was, and looking—so far as he could tell—exactly as it had back in the day.

Billy joined him, sandwich in one hand. "We've still got seventy-five miles ahead of us, Danno. Best we get our asses up the pass."

"Right," Dan said, then went on looking at the building with the peeling green paint. Once a little boy had lived here; once he had sat on the very piece of curbing where Billy Freeman now stood munching his chicken footlong. A little boy waiting for his daddy to come home from his job interview at the Overlook Hotel. He had a balsa glider, that little boy, but the wing was busted. It was okay, though. When his daddy came home, he would fix it with tape and glue. Then maybe they would fly it together. His daddy had been a scary man, and how that little boy had loved him.

Dan said, "I lived here with my mother and father before we moved up to the Overlook. Not much, is it?"

Billy shrugged. "I seen worse."

In his wandering years, Dan had, too. Deenie's apartment in Wilmington, for instance.

He pointed left. "There were a bunch of bars down that way. One was called the Broken Drum. Looks like urban renewal missed this side of town, so maybe it's still there. When my father and I walked past it, he'd always stop and look in the window, and I could feel how thirsty he was to go inside. So thirsty it made *me* thirsty. I drank a lot of years to quench that thirst, but it never really goes away. My dad knew that, even then."

"But you loved him, I guess."

"I did." Still looking at that shambling, rundown apartment house. Not much, but Dan couldn't help wondering how different their lives might have been if they had stayed there. If the Overlook had not ensnared them. "He was good and bad and I loved both sides of him. God help me, I guess I still do."

"You and most kids," Billy said. "You love your folks and hope for the best. What else can you do? Come on, Dan. If we're gonna do this, we have to go."

Half an hour later, Boulder was behind them and they were climbing into the Rockies.

CHAPTER NINETEEN

GHOSTIE PEOPLE

1

Although sunset was approaching—in New Hampshire, at least—Abra was still on the back stoop, looking down at the river. Hoppy was sitting nearby, on the lid of the composter. Lucy and David came out and sat on either side of her. John Dalton watched them from the kitchen, holding a cold cup of coffee. His black bag was on the counter, but there was nothing in it he could use this evening.

"You should come in and have some supper," Lucy said, knowing that Abra wouldn't—probably couldn't—until this was over. But you clung to the known. Because everything looked normal, and because the danger was over a thousand miles away, that was easier for her than for her daughter. Although Abra's complexion had previously been clear—as unblemished as when she was an infant—she now had nests of acne around the wings of her nose and an ugly cluster of pimples on her chin. Just hormones kicking in, heralding the onset of true adolescence: so Lucy would have liked to believe, because that was normal. But stress caused acne, too. Then there was the pallor of her daughter's skin and the dark circles beneath her eyes. She looked almost as ill as Dan did when Lucy had last seen him, climbing with painful slowness into Mr. Freeman's pickup truck.

"Can't eat now, Mom. No time. I probably couldn't keep it down, anyway."

"How soon before this happens, Abby?" David asked.

She looked at neither of them. She looked fixedly down at the river, but Lucy knew she wasn't really looking at that, either. She was far away, in a place where none of them could help her. "Not long. You should each give me a kiss and then go inside."

"But—" Lucy began, then saw David shake his head at her. Only once, but very firmly. She sighed, took one of Abra's hands (how cold it was), and planted a kiss on her left cheek. David put one on her right.

Lucy: "Remember what Dan said. If things go wrong—"

"You should go in now, guys. When it starts, I'm going to take Hoppy and put him in my lap. When you see that, you can't interrupt me. Not for *anything*. You could get Uncle Dan killed, and maybe Billy, too. I might fall over, like in a faint, but it won't be a faint, so don't move me and don't let Dr. John move me, either. Just let me be until it's over. I think Dan knows a place where we can be together."

David said, "I don't understand how this can possibly work. That woman, Rose, will see there's no little girl—"

"You need to go in *now*," Abra said.

They did as she said. Lucy looked pleadingly at John; he could only shrug and shake his head. The three of them stood at the kitchen window, arms around one another, looking out at the little girl sitting on the stoop with her arms clasped around her knees. There was no danger to be seen; all was placid. But when Lucy saw Abra—her little girl—reach for Hoppy and take the old stuffed rabbit on her lap, she groaned. John squeezed her shoulder. David tightened the arm around her waist, and she gripped his hand with panicky tightness.

Please let my daughter be all right. If something has to happen . . . something bad . . . let it happen to the half brother I never knew. Not to her.

"It'll be okay," Dave said.

She nodded. "Of course it will. Of course it will."

They watched the girl on the stoop. Lucy understood that if she *did* call to Abra, she wouldn't answer. Abra was gone.

2

Billy and Dan reached the turnoff to the True's Colorado base of operations at twenty to four, Mountain Time, which put them comfortably ahead of schedule. There was a wooden ranch-style arch over the paved road with WELCOME TO THE BLUEBELL CAMPGROUND! STAY AWHILE, PARTNER! carved into it. The sign beside the road was a lot less welcoming: **CLOSED UNTIL FURTHER NOTICE**.

Billy drove past without slowing, but his eyes were busy. "Don't see nobody. Not even on the lawns, although I suppose they coulda stashed someone in that welcome-hut doohickey. Jesus, Danny, you look just awful."

"Lucky for me the Mr. America competition isn't until later this year," Dan said. "One mile up, maybe a little less. The sign says Scenic Turnout and Picnic Area."

"What if they posted someone there?"

"They haven't."

"How can you be sure?"

"Because neither Abra nor her uncle Billy could possibly know about it, never having been here. And the True doesn't know about me."

"You better hope they don't."

"Abra says everyone's where they're supposed to be. She's been checking. Now be quiet a minute, Billy. I need to think."

It was Halloran he wanted to think about. For several years following their haunted winter at the Overlook, Danny Torrance and Dick Halloran had talked a lot. Sometimes face-to-face, more often mind-to-mind. Danny loved his mother, but there were things she didn't—couldn't—understand. About the lockboxes, for instance. The ones where you put the dangerous things that the shining sometimes attracted. Not that the lockbox thing always worked. On several occasions he had tried to make one for the drinking, but that effort had been an abject failure (perhaps because he had *wanted* it to be a failure). Mrs. Massey, though . . . and Horace Derwent . . .

There was a third lockbox in storage now, but it wasn't as good as the ones he'd made as a kid. Because he wasn't as strong? Because what it held was different from the revenants that had been unwise enough to seek him out? Both? He didn't know. He only knew that it was leaky. When he opened it, what was inside might kill him. But—

"What do you mean?" Billy asked.

"Huh?" Dan looked around. One hand was pressed to his stomach. It hurt very badly now.

"You just said, 'There isn't any choice.' What did you mean?"

"Never mind." They had reached the picnic area, and Billy was turning in. Up ahead was a clearing with picnic benches and barbecue pits. To Dan, it looked like Cloud Gap without the river. "Just . . . if things go wrong, get in your truck and drive like hell."

"You think that would help?"

Dan didn't reply. His gut was burning, burning.

3

Shortly before four o'clock on that Monday afternoon in late September, Rose walked up to Roof O' the World with Silent Sarey.

Rose was dressed in form-fitting jeans that accentuated her long and shapely legs. Although it was chilly, Silent Sarey wore only a housedress of unremarkable light blue that fluttered around stout calves clad in Jobst support stockings. Rose stopped to look at a plaque which had been bolted to a granite post at the base of the three dozen or so stairs leading up to the lookout platform. It announced that this was the site of the historic Overlook Hotel, which had burned to the ground some thirty-five years ago.

"Very strong feelings here, Sarey."

Sarey nodded.

"You know there are hot springs where steam comes right out of the ground, don't you?"

"Lup."

"This is like that." Rose bent down to sniff at the grass and wildflowers. Below their aromas was the iron smell of ancient blood. "Strong emotions—hatred, fear, prejudice, lust. The echo of murder. Not food—too old—but refreshing, all the same. A heady bouquet."

Sarey said nothing, but watched Rose closely.

"And *this* thing." Rose waved a hand at the steep wooden stairs leading up to the platform. "Looks like a gallows, don't you think? All it needs is a trapdoor."

Nothing from Sarey. Out loud, at least. Her thought

(*no rope*)

was clear enough.

"That's true, my love, but one of us is going to hang here, just the same. Either me or the little bitch with her nose in our business. See that?" Rose pointed to a small green shed about twenty feet away.

Sarey nodded.

Rose was wearing a zipper pack on her belt. She opened it, rummaged, brought out a key, and handed it to the other woman. Sarey walked to the shed, grass whickering against her thick flesh-colored hose. The key fitted a padlock on the door. When she pulled the door open, late-day sunshine illuminated an enclosure not much bigger than a privy. There was a Lawn-Boy and a plastic bucket holding a hand-sickle and a rake. A spade and a pickax leaned against the back wall. There was nothing else, and nothing to hide behind.

"Go on in," Rose said. "Let's see what you can do." *And with all that steam inside you, you should be able to amaze me.*

Like other members of the True Knot, Silent Sarey had her little talent.

She stepped into the little shed, sniffed, and said: "Dusty."

"Never mind the dust. Let's see you do your thing. Or rather, let's *not* see you."

For that was Sarey's talent. She wasn't capable of invisibility (none of them was), but she could create a kind of *dimness* that went very well with her unremarkable face and figure. She turned to Rose, then looked down at her shadow. She moved—not much, only half a step—and her shadow merged with the one thrown by the handle of the Lawn-Boy. Then she became perfectly still, and the shed was empty.

Rose squeezed her eyes shut, then popped them wide open, and there was Sarey, standing beside the mower with her hands folded demurely at her waist like a shy girl hoping some boy at the party will ask her to dance. Rose looked away at the mountains, and when she looked back again the shed was empty—just a tiny storage room with nowhere to hide. In the strong sunlight there wasn't even a shadow. Except for the one thrown by the mower's handle, that was. Only . . .

"Pull your elbow in," Rose said. "I see it. Just a little."

Silent Sarey did as she was told and for a moment she was truly gone, at least until Rose concentrated. When she did that, Sarey was there again. But of course she knew Sarey was there. When the time came—and it wouldn't be long—the bitchgirl wouldn't.

"Good, Sarey!" she said warmly (or as warmly as she could manage). "Perhaps I won't need you. If I do, you'll use the sickle. And think of Andi when you do. All right?"

At the mention of Andi's name, Sarey's lips turned down in a moue of unhappiness. She stared at the sickle in the plastic bucket and nodded.

Rose walked over and took the padlock. "I'm going to lock you in now. The bitchgirl will read the ones in the Lodge, but she won't read you. I'm sure of it. Because you're the quiet one, aren't you?"

Sarey nodded again. She was the quiet one, always had been.

(*what about the*)

Rose smiled. "The lock? Don't you worry about that. Just worry about being still. Still and silent. Do you understand me?"

"Lup."

"And you understand about the sickle?" Rose would not have trusted Sarey with a gun even if the True had one.

"Sicka. Lup."

"If I get the better of her—and as full of steam as I am right now, that should be no problem—you'll stay right where you are until I let you out. But if you hear me shout . . . let's see . . . if you hear me shout *don't make me punish you,* that means I need help. I'll make sure that her back is turned. You know what happens then, don't you?"

(*I'll climb the stairs and*)

But Rose was shaking her head. "No, Sarey. You won't need to. She's never going to get near the platform up there."

She would hate to lose the steam even more than she would hate losing the opportunity to kill the bitchgirl herself . . . after making her suffer, and at length. But she mustn't throw caution to the winds. The girl *was* very strong.

"What will you listen for, Sarey?"

"Don't make me punish lu."

"And what will you be thinking of?"

The eyes, half-hidden by the shaggy bangs, gleamed. "Levenge."

"That's right. Revenge for Andi, murdered by that bitchgirl's friends. But not unless I need you, because I want to do this myself." Rose's hands clenched, her nails digging into deep, blood-crusted crescents they had already made in her palms. "But if I need you, *you come.* Don't hesitate or stop for anything. Don't stop until you've put that sickle blade in her neck and see the end of it come out of her fucking throat."

Sarey's eyes gleamed. "Lup."

"Good." Rose kissed her, then shut the door and snapped the padlock closed. She put the key in her zipper pack and leaned against the door. "Listen to me, sweetheart. If all goes well, you'll get the first steam. I promise. And it will be the best you ever had."

Rose walked back to the lookout platform, took several long and steadying breaths, and then began to climb the steps.

4

Dan stood with his hands propped against one of the picnic tables, head down, eyes closed.

"Doing it this way is crazy," Billy said. "I should stay with you."

"You can't. You've got your own fish to fry."

"What if you faint halfway down that path? Even if you don't, how are you going to take on the whole bunch of them? The way you look now, you couldn't go two rounds with a five-year-old."

"I think pretty soon I'm going to feel a whole lot better. Stronger, too. Go on, Billy. You remember where to park?"

"Far end of the lot, by the sign that says kids eat for free when the Colorado teams win."

"Right." Dan raised his head and noted the oversize sunglasses Billy was now wearing. "Pull your cap down hard. All the way to your ears. Look young."

"I might have a trick that'll make me look even younger. If I can still do it, that is."

Dan barely heard this. "I need one other thing."

He stood up straight and opened his arms. Billy hugged him, wanting to do it hard—fiercely—and not daring.

"Abra made a good call. I never would have gotten here without you. Now take care of your business."

"You take care of yours," Billy said. "I'm counting on you to drive the Thanksgiving run out to Cloud Gap."

"I'd like that," Dan said. "Best model train set a boy never had."

Billy watched him walk slowly, holding his hands against his stomach as he went, to the signpost on the far side of the clearing. There were two wooden arrows. One pointed west, toward Pawnee Lookout. The other pointed east, downhill. This one read TO BLUEBELL CAMPGROUND.

Dan started along that path. For a little while Billy could see him through the glowing yellow leaves of the aspens, walking slowly and painfully, his head down to watch his footing. Then he was gone.

"Take care of my boy," Billy said. He wasn't sure if he was talking to God or Abra, and guessed it didn't matter; both were probably too busy to bother with the likes of him this afternoon.

He went back to his truck, and from the bed pulled out a little girl with staring china blue eyes and stiff blond curls. Not much weight; she was probably hollow inside. "How you doin, Abra? Hope you didn't get bumped around too much."

She was wearing a Colorado Rockies tee and blue shorts. Her feet were bare, and why not? This little girl—actually a mannequin purchased at a moribund children's clothing shop in Martenville— had never walked a single step. But she had bendable knees, and Billy was able to place her in the truck's passenger seat with no trouble. He buckled her seatbelt, started to close the door, then tried the neck. It also bent, although only a little. He stepped away to examine the effect. It wasn't bad. She seemed to be looking at something in her lap. Or maybe praying for strength in the coming battle. Not bad at all.

Unless they had binoculars, of course.

He got back in the truck and waited, giving Dan time. Also hoping he wasn't passed out somewhere along the path that led to the Bluebell Campground.

At quarter to five, Billy started the truck and headed back the way he had come.

5

Dan maintained a steady walking pace in spite of the growing heat in his midsection. It felt as though there were a rat on fire in there, one that kept chewing at him even as it burned. If the path had been going up instead of down, he never would have made it.

At ten to five, he came around a bend and stopped. Not far ahead, the aspens gave way to a green and manicured expanse of lawn sloping down to a pair of tennis courts. Beyond the courts he could see the RV parking area and a long log building: Overlook Lodge.

Beyond that, the terrain climbed again. Where the Overlook had once stood, a tall platform reared gantrylike against the bright sky. Roof O' the World. Looking at it, the same thought that had occurred to Rose the Hat

(*gallows*)

crossed Dan's mind. Standing at the railing, facing south toward the parking lot for day visitors, was a single silhouetted figure. A woman's figure. The tophat was tilted on her head.

(*Abra are you there*)

(*I'm here Dan*)

Calm, by the sound. Calm was just the way he wanted it.

(*are they hearing you*)

That brought a vague ticklish sensation: her smile. The angry one.

(*if they're not they're deaf*)

That was good enough.

(*you have to come to me now but remember if I tell you to go YOU GO*)

She didn't answer, and before he could tell her again, she was there.

6

The Stones and John Dalton watched helplessly as Abra slid sideways until she was lying with her head on the boards of the stoop and her legs splayed out on the steps below her. Hoppy spilled from one relaxing hand. She didn't look as if she were sleeping, nor even in a faint. That was the ugly sprawl of deep unconsciousness or death. Lucy lunged forward. Dave and John held her back.

She fought them. "Let me go! I have to help her!"

"You can't," John said. "Only Dan can help her now. They have to help each other."

She stared at him with wild eyes. "Is she even breathing? Can you tell?"

"She's breathing," Dave said, but he sounded unsure even to himself.

7

When Abra joined him, the pain eased for the first time since Boston. That didn't comfort Dan much, because now Abra was suffering, too. He could see it in her face, but he could also see the wonder in her eyes as she looked around at the room in which she found herself. There were bunk beds, knotty-pine walls, and a rug embroidered with western sage and cactus. Both the rug and the lower bunk were littered with cheap toys. On a small desk in the corner was a scattering of books and a jigsaw puzzle with large pieces. In the room's far corner, a radiator clanked and hissed.

Abra walked to the desk and picked up one of the books. On the cover, a small child on a trike was being chased by a little dog. The title was *Reading Fun with Dick and Jane*.

Dan joined her, wearing a bemused smile. "The little girl on the cover is Sally. Dick and Jane are her brother and sister. And the dog's name is Jip. For a little while they were my best friends. My only friends, I guess. Except for Tony, of course."

She put the book down and turned to him. "What *is* this place, Dan?"

"A memory. There used to be a hotel here, and this was my room. Now it's a place where we can be together. You know the wheel that turns when you go into someone else?"

"Uh-huh . . ."

"This is the middle. The hub."

"I wish we could stay here. It feels . . . safe. Except for *those*." Abra pointed to the French doors with their long panes of glass. "They don't feel the same as the rest." She looked at him almost accusingly. "They weren't here, were they? When you were a kid."

"No. There weren't any windows in my room, and the only door was the one that went into the rest of the caretaker's apartment. I changed it. I had to. Do you know why?"

She studied him, her eyes grave. "Because that was then and this is now. Because the past is gone, even though it defines the present."

He smiled. "I couldn't have said it better myself."

"You didn't have to say it. You thought it."

He drew her toward those French doors that had never existed. Through the glass they could see the lawn, the tennis courts, the Overlook Lodge, and Roof O' the World.

"I see her," Abra breathed. "She's up there, and she's not looking this way, is she?"

"She better not be," Dan said. "How bad is the pain, honey?"

"Bad," she said. "But I don't care. Because—"

She didn't have to finish. He knew, and she smiled. This togetherness was what they had, and in spite of the pain that came with it—pain of all kinds—it was good. It was very good.

"Dan?"

"Yes, honey."

"There are ghostie people out there. I can't see them, but I feel them. Do you?"

"Yes." He had for years. Because the past defines the present. He put his arm around her shoulders, and her arm crept around his waist.

"What do we do now?"

"Wait for Billy. Hope he's on time. And then all of this is going to happen very fast."

"Uncle Dan?"

"What, Abra."

"What's inside you? That isn't a ghost. It's like—" He felt her shiver. "It's like a *monster*."

He said nothing.

She straightened and stepped away from him. "Look! Over there!"

An old Ford pickup was rolling into the visitor's parking lot.

8

Rose stood with her hands on the lookout platform's waist-high railing, peering at the truck pulling into the parking lot. The steam had sharpened her vision, but she still wished she had brought a pair of binoculars. Surely there were some in the supply room, for guests who wanted to go bird-watching, so why hadn't she?

Because you had so many other things on your mind. The sickness . . . the rats jumping ship . . . losing Crow to the bitchgirl . . .

Yes to all of that—yes, yes, yes—but she still should have remembered. For a moment she wondered what else she might have forgotten, but pushed the idea away. She was still in charge of this, loaded with steam and at the top of her game. Everything was going exactly as planned. Soon the little girl would come up here, because she was full of foolish teenage confidence and pride in her own abilities.

But I have the high ground, dear, in all sorts of ways. If I can't take care of you alone, I'll draw from the rest of the True. They're all together in the main room, because you thought that was such a good idea. But there's something you didn't take into consideration. When we're together we're linked, we're a True Knot, and that makes us a giant battery. Power I can draw on if I need to.

If all else failed, there was Silent Sarey. She would now have the sickle in her hand. She might not be a genius, but she was merciless, murderous, and—once she understood the job—completely obedient. Also, she had her own reasons for wanting the bitchgirl laid out dead on the ground at the foot of the lookout platform.

(Charlie)

Token Charlie hit her back at once, and although he was ordinarily a feeble sender, now—boosted by the others in the main room of the Lodge—he came in loud and clear and nearly mad with excitement.

(I'm getting her steady and strong we all are she must be real close you must feel her)

Rose did, even though she was still working hard to keep her mind closed off so the bitchgirl couldn't get in and mess with her.

(never mind that just tell the others to be ready if I need help)

Many voices came back, jumping all over each other. They were ready. Even those that were sick were ready to help all they could. She loved them for that.

Rose stared at the blond girl in the truck. She was looking down. Reading something? Nerving herself up? Praying to the God of Rubes, perhaps? It didn't matter.

Come to me, bitchgirl. Come to Auntie Rose.

But it wasn't the girl who got out, it was the uncle. Just as the bitch had said he would. Checking. He walked around the hood of the truck, moving slowly, looking everywhere. He leaned in the passenger window, said something to the girl, then moved away from the truck a little. He looked toward the Lodge, then turned to the platform rearing against the sky . . . and waved. The insolent bugger actually waved at her.

Rose didn't wave back. She was frowning. An uncle. Why had her parents sent an uncle instead of bringing their bitch daughter themselves? For that matter, why had they allowed her to come at all?

She convinced them it was the only way. Told them that if she didn't come to me, I'd come to her. That's the reason, and it makes sense.

It did, but she felt a growing unease all the same. She had allowed the bitchgirl to set the ground rules. To that extent, at least, Rose had been manipulated. She had allowed it because this was her home ground and because she had taken precautions, but mostly because she had been angry. So angry.

She stared hard at the man in the parking lot. He was strolling around again, looking here and there, making sure she was alone. Perfectly reasonable, it was what she would have done, but she still had a gnawing intuition that what he was really doing was buying time, although why he would want to was beyond her.

Rose stared harder, now focusing on the man's gait. She decided he wasn't as young as she had first believed. He walked, in fact, like a man who was far from young. As if he had more than a touch of arthritis. And why was the little girl so still?

Rose felt the first pulse of real alarm.

Something was wrong here.

9

"She's looking at Mr. Freeman," Abra said. "We should go."

He opened the French doors, but hesitated. Something in her voice. "What's the trouble, Abra?"

"I don't know. Maybe nothing, but I don't like it. She's looking at him really *hard*. We have to go right now."

"I need to do something first. Try to be ready, and don't be scared."

Dan closed his eyes and went to the storage room at the back of his mind. Real lockboxes would have been covered with dust after all these years, but the two he'd put here as a child were as fresh as ever. Why not? They were made of pure imagination. The third—the new one—had a faint aura hanging around it, and he thought: *No wonder I'm sick.*

Never mind. That one had to stay for the time being. He opened the oldest of the other two, ready for anything, and found . . . nothing. Or almost. In the lockbox that had held Mrs. Massey for thirty-two years, there was a heap of dark gray ash. But in the other . . .

He realized how foolish telling her not to be scared had been.

Abra shrieked.

10

On the back stoop of the house in Anniston, Abra began to jerk. Her legs spasmed; her feet rattled a tattoo on the steps; one hand—flopping like a fish dragged to a riverbank and left to die there—sent the ill-used and bedraggled Hoppy flying.

"What's wrong with her?" Lucy screamed.

She rushed for the door. David stood frozen—transfixed by the sight of his seizing daughter—but John got his right arm around Lucy's waist and his left around her upper chest. She bucked against him. "Let me go! I have to go to her!"

"No!" John shouted. *"No, Lucy, you can't!"*

She would have broken free, but now David had her, too.

She subsided, looking first at John. "If she dies out there, I'll see you go to jail for it." Next, her gaze—flat-eyed and hostile—went to her husband. "You I'll never forgive."

"She's quieting," John said.

On the stoop, Abra's tremors moderated, then stopped. But her cheeks were wet, and tears squeezed from beneath her closed lids. In the day's dying light, they clung to her lashes like jewels.

11

In Danny Torrance's childhood bedroom—a room now made only of memory—Abra clung to Dan with her face pressed against his chest. When she spoke, her voice was muffled. "The monster—is it gone?"

"Yes," Dan said.

"Swear on your mother's name?"

"Yes."

She raised her head, first looking at him to assure herself he was telling the truth, then daring to scan the room. "That *smile*." She shuddered.

"Yes," Dan said. "I think . . . he's glad to be home. Abra, are you going to be all right? Because we have to do this right now. Time's up."

"I'm all right. But what if . . . it . . . comes back?"

Dan thought of the lockbox. It was open, but could be closed again easily enough. Especially with Abra to help him. "I don't think he . . . *it* . . . wants anything to do with us, honey. Come on. Just remember: if I tell you to go back to New Hampshire, you *go*."

Once again she didn't reply, and there was no time to discuss it. Time was up. He stepped through the French doors. They gave on the end of the path. Abra walked beside him, but lost the solidity she'd had in the room of memory and began to flicker again.

Out here she's almost a ghostie person herself, Dan thought. It brought home to him just how much she had put herself at risk. He didn't like to think about how tenuous her hold on her own body might now be.

Moving rapidly—but not running; that would attract Rose's eye, and they had at least seventy yards to cover before the rear of the Overlook Lodge would block them from the lookout platform—Dan and his ghostie-girl companion crossed the lawn and took the flagstone walk that ran between the tennis courts.

They reached the back of the kitchen, and at last the bulk of the Lodge hid them from the platform. Here was the steady rumble of an exhaust fan and the spoiled-meat smell of garbage cans. He tried the rear door and found it unlocked, but paused a moment before opening it.

(are they all)

(yes all but Rose   she   hurry up Dan you have to because)

Abra's eyes, flickering like those of a child in an old black-and-white movie, were wide with dismay. "She knows something's wrong."

12

Rose turned her attention to the bitchgirl, still sitting in the passenger seat of the truck, head bowed, still as could be. Abra wasn't watching her uncle—if he *was* her uncle—and she was making no move to get out. The alarm meter in Rose's head went from Danger Yellow to Condition Red.

"Hey!" The voice came floating up to her on the thin air. "Hey, you old bag! Watch this!"

She snapped her gaze back to the man in the parking lot and stared, close to flabbergasted, as he raised his hands over his head and then turned a big, unsteady cartwheel. She thought he was going to go on his ass, but the only thing that fell to the pavement was his hat. What it exposed was the fine white hair of a man in his seventies. Maybe even his eighties.

Rose looked back at the girl in the truck, who remained perfectly still with her head bent. She had absolutely no interest in the uncle's antics. Suddenly it clicked and Rose understood what she would have seen right away, had the trick not been so outrageous: it was a mannequin.

But she's here! Token Charlie feels her, all of them in the Lodge feel her, they're all together and they know—

All together in the Lodge. All together in one place. And had that been Rose's idea? No. That idea had come from the—

Rose broke for the stairs.

13

The remaining members of the True Knot were crowded together at the two windows looking down at the parking lot, watching as Billy Freeman turned a cartwheel for the first time in over forty years (and the last time he'd done this trick, he'd been drunk). Petty the Chink actually laughed. "What in God's name—"

With their backs turned, they didn't see Dan step into the room from the kitchen, or the girl flickering in and out of view at his side. Dan had time to register two bundles of clothes on the floor, and to understand that Bradley Trevor's measles were still hard at work. Then he went back inside himself, went deep, and found the third lockbox—the leaky one. He flung it open.

(*Dan what are you doing*)

He leaned forward with his hands on his upper thighs, his stomach burning like hot metal, and exhaled the old poet's last gasp, which she had given him freely, in a dying kiss. From his mouth there came a long plume of pink mist that deepened to red as it hit the air. At first he could focus on nothing but the blessed relief in the middle of his body as the poison remains of Concetta Reynolds left him.

"*Momo!*" Abra shrieked.

14

On the platform, Rose's eyes widened. The bitchgirl was in the Lodge.

And someone was with her.

She leaped into this new mind without thinking about it. Searching. Ignoring the markers that meant big steam, only trying to stop him before he could do whatever it was he intended to do. Ignoring the terrible possibility that it was already too late.

15

The members of the True turned toward Abra's cry. Someone—it was Long Paul—said: "What in the hell is *that?*"

The red mist coalesced into a shape of a woman. For a moment— surely no more than that—Dan looked into Concetta's swirling eyes and saw they were young. Still weak and focused on this phantom, he had no sense of the intruder in his mind.

"*Momo!*" Abra cried again. She was holding out her arms.

The woman in the cloud might have looked at her. Might even have smiled. Then the shape of Concetta Reynolds was gone and the mist rolled at the clustered True Knot, many of them now clinging to one another in fright and bewilderment. To Dan, the red stuff looked like blood spreading in water.

"It's steam," Dan told them. "You bastards lived on it; now suck it in and die on it."

He had known ever since the plan's conception that if it didn't happen fast, he would never live to see how well it succeeded, but he had never imagined it would occur as rapidly as it did. The measles that had already weakened them might have had something to do with it, because some lasted a little longer than others. Even so, it was over in a matter of seconds.

They howled in his head like dying wolves. The sound appalled Dan, but this was not true of his companion.

"*Good!*" Abra shouted. She shook her fists at them. "*How does it taste? How does my momo taste? Is she good? Have as much as you want! HAVE ALL OF IT!*"

They began to cycle. Through the red mist, Dan saw two of them embracing with their foreheads pressed together, and in spite of all they had done—all they were—the sight moved him. He saw the words *I love you* on Short Eddie's lips; saw Big Mo begin to reply; then they were gone, their clothes floating to the floor. It was that quick.

He turned to Abra, meaning to tell her they had to finish it at once, but then Rose the Hat began to shriek, and for a few moments—until Abra could block her—those cries of rage and maddened grief blotted out everything else, even the blessed relief of being pain-free. And, he devoutly hoped, cancer-free. About that he wouldn't know for sure until he could see his face in a mirror.

16

Rose was at the head of the steps leading down from the platform when the killing mist rolled over the True Knot, the remains of Abra's momo doing its quick and lethal work.

A white sheet of agony filled her. Screams shot through her head like shrapnel. The cries of the dying True made those of the Cloud Gap raiding party in New Hampshire and Crow in New York seem puny by comparison. Rose staggered back as if she had been hit with a club. She struck the railing, rebounded, and fell down on the boards. Somewhere in the distance, a woman—an old one, by the wavering sound of her voice—was chanting *no, no, no, no, no.*

That's me. It has to be, because I'm the only one left.

It wasn't the girl who had fallen into the trap of overconfidence, but Rose herself. She thought of something

(*hoisted on your own petard*)

the bitchgirl had said. It scalded her with rage and dismay. Her old friends and longtime traveling companions were dead. Poisoned. Except for the cowards who had run, Rose the Hat was the last of the True Knot.

But no, that wasn't true. There was Sarey.

Sprawled on the platform and shivering under the late-afternoon sky, Rose reached out to her.

(*are you*)

The thought that came back was full of confusion and horror.

(*yes but Rose are they can they be*)

(*never mind them just remember Sarey do you remember*)

(*"don't make me punish you"*)

(*good Sarey good*)

If the girl didn't run . . . if she made the mistake of trying to finish her murderous day's work . . .

She would. Rose was sure of it, and she had seen enough in the mind of the bitchgirl's companion to know two things: how they had accomplished this slaughter, and how their very connection could be turned against them.

Rage was powerful.

So were childhood memories.

She struggled to her feet, reset her hat at the proper jaunty angle without even thinking about it, and walked to the railing. The man from the pickup truck was staring up at her, but she paid scant attention to him. His treacherous little job was done. She might deal with him later, but now she had eyes only for the Overlook Lodge. The girl was there, but also far away. Her bodily presence at the True's campground was little more than a phantom. The one who was whole—a real person, a rube—was a man she had never seen before. And a steamhead. His voice in her mind was clear and cold.

(*hello Rose*)

There was a place nearby where the girl would cease to flicker. Where she would take on her physical body. Where she could be killed. Let Sarey take care of the steamhead man, but not until the steamhead man had taken care of the bitchgirl.

(*hello Danny hello little boy*)

Loaded with steam, she reached into him and swatted him to the hub of the wheel, barely hearing Abra's cry of bewilderment and terror as she turned to follow.

And when Dan was where Rose wanted him, for a moment too surprised to keep his guard up, she poured all her fury into him. She poured it into him like steam.

CHAPTER TWENTY

HUB OF THE WHEEL, ROOF O' THE WORLD

1

Dan Torrance opened his eyes. Sunlight shot through them and into his aching head, threatening to set his brains on fire. It was the hangover to end all hangovers. Loud snoring from beside him: a nasty, annoying sound that could only be some drunk chick sleeping it off at the wrong end of the rainbow. Dan turned his head that way and saw the woman sprawled on her back beside him. Vaguely familiar. Dark hair spread around her in a halo. Wearing an oversize Atlanta Braves t-shirt.

This isn't real. I'm not here. I'm in Colorado, I'm at Roof O' the World, and I have to end it.

The woman rolled over, opened her eyes, and stared at him. "God, my head," she said. "Get me some of that coke, daddy. It's in the living room."

He stared at her in amazement and growing fury. The fury seemed to come from nowhere, but hadn't it always been that way? It was its own thing, a riddle wrapped in an enigma. "Coke? Who bought coke?"

She grinned, revealing a mouth that contained only a single discolored tooth. Then he knew who she was. "*You* did, daddy. Now go get it. Once my head's clear, I'll throw you a nice fuck."

Somehow he was back in this sleazy Wilmington apartment, naked, next to Rose the Hat.

"What have you done? How did I get here?"

She threw her head back and laughed. "Don't you like this place? You should; I furnished it from your own head. Now do what I told you, asshole. Get the fucking blow."

"Where's Abra? What did you do with Abra?"

"Killed her," Rose said indifferently. "She was so worried about you she dropped her guard and I tore her open from throat to belly. I wasn't able to suck up as much of her steam as I wanted, but I got quite a lo—"

The world went red. Dan clamped his hands around her throat and began to choke. One thought beat through his mind: *worthless bitch, now you'll take your medicine, worthless bitch, now you'll take your medicine, worthless bitch, now you'll take it all.*

2

The steamhead man was powerful but had nothing like the girl's juice. He stood with his legs apart, his head lowered, his shoulders hunched, and his fisted hands raised—the posture of every man who had ever lost his mind in a killing rage. Anger made men easy.

It was impossible to follow his thoughts, because they had turned red. That was all right, that was fine, the girl was right where Rose wanted her. In Abra's state of shocked dismay, she had followed him to the hub of the wheel. She wouldn't be shocked or dismayed for much longer, though; Bitchgirl had become Choked Girl. Soon she would be Dead Girl, hoisted on her own petard.

(*Uncle Dan no no stop it's not her*)

It is, Rose thought, bearing down even harder. Her tooth crept out of her mouth and skewered her lower lip. Blood poured down her chin and onto her top. She didn't feel it any more than she felt the mountain breeze blowing through her masses of dark hair. *It is me. You were my daddy, my barroom daddy, I made you empty your wallet for a pile of bad coke, and now it's the morning after and I need to take my medicine. It's what you wanted to do when you woke up next to that drunken whore in Wilmington, what you would have done if you'd had any balls, and her useless whelp of a son for good measure. Your father knew how to deal with stupid, disobedient women, and his father before him. Sometimes a woman just needs to take her medicine. She needs—*

There was the roar of an approaching motor. It was as unimportant as the pain in her lip and the taste of blood in her mouth. The girl was choking, rattling. Then a thought as loud as a thunderclap exploded in her brain, a wounded roar:

(*MY FATHER KNEW NOTHING!*)

Rose was still trying to clear her mind of that shout when Billy Freeman's pickup truck hit the base of the lookout, knocking her off her feet. Her hat went flying.

3

It wasn't the apartment in Wilmington. It was his long-gone bedroom at the Overlook Hotel—the hub of the wheel. It wasn't Deenie, the woman he'd awakened next to in that apartment, and it wasn't Rose.

It was Abra. He had his hands around her neck and her eyes were bulging.

For a moment she started to change again as Rose tried to worm back inside him, feeding him her rage and augmenting his own. Then something happened, and she was gone. But she would be back.

Abra was coughing and staring at him. He would have expected shock, but for a girl who had almost been choked to death, she seemed oddly composed.

(*well . . . we knew it wouldn't be easy*)

"I'm not my father!" Dan shouted at her. "*I am not my father!*"

"Probably that's good," Abra said. She actually smiled. "You've got one hell of a temper, Uncle Dan. I guess we really *are* related."

"I almost killed you," Dan said. "It's enough. Time for you to get out. Go back to New Hampshire right now."

She shook her head. "I'll have to—for awhile, not long—but right now you need me."

"Abra, that's an order."

She folded her arms and stood where she was on the cactus carpet.

"Ah, Christ." He ran his hands through his hair. "You're a piece of work."

She reached out, took his hand. "We're going to finish this together. Now come on. Let's get out of this room. I don't think I like it here, after all."

Their fingers interlaced, and the room where he had lived for a time as a child dissolved.

4

Dan had time to register the hood of Billy's pickup folded around one of the thick posts holding up the Roof O' the World lookout tower, its busted radiator steaming. He saw the mannequin version of Abra hanging out the passenger-side window, with one plastic arm cocked jauntily behind her. He saw Billy himself trying to open the crumpled driver's side door. Blood was running down one side of the old man's face.

Something grabbed his head. Powerful hands twisting, attempting to snap his neck. Then Abra's hands were there, tearing Rose's away. She looked up. "You'll have to do better than that, you cowardly old bitch."

Rose stood at the railing, looking down and resetting her ugly hat at the correct angle. "Did you enjoy your uncle's hands around your throat? How do you feel about him now?"

"That was you, not him."

Rose grinned, her bloody mouth yawning. "Not at all, dear. I just made use of what he has inside. You should know, you're just like him."

She's trying to distract us, Dan thought. *But from what? That?*

It was a small green building—maybe an outside bathroom, maybe a storage shed.

(*can you*)

He didn't have to finish the thought. Abra turned toward the shed and stared at it. The padlock creaked, snapped, and fell into the grass. The door swung open. The shed was empty except for a few tools and an old lawnmower. Dan thought he'd felt something there, but it must only have been overwrought nerves. When they looked up again, Rose was no longer in view. She had retreated from the railing.

Billy finally managed to get the door of his truck open. He got out, staggered, managed to keep his feet. "Danny? You all right?" And then: "Is that Abra? Jesus, she's hardly there."

"Listen, Billy. Can you walk to the Lodge?"

"I think so. What about the people in there?"

"Gone. I think it would be a very good idea if you went *now*."

Billy didn't argue. He started down the slope, wallowing like a drunk. Dan pointed at the stairs leading to the lookout platform and raised questioning eyebrows. Abra shook her head

(*it's what she wants*)

and began leading Dan around Roof O' the World, to where they could see the very top of Rose's stovepipe hat. This put the little equipment shed at their backs, but Dan thought nothing of this now that he had seen it was empty.

(*Dan I have to go back now just for a minute I have to refresh my*)

A picture in his mind: a field filled with sunflowers, all opening at once. She needed to take care of her physical being, and that was good. That was right.

(*go*)

(*I'll be back as soon as*)

(*go Abra I'll be fine*)

And with any luck, this would be over when she came back.

5

In Anniston, John Dalton and the Stones saw Abra draw a deep breath and open her eyes.

"Abra!" Lucy called. "Is it over?"

"Soon."

"What's that on your neck? Are those bruises?"

"Mom, stay there! I have to go back. Dan needs me."

She reached for Hoppy, but before she could grasp the old stuffed rabbit, her eyes closed and her body grew still.

6

Peering cautiously over the railing, Rose saw Abra disappear. Little bitchgirl could only stay here so long, then she had to go back for some R & R. Her presence at the Bluebell Campground wasn't much different from her presence that day in the supermarket, only this manifestation was much more powerful. And why? Because the man was assisting her. *Boosting* her. If he were dead when the girl returned—

Looking down at him, Rose called: "I'd leave while you still have the chance, Danny. Don't make me punish you."

7

Silent Sarey was so focused on what was going on at Roof O' the World—listening with every admittedly limited IQ point of her mind as well as with her ears—that she did not at first realize she was no longer alone in the shed. It was the smell that finally alerted her: something rotten. Not garbage. She didn't dare turn, because the door was open and the man out there might see her. She stood still, the sickle in one hand.

Sarey heard Rose telling the man to leave while he still had the chance, and that was when the shed door began swinging shut again, all on its own.

"Don't make me punish you!" Rose called. That was her cue to burst out and put the sickle in the troublesome, meddling little girl's neck, but since the girl was gone, the man would have to do. But before she could move, a cold hand slid over the wrist holding the sickle. Slid over it and clamped tight.

She turned—no reason not to now, with the door closed—and what she saw by the dim light filtering through the cracks in the old boards caused a scream to come bolting out of her usually silent throat. At some point while she had been concentrating, a corpse had joined her in the toolshed. His smiling, predatory face was the damp whitish-green of a spoiled avocado. His eyes seemed almost to dangle from their sockets. His suit was splotched with ancient mold . . . but the multicolored confetti sprinkled on his shoulders was fresh.

"Great party, isn't it?" he said, and as he grinned, his lips split open.

She screamed again and drove the sickle into his left temple. The curved blade went deep and hung there, but there was no blood.

"Give us a kiss, dear," Horace Derwent said. From between his lips came the wiggling white remnant of a tongue. "It's been a long time since I've been with a woman."

As his tattered lips, shining with decay, settled on Sarey's, his hands closed around her throat.

8

Rose saw the shed door swing closed, heard the scream, and understood that she was now truly alone. Soon, probably in seconds, the girl would be back and it would be two against one. She couldn't allow that.

She looked down at the man and summoned all of her steam-amplified force.

(choke yourself do it NOW)

His hands rose toward his throat, but too slowly. He was fighting her, and with a degree of success that was infuriating. She would have expected a battle from the bitchgirl, but that rube down there was an adult. She should have been able to brush aside any steam remaining to him like mist.

Still, she was winning.

His hands went up to his chest . . . his shoulders . . . finally to his throat. There they wavered—she could hear him panting with effort. She bore down, and the hands gripped, shutting off his windpipe.

(that's right you interfering bastard squeeze squeeze   and SQUEE)

Something hit her. Not a fist; it felt more like a gust of tightly compressed air. She looked around and saw nothing but a shimmer, there for a moment and then gone. Less than three seconds, but enough to break her concentration, and when she turned back to the railing, the girl had returned.

It wasn't a gust of air this time; it was hands that felt simultaneously large and small. They were in the small of her back. They were pushing. The bitchgirl and her friend, working together—just what Rose had wanted to avoid. A worm of terror began to unwind in her stomach. She tried to step back from the rail and could not. It was taking all her strength just to stand pat, and with no supporting force from the True to help her, she didn't think she'd be able to do that for long. Not long at all.

If not for that gust of air . . . that wasn't him and she wasn't here . . .

One of the hands left the small of her back and slapped the hat from her head. Rose howled at the indignity of it—nobody touched her hat, *nobody*!—and for a moment summoned enough power to stagger back from the railing and toward the center of the platform. Then those hands returned to the small of her back and began pushing her forward again.

She looked down at them. The man had his eyes closed, concentrating so hard that the cords stood out on his neck and sweat rolled down his cheeks like tears. The girl's eyes, however, were wide and merciless. She was staring up at Rose. And she was smiling.

Rose pushed backward with all her strength, but she might have been pushing against a stone wall. One that was moving her relentlessly forward, until her stomach was pressing against the rail. She heard it creak.

She thought, for just a moment, of trying to bargain. Of telling the girl that they could work together, start a new Knot. That instead of dying in 2070 or 2080, Abra Stone could live a thousand years. *Two* thousand. But what good would it do?

Was there ever a teenage girl who felt anything less than immortal?

So instead of bargaining, or begging, she screamed defiance down at them. *"Fuck you! Fuck you both!"*

The girl's terrible smile widened. "Oh, no," she said. *"You're* the one who's fucked."

No creak this time; there was a crack like a rifleshot, and then Rose the Hatless was falling.

9

She hit the ground headfirst and began to cycle at once. Her head was cocked (*like her hat,* Dan thought) on her shattered neck at an angle that was almost insouciant. Dan held Abra's hand—flesh that came and went in his own as she did her own cycling between her back stoop and Roof O' the World—and they watched together.

"Does it hurt?" Abra asked the dying woman. "I hope it does. I hope it hurts a lot."

Rose's lips pulled back in a sneer. Her human teeth were gone; all that remained was that single discolored tusk. Above it, her eyes floated like living blue stones. Then she was gone.

Abra turned to Dan. She was still smiling, but now there was no anger or meanness in it.

(*I was afraid for you I was afraid she might*)
(*she almost did but there was someone*)

He pointed up to where the broken pieces of the railing jutted against the sky. Abra looked there, then looked back at Dan, puzzled. He could only shake his head.

It was her turn to point, not up but down.

(*once there was a magician who had a hat like that his name was Mysterio*)

(*and you hung spoons on the ceiling*)

She nodded but didn't raise her head. She was still studying the hat.

(*you need to get rid of it*)

(*how*)

(*burn it Mr. Freeman says he quit smoking but he still does I could smell it in the truck he'll have matches*)

"You *have* to," she said. "Will you? Do you promise?"

"Yes."

(*I love you Uncle Dan*)

(*love you too*)

She hugged him. He put his arms around her and hugged her back. As he did, her body became rain. Then mist. Then gone.

10

On the back stoop of a house in Anniston, New Hampshire, in a dusk that would soon deepen to night, a little girl sat up, got to her feet, and then swayed, on the edge of a faint. There was no chance of her falling down; her parents were there at once. They carried her inside together.

"I'm okay," Abra said. "You can put me down."

They did, carefully. David Stone stood close, ready to catch her at the slightest knee-buckle, but Abra stood steady in the kitchen.

"What about Dan?" John asked.

"He's fine. Mr. Freeman smashed up his truck—he had to—and he got a cut"—she put her hand to the side of his face—"but I think he's okay."

"And them? The True Knot?"

Abra raised a hand to her mouth and blew across the palm.

"Gone." And then: "What is there to eat? I'm really hungry."

11

Fine might have been a bit of an overstatement in Dan's case. He walked to the truck, where he sat in the open driver's side door, getting his breath back. And his wits.

We were on vacation, he decided. *I wanted to visit my old stomping grounds in Boulder. Then we came up here to take in the view from Roof O' the World, but the campground was deserted. I was feeling frisky and bet Billy I could drive his truck straight up the hill to the lookout. I was going too fast and lost control. Hit one of the support posts. Really sorry. Damn fool stunt.*

He would get hit with one hell of a fine, but there was an upside: he would pass the Breathalyzer with flying colors.

Dan looked in the glove compartment and found a can of lighter fluid. No Zippo—that would be in Billy's pants pocket—but there were indeed two books of half-used matches. He went to the hat and doused it with the lighter fluid until it was soaking. Then he squatted, touched a match, and flicked it into the hat's upturned bowl. The hat didn't last long, but he moved upwind until it was nothing but ashes.

The smell was foul.

When he looked up, he saw Billy trudging toward him, wiping at his bloody face with his sleeve. As they tromped through the ashes, making sure there wasn't a single ember that might spark a wildfire, Dan told him the story they would tell the Colorado State Police when they arrived.

"I'll have to pay to have that thing repaired, and I bet it costs a bundle. Good thing I've got some savings."

Billy snorted. "Who's gonna chase you for damages? There's nothing left of those True Knot folks but their clothes. I looked."

"Unfortunately," Dan said, "Roof O' the World belongs to the great State of Colorado."

"Ouch," Billy said. "Hardly seems fair, since you just did Colorado and the rest of the world a favor. Where's Abra?"

"Back home."

"Good. And it's over? Really over?"

Dan nodded.

Billy was staring at the ashes of Rose's tophat. "Went up damn fast. Almost like a special effect in a movie."

"I imagine it was very old." *And full of magic*, he didn't add. *The black variety.*

Dan went to the pickup and sat behind the wheel so he could examine his face in the rearview mirror.

"See anything that shouldn't be there?" Billy asked. "That's what my mom always used to say when she caught me moonin over my own reflection."

"Not a thing," Dan said. A smile began to break on his face. It was tired but genuine. "Not a thing in the world."

"Then let's call the police and tell em about our accident," Billy said. "Ordinarily I got no use for the Five-O, but right about now I wouldn't mind some company. Place gives me the willies." He gave Dan a shrewd look. "Full of ghosts, ain't it? That's why they picked it."

That was why, no doubt about it. But you didn't need to be Ebenezer Scrooge to know there were good ghostie people as well as bad ones. As they walked down toward the Overlook Lodge, Dan paused to look back at Roof O' the World. He was not entirely surprised to see a man standing on the platform by the broken rail. He raised one hand, the summit of Pawnee Mountain visible through it, and sketched a flying kiss that Dan remembered from his childhood. He remembered it well. It had been their special end-of-the-day thing.

Bedtime, doc. Sleep tight. Dream up a dragon and tell me about it in the morning.

Dan knew he was going to cry, but not now. This wasn't the time. He lifted his own hand to his mouth and returned the kiss.

He looked for a moment longer at what remained of his father. Then he headed down to the parking lot with Billy. When they got there, he looked back once more.

Roof O' the World was empty.

UNTIL YOU SLEEP

FEAR stands for face everything and recover.

—Old AA saying

ANNIVERSARY

1

The Saturday noon AA meeting in Frazier was one of the oldest in New Hampshire, dating back to 1946, and had been founded by Fat Bob D., who had known the Program's founder, Bill Wilson, personally. Fat Bob was long in his grave, a victim of lung cancer—in the early days most recovering alkies had smoked like chimneys and newbies were routinely told to keep their mouths shut and the ashtrays empty—but the meeting was still well attended. Today it was SRO, because when it was over there would be pizza and a sheet cake. This was the case at most anniversary meetings, and today one of their number was celebrating fifteen years of sobriety. In the early years he had been known as Dan or Dan T., but word of his work at the local hospice had gotten around (the AA magazine was not known as *The Grapevine* for nothing), and now he was most commonly called Doc. Since his parents had called him that, Dan found the nickname ironic . . . but in a good way. Life was a wheel, its only job was to turn, and it always came back to where it had started.

A real doctor, this one named John, chaired at Dan's request, and the meeting followed its usual course. There was laughter when Randy M. told how he had thrown up all over the cop who arrested him on his last DUI, and more when he went on to say he had discovered a year later that the cop himself was in the Program. Maggie M. cried when she told ("shared," in AA parlance) how she had again been denied joint custody of her two children. The usual clichés were offered—time takes time, it works if you work it, don't quit until the miracle happens—and Maggie eventually quieted to sniffles. There was the usual cry of *Higher Power says turn it off!* when a guy's cell phone rang. A gal with shaky hands spilled a cup of coffee; a meeting without at least one spilled cup of joe was rare indeed.

At ten to one, John D. passed the basket ("We are self-supporting through our own contributions"), and asked for announcements. Trevor K., who opened the meeting, stood and asked—as he always did—for help cleaning up the kitchen and putting away the chairs. Yolanda V. did the Chip Club, giving out two whites (twenty-four hours) and a purple (five months—commonly referred to as the Barney Chip). As always, she ended by saying, "If you haven't had a drink today, give yourself and your Higher Power a hand."

They did.

When the applause died, John said, "We have a fifteen-year anniversary today. Will Casey K. and Dan T. come on up here?"

The crowd applauded as Dan walked forward—slowly, to keep pace with Casey, who now walked with a cane. John handed Casey the medallion with XV printed on its face, and Casey held it up so the crowd could see it. "I never thought this guy would make it," he said, "because he was AA from the start. By which I mean, an asshole with attitude."

They laughed dutifully at this oldie. Dan smiled, but his heart was beating hard. His one thought right now was to get through what came next without fainting. The last time he'd been this scared, he had been looking up at Rose the Hat on the Roof O' the World platform and trying to keep from strangling himself with his own hands.

Hurry up, Casey. Please. Before I lose either my courage or my breakfast.

Casey might have been the one with the shining . . . or perhaps he saw something in Dan's eyes. In any case, he cut it short. "But he defied my expectations and got well. For every seven alcoholics who walk through our doors, six walk back out again and get drunk. The seventh is the miracle we all live for. One of those miracles is standing right here, big as life and twice as ugly. Here you go, Doc, you earned this."

He passed Dan the medallion. For a moment Dan thought it would slip through his cold fingers and fall to the floor. Casey folded his hand around it before it could, and then folded the rest of Dan into a massive hug. In his ear he whispered, "Another year, you sonofabitch. Congratulations."

Casey stumped up the aisle to the back of the room, where he sat by right of seniority with the other oldtimers. Dan was left alone at the front, clenching his fifteen-year medallion so hard the tendons stood out on his wrist. The assembled alkies stared at him, waiting for what longtime sobriety was supposed to convey: experience, strength, and hope.

"A couple of years ago . . ." he began, and then had to clear his throat. "A couple of years ago, when I was having coffee with that gimpy-legged gentleman who's just now sitting down, he asked me if I'd done the fifth step: 'Admitted to God, ourselves, and another human being the exact nature of our wrongs.' I told him I'd done most of it. For folks who don't have our particular problem, that probably would have been enough . . . and that's just one of the reasons we call them Earth People."

They chuckled. Dan drew a deep breath, telling himself if he could face Rose and her True Knot, he could face this. Only this was different. This wasn't Dan the Hero; it was Dan the Scumbag. He had lived long enough to know there was a little scumbag in everyone, but it didn't help much when you had to take out the trash.

"He told me that he thought there was one wrong I couldn't quite get past, because I was too ashamed to talk about it. He told me to let it go. He reminded me of something you hear at almost every meeting—we're only as sick as our secrets. And he said if I didn't tell mine, somewhere down the line I'd find myself with a drink in my hand. Was that the gist of it, Case?"

From the back of the room Casey nodded, his hands folded over the top of his cane.

Dan felt the stinging at the back of his eyes that meant tears were on the way and thought, *God help me to get through this without bawling. Please.*

"I didn't spill it. I'd been telling myself for years it was the one thing I'd never tell anyone. But I think he was right, and if I start drinking again, I'll die. I don't want to do that. I've got a lot to live for these days. So . . ."

The tears had come, the goddam tears, but he was in too deep to back out now. He wiped them away with the hand not fisted around the medallion.

"You know what it says in the Promises? About how we'll learn not to regret the past, or wish to shut the door on it? Pardon me for saying so, but I think that's one item of bullshit in a program full of true things. I regret plenty, but it's time to open the door, little as I want to."

They waited. Even the two ladies who had been doling out pizza slices on paper plates were now standing in the kitchen doorway and watching him.

"Not too long before I quit drinking, I woke up next to some woman I picked up in a bar. We were in her apartment. The place was a dump, because she had almost nothing. I could relate to that because *I* had almost nothing, and both of us were probably in Broke City for the same reason. You all know what that reason is." He shrugged. "If you're one of us, the bottle takes your shit, that's all. First a little, then a lot, then everything.

"This woman, her name was Deenie. I don't remember much else about her, but I remember that. I put on my clothes and left, but first I took her money. And it turned out she had at least one thing I didn't, after all, because while I was going through her wallet, I looked around and her son was standing there. Little kid still in diapers. This woman and I had bought some coke the night before, and it was still on the table. He saw it and reached for it. He thought it was candy."

Dan wiped his eyes again.

"I took it away and put it where he couldn't get it. That much I did. It wasn't enough, but that much I did. Then I put her money in my pocket and walked out of there. I'd do anything to take that back. But I can't."

The women in the doorway had gone back to the kitchen. Some people were looking at their watches. A stomach grumbled. Looking at the assembled nine dozen alkies, Dan realized an astounding thing: what he'd done didn't revolt them. It didn't even surprise them. They had heard worse. Some had *done* worse.

"Okay," he said. "That's it. Thanks for listening."

Before the applause, one of the oldtimers in the back row shouted out the traditional question: "How'd you do it, Doc?"

Dan smiled and gave the traditional answer. "One day at a time."

2

After the Our Father, and the pizza, and the chocolate cake with the big number XV on it, Dan helped Casey back to his Tundra. A sleety rain had begun to fall.

"Spring in New Hampshire," Casey said sourly. "Ain't it wonderful."

"Raineth drop and staineth slop," Dan said in a declamatory voice, "and how the wind doth ram! Skiddeth bus and sloppest us, damn you, sing goddam."

Casey stared at him. "Did you just make that up?"

"Nah. Ezra Pound. When are you going to quit dicking around and get that hip replaced?"

Casey grinned. "Next month. I decided that if you can tell your biggest secret, I can get my hip replaced." He paused. "Not that your secret was all that fucking big, Danno."

"So I discovered. I thought they'd run from me, screaming. Instead, they stood around eating pizza and talking about the weather."

"If you'd told em you killed a blind gramma, they'd have stayed to eat the pizza and cake. Free is free." He opened the driver's door. "Boost me, Danno."

Dan boosted him.

Casey wriggled ponderously, getting comfortable, then keyed the engine and got the wipers to work on the sleet. "Everything's smaller when it's out," he said. "I hope you'll pass that on to your pigeons."

"Yes, O Wise One."

Casey looked at him sadly. "Go fuck yourself, sweetheart."

"Actually," Danny said, "I think I'll go back in and help put away the chairs."

And that was what he did.

UNTIL YOU SLEEP

1

No balloons or magician at Abra Stone's birthday party this year. She was fifteen.

There *was* neighborhood-rattling rock music slamming through the outdoor speakers Dave Stone—ably assisted by Billy Freeman—had set up. The adults had cake, ice cream, and coffee in the Stone kitchen. The kids took over the downstairs family room and the back lawn, and from the sound of them, they had a blast. They started to leave around five o'clock, but Emma Deane, Abra's closest friend, stayed for supper. Abra, resplendent in a red skirt and off-the-shoulder peasant blouse, bubbled with good cheer. She exclaimed over the charm bracelet Dan gave her, hugged him, kissed him on the cheek. He smelled perfume. *That* was new.

When Abra left to accompany Emma back to her house, the two of them chattering their way happily down the walk, Lucy leaned toward Dan. Her mouth was pursed, there were new lines around her eyes, and her hair was showing the first touches of gray. Abra seemed to have put the True Knot behind her; Dan thought Lucy never would. "Will you talk to her? About the plates?"

"I'm going outside to watch the sun go down over the river. Maybe you'll send her to visit with me a little when she gets back from the Deanes'."

Lucy looked relieved, and Dan thought David did, as well. To them she would always be a mystery. Would it help to tell them she would always be one to him? Probably not.

"Good luck, chief," Billy said.

On the back stoop where Abra had once lain in a state that wasn't unconsciousness, John Dalton joined him. "I'd offer to give you moral support, but I think you have to do this alone."

"Have you tried talking to her?"

"Yes. At Lucy's request."

"No good?"

John shrugged. "She's pretty closed up on the subject."

"I was, too," Dan said. "At her age."

"But you never broke every plate in your mother's antique breakfront, did you?"

"My mother didn't have a breakfront," Dan said.

He walked down to the bottom of the Stones' sloping backyard and regarded the Saco, which had, courtesy of the declining sun, become a glowing scarlet snake. Soon the mountains would eat the last of the sunlight and the river would turn gray. Where there had once been a chainlink fence to block the potentially disastrous explorations of young children, there was now a line of decorative bushes. David had taken the fence down the previous October, saying Abra and her friends no longer needed its protection; they could all swim like fish.

But of course there were other dangers.

2

The color on the water had faded to the faintest pink tinge—ashes of roses—when Abra joined him. He didn't have to look around to know she was there, or to know she had put on a sweater to cover her bare shoulders. The air cooled quickly on spring evenings in central New Hampshire even after the last threat of snow was gone.

(*I love my bracelet Dan*)

She had pretty much dropped the uncle part.

(*I'm glad*)

"They want you to talk to me about the plates," she said. The spoken words had none of the warmth that had come through in her thoughts, and the thoughts were gone. After the very pretty and sincere thank-you, she had closed her inner self off to him. She was good at that now, and getting better every day. "Don't they?"

"Do *you* want to talk about them?"

"I told her I was sorry. I told her I didn't mean to. I don't think she believed me."

(*I do*)

"Because you *know*. They don't."

Dan said nothing, and passed on only a single thought:

(?)

"They don't believe me about *anything*!" she burst out. "It's so unfair! I didn't know there was going to be booze at Jennifer's stupid party, and I didn't have any! Still, she grounds me for *two fucking weeks*!"

(? ? ?)

Nothing. The river was almost entirely gray now. He risked a look at her and saw she was studying her sneakers—red to match her skirt. Her cheeks now also matched her skirt.

"All right," she said at last, and although she still didn't look at him, the corners of her lips turned up in a grudging little smile. "Can't fool you, can I? I had one swallow, just to see what it tasted like. What the big deal is. I guess she smelled it on my breath when I came home. And guess what? There *is* no big deal. It tasted *horrible*."

Dan did not reply to this. If he told her he had found his own first taste horrible, that he had also believed there was no big deal, no precious secret, she would have dismissed it as windy adult bullshit. You could not moralize children out of growing up. Or teach them how to do it.

"I really didn't mean to break the plates," she said in a small voice. "It was an accident, like I told her. I was just so *mad*."

"You come by it naturally." What he was remembering was Abra standing over Rose the Hat as Rose cycled. *Does it hurt?* Abra had asked the dying thing that looked like a woman (except, that was, for the one terrible tooth). *I hope it does. I hope it hurts a lot.*

"Are you going to lecture me?" And, with a lilt of contempt: "I know that's what *she* wants."

"I'm out of lectures, but I could tell you a story my mother told me. It's about your great-grandfather on the Jack Torrance side. Do you want to hear it?"

Abra shrugged. *Get it over with,* the shrug said.

"Don Torrance wasn't an orderly like me, but close. He was a male nurse. He walked with a cane toward the end of his life, because he was in a car accident that messed up his leg. And one night, at the dinner table, he used that cane on his wife. No reason; he just started in whaling. He broke her nose and opened her scalp. When she fell out of her chair onto the floor, he got up and *really* went to work on her. According to what my father told my mom, he would have beaten her to death if Brett and Mike—they were *my* uncles—hadn't pulled him away. When the doctor came, your great-grandfather was down on his knees with his own little medical kit, doing what he could. He said she fell downstairs. Great-Gram— the momo you never met, Abra—backed him up. So did the kids."

"Why?" she breathed.

"Because they were scared. Later—long after Don was dead— your grandfather broke my arm. Then, in the Overlook—which stood where Roof O' the World stands today—your grandfather beat my mother almost to death. He used a roque mallet instead of a cane, but it was basically the same deal."

"I get the point."

"Years later, in a bar in St. Petersburg—"

"Stop! I said I *get* it!" She was trembling.

"—I beat a man unconscious with a pool cue because he laughed when I scratched. After that, the son of Jack and the grandson of Don spent thirty days in an orange jumpsuit, picking up trash along Highway 41."

She turned away, starting to cry. "Thanks, Uncle Dan. Thanks for spoiling . . ."

An image filled his head, momentarily blotting out the river: a charred and smoking birthday cake. In some circumstances, the image would have been funny. Not in these.

He took her gently by the shoulders and turned her back to him. "There's nothing to get. There's no point. There's nothing but family history. In the words of the immortal Elvis Presley, it's your baby, you rock it."

"I don't understand."

"Someday you may write poetry, like Concetta. Or push someone else off a high place with your mind."

"I never would . . . but *Rose* deserved it." Abra turned her wet face up to his.

"No argument there."

"So why do I dream about it? Why do I wish I could take it back? She would have killed *us,* so why do I wish I could take it back?"

"Is it the killing you wish you could take back, or the joy of the killing?"

Abra hung her head. Dan wanted to take her in his arms, but didn't.

"No lecture and no moral. Just blood calling to blood. The stupid urges of wakeful people. And you've made it to a time of life when you're completely awake. It's hard for you. I know that. It's hard for everyone, but most teenagers don't have your abilities. Your weapons."

"What do I do? What can I do? Sometimes I get so angry . . . not just at *her,* but at teachers . . . kids at school who think they're such hot shits . . . the ones who laugh if you're not good at sports or wearing the wrong clothes and stuff . . ."

Dan thought of advice Casey Kingsley had once given him. "Go to the dump."

"Huh?" She goggled at him.

He sent her a picture: Abra using her extraordinary talents—they had still not peaked, incredible but true—to overturn discarded refrigerators, explode dead TV sets, throw washing machines. Seagulls flew up in startled packs.

Now she didn't goggle; she giggled. "Will that help?"

"Better the dump than your mother's plates."

She cocked her head and fixed him with merry eyes. They were friends again, and that was good. "But those plates were ug-*lee*."

"Will you try it?"

"Yes." And by the look of her, she couldn't wait.

"One other thing."

She grew solemn, waiting.

"You don't have to be anyone's doormat."

"That's good, isn't it?"

"Yes. Just remember how dangerous your anger can be. Keep it—"

His cell phone rang.

"You should get that."

He raised his eyebrows. "Do you know who it is?"

"No, but I think it's important."

He took the phone out of his pocket and read the display. RIVINGTON HOUSE.

"Hello?"

"It's Claudette Albertson, Danny. Can you come?"

He ran a mental inventory of the hospice guests currently on his blackboard. "Amanda Ricker? Or Jeff Kellogg?"

It turned out to be neither.

"If you can come, you better do it right away," Claudette said. "While he's still conscious." She hesitated. "He's asking for you."

"I'll come." *Although if it's as bad as you say, he'll probably be gone when I get there.* Dan broke the connection. "I have to go, honey."

"Even though he's not your friend. Even though you don't even like him." Abra looked thoughtful.

"Even though."

"What's his name? I didn't get that."

(*Fred Carling*)

He sent this and then wrapped his arms around her, tight-tight-tight. Abra did the same.

"I'll try," she said. "I'll try real hard."

"I know you will," he said. "I know you will. Listen, Abra, I love you so much."

She said, "I'm glad."

3

Claudette was at the nurses' station when he came in forty-five minutes later. He asked the question he had asked dozens of times before: "Is he still with us?" As if it were a bus ride.

"Barely."

"Conscious?"

She waggled a hand. "In and out."

"Azzie?"

"Was there for awhile, but scooted when Dr. Emerson came in. Emerson's gone now, he's checking on Amanda Ricker. Azzie went back as soon as he left."

"No transport to the hospital?"

"Can't. Not yet. There was a four-car pile-up on Route 119 across the border in Castle Rock. Lots of injuries. Four ambos on the way, also LifeFlight. Going to the hospital will make a difference to some of them. As for Fred . . ." She shrugged.

"What happened?"

"You know our Fred—junk food junkie. Mickey D's is his second home. Sometimes he looks when he runs across Cranmore Avenue, sometimes he doesn't. Just expects people to stop for him." She wrinkled her nose and stuck out her tongue, looking like a little kid who's just gotten a mouthful of something bad. Brussels sprouts, maybe. "That *attitude*."

Dan knew Fred's routine, and he knew the attitude.

"He was going for his evening cheeseburger," Claudette said. "The cops took the woman who hit him to jail—chick was so drunk she could hardly stand up, that's what I heard. They brought Fred here. His face is scrambled eggs, his chest and pelvis are crushed, one leg's almost severed. If Emerson hadn't been here doing rounds,

Fred would have died right away. We triaged him, stopped the bleeding, but even if he'd been in peak condition . . . which dear old Freddy most definitely ain't . . ." She shrugged. "Emerson says they *will* send an ambo after the Castle Rock mess is cleaned up, but he'll be gone by then. Dr. Emerson wouldn't commit on that, but I believe Azreel. You better go on down there, if you're going. I know you never cared for him . . ."

Dan thought of the fingermarks the orderly had left on poor old Charlie Hayes's arm. *Sorry to hear it*—that was what Carling had said when Dan told him the old man was gone. Fred all comfy, rocked back in his favorite chair and eating Junior Mints. *But that is what they're here for, isn't it?*

And now Fred was in the same room where Charlie had died. Life was a wheel, and it always came back around.

4

The door of the Alan Shepard Suite was standing half-open, but Dan knocked anyway, as a courtesy. He could hear the harsh wheeze-and-gurgle of Fred Carling's breathing even from the hall, but it didn't seem to bother Azzie, who was curled up at the foot of the bed. Carling was lying on a rubber sheet, wearing nothing but bloodstained boxer shorts and an acre of bandages, most of them already seeping blood. His face was disfigured, his body twisted in at least three different directions.

"Fred? It's Dan Torrance. Can you hear me?"

The one remaining eye opened. The breathing hitched. There was a brief rasp that might have been *yes*.

Dan went into the bathroom, wetted a cloth with warm water, wrung it out. These were things he had done many times before. When he returned to Carling's bedside, Azzie got to his feet, stretched in that luxurious, bowed-back way cats have, and jumped to the floor. A moment later he was gone, to resume his evening's patrol. He limped a little now. He was a very old cat.

Dan sat on the side of the bed and gently rubbed the cloth over the part of Fred Carling's face that was still relatively whole.

"How bad's the pain?"

That rasp again. Carling's left hand was a twisted snarl of broken fingers, so Dan took the right one. "You don't need to talk, just tell me."

(*not so bad now*)

Dan nodded. "Good. That's good."

(*but I'm scared*)

"There's nothing to be scared of."

He saw Fred at the age of six, swimming in the Saco with his brother, Fred always snatching at the back of his suit to keep it from falling off because it was too big, it was a hand-me-down like practically everything else he owned. He saw him at fifteen, kissing a girl at the Bridgton Drive-In and smelling her perfume as he touched her breast and wished this night would never end. He saw him at twenty-five, riding down to Hampton Beach with the Road Saints, sitting astride a Harley FXB, the Sturgis model, so fine, he's full of bennies and red wine and the day is like a hammer, everybody looking as the Saints tear by in a long and glittering caravan of fuck-you noise; life is exploding like fireworks. And he sees the apartment where Carling lives—lived—with his little dog, whose name is Brownie. Brownie ain't much, just a mutt, but he's smart. Sometimes he jumps up in the orderly's lap and they watch TV together. Brownie troubles Fred's mind because he will be waiting for Fred to come home, take him for a little walk, then fill up his bowl with Gravy Train.

"Don't worry about Brownie," Dan said. "I know a girl who'd be glad to take care of him. She's my niece, and it's her birthday."

Carling looked up at him with his one functioning eye. The rattle of his breath was very loud now; he sounded like an engine with dirt in it.

(*can you help me   please doc   can you help me*)

Yes. He could help. It was his sacrament, what he was made for. It was quiet now in Rivington House, very quiet indeed. Somewhere close, a door was swinging open. They had come to the border. Fred Carling looked up him, asking *what*. Asking *how*. But it was so simple.

"You only need to sleep."

(*don't leave me*)

"No," Dan said. "I'm here. I'll stay here until you sleep."

Now he clasped Carling's hand in both of his. And smiled.

"Until you sleep," he said.

May 1, 2011–July 17, 2012

AUTHOR'S NOTE

My first book with Scribner was *Bag of Bones,* in 1998. Anxious to please my new partners, I went out on tour for that novel. At one of the autographing sessions, some guy asked, "Hey, any idea what happened to the kid from *The Shining?*"

This was a question I'd often asked myself about that old book—along with another: What would have happened to Danny's troubled father if he had found Alcoholics Anonymous instead of trying to get by with what people in AA call "white-knuckle sobriety"?

As with *Under the Dome* and *11/22/63,* this was an idea that never quite left my mind. Every now and then—while taking a shower, watching a TV show, or making a long turnpike drive—I would find myself calculating Danny Torrance's age, and wondering where he was. Not to mention his mother, one more basically good human being left in Jack Torrance's destructive wake. Wendy and Danny were, in the current parlance, codependents, people bound by ties of love and responsibility to an addicted family member. At some point in 2009, one of my recovering alcoholic friends told me a one-liner that goes like this: "When a codependent is drowning, somebody else's life flashes before his eyes." That struck me as too true to be funny, and I think it was at that point that *Doctor Sleep* became inevitable. I had to know.

Did I approach the book with trepidation? You better believe it. *The Shining* is one of those novels people always mention (along with *'Salem's Lot, Pet Sematary,* and *It*) when they talk about which of my books really scared the bejeezus out of them. Plus, of course, there was Stanley Kubrick's movie, which many seem to remember—for reasons I have never quite understood—as one of the scariest films they have ever seen. (If you have seen the movie but not read the novel, you should note that *Doctor Sleep* follows the latter, which is, in my opinion, the True History of the Torrance Family.)

I like to think I'm still pretty good at what I do, but nothing can live up to the memory of a good scare, and I mean *nothing*, especially if administered to one who is young and impressionable. There has been at least one brilliant sequel to Alfred Hitchcock's *Psycho* (Mick Garris's *Psycho IV*, with Anthony Perkins reprising his role as Norman Bates), but people who've seen that—or any of the others—will only shake their heads and say *no, no, not as good*. They remember the first time they experienced Janet Leigh, and no remake or sequel can top that moment when the curtain is pulled back and the knife starts to do its work.

And people change. The man who wrote *Doctor Sleep* is very different from the well-meaning alcoholic who wrote *The Shining*, but both remain interested in the same thing: telling a kickass story. I enjoyed finding Danny Torrance again and following his adventures. I hope you did, too. If that's the case, Constant Reader, we're all good.

Before letting you go, let me thank the people who need to be thanked, okay?

Nan Graham edited the book. *Righteously*. Thanks, Nan.

Chuck Verrill, my agent, sold the book. That's important, but he also took all my phone calls and fed me spoonfuls of soothing syrup. Those things are indispensable.

Russ Dorr did the research, but for what's wrong, blame me for misunderstanding. He's a great physician's assistant and a Nordic monster of inspiration and good cheer.

Chris Lotts supplied Italian when Italian was needed. Yo, Chris.

Rocky Wood was my go-to guy for all things *Shining*, providing me with names and dates I had either forgotten or plain got wrong. He also provided reams of info on every recreational vehicle and camper under the sun (the coolest was Rose's EarthCruiser). The

Rock knows my work better than I do myself. Look him up on the Web sometime. He's got it going on.

My son Owen read the book and suggested valuable changes. Chief among them was his insistence that we see Dan reach what recovered alcoholics call "the bottom."

My wife also read *Doctor Sleep* and helped to make it better. I love you, Tabitha.

Thanks to you guys and girls who read my stuff, too. May you have long days and pleasant nights.

Let me close with a word of caution: when you're on the turnpikes and freeways of America, watch out for those Winnebagos and Bounders.

You never know who might be inside. Or *what*.

Bangor, Maine

Turn the page

for a sneak peak

at Stephen King's

exciting novel

Revival

I

Fifth Business. Skull Mountain. Peaceable Lake.

In one way, at least, our lives really are like movies. The main cast consists of your family and friends. The supporting cast is made up of neighbors, co-workers, teachers, and daily acquaintances. There are also bit players: the supermarket checkout girl with the pretty smile, the friendly bartender at the local watering hole, the guys you work out with at the gym three days a week. And there are thousands of extras—those people who flow through every life like water through a sieve, seen once and never again. The teenager browsing graphic novels at Barnes & Noble, the one you had to slip past (murmuring "Excuse me") in order to get to the magazines. The woman in the next lane at a stoplight, taking a moment to freshen her lipstick. The mother wiping ice cream off her toddler's face in a roadside restaurant where you stopped for a quick bite. The vendor who sold you a bag of peanuts at a baseball game.

But sometimes a person who fits none of these categories comes into your life. This is the joker who pops out of the deck at odd intervals over the years, often during a moment of crisis. In the movies this sort of character is known as the fifth business, or the change agent. When he turns up in a film, you know he's there because the screenwriter put him there. But who is screenwriting our lives? Fate or coincidence? I want to believe it's the latter. I want that with all my heart and soul. When I think of Charles Jacobs—my fifth business, my change agent, my nemesis—I can't bear to believe his presence in my life had anything to do with fate. It would mean that all these terrible things—these *horrors*—were meant to happen. If that is so, then there is no such thing as light, and our belief in it is a foolish illusion. If that is so, we live in darkness like animals in a burrow, or ants deep in their hill.

And not alone.

Claire gave me an army for my sixth birthday, and on a Saturday in October of 1962 I was gearing up for a major battle.

I came from a big family—four boys, one girl—and as the youngest I always got lots of presents. Claire always gave the best ones. I don't know if it was because she was the eldest, because she was the only girl, or both. But of all the awesome presents she gave me over the years, that army was by far the best. There were two hundred green plastic soldiers, some with rifles, some with machine guns, a dozen welded to tubelike gadgets she said were mortars. There were also eight trucks and twelve jeeps. Perhaps the coolest thing about the army was the box it came in, a cardboard footlocker in camouflage shades of green and brown, with PROPERTY OF U.S. ARMY stenciled on the front. Below this, Claire had added her own stenciling: JAMIE MORTON, COMMANDER.

That was me.

"I saw an ad for them in the back of one of Terry's comic books," she said when I was done screaming with delight. "He didn't want me to cut it out because he's a booger—"

"That's right," Terry said. He was eight. "I'm a big brother booger." He made a fork with his first two fingers and plugged his nostrils with them.

"Stop it," our mother said. "No sibling rivalry on birthdays, please and thank you. Terry, take your fingers out of your nose."

"Anyway," Claire said, "I copied the coupon and sent it in. I was afraid it might not come in time, but it did. I'm glad you like it." And she kissed me on the temple. She always kissed me there. All these years later, I can still feel those soft kisses.

"I love it!" I said, holding the footlocker against my chest. "I'll love it forever!"

This was after breakfast, which had been blueberry pancakes and bacon, my favorite. We all got our favorite meals on our birthdays, and the presents always came after breakfast, there in the kitchen with its woodstove and long table and our hulk of a washing machine, which was always breaking down.

"Forever for Jamie is, like, five days," Con said. He was ten, slender (although he bulked up later), and of a scientific bent, even then.

"Nice one, Conrad," our father said. He was dressed for work in a clean coverall with his name—RICHARD—stitched in gold thread on the left breast pocket. On the right breast it said MORTON FUEL OIL. "I'm impressed."

"Thanks, Daddy-O."

"Your silver tongue wins you the opportunity to help your mother clean up breakfast."

"It's Andy's turn!"

"It *was* Andy's turn," Dad said, pouring syrup on the last pancake. "Grab a dishtowel, Silver Tongue. And try not to break anything."

"You spoil him rotten," Con said, but he grabbed a dishtowel.

Connie wasn't entirely wrong about my concept of forever. Five days later, the Operation game Andy gave me was gathering dust bunnies under my bed (some of the body parts were missing, anyway; Andy got it at the Eureka Grange rummage sale for a quarter). So were the jigsaw puzzles Terry gave me. Con himself gave me a ViewMaster, and that lasted a little longer, but it eventually wound up in my closet, never to be seen again.

From Mom and Dad I got clothes, because my birthday falls near the end of August, and that year I was going into first grade. I found new pants and shirts about as exciting as a TV test pattern, but tried to say thanks with enthusiasm. I imagine they saw through that with no trouble; false enthusiasm does not come easily to six-year-olds . . . although, sad to say, it's a skill most of us learn fairly rapidly. In any case, the clothes were washed in the hulk, hung on the clothesline in the side yard, and finally folded away in my bureau drawers. Where, it's probably needless to add, they were out of sight and mind until September came and it was time to put them on. I remember there was a sweater that was actually pretty cool—it was brown with yellow stripes. When I wore it I pretended I was a superhero called the Human Wasp: evildoers, beware my sting!

But Con was wrong about the footlocker with the army inside. I played with those guys day in and day out, usually at the edge of the front yard, where there was a dirt strip between our lawn and Methodist Road, which was itself dirt in those days. With the exception of Route 9 and the two-lane leading to Goat Mountain, where there was a resort for rich people, all the roads in Harlow were dirt back in those days. I can remember my mother on several occasions weeping about all the dust that got into the house on dry summer days.

Billy Paquette and Al Knowles—my two best friends—played army with me on many afternoons, but on the day Charles Jacobs appeared in my life for the first time, I was on my own. I don't remember why Billy and Al weren't with me, but I do remember I was happy to be by myself for a change. For one thing, there was no need to split the army into three divisions. For another—this was more important—I didn't have to argue with them about whose turn it was to win. In truth, it seemed unfair to me that I should ever have to lose, because they were *my* soldiers and it was *my* footlocker.

When I advanced this idea to my mother one hot late-summer day shortly after my birthday, she took me by the shoulders and looked into my eyes, a sure sign that I was about to receive another Lesson in Life. "That *it's-mine* business is half the trouble with the world, Jamie. When you play with your friends, the soldiers belong to all of you."

"Even if we play-fight different sides?"

"Even if. When Billy and Al go home for their dinner and you pack the soldiers back into the box—"

"It's a *footlocker*!"

"Right, the footlocker. When you pack them away, they're yours again. People have many ways to be lousy to one another, as you'll find out when you're older, but I think that all bad behavior stems from plain old selfishness. Promise me you'll never be selfish, kiddo."

I promised, but I still didn't like it when Billy and Al won.

On that day in October of 1962, with the fate of the world dangling by a thread over a small tropical spit of land called Cuba, I was fighting both sides of the battle, which meant I was bound to come out on top. The town grader had been by earlier on Methodist Road ("Moving the rocks around," my dad always grumbled), and there was plenty of loose dirt. I scraped enough together to make first a hill, then a big hill, and then a *very* big hill, one that came up almost to my knees. At first I thought of calling it Goat Mountain, but that seemed both unoriginal (the real Goat Mountain was only twelve miles away, after all) and boring. After consideration, I decided to call it Skull Mountain. I even tried to poke a couple of eye-like caves in it with my fingers, but the dirt was dry and the holes kept caving in.

"Oh, well," I told the plastic soldiers tumbled in their footlocker. "The world is hard and you can't have everything." This was one of my father's favorite sayings, and with five kids to support, I'm sure he had reason to believe it. "They'll be pretend caves."

I put half of my army on top of Skull Mountain, where they made a formidable crew. I especially liked the way the mortar guys looked up there. These were the Krauts. The American army I arranged at the edge the lawn. They got all the jeeps and trucks, because they would look so groovy charging up the steep slope of the mountain. Some would turn over, I was sure, but at least a few of them would make it to the top. And run over the mortar guys, who would scream for mercy. They wouldn't get it.

"To the death," I said, setting up the last few of the heroic Americans. "Hitsmer, you are next!"

I was starting them forward, rank by rank—and making comic-book-style machine-gun noises—when a shadow fell over the battlefield. I looked up and saw a guy standing there. He was blocking the afternoon sun, a silhouette surrounded by golden light—a human eclipse.

There was stuff going on; at our house on Saturday afternoons, there always was. Andy and Con were in our long backyard, playing three-flies-six-grounders with a bunch of their friends, shouting and laughing. Claire was up in her room with a couple of *her* friends, playing records on her

Imperial Party-Time turntable: "The Loco-Motion," "Soldier Boy," "Palisades Park." There was hammering from the garage, too, as Terry and our dad worked on the old '51 Ford Dad called the Road Rocket. Or the Project. Once I heard him call it a piece of shit, a phrase I treasured then and still use now. When you want to feel better, call something a piece of shit. It usually works.

Plenty going on, but at that moment everything seemed to fall still. I know it's only the sort of illusion caused by a faulty memory (not to mention a suitcase loaded with dark associations), but the recollection is very strong. All of a sudden there were no kids yelling in the backyard, no records playing upstairs, no banging from the garage. Not a single bird singing.

Then the man bent down and the westering sun glared over his shoulder, momentarily blinding me. I raised a hand to shield my eyes.

"Sorry, sorry," he said, and moved enough so I could look at him without also having to look into the sun. On top he was wearing a black for-church jacket and a black shirt with a notched collar; on the bottom blue jeans and scuffed loafers. It was like he wanted to be two different people at the same time. At the age of six, I put adults into three categories: young grown-ups, grown-ups, and old people. This guy was a young grownup. He had his hands on his knees so he could look at the opposing armies.

"Who are you?" I asked.

"Charles Jacobs." The name was vaguely familiar. He stuck out his hand. I shook it right away, because even at six, I had my manners. All of us did. Mom and Dad saw to that.

"Why are you wearing that collar with the hole in it?"

"Because I'm a minister. When you go to church on Sundays from now on, I'll be there. And if you go to Thursday night MYF, I'll be there, too."

"Mr. Latoure used to be our minister," I said, "but he died."

"I know. I'm sorry."

"It's okay, though, because Mom said he didn't suffer, only went straight to heaven. He didn't wear a collar like that, though."

"Because Bill Latoure was a lay preacher. That means he was sort of a volunteer. He kept the church open when there was no one else to do it. That was very good of him."

"I think my dad knows about you," I said. "He's one of the deacons in the church. He gets to take up the collection. He has to take turns with the other deacons, though."

"Sharing is good," Jacobs said, and got down on his knees beside me.

"Are you going to pray?" The idea was sort of alarming. Praying was for church and Methodist Youth Fellowship, which my brothers and sister called Thursday Night School. When Mr. Jacobs started it up again, this would be my first year, just like it was my first year at regular school. "If you want to talk with my dad, he's in the garage with Terry. They're putting a new clutch in the Road Rocket. Well, my dad is. Terry mostly hands him the tools and watches. He's eight. I'm six. I think my mom might be on the back porch, watching some guys play three-flies-six-grounders."

"Which we used to call rollie-bat when I was a kid," he said, and smiled. It was a nice smile. I liked him right away.

"Yeah?"

"Uh-huh, because you had to hit the bat with the ball after you caught it. What's your name, son?"

"Jamie Morton. I'm six."

"So you said."

"I don't think anyone ever prayed in our front yard."

"I'm not going to, either. What I want is a closer look at your armies. Which are the Russians and which are the Americans?"

"Well, these ones on the ground are Americans, sure, but the ones on Skull Mountain are Krauts. The Americans have to take the mountain."

"Because it's in the way," Jacobs said. "Beyond Skull Mountain lies the road to Germany."

"That's right! And the head Kraut! Hitsmer!"

"The author of so many evils," he said.

"Huh?"

"Nothing. Do you mind if I just call the bad guys Germans? Krauts seems kind of mean."

"No, that's great, Krauts are Germans and Germans are Krauts. My dad was in the war. Just the last year, though. He fixed trucks in Texas. Were you in the war, Mr. Jacobs?"

"No, I was too young. For Korea, too. How are the Americans going to take that hill, General Morton?"

"Charge it!" I shouted. "Shoot their machine guns! Pow! Budda-budda-budda!" Then, going down way low in my throat: "Takka-takka-takka!"

"A direct attack on the high ground sounds risky, General. If I were you I'd split your troops . . . like so . . ." He moved half of the Americans to the left and half to the right. "That creates a pincers movement, see?" He brought his thumb and forefinger together. "Drive on the objective from both sides."

"Maybe," I said. I liked the idea of a head-on attack—lots of bloody action—but Mr. Jacobs's idea appealed to me, just the same. It was sneaky. Sneaky could be satisfying. "I tried to make some caves, but the dirt's too dry."

"So I see." He poked a finger into Skull Mountain and watched the dirt crumble and bury the hole. He stood up and brushed the knees of his jeans. "I've got a little boy who'd probably get a kick out of your soldiers in another year or two."

"He can play right now, if he wants to." I was trying not to be selfish. "Where is he?"

"Still in Boston, with his mother. There's lots of stuff to pack up. They'll be here Wednesday, I think. Thursday at the latest. But Morrie's still a little young for soldiers. He'd only pick them up and throw them around."

"How old is he?"

"Just two."

"I bet he still pees his pants!" I yelled, and started laughing. It probably wasn't polite, but I couldn't help it. Kids peeing their pants was just so funny.

"He does, at that," Jacobs said, smiling, "but I'm sure he'll grow out of it. Your father's in the garage, you say?"

"Yeah." Now I remembered where I had heard the man's name before—Mom and Dad at the supper table, talking about the new minister that was coming from Boston. *Isn't he awfully young?* my mother had asked. *Yes, and his salary will reflect that*, my dad replied, and grinned. They talked about him some more, I think, but I didn't pay any attention. Andy was hogging the mashed potatoes. He always did.

"You try that enfilading maneuver," he said, starting away.

"Huh?"

"Pincers," he said, tweezing his thumb and finger together again.

"Oh. Yeah. Great."

I tried it. It worked pretty good. The Krauts all died. The battle wasn't what I'd call spectacular, though, so I tried the frontal assault, with trucks and jeeps tumbling off the steep slope of Skull Mountain, plus Krauts tumbling off the back with deathcries of despair: "*Yaaaahhh!*"

Mom, Dad, and Mr. Jacobs sat on the front porch while the battle raged, drinking iced tea and talking about churchy things—in addition to my dad being a deacon, my mom was in the Ladies Auxiliary. Not the boss of it, but the next-to-boss. You should have seen all the fancy hats she had in those days. There must have been a dozen. We were happy then.

Mom called my brothers and sister, along with their friends to meet the new minister. I started to come, too, but Mr. Jacobs waved me back, telling Mom we'd already met. "Battle on, General!" he called.

I battled on. Con, Andy, and their friends went out back again and played on. Claire and her friends went back upstairs and danced on (although my mother told her to turn the music down, please and thank you). Mr. and Mrs. Morton and the Reverend Jacobs talked on, and for quite awhile. I remember often being surprised at how much adults could yak. It was tiring.

I lost track of them because I was fighting the Battle of Skull Mountain over again in several different ways. In the most satisfying scenario—adapted from Mr. Jacobs's pincers movement—one part of the American army kept the Germans pinned down from the front while the rest looped around and ambushed the Germans from behind. "*Vat is zis?*" one of them cried, just before getting shot in the head.

I was starting to get tired of it and was thinking of going in for a slice of cake (if Con and Andy's friends had left any), when that shadow fell over me and my battlefield again. I looked up and saw Mr. Jacobs, holding a glass of water.

"I borrowed this from your mother. Can I show you something?"

"Sure."

He knelt down again and poured the water all over the top of Skull Mountain.

"It's a thunderstorm!" I shouted, and made thunder noises.

"Uh-huh, if you like. With lightning. Now look." He poked out two of his fingers like devil horns and pushed them into the wet dirt. This time the holes stayed. "Presto," he said. "Caves." He took two of the German soldiers and put them inside. "They'll be tough to root out, General, but I'm sure the Americans will be up to the job."

"Hey! Thanks!"

"Add another glass if it gets crumbly again."

"I will."

"And remember to take the glass back to the kitchen when you finish the battle. I don't want to get in trouble with your mother on my first day in Harlow."

I promised, and stuck out my hand. "Put er there, Mr. Jacobs."

He laughed and did so, then walked off down Methodist Road, toward the parsonage where he and his family would live for the next three years, until he got fired. I watched him go, then turned back to Skull Mountain.

Before I could really get going, another shadow fell over the battlefield. This time it was my dad. He took a knee, being careful not to squash any American soldiers. "Well, Jamie, what did you think of our new minister?"

"I like him."

"So do I. Your mother does, too. He's very young for the job, and if he's good, we'll only be his starter congregation, but I think he'll do fine. Especially with MYF. Youth calls to youth."

"Look, Daddy, he showed me how to make caves. You only have to get the dirt wet so it makes kinda almost mud."

"I see." He ruffled my hair. "You want to wash up good before supper." He picked up the glass. "Want me to take this in for you?"

"Yes, please and thank you."

He took the glass and headed back to the house. I returned to Skull Mountain, only to see that the dirt had dried out again and the caves had collapsed. The soldiers inside had been buried alive. That was okay with me; they were the bad guys, after all.

These days we've become gruesomely sensitized to sex, and no parent in his or her right mind would send a six-year-old off in the company of a grown man who was living by himself (if only for a few days), but that is exactly what my mother did the following Monday afternoon, and without a qualm.

Reverend Jacobs—Mom told me I was supposed to call him that, not Mister—came walking up Methodist Hill around quarter to three and knocked on the screen door. I was in the living room coloring on the floor while Mom watched *Dialing for Prizes*. She had sent her name in to WCSH, and was hoping to win that month's grand prize, an Electrolux vacuum cleaner. She knew the chances weren't good, but, she said, hope springs infernal. That was a joke.

"Can you loan me your youngest for half an hour?" Reverend Jacobs asked. "I've got something in my garage that he might like to see."

"What is it?" I asked, already getting up.

"A surprise. You can tell your mother all about it later."

"Mom?"

"Of course," she said, "but change out of your school clothes first, Jamie. While he does that, would you like a glass of iced tea, Reverend Jacobs?"

"I would," he said. "And I wonder if you could manage to call me Charlie."

She considered this, then said, "No, but I could probably manage Charles."

I changed into jeans and a tee-shirt, and because they were talking about adult things when I came back downstairs, I went outside to wait for the schoolbus. Con, Terry, and I attended the one-room school on Route 9—an easy quarter-mile walk from our house—but Andy went to Consolidated Middle and Claire all the way across the river to Gates Falls High, where she was a freshman. ("Just don't be a fresh *girl*," Mom told her—that was also a joke.) The bus dropped them off at the intersection of Route 9 and Methodist Road, which was called Methodist Corner.

I saw them get off, and as they came trudging up the hill—squabbling as always, I could hear them as I stood waiting by the mailbox—Reverend Jacobs came out.

"Ready?" he asked, and took my hand. It seemed perfectly natural.

"Sure," I said.

We met Andy and Claire halfway down the hill. Andy asked where I was going.

"To Reverend Jacobs' house," I said. "He's going to show me a surprise."

"Well, don't be too long," Claire said. "It's your turn to set the table." She glanced at Jacobs, then quickly away again, as if she found him hard to look at. My big sister had a wicked crush on him before the year was out, and so did all her friends.

"I'll have him back shortly," Jacobs promised.

We walked down the hill hand in hand to Route 9, which led to Portland if you turned left, to Gates Falls, Castle Rock, and Lewiston if you turned right. We stopped and looked for traffic, which was ridiculous since there were hardly any cars on Route 9 except in the summer, and then walked on past hayfields and cornfields, the stalks of the latter now dry and clattering in a mild autumn breeze. Ten minutes brought us to the parsonage, a tidy white house with black shutters. Beyond it was the First Methodist Church of Harlow, which was also ridiculous since there was no other Methodist church in Harlow.

The only other house of worship in Harlow was Shiloh Church. My father considered the Shilohites moderate to serious weirdos. They didn't ride around in horse-drawn buggies, or anything, but the men and boys all wore black hats when they were outside. The women and girls wore dresses that came down to their ankles, and white caps. Dad said the Shilohites claimed to know when the world was going to end; it was written down in a special book. My mother said in America everyone was entitled to believe what they liked as long as they didn't hurt anybody . . . but she didn't say Dad was wrong, either. Our church was larger than Shiloh, but very plain. Also, it had no steeple. It did once, but a hurricane came along back in olden days, 1920 or so, and knocked it down.

Reverend Jacobs and I walked up the parsonage's dirt driveway. I was interested to see that he had a blue Plymouth Belvedere, a very cool car. "Standard shift or push-button drive?" I asked.

He looked surprised, then grinned. "Push-button," he said. "It was a wedding present from my in-laws."

"Are in-laws like outlaws?"

"Mine are," he said, and laughed. "Do you like cars?"

"We all like cars," I said, meaning everyone in my family . . . although that was less true of Mom and Claire, I guessed. Females didn't seem to understand the basic coolness of cars. "When the Road Rocket's fixed up, my dad's going to race it at the Castle Rock Speedway."

"Really?"

"Well, not him, exactly, Mom said he couldn't because it's too dangerous, but some guy. Maybe Duane Robichaud. He runs Brownie's Store
along with his mom and dad. He drove the nine-car at the Speedway
last year, but the engine caught on fire. Dad says he's looking for another
ride."

"Do the Robichauds come to church?"

"Um . . ."

"I'll take that as a no. Come in the garage, Jamie."

It was shadowy and musty-smelling. I was a little afraid of the shadows
and the smell, but Jacobs didn't seem to mind. He led me deeper into the
gloom, then stopped and pointed. I gasped at what I saw.

Jacobs gave a little chuckle, the way people do when they're proud of
something. "Welcome to Peaceable Lake, Jamie."

"Wow!"

"I got it set up while I'm waiting for Patsy and Morrie to get here. I
should be doing stuff in the house, and I *have* done a fair amount—fixed
the well-pump, for one thing—but there's not a whole lot more I *can* do
until Pats gets here with the furniture. Your mom and the rest of the
Ladies Auxiliary did a terrific job of cleaning the place up, kiddo. Mr.
Latoure commuted from Orr's Island, and no one's actually lived here
since before World War II. I thanked her, but I wouldn't mind if you
thanked her again."

"Sure, you bet," I said, but I don't believe I ever passed that second
thanks on, because I barely heard what he was saying. All my attention was
fixed on a table that took up almost half the garage space. On it was a rolling green landscape that put Skull Mountain to shame. I have seen many
such landscapes since—mostly in the windows of toyshops—but they all
had complicated electric trains running through them. There was no train
on the table Reverend Jacobs had set up, which wasn't a real table at all, but
sheets of plywood on a rank of sawhorses. Atop the plywood was a countryside in miniature, about twelve feet long and five feet wide. Power pylons
eighteen inches high marched across it on a diagonal, and it was dominated
by a lake of real water that shone bright blue even in the gloom.

"I'll have to take it down soon," he said, "or else I won't be able to get
the car in the garage. Patsy wouldn't care for that."

He bent, planted his hands above his knees, and gazed at the rolling
hills, the threadlike power lines, the big lake. There were plastic sheep
and cows grazing near the water (they were considerably out of scale, but
I didn't notice and wouldn't have cared if I had). There were also lots of
streetlamps, which was a little peculiar, since there was no town and no
roads for them to shine on.

"I bet you could have quite a battle with your soldiers here, couldn't you?"

"Yeah," I said. I thought I could fight an entire war there.

He nodded. "That can't happen, though, because in Peaceable Lake, everyone gets along and no fighting is allowed. In that way it's like heaven. Once I get MYF going, I plan to move it to the church basement. Maybe you and your brothers would help me. The kids would like it, I think."

"They sure would!" I said, then added something my father said. "You betchum bobcats!"

He laughed and clapped me on the shoulder. "Now do you want to see a miracle?"

"I guess," I said. I wasn't actually sure I did. It sounded like it might be scary. All at once I realized the two of us were alone in an old garage with no car in it, a dusty hollow that smelled as if it had been closed up for years. The door to the outside world was still open, but it seemed a mile away. I liked Reverend Jacobs okay, but I found myself wishing I had stayed home, coloring on the floor and waiting to see if Mom could win the Electrolux and finally get the upper hand in her never-ending battle with the summer dust.

Then Reverend Jacobs passed his hand slowly above Peaceable Lake, and I forgot about being nervous. There was a low humming sound from under the makeshift table, like the sound our Philco TV made when it was warming up, and all the little streetlights came on. They were bright white, almost too bright to look at, and cast a magical moony glow over the green hills and blue water. Even the plastic cows and sheep looked more realistic, possibly because they now cast shadows.

"Gosh, how did you do that?"

He grinned. "Pretty good trick, huh? 'God said Let there be light, and there was light, and the light was good.' Only I'm not God, so I have to depend on electricity. Which is wonderful stuff, Jamie. Such a gift from God that it makes us feel godlike every time we flip a switch, wouldn't you say?"

"I guess so," I said. "My grandpa Amos remembers before there were electric lights."

"Lots of people do," he said, "but it won't be long before all those people are gone . . . and when that happens, nobody will think much about what a miracle electricity is. And what a mystery. We have an idea about how it works, but knowing how something works and knowing what it *is* are two very different things."

"How did you turn on the lights?" I asked.

He pointed to a shelf beyond the table. "See that little red bulb?"

"Uh-huh."

"It's a photoelectric cell. You can buy them, but I built that one myself. It projects an invisible beam. When I break it, the streetlights around Peaceable Lake go on. If I do it again . . . like so . . ." He passed his hand above the landscape and the streetlights dimmed, faded to faint cores of light, then went out. "You see?"

"Cool," I breathed.

"You try it."

I reached my hand up. At first nothing happened, but when I stood on tiptoe my fingers broke the beam. The humming from beneath the table started up again and the lights came back on.

"I did it!"

"Betchum bobcats," he said, and ruffled my hair.

"What's that humming? It sounds like our TV."

"Look under the table. Here, I'll turn on the overhead lights so you can see better." He flipped a switch on the wall and a couple of dusty hanging lightbulbs came on. They did nothing about the musty odor (and I could smell something else as well, now—something hot and oily), but they banished some of the gloom.

I bent—at my age I didn't have to bend far—and looked beneath the table. I saw two or three boxy things strapped to the underside. They were the source of the humming sound, and the oily smell, too.

"Batteries," he said. "Which I also made myself. Electricity is my hobby. And gadgets." He grinned like a kid. "I love gadgets. Drives my wife crazy."

"My hobby's fighting the Krauts," I said. Then, remembering what he said about that being kind of mean: "Germans, I mean."

"Everyone needs a hobby," he said. "And everyone needs a miracle or two, just to prove life is more than just one long trudge from the cradle to the grave. Would you like to see another one, Jamie?"

"Sure!"

There was another table in the corner, covered with tools, snips of wire, three or four dismembered transistor radios like the ones Claire and Andy had, and regular store-bought C and D batteries. There was also a small wooden box. Jacobs took the box, dropped to one knee so we'd be on the same level, opened it, and took out a white-robed figure. "Do you know who this is?"

I did, because the guy looked almost the same as my fluorescent night-light. "Jesus. Jesus with a pack on his back."

"Not just any pack; a battery pack. Look." He flipped up the top of the pack on a hinge not bigger than a sewing needle. Inside I saw what looked like a couple of shiny dimes with tiny dots of solder on them. "I made these, too, because you can't buy anything this small or powerful in the stores. I believe I could patent them, and maybe someday I will, but . . ." He shook his head. "Never mind."

He closed the top of the pack again, and carried Jesus to the Peaceable Lake landscape. "I hope you noticed how blue the water is," he said.

"Yeah! Bluest lake I ever saw!"

He nodded. "Kind of a miracle in itself, you might say . . . until you take a close look."

"Huh?"

"It's really just paint. I muse on that, sometimes, Jamie. When I can't sleep. How a little paint can make shallow water seem deep."

That seemed like a silly thing to think about, but I didn't say anything because he didn't really seem to be talking to me. Then he kind of snapped to, and put Jesus down beside the lake.

"I plan to use this in MYF—it's what we call a teaching tool—but I'll give you a little preview, okay?"

"Okay."

"Here's what it says in the fourteenth chapter of Matthew's Gospel. Will you take instruction from God's Holy Word, Jamie?"

"Sure, I guess so," I said, starting to feel uneasy again.

"I know you will," he said, "because what we learn as children is what sticks the longest. Okay, here we go, so listen up. 'And straightaway Jesus constrained his disciples'—that means he commanded them—'to get into a ship, and to go before him to the other side of the water while he sent the multitudes away. And when he had sent the multitudes away, he went up into a mountain to pray—' Do *you* pray, Jamie?"

"Yeah, every night."

"Good boy. Okay, back to the story. 'When evening was come, he was there alone. But the ship was now in the midst of the sea, tossed with waves, for the wind was contrary. And in the fourth watch Jesus went unto them, walking on the sea. And when the disciples saw him walking on the sea, they were troubled, saying, It is a spirit; and they cried out for fear. But straightway Jesus spake unto them, saying, Be of good cheer; for it is I; be not afraid.' That's the story, and may God bless his Holy Word. Good one, huh?"

"I guess. Does *spake* mean he talked to them? It does, right?"

"Right. Would you like to see Jesus walk on Peaceable Lake?"

"Yeah! Sure!"

He reached under Jesus's white robe, and the little figure began to move. When it reached Peaceable Lake it didn't sink but continued serenely on, gliding along the top of the water. It reached the other side in twenty seconds or so. There was a hill there, and it tried to go up, but I could see it was going to topple over. Reverend Jacobs grabbed it before it could. He reached under Jesus's robe again and turned him off.

"He did it!" I said. "He walked on the water!"

"Well . . ." He was smiling, but it wasn't a funny smile, somehow. It turned down at one corner. "Yes and no."

"What do you mean?"

"See where he went into the water?"

"Yeah . . ."

"Reach in there. See what you find. Be careful not to touch the power lines, because there's real electricity running through them. Not much, but if you brushed them, you'd get a jolt. Especially if your hand was wet."

I reached in, but cautiously. I didn't think he'd play a practical joke on me—as Terry and Con sometimes did—but I was in a strange place with a strange man and I wasn't completely sure. The water looked deep, but that was an illusion created by the blue paint of the reservoir and the lights reflecting on the surface. My finger only went in up to the first knuckle.

"You're not quite in the right place," Reverend Jacobs said. "Go a little bit to your right. Do you know your right from your left?"

I did. Mom had taught me: *Right is the hand you write with.* Of course that wouldn't have worked with Claire and Con, who were what my dad called southpaws.

I moved my hand and felt something in the water. It was metal, with a groove in it. "I think I found it," I told Reverend Jacobs.

"I think so, too. You're touching the track Jesus walks on."

"It's a magic trick!" I said. I had seen magicians on *The Ed Sullivan Show*, and Con had a box of magic tricks he got for his birthday, although everything but the Floating Balls and the Disappearing Egg had been lost.

"That's right."

"Like Jesus walking on the water to that ship!"

"Sometimes," he said, "that's what I'm afraid of."

He looked so sad and distant that I felt a little scared again, but I also felt sorry for him. Not that I had any idea what he had to feel sad about when he had such a neat pretend world as Peaceable Lake in his garage.

"It's a really *good* trick," I said, and patted his hand.

He came back from wherever he'd gone and grinned at me. "You're right," he said. "I'm just missing my wife and little boy, I guess. I think that's why I borrowed you, Jamie. But I ought to get you back to your mom now."

When we got to Route 9, he took my hand again even though there were no cars coming either way, and we walked like that all the way up Methodist Road. I didn't mind. I liked holding his hand. I knew he was looking out for me.

Mrs. Jacobs and Morris arrived a few days later. He was just a little squirt in didies, but she was pretty. On Saturday, the day before Reverend Jacobs first stood in the pulpit of our church, Terry, Con, and I helped him move Peaceable Lake to the church basement, where Methodist Youth Fellowship would meet every Thursday night. With the water drained, the shallowness of the lake and the grooved track running across it were very clear.

Reverend Jacobs swore Terry and Con to secrecy—because, he said, he didn't want the illusion spoiled for the little ones (which made me feel like a big one, a sensation I enjoyed). They agreed, and I don't think either of them peached, but the lights in the church basement were much brighter than those in the parsonage garage, and if you stood close to the landscape and peered at it, you could see that Peaceable Lake was really just a wide puddle. You could see the grooved track, too. By Christmas, everyone knew.

"It's just a big old fakearoonie," Billy Paquette said to me one Thursday afternoon. He and his brother Ronnie hated Thursday Night School, but their mother made them go. "If he shows it off one more time and tells that walking-on-water story, I'm gonna puke."

I thought of fighting him over that, but he was bigger. Also my friend. Besides, he was right.